The University of Oxford

The University of Oxford
A History

L. W. B. Brockliss

OXFORD
UNIVERSITY PRESS

OXFORD
UNIVERSITY PRESS

Great Clarendon Street, Oxford, OX2 6DP,
United Kingdom

Oxford University Press is a department of the University of Oxford.
It furthers the University's objective of excellence in research, scholarship,
and education by publishing worldwide. Oxford is a registered trade mark of
Oxford University Press in the UK and in certain other countries

Published in the United States of America by Oxford University Press
198 Madison Avenue, New York, NY 10016, United States of America

British Library Cataloguing in Publication Data
Data available

Library of Congress Control Number: 2015945827

ISBN 978-0-19-924356-3

Printed in Great Britain by
Clays Ltd, St Ives plc

To the Memory of Henry Richard Brockliss (1920–1975)
and Rosemary Brockliss, née Beaumont (1920–1989),
Their parents, their parents' parents, their parents' parents' parents...
Who never went to university.

And some there be, which have no memorial; who are perished, as though they had never been; and are become as though they had never been born; and their children after them. But these were merciful men, whose righteousness hath not been forgotten....

Their bodies are buried in peace; but their name liveth for evermore.

(Ecclesiasticus 44: 9–10, 14)

PREFACE

This is a history of an English institution nearly as old as the monarchy. Although the oft-touted claim before the nineteenth century that the University of Oxford was founded by Alfred the Great is a myth, there was certainly a school of higher learning of some sort in the city from the turn of twelfth century, and from 1214 it has had a permanent institutional existence. The University is thus as old as the common law, predates Magna Carta, is older than parliament, and far older than the Church of England. Like the monarchy, too, Oxford is not only a venerable institution but one that has nearly always been able to hold its head high. By the end of the fourteenth century, it was one of only a handful of the forty or so universities that had by then been established in Europe that could boast an international reputation, thanks to the originality and contentiousness of its leading philosophers and theologians. At the beginning of the twenty-first century, in a world which contains an estimated 17,000 universities, Oxford is still considered to be in the top ten in terms of its teaching and research. Even in the eighteenth and first part of the nineteenth century, when it had been reduced to little more than a finishing school for well-heeled Anglicans, it continued to be viewed with respect from the other side of the Channel. Indeed, Oxford, like the monarchy, has survived the vicissitudes of English and later British history across the last eight centuries with surprising ease. For a university located in a small market town in a rural shire, it has managed to adapt to the modern research world of 'big' science and even 'bigger' medicine much more successfully than most of its rivals snugly embedded in large industrial and commercial hubs and national capitals. Oxford and her products are frequently accused of effortless superiority but her position at the top table was far from pre-ordained. What makes the University's history worth telling is that it is an improbable story. Oxford, and her slightly younger sister, Cambridge, ought to have gone the way of most of the other late medieval universities founded in out-of-the way towns that the modern world passed by. In the sixteenth century, Alcalá was a centre of European humanism, Wittenberg produced Luther and the Reformation, and Bourges was the most intellectually vibrant university for law. But who has heard of these universities today? Bourges was shut by the French revolutionaries, and Alcalá and Wittenberg subsumed by larger neighbours in the early nineteenth century. Yet Oxford and Cambridge did not just survive the economic, social, and cultural transformations brought about by the Industrial Revolution, the rise and fall of the British Empire, and the emergence of the democratic welfare state: they flourished.

The first historian of the University of Oxford of consequence was the antiquarian Anthony Wood, who graduated as an MA in 1655, and dedicated his adult life to recovering the history of his alma mater from its first centuries and chronicling in detail her more recent past. Much of Wood's research remained in manuscript form until the turn of the nineteenth century, and it was only after 1850 that the history of the University became the focus of serious enquiry. For the last century and a half, virtually every aspect of Oxford's past has been examined in the most minute detail by a galaxy of historians and their works placed before the public, frequently with the help of the Oxford Historical Society, founded in 1884. Cordeaux and Merry's *Bibliography of Printed Works relating to the University of Oxford*, which appeared in 1968, contains reference to nearly 9,000 books and articles, and many thousands more have been written since. Condensing the fruits of this research has proved understandably daunting. In the two decades before the First World War, virtually all the colleges, even the most recent foundations, found their historian, but there was no full-length account of the University before the Liberal politician Sir Charles Mallet published his three-volume history in 1924–7, which took the reader from the beginning through to 1887 with a short coda. Over the next fifty years, however, no one attempted to repeat his achievement and bring the story up to date, until the rector of Lincoln, V. H. H. Green, produced a short overview in 1974. By then the University had decided to remedy the deficiency by publishing an eight-volume, multi-edited and multi-authored history, which would draw wherever possible on existing work but would also be based firmly on original research. Launched in 1968 by Lord Bullock, 'The Project for the History of Oxford' was the most ambitious attempt to write an account of a university's past hitherto. The first volume appeared in 1984, the last in 2000. As a rigorous piece of scholarship, it is hard to imagine that *The History of the University of Oxford* will ever be bettered. Along with the growing number of equally scholarly new college histories that have been published between 1979 and 2015, it stands as a monument to Oxford's interest in and care for its past, not out of any misplaced sense of veneration but from a desire to understand how an institution of such antiquity and importance has shaped and been shaped by the socio-cultural context in which it has been embedded.

The invitation to write this present history of Oxford University came out of the blue. One day in the late 1990s, I was invited to lunch by Sir Keith Thomas, then president of Corpus Christi College, and asked if I would consider undertaking the task in the light of my broader interests in the history of higher education. The committee in charge of 'The Project for the History of Oxford' had decided it should be crowned with a one-volume, single-authored history, which would draw on the wealth of scholarship now available to produce an account of the University's past which would be accessible to general readers. This was a request I could not refuse. To be asked to write the history of one's own university is an honour and privilege, especially when, in my case, I had been educated at the university in the Fens. This volume has been long in the gestation. Since agreeing to take up the burden, I have been sidetracked down other avenues, not least overseeing the history of my own college, Magdalen, which was published to coincide with its 550th anniversary in 2008. I only hope that readers will feel that it has been worth the wait.

The volume is divided into four parts. This reflects my belief that the University's history has been one of discontinuity as much as continuity. When the members of the University assemble in their regalia and process through the streets of the city to the Sheldonian at particular moments of the year, an onlooker would be forgiven for thinking that the University existed outside time and, like Hardy's man harrowing clods, things 'go onward the same/Though dynasties pass'. And in important ways this is true. In many respects an umbilical cord connects the Oxford today with the Oxford of previous centuries, and those who attempt to break it do so at their peril. The offices of the Chancellor and the Proctors go back to the first half of the thirteenth century, as does the role of Congregation as the supreme legislative body of the University, while Oxford's hallowed tutorial system developed in the century following the Reformation. There is a visceral attachment within the University to Oxford's traditional institutions, however out of kilter with contemporary views of 'sector norms', and wise reforming heads recognize the need to work with the institutional grain. On the other hand, it would be completely wrong to see these institutions and their role as unchanging over the centuries: the tutorial system, for one, has always been in a state of evolution. Nor should the elements of continuity be allowed to hide the fact that the University has survived through the ages by prudent adaptation of its *raison d'être* in the light of changing circumstances. In my view there have been three decisive turning points in the University's history and these determine the structure of the book. The first occurred in the middle of the sixteenth century, when Oxford moved from being a catholic to a protestant university and began to welcome laymen as well as clerics. The second dates from the mid-nineteenth century when the University ceased to be an Anglican monopoly and developed into a largely secular institution with a *mission civilisatrice* which extended beyond England and Britain to the empire and the United States. The third change was accelerated by the Second World War and the social and technological revolution that followed in its wake: Oxford embraced the new agenda of social equality and transformed itself from being a high-quality liberal arts college into a modern research university.

In each case, change was forced upon the University, sometimes directly, from outside. But equally in each case, change had enough support within Oxford to ensure that there was a willingness to collaborate with the new world and for the University to have some control over the agenda and even force the pace. Change was not achieved without a fight and, in the mid-sixteenth century, not without martyrs on either side. But had Oxford sheltered only conservatives, its history at moments of crisis would have been very different. If there had been no Jowett of Balliol and Pattison of Lincoln in the Oxford of the mid-nineteenth century but only clones of Martin Routh, Magdalen's nonagenarian head of house who still wore a wig, the University could easily have become the home of lost causes indeed. Like

Matthew Arnold's 'Sea of Faith', all that might have been heard of an Oxford locked in its confessional past in the second half of the nineteenth century would have been 'its melancholy, long, withdrawing roar'. This still may be the fate of the University in the second half of the twenty-first century if that reforming impulse is allowed to atrophy. I suggest, in the Conclusion, that digitalization and the new information technology threaten to make the present structure of Oxford redundant, and that what is needed is an imaginative and radical response to the threat, arguably a fourth refounding. The problem in the modern era is that the calls on a don's time through the pressures of teaching, research and administration make it difficult for academics to step back and think about the University in the long term. Reform and restructuring is left to the University's administrators, who exist in their own well-meaning world of managerialism and government diktat and are as unlikely to provide a blueprint for revolutionary change as members of the fifteenth-century papal curia were to carry through the Reformation.

Oxford is and always has been an exceptional university compared with its peers. Although Cambridge's history has been very similar, England's two ancient universities have never been exactly the same institutions and Thackeray's coinage of the term 'Oxbridge' in 1849 created an unfortunate neologism. To calibrate that exceptionalism and to ensure that the pudding is not over-egged, the book endeavours to place the University in the broader context of the history of higher education *tout court*, something the eight-volume history was not always careful to do. Each of the four parts is prefaced and rounded with a short section which introduces the reader to the history of higher education across the period under review, and puts the experience of Oxford (and Cambridge, too) in a wider context. Throughout the individual chapters as well, especially in Part I of the book, there are frequent references to analogous developments on the continent of Europe. Placing Oxford in context is particularly difficult in Part IV as it covers the history of the University from 1945. The university system around the world was by then so vast and the relationship between Britain's higher-educational system and the British state so much more complex than hitherto (particularly from 1987) that it is impossible to summarize developments in a few paragraphs, and readers may feel the introduction to Part IV moves too far away from the history of Oxford. All I can say in my defence is that, fifty years from now, if this book is still read, the readership will know next to nothing about the 'nationalization' of the British university system by recent Conservative and Labour governments. Readers will need to be properly informed of the events of the last twenty-five years if they are to understand the new pressures that Oxford and the other institutions of higher education of the United Kingdom had to learn to live with at the turn of the twenty-first century.

The first three parts of the book depend heavily on the eight-volume *History of the University of Oxford*. Readers of this book who seek further knowledge about individuals and developments discussed in its pages are well advised to turn to the relevant volume or chapter in the earlier publication. Part IV of the book is extensively based on my own research. Although the eighth volume of the *History of the University of Oxford* extends to the mid-1960s and a final chapter takes the story through to 1990, so much has happened since then that the period since the end of the Second World War had to be written almost *ab initio*. I am only too well aware that much in Part IV will need revision in the course of time. I am also aware that my account of Oxford's contribution to the arts and science since 1970 only skims the surface. Given the sheer size of the modern research university and the impossibility, as yet, of gauging the real significance of the work done in recent decades, I have limited myself to a broad brush analysis.

Besides the many administrative and academic documents I have personally collected over the years since coming to Oxford in 1984, two sources have been particularly useful in writing the recent history of the University: the *Oxford Magazine* and the *Oxford Times*. The first, as the voice of the dons (albeit increasingly the retired and the exercised) not the university establishment, provides the historian with a running, often historical, commentary on the major initiatives that have emerged from the central administration (and central government) over past decades. The second is often the only source of solid information about town–gown relations, intercollegiate squabbling, and important Oxford anniversaries. The city is fortunate to have a weekly newspaper of its quality.

This book is dedicated to my forebears. My Brockliss ancestors for the three centuries from the Reformation to the mid-nineteenth century were solid members of the rural middling sort who dwelt on the Oxfordshire–Northamptonshire border. The last of the breed died in the village of Moreton Pinkney during the Second World War. They were acutely aware of their middling status and had no desire to change it. Sons were purposely given middle names denoting the occupations they could be expected to follow: yeoman, miller, wheelwright, weaver, and so on. None appears to have dreamt of elevating the family socially in the seventeenth century by sending one of their number off to Oxford or Cambridge to be a servant to the local squire's son in the hope he might enter the ministry. My Brockliss ancestors were stolidly suspicious of higher education and remained so to the last generation. They valued calloused hands, not subtle minds. A good dose of their scepticism runs in my own genes. Just like its eight-volume predecessor, this book is no hagiography but an attempt to produce a balanced account of Oxford's place in the nation, from its foundation to the present day. Nonetheless, were my ancestors able to read it, I believe that they would emerge from its pages with a more positive view of one of Europe's oldest universities. Oxford did and does matter, a text that needs to be continually preached in an age when, both inside and outside the British establishment, there are many, including a recent prime minister, who appear to feel that the University is a parasite on the national oak.

If today's dons were asked to explain the way in which Oxford matters, most would almost certainly proudly cite the University's contribution over the last century to research in the arts and sciences. If the same question were put to outsiders, they would be just as likely to cite, though with less enthusiasm, the continual domination by Oxford graduates of the higher echelons of the civil service, the bar, the media, the world of banking, and the country's political parties. In fact, over the centuries and even today, neither response properly captures Oxford's importance to the commonweal. For perhaps five hundred of its eight hundred years (from 1400 to 1900) Oxford's contribution to the advancement of human knowledge was limited, while only a very small proportion of its alumni, however significant and influential in the nation's history, have ever found their way to the top table. Until 1850, the majority of Oxford's undergraduates and graduates lived out their lives as country parsons, or, in the centuries following the Reformation, returned to their family's estate. Even in the last hundred years, if Oxford's men and women have spread their wings and graced a multitude of different professions, they have mainly served as subalterns in charge, at best, of small platoons. And herein lies their deeper importance. From the reign of Elizabeth, some Englishmen had deliberately gone abroad to be educated for confessional or professional reasons; in the eighteenth and early nineteenth century, others had attended the academies set up by non-conformists, while still others had travelled to Scotland. But before the expansion of the new University of London and the establishment of a growing number of provincial colleges in the reign of Victoria, the alumni of Oxford and Cambridge always formed the large majority of the English nation who had received a higher education.

However deficient the experience might often seem, the two universities gave their junior members access to a rich European cultural inheritance, of the present as well as the past, which only the most dedicated autodidact would ever acquire. In the countryside in particular, where the majority of the population lived before 1850, such alumni would normally have been the only resident figures whose horizons extended beyond the customary and the local. As such, their significant role in facilitating change, not just in religion but in all manner of fields, can too easily be overlooked. It is a commonplace to see the Industrial Revolution as an event completely outside Oxford and Cambridge. But even here the alumni of the two universities were far from being absent. One of my Brockliss collateral ancestors, John Brockliss from Sulgrave, a village a couple of miles from Moreton Pinkney, was a miller who, in 1788, purchased a steam engine from Boulton and Watt in Birmingham to run his mill. It is hard to see how a miller, albeit literate, could have had his mind opened to the possibilities of steam power and found the money (borrowed in London) to make his dreams a reality without the assistance and encouragement (indeed, the incitement) of the local parson and squire. Boulton and Watt demanded money in advance and screened all potential purchasers of their engine.

In writing this book, I am primarily indebted to the editors and authors of the eight-volume history. Without their Herculean reconstruction of Oxford's history, based on the most exemplary archival research, this present work would have been impossible. I would also like to thank three individuals in particular for their assistance in bringing this volume to fruition: Andrew Hegarty, Robin Darwall-Smith, and Jane Eagan. Andrew, over the years, has constantly refreshed my knowledge of the broader history of higher education with his observations and discoveries; Robin, Magdalen and University College's archivist, has done the same for Oxford; while Jane, head of the University's Conservation Consortium, has been indispensable in collating the volume's illustrations. Needless to say, a special thanks must also go the history team at Oxford University Press. The personnel has changed completely since Ruth Parr commissioned the volume in 2000, but I have always been greeted with the same unfailing patience and courtesy, despite the book falling ever further behind schedule. I thank them for keeping faith with the project. Special thanks too are due to Brian Harrison for his detailed and insightful comments on the first draft of the book. Finally, I would like to thank Keith Thomas and the late Michael Brock for their continual confidence in my ability to write this history of Oxford's first eight hundred years. I hope I have repaid their trust.

LWBB
Wootton
December 2013

CONTENTS

ILLUSTRATIONS

ABBREVIATIONS

Adams	Pauline Adams, *Somerville for Women: An Oxford College 1879–1993* (Oxford, 1996)
AEW	Association for Promoting the Higher Education of Women in Oxford
BA	bachelor of arts
BAAS	British Association for the Advancement of Science
BCL	bachelor of civil law
BCnL	bachelor of canon law
BD	bachelor of divinity
BEd	bachelor of education
BFA	bachelor of fine art
Bill	E. G. W. Bill, *Education at Christ Church Oxford 1600–1800* (Oxford, 1988)
BLitt	bachelor of letters
BM	bachelor of medicine
BMus	bachelor of music
BP	*Blueprint*, University of Oxford staff magazine
BPhil	bachelor of philosophy
Brockliss	L. W. B. Brockliss (ed.), *Magdalen College Oxford: A History* (Oxford, 2008)
Brooke	Christopher N. L. Brooke, *A History of the University of Cambridge*, vol. 4: *1870–1990* (Cambridge, 1993)
BSc	bachelor of science
BT	bachelor of theology
Buxton and Williams	John Buxton and Penry Williams (eds), *New College Oxford 1379–1979* (Oxford, 1979)
CATs	Colleges of Advanced Technology
Catto	Jeremy Catto (ed.), *Oriel College: A History* (Oxford, 2013)
CNAA	Council for National Academic Awards
Commission (1852)	*Royal Commission appointed to enquire into the state, discipline, studies and revenues of the University and Colleges of Oxford, Report and Evidence*: PP 1852 (1482), xxii
Commission (1873)	*Royal Commission appointed to inquire into the property and income of the universities of Oxford and Cambridge, and of the colleges and halls therein, Report and Evidence*: PP 1873 xxxviii C.856, pts 1–3
Commission (1881)	*University of Oxford Commission, appointed 10 Aug. 1877, evidence, circulars etc.*: PP 1881 lvi C. 2868

Crook	J. Mordaunt Crook, *Brasenose: The Biography of an Oxford College* (Oxford, 2008)
CUF	Common University Fund or Common University Fund Lecturer
CUFs	Common University Fund lecturers
Curthoys	Judith Curthoys, *The Cardinal's College: Christ Church, Chapter and Verse* (London, 2012)
Darwall-Smith	Robin Darwall-Smith, *A History of University College Oxford* (Oxford, 2008)
DCL	doctor of civil law
DD	doctor of divinity
Dearing	The National Committee of Inquiry into Higher Education, *Higher Education in the Learning Society: Report of the National Committee. Main Report* (London, 1997)
DLitt	doctor of letters
DM	doctor of medicine
DMus	doctor of music
DPhil	doctor of philosophy
DSc	doctor of science
EPSC	Educational Policy and Standards Committee
EU	European Union
Franks	University of Oxford, *Report of Commission of Inquiry* (2 vols; Oxford, 1966)
GDP	Gross Domestic Product
GNP	Gross National Product
Green	Vivian H. H. Green, *The Commonwealth of Lincoln College 1427–1977* (Oxford, 1979)
Hearne, i–xi	*Remarks and Collections of Thomas Hearne*, ed. C. E. Doble, R. W. Rannie, H. E. Salter, and others (11 vols; Oxford Historical Society: Oxford 1885–1921)
HEFCE	Higher Education Funding Council for England
HEI	higher education institution
HESA	Higher Education Statistical Agency
Hopkins	Clare Hopkins, *Trinity: 450 Years of an Oxford College Community* (Oxford, 2005)
HT	Hilary Term
HU	*History of Universities* [journal]
HUIE, i–iv	*A History of the University in Europe*, general editor, Walter Rüegg; vol. 1, *Universities in the Middle Ages*, ed. H. de Ridder-Symoens (Cambridge, 1992); vol. 2, *Universities in Early Modern Europe*, ed. H. de Ridder-Symoens (Cambridge, 1996); vol. 3, *Universities in the Nineteenth and Early Twentieth Centuries (1800–1945)*, ed. Walter Rüegg (Cambridge, 2004); vol. 4, *Universities since 1945*, ed. Walter Rüegg (Cambridge, 2011)
HUO, i–viii	*The History of the University of Oxford*, vol. 1: *The Early Oxford Schools*, ed. J. I. Catto (Oxford, 1984); vol. 2: *Late Medieval Oxford*, ed. J. I. Catto and T. A. R. Evans (Oxford, 1992); vol. 3: *The*

	Collegiate University, ed. James McConica (Oxford, 1986); vol. 4: *Seventeenth-Century Oxford*, ed. Nicholas Tyacke (Oxford, 1997); vol. 5: *The Eighteenth Century*, ed. L. S. Sutherland and L. G. Mitchell (Oxford, 1986); vol. 6: *Nineteenth-Century Oxford, Part 1*, ed. M. G. Brock and M. C. Curthoys (Oxford, 1997); vol. 7: *Nineteenth-Century Oxford, Part 2*, ed. M. G. Brock and M. C. Curthoys (Oxford, 2000); vol. 8: *The Twentieth Century*, ed. Brian Harrison (Oxford, 1994)
ICI	Imperial Chemical Industries
ICS	Indian Civil Service
James	*Letters of Richard Radcliffe and John James of Queen's College, Oxford, 1755–83: with additions, notes and appendices* (Oxford Historical Society, vol. xxxiv: Oxford, 1888)
JCR	junior common room
Jones	John Jones, *Balliol College: A History*, 2nd edn (Oxford, 1997)
JR	The John Radcliffe Hospital, Headington
JRAM	Joint Resource Allocation Model
JRF	junior research fellow
Laudian Statutes	*Statutes of the University of Oxford codified in the year 1636 under the authority of Archbishop Laud, Chancellor of the University*, ed. J. Griffiths (Oxford, 1888).
LEA	Local Education Authority
Leader	Damian R. Leader, *A History of the University of Cambridge*, vol. 1: *The University to 1546* (Cambridge, 1988).
Lit. Hum.	the School of Literae Humaniores
LMH	Lady Margaret Hall
LSE	London School of Economics
MA	master of arts
Mallet	Charles Edward Mallet, *A History of the University of Oxford*, vol. 1: *The Medieval University and the Colleges founded in the Middle Ages*; vol. 2: *The Sixteenth and Seventeenth Centuries*; vol. 3: *Modern Oxford* (London, 1927).
MBA	master of business administration
MC	Military Cross
MCA	Magdalen College Archives
MCR	middle common room
Mods	a classified examination taken in some Oxford schools by undergraduates at the end of their first, or during the course of their second, year
Morgan	Victor Morgan, *A History of the University of Cambridge*, vol. 2: *1546–1750* (Cambridge, 2004).
MPLS	Division of Mathematical, Physical and Life Sciences
MSc	master of science
MStud	master of studies
MT	Michaelmas Term
NHS	National Health Service

North	University of Oxford, *Commission of Inquiry Report* (Oxford, 1997)
NYU	New York University
OECD	Organisation for Economic Co-operation and Development
OED	*Oxford English Dictionary*
OFFA	Office for Fair Access
OHS	Oxford Historical Society
OM	*Oxford Magazine*
OT	*Oxford Times*
OTS	Officer Training Corps
OUA	Oxford University Archives
OUC	Oxford University Calendar
OUDS	Oxford University Dramatic Society
OUG	*Oxford University Gazette*
OUP	Oxford University Press
OUS	*Oxford University Statutes* (2 vols; London, 1845–51); vol.1, containing the Caroline Code or the Laudian Statutes, promulgated AD 1636, translated by G. R. M. Ward; vol. 2, containing the University Statutes from 1767 to 1850, translated to 1843 by G. R. M. Ward and completed under the superintendence of James Heywood
OUSRC	Oxford University Students Representative Council
OUSU	Oxford University Students' Union
PGCE	Postgraduate Certificate of Education
PGR	postgraduate research
PGT	postgraduate taught
PP	Parliamentary Papers
PPE	the School of Philosophy, Politics and Economics
PPH	permanent private halls
PPP	the School of Psychology, Philosophy and Physiology
PRAC	Planning and Resources Allocation Committee
QAA	Quality Assurance Agency
RAE	Research Assessment Exercise
RAM	Resource Allocation Model
REF	Research Excellence Framework
Report (1853)	*Report and Evidence upon the Recommendations of Her Majesty's Commissioners for inquiring into the state of the University of Oxford presented to the Board of the Heads of Houses and Proctors December 1 1853* (Oxford, 1853).
Robbins	Committee on Higher Education, *Higher Education: Report of the Committee appointed by the Prime Minister under Lord Robbins* (London, 1963)
ROQ	the Radcliffe Observatory Quarter
SCR	senior common room
Searby	Peter Searby, *A History of the University of Cambridge*, vol. 3: *1750–1870* (Cambridge, 1997)

Select Committee (1867)	*Select Committee on the Oxford and Cambridge Universities Education Bill*: PP 1867 (497), xiii. 183–560
Soares	Joseph A. Soares, *The Decline of Privilege: The Modernisation of Oxford University* (Stanford, CA, 1999)
Statuta	*Statuta antiqua universitatis Oxoniensis*, ed. Strickland Gibson (Oxford, 1931)
Statutes	*Statutes of the Colleges of Oxford with royal patents of foundation, injunctions of visitors, and catalogues of documents relating to the University preserved in the Public Record Office, printed by desire of Her Majesty's Commissioners for inquiring into the state of the University of Oxford* (3 vols; London, 1853)
TNA	The National Archive, Kew
TT	Trinity Term
TUC	Trades Union Congress
UCCA	Universities Central Council on Admissions (founded 1961; now Universities and Colleges Admissions Service)
UCL	University College London
UFC	Universities Funding Council
UGC	University Grants Committee
ULNTF	University Lecturer and Non-Tutorial Fellow
ULTF	University Lecturer and Tutorial Fellow
UMIST	University of Manchester Institute of Science and Technology
USS	Universities Superannuation Scheme
VC	Victoria Cross
WAAF	Women's Auxiliary Air Force
WEA	Workers Educational Association
Wood, *Life*	*The Life and Times of Anthony Wood, Antiquary of Oxford, 1632–1695, described by himself*, ed. A. Clark (5 vols; OHS, xix, xxii, xxvi, xxx, and xl; Oxford, 1891–1900).
Wood, *History*	Anthony Wood, *The History and Antiquities of the University of Oxford*, ed. J. Gutch (2 vols; Oxford, 1792–6).
Woodforde	*Woodforde at Oxford, 1759–76*, ed. W. N. Hargreaves-Mawdsley (Oxford, 1969)

NOTE ON PROPER NAMES

The birth and death dates of individuals mentioned in the text, where they are known, are given after the relevant entry in the *Index of Persons*.

NOTE ON REFERENCES

Where information has been taken from Mallet or the recent eight-volume *History of the University of Oxford*, or one of the several college histories, or monographs on some aspect of the University's history published since 1960, reference is made to the fact in the footnotes only where the text cites from a quotation that appears in one of these volumes. A list of these works that have been invaluable in writing this book appears under *Further Reading*, 'University of Oxford'.

Documents referenced in Part IV of the book without any indication of their location in a library or archive are papers in my personal collection.

A few URLs cited in the notes to Chapters 13 to 15 and to the tables are no longer live, and these are signalled. Every effort has been made to cite only URLs that could be accessed at the time that the book went to press. Readers should be warned, however, that the University of Oxford frequently changes the address to links through its home page and that the statistical information it provides on its sites is impermanent.

NOTE ON TERMS

Oxford's nomenclature can be very confusing. It includes terms that have a common everyday meaning as well as a specific Oxford usage, and terms that have evolved over the centuries; even spellings can vary. The list here contains brief definitions of some frequently encountered terms in the text which may cause readers confusion. The best account of Oxford's complex vocabulary is Andrew Hegarty, 'A Select Glossary', in L. W. B. Brockliss (ed.), *Magdalen College Oxford: A History* (Oxford, 2008).

battels: Oxford term for a college bill presented to a college member; the book uses the most common spelling

commoner: historically a member of a college who was not a *foundationer* and who paid for his board and lodging: the term refers to the custom of taking meals in common. Commoners were themselves divided into different categories according to status and amount. Today, the term is used only for undergraduates who have not been awarded a scholarship or exhibition

Congregation: initially the assembly of the newly created MAs or doctors of theology, law, and medicine residing and teaching in the University; today the University's sovereign legislative body, some 4,000-strong, comprising postholders, other college fellows, and senior administrators

determine: in the late middle ages and early modern period, to become a bachelor in one of the five faculties

dons: used since the nineteenth century as collective term for college fellows; used in the text to refer collectively to Oxford fellows from 1700

exhibition: traditionally a sum of money given to an indigent student, usually by his college, to help him support his studies; some exhibitions were endowed by benefactors; today a prize for good work

exhibitioner: the beneficiary of an exhibition

fellow: full member of the foundation of a college who is part of the governing body; historically, fellows enjoyed free board and lodging and a stipend of some kind but today many fellows are non-stipendiary. The fellows of Christ Church have always been known as students. Here individual fellows are referred to as student and fellow to avoid confusion

foundationer: used in the book to denote someone formally on the foundation of a college, such as the head of house, fellow, scholar, etc.

House (the): common Oxford term for Christ Church

incept: in the late middle ages and early modern period, to become a master or doctor in one of the five faculties

junior members: a modern collective term for all undergraduate and postgraduate members of the University who are not members of a senior common room or university or college employees. Used in the first three parts of the book as a shorthand for members of the University who had not yet taken their MA

matriculation: act by which a person is formally admitted into Oxford by the Vice-Chancellor and becomes an undergraduate or postgraduate and historically became entitled to the privileges of the University

postholder: an academic employee of the University with a permanent position and teaching responsibilities

scholar: when the name is used in the book to refer to a member or members of a college, the term specifically refers to those on the foundation studying for their BA or MA who are supported in their studies but are not members of the governing body; scholars in some colleges have idiosyncratic names. The term in the first two parts of the book is also used to refer to the whole academic community, both students (those following a course in the arts) and masters (those who have completed a course in the arts and taken the degree of MA). The term is further used in the book to mean someone engaged in research or an author of a scholarly work, usually in the arts

scholarship: a college bursary supporting a *scholar*. Before the Reformation, a scholar received enough in kind or money from his scholarship to survive at Oxford; since then, the value has been eroded by inflation and today scholarships are little more than honorific

Schools: since the early nineteenth century, the common term for the final examination taken by undergraduates to qualify for a BA

senior members: in the modern era, synonymous with membership of Congregation. The term is used in Parts I–III to denote MAs resident in the University, after 1650 mainly fellows

'*smalls*': student term for Responsions, a sort of pass qualifying exam sat by undergraduates in the nineteenth century

student: used in the first three parts of the book to refer to any member of the University who has yet to take his MA; in the fourth part, it refers to both undergraduates and postgraduates up to doctoral level. Pre-1960 postgraduates at Oxford were known as advanced students

undergraduate: used in the last two centuries for someone who has not yet taken their BA; used as such throughout the book

University Chest: used to denote Oxford's finance department; it refers to the chest where the University kept its money in the late middle ages

PART I

The Catholic University: c.1100–1534

Introduction

The First Universities

ACCORDING to the fourteenth-century *Polychronicon* of the Benedictine monk Ranulph Higden, the University of Oxford was founded *c.*873 by Alfred the Great, king of Wessex, an Anglo-Saxon monarch famed for his interest in education. Although the story gained warranty through its inclusion by the Elizabethan antiquarian William Camden in the 1600 edition of his *Britannia*, and was still championed in the eighteenth century, the hollowness of the claim was soon exposed once serious research was undertaken into the University's origins in the second half of the nineteenth century.[1] As a result, it has long been recognized that there were no schools of higher learning in Oxford before the end of the eleventh century and that the existence of the University as a legal and collective entity cannot be identified before 1214. Oxford was also just one of a number of universities which evolved in the late twelfth and early thirteenth centuries in towns where there was already a cluster of advanced schools, so its emergence as a centre of higher education can be understood only in the broader European context.

The first universities in Roman Christendom (and the world) were the belated fruits of a revival of learning that began about the time of the Norman Conquest of England. The Dark Ages were never as dark as historians used to depict them, but there can be no doubt that the fall of the Roman Empire in the west in AD 410 was quickly followed by a rapid decline in interest among the new lay elites in the Graeco-Roman philosophical, medical, and legal inheritance, and by the church largely turning its back on the speculative theology which had been a hallmark of its early centuries. Although some contact with the cultural achievements of classical antiquity was maintained in Benedictine monasteries, and Charlemagne, the first emperor of the post-classical era at the beginning of the ninth century, encouraged the creation of Latin schools where priests could be properly trained in the language

---

[1] The legend was effectively laid to rest in James Parker, *The Early History of Oxford, 727–1100* (OHS: Oxford, 1885), ch. 2.

of the church, the spirit of enquiry effectively died in Roman Christendom until the middle of the eleventh century. It was only then that a new type of school for clerics began to appear all over western Europe in which students once again had access to classical philosophy, law, and medicine (albeit only to an extent), and where textual, especially biblical, conundrums were illuminated, and philosophical and theological problems analysed using the tools of logic.[2]

These schools of higher learning could be found in monasteries, attached to cathedrals or run by private masters. They might be located in isolated spots such as the monastery of St Gall in Switzerland, perched on top of a hill, as at Laon in northern France, or encountered in large, bustling centres of commerce and administration, such as Paris and Bologna. Those in the Italian peninsula tended to be schools of law, or, in the peculiar case of Salerno, medicine. Those in northern Europe predominantly concentrated on philosophy and theology. Their establishment was made possible by the growing commercial and military contact between Roman Christendom and the Byzantine and Muslim worlds, where classical learning had always remained prized and continually refined. In the course of the twelfth century, thanks to these contacts, figures like James of Venice and Gerard of Cremona were able to introduce into western Europe, in Latin translation, numerous 'lost' texts of Greek antiquity, including significant parts of the Aristotelian corpus, and the most important fruits of Arabic scholarship.[3] The new schools, however, could never have flourished and spread had not their value been quickly appreciated by the powers that be. In the first era of real economic growth and urbanization since the fall of the Roman Empire, the mercantile elites who controlled the expanding towns of northern Italy realized that the Roman law of contract was a valuable tool in securing a stable commercial environment. The Holy Roman emperors, too, in their desire to quell the independence of these nascent centres of wealth and assert their authority over a revivified papacy anxious to emphasize the autonomy of the spiritual realm, appreciated the concept of absolute political power embodied in the civil law. The popes, in their turn, sensed that the new schools were the key to Christian unity and papal supremacy in the church, and would help to consolidate a celibate clerical estate properly separated from the laity. The principles of the Roman *Corpus Iuris* could be effectively used to bring order to canon law, while the new philosophy and theology schools could hammer out a common position on dogma and ritual. Thereby, Christendom would no longer be bedevilled by regional traditions and the whims of secular rulers and nobles, but be governed by an independent, educated clerical elite under the pope's thumb.

---

[2] P. Riché, *Les Écoles et l'enseignement dans l'occident chrétien de la fin du V*e *au milieu du XI*e *siècle* (Paris, 1979); R. N. Swanson, *The Twelfth-Century Renaissance* (Manchester, 1999) ; Richard Southern, *Scholastic Humanism and the Unification of Europe*, vol. 1: *Foundation* (Oxford, 1995).

[3] Among the Aristotelian works which now became available were his *Metaphysics*, his physical and ethical works, and a number of logical treatises. Many of these works had been translated into Latin by Boethius in the early sixth century but had been forgotten. For the translators and their work, see Gordon Leff, 'The Trivium and the Three Philosophies', in *HUIE*, i. 316–19.

In the beginning, the reputation of these new schools rose and fell according to the perceived ability of individual masters. Pupils would flock to one school at one moment, only to desert it the next as a master died or moved on. By the middle of the twelfth century, however, a number, usually those located in large, prosperous towns, had become predominant. Most famous of all were the schools of Bologna and Paris, the one for law, primarily canon law, the other for philosophy and theology. Both groups of schools were located in important commercial and administrative centres—Bologna was an independent commune, Paris at the heart of the burgeoning Capetian monarchy. Both boasted a number of flourishing schools and both played host to a growing contingent of foreign students. At Paris, one school was run by the bishop and two by the abbots of Saint-Victor and Sainte-Geneviève, while others were the result of private initiative and were established on the left bank of the Seine in today's Latin Quarter by masters who included the self-confident and controversial Peter Abelard, author of the *Sic et Non*, a pioneering methodology for reconciling textual disagreements.[4]

Generally speaking, the dominant schools of the mid-twelfth century became Europe's first universities, while the others gradually disappeared. A university or *studium generale*, as such institutions were normally called in the thirteenth or fourteenth centuries, largely explored the same texts with the same exegetical method as the school or schools from which it had directly or indirectly emerged but it was a new educational animal. It was neither a private business venture nor the property of a bishop or a monastery. Rather, it was a self-governing ecclesiastical corporation of masters and students whose existence and organization were usually given initial legal recognition by the local municipal, state, or ecclesiastical authorities, and then confirmed by the pope or emperor, the highest authorities of all, through a grant of statutes. As the original meaning of the Latin word *universitas* or corporation suggests, the emergence of the university as an organization cannot be divorced from the concomitant development of the first urban guilds and town councils, whose structures it mimicked. What encouraged the metamorphosis was the very success of the leading schools. So many students were flocking to sit at the feet of their masters that the local civic authorities feared a breakdown in public order. At the same time, masters in thrall to a bishop or monastery were puffed up with their celebrity as intellectual superstars and wanted their independence. The obvious solution in the context of the emerging guild system was for individuals to join together in a corporation, obtain legal recognition, and run their own affairs. The pope or emperor were only too happy to oblige in that they became the de iure protectors of the new educational institution, which enhanced their chances of using learning to boost their own power.

---

[4] Girolamo Arnaldi, 'L'università di Bologna', in Gian Paolo Brizzi and Jacques Verger (eds), *Le università dell'Europa. La nascità delle università* (Milan, 1990), pp. 87–115; S. C. Ferruolo, *The Origins of the University: The Schools of Paris and their Critics, 1100–1215* (Stanford, CA, 1985).

It can be assumed that a number of schools or groups of schools were beginning to develop into universities from the middle of the twelfth century, but there is no documentary evidence of this embryonic corporate identity for a further thirty years. The first indications of the gestation of a scholars' guild comes from Bologna in 1189 when the commune forced the masters to swear not to transfer the *studium* to another town. Thereafter, evidence confirming that Bologna had become a *universitas* and announcing similar developments elsewhere proliferate. The collective identity of the many Paris schools received some sort of official recognition in 1194 when their scholars were implicitly given a grant of clerical immunity by Pope Celestine III, which was confirmed six years later by the king, Philip II. By 1208, a university had definitely begun to take shape. In that year the city's bishop, who claimed the right to license private teachers and interfere in their teaching, accepted that the masters could form an autonomous guild and police themselves, albeit under his ultimate control. In 1215, the pope blessed this arrangement by granting the fledgling university its first statutes.

By the end of the thirteenth century there were at least sixteen further *studia generalia* scattered across western Europe, including Oxford and Cambridge.[5] By 1378, when western Christendom was ripped asunder by the Great Schism, the number had risen to thirty-one. The oldest, in the manner of Bologna and Paris, emerged by fits and starts: an approximate date of foundation can be gained from documents revealing some form of corporate identity but their independence and self-government was usually formally ratified many decades later. No statutes seem to have been promulgated for Bologna, for instance, regarding its organization, before 1253, and its relationship with the city commune remained contested until 1321. Increasingly, however, the newer *studia generalia* were the result of political fiat rather than slow evolution, in itself testimony to the appeal of the new institution to Europe's rulers. The University of Naples was deliberately founded as early as 1224 by the Emperor Frederick II, who was anxious to establish a *studium* in his own lands which would compete with Bologna and train the jurists he required. The pope too was soon directly sponsoring universities. In 1229, Gregory IX founded a university at Toulouse in the aftermath of the crusade launched by Louis IX of France against the Cathars in the Midi, while Innocent IV erected a *studium* in the papal curia at Rome in 1244 or 1245. Less elevated secular rulers were also quick to join in. Alfonso IX of Léon may have created a *studium generale* at Salamanca as early as 1218–19, although the royal privileges confirming its existence date only from 1254. On the eve of the Reformation the number of universities had leaped to seventy-five (see Map 1). Universities were to be found from one end of the continent to the other. If some universities, like Buda, proved short-lived, every petty prince in the fifteenth century wanted one within his dominions. Even towns sought to establish one in their midst, perceiving commercial advantages. When Pope Martin V was lobbied to

---

[5] For the location of Europe's medieval universities, see Jacques Verger, 'Patterns', in *HUIE*, i. 62–4 and 68–74 (list and maps).

found a university at Louvain in 1425, it was the city council that led the campaign for its installation.[6]

Just like any other set of corporate bodies fulfilling the same function, Europe's late medieval universities had their own idiosyncratic customs and administrative forms, the product of location, history, and chance. Historians have often tried to corral them into two types: the Bologna model, where the masters were subservient to the students who elected the head of the university, the rector; and the Paris model, where the masters or licensed teachers in residence dominated and the students had no voice. This, though, is to oversimplify a complex phenomenon and does not even do justice to the structure of the two universities identified as the inspiration for the others.[7] Behind the institutional diversity, however, lay a number of common characteristics that gave the early universities (and their successors) their defining and common identity. Besides the right of self-government, every university had the right of testing the sufficiency of students who had passed through its hands and licensing them to teach in its own and, in theory, other *studia*. While the actual degree or dignity was usually bestowed by the pope or the local bishop's representative, it was the university which judged the student's capacity. At the same time, all members of the university (masters, scholars, and various hangers-on, such as parchment makers and scribes) were given privileges which marked them off from the rest of the community in which they lived. These might be fiscal or judicial, but they emphasized the fact that members of the university were part of a separate estate, even if they had not yet been ordained.

Initially, the external authorities sometimes attempted to limit what the universities could teach. Before 1350, the popes forbade all but a handful of *studia* headed by Paris to teach theology, a science which the papacy had an obvious interest in policing. Eventually, however, virtually all universities gained the right to teach and license scholars in four recognized subject areas or faculties: the arts, theology, law (civil and canon), and medicine. The first, comprising the seven liberal arts (grammar, rhetoric, dialectic or logic, arithmetic, geometry, astronomy, and music) and the three philosophies (ethics, physics, and metaphysics), was considered propaedeutic to the other three, which, in consequence, became known as the higher faculties. Each subject area or faculty awarded three different degrees: the baccalaureate, which was granted on the completion of a preliminary period of study, the licence, which bore witness to a scholar's command of the discipline, and the master's or doctor's degree, which admitted a student to the community of teachers.[8] Over time the faculties generally developed their own corporate identity, though in most universities only one or two were really flourishing institutions.

---

[6] E. de Maesschalck, 'The Relationship between the University and the City of Louvain in the Fifteenth Century', *HU*, ix (1990), 45–71.

[7] For the complexity of the so-called Paris model, see Thierry Kouané, '*Ex communi consensus omnium magistrorum*: Enjeux et fonctionnement des *congregationes* dans les universités de type parisien (XIIIᵉ–XVᵉ siècles)', in Martine Charageat and Corinne Leveleux-Teixeira (eds), *Consulter, délibérer, décider: Donner son avis au moyen âge (France-Espagne, VIIᵉ–XVIᵉ siècles)* (Paris, 2010), pp. 223–52.

[8] In the arts faculty, the licence and master's degree were often conflated.

Universities usually had a bias in the direction of one subject area rather than another, a reflection very often of the bias of the schools from which they had emerged. Bologna was always essentially a university for law, Paris for philosophy and theology, and Montpellier, whose first statutes date from 1220, for medicine. There were very few universities that specialized completely. Orléans, created by a student emigration from Paris in 1229–31, only ever offered tuition in civil law, but this reflected the fact that, from 1219, teaching the science in the French capital had been banned by Pope Honorius III. Orléans acted then as an extension of the University of Paris.

University teachers in the older foundations of northern Europe usually survived on the fees they received from their pupils (and a share of the money graduands had to hand over when they took a degree). If they could, they augmented their income by acquiring a benefice. In the Italian, Spanish, and newer universities, teachers normally received salaries which were paid by the church, the prince, and some-times the municipality.[9] The students themselves were dependent on their own resources or charity. They lodged where they could: at home, with local townsmen, or in student lodging houses. The lucky few belonged to communities of scholars whose needs were met by a scholarship fund. Endowed hostels or colleges for poor scholars had first been established at Paris in the middle of the thirteenth century and the custom had quickly spread. By 1500, most universities had one or two such foundations and a handful many more. The colleges were often a powerful force in the university because they were independent corporate entities and usually sup-ported older students in the higher faculties. Nonetheless, they only ever sheltered a minority of students, even at the University of Paris, where there were forty colleges by the end of the fifteenth century.[10]

It is customary to credit Oxford with being Europe's third oldest university—after Bologna and Paris. But this merely reflects the fact that the first definite evidence for its corporative existence dates from a little later than that for the other two and predates that of other early foundations. Across the first three centuries of its existence Oxford was a typical northern European university: it was a privileged corporation of masters; it maintained teaching in four faculties (or five, since Oxford, like several other universities, distinguished between civil and canon law); it awarded the usual degrees; its masters largely relied on student fees; and by 1500 fifteen colleges had been founded to house poor students and monks. On the other hand, Oxford had distinctive features that always made it stand out. First, it was always one of the most frequented universities, even if it was never an international *studium* like Paris and its numbers fell after 1400. Secondly, England's reliance on

---

[9] E.g. Pavia, where the professors were dependent on the bounty of the dukes of Milan: D. Zanetti, 'A l'université de Pavie au XVe siècle: les salaires des professeurs', *Annales, économies, sociétés et civilisations*, 17 (1962), 421–33.

[10] Jean Dunbabin, 'Meeting the Costs of University Education in Northern France, c.1240–c.1340', *HU*, X (1990), 1–27; A. L. Gabriel, 'The College System in the Fourteenth-Century Universities', in F. L. Utley (ed.), *The Forward Movement of the Fourteenth Century* (Columbus, OH, 1961), 79–124.

common and not civil law meant that legal studies had neither the attraction nor the prestige that they often had elsewhere, which affected the balance of attendance in the higher faculties. Thirdly, the University was located in a small market town which made town–gown relations particularly difficult because the students and masters always formed a large and privileged minority. Fourthly, although Oxford mirrored the Paris model, its governance was noticeably different, as we shall see in Chapter 1. Fifthly, its colleges eventually enjoyed a much higher profile than their continental counterparts: a number were much grander and more securely endowed, and by the mid-sixteenth century, if not before, the colleges housed the majority of students. Finally and most importantly, for the previous points equally characterized Cambridge, Oxford had a high intellectual profile, second only to Paris among the universities north of the Alps. In the late thirteenth and fourteenth centuries, Oxford was the alma mater of a number of Europe's most innovative and controversial philosophers and theologians whose ideas spread round the continent. Oxford did not invent the distinctive academic culture of the late middle ages which historians call scholasticism but it left a profound imprint on its content and development.

CHAPTER 1

Foundation and Institutionalization

A. The Creation of Oxford

THERE seem to have been masters offering instruction in aspects of higher learning in Oxford from the late eleventh century, but they left little personal trace. The first master known to have been based in the town was the itinerant Frenchman Theobald of Étampes, who apparently taught the liberal arts or philosophy from about 1095 to the early 1120s. The second was Robert Pullen, of a Dorset family of small landowners, who lectured in theology at Oxford from 1133 to 1139. An ambitious and talented figure, he then moved to Paris, whence he was summoned to Rome in 1144 to become chancellor of the Roman see and cardinal. From 1139, however, the trail runs cold until the reign of Richard I, when it becomes clear that there was not just one but several masters holding schools in the town. These included Alexander Neckham, who reportedly taught theology from 1193 to 1197 before becoming an Augustinian canon at Cirencester; Robert Grosseteste, the future bishop of Lincoln; and the law teacher John of Tynemouth, later archdeacon of Oxford.[1] In the first part of the reign of Richard's brother, John, the number of schools appears to have grown rapidly. The most important master in the first decade of the thirteenth century was Edmund of Abingdon, future archbishop of Canterbury and saint, who taught arts at Oxford from c.1202 to c.1208 and was possibly the first Oxford professor to lecture on Aristotle's *Sophistici elenchi*, one of his logical texts reintroduced into Europe in the twelfth century.

Unlike its sisters, the town of Oxford was an improbable site for one of Europe's first universities in that it was not a peculiarly important administrative or commercial centre. There was no bishop of Oxford—until the Reformation the town was in the large diocese of Lincoln—and it had never been a vital hub of Anglo-Saxon, Norman, or Angevin government. The town itself appears to have been founded about 890 on the north bank of the Thames at a point easily forded by cattle, where a north–south track crossed the river. Built in the defensible fork of the

---

[1] Grosseteste's presence at this date is disputed.

Thames and the Cherwell, Oxford sat uncomfortably on the border of Wessex and Mercia until the creation of the kingdom of England in the tenth century. Although it grew in significance after it had been seized by Edward the Elder, second son of Alfred the Great, in 912, it was hardly thriving at the time of the Norman invasion. According to the Domesday Book, it contained 946 houses, 600 within the walls and 346 outside, but 478 were described as decayed or destroyed. It was only from the end of the eleventh century that Oxford began to develop as a strongpoint and ecclesiastical centre. The Norman castle was begun in 1072 and a secular community of clerics installed in its chapel of St George two years later; a new parish church, St Giles, was constructed in the northern suburbs; Augustinian canons replaced seculars in the former Saxon religious house of St Frideswide in the south of the town in 1122, then, seven years later, occupied a new and finer priory (later an abbey) at Oseney outside the walls; meanwhile, Henry I, who enjoyed hunting in the nearby forest of Woodstock, built a royal residence, called Beaumont, beside the north wall.

Nor was Oxford an isolated bastion of the revival of learning in the twelfth-century kingdom of England. Rather, it was only one of several towns where new schools were established. There were flourishing cathedral schools at Exeter, York, Lincoln, and Hereford—the last particularly noted as a centre for studying the seven liberal arts—whilst in London not only was a school attached to St Paul's and to the churches of St Martin-le-Grand and St Mary Arches, but there were also independent masters teaching law.[2] In addition, Northampton—another town in the centre of England without a bishop—boasted a particularly successful school in the second half of the century. It was to Northampton, not to Oxford, that the few foreign masters who worked in this country would gravitate in search of a chance to teach, such as the Bologna-trained lawyer Vacarius, who, in the middle of the twelfth century, served in the households of both the archbishops of York and Canterbury. It was at Northampton too where the first student riots in England were recorded in the 1180s, a sure sign that its school was attracting a sizeable clientele.

This is not to deny that Oxford's schools had a continual existence during the twelfth century, nor that they lacked reputation. But it suggests that the number of students and masters must have been small. The situation may have improved towards the end of Henry II's reign because, for three days in 1187 or 1188, Gerald of Wales, a canon of the castle church of St George, found a large enough resident body of students and masters in different disciplines to gather together an audience to hear him reading his recently finished *Topographia hibernica*. All the same, it was probably the case that student numbers grew only after 1193 when the uninterrupted eleven-year war with France stopped English clerics from travelling to Paris as they had traditionally done.

Admittedly, Oxford had certain advantages from the mid-twelfth century which made it more attractive to masters and students and its schools more competitive.

[2] K. Edwards, *English Secular Cathedrals in the Middle Ages*, 2nd edn (Manchester, 1967), *passim*.

To begin with, it grew in importance as a legal centre. Although, like Northampton, only the seat of an archdeacon, it became a centre for hearing cases referred back from the papal curia as well as judging cases involving local abbeys. At the same time, Henry II visited the town frequently, two of his sons—Richard and John— were born there, and his grandfather's palace became one of the hubs of the English administration. It was presumably for this reason that Richard I granted the inhabitants of Oxford a charter in 1199 and the town became a corporation (albeit ten years after Northampton). In consequence of these developments, Oxford became a place where ambitious clerics might seek patronage as well as education, while some of the lawyers and judges who earned their living in the town also enriched its schools by offering courses in law as a sideline.

Yet if this helps to account for Oxford's vitality at the turn of the thirteenth century, it does not explain why its schools became England's first recognized university during the reign of King John. By this date there were a number of towns whose schools were flourishing enough to have begun to develop an embryonic corporative identity and collective organization, but Oxford's alone made the transition. The answer lies, at least in part, in the fortunate fall-out from a murder, which initially put town and gown at irrevocable odds and threatened to put an end to the schools for good. Towards the end of 1209, a student killed a woman (presumably his mistress) in Maiden Hall, a house probably today within the bounds of New College. The malefactor fled, but the town had its revenge by arresting two other students living in the property and immediately hanging them. In response, the majority of the masters and students, either out of disgust, fear, or the realization that their departure would harm the town's economy, decamped— an easy option when there was no university 'plant': a master's classroom was simply a room in a rented house. Some went to Reading, others to Cambridge, Maidstone, Canterbury, and Paris, and there they remained for the next five years.[3] In normal circumstances, a suitable arbitrator would have been found and the quarrel soon resolved with honours even. At this particular juncture, however, such a solution was not to hand. Since the king sided with the town and the whole kingdom was at that moment under a sentence of excommunication because of John's quarrel with the papacy, there was no higher authority to whom the two parties could look for mediation. The schools therefore remained shut until the interdict was lifted. By then the town was desperate to get back its student market, so it went down on bended knee before the papal legate, expressed deep regret for its temerity, and begged him to produce a settlement which would satisfy the scholars. This Nicholas de Romanis, Cardinal Bishop of Tusculum, duly did in a judgement dated 20 June 1214.

The deed of 20 June made four separate provisions. In the first place, the legate ordered that, for the next twenty years, student rents were to be determined by their

---

[3] The background to the 1209 dispersion is only scantily recorded in contemporary chronicles, so the actual events remain hazy.

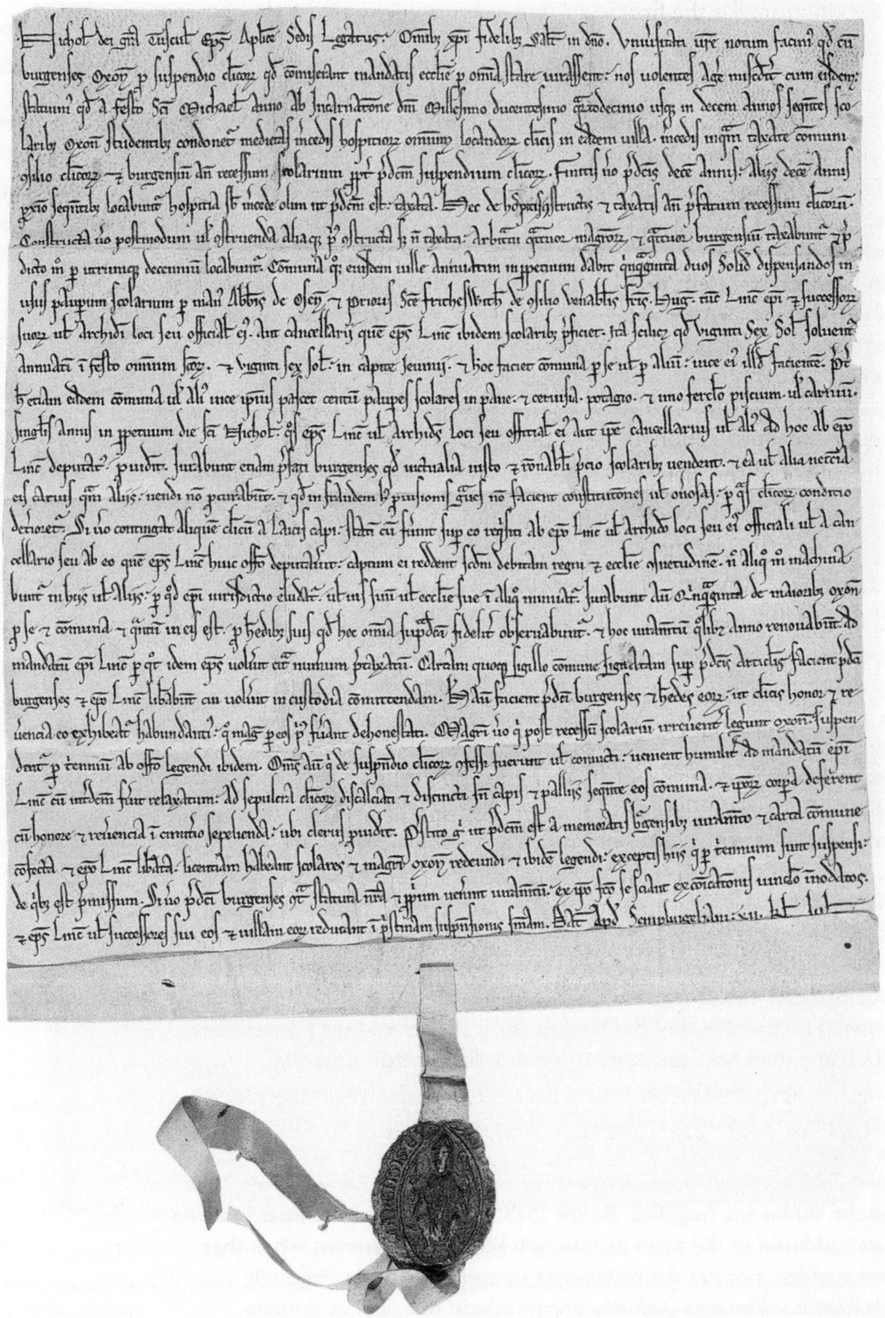

FIGURE 1.1 Bull of Nicholas de Romanis, cardinal bishop of Tusculum and papal legate in England, 20 June 1214. The bull formally settled the dispute between townsmen and students that had begun in 1209 and contains the first mention of a scholars' chancellor.

rate in 1209: for the first ten they were to be set at half their previous value, for the next maintained as they had been. The second provision demanded that the town pay a yearly fine of fifty-two shillings for the support of poor students and lay on an annual feast for a hundred of their number on St Nicholas' Day, probably the day on which the students had been hanged. Thirdly, the mayor was ordered to ensure that, thereafter, victuals and other necessities were available for students at a just price, and, fourthly, scholars were given immunity from lay jurisdiction:

> If a [scholar] cleric is arrested by laymen, they will immediately hand him over when it is demanded by either the bishop of Lincoln, the archdeacon of the town, his official, the chancellor or the person the bishop of Lincoln has deputed to this office.

This was an important provision, for it laid down that the schools' scholars were under the protection of the church and were to enjoy the primary privilege of members of the clergy. Oxford scholars thereby gained the same rights their Paris cousins had enjoyed for the previous twenty years. The deed concluded by demanding that fifty citizens swore, on behalf of the town and their heirs, to uphold the provisions, an oath which was to be retaken annually. In addition, as a sign of repentance, the town had to honour the bodies of the executed students by reburying them properly (see Figure 1.1).[4]

The significance of the document cannot be exaggerated. On the one hand, it makes clear that Oxford's schools must have had some rudimentary collective identity before 1209 because it talks of student rents before the exodus being decided 'by common agreement of the clerks and townsmen'. On the other hand, more importantly, the legate ensured that a fully-fledged *studium generale* would develop in the future. In that the rents of new lodging houses were to be assessed thereafter by a standing committee of four masters and four burgesses, the new university gained its first legally recognized officials. At the same time, through the annual fine, it received an income, if only one that had to be used to support students in need. Above all, by granting the students clerical immunity, the legate all but ensured that the university would develop its own judicial organization for dealing with malefactors. The deed stipulated various individuals to whom student criminals might be delivered, but the bishop would have been too distant and the archdeacon and his official too busy to police the schools. This left the chancellor or his deputy, who presumably resided in Oxford. The chancellor was definitely seen as a university not a diocesan official. Earlier in the document, when the legate discussed the procedure for disbursing the annual fine, he included among those to be consulted, 'the chancellor whom the bishop of Lincoln has put in charge of the scholars'; and the scholars' chancellor was again referred to in the clause establishing the annual fine.

---

[4] The document is transcribed in H. E. Salter, *Medieval Archives of the University of Oxford* (2 vols; OHS, lxx and lxxiii; Oxford, 1920–1), i. 2–4. A new transcription of the deed of 20 June is published in *Charters of Foundation and Early Documents*, ed. J. M. M. Hermans and Marc Nelissen (Groningen, 1994), pp. 106–7.

The office of scholars' chancellor may have been created for the first time as a result of the deed and be further evidence of the legate's role in promoting the institutionalization of the Oxford schools. The text is unclear whether bishops of Lincoln had already made such an appointment or whether they were being exhorted to do so in the future. A theologian called John Grim is described as *magister scholarum Oxonie* in the first decade of the thirteenth century, and may have held some sort of supervisory office in the gift of the bishop. But there is no mention of a scholars' chancellor in any record before the judgement of 1214. What is certain is that the bishop quickly took advantage of the terms of the deed to appoint an official who was given this title. Probably as early as September 1215 a scholar's chancellor was in post, in the person of Master Geoffrey de Lucy, who may have been the illegitimate son of the bishop of Winchester of that name. Lucy presided over the Oxford schools for only a couple of years before becoming a canon in London, and may not have been immediately replaced. From 1224, however, the new office was continually filled.

The appointment of a permanent episcopal chancellor was a major step in turning a collection of schools into a university. Doubtless the bishop's archdeacon had kept a weather eye on the town's schools in the twelfth century for signs of unorthodoxy, but he never attempted to take control. The new appointment gave the schools a visible head and a collective identity as an ecclesiastical institution under the bishop of Lincoln's tutelage. Presumably, the legate drew on his knowledge of what had happened at Paris, where the bishop was already exerting his authority over the nascent university through his personal diocesan chancellor. Unable to give Lincoln's chancellor a similar role, as Oxford was over a hundred miles from the bishop's seat, the legate had to invent a separate official to preside over the Oxford schools on the bishop's behalf. The appointment did the trick. By the second quarter of the thirteenth century the schools were being described as a *studium generale*, and by its end the Chancellor, long since a figure of real authority and status, was sealing documents with a seal bearing the inscription 'Sigillum officii cancellarii et Universitatis Oxonie' (see Figure 1.2).[5]

Although the deed threatened the town of Oxford with excommunication if its provisions were not maintained, the dispute of 1209 proved to be only the first in a long line of recorded moments of breakdown between town and gown in the thirteenth and the first half of the fourteenth century. Altercations and violence between citizens and scholars were commonplace during this period, culminating in the three days of mayhem that began on 10 February 1355, St Scholastica's Day. The spark on this occasion was a pub quarrel between the vintner and a party of clerks drinking in the Swyndlestock Tavern near Carfax. The vintner was hit over the head with a quart pot, the quarrel spilled over into the streets, and town and gown were soon at each other's throats. Unusually, the fighting did not fizzle out as

---

[5] The University had a common seal by 1249. The seal initially used carried the inscription *sigill' cancellarii Oxonie*. This was still being used in 1284 but was changed shortly afterwards: *HUO*, i. 33n.

FIGURE 1.2 The University's seal in use from the late thirteenth century until 1902. It depicts the Chancellor seated holding a book with three scholars on each side sat on a bench under a canopy. In front of the Chancellor are six other scholars seated on tiered benches, the two on the lower tier holding a book. See *Charters of Foundation*, p. 70.

night fell, but was renewed with increased violence the next day, when the citizens were reinforced by countrymen pouring in through the town gates, and the students were forced to take refuge in their lodgings. Their strategic retreat was to no avail. Their opponents began to set fire to the lodgings. On 12 February the bloodletting continued. The townsmen set about beating, wounding, and killing the occupants, pursuing them through the streets and dragging them from the churches where they sought sanctuary.

At no point, however, was the fledgling university's existence ever in danger, even when the violence was transparently the scholars' fault. Rather, as a privileged, corporate body it went from strength to strength. On such occasions, the king's chancellor would order a cessation of lectures, the clerks would leave, then the diocesan, or increasingly the king, would intervene to restore harmony and re-establish the schools by punishing the townsmen for their temerity. In the course of the thirteenth century, the new university became the favoured child of both church and state and everything was done to foster, not diminish, its independence. The king was particularly generous in releasing clerks from the need to appear in his or the town's courts. From 1244, the University's Chancellor was specifically given the power to oversee all cases involving contracts and loans between the scholars and citizens, a measure which particularly affected Oxford's flourishing Jewish community, from whom the clerks borrowed money. From 1251, it was agreed that the Chancellor's jurisdiction extended to all crimes committed by students, except the most heinous, which would be tried by the royal courts, a decision which was confirmed in 1258 when the king's justices itinerant in Oxford handed over to the University three scholars accused of seriously assaulting two laymen. More importantly, from 1290, with the exception of murder and riot, the Chancellor was empowered to oversee all criminal cases concerning scholars, even when the accused were citizens. The papacy, too, demonstrated its support for the young institution. From 1254, initially for a period of five years, Oxford scholars gained the right of *ius non trahi extra*. This was a privilege already ceded to Paris clerks nine years before and guaranteed that members of the University could not be summoned to appear as a witness or defendant for any reason whatsoever before an ecclesiastical court outside the town.

In the first half of the fourteenth century, the Chancellor's jurisdiction began to intrude even further on the powers of the town council in matters affecting the student body. In 1328, he gained the right to share with the mayor the latter's customary role of assaying the price of food and drink sold in the city, a right extended to produce marketed in the suburbs in 1336. Then, as a result of the St Scholastica Day riots, Edward III, by a royal charter of 27 June 1355, virtually handed the town over to the Chancellor altogether. The mayor and the corporation lost the right to play any part in taxing bread and drink, and the Chancellor was also put in charge of assaying the weights and measures used in the town and suburbs. Even keeping houses clean and streets repaired was brought within his purlieu. It was the king's view that a 'university peopled with so many nobles, foreigners and natives' needed a clean environment to thrive, and the Chancellor was empowered to compel the inhabitants to keep the town decent under threat of ecclesiastical censure.[6] The town council therefore was left only with jurisdiction over cases where both plaintiff and defendant were burgesses. It was also required to atone for its part in the riots by an annual show of submission to the University in St Mary's, the University's church.

Just as importantly, church and state allowed only one other centre of learning in thirteenth- and fourteenth-century England to develop into a *studium generale*. The emergence of Cambridge as a university, it must be said, is even more difficult to explain than Oxford's foundation, since there seem to have been no schools of importance in the Fenland town before the Oxford migration of 1209 and the town itself was insignificant. Still, whatever the reason—and it must have been connected in some way with the influence of the local diocesan, the bishops of Ely—Cambridge quickly developed similar institutions to those of its alma mater. It had a chancellor by 1225 and was recognized as a corporation of scholars by the pope as early as 1233. Thereafter, it too gradually developed into an independent enclave, gaining the right to police townsmen as much as students. Indeed, in 1318, on Edward II's request, the pope, John XXII, even published a bull formally giving Cambridge the status of a *studium generale*, an honour that Oxford never received.[7]

---

[6] Salter, *Medieval Archives*, i. 152–7 (charter, 27 June 1355).

[7] A. B. Cobban, 'Edward II, Pope John XXII and the University of Cambridge', *Bulletin of John Rylands Library*, xlvii (1964), 49ff. Papal confirmation of a university's status as a *studium generale* formally gave its graduates the right to teach in any other university without being examined. At the turn of the fourteenth century, the king and several bishops attempted to get the pope to grant the title to Oxford.

Cambridge's elevation, however, was an exception. In 1261, Henry III seems to have given permission to the still flourishing schools of Northampton to develop a corporate identity, but the king changed his mind three years later after the scholars had supported Simon de Montfort in the Second Barons' War. No other schools received any encouragement. In 1334–5, discontented northern students left Oxford and tried to set up a rival university at Stamford. The Chancellor and masters of Oxford complained to Edward III and the king immediately stepped in to preserve the monopoly position of the two extant universities. The schools of Northampton and Stamford were both in the diocese of Lincoln and their cause was unlikely to be championed by the bishop, who, from the beginning of the thirteenth century, had clearly decided to promote the Oxford *studium*, even at the expense of the schools in his own diocesan seat. Without royal or episcopal favour, rivals were inevitably doomed.

B. Organization

As the University of Oxford developed in the course of the thirteenth and the first half of the fourteenth centuries under the control of its ever more powerful Chancellor, it slowly acquired an administrative apparatus through which teaching could be organized and controlled and the student body policed. As befitted an institution which owed its inspiration to the nascent guild system, the University's heart was the assembly of regent or teaching masters, or Congregation, whose original function in the early thirteenth century was the inception of qualified students into the teaching fraternity. By about the 1230s, this body had become the supreme governing council of the *studium generale* and was meeting periodically to make new rules and regulations or statutes and choose at intervals the University's growing number of officials. From the early fourteenth century it divided in two. An enlarged body, which contained non-regent masters as well, assumed the role of the University's sovereign lawmaker and met occasionally as the *congregatio magna*, while the regent masters continued to meet regularly to deal with mundane academic business in the *congregatio minor*. At no stage did students have any say in decision-making, unless they were already masters of arts and were following courses in the higher faculties.

Regent masters in Congregation sat and voted by faculty, while the non-regents formed a separate block. Oxford in the late middle ages possessed five faculties—arts, theology, civil law, canon law, and medicine—but in reality there were only four, since masters in medicine were virtually non-existent. Of these, the most numerous were the masters of arts, who were also usually younger than the teachers in other faculties, given that arts were studied before other disciplines and few regents taught for long. The numerical power of the masters of arts was displayed in the fact that, by 1325, they met together separately in what was called the Black Congregation after the colour of their habits, and deliberated matters of concern apart from the other faculties. The arts' masters would have liked to obtain the right to veto decisions in the full Congregation that they disliked, but this was specifically denied them in 1357, although there seems to have been a gentlemen's agreement that nothing would be passed which the whole faculty was against.

In the first century and a half of the University's existence, Congregation principally legislated on matters of student discipline and granted graces to graduands who wanted to be released from some rule or other governing their admission to a degree. Oxford never had a proper constitution and was governed from the beginning by a set of customs, which slowly evolved and changed. Only from time to time was it felt necessary to turn these customs into written law. The first known statute dates from some time before 1231 and made it compulsory for students to matriculate under a regent master. Presumably, the nascent University was playing host to too many pseudo-scholars. The earliest datable statute, however, was only passed on 12 March 1253 and concerned the need for a master (or doctor) in theology to have first regented in arts in order to become eligible for the higher degree. Thereafter, statutes were promulgated fairly regularly but there was no attempt to register them in a specific book until 1313, during the chancellorship of Henry Harclay. Unfortunately, Harclay's collection is incomplete and few of the recorded statutes bear the date of their acceptance.

The most important of the officers of the University whom Congregation elected was the Chancellor, who normally acted for two years under a statute of 1322.[8] This official was intended to be an episcopal appointee, but, early on in the office's history, he became the University's nominee, chosen from among the resident regents in theology and law by a committee of regent masters drawn from the five faculties. Until the end of the thirteenth century, it was customary for the University to make its choice, then visit the bishop of Lincoln to seek his approbation. The appointment thus remained in the bishop's hands and no one could be foisted upon him. In 1295, when the University's representative informed Bishop Oliver Sutton that the committee had elected a new head, he was tartly told 'that chancellors hitherto had been only nominated not elected'.[9] In the course of the following century, however, the bishop was forced to accept that the choice was effectively in the hands of the University, as higher ecclesiastical authority undermined his position. When Bishop John Gynwell refused to confirm the appointment of William of Polmorva as Chancellor in 1350, the University appealed to the archbishop of Canterbury, who eventually admitted him himself. Finally, the pope came down on the side of the University, too, and in 1367 Urban V declared that episcopal confirmation was no longer necessary.

The Chancellor was thereafter the University's official alone and not part of the bishop of Lincoln's administrative bureaucracy. He was also, by this date, completely independent of the diocesan representative in the town, the archdeacon. The latter seems to have accepted that the Chancellor had jurisdiction over the University, including power of probate over the wills of scholars who died within its

[8] *Statuta*, pp. 121–2. He had to demit formally the day before Pentecost.   [9] *HUO*, i. 35, n.1.

precincts. The archdeacon continued, however, to claim authority over laymen who enjoyed the University's privileges because of their profession, such as scribes and parchment makers, and scholars with cure of souls in the town. Matters came to a head in the early fourteenth century, when the archdeacon, Cardinal Gaillard de la Motte, was an absentee and his powers were exercised by rapacious substitutes. The University began an action to ascertain where exactly the boundary between the two jurisdictions lay, and in 1345 accepted a judgement which confirmed the Chancellor's rights over all the University's members.

Next in importance among the officials appointed by Congregation were the Chancellor's right-hand men, the two Proctors, who were elected annually. They probably came into existence with the University but until the mid-thirteenth century were called rectors. Their duties were many and varied. They supervised the teaching and examinations; organized the ceremonial life of the University, hunted out and reported wrong-doing, and liaised with the town authorities over matters of mutual concern. They also looked after the University's finances, insignificant though they were at this date, and drew up an annual account for Congregation's perusal. The first Proctor who can be identified by name is Roger of Plumptone, who served in 1267–8. Both Proctors were elected annually by a complex and indirect system of voting from among the regents of arts, which ensured that the electoral committee represented a broad geographical constituency. As a result, the two Proctors tended to come from different parts of the kingdom, but neither was superior to the other by virtue of their place of origin: the title 'Senior' or 'Junior' Proctor was bestowed according to academic seniority. The Proctors not only served the Chancellor but kept an eye on his behaviour, and, by the statute of 1322, if not before, acquired the right to summon Congregation independently.[10]

Congregation also appointed the Proctors' permanent agents, the University's Bedels. By 1346 these were six in number, two each for the faculties of arts and theology and two for the combined faculties of law. Even more than the Proctors their duties were multifarious. On the one hand, they were the University's clerical officers and bailiffs, compiling lists, serving writs, and collecting fees. On the other, they were university servants, acting as ushers in the Chancellor's court or waiting at table when an incepting master gave a feast. Unlike the Chancellor and Proctors, they were paid for their services and were usually married laymen, whose whole family enjoyed the privileges of the University. As they served for long periods of time, they were the element of continuity in the University administration. One Nicholas of Kingham, for instance, held the position for twenty years in the mid-thirteenth century.

In addition, by 1350, the regent masters were expected to elect or appoint a bevy of less important administrators. The two Taxors, who determined the rents to be charged by the town's lodging houses, were again chosen from their own ranks. Arguably the oldest officials of the University, in that the office already existed in

---

[10] *Statuta*, pp. 123–5.

1209, they may also have doubled as proctors until the mid-thirteenth century. The Chaplain, who was responsible for saying the masses prescribed from time to time in the University's calendar, was also a regent master, as were the elected keepers of the ever growing number of university loan chests. Yet other regents served on examination boards or the annual judicial enquiry into student discipline and morality throughout the University, which had become customary by 1280. The University's four stationers, conversely, whose existence dates from at least 1346, were elected annually from within the town. Their primary duty was to ensure a supply of exemplars (called *peciae*) of the texts used in the schools, which they would lend to scholars. But they may also have supervised the whole bookmaking trade in Oxford.

In its broad outline, Oxford's nascent administrative apparatus mirrored the system of governance developing at a similar date in the University of Paris, which was scarcely surprising given the latter's greater academic significance and the number of English scholars who moved to and fro between the two. Oxford, however, was not a clone of the French university. In the first place, the University of Paris did not have its own independent chancellor. As its chancellor was also the bishop's chancellor, he was never an elected official but always an episcopal appointee, and his authority in the University of Paris was much reduced. Although his right to license its masters was never questioned, he always remained the bishop's man and was never considered to be the head of the corporation. Instead, this honour, in the course of the thirteenth century, fell to an official that Oxford and Cambridge never knew—the rector—elected every three months. Nor, as a result, did the clerks of the University of Paris ever enjoy immunity from outside ecclesiastical and secular jurisdictions. There was no equivalent of the Oxford Chancellor's court with its wide powers. Paris students could not even claim immunity from the secular arm in civil and criminal cases. Their only right was not to be subject to the justice of the city corporation but to appear before the Châtelet, the king's court of first instance in the French capital.

A second crucial distinction between Oxford and Paris lay in their respective faculty organizations. In Oxford, although there were distinctive subject faculties into which masters were incepted, the faculties had no separate corporative existence. There were no separate faculty boards with their own seal and finances, issuing statutes on behalf of their discipline. At Oxford, even if the masters of the faculty of arts might meet separately, there was only one corporation, embodied in Congregation. At Paris the position was very different. In the course of the first centuries of the French university's existence, the four subject areas—there was no faculty of civil law—gradually developed their own independent organization with their own officials and statutes. The university's unity was maintained through the rector and the rectoral committee, but the rectoral committee was quite unlike Congregation. It consisted simply of the three deans of the three higher faculties and four representatives of the faculty of arts, who met together regularly to discuss matters of mutual concern. The rector, too, could be a source of disunity as well as unity, for he wore two hats. Elected by the rectoral committee, he could only be a master of arts, even if he were studying in another faculty, and during his term of office he was also the head of the faculty of arts. This reflected the fact that at Paris, as at Oxford, the faculty of arts in the late middle ages was always the most populous.[11]

Thirdly, Oxford had no nations. Most of the first universities drew their students from a wide geographical area and from different kingdoms and duchies. For their own protection and welfare, foreign students in particular tended to live and mix with clerks from their own regions, and in time these loose associations developed into corporations. These were called nations for an obvious reason and might be societies of students or masters. Paris, the masters' university *par excellence* and with a peculiarly international profile, quickly established four for its masters of arts: the nations of Gaul (for students from France south of Paris and the Mediterranean world), Normandy, Picardy, and Germany (for students from northern Europe, including the British Isles). Each was headed by an elected proctor, who represented the nation to the outside world, organized lectures in the nation's 'schools', and occupied one of the four seats of the faculty of arts on the rectoral committee. Oxford, on the other hand, never officially recognized any geographical distinction between its scholars and remained a unified and homogeneous university. Nations threatened to develop in its early years, for there is evidence that, by the mid-thirteenth century, the students had divided themselves into two rival blocks—northerners and southerners (the latter including the Irish and the Welsh)—who frequently came to blows, notably in 1252. These student societies, however, never evolved into fully blown nations with visible officials, and in 1274 they were ordered to amalgamate to spare the University further violence. Although feuding between northerners and southerners did not immediately disappear, the sting in their regional rivalry was effectively drawn thereafter, by ensuring that the University's officials were elected from a broad regional base. The two Proctors, for instance, were nearly always a northerner and a southerner, although it would be wrong to see the office as developing out of these unofficial societies or in any respect analogous to the heads of the Paris nations.[12]

C. Consolidation, 1350–1530

After a century and a half's slow gestation, Oxford by the mid-fourteenth century was a fully fledged *studium generale*, and was already a peculiar English creation. An ecclesiastical institution like its continental sisters, it was yet remarkably in-dependent of its diocesan overlord and his officials, primarily the result of it taking root in a relatively unimportant town many miles distant from Lincoln. At the same time, thanks to the connivance of the king, it was largely protected from

[11] For the constitution and privileges of the University of Paris, see Hastings Rashdall, *The Universities of Europe in the Middle Ages*, ed. F. M. Powicke and A. B. Emden (3 vols; Oxford, 1936), i. 398–433.
[12] Pearl Kibre, *The Nations in the Medieval Universities* (Cambridge, MA, 1948).

secular authority, both municipal and royal. Oxford University was essentially an ecclesiastical liberty, a town within a town or a state within a state; its Chancellor in many respects enjoying a jurisdiction and authority analogous to the vast powers of the palatine bishops of Chester and Durham. Since Oxford's organizational structure was largely aped by Cambridge, it becomes possible to speak of the emergence, by 1350, of a specifically English university model, independent and self-contained, with its own institutional identity.

In the century and three-quarters from the death of Edward III (1377) to the start of the Henrician Reformation (1529), Oxford's governance underwent little further development. Largely untrammelled by the topsy-turvy of the bitter dynastic politics of the period, it remained an independent ecclesiastical enclave, even able to keep the archbishop of Canterbury at bay, except when a regent appeared to have stepped beyond the bounds of religious orthodoxy, such as John Wyclif.[13] The one significant change occurred in the role of the Chancellor. It had been anticipated in the 1214 judgement that the Chancellor might need a deputy, and it had become common practice for the Chancellor to appoint commissaries from time to time to help him process cases before his court, especially in his temporary absence.[14] Halfway through the fifteenth century, however, the office of Chancellor's commissary took on a novel and permanent status. Hitherto, the Chancellors had been resident masters who had held the office for two years. But in the second half of the fifteenth century, though still elected in due form, several became non-resident servants of the crown and served for long periods of time. The first non-resident was George Neville, archbishop of York, king's chancellor, and brother of Warwick the Kingmaker, who served as Chancellor of Oxford, with a short intermission, from 1461 to 1472. The first Chancellor to hold the office for life was John Russell, king's chancellor and bishop of Lincoln, who was elected in 1483. This development seems to have been initially generated by the belief that, in the troubled times following the overthrow of the Lancastrian dynasty and the death of Edward IV, there was a need to have a permanent representative of some stature near the king. Whatever the cause, it eventually became the normal state of affairs once the Tudors were on the throne, and necessitated the appointment of a permanent deputy, who soon became known as the Vice-Chancellor, even though the term was not officially adopted by the University until 1549.

Apart from the gradual establishment of the Vice-Chancellor as the University's chief official, the structure of governance remained largely unaltered after 1350. Although much more is known about how the University functioned after 1448, owing to the survival of Congregation's minute books, there were no other significant changes in the second half of the fifteenth and early sixteenth centuries.[15] In

---

[13] See, pp. 113–14, this volume.

[14] The legatine judgement had assumed the deputy would be appointed by the bishop of Lincoln, but as the Chancellor's power and independence grew this became inconceivable, whatever might have happened in the first half of the thirteenth century.

[15] The register survives from 1448–63 and from 1505 onwards.

fact, the University became an even more homogeneous institution. Not only did the faculties fail to develop further and challenge Congregation's authority, but Congregation's position was actually enhanced after 1450 since the Black Congregation of the Faculty of Arts declined in importance.[16] Grey areas were also clarified. That the *congregatio magna* and the *congregatio minor* had different functions was made clear from the beginning of the sixteenth century, when the former began to be called Convocation and its legislative sovereignty was confirmed.

This ever closer corporate unity was symbolized in the adoption of the coat of arms that the University still boasts today, which seems to have been in use from the late thirteenth century. The exact meaning of the design on the shield—an open book bearing the motto *dominus illuminatio mea* and seven seals between three crowns on a blue background—remains unclear. The book and its motto are self-evident but the seals may or may not refer to their counterpart in the Book of Revelation, and the crowns, which appeared on the arms of the king and martyr St Edmund, to the fictitious Anglo-Saxon origin of the University. The meaning of the design, however, is largely irrelevant. What is significant is the self-confidence that the adoption of a coat of arms displayed. All the first universities had their seals by which they authenticated their written acts, like any other corporation. But Oxford seems to have been the first *studium generale* to make such an aristocratic gesture as devising a coat of arms.

The University's privileged position as an ecclesiastical liberty similarly remained largely unchanged in the century and a half before the Reformation. Subsequent kings confirmed its jurisdictional autonomy, and Henry IV, in 1406, even accepted that felons and traitors should appear before a university officer rather than a royal judge, in this case the shadowy figure of the University's Steward, who was empowered to try scholars accused of major crimes in the town's guildhall with a jury chosen half by local royal officials and half by the University's Bedels.[17]

Unsurprisingly, the University's privileges were not always respected, for citizens continually objected to being subjected to the Chancellor's authority. During the chancellorship of Thomas Chace (1426–31), for instance, the University found itself cited before the king's Court of Common Pleas at Westminster, when its presiding official attempted to enforce his right to clean up the city's streets. However, despite the tendency of royal judges after 1400 to undermine ecclesiastical immunities wherever they could, the University's privileges held firm thanks to the backing of the crown. To all intents and purposes, until the Battle of Bosworth in 1485, the University continued to bask in the sun of royal pleasure, whoever was on the throne during the Wars of the Roses. In particular, the deposition of the House of Lancaster by Edward IV in 1461 had no adverse repercussions, in spite of the favour shown the University by members of the previous dynasty. Thanks, above all, to the

---

[16] On the assemblies in the second half of the period, see W. T. Mitchell (ed.), *Register of Congregations 1505–1517* (2 vols, OHS, new series, xxxvii; Oxford, 1998), i. 1–17.

[17] Salter, *Medieval Archives*, i. 231–4: charter, 2 June 1406. The Steward was usually a prominent layman.

astute election of George Neville as chancellor in 1461, the University suffered none of the problems faced by its Cambridge sister, which was seen as a Lancastrian bastion. Indeed, even when the Neville family fell foul of the king, ten years later, Edward's favour did not falter. While writing to the University in May 1472 telling them he was removing Neville as his own chancellor and asking the University to do the same, the king insisted that they had no need to make another political appointment for he wished to become their one and only protector.

All the same, the second half of the fourteenth century and the whole of the fifteenth century was an important period in Oxford's development as a university for it was then that it put down firm physical roots. In the twelfth and early thirteenth centuries the University had been a corporation of masters who happened to be based in the city of Oxford. The University owned no property in the town; lectures were given in rooms in private houses rented for the purpose; and the University held its meeting, debates, and examinations in the church of St Mary the Virgin or the chapter house of St Frideswide's Priory. This position changed only after 1320 when a meeting place for Congregation with a library above it was built on the north side of the chancel of St Mary's, thanks to the generosity of Thomas Cobham, bishop of Worcester (see Figure 1.3). This gave the University somewhere to meet in private and keep its records and chests, but it long remained the University's sole possession. It was not until a century later that the first moves

FIGURE 1.3 The original Congregation House in the church of St Mary the Virgin, built in the 1320s. Today it houses a café, and the present building is shorter than the original.

were taken to construct the University's own classrooms, when it was decided in 1423 to build a divinity school and launch an appeal for funds. Although the land for the building was acquired in 1427, the school took more than fifty years to complete and was not finally finished until 1488. By then, though, it was a much finer edifice than had ever been originally envisaged and was a powerful physical statement of the University's importance. Originally only intended to be a one-storey building, the decision was taken in 1444 to construct a library above the school, since the room provided a hundred years before could no longer house the University's growing number of manuscript books, which now included the 250 recently given by Duke Humfrey of Gloucester, the uncle of Henry VI. The task of completing the library and erecting the vault which would bear the load of its floor was eventually entrusted to one of Oxford's own master masons, William Orchard, in 1479. In the following nine years, Orchard created a late perpendicular masterpiece, which would provide sufficient space to house the University's manuscripts and books for the whole of the Tudor era (see Figure 1.4).

FIGURE 1.4 The Divinity School vault, completed in the late 1480s by William Orchard of Oxford. The School with its large windows and fan vault is a particularly fine example of the late perpendicular style then in vogue.

It was in this period too that Oxford's colleges made a visible imprint on the urban landscape. Oxford's first colleges were established in the third quarter of the thirteenth century and by 1350 there were eight: six for poor students and two for Benedictine monks. They had all been set up, however, in existing properties and were not obviously different from all the other houses, halls, and hostels in which townsmen and scholars could be found. Only Merton College, established in 1274, had begun to erect new buildings on its site in St John's Lane. With the foundation of New College towards the end of the fourteenth century, the situation radically changed, for its founder, William of Wykeham, bishop of Winchester, provided his scholars with two specially constructed quadrangles and a purpose-built chapel, dining hall, and library from the beginning.[18] New College set the tone for Oxford's collegiate architecture thereafter, and by the time of the Henrician Reformation, Oxford's richest colleges completely outshone the University in terms of the grandeur and visibility of their buildings.

Nonetheless, Oxford's stability and prosperity in the fifteenth century should not be exaggerated. In the first place, the University was no longer as free from the winds of competition as it had been in the first century of its existence. At the turn of the sixteenth century, Cambridge was still the junior partner but it was a much more important institution than it had been hitherto and it had finally escaped from Oxford's shadow. Moreover, there were no longer only two universities in the British Isles. Although there were still only two *studia generale* in the dominions of the king of England, three had been founded in Scotland through the initiative of local bishops: St Andrews (1411), Glasgow (1451), and Aberdeen (1495). Indeed, had the Lancastrian settlement of northern and western France gone to plan, Oxford would have been only one of four universities under an English prince. In order to encourage his French subjects to study within his dominions, Henry VI had established new universities at Caen (1432) and allowed the archbishop to establish a papal *studium* at Bordeaux (1441).[19] Given the fact, too, that the English occupied Paris in the first half of the 1430s, there must have been a time in the second quarter of the fifteenth century when the masters of Oxford feared that the status of their university was under threat. In consequence, they must have secretly rejoiced at the rapid collapse of the Lancastrian position in France in the early 1450s.

Secondly, the University's fiscal position was always shaky. It had no endowment as such, besides a few houses in the city it had been left, and its income came chiefly from the fines paid by those incepting for degrees, seeking graces, or making amends for breaches of discipline. In the early thirteenth century, when virtually the only source of revenue was the annual tribute offered by the town under the settlement of 1214, the University's income was £5 at the most. In the following

---

[18] See Chapter 3, section C, this volume.
[19] Lyse Roy, *L'Université de Caen aux XVe et XVIe siècles: identité et représentation* (Education and Society in the Middle Ages and the Renaissance, 24; Leiden and Boston, 2006), ch. 1.

centuries, receipts rose but the amount collected was never large. Even in the second half of the fifteenth century, for which there are accurate figures, the University's income hardly ever topped £100 and sometimes dropped below £40, as in 1471/2, the year the Lancastrians made their final bid to unseat Edward IV, when receipts fell to £13. Such sums were paltry. For all its pretensions as an ecclesiastical liberty, the University cut a poor figure compared with a bishop or abbot. The local abbot of Abingdon enjoyed a far larger income.[20]

As far as the day-to-day life of the University was concerned, this relative penury did not matter. Beyond wining and dining visiting dignitaries, Oxford had few expenses since its officials were paid by receiving a portion of the fines and fees they collected. In normal years, therefore, the University ran a surplus. Problems arose, however, as soon as the masters were confronted with extraordinary expenditure. The Divinity School took so long to complete because the University could not finance the structure itself. It relied almost entirely on donations to complete the project and these were difficult to solicit. Work on the building got off the ground in the 1450s thanks to the £333 6s. 8d. which the University received from the estate of Cardinal Beaufort, Henry VI's step-uncle. But this proved insufficient and the construction was only finished when Thomas Kempe, bishop of London, made a large gift in 1478. Obviously, the University could not afford to become entangled in lengthy and costly litigation in defence of its privileges. Penury was of little significance provided the crown protected the University against lay plaintiffs and the inclinations of his own common-law judges. If the king ever withdrew his favour, the University could soon be in serious trouble.

This was what threatened to happen in the reign of Henry VII. The first Tudor was a usurper who was highly suspicious of any institution or jurisdiction that claimed to be outside the king's law, especially if his enemies took shelter within its boundaries. Thus, in 1487, when Robert Stillington, bishop of Bath and Wells, took refuge in Oxford after being accused of plotting to depose the new king, the University found itself subject to the full force of Henry's wrath. On this occasion, the king did not invade an ecclesiastical liberty, as he had done two years before, when he had two lords who were under the protection of the abbot of Abingdon apprehended. Nonetheless, he made it clear that the University would forfeit its privileges, unless it immediately released the prelate into his custody:

> [Y]ff ye of obstynacye refuse to obeye thys our commaundement, we shall not only send thyther such power as oure entent in thys partie shalbe undowtly executed and fulfyulled, but also provide for the punnishment off your disobeissaunce in suche sharpe wyse as shalbe to the ferfull example of them so presumyng or attemptyng heeaftyr.[21]

---

[20] When dissolved by Henry VIII, the revenue of Abingdon Abbey was judged to be £1,876 10s. 9d.

[21] Henry Anstey, *Epistolae academicae Oxon. (Registrum F): a collection of documents illustrative of academical life and studies at Oxford in the fifteenth century* (2 vols, OHS, xlix; Oxford, 1898), ii. 517: 22 Mar. 1487.

Although the University initially tried to stand firm, it could see the way the wind was blowing under the new dynasty and eventually gave way. Stillington was escorted to Windsor Castle by the University's Steward.

Henry VII was also keen to ensure that the University elected officials to his liking. The incumbent Chancellor was another Yorkist bishop, Russell of Lincoln, and when he eventually died in 1494, the king told the University to elect in his place either the bishop of Chester or the bishop of Rochester, 'sithens they both be of yow and browght upp amonge yow'.[22] This time, however, the masters defied the king, as they did on other occasions when he tried to dictate their choice of officer. Instead, they elected another alumnus, Cardinal John Morton, the king's own chancellor, to head the University, doubtless assuming he would be just as acceptable and a far better protector at court. In the short term their defiance had no obvious repercussions. But Tudor monarchs had long memories and Henry would have stored up this and other slights to his authority. In 1506, the masters' earlier tenacious defence of their independence almost led to the scholars being exiled and the University closed. In that year, northerners and southerners came to blows and three students were killed, leading the king's council to contemplate dramatic action. That the royal hand was stayed seems to have been due to the influence of Morton's successor as the University's Chancellor, Archbishop William Warham of Canterbury, who also held the king's official seal.[23] If it were useful in the Yorkist era to keep a permanent representative at court, it was essential once the Tudors were on the throne.

---

[22] Ibid., p. 624.
[23] Warham reminded the University of his role in an exchange of letters in 1522: W. T. Mitchell (ed.), *Epistolae academicae, 1508–1596* (OHS, new series, xxxiii; Oxford, 1980), pp. 138–41.

CHAPTER 2

A University of Clerics

A. The Scholars

THE privileges enjoyed by Oxford's students and masters reflected the fact that the University, in the first centuries of its history, was an ecclesiastical institution primarily serving the needs of the Catholic Church in England. As a result, those attending its schools were called clerks and were expected to sport the tonsure as a mark of their clerical status. This is not to say that laymen were never to be found in the University's midst. Indeed, a legend has it that Oxford was even attended by no less a person than Edward I. But lay students were few in number and scarcely visible in the pre-Reformation era. Some students deserted their clerical calling in later life, usually when a turn of fortune's wheel left them heir to a large estate. The marcher lord Edmund Mortimer, for instance, was an Oxford student before he unexpectedly inherited his family's lands in 1282. Usually, though, members of the late medieval university came to Oxford expecting to spend their lives in the service of the church, even if, in the end, many never entered the priesthood, and a small number, whatever their status, swapped masters and served the crown.

Oxford's clerics were divided into two groups: seculars and regulars. When Oxford first began to develop as a centre of learning in the twelfth century, the student population would have overwhelmingly belonged to the secular clergy. The regular orders in catholic Europe showed little interest in supporting the new schools springing up across the continent from about 1050, and the Austin canons at St Frideswide's and Oseney were no exception. From the second quarter of the thirteenth century, however, the position quickly changed. The foundation of the orders of friars—monks who would go out into the world to preach, teach, and heal—heralded the arrival of a new type of regular cleric with an enthusiasm for learning, only too willing to set up their convents in university towns. Dominicans were to be found in the University from 1221, the Franciscans three years later, the Carmelites from 1256, and the Austin friars from 1266–7. Inspired by their example, the contemplative orders also began to send intellectually promising monks to Oxford towards the end of the thirteenth century, and, from 1339, the larger houses of the Austin canons were expressly required to do so by the pope.[1] Although their numbers never seem to have matched the friars', several contemplative orders were eventually well represented in the University, especially the Benedictines. As a section of the student community with a peculiar commitment to the holy life through their vows, the regulars inevitably formed a group apart. We know the names of some 15,000 scholars who passed through Oxford between 1200 and 1500. On average, 17 per cent were monks, a figure that rose to 24 per cent in the years 1360 to 1420.[2]

The secular clerics were divided in turn between the majority in minor and the minority in major orders. The former were generally clerks who went up to Oxford in their late teens and entered the priesthood, if at all, only when they eventually left the University. The latter were normally older scholars studying in the higher faculties who had been ordained during the course of their stay, or clergymen who had decided to gain a higher education mid-career. According to the constitution *Cum ex eo*, of Pope Boniface VIII in 1298, all priests had the right to study and ask their bishop to be relieved of their parish duties for a few years. Although the English parish clergy did not avail themselves of this opportunity in large numbers, there seems to have always been a steady trickle from every diocese. Bishop Thomas Hatfield of Durham, for one, allowed thirty of his clergy to take study leave during his episcopate in the third quarter of the fourteenth century.[3]

Establishing how many clerks there were at Oxford at any one time during the first three centuries of its history is impossible. The University did not record matriculands before the late sixteenth century, and before 1500 even a partial annual degree list can be constructed only between 1448 and 1463 due to the loss of Congregation's registers apart from those years.[4] It has been customary to claim that numbers rose steadily over the thirteenth century to reach a high point of some 1,500 around 1300, and that they then declined to about 1,000 in 1450, thanks principally to the effect of the Black Death of 1348, which reduced the English population by at least a third.[5] As the population continuously fell prey to fresh attacks of the disease across the following century, and did not probably begin to recover until the late 1400s, it must have been difficult for Oxford to rebuild its numbers. On the other hand, it is now thought that the second figure is too low and that there may have been as many as 1,700 scholars at Oxford in the mid-fifteenth century, or even more, since this figure does not include those living in monastic houses or seculars not dwelling in halls and colleges, as they were supposed to do from the early fifteenth century.[6] If so, and there really was a decline from the first part of the fourteenth century, there must have been far more than 2,000 clerks in the University on the eve of the Black Death. This is

---

[1] Simon Forde, 'The Educational Organisation of the Augustinian Canons in England and Wales and their University Life at Oxford, 1325–1448', *HU*, XIII (1994), 26–7.

[2] T. H. Aston, 'Oxford's Medieval Alumni', *Past and Present*, 74 (1977), 16–17.

[3] Even schoolmasters in minor orders were sometimes given permission to intercalate for a few years. One Boryngton, master of the high school at Exeter, was allowed to go to Oxford for two years in 1438: see Nicholas Orme, *English School Exercises, 1420–1530* (Toronto, 2013), p. 149.

[4] Aston, 'Oxford's Alumni', pp. 4–5.   [5] H.E. Salter, *Medieval Oxford* (Oxford, 1936), pp. 107–10.

[6] Aston, 'Oxford's Alumni', pp. 6–8.

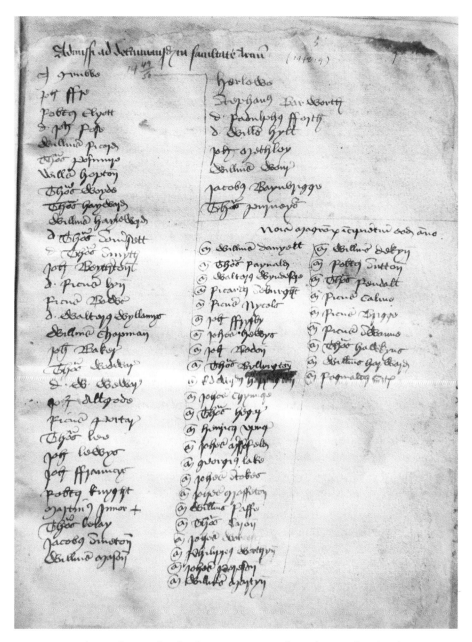

FIGURE 2.1 The graduation list for the year 1449–50, the only complete list that survives for the University before 1500. The illustration depicts the names of those determining and incepting in the faculty of arts.

plausible in that Cambridge, at this date, offered little competition. In the late fourteenth century, it seems to have contained only 400 to 700 scholars, but then suddenly experienced a burst of growth, taking numbers to 1,500 in about 1450.[7]

[7] T. H. Aston, G. D. Duncan, and T. A. R. Evans, 'The Medieval Alumni of the University of Cambridge', *Past and Present*, 86 (1980), 26–7.

A *studium generale* of 1,700 students was a large university in the late middle ages, and both Oxford and Cambridge in the fifteenth century must have been two of the most populous universities in Europe. The new *studia* created after 1350 often had only a couple of hundred scholars and many of the original foundations were not large institutions, even before the ravages of the Black Death. However, the English universities were far from being the most frequented on the eve of the Reformation and were dwarfed by the University of Paris. In the hundred years between 1450 and 1550 as many scholars matriculated at Paris each year as Oxford could boast *in toto*. In the period 1520–50 the number oscillated between 1,550 and 1,750, and in 1464 it was as high as 2,200. The disparity is confirmed when the number of scholars taking a degree in the two universities is compared. At Oxford in 1449–50—the one year before 1500 for which we have a complete list from all five faculties—there were twenty-six MAs, forty-one bachelors in either civil or canon law, fourteen bachelors in theology, and one in medicine (see Figure 2.1). At Paris in the second half of the fifteenth century, the numbers taking the baccalaureate in the higher faculties were not considerably higher: on average some sixteen in theology, fifty in canon law, and three in medicine. But there were far more MAs awarded per annum—usually around 200. Even making allowances for the fact that the Paris records of graduation exist in their entirety and 1449/50 may be an unrepresentative year, it is hard not to conclude that Paris, at least as an arts university, was in a league of its own.[8]

It can be assumed, too, that Oxford was always the smaller of the two universities throughout the first three centuries of their existence. Oxford's size was limited by its intake. The evidence from the list of the 15,000 scholars known to have passed through the University in the late middle ages reveals that Oxford's students and masters were predominantly English. A small proportion came from Ireland and Wales, and a few from Scotland (4 per cent in total), but hardly anyone visited the University from the continent of Europe, the largest contingent being chiefly from Italy and mainly friars. The scholar who travelled the farthest was probably the Franciscan Peter de Candia, who came from Crete and ended his days as Pope Alexander V in 1410.[9] In fact, Oxford was not just an English university, but a regional one, in that it drew its clientele predominantly from the south and west of the country, while Cambridge took the lion's share from the north and east. It is not surprising then that the northerners and southerners did not develop into separate nations: there must have been too few northerners after 1300 to make this a real possibility. Paris, in contrast, was a truly international university on the eve of the Reformation. Although about 80 per cent of matriculands and graduates in arts came from northern France, there were always a significant number of scholars from the Midi and other countries. At least 10 per cent of bachelors in canon law, for instance, came from outside France in the fifteenth century.[10] Admittedly, the

[8] L. W. B. Brockliss, 'Patterns of Attendance at the University of Paris, 1400–1800', *Historical Journal*, 21: 3 (1978), 512–15 (tables, all faculties).
[9] Aston, 'Oxford's Alumni', pp. 21–2.   [10] Brockliss, 'Attendance', pp. 500 and 502.

majority of foreigners came from northern Europe, especially the Netherlands, where there was no university before the foundation of Leuven in 1425.[11] Nonetheless, there can be no gainsaying the fact that Paris recruited its students from all over the continent on the eve of the Reformation: in the period 1494–1531, its arts graduates even included twenty-four Hungarians.[12] In earlier centuries, when the number of European universities was far fewer, its international profile must have been much greater.

On the other hand, if the English universities were in reality regional institutions, their significance among Europe's medieval *studia generalia* is emphasized by the fact that, for the most part, they retained the students they attracted. Many of Europe's *studia* were staging posts on the ambitious scholar's educational odyssey. He would attend his local university for a couple of years before moving on to one of the handful of highly respected academies. The phenomenon of the wandering medieval scholar should not be exaggerated, but the *peregrinatio academica* did exist.[13] The English universities, however, lost few of their clerks. Only 735 of Oxford's 15,000 recorded scholars in the late middle ages attended another institution, even to give a lecture. In the twelfth century, Englishmen had flocked in particular to Paris to taste the learning of its schools, but, thereafter, crossing the English Channel gradually lost its appeal. Although a number of prominent Oxford masters transferred to Paris in the thirteenth and early fourteenth centuries, such as Duns Scotus, the Hundred Years War seems to have severed the links almost entirely. In 1488–99, 137 scholars proceeded from Oxford to another university, compared with sixteen who came to it from elsewhere. Barely any went to Paris. Thirty-eight moved to one of the Italian *studia*, mainly Bologna, to study law. But most went off to Cambridge—further indication of the Fenland university's growing importance.[14]

Oxford and Cambridge, then, were largely self-contained universities in the first centuries of their existence. In this respect, they were entirely different from the new Scottish universities of the fifteenth century whose students frequently finished their education elsewhere. It was the Scots, not the English, who were to be found in Paris in considerable numbers in the years after 1450. Understandably reluctant to pursue their studies in the universities of the 'auld' enemy, they moved on from St Andrews, Glasgow, and Aberdeen to the Latin Quarter, and became the dominant group in the German nation. In the century and a quarter before 1554, 772 scholars from the British Isles appear in the extant matriculation and graduation registers of the University of Paris, the large majority studying arts. Of these, 696 were Scots, seventy-one English, and five Irish, the Scots, in other words, forming 90 per cent of the cohort, despite the fact that the population of their homeland (about half a million) was only a fifth of England's. In the same period, too, a largely different

---

[11] Leuven was the one new foundation with a large number of students: it had 1,821 scholars in 1526: Edward de Maeschalck, 'The Relationship between the City of Louvain in the Fifteenth Century', *HU*, IX (1990), 57.

[12] A. L. Gabriel, *The University of Paris and its Hungarian Students and Masters during the Reign of Louis XII and François Ier* (Texts and Studies in the History of Medieval Education, XVII; Notre Dame, IN, 1986).

[13] Hilde de Ridder-Symoens, 'Mobility', in HUIE, i, ch. 9. [14] Aston, 'Oxford's Alumni', pp. 25–7.

group of Scots also studied at the new University of Leuven, although in this case their preponderance among visitors from the British Isles was not as great. From 1426 to 1554, 357 Scots appear in the Leuven matriculation register compared with 176 Englishmen and nine students from Ireland. The sheer size of the Scottish exodus suggests attending a university on the continent was a necessary career move on the part of ambitious Caledonians, and this is confirmed by what can be known about their future lives. Of the 696 Scots at the University of Paris, 156 gained an important ecclesiastical office in the Scottish church, twenty-four becoming bishops, and one Robert Blackadder (or Blacader), who took an MA in the French capital in 1465, archbishop of Glasgow. The English contingent, conversely, seems to have benefited little from their sojourn abroad. The only one of the seventy-one to become a bishop was the Oxford MA Richard Pate, who was appointed to the diocese of Worcester by the pope in 1541 and eventually deprived by Elizabeth.[15]

Little is known precisely about the social origins of Oxford scholars in the late middle ages but the majority must have come from families with sufficient surplus income each year to bear the loss of a young adult's labour and pay for his upkeep without undue hardship. In the fifteenth century, when the wage of an artisan ranged from 2d. to 5d. a day, a scholar would need from £2 to £3 a year to stay at the University.[16] On the other hand, few scholars appear to have come from the top of the social ladder. The sons of the landowners of England in particular ought to have left plenty of traces of their presence at the University. But this was not the case. Sons of titled noblemen were particularly thin on the ground. Aristocrats who did pass through Oxford in the late middle ages, such as George Neville, mentioned in Chapter 1, were a rare species. Between 1307 and 1485, less than a hundred sons of peers are known to have attended Oxford. Even the sons of wealthy townsmen were not particularly prominent. The one detailed account of the social background of Oxford's students in the late middle ages is based on a study of the 937 scholars who passed through New College in the years c.1380–c.1500. Even though it is assumed that New College fellowships, like those in other late medieval colleges, were held by scholars who were a cut above the rest, still only 12.5 per cent of the cohort came from the gentry and 21.7 per cent from the middle to upper ranks of townsmen.[17] The University can never have been teeming with figures such as the future

[15] L. W. B. Brockliss, 'British Catholic Students in Paris', in Dominique Julia and Jacques Revel (eds), *Les universités européennes du XVIe au XVIIIe siècle. Histoire sociale des populations étudiantes*, vol. ii (Paris, 1989), pp. 578–9, 607 (n.14); E. J. H. Reusens, J. Wils, and A. H. Schillings, *Matricule de l'université de Louvain, 1425–1797* (Brussels, 1903–58), vols i–v.

[16] J. M. Fletcher and C. A. Upton, 'The Cost of Undergraduate Study at Oxford in the Fifteenth Century: The Evidence of Merton College "Founder's Kin"', *History of Education*, xiv (1985), 1–20.

[17] Guy F. Lytle, 'The Social Origins of Oxford Students in the Late Middle Ages: New College, c.1380– c.1510', in J. Ijsewijn and J. Paquet (eds), *The Universities in the Late Middle Ages* (Louvain, 1978), pp. 426–54. According to the statutes of foundation, college fellowships and scholarships were supposed to be for poor students but this did not mean scholars from the bottom of society. Given the preference accorded to founders' kin, it can be assumed they were meant to be drawn from families of influence but limited wealth. There were also very few places on the college foundations compared with the number of scholars thought to be at Oxford in the late middle ages: competition would have been fierce and influence and patronage essential to secure a vacant position. On the size of college fellowships, see pp. 68 and 76–7, this volume.

archbishop of Canterbury, John Stratford, a DCL about 1312, who was the son of a leading townsman of Shakespeare's birthplace.

The majority of scholars, in consequence, would have been the sons of prosperous yeomen and husbandmen. Before the Black Death some would even have been bondmen, given the fact that serfs were sometimes richer than freemen. Although, in theory, the unfree could not take minor orders, let alone pursue a clerical career, such students would have gambled on being released from servitude in the fullness of time, as happened in 1312 to Walter of Heighington, a fellow of Merton College and erstwhile bondman of the bishop of Durham. After the Black Death and the subsequent collapse of serfdom, most scholars would have had fathers who were small landowners or bailiffs, reeves, and manorial lessees.

Some scholars from a poorer background did manage to attend the University but they did so only by attracting support from outside their family. Some enjoyed the favour of a local patron. Richard of Wallingford, for instance, later Benedictine abbot of St Albans, was the son of a blacksmith who died when he was 10. He came to Oxford about 1310 with the help of the local Benedictine prior, William Kirkby, who, in return, seems to have expected him to enter the order. Other students from poor families managed to get to Oxford by becoming servants to the well-to-do, while others found employment in hostels and halls and in the growing number of colleges. Until the reign of Henry VIII, some poor seculars even took a leaf from the mendicants' book and survived by begging. Provided such students were licensed and were genuine scholars this was a strategy given the University's seal of approval.[18]

Genuinely poor students at Oxford would have always struggled to keep a toehold in the University. Unlike many of the new universities in the Holy Roman Empire, the two English *studia* made no special provision for the indigent. In Germany, the poor were treated as a special category and given remission from lecture and graduation fees, provided they reimbursed the university when they once had the means. At Freiburg, Erfurt, and Vienna they were also provided with cheap lodgings.[19] Nothing similar was done for the indigent at Oxford and Cambridge. At best there was a cushion for those temporarily down on their luck. Initially, the financially embarrassed had little recourse except to the pawnbroker and the loan shark, for the University had no resources of its own, apart from the loan chest set up in 1240 by Bishop Grosseteste from the proceeds garnered from the fine levied on the town by the papal legate in 1214. After the expulsion of the Jews in 1290 and the consequent loss of short-term credit, the situation improved: fourteen loan chests were founded over the next seventy years, followed by a further four between 1432 and 1457. The donation of loan chests was one way in which women played a part in the late medieval university, as a number were set up

---

[18] *Registrum cancellarii oxoniensis, 1434–1469*, ed. H. E. Salter (2 vols, OHS xciii–iv; Oxford, 1932), ii. 40: example from 1461.

[19] J. M. Fletcher, 'Wealth and Poverty in the Medieval German Universities', in J. R. Hale, J. R. L. Highfield, and B. Smalley (eds), *Europe in the Late Middle Ages* (Evanston, IL, 1965), pp. 410–36.

by widows, notably Ela Longespee, dowager countess of Warwick, who endowed the Warwick chest in 1293. Yet, however welcome such chests, they could only be used by students with a modicum of material property: beneficiaries had to leave, as pledges, items worth more than the amount they borrowed.[20]

The majority of Oxford's scholars, whatever their background or status, would have been studying arts. Although it would be expected that scholars who engaged in a higher study would have left the deeper trace, they form only 31 per cent of Oxford's 15,000 recorded alumni. In reality, then, the percentage must have been much lower, perhaps no more than 20 per cent. Late medieval Oxford—like Cambridge, Paris, and most northern European universities with the obvious exception of Orléans—was essentially an arts *studium*.[21] Moreover, at Oxford, as at its sister universities, the large majority of arts students (perhaps as many as five-sixths) left without ever taking even their first degree, the BA, let alone staying on to become a magister.[22] Only Oxford's friars were attracted to higher studies in significant numbers, a reflection of the fact they had often read arts elsewhere, at another university or in their convent. Attendance in Oxford's four higher faculties was also unbalanced. The most populous was theology, followed a long way behind by civil and canon law, while the faculty of medicine scarcely existed.

In the universities of Italy and France south of the Loire, it was the law rather than the arts faculty which usually had the largest number of scholars.[23] But in that part of Europe the civil law was the law of the land. England and northern Europe were common-law areas, and the common law was not a university discipline. Although in the thirteenth and fourteenth centuries common lawyers could learn at Oxford the basic clerical skills they needed for drawing up deeds and documents, the common-law as such was never taught. The Oxford law schools always had a clientele, for there were still many openings for canon and civil lawyers in the administration of church and state. Indeed, when the canonists and civilians were grouped together, they slightly outnumbered the theologians. But lawyers never formed more than 10 per cent of the total. Nor, as in many northern European universities on the continent, did their presence increase towards the end of the period. In the course of the fifteenth century, would-be common lawyers in northern Europe were encouraged to see the civil law as a law of reason or equity which would assist in the interpretation of their own customary and state law, with the result that the number of laymen studying in the law faculties started to grow. In England, on the other hand, there was never a comparable attempt to subordinate

---

[20] A. B. Cobban, 'English University Benefactors in the Middle Ages', *History*, 86: 283 (2001), 299–301.

[21] Aston, 'Oxford Alumni', p. 8. At Cologne in the fifteenth century, 20 per cent of the matriculated students were in the higher faculties; in Paris, the figure may have been as low as 5 per cent: Rainer C. Schwinges, *Deutscher Universitätsbesucher im 14. Und 15. Jahrhundert: Studien zur Sozialgeschichte des alten Reiches* (Stuttgart, 1986), p. 468; Brockliss, 'Attendance', pp. 513–15. For Orléans, see p. 8, this volume.

[22] In 1449/50, only forty nine students became a BA. Even where students in arts were on a college foundation, so had their studies paid for, there was significant drop out: two in seven New College fellows left before their BA and between a quarter and a third of the BAs never became a master.

[23] With the exception of Montpellier, which specialized in medicine: see L. Dulieu, *La Médecine à Montpellier*, vol. 1: *Le moyen âge* (Avignon, 1975).

common law to Roman jurisprudence, and barristers and judges in the crown's courts at the end of the middle ages were not expected to have a law degree. In the fifteenth century, those wanting instruction in the common law could find it in London at the Inns of Court and had no need to attend Oxford and Cambridge.[24]

The dominance of the Oxford arts faculty meant that the University was primarily filled with young men in their late teens and early twenties. Although the University never laid down any regulations about the age of entry, it is clear from the restrictions included in college statutes and enacted at Cambridge that undergraduates in arts were young men rather than children. Robert Hungerford, later Lord Hungerford and Moleyns, who attended Oxford in 1437/8 when 6 or 7, was an exception. The law contingent was also relatively young. Students of theology and medicine were expected to be masters of arts and would thus have been in their mid- to late twenties. Civil and canon lawyers, in contrast, could in theory begin their studies without passing through the faculty of arts at all. It is probable that most spent a couple of years there, but not the seven years required to gain an MA.[25] Oxford and Cambridge were ecclesiastical liberties full of adolescents.

B. Student Life

Entrants to the University had to be proficient in Latin grammar—otherwise, it would have been impossible for them to follow the lectures and disputes. Presumably, the more affluent would have been tutored at home, while others would have learnt their Latin with a parish priest. But many would have spent several years at a local school, either one of the old cathedral schools or one of the new grammar schools, specifically established in the second half of the period to provide pre-university education. The most important of the new foundations—Winchester and Eton (set up in 1387 and 1440/1)– were large, endowed boarding establishments intended as feeder schools to New College, Oxford, and King's College, Cambridge, respectively. Most, though, were modest establishments with a single master providing cheap education for day boys. The University itself employed two grammar masters to instruct local children, but these became redundant in the late fifteenth century with the creation of Magdalen College School, founded by William Waynflete, bishop of Winchester. Thereafter, Oxford had her own grammar school, which quickly gained a reputation as a centre of humanist studies.[26]

A scholar's arrival at Oxford in these early centuries was not marked by any ceremony, since at this date he did not matriculate. All that was demanded was that he enter his name on the register of the master whose lectures he intended to

---

[24] J. H. Baker, 'The English Legal Profession, 1450–1550', in W. Prest (ed.), *Lawyers in Early Modern Europe and America* (London, 1981), pp. 16–41.

[25] For the length of time required to gain a degree in each faculty, see pp. 87–8 and 90, this volume.

[26] Nicholas Orme, *Medieval Schools from Roman Britain to Renaissance England* (London, 2006). For Magdalen College School, see pp. 82–3 and 119, this volume.

follow.[27] Nor were scholars required to dress in a particular way. As clerks they were expected to adopt sober garb, but there were no specific regulations as to the colour and cut of the robe. Over the course of time, graduates became distinguished by the trimmings attached to their gowns, but simple students were hard to distinguish from ordinary citizens. It was only in the sixteenth century that members of the University were required to appear in black. Until then, what marked out a scholar was the tonsure without which he could not claim any of the privileges associated with his status. Oxford students in the late middle ages could be as fashion-conscious as any courtier. In about 1313, a statute had to be passed banning masters from lecturing in extravagant footwear, while twenty years later the archbishop of Canterbury denounced clergy and students alike for powdering and curling their hair, bedecking their fingers with rings, and wearing luxurious cloaks and girdles.[28]

In the thirteenth century, Oxford's students and teachers found lodgings where they could in and around the town. Regent masters tended to live within the city walls, while many students congregated outside the north gate, where rents were cheap and the University's schools within easy reach. Most students, whatever their age, lived unsupervised. They might rent a room in a townsman's house; or a group, usually students from the same region, might take over the whole property. Either way, they were known as 'chamberdeacons'. From the beginning, however, some students lived with a graduate master, who presumably exercised some sort of oversight of their lives and was also probably their teacher. By the end of the thirteenth century, this arrangement had become common. These embryonic student hostels became known as halls (aulae)—after the large, high room where the inhabitants met together for meals and other activities—and the graduate lessee, the principal. A similar development took place at Paris and Cambridge, where the hostels were called paedagogia and hospicia, and in many other universities north of the Alps.[29] An Oxford master would rent a house or a block of houses from an urban landlord, and be licensed by the University to hire out the rooms to younger students. The University allowed the principal to make a profit, but in return required him to ensure his tenants' general well-being, discipline them if necessary, and keep an eye on their academic progress. From the beginning of the fifteenth century, the University expected the large majority of its scholars to live in licensed halls. About 1410, it made lodging in private houses an offence (see Figure 2.2).[30] The only members of the University who could live elsewhere were those who dwelt in a college or a mendicant convent. In the first half of the fifteenth century, when only

[27] This was one of the oldest Oxford statutes and dated from before 1231: *Statuta*, p. 107.
[28] A. B. Cobban, *The Medieval English Universities: Oxford and Cambridge to c.1500* (Berkeley and Los Angeles, CA, 1988), p. 372. For the development of academic dress, see W. N. Hargreaves-Mawdesley, *A History of Academical Dress in Europe until the End of the Eighteenth Century* (Oxford, 1963).
[29] J. B. Mullinger, *The University of Cambridge* (3 vols; Cambridge, 1873–1911), i. 218–21, 638–40; Rainer C. Schwinges, 'Student Education, Student Life', in HUIE, i. 218–22.
[30] *Statuta*, pp. 208–9. The requirement was repeated in the articles imposed on the University by Henry V on 29 March 1420: ibid., pp. 226–7.

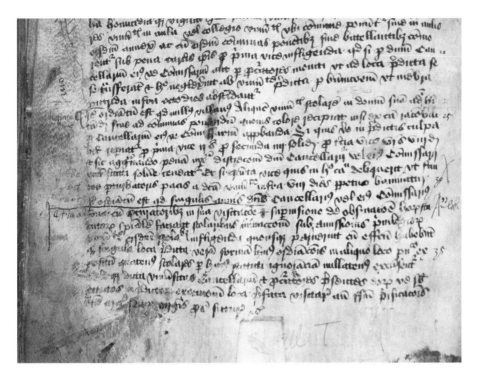

FIGURE 2.2 University statute, c.1410, known as 'De Pace'. Towards the end of the statute, scholars were ordered henceforth to live in halls or colleges and townsmen forbidden from renting out rooms to 'Chamburdekenys'.

those who were supported on the foundation lived in the nine colleges hitherto founded, the latter housed no more than 10 per cent of the total. A century later, however, when the number of colleges had grown and it had become common-place for the fellows to hire out rooms to other scholars, the colleges contained the lion's share of the student body.[31]

The amount of time the late medieval scholar devoted to matters academic was obviously affected by his aptitude and interest. Given the fact there were no statutory entrance requirements to Oxford, many students must have arrived ill-prepared and soon abandoned serious study before dropping out. But even under-graduates equipped to stay the course were under little compulsion to study hard. Graduates had little time on their hands. Oxford relied totally on its graduates to maintain teaching. Bachelors and masters in all faculties, even when they were pursuing their studies in another discipline, were caught up in a constant whirl of lecturing, disputing, and examining. At the same time, regent masters were admin-istrators, attending Congregation and taking their turn as office holders. If they were college fellows, too, they had extra academic and administrative duties to fulfil. The undergraduates' lot, in contrast, was undemanding. In the thirteenth and fourteenth

[31] See p. 84, this volume.

centuries, the one formal academic call on their time was the daily lecture of their chosen master. By the late fifteenth century, as student life became more institutionalized, they also had to attend the supplementary lectures given each morning in their halls, be catechized in the afternoon on what they had learnt, and take part in occasional disputes. But this would still have left plenty of leisure time. Before the invention of printing, undergraduates owned few books except their lecture notes, and they had next to no access to the University or college libraries. Having no role in university administration either, they were largely left to their own devices.

The inevitable consequence was that undergraduates got up to mischief. As clerks, they were expected to live as well as dress soberly and decently. As young adolescents living away from home with little supervision, they had energy to burn and little to constrain them from behaving any differently from other youths of their age. Some may have lived like Chaucer's clerk of Oxenford, who would 'lever have at his beddes heed/Twenty bookes, clad in blak or reed,/Of Aristotle and his philosophye,/than robes riche, or fithele, or gay sautrie'.[32] But there can have been few dedicated ascetics. Chaucer's Nicholas, the sweet-smelling, music-loving astrologer of the Miller's Tale, who uses his cunning and knowledge to seduce the wife of his landlord, was a more plausible literary creation. From the activities banned in university and college statutes, the initiatives of different Chancellors, and the cases brought before their court in the fifteenth century, undergraduates clearly let off steam in all manner of ways unacceptable to the University and church establishment. They made music, played cards, gamed with dice, hunted, practised armed combat, and continuously haunted taverns and brothels.

Student obsession with the opposite sex was a perpetual bone of contention. Oxford's red-light district in the late middle ages was around the site of the original royal palace of Beaumont. Undergraduates, however, roved all over the town and the surrounding district in search of the delights of female company, even finding solace in the arms of the sisters of the Benedictine nunnery of Godstow, a few miles to the north-west of Oxford.[33] In a visitation conducted by the bishop of Lincoln in 1445, for instance, the abbess complained of scholars continually invading her nunnery, and several nuns waxed indignant about the conduct of a certain Hugh Sadler, a student in priest's orders:

> [Dame Amy Hardelle] says that dame Alice Longspey used to hold parley after an exceedingly suspicious fashion in the church of the convent with sir Hugh Sadylere, priest, despite the prohibition of the abbess, for which there was enjoined upon her the penance of imprisonment and of discipline according to the rule [i.e. scourging] and to keep the frater and cloister for a year.[34]

Sadler justified his visits on the grounds he was Sister Alice's kinsman. It is unlikely, however, that his intentions were honest, whatever his affinity to the lady, for

[32] *General Prologue*, ll. 293–6.   [33] Founded 1122.
[34] A. Hamilton Thompson (ed.), *Visitations of Religious Houses in the Diocese of Lincoln* (2 vols in 3, Canterbury and York Society, 17, 24, and 33; London, 1915–27), ii. 114; editor's trans.

FIGURE 2.3 Confirmation of the University's privileges, 3 July 1461. It was customary for each king to renew and sometimes extend the University's privileges at the beginning of his reign. The illustration shows the end of the document where the Chancellor is given a new power to exile 'omnes pueras meretrices et mulieres incontinentes'.

he was a notorious student-pimp. Only the year before, he had been caught up in Chancellor Thomas Gascoigne's valiant attempt to close down prostitution in Oxford for good and had appeared before the University court.[35] But there was little that the authorities could do to end the trade. The Chancellor's register reveals that, in the mid-fifteenth century, prostitutes were imprisoned, fined, banished, and put in the pillory, but there was no diminishment in the number of women, many married, ready to offer students their services. In 1461, the crown gave the Chancellor the right to banish prostitutes to towns ten miles from Oxford, but this only helped to displace the trade to Abingdon, where it would become rooted in later centuries (see Figure 2.3).[36]

Students in the thirteenth and fourteenth centuries also collectively got out of hand. The extent to which late medieval Oxford was the scene of riot can be exaggerated since it is the moments of gross disorder which have left the most visible trace in the records. Nonetheless, prolonged and bloody bouts of fighting did periodically occur between students themselves, students and bourgeois, and

[35] *Registrum cancellarii*, i. 97.
[36] H. E. Salter, *Medieval Archives of the University of Oxford* (2 vols, OHS, lxx and lxxiii; Oxford, 1920–1), i. 251 (letters patent, 3 July 1461).

students and outsiders. This was an era of limited self-control when life was cheap and an insignificant quarrel could easily lead to violence, which could just as easily spread. A friendly crowd could turn into a murderous mob in minutes. In April 1238, the papal legate, Cardinal Otto, visited the area and was staying in Oseney Abbey with his Italian entourage. A party of scholars (who included some masters) went to the abbey to pay their respects, but was refused admittance by the door-keeper. The students then rushed the door and got into a fight with the legate's attendants. At this point, the invaders learnt that another student, a poor Irish chaplain, had been begging food from the legate's cooks but had had boiling water thrown at him for his pains by the cardinal's head chef. As a result, they headed to the kitchen to exact revenge:

> At this injury to the poor man, one of the clerks, a native of the Welsh borders, cried out, 'Shame on us to endure anything like this'; and drew a bow which he carried (for, as the tumult had increased, some of the clerks had seized on whatever arms came to hand), and by an arrow discharged from it, himself pierced the body of the cook, and on the fall of the dead man a cry was raised, at hearing which the legate was astounded and struck with fear ... and he betook himself to the tower of the church, clad in his canonical hood, and secured the doors behind him.[37]

On this occasion, the king, who must have been nearby at Woodstock, restored order by sending the earl of Warenne with a band of armed men to rescue the legatine party and arrest the culprits. Normally, though, little could be done to control the situation until the violence had fizzled out. Even in the fifteenth century, when students were fewer in number and the majority were institutionalized in halls, affrays continued. To a certain degree the north–south quarrels that had divided the student body in the thirteenth and early fourteenth centuries were replaced by inter-hall rivalries in the fifteenth. The resulting bloodshed led the University, on several occasions, to promulgate a statute concerning breaches of the peace, which laid down heavy fines for bearing arms and inflicting injury: carrying a bow and shooting arrows with intent to harm carried a hefty fine of 20 shillings.[38] But the regulations had limited effect. This was still a very violent age, and encounters could be murderous. In 1452, the Junior Proctor, Thomas Reynold, was fatally wounded when he intervened in a fight between the inmates of Peckwater Inn and St Edward Hall.[39]

The growing institutionalization of students in halls and colleges equally did not bring a speedy end to all the other breaches of clerical discipline of which students were continually guilty. This had clearly been the intention. The justification for forcing the chamberdeacons into a hall was that they were out of control: 'they

---

[37] Matthew Paris, *English History from the Year 1235 to 1273*, trans. J. A. Giles, vol. 1 (London, 1852), pp. 126–7. For an analysis of the incident, see David L. Sheffler, 'An Early Oxford Riot: Oseney Abbey, 1238', *HU*, XXI: 1 (2006), 1–32.

[38] *Statuta*, pp. 204–5 (c.1410) and 242–3 (24 May 1432).

[39] Hannah Skoda, 'Student Violence in Fifteenth-Century Paris and Oxford', in Jonathan Davies (ed.), *Aspects of Violence in Renaissance Europe* (Farnham, 2013), pp. 17–40.

sleep by day, and at night haunt taverns and brothels, intent on pillage and murder'. They were a 'putrid limb' that needed to be disciplined by communal living.[40] Keeping adolescents out of trouble, however, even when no longer free to roam as they chose, was not easy. Even college fellows, who were generally graduates and had taken an oath to live an exemplary life on their admission, were seldom pillars of virtue. College fellows were expected to live in harmony, avoid the temptations of the flesh, avoid all forms of indecorous behaviour, and keep gate-hours. This, though, they frequently failed to do. Fellowships were continually split by bitter rivalries and individuals repeatedly broke the rules, or were accused of doing so. Magdalen College, only founded in 1458, seems to have been in a state of anarchy by the first decade of the sixteenth century. When the commissary of Bishop Fox of Winchester, John Dowman, inspected the college in January 1507, he was regaled with a list of unedifying tales of mutiny, absenteeism, gambling, and thieving. John Stokesley, the future bishop of London, was singled out for particular condemnation. Among other sins, he was accused by his colleagues of heresy, adultery, and receiving stolen goods. One fellow even claimed Stokesley indulged in black magic:

> [Gold deposed] that he had heard it said by someone who could be trusted that Master Stokesley had performed illicit spells in baptizing a cat while back in his homeland the previous year. He had been denounced in the presence of the bishop of Lincoln and had not yet done penance for his crime which brought great shame on himself and the college.[41]

On the other hand, the growing subjection of the younger students to the immediate discipline of the hall principal or the college head must have had some effect in the decades preceding the Reformation. As we will see in Chapter 3, the rules concerning behaviour were strict and punishment could be severe.[42] Based closely on the disciplinary statutes of cloistered monks and nuns, the rules were arguably too harsh for secular clerks, who were generally only in minor orders, and thus must have been frequently counterproductive. All the same, the fact that the rules existed and were known to the students must have gradually led to their internalization. On the eve of the Reformation, church and state were more worried about religious subversion in the University than moral delinquency.[43]

The behaviour of Oxford students in the late middle ages was no different from that of scholars in other universities. Cambridge clerks were just as violent and ill-disciplined before they too were incarcerated in halls or colleges from the late fourteenth century. Indeed, enforcing clerical discipline in many universities on the continent could be even more difficult. At least at Oxford, affrays were spasmodic and unpredictable. Elsewhere they were recurrent, annual events, as the scholars turned key days in the Christian calendar, in particular Epiphany, into moments of licensed mayhem. If Oxford scholars let off steam on such occasions, they did so

---

[40] *Statuta.*, p. 208.
[41] W. D. Macray, *A Register of the Members of St Mary Magdalen College* (8 vols; Oxford, 1894–1915), i. 47–8. The bishop of Winchester was the college visitor. For this office, see pp. 62–3 and 74, this volume.
[42] See pp. 59–60 and 71–3, this volume.   [43] See p. 127, this volume.

relatively sedately behind the walls of halls and colleges. In other universities, furthermore, where scholars were never institutionalized in any numbers during the period, large-scale town–gown violence continued unabated into the sixteenth century. The St Scholastica riots of 1355 were the last pitched battles fought between scholars and burgesses: thereafter there were only minor flair-ups and individual altercations. In Paris, in contrast, where the population of the city and the university was much larger, town and gown were still at each other's throat two hundred years later. In 1557, a scholar exercising on the Pré-aux-Clercs, an open space to the west of the Latin Quarter set aside for the university members' recreation, was killed by a citizen. On hearing the news, his fellow students went on the rampage and sacked the town in a three-day orgy of violence. In the end, it took a royal army of 200 archers to quell the disturbance.[44]

C. Careers

Regulars from abroad who came to study in the higher faculties would have been attracted to Oxford by its burgeoning reputation as an intellectual centre. Other regulars would have been sent there by their superiors in the hope that their experience would raise the intellectual and moral calibre of their order. A similar expectation in regard to the good of the church in general may well have brought many seculars to the University who were dependent on a patron for their advancement or were dispensed from their parochial duties by their bishop. When Bishop Walter Reynolds of Worcester gave one of his clergy permission to attend a university in the early fourteenth century, the licence was expressly given, 'so he may acquire the pearl of knowledge, and more healthfully rule the cure committed him'.[45] It is unlikely, though, that the large majority of scholars at Oxford in the later middle ages attended the University out of love of study or a desire to be more effective monks or priests. Coming, as they seem to have done, from the yeomanry—small freeholders and affluent tenant farmers—and largely supported by their own families, they had been sent to Oxford for a more worldly purpose. The money invested in their education was intended to pay a social dividend. Appreciating that the church, and increasingly the crown, placed a value on learning, the rural elite all over Europe sent sons to universities in the hope that study would be a gateway to a lucrative career and future family advancement. If fortune really smiled, the scholar would repay the investment handsomely by ultimately endowing the family with landed estates. At the very least, if he returned to his native hearth as a learned parish priest, he would enhance the status of his family in the locality.

Discovering what actually happened to Oxford clerics in the late middle ages is extremely difficult, but, for some scholars, attendance at university was definitely a smart career move. As the period wore on, the higher echelons of the English clergy

[44] J. B. L. Crévier, *Histoire de l'université de Paris* (7 vols; Paris, 1761), vi. 29–49.   [45] *HUO*, i. 567.

were increasingly drawn from university graduates. In the first twenty-five years of the fourteenth century, only 52 per cent of collations to prebends in the dioceses of Lichfield, London, and York were in favour of university men; in the years 1476 to 1500, the figure rose to 90 per cent. Bishops and cathedral deans were particularly likely to have had a university education, and most passed through Oxford. In the fifteenth century, the University educated 72 per cent of the bishops and 70 per cent of the deans in England, Cambridge only 19 and 15 per cent. Across the period as a whole, Oxford's significance in providing the leadership of the English church was overwhelming. Of English bishops appointed in the years 1216–1499, 57 per cent were Oxford men, compared with 10 per cent who had attended its rival in the Fens. In this respect, Oxford far surpassed in importance its larger rival across the English Channel. Paris may have been the great international *studium* of northern Europe but it did not dominate the French episcopate. In fact, French bishops were notoriously ill-educated on the eve of the Reformation. It would be the seventeenth century before the French hierarchy was filled with learned men.[46]

Many more Oxford clerics found billets in diocesan administration as lawyers and judges. In the early twelfth century, when episcopal jurisdiction was still rudimentary, bishops' households contained few graduates. While the Oxford-educated St Edmund of Abingdon was archbishop of Canterbury (1233–8), he employed only one magister as chancellor, three as officials, and eleven as clerks. By the mid-thirteenth century, when the Benedictine Simon Langham was metropolitan, the position had changed dramatically, thanks in particular to the emergence of the court of arches as the high court of the Canterbury province. Langham served for only two years (1366–8), but he appointed thirteen graduates just to this one court: an official, commissary and dean, four advocates, four graduate examiners, and two proctors. Opportunities increased even more in the fifteenth century, since, from 1432, according to a decision of Archbishop John Stratford, only graduates could exercise jurisdiction in the southern province.

The regular clerics did particularly well. Besides becoming bishops, a large proportion—some 25 per cent across the three centuries—became heads of monastic houses, while others served their host community as legal councillors. The handful of Oxford men who spent time at the papal court were also usually monks. In the course of the late thirteenth and fourteenth centuries, all but one of the six or seven Oxford scholars who became cardinals were regulars, and others benefited from their elevation. When the cardinals made their customary visit to Avignon (where the papacy was based for over a century), they took several monks of their order with them. Langham's elevation to the cardinalate, for instance, led to the migration south of several other Benedictines, including the Oxford scholar Adam Easton, who himself was later raised to the purple. Only one Oxford master, regular or secular, however, is known to have become permanently part of the papal bureaucracy. This was Hugh Pelegrin DCL, a Gascon, who spent four years at the

---

[46] Joseph Bergin, *The Making of the French Episcopate, 1589–1661* (London, 1996), ch. 6.

University before replacing his brother in 1349 as papal nuncio in England and Ireland. He held this post for fourteen years and became a spectacular pluralist, drawing an income of £300 from his many benefices in the province of Canterbury. Normally, Oxford men spent only a few years in papal service before returning to the bosom of the English church. Typical in this respect was another secular and DCL, John Lydford, whose career can be followed particularly closely. Lydford practised as an advocate in the papal court at Avignon in the 1370s before returning to Canterbury to perform the same function in the court of arches. Thereafter, his reputation as an ecclesiastical lawyer secure, he became official to the bishop of Winchester, before ending his days as archdeacon of Totnes and a member of the Exeter chapter.[47]

A steady flow of Oxford clerics was also employed in the service of the crown. Although scholars were supposed to be in minor orders, there was nothing to stop them pursuing a secular career and many were still not priests when they left the University, or did not become so for many years. The future Archbishop Warham was not even a subdeacon when he graduated as a DCL. While England's kings largely used the common law, and, from the fourteenth century, parliamentary statute, to enforce their authority, they still had need of university-trained lawyers. There were a number of areas of government where knowledge of common law was of little value. The conduct of diplomacy required servants trained in civil law. So did the admiralty and chivalry courts, which often heard suits concerning foreigners and became steadily more important during the Hundred Years War, with the growing number of cases involving captured French goods and prisoners' ransoms. Above all, civil lawyers were needed to staff the court of chancery, where decisions were based on equity not custom. In the royal chancellor's court property cases were dealt with speedily and fairly, and its business expanded dramatically in the first half of the fifteenth century, as England's landowners, large and small, sensed its value in solving their grievances.

As a result, a number of Oxford lawyers were important figures in royal government across the period. Edward I used the Oxford DCL Robert Pickering to justify his assumption of the Scottish crown, while his successors relied heavily on the diplomatic skills of another Oxford civilian, John of Shoreditch. As Anglo-French relations deteriorated in the 1320s, Shoreditch visited the French court on many occasions to discuss the English king's need to give homage for the duchy of Guyenne (in English hands since the marriage of Henry II with Eleanor of Aquitaine). Then in 1339, having been knighted six years before for his pains and given a pension, he was entrusted with the impossible task of explaining to Philip VI why his royal master, Edward III, had now decided to declare himself king of France. Admittedly, Oxford scholars did not generally get their hands on the high offices of state, which frequently went to clerics but not to university men. On the other hand,

---

[47] The details of his career are to be found in *John Lydford's Book*, ed. D. M. Owen (Devon and Cornwall Record Society, new series, xx; London, 1975), pp. 5–11.

Oxford did provide the king with his chancellors as the jurisdiction of his chief judicial officer grew. Between 1330 and 1515, fifteen holders of the position had attended the University, including Magdalen's founder, William Waynflete, bishop of Winchester, who was royal chancellor under Henry VI.

There were also numerous less prestigious posts in the royal bureaucracy for Oxford men, as the administration expanded from the late thirteenth century. Given the shortage of educated laymen, the crown was keen to employ university clerics as letter writers, document keepers, and tax collectors, not just roving ambassadors, advisers, and propagandists. It was from this relatively humble milieu that high-flyers, such as Pickering, often appeared. Edward I employed perhaps as many as 1,500 scholars as proto-civil servants, and royal clerks continued to be primarily recruited from university men throughout the fourteenth and early fifteenth centuries. The favoured were handsomely rewarded for their service from the many lucrative benefices in the royal gift, including bishoprics. Thereafter, it would seem the royal bureaucracy was increasingly laicized and the opportunities for scholars declined. Nonetheless, university clerics were still finding their way into the royal administration on the eve of the Reformation, while others were taking up similar positions in the households of the aristocracy. In the early sixteenth century, Edward Stafford, duke of Buckingham, was particularly keen to use scholars to manage his estates and organize his affairs. Among those he tempted into his service through his wide ecclesiastical patronage were several former fellows of Magdalen, such as the priest and MA Robert Gilbert, who became his chancellor in about 1500. Gilbert quickly became the duke's right-hand man: he guaranteed his debts and began actions for him in court.

Many of Oxford's clerks who had a successful career in church and state owed their advancement to family background. It did not take elites long to sense the need to adjust their behaviour in order to hold onto their customary power base. Once it became clear, by the early fourteenth century, that the king and the pope wished to appoint learned men to high office, they ensured that some suitable candidates were available from their own ranks. The number of the sons of aristocrats who passed through Oxford may have been small, but most were destined for high-powered careers. Edward III could ask the pope in good conscience to appoint fifteen members of aristocratic families to bishoprics because fourteen of them had degrees and at least two were doctors. Nevertheless, there was also a considerable number of successful university men in this period who came from humble backgrounds. The market for learned, educated men was growing, and England's landowning elite was neither large enough nor sufficiently committed and perspicacious to meet the demand with its own relatives and clients. Had this not been the case, the investment and expectations of thousands of yeomen and well-to-do husbandmen who sent their sons to Oxford and Cambridge to make the family's fortune would have been inexplicable. Such figures were largely propelled onto the bottom rungs of the career ladder by being noticed. Before the middle of the nineteenth century (and even then), it was hard to be upwardly mobile without the right patron. Bishops, princes, and aristocrats must have always had their scouts in the universities looking out for new talent to patronize. A rich pupil's praise, a master's warm word of recommendation in a sympathetic ecclesiastical ear, or a precocious performance in a university dispute would have been the starting point for many stellar careers.

The background of most humble achievers has gone unrecorded. It is the fact that nothing is known about Grosseteste's origins that confirms he was a self-made man. Towards the end of the period, however, a few low-born scholars have left firmer footprints of their past, including the most famous and infamous of them all: Thomas Wolsey, bishop of Winchester, cardinal-archbishop of York, spectacular pluralist, and Henry VIII's chancellor from 1515 to 1529. Wolsey, according to his gentleman usher and first biographer, George Cavendish, was 'an honest poor man's son'. In fact, as his political rivals at court continually reminded him, he was the son of an Ipswich butcher, albeit a man of some property, called Robert Wulcy. His father, who died shortly before Wolsey was ordained in 1498, must have believed he had a prodigy on his hands for his son was sent to Oxford at an exceptionally early age and took his BA when only 15. Known in the University as the 'boy bachelor', he thereafter seems to have vegetated, probably studying theology and presumably searching for openings, and did not take his MA for a further seven years until he was elected a fellow of Magdalen. This election in itself suggests that he had by then found patrons in the University and he did not allow his good fortune to go to waste. Doubtless because of his academic abilities, he was soon appointed master of the flourishing grammar school attached to the college. His new position brought him into contact with at least one prominent layman, Thomas Grey, first marquess of Dorset, whose sons had been sent to the school. Thus, when he left Magdalen under a cloud in 1500 for squandering college funds while bursar, he was immediately presented with one of the marquess' livings at Limington in Somerset. Once on the lower rung of preferment, he was passed on ever upwards by a succession of patrons who grasped his potential or appreciated his spiritual council. Via the archbishop of Canterbury and the deputy warden of Calais, he arrived in the king's service in 1507 as a chaplain, and was soon involved in diplomatic and administrative work. In subsequent years, Wolsey became notoriously rich and eventually celebrated his arrival in the most ostentatious manner possible by building Hampton Court. He never forgot, though, that it was Oxford that had given him his start in life by affording him the chance to shine. In 1510, he dutifully supplicated for the degrees of BD and DD, then in 1525 used his vast power in church and state, if not his own vast wealth, to endow Cardinal College, the most grandiose Oxford foundation to date.

Of course, Wolsey's career was so extraordinary that no ambitious father from the middling sort could ever have entertained the thought that his Oxford-educated son might match it. The cardinal's fate—the fact that he abjectly handed over all his worldly possessions to the king when he fell from grace over his failure to gain Henry's divorce—also emphasized the dangers of rising too high. The majority of fathers probably dreamed only of their children gaining a humdrum administrative post in church or state. In the large majority of cases, however, even this was out of the question. The fact that some low-born scholars did extremely well for themselves must not obscure the reality. From what is known about the careers of the 15,000 scholars recorded as passing through Oxford in the late middle ages, the chances of using the University as a springboard for family advancement were only ever moderately good and may possibly have worsened over the period. In the thirteenth century, 26 per cent of secular scholar clerics who have left any trace gained a position in royal, episcopal, noble, or papal service; in the fifteenth century, when admittedly the names of far more unremarkable students are known, the figure was only 8 per cent. Clerks who spent time in the higher faculties always did better than simple arts students, yet they too were seldom destined for greatness: 48 per cent gained administrative posts in the thirteenth century but only 20 per cent two centuries later. Even the lawyers, who did best of all, saw their ability to land a bureaucratic position dramatically decline over time. In the first century of the University's existence, 62 per cent of their number found administrative employment, yet in their case, too, the percentage fell to 20 per cent in the fifteenth century. The percentage finding a state job dropped even further: from 38 to 9.[48] By then there was no greater benefit to studying law than theology except for the shorter amount of time it took to gain a degree. A law degree was always a good investment for scholars from whatever background who set their sights on a bishop's mitre. It was only in the reign of Henry VI that the king showed a preference for theologians.[49] In the fifteenth century, however, it no longer seems to have opened many doors in the state apparatus, which presumably was increasingly invaded by lay clerks trained in the Inns of Court.

In fact, the largest group of Oxford clerics in the late middle ages, whatever their dreams, would have ended up as parish priests, often deep in the countryside. Even this, though, would not have been automatic. There were 9,000 parishes in England on the eve of the Reformation and about 450 fell vacant each year.[50] If Oxford and Cambridge between them sheltered some 3,000 scholars in the second half of the fifteenth century, who, on average, stayed for only three years and then left without taking a degree, there may well have been twice as many university-educated clerics each year hoping to put a foot on the ecclesiastical ladder by obtaining a living as there were available places.[51] Nor were they necessarily first in the queue. The patrons who chiefly presented priests to parish cures—the crown, local gentry, and especially the local monasteries—were normally under no compulsion to appoint the alumni of the two universities. Little

---

[48] Aston, 'Oxford's Alumni', pp. 29–30. [49] Cobban, *Medieval English Universities*, pp. 394–5.

[50] On the assumption incumbents held the cure for twenty years; the number would have been lower when pluralism is taken into account.

[51] The figure may have been higher. Four years' residence was required to be eligible for a BA. However, as so few scholars ever took the degree, probably most arts students stayed only a couple of years. Even when scholars enjoyed free board and lodging, many soon left: at New College one in seven had gone within two years.

was required of the late medieval parish priest beyond a basic knowledge of Latin grammar and the fundamentals of Christian theology and ethics. Scholars were, by definition, overqualified. It made more sense for a patron to strengthen his power in the local community by bestowing a benefice in his gift on a client or servant with a modicum of learning rather than wasting his largesse on 'foreign' graduates.

Even those who stayed many years at the two universities and emerged with an MA or a doctorate in one of the higher faculties may have had difficulty landing a parish. From the limited information we have about the number of graduates at the two universities, it would seem that only about seventy scholars at Oxford and Cambridge incepted as an MA or doctor in a higher faculty each year.[52] This should have been a small enough number for all of them to have secured a cure with ease, regardless of the competition, but in many dioceses it would seem that *magistri* were always thin on the ground among parish priests. In the late thirteenth and early fourteenth centuries, the proportion ranged from a healthy 26 per cent in the diocese of Worcester to a paltry 7 per cent in neighbouring Hereford. In the late fifteenth and early sixteenth centuries the situation was little different: from a fifth to a sixth of the parish clergy were *magistri* in the dioceses of Canterbury and Norwich, but none at all in the large archdeaconry of Richmond in Yorkshire. Frequently, then, those who had invested heavily in their education in time and money must have found it difficult to acquire a living in the region from which they hailed. Many therefore would have had to serve for a time as a curate, chantry priest, or household chaplain before moving to a living. Even if the city of London can hardly be taken as representative of the rest of the country, it is still worthy of note that a sixth of its unbeneficed clergy in 1522 were *magistri*.[53]

In the fourteenth century an attempt was made to force patrons to promote university graduates of all kinds, not just *magistri*. Starting in 1317, Oxford copied Paris in presenting to the pope from time to time a list of the University's graduates and the benefices they sought to acquire. Once the petition was accepted, the pope wrote to the patrons concerned ordering them to appoint the suppliant to the position when it next fell vacant, in the expectation they would obey.[54] If the initiative ever worked, however, it did not prosper for long. The passage of the two

[52] The figure is based on the assumption that Oxford and Cambridge graduated the same number of masters and doctors each year: in 1449/50, Oxford incepted eight doctors in the higher faculties besides the twenty-six MAs and fifty-six bachelors in theology, law, and medicine referred to on p. 34, this volume.

[53] Peter Heath, *The English Parish Clergy on the Eve of the Reformation* (London, 1969), ch. 5; Guy F. Lytle, 'The Careers of Oxford Students in the Later Middle Ages', in J. M. Kittelson and P. J. Transue (eds), *Rebirth, Reform and Resilience: Universities in Transition 1300–1700* (Columbus, OH, 1984); R. N. Swanson, 'University Graduates and Benefices in Later Medieval England', *Past and Present*, 106 (1985), 28–61; R. N. Swanson, 'Learning and Livings: University Study and Clerical Careers in Later Medieval England', *HU*, VI (1986–7), 81–104. The information is based on surviving diocesan registers. Unfortunately, these only identify the *magistri* who became parish priests; incumbents who may have had the lesser degree of BA, BCL, or BCnL, or merely attended a university, are not distinguished from those who had had no higher education. Swanson is particularly pessimistic about the difficulties *magistri* faced.

[54] W. J. Courtenay, 'The Earliest Oxford Supplication List for Papal Provisions', *HU*, XVI (2000), 1–15. For the system of papal provisions at the University of Paris, see Hastings Rashdall, *The Universities of Europe in the Middle Ages*, ed. F. M. Powicke and A. B. Emden (3 vols; Oxford, 1936), i. 555–8.

statutes of provisors in 1351 and 1390 effectively limited the efficacy of papal provisions, since henceforth all such supplications had to be acceptable to the crown. Similarly, initiatives on the graduates' behalf by the two metropolitans in the early fifteenth century bore little fruit. In 1421, Henry Chichele of Canterbury got clerical patrons in the southern province to agree to present a graduate to the next benefice to fall vacant in their gift, and thereafter one in three, while his counterpart of York issued a similar ordinance the following year. But their intervention did not lead to any permanent change in behaviour.[55] At the turn of the sixteenth century in the diocese of Lincoln, some clerical patrons, such as the abbot of Ramsey, did privilege *magistri*, but others made no attempt at all.[56]

It was probably the even greater difficulty that scholars who had not taken a degree encountered in gaining a parish that explains why an estimated 40 per cent of all Oxford scholars in the second half of the fifteenth century never became priests. Doubtless they entered the University with the hope of gaining a parish living at the very least, but on going down and failing to secure patronage, they abandoned the idea of being ordained.[57] What career they pursued instead largely remains a mystery. There was as yet no university teaching profession as such— lectures were largely provided by bachelors and incepting masters—so there was little chance of unordained scholars staying in Oxford for the rest of their lives. The only positions with any permanence were the headships of halls and colleges, and these were generally held by beneficed clergymen. Obviously some unordained Oxford men would have found employment with the king and his nobility as clerks and bureaucrats, while others would have sensed there were better opportunities to be had in the common law and moved onto the Inns of Court. Given the expense, however, those who looked to set themselves up in London could only have come from the wealthier and better-connected families.[58] Many of the less well-to-do probably became teachers at grammar schools or took advantage of the landowning elite's growing interest in letters in the decades before the Reformation to become private tutors. It is unlikely, however, that education sopped up a third of Oxford's intake in the fifteenth century. Perhaps many students went home after a few years with their tails between their legs and re-entered the rural elite as bailiffs, reeves, and so on.[59]

---

[55] The king also took an interest on one occasion in furthering graduate opportunities. In 1401–2 Henry IV backed a plan to form a committee of bishops which would keep an eye on ecclesiastical patrons and ensure graduates were given their due.

[56] Margaret Bowker, *The Secular Clergy in the Diocese of Lincoln* (Cambridge, 1968), ch. 2. There was some change in the behaviour of lay patrons in the diocese across the fifteenth century; 3.5 per cent promoted *magistri* in 1421–31 and 11.5 per cent in 1495–1520 (pp. 44–5).

[57] The canonical age of ordination was 25, so many Oxford scholars left the University while still in minor orders. It was also customary for a bishop to ordain candidates for the priesthood only when they could demonstrate they had secured the promise of a cure.

[58] In the mid-fifteenth century, it was thought that a year at a London inn would cost £13 6s. 8d.

[59] Some took advantage of being only in minor orders to marry, like the fifth husband of Chaucer's 'Wife of Bath'; others unexpectedly inherited estates.

FIGURE 2.4 Misericord, New College Chapel, late 1380s. The misericord depicts the founder, William of Wykeham, welcoming scholars to his new college. On the right they depart to various positions in the church, emphasizing the religious purpose of the foundation. The reality may have been less rosy.

All this is speculation. But the conclusion receives support from the prosopographical study of the fellows of New College alluded to earlier.[60] Between 1386 and 1547, 312 became beneficed clergymen (the majority of whom remained rectors or vicars), eighty taught at Winchester (the college's feeder school) and forty elsewhere, seventy entered royal, aristocratic, or episcopal employment, twenty-two became common and twenty ecclesiastical lawyers, and thirteen entered a regular order. These, though, were only a minority of the fellows who passed through the college portals. A similar number—533—have left no trace of their future state, while 254—over 20 per cent—had the misfortune to die in the course of their studies. Evidently few fellows of New College hit the occupational jackpot, despite (one would think) having a better chance of attracting patronage than ordinary scholars. The college founder, William of Wykham, expected his fellows to become leading lights of the English church but most of the cohort disappeared into obscurity (see Figure 2.4).

Clearly, sending a son to Oxford must have often proved a wasted investment. It is testimony to the temporal ambition and optimism of England's middling sort in the late middle ages—undiminished it would seem by the psychological trauma of repeated visits of the plague after 1350—that so many yeomen and petty tradesmen were willing to gamble their hard-earned capital on such limited prospects of success. What the deeper consequences were of the fact that so many Oxford men gained little material benefit from their university education in the fifteenth and early sixteenth centuries can only be guessed at, but they are likely to have been significant. The failure of large numbers of scholars in the fifteenth and early sixteenth centuries to become priests meant that there were far more educated

[60] See n. 36.

laymen in pre-Reformation society than might be thought. Their existence cannot be unconnected with the well-documented rise in the laity's interest during this period in religious literature and private devotion.[61] Among some students, moreover, the collapse of youthful hopes may have led them in less orthodox directions. Disappointment may have led to religious disaffection. It would be naive to assume that the only social motor of Lollardy and the English Reformation was the frustrated careerism of Oxbridge students. All the same, the presence in this country, and doubtless in many others, of a large group of underachieving, disappointed scholars with a grievance against the church may well have played an important part in fanning the flames of reform.

---

[61] Eamon Duffy, *The Stripping of the Altars: Traditional Religion in England, c.1400–c.1580* (London, 1992), chs 6–8.

CHAPTER 3

Community Living

Halls, Convents, and Colleges

A. Halls

IN the thirteenth and fourteenth centuries, Oxford's clerics were free to live where they liked but a growing number resided in licensed halls. In the fifteenth century, after the University's decision in around 1410 to ban scholars from lodging with private citizens, the halls housed at least three-quarters of the University's residents. For the vast majority of scholars, until the eve of the Reformation, their academic hall became the focal point of their day-to-day existence and provided a communal framework in which they could live and work under the watchful eye of the resident principal.

As was noted in Chapter 2, academic halls were institutions run by individuals, usually non-regent masters, for profit.[1] Although principals might hold a lease for many years, and some halls had a continual existence that lasted several centuries, few documentary traces have been left. The names of many of the principals are recorded in surviving contracts and university records, but information about the individual members of a hall is scarce, save for the odd occasion when they surface in the registers of the Chancellor's court. According to a list made in the mid-1440s by the antiquarian John Rous, principal of Sekyll Hall off St Mildred's Lane (the modern Turl), there were sixty-six halls in the mid-fifteenth century. But the number had been much larger in the previous century. The names of 123 are known from the early fourteenth century and there must have been at least a hundred in the years preceding the Black Death. The sharp reduction by Rous' day was the result of several factors: the drop in numbers attending the University, the amalgamation of many small establishments into 'super halls', and the takeover of many others by the first collegiate foundations. Six, for instance, were swallowed up when All Souls was built in the first part of the fifteenth century.

[1] See p. 40, this volume.

Many of the halls were owned by local ecclesiastical landowners, notably Oseney Abbey and St John's Hospital, who between them let out more than thirty properties, the former renting houses to scholars from at least 1280. They were primarily located on either side of the High Street and to the west of Fish Street (today's St Aldate's), and tended to house students studying the same subject. In Rous' day six were for grammarians, twenty-five for arts students, thirty-three for lawyers, one for both arts students and lawyers, two for theologians, and four unclassified. But theology and medical students tended to stay in the halls that they had lived in when studying arts, so in reality probably half contained scholars from several faculties and of widely differing ages. By origin, most academic halls were town houses let out to graduate masters, but some may actually have been purpose built for the academic market, such as Tackley's Inn, a grammar hall on the south side of the High Street, just west of Oriel (see Figure 3.1). Whatever their origin, the halls appear

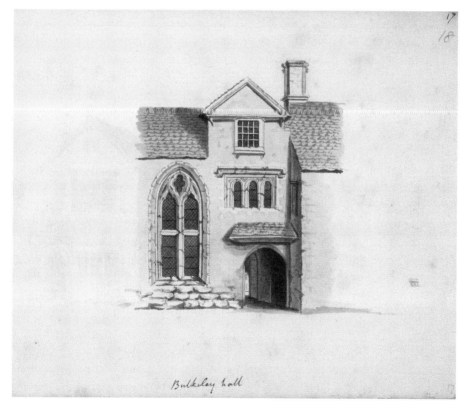

FIGURE 3.1 Tackley's Inn, built *c.*1291–1300, from a mid-eighteenth century drawing. Situated on the High Street, the inn was one of more than a hundred small residential halls at the beginning of the fourteenth century. Built by Roger le Mareschal, incumbent of Tackley in Oxfordshire, ownership was transferred to the new college of Oriel in the 1320s. In the mid-fifteenth century it served both as a grammar hall (Bulkeley Hall) and a tavern. The Illustration shows the *aula* to the left and the living quarters to the right; the passage way leads onto the High Street.

to have displayed a common footprint. An academic hall frequently consisted of an L-shaped building with a narrow frontage abutting the street and a long two-storey wing at right angles, part of which would contain the single-storey communal hall itself, rising to the level of the roof. Sometimes the street frontage would contain shops.[2] Normally, halls would house from ten to thirty students, and from two to four students would share a room. Boarders divided between them the annual room rent of about 4s. per room, and contributed a weekly sum towards the common table—usually between 8d. and 1s. 6d. per person—which was organized by the hall manciple. There were other costs that had to be met, but residents in the early fifteenth century could spend as little as 16s. 4½d. a term. The legal halls seem to have been the best appointed: commons were more expensive and rooms were less crowded.[3]

About 1290, the University laid down a series of conditions, some described as already the custom, that were to pertain when graduates took out a lease on a hostel or school. Although rents had been fixed each year by a joint town–gown committee since 1214, the policing arrangements had apparently been frequently circumvented in pursuit of profit. The new regulations forbade principals to do private deals with landlords that broke the agreed rate, insisted that leases should be renegotiated annually, made it an offence on pain of excommunication to swap or sell leases during the year, and demanded the lessee remained in residence. In return, in normal circumstances, a principal could no longer be ejected by his landlord at the end of the contracted term, provided that, 'before the six o'clock bell on the morning after the birth of the blessed Virgin', he had 'given security for the payment of his rent to the owner of the property, or in his absence, the Chancellor or his deputy'.[4] This last condition eventually evolved into a university ceremony, giving the halls a form of collective identity. Every 9 September, the day following the Virgin's nativity, the principals would repair to St Mary's church to renew their pledge, either in the form of a guarantor, a sum of money, or an object of value. This was often a book: in 1311 the principal of the hall of Reginald the Bedel in Schidyard (now Oriel Street) deposited a copy of the Sentences of Peter Lombard, the chief theological textbook.[5]

Only the history of St Edmund Hall is known in any detail, the one hall that survived until recent times before becoming a college.[6] There is no reason to believe it was atypical. The hall was named after St Edmund of Abingdon, who had purportedly rented a house on the site when a master regent at the beginning of the thirteenth century. Situated in a tenement lying at the east end of the present college quadrangle, the hall was owned by the monks of Oseney Abbey, who had

[2] W. A. Pantin, 'The Halls and Schools of Medieval Oxford: An Attempt at Reconstruction', *Oxford Studies Presented to Daniel Callus* (OHS, new series, xvi; Oxford, 1964).

[3] A. B. Emden, *An Oxford Hall in Medieval Times: Being the Early History of St Edmund Hall* (Oxford, 1927), pp. 40−3, 50, 193−4.

[4] *Statuta*, pp. 78−81, 'De domibus et scholis'.   [5] Emden, *Oxford Hall*, p. 26n.

[6] Anthony Wood, *The History and Antiquities of the Colleges and Halls in the University of Oxford*, ed. J. Gutch (Oxford, 1786), has a chapter on each of the halls that survived into the second half of the seventeenth century.

bought it around 1270 from the vicar of Cowley. The first documentary evidence of its existence comes from 1317/18, when a Cornishman established a hall in the property for a rent of £1 15s., which, six years later, was raised to £2 6s. 8d. Initially, it probably welcomed less than a dozen boarders. Over the next two centuries St Edmund Hall expanded in size, taking out leases on several adjacent properties owned by the abbey and St John's Hospital. By the late fifteenth century, these had been turned into two other halls—White Hall and St Hugh Hall (today 42–46 High Street). This allowed John Thamys, principal c.1438–60, to run a much larger establishment. St Edmund and White Halls offered board and lodging to students in arts (and presumably some theologians), while St Hugh was designated a grammar hall and used as a feeder institution. Under the University's rules a principal could only control directly one hall, so Thamys employed two masters to look after the scholars in the other properties. Virtually nothing is known about the everyday life of the student hostel, but the hall was kept in good condition. It was the duty of the owner to maintain the fabric, and Oseney Abbey was a conscientious landlord. In the 1450s, the monks were spending 13 per cent of the rent they received from the principal on repairs.[7]

It can be assumed that, over the fourteenth and fifteenth centuries, individual principals drew up sets of regulations governing the conduct of their charges. But it was not until the 1480s, during the chancellorship of John Russell, that a set of university-wide regulations governing internal discipline in the halls was issued.[8] Known as the Aularian statutes, they presumably reflected what was considered as contemporary best practice, and give a good idea how the hall had developed as an agent of student control over the previous two centuries.

The tenants were expected to hear mass every day and attend other religious services on feast days in the local church.[9] Their conversation was to be honest, their deportment seemly, they had to speak in Latin (except on major feast days), and they were not to sport side arms. They were to accept the room allocated, eat in hall, come to meals on time, and eat quietly while listening to a Bible reading. They were not stay out overnight, had to keep gate-hours (8 p.m. in winter, 9 p.m. in summer), and, if forced to leave Oxford for some reason, had to inform the principal. They were not to run on the grass, keep pets, or relieve themselves in the courtyard or garden. Inmates were also not to call each other names, tell tales, disturb others' study or sleep by loud noises or playing musical instruments, or strike each other—for which the fine, if blood was shed, was a colossal 6s. 8d. Breaks from study were permitted but scholars were not allowed to spend their leisure as they liked. Members of the hall were to take recreation in the surrounding country-side at times laid down by the principal, and could not play unsuitable games inside or outside the hall:

---

[7] Emden, *Oxford Hall*, chs 6–8.
[8] *Statuta*, pp. 574–88. No set of regulations drawn up for an individual hall has been discovered.
[9] Only Broadgates Hall had its own chapel: Emden, *Oxford Hall*, p. 50.

> Likewise, no student is to indulge in games of chance or dice, hand-ball, sword play (with either a two-handed sword or a sword and buckler), or any other dishonest game that disturbs the peace or distracts from study under pain of a fine of 4d, irrespective of persons.[10]

On entry a boarder had to swear that he would uphold the Aularian statutes. The principal was given the paramount role in disciplining the recalcitrant but was helped by an *impositor* elected from the lodgers each week, whose job was to report delicts. Breaches in discipline were dealt with publicly on Sunday evenings and could lead not just to fines but corporal punishment. Failure to comply led to expulsion, as did failure to pay rent at the due time or contribute to the expenses of the manciple. Expulsion and even denunciation to the Chancellor as a rebel would also follow treating the principal with disrespect. Everyone in the hall was 'to show honour to the principal as his superior and governor'. He was not to be maligned 'by any gesture, word, sign or deed'.[11]

The Aularian statutes further demonstrate that a rudimentary tutorial system had come into being in the halls over the years. A document from 1424, probably relating to St Mildred Hall, suggests that principals, by the beginning of the fifteenth century, were acting in loco parentis towards younger boys or at least acting as their 'creditor', someone who managed their money and disbursed payments when needed. It also reveals that some halls were employing teachers, for it refers to an agreement made with a John Burwyke to provide unspecified in-house lectures, 'on the understanding that he receives 10 shillings a term for three terms, if there are twenty-two scholars to be taught'.[12] By the late fifteenth century both practices had evolved. Other older boarders, not just the principal, were now acting as creditors; they were looking after the morals of their charges as well as their purse, and had the power to chastise. Teaching within the halls had, meanwhile, become commonplace. The new statutes ordered the *aularii* not only to attend the public lectures and disputations laid on by their faculty, but also the morning lecture in their hall, the afternoon recitations where they would be quizzed on what they had heard, and any disputation organized by the principal.[13]

B. The Mendicant Convents

Among the 25 per cent or so Oxford scholars who did not live in a hall in the first part of the fifteenth century, perhaps a half belonged to the mendicant orders, the new religious societies set up at the beginning of the thirteenth century to go out into the world to preach the Word, heal the sick, and succour the poor. Mendicant students lived and received instruction in their respective priories, which began to

[10] *Statuta*, p. 576.   [11] Ibid., pp. 577–8,
[12] Emden, *Oxford Hall*, pp. 192–6; H. E. Salter, 'An Oxford Hall in 1424', in H. W. C. Davis (ed.), *Essays in History presented to R. L. Poole* (Oxford, 1927), pp. 421–35.
[13] *Statuta*, pp. 576 and 579–80.

be established outside the city's walls within a few years of the first orders being founded. The Dominicans, the Order of Preachers or Black Friars, arrived in Oxford in 1221 and settled on a site in modern Grandpont to the south-west of the causeway.[14] They were followed three years later by the Franciscans, the Order of Friars Minor or Grey Friars, who built their convent a little further to the west, on the north bank of the Thames, straddling the city limits. The Carmelites arrived in 1256 and the Austin Friars in 1266–7. Early in the fourteenth century, the former took over the royal palace of Beaumont in the north-west suburbs, while the latter established themselves beyond Smithgate, where Wadham stands today. Later in the fifteenth century, several smaller mendicant orders also set up in Oxford, notably the Trinitarians, who occupied a small site outside Eastgate on the south side of the London road.

The mendicant orders placed a great emphasis on education. Every priory was a school where young friars were taught their letters. The promising were then sent off for more detailed instruction to convents that had been selected to provide higher learning. The Dominicans' system, copied in some form by the other mendicant orders, was especially complex. Able pupils passed first to a priory where they studied Latin grammar for two years, then to one that offered three years' instruction in the different parts of philosophy. After that, the best students moved on to a *studium particulare* where they studied the *Sentences* of Peter Lombard, and finally they transferred to a *studium generale* to finish their theological studies. As befitted a university town, the Oxford priories of the Black and Grey Friars were designated *studium generale*, but the English Carmelites gave this status to their London convent. At each level the friars would be taught within their own house by masters of the order, which, in university cities, inevitably caused friction, especially when mendicants wanted to take degrees in theology without jumping through the usual hoops.

In 1376–7 there may have been as many as 279 friars in Oxford's four mendicant convents: 103 Franciscans, 70 Dominicans, 57 Carmelites, and 49 Austins. The convents, however, served several functions, so it is impossible to know how many of these friars were scholars, or, indeed, how many, even if scholars, were involved in university-level studies. In fact, little specific is known about the daily life of the priories, for they have left few records. As their buildings no longer survive, we equally know little about their ground plan, apart from the fact that the Blackfriars and Greyfriars churches had very large naves, presumably to accommodate outsiders who came to hear sermons. Oxford's convents as institutions appear to have been principally financed through small bequests from townspeople. Only the Carmelites had a more centralized system, demanding that each house contributed 10 per cent of its income to a pooled educational fund that could support the order's scholars. As friars had no personal income and survived on

---

[14] As the road south of Folley Bridge was subject to flooding, the Normans constructed a causeway under the modern Abingdon Road.

alms, presumably their Oxford brethren lived a hair-shirt existence. Scholar friars, however, do seem to have had some privacy: the Dominicans replaced the monastic dormitory with private cells with space for benches for books.

Mendicant masters seldom taught in a convent for very long: Oxford's Greyfriars employed 67 regents in its first 125 years. Nonetheless, in the thirteenth and fourteenth centuries, the *studia* of the Oxford Dominicans and Franciscans, if not the other mendicant orders, were intellectually vibrant, and their influence in the University in the first centuries of its history far outweighed their numbers. The academic development of mendicant scholars was greatly enhanced by the fact that they had easy access to texts, unlike most secular clerics living in halls. When a friar died, the books he owned were given to the order and then distributed to priories in need. At Oxford, the Greyfriars library was of particular importance. Its basis was the large collection of books owned by Bishop Grosseteste. Although never a Franciscan, he had been the priory's theological *lector* in its early years and had bequeathed his library to the Oxford convent on his death in 1253.

C. The Early Colleges

The remaining scholars domiciled outside the halls in the years following the early fifteenth-century decree about residence lived in the University's first colleges. At this date these housed about 200 scholars, a mix of arts students and masters of arts studying for a higher degree. Colleges resembled Oxford's licensed academic halls in that they contained a small group of students living communally under the charge of a superior and in obedience to a set of rules. Yet they were very different, for they were endowed institutions with a corporate identity and their primary purpose was to provide free board and lodging either for scholar monks of a particular order or for secular clerks with limited means, usually drawn from a particular place, region, or family. Scholars supported on the foundation were known as *socii* or, in English, fellows. They were usually given a weekly or annual allowance from which they paid the cost of their commons. To enhance collegiality and discourage the amount of time fellows would spend in the town, most colleges had their own chapels so that the *socii* could worship together and not have to attend religious services at the local parish church. The chapel emphasized the fact that the college had a dual educational and religious function. The original and subsequent benefactors in establishing and enhancing a college hoped to benefit both the church and shorten their time in purgatory: by providing poorer students with the chance to study without worrying about the cost, they hoped to raise the quality of the parish clergy; at the same time, the colleges were set up as chantries, and most foundations supported at least one chaplain who maintained divine service and said masses for their own and their family's souls. The colleges also offered other marks of their religious status. Like monastic communities, they usually built up a communal library. And like religious communities and parish churches, they had patrons who acted as visitors and ensured that the regulations governing the institution were upheld. Finally, they were distinguished from academic halls by dint of the fact that they had a definite moment of foundation: this was either the date on which the college was given its first statutes by the founder, or, more usually in England from the early fourteenth century, the date on which the founder was given permission by the crown to establish an endowed hostel.[15]

The first educational institution of this kind was founded in 1180 at Paris and predated the official existence of the French university. It was the gift of a Josse de Londres on his return from Jerusalem and was intended as a hostel for young clerics, presumably arts students, who would be under the authority of the chapter of Notre Dame. Dedicated to the Virgin, it became known as the Collège des Dix-Huit after the original number of scholars supported on the foundation.[16] Other colleges were created on the left bank of the Seine in the thirteenth century, notably the Collège des Prémontrés, established in 1252 for Premonstarians, and the Collège de la Sorbonne, founded in 1257 by a royal chaplain from the Ardennes, Robert de Sorbon, as a refuge for an indeterminate number of secular clerics studying theology.[17] From the beginning of fourteenth century the number of Paris foundations exploded, as bishops and administrators vied with each other to make provision for the studious poor. In 1540, the Latin Quarter contained more than forty colleges of varying size, offering sustenance to about 680 students.[18] The largest was the Collège de Montaigu, which supported seventy-two arts students and twelve theologians, a number that supposedly corresponded to the number of Christ's disciples and apostles. Initially founded by Gilles Aicelin de Montaigu, archbishop of Rouen, in 1314, then re-established on a much broader scale under the principal, Jean Standonck of Malines, in the late fifteenth century, it had a reputation for austerity that Erasmus in particular found irksome.[19] In imitation of Paris, colleges for indigent scholars were founded in many European universities. Most boasted only one or two but the leading *studia* often attracted a clutch of endowments. By 1500 Padua had seen fifteen foundations, Toulouse fourteen, and Bologna nine.[20] From this perspective, the flurry of foundations at Oxford and Cambridge in the late

---

[15] The crown also often endorsed the statutes.

[16] Marie Madeleine Compère, *Les Collèges français. 16e–18e siècles. Répertoire 3: Paris* (Paris, 2002), pp. 155–9.

[17] André Tuilier, *Histoire de l'université de Paris et de la Sorbonne* (2 vols; Paris, 1994), i. ch. 5.

[18] Marie-Madeleine Compère, 'Les Collèges de l'université de Paris au XVIᵉ siècle: Structure institutionelle et fonctions éducatives', in Domenico Maffei and Hilde de Ridder-Symoens (eds), *I Collegi universitari in Europa tra il XIV e il XVII secolo* (Milan, 1991), p. 102. Short histories of all the Paris foundations can be found in Compère, *Collèges*. The foundations are listed in chronological order in Hastings Rashdall, *The Universities of Europe in the Late Middle Ages*, ed. F. M. Powicke and A. M. Emden (3 vols; Oxford, 1936), i. 536–9. The most recent detailed studies are Nathalie Gorochov, *Le Collège de Navarre de sa fondation (1305) au début du XVe siècle (1418): histoire de l'institution, de sa vie intellectuelle et de son recrutement* (Paris, 1997); Cécile Fabris, *Etudier et vivre à Paris au moyen âge. Le collège de Laon (XIVᵉ–XV siècles)* (Paris, 2005); Marion Bernard, 'Le collège de Notre-Dame de Bayeux, dit Maître Gervais. Centre intellectuel et lieu de vie à Paris (XIVᵉ et XVᵉ siècles)', thèse de l'école des chartes, 2 vols, 2010; and Thiery Kouamé, *Le collège de Dormans-Beauvais à la fin du Moyen Age. Stratégies politiques et parcours individuels à l'université de Paris (1370–1458)* (Leiden, 2005).

[19] William J. Courtenay, 'The Collège de Montaigu before Standonck', and Paul J. J. M. Bakker, 'The Statutes of the Collège de Montaigu: Prelude to a Future Edition', both in *HU*, XXII: 2 (2007), 54–111.

[20] Peter Denley, 'The Collegiate Movement in Italian Universities in the Late Middle Ages', *HU*, X (1991), 29–92; Rashdall, *Universities*, ii. 172–3; Jacques Verger, 'Patterns', in *HUIE*, i. 60–2.

middle ages was not unusual. What has marked out the two English universities from the rest is that their medieval collegiate foundations have largely survived.[21]

In 1400 Cambridge had eight colleges for secular clerks and Oxford seven, plus three for Benedictine monks.[22] Arguments have raged over the centuries over which was the first Oxford foundation, though the accolade is normally accorded to University College, which was founded with money left by William of Durham, who died in 1249. William was a doctor of theology of the University of Paris, who was a resident prebend of Rouen Cathedral, but he always retained some association with his home county for he was also rector of Wearmouth. In his will, he left 310 marks to the masters of the University of Oxford with instruction to spend the money on real estate and use the annual rent to support the higher studies of a number of masters. His aim in the first instance was to sustain a group of four masters studying theology. The number was to grow as the money available increased, and they were to be chosen, by preference, from students born in the Durham area. The inspiration for William's generosity was doubtless the Paris Collège des Dix-Huit, for the Sorbonne had yet to be founded. But it is possible Durham moved in a circle in France where further foundations were being mooted. William may well have come across Robert de Sorbon, and he would definitely have known Guillaume de Sâone (or Saane), the Rouen Cathedral treasurer, who established another Paris college, Le Trésorier, in the 1260s, for theology students from the local diocese and city.[23]

The University, however, moved slowly. The benefaction was deposited in the University's coffers and part of the sum was spent on buying property that the University rented out as halls. It was only three decades later, in 1280, that a university commission drew up statutes inaugurating a college. These allowed for the establishment of a body of four scholars living together in a house in Schools Street, who would each receive an allowance of £2 10s. a year out of a small endowment that they would administer. Twelve years later the embryonic college was given further definition with the promulgation of a set of disciplinary statutes, although as yet the institution had no name. It was only at the beginning of the thirteenth century that the ground began to be laid for its present appellation, as documents started to call the foundation 'the Hall of the University of Oxford'. Further statutes followed in 1311, which limited the holding of a fellowship to seven years, and, as a result of additional benefactions, the fledgling institution became the owner of several halls on the south side of the High Street. In 1330, the incumbent fellows transferred to one of these, Spicer Hall, on the present site of the college, and by 1340 their number had increased to seven.

By then Oxford already boasted seven other colleges, one of which, Balliol, had actually opened its doors twenty years before William's foundation. Its founder,

[21] By 1500, 145 colleges had been founded in university towns: see A. L. Gabriel, *The College System in the Fourteenth-Century Universities* (Baltimore, MD, n.d.), p. 5.

[22] For the foundations, see A. B. Cobban, *The Medieval English Universities* (Berkeley, CA, 1988), ch. 4.

[23] Compère, *Collèges*, pp. 353–6.

John Balliol, was a leading mid-thirteenth-century northern landowner who agreed with the bishop of Durham to perform charitable acts as a penance after an affray concerning his retainers. About 1260, doubtless on the bishop's prompting, Balliol hired a house outside the city walls on Horsemonger Street near the church of St Mary Magdalen, which he turned into a hostel for sixteen poor scholars who each were given 8*d.* per week for their board. When Balliol died in 1268 the hostel had no endowment but his work was completed by his wife, Dervorguilla of Galloway, a descendant of David I of Scotland. Dervorguilla provided the college with its first statutes in 1282, assigned land in Northumberland to the new institution the following year so that it thereafter had its own income, then in 1284 transferred the scholars to houses purchased close by the hostel, which became known as New Balliol Hall. In subsequent decades the new college added to its property portfolio. In 1294 it gained the advowson of St Lawrence Jewry in London, and in the early fourteenth century it acquired property in St Aldate's.[24] It was only in 1340, however, that Balliol was solidly underpinned, thanks to the generosity of Sir Philip Somervyle, a Northumberland knight. Somervyle increased the number of scholars on the foundation to twenty-two and raised their weekly allowance to 11*d.* Six were henceforth to be students of theology; the remainder were to study arts.

Balliol's endowed hostel was followed in the next decade by the foundation of Merton. The college began life about 1264 as a religious house. The founder, Walter de Merton, bishop of Rochester and a key royal administrator—as the king's chancellor he virtually ruled England in 1272–4 while Henry III was on crusade—initially set up a community of secular clerics on his manor of Malden in Surrey. Two or three of its members were to be resident chaplains who would spend their life in a continual round of prayer. Twenty others were to be scholars living at Oxford or a similar place of learning. In 1266–8, Walter began buying property in Oxford and was given the advowson of St Peter in the East and the wealthy manor of Holywell by the king. By 1270, the Malden community was extremely well endowed and was also supporting a hospital for elderly scholars at Basingstoke. Finally, in 1274, three years before he died, Walter moved his Malden college to Oxford and turned it into an endowed academic hall, controlling its own property. To begin with, Merton's scholars were housed in Bull Hall on the north side of modern Pembroke Street. When the college was relocated in Oxford, it was established on its present site, in the street then called St John's Lane, where Walter had purchased a number of buildings, including the parish church of St John. Merton can thus lay claim to being the first functioning Oxford college, even if it was not the first to be conceived. Under the 1274 statutes, the size of the fellowship was to depend on the number that could be supported on the endowment with a per capita allowance of 50*s.* per annum. The majority, in the first instance, were to be arts students with the assumption that they would move on, if capable, to study theology, although four

---

[24] Notably Burnell's Inn, founded by Robert Burnell, bishop of Bath and Wells, who died in 1292. It was one of two mooted endowed halls that failed to get off the ground before 1400.

FIGURE 3.2 Monastic cells, Gloucester College, probably early fifteenth century. The chambers off each staircase housed Benedictine monks from a different abbey. Today part of Worcester College, the chambers are the most visible surviving sign of the University's medieval regular colleges and convents.

or five might be permitted to study canon law. According to statutes given to the community four years before, preference was to be given to the founder's kin, then to scholars from the diocese of Winchester, and finally to those from the diocese where the college had estates.[25] Besides the head of house, the fellows, and their servants, the new foundation was also to contain a number of *parvuli* or young boys, to a maximum of thirteen, who would be members of the founder's family studying grammar under a master.[26] In reality, for at least the next half-century, Merton supported a number of other grammarians on the foundation. The founder's kin among them were placed in the adjacent Nun's Hall, which was later attached to the college, the other boys in the vacated Bull Hall some distance away. By the mid-fourteenth century, however, the grammarians had disappeared. A further community of twelve junior scholars was attached to the foundation in 1380 through the munificence of John Wyliot, chancellor of Exeter Cathedral. But Wyliot's bursaries were reserved for scholars capable of following the arts course and were not for Latin beginners. Called *portioniste*, due to the fact they were given a weekly allowance or *portio*, the scholars eventually became known as postmasters after the name of the hall in which they resided in the sixteenth century.

[25] Statutes, vol. 1, *Statutes of Merton College*, p. 10.   [26] Ibid., pp. 36–7.

The final colleges to be established in the thirteenth century were the Benedictine colleges of Durham and Gloucester, the first in 1289, the second, which had had some sort of existence from 1283, in 1298. Unlike the friars, the older contemplative orders were less interested in university education. For most of the thirteenth century, the small number of monks who did attend Oxford either lodged in the growing number of secular halls or, in the case of Augustinian and Cistercian scholars, found space in the local abbeys that belonged to their order: St Frideswide's within the walls and Oseney and Rewley without.[27] By the end of the century, however, the Benedictines, who had been mainly responsible for keeping learning alive after the collapse of the Roman Empire, had realized that they could no longer ignore the new developments in philosophy and theology that the universities had spawned. Durham College, established on the present site of Trinity, was for the monks of the Durham Cathedral chapter. When fully established towards the end of the fourteenth century, it was to shelter eight monks and eight secular clerics. In the century and a half before the Reformation, the foundation allowed probably a third of Durham's monks to spend some time at Oxford. Gloucester, where Worcester College now stands, was intended to serve the Benedictine order in England *tout court*. The original Benedictine cell was put under the control of the Malmesbury monastery in 1298, and thereafter individual abbeys were encouraged to send promising monks to the college on the understanding the mother house would support their sojourn. Gloucester was never a proper college because it lacked an endowment and had no seal. Its life as a community also took time to organize. Eating in common was still not automatic in 1360 and it had no statutes until 1363. But some forty Benedictine houses sent monks there between 1370 and 1530, and several had permanent units of accommodation built (see Figure 3.2).[28]

Three more secular colleges were founded in the early fourteenth century: Exeter (c.1314), Oriel (1324), and Queen's (1341). Each was founded on part of the site it still occupies. Exeter was the gift of the king's treasurer and local bishop, Walter de Stapledon, and his brother, who established a college for twelve students of philosophy: eight were to come from Devon and four from Cornwall. It differed from the earlier secular foundations in that its income was collected on its behalf by the Exeter chapter and then handed over. Oriel was the first endowed hall where the word *collegium* was used in its foundation statutes.[29] It was founded by Adam of Brome, a royal almoner, and was initially to support ten theologians,

[27] The Cistercians' house at Rewley was only founded in 1281.

[28] W. A. Pantin (ed.), *Documents Illustrating the Activities of General and Provincial Chapters of the English Black Monks, 1215–1540*, vol. iii (Camden series, vol. liv; London, 1937), pp. 30–1: abbot of Glastonbury to a student monk, c. Nov. 1360. For an overview of the order in the University in the late middle ages, see Henry Wansbrough and Anthony Marett-Crosby (eds), *Benedictines in Oxford* (London, 1987), chs 3–6.

[29] Statutes, vol. 1, *Statutes of Oriel College, Oxford* (1326, 1329), pp. 5–16. Until then, as in the case of University College and Balliol, Oxford did not distinguish between unendowed and endowed halls. Exeter College was initially called Stapledon Hall. In medieval Cambridge where halls were called *hospicia*, the word *aula* continued to be used as a synonym for *collegium* throughout the period and beyond: e.g. Trinity Hall, Gonville Hall (now Gonville and Caius College), King's Hall (now King's College). The Oriel statutes speak of 'a college of scholars' but still call the community a house (*domus*) or hall (*aula*).

though up to seven of their successors could be canon lawyers. The singular name by which the college was eventually called came from La Oriole, the name of the Oxford messuage on which the new institution was chiefly situated, that was given to Brome by a kinsman of Queen Eleanor of Castile. Queen's founder, Robert of Eglesfield, was also a member of the royal household. As almoner to Edward III's queen, he attempted to associate Philippa with the foundation by naming it after her. Eglesfield, who endowed his college with property in the north-west of England, was ambitious. He envisaged an institution which might eventually support twelve fellows and thirteen chaplains and also fund the education of seventy-two boys studying grammar. Founder's kin were to be preferred; otherwise, fellows were to come, in the first instance, from Cumberland and Westmorland, 'because of the devastation of the area, the poverty of a greater number of people in the same, and the rarity of letters there'.[30] But Eglesfield failed to endow the new college sufficiently. There were usually fewer than ten fellows in the fourteenth century, the grammarians seem to have disappeared from the picture, and after the Black Death the numbers in college sank to three.

While Merton, in the first half of the fourteenth century, supported forty scholars of some kind, of whom perhaps thirty were fellows, the other secular colleges founded before 1350 could barely muster sixty between them. The number living in the endowed halls virtually doubled overnight with the foundation of New College in 1379 on a site in the north-east of the city, abutting the walls, which likewise became its permanent home. Apart from Canterbury College, established in 1363 immediately north of St Frideswide's as a refuge for Benedictine monks of the chapter of Canterbury Cathedral,[31] New College was the only collegiate foundation in the second half of the fourteenth century. Its founder, William of Wykeham, was a man of humble background who rose to become the king's chancellor and bishop of Winchester. His college was dedicated to Christ's mother, to whom he had been particularly devoted since a boy, but it soon became known as New College to distinguish it from Oriel, which was originally called the House or Hall of the Blessed Virgin.[32] New College was to have seventy fellows in perpetuity: the scholars were to enter the community between the age of 15 and 20 to study arts; most would then move on to theology, although twenty could be lawyers, and two were allowed to study medicine and two astronomy. This was one of the largest foundations thus far in Europe, and reflected Wykeham's fears that the number of ordinands had fallen as a result of the Black Death. Its size was the same as the Paris Collège de Navarre founded in 1304, though Navarre comprised a community of grammarians as well as arts students and theologians. New College's establishment also broke new ground. Rather than simply making provision for the conduct of divine service and ensuring that masses could be said for the souls of the founder and other benefactors,

---

[30] Statutes, vol. 1, *Statutes of Queen's College*, p. 12.
[31] Canterbury was initially a mixed college for monks and seculars, then a secular college, 1365–69, and finally a college for monks alone. It was located on the site of Christ Church's Canterbury Quad.
[32] Statutes, vol. 1, *Statutes of Oriel College*, p. 6.

Wykeham established a full choral foundation where as many as ten chaplains were supported by three clerks and sixteen choristers. Recruitment was especially restrictive. Once again founder's kin were privileged. More importantly, no one could become a fellow of New College who had not previously studied at the grammar school for poor boys that Wykeham had established at Winchester in 1373. This was completely novel. None of the existing colleges at Oxford and Cambridge had an organic link with a feeder grammar school, even if King's Hall, Cambridge, founded in 1337 and often described as the template for New College, drew many of its fourteenth-century fellows from the grammar school of the Chapel Royal.[33]

The endowed halls varied greatly in their income. Even though all the colleges gradually acquired extra property through benefactions, most were poor and had difficulty balancing the books. University, Balliol, Exeter, and Oriel had rent rolls of £30–£50 per annum in the mid- to late fourteenth century, which placed them among the poorest of England's religious institutions. Queen's was better endowed—it had an income from property of £66 6s. 5d. in 1350—but only Merton and New College were rich. Besides properties in Oxford, Walter de Merton assigned his college ten manors and ten appropriated churches, plus the advowsons of four that were unappropriated. He also left the fellows 1,000 marks to build up the portfolio. Unlike the smaller foundations, the rural properties were all in the south of England and thus the rent was relatively easy to collect as tenants lived for the most part within reach. In 1330–50, in good years, the college had an income of £330–£350. New College was of a different order altogether. Wykeham endowed his foundation with twenty-one manors, with the advowson rights to thirteen or fourteen of these. He further provided the college with a cash reserve of £2,000, nearly half of which was spent on gaining the confiscated priory of Newton Longueville, Buckinghamshire, in 1441. From the outset, New College enjoyed an annual rental income of about £630. It was still not, though, in the big league of the country's religious houses. The large monastic foundations had incomes of £2,500 per annum.

The size of income not only determined the number of fellows who could be supported, but also affected the speed with which the first endowed halls could build anew on the sites they occupied. Before 1350, Oxford's colleges were not established in new buildings but set up in town houses and existing academic halls that their founders had purchased. Unsurprisingly, Merton was the first to make alterations to its site. Even before Malden College moved to St John's Lane, the founder had begun the construction of the present dining hall, which measured 80 feet by 30 feet and, at the end of the thirteenth century, was the largest secular building in Oxford after the castle. Then, in the 1280s, the college began work on a new chapel, which consisted initially of the present chancel, plus a space at the west end for parishioners. In the early 1330s, it was further enhanced by the building of the chapel crossing and a start was made on the two transepts. With the new chapel,

---

[33] A. B. Cobban, *The King's Hall within the University of Cambridge in the Later Middle Ages* (Cambridge Studies in Medieval Life and Thought, 3rd series, 1; Cambridge, 1969).

FIGURE 3.3 Mob Quad, Merton College, mid-fourteenth century. The photograph shows one-side of the L-shaped library created a little later on the first floor of the south and west sides. The dormers are a later addition.

St John's Church was redundant as a place of worship. It was pulled down and in its place was erected the present Mob Quad, the first purpose-built Oxford quadrangle (see Figure 3.3). Merton also created the first secular college library. The college's books were originally kept in a chest, but as early as 1284 a chained library had been constructed, though its location is unknown. Within a few generations, however, the room was not big enough for the college's needs, so, in the final quarter of the fourteenth century, a second library was built through the generosity of Bishop Rede of Chichester, an erstwhile fellow. Erected on the first floor of the south and west wings of Mob Quad, this new library, today's old library, had room for fifty readers. The lecterns were placed in the window bays and books chained beneath.[34]

The other early colleges were unable to follow suit. The most that they achieved was to adapt existing space for a chapel and small library. Exeter had a licence to build a chapel by 1311; Balliol had a chapel from 1325, University from 1370, and Queen's from 1382. Queen's set up a library in 1372–3; Exeter had one from 1374; and Balliol had some sort of library room by the end of the fourteenth century. The foundation of New College, however, soon put Merton's building spree in the shade. At the time of the official foundation of the college, Wykeham was already housing as many as sixty

[34] The first college quadrangle in England was built at Corpus Christi, Cambridge, and begun in 1352. Cambridge quadrangles became known as courts.

scholars in contiguous halls along what is now New College Lane. The fellows lived there until 1386, when they transferred to a completely new set of buildings erected close by. Wykeham had been buying property in the rundown and depopulated north-east of the city from 1369. The site was cleared, and in 1380, a year after the college's inauguration, the foundation stone of the new college was laid. In 1386, the fellows took possession of the first of what would be two adjoining two-storey quadrangles built in the new perpendicular style and using, for the first time in Oxford, Headington hardstone for walling. This, the larger and more easterly quad, housed on the western side of the north range the chapel, and on the eastern the first-storey dining hall, so that the east end of the chapel abutted the west end of the hall. The chapel was T-shaped, the crossing and the transepts running north–south along the west side and forming an antechapel decorated with sumptuous stained glass, the work of Thomas Glazier of Oxford. At the corner of the northern and eastern ranges was built a muniment tower, and on the first storey of the eastern range the library, while most of the ground floor of this range and the whole of the southern side of the quadrangle contained rooms for the fellows. The smaller quadrangle, built between 1396 and 1403, took the form of a cloister with a bell tower on its northern side (finished in 1405), surrounding what became a cemetery. Access to the college was through a three-storey gatehouse that gave onto New College Lane and where the head of house was lodged (see Figure 3.4). New College's design, which owed much to the mason William Wynford, borrowed heavily from recently constructed sets of buildings at Windsor Castle, the London Charterhouse, and two collegiate churches in Kent and Sussex. It was modern, serviceable, and distinctive, and inevitably became the blueprint for college architecture for centuries to come. In the course of the fifteenth century the earlier foundations imitated its magnificence as far as they were able. With the help of numerous small gifts and benefactions, Merton added a gatehouse to Mob Quad in the early 1420s, and from 1488 to 1450 completed its huge chapel by the addition of the tower, while both Balliol and University College managed to erect their own quadrangle, entrance tower, and library by the 1460s.

The rules governing internal discipline laid down in the first colleges' statutes anticipated the provisions of the Aularian statutes of the 1480s. This is unsurprising, once it is accepted that the college statutes would have mirrored those already drawn up by individual principals for their halls, just as the principals would have drawn on monastic precedents. Fellows were to remember they were clerks and live accordingly. The University College statutes of 1292 put it succinctly:

> [Fellows are to live] as befits holy men, not fighting, not uttering scurrilous or abusive words, not narrating, singing or eagerly listening to songs or tales about mistresses and loose-living people, or inclining them to lust; they are not to mock someone or rouse him to anger, and not to make a noise, so that those studying are hindered in their study or quiet.[35]

---

[35] Darwall-Smith, p. 19.

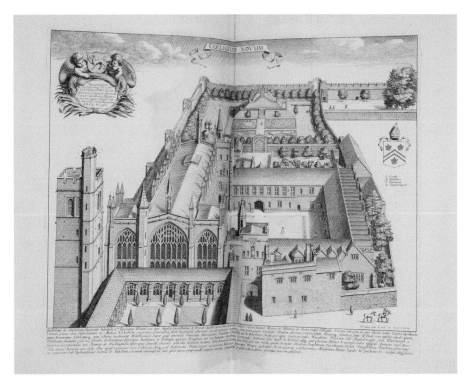

FIGURE 3.4 New College, late fourteenth century: David Loggan, *Oxonia Illustrata*, 1675. The engraving shows the original quadrangle with its chapel on the north side and the separate cloister and bell tower. The Danzig-born Loggan, engraver to the University, provided the first accurate three-dimensional maps of the colleges and the University's buildings.

Fellows in all colleges were forbidden to frequent taverns, stay out overnight without permission, play dishonourable games, eat on their own or outside college, or keep pets—the New College statutes of 1400 specifically mentioned dogs, ferrets, and birds of prey.[36] At meals fellows were to listen attentively to the Bible reading and speak only in Latin, except at Queen's and Exeter where French was allowed, or, occasionally, English if prominent guests were present.[37]

However, the college statutes had various distinctive features that reflected the fact that they were charitable institutions. Fellows were not supposed to be rich, even if few can have hailed from really humble families,[38] and were expected to demit their bursary if they had an income over a certain amount: at Balliol, for instance, under the 1340 statutes, the sum was £5.[39] In consequence, it was hardly reasonable to fine a 'poor' scholar for committing a misdemeanour. Instead, he was 'discommoned' for a number of days, which presumably meant he had the choice of starving or

[36] Statutes, vol. 1, *Statutes of New College*, p. 48. [37] Ibid., *Statutes of Queens*, p. 14.
[38] See Chapter 2, n.17, this volume.
[39] Statutes, vol. 1, *Statutes of Balliol College*, 'Sir Philip Somerville's Statutes', p. xiii. Demitting was not usually mentioned in the statutes but was the customary practice.

purchasing food and drink from the college kitchen out of the residue of his meagre allowance. The religious character of the foundations was stressed by the emphasis on daily spiritual exercises. At New College, where the statutes laid down with particular precision how the fellows should deport themselves, members of the foundation were required to recite a special antiphon in honour of the Trinity on rising and before going to bed. Each day, too, they were to say prayers for the soul of the benefactor, his family, and members of the royal family, hear or say mass (if they were priests), and during the service or separately 'say on bended knee fifty times over, as devoutly as possible, the angelic salutation [to the Blessed Virgin], interspersed on each occasion with the Lord's Prayer'.[40] Attempts were also made to enhance collegiality by closely prescribing dress. At New College, the fellows were expected to dress uniformly and each Christmas were given a livery of cloth that came to about one-sixth of the annual expenditure. They were forbidden to carry weapons inside and outside the college, and to grow their hair long, or wear 'red or green hose, pointed shoes and knotted head-gear'.[41] At Queen's, the doctors of theology and law were to appear at lunch and dinner in 'a purple cloak split at the collar, edged with black fur', as a mark of their status 'and in memory of the robe and blood of Christ'. The other fellows were to wear a plainer cloak of the same colour.[42]

Above all, the college statutes were more complex because they were not simply concerned with the fellows' behaviour but dealt with the general running of the institution. The colleges were self-governing bodies in charge of choosing a head of house, filling vacancies in the fellowship and chaplaincies, and periodically appointing one or more of the fellows as bursars or deans to look after the finances, manage the day-to-day expenses, and assist the head in maintaining discipline. The statutes expatiated at length on how this was to be done and described in more or less detail the rights and duties of the different members of the foundation.[43] All those described as fellows or *socii* in the statutes were expected to play a part in governing the college; only grammarians on the foundation or young scholars given a different designation, like Merton's *portioniste*, had no administrative responsibilities.

To distinguish the colleges from the academic halls and confirm that the college was a religious institution, only University College's head of house was called a principal. The others were given suitably ecclesiastical titles: master (Balliol), warden (Merton and New College), rector (Exeter), and provost (Oriel and Queen's). All, once elected by the fellows or the senior part of the fellowship, served for life or until they resigned. They had much in common with monastic heads. They were usually assigned a particular part of the college for their lodging, as at New College, and they often had the right to a separate table in or even apart from the hall so they could entertain guests.[44] They were also given a stipend on top of their fellow's

---

[40] Ibid., *Statutes of New College*, pp. 67–8.   [41] Ibid., p. 46.   [42] Ibid., *Statutes of Queen's*, p. 14.

[43] The period of election was not usually stipulated in the statutes, but became the custom across the fourteenth century: see ibid., *Statutes of New College*, p. 38 (on the deans).

[44] New College's warden had his own kitchen.

allowance,[45] and permitted to have a servant or servants and keep a small stable so they could regularly inspect the condition of the college's properties. Fellows, on the other hand, elected according to the idiosyncratic limitations of each institution, were birds of passage. They were expected to vacate the fellowship either after a set number of years or once they had gained a higher degree. Unlike the heads of house, theirs was a no-frills existence. They had to share a room, though for obvious reasons not a bed, and were not allowed personal servants. Privacy was at a premium. In New College, fellows on the top floor were to sleep three, and on the ground floor four, to a room, and scholars studying different disciplines were to be mixed indiscriminately together, so that one of the group 'with a greater maturity, discretion and knowledge than the others' might look after the rest, and, when necessary, report 'on their morals, conversation and scholarly progress' to the warden and his deputies.[46]

If the statutes were being ignored or the college was beset with a problem that could not be resolved in-house, then the head and the fellows, either individually or collectively, could appeal to the visitor. The statutes indicated who the visitor was to be and laid down his powers. In the case of University College, the visitor was the Chancellor of the University assisted by the Proctors and the doctors of theology usually, it was an appropriate bishop or the crown. The visitor was always the official of last resort, however. His only formal role in the government of the college was to confirm the election of the head of house. And in this regard, the early colleges of both Oxford and Cambridge developed in a different way from their sister institutions in Paris. Colleges in Paris looked after their own endowment and elected a *procureur* to administer the finances. But they only occasionally chose their own head of house and they seldom elected to vacancies in the community. The principal and *boursiers*, as they became known, were appointed by the college visitor or, in the second case, whoever the founder of the scholarship had designated should have the right to nominate.[47] They were not then fully self-governing institutions. It would be naive to assume that Oxford colleges were free to elect whom they would to the foundation. It is evident from a later period that influence was frequently brought to bear by the great and good on behalf of their clients and could be difficult to resist. The principle of free election, though, was not a hollow one, and once established would normally be acknowledged in future centuries, even by those who sought to pervert it. Outsiders would usually recommend rather than demand the election of a candidate. Oxford and Cambridge colleges were not automatically in the king's or anyone else's pocket.[48]

---

[45] At Queen's, initially 5 marks: Statutes, vol. 1, *Statutes of Queen's College*, p. 11.

[46] Ibid., *Statutes of New College*, pp. 88–9.

[47] Merton initially did not appoint its own warden but offered the visitor three names: ibid., *Statutes of Merton College, 1274*, p. 33.

[48] Thierry Kouamé, 'Rex Fundator. Royal Interventions in University Colleges: Paris, Oxford, Cambridge (Fourteenth–Fifteenth Centuries)', *HU*, XXV: 1 (2010), 1–25. For the situation in later centuries, see pp. 153–8.

D. The Later Colleges

Eight more colleges were founded at Oxford between 1400 and Henry VIII's break with Rome in the 1530s: six secular and two regular. The two regular colleges were established in 1424 and 1437. The first, Frewen Hall, was a property in the city given to the Augustinian canons for their students; the second, St Bernard's College, was founded for Cistercian scholars out of several houses on St Giles, purchased thanks to a gift from Henry Chichele, archbishop of Canterbury.[49] Neither institution had the funds to develop their sites for many years. The Cistercians eventually built a new hall, chapel, and quadrangle at the turn of the sixteenth century, which was paid for by Abbot Marmaduke Huby of Fountains Abbey. Half a century later, the quadrangle would be incorporated into the new foundation of St John's College. The Austins, on the other hand, were forced to throw in the towel: in 1518, they handed over management of the college to Cardinal Wolsey, who used his great wealth to construct them a set of buildings.[50]

The first of the six secular colleges to be founded was Lincoln in 1427, on a site to the south of Exeter on the east side of St Mildred's Lane, which was the gift of the then bishop, Richard Fleming, anxious to make amends for his earlier flirtation with the heresies of Wyclif. This was followed by All Souls, established on the north side of the High Street to the east of St Mary the Virgin in 1438, founded by Chichele only a year after he had helped to set up St Bernard's. The archbishop of Canterbury equally hoped to create a foundation that would strengthen orthodoxy. A close ally of the Lancastrian dynasty, he dedicated his college to the souls of the faithful who had been killed fighting in the ongoing war against France.[51] The third secular foundation, Magdalen, was established in 1448, when its founder, William Waynflete, the recently appointed bishop of Winchester, installed a number of scholars under a president (a new name for an Oxford head of house) in properties on the south side of the High Street. Named rather oddly after Christ's most famous female follower, Mary Magdalene, a reformed prostitute, the new foundation was christened in English, Maudeleyn Hall, evidence that the modern pronunciation of the college was used from the beginning. Ten years later Waynflete issued a foundation charter for his new college on the strength of a royal licence, and transferred his scholars to its present site outside the east gate formerly occupied by the Hospital of St John, which the bishop had persuaded the king to secularize. Waynflete's influence with Henry VI stemmed from the role he had played as the first provost of the king's new grammar school at Eton. Although a schoolmaster cleric—he had initially been the head grammar teacher at Winchester—he proved an able political operator. The king's chancellor from 1456 to 1460 as well as bishop of Winchester, he was a Lancastrian

---

[49] The Cistercians had been hiring an academic hall in the city since the late fourteenth century.

[50] With the foundation of St Mary's Priory outside the city in the late fourteenth century, the Austins had three possible refuges besides their new college. It seems, though, that many lodged in halls. Members of the two orders were much more visible at Oxford from the turn of the sixteenth century.

[51] Jeremy Catto, 'The World of Henry Chichele and the Foundation of All Souls', in *Unarmed Soldiery: Studies in the Early History of All Souls College Oxford* (The Chichele Lectures 1993–1994; Oxford, 1996), pp. 1–13.

prelate who had an enviable ability to navigate the shoals of the Wars of the Roses and ensure his foundation flourished: in 1480, the first royal visitor to grace the portals of his new college was the Yorkist king Edward IV.[52]

After Magdalen's foundation, no more colleges were set up at Oxford until 1509, when Brasenose came into existence, named supposedly after the knocker on the front gate. Brasenose Hall, close by the University's schools, had existed since at least 1381 on a site leased from University College as a hall for lawyers. In the following century and a quarter, under a series of ambitious principals, Brasenose extended its size by taking over neighbouring halls: by 1500 it had incorporated ten. At the start of the sixteenth century, William Smith, bishop of Lincoln and a royal administrator, decided to turn the 'super hall' into a college by acquiring the site, installing the hall's former principal, Matthew Smyth, as his head of house, and gaining royal letters patent in 1512. The next and fifth foundation occurred five years later when Richard Fox, another bishop of Winchester, established Corpus Christi College, on land to the west of Merton. The pre-Reformation creations were then completed in 1525 by the foundation of Cardinal College on the site of St Frideswide's. This was the legacy to the University of Cardinal Wolsey, who had arranged to have the priory dissolved, just as Waynflete had earlier gained control of St John's Hospital. When Wolsey fell in 1529, his college, along with the rest of his property, was taken over by the king. In 1532, the institution was temporarily replaced by the much smaller King Henry VIII's College, which seems to have been more like a collegiate church than an endowed academic hall. In 1546 this became, in turn, the home of the cathedral church of the new diocese of Oxford, dedicated to Christ, which had been set up initially in 1542 in the former Oseney Abbey. By 1547, however, it had become the modern Christ Church, a cathedral chapter with an academic college attached whose head of house was the dean.[53]

Lincoln and Brasenose were small foundations. The first was set up to support seven theology students and a rector. It had a small endowment, and the first surviving accounts from 1455/6 reveal that it had an income in its first years of £70. Thanks to further benefactions—notably from another bishop of Lincoln, Thomas Rotherham, in the 1470s—the number of fellows had risen to twelve on the eve of the Reformation. But the college was never rich. Brasenose was initially even poorer. Smith had wanted to found a college for sixty scholars, but Richard Sutton, an Inner Temple lawyer, who had helped the founder get the college off the ground, wisely reduced the number to twelve philosophers and theologians. Until a new benefaction was received in 1515 from Elizabeth Morley, the wife of a London vintner and draper, the new college had had an income of only £47. All Souls was a college on a par with Merton. Under the 1443 statutes, it was to house forty fellows: sixteen lawyers, and twenty-four arts students who might proceed to

---

[52] On Waynflete's career, see Virginia Davis, *William Waynflete: Bishop and Educationalist* (Woodbridge, 1993).
[53] Another, albeit small, local religious institution secularized to fund Cardinal College was the Benedictine nunnery at Littlemore to the south of Oxford, closed in 1525 on the grounds the nuns were out of control.

study theology; and it had an annual income of some £400. Corpus was of similar size. Its foundation was intended to support a president, twenty fellows of the status of BA or above, and twenty undergraduate *discipuli*, who might go on to succeed their seniors. In the 1520s, the college had an income of some £350 per annum, which had risen to £500 by the mid-sixteenth century in line with inflation.

In comparison, Magdalen and Cardinal College were massive foundations. Waynflete's college was set up with forty fellows and thirty demies: the fellows were to be BAs or MAs committed to theological studies, though in exceptional circumstances some might be allowed to study law and medicine; the demies, so-called because they received half commons, were to be undergraduate scholars between the ages of 12 and 25 studying grammar or the different parts of philosophy, and would play no part in the government of the institution.[54] Magdalen was also, like New College, a choral foundation. Besides four chaplains, the college supported eight singing clerks and sixteen choristers. Cardinal was conceived in the same spirit but was more ambitious. It was set up to sustain 100 fellows who were to be secular canons: the sixty seniors would already have a BA degree and intend to go on to study in a higher faculty; the juniors were to be undergraduates of 15 or over, learned in grammar. Cardinal's chapel retinue outshone all others, boasting thirteen chaplains as well as a very large choir. Christ Church, once established, was of the same order: according to the draft Edwardian statutes, the cathedral chapter and the college were to comprise the dean, eight canons, and 100 students or fellows: twenty scholars pursuing theology, forty BAs (*philosophi*), and forty undergraduates.[55]

Both colleges were rich. In the last thirty years of his life, Waynflete had secured land for his college in many different parts of England through pressure and purchase: above all, he had persuaded the chief executor of the will of Sir John Fastolf, who had made money in the French wars, to pass the knight's fortune to Magdalen rather than found a collegiate church as the testator had desired. In consequence, at the end of the fifteenth century, the college had an income of £600, certainly as much as New, and greater than any Cambridge college except King's; by the mid-sixteenth century this figure had kept abreast of inflation and doubled. Cardinal was wealthier still. Wolsey had been given the right to endow his college with lands held in mortmain to the annual value of £2,000.[56] This may not have been its initial rent roll, but it was deemed to be the revenue of Christ Church in 1566, at which date the median income of all Oxford colleges was about an eighth of this sum.

Whatever the size of the new secular foundations, all, unlike the early colleges, very quickly acquired a distinctive physical character that marked them out as

---

[54] They are called 'Demyes' in the 1480 statutes: Statutes, vol. 2, *Statutes of Magdalen College, Oxford*, pp. 15–16. Corpus' *discipuli* also played no part in college government.

[55] The Edwardian statutes were never implemented. Christ Church was never given foundation statutes and the college was governed by orders of the chapter for the next three hundred years. It was therefore the one Oxford college not run by its fellows.

[56] Mortmain: property which could not be alienated or repossessed by original owners.

FIGURE 3.5 Entrance and tower, Brasenose College, *c*.1520. The new colleges of the late fifteenth and early sixteenth centuries were quick to make their mark on the Oxford land-scape. Although not a wealthy foundation, Brasenose immediately put itself on the architec-tural map by erecting a colossal late perpendicular gateway.

endowed rather than unendowed halls. In providing New College with its brand-new buildings, Wykeham had thrown down a gauntlet that later foundations had perforce to pick up. Each had to have its own quadrangle and gatehouse built in the fashionable perpendicular style. With the help of a generous gift from John Forest, dean of Wells, humble Lincoln had completed an entrance gateway and tower and three sides of a new quadrangle containing a dining hall, chapel, and library by the death of its second rector in 1465. Brasenose, too, quickly constructed an irregular two-storey quadrangle in the 1510s with a chapel and library, and by about 1520 had erected its distinctive three-storey battlemented gate tower (see Figure 3.5), although it never had a hall worthy of the name until the late seventeenth century. All Souls' and Corpus' buildings, in contrast, were erected before the college site was occupied.

FIGURE 3.6 Entrance vault, Corpus Christi College, *c.*1517. Bishop Fox equally intended that Corpus should cut a dash from its foundation. He had the mason William Vertue suspend Corpus's more modest gate tower on a peerless van fault.

All Souls' quadrangle, built of Burford stone, and notable for its T-shaped chapel with a hammer-beam roof, took five years to complete and was principally the work of Richard Chevynton, the master mason of Abingdon Abbey. It was not ready for occupation until 1442, and in the meantime Chichele's scholars were housed in Charlton's Inn.[57] Bishop Fox, on the other hand, had begun to build his college quadrangle and gatehouse four years before Corpus was founded, and the fellows were able to take possession immediately. The work was overseen from a distance by the prestigious William Vertue, one of the king's masons, who presumably was responsible for supporting the entrance tower with a fan vault, the first time this form of vaulting had been used for this purpose at Oxford (see Figure 3.6).

[57] E. F. Jacob, 'The Building of All Souls College 1438–1443', in J. G. Edwards, V. H. Galbraith, and E. F. Jacob (eds), *Essays in honour of James Tait* (Manchester, 1933), pp. 121–35.

Unsurprisingly, Magdalen and Cardinal/Christ Church were given the most sumptuous buildings. Magdalen occupied a huge area outside the city walls and Waynflete began by erecting a wall round the whole site west of the Cherwell. Using as his architect William Orchard, who would go on to build the University's Divinity School, Waynflete then set about constructing a large quadrangle which was finished in 1480. It took seven years to complete and cost in excess of £5,000. The quadrangle contained on its south side the chapel and abutting first-floor hall, and on the west (from north to south) a first-floor library, a three-storey gatehouse, which formed part of the president's lodgings, and a muniment tower over the entrance porch to the north door of the chapel. All the buildings were richly decorated anticipating the less austere 'Tudor' gothic, and topped off with battlements and pinnacles. The quadrangle's most original feature was that it incorporated on three sides (later four) a cloister. The college was also peculiar in that the gatehouse did not immediately give on to a street. The quadrangle was set back from the surrounding wall and visitors entered the college through a smaller gatehouse opposite the west door of the chapel that gave onto a large, open courtyard through which dignitaries could process before reaching the main buildings. The wall fronting the London road (today's High Street) initially contained buildings that earlier formed part of the hospital. Most of these were swept away at the turn of the century to construct a second quadrangle, Chaplain's Quad, which was enhanced at its south-east corner by a 144-foot late perpendicular bell tower. Commanding views over the city and surrounding countryside, the additional tower served no obvious purpose beyond advertising to the world the college's wealth and academic pretensions (see Figure 3.7).

FIGURE 3.7 Magdalen College, the Tower and High Street façade, c.1500: oil painting, early seventeenth century. Magdalen was the richest college to be founded before Christ Church. Twenty years after the erection of its original quadrangle, it spent a large sum of money building a second and erecting its beautiful late perpendicular tower fronting the High Street.

Cardinal College was planned on a gargantuan style with a huge quadrangle and a gateway to rival a royal palace. The chapel and hall were to face each other in the north and south ranges, and the whole quadrangle, as at Magdalen, was to have a cloister walk. However, despite an outlay of nearly £9,000 on its construction in the three years from January 1525, the quadrangle was still a truncated shell when Wolsey fell, and would be finally finished, minus the cloister, only in the 1660s. Even the 300-foot front range, containing the gatehouse, was only two-thirds complete and missing most of its north wing. The site eventually occupied by Christ Church was not short of buildings the new college could use. Besides the surviving monastic church and other remnants of St Frideswide's, the new institution incorporated the Benedictines' Canterbury College, dissolved at the Reformation. But it was not the perfect endowed hall Wolsey had envisaged. Until 1563 it appears it did not even have a library.[58]

The statutes given the new foundations of the fifteenth and early sixteenth centuries largely reprised the clauses of the earlier sets concerning governance and behaviour, and in their detail mimicked Wykeham's meticulous provisions for New College. For the most part, care continued to be taken not just to limit the subject a fellow might study but also to place restrictions on his background. Chichele was the only one to insist that founder's kin should have preference.[59] But all the colleges placed geographical constraints on the choice of fellows. Under the statutes given to Lincoln by Thomas Rotherham in 1480, one fellow was to come from the bishopric of Wells and the rest from Lincoln and York, on the grounds that other colleges drew few of their fellows from either diocese.[60] Brasenose, in contrast, favoured the dioceses of Coventry and Lichfield, but also gave 'preference to the sons of Lancashire and Cheshire, especially the natives of Prestbury and Prescott', the birthplaces of William Smith and Richard Sutton.[61] The restrictions Waynflete laid on the Magdalen fellowship were particularly complex. Like several of the foundations, the fellows and demies were to be taken from the parts of the country where the college had estates. In the demies' case there were no further stipulations, but each fellowship was specifically allotted to one of fourteen counties and five dioceses and could only be given to a native. The distribution was uneven: there could be only one fellow from Buckinghamshire, but seven from Waynflete's home county of Lincoln.[62] Similar limiting clauses were inserted into the statutes of Corpus Christi and Cardinal. In Wolsey's case, even the junior canons, analogous to Magdalen's demies, could not be admitted indiscriminately from the fifteen dioceses that were specifically designated: rather they were to be the products of the grammar schools he intended to found in these bishoprics.[63]

---

[58] Eventually a library was constructed out of the old St Frideswide's refectory: see the drawing in Curthoys, p. 284.

[59] Statutes, vol. 1, *Statutes of All Souls*, p. 2. [60] Ibid., vol. 1, *Statutes of Lincoln*, pp. 12–13.

[61] Ibid., vol. 2, *Statutes of Brasenose*, p. 2. [62] Ibid., vol. 2, *Statutes of Magdalen*, p. 17.

[63] Ibid., vol. 2, *Statutes of Cardinal College*, pp. 19–21. According to the Edwardian draft statutes, the undergraduates on the Christ Church foundation were also to be drawn from specified schools.

The statutes of Magdalen, Corpus Christi, and Cardinal, however, suggest that the concept of the academic college was undergoing revision. Waynflete's foundation was innovatory in three ways. In the first place, his statutes of 1480 specifically permitted scholars not on the foundation to reside in the college. A small group of students described as the 'sons of the friends of the college', no more than twenty in number and the offspring 'of noblemen and worthy commoners', were allowed, on the president's discretion, to join the Magdalen community as paying guests. The statutes also required that the best first-floor chambers on the north-eastern side of the Cloister quadrangle were to be reserved for their use. There was no insistence that the lodgers should be bound for a career in the church, though presumably Waynflete expected that they would be scholar clerks.[64] Scholars not on the foundation had lodged in Oxford colleges at an earlier date. University College rented out rooms to outsiders under a provision in its 1292 statutes, and its late fourteenth-century lodgers included Richard Fleming, the founder of Lincoln. But Magdalen was the first Oxford college to permit a large number of resident guests. Waynflete may have been aware that King's Hall, Cambridge, had been freely admitting outsiders from the 1430s, or he may have been building on the practice of the two foundation boarding schools with which he had been earlier associated, where fee-payers were also welcomed.[65]

Secondly, Waynflete established three stipendiary college lecturers in divinity, natural philosophy, and ethics and metaphysics. These daily lectures were to be available to scholars living outside the college as well as in. Waynflete also made provision for a fourth lecturer in logic and sophistry, who was to be employed for the benefit of the younger fellows and demies alone. But he was clearly distinguished in stipend and status from the three *praelectores*, who had a wider remit.[66] The establishment of lectures of any kind within a college was an innovation. Colleges must have long arranged extra-curricular disputations and other exercises to keep the fellows on their toes, whilst it had also become the custom in some colleges, such as New, that seniors should oversee the studies of beginners.[67] No earlier statutes, however, had established in-house lectures. The establishment of public lectures further distinguished Waynflete's initiative from the practice in the halls. Aularian lectures were being given by 1480, as we have seen in the first section of this chapter, but they were closed.

Thirdly, Magdalen's statutes established a free grammar school on the college site, which was set up in a new two-storey building, measuring 70 feet by 24 feet, erected on a north–south elevation to the west of the college courtyard. The schoolroom had space for about a hundred boys and the endowment supported two masters. The school's pupils would have included the younger demies and presumably the

---

[64] Ibid., vol. 2, *Statutes of Magdalen*, pp. 60 and 73.
[65] Nicholas Orme, *Childhood to Chivalry: The Education of English Kings and Aristocracy 1066–1530* (London, 1984), p. 74.
[66] Statutes, vol. 2, *Statutes of Magdalen College*, pp. 47–8 and 78.
[67] Ibid., vol. 1, *Statutes of New College*, p. 54.

choristers, but like the college lectures, it was open to the wider world (both town and gown). Its *raison d'être* appears to have been to teach the young to write and speak a purer Ciceronian Latin, as advocated by the fifteenth-century humanists, whose campaign for the complete renovation of the study of classical languages, philosophy, and Scripture had not yet made a profound impact in England outside a small circle at the royal court.[68]

Magdalen was the only Oxford college to found its own on-site grammar school in the following decades, though Jesus, Cambridge, established at the turn of the sixteenth century, was both a school and a college for its first sixty years.[69] Later foundations, on the other hand, did make specific room for paying guests: Brasenose was to make space for six; Corpus four to six; and Cardinal copied Magdalen's statutes virtually word for word.[70] Corpus and Cardinal also built on Magdalen's introduction of in-house teaching. Magdalen's grammar school may have taught pupils the new humanist Latin, but it does not appear to have taught Greek or provided instruction in the art of rhetoric, so it was only teaching a small part of the humanists' linguistic programme. Bishop Fox, a friend of Erasmus, was anxious that Oxford scholars should have the chance to study the Latin and Greek humanities in their entirety and aimed to fill the gap with his collegiate foundation. Corpus was to have college lectureships in Latin rhetoric (which was to be taught through specified classical authors) and in Greek grammar and literature. In addition, it was to have a lecturer in theology who would explicate the Scriptures according to the ancient doctors of the church rather than recent commentators.[71] Cardinal College, in contrast, was set up to provide lectures in the new learning as well as the traditional parts of the university curriculum. Wolsey was already supporting public lectures in the humanities and theology in the late 1510s. His new institution was to extend the provision. He envisaged six lecturers: in Latin and Greek literature, philosophy, theology, canon law, civil law, and medicine.[72] When Henry VIII refounded the college as Christ Church in 1546, Wolsey's plan was taken a step further. The king set up three public readers in theology, Hebrew, and Greek, and six domestic lecturers, two in dialectic, the others in rhetoric, natural philosophy or mathematics, and ethics.

E. The Decline of the Halls

Thanks to the new collegiate foundations across the fifteenth and the early sixteenth centuries, the number of scholars on bursaries more than doubled. In the mid-sixteenth century, Oxford's colleges provided free board and lodgings for some

---

[68] Ibid, vol. 2, *Statute of Magdalen College*, p. 76; Nicholas Orme, *Education in Early Tudor England: Magdalen College and its School 1480–1540* (Oxford, 1998). For humanism in England and Oxford, see pp. 119–23, this volume.

[69] Peter Glazebrook, 'Grammar School and College: Jesus' First Sixty Years', *Jesus College Annual Report* (2009), 7–29. Although there appears to have been grammarians on the foundation of Christ Church in 1547, there is no evidence of a school within its grounds, even if one was envisaged.

[70] Statutes, vol. 2, *Statutes of Brasenose*, p. 12; *Statutes of Corpus Christi*, p. 80; *Statutes of Cardinal College*, pp. 103–4.

[71] Ibid., *Statutes of Corpus Christi*, pp. 48–54.   [72] Ibid., *Statutes of Cardinal College*, pp. 122–32.

450 graduates and undergraduates. This was still fewer than the number of scholarships available at the University of Paris, but Oxford was a much smaller university. By this date, too, there was a fast increasing number of paying guests residing in the endowed halls. The readiness of the founders of Magdalen and the three early sixteenth-century colleges to give statutory warranty to the practice of taking in outsiders seems to have encouraged the older colleges to open their gates more widely than hitherto. Balliol was given a new set of statutes in 1507 by Bishop Fox of Winchester. These made clear that the reception of outsiders was, by then, a commonplace at the college, and that they were given the best rooms. The main concern of the bishop was that the *extranei*, on their admission, should be made to swear to obey the provisions of the statutes with regard to good behaviour whether in hall, at table, in chapel, or at in-house disputations.[73]

In the course of the first half of the sixteenth century, moreover, the colleges abandoned any attempt to limit the number of outsiders living in the midst, although it is impossible to know whether this happened before or after the break with Rome. So many students were 'rooming' in colleges by the mid-sixteenth century, that the halls no longer housed the majority of scholars. In 1552, towards the end of Edward's VI's short reign, the Vice-Chancellor ordered a head count of the numbers in Oxford's halls and colleges, partly to discover how many students in residence had not taken the oath to 'observe the statutes, privileges, customs and liberties' of the University.[74] This revealed that, in a period of rapid religious change, numbers overall had fallen by about a third to little more than a thousand. It also revealed that the halls now accommodated only a quarter of the total and that their number had fallen to eight. With one exception, the surviving halls were still substantial institutions: the largest, Hart Hall, on New College Lane to the west of Wykeham's foundation, sheltered forty-five students.[75] But the colleges were clearly admitting *extranei* in some numbers, especially Brasenose. Although it was a foundation for eighteen scholars, in 1552 it had seventy names on its books, including forty-nine arts students.[76]

It would be wrong to conclude that the novel dominance of Oxford's colleges in the mid-sixteenth century (and at Cambridge too where the same development can be observed) is evidence that the academic hall was a flawed institution. The more common view today is that the hall was the victim of its own success. As a vehicle for policing students and providing them with extra-curricular tuition, it provided a model that the colleges after 1450 would adopt and adapt.[77] Once the colleges, with

---

[73] Ibid, vol. 1, *Statutes of Balliol*, pp. 19 and 20.

[74] C. W. Boase (ed.), *Register of the University of Oxford*, vol. 1 (Oxford, 1885), pp. xxii–xxv. Some of the names recorded were servants.

[75] Hart(e) Hall appears to have been one of the few late medieval halls to have a library. For its pre-1550 history, see Sidney G. Hamilton, *Hertford College* (London, 1903), ch. 1.

[76] Brasenose had been endowed with six more scholarships in 1538.

[77] Jeremy Catto, 'The Triumph of the Hall in Fifteenth-Century Oxford', in Ralph Evans (ed.), *Lordship and Learning: Studies in Memory of Trevor Aston* (Woodbridge, 2004), ch.13. Catto's article has completely transformed the way historians think about the academic hall.

their elegant, purpose-built quadrangles, became more numerous, larger, and expanded their remit, they were guaranteed to supplant the halls. But this does not belittle the hall's contribution to structuring student life. It is better, therefore, to see the two institutions as manifestations of the same idea. Indeed, until the end of the fifteenth century, the halls, though now far fewer in number through amalgamation and closure, were flourishing. A new hall, one that would have a long history, was even established about 1490. This was Magdalen Hall. Located within the curtilage of Magdalen College, fronting the London road and abutting the college school to the west, it had thirty-five inhabitants in 1552. It seems likely that the hall was initially established to house pupils of the school, who apparently, in its early years, came from a wide provenance, attracted by the humanist slant of its teaching. After 1500, when other schools in England were also teaching the new Latin, the hall may principally have been filled with undergraduates who hoped in the course of time to become Magdalen demies.[78] Whatever its specific purpose, Magdalen Hall flourished in the decades before the Reformation and was extended further westwards in 1518. Its success gives the lie to the idea that the hall by then was a redundant concept.[79]

---

[78] Other surviving halls often had a close relationship with a neighbouring college. St Mary Hall, on the south side of the High Street to the north of Oriel, had taken over the adjacent Bedel Hall at the end of the fifteenth century. After 1500, it became, in all but name, an undergraduate wing of the college.

[79] For the other surviving halls in the mid-sixteenth century, see p. 144, this volume.

CHAPTER 4

Teaching and Learning

A. The Curriculum

As is the case for most of the first universities, Oxford's curriculum is impossible to reconstruct perfectly before the early fourteenth century. University statutes are difficult to date before 1350, and those concerning the organization of teaching and examining are relatively few.[1] What is evident is that, by the mid-fourteenth century, there were clear rules about the years of study needed to proceed to a degree, the content of the course, and the process of examination. The curriculum was text-based and the lectures given by masters or doctors fell into two principal categories: ordinary and extraordinary. The first were lectures on compulsory texts given in the morning; the second, on approved but less important ones, given in the afternoon. Each lecture would consist of a detailed exposition of a passage or passages of a set text that the lecturer would initially read out to the class, an essential ritual when students did not always have their own copies. The exposition would be built round a series of *quaestiones*, where the lecturer would take a word or phrase from the text, then propose and refute a number of possible meanings before settling on his preferred answer. In so doing, the lecturer might move a long way from the text itself and discuss problems that the author had barely touched on. As paper was expensive, most students would have sat and listened rather than transcribed lecturer's words or taken notes. A good memory was essential. This method of exposition, to the extent it was associated specifically with the 'schools' of the universities, became known to later opponents and historians as scholasticism.[2]

To become a bachelor usually required that a student had simply studied under a master for the requisite number of years and listened to lectures on the right texts. To qualify to be a licentiate, and then a master or doctor, however, was much more onerous and helps to explain why so few scholars ever incepted. To progress to a higher level the bachelor had to display his debating skills in a number of

---

[1] For an attempt to bring some precision, see G. Pollard, 'The Oxford Statute Book of the University', *Bodleian Library Record*, 8 (1967–72), 69–91.

[2] Richard Southern (with notes and additions by Lesley Smith and Benedicta Ward), *Scholastic Humanism and the Unification of Europe*, vol. 2: *The Heroic Age* (Oxford, 1995). At Oxford, the format for arts lectures was prescribed in a statute of 1431: *Statuta*, p. 236.

disputations on selected topics with his peers and other masters. The disputes mirrored the format of the *quaestio*. Under the watchful eye of a presiding master, a bachelor would 'oppose' or put forward his solution; others would then be called on to respond; and the *quaestio* would be knocked to and fro until the master brought the disputation to a close. In the higher faculties especially these could be occasions where the bachelor could display originality and ingenuity and even come to the attention of the outside world. Becoming a master or doctor, however, was not the final staging post on an Oxford scholar's academic *cursus*. A primary concern of the University was to ensure continuity in teaching. The regular convents employed their own lecturers from the beginning, and eventually the halls and some colleges hired teachers to cover part of the curriculum, but until the turn of the sixteenth century and the creation of the Lady Margaret chair in divinity in 1497 by Henry VII's mother, Lady Margaret Beaufort, Oxford had no stipendiary university professors. New masters, therefore, were expected to lecture for a few years before becoming full doctors and moving on.

The arts curriculum was built around the works of Aristotle and other ancient authors. The first regulations were laid down in a statute of 1268, which set out the texts that a bachelor had to have heard expounded before he could determine or receive his degree. These texts comprised Priscian's grammar and Donatus' rhetorical work, the *Barbarismus*, the so-called old logic (the first three books of Boethius' *Topics*, and his translations of Porphyry's *Universals* and Aristotle's *Predicaments* and *De interpretatione*), the recently rediscovered new logic (Aristotle's *Topics*, *Elenchi*, and the *Prior* and *Posterior Analytics*, which dealt with the syllogism and constructing an argument), and three of Aristotle's books on natural philosophy (the *Physics*, *De generatione et corruptione*, and *De anima*). The statute gave no indication of how long a student was to spend in listening to lectures on these texts, although it did insist he heard lectures on some texts twice.[3] At some time before 1350, possibly in 1313, the regulations were further formalized in a second statute that declared no one could determine as a bachelor, 'unless he has confirmed with his own oath that he has heard lectures in arts for four years in schools where there is a *studium generale*'.[4]

A further statute, probably of the same date, revealed that before being licensed a student had next to hear the other works on physics by Aristotle, as well as his *Ethics* and *Politics*, Boethius' fourth book of *Topics* (on rhetoric), more Priscian, six books of Euclid, Boethius' *Arithmetic*, and the simple but extremely widely circulated mathematical and astronomical works of the thirteenth-century John of Holywood (Sacrobosco). The only Aristotelian text of significance which was not stipulated was his *Metaphysics*, though this was a book that was certainly being expounded in the early fourteenth century, according to information in a Merton manuscript.[5] Other, usually undatable, statutes established further details about the path to the

---

[3] *Statuta*, pp. 25–6. Priscian, Donatus, and Boethius were authors of the late Roman Empire.
[4] Ibid., p. 24. The regulation was repeated in 1409.
[5] *Statuta*, pp. 32–3. On the ubiquity of Sacrobosco, see John North, 'The *Quadrivium*', in *HUIE*, i. 339, 348–9.

licence. This second period of study was to last three years. During this time the bachelor would have to give so-called cursory lectures of his own on works of logic and physics, which probably entailed no more than reading out the text and offering a short commentary. He was also expected to participate in a number of disputations (four with masters, and, from 1346, two per year with his fellow bachelors), then deliver an ordinary lecture before a group of masters, who would sit in judgement on his performance and his ability to handle the succeeding dispute. The bachelors would then qualify for the licence and be given leave to incept as a master. This time the interval between the two was short. After two more disputations (one where he acted as the proponent, the other as the respondent) and a feast, the licentiate became a regent master. For the rest of the year and the year following, he was a 'necessary regent', who had to give ordinary lectures and attend disputations when required. Only after this could he start studying in a higher faculty, if he so wished.

The formal structure of the arts course that had crystallized by 1350 remained broadly unchanged over the coming centuries and would be confirmed by the Laudian statutes of the 1630s.[6] The official content of the curriculum, however, did not stay the same. It was reorganized, strengthened, and clarified by a statute issued in December 1431 (see Figure 4.1).[7] This statute appears to have intended that, in future, the seven liberal arts should be studied before, and the three philosophies after, a student became a bachelor. It also laid down how many terms were to be spent on each sub-discipline, confirmed that Aristotle's *Metaphysics* was now an official part of the curriculum, and greatly extended the attention to be paid to rhetoric and the quadrivium.[8] An important influence within the University at this date was Humfrey, duke of Gloucester, who was one of the first to take an interest in the attempt by Italian humanists to breathe new life into the art of public speaking by creating a new rhetoric based on classical texts. It was Humfrey, it seems, who persuaded the University to make the subject a serious part of the curriculum.[9] Donatus was replaced and, in its stead, masters over three terms were to read either the *Rhetoric* of Aristotle, the fourth book of Boethius' *Topics*, the pseudo-Ciceronian *Rhetorica ad Herennium*, or (particularly novel) Ovid's *Metamorphoses* and the poetry of Virgil. In contrast to the earlier period, the quadrivium was now represented in its entirety. Boethius' *Arithmetic* was to be read for a term, then his *Musica* for another, followed by either Euclid's geometry or the works on optics of Alhazen (Ibn al-Haytham) or the thirteenth-century Silesian Witelo. Astronomy was also to be studied for the same amount of time and in a much more sophisticated way, using either the *Theorica planetarum* (a thirteenth-century anonymous exposition of

---

[6] See pp. 234–6, this volume   [7] *Statuta*, pp. 234–6.
[8] It also introduced Aristotle's *Economics* to the curriculum. Both his *Politics* and his *Economics* had only been translated into Latin in the mid-thirteenth century. The quadrivium was the collective name for the four mathematical liberal arts; grammar, rhetoric, and logic were called the trivium.
[9] On Humfrey and the University Library, see p. 27, this volume.

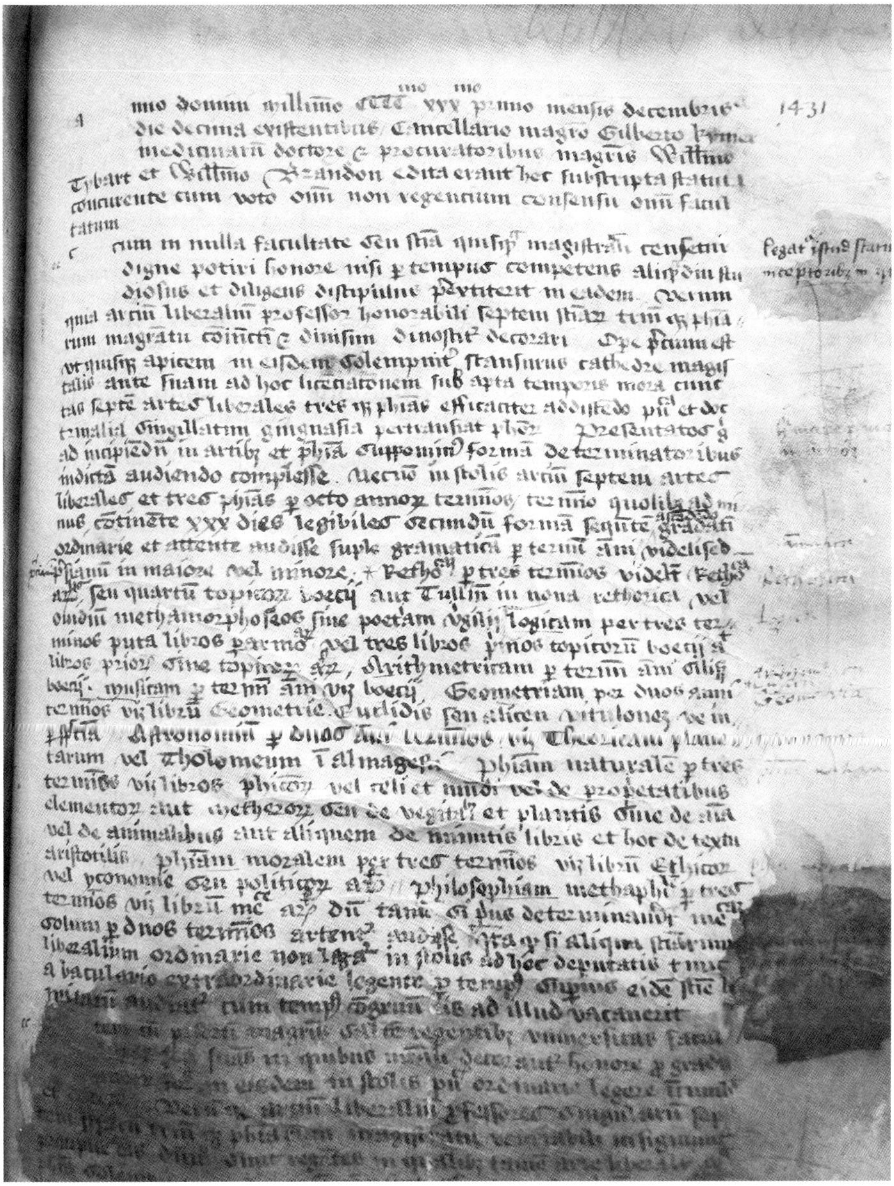

FIGURE 4.1 The arts course as laid down in the statute of 1431, promulgated during the chancellorship of Gilbert Kymer MD. According to its preamble, the course needed to be laid out in detail to ensure that no one was licensed in the arts who had not studied all of the seven liberal arts and three philosophies.

planetary theory) or (an extremely ambitious choice) Ptolemy's *Almagest*, rather than the simplistic John of Holywood. Time was saved, so that this extended curriculum could be followed in seven years, by allowing students to select which works of logic and physics they wanted to study, and the removal from the course altogether of Aristotle's *Posterior Analytics*.

The path to the doctorate in theology, law, or medicine was never mapped out with the same precision but was basically similar. By the early fourteenth century, when their first statutes were promulgated (probably at the same time as the regulations for incepting as an MA), each of the higher faculties had evolved a detailed programme of study and examination. Becoming a doctor of theology could take many years. A scholar could supplicate to become a bachelor only after four years' initial study, for it was only in his fifth year in the faculty's schools that he was permitted to oppose in a disputation. As a theologian was not allowed to give his cursory lectures until he had completed his seventh year of study—or his ninth if he had not already gained the MA that he would need before he was licensed—fulfilling the requirements for the doctorate must have frequently taken ten years or more. Even after finishing lecturing, a scholar was expected to undergo a further two years of study.[10] Becoming a doctor of law or medicine still took time but was comparatively swift. The statutes of the two faculties did not lay down a compulsory period of study that had to be completed before a student could dispute or lecture. Rather, they simply stipulated the number of years of study that must be undertaken before supplicating for the licence, thus allowing students towards the end of the course to fulfil their lecturing and disputing obligations concurrently. Civil lawyers who had an arts degree had to study in the faculty's schools for four years; otherwise they had to sit on the benches for six. Canonists, who had not already taken a civilian degree, were required to listen to lectures for eight years: three years of civil law, two on the Bible, and three at least on the law of the church. Medical students could be licensed after six years of study if they were masters of arts, eight if they were not.[11]

The course in theology and the two laws was structured, from the late thirteenth century, around an unchanging corpus of texts that were standard across Europe. Students in theology had to listen to two sets of lectures: one on the Bible (for three years); the other on the *Sentences* of Peter Lombard, a twelfth-century work composed by a master of the cathedral school of Notre-Dame de Paris, which used rational argument to explicate and resolve a series of *quaestiones* dealing with key points of doctrine.[12] Licensiands, it would appear, were expected to lecture on both of these texts, albeit only on one book of the Bible and one of the four volumes of the *Sentences*.[13] A bachelor's lectures on the Bible were not supposed to be controversial but to concentrate on 'the literal meaning'.[14] Conversely, there seem to have been no restrictions on how the text of the *Sentences* was handled, even though this was customarily read first, in contrast to the practice at Paris.[15]

[10] *Statuta*, pp. 48–9. All Oxford licentiates in theology had to be an MA of some university from 1253.
[11] Ibid., pp. 41–2, 43, and 47.
[12] The first Oxford master to leave a commentary on the *Sentences* was the Dominican Richard Fishacre, d. 1248.
[13] The books dealt with God and the Trinity, Creation, the incarnation and the virtues, and the sacraments and the Last Judgement. Lombard's text was the most complete of a number of scholastic *sententiae* produced in the twelfth century: Monika Asztalos, 'The Faculty of Theology', in *HUIE*, i. 411–12.
[14] *Statuta*, p. 50.
[15] The friars objected to this in 1311. See H. Rashdall, 'The Friar Preachers versus the University', in M. Burrows (ed.), *Collectanea II* (OHS; Oxford, 1890), pp. 195–273.

The chief civil law texts were the *Digest*, a collection of judgements of Roman jurisconsultants, and the sixth-century *Code* that was drawn up for the Emperor Justinian from the decisions of his predecessors and became the law of Byzantium. Canon law was primarily taught from Gratian's *Decretum*, a collection of church pronouncements from different bodies that the twelfth-century Bolognese jurist had attempted to reconcile and clarify using rational and historical analysis, and the *Decretals*, five volumes of papal bulls and rescripts collected on behalf of Pope Gregory IX and issued as church law in 1234. The civilians ensured the ground was adequately covered by a simple division of labour. The most important parts of the civil law collections, the so-called *Old Digest* and the first nine books of the *Code*, were read in alternate years by one or more regent doctors; other civil law books, such as the *Institutes*, an introduction to Roman law, were read by the bachelors as cursory or extraordinary lectures. The regent and the bachelors probably worked as a team.[16] The canon law course, on the other hand, remained the property of the doctors regent. Next to nothing is known about the course on the *Decretum*, but until 1333 the *Decretals* were taught in a single year, with the result that the course could not be finished. Thereafter, its explication became part of a two-year cycle of ordinary lectures that covered books 1 and 3–5 and two later collections of papal bulls, the *Sextus* (1298) and the *Clementines* (1317). Before supplicating for the licence, bachelors of canon law were expected to have read one book of the *Decretals* and to have lectured on two of three specified themes: simony, consecration, and peni- tence. These lectures were called extraordinary, not cursory, but they were not a vital part of the official curriculum. Unlike their peers in civil law, the bachelors' teaching supplemented rather than complemented the regents' lectures.[17]

The medical course, in contrast, appears to have never been based on a set of prescribed texts, perhaps because this was a science in the making across the middle ages, and its text base was far from stable. The curriculum would have been built around the extant oeuvre of the classical doctors, Galen and Hippocrates, and the works of medieval Jewish and Arab physicians. But the statutes offer no clue as to the books that were normally read. Presumably, the principal texts commented on were the three studied in all medical faculties: Galen's *Tegni*, a brief compendium also called the *Ars parva* or *Microtechne*, Hippocrates' *Aphorisms*, a text that would remain essential study for medical students until the late eighteenth century and beyond, and the *Canon* of the Muslim philosopher Avicenna, the most complete post-classical medical textbook. Certainly one of the first two had to be read by bachelors before they incepted under the faculty's statutes, which required licen- siands to have lectured on a book of theoretical and a book of practical medicine. Under the second head, the bachelor was offered three choices, all again favourite medical texts in the late medieval university: Hippocrates' *De regimine acutorum*, the *Librum febrium* of the Jewish physician Isaac Israeli, and the *Antidotarium* of Nicolas of

Salerno, the standard pharmaceutical text written by a doctor of medieval Europe's first medical school.[18]

Faculty lectures were normally given in the faculty schools, which were buildings owned by townsmen, religious houses, or colleges, and specifically set aside for this purpose. Regents had to hire their school from the owner. Faculty disputations, on the other hand, were held in various venues. By 1346 it was the convention that bachelors of arts disputed with each other at the Austins' friary, while the vespers—the disputation held immediately prior to their becoming masters—took place in St Mildred's Church until it was absorbed, in the early fifteenth century, into Lincoln College. The arts and theology faculties' schools formed a complex of buildings at the north end of what came to be called School Street, which ran from the High Street, west of St Mary's, to the city wall (following a line that today would go through the west side of Radcliffe Square and the Bodleian quadrangle). Initially, the civilians and canonists shared the same school that was situated to the north-west of St Edward's Church—the civilians had one classroom, the canonists two—in 1465, however, the civilians moved to a new site to the north of Jury Lane. The location of the medical school is a mystery but lectures in the early fourteenth century were possibly delivered in Tingewick Inn or Corbet Hall, on the east side of Cat Street.[19] (See Map 2.) Given the relative size of the different faculties and the small number of students who became doctors in the higher faculties, the majority of masters regenting in the University's schools would have been lecturing in arts.

Regents were under no compulsion to be innovative. In an age when access to books was limited, lecturers were principally expected to ensure their students were introduced to the range of existing opinions on a subject rather than dazzle them with their own. The late medieval university was not a research institution pushing forwards the frontiers of knowledge but an arm of the church in its struggle to create unity, uniformity, and good order. The fact, too, that most regents were novice masters and doctors who would only teach for a couple of years limited the likelihood of their having something fresh to say. Nonetheless, there were no restrictions placed on originality, provided a lecturer did not sin egregiously against religious orthodoxy, and most universities supported the odd original mind across the period. The institutions that gained and maintained an international reputation were those whose regents consistently added to the interpretative literature, and developed out of the *quaestio* format completely new avenues of thought which were committed to writing, and copied and disseminated around the continent.

The paucity of surviving manuscripts relating to the lectures and disputations given in the legal and medical schools suggests that three of Oxford's five faculties

---

[18] *Statuta*, p. 41. For the standard medical curriculum, see Nancy Siraisi, 'The Faculty of Medicine', in *HUIE*, i. 366, 374, and 378–9. Both the *Tegni* and the *Aphorisms* were part of a collection of introductory medical texts which had been brought together by the early twelfth century by doctors at Salerno under the title of the 'articella'.

[19] W. A. Pantin, 'The Halls and Schools of Medieval Oxford: An Attempt at Reconstruction', in *Oxford Studies presented to Daniel Callus* (OHS, new series, xvi; Oxford, 1964), pp. 90–8. Faculty lectures in other disciplines were also sometimes given in halls.

were intellectually humdrum. Though they doubtless provided their students with a solid working knowledge of the state of contemporary scholarship, there is equally no reason to believe that the quality of their teaching rose above the mundane. Oxford's law schools could never hold a torch to those of Bologna and Paris, or even to schools of more recent foundation such as Orléans and Toulouse.[20] The University, once established, never sheltered a single civilian or canonist teacher of international note. In the fifteenth century, moreover, when many of Oxford's lawyers were finding lucrative billets in the administrations of church and state, standards in both faculties slipped: licensiands were frequently allowed by the University to dispense with giving their cursory lectures or studying in the schools for the requisite number of years.[21] Oxford's small medical faculty was singularly unimpressive. While Europe's leading medical faculties from the end of the thirteenth century—Montpellier, Paris, Bologna, and Padua—were producing novel commentaries on the texts of the Greeks and the Arabs, writing treatises on specific diseases, and developing an interest in anatomical dissection and surgery, Oxford scholar physicians seem to have been content to build up medical libraries rather than compose their own books or do their own investigations. Only two notable medical works were produced by Oxford scholars in the fourteenth and fifteenth centuries, both written by fellows of Merton. The better known, John of Gaddesden's *Rosa angelica medicinae*, probably composed in the 1310s, demonstrated wide reading but got short shrift from the great Montpellier surgeon Guy de Chauliac, who dismissed it fifty years later in the opening chapter of his own *magnum opus* as 'insipid'.[22]

Oxford's arts and theology faculties, in contrast, were of an entirely different order. Before the end of the thirteenth century, neither faculty caused much of a stir on the continent, though some Englishmen with an Oxford association gained an intellectual reputation while teaching abroad and others left interesting works. In the first two-thirds of the fourteenth century, however, Oxford produced a bevy of scholars who developed aspects of Aristotelian logic and physics in a novel direction that took Europe by storm. As logicians, Oxford's philosophers were primarily 'terminists' who were interested in the slippery meaning and truth content of words and phrases, while, as natural philosophers, they particularly studied the physics of motion. Many of the same figures also turned their attention to theological speculation and made significant contributions to the late medieval understanding of free will, grace, and authority. Oxford's philosophers and theologians did not begin *ex novo*: their work largely built on thirteenth-century commentaries that had been chiefly written at the University of Paris. Nor was there an Oxford 'School': the creative tension stemmed from the fact that the masters and bachelors were frequently at loggerheads; even within the same religious order there could be profound differences of opinion. But collectively Oxford's philosophers and theologians put the University on the

---

[20] Antonio Garcia y Garcia, 'The Faculties of Law', in *HUIE*, i, ch. 12.
[21] E.g. the dispensation given to John Wanflete, the founder of Magdalen's brother, in Mar. 1449: *Register of the University of Oxford*, vol. 1: *1449–1463, 1506–1571*, ed. C. W. Boase (OHS, i; Oxford, 1885), p. vii.
[22] Siraisi, 'Medicine', pp. 380–2.

intellectual map, and for the next two centuries many of their manuscripts were continually recopied and circulated around the university world. The burst of intellectual activity did not, however, last, and Oxford philosophy and theology in the fifteenth and early sixteenth centuries lost their international élan. Yet the achievements of the fourteenth century left a permanent legacy: they gave the University a reputation as a pre-eminent centre of learning that it was able to trade on thereafter.

B. The Paris Inheritance, Scotus, and Ockham

Masters at the University of Paris began commentating on the newly recovered Aristotelian corpus at the turn of the thirteenth century. Their teaching immediately came under close scrutiny from the church. Aristotle's physical works ran counter to Christian orthodoxy in that they taught the eternity of the world and the mortality of all living creatures. They smacked of materialism, even when read with the aid of the commentaries of the Persian Arab philosopher Avicenna, who, as a pious Muslim, upheld the immortality of the human soul, if not the resurrection of the body.[23] As a result, the Council of Sens, in 1210, banned both public and private lectures on Aristotle's natural philosophy and commentaries on the texts, a ban that was repeated five years later and extended to the *Metaphysics* by the papal legate, Robert de Courson, when he drew up the first regulations for the Paris arts faculty. In the following decades, the church tempered its position. In 1231, Pope Gregory IX confirmed the ban, but only until the texts were sufficiently purged of error. This ruling opened the door to the study of the texts once again, and from 1255, when the Paris arts syllabus was revised, virtually every Aristotelian natural philosophical text, as well as the *Metaphysics*, became a set book.[24] Paris, in the second half of the thirteenth century, became a dynamic and fertile centre of Aristotelian commentary. Its teaching masters came from all over Europe and included the two founding fathers of late medieval philosophy, both Dominicans and both eventually beatified: the German Albert the Great and his pupil, Thomas Aquinas. Albert and Thomas did not distance them-selves from Aristotle where he appeared unchristian. Rather, they found ways of reconciling Aristotle and Christianity, principally by redefining the Aristotelian doc-trine of form. Aristotle believed that all natural bodies consisted of two parts, matter and form; though he appeared to see form as something more than the sum of the parts, there was no suggestion that form was anything other than a material entity. Aquinas, on the other hand, declared that forms were substantial, individual, and spiritual, thereby explaining how the form of the human body, the soul, or the mind (*anima*), could be immortal.[25]

[23] F. C. Copleston, *A History of Medieval Philosophy* (London, 1977), pp. 110–15.

[24] Hastings Rashdall, *The Universities of Europe in the Middle Ages*, ed. F. M. Powicke and A. B. Emden (3 vols; Oxford, 1936), i. 353 69; Gordon Leff, 'The *Trivium* and the Three Philosophies', in *HUIE*, i. 320–1; and Asztalos, 'Theology', pp. 420–2.

[25] Albert taught at the Paris convent from 1243–48 and Thomas from 1252–59. Albert's commentaries were written after he moved to the Cologne convent in 1248. On Dominican thought: Copleston, *Medieval Philosophy*, ch. 12.

The successful Christianization of Aristotle did not leave the French university free from church scrutiny. The traditional view of God and man that had held sway in the western church since the fifth century was the position of St Augustine of Hippo that man was a fallen creature and God all-powerful and inscrutable. There was a widespread suspicion that Aquinas, for all his philosophical brio, had placed far too much emphasis on human potential by subjecting the mysteries of faith to rational enquiry. The teaching of some of Aquinas' younger contemporaries in the final third of the thirteenth century, notably Siger of Brabant, only confirmed the church's worst suspicions. Siger, unlike Aquinas, was captivated by the second great Arab commentator of Aristotle, Averroes, whose commentaries were available in Latin from about 1230. Averroes, a Spanish Muslim, was far more threatening to Christian orthodoxy than Avicenna, in that he appeared to deny the immortality of the human soul as well as the body. In his opinion, every human being had an 'imaginative' intellect which stored images received from sense impressions, but the 'active' intellect that turned these images, our very personal cache of experiences, into knowledge was not individuated, and the 'material' intellect in which this knowledge was contained had no form and was similarly common to all. Although both the active and material intellect were eternal, the 'acquired' intellect—the individual's singular collection of thoughts—was not, so there could be no individual salvation. To the church, Averroism was a heresy, all the more that the Cordovan philosopher taught that the Koran (and by extension the Bible) was not to be taken as literally true; rather it had been composed in a way that would bring enlightenment to simple minds who could only grasp a message that was presented in picture form.[26] In an attempt to rid the university of all materialist teaching, the bishop of Paris, Étienne Tempier, in 1270 and again in 1277 listed a number of 'errors' that could no longer be taught. All told, in 1277, 219 propositions were outlawed, which included the denial of the Creation, the Trinity, and the immortality of the soul, and a belief in the influence of the heavens over events and actions on the earth.[27]

In contrast, Oxford's philosophy teaching in the thirteenth century largely remained immune from church intervention. In the first part of the century this reflected the slow absorption of the recovered Aristotelian corpus. The future Oxford Chancellor and bishop of Lincoln, Robert Grosseteste, had completed a commentary on the *Posterior Analytics* as early as 1220, and then moved on to study the *Physics* while part of the Hereford cathedral school. But Grosseteste's relocation to the new Oxford *studium* about 1225 to teach theology did little to spark interest in the new Aristotelian texts.[28] Although the new logic and two of the three philosophies were officially part of the curriculum from 1268, no one lectured at Oxford on

---

[26] Copleston, *Medieval Philosophy*, pp. 117–24.

[27] *Chartularium Universitatis Parisiensis*, vol. 1, ed. H. Denifle and A. Chatelain (Paris, 1899), pp. 543–58 (no. 473); Asztalos, 'Theology', pp. 424–6; E. Grant, 'The Condemnation of 1277, God's Absolute Power, and Physical Thought in the Late Middle Ages', *Viator*, 10 (1979), 211–44; J. F. Wippel, 'The Condemnations of 1270 and 1277 at Paris', *Journal of Medieval and Renaissance Studies*, 7 (1977), 169–201.

[28] J. McEvoy, *The Philosophy of Robert Grosseteste* (Oxford, 1982); and R. W. Southern, *Robert Grosseteste and the Growth of an English Mind in Medieval Europe* (Oxford, 1986).

the complete run of the newly translated works before Adam of Buckfield in the 1240s. In the second half of the century, Oxford steered clear of trouble because none of the masters was tempted to identify with the more suspect aspect of Averroes' teaching. The Muslim's commentaries were available in Oxford shortly after they were known in Paris. Buckfield referred to them continually. But Oxford masters were not made of the stuff of Siger of Brabant. They were never accused of materialism, or even sustaining materialist positions philosophically. If the Oxford masters of the thirteenth century did discuss the Averroist doctrine of the intellect, they can have only outlined it as a possible position before proceeding to reject it in bringing the *quaestio* to a close.

Yet this did not mean that the masters' teaching completely passed muster. The same year, 1277, in which Tempier censured the Paris faculty for a second time, the archbishop of Canterbury, Robert Kilwardby, took issue with a number of positions in grammar, logic, and philosophy being taught in the Oxford schools. The grammatical and logical positions attacked seem to reflect Kilwardby's desire to enforce the view that statements that are grammatically incorrect, even if their sense can be understood, are still wrong, and that statements that seem logically right can also be wrong if the proper distinctions are not made. Only one position—'that every true proposition about the future is necessary'—bore any relation to the contemporary concerns of the bishop of Paris.[29] The philosophical positions, in contrast, had a clear point of reference. The target was certain opinions of Thomas Aquinas. In the 1250s and 1260s Oxford masters appear to have been primarily influenced by the Paris teachers before Albert and Thomas, who had taken Aristotle as the foundation of their science of philosophy but had used Augustine and other church sources to keep on the right side of orthodoxy. In this they were following in the footsteps of Grosseteste himself several decades before. In the 1270s, however, Aquinas' version of Aristotelianism began to be taught at the University and was particularly championed by the Dominican Thomas Sutton. Kilwardby was especially incensed by the Thomist belief in the unity of the human soul. The earlier view that still continued to be supported in Franciscan circles at Paris and had been taught by Buckfield and others at Oxford was that human beings had three separate souls or forms: the vegetative dealt with growth and nutrition, the corporeal with movement, and the rational with thought; only the rational was immortal. Critics declared that if this were not the case then Christ's body on the cross and in the tomb could not be one and the same. Kilwardby himself belonged to the Order of the Preachers and had studied in Paris but this did not make him an automatic supporter of Aquinas. Probably pushed into action by conservative regents worried by the dissemination of Thomism in the University, he convened a congregation of regent masters, and had this and other Thomist positions condemned as irrational and contrary to faith.

[29] The propositions are cited in *HUO*, i. 419–20, n. 5.

Grammatical and logical treatises that survive from the following decades suggest that Kilwardby succeeded in imposing a party line. He was much less successful with Thomism. His successor in the Canterbury see was the Franciscan John Pecham, who had taught at Oxford in the 1250s, then prepared important philosophical treatises for use in the Franciscan convents two decades later. Pecham was equally hostile to the Thomist view of the soul, and in 1284 he reissued Kilwardby's condemnation of the philosophical theses, this time without consulting the University. On this occasion, the condemnation met with considerable opposition. Pecham managed, by having recourse to a convocation of bishops, to silence one of the leading Thomists, the Dominican Richard Knapwell, who was excommunicated, but this was the culmination of his campaign. The growing veneration for Aquinas in the broader church made it impossible for the primate or his successors to repeat the censure, and in the following decades Dominicans were left free to espouse Thomist Aristotelianism in the University unchallenged. However, the Thomists did not dominate the philosophical landscape. Indeed, the dominant figure of interest in the Oxford schools after 1290 was not Aquinas but another Parisian master, Henry of Ghent, one of the Paris theologians who drew up the 1277 condemnation for Tempier and championed St Augustine above St Thomas.[30] At Oxford, Henry had no supporters: he raised the hackles of both the Franciscans and the Dominicans. But his works were widely read and critiqued, and they became the starting point for the first internationally significant contribution of an Oxford man to scholastic philosophy and theology.

Duns Scotus became one of the most influential philosophers and theologians of the late middle ages, and in the era of the Reformation would become a byword for scholastic logic-chopping. He was a native of the Scottish borders and joined the Franciscan order when he was young. Very little is known about his connection with Oxford, except that he seems to have studied theology at the University in the 1290s and lectured on the *Sentences* in 1298–9 (see Figure 4.2). He then moved to Cambridge where he read the Lombard again in 1301–2, before transferring to Paris, lecturing on the *Sentences* for a third time, and gaining his doctorate in theology in 1305. From there, he went to the Franciscan convent at Cologne (not yet a university town), where he died a few years later. Scotus perished too young to produce a magisterial summa, but he left behind him a large quantity of commentaries and *quaestiones*, including a study of Aristotle's *Metaphysics* that lecturers and students all over Europe would continually refer to in future centuries in their courses and disputations. As a tribute to his analytical rigour he became known as 'the subtle doctor'.

Scotus, in many respects, belonged to a Franciscan tradition: he supported the pre-Thomist position of the plurality of souls, for instance. But in engaging, like other Oxford schoolmen of his era, with the writings of Henry of Ghent, he moved a considerable distance from the Augustinian views of earlier members of his order. Scotus did not always disagree with Henry. Aquinas had insisted that the mind's object

---

[30] Roland J. Teske, *Essays on the Philosophy of Henry of Ghent* (Milwaukee, WI, 2012).

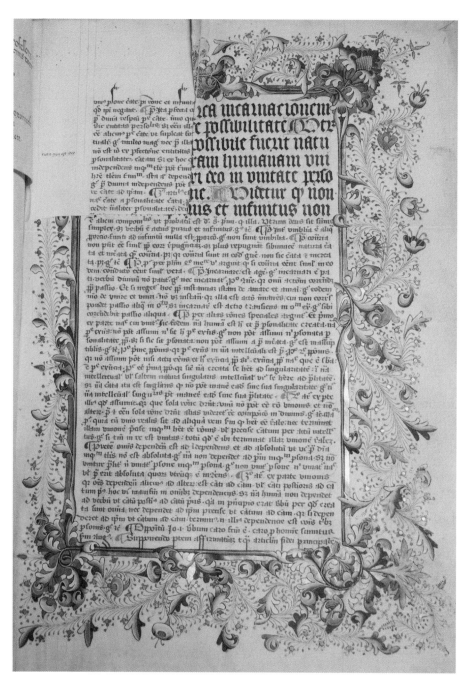

FIGURE 4.2 Johannis Duns Scoti, 'In Sententiarum librum tertium lectura in universitate Oxoniensis habita', transcribed by Johann Reynbold, first page. Scotus' commentary on the *Sentences* of Peter Lombard was one of the most important philosophical and theological works of the late middle ages. The third book dealt with the Incarnation. Reynbold was a German scribe who worked at Oxford in the mid-fifteenth century. He transcribed a number of Scotist works for the Merton fellow and theologian Richard Scarburgh, who then sold them to his colleague, the MD Thomas Bloxham. The first seven lines of this beautifully ornamented copy of Scotus' commentary have been vandalized by a collector who wanted to own the large illuminated first letter: the next folio can be seen underneath.

was natural phenomena. Duns had a more extensive vision and insisted with Ghent that all being was the mind's province, including possible beings that God could create if He had a desire to do so. Usually, though, Scotus placed much greater emphasis on human potential and dignity than Ghent had done. He particularly disliked Ghent's belief that a divine illumination of the mind was needed for a human being to gain certain knowledge. Although this was a position maintained by the Franciscans' leading thirteenth-century philosopher, Bonaventura, and seemed to be upheld by Augustine, Scotus thought it pointless. Duns had a passionate and very unAugustinian belief in the freedom of the will, placing it as a faculty of the mind above the intellect. The intellect could not determine what a man did, for humans frequently acted contrary to what their reason told them to do. The will, then, was the principal faculty, even if Aristotle had argued differently. It also deserved this status because it was the seat of love. To Scotus, as a Christian, the good life consisted in obeying the Decalogue out of love of God; it did not, as it had for Aristotle, consist in intellectual contemplation. Scotus was always impeccably orthodox, and never forgot that man was a fallen creature who had lost his original sense of justice. It was for this reason he promoted the doctrine of the immaculate conception of the Virgin Mary; Christ's mother had to be pure. But Duns was much closer to Aquinas than earlier Franciscans and their allies, in his readiness to accept that the man who uses his reason can turn away from evil with God's help.

There was much, however, that separated Duns from Aquinas, especially where they drew the boundary between faith and reason. For Aquinas, the Christian God was knowable by reason. For Scotus God was ultimately unknowable. His existence could be proved, though he disliked the physical argument based on the need for a first mover. So too could some of God's properties: his infiniteness and his power to do all that was logically possible. Duns also accepted with Aquinas that God could not act irrationally: rationality was part of his definition; God could not make a square circle. But the attributes of the Christian God—especially that he was just and merciful—were truths of faith that were not understandable by reason. God might also have made the world in a different way. His activity could not be circumscribed by what existed. Thus, the rules of the Decalogue could be deduced rationally in that they made for a secure and prosperous society. But God could have decided to command our obedience to other rules that equally made sense: he could have ordered goods to be held in common, for instance. God could also command men to break his own rules and men would have to obey, as when Abraham was ordered to sacrifice Isaac. Duns also believed, in opposition to Aquinas, that it was impossible to prove the soul's immortality. Human beings may well have a desire to survive death, but this did not mean that desire was well founded. Much more than Aquinas, then, Duns placed limits on the possibility of reconciling Aristotle and his commentators with Christian dogma.[31]

---

[31] Copleston, *Medieval Philosophy*, ch. 14; M. B. Ingham and Oleg Bychkov (eds), *John Duns Scotus Philosopher* (Münster, 2010).

Scotus quickly became accepted by the Franciscans throughout Europe as 'their' philosopher, even though he had moved a long way from the Augustinianism of the early masters of the order. Duns would also have long influence on Oxford, but from the beginning his ideas were criticized. Some followed the secular Henry Harclay, Chancellor in 1312, in believing that Scotus did not distinguish carefully enough between the realms of faith and reason. Others thought some of his positions were suspect: in 1315, the theology faculty condemned his views on the relationship between the persons of the Trinity and their role in the Creation.[32] Even the Franciscans did not embrace their pupil totally. As early as 1306–8, Duns' idea of the univocity of being—that the term good, when applied to God or ourselves, for instance, had exactly the same meaning—was attacked by the order's lector, Peter Sutton, while ten years later the underpinning of his whole philosophy was challenged by the precocious William of Ockham. The Franciscan Ockham, born in Surrey, was the University's second philosopher of international stature. Ockham began to study theology at Oxford about 1309, and lectured on the Bible from 1313 to 1315 and the *Sentences* from 1317 to 1319, reversing the traditional order. In 1323, the Chancellor of the University, John Lutterel, submitted to the pope that aspects of Ockham's teaching on the *Sentences* were suspect. As a result, he was summoned to the papal court at Avignon in 1324 to answer the charges and never became a doctor. While there, he got involved in the argument between the papacy and the Franciscans over the order's commitment to evangelical poverty and was forced to flee the city in 1328 with the order's minister-general. He found refuge in the Bavarian court and died in 1349, probably of the Black Death.[33]

Both Aquinas and Scotus believed that collective terms, such as man and woman, were real entities that in some way were manifest in individual exemplars. Ockham rejected this and claimed that such words were human constructions that had no ontological status: they were convenient labels that allowed apparently similar things to be brought under a single head. Universals did not exist outside the mind. Indeed, there was no guarantee that our perceptions of individual phenomena were of the things that really existed. It was quite possible for God to permit 'intuitive apprehension' of an object that was not present. Ockham did not deny that abstract and causal knowledge existed, provided it was grounded on right reasoning, but he inevitably considered there was an element of contingency in all judgements, however properly constructed. In consequence, to later philosophers Aquinas and Scotus were 'realists', Ockham a 'nominalist'. Ockham also objected to multiplying entities unnecessarily: in the name of economy, philosophers should wield a razor to remove what was unverifiable by experience or could not be

---

[32] J. T. Paasch, *Divine Production in Late Medieval Trinitarian Theology: Henry of Ghent, Duns Scotus and William of Ockham* (Oxford, 2012); William Courtenay, 'The Articles Condemned at Oxford Austin Friars in 1315', in H. A. Oberman and Frank A. James III, with Eric L. Saak (eds), *Via Augustini. Augustine in the Later Middle Ages, Renaissance and Reformation: Essays in Honour of Damasus Trapp, OSA* (Leiden, 1991), pp. 5–18.

[33] Copleston, *Medieval Philosophy*, pp. 236–7. The Franciscans claimed that they not only could not own property but they did not even have the right to use temporal things, such as food and clothing, even if in fact they did: the pope thought this position absurd (ibid., pp. 255–6).

deduced by reason. Aristotle identified ten different sorts of thing that existed: he called these the ten categories. Aquinas and Scotus concurred. Ockham reduced Aristotle's categories to two. Only substances and qualities (both physical and spiritual) existed in reality, or for as long as God allowed them to do so. All the other categories that Aristotelians accepted as real—quantity, time and place, motion, and so on—were merely terms used by the mind to stand for something the mind apprehended but had no objective reality.

Behind Ockham's nominalism was a view of God that went much further than Scotus had done in declaring the divine unknowable. Ockham could just about accept that God's existence could be demonstrated rationally because there was a need for an ultimate conserving cause. Human beings, however, could know nothing of his attributes, apart from what was revealed in Scripture. Ockham's God was both omnipotent and unconstrained by human reason. The only restraint on his power was that he could not make a contradiction, such as a square circle. Neither was it possible to prove the immortality of the soul. Attempts to make sense of church dogma were therefore pointless, and the sciences of philosophy and theology had to be kept completely apart. This did not stop Ockham himself from wandering down speculative alleys, as his summons to Avignon makes clear, and he promoted several controversial theological ideas. One of the most difficult dogmas of the church to explain rationally was transubstantiation. The usual view was to distinguish the substance of bread and wine from their accidents. In the miracle of the eucharist the substance was changed into the body and blood of Christ but the accidents (shape, taste, texture) remained. Ockham developed another argument in his Oxford *Sentences*. As God could annihilate quantity or reduce matter to a point, Ockham preferred to believe that Christ was present in the bread and wine without extension.[34]

It was not this view, though, that got Ockham into trouble. Lutterel, a dogmatic Thomist, accused him of Pelagianism. The catholic church throughout the middle ages believed that men as fallen creatures were naturally damned. Entry to heaven could be obtained only through faith in the redemptive power of Christ and the performance of good works in this life that had won merit in God's sight. There was disagreement, however, over the definition of a meritorious work. At the turn of the fifth century, the British or Irish cleric Pelagius had argued that a good act freely performed was deserving of merit. Augustine, on the other hand, believed that a good act was meritorious only if performed with the assistance of divine grace. Augustine's position was adopted by the church. Thereafter, though theologians would argue incessantly over whether meritorious acts required a special grace and whether that grace were given before, during, or after the act's performance, Pelagius' view was considered a heresy: it gave too much power to fallen humans to

---

[34] Ibid, pp. 238–52; Jenny E. Pelletier, *William Ockham on Metaphysics: The Science of Being and God* (Leiden, 2013); Marilyn McCord, *Some Later Medieval Theories of the Eucharist: Thomas Aquinas, Giles of Rome, Duns Scotus and William Ockham* (Oxford, 2010).

determine their fate. In fact, Ockham was not a Pelagian. As much as Scotus, he believed in the freedom of the will and our ability to follow God's law from love. But he never claimed with Pelagius that God had to give us merit for all our freely performed good acts. Rather, he insisted that no good act, whether performed with or without divine aid, was ipso facto acceptable by God. It was up to God to decide. On the other hand, he did believe that God might decide to award merit to an act performed naturally, which devalued the customary role prescribed to grace. The commission at Avignon thought this position was worse than the Pelagian one. At least the Pelagians had believed that an act performed with grace might win merit more easily.

While Ockham himself never taught at Paris, his ideas soon gained supporters on the other side of the Channel. Although his works were temporarily banned in the French university on two occasions, from 1339 to 1342 and from 1474 to 1481, for the next century and a half Paris sheltered a number of nominalists who shared Ockham's belief that most Christian dogmas were mysteries that could not be explored by reason. The most famous was the formidable theologian Jean Gerson, Paris chancellor at the turn of the fifteenth century, who wanted members of the arts faculty to steer clear of theological issues and attacked theologians for seeking to know what was beyond knowledge. Nominalism was also promoted in the new German universities of the early fifteenth century, such as Vienna, Heidelberg, and Cologne, where it was taken by scholars who had to leave Paris because of the Papal Schism.[35] In Oxford, however, Ockham's supporters were limited. For the most part Oxford's philosophers remained wedded to realism or the *via antiqua*, as it was called. Ockham's *via moderna* did have its disciples among the Franciscan order, and his ideas were discussed in a number of the order's convents in England, most notably by Adam Woodham, who lectured on the *Sentences* at Oxford in 1330−2. But even Woodham's was a critical voice, accepting Ockham's views of universals and categories but attacking aspects of his epistemology and psychology. Virtually all Oxonians distanced themselves from Ockham's view of meritorious action. One particularly strident opponent, the Merton fellow Thomas Bradwardine, took on not just Ockham but what he saw as the general 'Pelagian' drift in Oxford philosophy and theology since the turn of the century. Bradwardine was part of an Augustinian revival in Oxford in the 1330s and 1340s. In his *De causa Dei*, which was completed in 1344 and became famous throughout the university world, Bradwardine anticipated Calvin in giving no place at all to individual initiative in determining personal salvation. God predestines to heaven and hell by his eternal decree, which is purely arbitrary and not even based on foreseen merits. Bradwardine's views found little favour in Oxford but they testify to the spectrum of philosophical and theological beliefs that could be encountered in the University

---

[35] William J. Courtenay, *Ockham and Ockhamism: Studies in the Dissemination and Impact of His Thought* (Leiden, 2008). Between 1378 and 1418, two and, at one point, three rival popes claimed the right to wear the papal tiara; secular rulers took sides and scholars at their universities from states supporting the 'wrong' pope were ejected.

in the mid-fourteenth century. Even among the realists, while the Dominicans largely favoured Thomas and the Franciscans Duns, no single school of thought was ever dominant or in the ascendant for long.[36]

C. Mertonians, Mathematicians, and Roger Bacon

Ockham's most positive contribution to ongoing debate in Oxford lay in logic rather than the three philosophies or theology. He was not the first Oxford terminist but he certainly helped to consolidate terminist logic as a peculiar Oxford concern. Terminist logic explored the complex role and meanings of words as they were put to use in particular contexts. It could focus on *suppositiones* or propositional subjects, where the same word might have a singular or universal meaning, such as the word 'man'; or it could deal with *syncategoremata*, words that have no meaning on their own, such as 'not', 'if', and 'from'. It was particularly concerned with *insolubilia*, paradoxical statements that appear to be nonsense when they stand alone. The phrase 'what I am saying is false', for instance, is meaningless if it has no point of reference outside itself. The first widely distributed textbook of logic to deal with terms was the *Summulae logicales* of the Portuguese Peter of Spain, later Pope John XXI, who studied at Paris in the mid-thirteenth century. But Peter was not the only terminist at this date at the French university. A more fertile logician was one of his probable teachers, William of Sherwood or Shyreswood, who had taught at Oxford before crossing the Channel, and left a specific study of *syncategoremata*. At Paris, however, terminist logic never became part of the official curriculum. Possibly because the masters' principal focus was on establishing the absolute truth of metaphysical and theological positions, Paris logicians became interested in 'modist' logic. Modists looked at language outside of time and context: they assumed that words had a formal unchanging meaning according to their position in a sentence and were modes of signification (*modi significandi*), which related directly to concepts (*modi intelligendi*) and objects (*modi essendi*). Once understood, they could be confidently used in the search for philosophical and theological knowledge.[37]

At Oxford, terminist logic exerted a fascination from the moment the treatises of Peter of Spain and William of Sherwood were known in England, while the Parisian modists were largely ignored. This in part reflected the relative philosophical conservatism of the University in the second half of the thirteenth century. Oxford philosophers were more interested in the old logic, with its emphasis on deconstructing the parts of a sentence, than the new logic, which emphasized the construction of watertight arguments. Kilwardby was one of the first Oxford men to take an interest in Peter's *Summulae* and write a commentary on the text.

---

[36] William J. Courtenay, *Schools and Scholars in Fourteenth-Century England* (Princeton, NJ, 1987), pp. 151, 216–18, and chs 9–10. Bradwardine was temporarily archbishop of Canterbury at the end of his life. Like Ockham, he appears to have died of the plague.

[37] Copleston, *Medieval Philosophy*, pp. 234–6; Courtenay, *Schools and Scholars*, pp. 224–7.

Although his work was written while he was in Paris, he carried his interest back home, and his concern with the use of terms arguably manifested itself in particular in his archiepiscopal condemnation in 1277 of certain grammatical and logical positions, which was referred to in the previous section of this chapter. It was only in the early thirteenth century, however, that Oxford logicians began to make a positive contribution to terminist logic and develop an interest in analysing a much wider variety of types of statements. The first significant figures were Richard of Campsall, Walter Burley or Burleigh, and Ockham.

Campsall left little except an analysis of the liar paradox: he appears to have been fascinated by temporal propositions (ones that used different tenses) and modal propositions (ones that concerned necessity, contingency, or possibility). Burley, on the other hand, was the author of a large number of specialist treatises which covered the gamut of terminist interests. His works included treatises on suppositions, *syncategoremata*, and insolubles, and on various forms of proposition: conditional propositions or 'consequences', propositions with relative clauses, and propositions concerning the division of the continuum (*de finite et infinito* and *de toto et parte*). He also wrote a treatise on 'obligations', a favourite academic exercise whereby the aim was to make the respondent end up contradicting himself.[38] Ockham's contribution was as a synthesizer. He produced the first textbook of logic where terminist logic was fully integrated into the course rather tacked on to existing concerns. His *Summa logicae*, composed by mid-1324, reorganized the old and new logic into four parts: terms, propositions, syllogisms, and fallacies. Each part was interpreted from the terminist position, thus showing that terminist logic had an important place in constructing right argument as well as making clear statements. He also overlaid his logic with his nominalist views, which inevitably led him into conflict with the guardians of realism, such as Lutterel. But terminism was never synonymous with nominalism. Indeed, Burley was an ardent realist, who soon clashed swords with Ockham in his *De puritate artis logicae*; so too was the first Parisian of significance to latch on to terminist logic in the 1340s, Jean Buridan, who successfully undermined the hitherto untroubled reign of the modists.[39]

Ockham's logic and the treatises of Walter Burley spread all over Europe. At home they inspired a new generation of logicians, who took the examination of terminist problems much further. As many, like Campsall before them, were secular clerics associated with Merton College, they have come to be known as the Mertonians. Bradwardine has already been introduced. The other Mertonians of note were William Heytesbury, John Dumbleton, William Sutton, Richard Kilvington, and Richard Swineshead or Swyneshed.[40] Between them, they produced a large

---

[38] A respondent answered positively or negatively to a proposition in the first instance, then had to continue to respond in a similar vein whenever the proposition was repeated in a different context, ultimately forcing him to contradict his position or accept an absurdity.

[39] Courtenay, *Schools and Scholars*, pp. 229–33; Copleston, *Medieval Philosophy*, pp. 244–8.

[40] Identifying the works of Richard is difficult because there were three Oxonians from the village of Swineshead in the fourteenth century. Campsall became a fellow of Merton in 1305. Kilvington was one of the first fellows of Oriel.

number of widely disseminated treatises which formed what the continent called the *logica anglicana* or *logica moderna*. Many of these were on specialist topics such as *insolubilia*, the truth content of propositions, obligations, and consequences, but many were simply on suppositions, a subject which was now greatly extended to cover a wide variety of problems, including *syncategoremata*. Lying behind the logicians' work was the belief that many of the problems that divided philosophers and theologians stemmed from the ambiguous use of language and the failure to use rules of argumentation and inference properly. By the middle of the fourteenth century, this claim had won general approval, and the new logic was standard undergraduate fare, and had been incorporated into a new set of elementary textbooks.[41]

One of the topics pursued by this second generation of terminists concerned propositions about motion and change which took them into the realm of physics. It was here that they displayed their greatest creativity. Unlike earlier logicians, the terminists drew inspiration from classical mathematics: they used symbols as short-hand, and their adoption of an axiomatic approach in presenting their arguments was probably inspired by Euclid as much as Aristotle's *Topics* or *Sophistical Refutations*. When discussing motion, they went one step further and used Euclidian geometry as an analytical tool to bring greater accuracy and precision to their account. The inspiration for the work of the group was Bradwardine's *De proportionibus velocitatum in motibus*, which was written in 1328. In this treatise, the Merton fellow studied a number of aspects of bodies in motion that had hitherto been ignored: he differentiated between initial speed and velocity after a period of time, and began discussion about the relationship between force and distance travelled. Most famously, he took issue with Aristotle's claim that velocity was proportional to changes in force or resistance, demonstrating instead that velocity increased or decreased arithmetically as the ratio of force to resistance increased or decreased geometrically. Bradwardine was not the most ambitious of the group, however. This honour fell to Swineshead, who wrote a number of important mathematical treatises, especially his *Liber calculationum*, composed between 1345 and 1355. Swineshead made significant contributions to the study of local motion. He is credited in particular with offering the first proof of the mean speed theorem: that a body with a uniform speed will travel the same distance over a given period of time as a uniformly accelerating body with the same average speed as the first. But Swineshead stands out above all because he wanted to develop the use of mathematics beyond the realm of local motion. Like Aristotle, the terminists had a broad understanding of the term 'motion': it included the intension and remission of qualities (such as the loss or gain of heat) as well as changes of place, and covered the human emotions and even divine grace. Swineshead believed that qualitative change could be envisaged as a distance that had to be achieved or a space that had to be crossed and could therefore be ascribed a mathematical quantity. In his *Liber*

---

[41] Courtenay, *Schools and Scholars*, pp. 234–40.

he dealt mathematically with changes in intensity of various qualities, and explored inter alia how different qualities (such as heat and humidity) might interact when two bodies with these characteristics came into contact with each other. For his efforts, he gained the nickname of the 'Calculator'.[42]

The Mertonians' work was developed further at Paris in the 1340s and 1350s, particularly by Buridan and Nicolas Oresme. The first exploded Aristotle's explanation for the maintenance of projectile motion by relating this to an impetus initially conveyed to the moving object, and not to the pressure of the air through which the object passed; the second invented a graphical method of describing motion. By the end of the fourteenth century, the Mertonians' books were widely read all over the continent. Bradwardine's *De Proportionibus* was a prescribed text at Vienna in 1399 and three copies can be found in the library of the University of Cracow, while Swineshead's *Liber* was well known in the north Italian universities of the early Renaissance.[43] It should not be thought, however, that either the Mertonians or their followers anticipated Galileo in developing a mathematical science of dynamics. For all their originality, they remained firmly wedded to the Aristotelian tradition of motion. Unsurprisingly, then, despite their debt to Euclid, the Mertonians made little contribution to mathematics themselves. Early on in his career, in the 1320s, Bradwardine produced a *Geometria speculativa* which contained a number of theorems not in Euclid, but he was exceptional.

Indeed, Oxford, while clearly teaching the quadrivium and in touch with what was happening elsewhere, produced only a handful of significant mathematicians in the late middle ages. The most fertile work was in the field of astronomy. Thanks to the so-called Alfonsine tables drawn up in Castile between 1263 and 1272, European astronomers no longer had to work from the outdated data compiled in eleventh-century Toledo, probably by Al-Zarqali. The new tables reached Oxford about 1330 where they were adapted to the University's longitude by the Merton fellow William Rede. A century later the tables were revised again by another Merton fellow, John Killingworth, who somehow or other developed an equation for identifying the daily position of planets from their mean position. But neither astronomer was of European significance, and the most important observational updating of the astronomical tables at the end of the fifteenth century would take place in Vienna— with the work of Regiomontanus and Peuerbach—just as the first stirrings of the later astronomical revolution would occur at Cracow where Copernicus was based.[44] Oxford, however, did produce talented instrument makers and a number of their instruments can still be seen (see Figure 4.3). The most gifted was the Benedictine Richard of Wallingford, who lived in Gloucester Hall in the first decades of the fourteenth century. Richard was a good mathematician and wrote Europe's first trigonometry textbook, probably in the late 1320s, which contained in

---

[42] Ibid., pp. 241–9.
[43] Marshall Clagett, *The Science of Mechanics in the Middle Ages* (London, 1961), chs 6–11, *passim*; North, 'Quadrivium', p. 351.
[44] North, 'Quadrivium', pp. 355–7.

FIGURE 4.3 Oriel astrolabe, fourteenth century. Astronomy was the one mathematical science that flourished in late-medieval Oxford. The astrolabe depicted may have been part of a bequest to Oriel by Simon Bredon MD, a fellow of Merton in the 1330s and 1340s, who died in 1372.

its fourth part a treatise on spherical surfaces that was intended to assist astronomers in their calculations. Richard's most famous instrument was his *albion*, an *equatorium* that he designed in 1327, which, in a revised form, was still being used in southern Europe in the seventeenth century. This was a sort of cosmological slide rule, a series of circular discs with a complicated graduated scale that could be used to simulate the movements of the planets and obviate the need to make complex calculations. Richard was also a clock maker. Robert Anglicus, in his commentary on Sacrobosco in 1271, mentioned early attempts to create mechanical clocks, but Richard was the first Oxonian to have the necessary mechanical flair to design one. The astronomical clock he constructed for the convent of St Albans, where he became abbot, is the first for which we have a detailed account. It was working by the time of his death and would not be surpassed in England for two centuries.[45]

The Mertonian physicists were equally uninterested in testing their mathematical deductions by experimentation. Although as Aristotelians they believed that all

[45] J. D. North (ed.), *Richard of Wallingford: An Edition of His Writings* (3 vols; Oxford, 1976): includes an English translation and commentary.

107

knowledge ultimately came through the senses, theirs was not a science under-pinned by careful observation. The only Oxford philosopher in the late middle ages who has been traditionally associated with modern experimental science was the thirteenth-century friar Roger Bacon.[46] Bacon probably began his arts course at Oxford in the early 1230s. He never taught at the University but moved, like so many others, to Paris to finish his degree, and it was at Paris that he lectured on Aristotle. At this stage, there was nothing original in his philosophy: his lectures closely mirror others given in the French capital by pre-Thomist Aristotelians. Having stopped teaching at Paris about 1247, however, he developed in a much more radical direction, spending ten years in private study, probably at Oxford, where he engaged in alchemical, optical, and other experiments. This led him to discard the learning of the schools and develop his own science of physics, which he outlined in his *De multiplicatione specierum* of *c*.1262. Building on the insights of Arab optical philosophers, such as al-Kindi and Alhazen, this work posited the existence of a number of radiating forces, most obviously light, emanating from physical and spiritual substances, which, in Bacon's view, would explain everything, including the ability to bewitch. Five years later, on the request of a sympathetic pope, Bacon produced his *Opus maius*, where he argued a new philosophy had to be built from the widest possible range of ancient texts (for whose study a knowledge of Greek, Hebrew, Chaldean, and Arabic, not just Latin, was necessary), mathe-matics (especially the science of perspective), and personal experience (*scientia experimentalis*). Mathematics in particular would be a powerful weapon in the armoury of Christian evangelism: by making it possible to calculate more precisely latitude and longitude and to overhaul the calendar, missionaries would be sped on their way overseas and would no longer be discomfited by the uncertainties surrounding establishing the date of Easter.[47]

Bacon's later life is obscure. About 1257 he joined the Franciscans and spent a further long period abroad. But he seems to have been back in England from 1270 and, according to tradition, eventually died at Oxford. Bacon's works were quickly known and considered dangerous, despite the fact that he always remained highly respectful of Aristotle. While believing that, by experimentation, it would be possible to increase man's control over nature, he was also an astrologer who gave a much greater power to the heavens in human affairs than the late medieval church would countenance, even believing that national customs were shaped by the planets. As a result, he was viewed in the following centuries with suspicion as the embodiment of the satanic philosopher who dabbled in magic and peddled forbidden knowledge. The fact that he had been vilified in the late middle ages, on the other hand, guaranteed that his memory, if not his works, would be seized upon by a later age that rejected the Aristotelianism of the schools as worthless pedantry.

---

[46] The most recent study in English is Brian Clegg, *The First Scientist: A Life of Roger Bacon* (London, 2003).
[47] Bacon wrote Greek and Hebrew grammars.

After the Reformation, Bacon was turned into an English intellectual hero and his credentials burnished by succeeding centuries who came to see him, quite wrongly, as a precursor of seventeenth-century experimental philosophy. Bacon came to be seen as one of the two beacons that had shone in the medieval darkness: the other was Wyclif.[48]

D. Wyclif

Although the church was always on the lookout for signs of heterodoxy in Europe's universities, it seldom ever censured teaching on its own initiative. Rather, intervention by the ecclesiastical authorities usually followed an appeal from disgruntled masters who demanded action. For the first century and a half of its existence, Oxford's teaching largely escaped censure by the pope or English hierarchy, which would suggest, in an easily scandalized age, that internal divisions of opinion were relatively muted.[49] In the second half of the fourteenth century, in contrast, the University contained several provocative individuals who promoted positions that seriously antagonized one group or other in Congregation. Sometimes the offenders were successfully dealt with in-house. In 1358, an Augustinian friar, John Kedington, was suspended by the University after complaints that he had questioned the probity and independence of the secular clergy: the friar had argued in a debate that mendicants had a greater right to tithes than rectors, and that the king could deprive ecclesiastics of their livings for moral misconduct. Some twenty years later, a Franciscan was forced to recant for teaching that the church was corrupt and had forsaken poverty. On two occasions, however, internal disputes led to outside intervention. In 1366, the Benedictine John Uthred of Boldon became embroiled in a quarrel with the Dominicans over his claim that pagans might be granted the divine vision and that salvation was dependent on how the soul reacted to the vision of God on the moment of death. Two years later, Uthred was denounced to the archbishop of Canterbury, Simon Langham, a fellow Benedictine, who responded by censuring the teaching of Uthred but also condemning certain positions attributed to the Dominican William Jordan, who had probably instigated the complaint. Nine years later, Langham's successor was again forced to move against a controversial Oxford theologian. In early 1377, Archbishop Simon of Sudbury summoned the secular theologian John Wyclif to London to answer charges of seditious preaching regarding the relationship between the temporal and spiritual realms. Wyclif's putative errors were of a different order from those of Uthred. As his views seemed to threaten the very integrity of the church, the pope was also alerted—probably by the Oxford Benedictine Adam Easton, who was then

---

[48] Cf. the laudatory account of his life and works in Wood, *History*, i. 332–44. Bacon was still hailed as a harbinger of modern science in the early twentieth century: see Robert Gunther, *Early Science at Oxford*, vol. 1 (Oxford, 1923), pp. 1–3.

[49] There were only two clear-cut examples of outside intervention in this period: Kilwardby's move against Thomism in 1277 and the papal commission set up to investigate Ockham in 1324.

at the papal court—and in May 1377, Pope Gregory XI issued five bulls denouncing the Oxford teacher, which arrived in England at Christmas. The University was ordered not to allow any propositions to be taught that were contrary to faith and have Wyclif arrested. In this case, however, academic peace was not to be restored by simple ecclesiastical fiat. The pope's intervention, although backed by the archbishop, succeeded only in raising a storm in the University which would take thirty years to blow over.[50]

Wyclif came from Yorkshire and studied arts at Oxford in the 1350s.[51] Once a bachelor, he became a fellow of Merton in 1356, then, on taking his MA, served temporarily as master of Balliol about 1360. From 1361 to 1363 he was rector of Fillingham in Lincolnshire before returning to Oxford to study theology. For the next eighteen years, he appears to have lived in Queen's, though he was warden of Canterbury College from 1365 to 1369 when it was briefly turned into an endowed hall for seculars. Wyclif almost certainly lectured on the *Sentences* in 1369–70, and then on the Bible, before becoming a DD in 1372. He next continued his lectures on the Scriptures for a further four years, so that by 1376, a year before he came under attack, he had taught the whole text. This immediately marked him out from his contemporaries, regardless of the content of his lectures. Oxford had produced several notable biblical exegetes earlier in the century, especially the Dominican Robert Holcot, whose lectures on the Book of Wisdom in the 1330s had circulated around Europe. No Oxonian before Wyclif, however, had lectured on the whole of the Bible. In fact, he was the first European scholar to do so since the Paris Franciscan Nicholas of Lyra, in the early fourteenth century, and the first secular to ever attempt the feat. Like most doctors of theology in late medieval Europe before 1450, Wyclif was particularly interested in unravelling the hidden meaning in the text. While Oxford's bachelors were expected to render a literal account, older exegetes searched for an allegorical, tropological, or anagogical meaning. In the first case, a passage or word was thought to represent an event or person depicted in the New Testament; in the second, a moral state; and in the third the church or eternal felicity. Wyclif was interested in the second.

Wyclif's early writings, presumably written after he became an MA in about 1358, were on logic, and showed him to be an able, if unoriginal, terminist. His *Tractatus de logica* (composed c.1370) was a synthesis of the ideas of the Mertonian school, which was intended for use as a textbook. But like many earlier 'Mertonians', Wyclif was not an Ockhamist and came out strongly in favour of the reality of universals, arguing in his *De universalibus* (c.1373–4) that the universal was inherent in every substance. For this reason, he believed that substances could not be annihilated, since this would be to destroy an eternal and intelligible being. Indeed, so ardent a supporter of realism was Wyclif that, in one important regard, he broke with his terminist

---

[50] Andrew E. Larsen, 'Academic Condemnations and the Decline of Theology at Oxford', *HU*, XXIII/1 (2008), 1–32, at pp. 6–9.
[51] The most recent accounts of his life and thought are Stephen E. Lahey, *John Wyclif* (Oxford, 2009), and G. R. Evans, *John Wyclif* (Oxford, 2007).

contemporaries, refusing, in his metaphysical treatise *De ente* (*c.*1372–3) to accept that the truth value of tensed propositions could change according to circumstances: in his view this suggested that what God knows or wills would be always in flux. As a result, in his own mind at least, he was the first genuine realist in Oxford since Grosseteste, and completely discounted the fact that nominalism had never taken root in the University. He was also at times impatient with terminist quibbles, especially in the obligation exercises. The study of logic had to be focused and its purpose was as a handmaid of theology.[52]

These were the sentiments of a man who was first and foremost a theologian, and it was as a theologian that Wyclif demonstrated his originality and potential to alarm. Wyclif's theology was heavily influenced by Bradwardine. God was all-powerful and all-knowing, and the human soul was predestined to heaven or hell. He had no time for the neo-Pelagianism which had so recently reared its head yet again in the teaching of Uthred. But he kept on the right side of orthodoxy by making room for free will. He did this by distinguishing between eternal and chronological time. God occupied eternal time where everything was in the present. Man lived in a different time zone and was at liberty to choose how he acted, even to the extent of being able to determine God's decree, which was only settled in eternal not future time. Humans, even babies who died immediately after baptism, had to have freely sinned in order to be justly condemned by God's prior decree. In consequence, if Wyclif was scarcely an optimist about the human condition, he was not a one-dimensional predestinarian as Calvin would later be.[53] It was not then for his predestinarianism that Wyclif raised ecclesiastical ire in 1377. It was rather for his views on the power and possessions of the church, which he set out in a number of treatises and sermons from the 1370s, especially in his *De civili dominio*, that began life as series of lectures in 1375–6. The predominant influence on him in this case appears to have been the Irishman Richard Fitzralph, former Chancellor of Oxford and archbishop of Armagh, 1347–60, who, in the 1350s, waged a campaign at the papal court against the privileges of the mendicant orders. Believing that their power to operate unsupervised in his metropolitan diocese was a subversion of his authority, Fitzralph developed an account of lordship before and after the Fall to demonstrate that the friars' privileges, albeit derived from the pope, were illegitimate.

Fitzralph's ideas were well known in Oxford in the second half of the fourteenth century, and much debated. The tension that arose between the friars and the other theologians as a result helps to explain the growing willingness of the different factions to invite interference from outside. Wyclif himself was not a party to the attack on the friars' rights but had earlier been their supporter, despite his secular status. He was not interested therefore in using Fitzralph's ideas to continue to beat the mendicants' backs. Rather, he developed them in a different and more danger-ous direction. According to Wyclif, dominion in this world was only temporary: it

---

[52] Courtenay, *Scholars and Schools*, pp. 348–52.
[53] Anthony Kenny, *Wyclif* (Oxford, 1986), pp. 31–41.

depended on the owner remaining in a visible state of grace. The property that the church had received from the laity therefore was not alienated in perpetuity. It could be revoked and resumed if the clergy misbehaved or even if the original donor was in need. Wyclif's doctrine had consequences for temporal as well as spiritual dominium, as he demonstrated in a number of sermons in the second half of the 1370s that attacked the nobility for warmongering. But the immediate target, as the pope understood only too well, were the higher clergy, whose lifestyle and riches were already the subject of criticism at the royal court and in parliament. Wyclif had already been advising a crown desperate for money to fight its French wars on its right to revoke clerical property. In addition, Wyclif's views threatened the spiritual power of the church. According to his theory of dominion, only sacraments administered by a righteous cleric had any efficacy: an unholy priest, including the pope, lost his God-given power to bind and loose.[54]

The year 1377 saw the death of Edward III and the inauguration of the boy king, Richard II, but the new government was no less covetous than the old. Knowing that he had powerful patrons at court, particularly John of Gaunt, the new king's uncle, Wyclif was not cowed by papal criticism. Instead, he became more radical and began to undermine the church even further. In 1377–8 he composed the tract *De veritate sacrae scripturae*, where he argued that the Bible contained a hidden truth and rule of life that was revealed to the individual mind, and that that truth might be preached by the good layman. In 1378 he also suggested that the church comprised only the predestined, and began to speculate on the legitimacy of kings and popes, in the light in that year of the election of two rival pontiffs, which heralded the beginning of the Papal Schism. In the next few years, he became ever more strident, attacking moral evils in the church, particularly simony, and rejecting the doctrine of transubstantiation on the grounds that substances could not be annihilated and accidents independent of their subject: the body and blood of Christ were present in the eucharist only figuratively or symbolically. Wyclif's style also became more evangelical: though continuing to write in Latin, he abandoned the standard scholastic form of argumentation in favour of apodictic polemic. By the early 1380s, however, he had lost his backers at court, and was under growing pressure to recant. In 1381, parts of southern England had been turned upside down by the Peasants Revolt and the king and council no longer felt so kindly towards a man who preached the limits of authority. Not wishing to be ground between both church and state, Wyclif prudently withdrew from the University and spent the remainder of his life in his living at Lutterworth in Leicestershire.

Wyclif in the 1370s had gathered around him a coterie of Oxford supporters. But he also had many intellectual enemies, especially among the friars and the monks, who now came together to develop an intellectual case against the secular theologian. The leading apologist was a Franciscan, William Woodford, who wrote

[54] Joseph Canning, *Ideas of Power in the Late Middle Ages, 1296–1417* (Cambridge, 2011).

a powerful defence of the church's rights based on tradition. Opponents made limited headway while Wyclif had royal protection. When the papal bulls arrived in Oxford, some attempt was made to comply, but there were objections in Congregation to imprisoning an Englishman on the strength of a papal letter, and the University's Chancellor, Adam Tonworth, was careful not to antagonize the secular power. Having canvassed the regent theologians on the soundness of the papal condemnation, he diplomatically concluded that the positions condemned by the papacy 'were true but sounded badly to those who heard them'.[55] By 1381, however, the University knew the wind was changing, and even before the Peasants Revolt broke out, another Chancellor, William Barton, had succeeded in having a number of Wyclif's positions, especially his views on transubstantiation, outlawed. With Wyclif's subsequent retirement, the pressure mounted on his Oxford friends. Sudbury's murder by the peasants led to the elevation of a new archbishop, the Oxford doctor of both canon and civil law, William Courtenay, a much tougher character. In May 1382, Courtenay held a council at the Dominican convent in London which condemned all the conclusions that Wyclif drew from his theory of dominion as well as his doctrine of the eucharist and certain positions that he had never held, such as that 'God must obey the devil'. The condemnation was signed by a clutch of bishops and representatives of the four orders of friars. Courtenay's actions were supported by the king's chancellor, Lord Scrope, and the new Oxford Chancellor, Robert Rygge, was ordered to root out Wyclif's associates. Rygge attempted to withhold publication of the condemnation on the grounds that the primate had no jurisdiction over the University and was thus acting *ultra vires*, but was soon forced to submit by the combined weight of church and state. The extent to which Oxford was now under the hierarchy's thumb was made clear in November 1382 when Archbishop Courtenay summoned a meeting of the southern convocation to St Frideswide's, which promptly set up a joint committee of bishops and regent masters to investigate heresy in the University.[56]

Although Wyclif died within a few years of settling in Lutterworth, his critique of the worldliness of the church and his collapse of the traditional boundaries between the clergy and the laity struck a chord in the world beyond Oxford. Future decades would demonstrate that he was not just an academic theologian but the founder of a religious movement, albeit one that had to live underground and suffer periodic persecution. Initially, Oxford played an important part in the popularization of Lollardy, as Wyclif's ideas came to be known.[57] There were still a number of his supporters in the University in the 1380s and 1390s, principally located in Merton and Queen's, and their role in the dissemination of the master's ideas among the

---

[55] *Oxford Dictionary of National Biography, sub* Wyclif, John.

[56] Each of the two English metropolitans called together representatives of their province to discuss important issues: like the University's *congregatio maior* from 1500, these meetings were called convocation.

[57] Probably from the Middle Dutch word 'lollaerd', a mumbler or mutterer. Wyclif's popular followers were thought to be semi-literates who stumbled over words as they read out aloud Wycliffite texts.

laity was crucial. Although the history of the production of Lollard texts remains shrouded in mystery, it appears to have been at Queen's that a Wycliffite scriptorium translated the Bible into English and prepared a number of other spiritual texts, which were intended to provide the laity at large with the resources to rejuvenate church and state from below.[58]

Lollardy's presence in the University, however, was short-lived. There were still Lollards at Oxford in the first decade of the fifteenth century for, as late as 1406, two Prague masters visiting Oxford were able to take away with them a letter extolling Wyclif, which bore the University's seal.[59] But thereafter the history of Lollardy and the history of Oxford divide. Wycliffism after 1420 was principally a religion of artisans. Its following at court and among the gentry was quickly snuffed out when the House of Lancaster usurped the throne in 1399. The parvenu dynasty was anxious to curry favour with the church, so was happy to give its support to rooting out unorthodoxy, most notably by having parliament make heresy a capital crime in 1401.[60] Six years later, another archbishop of Canterbury, Thomas Arundel, who was also the king's chancellor, issued constitutions for the University and his archiepiscopal diocese that were tantamount to a series of gagging orders on free theological enquiry. Oxford's Wycliffites were doomed. No one in the University was to propose, dictate, or communicate 'conclusions or propositions that sound contrary to the catholic faith or good morals...with or without a prefatory protestation'. Congregation was forced to set up a committee of theologians that would inspect the halls and colleges every month for signs of unorthodoxy.[61] Four years later, Arundel decided to see for himself if the prohibition had had the desired effect and announced an official visitation to Oxford, which, following the king's wishes, would limit its scope to the investigation of heresy. Part of the University jibbed on the grounds that, after Rygge's humiliation, the scholars had won a bull from Pope Boniface IX in 1395 exempting Oxford from ecclesiastical jurisdiction, but the visitation was carried out and the bull was revoked by John XXIII. Standing on privilege got nowhere, and in 1412 the University enacted a statute requiring future graduates to take an oath denouncing Lollardy, and heads of halls and colleges to swear each year to admit no one, not even a servant, 'who may in all likelihood be guilty of heretical . . . depravity' (see Figure 4.4).[62] The odd Lollard still hung on, but the trial of Sir John Oldcastle and the Lollard knights in 1414, who had risen up against the new king, Henry V, saw them pack their bags. One of the last to leave was Peter Payne, principal of St Edmund Hall, who left for Prague to promote Wyclif's ideas in Bohemia.[63]

---

[58] Anne Hudson, *Studies in the Transmission of Wyclif's Writings* (Aldershot, 2008); Mary Dove, *The First English Bible: The Text and Context of the Wycliffite Versions* (Cambridge, 2007).

[59] It was possibly purloined.

[60] For Lollardy in fifteenth-century England, see Richard Rex, *The Lollards* (Basingstoke, 2002).

[61] Larsen, 'Academic Condemnations', pp. 24–5.   [62] *Statuta*, pp. 221–2.

[63] A. B. Emden, *An Oxford Hall in Medieval Times: Being the Early History of St Edmund Hall* (Oxford, 1927), pp. 124–54. It is likely that another principal of St Edmund Hall, William Taylor, principal 1405–6, was a Lollard martyr, burnt at Smithfield in 1423.

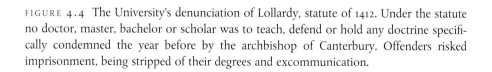

FIGURE 4.4 The University's denunciation of Lollardy, statute of 1412. Under the statute no doctor, master, bachelor or scholar was to teach, defend or hold any doctrine specifically condemned the year before by the archbishop of Canterbury. Offenders risked imprisonment, being stripped of their degrees and excommunication.

E. The Fifteenth Century: Reorientation and the Challenge of Humanism

Wyclif's ideas were warmly welcomed by the Czech minority at the University of Prague, who were engaged in their own campaign against worldly clerics. His realism was embraced as a counterweight to the nominalism espoused by the German majority, and his theological and ecclesiological ideas used to underpin their reform movement. The leading Prague reformer, Jan Hus, borrowed heavily from the English theologian's works in his own *De ecclesia*, finished in 1413, and when, two years later, he was condemned by the Council of Constance to be burnt for heresy, Wyclif was deemed to be his teacher.[64] Wyclif, however, was to be the last Oxford master whose name would resonate on the continent for many years. Although the arts and theology curriculum underwent little alteration and the commentators of an earlier age continued to be studied and admired, the teaching of speculative philosophy and theology in fifteenth-century Oxford lost much of its vitality. The regents remained true to the non-dogmatic Scotist and realist tradition they had inherited but added nothing of significance to the work of their predecessors. Teachers in logic appear to have been content with rehearsing the arguments of the fourteenth-century terminists and took no interest in developments in logic elsewhere. Oxford theologians similarly showed little enthusiasm for exploring the connections between faith and reason more deeply, and became more concerned with preparing students to be effective preachers and pastors. Instead, the more creative minds developed a novel enthusiasm for scriptural exegesis on the grounds that what the clergy needed to sustain and foster the faith of the laity in an age of growing urban literacy was a better understanding of the Bible.

Oxford's new-found caution made obvious sense in the Lancastrian era. There can be no doubt that the University was anxious to purge itself of any association with Wyclif and heresy, if only to ensure that church and crown did not withdraw their patronage. The easiest way was to avoid further controversy.[65] Subsequent events suggest the policy paid dividends and that the crown was quickly mollified. Henry VI may have decided to found his own college of King's at Cambridge in 1441, but neither he nor his regency council stopped three of the country's leading prelates, including his chancellor, Waynflete, from establishing colleges at Oxford during his reign and granting them the right to hold lands in mortmain. Moreover, the king's uncle, Humfrey, duke of Gloucester, no friend of the Lollards, remained a sterling supporter of the University until his death in 1447.

It would be wrong, however, to attribute Oxford's fifteenth-century intellectual change of tack to prudence, for it takes no account of the wider context which alone explains the new interest in pastoral education. The decline in the vitality of

---

[64] Gordon Leff, *Wyclif and Hus: A Doctrinal Comparison* (Manchester, 1868).

[65] Oxford graduates, once they had left the University, also helped formulate the church's defence against Lollardy, notably the Carmelite Thomas Netter or Walden, author of the *Doctrinale antiquitatum fidei ecclesiae catholicae* in the 1420s.

speculative philosophy and theology was a European-wide phenomenon. There were virtually no scholastic scholars of note in any fifteenth-century university, especially in the second half of the century. The nominalist Gabriel Biel at Tübingen,[66] and the Dominican Thomas de Vio (Cardinal Cajetanus) at Padua, and Pavia, author of important commentaries on the *Summa theologica* of Thomas Aquinas,[67] were singular exceptions. Instead, theologians, all over Europe redirected their energies to producing guides and manuals which could be used by the parish clergy, graduate and non-graduate alike, to improve their ministry.[68] Developments in Oxford were part of a wider belief championed in both church and state: that universities had forsaken their primary role, which was to raise the calibre of the priesthood, and were producing philosophical wranglers, not useful servants of God. Even before Wyclif and Hus upset the ecclesiastical apple cart, there were attempts at Paris to stop lecturers on the Bible and the *Sentences* from departing from the text to explore extraneous logical and philosophical questions, and the restrictions were repeated in the statutes of the faculties of theology set up in new universities from the end of the fourteenth century. Speculation was now feminized and dismissed as curiosity, the sin of Eve. According to the Paris theologian Jean Gerson, in a work of 1402, the theology curriculum had to be overhauled, so that biblical exegesis not philosophical speculation would be placed centre stage.

The change in emphasis, if never complete, had a positive effect on the wider church all around Europe. In England in particular, it quickly led to the appointment in the cathedral chapters and urban parishes of a growing number of competent and committed preachers, exemplified in the second quarter of the fifteenth century by the Cambridge DD William Lichefeld, incumbent of All Hallows-the-Great in London, who, on his death in 1447, purportedly left over 3,000 sermons in English. In Oxford, the new direction was spearheaded by Thomas Gascoigne, a Yorkshire gentleman's son, who became a doctor of theology in 1434 and spent the next twenty years or so living as a paying guest in Oriel perfecting his knowledge of Scripture.[69] Gascoigne strove to recover the literal meaning of the Bible, *secundum ordinem textus*. He turned his back on the hunt for the hidden sense espoused by Wyclif and earlier scholastics and looked for enlightenment in the biblical commentaries of the church fathers and the relatively small number of more recent exegetes who had simply set out to clarify obscure or contradictory passages. His favourite authors were St Jerome, at that date largely ignored, St Augustine, Oxford's Grosseteste, and the thirteenth-century French Dominican Hugo of Vienne, author of the first complete biblical concordance.[70] Gascoigne's approach

---

[66] H. A. Oberman, *The Harvest of Medieval Theology: Gabriel Biel and Late Medieval Nominalism* (Cambridge, 1963).

[67] After 1450, first in Germany and then in Italy, faculties of theology replaced Peter Lombard with Aquinas as the core text of speculative theology: Asztalos, 'Theology', p. 440.

[68] R. Emmet McLaughlin, 'Universities, Scholasticism, and the Origins of the German Reformation', *HU*, IX (1990), 1–43.

[69] R. M. Ball, *Thomas Gascoigne, Libraries and Scholarship* (Cambridge Bibliographical Society, 14; Cambridge, 2006).

[70] This was eventually published in seven volumes at Basel between 1497 and 1502.

was scholarly and thorough. He trawled the University's college and conventual libraries looking for manuscripts; then pursued his quest further afield, visiting most of the larger monasteries and friaries in the hope of finding the commentaries that Oxford lacked. But from the beginning Gascoigne intended his researches would profit the new community of preachers. In the course of his studies he put together an extensive collection of extracts from the Bible and his favourite authors, interlaced with personal comments, which was organized alphabetically under easy-to-use headings and covered obvious sermon topics. When he died in 1458, he left his *Liber seu scriptum de veritatibus collectis ex sacra scriptura et ex scriptis sanctorum et doctorum* to the monks of the Bridgettine monastery of Syon, one of the spiritual centres of fifteenth-century England, in the hope they would ensure it was copied and circulated.[71] Gascoigne also led by example. Although he opted to live out his life in Oxford rather than take up a cure of souls, he delivered many notable sermons and lent his weight to the campaign waged by other leading preachers against his fellow Orielensis, Reginald Pecock, bishop of Chichester, after the latter claimed in 1447 that a bishop should not be expected to appear in the pulpit.[72]

By the turn of the sixteenth century, the spread of the humanist movement had further pulled the rug from under speculative enquiry in Europe's institutions of higher education. This was a movement which developed in fifteenth-century Italy outside the universities, and whose promoters stressed the need for laymen as well as clerics to receive a higher education if they were to be successful administrators and communicators. The humanists felt the learning of the schools was sterile, incestuous, and obsolete. In the 'real' world of the parish church, courtroom, and council chamber, clergymen, lawyers, and administrators needed to be effective rhetoricians who could write and speak both in Latin and in the vernacular in a way that would entertain and convince. Years spent studying speculative philosophy and theology was professionally pointless, even for clerics. What was needed was a new form of higher study where students were initially thoroughly immersed in the language and literature of ancient Rome and Greece before they went on to clearly focused professional training. Thereby, students would not only learn good rather than 'dog' Latin, but also would benefit from the moral and civic wisdom contained in classical poetry and history. The humanists were as hostile as many fifteenth-century theologians to scholastic exegesis, but took the critique much further and developed new scholarly tools of textual analysis. All texts, not just the Bible, should be read in order to understand the meaning of the author, and not as starting points for extraneous discussion. The right way to study a work of classical literature, the

---

[71] Gascoigne was deeply committed to the cult of the Swedish mystic St Bridget. The monastery, with separate accommodation for men and women, was founded by Henry V. Gascoigne's book was very long and only a few copies exist.

[72] Pecock got his comeuppance for standing out against the new interest in preaching. Although the author of significant attacks on Lollardy, he himself ended up being accused of heresy for claiming inter alia that the church could err, and he was forced to resign his bishopric in 1458.

Aristotelian corpus, the Civil Code, or Scripture was through careful linguistic and historical analysis of the surviving manuscript copies.[73]

The humanist movement did not carry all before it. However, patronized by the papacy as well as by Italian principalities and city states, and part of a larger cultural movement we call the Renaissance, it represented a new Zeitgeist, the *aetas Ciceroniana*, which inevitably impacted on the universities to some degree. By the 1520s, virtually every *studium* had come under the influence of the humanist programme in regard to teaching the liberal arts. In some universities, private lecturers had been allowed to give lectures on the new rhetoric or to teach specific texts using the humanists' exegetic methods.[74] In others, where there were residential colleges, as at Paris, enterprising heads had set up courses in the new Latin for their own and outside scholars.[75] Leuven, from 1517, even had a specialist humanist school, the *collegium trilingue*, founded by Jérôme de Busleyden, which offered instruction in Hebrew as well as Latin and Greek.[76] On the other hand, on the eve of the Reformation, the humanists' critique had had little effect on the teaching of philosophy and the higher sciences. In Spain in 1499, Cardinal Ximenes de Cisneros had set up a new *studium*, the University of Alcalá de Henares, where the new learning was introduced into faculty instruction at all levels. But the only old university where any part of the traditional course had been touched by humanism was Padua. In the northern Italian university in the early sixteenth century, professors of philosophy no longer used the old Latin translations as a starting point for long-rehearsed *quaestiones*. Instead, the emphasis was placed on understanding the meaning of the Aristotelian text in the original Greek.[77]

Oxford's reception of the new learning displayed the same characteristics as elsewhere. Although, under the influence of Humfrey of Gloucester, the University partially opened its doors to the study of classical rhetoric as early as 1431, this was as far as it went for the next fifty years. The odd scholar showed some interest in the humanists' wider concerns. Thomas Chaundler, for instance, New College's warden from 1454 to 1475, was close to the fledgling humanist coterie at the court of Henry VI, and believed strongly that university study should provide a moral as well as intellectual education and prepare students for a life of public service. The Balliol fellow Alexander Bell, who died in 1472, showed an interest in classical rhetoric (see Figure 4.5). But the humanist presence, for most of the fifteenth century, was

[73] Paul O. Kristeller, *Renaissance Thought: The Classic, Scholastic and Humanistic Strains* (New York, 1961); Paul O. Kristeller, *Renaissance Thought and Its Sources* (New York, 1979).

[74] Anja-Silvia Goeing, 'Paduan Rhetoric 1489: MS lat. 86 (Bibliothèque de Genève)' (MStud dissertation, Oxford, 2009).

[75] L. W. B. Brockliss, 'The University of Paris in the Sixteenth and Seventeenth Centuries' (PhD dissertation, Cambridge, 1976), pp. 115–25.

[76] Henry de Vocht, *History of the Foundation and Rise of the Collegium Trilingue de Lovaniense, 1517–1550* (4 vols; Louvain, 1951–5).

[77] M. Bataillon, *Érasme et l'Espagne: recherches sur l'histoire spirituelle du XVI siècle* (Paris, 1937); John H. Randall, *The School of Padua and the Emergence of Modern Science* (Padua, 1961). On the struggle between the ancients and moderns at Cologne, see a number of the essays in Charles G. Nauert, *Humanism and Renaissance Civilisation* (Farnham, 2012).

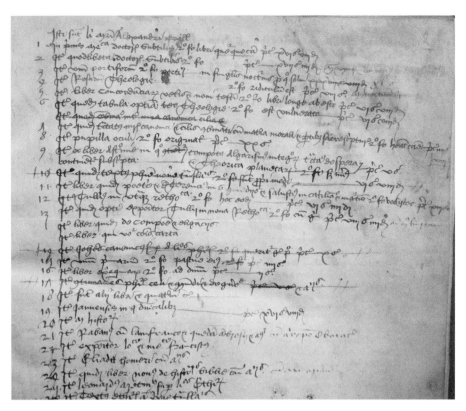

FIGURE 4.5 The library of Alexander Bell, fellow of Balliol, in Johannis Duns Scoti, 'Super Aristotelis Metaphysica quaestiones lxxxi', f. 2v. Bell died in 1472 and left his collection of thirty-four MS books to his college. The list reflects the University's fifteenth-century commitment to practical theology. Besides several volumes of Duns Scotus, there are no significant works from the heyday of Oxford scholasticism but a number of works relating to biblical exegesis. On the other hand, Bell was much more interested in the new learning than most of his colleagues. Besides Cicero's rhetorical works, he owned the plays of Terence, Sallust's histories, Homer's *Iliad* (presumably in a Latin version), and Leonardo Bruni's translation of Aristotle's *Ethics* (nos 11, 23 and 25).

muted. Gascoigne for one remained completely untouched by the movement. The situation began to change only with the establishment of Magdalen College School in 1480. Waynflete made no reference to the humanist programme in the founding statute but there can be no doubt that it was intended to provide an education in classical rather than contemporary Latin. The first master of the school, John Anwykyll, appointed by Waynflete, was a supporter of the new pedagogy, albeit a relatively conservative version, and used Terence, one of the humanists' favourite authors, as a vehicle for teaching grammar.[78]

From 1480, too, a small but steady stream of Oxford graduates can be found heading south to seek humanism in its native land. These included two of the

[78] Nicholas Orme, *Education in Early Tudor England: Magdalen College and its School 1480–1549* (Oxford, 1998).

leading figures of English humanism in the early sixteenth century, John Colet, later dean of St Paul's, and the physician Thomas Linacre. Colet passed most of the 1490s in France and Italy where he mixed in humanist circles and became a devotee of the neoplatonist Florentine scholar Ficino, while Linacre left All Souls in 1493 to pursue his studies at Padua, which was a centre of medical as well as philosophical humanism.[79] When Colet returned he shared his new scholarly insights with his alma mater. In 1498 he gave private lectures at Oxford on Paul's Epistle to the Romans. Colet was at one with the University's belief that the aim of a theological education was to produce a good and effective pastor. But, as a humanist, he believed that this could be achieved only by a careful study of Scripture. In his lectures he ignored traditional commentaries and avoided speculative questions, concentrating instead on providing an exposition of the literal meaning of the text and the moral lessons that it contained, which he illuminated using Plato and neoplatonist authors.[80]

However, the presence of a school teaching the new Latin and a growing number of old members, often in high places, with a taste for humanist learning did not lead to the University committing more deeply to the humanists' programme in the early sixteenth century. Even once humanism moved from being on the fringe to the centre of the court with the accession of Henry VIII in 1509, Oxford made no effort to change its method of teaching philosophy and the higher sciences. When the greatest humanist of northern Europe, Erasmus, came to England on a visit in 1498, he spent much of his time at Oxford with Colet. Significantly, on his two subsequent visits, including his long stay in the first part of the reign of Henry VIII, he ignored the University completely. When he agreed to take up a teaching post, he did so at Cambridge, where, on and off, he taught both Greek and divinity from 1511 to 1514. Cambridge had been no more ready than Oxford to abandon the old learning, but at least it saw stirrings of reform at the end of the first decade of the sixteenth century. Two new colleges, Christ's and St John's, were in the process of being set up by benefactors sympathetic to the new learning.[81]

Part of the reason for the University's relative disregard of the new learning must have been institutional hauteur. If there was one aspect of scholasticism humanists particularly deplored it was terminist logic: Oxford, in their eyes, was the home of the *barbari*. Arguably, the majority of masters, piqued at being the butt of foreign satire, dug their heels in and turned their back on the movement. Whatever the cause, the only way for the new learning to make headway was by direct intervention from outside. As at Cambridge, the surest route was to establish a new college which could be filled with sympathetic fellows. The initial step was taken in 1517

[79] Jonathan Woolfson, *Padua and the Tudors: English Students in Italy, 1485–1603* (Cambridge, 1998); C. B. Schmitt, 'Thomas Linacre and Italy', in Francis Maddison, Margaret Pelling, and Charles Webster (eds), *Essays on the Life and Work of Thomas Linacre, c.1460–1524* (Oxford, 1977).

[80] Jonathan Arnold, *Dean John Colet of St Paul's: Humanism and Reform in Early Tudor England* (London, 2007).

[81] At Cambridge, Erasmus held the Lady Margaret chair for divinity. Henry VII's mother had endowed a theology chair at both universities. For the first stirrings of the new learning in two Cambridge colleges, Christ's and St John's, see Leader, pp. 281–90.

when one of the leading supporters of humanism within the church, Bishop Fox of Winchester, was granted a royal charter for his new college of Corpus Christi, and drew up statutes which made provision for public lectures in the new learning.[82]

The traditionalists were not amused and tried to scupper the initiative before it got off the ground, much to the annoyance of the king's friend, Sir Thomas More. The humanist and courtier was so incensed that, in March 1518, he penned a caustic letter to the University, reproaching the masters for allowing one of their number to 'babble' in a Lenten sermon 'against not only Greek but Roman literature, and finally against all polite learning'. The offender, claimed More, belonged to a society of so-called 'Trojans', who, 'whether as a joke, or a piece of anti-Greek academic politics, begin to pour ridicule on the study of Greek'. More, an alumnus of St Mary Hall, who had possibly learnt Latin grammar at Magdalen College School, was horrified, and threatened the University with the wrath of Wolsey, Wareham, the archbishop of Canterbury, and the king himself, who all, he reminded the masters, valued the new learning as a support for theology.[83]

Wolsey duly rode to the rescue. Evidently feeling it was time to show the University where his loyalties lay, the king's chief minister made it clear that Fox's initiative had his and the crown's blessing. By the start of Michaelmas Term 1518, he had personally endowed a public lectureship in the humanities, which he filled over the next seven years with a number of leading humanists, including the Spaniard Juan-Luis Vives, who came to Oxford in 1523. By 1524–5, Wolsey was determined on a more grandiose gesture. Like Fox, he understood that the best support for the new learning was a new college. But he was intent on putting his episcopal rival in the shade and in 1525, in founding Cardinal College, established a mini-university.[84]

Both Fox and Wolsey saw their colleges as vehicles for institutionalizing the study of Latin eloquence and Greek in the University in the manner of Busleyden's foundation at Leuven, although neither envisaged a lectureship in Hebrew.[85] Fox, in addition, was keen to build on Colet's biblical lectures twenty years before, and expected his theology lecturer to promote a new form of Scriptural exegesis. Emphasis was to be given to the views of the fathers of the early church, not 'ignorant' moderns such as Nicholas of Lyra, whose biblical commentaries were the first to be put into print and were to be found in most Oxford college libraries.[86] Neither ecclesiastic, however, was a revolutionary. They did not intend to overturn the old learning but rather integrate new and old. Fox's statutes for Corpus made it clear that his fellows, according to their status, were to attend the scholastic lectures

---

[82] See p. 83, this volume.

[83] Thomas More, *Selected Letters*, ed. Elizabeth Francis Rogers (New Haven, CT, 1961), pp. 96–7. More was purportedly at St Mary Hall from 1490 to 1492.

[84] See p. 83, this volume. Vives was also appointed tutor to the Princess Mary. He was forced to leave England when he opposed the annulment of the king's marriage.

[85] Greek was taught occasionally in the University before Fox's foundation. It was 1518 before it was also taught regularly at Cambridge with the appointment of Richard Croke.

[86] Statutes, vol. 2, *Statutes of Corpus Christi*, pp. 50–1. Lyra's *Postillae perpetuae in universam S. Scripturam* was published in 1471.

in philosophy and theology given at Magdalen, while the theologians among them were also to sit at the feet of the recently appointed Lady Margaret professor.[87] Wolsey, too, was anxious not to offend the Trojans. He was adamant that his professor of Latin should teach rhetoric through the orations of Cicero and that his Greek professor should teach the language through literary texts. But he was no humanist theologian. His professor of theology was to alternate between lecturing 'clearly and elegantly' on Scripture and introducing his charges to 'the subtle scholastic questions' of Duns Scotus. Wolsey was aware that the church in the 1520s had a new foe in Martin Luther and was convinced that the old learning was necessary 'to confute heresy'. His great fear was that 'scholastic erudition', once neglected, would be despised.[88]

---

[87] Statutes, vol. 2, *Statutes of Corpus Christi*, p. 54.

[88] Ibid., *Statutes of Cardinal College*, vol. 2, pp. 127–8. His views were shared by Bishop Longland of Lincoln, who had been brought up on the new grammar at Magdalen College School. In 1531 he instructed the bachelors of arts in Oriel to abandon Latin poetry and the Latin classics and concentrate on the writings of the ancient doctors, 'which they can employ more usefully in their ordinary disputations': Catto, pp. 75–6.

Conclusion

The Coming of the Reformation

O XFORD in the twelfth century was just one of many towns in western Christendom where schools were to be found offering tuition in some aspect of the liberal arts, philosophy, or the three higher sciences. A century later, it was one of the few centres of learning whose school or schools had developed into an entirely new educational institution which soon became known as a *studium generale* or *universitas*. The old schools and the new universities were very different institutions even if they taught the same subjects. The schools had no independent existence: they were the property of self-appointed masters and lasted as long as the teacher was able to attract pupils or cared to stay in the town. Universities, on the other hand, were self-governing corporate bodies whose legal existence and privileges were recognized and protected by the pope, emperor, and local ruler. Above all, they had the peculiar right to offer scholars who had demonstrated their ability to debate and lecture in one of the four subject areas or faculties a formal, written attestation of their competence. These marks of competence or degrees of bachelor, licentiate, and doctor were universally acknowledged badges of status: they allowed the holder, in theory at least, to teach in any university in Christendom.

Although, between the beginning of the thirteenth century and the sixteenth century, universities came to be founded all over Europe, the Oxford *studium* always remained one of the most prominent. This was not simply because of its antiquity but because of its size and reputed intellectual significance, even if its academic credentials in the fifteenth century were somewhat tarnished. It was also, along with its Cambridge sister, a distinctive university in terms of its organization, which differentiated it from the other universities of northern Europe, which were closely modelled on the University of Paris. Oxford and Cambridge were headed by a chancellor not a rector; their faculties were not independent corporations; there were no nations; and their scholars, from the turn of the fifteenth century, had to reside in halls or colleges. The English universities even invented a separate degree subject. As one of the seven liberal arts, music was traditionally taught, albeit perfunctorily, as part of the arts curriculum: it was a purely mathematical subject based on the study of Boethius.[1] In the second half of the fifteenth century, Cambridge, then Oxford, began to offer a specific degree in the art to those who were accomplished performers and composers.

Nonetheless, however distinctive, Oxford and Cambridge in the late middle ages were always part of a single university system. Like every other *studium*, they were first and foremost ecclesiastical institutions. They owed their existence to the fact that the Roman church, in its desire to create unity and uniformity in western Christendom, grasped the value of sustaining a formal network of institutions of higher education which could provide it with a solid coterie of educated clergy. Until the turn of the sixteenth century, when a growing number of laymen intent on a career in law began to invade continental universities, the vast majority of scholars in all *studia* were clerics who hoped, often in vain, to turn the church's agenda to their own material advantage. Oxford and Cambridge were ultimately cogs in the papal machine, even if the English crown soon realized that the universities' scholars would make efficient secular administrators as well. The state might become involved in Oxford's affairs at moments of civil disorder but the archbishop of Canterbury was entrusted with keeping scholars on the intellectual straight and narrow: hence the primate's growing intervention in Oxford's life in the fourteenth century. Intellectual curiosity and creativity had to be held in check in order that the church's spiritual and material power was not threatened by an institution that was principally there to enhance its authority.

In the course of the first half of the sixteenth century, however, the idea that Europe's universities shared a common purpose came under intolerable strain when the church itself fell apart as a result of theological divisions which could not be resolved by discussion or force. Wyclif and Hus had taken issue with many aspects of the church of their own day, but they had never challenged its fundamental salvation theology that humans were fallen creatures destined for hell who might be saved through a combination of faith in the redeeming power of Christ's sacrifice and the performance of good works pleasing to God. From the turn of the sixteenth century, this soteriology came under rigorous scrutiny. Erasmus and his humanist friends accepted that man was saved through a mix of faith and good works but felt that good works needed radically defining in line with their view of the centrality of the active moral life. To the late medieval church, a good work was not limited to acts of neighbourly charity: it could be a life of prayer and abstinence, taking the sacraments, any form of spiritual or penitential exercise, such as going on a pilgrimage, or even a donation to church funds. To Erasmus, such practices had nothing to do with being a Christian and were instruments of church enrichment and extortion which should be discouraged and even abolished. Martin Luther, a professor of theology at the University of Wittenberg, went much further. In 1517, he nailed ninety-five theses or positions for debate to the door of the town's parish church in which he took issue with a salvation theology which found a place for

---

[1] John North, 'The Quadrivium', in *HUIE*, i. 343–4.

good works at all. He agreed with everything Erasmus had to say about the pointlessness of much late medieval piety, but also believed that acts of neighbourly charity would not win favour with God. Humans were so corrupted as a result of the Fall that imitating Christ was impossible: even acts of kindness were done from love of ourselves, not love of God. We performed good works of any kind because we sought to curry favour with our maker. There was only one way to be reconciled with God and that was to believe in the fullness of Christ's sacrifice. Christ's merits, on their own, would lead God to look kindly on us at the hour of our death. The doctrine of justification by faith alone threatened the late medieval church in its entirety. Erasmus' critique sanctioned the abolition of monasteries, the desecration of shrines, and a large reduction in the number of priests. Luther wanted the church to be completely restructured: popes, bishops, and priests were no longer a caste apart, miracle workers who acted as the intermediaries between God and man, but professional functionaries whose primary role was to teach and help the laity to read the Bible in their mother tongue.

Between them, Erasmus and Luther laid the foundations of the Reformation, the movement for church reform that swept through Europe in the second quarter of the sixteenth century and ultimately divided western Christendom into warring confessional camps. Luther was no humanist—he initially knew no Greek and had developed his salvation theology through studying the New Testament in the Latin translation of St Jerome, which had been used in the church for centuries.[2] But he quickly understood that humanist exegetic techniques could help his cause, and many humanists, though not Erasmus and Thomas More, enlisted under his banner, convinced that his salvation message was correct.[3] Luther also knew how to spread his ideas beyond a small group of intellectuals. Rebuffed by other university theologians and the papacy, he took his critique to the laity through a creative use of the vernacular printing press, a tool unavailable to Wyclif and Hus a century before and whose mass-marketing potential had hitherto not been fully exploited. The political juncture was also apposite. The University of Wittenberg had been founded by the local ruler, Frederick the Wise, elector of Saxony, only in 1502, and the elector's pride in his new foundation was an important factor in Luther's early survival. Although, within a few years, Luther had been condemned as a heretic by the pope and outlawed by the Holy Roman Emperor, he remained safe under the elector's protection. Frederick had little sympathy with Luther's theology but he wanted to place his new university on the map and the reformer's presence gave his foundation the notoriety and élan he craved. As the elector's overlord, the Emperor Charles V was too busy securing his Spanish throne, then fighting the Turks and the French, to bring his own weight to bear. Luther and his supporters thus had more

---

[2] On the new learning at Wittenberg, see M. Grossman, *Humanism at Wittenberg 1485–1517* (Nieuwkoop, 1975).
[3] Erasmus claimed that the New Testament did not contain a straightforward salvation theology. Unlike More, who thought heretics should be burnt, he did not believe that Luther should be persecuted.

than twenty years to win the hearts and minds of the princes and people of northern Germany and Scandinavia.[4]

Luther's ideas quickly found their way to all parts of Europe, where the implications of his fundamental doctrine of solafideism were explored and refined by other intellectuals, such as Jean Calvin, the Genevan reformer whose influence on the English Reformation in the second half of the sixteenth century was particularly strong. Calvin, though tonsured when young, was not even a theologian. Educated in the Latin humanities at the Parisian Collège de Sainte-Barbe in the early 1520s, he later moved on to Orléans and Bourges to study civil law, before dedicating his life to renewing the church.[5] Lutheran or quasi-Lutheran cells were soon established in many universities. Oxford's first Protestant reformer of significance was the martyr William Tyndale, who was at Magdalen Hall in the 1510s, where he developed a passion for biblical study. It is likely, though, that his interest in Luther and his decision to translate the Bible into English developed after he had gone down, for initially Oxford seems to have been less affected than Cambridge by the burgeoning movement.[6] By late 1527, however, the University had spawned its own coterie of reforming intellectuals, many of them connected to Wolsey's new foundation of Cardinal College. When their presence was discovered in the following year, the horrified prelate swiftly moved to root them out. The ringleader, Thomas Garrett, an erstwhile fellow of Magdalen but then based in London, was arrested for disseminating protestant literature in the University, tried as a heretic in St Mary's, and made to recant. Many of the others were rounded up, marched through the streets, and ordered to throw one of the offending works on a bonfire at Carfax as a sign of repentance.[7] Within a few months, the cardinal was confident that at Oxford at least the threat had been nipped in the bud.

Given that Henry VIII was totally hostile to Luther—indeed, the king had been given the title Defender of the Faith by the pope for writing a book against the reformer in 1521—there was no reason to think that the menace could not be contained thereafter. But Henry's desperate need for a male heir completely changed the situation. The king's request in 1527 for an annulment of his marriage to Catherine of Aragon so that he could marry again put Henry at odds with the pope, led to Wolsey's removal two years later for failing to do his master's will, and eventually brought to prominence in government a Lutheran sympathizer in Thomas Cromwell. It also caused friction in the relationship between Henry and the

---

[4] In contrast with most other European states, the princes or magnates of the Holy Roman Empire were all but sovereigns in the regions over which they claimed jurisdiction, and the emperor had no way of enforcing his will except by force, which he was seldom in a position to exercise. The imperial title was elective and those German princes who formed the electoral college were known as electors.

[5] Sainte-Barbe was a Paris college at the forefront of teaching a course in the Latin humanities in the early sixteenth century: see L. W. B. Brockliss, 'The University of Paris in the Sixteenth and Seventeenth Centuries' (PhD dissertation, Cambridge, 1976), p. 120.

[6] On Tyndale at Oxford: see John Foxe, *Actes and Monuments, with a life and defence of the martyrologist by the late Rev. George Townsend DD* (3rd edn (6 vols; London, 1870), iv. 115. Tyndale's translation of the New Testament was published abroad in 1526. He was burnt in 1536 in the Netherlands.

[7] Ibid., pp. 421–9. Garrett was burnt in 1540.

University. In order to convince the pope that he had right on his side, Henry sought the support of the leading universities of Europe. Oxford, however, when asked to confirm that marriage to a dead brother's widow was unlawful, was less than forthcoming. Initially, Congregation stalled and the masters dug in their heels. The king subsequently got the endorsement he demanded but only by a constitutional sleight of hand. It was agreed that the majority opinion of the doctors of theology could stand for the opinion of the University as a whole.

As the quarrel dragged on, the masters must have fervently hoped that a compromise could be found that would safeguard the honour of both sides. This, though, was not to be. In 1533, Henry abandoned his search for the pope's blessing and had his marriage annulled by his new archbishop of Canterbury, Thomas Cranmer, a Cambridge man, who was a closet reformer. A year later, Cromwell pushed the Act of Supremacy through parliament, which severed the country's ties with Rome and set up the king as head of the English church. Thereby, the first period of the University's history was brought to an abrupt close. For the first three centuries of their history, Oxford and Cambridge had been part of the higher-education system of catholic Christendom. For the next three centuries, except for a few years under Mary, they became confessional universities, principally dedicated to upholding the state's religion and answerable to the state if they stepped out of line.

PART II

The Anglican University: 1534–1845

Introduction

The Age of Confessionalism

THE masters of Oxford University did not have to wait long after the passage of the Act of Supremacy to learn that they were in a new age. Henry VIII appointed Cromwell his vicegerent in spirituals and, in the late summer of 1535, the king's secretary sent commissioners to Oxford and Cambridge to get members of the two universities to swear to the legality of the break with Rome, which they sensibly did.[1] As Cromwell and the other religious reformers at court were ardent supporters of the humanist movement, the commissioners were further empowered to put the new learning on a solid footing. On their arrival at Oxford, Cromwell's men found only two colleges with permanent teaching in classical languages: Magdalen and Corpus. By the time they had left, the commissioners had established Latin and Greek lectureships at All Souls and New College, a Greek lectureship at Magdalen, and Latin lectureships at Merton and Queen's. The other colleges were judged too poor to bear the burden. The commissioners also reported to Cromwell that they had successfully weaned the University off its taste for scholastic debate. Duns Scotus, they declared, had been confined to Oxford gaol, and been banished from the University for ever, 'and is now made a common servant to every man fast nailed up upon posts in all common houses of easement'. New College, it seems, had led the way. When the commissioners visited the college a second time, they found the quadrangle filled with the leaves of Duns' manuscripts, and a Buckinghamshire gentleman called Grenefelde gathering them up for 'sewelles or blawnsherres to keep the deer within the wood, and thereby have the better cry with his hounds'.[2]

The need to ensure Oxford and Cambridge's loyalty to the new order was essential if the English clergy of the future were to be firmly behind the new Church of England. Similar visitations occurred in all the other universities of Europe

---

[1] The University had already agreed, after royal prompting, on 27 June 1534, that the bishop of Rome possessed no authority in England.
[2] *Letters and papers, Foreign and Domestic, of the Reign of Henry VIII*, vol. 9, 1535, p. 117 (no. 350): Richard Layton to Cromwell, 12 Sept. 1535. A 'sewelle' is an object set up to scare deer from passing.

that lay in territories that embraced the Reformation. Where no university existed or the ability of existing institutions to train sufficient godly ministers and administrators was distrusted, then new *studia* were founded in the following years. The University of Edinburgh was established in 1582 to ensure that Scotland, a country divided politically and religiously, had a university directly under the king's nose; Elizabeth belatedly founded an Irish university in Dublin in 1592; while in the Calvinist United Provinces a university was eventually set up in each of its parts, beginning with Leiden in 1575. Everywhere, the establishment of a protestant university also led to the introduction or consolidation of humanist ideas about language teaching and textual exegesis, even if the traditional scholastic approach was never completely abandoned. By the seventeenth century, moreover, it was judged insufficient to be proficient only in classical Latin and Greek, and ancient history, Hebrew, and sometimes other oriental languages deemed useful for the study of early versions of Scripture and ancient philosophy and medicine were added to the curriculum of the faculty of arts.[3]

Europe's catholic universities adopted these curricular changes more slowly. Initially there was great suspicion of promoting the new learning any further, for many theologians and intellectuals who remained loyal to Rome blamed humanism for Luther's revolution. But views eventually changed. In the 1540s, the pope convened a council of bishops at the Italian city of Trent to strengthen the church against the protestant threat. By 1563, when the council declared that the way forward was to reaffirm the role of good works and the sacraments in gaining salvation and cut the protestants adrift, catholic attitudes to the humanist agenda had softened. The Jesuits in particular, a new order founded in 1540 to convert the heathen and reconvert the heretic, had come down forcefully in its favour, recognizing that the failure of the Catholic Church to embrace the new learning wholeheartedly was one of the chief reasons that elites all over Europe were deserting the fold. In the catholic world, however, the integration of humanist language teaching into the arts curriculum had a profound impact on the structure of the university system. In protestant Europe, boys entered the faculties of arts with a good knowledge of Latin and some proficiency in Greek that they had learnt in feeder schools. They then perfected that knowledge during their first years at university before going on to study philosophy. In general, in catholic Europe, the feeder schools, many run by the Jesuits, came to provide a complete course in the Latin and Greek humanities, and often in the four parts of philosophy as well. In the catholic world, therefore, the faculties of arts frequently did little but examine, and the universities were reduced to teaching the higher studies. The feeder schools might be a part of the local university, as at Paris, where a number of the colleges began to usurp the

---

[3] For a good indication of the richness of the pre-philosophy arts curriculum in arguably protestant Europe's leading university, see T. H. Lunsingh Scheurleer and G. H. M. Posthumus Meyjes (eds), *Leiden University in the Seventeenth Century: An Exchange of Learning* (Leiden, 1975). The United Provinces, the modern Netherlands, was part of the Spanish Empire until the region rebelled in the mid-1560s. The local university had been Leuven in Flanders.

teaching function of the faculty of arts from the 1520s. But this only masked the fact that the arts were no longer a university discipline.[4]

In the course of the hundred years from 1550 to 1650, the protestant and catholic systems became segregated as well as distinctive. The extent to which students moved around in the late middle ages can be exaggerated, but they were largely free to roam where they would. The division of Europe into confessional blocks made travel less easy. Many rulers, such as Philip II of Spain in 1559, positively forbade their subjects from studying outside their dominions. Until the mid-seventeenth century, protestants from many parts of Europe could be found attending the catholic law faculty at Orléans or receiving a medical education at Padua. But this, thereafter, all but ceased.[5] In the eighteenth century, virtually all universities were confessionally closed and even interstate student migration between universities of the same denomination became much less common. Only the odd faculty, renowned as a centre of excellence or notorious for awarding degrees on demand, could attract foreigners.[6] The young continued to travel abroad in the eighteenth century in pursuit of knowledge. Indeed, there were more on the road than ever before, and most were oblivious to confessional boundaries. But they were young men seeking an education that Europe's universities could not supply. Medics who had gained a degree in their home country flocked to Paris for high-quality hands-on tuition in anatomy and surgery that was supplied by private teachers;[7] future military officers, like the duke of Wellington, went to Angers to study in the town's military academy; while countless thousands from northern Europe headed for Italy on the Grand Tour to absorb classical culture *in situ* and gawp at Renaissance art and architecture.[8]

Towards the end of the eighteenth century, thanks to a bevy of foundations in both catholic and protestant countries, there were some 180 universities in Europe, more than double the number in 1517.[9] The percentage of the male population in its

---

[4] For this development in one catholic state, see R. Chartier, M.-M. Compère, and D. Julia, *L'Education en France du XVIe au XVIIIe siècle* (Paris, 1976), chs 5 and 6. The change did not occur in modern-day Belgium, where philosophy teaching always remained a monopoly of the University of Leuven. In both protestant and catholic states, many of the feeder schools were new foundations in the sixteenth and early seventeenth centuries.

[5] Michel Bideaux and Marie-Madeleine Fragonnard (eds), *Les Echanges entre les universités européennes à la Renaissance* (Geneva, 2003); Ad Tervoort, *The iter italicum and the Northern Netherlands: Dutch Students at Italian Universities and their Role in the Netherlands' Society (1426–1575)* (Leiden, 2005); Hilde de Ridder-Symoens, 'The Mobility of Medical Students from the Fifteenth to the Eighteenth Centuries: The Institutional Context', in O. P. Grell, A. Cunningham, and Jon Arrizabalga (eds), *Centres of Medical Excellence? Medical Travel and Education in Europe, 1500–1789* (Farnham, 2010), ch. 3 (esp. pp. 79–89, tables). Philip II did let scholars out of Spain to study in 'safe' Italian universities, mainly in parts of the peninsula he directly controlled.

[6] Willem Frijhoff, 'Surplus ou déficit? Hypothèses sur le nombre réel des étudiants en Allemagne à l'époque moderne (1576–1815)', *Francia, 7* (1979), esp. p. 201; Willem Frijhoff, *La Société néerlandaise et ses gradués, 1575–1811* (Amsterdam, 1981), pp. 83–94.

[7] For a good account of a Swiss student's experience, see *Johannes Gesners Pariser Tagebuch 1727*, ed. U. Boschung (Bern, 1985). The classic study is Toby Gelfand, *Professionalising Modern Medicine: Paris Surgeons and Medical Science and Institutions in the Eighteenth Century* (London, 1980).

[8] Studies of the Grand Tour are legion: for an introduction, see Jeremy Black, *The British Abroad: The Grand Tour in the Eighteenth Century* (Stroud, 2003).

[9] Willem Frijhoff, 'Patterns', in HUIE, ii. 97–105 (maps).

late teens and early twenties attending university was still very small in all parts of Europe—only very occasionally more than 3 per cent, usually less than 1.[10] But the social significance of Europe's universities had grown considerably across the intervening period. Traditionally, they had been ecclesiastical institutions almost exclusively preparing people for the church. This still remained an important part of their *raison d'être*, but by the end of the eighteenth century, more than half of the students in most universities were laymen destined for a career in the secular courts or state administration. At the beginning of the sixteenth century, the number of secular lawyers who had attended a law faculty was in the ascendant, but the majority of law students would still have been destined for the ecclesiastical courts. On the eve of the French Revolution, the situation was very different. In most parts of Europe the size and power of the state had grown considerably in the interim and, with it, the number and scope of the state's courts, usually at the expense of ecclesiastical jurisdiction. As rulers had been persuaded that consistent and reliable justice depended on secular judges and barristers having a good grounding in civil law, the law faculties had filled up with laymen, even in areas in northern Europe governed by local customs.[11] By the end of the period, too, a growing percentage of students were laymen studying medicine, even if medics were only ever a significant proportion of the total in a handful of universities. Graduate physicians in orders had virtually disappeared by the end of the sixteenth century as a result of a growing belief that it was unseemly for a clergyman to minister to the body as well as the soul. In consequence, in the eighteenth century, when growing wealth and a novel concern about health offered much more employment for graduate physicians, a new cohort of laymen appeared in the higher faculties and carried laicization further.[12]

The two groups, however, continued to form a single university community. What principally united clerical and lay students within this expanding university system and once they had left was their common grounding in the Latin, and to a less extent, Greek humanities. Latin remained the language of formal university lectures and disputations until the end of the eighteenth century, and every university student spent seven or eight years learning to read, write, and speak the classical tongue before embarking on the study of philosophy and the higher sciences. Only mathematics, which was a much more sophisticated discipline in

---

[10] Maria Rosa di Simone, 'Admission', in ibid., p. 311 (table).

[11] Once the University of Paris was allowed to teach civil law from 1679, numbers in the law faculty almost trebled, from 250 to 700. The overall number of law students in France rose from 2,000 to 3,000 across the eighteenth century: see L. W. B. Brockliss, 'Patterns of Attendance at the University of Paris', *Historical Journal*, 21: 3 (1978), 514; R. Kagan, 'Law Students and Legal Careers in Eighteenth-Century France', *Past and Present*, 68 (1975), 62–3.

[12] In France there was a threefold expansion in the number of medical graduates across the eighteenth century: L. W. B. Brockliss and Colin Jones, *The Medical World of Early Modern France* (Oxford, 1997), pp. 517 and 520 (tables). For an idea of the distribution of medical students around Europe, see L. W. B. Brockliss, 'Medical Education and Centres of Excellence in Eighteenth-Century Europe: Towards an Identification', in Grell, Cunningham, and Arrizabalga, *Centres of Medical Excellence*, ch. 2.

1750 than in 1500, began to be taught in the vernacular, because of the difficulty of expressing large numbers in Latin.[13]

On the other hand, the universities lost much of their former intellectual dynamism as the period wore on. In the late middle ages, the dominant intellectual tradition of the era, scholasticism, had been engendered in their midst. Thereafter, the universities largely surrendered their cultural leadership. The period between the birth of the Reformation and the French Revolution witnessed the emergence of three successive, interlocking, and ongoing intellectual movements which all but swept the scholastic inheritance aside. From the turn of the sixteenth century, scholars both north and south of the Alps took Renaissance humanism to a new critical level. By subjecting the textual inheritance of antiquity and a growing number of other ancient and medieval books, documents, and artefacts to ever more careful philological and contextual exegesis, they were able to establish their authorial meaning, date them more accurately, and ultimately permit the construction of a novel, critical, and evolving account of man's past.[14] In the seventeenth century, a new group of intellectuals, who called themselves experimental philosophers, largely jettisoned the study of texts and began to extend and reconceptualize Europe's understanding of the natural world by accumulating more and more information of its fecundity through observation and experiment. In a movement known to historians as the Scientific Revolution, Aristotelian explanations based on matter and form were abandoned and a new particulate and mathematical science of physics developed, which built on the alternative classical traditions of Pythagoras, Epicurus, and Plato, and allowed humans to manipulate nature not simply admire it.[15] Finally, in the eighteenth century, a mixed group of men of letters and philosophers transferred the observational methodology of the new science to the study of man, and created a movement dubbed today the Enlightenment. Developing an earlier seventeenth-century idea that a science of man might be built from scratch without reference to the Bible or the wisdom of the ancients, they laid the foundations of modern secular social science by rejecting the Christian notion of the inevitability of human imperfection and suggesting ways in which mankind might improve morally and materially. The most radical among them, known as the philosophes, equally denied that the Bible was divinely inspired, and rejected most or all aspects of Christian theology as unknowable.[16]

None of these movements originated within the confessional university, and the last seriously aimed to undermine it by attacking confessionalism and calling for dramatic changes in the content and structure of a university education. Many aspects of the movements' critique of traditional learning were eventually integrated

---

[13] Teaching mathematics in Latin began to be abandoned in France from the 1730s.

[14] The leading living scholar of the movement is Anthony Grafton. Among his many works, see *Defenders of the Text: The Traditions of Scholarship in an Age of Science, 1450–1800* (London, 1991).

[15] For a brief overview, see John Henry, *The Scientific Revolution and the Origins of Modern Science* (Basingstoke, 1997).

[16] The best introduction remains Peter Gay, *The Enlightenment: An Interpretation* (2 vols; New York, 1966–9).

into the curriculum, and individuals within the universities continually assisted in their development, especially in the field of humanist scholarship across the period. Yet, by and large, the movements took shape and root beyond the *studia*. The exegetes, antiquarians, experimental philosophers, and men of letters who fashioned these movements were nearly always the beneficiaries of higher education. But most were not involved in teaching of any kind: they were drawn from a broad cross-section of the socio-professional elite and included incumbent ecclesiastics, practising lawyers and physicians, courtiers, and gentlemen living on their estates. What linked the practitioners together was their membership of the Republic of Letters, a virtual polity invented by Erasmus at the dawn of the Reformation age, whose citizens were devoted to expanding man's knowledge of himself and the natural world through collaboration and mutual exchange, irrespective, in theory, of country or confession.[17]

Initially, in the sixteenth century, the Republic had been a small isolated group of intellectuals, frequently viewed with suspicion by Augustinian-minded religious establishments who disliked their commitment to improvement.[18] By the eighteenth century, however, in a more tolerant age, the Republic was populated by many thousands, including, for the first time, a large number of former army and navy officers. It had also finally begun to take institutional shape with the establishment of the learned academy or society, which brought members of the Republic together to present their work and discuss each other's ideas. Private literary and musical academies had existed in Italy and the Netherlands from the fifteenth century, while the first state-supported academies devoted wholly to the new experimental philosophy—the Royal Society and the Parisian Académie des sciences—were founded in 1660 and 1666. In the eighteenth century, the state's investment in the new institutions mushroomed, and by the outbreak of the French Revolution some hundred had been created. Most official academies catered for both the arts and sciences but they shared a common commitment to expanding the boundaries of knowledge. Virtually all set annual essay questions where members of the public were invited to send in their solutions to current scientific, social, economic, and educational problems. Although some academies offered instruction, most did not. Their *raison d'être* was completely different from the universities'.[19]

Oxford and Cambridge, between the Reformation and the French Revolution, shared the chief characteristics of their sister institutions.[20] They were always solidly

---

[17] Hans Bots and Françoise Wacquet, *La République des lettres* (Paris, 1997); Ann Goldgar, *Impolite Learning: Conduct and Community in the Republic of Letters, 1680–1750* (London, 1995).

[18] Like the scholastic philosophers of the fifteenth century they were accused by the church of the feminine vice of curiosity: see L. W. B. Brockliss, 'Culture', in J. Bergin (ed.), *The Seventeenth Century: Europe 1598–1715* (Oxford, 2001), pp. 152–60.

[19] James E. McClellan III, *Science Reorganized: Scientific Societies in the Eighteenth Century* (New York, 1985); Daniel Roche, *Le Siècle des lumières en province: Académies et académiciens provinciaux, 1680–1789* (2 vols; Paris, 1978); Jeremy Caradonna, *The Enlightenment in Practice: Academic Prize Contests and Intellectual Culture in France, 1670–1794* (Ithaca, NY, 2012).

[20] For Cambridge during this period, see Morgan and Searby.

confessional universities and a significant proportion of their students would end up as clergymen. But by the end of the sixteenth century, they had ceased to be solely clerical institutions as more and more students came up who had no intention of taking orders or entering the church. Equally, even if Cambridge could boast Newton among its masters in residence, neither university could claim to have made a continual and consistent contribution to the great intellectual movements of the age. Oxford and Cambridge were also unequivocally part of the protestant university world, once England's allegiance to the Reformation had been finally confirmed with the accession of Elizabeth in 1558, for the two English universities always retained an active faculty of arts, and what student migration they experienced was nearly always to and from other protestant universities.

Yet, even more than in the late middle ages, Oxford and Cambridge were peculiar universities. In the first place, laicization had nothing to do with an influx of law students looking for a career in the crown's courts. Not only did the secular legal system in England remain based on common law but, just as in the earlier period, no attempt was made to make entry to the English bar dependent on holding a degree in civil law. To the extent that barristers, judges, and justices of the peace received any formal professional training during the period, they obtained it, as in the past, by attending the London Inns of Court.[21] The influx of lay students occurred instead in the faculty of arts, and was principally due to a decision taken by the landowning elite to send their sons to the two universities for the first time. By the middle of the sixteenth century, humanist educationalists had convinced the English elite that a gentleman, whatever his future life, needed an acquaintance with the Latin and Greek humanities and a smattering of philosophy to justify his status and wealth. In other countries, where the elites fell less completely under the humanist spell, there was no need to go to a university to acquire the necessary scholarly patina, since the feeder schools, especially in catholic Europe, provided all the education a gentleman desired. Even would-be secular lawyers could bypass the arts faculty on the continent. As they seldom needed an arts degree to graduate in law, they could go straight from school to the law faculty. In England, however, the grammar schools, apart from the very best like Westminster, taught little but Latin grammar, and the universities were the primary source of instruction in the broader classical humanities.[22] Having been won over to the new conception of the gentleman, the landowning elite had little choice but to send their sons to Oxford and Cambridge to study arts, even if most had no intention of completing the whole course and taking a degree.

---

[21] W. Prest, *The Rise of the Barristers: A Social History of the English Bar 1590–1640* (Oxford, 1991); W. Prest, *Legal Education of the Gentry at the Inns of Court 1590–1640* (Oxford, 1967). Barristers and judges who served in the king's high courts and county assizes had to be members of an Inn. Justices of the peace were usually local notables who did not practise law.

[22] Ian Green, *Humanism and Protestantism in Early Modern English Education* (Farnham, 2009), chs 2 and 3. On the conversion of Europe's nobility to the humanist programme, see J. H. Hexter, 'The Education of the Aristocracy in the Renaissance', in J. H. Hexter, *Reappraisals in History* (London, 1961), pp. 45–70.

In the second place, much more than in other protestant universities, the arts faculties continued to have the lion's share of the students. Elsewhere, not only the faculties of law but the faculties of theology expanded fast following the Reformation. Protestant reformers believed that the decadence they identified in the old church could be put down, in part, to the fact that the clergy were relatively poorly educated. In consequence, ministers in the reformed churches were expected to have a degree in theology. This was never the case in the new Church of England, however. All that was required for ordination was an MA, so most future ministers left university after completing their arts course. Most bishops had a higher degree but not the mass of the clergy. In this respect, Anglican ministers had often had less formal theological training than their catholic counterparts. Although the Catholic Church, after the Council of Trent, usually expected only the higher clergy and urban parish priests to have a theology degree, it was normally the case, by the eighteenth century, that all ordinands had spent some time in a seminary. There was equally no formal reason for prospective medical practitioners in England to engage themselves in higher study at Oxford and Cambridge. The art of medicine in the early modern era embraced three distinctive professions: physic, surgery, and pharmacy. In most parts of western and central Europe by 1700, no one could practise physic without a medical degree. In England, on the other hand, no formal qualifications were required to practise any branch of medicine, so there was no legal distinction between the graduate physician and the popular healer.[23]

Thirdly, Oxford and Cambridge were Europe's only universities where town and gown were segregated: as in the fifteenth century, all members of the two universities had to reside in a college or hall. This had a profound effect on the way arts tuition developed across the period. In all protestant *studia* by 1650, the use of temporary regent masters to deliver the curriculum, already in abeyance in some universities before 1500, had been abandoned in favour of permanent stipendiary lecturers or professors. Oxford and Cambridge were no different in this regard, but teaching posts were established in their colleges as well as the two universities. The colleges appointed their own lecturers in the main branches of the course, especially in the subjects covered by the BA curriculum, and insisted that each undergraduate was looked after by a personal tutor. The Oxbridge tutorial system that had come into being by the end of the sixteenth century was unique. In all universities there was a host of *répétiteurs* and private teachers offering extra-curricular coaching for a price. But only at Oxford and Cambridge was every student following the first part of the arts course put under the care of an older member of the university, who was supposed to police his behaviour, look after his finances, and closely supervise his academic progress.

---

[23] On the comparatively inchoate structure of the English professions before the second half of the nineteenth century, see W. Prest (ed.), *The Professions in Early-Modern England* (London, 1987); and Penelope Corfield, *Power and the Professions in Britain 1700–1850* (London, 2000).

Oxford and Cambridge's distinctiveness did not mean that they ceased to be among Europe's most populous universities. The demand for an arts education and the absence of any rival institutions before the foundation of the dissenting academies in the eighteenth century meant that recruitment, if subject to peaks and troughs, was buoyant.[24] In both universities, for nearly all of the period under review, the total number of students in arts, students seriously or theoretically engaged in higher study, and masters simply resident was seldom less than 1,750, and at a high point in the early seventeenth century was over 3,300. Even the lower total was a large number in European terms. A handful of universities boasted larger rolls at one point or other in the period: Salamanca, around 1600, registered 7,000 students; Coimbra, in the 1760s, had 4,000.[25] But few universities that depended in large part or wholly on their ability to attract students to their higher faculties had more than 1,000 on their books. Thus, Paris, almost certainly one of the largest catholic universities, could muster only some 1,300 students in theology, law, and medicine on the eve of the French Revolution, while its feeder schools in the city may have contained as many as 5,000 pupils.[26] Indeed, there were so many universities in continental Europe by the eighteenth century that the butter was spread very thinly. Only four of Germany's twenty-eight universities had more than five hundred students and four had less than a hundred. The situation did not change greatly in the first half of the nineteenth century, when the conception of a German university was rapidly evolving.[27] Numbers rose, partly because a third of the universities were shut by Napoleon and his allies, by about 1850 there were still only two with more than 1,300 students and as many as ten with less than 500.[28]

However, if Oxford and Cambridge were distinct from other universities, they were not identical by the end of the eighteenth century. Although their undergraduate arts courses were theoretically similar, in reality they had diverged. While Oxford after 1700 gave pride of place to the study of the Latin and Greek humanities, logic, and ethics, Cambridge—perhaps in deference to the iconic status of Newton—began to privilege mathematics, to the despair of undergraduates like the young William Wordsworth at St John's, who found the subject uncongenial. The rising status of mathematics at Cambridge was confirmed by the 1740s, when the examination which concluded the round of tests for the BA was devoted almost entirely to the subject and took on a new order of importance. Thereafter, this became an increasingly competitive contest, and the best candidates spent several days tackling more and more complex mathematical problems until a ranking based on their relative prowess emerged.[29] Oxford eventually produced its own competitive BA exam in 1800, but pointedly distinguished it from the Cambridge

[24] For these, see pp. 215–16, this volume.   [25] Di Simone, 'Admission', pp. 306–7.
[26] Brockliss, 'Attendance', pp. 512–15 (tables) and 518–19.   [27] For this, see pp. 325–7, this volume.
[28] Di Simone, 'Admission', p. 304; Ulrich Schneider, 'The Teaching of Philosophy at German Universities in the Nineteenth Century', *HU*, XII (1993), 207.
[29] Searby, pp. 154–63 and 564–71 (on Wordsworth); J. Gascoigne, 'Mathematics and Meritocracy: The Emergence of the Cambridge Mathematical Tripos', *Social Studies of Science*, 14 (1984), 547–84.

version by all but omitting mathematics. The distinction was only reinforced in the following years when both universities moved to allow the competitive to demonstrate their prowess in other parts of the arts course. Oxford, from 1807, allowed the best undergraduates to show their paces in mathematics and natural philosophy as well as the humanities, logic, and ethics, while Cambridge introduced a competitive examination in classics in 1822.[30] It became customary in both universities, though, for takers to be examined separately and participation was never mandatory for those seeking the BA degree. The die was therefore cast. A perception took root that pertains to the present day: Cambridge was a science, Oxford an arts university.

Oxford and Cambridge also had different political and religious loyalties in the eighteenth and the first half of the nineteenth century. Until the execution of Charles I, sovereignty in England lay with the crown. In the following half-century it was gradually transferred to parliament, a development cemented after the Glorious Revolution of 1688 when the need for money to wage war against France forced William III, then Anne, to call the two houses every year.[31] Thereafter, power in the new British state belonged to the propertied elite and their clients, who dominated local and central government and were themselves divided into two parties: Tories and Whigs. The Tories were descendants of the king's supporters during the Civil War: they remained committed to the power and mystique of monarchy; they strongly approved of the confessional state established under the 1673 and the 1678 Test Acts, which allowed only members of the established church to be MPs or office holders; and they opposed parliamentary reform when this became an issue from the 1780s. The Whigs were descendants of those who had fought for parliament: they were suspicious of royal authority; they were ready to give much more room religiously and politically to non-conformists; and they were the architects of the 1832 Reform Act, which gave new cities, like Birmingham and Manchester, representation and doubled the number of voters.[32] The parties' views and support base shifted over the years. The Tories' position on kingship mellowed once their Jacobite wing had gone into exile when the Hanoverians inherited the throne in 1714, while many Whigs moved towards the Tories during the French Revolution.[33] But the religious differences always remained. Although a Tory administration

---

[30] Searby, pp. 166–7. The Cambridge mathematical exam was initially called the Senate House Examination, but became known as the Tripos because of the shape of the seat on which candidates had been placed for their viva. The Oxford 1800 exam became known as Schools: see p. 237, this volume.

[31] Until 1660, parliament had met only occasionally and the crown largely paid for the cost of running the state from its own resources. From 1688, parliament became an annual event, and the king's government—henceforth heavily committed on the international stage as Britain became a leading European and world power—relied on the passage of an annual money bill to pay a burgeoning bureaucracy and army.

[32] The two sides had gained the sobriquet 'Tory' and 'Whig' during the Exclusion Crisis of 1679–81, when the latter tried to stop Charles II's brother, the catholic convert James, duke of York, inheriting the throne. They were terms of abuse used by their opponents: a Tory was an Irish bandit, and a Whig a hard-line Scottish Presbyterian.

[33] The Hanoverians had only a very weak claim to inherit the throne after the Stuart line died out with Anne. They inherited through an Act of Parliament of 1701, which deliberately banned more direct descendants of James I on the grounds they were catholics. Jacobites wanted the throne to pass to Anne's nephew, James, the son of the catholic James II, who had been a baby when her father fled in 1688 in the face of the invasion by William of Orange to deliver the country from 'papist tyranny'.

was forced to dismantle the confessional state in the late 1820s in the light of the growing strength of protestant and catholic non-conformity in the new industrial-izing union state of Britain and Ireland, the party's traditional supporters steadfastly continued to oppose further steps towards disestablishment.

Oxford and Cambridge were confessionally closed universities from the 1570s, and until the end of the period welcomed only members of the Church of England.[34] Nevertheless, after 1688 the two universities took different religious and political sides. Oxford, for the most part, was Tory, and Cambridge moderately Whig. As Whigs of some description were in control of the machinery of state from 1714 to 1801, and again for most of the 1830s, relations between Oxford and the government of the day were frequently strained, especially until 1760 when the accession of George III brought a Tory-leaning monarch to the throne.[35] The contrasting alle-giance of the two universities was highlighted by the profiles of the men they sent to parliament. From 1603, both Oxford and Cambridge had the right to elect two members of parliament apiece. Oxford was nearly always represented by two stalwart Tory backwoodsmen, like Sir Roger Newdigate, who served from 1750 to 1780. Cambridge elected Whigs or reform-minded Tories, and their MPs from the late eighteenth century included two figures at the heart of British political life, William Pitt the Younger and Palmerston.[36]

---

[34] At Oxford, students had to take an oath swearing allegiance to the established church when they matriculated; at Cambridge when they took a degree.

[35] The first two Georges suspected the Tories of Jacobitism so gave office to their opponents. Once in government the Whigs were difficult to dislodge, as George III discovered. Although the majority of the small electorate were Tory, the Whigs in office used bribery and patronage power to ensure they maintained a majority in parliament.

[36] Searby, ch. 11; John Gascoigne, *Cambridge in the Age of the Enlightenment: Science, Religion and Politics from the Restoration to the French Revolution* (Cambridge, 1989). Although Pitt is usually seen as the founder of the modern Tory party, he was a Whig by background and resigned as prime minister in 1801 when George III refused to back catholic emancipation in Ireland.

CHAPTER 5

The University and the Colleges

A. Governance

THE University, in the three centuries following the Reformation, remained, in important respects, the Oxford of the late middle ages. As in the pre-Reformation era, early modern Oxford was a self-governing corporation of masters whose public representative was the Vice-Chancellor, the resident deputy of the elected absentee Chancellor, who was usually someone with influence in government. The Vice-Chancellor looked after the day-to-day administration and discipline of the University, assisted by the two elected Proctors, while matters of major concern were the province of Congregation and Convocation. The first dealt primarily with educational matters; the second considered missives from agents of the state or church, made new disciplinary statutes, acted as a court of appeal, and elected the University's officials. Both came to have a more extended constituency than hitherto. Congregation, from the end of the sixteenth century if not before, could be attended by all resident masters and doctors, while Convocation, in the course of the eighteenth century, came to include the majority of Oxford MAs, wherever based.[1] As in previous centuries, the University continued to have a wide range of privileges vis-à-vis the city of Oxford, which were confirmed by an Act of Parliament in 1571 and augmented in a charter conferred on the University by Charles I in 1636.[2] In particular, the Vice-Chancellor's court was always the civil and criminal court of first instance, both in cases concerning members of the University alone and in cases concerning both scholars and citizens. From time to time the city attempted to persuade the state to reduce the University's privileges, but with no permanent success before the second half of the nineteenth century. Even the annual obeisance at St Mary's in penance for the St Scholastica Day massacre in 1355 was exacted until 1825.

Oxford's students and masters also had to continue to live in a hall or college. In the mid-sixteenth century, after the closure of the regular colleges following the

---

[1] For the composition of these two bodies in the late middle ages, see pp. 19–20 and 24–5, this volume. The changes in the membership of Congregation reflected the fact that the traditional distinction between regent and non-regent masters in residence no longer pertained by 1600.

[2] L. L. Shadwell (ed.), *Enactments in Parliament specially concerning the Universities of Oxford and Cambridge etc.* (4 vols; Oxford, 1912), i. 183–8.

abolition of the monasteries in 1536 and 1539 and the refoundation of Cardinal College as Christ Church, there were thirteen colleges in Oxford. By 1850 this number had risen to nineteen, with the addition of Trinity and St John's in 1555, Jesus in 1571, Wadham in 1610, Pembroke in 1624, and Worcester in 1714. Jesus was established by a prebendary of Rochester Cathedral of Welsh extraction, Hugh Price; Trinity was the gift of a government administrator, Sir Thomas Pope; Wadham and Worcester were founded by affluent members of the gentry, Nicholas and Dorothy Wadham and Sir Thomas Cookes; while St John's and Pembroke were the result of the bounty of a cloth merchant and a maltster, Sir Thomas White of London and Thomas Tesdale of Abingdon. All but St John's were medium-sized colleges supporting some twenty to thirty graduate fellows and undergraduate scholars: the fellows were chosen from among the scholars and the scholars were a mix of founder's kin and boys drawn from specific schools or regions where the founder had estates.[3] St John's, on the other hand, was a distinctive foundation. It was set up for fifty fellows, its fellows included boys straight from school, and, in imitation of New College, Magdalen, and Christ Church, it was intended to have a small choral foundation. Moreover, most of the fellows were not elected by the fellowship, as was the custom, but were the nominees of particular schools, above all Merchant Taylors' in London, which, from 1566, was to provide thirty-seven of the foundationers.[4] The halls, in contrast, continued their late medieval decline. In 1552 there were eight: Broadgates, New Inn, White, Hart, St Mary, St Alban, St Edmund, and Magdalen. In 1842 there were only five: Magdalen, New Inn, St Alban, St Mary, and St Edmund. Broadgates had been transformed into Pembroke College; White or Great and Little White Halls, an old lawyers' hall, had been swallowed by Jesus; and Hart had become Oxford's short-lived twentieth college, Hertford, which was established in 1739 by its principal, Dr Richard Newton, and dissolved in 1816 because it had no fellows or students.[5] How far all scholars attending the University did reside within the walls of a college or hall will never be known, but from the moment in 1581 when every scholar had to matriculate formally, it became impossible to become a member of the University and enjoy its privileges without this institutional attachment.

The continuity between the pre- and post-Reformation eras was given formal expression in the Laudian statutes of 1636, under which the University would be governed until the mid-nineteenth century (see Figure 5.1).[6] These were not new statutes as such, but a codification of the University's existing statutes and customs that had hitherto never been brought together in a single compilation. William Laud, archbishop of Canterbury from 1633 and Charles I's favourite divine, has been remembered by posterity principally for his desire to move the protestant Church

---

[3] As at Corpus and Magdalen, the scholars on the foundation played no role in college government.
[4] Statutes, vol. 3, *Statutes of St John's College*, pp. 12–13 and 115–19.
[5] Sidney Graves Hamilton, *Hertford College* (London, 1903), chs 3–5.
[6] *Statutes of the University of Oxford codified in the year 1636 under the authority of Archbishop Laud, Chancellor of the University*, ed. J. Griffiths (Oxford, 1888); OUS, vol. 1 (English translation).

FIGURE 5.1 *Corpus Statutorum Universitatis Oxon.*, 1636, MS, title page bearing the signature of the Chancellor, Archbishop Laud. The Corpus, or Laudian Code as it became known, was the first compilation and rationalization of the University's statutes and confirmed the power of the Hebdomadal Board over Convocation and Congregation.

of England in a more ceremonial direction. But he was first and foremost a man who loved neatness and order. Having been elected Chancellor in 1630 (not without difficulty given his well-known religious views), he grasped the opportunity to push for the completion of a project that had been on the University's agenda since Wolsey's day. The task of compilation was principally entrusted to the University's leading antiquarian, Brian Twyne of Corpus, and Laud's chief Oxford lieutenant, Peter Turner of Merton.[7] Once finished, Convocation somewhat surprisingly agreed

---

[7] Twyne later became the University's first archivist. Turner was Savilian professor of geometry: see pp. 239–40, this volume (chair's foundation).

that the draft should be left entirely to the archbishop to perfect. This Laud duly did. Printed copies of the compendium were distributed around the University in 1634, but the archbishop was still not satisfied. The final authentic version in an impressively bound manuscript was only ready for presentation to Convocation in 1636. The singular weight that was to be given to this compilation was made evident by the seals that the manuscript bore on its delivery by the royal secretary, Coke, as Francis Cheynell of Merton, no lover of Laud, was quick to report to his family:

> Our greate Chauncellour had sent [the statutes] downe under the seale of his province and the seale of his chauncellourship, but that they might bee like the Lawes of the Medes and the Persians irrevocable, his Majesty for to give the University more honour, and the Statutes more Authority, had sent them to confirme them under the Great Seale of England.[8]

The Laudian code, however, also confirmed the fact that the University of the 1630s was no longer the Oxford of the century before. While its structure might look unaltered, there had been a substantial shift in the balance of power between the Chancellor, his Vice-Chancellor, and the corporation of masters, which had begun in the reign of Elizabeth. The queen's favourite, the earl of Leicester, was Chancellor from 1564 to 1588: he took the task seriously, not only admonishing the University about its inadequacies from afar but personally visiting his charge on six occasions. During his tenure, he initiated one important innovation and encouraged another. In the first place, from 1570, Congregation lost its right to elect the Chancellor's deputy; thereafter the earl appointed his own Vice-Chancellor from among the heads of house and canons of Christ Church, and this became the default procedure.[9] Secondly, Leicester began to erode the authority of Congregation and Convocation more generally. The year before, in 1569, he ordered that nothing should come before either body that had not been first approved by the Vice-Chancellor, Proctors, heads of house, and doctors of the three higher faculties. As the last were few in number, this increasingly meant that the business of Congregation and Convocation was controlled by the heads of house. In 1631, the arrangement was given formal recognition with the establishment, on royal command, of the Hebdomadal Board, a council of the Vice-Chancellor and heads of house that was supposed to meet every Monday at 1 p.m. to discuss university business and bring forward legislation if needed.[10] For the first three years of the board's existence, Convocation had no direct influence at all on its deliberations, for the Proctors were not members. This was changed in 1634, but by then the Proctors had already been effectively corralled. Six years before, in 1628, the Chancellor and the heads

---

[8] Cited in Andrew Hegarty, 'The University and the Press 1584–1780', in *History of Oxford University Press*, vol. 1: *Beginnings to 1780*, ed. Ian Gadd (Oxford, 2013), p. 166. Hegarty's account of the relationship between the University and the Press before 1800 contains the most careful description of the creation of the Laudian statutes to date.

[9] Under the Laudian statutes, the Chancellor's nominee had to be formally accepted by Convocation: Title XVII, section 3, ch. 1 (pp. 167–8).

[10] *Statuta*, p. 570: 15 Dec. 1631. Virtually no minutes of the Hebdomadal Board survive.

announced that the Proctors were no longer to be indiscriminately elected each year from the body of masters and doctors but from two specified colleges, arranged in an electoral cycle, and by those colleges' graduate fellows. This gave the heads much closer control over the elections, especially as college fellows were usually beholden to the head of house for advancement.[11]

Convocation's wings were further clipped by the appointment of delegacies. These were ad hoc committees of Convocation, whose membership was in the gift of the Proctors, and which began to be set up from the late sixteenth century to expedite some of Convocation's routine duties, such as auditing university officials' accounts. The Laudian code recognized their existence but also suggested that, for convenience sake, the audit committee should become a standing delegacy whose members in the future would be appointed by the Vice-Chancellor as well as the Proctors. Thereby, the way was paved for the creation of other standing delegacies, such as the management committee of the new University Press, while the power of the Vice-Chancellor to control the business of the University was greatly increased.[12]

On the other hand, the 1636 statutes firmly established for the first time that it was Convocation and not Congregation that was the more important of the two assemblies of masters and doctors, whatever ambiguities there might have been in their respective roles hitherto. In future, only Convocation was to deal with 'business of great moment', while Congregation's role was limited to day-to-day academic affairs. This left Congregation with relatively few responsibilities. In the late middle ages Congregation had played a central role in the delivery of the curriculum through ensuring that enough of the newly incepted masters and doctors spent the next one or two years of their lives lecturing on the set texts in the faculties' schools. During the sixteenth century, however, most arts teaching for the BA degree migrated to the colleges, which established a number of permanent lectureships, and the need for regent masters to cover the undergraduate course disappeared. Teaching for the MA and higher degrees remained the province of the University, but there too the regent masters became redundant, as the crown and other benefactors founded a series of endowed chairs to cover the lecturing needs.[13] Under the Laudian statutes, therefore, Congregation had little to do except grant graces and dispensations allowing graduands to proceed to a degree. It had no control either over the organization of the different proofs of attainment graduands had to fulfil to qualify for a degree, for this was the prerogative of the Proctors.[14]

The constraints placed on the masters' and doctors' right to self-government during the Elizabethan and early Stuart era reflected the desire of state and church, in a period when the religious settlement of 1559 did not command universal support, that Oxford should toe the party line. The emasculation of Convocation's electoral power, the introduction of what today would be dubbed a

---

[11] Ibid., pp. 561–5: 31 Dec. 1628; every four to five years in the cycle a Proctor was nominated from a hall.

[12] Laudian Statutes, 'De magna congregatione, sive convocatione magistrorum regentium et non regentium', pp. 136–8 (Title X, section 2, clause 7). For the University Press, see Chapter 8, section F.

[13] See pp. 239–40 and 243–5, this volume.   [14] Laudian Statutes, pp. 85–138 (Titles IX and X).

senior management structure, and the device of the standing delegacy made it much easier to police the corporation of masters and scholars. The power of the Vice-Chancellor was further enhanced by the customary extension of his period of office from a two- to a four- or five-year term. To all intents and purposes, he became the *de iure* head of a small oligarchy that ran the University. Unsurprisingly, similar developments occurred at Cambridge, where the legislative body remained the senate, comprising all the University's resident MAs, but where real power came to lie with the caput, the council of the Vice-Chancellor and heads.[15]

A concern to maintain the Hebdomadal Board's top-down authority explains a less significant but highly symbolic change to the University's calendar that occurred long after the heads had taken control. The high point of the university year in the sixteenth and seventeenth centuries was the annual Act, the moment when masters and doctors incepted. At the beginning of the eighteenth century the Act was replaced by the present Encaenia, where the blessings bestowed by the University's several benefactors were and are publicly remembered. On one level, this reflected changing needs and taste. The Act consisted of a series of academic disputations and speeches in Latin where each faculty showed off its credentials. It was a form of celebration suited to a gathering of intellectuals. Encaenia, in contrast, was an entertainment of witty speeches in English and musical interludes, much more in keeping with eighteenth-century ideas of polite society, and an ideal occasion to bestow honorary degrees on visiting dignitaries and celebrities.[16] But replacing the Act also put an end to the antics of the *terrae filii*, the pair of student jesters selected each year to spice up proceedings.

It had become the custom in the Elizabethan period for the University to emphasize its protestant allegiance by appointing one or two university graduates to enliven the Act with an anti-catholic tirade. From the beginning of the seventeenth century, however, the *terrae filii* often used the occasion to mount scurrilous attacks on unpopular opinions and dons or poke fun at Cambridge, and in the 1660s they began to target the heads of house. In 1669, Henry Gerard of Wadham even attacked their wives.[17] Not surprisingly, the heads did not see the *terrae filii*'s insults as harmless fun but an affront to their dignity and authority, and frequently made examples of the worst offenders. In 1714 they were finally left off the programme altogether, and a decision appears to have been taken by the Hebdomadal Board to turn the Act into a less academic and acrimonious occasion. There was an attempt to revive it in 1733, but thereafter it was permanently replaced by Encaenia, by which time the University had secured a benefaction from Nathaniel Crewe, bishop of Durham, which funded an annual oration given alternately by the public orator and the professor of poetry to commemorate Oxford's benefactors.[18]

---

[15] Morgan, pp. 84–8; Searby, pp. 47 and 53.   [16] For honorary degrees, see pp. 182–3, this volume.
[17] Kristine Haugen, 'Imagined Universities: Public Insult and the *Terrae Filius* in Early Modern Oxford', *HU*, XVI: 2 (2000), 1–31, and Felicity Henderson, 'Putting the Dons in their Place: A Restoration *Terrae Filius* Speech', *HU*, XVI: 2 (2000), 32–64.
[18] Secured in 1731.

Convocation, however, was only neutered under the Laudian statutes: its electoral and legislative power was never abolished. From the beginning of the Hanoverian era, while never breaking free from the control of the Vice-Chancellor and the heads of house, it began to reassert itself. The large majority of Oxford's junior and senior members in 1714 were rabid Tories, who disliked the way the line of succession had been arbitrarily changed and feared that the new dynasty and its Whig ministers would end the Church of England's monopoly over civic life. The more intemperate in the first years of the Hanoverian era openly displayed their alienation on the streets and vented their spleen in an avalanche of satirical plays and poems. The attempt by a small group of Oxford Whigs to celebrate George I's birthday on 28 May 1715 by lighting a bonfire in the street led to two days of rioting and the destruction of the Presbyterian meeting house.[19] The majority, on the other hand, used their power as electors in Convocation to show their political colours. In 1715 a new Chancellor had to be elected because the old, the duke of Ormonde, an open Jacobite, had been attainted for treason and gone into exile. The dons pointedly elected his brother, the earl of Arran, as his replacement.[20] The heads of house were immediately unnerved. Anxious to keep on good terms with the government of the day, they endeavoured to prevent similar acts of provocation in the future by putting up their own moderate candidates whenever there was a chance the insult might be repeated. Parliamentary elections, in consequence, especially before the accession of the Anglican traditionalist, George III, in 1760, often became bitter contests, where the Hebdomadal Board's candidate was not guaranteed success. Convocation never elected an avowed Jacobite but, as late as 1751, it preferred the hardliner Sir Roger Newdigate over two moderate Tories.[21]

The board's task was made harder by divisions and jealousies among the heads themselves. There was always a handful of heads who supported the Whig interest, and the odd intemperate Tory who was willing to go out on a limb with the diehards in Convocation.[22] In elections, too, there could be bitter divisions of opinion over a candidate's worth, based on nothing deeper than college rivalries that pulled both heads and Convocation apart. Magdalen and Christ Church, who between them controlled a fair proportion of the votes in the dons' parliament, would usually never support candidates associated with the other.

The enlargement of Convocation's membership in the course of the century only encouraged the conservative tendency. The Laudian statutes began the expansion by giving the vote to non-resident as well as resident MAs, but they did not specify

---

[19] The Hanoverian loyalists were chiefly to be found in Oriel, Merton, and New College, and banded together to form the Constitution Club. Their opponents continually ridiculed the new king in print. Thomas Warton's account of George I as 'The Turnip Hoer', which circulated in 1717–18, was a classic in the genre. Warton, a fellow of Magdalen, became the second professor of poetry in 1718.

[20] James Butler, 2nd Duke of Ormonde, was the recognized leader of the Jacobites in London on George's accession.

[21] As it was the tradition that a university MP who sought re-election would be returned unopposed, parliamentary elections could sometimes pass off without too much conflict.

[22] Merton, Wadham, Exeter, Jesus, and Christ Church, where the dean was a royal appointment, usually had Whig-leaning heads.

whom exactly the former comprised. A tradition developed that any MA who kept his name on his college's buttery book (for a fee) was eligible, irrespective of whether he was pursuing higher studies. Until 1760 this interpretation remained moot. When the University passed a statute in that year affirming that this was the case, it gave interested graduates a permanent stake in university business and swelled the electorate for important elections and debates.[23] There were probably 400 members of Convocation in 1700, but 2,500 in the 1830s. As most of these extra members were backwoods clergymen, their presence invariably strengthened the conservative phalanx whenever issues of university reform or theological heterodoxy were discussed.

Before the late 1820s, the Hebdomadal Board normally got its own way, outside elections, and relations between the board and Convocation were particularly harmonious in the era of the Revolutionary and Napoleonic Wars, when virtually everyone in the University was on the side of the status quo. Thereafter, the two fell out in an unprecedented fashion. In 1829 parliament passed the Catholic Emancipation Act, which repealed the Penal Laws and gave Roman Catholics the right to hold public office. One of the University's two MPs, Robert Peel, who had previously been elected on a 'no popery' ticket, voted in favour of the bill, and felt it his duty to resign his seat and stand for re-election. In the ensuing contest, the heads, for the most part, shared his conviction that there was a need to show flexibility in the face of the prevailing winds of reform. The majority in Convocation, on the other hand, were still viscerally supportive of the confessional state and voted for Peel's opponent. For the next twenty years, the conservatives resisted all attempts by the heads or any other constituency in the University to place Oxford on the side of modernity. Their key to success was the organizing skills of the Tractarians, a party in the University interested in moving the Church of England in a more exclusive, authoritarian, and catholic direction in the name of religious renewal. In a succession of set-piece struggles with a modernizing Hebdomadal Board, Convocation watered down moves to liberalize the curriculum, stopped any concession to weakening the Anglican character of the University, saved the Tractarians' leader, John Henry Newman, from being condemned as a heretic, and eventually elected a Tractarian fellow traveller, William Ewart Gladstone, as an MP.[24]

B. Outside Interference

The establishment of a more hierarchical university of masters certainly helped to ensure that Oxford marched in time with the religious regime of the day in the troubled century and a half that followed the Elizabethan Settlement. The control of

---

[23] The colleges were anxious to keep as many MAs on the college books as possible; thereby they could maintain contact with old members and approach them for donations from time. The buttery book was the college ledger detailing each student's expenses. Their name was entered on the ledger when they arrived and the account usually closed when they left.

[24] For the religious divisions in the University in the first half of the nineteenth century, Chapter 6, section D, this volume.

the heads of house also helped to cool the temperature in the first part of the Hanoverian era when many younger dons and students expressed their disenchantment with a Lutheran as their king by flirting with Jacobitism. At moments of regime change, however, the better policed and the more conformist the University, the more difficult a nut it became for root-and-branch reformers to crack. Cracked, though, it had to be. Oxford and Cambridge's primary role from the mid-sixteenth century was to train the next generation of English protestant clergy. But neither institution was any longer simply a university of clerics, for, from the mid-sixteenth century, they were also educating an increasing number of scholars, especially sons of the gentry and nobility, who had no intention of entering the church.[25] It was impossible, therefore, for a revolution in church or state to be effected without first establishing the loyalty of the universities. Solid opponents of change had to be weeded out and persons of the right calibre intruded before the forces of hierarchy could work for the new regime and not against it. Such was the political and religious instability of the country that the post-Reformation era was characterized by frequent bursts of state interference in both universities' affairs.

Cromwell's 1535 visitation of Oxford was only the first of a series that stretched into the early eighteenth century. Further twists in the country's religious politics brought commissioners back to the University in 1548 in Edward's reign, in 1556 under catholic Mary (appropriately in the guise of a legatine not a royal visitation), in 1559 under her protestant successor, in 1648 after parliament had won the Civil War, and in 1662 on the restoration of Charles II. On each occasion the visitors sought to establish that the University and colleges were religiously sound. In the seventeenth and early eighteenth centuries, when the state came under the control of foreigners or usurpers, commissioners also returned on several occasions to test the University's secular loyalties. The Scottish James I imposed an oath of loyalty on Oxford in 1610; so too did the republican Rump in 1650 after the execution of Charles I; while the regimes of William and Mary in 1689 and the Hanoverian George I did the same in 1689 and in 1715.[26] Indeed, between 1648 and 1662 there was a state visitation almost permanently in session. The successive regimes of the Interregnum were anxious to keep careful watch over a university suspected of continuing to harbour the religiously and politically disaffected. Charles II, on the other hand, appointed commissioners as soon as he was safely installed in 1660 to remove diehard republicans and reinstate fellows and officials deprived twelve years before, who were still eligible for their position.[27]

Even in the absence of a state visitation, Oxford in the Tudor and Stuart era was seldom far from central government's thoughts. Fears for discipline, good order,

---

[25] See section C, this chapter.

[26] James' oath was particularly wide-ranging, for it seems that every member of the University was expected to subscribe. The later loyalty tests, in contrast, merely targeted college foundationers and university post-holders. These included the growing number of stipendiary professors and readers.

[27] The 1660 commissioners sat for two years and eventually formed the commission which tested loyalty to the new religious settlement of 1662.

and religious orthodoxy frequently moved the crown or the Privy Council to send down admonitions from Whitehall, calling on the University to attend to its reported failings, such as the order issued to the Vice-Chancellor in 1577 that he identify catholic fellow travellers by conducting a religious census. The reward for compliance was a ceremonial visit from the crown, an official rather than an officious visitation, where, for a short time, the monarch of the day graced his or her loyal university with his or her regal presence. Elizabeth came to Oxford in 1566 and 1592, and on each occasion endured a strenuous round of academic disputations and theatrical performances. James I showed his affection for both universities immediately on his succession by granting them representation in parliament. He then visited Oxford one year later in 1605, bringing with him his queen and his elder son, and demonstrating his pleasure by having Prince Henry matriculated as an undergraduate; he was back again in 1614. His successor, Charles I, always careful with his royal dignity, had more circumspection and waited four years to show his face to the scholars in 1629. But he also soon returned, in 1636, and took up permanent residence in the University in 1642 when he made Oxford his head-quarters during the Civil War.[28] Similarly, Charles II, though scarcely enamoured with things of the mind, did not forget to grace the University with his presence from time to time, holding several sessions of parliament in the city. Only his brother, the catholic convert, James II, always at odds with his kingdom's customs and prejudices, misunderstood that a royal visit was an occasion for monarch and University to show their mutual appreciation. After a highly successful visit in 1683 as duke of York, he was back again in 1687 as the king to vent his spleen on Magdalen for refusing to follow the royal will.[29]

As far as the colleges and halls were concerned, periodic subjection to state-appointed visitors was only one aspect of outside interference in their affairs after 1530. Once convinced that those most hostile to the latest religious settlement had been removed or silenced and some effort at compliance was being made, the crown's agents departed. The task of keeping a college or hall on the straight and narrow was left to the official visitor, usually an ecclesiastic.[30] Visitors had occa-sionally inspected the institutions under their care in the pre-Reformation era. But they became much more visible following the establishment of a lasting religious settlement in 1559. Although many bishops of the new Church of England did not always see eye to eye with the crown's religious policies, they were fervent suppor-ters of a reformed church and were keen to ensure that their colleges removed all traces of popery. Where colleges dragged their feet, the bishop's visitors could return repeatedly. New College, which harboured papists long after the Elizabethan Settlement, had to be inspected on three occasions in the first fifteen years of the

---

[28] The first two Stuarts were also frequently at nearby Woodstock, where they would invariably receive a university delegation.

[29] See pp. 208–9, this volume. James went on from Magdalen to University College, where he showed his gracious side.

[30] The halls did not have an official visitor but were subject to inspection by the Vice-Chancellor.

reign before it was given a clean bill of health. Once the Elizabethan Settlement was successfully established, college visitations became less frequent but they never completely stopped, even after 1662 when the protestant character of the national church was finally settled. Colleges were never perfectly governed institutions and there were always problems for a conscientious visitor to address. In 1670 and 1671, Balliol's visitor, the bishop of Lincoln, thought that neglect of the statutes and fiscal maladministration had reached such pass that he turned up in person to tackle the mess. College visitations in the Tudor and Stuart era ceased altogether only during the Interregnum when the episcopate was abolished, and the Republic's own commissioners were a permanent fixture.

The colleges, moreover, had to put up with the continual intrusion of outsiders whenever they elected a head of house or a new foundationer. This, too, had a religious dimension. The crown and its councillors were anxious that colleges would be led by individuals who supported their religious agenda. But more commonly, especially in the Stuart era, it reflected the exigencies of a society held together by patronage. To the crown, councillors, courtiers, bishops, and the simply high born, positions on a college foundation were patronage plums that they sought to bestow on relations, friends, and clients. The colleges must have come under pressure to favour the nominees of the great and good in the late middle ages, but they would have been unlikely to have been endlessly importuned by the leading lights of English society to find a place for people in their immediate circle. Fellowships, when originally endowed, were primarily intended to cover only the board and lodging of the relatively indigent scholar and brought little direct financial benefit, whatever their value as a stepping stone to a successful ecclesiastical or political career.[31] In the seventeenth century, in contrast, college positions began to become fiscally attractive, while rapid inflation made a nonsense of statutory restrictions on a fellow's private income, and made it easier to admit the affluent.[32] The vultures therefore circulated in growing numbers.

The upshot was that the competition for places could be so strong that the college was sometimes free to pick and choose which patron to gratify. Even the king could be snubbed. When, in 1623, James I asked Magdalen 'to admit Edward Hyde [later earl of Clarendon], who is well born and deserving, to a Demy's place', President William Langton declined, claiming that the demyships were 'far bespoken'. Even an admonitory letter from the king's secretary, Edward Conway, threatening royal displeasure, had no immediate effect. The candidate was simply promised the first vacancy.[33] But royalty was harder to put off when a prestigious post was at stake.

---

[31] In an earlier period, it can be assumed that the influential, especially churchmen, played a central role in 'discovering' potential candidates, but it is unlikely they ever championed the well born who were not founder's kin.

[32] For the value of fellowships, see pp. 282–3, this volume.

[33] *Calendar of State Papers Domestic, 1623–25* (James I), p. 120; J. R. Bloxam, *A Register of the President, Fellows, Demies, Instructors in Grammar and in Music, Chaplains, Clerks, Choristers and Other Members of St Mary Magdalen College in the University of Oxford, from the Foundation to the Present Time* (7 vols; Oxford, 1853–81), v. 84–5. Hyde never became a Magdalen demy.

In 1590, when a previous Magdalen president, Laurence Humphrey, died, Elizabeth wrote to the college indicating her preference as his successor. The queen recognized that the fellows were bound by oath to choose the one amongst them whom they judged most worthy, but moved by 'the special care we have of the state of that House to be preserved by good order', she had decided to give them a steer:

> [F]or your better direction, we do specially recommend to you before any other our well-beloved Servant, Dr Bond, one of our ordinary chaplains, a man well approved of Us for his good parts, and well known to you as Fellow of that House by the space of many year.

The fellows, however, failed to take the hint. The college had strong puritan leanings and the queen's chaplain was not one of the godly. Instead the fellowship elected Ralph Smith. The queen was incandescent and appointed Nicholas Bond by royal fiat, pretending that Smith's election was null and void because it had not taken place within the time limit set by the statutes.[34] Thereafter the college wisely did as it was told. Every presidential election about which details are known until the reign of James II, including Langton's, was won by a royal nominee, although it did take two letters from Charles II to win the day for Thomas Pierce in 1661.[35]

After 1715, state intervention, both direct and indirect, in the University's affairs was greatly reduced. For the whole of the Hanoverian era, no royal commissioners descended on Oxford and there were no more angry missives from above or demands that a favoured candidate be elected. The government of the day occasionally put its weight behind a candidate in a contest for the chancellorship or one of the University's two parliamentary seats. But it did so relatively gently and never challenged the result if the candidate was rejected.

The hands-off approach of the Hanoverians did not mean that Oxford in the eighteenth and the first half of the nineteenth century disappeared off the government's radar. The two English universities always remained the training ground of the nation's clergy, even if, for a time in the eighteenth century, they educated a smaller proportion of the landed elite than in the previous century and a half.[36] As a result, they were always an object of interest. Oxford, too, obviously gave particular cause for concern in that its religious and political values were out of step with the views of the Whig ministries that dominated British political life for virtually all of the period. Indeed, there was a government plan in 1717, in response to ongoing anti-Hanoverianism at Oxford, to introduce a bill in parliament which would hand over to crown commissioners the power of appointing candidates to all university and college posts, including fellowships.

---

[34] W. D. Macray, *A Register of the Members of St Mary Magdalen College, Oxford* (8 vols; Oxford, 1894–1915), II. 172–3: Elizabeth's original letter; MCA, EL/7, fs 279b–282b: the queen's second letter.
[35] Some colleges did defy the crown's demands successfully over the appointment of heads. In 1614, Brasenose elected as principal the puritanical Samuel Radcliffe rather than the king's conformist candidate.
[36] See pp. 164–5, this volume.

That the University escaped state intervention in the Hanoverian era can be attributed, until 1832, chiefly to the peculiar structure of the British political system. Although the government was generally run by Whigs of some colour, thanks to their ability, once in power, to manipulate parliamentary elections, the Tories had a natural majority, not just in the electorate but beyond, and were not averse to taking politics to the streets. The British state had no standing army large enough with which to enforce its will, so was always unwilling to pursue policies that might lead to civil unrest: any attack on the guardian of the Tory interest before the 1820s was a game not worth the candle. The horrors of the French Revolution in the 1790s only pointed up the dangers of rocking the boat in any direction.

Oxford also helped its own cause, for, from the beginning of the reign of George III, it appreciated the need of keeping a line of communication open with the government. The University did its best to please when first George and then his son paid an official visit in 1786 and 1814 (see Figure 5.2), and it showed political nous in its choice of Chancellors. The election of the then prime minister, Lord North, to the office in 1772 did not demand too much soul-searching, for he had earlier attended the University and was a fairly conservative Whig. On the

FIGURE 5.2 Reception of the Prince Regent, June 1814: painting by George Jones. The painting depicts Prince George being greeted by the dignitaries of the University and the city in the High Street outside Queen's. The visit bore witness to the University's steadfast loyalism during the twenty-year war against France. The Prince Regent was accompanied by the king of Prussia and the emperor of Russia. Both received an honorary degree, along with the Prussian general Marshal Blücher.

other hand, the election of the erstwhile prime minister Lord Grenville, in 1809, was achieved only by many dons holding their nose: although an Oxford man like North, Grenville was besmirched by his support for catholic emancipation as a way of reconciling Ireland to the 1801 Act of Union. After the confessional state had been demolished and parliament reformed in the late 1820s and early 1830s, the Tory University became more exposed, and once again was faced with the threat of state intervention. Even then the University made sure it was not left to fight its corner alone. When Grenville died in 1834 and the University reverted to type and elected a Tory, it had the good sense to place its fortunes in the hands of a national institution, the venerable duke of Wellington.

There is little sign either that the government tried to interfere with college elections in the Hanoverian era, even though it must have been tempting at times to try to fix the appointment of heads of house, especially in the large colleges. The field was thus left free to private patrons, who strove manfully throughout the eighteenth century to secure positions for the sons of clients. Success, though, was never guaranteed. Fellowships were, by then, much more valuable financially and socially and it was a sellers' market. Appointments of heads of house were all but impossible to fix, even at the beginning of the Hanoverian era, as the protracted election of a new master of University College in 1722 demonstrated. The two candidates for the vacant post were William Denison, the senior resident fellow, and a former junior member of the college, Thomas Cockman, vicar in a Kent parish. Denison apparently held all the aces because his tutorial pupil was the young duke of Beaufort. But he had been close to the previous master, who had been heartily disliked by a number of the college's small fellowship, and ducal patronage counted for little. As a result, the vote was inconclusive and was appealed to the visitor, in this case the Vice-Chancellor. When the Vice-Chancellor ordered a rerun of the contest which went in Denison's favour, to the young duke's delight, Cockman petitioned the king. Arguing that, as the founder of University College was Alfred the Great, the crown not the University was the true visitor, he called on the government to judge the dispute. This it eventually did by appointing a visitation commission which duly found for the appellant, but only in 1729.

Understandably, by the turn of the nineteenth century, most patrons had given up the struggle. Colleges still received recommendations in favour of candidates, especially for scholarships, but the fellows exercised a free choice. The eighteenth century therefore ushered in a new age of college autonomy. Even the colleges' official visitors largely left them alone. After the 1729 visitation of University College, there was only one other full-scale visitation of an Oxford college in the eighteenth century—at Merton in 1738—where Warden Wyntle called in Archbishop John Potter of Canterbury to settle his dispute with the fellows over a wide range of issues, including their ownership of troublesome dogs. Visitors normally became involved in the life of a college in the Hanoverian era only when there were disputed fellowship elections. In most colleges, fellowships were attached to particular geographical regions or were to be given in preference to descendants of the founders' families. In the eighteenth century, these limitations were sometimes ignored. All Souls, for instance, had to be reminded by Archbishop William Wake in 1722 that it was supposed to privilege Chichele's kin. A gentleman commoner at Christ Church, Robert Wood, related to the founder, had been passed over for a fellowship in favour of two other candidates on the grounds he was intellectually feeble and 'did not appear to understand the Common Syntax in the Greek or Latin tongues'.[37] Wake judged him sufficient, had him installed, and declared the election of the successful pair void. In no instance were college visitors interested in making college statutes more open or meritocratic. They were simply intent on upholding the letter of the statute. From the late eighteenth century, the number of founder's kin at All Souls actually mushroomed as another visitor in 1777, Archbishop Frederick Cornwallis, instructed the college to reserve at least 25 per cent of its fellowships to Chichele's blood line.

After 1800, outside interference was further reduced when several leading members of the University began to recognize that the world was changing and that meritocracy was now the order of the day. Whatever the influence brought to bear on an election, there had always been some attention, however perfunctory, paid to the capacity of the successful candidate. In the 1790s, Provost John Eveleigh of Oriel became convinced that this should be given much greater weight. With the outbreak of the French Revolution, sectarianism and philosophical scepticism appeared to have been given their head, and Eveleigh was anxious to fill the University with intellectual heavyweights who could fight the Church of England's corner.[38] Taking advantage of the fact that only four of the college's eighteen fellowships had geographical or other restrictions attached to their disposal, he decreed that fellowship contests were to be settled in future by a competitive examination. As a result, under Eveleigh and his like-minded successor, Edward Copleston, who held office from 1814 to 1828, Oriel boasted the most intellectually vibrant fellowship in Oxford. Its fellows included a cluster of stars, such as John Keble, John Henry Newman, Thomas Arnold, Nassau Senior, and Baden Powell, whose influence would extend far beyond the college and the University.[39] In the first half of the nineteenth century, Oriel's initiative found few imitators. Elsewhere, only Balliol, another college with no restrictions on its fellowships, immediately followed Oriel's lead and looked to limit its elections to the intellectually respectable.[40] If, by the end of the period, all colleges paid greater attention to merit than

---

[37] John Davis, 'Founder's Kin', in S. J. D. Green and Peregrine Horden, *All Souls under the Ancien Regime: Politics, Learning, and the Arts, c. 1600–1850* (Oxford, 2007), p. 238. For gentlemen commoners, see p. 226, this volume.

[38] Eveleigh first publicly demonstrated his commitment to defending the religious status quo in the Bampton lectures he delivered in Oxford in 1792. For this annual series of theological lectures, see pp. 220 and 276 this volume.

[39] In the late 1820s, these and other less well-known fellows of Oriel of the Eveleigh and Copleston eras began to divide into two bitterly opposed theological camps: see Chapter 7, section D.

[40] In Balliol's case, the move to a competitive contest was the work of John Parsons, master of the college from 1798 to 1819.

hitherto in the selection of fellows, a thoroughgoing revolution would occur only after 1850. Nonetheless, the significance of the move cannot be gainsaid. Under Eveleigh, albeit for conservative reasons, a part of the University had deliberately turned its back on the old world of jobbery and firmly embraced talent as the sole criterion of election.[41]

C. Patterns of Attendance

The Oxford presided over by Chancellor Laud was a much more populous university than its late medieval predecessor. The size of pre-Reformation Oxford will never be known as totals were never recorded but, at most, the fifteenth-century University contained 1,700 scholars. From the mid-sixteenth century, information becomes firmer due to the interest of the protestant state and its surrogates in maintaining order in its two universities and establishing the political loyalty and religious reliability of the scholars. A census taken in 1552 by the Vice-Chancellor's deputy, the first of its kind, recorded a resident population, both seniors and juniors, of only 1,015, suggesting, understandably, that numbers had fallen following the closure of the regular colleges in the late 1530s and the uncertainty regarding the religious direction the country was taking. A second private enumeration in 1566, occasioned by Elizabeth's first visit to the University, revealed that Oxford had recovered the lost ground and now boasted a resident membership of 1,764 (see Table 1).

Thereafter numbers continued to rise. Various head counts in the early Stuart era give totals of 2,254 in 1605, 2,920 in 1612, and 3,305 in 1634. None of these figures is likely to be entirely accurate: the 1552 total is probably too low, while the later ones are inflated by the inclusion of some 200 college servants, who were not necessarily involved in study. There can be no doubt, however, that the general upward trend is reliable. From 1565, the University kept a matriculation register on which the names of all scholars were to be entered within a week of their arrival (see Figure 5.3). Those presenting themselves also had to promise to observe the University's statutes, and from 1581 take an oath subscribing to the royal supremacy and the articles of religion.[42] A proportion of students always avoided matriculating, especially those who came up under the age of 16 and were too young to take an oath, and those with religious scruples. But the halls and colleges were expected to ensure that their charges duly appeared before the University's clerk, and there is no reason to think that the information in the register is misleading from the 1580s. The register confirms the impression given in the different censuses but with more precision. Matriculations rose slowly from the moment of their introduction from some 250 to 320 a year in the 1580s. They then fell back in the 1590s to their starting point,

---

[41] In contrast, election to scholarships became much more meritocratic in the first part of the nineteenth century: see pp. 229–30, this volume.
[42] *Statuta*, pp. 391–5 and 421. The introduction of subscription was part of the campaign to root out the last remnants of catholicism from the University.

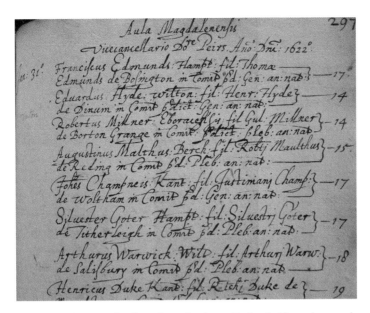

FIGURE 5.3 Matriculation of Edward Hyde, later Earl of Clarendon and university Chancellor, 31 January 1623 (or 1622 old style). The University matriculation register, started in 1565, listed matriculands by hall or college and gave their place of birth, father's name, status and age. As Hyde, from Dinton in Wiltshire, was only 14 when he came up to Oxford, he was comparatively young.

remained stable for twenty years, and then steadily rose again to reach a high point of 460 per year in the 1630s, nearly double the figure in the 1560s.[43]

The 1630s, however, was the high point in attendance. Later enumerations of the student population are few and difficult to use but the matriculation register continued to be carefully maintained, so the trend over the next century and a half can be easily reconstructed. Matriculations fell dramatically during the Civil War, when the king and the court were in residence in the University and troops roamed the street, but they picked up again in the 1650s and continued to climb after the Restoration, coming close, by 1680, to their peak fifty years earlier. Thereafter attendance began to decline, and by 1700 Oxford's population was probably in the region of 1,850. The nadir was reached in the 1750s. In that decade, matriculations slumped to 200 per annum, and Oxford probably contained fewer scholars than it had done two centuries before. The second half of the eighteenth century saw a modest increase in the annual intake to 250 and the momentum was sustained at a quickening pace after 1800. In the 1820s there was an average of 364 new matriculands per year. Thereafter progress stalled once more, with the

---

[43] Lawrence Stone, 'Educational Revolution in England, 1560–1640', *Past and Present*, 28 (1964), p. 51. Stone gives slightly different figures in his 'The Size and Composition of the Oxford Student Body 1580–1910', in Lawrence Stone, *The University in Society*, vol. 1: *Oxford and Cambridge from the 14th to the Early 19th Century* (Princeton, 1975), p. 91. Stone believes there is a need to inflate the figures by as much as 40 per cent in some decades to account for under-registration.

consequence that, in 1850, Oxford was still a smaller university than it had been on the eve of the Civil War, although England's population was more than three times as high. At this stage there were probably about 550 senior members based in the University, and an undergraduate population of little more than 1,200, which was the number reported to be in residence in 1842.[44]

Much the same pattern can be observed in individual colleges and halls, though they varied greatly in size. Christ Church, Exeter, and Brasenose were always well attended and can never have sheltered fewer than a hundred undergraduates. Corpus, on the other hand, was always tiny and probably never housed more than a couple of dozen. The pattern of college attendance, however, did not always follow the general trend. One or two colleges saw their numbers collapse across the period. In the early seventeenth century, Magdalen was the second most frequented hall or college, welcoming between sixteen and twenty new members a year: in the reign of James I the college contained from 200 to 250 residents. But in the 1670s the number of new admissions fell fast and never recovered. Not only did they fail to rise after 1760, but they bounced along at the same low level in the first half of the nineteenth century, too. For a century and a half Magdalen consistently welcomed between five and ten new faces a year. Conversely, a few societies saw a dispropor-tionate rise in numbers after 1760. Balliol was a medium-sized college in the early Stuart era; in 1842, it was fifth in the ranking. Magdalen in that year had only thirteen undergraduates in residence; Balliol had seventy-three. Yet other colleges bucked the secular trend for a decade or so. University College, for instance, experienced the common trough in the mid-eighteenth century, but its numbers rose swiftly in the late 1760s and 1770s, only to fall back just as quickly before sharing in the general early nineteenth-century expansion. Lincoln, in contrast, hit its low point in the 1800s under its unpopular rector, Edward Tatham. Numbers in the surviving halls could also be particularly volatile. In the early seventeenth century, the most populated was Magdalen Hall. In the 1630s it supplied the second largest number of matriculands in the University. Its numbers, however, declined rapidly after the Restoration and it became insignificant until it enjoyed a revival right at the end of the Hanoverian period.[45]

The picture at Cambridge, where a matriculation register was introduced in 1544, was also largely identical and similarly repeated, to a greater or lesser extent, in the history of individual colleges. The differences were one of degree. In Elizabeth's reign, Cambridge, probably for the first time in its history, was the larger university, but its matriculations peaked in the 1620s and Oxford was once more the more populous of the two on the eve of the Civil War. Oxford retained this position until

---

[44] Stone, 'The Oxford Student Body', pp. 6 and 91 (graph and table)

[45] Only the numbers at Magdalen and University College have been studied in detail across the period. Attendance at Christ Church has been analysed between 1660 and 1800. For Exeter's membership before and after the Civil War, see K. P. J. Padley, 'The Membership of Exeter College, Oxford, 1500–1640' (BA dissertation, Oxford, 2000); and Anon., 'The Membership and Character of Exeter College, Oxford, 1640–90' (BA dissertation, Oxford, 2002).

the end of the eighteenth century. If Cambridge's numbers never collapsed as far in the 1640s, they did not recover as fully after the Restoration, so entered the period of contraction at a lower level. On the other hand, Cambridge's recovery, which began about 1770, was more robust and its numbers climbed above Oxford's for a second time: by 1820 Cambridge was matriculating 450 students a year.[46]

The steep rise in the number of matriculated scholars at both universities in the late sixteenth and early seventeenth centuries reflected their changing constituency. The late medieval university had exclusively welcomed existing or future members of the clergy. Aspirant clerics came in even greater numbers after 1560, as the protestant episcopate sought to establish a new church where every one of England's 10,000 parishes would be staffed by a minister with a university degree in arts.[47] In the early seventeenth century, however, only half of Oxford and Cambridge's matriculands entered the church. Some of the remainder aimed at lay careers in medicine and law; others at some form of government service that could be best accessed by flaunting scholarly credentials. But a sizeable proportion of the lay cohort comprised elder sons of the landed elite who looked forward to an adult life spent on their country estates. They were not at university to gain a professional qualification, access practical skills, or demonstrate their employability. They came to make contacts and acquire a cultural veneer of varying degrees of thickness.

What brought such people to the English universities for the first time was a new conception of gentility, promoted by Renaissance humanists. Gentility in the late middle ages had been associated with military prowess and chivalric conduct and had had nothing to do with formal education. In contrast, humanists in the early sixteenth century, such as Erasmus of Rotterdam, had argued that true nobility came from imbibing the virtues of civility and charity embodied in classical literature and holy writ, and was only properly accessible to those who could read the texts in their original tongue. Gentlemen therefore had to be schooled in Latin and Greek before they learnt the art of war.[48] Henry VIII, who was himself a good Latinist, having been raised as a younger son probably bound for the church, took on board the humanists' educational programme more than most of his fellow sovereigns and ensured each of his children, especially Edward and Elizabeth, were raised as scholars. The 2,000-odd families who were the owners of England responded more slowly but had largely accepted the humanist case by the late sixteenth century. Early enthusiasts employed live-in tutors, as Henry had done. But in Elizabeth's reign it became more common for gentlemen to send their sons, after

---

[46] Stone, 'Educational Revolution', p. 91; Searby, pp. 63 and 727–8. Cambridge had 1,753 undergraduates in 1850. On the eve of the Civil War, it has been estimated that the two universities and the Inns of Court, taken together, were educating some 2.5 per cent of 17-year-olds (Stone, 'Educational Revolution', p. 57).

[47] But not theology: see p. 138, this volume. Theological training of sorts began to be provided at Oxford for future clergyman from the mid-eighteenth century: see pp. 279–80, this volume.

[48] Eugenio Garin, *L'Education de l'homme moderne, 1400–1600* (Paris, 1966). Erasmus hated war. Other, more realistic humanists, such as the Italian Castiglione, author of the much read *The Book of the Courtier*, recognized the need to integrate a programme of classical study with training in the courtly and martial arts.

a few years of study at home, to one of the universities for further instruction in classical letters and philosophy.

Why England's landed elite should have succumbed so completely to the humanists' propaganda is not immediately obvious, given that their cousins on the continent were much more circumspect.[49] Clearly the royal example was infectious, but there must have been other forces informing their conduct. Arguably, a humanist education was seen as a means of status consolidation in an age when the landed were fast losing both their monopoly over display and their *raison d'être* as a warrior class: too many London merchants now had the wealth to engage in conspicuous consumption, while both Elizabeth and James valued peace at home and abroad, so their reigns offered limited opportunities for noble derring-do.[50] Perhaps too the fact that the crown expected the landed elite to be capable, if called upon, of serving as judges of first instance in their localities, encouraged the conviction that a gentleman needed to have at least a smattering of arcane learning to overawe malefactors. Why the university replaced the tutor is a further conundrum. Most humanists in the sixteenth century emphasized the value of a live-in tutor, while Oxford and Cambridge, even in the post-Reformation era, integrated the humanist programme into the existing arts curriculum rather than embracing it wholeheartedly.[51] Perhaps the landed sent their teenage sons away because this is what they had always done: it was commonplace for young gentlemen to learn to be a chivalric knight in a stranger's household, just as the sons and daughters of farmers and artisans were sent into domestic service or apprenticed out.

The proportion of Oxford scholars who came from a gentle background in the period before the Civil War can be known with some accuracy. On matriculation, newcomers paid a fee according to their social circumstances. Although the categorization was crude in the extreme, those of gentle birth were carefully demarcated, and in the early seventeenth century comprised between 30 and 45 per cent of the intake, depending on the college.[52] Even though the cohort included many younger sons who had to make their way in the world, barely any of the group was destined for the church. Some younger sons might have been pushed towards the church in the pre-Reformation era, and the younger sons of the nobility in catholic countries continued to be so. But in protestant England they eschewed a clerical career, in part because most parishes were poorly endowed.

The non-gentle remainder registered, for the most part, as either clergymen's sons (a growing group from 1580, as more and more Anglican ministers were married) or plebeians, who made up 30 to 50 per cent of all matriculands in the early Stuart era. Presumably the plebeians came from families who hoped to improve their status by

---

[49] Some French aristocrats were purportedly semi-literate, even in the age of Richelieu.

[50] Ireland was the main theatre for the gentleman adventurer who did not seek service in a foreign army. The naval warfare of Elizabeth's reign was akin to piracy and hardly gentlemanly: Drake was the son of a farmer turned cleric.

[51] See pp. 234-6, this volume.

[52] For the purpose of matriculation, the 1565 statute divided the well born into five categories: sons of princes, dukes and marquesses, sons of counts or viscounts, sons of knights, sons of armorial gentlemen, and sons of simple gentlemen (*generosi*): *Statuta*, p. 394.

putting a son in the church, but as a social group they remain amorphous in the Oxford records: they are simply non-gentle. The evidence from the intake to two Cambridge colleges, however, that kept a more informative matriculation register—Caius and St John's—suggests that Oxford's plebeians in the first decades of the seventeenth century would have come from a broad cross-section of the middling sort and the lower orders, and not just the professional and mercantile classes. In the 1630s, 8 per cent of St John's students were sons of yeomen and farmers, and 15 per cent sons of artisans and shopkeepers, while others seemed to have come from even further down the social scale.[53] Certainly, a sizeable percentage of Oxford's non-gentle students were unable to support their studies on their own, and either survived on charity and handouts from richer students or college fellows, or acted as gentlemen's or fellows' servants, gaining an education while meeting their master's wants. Information from college documents which list the number of dependent students on their books reveals this group could form more than a quarter of the scholars in residence. Of the 246 members of Magdalen in 1612, 76 were servants or pauper scholars.[54] The fathers of such students must have had the means to place them for a few years in one of the growing number of English grammar schools where they could gain the basic facility in Latin needed to attend university. But how they actually got to Oxford and found a patron is a mystery.[55] What seems likely is that many would have been disappointed in their career aspirations. Only a third to two-fifths of all matriculands in the early seventeenth century were destined to enter the church and probably half of those were clergymen's sons. As in the late middle ages, England in the 1630s appears to have had too many adolescents from relatively humble homes at university. Supply was outstripping demand.[56]

From the Restoration, however, this legion of social aspirants began to disappear. Plebeians fell from 46 to 32 per cent of matriculands between 1660 and 1700, and then virtually abandoned the University altogether. They were only 9.6 per cent of the students admitted to Magdalen in the period 1769–1810, and a mere 1.2 per cent of those who entered University College in the years 1764–1807. The large majority of undergraduates now identified themselves as sons of clergyman (more than a third) or sons of gentlemen (as high as three-quarters).[57] To a certain extent, the information in the matriculation register needs to be treated with caution. From

---

[53] Stone, 'Educational Revolution', p. 66 (table). Sixteen per cent of St John's students are lumped together by Stone as the sons of husbandmen, plebeians, and people of small fortune.

[54] Each of the forty Magdalen fellows had a scholar servant in 1636 and the college seems to have maintained a further twenty-one scholar paupers: Macray, *Register*, iii. 42–3; Bloxam, *Register*, iii. 163.

[55] Unfortunately, only one student in a state of dependence, the Elizabethan magus Simon Forman, has left an account of his university days and this is scanty: Bodleian Library, MS Ashmole 208, f. 142r. Some students did matriculate as paupers or servants but very few.

[56] Based on studies of students at Magdalen and University College. The information comes from J. Foster, *Alumni Oxonienses: the members of the University of Oxford, 1500–1714; their parentage, birthplace and year of birth, with a record of their degrees; being the matriculation register of the University* (4 vols; Oxford, 1891–2). Foster's information is unlikely to be complete.

[57] For the whole University, plebeian matriculands were 17 per cent in 1760 and 1 per cent in 1810.

the second half of the seventeenth century many undergraduates from non-landed backgrounds began to record their fathers as *generosus* in response to the increasing contemporary dilution of gentle status to include simply the wealthy and well mannered. This, though, only partly explains the rapid fall in plebeian representation. There is no doubt that both Oxford and Cambridge in the eighteenth century not only became smaller but also much more socially exclusive institutions. This was chiefly because the landed classes, who had helped fuel the expansion in the late sixteenth century, began to use the universities in a new way.

From the end of the seventeenth century, elder sons became much less visible. New theories of education, peddled by John Locke and his eighteenth-century successors, challenged the long-standing Renaissance paradigm that learning was a mark of gentility. In their opinion, years of studying Latin and Greek created dry-as-dust pedants not practical, well-rounded, and polite men of the world, who needed to know modern languages, mathematics, and science. The universities in their present form should be left to training the clergy, lawyers, and doctors, and England's ruling class should once again be educated apart, either by tutors or in new schools with a broader, more relevant curriculum.[58] Just as in the sixteenth century, the landed quickly succumbed to the new educational pundits, if never entirely. Scared lest their precious heirs became sterile sticks, or perhaps in Oxford's case, even worse fanatical Jacobites, many landowners decided not to send their sons to university when they had reached the age of 17 or 18, but to pack them off with a tutor on the Grand Tour, a more exclusive and less cerebral rite of passage.[59] On the other hand, gentle families did not abandon the universities completely and continued to send their younger sons there. They did so because their attitude towards placing a son in the church had totally changed. In rural England a significant percentage of parish livings fell into the hands of gentry patrons after the dissolution of the monasteries.[60] Before the Civil War, this was a piece of patronage that the landowner was happy to bestow on a grateful client of lowly station. The popular disruption and rise of radical sectarianism in the 1640s and 1650s forced a rethink. The maintenance of social order seemed to depend on squire and parson being joined by the more viscous substance of blood rather than the rather watery oil of patronage ties. Increasingly, rural livings were kept for younger sons. Long before the end of the eighteenth century, the same family occupied the manor house and the vicarage in a manner familiar to the readers of Jane Austen.

---

[58] Nicholas Hans, *New Trends in Education in the Eighteenth Century* (London, 1951). Politeness, an ability to debate and inform without giving offence or boring was the cornerstone of eighteenth-century social life in a world divided into two antagonistic political parties: the ideal was outlined in Joseph Addison's periodical the *Spectator*, which appeared in 1711–12 and was briefly revived in 1714. Locke's *Some Thoughts Concerning Education* was first published in 1693. Locke had been a fellow of Christ Church; Addison a fellow of Magdalen.

[59] Jeremy Black, *The British Abroad: The Grand Tour in the Eighteenth Century* (London, 1992). Some elder sons went to university, then went on the Grand Tour. By the second half of the eighteenth century, well-to-do bourgeois were also to be found tasting the cultural delights of the continent, albeit usually in middle age.

[60] The large proportion of advowsons that had belonged to the monasteries came into the hands of the gentry when the crown sold off monastic land after the dissolution.

The gentry's new use of the universities dealt a double blow to the socially aspirant. As gentlemen now came to Oxford and Cambridge in smaller numbers, there was less of a need for scholar servants. To make matters worse, as the eighteenth century wore on, the custom of patronizing poor students in return for service seems to have become frowned upon. Poverty was no longer seen as a suitable attribute of learning but a mark of shame: one indigent scholar who did attend Oxford early in the century, the lexicographer Samuel Johnson, felt so humiliated by the holes in his shoes that he gave up going to lectures.[61] Colleges and halls therefore began to engage townsfolk to provide their young gentlemen with the services they required. This was good for employment in the town but not for social mobility.[62] More importantly, the new interest that younger sons took in the church affected the opportunities of the non-gentle in general. Younger sons now snapped up the scholarships and fellowships that they had formally disdained, and their monopoly of rural livings made the ministry a much less attractive career for the non-gentle aspirant. Just as the opportunities of securing a livelihood in the new reformed church drew the sons of the middling sort and below to the universities before 1640 (and to such an extent that the market became overcrowded), so their comparative exclusion from the clerical marketplace in the eighteenth century discouraged their attendance.

The less affluent students were not won back to Oxford and Cambridge after 1800, even though numbers rose once more. The expansion, and its limits, primarily reflected the greater numbers of gentlemen's and clergymen's sons coming up, plus a leaven of scions of the new industrial plutocracy.[63] This increase was partly caused by the larger families of the early nineteenth century, but it was principally the result of a further sea change in the landed class' relationship with the two universities. The social upheavals in Revolutionary France, the emergence in the 1790s of a popular radical movement in Britain and Ireland, and the renegade behaviour of certain peers seem to have convinced the ruling elite that its heirs needed a good dose of university discipline if church and state were to be safe in the hands of the next generation. Oxford's apologists only helped to confirm the belief by promoting the University as the training ground of good morals, right thinking, and a manly conformist spirit.[64] Little was done to change the curriculum in either university in the late Hanoverian period, but the landed were convinced once again of its character-building value. In some cases, too, it even proved possible to get gentlemen with no intention of entering the church to study hard for a degree. After

---

[61] James Boswell, *The Life of Samuel Johnson* (Ware, 1999), p. 38. Johnson was perhaps peculiarly sensitive and would also not accept charity. He was a student at Pembroke.

[62] Living-out bedmakers are encountered from the beginning of the eighteenth century. Their use only engendered comment when they were female.

[63] Most industrialists were non-conformists, so were uninterested in sending their sons to Oxford and Cambridge. Among admissions to Magdalen between 1810 and 1854, 4.8 per cent matriculated as plebeians, 19.8 per cent as sons of clergymen, and 70.9 per cent as to the manor born.

[64] The claim was forged in response to Whig critics who believed Oxford had outlived its usefulness: see pp. 334–6, this volume.

1800, a BA at both universities could be gained only after an intensive examination. Although competitive intellectual endeavour had never been the mark of an eighteenth-century gentleman, a sprinkling of their successors in the first half of the nineteenth century were not as coy. Christ Church's two future prime ministers, Robert Peel and Gladstone, were as eager to enter the lists and do well as Trinity's parson's son, the future Cardinal Newman.[65]

Oxford, in the first half of the nineteenth century, was thus a socially exclusive as well as an Anglican institution. Since the average clergyman's son would have also been related, however distantly, to gentry families, blue blood of some kind coursed through most undergraduate veins. The undergraduate population after 1800 was equally much more homogeneous in age. In the period before the Civil War, scholars had come up to Oxford as young as 10 and frequently in their early to mid-teens. In the course of the eighteenth century, the age of matriculation began to standardize around 17 and 18, and many freshmen were older. This reflected a further change in the gentry's relationship with schooling in the century following the Restoration. Few gentlemen came up to Oxford in the early nineteenth century straight from being tutored at home. Most passed through one of the country's small number of boarding grammar schools, such as Eton, Westminster, and Winchester, which would become the elite public schools of the second half of the nineteenth century. The change is graphically illustrated in the educational histories over the period of the Northamptonshire Ishams, who were one of Oxford's prominent dynasties. Before the Civil War, they came up to the university at a young age. Then, in the late seventeenth century, they were packed off in their early teens to nearby Rugby School instead. Consequently, eighteenth-century Ishams, including Euseby, seventh son of Sir Justinian and the long-serving rector of Lincoln College, arrived at Oxford as young men rather than children.[66] In the upper classes, secondary and tertiary education was beginning to be distinguished in a way that had not been the case in earlier centuries.[67]

D. Urban Footprints

Oxford in 1520 was a small market town of 3,000 inhabitants. On the eve of the Civil War, the population had expanded to 8–10,000. Thereafter, the population hovered about this level until the late eighteenth century, when it began to rise quickly. It was 16,446 in 1821 and 27,843 in 1851. To a certain extent, the city's population moved to a similar rhythm as the University's, but in the first half of the nineteenth century town and gown expanded at different rates. The medieval

---

[65] Both admittedly came from new blood: Peel's father was a manufacturer and Gladstone's a merchant. But both were from families that had been assimilated into the landed elite. The development of the BA examination at both universities is discussed on pp. 236–8, this volume.

[66] The other Isham who spent many years in the University was Edmund, demy and fellow of Magdalen; he was later an MP.

[67] Secondary and tertiary education, however, still formed a single system. Elementary schools were for those who wanted only to learn to read and write, and were not attended by the well-to-do.

university was never as populous as the city, but in term times students must have increased the number of residents by 40 per cent. In the middle of the nineteenth century, when junior and senior members combined numbered only 2,000, the University made up only 7 to 8 per cent of the town's population. It is understandable, therefore, why town and gown friction was so great in the medieval era: the University was a privileged community whose privileges enveloped the city; it was a much more violent age; and before the early fifteenth century many scholars were not segregated from the citizenry in halls and colleges. Conversely, even before the disproportionate expansion in the town's population, the incarceration of students in halls and colleges and the gradual gentrification of the University must have greatly reduced the tension. From the late seventeenth century especially, gentlemen came to Oxford with money in their pockets, and the growing number of tradesmen and shopkeepers saw the community of scholars in its midst as a never-ending source of income rather than an overbearing intruder. Citizens did not find the continued authority of the Vice-Chancellor's court a threat to their civic pride when it allowed them to pursue student debtors cheaply and quickly.[68] For large parts of the period, too, the University, halls, and colleges provided plenty of work for the local building trade, as they left an ever-extending physical mark on the urban landscape. By 1850, the colleges had either redeveloped or extended the buildings on their own sites and the University had spread into the suburbs (see Map 3).

Little new college building took place in the second half of the sixteenth century as the fellows in the immediate post-Reformation era turned their backs on grandiose building projects. The new colleges founded after 1540 merely occupied existing buildings and made them habitable. Christ Church was established on the unfinished site of Cardinal College; St John's was set up outside the city to the north in the old Cistercian college of St Bernard; Trinity took over the Benedictines' Durham College off present-day Broad Street; while Jesus, installed on the west side of the Turl, was formed out of two former halls. Existing colleges showed no more ambition. They dealt with the rapid increase in numbers simply by cramming in more scholars per set and by constructing cock lofts or attic rooms in existing ranges. The first attic rooms seem to have been built at New College in 1539, long before the expansion, but from the 1570s they began to frame the skyline everywhere. By 1587, half of University College's upper chambers had cocklofts; a year later three of eleven at All Souls had been converted. The new foundations, similarly short of space, followed suit.

From the last decade of the sixteenth century, however, attitudes changed and make-do and mend gave way to a period of competitive expansion (see Map 4). Over the next sixty years, Christ Church, Merton, Lincoln, Exeter, St John's, Trinity, Jesus, Queen's, and Magdalen refurbished and improved existing buildings and constructed additional quadrangles and ranges, while University College and Oriel

---

[68] The Vice-Chancellor's court was notoriously swift to reach a decision in civil cases. Harmony between town and gown was also fostered from the eighteenth century with the growing employment of living-out servants, who replaced the scholar servants of the late sixteenth and seventeenth centuries.

drew up grandiose plans to rebuild their establishments completely, which began to bear fruit from 1620 and 1634. Even Magdalen Hall got in on the act, Principal John Wilkinson extending one range and adding another at a personal cost of £3,000.[69] Not surprisingly, then, when Wadham was founded in 1610 on the site of the old Austin friary to the north-east of the city, which had lain vacant since the suppression of the monasteries, the founders, a childless West Country landowner and his wife, provided the huge sum of £10,900 to build an entirely new quadrangle. The result was that, on the eve of the Civil War, the colleges' footprint had grown extensively and Oxford boasted a clutch of handsome buildings in Renaissance gothic, the mixed late perpendicular and classical style much in favour in late Elizabethan and early Stuart England. First in the field, Merton's new Fellows Quad, erected between 1608 and 1610, set the standard for others to imitate. Its tower gateway, consisting of four storeys framed with fluted columns depicting the Doric, Ionic, and Corinthian orders, topped off with a free-standing pediment, would be copied, over the course of time, at Wadham, Oriel, and University College (see Figure 5.4).

In a number of cases the rebuilding programme included the construction, on a fresh site, of a completely new chapel, hall, or library, or a new set of lodgings for the head of house. But even where the existing facilities were deemed sufficient, the period saw widespread refurbishment of a college's principal interiors. Everywhere, these were deemed too spartan, insufficiently large, or simply too dilapidated to attract the gentle undergraduate or sustain a college's sense of its own importance. Libraries were refitted to make using the books easier; many chapels were embellished in the spirit of the new Laudian emphasis on the 'beauty of holiness';[70] and halls were decked out with fine panelling and a classical screen at the lower end to hide the comings and goings of the kitchen staff from the diners. Wainscotting had begun to be introduced into halls in the mid-sixteenth century, although probably only at the high table end. The hall screen, on the other hand, was first introduced at Wadham. The work of the Oxford joiner John Bolton, the Wadham screen consisted of two arched doorways framed with Corinthian pillars and fronting a small gallery that could accommodate musicians (see Figure 5.5). A similar design would be later adopted at Exeter, Jesus, and Magdalen. College life was not luxurious on the eve of the Civil War. But by then most rooms were heated and glazed, and Oxford colleges, both inside and out, were grand enough to house the king and his court and government during the subsequent conflict.

Only Merton, of Oxford's colleges, could afford to put up a new range or quadrangle or carry out large-scale refurbishments financed from its own income. The others needed outside help and even Merton did not pay for its own gateway. Some colleges relied on the munificence of their present or former heads of house: Ralph Kettell paid for Trinity's new range, while St John's was beholden to their former president, Laud. But colleges also showed enterprise and, for the first time, began to fund-raise. In mid-1617,

[69] Presumably Wilkinson hoped to recoup his costs from the hall's many tenants.
[70] See pp. 199–200, this volume.

FIGURE 5.4 Gateway, Fellows' Quad, Merton College, c.1608–10. Erected through the generosity of the warden, the mathematician and biblical scholar Sir Henry Savile, the gateway was the first in Oxford to be built in the classical style, unlike the Wadham gateway, which was constructed a few years later.

Griffith Powell, the principal of Jesus, always the poorest college, appointed agents to tour Wales, Oxfordshire, and London and solicit donations from the clergy and well-to-do towards a new hall. The initiative had only garnered £744 by 1620 but it was deemed enough of a triumph for Powell's successor, Sir Eubule Thelwall, to mount a further campaign in 1626 to build a new library as the first range of a new quadrangle. This raised more than £800 from the Welsh clergy alone by 1640. When all else failed it was sometimes possible to asset strip. University College was able to obtain two big donations towards rebuilding its quad in the 1630s but the majority of the cost was found elsewhere. All but £1,800 of the £5,400 spent on the project by 1642 came from the sale of timber on the large estate of Handley Park that the college had fortunately inherited in 1631 from a former pupil, Sir Simon Bennet.

Building work was inevitably curtailed during the Civil War but it began again in the mid-1650s, Magdalen Hall, Brasenose, and University College leading the way. Within a few years, Magdalen Hall had filled in the western side of its only

FIGURE 5.5 Hall screen, Wadham College, early 1610s. Hall screens began to appear in England in the reign of Elizabeth. The beautiful Wadham screen with its slender classical pillars was the first to be installed at Oxford. John Bolton, the joiner responsible, also built the college's fine chapel screen.

quadrangle with a range that contained a purpose-built library, while by the late 1660s Brasenose had had the architect-builder John Jackson, who had earlier finished St John's Canterbury Quad, construct an additional quadrangle containing a baroque chapel, library, and cloister. University College, meanwhile, slowly brought to a close the rebuilding of its original quadrangle, which had been begun in the 1630s, the fourth side being finally closed in 1675. The torch was then passed to Trinity, Christ Church, and New. Trinity, in 1665–8 and 1683–5, built two new residential blocks at right angles to one another in the same style, the first designed by the, as yet, little-known architect Christopher Wren, a former fellow of All Souls. Built to a purely classical design with a central protruding pediment and mansard roof, they signalled the end of Oxford's obsession with Renaissance gothic. The college then went on to build a completely new chapel in the classical style, consecrated in 1694 (see Figure 5.6). Wren's skills were also deployed at Christ Church in the 1680s, where Dean Samuel Fell finally brought to fruition Wolsey's grandiose vision by rebuilding and extending the college front and surmounting the gateway with a classical bell tower. Wren's cupola bell tower was ready by 1684, and Great Tom, a bell that had formerly hung in the cathedral, was transferred to its new and permanent location (see Figure 5.7). New College, on the other hand, did not see fit to use the services of the greatest architect in England when it heightened its main quadrangle to three storeys between 1670 and 1675. Nor did it turn to Wren

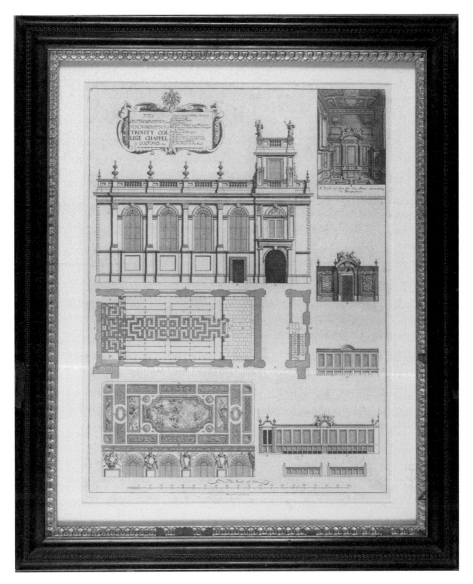

FIGURE 5.6 Chapel, Trinity College, 1694: engraving M. Burghers 1694. Possibly designed by Christ Church's Henry Aldrich, Trinity chapel was the first Oxford college chapel to be built completely in the classical style. Much of the interior woodwork may be by Grinling Gibbons. Burghers was a Dutch engraver who from 1676 engraved the plates for the University of Oxford's almanac.

when it had a new three-sided quadrangle, Garden Quad, erected to the west of the college in the 1680s. This was designed by the mason-carver William Byrd.[71]

All three developments were to prove the prelude to a building mania that affected the large majority of Oxford colleges in the sixty years after 1690, and

[71] Its two wings would be later extended in the early eighteenth century.

FIGURE 5.7 Tom Tower, Christ Church, 1684. Surmounting Christ Church's new classical frontage, Tom Tower on its completion immediately became an Oxford landmark. Designed by Sir Christopher Wren, who sensitively decorated its exterior with late gothic echoes, Tom Tower took its name from the great bell that was hung in its belfry.

mirrored the building explosion a hundred years before. The ball was set rolling by Queen's, which, in the mid-1690s, had an unknown architect erect a new library that had echoes of the classical edifice designed by Wren for Trinity College, Cambridge.[72] Then, between 1706 and 1710, Christ Church put up Peckwater Quad in a restrained and unadorned classical style that mimicked the Palladian country house, a vision of domestic living which, at that date, was just beginning to attract the attention of the English upper classes. The three-sided building was designed by the Christ Church dean, Henry Aldrich, who added a flair for Italianate architecture to his talents as a religious polemicist and musician. The fourth side was to be eventually partly closed by a new college library, again in a classical style, which

[72] J. R. Magrath, *The Queen's College*, vol. 2: *1646–1877* (Oxford, 1921), 69–72.

was not fully finished until 1762, and only finally completed seven years later when its open ground floor was filled in to form the Christ Church picture gallery. Aldrich probably had a hand in the construction of one other Oxford building begun at the same date, Corpus Christi's Fellows Quad. But his death in 1712 left the field open to another scholar architect, the All Souls fellow and university MP George Clarke.

Clarke's first Oxford commission was a new quadrangle begun at All Souls in 1715, which was principally built to house another new library. Classical but idiosyncratic, its striking design owed much to the assistance he received from the prestigious and versatile London architect Nicholas Hawksmoor. Clarke was next deeply involved in two grandiose projects at Queen's and the recently founded Worcester College: to erect a complete set of new college buildings in a much more conventional classical style. In both cases, however, the master plan took many decades to realize and Clarke never lived to see their completion. Rebuilding Queen's two existing quadrangles began in 1710. Though the first stage was finished by 1721, it would be 1760 before the southern quadrangle fronting the High Street—with its spectacular temple cupola over the entrance, based on a drawing by Hawksmoor—was finally completed (see Figure 5.8). Within two decades,

FIGURE 5.8 Gateway and cupola, front quadrangle Queen's College, 1733–6: architect, chiefly George Clarke. Queen's was the only medieval Oxford college to be completely rebuilt in the classical style. The statue under the cupola by Henry Chere is of George II's wife, Queen Caroline, who had contributed to the building fund. Queen's was a college with Whiggish tendencies. Once finally finished Hawksmoor's cupola gave the college a visual identity to match that of Magdalen and Christ Church.

moreover, the college had to spend further large sums on refurbishment after a fire destroyed most of the provost's lodgings.[73] Worcester replaced the medieval buildings of Gloucester College even more slowly, and the work reached conclusion only in the 1780s when the hall and chapel interiors were finished off by the neoclassical architect James Wyatt, whose designs reflected the partial rehabilitation of the gothic that marked the second half of the eighteenth century.[74] Clarke was not involved, on the other hand, in the building of University College's second quad between 1717 and 1719, which was the work of William Townesend, member of an Oxford dynasty of architect-builders, and deliberately built in the style of a century before. Nor was Clarke part of Magdalen's equally grandiose plans to replace its existing buildings with a classical quadrangle. The New Building to the north of the fifteenth-century cloister was the work of a former college demy and Jacobite, Edward Holdsworth. The north range, put up in the 1730s, was intended to be completed by two wings, but the project ran into the ground and nothing further was built, leaving the building with an unbalanced feel.[75]

The building work undertaken in all of Oxford's nineteen colleges in the first half of the eighteenth century cost at least £120,000. As in the era before the Civil War, the colleges lacked the means to finance large-scale building work from their own resources, and individual benefactors were again extremely important. Queen's new library owed much to a gift of £2,000 from Provost Timothy Halton;[76] Peckwater Quadrangle was largely paid for by the £3,000 bequest of a Christ Church canon; All Souls library existed because of a £6,000 legacy from a former fellow turned West Indian planter, Christopher Codrington; University College was able to build its second quadrangle thanks to a donation of £5,000 from an old member, the society physician John Radcliffe; while Worcester's rebuilding programme was revitalized by a £3,000 legacy from the architect Clarke. But, more so than in an earlier age, colleges also held out the begging bowl. Magdalen's New Building, which initially cost about £5,000, depended entirely on donations from old and current members. President Edward Butler opened a benefactors' book in 1720 and contributed the first donation of £105. By 1740, £6,400 had been given by some forty individuals, a mix of fellows, old and current, and well-to-do old members chiefly connected with the church. Butler himself had donated £600 by 1740, as had the fellow Matthew Frampton, while two former fellows—John Hough, bishop of Worcester, and Hugh Boulter, archbishop of Armagh—had given £500 apiece.[77]

---

[73] Magrath, *Queen's*, pp. 63–97 and 133; James, pp. 56–9, letters 18 and 21 Dec. 1778 (on the fire). The new library provided the alignment for the western range of the two quads. The only part of the old college that survived, though altered, was a short section of the east range of the north quad, which had been erected in the 1670s in the classical style with money from Sir Joseph Williamson: Magrath, *Queen's*, p. 47.

[74] At Worcester, Clarke also received help from Hawksmoor.

[75] Christine Ferdinand, *An Accidental Masterpiece: Magdalen College's New Building and the People Who Built It* (Oxford, 2010).

[76] Magrath, *Queen's*, p. 71.

[77] Ferdinand, *Masterpiece*, pp. 169–70 (list). The book was kept open and shows that £9,100 had been given by 1768, including a further £1,500 as a bequest by Butler.

Since Oxford's numbers were declining in the first half of the eighteenth century, the new buildings were not needed to absorb the additional students as they had been in the early Stuart era. Their erection rather reflected changing conceptions of comfort and living. Fellows and young gentlemen were no longer content to be cooped up with two or three others in a single bedroom with only their small partitioned study as a private space. Nor did they want to live in dark, low-ceilinged late medieval buildings often in need of repair. The eighteenth-century Oxford undergraduate and don liked their creature comforts, which were hard to enjoy in a quasi-monastic cell. The college had to become an extension of the country house. Whether the collapse in the attendance of elder sons would have been even greater without the rebuilding programme of the period is impossible to say. But there is no doubt that Aldrich's purpose in building Peckwater Quad at the beginning of the century was to provide lodgings fit for aristocrats. He also thought that the University should educate its charges in good taste as well as good morals. A few years spent in a Palladian villa would refine the architectural sensitivities of the scions of the Tory squirearchy, used to the beams and gables of a sixteenth- and seventeenth-century English manor house. The Christ Church portrait gallery, with its Renaissance grand masters, served a similar end in the latter part of the century: the gallery was meant to prepare young gentlemen in advance for the Grand Tour.[78] The eighteen colleges, though, were also repositories of English, and not just continental, sensibilities. The country-house illusion was taken one stage further by their abandonment of the formal garden in favour of the park-like vistas made increasingly fashionable as the century wore on by the likes of Capability Brown. New College's Garden Quad looked out onto an artificial mound through a delicate wrought-iron gate screen, moulded by Thomas Robinson in the 1710s. Magdalen, in the early eighteenth century, seeded over its bowling alley and formal walks in the Grove and created a deer park.[79]

Post-1750, the building boom fizzled out. There were lots of alterations to college interiors, especially college chapels in the light of changing religious taste. But there was only one significant addition to existing college buildings: Christ Church's Canterbury Quad, built from a design by Wyatt between 1775 and 1778 and notable for its Doric gateway giving on to Merton Street. Prices were rising in the second half of the eighteenth century and the building cost £7,438, a sum which was partly met by a donation from Richard Robinson, archbishop of Armagh. Some fellows and heads of house continued to dream of wholesale rebuilding, even in a period that began to appreciate gothic architecture again. At Magdalen, the fellows were still commissioning plans to build an entirely new college in the early nineteenth century, eliciting a response from Humphry and J.A. Repton in 1801, where the unfinished New Building quadrangle was replaced by a neo-gothic extravaganza

---

[78] Brian Young, 'Henry Aldrich and Christ Church', unpublished paper given at the conference 'Henry Aldrich (1648–1710): An Oxford Universal Man', Christ Church, 21 Jan. 2011.
[79] The presence of the deer was first mentioned in 1710.

with its open fourth side facing the River Cherwell and the college meadow turned into a large lake.[80] But the dreams got no further than the drawing board. The influx of students after 1800 could usually easily be accommodated within the extended premises created before 1750, and taste was no longer so monolithic.[81] Fellowships now favoured the gothic style again but were divided between modernizers and historicists. When, in the long vacation of 1822, the venerable head of Magdalen, Martin Routh, born in the 1760s, started to pull down the decrepit north and eastern ranges of the fifteenth-century quadrangle, to replace them with something more functional, he was stopped in his tracks by a college mutiny that put its weight behind a burgeoning press campaign to save Orchard's masterpiece. Magdalen, however, could claim one new building to its name. In 1822, Magdalen Hall was moved to a new site on Cat Street that had formerly housed the defunct Hertford, so that the college could extend, if necessary, westwards. Forced to foot the bill for a new building for the hall, Magdalen responded by constructing a quadrangle in an outmoded classical style. But it still cost the college a massive £60,000.[82]

In stark contrast to the pre-Reformation era, the expansion of the colleges' physical presence from the turn of the seventeenth century was matched and even out-trumped by the University. The University was far poorer than the colleges throughout the period. Although its income had been greatly increased by the return from the endowments underpinning the many subject specific chairs founded from 1540, it had only two sources of unhypothecated income: matriculation and graduation fees, and the revenue it received from three rectories it had been given by Mary I. Nonetheless, it was able to greatly improve its stock of buildings, thanks to a number of generous benefactors.

The first building to be erected was an extension to the Divinity School and the University Library, financed by the diplomat Sir Thomas Bodley, who had been a fellow of Merton in the early years of Elizabeth's reign. Anxious to revive the fortunes of Duke Humfrey's Library, which seems to have become totally rundown by the second half of the sixteenth century, Bodley, in 1598, promised the University to undertake its refurbishment: 'I will take the charge and cost upon me to reduce it again to [its] former use, and to make it fitte and handsome with seates and shelfes and deskes, and all that may be needed to stirre up other men's benevolence to helpe furnish it with bookes.'[83] The new library was opened in 1602 and so successful was Bodley's acquisition policy that the original building had to be enlarged in 1610–12, with the addition of a range abutting at right angles, whose upper storey served as an additional book repository and became known as the Arts End. This proved the catalyst for the University to consider Bodley's other desire: that not just divinity but the other arts and sciences should be taught in decent accommodation, rather than

[80] Roger White and R. Darwall-Smith, *The Architectural Drawings of Magdalen College, Oxford: A Catalogue* (Oxford, 2001), no. 87 and plate 13.

[81] The one college which did have to build a new quad because of its new-found popularity was Balliol. A new building, the work of the neoclassical architect George Basevi, was finished in 1826.

[82] Hamilton, *Hertford*, ch. 7.   [83] *HUO*, iv. 660.

the existing down-at-heel schools that straddled the space between his library and Cat Street. Bodley died in 1613, but the University was undeterred. Over the next nine years, 1613–24, Oxford conducted a well-targeted fund-raising campaign and raised enough money (more than £5,000) from the great and good to develop Bodley's new range into a closed quadrangle in the Renaissance gothic style. This comprised twelve lecture rooms or schools on two storeys, and accommodated each of the University's professors at that date except the professor of divinity.[84] The new Schools Quadrangle was ready for use in 1624. Its most prominent feature was its gateway topped by a tower that replicated Merton's tower of orders but on a much larger scale, and with a group of figures in the fourth storey representing the sovereign, James I, handing his collected works to the Bodleian in 1620 (see Figure 5.9).

The construction of the Bodleian and the Schools Quadrangle encouraged Laud to think of sweeping aside all of the buildings still standing in their vicinity and creating an academic precinct in the heart of the city which would stretch from St Mary's to Broad Street.[85] During his own chancellorship little was achieved. He disliked St Mary's, as a house of God, being used for university meetings, so had a two-storey building constructed to the west of the Divinity School, which was finished in 1640. Its lower floor became the Convocation House, its upper, in due course, the Selden End of Duke Humfrey's Library, after the books and manuscripts left to the University by the antiquarian John Selden, on his death in 1654, were housed there. Laud's vision, however, continued to be embraced by a number of Oxford fellows, and with the Restoration one of their number, the former warden of All Souls and the new archbishop of Canterbury, Gilbert Sheldon, was in a position to carry them forward.

In the early 1660s, Sheldon offered to give £1,000 towards the construction of a building that would serve as a stage for the University's set-piece annual gatherings, especially the Act. In the event, no other benefactors came forward, and the archbishop spent £13,000 of his own money on its erection and furbishment. The Sheldonian Theatre, opened in 1669, was built on a site to the north of the Schools Quadrangle, which had been opened up by the demolition of large sections of the city wall after the Civil War. Like Trinity's new block, completed a year earlier, it was the work of Christopher Wren, but it was a much more original classical building. Wren had spent time in Paris and seen Jacques Lemercier's new church of the Sorbonne built in the 1630s, in a style that would become known as French baroque. The circular theatre, with its raked seating, painted ceiling, and colossal dome was an attempt both to give Oxford a building that would match the best that Paris

---

[84] For the size of the university professoriate in the 1620s, see pp. 239–40, this volume. Divinity continued to be taught in the Divinity School.

[85] Peter Heylyn, *Cyprianus Anglicanus, or the history of the life and death of the most reverend and renowned prelate, William, by divine providence, Lord Archbishop of Canterbury* (London, 1668), p. 404. I am indebted to Andrew Hegarty for this reference.

FIGURE 5.9 Schools Quadrangle, completed 1624. (A) East side: the tower and gateway; the flanking columns depict all five of the Greek orders; the statue of James I in the fourth storey has an angel to its left which suggests the works the king is donating to the University are divinely inspired. (B) West side: the new entrance to Bodley's library and the divinity school with the Arts' end above; the doors on the left and the right side of the photograph give onto staircases leading to the schools of jurisprudence (north side) and medicine (south side).

FIGURE 5.10 Sheldonian Theatre, 1669. A Wren masterpiece and named for the theatre's benefactor, Gilbert Sheldon, archbishop of Canterbury, the Sheldonian provided the University with its own large public space where outsiders could gather with junior and senior members to celebrate the annual degree-giving ceremony.

could offer and to place the University in the van of English architecture. It was Wren's rehearsal for the rebuilding of London's churches (see Figure 5.10).[86]

The Sheldonian was soon followed by the erection of a second classical edifice on the precinct site. In 1683, a building, possibly again by Wren, was opened to the west of the theatre, to house the collection of curiosities left to Oxford by Elias Ashmole. Paid for entirely by the University and costing £4,540, the Ashmolean was the world's first public museum, and its opening a great public event graced by the heir to the throne, James, duke of York.[87] There was then a hiatus until 1710–13, when the Clarendon Building was erected on a site to the north-west of the Sheldonian, according to a design by Hawksmoor. Clarendon, Charles II's chief minister in the 1660s and Oxford's first Chancellor after the Restoration, had bequeathed to the University the profits that would eventually accrue from his *History of the Rebellion*, an account of the Civil War. Posthumously published in 1702–3, the

---

[86] The ceiling was painted by Streater to give the illusion of the building being open to the sky. Special seating was provided for university dignitaries, which emphasized the concept of hierarchy enshrined in the Laudian statutes. For Lemercier and the French baroque, see Anthony Blunt, *Art and Architecture in France*, 2nd edn (Harmondsworth, 1970), pp. 117–45.

[87] R. F. Ovenell, *The Ashmolean Museum 1683–1894* (Oxford, 1986), pp. 21 and 25–7. Until the mid-nineteenth century, the Ashmolean also served as a science laboratory.

work was so successful that, within a few years, the University could contemplate putting up a new building, specifically to house its burgeoning press.[88] With the Clarendon Building, an attempt was made to pull the gothic and classical elements of the university precinct together, by aligning its arched gateway passage with the northern and southern entrances of the Schools Quadrangle. Eventually, it was hoped that it would be possible to see right through the precinct from Broad Street to St Mary's, but the aspiration was undermined in 1748 with the completion of the last building on the central site, the Radcliffe Camera. When the physician John Radcliffe died in 1714, he left £88,000 in trust for the benefit of the University and the town. A total of £40,000 was to be devoted to clearing the site between St Mary's and the Schools Quadrangle and building a new library. The trustees moved slowly, but by the early 1730s were ready to construct another architectural gem. From the planning stage to the opening ceremony took a further thirteen years. Initially the commission had been given to Hawksmoor, but the architect died in 1736 and the work was entrusted to his erstwhile rival, James Gibbs, famous as the designer of the unfinished quadrangle at King's, Cambridge. The Camera, another circular, domed building, consciously echoed and balanced the Sheldonian. But no attempt was made to align its entrance with other buildings on the precinct. Unlike the others too, it was a vanity project. The University had no need for more library space at this juncture, and the collection housed in the Camera remained ill-defined and unspectacular until the end of the century.

Thereafter, the University began to extend its physical footprint beyond the central site. Before 1750, the University occupied only one piece of land outside the city walls. This was the five-acre site opposite Magdalen, which formed the University's botanical garden and had been a gift of Lord Danvers. Danvers had leased the land from Magdalen in 1621, improved its quality, surrounded it with a wall in the early 1630s, and constructed the imposing baroque entrance gate, the first of several small-scale classical edifices erected in Oxford before the Civil War.[89] In the second half of the eighteenth century, the University began to expand in a northerly direction. Radcliffe's trustees acquired a site to the north of St Giles on the west side of the Woodstock Road and used the rest of the money to build the Radcliffe Infirmary and the Radcliffe Observatory. The first was opened in 1770 and the second, designed by James Wyatt in imitation of the Temple of Winds at Athens, was largely completed by 1776, although not fully operational till the end of the century.[90] The next university building was even further away. By the early nineteenth century, the University Press was too large an enterprise for the Clarendon Building and, in 1825, the delegates decided to move to new premises. A site was found in the north-western suburbs on what is now Walton Street, and within two

---

[88] For the development of the University Press, see pp. 318–19, this volume.

[89] Two other classical constructions were Magdalen's stand-alone baroque entrance gate (no longer in existence) and the incongruous baroque porch attached to St Mary's.

[90] The infirmary never belonged to the University, though one of its medical professors was attached to the institution from the late eighteenth century. The Observatory eventually cost £31,700.

years the building was ready for use. Remaining loyal to the tradition of the previous century, the delegates ignored the contemporary passion for the gothic and commissioned a classical building, replete with a gateway in the form of a Roman triumphal arch.[91]

The classical style also continued to be favoured, albeit in a mixed Italianate-Grecian form, for the final building set up by the University before 1850 that was located somewhat closer to the University's heartland. The eighteenth-century sculptor Sir Robert Taylor had no connection with Oxford, but when he died in 1788 he left the residue of his estate to further the study of modern languages. When the University eventually received a sum of £65,000 on the death of his son in 1835, it used the money to build a three-sided neoclassical quadrangle on the corner of St Giles and Beaumont Street, on land purchased from Worcester. The building was designed by C. R. Cockerell, cost £49,300, and was opened in 1845. The east-facing range became the Taylorian, comprising a library and lecture rooms. The rest of the building, with its Beaumont Street frontage, was given over to house a new university art gallery, which, it was hoped, would eventually hold a world-class collection. Initially, it merely contained the University's current small collection of pictures, and the busts and statues given to Oxford by the Countess of Pomfret in 1755 (both hitherto kept in the Bodleian).

E. A Mecca for Tourists and Celebrities

Oxford's new quads and buildings, designed by some of England's leading architects and constructed in the latest architectural styles, gave the University and its colleges a new cachet. Irrespective of its academic credentials, Oxford, from the late seventeenth century, was on the architectural map. The University itself did its best to broadcast its physical charms. Pre-classical Oxford was lovingly embalmed in a series of engravings published by David Loggan, engraver to the University, in 1675.[92] Then, from the beginning of the eighteenth century, the University used the upper half of its almanac, an annual folio published from 1673, with a print run of 30,000, to advertise its changing face more widely. No distinction was made between buildings completed and those still on the drawing board. When Magdalen planned to replace its old buildings with a completely new classical quadrangle, it had its intentions publicized in the *Almanack* in two separate engravings. In 1730, George Vertue presented a bird's-eye view of the existing college with a group of four people bottom right, one an architect holding dividers, poring over the plans

---

[91] Simon Eliot, 'Machines, Materials and Money', *The History of Oxford University Press, vol. 2: 1780–1896* (Oxford, 2013), pp. 142–9. The press employed a large workforce in the early nineteenth century. It was another way in which town and gown were joined together. The press's contribution pre-1850 to the scholarly and scientific life of the University is discussed on pp. 321–2, this volume.

[92] David Loggan, *Oxonia illustrata, sive, Omnium celeberrimæ istius universitatis collegiorum, aularum, bibliothecæ Bodleianæ, scholarum publicarum, Theatri Sheldoniani, nec non urbis totius scenographia* (Oxford, 1675). The engravings, though clear and detailed, are not necessarily accurate. University College had the engraver draw its as yet unfinished quad as complete.

for the future. The following year, Vertue engraved another drawing, this time of the college as it would look once remodelled by Holdsworth. As a result, Oxford became a city to see.[93] In the first serious age of cultural tourism, where English travellers moved south to contemplate the ruins of antiquity, and a smaller number of continental Europeans made their way north to view the splendours of a civilization on the rise, Oxford was part of the Grand Tour. While the University continued to be visited by the occasional scholar who wished to use the library resources of the Bodleian or talk with learned fellows, it was assailed, for the first time, by increasing numbers of tourists of both sexes from Britain and overseas. Although they were seldom interested in Oxford's late medieval buildings, they were usually extremely impressed with the classical structures put up after 1660. Jean-François Séguier was a French antiquarian from Nîmes who visited the University with his friend and patron, the Marchese di Maffei, in 1736. He admired the Sheldonian, Ashmolean, and Botanic Garden, looked approvingly on the building work going on at Christ Church and Queen's, but was particularly taken with the cedar-wood finish of Trinity's new chapel and its well-maintained gardens. For a cultural tourist like Séguier, visiting Oxford was as essential a part of the tour of southern England as seeing Windsor Castle and Stonehenge.[94]

Oxford's experience was shared with Cambridge. Just as its sister university witnessed similar changes in its relations with the state and in its internal structure and pattern of attendance, so it too underwent a building explosion across the period that made it a tourist Mecca. The two English universities were unique. Although several of the leading universities on the continent came to boast elegant and architecturally interesting buildings, none possessed the number and variety that would turn them into tourist attractions.[95] Tourists flocked to Paris, for instance, in the eighteenth century, but few bothered to visit the university in the Latin Quarter, which was still architecturally much the same as it had been in 1500. Some rebuilding of the medieval university had occurred under the Bourbons, but on the eve of the Revolution only the Sorbonne and the new Collège de Mazarin, today the Institut, were worthy of note.[96] When Dr Johnson went to Paris in 1775 he visited all the city's many cultural monuments, civil and ecclesiastical, but he never graced any part of the university with his presence.[97]

Neither university let its new-found fame go to waste. Once it became clear that it had the power to entice foreign princes and celebrities to enter its portals, Oxford

[93] A collected edition of the *Almanack's* illustrations can be found in H. M. Petter, *The Oxford Almanacks* (Oxford, 1974). The *Almanack's* illustrators were talented draughtsmen. At the turn of the nineteenth century, a number were the work of J. M. W. Turner.

[94] Bibliothèque Municipale Nîmes, MS 286, pp. 58–9. On Séguier, see Gabriel Audosio and François Pugnière (eds), *Jean-François Séguier. Un Nîmois dans l'Europe des Lumières* (Aix-en-Provence, 2005).

[95] Guides to Europe's institutions of higher education at the end of the eighteenth century were based on the extent of their scientific plant not their aesthetic merits: e.g. Friedrich Colland, *Kurzer Inbegriff von dem Ursprunge der Wissenschaften, Schulen ... und Universitäten in ganz Europa, besonders der Akademien ... zu Wien* (Vienna, 1796).

[96] Both had chapels that were outstanding examples of the French baroque. Mazarin, founded with a bequest from the cardinal, was opened in 1690.

[97] Boswell, *Johnson*, pp. 455–63. On things to see in Paris, see the annual *Almanach royal* (Paris, 1700–92).

took advantage of their visits to add to its own lustre. The University had long curried favour with the great and good by occasionally giving honorary degrees to the powerful at court: the first recipient was probably Lionel Woodville, bishop of Salisbury, elected Oxford's Chancellor in the late 1470s. From the turn of the eighteenth century, the practice became a commonplace and the list of honorands was extended to visiting royalty and foreign dignitaries of all kinds, while the Act, and later Encaenia, was used as a grand ceremonial moment to welcome them into the fold. In 1791, the University even felt moved to recognize the distinction of a simple musician, Josef Haydn. Honorary degrees were especially used to associate the University with national politicians and prominent cultural figures, including those from outside the national church. In 1741, Alexander Pope, though raised a catholic, was in line to be given a degree with his friend the latitudinarian bishop William Warburton, a Cambridge man. It was only because Pope took offence when Warburton was blackballed for his liberal religious views that the poet was never inscribed on the university register.[98] The celebration of blood and talent in the Age of Enlightenment served a useful purpose. It covered Oxford's naked confessionalism with a fig-leaf of religious pluralism, and conned many foreigners, who failed to look beneath the surface, into believing that the Anglican University was a beacon of enlightened modernity.

[98] Handel was offered a degree in 1733 but also refused.

CHAPTER 6

Church and State

A. Catholics and Protestants

AFTER the Cromwellian visitation of 1535 and the University's acceptance of the oath of supremacy, Oxford ceased to be a major concern to the Henrician state. The University, for the most part, retained a steadfast allegiance to the doctrine and liturgy of the traditional church, but there was no chance its conservatism would induce royal opprobrium, as long as it remained loyal. Prompted by greed and the humanist entourage at court, the king was moved, in the second half of the 1530s, to dissolve the monasteries and outlaw pilgrimages and other purportedly idolatrous practices of the late medieval church, but he had no wish to see fundamental reform, especially once released from the influence of the more reform-minded Cromwell, executed in 1540. Henry until his death remained wedded to the catholic doctrine of works: he had no truck with the protestant theory of justification by faith alone, and in his last years was more interested in rooting out avowed protestants than investigating the beliefs of traditional catholics. Oxford did not escape unscathed from the Henrician Reformation. The houses and colleges of the regular orders both in and around the city were closed as part of the process of dissolution, the shrine of St Frideswide destroyed, and the teaching of canon law forbidden by Cromwell's visitors. But otherwise there was no material damage. Oxford and Cambridge were momentarily threatened at the end of the reign when it looked as if the king had cast his covetous eyes on the college endowments in his search for further religious foundations to secularize in order to fund his war with France. However, the universities were saved from despoliation by the good offices of Henry's sixth and evangelical queen Catherine Parr, and both Oxford and Cambridge had cause to thank rather than curse the king on his death in 1547, for the final years of his reign brought a number of royal benefactions. In 1540 Henry put aside funds to establish five permanent regius chairs in the two universities in theology, medicine, civil law, Greek, and Hebrew. These were intended to ensure high-quality tuition in the three higher sciences and guarantee a permanent place in the arts curriculum for the two ancient languages particularly dear to the humanists. Then, in 1546, he founded two new colleges,

Trinity, Cambridge, and Christ Church, Oxford, to which the chairs in theology, Greek, and Hebrew were attached.[1]

Supporters of a more radical Reformation existed at Oxford in the years after the Cromwellian visitation but they largely lay low or, if fellows, demitted their fellowship rather than take holy orders. When Edward VI came to the throne, however, the protestants were given their head. The boy-king's regency council, headed by Protector Somerset, was intent on fuller reformation and, as early as Easter 1548, ordered that an English service of communion in both kinds be inserted into the Latin of the Sarum mass. For the most ardent reformers this was the green light to speed up reform. The lead was taken at Christ Church, where Henry had appointed as its first dean his son's tutor, the reformer Richard Cox, who was now elected Oxford's Chancellor.[2] But it was at Magdalen where the full fervour of protestantism was exposed to the public gaze. Magdalen in the early 1540s sheltered a number of earnest reformers who would become prominent figures in the future Elizabethan church, including the martyrologist John Foxe, who had diplomatically vacated his fellowship in 1545 after incurring his head of house's disapproval for reading the Scriptures in the vernacular. His successors now felt free to throw caution to the wind, and on the evening of Whitsunday 1548, staged a series of 'events' in the college chapel:

> Thomas Bickley, a young man of Magdalen College...presumed on Whitsunday Even, in the middle of divine service, to go to the High Altar there, and before the face of a great multitude most irreverently to take away the Sacrament and to break it in pieces, to the great offence of many, whereof not a few were strangers that came at the time to hear divine Service. Henry Bull also of the same College...did with the help of Thomas Bentham openly in the Choir snatch the Censer out of the Priest's hands who was about to offer incense therein.
>
> Besides this also, one Thomas Willyams, a Bachelor of Arts, pulled a priest from the Altar after he had said the Gospel, and flung away his book...Furthermore also, he with other young people not contenting themselves with these zealous insolencies, did borrow hatchets and went into the Choir and chopped in pieces such books that were not bought forty pound.[3]

Bickley and his friends' vandalism went further than anything the royal council had intended. Cranmer's first English prayer book, which parliament would sanction for use in the following year, still retained the traditional belief in the communion service as a sacrifice. But the council appears to have protected the radicals from their conservative colleagues' ire, merely urging the president and fellows to take a leaf out of Dean Cox's book and become part of the vanguard initiating a godly reformation.[4]

---

[1] For developments at Cambridge, see Leader, pp. 332–8 and 343–9.
[2] Cox of Eton and Cambridge had been a junior canon of Cardinal College.
[3] Wood, *History*, ii. 105.   [4] Bickley would eventually be warden of Merton.

By November 1548, the council felt the need to force the pace themselves, and appointed royal commissioners to visit Oxford and Cambridge in the following year, who were to take the pulse of the academic and religious health of the two universities and ensure they conformed to government thinking. Oxford's commissioners, who included Cox, duly arrived in May 1549 and set to work. First, they drew up new university statutes which covered all areas of teaching and discipline; then they moved on to the individual colleges, where they backed up their recommendations with specific injunctions about religious worship. Everywhere, war was waged on fasting, masses for the dead, and the old daily array of 'papistical' services. At All Souls, for instance, fellows were ordered to 'have only one altar or Lord's table in the chapel', while 'secondary altars, images, statues, tabernacles and what are called organs' were 'to be immediately removed, along with all other monuments to superstition and idolatry'.[5]

The visitation was also used for a great set piece of academic theatre. To emphasize that the religious changes carried through to date were only a beginning, the king's council removed the incumbent regius professors of theology and replaced them with hardened reformers from abroad. Oxford's new regius was the Italian protestant Peter Martyr, who had been giving explicitly protestant lectures, emphasizing justification by faith alone, from the spring of 1548. Martyr was a protestant enfant terrible, much more radical than either Luther or Calvin when it came to the significance of communion, where he followed the Swiss reformer, Zwingli, in seeing the service as a simple commemoration. Over the four days of 28 May to 1 June the visitation climaxed at St Mary's with a theological dispute where Martyr, backed by Cox, who was in the chair, debated his radical eucharistic doctrine with his conservative opponents, who included William Tresham, canon of Christ Church, and William Chedsey of Corpus.[6] Martyr showed a formidable acquaintance with patristic scholarship as well as Scripture, but the traditional position was ably defended and both sides emerged claiming victory. Nonetheless, the religious direction of the regime was henceforth clear, even if it would be another three years before Cranmer's second English prayer book, with its clear-cut Zwinglian eucharistic emphasis, would be enacted into law.

In the meantime, the government put pressure on Oxford to endorse the new religious order more firmly. In mid-1549, despite the best endeavours of the visitors, probably only two college heads—Cox and William More of Exeter—were enthusiastic reformers. While Cambridge seems to have swung behind the regime relatively quickly, Oxford continued to dig in its heels.[7] There was no move to purge Oxford of conservatives—perhaps the new regency council headed by Northumberland was unnerved by the catholic riots that occurred in the city on

---

[5] Statutes, vol. 1, *Statutes of All Souls College*, p. 87, 'Ordinances of Royal Visitors, 1549', article 19.

[6] Tresham had been a canon of King Henry VIII College.

[7] H. C. Porter, *Reformation and Reaction in Tudor Cambridge* (Cambridge, 1958), pp. 67–9 (on refashioning Cambridge college chapels); Richard Rex, 'The Sixteenth Century', in Peter Linehan, *St John's College Cambridge: A History* (Woodbridge, 2011), pp. 44–9.

the fall of Protector Somerset in the winter of 1549/50—but some of the more prominent senior members were silenced. Corpus, though the college of two vocal reformers in John Jewel, the later Anglican apologist, and William Cole, a future head of house, was particularly targeted. Chedsey was locked up in London's Fleet Prison in Lent 1550 for preaching sedition, as were the president, Robert Morwent, and two other fellows in June 1551, following accusations that they had listened to the old service of the mass on Corpus Christi Day. In other colleges prominent conservatives were lent on to resign. Magdalen's head of house from 1538, Owen Oglethorpe, was a religious moderate, ready to swim with the tide. But the radical reformers in the college on several occasions tried to unseat him by complaining to the regency council of his lack of enthusiasm, and he was eventually persuaded to depart in the summer of 1552. The council took advantage of the subsequent election to impose on the college a Cambridge outsider and civil lawyer, Walter Haddon.

Doubtless with time Oxford would have put itself behind the Edwardian Reformation, or the regime would have felt strong enough to impose its will, but time was not on the latter's side. The teenage king died in July 1553 and was replaced after a short interlude by his catholic sister, Mary. The new queen was as keen as her half-brother's council that the English universities should embrace the true faith and immediately ordered that the colleges should observe and live by their ancient statutes, which had been current in the reign of her father. Cambridge took time to bring to heel but at Oxford, where the commitment to Edwardian reform had always been partial, the old religion was restored with little difficulty. Most colleges did not wait to be commanded to return to the old ways. As their banished vestments and ornaments had frequently been hidden rather than destroyed, they were quickly rediscovered, the statues returned to their niches, and the mass was reinstituted. There was little need either to clear out the protestant phalanx. Only three college heads had to be expelled. Except at Corpus, Christ Church, and Magdalen, most reformers did not wait to be officially deprived of their fellowship by the college visitor but prudently departed for the continent, led by Cox and Martyr. The primary task of the queen and her new archbishop of Canterbury, the papal legate and former Magdalen commoner Cardinal Reginald Pole, was to confirm rather than reconstitute the University's catholic allegiance.[8]

Presumably this was the reason why church and state decided to use Oxford as the stage on which to try the leading episcopal lights of the previous regime for heresy. Edward's regency council had deprived recalcitrant bishops, like Stephen Gardiner of Winchester, but they had not moved to destroy them. Mary and Pole were more vindictive. The campaign began in April 1554 when the erstwhile bishops Hugh Latimer and Nicholas Ridley and the deposed Archbishop Cranmer were

---

[8] Elizabeth Russell, 'Marian Oxford and the Counter Reformation', in C. M. Barron and C. Harper Bill (eds), *The Church in Pre-Reformation Society: Essays in Honour of F. R. H. Du Boulay* (Woodbridge, 1985). Pole had been part of a humanist and reforming circle in Italy in the 1530s but had never broken with the church: see Dermot Fenlon, *Heresy and Obedience in Tridentine Italy: Cardinal Pole and the Counter Reformation* (Cambridge, 1972).

FIGURE 6.1 Burning of Thomas Cranmer, archbishop of Canterbury, 1556: engraving in John Foxe, *Actes and Monuments*, 4th edn 1583. A copy of the Book of Martyrs was to be found in every parish church and it was the second most widely read book in early modern England after the Bible. The engraving depicts one of the founding moments in English protestantism when Cranmer holds out to the flames the hand which had signed his recantation.

taken from prison in London and forced to participate in a second three-day debate on the eucharist in St Mary's. The catholic position was again sustained by Tresham and Chedsey, assisted by Richard Smith, the restored regius professor of divinity. This time the traditionalists were on the offensive and the three Edwardian reformers were declared to be heretics at the end of the proceedings. At this stage, however, no action could be taken against them because the Edwardian regime had repealed the early fourteenth-century legislation which had made heresy a capital crime. Once new legislation had been passed by parliament in December 1554, Mary and Pole were free to act. As the reformers refused to apostatize, the way was clear for their trial. Latimer and Ridley were tried in St Mary's in autumn 1555; convicted as heretics and refusing to recant, they were burnt at the stake outside Balliol on 15 October. Cranmer followed on 21 March 1556. The author of a tract on the necessity of obedience to the sovereign even when the crown ordered something contrary to conscience, he was initially convinced that consistency demanded that he accept the new regime. When it became clear that Mary wanted him to burn anyway, instead of publicly recanting, as he had promised, he stood in the pulpit of St Mary's and passionately reaffirmed his protestant faith. He met death with an impressive courage and a gesture that would become thereafter cemented in the English protestant imagination. Having originally signed a document confessing to heresy, as the queen required, he atoned for his weakness by turning his execution into a *coup de théâtre*:

> And when the wodde was kindled, & the fyre began to burn nere him, stretching out his arms, he put his right hand in ye flame, which he held so stedfast and immovable (saving ye once with the same hande he wiped his face) that all men might see his hand burned before his body was touched. His body did so abide the burning of the flame, with such constancie and stedfastnes, that standing always in one place without moving of his members, he seemed to move no more than the stake to which he was bound: his eyes were lifted up to heaven, & oftentimes he repeted his unworthy right hand, so long as his voyce would suffer him. (See Figure 6.1)[9]

By the time Cranmer went to the pyre, Pole was busy rebuilding as well as pulling down. His first official act as papal legate, with regard to the University, was to issue a general dispensation and faculty in March 1555 reconciling its members to the catholic faith after their temporary lapse into heresy in the previous reign.[10] His attention then turned to the need to improve the quality of theology teaching at the two universities. Like Edward's councillors, Pole looked abroad, and in October 1555 brought to Oxford a Spanish Dominican with impeccable intellectual credentials, Juan de Villa Garcia. Initially he was given the theology praelectorship of Pole's old college; then the following year he was elevated to the regius chair on the demission of Richard Smith. At the same time, Pole inserted another Spanish Dominican, Pedro de Soto, into the regius chair of Hebrew, which was converted temporarily into a professorship of scholastic theology.[11] With theological instruction in good hands, the legate next moved to restore university discipline generally, which he presumably felt had decayed in the preceding years despite the efforts of the Edwardian commissioners. At the turn of 1556 he announced his own legatine visitation of the two universities, which began its work in Oxford in July. The commissioners appear to have found little amiss. Certainly they had little joy in hunting out heretics and had to be satisfied with ordering the exhumation of the body of Peter Martyr's wife from Christ Church Cathedral and having it tossed on a dunghill. Pole, however, wanted to leave his mark, and in the autumn of 1556,

---

[9] John Foxe, *Actes and Monuments* (London, 1563), p. 1503. There is no reason to doubt the accuracy of Foxe's account. For a modern account of the archbishop's trial and execution, see Diarmaid MacCulloch, *Thomas Cranmer* (London, 1996), ch. 13.

[10] Bodleian Library, OUA, WPBeta/M/22.

[11] For the two Dominicans, see Andrew Hegarty, 'Bartolomé Carranza and the English Universities', in John Edwards and Ron Truman (eds), *Reforming Catholicism in the England of Mary Tudor: The Achievement of Friar Bartolomé Carranza* (Aldershot, 2005).

having become the University's Chancellor, promulgated a new set of statutes, which made it quite clear that orthodoxy and good discipline went hand in hand. Lumped together into a blanket category of undesirables whom the University must purge were 'heretics, those who view the catholic faith not quite correctly, all those living badly and dishonestly, the scandalous, the conspiratorial, disturbers of the peace, the useless and those who make no progress in their studies'. Similarly, it was not just heretical books and manuscripts that were banned but any work that 'corrupts the true teaching of the faith and perverts honest and good morals'.[12]

The foundation in 1555 of two new Oxford colleges specifically dedicated to maintaining the catholic faith—Trinity and St John's—was a strong sign that those outside as well as inside the University felt that the future lay with Rome not Wittenberg or Geneva. Mary died in 1558, however, and her Counter or Catholic Reformation was nipped in the bud. Latimer had strengthened Ridley's resolve at their execution by claiming that by their death they would light 'such a candle, by God's grace in England, as I trust shall never be put out'. With the accession to the throne of the protestant Elizabeth in November 1558, the candle's faltering flame sprang into life. Mary's younger sister had been reared in the Edwardian church. Though she failed in her attempt to make her first parliament embrace Cranmer's second English prayer book, she obtained a religious settlement in the spring of 1559, backed up four years later by the Thirty-Nine Articles, that was protestant enough for the new Church of England to be recognized as part of the Calvinist family of churches. This inevitably meant that the universities had once again to be brought into line with the new religious order. This time, however, the Oxford climate was decidedly inclement. Whereas the traditionalist majority had, albeit reluctantly, accepted the Edwardian changes, their Marian successors were more robust. The intruded Spanish theologians seem to have been particularly effective in strengthening the old faith. Both, according to the new bishop of Salisbury and former Corpus fellow John Jewel, who had spent Mary's reign in exile in Zurich, had proved gifted teachers. In a letter of 22 May 1559 written to the Swiss reformer Henry Bullinger, Jewel declared that Oxford was lost to the cause. The Dominicans had 'torn up by the roots all that Peter Martyr had so prosperously planted' and 'reduced the vineyard of the Lord into a wilderness'.[13]

The early years of Elizabeth's reign suggests that Jewel was not exaggerating. Cambridge once again swung behind the regime fairly easily, but Oxford was a tougher nut to crack.[14] The regime, like its Edwardian predecessor, moved carefully, recognizing the potential opposition. A royal visitation descended on the University in 1559 and administered the new oath of supremacy that caught the

[12] *Statuta*, p. 364. For developments in both universities, see C. Cross, 'The English Universities, 1553–58', in Eamon Duffy and David Loades (eds), *The Church of Mary Tudor* (Aldershot, 2006), pp. 57–76.
[13] Hegarty, 'Carranza', p. 160.
[14] Porter, *Reformation*, ch. 5; Rex, 'Sixteenth Century', pp. 58–63 (on Pilkington's protestantization of St John's). Gonville and Caius was the one Cambridge college where crypto-catholics were still to be found into the 1570s.

most uncompromising catholics. But there was no government witch hunt, and it was left to college visitors, usually newly appointed protestant bishops, to prise out catholic non-conformists. In the case of some of the small colleges this was achieved quickly: University College had completely renewed its fellowship by 1563 and thereafter was no cause for concern. The larger foundations, however, were much less malleable. When Bishop Robert Horne of Winchester visited the four colleges under his jurisdiction in 1561, he found three—New College, Corpus Christi, and Trinity—full of papists. Only Magdalen flew the protestant flag, thanks to a large number of younger fellows who had been elected towards the end of Mary's reign and had somehow kept their religious beliefs concealed from the catholic president, Thomas Coveney. Horne attempted to remove the most recalcitrant, depriving both college heads and fellows and encouraging the election of godly successors. But his success was limited. New College proved a particular thorn in his flesh. Its Marian warden, Thomas Whyte, managed to cling on to his office until 1573, despite the objections of reformers. While he did so, religious progress was slow. For fifteen years of the reign of a protestant queen he presided over a residual catholic community whose most ardent members were periodically forced into exile. In total, during Whyte's stewardship, the college lost thirty-nine fellows to recusancy, twenty-nine elected under Mary, and ten from the Elizabethan intake. New College had lost much of its papist image by 1571, but it was 1576 before a later bishop of Winchester was convinced it was fully conforming.[15] Even in a college where the fellows had apparently fallen in line by the mid-1560s, thoroughgoing reformation could still take time. Trinity's fellowship accepted the Thirty-Nine Articles in 1566, but it was in trouble four years later with both the bishop and the queen for failure to deface 'certain monuments tending to idolatry and popish or devil's service, as crosses, censers, and such like filthy stuff'.[16]

According to a religious census held by the Vice-Chancellor in 1577 on the orders of the Privy Council, catholics, by then, were to be found only in Balliol, Exeter, Queen's, and All Souls. However, there were still supposedly many recusants sheltering in the surviving halls, where religious discipline was much less strict, especially in Gloucester Hall, and Convocation recognized more had to be done to guard against the corruption of the young. In January 1579, the University's resident masters and doctors ordered that the colleges and halls should arrange catechetical instruction for their charges based on Calvin's *Institutes* and the Heidelberg Confession,[17] and set up a mechanism for checking the undergraduates' progress each term. This was followed up a month later by a statute forbidding students from

---

[15] New College lost the most fellows, but it did not provide the most catholic martyrs: here the honour was shared by St John's and Brasenose. St John's was also under the bishop of Winchester but for the first part of Elizabeth's reign was outside his jurisdiction.

[16] Hopkins, p. 50.

[17] Heidelberg was the capital city of the Palatinate, one of the few German principalities to embrace Calvinism. The catechism was drawn up on the orders of the ruler by the local university and sanctioned for use in 1563. It was recognized to be the best of the Calvinist catechisms on the market and was translated into several languages.

taking a degree unless their heads of house had 'confirmed that they had been sufficiently instructed in the catechism'.[18] Then, in late 1581, as part of a wider move by the government against catholic survivalism, an attempt was made to remove the problem of recusancy for good. In a letter to the University written in the October of that year, the incumbent Chancellor, the earl of Leicester, expressed concern about the 'many papists' who 'have heretofore and may hereafter lurk among you, and be brought up by corrupt tutors', and ordered a crackdown. In consequence, the University promulgated a new matriculation statute requiring all those coming into residence 'of 16 or upward' to subscribe to the royal supremacy and the articles of religion as well as promise fidelity to the University's acts and statutes.[19] Thereafter, only catholic boys in their early teens could survive at Oxford unpressurized, and the last recusants disappeared.

The slow pace of enforcing conformity in Elizabethan Oxford is evident in the educational background of many of the catholic priests who returned to England in the second half of the reign in an attempt to keep the Roman faith alive. The driving force behind their campaign was a former fellow of Oriel and principal of St Mary Hall, William, later Cardinal, Allen, who in 1568 established a seminary at Douai to train priests for the English mission. Allen himself had left Oxford at the beginning of Elizabeth's reign, but among the several hundred students who passed through his hands at the English college over the next twenty-five years, there were several who had been either confirmed in their catholic beliefs or won back to the old religion while studying in an ostensibly protestant university.[20] The catholic controversialist and Jesuit Edmund Campion, a former fellow of St John's who would be eventually executed for treason, had been a much admired disputant in front of the queen when she visited Oxford in 1566. His more cantankerous confederate, Robert Parsons, a fellow of Balliol, did not arrive in Oxford until 1564 and only took the decision to decamp for the continent ten years later.[21] Protestant Oxford, in its first flush of youth, had not been successful at winning the hearts and minds of some of its most brilliant alumni.

B. Protestant Quarrels

The three hundred English protestants who went into exile during Mary's reign rather than face persecution, and returned in 1558, divided into two camps. The 'Coxians' (named after the Christ Church dean, Richard) wanted the restoration of

---

[18] *Statuta*, pp. 413–14.

[19] HUO, iii. 413. *Register of the University of Oxford*, vol. 2, part 1: *Introductions*, ed. Andrew Clark (OHS; Oxford, 1887), pp. 167–8: the statute is ambiguous; it is unclear whether boys between 12 and 16 also had to subscribe.

[20] Allen was excluded from his Oriel fellowship on grounds of absenteeism only in 1565. Douai, where Allen was professor of theology, was a new university in the Spanish Netherlands. In 1578, the English college moved to Reims in France when the whole of the territory was temporarily in the hands of the mainly Dutch protestant rebels who had rebelled against Philip II of Spain. The college returned to Douai in 1593.

[21] The 1581 clampdown was probably inspired by the discovery in St Mary's of copies of one of Campion's pamphlets, left on the benches before a meeting of Convocation.

the 1552 Settlement. The 'Knoxians', named after the later Scottish reformer, John Knox, wanted a more thorough reformation that would do away with so-called popish remnants in the liturgy, such as making the sign of the cross in baptism, outlaw wearing vestments, and set in motion a clean-up of the country's morals. Some Knoxians also favoured the replacement of the traditional hierarchy with a presbyterian system of church government, as used in Geneva. The queen was a Coxian by conviction, and though unable to establish the exact religious settlement she wanted, refused to budge thereafter, her conscience reinforced by political calculation. If a country with no standing army and little bureaucracy was ever to be won away from traditional catholicism, then the purity men or puritans, as the Knoxians came to be called by their enemies, could not be given their head.[22]

Yet if the queen found the puritans tiresome, she could not do without them. They were the most committed and zealous of her protestant subjects, and throughout her reign, particularly at the beginning when genuine protestants were thin on the ground, she needed their assistance and was forced to promote them. Puritans were to be found on her Privy Council, on the bench of bishops, and in many Oxford and Cambridge colleges. Of the two universities, Cambridge was always the more profoundly infiltrated by radical religious reformers. It was there that Thomas Cartwright, Lady Margaret professor of divinity, publicly launched the campaign to end episcopacy in 1570. It was there, too, that puritanism was institutionalized with the foundation of Emmanuel and Sidney Sussex in 1584 and 1596, two colleges deliberately set up to shelter and sustain the 'hotter sort' of protestant.[23] Oxford's contribution to Elizabethan puritanism, however, should not be undersold. The very fact that committed protestants were in a minority in the first years of the reign guaranteed that most were zealots.

In the 1560s and 1570s the most visible Oxford puritan was Laurence Humphrey. Humphrey had been a protestant fellow of Magdalen who had been given permission to leave Oxford in September 1553, and had spent Mary's reign in Strasbourg and Zurich. Returning home, he was rewarded with the regius chair of divinity in the summer of 1560, then the following year, on the prompting of one of Elizabeth's protestant councillors, the earl of Bedford, elected president of his former college in succession to the deposed Coveney. He was to hold both posts until his death in 1589. Humphrey quickly turned Magdalen into a puritan seminary and was instrumental, through his protestant friends at court, in getting the queen to appoint another hardliner, Thomas Sampson, as dean of Christ Church. Both Humphrey and Sampson were particularly irked by the liturgy's requirement that ministers of religion should conduct divine service in traditional vestments. For the first half of the 1560s they refused to conform and encouraged the two fellowships to follow

[22] C. H. Garrett, *The Marian Exiles: A Study in the Origins of English Protestantism* (Cambridge, 1938); Patrick Collinson, *The Elizabethan Puritan Movement* (London, 1967); Peter Lake, *Moderate Puritans and the Elizabethan Church* (Cambridge, 1982); Peter Lake, *Anglicans and Puritans? Presbyterianism and English Conformist Thought from Whitgift to Hooker* (London, 1988).

[23] Porter, *Reformation*, chs vii, viii, and x; S. Bendall, C.N.L. Brooke, and P. Collinson, *A History of Emmanuel College, Cambridge* (Woodbridge, 1999), esp. ch. 6; Rex, 'Sixteenth Century', pp. 84–91.

FIGURE 6.2 Portrait of John Rainolds, president of Corpus Christi College, by an anonymous artist. Rainolds was one of Oxford's most prominent puritans. The portrait is of Rainolds as a young man, probably painted shortly after he became a fellow of Corpus in 1566. The motto says that Christ is his all.

suit. There was a limit, however, to the extent to which Elizabeth could be defied, and in March 1565 she ordered the archbishop of Canterbury, Matthew Parker, to get them to change their minds. Humphrey and Sampson were summoned to London and their behaviour investigated. But this only led them to agitate against wearing the surplice in the capital. Sampson's stubbornness led to his deprivation by his royal mistress. Humphrey, equally unrepentant, escaped a similar fate because Magdalen's visitor, Bishop Horne, to whom he was referred for disciplining, was a puritan sympathizer and refused to silence him. But the queen never forgave a slight. When she visited Oxford the following year and was greeted by the heads of house decked out in their doctoral finery, Magdalen's president suffered a tart rebuke, as he stooped to kiss her hand: 'Dr Humphrey methinks this gown and habit becomes you very well, and I marvel you are so straitlaced in this point; but I come not now to chide.'[24]

Humphrey mellowed with age and judicious ecclesiastical patronage, and in the 1570s he was considered a safe enough pair of hands by Chancellor Leicester to be appointed his deputy for a six-year term. Magdalen, however, remained the

[24] Brockliss, p. 162. There are several versions of the royal put-down.

haunt of puritans. A younger generation of fellows in the 1570s and 1580s were more and more irritated by their president's time-serving, and on two occasions complained of his governance of the college to the visitor in the hope of having him removed. He was even accused in 1585 of protecting papists in the college. The most radical of this new generation was Edward Gellibrand, fellow in 1573. A prominent member of the underground 'classis' movement that, in the middle of Elizabeth's reign, tried to push the country in a presbyterian direction, he was in constant communication with its leader, John Field, a former Christ Church man, and was probably responsible for circulating in Oxford the English translation of the party's reform manifesto, *De Disciplinis*, in 1587. But Gellibrand was only one of a number of notorious Oxford puritans in the 1580s. By then, Brasenose, Queen's, and particularly Corpus, home to the formidable John Rainolds, were also producing a string of puritan ministers. Rainolds was an Oxford fixture for thirty years and another theologian with presbyterian leanings (see Figure 6.2). Although, from 1584, Elizabeth had a new archbishop of Canterbury, John Whitgift, charged with rooting out all forms of non-conformity, Rainolds was always relatively safe from ecclesiastical persecution thanks to the protection of one of Elizabeth's puritan councillors, Francis Walsingham. The latter thought highly of his talents and, from 1586, paid for him to give annual lectures on theological controversy in the University.

It would be wrong, however, to see late Elizabethan Oxford as deeply divided between conformists and puritans. For all their differences, the two groups lived together peaceably for the most part, united in the understandable conviction that the principal enemy was catholicism, whose machinations had to be countered by word and deed. Humphrey wrote polemics against popery, not critiques of the Elizabethan church.[25] In the 1590s, moreover, Oxford puritanism became less of a concern to the authorities. The unreconcilable went abroad. Gellibrand, having married, left as early as 1589 to serve as pastor to the English church at Middelburg in Calvinist Holland. Others toned down their views. Rainolds had been present at an illegal presbyterian convention held in Oxford in 1587 but he must have trimmed his views in subsequent years or the queen would have stopped him becoming president of Corpus in 1599. Even Magdalen conformed, once the queen had made the fellows accept Nicholas Bond as Humphrey's successor. Bond ran a tight ship and finally got the fellows to wear surplices.[26]

Cambridge's puritans had also mellowed by 1590 as the radicals learnt to temper their anti-episcopalian rhetoric.[27] At the end of the day, conformists and puritans had a common ground. With a few exceptions, they were all theologically Calvinist, and believed that men and women had been predestined to heaven and hell by a

---

[25] E.g. *De religione conservatione et reformatione* (1559); *Jesuitismi* (1584); and *A View of the Romish Hydra and Monster* (1588).

[26] See p. 154, this volume.

[27] The stand-off between conformists and puritans at Cambridge was principally limited to the years 1567–77 when Whitgift, who was master of Trinity, regius professor of divinity, and eventually Vice-Chancellor, burnished his credentials for a bishopric by cutting the presbyterians down to size. He left the university in 1577 to become bishop of Worcester: Porter, *Reformation*, pp. 170–8.

foreseeing and omnipotent God from the beginning of time. An individual played no part in his or her salvation: faith alone saved and Christ died for God's chosen, not mankind as a whole. Faced by the twin threat of Spanish invasion and the catholic mission, all the more fearful by dint of its being hidden from view, conformists and puritans in both universities joined hands to protect protestant England. The 1580s was the high-water mark of Oxford puritanism, but it also saw a number of colleges building on the 1579 statute and establishing a catechetical lecturer to make sure undergraduates left their care as good protestants: New College in 1580, University in 1583, Oriel in 1585, and Merton in 1589.

The accession of a Scottish king in 1603 did nothing to arrest the relative harmony. Scotland had had a much more thoroughgoing Calvinist Reformation, which had left it with a limited form of presbyterian church government, but James VI had fought a long campaign to retain some element of episcopacy in the Scottish kirk and he had no intention of remodelling the Church of England. The English puritans were temporarily heartened when James called a conference at Hampton Court to discuss religious change in response to a petition calling for minor reforms to the liturgy. But their hopes were dashed when James failed to distinguish between moderates and radicals and equated presbyterianism with anti-monarchism. As a result, the Elizabethan Settlement was confirmed and the new archbishop of Canterbury, Richard Bancroft, was allowed to hunt down non-conformist ministers. Despite James' uncompromising stance, Hampton Court only further consolidated religious harmony in the two universities, owing to a decision by the delegates, prompted by Rainolds of Corpus, to instigate a new translation of the Bible. A knowledge of ancient languages was not a monopoly of any religious party, and for the next seven years groups of protestant scholars from Oxford, Cambridge, and London, puritans as well as conformists, worked together to produce the Authorized Version, first published in 1611.[28]

Harmony at both universities began to break down seriously only when Charles I came to the throne in 1625. From the late 1590s, a handful of Oxford and Cambridge theologians had begun to question the Calvinist status quo. While remaining wedded to the protestant doctrine of justification by faith alone, they challenged the idea that men and women had no role in their salvation, claiming instead that the faith that saves was freely offered to everyone and could be accepted or rejected. Traditional Calvinists called supporters of the doctrine Arminians after the Dutch theologian Arminius, who taught a similar position at the University of Leiden. But English and Dutch Arminians need to be separated. In England, as interest in this more human-orientated version of Calvinism grew in the early seventeenth century, its supporters also championed a variety of unorthodox ecclesiological and liturgical positions: they argued that the order of bishops was

---

[28] For more details see p. 305, this volume. The principal translation used by English Protestants hitherto had been the Geneva Bible, put together by the Marian exiles and published for the first time in 1560. It went through at least 150 editions, the last as late as 1644.

divinely constituted and not an administrative convenience; they placed a new emphasis on frequent communion as the vehicle of divine grace; they called for churches to be once more visually stunning places of worship where the eucharist was conducted with due reverence and the communion table placed altar-wise at the east end; they aspired to free the church from economic dependence on the laity; and they claimed that the Church of England, as established, was the only true church. To complicate matters further, a number of the new ritualists remained traditional Calvinists.[29]

The first Oxford-bred theologian to support Arminianism was probably the Corpus-educated Richard Hooker, author of the *Laws of Ecclesiastical Politie*, a famous defence of England's protestant church and state published in 1594 and 1597. But Hooker developed his ideas outside the University and anti-predestinarians were more visible at Cambridge than at Oxford when Elizabeth died.[30] The situation changed dramatically in the first part of James' reign, when several of Oxford's more prominent anti-Calvinists, notably John Howson, canon of Christ Church, and William Laud, fellow of St John's, began to air their views in public. Howson caused a stir as early as November 1602 when, as Vice-Chancellor, he preached an accession sermon that paradoxically criticized the Calvinist obsession with the pulpit. But it was Laud who particularly raised the temperature in the University when he publicly signalled his move away from the religious status quo in June 1608 by arguing, in his doctoral thesis sustained at the Act, that only bishops could ordain. This confirmed suspicions in the University that Laud was theologically unsound, and when he was elected president of St John's in 1611, the election was appealed to the visitor. The then bishop of Winchester, however, had little political influence, while Laud had an Arminian patron at court in Bishop Richard Neile of Lichfield, who had the election confirmed by the king.[31] There was a limit, though, to James' support for the Arminian party at Oxford. Laud was elevated to the distant bishopric of St David's in 1617 and Howson to Oxford two years later, while another member of their party, Richard Corbet, was made dean of Christ Church. But James never prevented the Calvinist majority from making its position clear in lectures and disputations, or using the Act, as Laud had done, to give their views public exposure. Indeed, in 1618, James firmly nailed his colours to the Calvinist mast. When representatives of the Calvinist churches met at Dort in the United Provinces to discuss the theological positions of Arminius, the king instructed his delegates to vote in favour of Calvinist orthodoxy. In consequence, in the final years of James' reign, with Laud out of the way and the University's chancellorship in the safe hands of a Calvinist, William Herbert, earl of Pembroke, Oxford was free from religious divisions.

---

[29] Nicholas Tyacke, *Anti-Calvinists: The Rise of English Arminianism*, c. 1590–1640 (Oxford, 1987).

[30] Porter, *Reformation*, chs xv, xvii, and xviii.

[31] Laud had been elected by one vote over his opponent John Rawlinson, a former fellow and principal of St Edmund Hall, and there had been an unseemly altercation in chapel: W. C. Costin, *The History of St John's College Oxford 1598–1860* (OHS, new series, xii; Oxford, 1958), pp. 27 and 30.

Charles' accession immediately destabilized the new *modus vivendi*. Charles, convinced that his father had been a hands-off king who had allowed law and order to break down in his dominions, was a committed supporter of the Laudians' campaign to restore hierarchy and ceremony in the church. As the Laudians were also willing to promote royal authority (in a way Hooker had never done), the new king was happy to give them their head and appoint them to bishoprics as fast as they fell vacant. Laud himself would become bishop of London in 1628 and archbishop of Canterbury five years later, on the death of the Balliol-educated George Abbot, Bancroft's successor since 1610 and an orthodox Calvinist. No longer constrained, the Laudians were free to impose their agenda of the 'beauty of holiness' on the church as a whole, with greater or less circumspection according to the bishop involved. In virtually every parish by 1640, the communion table had been moved from a side aisle and once more placed altar-wise at the east end, and parishioners no longer took communion standing or sitting in the centre of the church but decorously kneeling at the newly installed altar rails.[32]

The first sign that a new era had dawned in the universities occurred in 1626. The king's views on predestination are unclear but he quickly moved to dampen down further controversy by ordering, the year after his succession (an order repeated two years later), that the subject was to be no longer debated. This effectively silenced the Oxford Calvinists, while allowing their opponents to emerge from the shadows. While neither side could push their views on official occasions, as the Calvinists had done in the previous reign, especially at the annual Act, the Arminians were free to preach and publish in a private capacity. They were also free to use disputations to raise their opponents' hackles over other issues which divided them, as happened in 1628 when the future archbishop of Canterbury, Gilbert Sheldon, shocked his Oxford audience by denying one of the most treasured beliefs of the Calvinist majority, that the pope was antichrist. All that the orthodox could do was direct their ire at other targets. The regius professor of divinity when Charles came to the throne was the Calvinist John Prideaux of Exeter. He was not deprived by the new king but he was careful to keep out of trouble. Three years before Charles' accession, he turned from attacking Arminians at the Act to denouncing papists, a sign of growing protestant disquiet at the catholic success in the religious war that had broken out in Germany in 1618, when James' son-in-law, Frederick the Calvinist Elector Palatine, had snatched the Bohemian throne from the Holy Roman Emperor.[33] In the 1630s, perhaps mindful that Charles had a catholic queen, Henrietta Maria of France, Prideaux prudently moved his sights once again. This time he attacked the

---

[32] For an overview, see J. Davies, *The Caroline Captivity of the Church: Charles I and the Remoulding of Anglicanism* (Oxford, 1992).

[33] Puritans, who often held millenarian views, believed the war was Armageddon. Known as the Thirty Years War, it lasted until 1648 and steadily became more to do with dynastic rivalry and power politics than religion. Bohemia had been a possession of the imperial family for a century but the crown was elective not hereditary, and in 1618 Bohemia's protestant nobility feared the new emperor would clamp down on heresy and decided to offer it to the ruler of the Palatinate. James warned him not to take it.

Socinians, the anti-Trinitarian sect that had emerged in central Europe towards the end of the sixteenth century and had no evident support in the Oxford of his day. He also eschewed religious dogmatism. When a former fellow of Trinity, William Chillingworth, wrote a defence of protestantism in 1637 that called on all sides to remember what they shared in common rather than their differences, and looked to reunite the churches around the essentials of Christian doctrine, Prideaux was one of those who testified to its orthodoxy.[34]

The advent of the Laudians to power affected Oxford much more profoundly than Cambridge. Pembroke died in 1630, and Laud, as we saw in Chapter 5, was elected its Chancellor.[35] Although presumably an election desired by the king, the leading promoters of his cause in the University were two heads of house: the Vice-Chancellor, Accepted Frewen of Magdalen, and Brian Duppa, dean of Christ Church. Both were convinced supporters of the Laudian programme, though Frewen was a recent convert. As his Christian name reveals, he came from a puritan background, and his surviving theological statements, including his doctoral thesis of 1626, suggest he was an orthodox Calvinist.[36] In 1630 they were powerful figures in the University but their views commanded limited support. Ten years later, the Laudians ruled the roost as more and more heads, such as Christopher Potter of Queen's, joined the archbishop's party. By 1640, anti-Laudians were to be found in significant numbers only in Merton, Exeter—where Prideaux was rector—and two of the halls, Magdalen and New Inn, run by the puritanically inclined John Wilkinson and Christopher Rogers.

The visible sign of the Laudian revolution lay in the refurbishment of a number of college chapels. The Elizabethan Reformation had eventually led to the removal of all forms of traditional decoration, such as wall paintings, statues, rood screens, and crosses. Essentially, college chapels in the early Stuart period were white-washed shells with pulpits and pews. By the late 1630s, they had been transformed. Everywhere the communion table had been placed at the east end and railed off, while many colleges had repaved their chapels with fashionable black-and-white marble tiles, replaced the plain with painted glass in the windows, hung tapestries of an episode from the life of Christ above the altar, and renewed the stalls.[37] The first embellishments predated Charles' reign. Wadham's chapel, consecrated in 1613, had painted glass in the chancel containing images of the prophets and Christ and his apostles from its inception; then in 1622 a new east window was constructed depicting ten images of the passion painted by the Dutchman Bernard van Linge. St John's too had painted windows in its chapel by the early 1620s, thanks to the

[34] William Chillingworth, *The Religion of Protestants a safe way to salvation...* (Oxford, 1638). Chillingworth was a suspect figure because, in 1629, he had temporarily converted to Roman Catholicism and left England. He was also a close friend of Laud.

[35] See p. 144 ff., this volume (on Laud and the reform of the University's statutes).

[36] T. Cochran, 'An Investigation into the Development of Accepted Frewen's Religious Beliefs and Practices up to 1640' (BA dissertation, Oxford, 2005).

[37] G. Parry, *The Arts of the Anglican Counter-Reformation: Glory, Laud and Honour* (Woodbridge, 2006), pp. 59–76.

FIGURE 6.3 East window, Lincoln College chapel, *c.*1630. Painted by Abraham van Linge, the window exemplified Oxford's commitment to the 'beauty of holiness' movement in the Laudian era. The upper half of the window depicts scenes from the life of Christ centred on the crucifixion and resurrection, the lower half scenes from the Old Testament in which they were prefigured.

munificence of Laud. But the real revolution began in 1629 when Lincoln decided to build a completely new chapel and deck it out in the new fashion, entrusting the task of providing the painted glass for the windows to Bernard's brother, Abraham (see Figure 6.3). The work was paid for by the visitor, Bishop John Williams, who was no lover of Laud but shared his ideal of the beauty of holiness. Lincoln Chapel set the standard. In the course of the 1630s, the Van Linge brothers provided painted glass for the chapels of Balliol, Queen's, Christ Church, and University College (where the chapel was completely rebuilt in the late 1630s as part of the new quad). Only Magdalen, which commissioned a new organ in addition to the usual embellishments, used a different artist. When the college, as part of its refurbishment programme, overseen and largely paid for by Frewen, decided to reglaze its windows in 1637, it gave the commission to Richard Greenbury, whose pièce de résistance was his painting of the Last Judgement in the great west window.[38]

---

[38] In the 1630s Magdalen also revived its choral tradition, largely supine since the Reformation.

Laud's influence at Oxford, however, waned swiftly once Charles I was forced to place himself in the hands of the Long Parliament, which met in November 1640 following the king's defeat by the Scots, who had been so incensed by the extension of Laudian reform to their own Calvinist church that they had taken up arms.[39] Most members of both houses were unhappy with Laud's stewardship of the church, and even those, such as Edward Hyde, future earl of Clarendon, who had some sympathy for the 'beauty of holiness' programme, were antagonized by the Laudians' support for divine right absolutism and their desire to free the church from gentry control. Laud and like-minded bishops were therefore imprisoned, and many MPs and their London allies began to embrace demands for radical religious reform and cast aspersions on Oxford's protestant integrity. This immediately revitalized the University's anti-Laudians. Even before the Long Parliament met, Oxford's Calvinists had reasserted themselves. As early as 6 September 1640, Henry Wilkinson, a member of Magdalen Hall and John's cousin, had made his views of the liturgical changes crystal clear in a sermon in which he accused the Laudians of 'inclining to favour Romish superstitions' and encouraging religious hypocrisy:

> These lukewarm Men can be content to afford Christ a cap and a knee, but they will not give him their heart, nay they are very scrupulous in mint and rue, and very exact in the Ceremony; and (as if Religion were a Comedy) they will in voyce, and gesture act divine duties, though in their hearts they renounce; and in their lives deny the parts they play.[40]

Once the parliament was in session, the Oxford Laudians were on the back foot. The heads of house, Laudians and non-Laudians, had the stomach to defend themselves collectively against the wild accusation that they allowed mass to be said in the University. But they anticipated a religious reaction and began to backtrack: in April 1641, Magdalen and Queen's repositioned the communion table in the body of the choir. Two months later, the reaction duly arrived. Laud voluntarily laid down his chancellorship and was replaced by one of his vocal critics, Philip Herbert, earl of Pembroke, brother of his predecessor, who appointed as his Vice-Chancellor the long-standing puritan opponent of the archbishop, John Prideaux. Thereafter, the Laudian experiment might have been quickly brought to an end, had not Charles made Oxford his headquarters during the ensuing Civil War. While Cambridge, in the heart of parliament's Eastern Association, was quickly purged of its more limited Laudian innovations, the presence of the king and his court in Oxford colleges from October 1642 gave the anti-Calvinists a new lease of life.[41]

---

[39] The king summoned parliament to obtain the money he needed to pay off the Scottish army encamped in the north. It was called the Long Parliament because it sat until 1653 rather than for the customary couple of months. In 1641, the king agreed that it could sit until it dissolved itself.

[40] H. Wilkinson, *A Sermon against Lukewarmenesse in Religion: Preached at St Maries in Oxford, the Sixt of September 1640* (London, 1641), p. 11.

[41] Frewen of Magdalen was rewarded for his steadfastness and made archbishop of York in 1644.

Indeed, they had the field to themselves, as hard-line Calvinists, such as the Wilkinsons and Christopher Rogers, prudently withdrew. Colleges that had held out against the Laudian tide in the 1630s were made to pay for their temerity. Puritan Merton, whose warden, Nathaniel Brent, was another to decamp, was turned over to the catholic queen and her entourage, and had to suffer the indignity of mass being said within its walls in earnest.

The failure to dislodge the Arminians in the early 1640s guaranteed that the Oxford Calvinists' revenge would be swift once the king surrendered in 1646. In the interim, parliament's position on the religious question had clarified. In August 1643 it had outlawed all Laudian innovations by ordering that all altars and altar rails be demolished, all candlesticks removed from the communion table (which was no longer to be placed at the east end of the chancel), and all crucifixes and images or paintings of the saints and persons of the Trinity taken away. The following year, in May, it repeated the order about images, demanded that chancel pavements be levelled, and called for the removal of organs. By then, moreover, parliament was committed to establishing a presbyterian system of church government, once victorious, as the price that had to be paid for getting the Scots to enter the war on its side. Charles' defeat therefore signalled the dawn of a new religious era. By late 1646, most of the surviving Calvinist exiles were back and in their former positions, and one of their number, Francis Cheynell of Merton, who had been deprived of his fellowship in 1638 for refusing to bow to the altar, was entrusted with the task of using the University's press to wage a propaganda campaign in favour of presbyterianism. Doubtless aware that propaganda alone would have a limited effect, parliament, the following May, set up a commission to root out supporters of episcopacy and implement its religious decrees. Its membership was dominated by the former exiles. Headed by Warden Brent, now back in harness, the commission included Cheynell, another fellow of Merton, and the two Wilkinsons. Appropriately, when the commission finally met in Oxford in May 1648, Merton became its headquarters.

The commission's first act was to summon before it the 400 or so college foundationers and university postholders, and identify those who had not or would not subscribe to the Solemn League and Covenant, a document originally penned by the Scots in their quarrel with Charles in the late 1630s proclaiming loyalty to a presbyterian church. Only forty-five of the 379 summoned actually swore to uphold the Covenant, and many called before the committee had already left Oxford and did not appear. But the committee was surprisingly lenient and only half of the foundationers and postholders were deprived. Corpus, Wadham, and St John's suffered heavily, but a majority of Christ Church's fellows survived despite the college being viewed as particularly delinquent. As the case of the future antiquarian Anthony Wood reveals, stubbornness could be easily forgiven if a family had contacts. Wood was a Merton postmaster who refused to submit to the parliamentary visitors but kept his place thanks to his mother, who knew the warden and chief commissioner:

At length by the intercession of his mother made to Sir Nathaniel Brent (who usually cal'd her his little daughter, for he knew her, and us'd to set her on his knee when she was a girle and a sojourner in her husband's house during the time of his first wife) he was conniv'd at and kept in his place, otherwise he had infallibly gone to the pot.[42]

Initially, moreover, the commissioners did not attempt to replace all those excluded. In the summer of 1648, fifteen heads of house were intruded but only 128 fellows. Many of the new incumbents were found among former members of the two halls who had kept the puritan faith in the 1630s. Rogers was made a canon of Christ Church, John Wilkinson president of Magdalen, and cousin Henry a fellow. Others were parachuted in from puritan Cambridge. At most colleges, the intruded heads of house were barred from entry and the gate had to be broken down to gain admittance. At Christ Church, since the royalist dean, Samuel Fell, was already in custody in London, it was left to his wife to show resistance. She refused to leave her room when the commissioners arrived and had to be carried out of the college still sitting in her chair.[43]

The commission sat until 1652, principally ensuring that vacant fellowships and scholarships were filled with the godly and rusticating the occasional malefactor.[44] From the autumn of 1648, however, it lost its presbyterian *raison d'être* when protestants, whose power base was the parliamentary army and who favoured a more flexible and localist Calvinist church, seized power and put the king on trial for fomenting a second Civil War. A few more expulsions followed the execution of Charles I in January 1649 when the commissioners administered a second oath— this time to the new Republic.[45] But on this occasion there was no wholesale replacement of presbyterians by 'independents', as supporters of a decentralized church were called. Oliver Cromwell, the dominant figure in parliament and the army in the first years of the new state, and its head from 1653, was anxious to spare the University from further upheaval, so prominent presbyterians, such as Conant of Exeter, survived throughout the 1650s.[46] Independents, though, set the tone. Cromwell became Chancellor in 1651 and he appointed his like-minded chaplain, John Owen, formerly of Queen's, to the deanery of Christ Church to serve as his deputy. As Vice-Chancellor and member of a new government commission, established in 1653 and remodelled the following year to give it teeth, Owen struggled for six years to turn Oxford into a godly Calvinist commonwealth, ably assisted by Wilkinson's successor as president of Magdalen, the Cambridge-educated Thomas Goodwin. Owen identified several enemies who threatened his

[42] Wood, *Life*, i. 144.   [43] Wood, *History*, ii. 563–4.
[11] With the episcopacy abolished, most colleges no longer had a visitor to watch over discipline. One fellow removed for wrongdoing at Merton was Wood's brother, Edward: ibid., i. 166–7.
[45] The most significant casualty of this second purge was Brent of Merton.
[46] For the first years of the Republic, sovereignty lay with the Long Parliament, now known as the Rump because the monarchists in its midst had been purged by the army. But in 1653, the Rump was forcibly dissolved by the army's commander, Oliver Cromwell, who seized power later in the year and inaugurated the quasi-monarchical Protectorate, which lasted until 1659 when his son, Richard, was encouraged to stand down by the army's council of officers.

vision of the New Jerusalem. Protestant Europe, in his view, was awash with Arminians and Socinians whose ambitions had to be thwarted, while protestant England was assailed by sectarians who wanted an end to all forms of religious establishment.[47] Oxford, he believed, could play its part in defeating the twin threats by improving the scholars' behaviour and religious observance, and by subjecting the colleges to university control so that teaching could be more effectively organized and dissidents rooted out. He had some success with the former but the latter defeated him and he resigned in 1657, to be replaced not by a fellow independent but by the more consensual presbyterian Conant.

The continual independence of the colleges, despite the watchful presence of a series of university commissions, helps to explain why many of the embellishments to the college chapels in the Laudian era survived the radical decade. The fellows, presbyterians, independents, or fellow travellers, kept destruction to the minimum, whatever the views of the heads of house. At Magdalen some of the hangings at the east end seem to have been destroyed in either 1649 or 1651, but Greenbury's painted glass in the chancel and antechapel was spared, except for the image of Christ in the great west window.[48] Even the organ survived for many years, as the diarist John Evelyn, a product of Balliol, noted when he visited the college in 1654:

> Next we walked to Magdalen College: where we saw the Library and Chapell, which was likewise in pontifical order, the Altar onely I think turn'd Table-wise: and there was still the double Organ, which abominations (as now esteem'd) were almost universally demolish'd.[49]

Several colleges, too, as Owen must have been aware, continued to shelter royalists and episcopalians. Some were even to be found at Christ Church, presumably to the Vice-Chancellor's despair. But the favourite haunt of the malignant was Wadham. Wadham's warden in the 1650s was John Wilkins, an intruded head but a royalist sympathizer, despite being Cromwell's son-in-law. He went out of his way to attract undergraduates from all backgrounds, and both he and five of the fellows of his day would become bishops at the Restoration. Protestants who supported the 1559 Settlement were also to be found in the city, where several Oxford graduates had set up in medical practice, having chosen to study medicine rather than theology so as to avoid the need to seek ordination in an alien church. The most important member of this group was the physiologist and former undergraduate of Christ Church Thomas Willis, later Sedley professor of natural philosophy, who, in the 1650s, lived at Beam

---

[47] Oxford was the home of the notorious sectarians Reeve and Muggleton, who were tailors; the Quakers were there from 1654: see Wood, *Life*, i. 177 and 190–1. Numerous sectarian groups, whose leaders sometimes claimed to have had a new divine revelation, had sprung up in the 1640s as the mechanisms of ecclesiastical control atrophied during the Civil War. Cromwell tolerated the sects but did not like them. See Christopher Hill, *The World Turned Upside Down: Radical Ideas during the English Revolution* (Harmondsworth, 1991).

[48] The image of the devil survived: see Wood, *Life*, i. 161. For the level of destruction in these years in the colleges generally, see J. Spraggon, *Puritan Iconoclasm during the English Civil War* (Woodbridge, 2003).

[49] *The Diary of John Evelyn*, ed. E. S. de Beer (6 vols; Oxford, 1995), iii. 109. The organ was eventually taken away to Hampton Court.

Hall in Merton Street. Willis' medical practice was a cover for an Anglican cell. His house was home to several ejected Christ Church fellows, including John Fell, son of Samuel, who between them kept up the forbidden offices of the Elizabethan church day by day, purportedly attracting on Sundays a congregation of 300.

Royalism and episcopalianism seems to have struck a chord with the younger undergraduates, and as the Republican regime began to untangle after Cromwell's death in 1658, the dissidents became more visible in the University. By the Restoration in May 1660, heads with royalist and episcopalian sympathies had been successfully elected at four Oxford colleges: Queen's, New, Wadham (after Wilkins demitted in September 1659), and Trinity. In the last case, the successful candidate was an outsider, Seth Ward, later bishop of Salisbury. A loyalist refugee from Cambridge, who had been expelled for not taking the Solemn League and Covenant in 1644, Ward had resided at Wadham under Wilkins, and would have become principal of Jesus in 1657 had his election not been squashed by Cromwell. Two years later he was unanimously elected president of Trinity, his election engineered by his close friend, fellow Anglican and practising physician Ralph Bathurst (who would succeed Ward the following year). Other episcopalians were back in place by the time Charles II landed, notably John Oliver of Magdalen, elected president in 1644, expelled in 1648, then restored by the Convention Parliament a fortnight before the king returned.[50]

C. The Anglican Seminary

The Convention Parliament, which met at the beginning of 1660, had been summoned by the Republic's de facto ruler, General Monck, on the assumption it would oversee the country's return to a monarchy.[51] Although the MPs were keen to see the back of the Interregnum and military rule, they were generally from families who had fought against the king in the Civil War and were largely moderate puritans. Given the religious mood of the Convention, Charles II seems to have assumed that the price of his restoration would be a presbyterian church settlement. In the event, the parliament he called on his return, which, for the first time since 1640, was elected by the whole political nation, was dominated by hard-line episcopalians who wanted to put the clock back.[52] The settlement, passed into law by the Act of Uniformity of May 1662, restored the church of 1559 with a few minor alterations. It was not Laudian in that the liturgy did not specifically promote

---

[50] Another head of house, Robert Saye of Oriel, showed his conversion to royalism the year before the Restoration by allowing local Cavalier gentry to use his lodgings to plot an aborted military uprising.

[51] The Convention Parliament, so-called because it had not been summoned by the crown, met on 25 April 1660 with a mandate to solve the political crisis caused by Oliver Cromwell's death. Its convocation had been made possible by Monck, Cromwell's commander in Scotland, marching south, putting an end to the military rule that had eventually supplanted the Protectorate, recalling the Rump, and getting it to vote for its dissolution and issue writs for a new parliament.

[52] Royalists were banned from voting in the elections for the various assemblies called in the 1650s after Cromwell's dismissal of the Rump, including the Convention.

the 'beauty of holiness' and the new church remained theologically Calvinist and decoratively austere. But Laudians were comprehended within the episcopalian settlement in a way that other protestants, including presbyterians, were deliberately not. The existence, in the future, of a section of the protestant population who would not attend the national church was acknowledged: non-conformist protestants were not to be subject to recusancy fines, unlike residual catholics. But the Cavalier Parliament (as it was called) made clear in subsequent legislation that opponents of episcopacy would be wise to conform: above all, in the 1670s, by passing the Test Acts it made taking communion in the Anglican church essential for holding any secular office.[53]

The re-establishment of the old Church of England meant that the religious reliability of the two universities had to be once more put to the test, and every member in residence was asked to submit to the new Act of Uniformity in the summer of 1662. This time, though, Oxford suffered few casualties: only three heads of house (Conant, Rogers, and Henry Wilkinson Junior of Magdalen Hall), four fellows, seven graduates and undergraduates refused and were asked to leave.[54] This was because the University had already been effectively purged by a commission Charles II had appointed almost immediately on his succession to investigate the legal position of incumbent foundationers and postholders. Its task had been to search out and remove any member of the University whose position had been obtained at the expense of another. The latter, if still alive and eligible to hold the position (many ex-fellows had married in the interim), was restored to his office; otherwise the position was declared vacant. As a result, eleven college heads and thirty-nine fellows had already left before the new Act of Uniformity came into law in August.[55] The purge at the Restoration was thus still dramatic even if the headcount was comparatively low. Except for the odd survivor, notably Paul Hood of Lincoln, who had managed to keep his place through every change of regime since 1621, the Hebdomadal Board was now in the hands of a new generation who had grown up during the Civil War and the Interregnum on the losing side and was ardently royalist.[56]

The re-emergence of Oxford as a bastion of episcopalian protestantism, however, did not put an end to old quarrels. The restored church was officially Calvinist but Arminians remained powerful within the hierarchy, and one of their number, the Oxonian Gilbert Sheldon, held the see of Canterbury. Oxford itself was split into two theological camps. The Calvinists were led by Thomas Barlow, the royalist head of Queen's, elected in 1657, who held the Lady Margaret chair of divinity and taught that baptism did not wash away original sin. The Arminians' champion was John Fell,

---

[53] Ian Green, *The Re-establishment of the Church of England, 1660–1663* (Oxford, 1978); John Spurr, *The Restoration of the Church of England, 1646–1689* (London, 1991).

[54] Henry Wilkinson was John Wilkinson's nephew.

[55] The commission's minutes are published in F. J. Varley (ed.), 'The Restoration Visitation of the University of Oxford and its Colleges', *Camden Miscellany*, 18 (London, 1948), last item of 3, separately paginated. Among undergraduates who left before the passage of the Act of Uniformity was the future Quaker William Penn, an undergraduate at Christ Church.

[56] Hood governed Lincoln from 1621 to 1668.

dean of Christ Church from 1662, who, even before taking up his office, had played an important part in restoring choral services to the cathedral, placing the communion table altar-wise and decorating it with flagons and plate, and introducing bowing at the name of Jesus, as the Laudians had earlier desired. Nonetheless, the two sides lived amicably together and both were free to promote their liturgical traditions.[57] The new regius professor of divinity, Richard Allestree, set the tone. Though an Arminian put into the chair by Sheldon to counter the Calvinist influence, he concentrated on relieving possible tension by avoiding thorny theological questions. Charles II, in October 1662, had repeated his father's injunction that predestination was not to be disputed in the universities and Oxford was happy to oblige. Throughout his reign, Oxford divines, in their theses, tracts, and sermons, targeted catholics and protestant dissenters rather than each other. There was a shared commitment to building the restored church around the Bible and the 1662 prayer book, and a growing emphasis on promoting practical religion rather than religious debate.

The University was also united in its royalism. Charles II strained its loyalty on two occasions when he attempted to remove the restrictions on non-conformist protestants by royal edict. But when the right of his brother James to inherit the throne was questioned by the conforming wing of the old parliamentary cause in the late 1670s on the grounds he was a declared catholic, the Anglican University rallied behind the monarch, all the more because the dons suspected that the exclusionists would next target the church.[58] It was no coincidence that the 1681 parliament that eventually scotched the attempt to disinherit James was held at Oxford. Two years later, when James himself visited the University to open the Ashmolean, he was greeted with enthusiasm, while the subsequent attempt on the king's life (the Rye House Plot) led to Convocation passing a decree emphasizing the inviolability of royalty. Professors, tutors, and catechists were to teach submission and obedience, and members of the University were forbidden to read books that preached resistance.[59] Moreover, any books of this kind that existed in the University were ordered to be sought out and burnt. A few days after the decree's passage, works by Thomas Hobbes, an Oxonian long suspected of atheism for his godless *Leviathan*, the puritan poet John Milton, defender of the Republic, and the Jesuit Robert Bellarmine, an apologist for the pope's right to depose secular rulers, were consumed by flames in the Bodleian quadrangle.[60]

---

[57] Calvinist Exeter, for instance, stolidly refused to place its communion table at the east end, and Pembroke had no chapel.

[58] It was at this moment that the terms Whig and Tory were spawned.

[59] *Judicium et decretum universitatis oxoniensis, latum in convocatione habita julii 21 an 1683, contra quosdam perniciosos libros et propositiones impias* (Oxford, 1683).

[60] Hobbes had been at Magdalen Hall in the early seventeenth century. His *Leviathan* (1651) rejected absolute morality and saw restraints on the will as useful conventions. Sovereign governmental power was based on its utility for maintaining social peace. Bellarmine's most notorious work was his *Tractatus de potestate summi pontificis in rebus temporalibus* (1610).

However, when James inherited the throne in 1685, the mood swiftly changed. James' intentions remain a subject of historical debate. He may have ultimately intended to replace Anglicanism by Roman Catholicism as the established religion of his lands, or he may simply have wanted to give his fellow catholics freedom of worship and the right to a civic life. What is certain is that his actions during the first two years of his short reign, when he dispensed individual catholics from the recusancy laws so that they could hold office, then issued a Declaration of Indulgence in April 1687 allowing non-Anglicans to worship openly, terrified his protestant subjects of all persuasions.[61] The first indication that the king was bent on undermining Oxford's confessional integrity came in March 1686. The master of University College, Obadiah Walker, had long harboured misgivings about Anglicanism. When he finally declared his conversion to Roman Catholicism, James obligingly exempted him from attending Anglican services. Walker's conversion hit Oxford hard, especially as he took a handful of fellows with him. When, in May, James permitted him to retain the mastership and gave him a licence to print specified catholic works, the University was scandalized. Worse was to follow. Walker had already created a private catholic chapel in his lodgings. In August, the king allowed Walker to use any rooms in the college for the purpose and the chapel was opened for public worship. A Jesuit was brought in to conduct mass, and catholic children began to haunt the college.

University College took the blow on the chin and, in February 1687, the fellows demonstrated their continual loyalty by putting up a statue of the king in the quadrangle. Emboldened, James moved to introduce catholics into other colleges. Dean Fell of Christ Church died in the summer of 1686, and in the following December the king appointed a fellow of Merton, John Massey, in his place. But Massey, who had been Walker's pupil in his youth, shared his tutor's religious misgivings and quickly announced his own conversion to Roman Catholicism. The largest college in Oxford now appeared to be in the royal pocket. James' next target was another large foundation, Magdalen.[62] On the death of President Henry Clerke in March 1687, the king demanded that the fellows appoint one Anthony Farmer, a catholic, in his stead. The fellows, however, refused and elected one of their own, John Hough. Faced by intransigence, James had to move more carefully. He declared Hough's election void, but in August compromised and offered the college a more suitable candidate in Samuel Parker, bishop of Oxford, a former student of Wadham and Trinity. The fellows still demurred, so Parker was admitted by force. When the college then refused to apologize for defying the king, the fellows and demies were summoned one by one to submit before royal commissioners sent to Oxford the following November (see Figure 6.4). Only three did so. The rest were expelled and debarred from all ecclesiastical preferment. The king now had a free hand to

---

[61] Even non-conformists, who benefited from the Declaration of Indulgence. The standard history is J. Miller, *James II: A Study in Kingship* (Hove, 1978).

[62] L. W. B. Brockliss, G. L. Harriss, and A. D. Macintyre, *Magdalen College and the Crown, Essays for the Tercentenary of the Restoration of the College 1688* (Oxford, 1988), esp. ch. 1.

FIGURE 6.4 *Expulsion of the President and Fellows of Magdalen College, 1687*: painting by Joseph Tonneau, 1884. James II's removal of the fellows for refusing to accept the bishop of Oxford as their head of house was seen as an attack on property rights. When James subsequently imposed a catholic head, his action was seen as part of his campaign to undermine English protestantism. Tonneau's painting depicts the scene in the college hall when the fellows' preferred candidate, Hough, is expelled by the king's commissioners led by the bishop of Chester.

bend the college to his will. In the coming months, James filled up the fellowship with a mix of catholics and malleable Anglicans, and in March 1688, when Parker conveniently died, he was replaced by a catholic, Bonaventure Giffard, who held a doctorate from the University of Paris. With Giffard in charge, the chapel became a centre of catholic worship.

Why Magdalen chose to stand up to James initially is understandable. Farmer was not only a catholic but a man with a tarnished reputation. Why the fellows opposed Parker as the compromise choice remains difficult to understand. Although the bishop of Oxford was ineligible under the statutes, in that he was not a Magdalen fellow, he was no papist and the college had always been happy to accept royal nominees before. Moreover, just like the majority of Magdalen's fellows, he was a keen supporter of the Anglican monopoly and was hostile to any move to accommodate the tender conscience of non-conformists.[63] Whatever the reason, the

---

[63] See his *A Discourse of Ecclesiastical Politie* (1669). On Parker's broader political and religious thought, see Jon Parkin, *Taming the Leviathan: The Reception of the Political and Religious Ideas of Thomas Hobbes in England, 1640–1700* (Cambridge, 2007).

consequence of the fellows' decision to elect and stand by Hough was momentous. By refusing to accept James' orders and being expelled for their temerity, the fellows, somewhat bizarrely, became national martyrs for the cause of the Anglican church at a time when it felt under attack. Their high-handed treatment and the subsequent developments in the college provided graphic copy for the growing number of Anglican pamphleteers both inside and outside the University. The centre of the Oxford campaign was Christ Church, where the canons, led by the sub-dean Henry Aldrich, had challenged Massey's appointment by indicting him for recusancy before the court of King's Bench in January 1687. When the manoeuvre inevitably failed, Aldrich and his friends took to anonymously waging a propaganda war in defence of protestantism and the national church, adding Oxford's weight to the flood of anti-catholic literature being published in the capital under the patronage of the erstwhile college canon Henry Compton, bishop of London.

Magdalen's ousted fellows were restored by the king one year later on 25 October 1688. What softened the royal anger was not the war of words but the imminent invasion of William of Orange, which led to James' overthrow and the confirmation of Anglicanism as the national church. However, the events of 1686–8 were a significant moment in the University's history. The royalist and Anglican University established at the Restoration had had to make a choice and it had chosen Anglicanism. *Pace* the 1683 decree, members of the University had resisted the lawful monarch, even if they had not taken up arms against him. And church continued to be placed before state thereafter. At the beginning of his reign, William hoped that the church, through its own parliament—which, since the Reformation, met by convention at the same time as the Lords and Commons—would adjust the 1662 settlement to allow protestant dissenters to be comprehended as a reward for joining Anglicans in opposition to James. The Oxford-educated clerics in its lower house, however, defeated the scheme.[64] William had to make do with passing through parliament the Act of Toleration, which gave protestant non-conformists the right to worship openly but left them still subject to the Test Acts, so unable to hold state or civic office. On the other hand, Oxford had little problem in accepting William and Mary as king and queen despite the fact that James was alive in France and now had a male heir. When Oxford's foundationers and postholders were asked to swear allegiance to the new monarchs, only seven fellows refused.

Admittedly, most English Tories found it easy to accept William and Mary, and all were enamoured of Anne when she eventually succeeded in 1702. James had forsaken his duty by running away to the continent and there was doubt over the legitimacy of the baby Prince of Wales.[65] But Oxford continued to show scant regard for the claims of the exiled Stuarts once parliament, in 1701, had responded to

[64] From the sixteenth century, the provinces of Canterbury and York no longer held separate convocations. The convocation of the Church of England had an upper house of bishops and a lower house elected from the diocesan clergy.

[65] Prince James, born in 1688, was rumoured to be a changeling, smuggled into the birth chamber in a warming pan.

Anne's childlessness by ignoring the hereditary line of succession and bestowing the crown on a distant protestant relative of the royal family, Sophia of Hanover. The only vocal Jacobite in the University in Anne's reign was the Magdalen fellow Henry Sacheverell, who made a name for himself in the mid-1700s preaching a series of sermons in Oxford attacking catholics, dissenters, and all who attempted to subvert the church's constitution. In one entitled 'In Perils against False Brethren', he also questioned the legitimacy of the Williamite invasion. When he repeated the sermon in St Paul's Cathedral in 1709, the Whig-dominated government of the day took umbrage and had him impeached for high crimes and misdemeanours before the House of Lords the following year. Sacheverell escaped with the lightest of penalties—he was merely banned from preaching for three years. But he owed his deliverance to the London Tory mob not his University, which practically disowned him. His own college did little more than prepare a testimonial on his behalf.[66] Not surprisingly then, when Sophia's son ascended the throne in 1714 as George I, there were once more few postholders and foundationers who refused to take an oath of loyalty to the new king when this was again demanded—the most notorious casualty being Bodleian's deputy librarian, Thomas Hearne of St Edmund Hall.[67]

There was no reason, therefore, to suspect Oxford of being viscerally anti-Hanoverian on George's accession. That many junior and senior members openly displayed Jacobite leanings even after the terminal defeat of the Stuart cause at the Battle of Culloden in 1746 can be chiefly put down to the political dominance of the Whigs under the new dynasty, which exacerbated long-standing differences within the national church. Anglicans from the Restoration had been divided between the orthodox or high-church majority who believed that the 1662 Restoration Settlement had established God's true church, and the latitudinarian or broad-church minority who were suspicious of dogmatism and looked to bring dissenting protestants within the fold or at least to offer them toleration.[68] In the reigns of William and Anne, broad-church Anglicans were to be found in several Oxford colleges, notably Pembroke, Oriel, Wadham, and Merton (still sporting its pre-Civil War colours). But the large majority of Oxford dons and students were always firmly in the camp of the orthodox.[69] The elevation of the Whigs to permanent power was, in consequence, a professional disaster for Oxford's high churchmen. As latitudinarians inevitably monopolized the plum jobs, there was little chance of an Oxonian gaining a bishop's mitre. Moreover, as Cambridge dons were much

---

[66] Geoffrey Holmes, *The Trial of Doctor Sacheverell* (London, 1973).

[67] Hearne continued to live in St Edmund Hall, and his diary, which runs from 1705 to 1735, is the best extant source for everyday life in early eighteenth-century Oxford. Hearne never formally demitted his office, nor was he sacked—he just no longer turned up to perform the duties relating to the office after he had refused to take the oath: see Hearne, v. 135–40 and 283–4.

[68] High church was a term invented by the dissenter Richard Baxter in 1650. On the problems of labelling, see P.B. Nockles, 'Church Parties in Pre-Tractarian Church of England 1750–1833', in John Walsh, Colin Haydon, and Stephen Taylor (eds), *Church of England c.1689–1833: From Toleration to Tractarianism* (Cambridge, 1993), pp. 334–59.

[69] The most famous broad church Oxonian at the turn of the eighteenth century was actually a fellow of Magdalen, the future editor of the *Spectator*, Joseph Addison.

more adaptable, the higher echelons of the church came to be dominated by graduates of Oxford's rival. Fellows in some Oxford colleges gradually came round to the new reality. Christ Church and Exeter both gained a reputation for whiggery and reaped the reward in patronage. But the majority of Oxford masters refused to bend before the broad-church wind, and found themselves ostracized.[70]

Even worse, as far as the steadfast majority was concerned, the Whigs were happy to promote latitudinarians, such as the Cambridge-educated Benjamin Hoadley, who appeared to be scarcely Christians at all in that they believed all dogmas should be tested on the anvil of reason and irrational ideas such as the Trinity discarded. Christian rationalists had first become an identifiable coterie in the national church in the 1690s when several anti-Trinitarians committed their ideas to print, including John Locke, previously a fellow of Christ Church and anonymous author of the 1689 *Two Treatises of Government*, which defended the people's right to overthrow a tyrant.[71] The University was scandalized, and in the reigns of William and Anne waged war both against those who questioned fundamental Christian dogmas and those who supported the abolition of the Licensing Act in 1696, which essentially put an end to censorship. The first anti-Trinitarian to be found in the University's midst was Arthur Bury, rector of Exeter, who was uncovered in 1690 and quickly removed. The second, Matthew Tindal, fellow of All Souls from 1678, whose *Rights of the Christian Church Asserted* was burnt on order of the House of Commons in 1710, proved impossible to dislodge. Thanks to government protection, Tindal survived at All Souls until his death in 1733, churning out a string of deistic pamphlets.[72] To many at Oxford during the reigns of the first two Georges, unaware that Whigs like Walpole were too politically astute to risk a major confrontation, it looked as if it were only a matter of time before the 1662 Settlement was completely unpicked.

Oxford's hostility to any move to weaken the 1662 Settlement meant that even Tory reformers received short shrift. Within the University, the most serious challenge to the religious status quo in the eighteenth century came not from the deists, who were largely an external threat, but the Wesleyans. John and Charles Wesley were the sons of a Lincolnshire rural rector and came up to Christ Church in the early 1720s. In 1726, John became a fellow of Lincoln, partly through the good offices of his father, and three years later was asked by the rector to act as a college tutor (see Figure 6.5). Both brothers thought Anglicanism should become a more active and demanding faith, and at the beginning of the 1730s joined together with a handful of like-minded souls to form an inchoate religious society. The Holy Club, as it was christened, promoted early rising, dedication to study, fasting, frequent communion, and good works that included visiting prisoners in the Castle gaol.

---

[70] In 1745, only five heads of house and senior university figures signed the association pledging to defend the dynasty to the death. Exeter was the alma mater of Archbishop Thomas Secker of Canterbury, who had been initially trained for the dissenting ministry.

[71] E.g. John Locke, *Reasonableness of Christianity* (1695). Locke had been expelled from Christ Church in 1683 because of his association with the Rye House Plot against Charles II.

[72] E.g. *Christianity as old as the Creation* (1730).

FIGURE 6.5 Portrait of John Wesley as a young man: anon., early 1730s? In the first half of the 1730s Wesley was a fellow of Lincoln and conscientious tutor. The portrait depicts him with his books, a sensitive scholar rather than a tub-thumping evangelist.

Some of the club's religious practices were redolent of catholic piety, but the Wesleys and their friends initially caused little stir. Nonetheless, the long-serving rector of Lincoln, Euseby Isham, became worried when John appeared to be exercising undue spiritual influence over his tutorial pupils, and gradually eased him out of his office. Discouraged, John and Charles, who was still in Christ Church, took ship for Georgia in December 1734 with the intention of converting the Native Americans.[73] John never resided in Oxford again, but he retained his fellowship until his marriage in 1751, and on his return from the colonies preached on and off when required in St Mary's.[74] His sermons were memorable occasions and he was nicknamed 'the methodist' because of their uncompromising tone.

After a conversion experience in the late 1730s, Wesley became convinced mankind could be saved only by the redeeming power of Christ's sacrifice and that works counted for nothing. But he was equally sure that those who had truly accepted the gift of faith would want to express their inner transformation in their outward lives. In consequence, the faithful had to be urged to repent before it was too late, including the faithful of his alma mater. Eighteenth-century

---

[73] V.H.H. Green, *The Young Mr Wesley, a Study of John Wesley and Oxford* (London, 1961).
[74] Fellows in orders had to take turns giving sermons in St Mary's.

Oxford was not a particularly godless community, but the dons liked to drink, many undergraduates idled away their days, and chapel attendance was often neglected or perfunctory. Wesley's sermons were intended to rouse the University from its spiritual torpor and he pulled no punches. On 24 August 1744, he overstepped the mark and, in an excoriating address in St Mary's, accused the whole University of sloth and debauchery, as the All Soul's lawyer, William Blackstone, revealed in a letter four days later:

> We were last Friday entertained at St. Mary's by a curious sermon from Wesley the Methodist. Among equally modest particulars he informed us, 1st that there was not one Christian among all the Heads of Houses, 2ndly, that pride, gluttony, avarice, luxury, sensuality and drunkenness were the general characteristics of all Fellows of Colleges, who were useless to a proverbial uselessness. Lastly, that the younger part of the University were a generation of triflers, all of them perjured, and not one of them of any religion at all.[75]

Many in the University were convinced that the earnest young don had become a puritan fanatic: theologians who overemphasized the heart were as bad as Socinians and deists who privileged the place of reason. Wesley never preached in St Mary's again and his intemperance coloured the University's attitude towards his future Oxford disciples. With the Wesleys' departure to the colonies, the Holy Club had broken up. But in the coming decades, as John's evangelical message struck a deepening chord in the church, especially among the young, the number of his Oxford followers began to grow. To many in the University the Wesleyans were a boil that had to be lanced: the movement's penchant for open-air revivalist meetings addressed by unlicensed preachers was only further evidence of its subversive intent. The Oxford Wesleyans therefore had to tread carefully. Those with evangelical sympathies were denied fellowships, sneered at when preached, occasionally pelted with stones, and sometimes rusticated. This was the fate which befell a group at St Edmund Hall in 1768. Seven members of the hall had become accustomed to attending Bible readings in the city in the house of a Mrs Durbridge. Nearly all were of modest extraction and they were known associates of leading evangelicals outside the city, such as the future anti-slavery campaigner John Newton, curate of Olney. Wesleyans were loathed by the hall's vice-principal and he denounced them as schismatic. Principal George Dixon, who in his youth had been associated with the Holy Club, would not touch them, but the Vice-Chancellor, as the hall's visitor, accepted the accusation, egged on by other college heads, and expelled them from the University. Figures within and without Oxford rallied to their side, notably President Thomas Fry of St John's, but without success. The Oxford Wesleyans' situation began to improve only in the 1780s, once their evangelical message found supporters within the religious and secular establishment and the more popular and

[75] Green, p. 349. For Blackstone and his commentaries on the common law, see p. 312, this volume. For the sinfulness of eighteenth-century Oxford, see pp. 268–70 and 289–93, this volume.

radical wing of the movement had started to take leave of Anglicanism altogether to set up the Methodist church. As a result, evangelicals eventually found space within the University as the century drew to a close, and laid the foundations for what became a distinctive 'low-church' presence at Oxford. Appropriately, in the first half of the nineteenth century, St Edmund Hall became their spiritual home. They were never particularly liked by the mainstream but they were welcomed aboard because they were virulently anti-catholic and anti-Socinian.[76]

D. Noetics, 'Drys', and Tractarians

Despite the Enlightenment critique of dogmatic Christianity and the long period of Whig political dominance, Oxford and Cambridge were still solidly confessional universities at the turn of the nineteenth century. Cambridge was the more open of the two, as subscription was demanded only of graduates, probably because pro-testantizing the university in Elizabeth's reign had proved an easier task. In addition, Cambridge had the more liberal air. In the reign of Charles II, it had been as Tory and religiously exclusive as Oxford, despite coming under parliamentary control at the beginning of the Civil War. From 1688, however, Cambridge was largely adminis-tered by Whig heads of house, and throughout the eighteenth century it was much more welcoming to the latitudinarians. Broadly speaking, it became the university of the liberal wing of the Church of England, and understandably the favoured child of the Hanoverians and their Whig ministers. But there was a limit to Cambridge's broadmindedness: it did not tolerate Socinians, and William Whiston, Newton's successor in the Lucasian chair of mathematics, was quickly shown the door in 1710 when he flaunted his anti-Trinitarian views too openly. Cambridge, moreover, seldom admitted non-conformists, for all its latitudinarian brio, for it too was a collegiate university and its colleges, just like their Oxford counterparts, expected their members to attend Anglican services in chapel.[77]

Both universities, then, were effectively closed, which is why protestant dissenters set up their own academies, as they were free to do under the Toleration Act of 1689. These purported to offer an equivalent education in the arts to the two traditional universities and occasionally engaged the services of talented minds, such as Joseph Priestley or Isaac Watts. But dotted around the country, frequently impermanent, and seldom attracting more than fifty students, they were hardly a threat to Oxford and Cambridge's monopoly of higher education in England and Wales in the eighteenth century. Their existence was rather a visible indictment of Oxford's and Cambridge's confessional narrowness. Even fellow protestants, who were theologically little different from the Anglican mainstream, used the

---

[76] In the 1830s, evangelicals were also present in numbers in Wadham. Elsewhere they tended to be isolated figures like Henry Bellenden Bulteel, fellow of Exeter in the 1820s, who eventually left the Church of England.

[77] John Gascoigne, *Cambridge in the Age of the Enlightenment: Science, Religion and Politics from the Restoration to the French Revolution* (Cambridge, 1989).

King James Bible, and venerated the same Marian martyrs, were unwelcome within their walls.[78]

In parliament, the representatives of the latitudinarian wing of the church first challenged subscription in the early 1770s. The MPs had some inside support at Cambridge where John Jebb (who later turned Unitarian) was a fierce proponent of change.[79] At Oxford, though, only one head of house, Hoare of Jesus, was in favour of abandoning the status quo. The most that the majority could accept was a modification of subscription that would allow matriculands simply to affirm they were members of the Church of England rather than swear approval of the Thirty-Nine Articles. But Convocation would have none of it and refused all compromise when the heads' proposals were debated on 4 February 1773, even though it was suspected that the University's new Chancellor, Prime Minister North, favoured some change. In the event, the move was also easily defeated in parliament the following year, where one of the University's long-serving Tory MPs, Sir Roger Newdigate, rallied the backwoodsmen in the Commons by raising the spectre of a new puritan revolution. Thereafter, the loss of the American colonies, closely followed by the French Revolution and the outbreak of the twenty-year war with France, put subscription on the parliamentary back burner for many years. The chaos unleashed across the Channel by the overthrow of the monarchy convinced all but the most radical Whigs in parliament that any change whatsoever to British institutions would result in anarchy. The king was particularly conservative and resolutely opposed any abridgement of the confessional state.

From the second half of the 1820s, however, in an era of liberal reform which affected virtually every area of society, subscription was once again on the agenda. The abolition of both the Test Acts and the penal laws against catholics in 1828–9 effectively put an end to the denominational state and immediately brought Oxford and Cambridge's confessional status into question. As early as 1834, a dissenting MP called George Wood put forward a bill to end subscription, which was followed a year later by a similar move in the Lords. This time the reformers could count on more support within the two universities. At Oxford, advocates of an end to subscription were chiefly to be found among the Noetics and their neo-Kantian successors. The first was a group of rationalist theologians in the 1820s and 1830s, principally associated with the Oriel Common Room, who took their cue from the eighteenth-century latitudinarian Bishop Joseph Butler, a former junior member of the college, and formed what became known as the broad-church party in the University.[80] While accepting much of the enlightenment critique of Christianity, they insisted that its core dogmas were empirically defensible and that the

---

[78] H. McLachlan, *English Education under the Test Acts: Being the History of the Nonconformist Academies, 1662–1820* (Manchester, 1931). For an idea of the dissenting academies' teaching, see Alan Sell, 'Philosophy in the Eighteenth-Century Dissenting Academies of England and Wales', *HU*, IX (1992), 75–122. For details on the academies and their teachers, see the ongoing database project, 'Dissenting Academies Online: Database and Encyclopedia', at <http://www.english.qmul.ac.uk/drwilliams/portal.html> (accessed 6 Nov. 2013).

[79] Searby, pp. 406–10. Cambridge undergraduates presented a petition calling for the end of subscription.

[80] Fellows had their own common room from the 1660s: see p. 288, this volume.

Bible could still be taken as true if read metaphorically rather than literally. Their number included Provost Edward Copleston, his long-serving successor Edward Hawkins, Richard Whately (later archbishop of Dublin), Thomas Arnold (until he left to become headmaster of Rugby), and Baden Powell, Savilian professor of geometry.[81] The second group emerged in the 1840s around figures like the young Balliol don Benjamin Jowett, elected to a fellowship in 1838. Rejecting any attempt to demonstrate the reasonableness of Christianity, they argued, like the German philosopher Kant and his followers in the German universities, that its truth value was a matter of simple faith and that the Bible should be treated as an ordinary text subject to the canons of literary and historical criticism. This being so, Oxford's insistence that the young subscribe to a series of articles that could not be rationally substantiated was nonsensical.[82]

The Noetics, in their heyday, were influential among the heads of house and the holders of chairs. Jowett and his friends, on the other hand, were initially more on the fringe. The Balliol fellow's existential view of Christianity fully came to the notice of the University only in 1855 when he published his commentary on the Pauline epistles. Neither group, however, was, in the slightest, representative of the University at large. Oxford's continued commitment to confessionalism was graphically emphasized in the 1829 by-election in the wake of catholic emancipation. Though the renegade Peel managed to poll a respectable 609 votes, his conservative opponent, Sir Robert Inglis, garnered 755 and roundly defeated the erstwhile member, thanks to the phalanx of Tory clerics, still on their colleges' books, who came up to Oxford in droves to register their disgust.[83] Peel's defeat only encouraged the Tory diehards to dig in their heels, and vehement opposition to ending subscription continued throughout the 1830s and 1840s. Much of this was a traditionalist riposte to a fast-changing era where Anglicanism seemed to be becoming marginalized. Always only the church of a small minority in Ireland, it was no longer the majority church even in England and Wales by 1850, thanks to the growth of non-conformity in the new industrialized cities. But Oxford's hostility to opening its doors to non-Anglicans also had its radical edge. Through the leadership the Tractarians brought to the opposition, Oxford's refusal to move with the times was enthusiastically embraced by the young as well as the superannuated. When Wood published his bill to abolish subscription, the protest petition drawn up by the University was signed not only by 1,900 of the 2,519

---

[81] General study: Richard Brent, *Liberal Anglican Politics: Whiggery, Religion and Reform* (Oxford, 1987). For Baden Powell's involvement, see Pietro Corsi, *Science and Religion: Baden Powell and the Anglican Debate, 1800–1860* (Cambridge, 1988).

[82] On similar developments in Cambridge, see Searby, pp. 357–77. Immanuel Kant held the philosophy chair at the University of Königsberg in the second half of the eighteenth century. His explorations of what is or is not rationally and completely knowable, in a series of works published across the 1780s, are sometimes seen as the culmination of the Enlightenment: see E. Cassirer, *The Philosophy of the Enlightenment* (Eng. trans., Boston, MA, 1964; original German edn, 1932).

[83] For the voting figures, see *An authentic copy of the poll for a member to serve in Parliament for the University of Oxford* (Oxford, 1829). For the background to the election, see p. 150, this volume.

members of Convocation, but also by 1,050 of the 1,200 undergraduates, and thousands of humble parishioners activated by their Oxford-educated parsons.[84]

The Tractarians also emerged from Oriel, but they had nothing in common with the Noetics beyond impatience with the pedestrian nature of Oxford high church-manship. Their leader, John Henry Newman, who had become a fellow of Oriel in 1822 after spending his undergraduate days in Trinity, came from an evangelical family and retained the evangelicals' earnestness. But evangelicals, as Gladstone found ten years later at Christ Church, were still looked down upon at Oxford, and Newman, perhaps in consequence, moved in the opposite direction.[85] What he and his supporters came to embrace was an Anglicanism that was both active in the community, especially among the poor, and radical in its devotional rituals. It was a religion of the heart rather than the head that drew inspiration from the seventeenth-century Laudians but pushed the liturgy in a much more Roman direction and favoured such unprotestant practices as genuflexion. While totally committed to Oxford's exclusiveness on the grounds that Canterbury was the true church, the Tractarians wanted to make Anglicanism a living faith rather than the dry creed of Oxford's high-church majority.[86] Initially Newman had been part of the reforming wing of the University, critical of many aspects of its undergraduate curriculum and involved in launching a subversive student newspaper. Then, in the second half of the 1820s, with two other like-minded Oriel fellows—Hurrell Froude and Robert Wilberforce—he had been a dedicated, if not always successful, tutorial teacher.[87] Deprived of his tutorial pupils in the summer of 1830, when he and his friends fell out with Provost Hawkins, Newman's energies were redirected towards creating the New Jerusalem, setting a pastoral example among his parishioners at Littlemore on the eastern fringes of Oxford, and using the pulpit of St Mary's, where he had been appointed vicar in 1827, to promote his moral message.[88] The establishment of the Tractarians as a visible party occurred three years later when John Keble, another Oriel fellow and the Oxford professor of poetry, preached, then published, an assize sermon at the university church, which attacked the government's recent suppression of a number of Irish bishoprics on the grounds they were surplus to requirements. This was quickly followed by the publication of the first 'Tract for the Times', in which Newman and his supporters set out to redefine the Anglican faith in the face of growing secularism.[89] The Tractarians saw themselves

---

[84] In 1834, sixty-two members of the Cambridge Senate petitioned for abolition; a counter-petition by residents and non-residents gained 1,200 signatories: Searby, pp. 495–7.

[85] E.J. Feuchtwanger, *Gladstone* (London, 1975), p. 11.

[86] Peter B. Nockles, *The Oxford Movement in Context: Anglican High Churchmanship 1760–1857* (Cambridge, 1994); Simon Skinner, *Tractarians and the Condition of England: The Social and Political Thought of the Oxford Movement* (Oxford, 2004); I. T. Ker, *John Henry Newman: A Biography* (Oxford, 2009); Frank M. Turner, *John Henry Newman: The Challenge to Evangelical Religion* (London, 2002).

[87] See pp. 248 and 254, this volume. Robert Wilberforce was the son of the evangelical opponent of the slave trade, William, who sent all three of his sons to Oriel.

[88] Littlemore was chaplaincy dependent on St Mary's.

[89] Hence their sobriquet. The title was first used in 1839: Peter Nockles, 'An Academic Counter-Revolution: Newman and Tractarian Oxford's Idea of a University', *HU*, X (1991), 182–3, n.11. Some historians date the

as launching a second reformation in order to reinvigorate Anglicanism and save the true church from itself, even if that meant falling out with the state, or perhaps ultimately separating church and state altogether. As alive as any secular radical to the importance of the press, the Tractarians even had their own newspaper from 1837, when Newman became editor of the quarterly *British Critic*.[90]

The Tractarians' commitment to a more elaborate liturgy did not take Oxford completely by surprise. Although post-Restoration Oxford high churchmanship was based firmly on the 1662 prayer book and, in the main, was an austere religion—college chapels had little ornamentation and services were generally conducted without singing or music—an alternative tradition had taken root at Magdalen in the second half of the eighteenth century, which, in some respects, anticipated the Tractarian agenda. President George Horne, elected head of house in 1768, had been a fellow of University College, where he had belonged to a small group of clergymen influenced by the ideas of John Hutchinson. Hutchinson was a devout Anglican layman and natural philosopher of limited education who published several books in the 1720s attacking Newton. Arguing that revelation had been endangered by Newtonian physics, he developed an alternative cosmology based on the Bible, which attributed natural events to the agency of spirits.[91] Horne also took from Hutchinson a more intense, almost mystical religiosity, which he transferred to his new college, where worship in chapel was already distinct from most other Oxford colleges because of its choir. Building on Magdalen's Laudian traditions, Horne encouraged fasting, placed candles on the chapel altar during the communion service, and sometimes practised private confession. As one undergraduate recalled, services at Magdalen in Horne's day were out of the ordinary: 'The President even bowed to the altar on leaving the chapel, without any dread lest the picture of Christ bearing the Cross [above the communion table]…should convict him of idolatry. Here we all turned towards the altar during the recital of the Creed.'[92]

When Horne departed to be bishop of Norwich in 1791, his innovations were continued by his successor, the patristic scholar Martin Routh, who headed Magdalen for the next sixty years. Politically, Routh was one of the most conservative figures in the University: he objected to change of any kind in church or state and in 1829 his name headed a letter to *The Times* signed by sixty members of Convocation opposing Peel's re-election. Religiously, he identified completely with the seventeenth-century Laudians and always kept a copy of Laud's *Devotions* to hand: he

---

foundation of the party to 1829 and the rejection of Peel, which Newman saw as an apocalyptic moment when Oxford turned its back on the secularizing tendencies of the present: ibid., 143–4.

[90] Skinner, *Tractarians*, pp. 33–64. The journal was founded in 1793.

[91] C. B. Wilde, 'Hutchinsonian Natural Philosophy and Religious Controversy in Eighteenth-Century England', *History of Science*, 18 (1980), 1–24; Brian Young, *Religion and Enlightenment in Eighteenth-Century England: Theological Debate from Locke to Burke* (Oxford, 1998), pp. 136–51.

[92] H. Best, *Four Years in France* (London, 1826), pp. 8–9. Horne had also been one of the first at Oxford to welcome church evangelicals and frequently had one of their principal female allies, Hannah More, to tea in the president's lodgings: A. Stott, *Hannah More: The First Victorian* (Oxford, 2003), esp. ch. 5 and pp. 135–6.

believed in the beauty of holiness, demanded decorum in the presence of the Lord, and objected to evangelicals who displayed an excess religious zeal, being particularly exercised by one gentleman commoner who used to turn up the whites of his eyes in chapel. The president also had great respect for the late medieval church, and in the late 1820s the college had Lewis Cottingham reconstruct the original fifteenth-century gothic reredos, complete with niches for statues, as part of a wider embellishment of the chapel.[93] Understandably, Routh's reaction to the Tractarians was positive, just as they appreciated his interest in the church fathers and his veneration of Laud. A number of Magdalen fellows joined the movement, notably John Bloxam, who served as Newman's curate at Littlemore in the second half of the 1830s and claimed to be first Anglican cleric to wear a stole when officiating.[94]

With the endorsement of a venerable and unimpeachably anti-catholic head of house, the Tractarians appeared initially to be in the Anglican mainstream. Forming an alliance with the high-church 'drys' and the conservative evangelicals, they spearheaded the campaign in the 1830s to keep the University religiously exclusive. In 1835, having led the defence against Wood's bill, the Tractarians defeated in Convocation an attempt by the Hebdomadal Board, led by Hawkins, to replace subscription by a simple test of conformity, claiming that even a minor change would put the church in danger. In Newman's eyes it was irrelevant whether the undergraduate understood the articles: subscription was a quasi-sacramental act of submission:

> The advantage of subscription (to my mind) is its witnessing to the principle that religion is to be approached with a submission of the understanding...Subscription to the Articles...actually does, I believe, impress upon the minds of young men the teachable and subdued temper expected of them. They are not to reason, but to obey; and this quite independently of the degree of accuracy, the wisdom, &c., of the Articles themselves.[95]

A year later, the Tractarians were back in the lists, this time standing up for 1662 Anglicanism against the subversive theology of the Oriel-educated Noetic Renn Dickson Hampden, principal of St Mary Hall. In 1832, Hampden had been chosen to give the Bampton lectures, an annual theological series set up under the will of the Salisbury prebendary John Bampton, formerly of Trinity, who had died in 1751. He used the occasion to argue that doctrinal positions laid down in the creed and the confessions of the different churches were imperfect deductions from Scripture

---

[93] At this stage the college did not put statues in the niches.

[94] Bloxam was the inventor of the present May morning celebrations at Magdalen. The Tractarians also had their precursors in the wider eighteenth-century church: see F. C. Mather, *High Church Prophet: Bishop Samuel Horsley (1733–1806) and the Caroline Tradition in the Later Georgian Church* (Oxford, 1992).

[95] H. C. G. Matthew, 'Noetics, Tractarians and the Reform of the University of Oxford in the Nineteenth Century', *HU*, IX (1990), 210. This is a very careful comparison of Noetic and Tractarian views on subscription in particular, which suggests they were not as far apart as appears at first sight.

FIGURE 6.6 Martyrs' Memorial, Sir George Gilbert Scott, 1843. Erected close to the spot where Latimer, Ridley, and Cranmer were burnt, the memorial was intended as an affirmation of Anglicanism's protestant credentials and a challenge to the Tractarians. The memorial was the particular inspiration of the former Oriel undergraduate Charles Pourtales Golightly, one of Newman's 'High and Drys'.

and should not be accorded the value of Christian truth.[96] The lectures caused little stir but two years later, when Hampden published an anti-subscription pamphlet where he argued that 'no conclusions of human reasoning, however correctly deduced, however logically sound, are properly religious truths', the Tractarians concluded they had a heretic in their midst.[97] Thus, when, in 1836, the Whig prime minister, Melbourne, appointed Hampden to the regius chair of divinity, they moved to clip his wings. Using Convocation once more, they passed a motion depriving the new regius of certain powers, including the right to select preachers. Even the octogenarian Routh turned out to vote.[98]

This, though, was the high point of Tractarian influence in the wider University. Thereafter, their public announcements revealed that the Church of England, which

[96] The lectures were published as *The Scholastic Philosophy considered in its relation to Christian Theology* (1833).
[97] The offending pamphlet was entitled *Observations of Religious Dissent* (1835).
[98] For the liberals' response to the vote, see David Roberts, *The Church Militant: Interpreting a Satirical Cartoon* (Magdalen College Occasional Papers 8: Oxford, 2013), an account of a drawing penned by Baden Powell.

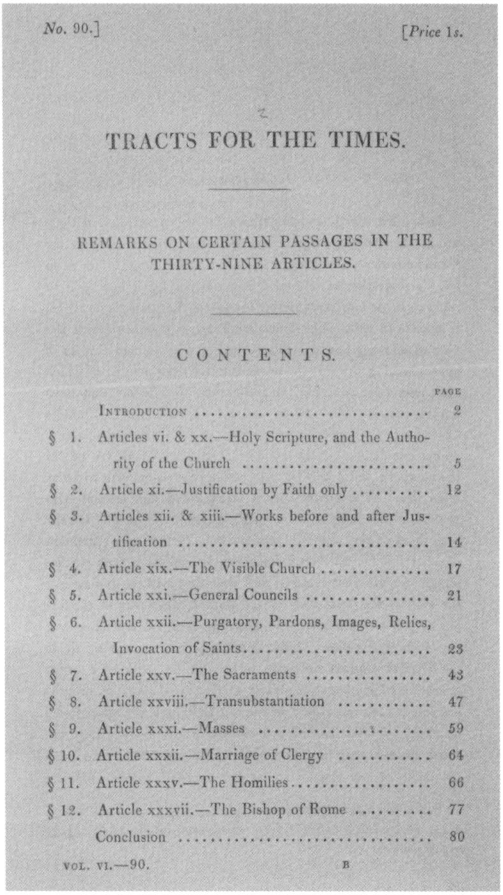

No. 90.]   [Price 1s.

TRACTS FOR THE TIMES.

REMARKS ON CERTAIN PASSAGES IN THE
THIRTY-NINE ARTICLES.

CONTENTS.

VOL. VI.—90.   B

FIGURE 6.7 John Henry Newman, *Remarks on Certain Passages in the Thirty-Nine Articles* (Tracts for the Times, no. 90, 1841), frontispiece. The most famous of the tracts published by Newman and his friends in their attempt to rejuvenate the Church of England. By allowing space for works in salvation, the pamphlet confirmed that Newman had left the Anglican mainstream and the hostility that it encountered hastened his conversion to Rome.

they expressed to support, was no longer the church of the Reformation but a Rome-leaning church of their own concoction. In 1838–9, they lost the support of the evangelicals with the publication of Froude's *Remains*, which expressed distaste for the English reformers of the sixteenth century and highlighted the importance of Laud.[99] In the same year, Oxford Anglicans more generally began to question the Tractarians' allegiance when they opposed plans to set up the martyrs' memorial in honour of Cranmer, Latimer, and Ridley (see Figure 6.6). Finally, in 1841, Newman scandalized all good protestants when he published Tract 90. In the eighteenth century, the University had become largely Arminian in its salvation theology; by 1800 there were few hard-line Calvinists left. But the 'drys' were as opposed to the

[99] Piers Brendon, 'Newman, Keble and Froude's *Remains*', *English Historical Review*, 87: 345 (1972), 697–716.

catholic doctrine of salvation by faith and works as the evangelicals. When Newman declared, therefore, that the Thirty-Nine Articles could be understood in a catholic sense, he raised establishment hackles (see Figure 6.7). The Hebdomadal Board, with the exception of Routh and Joseph Richards of Exeter, denounced Newman's position and accused him of encouraging undergraduates to equivocate when they subscribed. The Tractarians were now a marked group and their literary output was checked.[100] Initially, however, the heads mistook the level of hostility the Newmanites had engendered. When the board attempted to rehabilitate Hampden in 1842, Convocation refused, and when, in the following year, the heads suspended from preaching the Tractarian and regius professor of Hebrew, Edward Pusey, for delivering a controversial sermon on the spiritual benefits of taking communion, they found themselves isolated.[101] The Board was only able to carry Convocation with it in 1844 when it moved against one of the most notorious of the coterie, William George Ward, on the publication of his *Ideal of a Christian Church considered in comparison with existing practice*.

Ward was a fellow of Balliol, a college with a virulently anti-Tractarian master, Richard Jenkyns, as well as the home of Jowett. In the early 1840s he had been eased out of his college duties for fear lest he infect the undergraduates with his crypto-papist views, and when he argued in the *Ideal* that only the Roman Catholic church provided the discipline necessary to enlighten the religious conscience, he put himself beyond the pale. When the Hebdomadal Board called for Ward's book to be condemned and for him to be stripped of his degrees, Convocation duly complied. Its members, though, refused to condemn Tract 90, as the heads also wanted, revealing that Newman still commanded respect. Indeed, it was only the evangelicals and the 'drys' who were anxious to penalize the Tractarians for their unorthodoxy. The university liberals, for all the abuse that they had to suffer from Newman and his friends, turned their face against persecution in favour of freedom of speech.[102]

The quarrel between the Tractarians and their opponents devoured the University throughout the first half of the 1840s without definite resolution. A conclusion of sorts was reached only in October 1845, when Newman retired from Oxford and declared his conversion to Rome. With his departure, according to George Cox, the University's esquire bedell, the members of Convocation immediately regrouped and found a more material concern to absorb their energies: 'Speculative theology gave way to speculation in railroad shares . . . instead of High Church, Low Church and Broad Church, they talked of high embankments, the broad gauge and low dividends.'[103] This was an exaggeration. In the years 1841–7, only fifty-seven Oxonian members of the Tractarian movement converted. Perhaps ten times as many,

---

[100] Tract 90 was the last, and the *British Critic* closed in 1843.

[101] The title of the sermon was *The Holy Eucharist: A comfort to the penitent*. Pusey had also originally been a fellow of Oriel.

[102] Ward's book shocked sensibilities in much the same way as Wesley's diatribe a hundred years before.

[103] G. V. Cox, *Recollections* (London, 1868), p. 338.

principally those more interested in right ritual than right doctrine, remained in the University under Pusey's leadership.[104] In 1847, they exacted revenge on the heads of house by having the sympathetic Gladstone elected as a university MP.[105] This, though, was the movement's last hurrah. However much Tractarians within the church would contribute to the development of an entirely new form of high-church Anglicanism in the second half of the nineteenth century—Anglo-Catholicism—inside Oxford they were a spent political force.[106] The Tractarians had hoped to strengthen the Church of England in the life of the nation and consolidate Oxford's role as the church's educational arm.[107] Through their intolerance of opponents and their drift towards Rome, they merely succeeded in discrediting the University in the eyes of most British protestants, inside and outside the Anglican church, and providing the enemies of subscription with fresh reason to urge its abolition as part of a wider reform of Oxford and Cambridge in the mid-nineteenth century.[108]

[104] Pusey was also keen that undergraduates who fell under his spell appreciated the plight of the poor. During the Irish famine he encouraged undergraduates in Christ Church and Balliol to raise money for the victims by, among other things, giving up pudding, and in the New Year of 1847 backed a fact-finding mission to Skibbereen by two Christ Church undergraduates: Michael Moss, 'The High Price of Heaven: The 6th Earl of Glasgow and the College of the Holy Spirit on the Isle of Cumbrae', *Architectural Heritage*, xxii (2011), 81.

[105] Gladstone, though supportive of Tractarian views, claimed never to have read their works: P. Butler, *Gladstone: Church, State and Tractarianism: A Study of His Religious Ideas 1809–1859* (Oxford, 1982).

[106] It is a tribute to the underlying unity of the Anglican clergy, arguably founded on a common social background and a common university experience, that the church did not split after 1845. There was no Anglican equivalent to the Disruption that permanently divided the Church of Scotland in 1843: Matthew, 'Noetics', p. 200.

[107] There was a considerable party of Tractarians at Cambridge, led by J. M. Neale: Searby, pp. 340–3. Nonetheless, the fact that, to church historians, they became known as the Oxford Movement, emphasizes they were predominantly associated with one university.

[108] See Part III, 'Introduction: Reform and Resurrection'.

CHAPTER 7

Students and Teachers

A. The Junior Members

ARTS students at Oxford in the era of the confessional university fell into two groups: foundationers and non-foundationers. The former, a group several hundred strong, consisted of students whose board and lodging was provided by their college out of the endowment: either they received their commons free of charge or they were given an annual allowance and their subsistence charged to their battels. Arts students on the foundation at New College, Christ Church, and St John's had the status of junior fellows, whatever their academic standing. Elsewhere, only MAs or senior BAs were eligible to be fellows, and most arts students supported by a college, whether undergraduates or bachelors, were known as *scholari* not *socii*, and played no role in administering the institution. In a handful of colleges foundation scholars had their own idiosyncratic title: at Merton they were called postmasters; at Queen's, poor children if they were undergraduates and tabarders if they were BAs; at Corpus Christi, disciples; and at Magdalen and Trinity, demies.[1] Most scholarships dated from the original foundation, for it was usual, from the late fourteenth century, for founders to establish support for undergraduates as well as graduates. Others were the gift of later benefactors. At some colleges scholarships were open, but for the most part, like fellowships, they were closed. Preference was given to founder's kin or to undergraduates from a particular county, town, or even grammar school. New College's association with Winchester was built into Wykeham's original foundation but other links matured with time. Christ Church forged a connection with Westminster,[2] Pembroke with Roysse's school at Abingdon, and Brasenose with Manchester Grammar School. In the last case this was principally due to the bounty of Sarah, dowager duchess of Somerset, who gave the college enough land in the late seventeenth century to support up to twenty-two scholars each year, the majority of whom had to have been educated in Manchester, regardless of where they were born.[3]

---

[1] For the derivation of the word see p. 77, this volume.
[2] From the reign of Queen Elizabeth, Christ Church had to elect at least three Westminster boys to a studentship each year: E. G. W. Bill, *Education at Christ Church 1660–1800* (Oxford, 1988), pp. 93–4.
[3] The benefaction also supported students from Marlborough and Hereford Grammar School.

Normally scholarships were also restricted by age, but there is plenty of evidence to show that, by the eighteenth century, holders did not demit when expected to. This was because, either by statute or custom, scholars usually ended up on the foundation as fellows, and holders would retain their scholarship until there was a vacancy. This could be for a considerable time. William Bagshaw Stevens was a Magdalen demy from 1772 to 1794. He gained his scholarship when he was 16 and, according to the statutes, he should have resigned in 1781, two years after he took his MA. But at Magdalen, where the scholarships were open but the fellowships closed, there were no openings for a student from Stevens' county, Berkshire, for a further thirteen years. While he waited his turn, he left Oxford and became a schoolmaster at Repton, a job he loathed, continually on the lookout for an incumbent fellow to resign or die and frequently bemoaning his fate in his private diary.[4] But Stevens' case cannot have been uncommon after 1750. A statistical survey of the under-graduates in residence at Oxford and Cambridge in 1842 reveals that many junior fellows and scholars on the foundation were absent: at Magdalen, for instance, only five out of thirty demies were present.

The non-foundationers, by far the majority of junior members, were students in colleges and halls who in some way supported their own studies. Under the Laudian statutes they were meant to be clearly distinguished from the foundationers by their academic dress. Foundationers, both fellows and scholars, were to wear square caps, non-foundationers round ones. But if the distinction was maintained in the seven-teenth century, it largely broke down in the eighteenth when most undergraduates were allowed to sport a mortar board.[5] All non-foundationers were known as commoners in that they were expected to be present with the foundationers at the common college dinner each day. But before 1750 they were divided into four distinctive groups, which was reflected in the fees and caution money that they paid on entering a college or hall, the quality of their food and accommodation, the cost of their education, and the cut of their gowns (see Figure 7.1). The most highly honoured were the gentlemen or fellow commoners, who not only paid the highest entrance fee but were also expected to present the college with a piece of silver.[6] Below them came the simple commoners, followed by the batelers and last of all the *pauperi scholari*, many of whom had the title of servitor. The first two had enough funds to pay their way but those in the last category relied, either in part or totally, on charity.[7] Servitors, as we have seen in Chapter 5, paid for their studies by

---

[4] E.g. entry October 1792: G. Galbraith (ed.), *The Journal of the Rev. William Bagshaw Stevens* (Oxford, 1965), p. 52. According to Magdalen's original statutes, demies had no automatic right to a fellowship.

[5] Laudian Statutes, p. 144 (Title XIV, ch. 3). At Queen's, poor children seem to have worn square caps only from 1733: J. R. Magrath, *The Queen's College*, vol. 2: 1646–1877 (Oxford, 1921), p. 112.

[6] For a list of the silver presented to Magdalen in the early seventeenth century, which includes the tankard given by John Hampden, see MCA, LCD/3, isolated folio towards the end of the volume.

[7] The origin of term bateler, from which the modern word 'battels' or at Magdalen 'batells' is derived, is unclear. According to T. Salmon, *The Present State of the Universities and of the five adjacent counties*, vol. 1 (London, 1744), p. 423, commoners received the same meal or commons in hall as foundationers; batelers, on the other hand, bought what they wanted each day directly from the butler and cook. Salmon claimed some batelers were also servitors.

2 A noble graduate in full dress

3 A gentleman-commoner

4 A commoner

5 A servitor

FIGURE 7.1 Undergraduate academic dress, eighteenth century. The status of an under-graduate in the Hanoverian University who was not on a college foundation could be told by his cap and gown. Servitors, a fast disappearing group, wore a simple black sleeveless gown and no mortar board, commoners a similar gown but with braided streamers, a gentleman commoner one with sleeves covered in black tassels, and a nobleman a silk gown of his own devising. Servitors did not sport a mortar board but a simple cap, while gentlemen commoners and noblemen wore a black or gold tuft on their boards rather than the commoners' tassel.

acting as drudges to other members of the college community.[8] Some received a stipend from the college but the majority were personal servants, often serving more than one master. In return for help towards bed, board, and tuition, they performed all the menial tasks, such as carrying wood and emptying chamber pots, that even undergraduate scholars, by the late sixteenth century, found demeaning. According to Brian Twyne, a disciple of Corpus, to have performed them himself 'had bene worse than homely and beggarly'.[9] A non-foundationer's place in the college hierarchy usually closely matched the status he matriculated under in the university register. This, though, was not always the case, for families with limited means might choose to enter a son below his birthright to save money. Henry Fleming, who was at Queen's from 1677 to 1689, when he graduated as a DD, was a squire's younger son from Westmorland. He matriculated as a *generosus* but he joined the college as a batteler.[10]

Each category of non-foundationer wore a slightly different academic dress, so that their status could be immediately known outside the college, while, inside, their relative position was made particularly clear at dinner. Within the dining hall, there were separate tables for fellows and scholars (and sometimes for other members of the foundation, such as chaplains, clerks, or bursars). Gentlemen commoners sat with the fellows at the top end of the hall on a raised platform, while the ordinary commoners and battelers each had their own tables towards the screen end.[11] Servitors and poor scholars also had a separate table but did not sit down until dinner was over. During dinner, the servitors waited in hall and the poor scholars languished outside. Those who were hired by particular foundationers or non-foundationers looked after their masters; others hired by the college served the members of the college community in hall who were servant-less.[12] When the meal was over, both servitors and poor scholars sat down to devour the leftovers. All non-foundationers were batteled for what they had eaten but the poor scholars may well have had their battels paid by the college or a patron.[13]

This status hierarchy was at its most visible in the late sixteenth and seventeenth centuries, when junior members were drawn from a relatively broad social spectrum. As the social tone became more elevated in the eighteenth century, the distinctions were largely eroded. While poorer students continued to be employed as servants, there was always a sprinkling of low-status non-foundationers in every college, but the switch to domestic bedmakers and waiters in hall after 1750 ensured

---

[8] See, p. 163.   [9] HUO, iii. 724.

[10] *The Flemings in Oxford, being documents selected from the Rydal papers in illustration of the lives and ways of Oxford men 1650–1700*, ed. J. R. Magrath (3 vols; OHS; Oxford, 1904–24), i. 258. Fleming became a scholar at Queen's in 1678 but never a fellow.

[11] The number of tables varied from college to college: Brasenose had eight. Queen's had a separate table for gentlemen commoners.

[12] George Fothergill, at Queen's in the 1720s, was both a college servitor and personal servant to three commoners and one gentleman commoner: Magrath, *Queen's*, pp. 87–8. It is possible that battelers had to fetch their own food from the buttery: Anon., 'The Membership and Character of Exeter College, Oxford, 1640–90' (BA dissertation, Oxford, 2002), p. 12.

[13] When richer students entered a college they sometimes had to pay a fee to the poor scholars' fund.

their complete disappearance by 1800.[14] By then, the battelers had also ceased to exist. This left only the gentleman commoners and commoners. These remained distinctive categories, and until the end of the eighteenth century the social pecking order of the colleges was measured by the number of gentlemen commoners admitted. Magdalen and Christ Church would accept almost no one else.[15] But in all colleges the gap between the two categories began to close as the eighteenth century came to an end. Gentlemen commoners lost their right to dine at high table, use the senior common room, and occupy special seats in chapel, as well as other peculiar privileges that they had obtained over the years, such as, in Lincoln, not bowing to fellows. It appears, too, that a gift of silver came to be expected from all college entrants. The status distinction therefore ceased to have much meaning and, in the first half of the nineteenth century, most colleges started to refuse to admit undergraduates as gentlemen commoners, beginning with Trinity from 1808 and University College from 1813.[16]

The distinction between foundationers and non-foundationers was emphasized by their mode of admission. Except in the peculiar case of St John's where election was in the hands of corporate bodies external to the college, scholarships and junior fellowships were mainly in the gift of the governing fellows, who either exercised the right collectively or took turns.[17] In most colleges in the late sixteenth and seventeenth centuries, success was largely determined by nothing more than the influence that a candidate's patron could wield with electors.[18] But in the second half of the period, as the number of candidates for a vacancy increased, a simple request on a client's behalf was insufficient: fellows demanded some evidence of potential. At Magdalen, at the beginning of William and Mary's reign, a candidate displayed his credentials simply by writing an elegant if short letter of introduction to the president, and forwarding a copy of his certificate of baptism and a character testimonial.[19] By the 1830s, when there could be twenty or more candidates for every place rather than the previous two or three, a candidate was also expected to show his proficiency in translating a passage of English into Latin and compose an English essay. Balliol, the most academically ambitious college in the second quarter of the nineteenth century, went even further. Until 1827, individual fellows could nominate college scholarships in turn. Thereafter, the possibility of non-academic factors affecting choice was all but reduced by the introduction of a week-long

[14] Servitors waited in hall at Queens until 1796 and Brasenose until 1799: Magrath, *Queen's*, pp. 138–9. For the changing social background of undergraduates, see pp. 163–5, this volume.

[15] Bill, *Christ Church*, pp. 167–71 (entrance statistics).

[16] From its establishment in 1810, the respective numbers of gentlemen commoners and commoners were recorded each year in the *Oxford University Calendar*.

[17] At St John's, election chiefly lay in the hands of the Merchant Taylors' Company: see p. 144, this volume. There was frequent friction between the company and the fellowship over the choice: see H.B. Wilson, *History of the Merchant Taylors' School, from its foundation to the present time* (2 vols; London, 1812–14), *passim*.

[18] An exception were elections to Westminster studentships or fellowships at Christ Church, where candidates had to present various pieces of written work as early as 1660. Even here, patronage and the cultivation of the dean still played an important part. For the role of patronage in obtaining a place on a college foundation, see pp. 153–7, this volume.

[19] For the letter of introduction penned by the journalist Joseph Addison, demy in 1689, see MCA, MS 516/2.

scholarship examination held in the college every November, which involved testing Greek and Latin translations and composition, along with papers in English, mathematics, and divinity. The contest attracted candidates from the most academic public schools and the outcome was eagerly awaited. Arthur Stanley, erstwhile pupil of Dr Arnold's Rugby and a future dean of Westminster, was a successful candidate in 1833. He described the climax to his sister:

> We all assembled in the Hall and had to wait one hour—the room getting fuller and fuller of the Rugby Oxonians crowding in from various parts to hear the result. At last the Dean appeared in his white robes and moved up to the head of the table. He first began a long preamble—that they were well satisfied with all—that those who were disappointed were many in proportion to those who were successful, etc., etc.,—all this time everyone was listening in the most intense eagerness—and I almost bit my lips off—till 'the successful candidates are Mr Stanley'—I gave a great jump—and there was half a shout among the Rugby men...The Dean then took me into the Chapel, where was the Master and all the Fellows in white robes. And there I swore that I would not dissipate the property, reveal the secrets, or disobey the Statutes of the College—I was then made to kneel on the steps and admitted to the rank of Scholar...of Balliol College.[20]

Commoners, in contrast, were not expected to demonstrate any academic prowess before their admission. Admissions were initially haphazard, but by the eighteenth century, it was accepted that the power to admit lay with the head of house. Presumably prospective students' fathers wrote in advance to see if the college or hall had room, and if so, their sons duly appeared. Before 1700, there is no evidence that commoners were examined even once *in situ*. Thereafter, they were appraised, but only perfunctorily. When John Kenrick came up to Brasenose in October 1750, his encounter with Principal Francis Yarborough was scarcely taxing. He 'put a Horace in my hand, and then Virgil, and lastly Sophocles, where I read half a dozen lines...[Finally] he gave me a theme to make.'[21] No college before the mid-nineteenth century established an entrance examination for commoners, though Balliol did encourage would-be entrants to try its scholarship competition. As Balliol was an oversubscribed college in the second quarter of the nineteenth century, this allowed the master, Richard Jenkyns, to privilege the cleverer applicants who had attempted the exam but not been elected. Influence had little effect on his decisions, as Robert Peel, the University's ousted MP, but now firmly entrenched at the heart of the nation's political life, discovered in 1834, when he failed to get a friend's son admitted.

The difference between undergraduate foundationers and non-foundationers should not be exaggerated, however. In the first place, the vast majority of undergraduates in the period 1550 to 1850 came up to Oxford as some sort of commoner.

---

[20] Jones, p. 184. Rugby was just beginning to flourish under Thomas Arnold. Balliol's initiative was predated by Corpus and Trinity where solidly competitive scholarship examinations were introduced in 1815 and 1816, though at Corpus the traditional geographical restrictions pertained.

[21] Crook, p. 116. A theme was usually a Latin or Greek poem on a selected topic.

With most colleges before the mid-nineteenth century allowing their scholars to hang on for a fellowship, if they so desired, there was no guarantee that a suitable bursary would fall vacant just at the moment when an aspirant was ready to come into residence. Usually, then, scholarship-hopefuls would enter a college as a commoner, begin their studies, and start looking around for a vacancy. The initial choice of college was based on several factors—space, social tone, family connections, but above all regional background. Apart from the largest foundations, such as Magdalen, most colleges drew their fellows and scholars from a particular part of England—Brasenose from the north-west, University College from Yorkshire and the north, Jesus from Wales, Exeter from the West Country, and so on. By and large, their commoner entrants came from the same areas, understandably pulled towards colleges where they could mix with students from local families who spoke with the same accent and shared the same childhood memories.[22] But there was no unwavering loyalty to one's college of matriculation. Undergraduates who sought a scholarship were happy to move on if the opportunity arrived. Some could not wait to change. John James was a native of Westmorland who came up to Queen's as a commoner in October 1778 because of its local ties. When it was suggested that he put in for a Christ Church studentship in 1780, he declared he was only too ready to abandon an institution he had grown tired of for its 'farce of discipline' and 'freezing indifference'.[23] Like James, then, scholars frequently matriculated elsewhere. Between 1689 and 1854, some 40 per cent of Magdalen's cohort of thirty demies started their university life in another college: before 1730 most came from neighbouring Magdalen Hall; thereafter the majority came from Queen's.

In the second place, the social background of the two groups was more homogeneous than might be expected. Scholarships always met only a part of the cost of study: they were never intended for the destitute but for students of modest means who thereby got the chance to gain a BA, compete for a fellowship, and eventually enter the church.[24] Until 1640, most scholarships appear to have been filled appropriately. However, from the turn of the seventeenth century, the sons of the middling sort faced increasing competition from the offspring of gentry families, such as the Hydes of Wiltshire, who saw a scholarship as a useful contribution to the expense of educating their sons.[25] The gentrification of scholarships only got worse in the eighteenth century as the value of fellowships rose and the church became filled with younger sons. At Magdalen, in the second half of the seventeenth century, undergraduates who matriculated as plebeians were fast losing their grip on foundationer places but they still accounted for a third of the cohort. In the eighteenth century they disappeared from the ranks of the foundationers as fast as they did from the commoners' roll. The only section of the college in which plebeians

---

[22] E.g. Anon, 'Exeter College', p. 57 (appendix 4).

[23] James, p. 102. James' father claimed all colleges were the same and had only sent his son to Queen's because of its local ties: ibid., p. 97.

[24] See p. 36, n. 17 this volume.   [25] See p. 153, this volume.

remained a significant group, still a quarter in the first half of the nineteenth century, was among the choristers. But hardly any chorister became a fellow.

Undergraduates, too, rich or poor, who were not given their board and lodging by the foundation might still have their studies partly subsidized in various ways without having to labour in return like a servitor. Most colleges had exhibitions worth a few pounds that were given to the deserving (however defined), in some cases established when the funds set aside for obits (masses for the soul of dead benefactors) were secularized at the Reformation. Even halls that were unendowed and therefore had no foundationers could have funds at their disposal to support some of their undergraduates who met a benefactor's idiosyncratic whim. In 1723, the Reverend William Lucy left £2,000 to Magdalen Hall to provide an eight-year bursary for four boys who had spent three years or more attending the small grammar school of Hampton Lucy in Warwickshire.[26] Other undergraduates were the beneficiaries of external trust funds. More than half of the boys from the city of Worcester who attended Oxford in the years 1668–1700 held exhibitions of seven years' duration, worth £3 per annum, which were paid for by the Worfield charity, set up in 1650. Yet others were able to survive at the University thanks to personal patronage. The diarist Thomas Hearne, son of a parish clerk, owed his education at St Edmund Hall in the late seventeenth century to the bounty of Francis Cherry, who had also studied there.[27] In 1685, the Wesleys' father, Samuel, had his battels paid for him by a fellow student at Exeter.

Furthermore, undergraduate foundationers and non-foundationers largely studied together. Even if many non-foundationers had no intention of staying the course, undergraduates of all backgrounds were expected to follow a common curriculum. Some leeway was given to those who came up for only a year or two and could not possibly study the whole curriculum in detail, but there was never a separate cursus for non-foundationers who were birds of passage. Only gentlemen commoners and the titled were free, to some extent, from the constant round of lectures and disputations which formed the kernel of the student day. But even their freedom could be heavily circumscribed. When John Evelyn went up to Balliol in 1637, he found that 'Fellow-Communers...were no more exempted from Exercise than the meanest Scholars there.'[28] Admittedly, standards slipped after the Restoration, but they were gradually tightened once more in the second half of the eighteenth century, as the gentlemen commoners' other privileges were reined in. By the turn of the nineteenth century, any licence customarily given to the group was fast being withdrawn. At Trinity from 1797, they were expected not just to attend prayers like everyone else but 'do all other exercises with the same regularity as commoners'.[29]

---

[26] *History of the County of Warwick*, vol. 2, ed. William Page (London, 1909), p. 368. Lucy had been at Magdalen Hall. On the assumption that the principal was invested, this would have given Lucy scholars £20 per annum towards their studies and covered perhaps a quarter of their needs.

[27] *The Life of Thomas Hearne, of St Edmund's Hall, Oxford, …* (Oxford, 1772), pp. 2–8.

[28] *The Diary of John Evelyn*, ed. E. S. de Beer (6 vols; Oxford, 2000), ii. 17. [29] Hopkins, p. 226.

Lastly, there was always some form of college identity that bound members together whatever their status. Before the Restoration, undergraduates, on their arrival, were inducted into the college community by their peers. At Merton in the time of Anthony Wood, freshmen had to stand on a stool placed on a high table and deliver a mock declamation to the assembled undergraduates: '[I[f well done, the person that spoke it was to have a cup of cawdle and no salted drink; if indifferently some cawdle and some salted drink; but if dull, nothing was given him but salted drink or salt put in college beere.' Afterwards the senior college cook administered an oath to the freshman and admitted him into the fraternity.[30] Other moments of licence throughout the year helped to consolidate the sense of college identity that was thus engendered, especially at Christmas time. In the festive season, from St Nicholas' Eve to Epiphany, the community was treated to a round of plays and entertainments that its members would organize, and on 28 December, the day of the Holy Innocents, the world would be turned upside down and the college placed under the government of a boy bishop.[31] Less frequently, the young scholars had the chance to show off their rhetorical skills. College revels were usually in-house affairs, but when royal visitors came to town, they set up camp in Christ Church and expected to be entertained by players and orators from the different colleges, who thereby gained the chance to assert their collective honour. On such occasions, too, students were able to flaunt their mastery of their native tongue as well as Latin and Greek. In 1636, one of the plays performed before Charles I was William Cartwright's *The Royal Slave*, a tragi-comedy on the appropriate theme of the cares of kingship.[32]

From the second half of the seventeenth century, the ritual life of the college outside the chapel was greatly impoverished. A dislike of disorder, promoted by the Civil War as much as any residual puritanism within the University, meant that Christmas festivities ceased, college drama disappeared, and initiation rituals became mundane.[33] When Fleming joined Queen's in the late 1670s, freshmen were merely expected to show their bottle by braving the ban on attending alehouses and standing a round of drinks in a local hostelry.[34] As a result, the strength of an

---

[30] Wood, *Life*, i. 138–40. Unsurprisingly, his own oration was a masterpiece.

[31] W. C. Mellor, *The Boy Bishop and Other Essays on Forgotten Customs and Beliefs* (London, 1923); Robin Darwall-Smith, 'Magdalen and the Rediscovery of Christmas', *Magdalen College Record* (2001), 92–101; J. R. Bloxam, *Register of the Presidents, Fellows, Demies, Instructors in Grammar and in Music, Chaplains, Clerks, Choristers and Other Members of Saint Mary Magdalen College, in the University of Oxford, from the Foundation of the College to the Present Time* (7 vols; Oxford, 1853–81), v. 48–57 (citing the diary of Laud's biographer, Peter Heylyn).

[32] Published in 1639. Cartwright of Christ Church was the University's lecturer in metaphysics. Performances could bomb. In 1605, Magdalen played a drama in front of James and his court called *Ajax Flagellifer*, loosely based on the Sophocles play, 'which was very tedious and wearied all the companie': Marion Turner, 'Drama at Magdalen: 1458–1642', *Magdalen College Record* (2003), 87. Plays performed on less august occasions could have a subversive edge: William Poole, 'Rowing, Shopping and Plays? All Perversions', *OT*, 6 Mar. 2014.

[33] College drama had been attacked by puritans in the University from the 1590s. Throughout the decade, Oxford's leading Latin playwright of the day, Christ Church's William Gager, was embroiled in a lengthy pamphlet war with John Rainolds of Corpus, who was particularly exercised by male students playing female parts.

[34] Magrath, *Queen's*, p. 74. Fleming was caught and made to accept a whipping or be sent down. Initiation rituals seem to have disappeared in some colleges even before the Civil War. When the young Ashley Cooper,

undergraduate's college allegiance must have been correspondingly reduced, even if it never dissipated entirely, as the success of several college building appeals in the late seventeenth and eighteenth century reveals.[35] However, after 1820, the sense of college identity was reinvigorated and reached new heights with the development of competitive rowing. College regulations permitted only gentle games within the college precincts, so undergraduates traditionally had little opportunity to let off steam in-house: at best, colleges provided facilities for playing skittles or bowls. More vigorous exercise had always been allowed outside the walls but as this usually involved walking or riding, it was taken alone or in pairs.[36] The evolution of rowing on the Isis from a humdrum pastime into a serious sport, which was inherently adversarial and pitted college against college, opened up a completely new chapter in the history of college loyalty. The first Oxford and Cambridge boat race was rowed in 1829. The first eight-oar races between Oxford colleges took place as early as 1815, and intercollegiate competition was well established by the late 1830s.

On the other hand, sport at the end of the period was only beginning to show its potential for making an undergraduate his college's man for life. Some colleges were initially much more enthusiastic than others about taking to the water. Brasenose, with its large undergraduate population, was early in the lists, defeating Jesus to become head of the river in the very first contest and continually fielding a strong crew in subsequent years. Magdalen, which had few undergraduates, on the other hand, stayed aloof and only entered a boat of its own in the eights of 1846. It was also the case that other intercollegiate sports had barely begun to register on the University's seismograph. The first varsity cricket match took place two years before the first boat race, but the only intercollegiate matches in 1850 were between Brasenose and Christ Church.[37]

B. The Curriculum

Between 1534 and 1800, Oxford's arts course was closely modelled on the curriculum of the pre-Reformation University. In the century after the passage of the Henrician Act of Supremacy, a number of new statutes concerning arts teaching were promulgated, culminating in the provisions laid down in the Laudian code of 1636, but few substantial alterations were made to the existing structure. In the first place, the course remained unchanged in length: the Laudian statutes still required four years of study for the BA and a further three for the MA. In the second place,

---

future earl of Shaftesbury, came up to Exeter in the 1630s, he refused to play the game and ended up fomenting a riot. Prideaux, the puritanical head of house, used this as an excuse to ban the practice in future: W. D. Christie, *A Life of Anthony Ashley Cooper, First Earl of Shaftesbury* (London, 1871), pp. 14–18.

[35] See p. 174, this volume.

[36] Graham Midgley, *University Life in Eighteenth-Century Oxford* (London, 1996), chs 8–9 (licit and illicit pastimes). The Laudian statutes had banned football in the street, among other things: Laudian Statutes, pp. 150–1 (Title XV, ch. 7).

[37] Timothy J. Chandler, 'The Development of a Sporting Tradition at Oxbridge: 1800–1860', *Canadian Journal of the History of Sport*, 19: 2 (1988), 1–29.

while due attention was given to the Renaissance humanists' insistence on the importance of studying the languages and culture of the ancient world, the new subjects were subsumed within the traditional curriculum and in no way superseded it. On arrival, an undergraduate's first year was to be spent in studying grammar and rhetoric. Essentially, he had to get his reading and speaking knowledge of Latin up to scratch, so that he could follow lectures and take part in debates. In the seventeenth century, Latin was not just the language of the classroom but was still required to be used when dining in hall. The undergraduate was then to proceed to logic and ethics, which would be the core of his studies until he was eligible to become a BA. From the beginning of his third year he was also to study Greek and geometry. Once he had taken his BA, he spent the next three years studying natural philosophy and metaphysics, and astronomy and higher mathematics (optics, gnomonics, geography, and navigation). At the same time, he was required to develop his knowledge of ancient languages. He was to continue Greek until he took his MA, and in the course of the three years begin Hebrew and, from 1640, Arabic. Shortly before he became a master, he was finally to take up ancient history. The Laudian statutes equally largely confirmed the traditional system of graduation. Candidates for the BA had to have studied for the requisite number of years, formally disputed, and undergone an oral examination. Candidates for the MA had to have studied for the requisite number of years, formally disputed, and given a number of lectures.[38]

The Laudian statutes' commitment to the traditional curriculum was also mirrored at post-Reformation Cambridge where the arts course similarly remained seven years long, with the study of grammar, rhetoric, and philosophy at its core. Elsewhere in Europe, on the other hand, the arts course had been usually greatly shortened by the beginning of the seventeenth century, as it became commonplace for the first and second arts degrees to be taken within a few months of one another. At the Scottish universities, for instance, an MA could be obtained after only four years of study, while under the 1601 statutes of the University of Paris the degree could be obtained in as little as two. At Paris and many catholic universities, such a large reduction in the length of the course was partly made possible by narrowing rather than expanding the late medieval curriculum. Paris graduands were tested only on their knowledge of the four philosophical sciences; grammar and rhetoric were no longer part of the syllabus, and mathematics largely neglected.[39] Indeed, in

[38] Laudian Statutes, pp. 33–42 and 45–6 (Titles IV and VI, section 1, chs 1 and 2). In the eighteenth century, the emphasis on Latin as a vehicle of communication, inside and outside the classroom, began to decline: see pp. 134–5, this volume.

[39] In most catholic countries, it will be recalled, the faculties of arts were no longer involved in instruction and were little more than examining boards. The Latin and Greek humanities and philosophy were taught in colleges that might or might not be affiliated to the local university: see pp. 132–3, this volume. In the colleges, the humanities were not taught alongside philosophy as at Oxford, but beforehand. The last two years in the French collèges de plein exercice were devoted entirely to philosophy, which was taught in a different fashion and considered to have a much higher level of significance as a discipline. Some French colleges did offer sophisticated mathematics education but it was not seen as a central part of the MA course. See L. W. B. Brockliss, French Higher Education in the Seventeenth and Eighteenth Centuries: A Cultural History (Oxford, 1987), chs 3, 5, and 6.

some respects the Oxford course laid down in the code was peculiarly capacious. Many protestant universities would have expected their MAs to have some knowledge of Hebrew but none of Arabic, while most could not have matched Oxford's commitment to mathematics in the seventeenth century. The undergraduate geometry course under the Laudian statutes was particularly sophisticated. If founded on Euclid, it also included the study of conics and statics through the recently recovered texts of Apollonius and Archimedes.[40] In an earlier attempt to amend the curriculum in the post-Reformation era, mathematics had been given even greater prominence. According to the 1549 statutes delivered by Edward VI's commissioners, undergraduates on first coming up were to devote their first year exclusively to its study, though there is no way of knowing whether the requirement was ever actually followed.[41]

In the second half of the eighteenth century, voices were raised all over Europe about the narrowness of the university arts course in an age which placed a new emphasis on modern languages and modern history.[42] At Oxford, however, the main target of criticism before 1800 was the system of examination, which, it was felt, was both outmoded and no longer properly maintained. The disputations had become difficult to police; the viva voce exam for bachelors was perfunctory; while the requirement that BAs should give a series of lectures before incepting as masters was only honoured in the breach. All that was required in the last case was for the candidate to turn up at the appointed place and time. The series became known as 'wall lectures', for there was no audience and the lecturer was left to his own devices unless a proctor called in.[43] The French Revolution moved the Hebdomadal Board to act. Fearing that students who had little incentive to study hard would fall easy prey to revolutionary agitators, the heads promulgated a new examination statute in 1800 that was intended to keep adolescent noses to the grindstone. Its principal architect was Cyril Jackson, dean of Christ Church.[44]

Under the new statute, the curriculum for the BA and MA was left unaltered, but the BA exam was given more teeth. The six examiners were given the liberty of testing candidates on all parts of the course as they felt moved, but the viva was always to contain 'an examination in Humane Literature' based on at least three

---

[40] In 1619 the course was defined by the books to be taught by the new Savilian professor of geometry: Laudian Statutes, p. 36 (Title IV, ch. 6). On the level of mathematics teaching in the early modern university, see Laurence Brockliss, 'Curricula', in HUIE, ii. 570–92.

[41] *Statuta*, p. 344. Presumably the commissioners hoped that the grammar schools or private tutors would provide pupils with a good enough training in Latin to make the traditional study of grammar superfluous but that little or no attention would be paid to mathematics. The statutes still assume that Greek would be part of the undergraduate curriculum.

[42] See p. 324, this volume.

[43] The first public attack on the Oxford examination system appeared in Vicesimus Knox, *Essays Moral and Literary* (2 vols; London, 1782), i. 321–7. For an idea of the low quality of the BA viva at this date, see James, pp. 160–1. The Cambridge examination system had come under attack a few years before: see John Jebb, *Remarks upon the present mode of the education in the University of Cambridge*, 4th edn (Cambridge, 1774), pp. 37–40. But at Cambridge change was already under way: see p. 139, this volume.

[44] Another key figure was Eveleigh of Oriel, whose concern for the security of the established church and state has been noted in Chapter 6: see p. 157, this volume.

Greek or Roman authors selected by the candidate, an unseen prose translation (from English to Latin), and an examination on the elements of religion (taught through the Greek New Testament and the Thirty-Nine Articles). To encourage emulation, it was also made possible for a small group of twelve, who would be ranked according to merit, to take an extended examination and have their results made public.[45] Seven years later, in 1807, the new statute was revised. The MA examination was scrapped, and the degree henceforth awarded after a candidate had spent three years listening to public lectures and delivering a couple himself in Latin, while the BA examination was refined. The clauses relating to the examination in humane literature and religion and the Latin unseen were retained, but religion was now given pride of place (no degree could be awarded to those who were deemed to have failed it), and the Greek and Latin texts selected could be works of rhetoric, ethics, and logic, as well as literature. In addition, it was specified that every candidate had to be examined in mathematics and physics. Further thought was also given to allowing the best candidates to gain public recognition. The single published list of twelve was abolished and replaced by two lists, one for polite literature and the other for mathematical and physical sciences. Those so honoured were no longer limited in number but divided into two classes ranked alphabetically.[46] Thereafter, undergraduates hoping to be classified announced their intention in advance and presented the examiners with a much larger list of books to be tested on than their peers. The revision was followed the year after by the introduction of a further viva voce examination called Responsions, which was intended to be taken before the beginning of the third year and tested a candidate on at least two works of Greek and Latin, the rudiments of logic, and Euclid's *Elements*. This replaced the disputation element in the traditional BA (hence its name), and from 1809 had to be passed by anyone wishing to take a degree.[47]

After 1809, the statute governing the BA examination remained largely unchanged until the middle of the nineteenth century. The new exam quickly became known as 'Schools' after the Metaphysical and Music Schools in the Bodleian quadrangle in which they were held. Quite quickly, too, it became common for most candidates to be spared the mathematics and physics exam on the grounds that they were insufficiently prepared, and in 1825 this was given formal sanction when provision was made for those who wanted to be put through their paces in the two subjects to be tested by three separate examiners.[48] There was also pressure in the 1820s from the Noetics to extend the definition of humane literature, and this was satisfied to a certain extent in 1830 when students were allowed to select works of poetry, politics, and Greek and Roman history in addition to literature, rhetoric,

---

[45] OUS, ii. 31–7.   [46] Ibid., 61–5 and 83–6.

[47] Ibid, 76–80. A useful description of the examination system in its first years can be found in E. Copleston, *Reply to the Calumnies of the Edinburgh Review against Oxford containing an account of the studies pursued in that University* (London, 1810), pp. 137–44. For the attack launched by the *Edinburgh Review* against Oxford in the first half of the nineteenth century, see pp. 334–7, this volume.

[48] OUS, ii.124–5.

logic, and ethics. Furthermore, the 1825 and 1830 revisions saw the introduction of a third, then a fourth class in the honours list, so that ambitious candidates could be more carefully distinguished.[49]

In the 1580s, only 26 per cent of matriculands determined as BAs four years later. In the seventeenth and eighteenth centuries, the fraction was normally a half, but this was as high as it rose, and the number of matriculands incepting as an MA was never more than quarter. Indeed, during the Interregnum, the proportion determining temporarily fell back to its original level. The reluctance to graduate was scarcely surprising when only entrants to the church needed a degree, and a significant percentage of the intake were gentlemen's sons for whom Oxford was a finishing school. The changes to the BA examination instituted in 1800 gave a significant boost to numbers taking the degree. After 1800, the fraction of matriculands taking the degree rose rapidly and had reached nearly three-quarters of the total by the 1840s.[50] On the other hand, the percentage of undergraduates who entered for honours under the new statute remained comparatively small. Forming some 25 per cent of the cohort in 1810, it was still only 30 per cent in the 1850s. The majority of undergraduates who graduated in the first half of the nineteenth century left with a pass degree. Among the honours' candidates, too, some colleges were much better represented than others, and three—Christ Church, Balliol, and Oriel—nearly always produced the majority of Firsts. In the early years, when Firsts were few, Christ Church's undergraduates scooped the pool and took a third of the total. By the middle of the century, they still took more than 10 per cent but they had surrendered poll position to Balliol. Initially a college whose students made little impact on the class list, the latter was home to 20 per cent of the Firsts in the 1840s and had gained a reputation as the University's intellectual powerhouse.

As matriculations were also rising in the first part of the nineteenth century, the number of students presenting themselves for a BA doubled over thirty years. In consequence, the viva voce format became unworkable: the examiners found they were spending six months of the year processing candidates. Ambitious candidates were particularly demanding. When Sir William Hamilton presented himself to the examiners in 1810, it took two days to question him on all the books he offered for the humane literature exam. The solution, in operation by 1825, was to set written papers, which from 1828 were printed. Orals were not totally discontinued. The viva remained a central part of the examination throughout the nineteenth century but written papers were now the core (see Figure 7.2).[51]

[49] Ibid, 138, 166, and 174–5.

[50] Lawrence Stone, 'The Size and Component of the Oxford Student Body 1580–1910', in Lawrence Stone, *The University in Society*, vol. 1: *Oxford and Cambridge from the 14th to the early 19th Century* (Princeton, NJ, 1974), p. 95 (table). For the gentry's invasion of the University, see pp. 161–2, this volume.

[51] Christopher Stray, 'The Shift from Oral to Written Examination: Cambridge and Oxford', *Assessment in Education*, 8: 1 (2001), 43–4. Mathematics questions seem to have been solved on paper from the start.

FIGURE 7.2 'Examination of Candidates for the Degree of Bachelor of Arts [Oxford]': R. Buss, drawing, 1842. Buss' depiction of 'Schools' suggests a scene of chaos. Some undergraduates are in the process of taking a written examination; others look on nervously. The standing figure may be being viva'd.

C. Lecturers

In the pre-Reformation University the arts curriculum had been principally delivered by the regent masters, who were expected to spend one or two years after their inception lecturing. New MAs were still required to lecture in the old schools in the 1530s and 1540s. But they were continually given a grace to avoid compliance, and from the 1550s compulsory regenting was effectively abandoned. Instead, a team of nine lecturers was chosen from the pool of regent masters each year by Congregation; they were given the task of delivering the arts curriculum in return for a small stipend.[52] The Laudian statutes maintained the new system, but took the election out of the hands of Congregation, transferring it instead to four colleges in turn, supposedly in order to avoid faction fighting.[53] By the 1630s, however, regent lecturers had to be found to cover only a part of the curriculum. In 1540, Henry VIII had endowed chairs in Greek, Hebrew, theology, civil law, and medicine at both Oxford and Cambridge, which ensured permanent teaching in two of the components of the syllabus. The 1610s and 1620s witnessed the foundation of additional public chairs at Oxford, this time by private individuals, in natural philosophy, geometry, astronomy, ethics, history, and music. The first was the gift of Sir William Sedley in 1618, the second and third of Sir Henry Savile, warden of Merton, in 1619, the fourth of Thomas White, canon of Windsor, in 1621, the fifth of the antiquarian William Camden in 1622, and the last of William Heather, gentleman of the Chapel

---

[52] Presumably each member of the team was allotted a component of the curriculum to teach.
[53] Laudian Statutes, p. 33 (Title IV, section 1, ch. 1).

Royal, in 1626.[54] This left only grammar, rhetoric, logic, and metaphysics to be covered in the traditional way, and Laud hoped that, in time, they too would be taught by endowed lecturers. He himself showed the way forward by establishing a professorship in Arabic in 1640.

Under the 1549 statutes, regent lecturers were supposed to teach five days in seven. Under the Laudian code, arts professors, endowed or unendowed, had to appear in schools only twice in a week and their lectures were limited to forty-five minutes with a quarter of an hour for questions.[55] The code made attendance at appropriate lectures compulsory, under threat of a fine for absence, but this would have still left junior members with plenty of time on their hands. Seventeenth-century undergraduates, however, had no excuse to be idle, for a major part of the undergraduate curriculum was also delivered by the colleges. The first college to appoint in-house lecturers was Magdalen in the late fifteenth century; the first to set up stipendiary lecturers to teach the new humanist subjects was Corpus in the 1520s.[56] Thereafter, both old and new foundations established a growing number of lecturers in both the traditional and novel components of the arts curriculum, and in most cases eventually provided teaching in Greek, rhetoric (advanced Latin composition), logic, and philosophy (both moral and natural). The larger colleges even offered teaching in Hebrew. In the early seventeenth century, the language was taught at Magdalen (where a chair had been founded as early as 1566), Merton, New College, Brasenose, and Exeter.[57]

The innovation was encouraged by Thomas Cromwell's visitors, who ordered Greek and Latin lectureships to be established in a number of colleges, at a time when there were no university chairs in the new learning.[58] The Edwardian visitors can have had no problem with the development because the 1549 statutes assumed that third- and fourth-year undergraduates would be pursuing a number of arts subjects in their colleges while studying philosophy in the schools.[59] When Sir Thomas White set up lectureships in Greek, rhetoric, and logic on founding St John's in 1555, he explained that he did so for sound pedagogical reasons. Good pupils were only formed by good masters:

> Lest therefore anything may seem remiss in the diligent cultivation of our vine, were we to leave to the student's will and disposition the choice of a master to imitate in his formation, we wish certain outstanding masters in the art of speaking to be selected out of the body of our fellowship, who will diligently instruct the unskilled

---

[54] *Statuta*, pp. 528–44 and 556–8 (Savile, White, and Heather); Kevin Sharpe, 'The Foundation of the Chairs of History at Oxford and Cambridge: An Episode in Jacobean Politics', *HU*, II (1982), 127–37 (on Camden). The Sedley bequest took effect from 1621: <https://en.wikipedia.org/wiki/Sedleian_Professor_of_Natural_Philosophy> (accessed 12 June 2013). Camden had been at Magdalen, Broadgates Hall, and Christ Church; he became headmaster of Westminster School. White had been at Magdalen Hall; and Heather had an Oxford DMus.

[55] *Statuta*, p. 343; Laudian Statutes, pp. 40 and 42 (Title IV, section 2, chs 1 and 4).

[56] See pp. 82–3, this volume.

[57] Chairs were also established at Christ Church and Queen's in the second half of the seventeenth century.

[58] See p. 131, this volume.   [59] *Statuta*, p. 344.

in a good method of working. We will pick out among our vine three of the most excellent workmen in any age who will by their example spur on their minds and bring forth and tend the most useful and fruitful shoots.[60]

By the early seventeenth century, on the other hand, college teaching was a commonplace and no longer merited such an effusive defence. When lectures were established under Pembroke's statutes in 1622, their value was deemed to be disciplinary rather than pedagogical, for it was assumed they would act as a hedge against idleness.[61]

In the seventeenth century, college lecturers were usually expected to lecture for an hour every day except Sunday, so most undergraduates and BAs would have had at least two college lectures a day in addition to any they attended in the University's schools. In addition, they would also have had to attend a catechetical lecture on Sundays, which was established in many colleges in response to the University's demand of 1579 that the halls and colleges offer formal religious instruction.[62] On top of this, the colleges also took it upon themselves to lay on a constant round of student exercises from which only gentlemen commoners ever escaped. These took the form of weekly revision classes where the college lecturer would test his charges on what they had retained from his lectures, public declamations where undergraduates would take turns to show their skills in Latin prose composition, and frequent disputations where arts students of all levels could demonstrate their mental agility and acuity. In consequence, most students must have spent at least three or four hours a day, every day except Sunday, undergoing formal instruction in college.

Not all colleges provided tuition in every part of the curriculum and some college lecturers had a better reputation than others. As most college lectures were public and open, there was nothing to stop assiduous junior members shopping around to plug the gaps or listen to the best lecturers.[63] There was one subject, however, where official college tuition for most of the period was insufficient or non-existent. This was mathematics. Although mathematics was always an important part of the curriculum and valued for the mental training it provided, only three colleges established mathematics lecturers in the century before the Civil War—New College (1616), Merton (c.1620), and St John's (1636, courtesy of Archbishop Laud). The provision did not expand significantly in the aftermath of the war. Christ Church had an endowed mathematics lecturer from 1667, but he was expected to teach only once a week, and there is no evidence that the post was continually occupied. It was only with the establishment of a second lecturer, under the will of the society physician Matthew Lee in 1765, that mathematics teaching was firmly embedded in the House. Most colleges did not establish a stipendiary lecturer in the

---

[60] Statutes, vol. 3, *Statutes of St John's College*, p. 12.   [61] Ibid., *Statutes of Pembroke College*, p. 15.
[62] See p. 191, this volume.   [63] St John's lectures were closed.

subject until the creation, in 1807, of a separate mathematics class list. Magdalen, for instance, made its first appointment in 1813.[64]

The deficiency throughout the seventeenth and eighteenth centuries was made up by private teaching as much as by the University's professors. Private tuition in mathematics was readily available at Elizabethan and early Stuart Oxford, where a number of heads of house and other senior members took an interest in the subject.[65] The most famous teacher in the era before the Civil War was Thomas Allen of Gloucester Hall, who gave private lessons in mathematics for over sixty years, until his death in 1632. Allen was never a full-time teacher, though, and was particularly sought out by those who wanted advanced tuition. The first person to have gained a living teaching the discipline to junior members was Richard Holland, who began a fifty-year career teaching mathematics and geography in 1620. Holland's successor was John Caswell of Hart Hall, who eventually became the Savilian professor of geometry in 1709. Thereafter, there was no figure of similar prominence in the eighteenth century, but private teachers remained readily available.

In the second part of the period, arts students also sought out private tuition in experimental philosophy. Natural philosophy, as traditionally taught in Europe's universities, had been a logical and deductive science based on the physical works of Aristotle. Seventeenth-century experimental philosophers in Britain and on the continent constructed a new type of physics built on observation, experiment, and measurement, which, in the following century, divided into a series of sub-sciences. Neither the University nor the colleges made much attempt to accommodate the new development, even in the eighteenth century when an interest in experimental philosophy became part of the mark of an educated gentleman. In the course of the late seventeenth and eighteenth century, important aspects of the new mathematical science of motion found their way into the courses given by the two Savilian professors, but the only new professorship endowed in a specific branch of experimental philosophy was the Sherardian chair of botany, established in 1734.[66] As a result, private lecturers saw a market opportunity and filled the gap. Extra-curricular courses in chemistry were first offered in Oxford by the German Peter Stahl, who arrived in 1659 and set up his own laboratory. Then, with the opening of the Ashmolean Museum in 1683, a permanent location was provided for lectures in experimental philosophy, which gave them a quasi-official if never a public stamp.[67] In the mid-eighteenth century, the most popular lectures were given by Balliol's James Bradley. Bradley was Savilian professor of astronomy from 1722 and

[64] Bill, *Christ Church*, pp. 205–6 and 271–2. Balliol had an official lecturer from 1697. Lee had been at Christ Church and was a prominent doctor in Bath and London.

[65] Mordechai Feingold, *The Mathematicians' Apprenticeship: Science, Universities and Society in England, 1580–1640* (Cambridge, 1984), chs 3–4.

[66] The naturalist William Sherard, formerly of St John's, left the University a legacy on his death in 1728. A chair in botany had been established for the naturalist Robert Morison in 1669, but it was not refilled after his death in 1683.

[67] The University actually appointed the first keeper of the Ashmolean, Robert Plot, to be the University's professor in chemistry. But after he demitted in 1689, he had only one successor.

FIGURE 7.3 Ashmolean Museum, 1683. Built to house the collection left to the University by Elias Ashmole, possibly to a design by Wren, the present-day Museum of the History of Science also provided space for the teaching of chemistry and physics and from the beginning of the nineteenth century geology, mineralogy, and rural economy.

also Astronomer Royal. From 1729 to 1760 he gave three courses a year in experimental philosophy at the Ashmolean for a fee of three guineas per course. So frequented were his lectures that it has been calculated that, between 1746 and 1760, over 1,200 undergraduates attended his classes (see Figure 7.3).

The private lecturers disappeared only in the first decades of the nineteenth century when the University finally gave its official imprimatur to the new science in a flurry of endowments which matched the one two centuries before. The year 1803 saw the creation of a professorship in chemistry, 1810 a readership in experimental philosophy, 1813 a readership in mineralogy, and 1818 a readership in geology. The first was founded by George Aldrich, a Nottingham physician who also established several medical chairs; the second was originally provided in a further Crewe benefaction of 1749 but took sixty years to fund sufficiently; while the last two chairs were gifts of the Prince Regent.[68] The burst of activity was completed in 1840 with the foundation of a chair in rural economy. This had been gifted to the University in 1796 by the Sherardian professor, John Sibthorp, but the

---

[68] Nathaniel Crewe, bishop of Durham, had earlier underpinned Encaenia: see p. 148, this volume.

money had been initially used to publish his monumental Greek flora based on his extensive travels in the eastern Mediterranean.[69]

Modern languages was another subject not catered for by the University or colleges until the end of the period, and for which there was again considerable demand from the students. Gentlemen throughout the period needed some knowledge of Italian and French in particular if they intended to go on the Grand Tour, dreamed of a life at court or a diplomatic career, or simply wished to measure up to contemporary conceptions of gentility.[70] Young gentlemen had usually acquired some facility in a modern language before coming up, but their parents expected them to maintain their study while at Oxford. The assiduous studied modern languages on their own, but most, such as William Trumbull, who entered Magdalen in 1622, engaged a native speaker who could give them one-to-one tuition, sometimes as their companion. In the eighteenth century, the competition for a good teacher was strong and less affluent undergraduates unable to secure a permanent tutor could be disappointed. John James' father, a northern parson and schoolmaster who wanted his son to emerge from Oxford as a gentleman, expected John to begin French immediately on his arrival at Queen's in 1778 and hoped he would have three hour-long lessons a week. There was only one teacher hiring himself out in this way, however, a man called Chamberlain, and John was forced to hold back: 'It so happens that Chamberlain has, at present, his hands so full that he is engaged for every hour in the day, and will not be able to attend till the expiration of the Term...Till that time I must defer paying my compliments to Monsieur.'[71]

By then, James and others in his situation should have had their wants satisfied by the University. Oxford, in the eighteenth century, continued to develop its portfolio of ancient language professorships. In 1708 a chair of comparative poetry was set up thanks to the bequest of a former fellow of All Souls, Henry Birkhead;[72] a second chair of Arabic was established somewhat shakily six years later, known as the Lord Almoner's professorship; and a chair of Anglo-Saxon was endowed in 1755 by the non-juring bishop and collector Richard Rawlinson, although it was not to be filled for a further forty years.[73] But there was also a move in the first half of the eighteenth century to promote modern studies. In 1724, in an attempt to provide prospective diplomats with some useful knowledge, the crown created chairs in modern history at both Oxford and Cambridge. Part of the professors' duties was to sustain two teachers in modern languages. There is no evidence, however, that these university teachers were ever engaged at Oxford before Edward Nares was appointed to the professorship in 1813. Even then, public tuition in modern languages was not firmly cemented. It was

[69] *Flora graeca: sive plantarum rariorum historia, quas in provinciis aut insulis Graeciae legit, investigavit et depingi curavit Johannes Sibthorp, M.D* (10 vols; London, 1806–40).

[70] Spanish too was important before 1660, when Spain was the greatest European power.

[71] James, pp. 47, 51–2, 55. Chamberlain charged a guinea for twelve lectures.

[72] Joan Pittock Wesson, *Henry Birkhead, 1617–1696, Founder of the Oxford Chair of Poetry: Poetry and the Redemption of History* (Lampeter, 1999). Birkhead saw himself as the last of the Cavalier poets.

[73] An Anglo-Saxon lectureship temporarily existed at Queen's in the 1690s. For Anglo-Saxon studies at Oxford, see pp. 308–9, this volume.

not until the Taylorian was opened in the late 1840s that Oxford had a professor in modern languages and two permanent teachers in French and German. The first person to hold the chair was the Swiss F. H. Trithen, elected in 1848, who was actually a comparative philologist with an expertise in Sanskrit.[74]

The complex mix of university, college, and private teaching in the period 1550 to 1850 provided Oxford's undergraduates with a rich smorgasbord of intellectual delights from which to choose. In the early nineteenth century, even traditional subjects were being explored more deeply. The science of ethics was traditionally divided into the sub-sciences of politics and economics or the ethics of the household. There is not much sign that either had a place in the curriculum in the seventeenth and eighteenth century, though students were definitely warned off dangerous and ungodly examples of modern political theory and disputations and sermons occasionally had political themes.[75] In the second quarter of the nineteenth century, on the other hand, undergraduates often studied Aristotle's *Politics* in the college classroom, and any student could learn about the new science of economics created by Adam Smith and his successors by attending the university lectures of the holder of the Drummond chair of political economy, created in 1825.[76]

One of the additional qualities of Oxford's rich curriculum was the constantly changing ingredients with which each dish was fashioned. In most cases, the basic content of the courses given by the University's lecturers was set down in the Laudian code or in later documents of foundation. It was Laud's wish, for instance, that the lecturers charged with teaching the four sciences of philosophy should continue to build their course on the works of Aristotle. No reference was made in the code to other schools of ancient philosophy, such as Platonism, Stoicism, or Epicureanism, that had been given a new lease of life by humanist scholars.[77] Nonetheless, there was little attempt to police university teaching. Professors, after the Restoration, were free to teach what they liked as long as they stayed broadly within the remit of their subject. Those who held chairs in a discipline widely covered at college level were free to give up bread-and-butter teaching and lecture on their own scholarly interests. In the 1660s, Thomas Willis used the Sedley chair in natural philosophy to publicize his innovative ideas on the physiology of the brain, which married his experimental work with the anti-Aristotelian theories of the iatrochemists, who explained natural phenomena in terms of chemical reactions rather than in terms of their substantial forms.[78] Thirty years later, the

---

[74] Oxford did not have a Sanskrit chair until later in the nineteenth century. There had been a failed attempt to raise money for a Persian chair in the second half of the eighteenth century. The appointment of a German teacher reflected the contemporary significance of German scholarship.

[75] In 1622, a sermon was given at St Mary's claiming the right of inferior magistrates to resist tyrants: see Anon., 'The Study of Politics in the English Universities 1570–1600' (BA dissertation, Cambridge, 2013), pp. 54–5. Undergraduates would also have picked up some political theory from reading classical history.

[76] Its founder, Henry Drummond, had been an undergraduate at Christ Church and was a reform-minded MP.

[77] *The Cambridge History of Renaissance Philosophy*, ed. Charles B. Schmitt, Quentin Skinner, Eckhard Kessler, and Jill Kraye (Cambridge, 1988), esp. chs iv, vi, vii, and ix.

[78] For iatrochemistry in England, see Allen G. Debus, *The English Paracelsians* (London, 1965).

Scot David Gregory used the Savilian chair of astronomy to introduce Newton's mathematical theory of universal attraction as an explanation of planetary motion to an Oxford audience, only a few years after the Cambridge experimental philosopher had published the *Principia*.[79] College and private lecturers appear to have had a similar licence in the eighteenth and the first half of the nineteenth century to discuss the latest logical and ethical theories in their course. Lecturers, like Edward Bentham at Oriel, had no difficulty introducing Locke's psychology or the new moral sense school of ethics developed by Glasgow's Francis Hutcheson into their teaching.[80] Oxford was never a university that turned its back on new learning in the arts and sciences, as John Wilkins and Seth Ward were quick to point out in the early 1650s, when the University came under attack for obscurantism. The only requirement was that teaching did not threaten the established church or the dynasty.[81]

On the other hand, the smorgasbord may have tempted more than it delighted, for there was no guarantee that lecturers at any level were competent at their job. University lectures must have been frequently tedious before 1800. According to the Laudian code they were to be delivered at dictation speed and questions only asked at the end.[82] College lectures were probably always less formal but the lecturers must have been frequently bored by the elementary level of much of their teaching or just tired of teaching the same old thing year after year. In the eighteenth century, furthermore, there seems to have been a general drop in standards. University professors were often pluralists, so frequently failed to lecture, while fellows became less willing to maintain college lectures once the income from their fellowships rose. As a result, college courses were abandoned entirely or given less frequently. At Magdalen in the 1790s, where the tradition of college teaching had particularly decayed, the number of lecturers was reduced to three and the incumbents were expected to give a lecture only four times a year.[83] Even private lecturers, whose income depended on keeping their paying customers engaged, could be a sore disappointment. The young Jeremy Bentham at Queen's attended the experimental philosophy lectures of Nathaniel Bliss in the 1770s and was not amused:

> We have gone through the Science of Mechanics with Mr. Bliss, having finish'd on Saturday; and yesterday we began upon Optics; there are two more remaining; viz: Hydrostatics, and Pneumatics. Mr Bliss seems to be a very good sort of Man, but I doubt is not very well qualified for his Office, in the practical Way I mean, for he is oblig'd to make excuses for almost every Experiment they not succeeding according to expectation.[84]

---

[79] Gregory had been professor of mathematics at Edinburgh; in Oxford he was attached to Balliol.

[80] Edward Bentham was the author of an *Introduction to Moral Philosophy* (1745), which dealt with the new moral sense school of ethics developed by Hutcheson. Bentham was later the regius professor of divinity.

[81] Allen G. Debus, *Science and Education in the Seventeenth Century: The Webster–Ward Debate* (London, 1970).

[82] Laudian Statutes, pp. 41–2 (Title IV, section 2, ch. 4).

[83] For fellows' stipends, see pp. 282–3, this volume.

[84] *The Correspondence of Jeremy Bentham*, vo. 1: *1752–76*, ed. T. L. S. Sprigge (London, 1968), p. 67: Bentham to his father 15 Mar. 1763. Bliss was also Savilian professor of geometry.

The situation improved dramatically at all levels in the first half of the nineteenth century but the problem at college level was only ever partially solved. The rot was stopped towards the end of the eighteenth century when several determined heads of house took action to revive the quantity and quality of college lecturing. The lead was taken by Christ Church, with the appointment of the headmaster of Westminster, William Markham, to the deanship in 1767. Markham restored college lecturing to its full vigour, and at the House in the last third of the century there appear to have been as many as seven lecturers in post, including one in ancient history.[85] But Christ Church had a huge fellowship, and the average college could not restore the status quo ante. Most colleges, from the end of the eighteenth century, accepted the new reality and accommodated their teaching provision accordingly. By the 1830s and 1840s it was usual to employ a team of no more than three or four: one would concentrate on mathematics; the others would teach Latin and Greek literature, rhetoric, logic, and ethics. In some colleges the demand placed on the lecturers never retained its earlier intensity. At Merton, according to the evidence presented to the royal commission of 1850, each of the two lecturers in literature and philosophy were expected to give only thirty-five weekly classes a year. At other colleges, on the other hand, lecturing was once more hard work and students were attending several lectures a day, as Arthur Evans, uncle of the archaeologist, discovered when he went up to Brasenose in 1841: 'There are three tutors whose lectures, at least some of them, I am obliged to attend to the amount of 12–16 a week.'[86]

A system that entrusted the whole curriculum to three or four teachers was unlikely to provide adequate stimulation to the intellectually gifted. When lecturers had to race through the curriculum and classes contained a wide range of ability, the fare must have been frequently pedestrian. The schoolboy quality of the college class in the first half of the nineteenth century was only accentuated by a new emphasis on pupil–teacher interaction. As Richard Whately, archbishop of Dublin and erstwhile fellow of Oriel, pointed out in 1831 in response to critics, Oxford college lectures were not meant to be lectures in the traditional sense:

> If the subject of the lecture be a classical author, the several members of the class are called on in turn, to translate a portion; questions are put by the tutor, as occasion offers, and remarks are made by him, on points of grammar, philology and criticism, as well as on the subject-matter of the book, whether it be history, philosophy, or poetry. At the same time, directions are given, as often as may be needful, respecting the mode of preparing for these lectures, the books to be consulted, method of analysing and illustrating, and the like.[87]

---

[85] Markham had been college lecturer in rhetoric from 1747 to 1750. His appointment was backed by Secker, archbishop of Canterbury. Lincoln and University College also made moves to reinvigorate college teaching about 1770.

[86] Crook, p. 243. For the royal commission, see Chapter 9, section B, this volume.

[87] HUO, vi. 149.

At best, the experience could be enjoyable with an enthusiastic tutor, such as Arthur Stanley at University College, who knew how to hold the class's attention, albeit in rather infantile fashion:

> In treating a difficult book like the 'Politics' of Aristotle, he would recommend us carefully to note peculiarities with three varieties of coloured pencils under the following heads: truths for all time, red; truths for the time of Aristotle, blue; and the, with a humourous twinkle of his eye, truths for the schools, black.[88]

But many lecturers in the second quarter of the nineteenth century were still indifferent teachers. On coming up to Magdalen in 1826, the Tractarian William Palmer was required to attend the lectures of Edward Ellerton on Herodotus. He found that the lecture simply comprised members of the class taking it in turns to construe the text without any further illumination on the part of the teacher. The Tractarians themselves, for all their pulpit skills, were not necessarily good teachers either, as the later secretary to the 1850 royal commission, Goldwin Smith, recalled. At Magdalen in the 1830s, Smith attended the lectures of the Tractarian James Mozley. The latter's mind was 'rich and gifted'. But he was 'engrossed by the ecclesiastical movement, so that the lectures were little better than form'.[89] Newman was also an appalling lecturer and quite unable to keep order in class. At Oriel in the late 1820s, the undergraduates ran rings round him, moving their desks gradually forwards so that he got trapped in a corner and was forced to summon assistance from the porter by pulling the bell rope in the room. His pupils were soon wise to this and cut the bell rope.[90]

The inadequacy of college lectures in the first half of the nineteenth century encouraged the intellectually ambitious to seek deeper enlightenment from private teachers even in mainstream subjects. But recourse to a private coach would never have become as extensive as it did in this final part of the period but for the new examination system. The introduction of degree classification turned a rite of passage into a competitive struggle. For the ambitious and intelligent it was not enough to take honours; they wished to excel. But this was impossible without extra assistance. Newman at Trinity in the late 1810s was at a college where the lecture provision was good. In his first term he attended a class on Tacitus 'every morning but Thursday; one in Cicero on Wednesday, Mathematics three times a week'. But this was insufficient for an exceptionally precocious student, and he hired a senior scholar of the college, James Adey Ogle, as his coach in mathematics. Ogle saw him privately for two hours a day along with another student. In the term leading up to the BA examination, Newman relied particularly heavily on private coaching. John Wilson, one of the college's tutors, saw him on his own for at least two hours a day and sometimes five.[91]

---

[88] Comments of Arthur Butler, later headmaster of Haileybury: cited in Darwall-Smith, p. 358. Stanley became a fellow of University College after being an undergraduate at Balliol.

[89] Brockliss, p. 311.

[90] James Howard Harris, 3rd earl of Malmesbury, *Memoirs of an Ex-Minister*, 2nd edn (2 vols; London, 1884), i. 18.

[91] *The Letters and Diaries of John Henry Newman*, ed. I. T. Ker, vol. 1 (Oxford, 1978), pp. 43, 49, and 92. Ogle took a First in Mathematics and the physical sciences in 1813, and became regius professor in medicine in 1851.

Newman was ultimately defeated by overwork and nerves, and did not get the First he coveted, but the experience helped him to think of a way of making college lecturing a more useful preparation for the gifted pupil. At Oriel, he and his friends suggested to Provost Hawkins that the undergraduates should be grouped according to ability: dimmer pupils could then be placed into one large class, while the brighter ones could be given more personal tuition. As this, however, would inevitably mean that the most socially prestigious element in college would be condemned to the inferior class, the proposal fell on deaf ears and Newman lost his college post for his pains.[92]

D. Tutors

Faced with a smorgasbord of intellectual delights that were too rich for some and too bland for others, sometimes well prepared but often lacking in relish, and sometimes put on the menu then suddenly withdrawn from the table without notice, the early modern Oxford undergraduate, whatever the level of his intelligence, must have been frequently at a loss in making his curricular choices. Fortunately, from the late sixteenth century, he had a helpful maître d' to help him reach his decisions in the form of his personal college tutor. The undergraduate's tutor (not to be confused with the lecturers, official or private, whose courses he followed, though the roles could overlap) was the pivot around which an Oxford student life came to turn. Broadly speaking, the tutor played Mentor to the undergraduate Anchises. His exact role, however, was continually in a state of development and reinvention across the period, and it could be interpreted conscientiously or indifferently. Precisely identifying the typical early modern undergraduate tutorial experience is therefore well-nigh impossible.

The idea that undergraduates should be put under the care of more senior members of the University surfaces for the first time in the statutes of New College at the end of the fourteenth century. For their first three years at the college, young scholars studying arts or civil law were to be assigned an *informator* from among the other fellows who would look after their progress. The *informator*'s precise role, however, was not defined, and he may simply have provided extra instruction to a small group of youths.[93] The concept of a personal tutor did not begin to develop until a hundred years later with the admission of undergraduate commoners into the colleges. When the founder of Magdalen made provision in the 1480 statutes for the admission of twenty 'outsiders', he also insisted that none should come into residence who was not 'under the care and government' of somebody trustworthy, a *creditus* or a 'creancer'. This prescription was followed in the statutes of the next new foundation, Brasenose, except the English word 'creancer' was replaced by

---

[92] The provost admitted there was some evidence of it happening in other colleges. But he suspected Newman had a religious agenda.
[93] Statutes, vol. 1, *Statutes of New College*, p. 54.

tutor.[94] This term thereafter stuck. In the course of the second half of the sixteenth century, with commoners now admitted willy-nilly into all colleges, the principle was accepted everywhere, and in some cases, as at Balliol, incorporated into the statutes. The halls duly followed suit. By the early seventeenth century, even young foundationers had to have an official university guardian.

Some colleges always insisted that tutors were fellows, but this was never a universal requirement in the sixteenth and first half of the seventeenth century, and in the halls was obviously never the case.[95] While tutors were always, at the very least, a BA, there was no attempt to prescribe their specific graduate status. Some were not even based in their pupil's college or hall. When Edward Hyde, the future earl of Clarendon, came up in the early 1620s, he was a member of Magdalen Hall but his tutor was John Oliver, president of Magdalen College. Nor was the appointment of tutors regulated. An undergraduate commoner had to have a tutor but the choice was up to his father or guardian, who entered into a private arrangement with a member of the University of more senior status for an agreed fee. Tutors were usually people from the same part of the country as their undergraduate charges and they were often relatives. When Anthony Wood entered Merton in October 1648 as a postmaster, his tutor was his elder brother, Edward, who was then a scholar of Trinity: Edward only moved to Merton a month later when he became a fellow.[96]

The appointment of a tutor began to be more closely supervised in the 1650s. The University's visitors during the Interregnum expressed the wish that tutors be thereafter appointed by the heads of house so that only the religiously and morally appropriate would be given the position. Thanks to the Restoration, this initiative had limited effect in the first instance but it was gradually adopted over the following half-century. By the early eighteenth century, the heads of house controlled the appointment of tutors in virtually every college and hall, although the tutors continued to be paid for their services directly by their pupils.[97] The appointing power of the head of house led to a large reduction in the number of active tutors in any one college. In the late sixteenth and seventeenth centuries, most, if not all, the fellows of a college were tutors, including the head of house, who frequently monopolized the wealthiest and most honourable undergraduates. In 1575, seven of the fellows in Lincoln's small fellowship acted as tutors; in 1681–5 there were ten serving tutors at Jesus. From 1700, however, there were seldom more than two or three in a college. This inevitably meant that the number of tutorial pupils any one tutor might have was greatly increased. The Lincoln tutors, in 1575, had from one to six pupils each. In the years 1765 to 1775 at University College, all

---

[94] Ibid., vol. 2, *Statutes of Magdalen College*, p. 60; *Statutes of Brasenose College*, p. 12.
[95] Nothing was said about tutors being fellows in Magdalen's 1480 statutes, but it was college policy from 1547: ibid, *Statutes of Magdalen College*, p. 127 (decision of the president and senior fellows).
[96] Wood, *Life*, i. 129 and 147.
[97] Tracing the revolution with any precision in a college is impossible. Balliol seems to have been one of the last where it occurred.

but thirteen of the 175 undergraduates who passed through its portals were tutored or co-tutored by a single man, William Scott, the future Admiralty judge, Lord Stowell.[98] Tutors who were appointed by heads of house were also much more likely to serve for a long period of time, especially after 1800. Tommy Short of Trinity, who became a fellow in 1816, held the office for forty years.

The role of the tutor as initially conceived appears to have been primarily financial. The admission of commoners, especially in large numbers, was both a financial opportunity—it was usually the poorer colleges, such as Exeter and Brasenose, that took in the most—and a financial headache. Undergraduate commoners were batteled for their rooms and meals, and colleges were understandably anxious that they be paid promptly each quarter. The best way to guard against delay, be it the result of parental dilatoriness or youthful improvidence, was to ensure that each non-foundationer's debts were secured by a third party. As a Magdalen college order made clear in 1576, the tutor was first and foremost a guarantor: 'Item that no scholler be here without a tutor who shall answere for his battels and subscribe his name in the bursars book.'[99] Whether, for most of the sixteenth century, this was the limit of the tutor's financial obligations is impossible to know, but by the turn of the seventeenth century more was demanded of him. From being a guarantor, the tutor became an undergraduate's personal banker. It was the tutor to whom parents sent the funds that the undergraduate needed to survive, and it was the tutor who paid for all the many expenses that the undergraduate incurred, such as the purchase of books and clothing, and advanced him pocket money and credit.

Sir George Radcliffe, who came from a Yorkshire landed family, went up to University College in 1609, where his tutor was his cousin, the college fellow Charles Greenwood, with whom he was already familiar. Greenwood kept a careful tally of the expenditure of his young charge and made it clear to Radcliffe's father when more funds had to be sent. 'As I was sealing my letter,' wrote George to his mother in April 1611, 'my Tutor gave me the note herein enclosed, of such money as he had laide out for me, which was all (within one groate) that he had of mine, saving that of the last 5 L which was sent, there remained 8s, which I had.' Greenwood also saw it as his job to give young George some experience in handling money himself. In the same letter, Radcliffe informed his parents that his tutor was intending thereafter to let him manage his own funds, 'that I may learn to play the good husband before I goe to the Inns of Court'.[100]

The extension of the tutor's financial responsibilities seems to have led him to take on the wider role of *in loco parentis*, policing the undergraduate's morals as well as his purse and ensuring he pursued his studies with due diligence. This development

[98] There were some tutors with a large number of pupils pre-1700: e.g. James Parkinson at Lincoln supposedly had twenty in the latter years of Charles II's reign.
[99] MCA, EL/6, f. 276r.
[100] Robin Darwall-Smith, 'Letters to Mother: The Undergraduate Correspondence of Sir George Radcliffe', *University College Record*, 13: 2 (2002), 71 and 72.

made sense and largely explains why young undergraduate foundationers as well as commoners came to be placed in the care of an older member of the University by the early seventeenth century. It was obviously in the interests of college or hall that tutors undertook the discipline of their charges, as the number of undergraduate residents expanded. Keeping large numbers of teenage boys in line, whatever their status, would have been very difficult if it had been left to the head of house and the college deans. The tutor was also usually near at hand. Gentlemen commoners had their own accommodation, and some tutees might live in another college. But most, in the late sixteenth and seventeenth century, lodged in or above their tutors' rooms, occupying the many cocklofts that were installed from the late Tudor period.

From the early seventeenth century as well, tutors began to take on a much more active educational function. About half of the undergraduates in their care had no intention of taking a degree and many would spend only a couple of years at Oxford before proceeding to the Inns of Court, going abroad, or returning to the family estate.[101] Many too wanted to acquire various extra-curricular accomplishments while they were up. Young gentlemen were not just interested in learning modern languages at Oxford but sought to become proficient on a musical instrument and to improve their dancing, fencing, and equestrian skills. Gentle parents, on the other hand, were anxious that their offspring spent their time wisely and efficiently and received extra-curricular tuition from appropriate and skilful teachers. The tutor was the obvious figure to ensure this came to pass. As a result, he quickly metamorphosed into a director of studies, offering tuition himself if he had the capacity, finding private tutors where needed, suggesting books his charges should read, and increasingly taking his pupils singly or in small groups to quiz them on their personal studies and to give them direct instruction.

Before the establishment of the tutor as director of studies, the serious undergraduate was largely left to his own devices. Richard and Matthew Carnsew were two Cornish gentlemen who attended Christ Church in the 1570s. They worked their way on their own through a number of historical, rhetorical, logical, and ethical texts learning in tandem. When they felt they needed external help, as in mathematics, they hired a personal tutor.[102] Once under the control of a tutor, undergraduates had little opportunity to build their own course. Tutors in the early Stuart era principally offered advice on a student's private reading. There were many works appearing every day from the press that could be usefully perused as a supplement or corrective to the lectures a student followed in the college or University, and tutors provided guidance in navigating the bibliographical maze.[103] But from the mid-seventeenth century, they also offered their charges

---

[101] Young gentlemen were going on the Grand Tour from the beginning of the seventeenth century, though it was only in the eighteenth that it became almost de rigueur: see John Stoye, *English Travellers Abroad, 1604–1667: Their Influence in English Society and Politics* (London, 1952).

[102] The National Archive (Kew), SP 46/15, fs. 212–20: the Carnsews' diary.

[103] Some, such as Thomas Sixsmith of Brasenose, produced formidable reading lists; see 'Directions for my Scholers, what books to buy and read' (1638): Brasenose Archives, MPP 158 A1: discussed in Crook, pp. 47–8.

basic instruction in the key components of the undergraduate curriculum on the grounds that the lecture courses given in the colleges and University were too advanced for most students and they needed to be prepared for the ordeal. A few were given further language instruction. When Sackville Crow arrived in Oxford in 1654, his Greek was so poor that his tutor, Francis Mansell, principal of Jesus, felt it necessary to read Thucydides with him on a daily basis. More commonly, it became the tutor's task to introduce an undergraduate to key components of the under-graduate curriculum—rhetoric, logic, ethics, and mathematics.

The normal practice was for a tutor to take his tutees through an introductory compendium and then suggest particular works they should read on their own. The compendium might be one of his own composition, or one of the several printed and manuscript beginners' courses that had originally been penned years before by another tutor and circulated for many years thereafter. Some had an exceptionally long life, and compendia of logic and ethics composed before 1650 might still be in use a century later. This, though, was unusual, and over the years tutorial courses generally became more sophisticated and demanding, so that, by the mid-eighteenth century, the best could no longer be considered simply preparatory. This often made the official college lectures all but superfluous, a further reason for their disappearance or declining significance. It also made for unnecessary duplication, even if there were seldom more than two or three tutors per college. The problem was solved only at the beginning of the nineteenth century when a serious attempt was undertaken to restore college lectures to their former glory. The tutors' dis-ciplinary and educational roles were separated. The undergraduates were distributed among the college tutors as before. But the tutors now doubled as college lecturers and received each other's pupils in their class.

The dominance of the college tutor in all aspects of an undergraduate's life in the eighteenth century led to a growing emphasis on the peculiar significance of his role. To Edward Bentham, writing in 1760 with all the authority of one who had held the office at Oriel for twenty years, the tutor was the centre point of the undergraduate's life: 'One to whom the care of your health, your morals, your oeconomy, your learning, indeed your whole interests in this place are immediately consigned' (see Figure 7.4).[104] A century later, the Tractarians and their followers were even more effusive. In their eyes, and much to the suspicion of the high and dry, the tutor should turn the undergraduate into a new man. According to William Sewell, fellow of Exeter and White's professor of moral philosophy, a tutor's chief end was more than the communication of knowledge:

> We are...entrusted with the care of the young...and our consideration is to form and fashion and bring them to that model of human nature, which in our conscience we think is perfection...This model...we do not find, and therefore we will not place in the intellect.

[104] Edward Bentham, *Advices to a young man of fortune and rank upon his coming to the university* (Oxford, printed at the theatre, 1760), p. 19.

(22)

I need not use many words to shew what particular regards of respectfulness are due to your tutor, he to whom the care of your health, your morals, your œconomy, your learning, indeed your whole interests in this place are immediately consigned. If he does his duty by you, he well earns not only his stipend, but all the esteem and love that you can pay him. Neither will a tutor of this character be at all solicitous for the continuance of pecuniary advantages to himself, when, after a fair trial of your disposition, he finds that his tuition is no longer attended with credit to the college, or benefit to you. If he be an honest man, he will consider what the nature of his trust requires, what will be for your improvement, and not for your pleasure;---or rather, he will spare no pains to adjust them in perfect consistency

with

FIGURE 7.4 Edward Bentham on the respect owed to an undergraduate's tutor. Bentham was an Oriel tutor in the 1730s and 1740s who decided in later life that freshmen would be better prepared for Oxford if they were given some timely advice before they arrived. His *Advices to a young man of fortune and rank upon his coming to the university* appeared in 1760. His words of wisdom proved popular. His *Advices* went through three editions by 1775.

Newman, many years after leaving Oxford, equated the tutor with the priest:

When I was a Public Tutor of my college at Oxford, I maintained, even fiercely that my employment was distinctly pastoral. I considered that, by the Statutes of the University, a Tutor's profession was of a religious nature. I never would allow that, in teaching the classics, I was absolved from carrying on, by means of them, in the minds of my pupils, an ethical training; I considered a College Tutor to have care of souls.[105]

---

[105] P. B. Nockles, 'An Academic Counter Revolution: Newman and Tractarian Oxford's Idea of a University', *HU*, X, 153 (both quotations). Note how Newman conflates his role as lecturer and tutor.

How far Oxford tutors measured up to such an exalted billing is another matter. Long before the Tractarians turned the tutorial office into a calling, there were clearly assiduous tutors who were meticulous and honest bankers, saw their pupils regularly, carefully supervised their academic studies, and were proactive rather than reactive in safeguarding their moral well-being. One such in the pre-Civil War era was the puritanical John Oxenbridge, a tutor at Magdalen Hall in the 1630s. Not content with discouraging his students from reading lascivious and irreligious works, he got them to study sections of the Geneva Bible, John Ball's *Catechism*, the works of Richard Rogers, and, when sufficiently advanced, Calvin's *Institutes*, and tracts by William Bradshaw and William Pemble.[106] Two further examples in the later Stuart era were Ralph Rawson and Jeremiah Milles. The former, a tutor at Brasenose in the late 1670s, would read to his pupils twice a day, including Sundays; while the latter, a tutor at Balliol in 1701–2, made a strenuous effort to get to know his pupils personally, dining with them and sharing their leisure hours. Thereafter, the information becomes richer and a number of figures stand out in the collective college memory. None, though, came closer to the ideal articulated by Bentham than his near contemporary and tutor at Lincoln in the early 1730s, John Wesley. Put in charge of eleven pupils by the rector, he conscientiously took them through the customary introductory texts and corrected their declamations and exercises in logic. Like Milles he also supervised their leisure hours, accompanying them on walks in the countryside. Above all, and not surprisingly, he took a close interest in their religious and moral well-being. If he did not proselytize unduly, he certainly expected his pupils to be upstanding. According to one disenchanted gentleman commoner, he lectured 'scarce in anything but books of devotion'.[107]

On the other hand, if the satirical literature of the seventeenth and eighteenth centuries is to be believed, there were far more sinners than saints. Uncomplimentary generalized accounts of the Oxford tutor abound. One versifier from the Commonwealth era, himself clearly no angel, dismissed the whole fraternity as knaves, hypocrites, and fraudsters:

> This fellow sends unto our friends,
> To keep our money for his own ends;
> And there he locks it in his truncke,
> Whilst we must upon ticke be drunke.[108]

The satirists' negative stereotype, however, is confirmed by few portraits of actual tutors. And only one, drawn by the acerbic pen of Edward Gibbon, is irredeemably damning. The future historian, still only 14, came up to Magdalen in 1752 as a gentleman commoner after suffering the attentions of a string of private tutors. Gibbon was first entrusted to Thomas Waldegrave, whom he remembered as 'a

---

[106] The English authors were all leading puritans. On the Geneva Bible, largely based on Tyndale's translation, see p. 196, n.28, this volume. It was the version widely used by puritans in England until the Civil War.
[107] Green, p. 340 (letter from Richard Morgan to his father). [108] Ibid., pp. 159–60.

learned and pious man, of mild disposition, strict morals, and abstemious life'. But Waldegrave soon took up a college living, and the teenager, with Waldegrave's other pupils, was transferred to Thomas Winchester. His new tutor left him completely to his own devices:

> [Winchester] well remembered that he had a salary to receive, and only forgot that he had a duty to perform. Instead of guiding the studies, and watching over the behaviour of his disciple, I was never summoned to attend even the ceremony of a lecture; and, excepting one voluntary visit to his rooms, during the eight months of his titular office, the tutor and the pupil lived in the same college as strangers to each other.[109]

In the light of the uniqueness of Gibbon's portrait, it seems best to conclude that the average tutor was relatively conscientious most of the time, if seldom as hands-on as the famous few. Indeed, by the time Gibbon's account was published in 1796, tutors were probably more dedicated than they had ever been. In the seventeenth century, the colleges and halls took little direct interest in an undergraduate's education as long as his tutor kept him under control. From the turn of the eighteenth century, however, the colleges, if not the surviving halls, began to take on greater responsibility for their students' academic development. The tutorial system was slowly formalized. The first step, already encountered, was for the tutor to become an appointee of the head of house. The second was for the college's officers to monitor an undergraduate's progress through the institution of collections. These were a termly oral examination held in hall, where each student in turn presented the notes he had 'collected' from the books he had read and lectures attended during the term and was quizzed on their contents. The system was first introduced at Christ Church at the turn of the eighteenth century by Dean Aldrich, when it seems to have embraced only undergraduates on the foundation who had attended Westminster School and servitors. In the second half of the eighteenth century, however, collections were made compulsory and, at the turn of the nineteenth century under Dean Jackson, became much more inquisitorial. It was in this guise that they were adopted by other colleges. Trinity introduced collections in 1789; Magdalen had done so by 1796; while Balliol instituted them about 1800 and Brasenose in 1809 (see Figure 7.5).[110]

Taken together, the two developments went a long way to guaranteeing that college tutors stuck to their last. Invested by the head of house, tutors could have their pupils taken away if their performance was judged inadequate in any way, as

---

[109] *The Autobiographies of Edward Gibbon*, ed. J. Murray (London, 1896), pp. 77 and 81. Waldegrave took Gibbon on country walks. He had been tutored himself by Wesley. Winchester's name was omitted in the original 1796 edition.

[110] The history of collections at Christ Church can be fully reconstructed thanks to the survival of the college collection books, which record the development of the system across the eighteenth and early nineteenth century. The introduction of collections at Christ Church appears to have been the initiative of the two censors who had overall supervision of the arts students and specifically tutored both the holders of Westminster studentships and servitors.

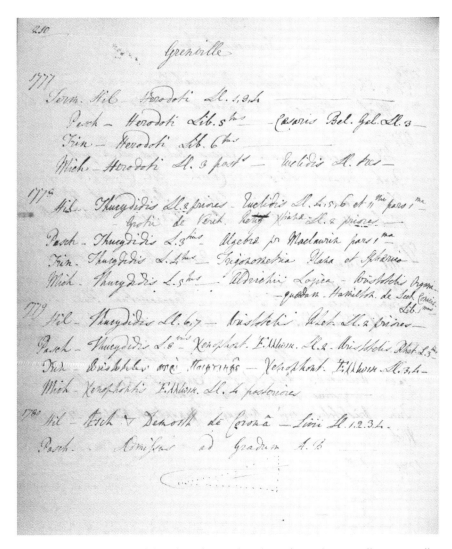

FIGURE 7.5 Books studied by the Christ Church undergraduate William Wyndham Grenville 1777–80. Thanks to the Christ Church collection books, it is possible to know what every undergraduate at the House studied with his tutor in the eighteenth century. Grenville, later prime minister and University Chancellor, principally studied the Greek historians and mathematics while he was up, proceeding as far as conic sections. He studied logic but does not appear to have read Aristotle's *Ethics*.

Newman discovered.[111] At the same time, collections kept the head abreast of what the tutor actually taught. Collections in their mature form were principally instituted to ensure that undergraduates, especially gentlemen commoners, did not fritter away their time. But they were a good way of testing the tutor as much as

---

[111] Wesley, for all his credentials as a tutor, also lost pupils when complaints were made about his religious extremism.

the student, especially in the early nineteenth century when the oral interview became much more intense. What the tutor 'read' to his charges also became much more closely policed, as several colleges, by the end of the eighteenth century, had compiled lists of prescribed authors for each undergraduate year. Here again Christ Church led the way, drawing up annual lists of approved authors from as early as 1717. Frequently revised as new editions or textbooks appeared on the market which seemed to be easier to use or provided a better digest of the present state of the discipline, the Christ Church lists ensured that the college's tutors took their students through a common curriculum, while allowing the more intelligent and committed undergraduate to read more widely.[112]

As colleges became more interested in achieving success in the new schools examination introduced in 1800, supervision of their tutorial staff can only have grown. What closer control could not guarantee, however, was that tutors were always competent teachers. Just as many lecturers were boring, so many tutors were uninspiring. In 1673, the infamous master of University College, Obadiah Walker, who had himself been a tutor, published a treatise on educating young gentlemen. In it he gave a clear idea of tutorial best practice in the second half of the seventeenth century, setting out how a class, some three hours long, should be organized:

> First an account of the former Lectures; then to read and write about half an hour; then to explicate about an equal time. Experience since hath an added an hour more for the Scholars conferring one with another in circles, in presence of their Reader, and disputing on questions given them the reading before. The hour that remains, the Master begins another Lecture, explains it to them, and gives them questions for their next disputations.[113]

An interactive approach to learning, however, was probably only ever championed by a minority of the tutorial fraternity. John James' tutor at Queen's, a century later, was a man called Thomas Nicholson. He seems to have been readily available to his students, provided them with the customary lectures on logic and ethics, and made them compose declamations. John saw him regularly. When he went up, he had to attend his tutor every day at 11 a.m. But Nicholson was pedestrian and dull. The introductory logic textbook Nicholson worked through with James was an old seventeenth-century favourite by Robert Sanderson of Lincoln College. The tutor did no more than ensure that his pupils understood the Latin: 'The Doctor construes a few chapters, which the next lecture we repeat to him. He does not explain a single term, and were I to rely only on the instructions I receive from him, I would find myself deficient.' The ethics text that James next moved onto was another seventeenth-century classic by Gerard Langbaine of Queen's. The

---

[112] For an idea of the range of authors taken up to collections at Christ Church at the turn of the nineteenth century, see the examples published in Bill, pp. 327–40.

[113] Obadiah Walker, *On Education* (Oxford, 1673), p. 122. 'Read and write': presumably a reference to a dictated lecture.

classroom experience was much the same. Nicholson construed the text with great solemnity, 'and if he meet with a sentence which seems peculiarly pointed at young men, he delivers it with so pompous a cadence that I am afraid it excites different ideas than what he could wish'. Nicholson was also an unimaginative disciplinarian, with the result that his pupils laughed at him and thought him a fool: 'By interposing too often in matters of trifling importance he has lost the power of exerting himself effectually where it is requisite.'[114] There is no reason to suspect that Nicholson's limited abilities as a tutor were peculiar. James' father had also been at Queen's and was not surprised by the inadequacy of the man placed over his son. In a letter to one of his friends about John's Oxford experiences, he waxed lyrical about the wholesome effect the '*genius* of the place' might have on a 'lad of spirit'. But he had no expectations that the tutors would make any difference: 'from the tutors, I verily believe, *nothing*'.[115]

That many, perhaps most, tutors were not inspiring teachers is scarcely surprising given their age and inclination. The large majority were always young fellows in their twenties, pursuing higher studies while waiting on a living. They agreed to tutor for its monetary reward rather than from any sense of vocation, *pace* Newman. But account must also be taken of the very different abilities of the undergraduates who came under their wing. Many undergraduates, especially the sons of the gentry for whom university was a rite of passage, were intellectually limited and little interested in their studies. Teaching a mixed ability group in a way that profited every member was possible when tutors had only two or three pupils. But once tutorial groups expanded in size, the abilities of the least distinguished must have determined the pace.[116] In fact, getting many undergraduates to work at all, especially in the eighteenth century when the value of an arts education for a country gentleman had been called into question, must have been a perennial headache. The tutor, at the end of the day, was a hired wage slave, frequently socially inferior to many of his charges, and with few disciplinary weapons at his command.

Keeping undergraduates on the straight and narrow in and out of the classroom must have been a thankless task at any time in the period, and doubtless explains why the shameless, like Winchester, ignored their tutees altogether: it was the easier option.[117] In the late sixteenth and seventeenth centuries, the tutor was largely on his own. In loco parentis, he had the power to punish his pupils for their intellectual and moral delicts but there would have been limits to how often a tutor could take the whip to a young teenager of blue blood. Before the colleges regulated the office, changing tutors was too easy. Close relatives could probably get away with being

---

[114] James, pp. 50, 55, and 56. Sanderson was first published in 1615 and Langbaine long after his death in 1698. There was one eighteenth-century edition in each case.

[115] James, p. 53.

[116] The problem would have been even greater in the early nineteenth century once the tutorial group had developed into the college class. Hence Newman's suggested reform.

[117] Gibbon must have been peculiarly difficult to teach given his chequered earlier educational cursus. As he himself admitted, he was both peculiarly ignorant and peculiarly erudite.

harsh disciplinarians but even then there were limits. Anthony Wood parted company with his brother in February 1650 and took up with another Merton fellow, Clinton Maund, because Edward was too violent:

> A. Wood's brother was pevish and would be ever and anon angry if he could not take or understand Logical notions as well as he. He would be sometimes so angry that he would beat him and turne him out of his chamber; of which complaining to his mother, she was therefore willing that Anthony should take another tutor.[118]

One ingenious solution, adopted by Oxenbridge of Magdalen Hall in late 1633, was to make tutees sign an oath of obedience. Oxenbridge's pupils had to promise to obey his commands in all matters relating to hair and clothing, studies, performance of religious duties, mixing with outside company, and recreation. They were also expected to confess their faults to their tutor and reveal what they knew about the delinquency of their peers. Oxenbridge, however, was soon in hot water for eliciting a private oath. A copy of the *sacramentum academicum* was sent to Archbishop Laud, which resulted in the tutor being called before Vice-Chancellor Duppa to explain himself in April 1634. Even before this, the principal of Oxenbridge's hall, John Wilkinson, had upbraided him for his temerity and had other copies of the offending oath burned in front of him.[119]

In the later Stuart era, some zealous heads of houses gave tutors much needed moral support by regularly visiting the undergraduates in person. Henry Aldrich of Christ Church, for instance, would look in on young gentlemen 'to see that they imploy'd their time in usefull and commendable Studies',[120] while Thomas Tully of St Edmund Hall supposedly visited student rooms every day in the 1670s. But it was only from the mid-eighteenth century, when the tutor became a quasi-college official, that he enjoyed real backing. Whereas colleges had previously intervened only when the offence was so heinous that it merited expulsion or the undergraduate was on the foundation, they now largely took over the tutor's disciplinary role. The tutor was no longer judge and jury in his own cause. He was free to report his charges for wrongdoing, and the instrument of vengeance was now the college dean. This scarcely made disciplining the delinquent easier, however. Most undergraduates now lived in separate sets and were no longer under the immediate wing of their tutors, so their misbehaviour outside the classroom could be difficult to detect.[121] Moreover, young men in their late teens and early twenties were too old to be beaten, while fining them was also to little purpose when they were rich young gentlemen. The favourite punishment therefore became the imposition, giving out lines, or demanding that the malefactor should write an essay in his own time.[122]

---

[118] Wood, *Life*, i. 162.

[119] *Calendar of State Papers, Domestic Series, of the Reign of Charles I*, vol. 6: 1633–4, pp. 563 and 571 (22 and 27 April 1634). Oxenbridge was ejected from the University. He had an eventful career as a non-conformist minister in England and the colonies.

[120] Hearne, iii. 89.   [121] See p. 262, this volume.

[122] Even in the harsher seventeenth century, corporal punishment could be exacted only on those under 18: see Laudian Statutes, pp. 146–55 (Title XV, *passim*).

An Oxford tutor's lot can never have been an entirely happy one at any time in the period. Continually the butt of provocation from the bored, the blue-blooded, and the simply bloody-minded, tutors who forged a lifelong bond of trust and affection with their charges, and many did, were clearly remarkable men who must have eventually become effective ministers of souls. Before the nineteenth century, however, a college tutorship was never the starting point for a highly successful career in the church. The first to achieve greatness, indeed to ascend right to the top of the greasy pole, was Archibald Tait, archbishop of Canterbury in 1869. Tait, a Balliol man, was a tutor in his college from 1835 to 1842. At a time when Balliol dominated the schools results, its master, Jenkyns, was anxious to maintain momentum by appointing only the best. Tait did not disappoint. Although never tempted down the Tractarian road, he was nonetheless the kind of tutor Newman and his friends approved of, as a later fellow of Balliol, W. C. Lake, attested:

> He gave me at once that impression of strength of spirit which I always associated with him through life. I soon became almost, or quite, his earliest College pupil; and felt at once his genuine kindness and interest in his pupils. In those days at Oxford… intimacies between tutors and pupils ripened rapidly. I was a companion on a short tour in Belgium and Germany in 1837, and again in 1839, and during my last undergraduate year in 1838 was constantly with him.[123]

E. Undergraduate Life

In the late middle ages, two to four college foundationers usually shared a room. They had individual partitioned-off studies but otherwise lived and slept together, albeit in separate beds. Presumably accommodation in the halls was organized along the same lines. The flood of lay commoners into the University in the century before the Civil War did not lead to any significant change in the customary arrangements. From the second half of the sixteenth century, old buildings were altered and new ones erected to accommodate the increased numbers but there were never enough rooms to allow individual occupation. Simple commoners, battelers, servitors, even sometimes scholars on the foundation, were crammed into the newly constructed cocklofts where they frequently lived cheek to jowl.[124] Gentlemen commoners were better lodged as befitted their dignity, and normally occupied the ground-floor rooms in a quadrangle, which were relatively spacious if often damp, as they were not always floored or wainscoted. But they too had to share, like the diarist John Evelyn, who roomed with his brother at Balliol in 1640.[125]

The rooms themselves would have had few pieces of furniture beyond bedsteads, chairs, and tables. Their occupants may have made some effort to make them more comfortable by purchasing curtains or other hangings, but in such cramped

---

[123] Jones, p. 190.
[124] Both Wood and his elder brother occupied cocklofts while they were scholars on the foundation: Wood, *Life*, i. 129 and 147.
[125] Evelyn, *Diary*. ii. 23. Fellows usually had the first-floor rooms, which were healthier.

conditions undergraduates had few possessions beyond what could be kept in a private trunk or on a bookstand. The inventories of undergraduates who died in the course of their studies prepared for the Vice-Chancellor's court suggest that their principal belongings were books, bedlinen, and clothes.[126] Radcliffe's letters home from University College confirm that even the well heeled had limited needs. His one extravagance was the purchase of a bass viol which cost 30 shillings and must have been difficult to keep safe. Otherwise, his chief request was for day-to-day apparel:

> I lose my handkerchiefs fast: if it shall please you to send me some…I shall rest so much more indebted to your motherly kindness.

> If you send my shirts I pray you let them be strong, or else they will do but little service; for my laundresses beat out all in the washing.[127]

After 1660, undergraduates began to enjoy more space. Much of the building boom in the late seventeenth and early eighteenth centuries was an attempt to meet a novel demand for privacy among the gentle classes and to attract gentlemen commoners: seven of the nine double rooms in New College's Garden Quadrangle, built in the 1680s, for instance, were reserved for this class of student and were intended for single occupancy. Meanwhile, rapidly falling numbers after 1720, coupled with the long periods of absence of many fellows, meant that few eighteenth-century undergraduates of any status were required to share, a state of affairs that continued to pertain when attendance grew again at the beginning of the following century. Better-off undergraduates could even afford to be choosy and wait for a room or rooms of the right quality to become available, while tutors would ingratiate themselves with parents by claiming to have secured the perfect accommodation for their offspring, as Walter Stanhope's father was told on his son's arrival at University College in 1766.[128]

Undergraduates in the eighteenth and first half of the nineteenth century also spent much more time and money making their rooms habitable. Lodged separately, part of a more consumer-orientated culture, and generally more affluent than their predecessors, most students were anxious to personalize their living space as soon as they arrived. Furniture tended to be handed down from one occupant to the next. On entering into residence, the existing pieces were valued, and the former occupant paid from a third to two-thirds of the sum to compensate for any additional purchases he might have made. Smaller and more decorative items, however, had to be bought anew: fireguards and tongs, a chimney glass, above all china and glasses had to be obtained in order to entertain guests. John James' mother, as anxious as his father that their son should become a man of taste, was

---

[126] OUA, Vice-Chancellor's court, wills and inventories: Microfilm HO235000, Reels 001–007. Judgement based on brief survey.

[127] Letters 27 July 1609 and 16 March 1610: cited in Darwall-Smith, 'Letters to Mother', p. 75.

[128] L. G. Mitchell, 'The Stanhopes at Univ.', *University College Record*, 13: 2 (2002), p. 86. On the long absences of fellows, see pp. 284–5, this volume.

adamant he spared no expense on arriving at Queen's in the late 1760s, even to the extent of purchasing green tea 'for genteeler company'.[129] By the first half of the nineteenth century, undergraduate rooms could be veritable Aladdin's caves full of exotic bric-a-brac: prints on the walls, card tables, peculiar gadgets associated with field or other sports, and the ubiquitous paraphernalia needed for the fashionable pastime of smoking.[130] The undergraduate wardrobe also became much more lavish as the richest undergraduates were keen to keep up with London and Bath. Since gowns were worn outside the room, these too had to be of the right cut and quality, as the young Viscount Lewisham explained to his friend, Walter Bagot, in 1720, who was on the point of joining him as gentleman commoner at Magdalen:

> You must have 12 yards of a rich black Damask, half Ell wide. 14 yards of a plain strong
> black silk to line it, half yard wide (If you don't buy a good silk for your lining, the
> damask will soon frett it out) 5 dozens of substantial loops & buttons, they must be
> gold ... the loops are a sort of open lace with a little gold fringe at the end, the buttons
> are in the shape of a barrel, with a little tuft at each end, the loops must be pritty rich
> or they dont look well att all, upon black. This is for your best gown, but you must
> have a gown for every day, of plain black silk, which you had better buy hear.[131]

The undergraduate day officially began and ended with attendance at prayers in the college chapel or the hall's *aula*.[132] In the seventeenth century, undergraduates had to rise early: morning prayers were at 6 a.m., evening prayers twelve hours later. By the second half of the eighteenth century, in contrast, the working day had been shortened by as much as three hours. Colleges gave students another hour in bed and brought forward evening prayers to 4 or 5 p.m. Trinity, in 1770, even allowed young gentlemen to get up at their leisure by having a 'second house' at a quarter to eight in the morning.[133] In-between these two acts of worship, undergraduates were expected to be involved in formal or informal academic study. Only the late afternoons and evenings were put aside for relaxation and the pursuit of what the University historically decreed to be suitable leisure activities. Sunday brought a different routine, but one more closely built around the chapel or the city churches. Undergraduates were never incarcerated in their college or hall. This would have been impossible when so much academic activity took place outside its walls, physical activity was deemed good for the soul, and so many undergraduates were gentlemen. But they were expected to be resident overnight. There was no official bedtime, but the gates of the city and the gates of the colleges and halls were

---

[129] James, p. 47: letter, 6 Nov. 1778.
[130] Cf. the description of Larkyns' room in Cuthbert Bede's extremely popular *The Adventures of Mr. Verdant Green: An Oxford Freshman*, 2nd edn (London, 1853), ch. 7 (with illustrations, pp. 57 and 59).
[131] MCA, P287/C3/6.
[132] In the halls' case, stipulated in a new set of Aularian statutes, issued in 1636: 'The statutes of the halls', section 2, clause 4, in OUS, i. 322. On Sundays and feast days inhabitants of the halls were expected to attend the local parish church or a college chapel (ibid., p. 321).
[133] Towards the end of the period, prayers had been put back as late as 8 a.m. This was the case at Oriel by 1778.

closed at 9 p.m. Any undergraduate outside his institution after that was in breach of the rules and was punished.[134]

Meals were supposed to be taken only inside the college or hall. In the eighteenth century, coffee houses, cooks' shops, and victuallers were all put out of bounds by order of the Hebdomadal Board.[135] Breakfast would be eaten before or after prayers and was an insubstantial meal consumed in the undergraduate's room. Initially, it was no more than bread and small beer obtained from the buttery, but the fare improved in the eighteenth century when undergraduates lived on their own and were better off. Breakfast set the tone for other meals taken in college rooms, which were never much more than snacks. Although, in the course of the eighteenth century, an undergraduate's room became a centre of sociability where large amounts of alcohol as well as tea and coffee might be consumed, it was never where an undergraduate was supposed to dine. Substantial meals were to be taken in common in hall, each undergraduate seated at a table that marked out his status.

Before about 1750 there were two common meals a day: dinner and supper. The first took place at the early hour of 11 a.m., the second about 6 p.m. In the second half of the eighteenth century, dinner was gradually put back to mid- to late afternoon, and by the turn of the nineteenth century was usually scheduled for 4 p.m. At the same time, the common supper was abolished, and foundationers received their daily allowance at one sitting.[136] Although attendance at common hall was always compulsory, little attempt was made to make the experience enjoyable. Filling but stodgy, the common dinner's essential ingredients were meat (boiled or roasted), vegetables, bread, and beer, and common supper's pottage. Occasionally the fare was enlivened by eggs and fish.[137] An undergraduate's status determined the quantity not the quality of the repast, which at times was so poor that the diners objected. At Queen's on 6 May 1748, the commoners found the boiled meat so unpalatable that they complained to the dean and, on receiving no redress, refused to attend hall. When the college attempted to starve the undergraduates into submission by preventing food coming in from outside, the commoners en bloc demanded permission to migrate to another college.[138] Even if the meal were edible, dinner can hardly have been a sparkling social event in the first half of the period when students had to converse in Latin or risk being fined.

How undergraduates filled their day depended on the level of their commitment to their studies. For most of the period the student community could be crudely divided into the studious and the relatively idle. The former were usually the less affluent undergraduates or younger sons, who looked to a career in the church,

---

[134] No official timetables exist; the information given is a composite from individual examples and theoretical writing.

[135] Magrath, Queen's, p. 231: order of 1766.

[136] Ibid., p. 135: Queen's ruling 1769.

[137] At Oriel about 1560 apparently no vegetables were served. Vegetables normally came from the college garden.

[138] Magrath, Queen's, pp. 207–12. The dean had declared the food was worse in the late cook's time.

though after the establishment of the new competitive BA examination in 1800, they could include the earnest of all backgrounds. In the first half of the nineteenth century they were known as 'reading men'. The idle were largely young gentlemen up at Oxford, if not to sow their wild oats, then to burnish their cultural credentials, make useful friends, and enjoy themselves. In the eighteenth century the most visible were called 'smarts' because of the interest they took in their attire, but the group was never limited to the sartorially distinguished and included any undergraduate with limited academic ability, pretensions, or commitment. Towards the end of the period, the idle included the 'boating men', whose primary interest was river racing.

In the seventeenth century, both groups spent long hours in each other's company. At this date, every undergraduate was expected to attend the gamut of scheduled college lectures, disputations, and declamations, and wait on his tutor when required, and the formal timetable covered most of the day. When John Harris was a scholar at Trinity in the early 1680s, he was free only in the evenings. His day began at 7 a.m. with a lecture in hall, and was a constant round of college and tutorial exercises until at least 6 p.m. In the eighteenth century, in contrast, the assiduous and the idle would have studied together less often. Colleges, for most of the century, allowed gentlemen commoners to escape disputations and the daily diet of official classes was less. Walter Stanhope at University College proved to be an academically minded gentleman commoner, but in February 1767 he was attending merely one college or tutorial lecture a day and college disputations twice a week.[139]

In the first half of the nineteenth century, when the official college curriculum expanded again, the two groups were once more thrust together for several hours a day. There was far less disputing and declaiming towards the end of the period, but the daily diet of college lectures mushroomed, as was noted in section C, and undergraduates were expected to compose a weekly essay or composition in English or Latin, which was often corrected in class. In the final part of the period, too, as collections became commonplace, it would have been difficult for the academically indifferent simply to go through the motions. Every student must have had to embrace the work ethic to some extent. Had this not been the case, the number of undergraduates taking a degree could not have risen in a period when the examination for the BA had become more onerous. According to James Pycroft of Trinity, there were many who got a BA in the 1830s who 'did not pretend to be studious or hard-reading men' but simply 'went quietly through the academical course'.[140]

What particularly divided the studious from the idle was their attitude to personal study and leisure. The former not only assiduously fulfilled their college and tutorial obligations but knuckled down to private reading when released from class, even if this meant rising early and working long hours in the evening. From

---

[139] The college at this date was attempting to reintroduce daily disputations.
[140] Hopkins, p. 232.

the mid-eighteenth century too, the most dedicated could go the extra mile and compete for the Chancellor's and Newdigate Prizes. The first were prizes in Latin verse and English prose composition instituted in 1769, the second an English poetry prize established in honour of the long-serving university MP, Sir Roger, in 1806.[141] Competing for a university prize, however, called for real dedication and even serious students found they had insufficient time. John James, the parson's son who went up to Queen's in 1778, was keen to enter for the Chancellor's in 1780 when the theme for the verse prize was the death of Captain Cook.[142] But he never got down to writing his Latin poem, chiefly because he was too much caught up in his personal studies. In his first years at Queen's, James waited on his tutor every day at 11 a.m. to study logic and ethics, and in the third year he had to attend disputations in the college hall at noon. Otherwise the rest of his day was his own. He initially appears to have spent two hours a day supplementing his tutor's inadequate lectures on Sanderson by reading independently the more up-to-date logic manuals by William Duncan and Isaac Watts, and finally Locke's *Essay concerning Human Understanding*.[143] But his real love was classical literature. Beginning work at 9 a.m., apparently half an hour before anyone else, he spent the first part of the day translating an English version of Cicero back into Latin. The afternoons he dedicated to a close perusal of other Latin and Greek classics that he also sometimes read in translation for comparative purposes. By the end of his time at Oxford he had been through most of Terence, Virgil, Livy, and Horace among the Latin authors, and Lucian, Pindar, Aristophanes, Anacreon, Xenophon, Plato, and Homer among the Greek, calling on friends for assistance where help was needed: 'If anything occurs difficult or worth observation, I talk it over with some of my acquaintance.' He further found time to follow a series of university and private lecturers—William Scott on ancient history, Benjamin Wheeler on divinity, and Martin Wall on chemistry. He even spent his moments of relaxation profitably: 'Now and then after supper, I sit with my friends, and seldom walk out without company, and, as our conversation is either literary or at least innocent and entertaining, I hope to receive benefit from it.' Rambles in the countryside became occasions to botanize.[144]

The idle, on the other hand, reneged on their academic contract and kept their personal study to a minimum, taking every chance to desert their books

---

[141] Chancellor Grenville added a Latin prose Chancellor's prize. In the early nineteenth century there could be fifty to sixty entrants for each: see Copleston, *Calumnies*, p. 153. Other prizes were established towards the end of the period: the Ellerton Theological Essay (1825); the Dean Ireland annual scholarship (1825); the university mathematical scholarships (1831); and the Boden Sanskrit scholarship (1831).

[142] James, pp. 107 and 122. Cook was killed on his third voyage in 1779. The prize was won by Lord Wellesley, a student and fellow of Christ Church.

[143] Watts published his manual in 1746, Duncan (professor of natural philosophy at Aberdeen) in 1748. Both went through many editions.

[144] James, pp. 51, 55, 68, 81–2, 92–4, 101, 110, 143, 146. Scott was the Camden professor, Wheeler the regius professor of divinity who lectured privately in the evening, and Wall a private chemistry lecturer. James did not think much of Wall. For a day-to-day account of the studies of a serious undergraduate towards the end of the period, see *The Gladstone Diaries*, vol. 1: *1825–1832*, ed. M. R. D. Foot (Oxford, 1968), pp. 204ff. Gladstone was at Christ Church from 1828 to 1831.

for pleasurable activities. According to the satirical portrait painted by Nicholas Amhurst in 1726, a 'smart' was a dainty dandy who was in the coffee house by 10 or 11 a.m. in a state of *academical undress*, cut college hall, and dined in his own room 'upon a *boil'd* chicken, or some *pettitoes*', spent an hour dressing in the afternoon before going out on the town, then, after chapel, drank 'Tea with some celebrated *toast*' before escorting her around Magdalen Grove or Paradise-Garden: 'He seldom eats any supper, and never reads any thing but *novels* and *romances*.'[145] The average malingerer was more hot-blooded. He ate copiously, drank to excess, and adored field sports and physical exercise. In Elizabeth's reign, he would have coursed hares and illegally hunted the queen's deer in Shotover forest, as the future astrologer Simon Forman claimed to have done;[146] in the first half of the nineteenth century, he would have spent every day on the river and belonged to the Phoenix, Oxford's first dining society, established at Brasenose in 1778, or one of the other rowdy drinking and eating clubs it spawned.[147] Such men were only academically lazy and quite capable of submitting to discipline when it came to burnishing their physical attributes. John Evelyn left next to no information for posterity about his academic activities at Balliol in the late 1630s, but he proudly noted the exact day on which he joined a dancing and vaulting school.[148]

In the late sixteenth and seventeenth century, the idle must have been the despair of their tutors. The rules of behaviour that governed members of the University throughout the period had largely been drawn up in the late middle ages and were modelled on monastic regulations. Foundationers and non-foundationers alike were banned from wenching, gaming, and drinking; they were expected to keep gate-hours; and they were allowed only to relax decorously. Making young gentlemen with time on their hands obey such rules would have been difficult, and not surprisingly there are many individual examples of wrongdoing. Some students were notorious lawbreakers, like William Finmore of St John's, who was habitually to be found in the alehouse in the early 1580s. Others, like Edmund Verney, up at Trinity a hundred years later and temporarily expelled for being absent from college at night, were independently minded teenagers seeing how far they might stretch the rules. But the extent and frequency of delinquency in the Tudor and Stuart era, whatever its form, can only be imagined. As breaches in discipline in college generally came under the purview of the tutors and there are no surviving proctorial records of external wrongdoing, examples of student misconduct come only from the occasional surviving letter or memoir. All that can be said with any certainty,

---

[145] N. Amhurst, *Terrae filius; or the secret history of the University of Oxford* (London, 1726), p. 255. Amhurst presents himself as a loyal Whig duty-bound to restore an ancient tradition and take the University and its members to task for their many shortcomings. Paradise-Garden was a riverside terrace attached to an inn near today's Park End Street. It was divided by cropped hedges into private drinking areas: see Zacharias Conrad von Uffenbach, *Oxford in 1710*, ed. W. H. and J. C. Quarrell (Oxford, 1928), p. 9.

[146] Bodleian Library, MS Ashmole 208, fo. 142r.

[147] In the eighteenth century, the lazy gentleman commoner would have repaired to the fellows' common room to drink away the afternoon. Peter and John Lovell, up at Oriel in the late 1770s, visited the common room virtually every day, and on particularly bibulous occasions would be batteled for six bottles of port.

[148] Evelyn, *Diary*, ii. 20–1.

given the relatively few instances of undergraduates being cited before the Vice-Chancellor's court for murder and mayhem after 1570, is that ill-disciplined undergraduates before and after the Civil War were boisterous and rowdy rather than homicidal.[149]

After 1700, when information is much fuller, rule-breaking of the most egregious kind seems to have fast disappeared altogether. In the first half of the eighteenth century, violence could flare when students were under the influence of alcohol. In the early 1720s, two young Magdalen bucks, Sir William Wheler and Wigley Statham, who had been drinking heavily at Trinity, got into a fight with a Jesus servitor and a servant near All Saints Church, which ended with the servant being stabbed and Statham being badly beaten up.[150] But such a serious fracas was uncommon, despite the fact that many undergraduates in the early Hanoverian era still had easy access to weapons. More typical was the brawl that ensued at Brasenose a few years later, when a drinking competition ended with one of the party being kicked down the stairs. Even brawling became infrequent after 1750 as teenage students appear to have completely internalized the Addisonian ethic of politeness and come to see interpersonal violence in the defence of injured pride as unbecoming and demeaning. While Proctor in 1774, the New College diarist, James Woodforde, caught many undergraduates in taverns or out after gating hours, but the miscreants were drunk rather than vicious and were sent on their way with a warning and imposition.[151] Within the walls of the college, too, undergraduates normally misbehaved outrageously only when they were in their cups, and then broke things rather than each other's heads. Even purported hell-raisers, such as the explorer Richard Burton, up at Trinity for two terms in 1840–1, were much more sedate than their memoirs have led future generations to believe. Burton arrived at Oxford from Italy rather than public school, and was already sexually experienced. His claim, though, that he got himself rusticated by attending a steeplechase illegally and attacking the fellows' honour seems to have been a fabrication.[152]

There are few traces either of gross academic delinquency in the later part of the period. It was certainly suspected that undergraduates were likely to cut college or tutorial lectures and absent themselves from in-house disputations, for students at Queen's in the second half of the eighteenth century had to swear that they would 'be

---

[149] More can be known about ill-discipline among the young foundationers, for their sins were recorded in college registers, but the evidence from the All Souls punishment book suggests that undergraduate scholars or fellows were surprisingly well behaved. Their chief sins were cutting prayers, missing meals in hall, and wearing their hair too long. The most egregious offender was Robert Gentilis (Gentili), son of the regius professor in law, who in 1604 was elected a fellow at the age of 14 in breach of the statutes, and was a perpetual nuisance for the eight years that he spent in the college. On 12 May 1607 he was put on bread and water for a day as a punishment for fighting: *The Warden's Punishment Book of All Souls College, Oxford, 1601–1850*, ed. Scott Mandelbrote and John H. R. Davis (OHS; Oxford, 2013), p. 8.

[150] Hearne, vii. 144.

[151] E.g. Woodforde, pp. 224–5 (the case of Taylor of Worcester and Duprée of Exeter).

[152] There were probably some undergraduates in the second half of the period, as in the first, who used the services of Oxford's and Abingdon's many prostitutes, but none has come to light. The only reference is a fictional one. The plot of Tobias Smollett's *Humphrey Clinker* (1771) turns on Squire Bramble unwittingly employing as his servant his bastard son, conceived while he was up at Oxford.

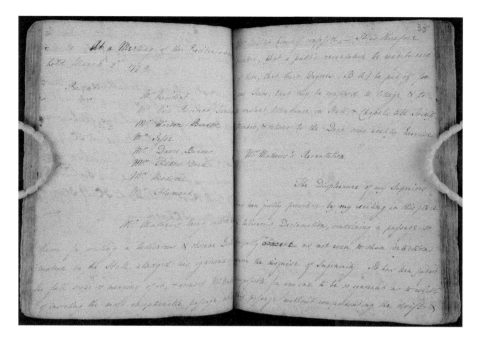

FIGURE 7.6 Punishment of William Matthews, undergraduate, Trinity College, 1779. The punishments meted out to Trinity undergraduates were carefully recorded in the surviving Dean's Book. After delivering a subversive declamation and trying to pin the blame on a fellow undergraduate, Matthews was forced to apologize in public and lost a term towards his degree. He was also gated, made to attend hall and chapel each day, and ordered to write a weekly exercise for the dean.

punctual in attending', unless they had a good excuse.[153] But there is no evidence that this was ever a serious problem, even once college exercises became compulsory for all students. The orientalist William Jones did not attend tutorial lectures once he became a scholar at University College in 1764, but this was because he was judged so advanced that he was allowed to study entirely on his own. Perhaps tutors and the college authorities made no effort to follow up malingering provided it was covered up by a suitable apology, as Gibbon discovered when he decided to miss one of Waldegrave's lectures as a test.[154] A bigger problem was students who turned up and disrupted or made a mockery of proceedings. This was always deemed unacceptable behaviour and dealt with severely, as William Matthews of Trinity discovered. In March 1779, he was forced to make a public apology in hall for 'reciting in this place a ludicrous declamation, containing a passage so palpably obscene as not even to shun detection under the disguise of ingenuity' (see Figure 7.6).[155]

What the deans continually stamped down upon after 1750 was non-attendance at chapel, improper dress, general rowdiness, keeping firearms and dogs, and staying out after the gates were closed. In the second half of the eighteenth and at

---

[153] 'Dr Smith's Rules and Orders for ye better Regulation of ye College': James, p. 243.
[154] Gibbon, p. 78.   [155] Hopkins, p. 200 (deans' book).

the turn of the nineteenth century, sensible colleges enforced the rules with a light touch. Queen's attitude to gate-hours was particularly lenient. The college only punished undergraduates who knocked up the porter after midnight and were serial offenders.[156] Undergraduates in all colleges were only sent down for unforgiveable offences. The expulsion of the poet Shelley and his friend Thomas Jefferson Hogg from University College after publishing anonymously *The Necessity of Atheism* in 1811 is the stuff of legend. But Shelley, an unconventional student who dressed in a slovenly fashion and played practical jokes, could easily have avoided his fate. His pamphlet shocked the university establishment but the college took time to investigate his involvement in its publication, and he was thrown a lifeline by the master and fellows that he refused to grasp: 'I was informed, that in case I denied the publication, no more would be said. I refused, and was expelled.'[157]

After 1815, colleges became more authoritarian. There was no longer any fear that undergraduates would become involved in radical politics, though students on the continent were increasingly caught up in anti-governmental agitation and Oxford students took an interest in university reform. The change rather reflected a new and peculiarly charged belief, associated perhaps with that contemporary Romantic emphasis on the vulnerability of youth, that undergraduates too easily fell prey to temptation and had to be kept out of harm's way. Particularly worrying was the thought, in the 1830s, that Oxford might soon be joined to London by a railway. In 1838, Vice-Chancellor Ashurst Turner Gilbert, principal of Brasenose, informed the House of Lords committee set up to look at the Great Western Railway Bill that such a junction would turn Oxford into a sink of vice and corruption as young men swarmed to the capital to waste their money gambling in the London clubs.[158] Doubtless it was for this reason that the colleges did little to prevent the development of college sport. If some tutors, like Tommy Short of Trinity, thought it disrupted study, most felt it kept the devil at bay.[159] But Oxford's undergraduates were now nearly all 18 when they matriculated, and the new tougher regime came close to treating them as schoolboys. Tutors who were sticklers for discipline in an earlier age, such as Nicholson of Queen's, had soon become laughing stocks. In the late Hanoverian era, pocket Hitlers brought the whole disciplinary system into disrepute. The result was growing frustration. Trinity was particularly rule-bound in the final decades of the period, when an undergraduate caught loafing around college in his hat could even be given an imposition. In 1831, its undergraduates finally rebelled. Antagonized by an overzealous dean who set impositions for the most minor offences, they smashed his windows in protest, and then, far from showing repentance, petitioned the president for redress.

[156] 'Dr Smith's Rules': James, p. 244.   [157] Darwall-Smith, pp. 339–42.

[158] PP 1837–8 House of Lords, XX, 'Oxford and Great Western Union Railway Bill', pp. 225–47 (Gilbert's evidence, esp. p. 234). Gilbert claimed (for effect?) that many young bloods were already a long way down the primrose path to perdition: they attended race meetings where gambling was rife and consorted with prostitutes in the neighbouring towns.

[159] Tommy Short stopped Trinity scholars from rowing. He called rowers 'hydro-maniacs'.

F. The Costs of Study

For both the assiduous and the idle, the cost of studying at Oxford was principally determined by status. The more privileged and better accommodated the undergraduate, the higher the charge for board, lodging, and tuition, and the greater the pressure to spend money on luxuries. During the period, for no category of student was study cheap, however, and costs rose faster than inflation. In the 1560s, a poor student needed some £4 to pursue his studies and a well-to-do commoner twice that amount. By the early seventeenth century, when prices had doubled and were still rising rapidly, the most lowly student needed £8 to survive reasonably well; a commoner, like George Radcliffe of University College, £16 minimum; and the new breed of gentlemen commoners probably £35–£45. In the second half of the seventeenth and the first half of the eighteen century, once inflation had peaked about 1640, each category would have needed three times these sums. A servitor, such as the innkeeper's son and future Methodist George Whitefield, at Pembroke in the 1730s, could get by on £24; a batteler needed about £40; and a gentleman commoner some £120.[160] In the first half of the nineteenth century, when virtually all undergraduates were commoners and prices had doubled again, it was possible to get by on £150, but a bill of £200–300 was not uncommon.[161] Extravagant undergraduates, generally gentlemen commoners, spent far in excess of this. The foppish Christopher Martyn of University College was annually consuming £20 as early as 1584, while the Newdigate brothers (John and Richard) at Trinity in the late 1610s were spending the same on their battels alone, plus a further £2 4s. a quarter for their tutor's services and 6s. 8d. for lessons on the lute. These, though, were small sums. In the second half of the seventeenth century, Sir Thomas Southwell got through £200 per annum at Christ Church; Lord Brooke £450 at Magdalen; while the future Chancellor, Lord James Butler, in one spectacular year at Christ Church, threw away £1,100.[162]

The conscientious also had difficulty in keeping expenses down. Serious scholars might not spend a great deal on fancy clothes or, in the eighteenth century, on stylish furnishings, but they coveted books, and their purchase, though the cost diminished comparatively over time, could make a large hole in the student budget. It was an expense, moreover, that was difficult to avoid. College (and hall) libraries were usually open only to senior members, gentlemen commoners, and undergraduates of three years' standing, while the Bodleian admitted no junior members at all except barons' sons. In the eighteenth century, only eight colleges—Trinity, Magdalen, Exeter, Wadham, Merton, Balliol, University College,

---

[160] An ordinary commoner could also get by on £40 a year if he lived frugally and inhabited one of the surviving halls. George Fleming, brother of Henry of Queen's, who was at St Edmund Hall in the late 1680s, got through on only £9 3s. 4d. in the autumn term of 1688–9: see *The Flemings of Oxford*, ii. 244–5. This collection contains the termly accounts of a number of members of the Fleming family who attended the University. For Henry, see p. 228, this volume.

[161] A middling middle-class family would have a yearly income of about £300 c.1850.

[162] When inflated to 2013 prices, this was equivalent to £135,000.

and Christ Church—had libraries specifically for undergraduate use, and most had a chequered history.[163] John James of Queens, in the late 1770s, coped by coming up with a serviceable collection of texts and getting other books he needed from the city's lending library for a small fee.[164] But most students throughout the period became clients of local booksellers. Bills of £4 to £8 per term were not uncommon in the Hanoverian age and serious scholars had to dip into their reserves or lean on their parents. This was as true of foundationers as non-foundationers. About 1770, a Magdalen demy would receive no more than £3 to £7 a year on top of his board and lodgings, and a junior Christ Church studentship was worth little more: though judged at this date to be worth £20 annually, a new fellow at the House had to pay his room rent out of the sum.[165]

From the beginning of the eighteenth century, moreover, it was becoming harder to live frugally, especially for the sensitive like Samuel Johnson. Tuition fees were rising fast. While the most affluent student would not have had to pay more than £1 a year in the sixteenth century, by the late eighteenth century a gentleman commoner at Merton would expect to pay £21. Private coaches, in particular, were an expensive accessory. Newman, in the late 1810s, paid his tutor 12 guineas per year, but two hours of private mathematics teaching a day cost him a further £30 in Michaelmas 1818. The colleges too were adding new charges to battels, as they took over the provision of bedmakers, shoe shiners, and waiters at table, and began to expect undergraduates to pay a small annual sum towards the college library (which they could not use) and even towards renovations.[166] Undergraduate personal needs had also grown, as was seen in section E.[167] In 1737, a Mr Charlton of Lincoln spent £7 8s. simply on maintaining his horse. Thirty years later he could easily have spent double the sum.

The result was that many of the idle and not so idle got themselves into debt. In 1847, a Worcester student, Edward Jennings, went bankrupt with liabilities of £2,200. He owed money to sixty-four creditors, most of them Oxford tradesmen, and was judged to have assets of only three shillings. At the subsequent hearing, the magistrate took pity on his weakness and declared it unreasonable that the spendthrift should be expected to decline 'every species of credit proffered for every species of extravagance'.[168] Young bucks like Jennings took indebtedness in their stride, but more sensitive souls could be destroyed by shame. Many undergraduates

---

[163] For the contents of the Magdalen undergraduate library, see Christine Ferdinand, 'The Mystery of Cooking and the Art of Wheedling: What Magdalen Undergraduates Read in the Eighteenth Century', *Magdalen College Record* (2006), 127–36, and Pia Gadkari, 'Cane's Catalogue and the Intellectual Life of Undergraduates at Magdalen College in Early Hanoverian England' (BA dissertation, Oxford, 2007).

[164] James, p. 82. The lending library may possibly have been the one run by James Fletcher, though this appears to have only opened about 1783: *A History of the County of Oxford*, vol. 4: *The City of Oxford* (Oxford, 1979), p. 440.

[165] We have next to no idea how many books a 'reading' man might accumulate during his years at Oxford. Some must have owned quite sizeable collections. As early as 1577, John Gray, an exhibitioner at Oriel, who died in his third year, had built up a library of forty works, mostly in Latin and related to the arts syllabus.

[166] James was batteled by Queen's for a charity donation at the set times of the year that he and other residents took communion in chapel.

[167] See, pp. 262–3.   [168] OT, 13 June 2013, p. 41.

FIGURE 7.7 Monument to John and Thomas Littleton, Magdalen College chapel. Many undergraduates died while at Oxford. The Littleton brothers, aged 13 and 17, were drowned in 1635 when the younger fell into the river and the elder tried to save him.

died in the course of their studies during the period. Most were struck down by disease;[169] others died by accident, like John and Thomas Littleton, commoners at Magdalen who drowned in the Cherwell in 1635 (see Figure 7.7). But an unhappy few died by their own hand. Robert Andrews was the son of an indigent Lancashire clergyman who went up to Brasenose from Rugby in 1807. Three years later after

---

[169] Illness within the University has not yet been studied in detail. As a starting point, see W.D. Churchill and J.D. Alsop, 'Prescribing Physicians and Sick Scholars of Oxford: Jeremiah Webbe's Apothecarial Notebook, 1653–54', *Vesalius*, 2 (2001), 73–7. Webbe had twenty-eight students on his books in the early 1650s, most with melancholy and consumption.

falling into debt attempting to keep up with the fast set, the 20-year-old committed suicide. A messenger sent by his father promising assistance arrived to find an inquest already in process over the corpse 'whose head was shattered to atoms by a pistol-ball'.[170] All students from modest families who passed through Oxford in the period came up with great expectations. Some, like John Potter, son of a Wakefield draper, who entered University College as a servitor in 1688 and rose to be archbishop of Canterbury, did their family proud; most were destined to disappoint; but none can have left as deep a cut in his father's heart as Robert Andrews, victim of Oxford's minority undergraduate culture of excess.

[170] Crook, p. 200.

CHAPTER 8

Masters and Learning

A. The Higher Faculties

THE Reformation had an immediate effect on the range of higher studies taught at Oxford, in that canon law, as the law of the Roman church, ceased to be part of the curriculum. Otherwise, the rules and regulations governing the higher faculties underwent little change with the coming of protestantism. In the reigns of Edward and Elizabeth, the demands placed on a bachelor or doctor before determining or incepting were modified to a degree, but no fundamental alteration was made to the late medieval structure. Under the Laudian code of 1636, it continued to take an MA seven years to become a doctor in law or medicine and eleven to become a doctor in theology.[1] The meat of the course, too, was little altered in the century following the break with Rome. The *Sentences* of Peter Lombard ceased to be part of the divinity curriculum, which came to be focused solely on the Bible as the reformers desired; but a course in civil or Roman law continued to be built on the study of the *Digest* and the *Code*, while Galen remained the dominant medical authority.[2] It was not until the late eighteenth century that any attempt was made to shorten the length of time it took to gain a higher degree. From 1781, a medical student could determine as a BM after one year's study and incept as a DM after a further three, while from 1789 it became possible for a civil lawyer who was not an Oxford MA to become a BCL in four years rather than five.[3]

From the start of the period, the delivery of the curriculum in the higher faculties ceased to be entrusted to those who had recently become doctors, just as in the faculty of arts it was taken out of the hands of the new masters. From 1564 to 1565, bachelors in all three faculties had to give a short course of lectures before they could supplicate for their doctorate, but doctors themselves were not expected to carry the curriculum as they had in the past. The most that was expected of doctors of theology, for instance, was that on graduating they gave a presentation of their

---

[1] *Statuta*, pp. 345–6 (Edwardian statutes, 1549) and pp. 378–81 (*Nova Statuta*, 1564–5); Laudian Statutes, pp. 59–65 (Title VI, sections 3–6).

[2] See above, pp. 91–2. There appears to have been no university instruction on Justinian's *Institutes* after the mid-sixteenth century. According to the Edwardian statutes, civil lawyers were to study the emperor's introductory textbook on their own prior to beginning their formal studies.

[3] OUS, ii. 16–17 and 25.

knowledge and skill in the form of a disputation, and that while they remained at Oxford they preached an annual sermon.[4] Instead, the teaching was handed over to stipendiary professors. Thanks to Henry VIII's establishment of the regius professorships in theology, law, and medicine, each faculty had a permanent university postholder to cover the teaching from 1540, while theology students were also able to attend the lectures of the Lady Margaret professor and the public courses given by the praelectors at Magdalen and Corpus.[5]

For the next two centuries, the teaching provision remained largely unchanged. Apart from the chair in theological controversy briefly subsidized by Walsingham in the late sixteenth century,[6] and the creation of the Tomlins reader in anatomy in 1623,[7] there were no additional posts created until 1750. The last century of the period, in contrast, saw a flurry of new foundations. The ball was set rolling in 1755 with the establishment of the Vinerian chair in common law jurisprudence, which allowed students in civil law the opportunity to hear lectures on English as well as Roman law.[8] This was followed by a significant expansion in the facilities for teaching practical medicine, with the opening of Dr Lee's anatomy school in Christ Church in 1770, the establishment of the Lichfield clinical chair attached to the new Radcliffe Infirmary in 1780, and the foundation of the Aldrichian professorships in medicine, anatomy, and chemistry in 1803.[9] The needs of the theologians were also not forgotten. While the courses given at Magdalen and Corpus seem to have been all but defunct by the end of the eighteenth century, the curriculum was strengthened with the foundation of the annual Bampton lectures in 1780, which offered students the chance to hear the country's leading divines debating current theological concerns.[10] Right at the end of the period, too, the teaching provision was further enhanced with the establishment of chairs in pastoral theology and ecclesiastical history in 1842, a reflection of a new belief that the leading lights of the nineteenth-century Anglican church needed to be more than biblically literate.

As in the late middle ages, the numbers studying for a higher degree at Oxford across the period never seem to have been large. In the two centuries following the Civil War, the combined number of bachelors determining in the three faculties each year was seldom more than 10 per cent of the total in arts. Few years could

---

[4] In the disputation they were supposed to show their ability to sustain the protestant case in an area of controversy with catholics.

[5] Above, pp. 82–3, this volume.   [6] Above, p. 195, this volume.

[7] Its founder, Richard Tomlins, was a lawyer who was a close friend of the then regius professor of medicine Thomas Clayton.

[8] Its founder was the jurist Charles Viner, formerly of Hart Hall, and the author of a twenty-three-volume *Abridgement of Law and Equity*. Under the Edwardian statutes of 1549, new doctors of civil law were encouraged to study the law of England once they had graduated, but there was no specific teaching provision. Faculties on the continent had begun giving lectures on customary and national law from the late seventeenth century; in France chairs were established by Louis XIV: see C. Chêne, *L'Enseignement du droit français en pays de droit écrit (1679–1793)* (Geneva, 1982).

[9] The Lichfield chair was created with a bequest from George Henry Lee, the third earl, late of St John's, who was the University's Chancellor, 1762–72. For Aldrich and Matthew Lee, see pp. 241 and 243, this volume.

[10] The Bampton lectures were established to provide a public defence of Anglicanism. For Bampton, see p. 220, this volume.

muster more than twenty-five. Medicine remained the smallest of the faculties, at best sending out half a dozen bachelors into the world each year and often only one or two; law graduated on average nine or ten; and theology only a couple more, except in the occasional year when upwards of twenty determined. The number of doctorates awarded was even fewer, in most years in the ratio of one to two or three to five to the number of bachelors. It would appear, too, that the attractions of a degree in medicine and law all but died away in the first half of the nineteenth century.[11]

Given England's tenacious attachment to the common law in the centuries following the Reformation, the relatively small numbers gaining a degree in civil law are unsurprising. Only those who intended to serve in courts which used civil law procedure, notably the ecclesiastical and maritime courts, needed to study it carefully. Many barristers, judges, and justices of the peace, during the period, attended Oxford or Cambridge as undergraduates, but they pursued their legal training in the London Inns of Court.[12] Indeed, the number of bachelors in civil law would almost certainly have been lower but for the fact that the degree was sometimes taken by undergraduates instead of a BA, which was judged to be more demanding. All that was required of the determining student was that he had studied for the requisite time and opposed and responded in two disputations.[13] The establishment of the Vinerian chair was an attempt to make the Oxford course more relevant to the future common lawyer, but seems to have had little effect beyond drawing the precocious Jeremy Bentham back to the University from Lincoln's Inn to listen to the lectures of its first incumbent, William Blackstone.[14] The senior degree of DCL was even less attractive. That a steady number continued to be awarded during the period was due to the fact that it began to be given as an honorary degree to celebrities and the great and good at Encaenia.[15]

The paucity of medical degrees, on the other hand, calls for an explanation. In the pre-Reformation era, few medical practitioners in England (or anywhere in Europe) were graduates. From the late seventeenth century, however, the picture changed.

[11] A catalogue of all graduates in divinity, law, medicine, arts and music, who have regularly proceeded or been created in the University of Oxford, between October 10, 1659, and December 31, 1850: to which is added, a list of Chancellors, High-stewards, Vice-chancellors, Proctors, heads of colleges and halls, and burgesses of the University; together with a statement of matriculations and regencies, ed. Philip Bliss (Oxford, 1851). Figures for BDs and DDs in the years 1580 to 1660 can be found in Lawrence Stone, 'The Size and Composition of the Oxford Student Body 1580–1910', in Lawrence Stone, The University in Society, vol. 1: Oxford and Cambridge from the 14th to the early 19th Century (Princeton, NJ, 1975), p. 94. Annual lists of graduates can be found in the OUC from its initial date of publication in 1810.
[12] See p. 137, this volume. Some were entered at an inn before they went to Oxford; e.g. Daniel Fleming, a Westmorland squire's son, who joined Gray's Inn in June 1650, then matriculated from Queen's the following month: The Flemings of Oxford, vol. 1: 1650–1680, ed. J. R. Magrath (OHS; Oxford, 1904), p. 3.
[13] Under the 1636 code, a civil lawyer without an MA was expected to have studied the arts for two years before beginning his law studies, which would have extended the length of the course to seven years, or six from 1789. Dispensations, though, were easy to acquire, especially towards the end of the period: OUC (1813), p. 6.
[14] Bentham had left Queen's as a BA in 1764, having already enrolled as a student of King's Bench in Westminster Hall the year before.
[15] The most prestigious beneficiary domiciled in England was Prince Albert, who was given a DCL on 19 March 1840.

Although there was no requirement for medics in Britain and Ireland to obtain a diploma of any kind before 1858, many began to do so, and between 1650 and 1800 the number of degrees awarded to medical students from the British Isles rose sixfold to some forty per annum.[16] Neither Oxford nor Cambridge benefited from the upsurge in interest, however. English medical students initially went to the continent in search of a medical degree, above all to Leiden, and then, from 1750, went off to Scotland. There were several reasons for this. In the first place, gaining a medical degree from an English university was a protracted business, while other universities were far less demanding: some favoured faculties with British practitioners, notably Reims, gave degrees on demand.[17] Secondly, neither English university had the requisite facilities until the end of the period. Medicine in the late middle ages had been a theoretical study. But from the beginning of the sixteenth century physicians were expected to have studied the practical arts of anatomy, surgery, plant recognition, pharmacy, and chemistry, and in the eighteenth century to have gained bedside experience prior to graduation.[18] Oxford, from the early seventeenth century, had a botanical garden and a rudimentary anatomical theatre in the new schools complex, and, with the opening of the Ashmolean laboratory, could offer courses in chemistry. Until the improvement in its practical facilities after 1770, however, it lacked the necessary kit.[19] Even then, its resources could not compare with the practical tuition available in the London hospitals and private medical schools, such as the renowned Windmill Street Academy run by William Hunter, especially as the chairs tended to be held by one man. Rather than go to Oxford and Cambridge, British and Irish medical students in the century after 1750 preferred to mix training in London with study and graduation at the new medical faculty of Edinburgh, which had first-rate medical professors and good practical facilities. The Edinburgh faculty, opened in 1726, also had no religious tests, which made the university particularly appealing to the large number of English and Irish religious non-conformists of all stripes, who chose medicine as a career because practitioners did not have to be members of the established church.[20]

---

[16] Laurence Brockliss, 'Les Etudiants en médecine des Iles britanniques en France sous l'Ancien Régime', in Patrick Ferté and Caroline Barrera (eds), *Etudiants de l'exil. Migrations internationales et universités refuges (XVIe–XXe siècles)* (Toulouse, 2009), pp. 81–104, esp. table, p. 102. Even greater numbers each year gained a diploma from one of the colleges of surgery in London, Edinburgh, or Dublin, or from the London Society of Apothecaries. On the continent, medical practitioners in the early modern period were divided between graduate physicians on the one hand, and surgeons and apothecaries, who did an apprenticeship and had little formal training before the eighteenth century, on the other. In the British Isles, the divisions were less clear-cut.

[17] Laurence Brockliss, 'Medicine and the Small University in Eighteenth-Century France', in G.P. Brizzi and Jacques Verger (eds), *Le universita minori in Europe (secoli XV–XIX) (Soveria Mannelli, 1998)*, pp. 239–72.

[18] As early as 1549, the need to move the faculty curriculum in a more practical direction was acknowledged. Under the Edwardian statutes, students of medicine and bachelors were expected to attend anatomies, and bachelors were forbidden to practise unless they had performed two anatomies and given practical demonstration of their therapeutic knowledge: *Statuta*, p. 346.

[19] With only three medical professors (including the Sherardian professor of botany) in the mid-eighteenth century, Oxford was a small faculty compared with the leading centres: the faculties of Paris and Montpellier had eight each.

[20] Susan Lawrence, *Charitable Knowledge: Hospital Pupils and Practitioners in Eighteenth-Century London* (Cambridge, 1996); Lisa Rosner, *Medical Education in the Age of Improvement: Edinburgh Students and Apprentices, 1760–1826* (Edinburgh, 1991), esp. ch. 6; G. Risse, *Hospital Life in Enlightenment Scotland: Care and Teaching at the Royal Infirmary*

The relatively low number of theology graduates is, at first sight, even more perplexing. Admittedly, as there was no need for a Church of England minister to have a theology degree, there was little point in a prospective ordinand going to the expense of continuing his studies in the theological faculty after he had gained his MA. There was no captive constituency, therefore, to swell the ranks of the faculty as in other protestant countries.[21] On the other hand, the large majority of college fellows were senior members who held their fellowship on the understanding that they would pursue theological studies. As there were 471 Oxford fellows in 1592, and 542 in 1850, the faculty ought to have contained, at the very least, from 350 to 450 scholars in any one year, and produced an annual crop of thirty to forty bachelors, three to four times the actual number.[22] Evidently this was not the case. The number of bachelors determining each year suggests there were never more than a hundred masters seriously engaged in theological studies.

The fact that so many fellows paid scant attention to the statutes under which they were elected reflects the changing nature of a college fellowship across the period. With the departure of the monks and friars, the closure of the canon law faculty, and the abolition of compulsory regenting for masters of arts, college fellows were virtually the only senior members left in the University from the beginning of the seventeenth century.[23] After the emergence of the Hebdomadal Board, they may have been less involved in university administration than resident masters in an earlier age, but many among them had a wider range of responsibilities at college level. Tutoring and lecturing could be a full-time occupation in term time, which made serious academic study all but impossible. It was also the case that, by the eighteenth century, fellowships were largely perceived to be sinecures. As we will see in section B, their monetary value rose quickly after 1700, so they were coveted and obtained by arts graduates destined for the church, who were frequently gentlemen's sons. They had little intention of knuckling down to theological studies but sought a comfortable billet where they could live, independent of their parents, until a suitable living became vacant.

Of course, had the crown insisted that ministers of the Church of England had a theology degree, as was the case in other protestant countries, then the theology faculty would have been quickly raised from its somnolence. This, though, was never mooted. Instead, the emphasis at Oxford in the second half of the eighteenth century was placed on ensuring that arts students bound for the ministry received some theological tuition before going down. It had long been the case that the best tutors attempted to prepare their charges for the ministry by setting for discussion

---

of Edinburgh (Cambridge, 1996). Non-conformists and catholics, however, could not become full members of the royal colleges of physicians in London, Edinburgh, and Dublin.

[21] See p. 138, this volume.

[22] Calculation based on the assumption that there would have been about a hundred fellows at any one time who were either undergraduates or permitted to study law or medicine, and that all fellows studying theology would have held their fellowship for the eleven years needed to become a doctor.

[23] There would always have been some MAs living in halls or renting a room in college, but they would have been few in number.

prominent works of protestant spirituality.[24] In the mid-eighteenth century, the University moved to formalize the process. When the long-serving Queen's tutor Edward Bentham was made regius professor of divinity in 1763, he immediately agreed to the suggestion of the archbishop of Canterbury, Thomas Secker, that he should lecture on divinity three times a week to BAs. Bentham was an orthodox and conservative divine—he even suggested his students should read Aquinas—but the course of seventy lectures was a great success and was repeated by his successors. The one drawback, according to George Valentine Cox, who attended the course in the 1790s, was that they were delivered in the evening, with the result that 'many of the class slept through the lecture, waking up now and then at the sound of a Greek quotation'. What most students took away with them was the syllabus handed out at the beginning and 'a formidable list of printed authors recommended for future reading'.[25] Only at the end of the period was it possible for the assiduous to give evidence of the fruits of their theological labours. In 1842, the University instituted the voluntary theological exam, which offered the new MA the chance to demonstrate his theological knowledge before taking up a living.

Introducing higher studies to undergraduates before they went down was also tried, at the same time, in law. Recognizing that many arts students would go on to serve as JPs or in the crown courts, Thomas Wood of New College published an *Institutes of the Laws of England* in 1720, which was intended to be read by gentlemen while they were up. It reached its tenth edition in 1772. The foundation of the Vinerian chair in 1755 further provided undergraduates with a lecture course in common law that they could and did attend.

B. The Fellows

Becoming a fellow has been explored in an earlier chapter.[26] Throughout the period, fellowships, apart from those at Oriel and Balliol in the first half of the nineteenth century, were closed under the terms of their foundation. They were either attached to a particular region or town, as at Magdalen, or had to be bestowed on scholars already on the foundation, as at Wadham. They were closed too in that, for most of the period, election depended on patronage and favouritism. Even in the first part of the nineteenth century, when far greater attention was paid to merit, fellows were not necessarily selected from the most able undergraduates, as defined by success in Schools. Oriel was one of the first colleges to privilege talent above connections in its elections, but it did not fill its fellowship with Firsts, believing its own fellowship examination was a better judge of ability. Had this not been the

---

[24] According to the Cambridge tutor Daniel Waterland, an undergraduate bound for the church should set aside Sundays and holidays for religious study: see Daniel Waterland, *Advice to a young student with a method of study for the first four years* (London, 1730), chs 5 and 6 (comments and booklist).

[25] G. V. Cox, *Recollections of Oxford*, 2nd edn (Oxford, 1870), p. 140. At that date the regius was John Randolph. John James of Queen's had attended the course given by the regius Wheeler in the 1770s.

[26] See pp. 153–8, this volume.

case, Newman, who had underperformed miserably in Schools, would never have joined its ranks. In fact, before the mid-nineteenth century, there were still not enough undergraduates taking Firsts to fill the thirty-five or so fellowships that annually fell vacant.[27]

Once a fellowship had been obtained, it could usually be held for life. Few statutes covering their foundation stressed that a fellow had to demit after a specific period of time. Incumbents, though, were not expected to stay for ever. Once admitted in their early twenties, it was assumed that fellows would complete their arts studies, if they had not already done so, enter the theology line (or another if it were permitted), become ordained at the earliest sanctioned age, proceed to a higher degree, then quit the University to begin a career, usually in the church, while still relatively young. The statistics concerning length of tenure in a number of colleges across the period suggest that, for most of the time, reality and theory were closely matched. There were always perpetual hangers-on who held their fellowships for most of their adult years and even ended up dying in college. When Oriel's James Davenant died in his rooms in 1716, he had been a fellow for fifty-four years and attached to the college for more than sixty.[28] But the lifelong fellow was an exception, albeit a highly visible one. There were inevitably differences between colleges, but the normal period of tenure from the late sixteenth century was some ten to eleven years, and a significant proportion of fellows departed relatively quickly: many remained for less than five. Only in the eighteenth century can large numbers of fellows be identified holding on until middle age: as at University College, where the average incumbent between 1689 and 1764 retained his fellowship for nineteen to twenty years.

There were two factors encouraging compliance. In the first place, if the Reformation permitted clerical marriage, it brought no change to the requirement that fellows should be celibate. Only heads of house could take a wife. If a fellow wanted to start a family while he remained relatively young, he had to quit the cloister betimes. More importantly, fellows who were happy to serve out their days as a country parson could usually count on their college to assist them in finding a parish in due course. Most colleges had several advowsons attached to the original foundation, and in the following centuries more were acquired by gift or purchase. In 1585, Oxford already owned some 200 advowsons; by 1699 the figure had risen to 273. Parliament was so alarmed by the continual accumulation of livings by colleges of both universities that, in 1737, it passed a mortmain act limiting the number each institution could hold to half its contingent of fellows. This reduced the rate of growth, but when the act was repealed in 1805, the expansion continued. Some colleges were particularly well endowed in livings: by the mid-nineteenth century Magdalen possessed thirty-nine, sixteen of which had been a gift from its founder,

---

[27] Oriel placed particular emphasis on how well candidates performed in the Latin prose and English essay papers.
[28] He never held a living. According to Hearne, 'He lov'd to live at his ease, as he did': Hearne, v. 332.

William Waynflete, eight were obtained in the sixteenth and seventeenth centuries, and no fewer than fifteen between 1689 and 1854.[29] Some too could offer other inducements to leave, for, besides parish livings, colleges frequently had grammar-school headships in their gift, which were also usually reserved for clergymen.

Obviously, the more patronage a college possessed the more easily and swiftly a fellow could be launched into the world. As long as nature did her work (and in the early modern period premature death was a constant occurrence), there was no reason to expect that a fellow would remain on the books much longer than his early thirties, even if competition could mean that obtaining a college benefice might take time and fellows had to lobby hard with their colleagues to get what they wanted. The clergyman diarist James Woodforde became a fellow of New College in 1763 and took orders. Ten years later he felt the urge to marry and hoped that the college would appoint him to the mastership of Bedford School, which was worth 200 guineas a year. This, though, it failed to do in the summer of 1773, and he had to wait until December 1774 before he netted the college living of Weston Longville. Even then, as his diary records, he did not secure the position without a fight:

> Dec: 15...We had a meeting of the whole House in the Hall at 12. o'clock to present a person to the Living of Weston Longville & to seal the remaining leases. The former came on first—Hooke [another fellow] & myself were the two Candidates proposed—Many learned & warm arguments started & disputed—and after 2. Hours Debate the House divided & it was put to the Vote—when there appeared for me 21 Votes, for Mr. Hooke 15. Only, on which I was declared & presented the Presentation of the Rectory.[30]

In the final century of the period, waiting a few years to obtain a position would have been a great hardship only to the desperately lovelorn, for fellowships, by the late eighteenth century, had become valuable pieces of property that many gently born clerics were happy to possess. In the second half of the sixteenth century, fellowships had limited value. The college provided free lodgings and free board, either in kind or via a weekly allowance which was adjusted to an extent to take account of rampant inflation.[31] In addition, some colleges gave their fellows a clothing allowance or small stipend of a few pounds. The fellows' prospects brightened, however, from the turn of the seventeenth century as they began to receive, at a varying rate according to seniority, a share of the fines paid by tenants on taking up or renewing a lease, and also a share in the profits if the annual accounts were in the black.[32] Initially the amount divided was not large, but by the late seventeenth century Magdalen fellows were receiving a respectable income of some £60 per annum. This placed them on a par with the 2,000 most affluent

---

[29] The number of livings owned by each college in the first half of the nineteenth century is listed annually in the OUC.

[30] Woodforde, pp. ix and x, and p. 265. Sadly he lost the girl. He would hold the living until 1803.

[31] Brasenose paid a weekly allowance of 8s. 5d. or £22 a year in 1639.

[32] The share varied from college to college: see the table in HUO, iii. 528. Fellows of University College did not receive a share of the fines until the 1670s.

parish ministers, according to Gregory King's famous 1688 division of the people of England by annual income.[33] From the mid-eighteenth century, the return from the fines and the dividend blossomed. In Lincoln in the early seventeenth century, fellows on average received less than £15 per annum besides their free room and some other fringe benefits. By 1750, resident fellows enjoyed incomes of £50 to £70; by 1837–8 the most senior were receiving four times as much, though prices had only doubled and actually fell after 1815. The situation was much the same in other colleges. An All Souls fellowship at the end of the eighteenth century was worth from £124 to £181, one at Queen's, between 1790 and 1804, £120 on average, and one at University College in 1807, £150. In the early nineteenth century, the figure could climb even higher, especially at Magdalen, where a fellowship, after 1700, was always comparatively lucrative. In 1820, during the depression following the Napoleonic Wars, the fellows of the college received between £185 and £324 a year, but by 1840, during a period of stable prices, the range was between £252 and £403. Moreover, as the orientalist Sir William Jones, a fellow of University College, pointed out in 1782, the real value of a fellowship was far greater than it appeared on the surface. At that date, he estimated the cash value of his fellowship to be about £100 per year. This, though, he judged to be equivalent to what £300 'could purchase out of the college' when advantages such as 'apartments' and servants were included.[34]

This was just the basic salary. Fellows who held college offices might expect to double their income, for the highest rewarded tutors at Balliol in the late eighteenth century were annually receiving £300 for their pains. Incumbents could also have a much larger independent income than hitherto and hold on to their fellowship. The foundation statutes of the late medieval colleges seldom allowed a fellow to have private income from a benefice or estate of more than £10 per annum. In the sixteenth and early seventeenth century, nothing was done to adjust this sum in line with inflation. Wadham was a late foundation but the largest annual income a fellow could draw from an outside source was £8. By the end of the eighteenth century, the sum had been inflated to a suitable level. Most colleges allowed their fellows to have a private income of £120 a year, and Magdalen in 1812 permitted James Hudson to continue to hold his fellowship despite having private property that brought him £275 a year. This was justified on the grounds that the disqualifying sum of £5 under the 1480 statutes had been equivalent to the value of a middle-ranking fellowship when the college was founded. As the average value of a Magdalen fellowship over the previous seven years had been about £294, Hudson's private income was judged within the statutory limits.[35]

---

[33] D. C. Coleman, *The Economy of England 1450–1750* (Oxford, 1977), p. 6.
[34] *The Letters of Sir William Jones*, ed. G. H. Cannon (Oxford, 1970), ii. 599.
[35] MCA, VP1/A1/3. Heads of house in the second half of the period were able to draw as large an income from private sources as they liked. At Oriel in 1770s the provost received some £140 from the college; the fellows £90–£100. The then provost, John Clark, however, had accumulated so many benefices by 1776 that he was receiving a further £920.

The rise in fellows' incomes in real terms, from the late seventeenth century, brought a new independence that encouraged absenteeism. Even if fellows were seriously engaged in study and looked to take a higher degree, it was only the statutory requirement that they resided in college that kept them in Oxford. All scholars, once they had taken their BA, were largely left to their own devices. The lecture provision in the higher faculties was perfunctory, and it was expected that a scholar in a higher faculty would study on his own during the long years of probation that were needed to qualify for a higher degree. In the sixteenth and early seventeenth centuries, the large majority of fellows spent no more than a few days away from their college each year, even though fellows were allowed to be absent if permission were granted by the governing body. With limited money in hand they had no alternative but to remain in Oxford, whatever their commitment to their studies. The many fellows, too, who were able to boost their income by serving as college officers and lecturers or taking tutorial pupils could hardly spend much time away from college if they took their administrative and teaching responsibilities even reasonably seriously. The only fellows who were likely to be absent for a long period of time were the notably studious, often medics, who were given permission to study abroad, and the lucky few who gained minor employment at court or in a noble household. In 1578, Henry Savile, for instance, was allowed to go off to the continent for three years to deepen his knowledge after demonstrating his humanist and mathematical credentials by lecturing in the University on Ptolemy's *Almagest* between 1570 and 1575. Once there, the future warden of Merton did not waste his time but took the opportunity to visit a number of centres of learning such as Prague, Breslau, and Padua. The college, however, gave him only a modest allowance of £6 13s. 4d., and he was able to travel so far afield solely because he was acting as chaperone to a pair of young gentlemen on the Grand Tour.

After the Restoration, however, as incomes improved, tutorial responsibilities were increasingly confined to a handful of fellows, and lecturing duties atrophied, the temptation to wander increased. At Magdalen, a college of forty fellows, there was only one fellow continually absent in the 1670s. This was the medical fellow, Henry Yerbury, who was given permission each year to travel abroad. A further ten to fifteen of his peers, however, were absent for three to six months. By the first decade of the eighteenth century, the college was beginning to empty out. In 1708, half the establishment was on leave, including the college's literary lion, Joseph Addison, and by the mid-eighteenth century there were only eight fellows permanently resident. In the second half of the eighteenth century, absenteeism was so commonplace and so acceptable that, from 1765, the college ceased to bother to grant permission for absence.[36] Magdalen fellows, though wealthier than most, were in no way exceptional in their behaviour. John Wesley retained his Lincoln

---

[36] MCA, VP/A1/2, vice-president's notebook (in which the names of those given permission to be absent were recorded).

fellowship for seventeen years after leaving Oxford to convert the world; Wood-forde spent ten of his fifteen years as a fellow of New somewhere else. Initially there was some resistance, especially if the absentee was a head of house. Trinity's President Bathurst, for one, was in trouble with the fellows in the late seventeenth century for being too frequently away from his post.[37] But absenteeism soon became endemic. In the second half of the eighteenth century even tutors and lecturers could be absent. At University College in the second half of the 1760s, Robert Chambers shared the undergraduates with William Scott. But he had been admitted to the Middle Temple in 1764 and had already forged a legal career for himself, becoming the second Vinerian professor of law in 1766. Unlike Scott, he was continually away on other business, as Walter Stanhope complained in a letter to his uncle in February 1767:

> When Chambers is here he gives us a lecture every Evening, as Scott does in ye Morning: but he has now been in London 3 weeks, & will be so a fortnight longer, in which time merely in ye place of his lectures, he has set one to read Rollin's Ancient History ... & to learn French in such a manner as to construe it with Readiness.[38]

Tutors in the first half of the nineteenth century were much more punctilious. But this was hardly true of fellows more generally. It was estimated in 1842 that only 192 of the 490 graduates among them (including BAs) were resident, suggesting that, at the end of the period, there was no more than one master actually living in Oxford for every six to seven undergraduates.[39]

Far better off than most parish clergymen, single, and free to come and go as he pleased, a fellow after 1700 was in an enviable position. Provided he was careful with his money, he could build up a tidy nest egg which would go a long way to attracting a suitable wife and ensuring that the happy couple would not be immured in too cold a vicarage and that their children could be decently educated. With such a comfortable life, it is surprising that more fellows did not hold onto their fellowships for good in the final decades of the period. This was certainly a prospect that was unnerving the long-serving Magdalen demy William Bagshaw Stephens as early as 1793, who expressed the fear in his diary that, with 'the increasing Value of Fellowships Senior Fellows will be less and less tempted every day to take College Livings'.[40] That fellowships continued to be demitted as frequently in the first half of the nineteenth as in the first half of the seventeenth century, and that thirty or so fellows a year joined the ranks of the parish clergy, suggests that the lure of mammon was always ultimately trumped by the calls of the flesh, if not the calls of conscience.

---

[37] He was also dean of Bath and Wells.

[38] L. G. Mitchell, 'The Stanhopes at Univ', *University College Record*, 13: 2 (2002), p. 87. Charles Rollin was principal of the Paris Collège de Beauvais in the first half of the eighteenth century. His multi-volume history of the ancient world, which appeared in French in the 1730s, was a synthesis of the surviving classical sources. It was immediately translated into English and went through numerous editions.

[39] There were 1,212 undergraduates at this date: see Table 1.

[40] *The Journal of the Rev. William Bagshaw Stevens*, ed. G. Galbraith (Oxford, 1965), p. 106. For Stephens' travails as a demy, see p. 226, this volume.

C. A Don's Life

In the century between the Henrician Reformation and the Civil War, when space in college was at a premium, the vast majority of masters in residence lived a cramped and confined existence. Senior members on the foundation or in a hall usually enjoyed slightly better conditions than the average junior scholar: their accommodation was on the first rather than the ground floor, where the rooms were prone to damp, and their chamber normally had a serviceable fireplace and glazing. But seniors, wherever based, were expected to live two to a room, and most masters shared their chamber not only with a scholar of a similar status but with several tutorial pupils and servitors, who would have constantly invaded the limited space even if they had a separate lodging in a cockloft above.[41] Admittedly, seniors were not completely without their private space since chambers were partitioned into a common sleeping area and individual studies. Nonetheless, only heads of house had a set of rooms at their disposal and even heads, if married with a large family, can have had little privacy. In consequence, seniors at Oxford who died *in situ* in the Elizabethan and early Stuart era left few possessions. Most masters possessed little furniture beyond a feather bed, a few trunks, a cupboard, desk, chairs, and stools, while their chief personal belongings were bed linen, clothes, and books. Their sole items of luxury were ordinarily a fireguard, tongs, a looking glass, and a commode. Some heads of house had large collections of books which they would have acquired over a lifetime—John Tatham of Lincoln left 900 in 1576 and John Rainolds of Corpus 2,232 in 1607. But the normal master in his twenties or thirties probably had no more than a hundred. Seniors who had better libraries were usually those rich enough to acquire a finer array of goods. Sampson Newton, an MA who rented a room in Magdalen, had over 600 books when he died in 1606, plus movable goods valued at £70. Newton was no hair-shirt scholar but a Renaissance man. His possessions included ten maps (eight without frames and two framed), sixteen small pictures, a pair of playing tables (presumably for cards or backgammon), and a viol.[42]

After the Restoration, and especially in the eighteenth century, the masters' lot improved considerably. As space was no longer a problem, with the erection of new quads and falling undergraduate numbers after 1700, the colleges and halls had no difficulty in responding to the age's growing desire for greater privacy, especially among the socially select. Tutors and tutees no longer wanted or had to live in close proximity, so masters usually had at least one room to themselves. The new classical-style buildings put up in many colleges from the end of the seventeenth century were deliberately designed to give fellows greater elbow room. High ceilinged, airy, and

---

[41] There was a ladder from the room to the cockloft and no separate staircase.

[42] OUA, Vice-Chancellor's Court, Inventories (Eaton-Ta), HYp B 16: M-O, f. 86 (microfilm HO235.000, Reel 006). In contrast, when John Hutton, fellow of New College, died in 1652 aged 24, he left goods only worth £13 1s. 2d., and fewer than 150 books: listed in William Poole, 'Book Economy in New College, Oxford in the Later Seventeenth Century: Two Documents', HU, XXV: 1 (2010), 90–102.

fashionably wainscoted, if often initially at the expense of the first incumbent, fellows in the richest colleges now lived in country-house grandeur.[43] The fellows of New College, where there were never more than a handful of commoners at any time in the period, were particularly favoured. From 1683, with the erection of the south range of the new Garden Quad, it was understood that fellows of MA status should have a two-room set. But the lucky few were even more liberally accommodated. When Celia Fiennes visited her nephew in the college at the end of the seventeenth century, she found that his tutor had a separate dining room, bedchamber, study, and room for a servant.[44] At this date, the servant was probably a servitor who received tuition in return for performing menial tasks. A century later, however, the scholar servant had been completely replaced by a professional domestic, called at this date a bedmaker, who lived out and was paid a wage for cleaning a senior's room, lighting his fire, emptying his chamber pot, and so on. James Woodforde, the diarist, who was a resident fellow of New College on and off from 1762 to 1776, was looked after initially by Thomas Dod, and then, when Dod gave up because he was too infirm, by Frank Pain, who received the princely sum of one shilling a week for his care. Helped by his two sons, Frank looked after Woodforde whenever he stayed in Oxford, providing a wide variety of services, including delivering his morning cream. The one service Pain did not provide was laundering, for which Woodforde had recourse to a local washerwoman, Elizabeth Hamlett, who was paid £1 14s. for six months washing and mending on 1 August 1774.[45]

As masters, particularly fellows, metamorphosed into ersatz country gentlemen, so they surrounded themselves with things, rather than a retinue of often rowdy teenage scholars. An early instance was Edward Drope, fellow of Magdalen and a member of a family that had constantly supplied fellows to the college over the previous century, who died in 1683. Drope was one of the few Magdalen fellows of the seventeenth century of enough wealth and significance to leave a will that was proved in the archiepiscopal court of Canterbury. Among the possessions he bequeathed to his family were a leather couch, four silver tankards, and four silver spoons.[46] Woodforde, in a much more comfort-loving age, sought to make his environment homely. In the course of 1774, he purchased five engravings by the London-based Francesco Bartolozzi (ready framed with glass), some briar shrubs in pots to stand in his window, a second-hand spring clock from a silversmith in the High Street for 5 guineas, and six cheap china bowls in which he doubtless served up the cocoa he liked to offer friends for breakfast.[47] He also indulged his taste for music. Having plenty of space, on 14 June he hired a new harpsichord. Ten days later he purchased six sonatas by Philip Hayes, soon to be the Magdalen organist, then

---

[43] Wainscotting private rather than public rooms began only with the Restoration.

[44] *The Journeys of Celia Fiennes*, ed. Christopher Morris (London, 1947), p. 37.

[45] Woodforde, pp. 7, 82, 87, and 243. At the turn of the eighteenth century, women were also used as bedmakers, but this seems to have raised eyebrows at Oxford, if not at Cambridge, with the result only men were employed thereafter.

[46] The National Archive, Prob/11/373.   [47] Woodforde, pp. 205, 220, 223, 252.

started taking lessons. By the end of the year, however, he suspected he had over-extended himself: six months' hire of the instrument had cost him two guineas, its tuning one, and the twenty lessons he had taken from the organist and composer, William Walond, a further two. As he was also spending £5 10s. 3d. on stabling a horse in the city, he was eating up his annual college income of £129 9s. 6d. rather quickly.[48]

The years following the Restoration, too, saw the creation of the seniors' own social space. Oxford's early modern colleges and halls were hierarchical institutions where academic and social distinctions were clearly visible. But if seniors could be identified by their dress, the separate table or tables they occupied at dinner, and probably the place they sat in chapel, before the Civil War they had no common space where they could gather to talk and relax. This ceased to be the case in 1661, when Merton established the first fellows' common room. It was evidently an idea whose time had come because, by the 1680s, a further seven colleges had followed suit, including Balliol, Magdalen, and Trinity. Whether other seniors resident in a college but not on the foundation were members of the fellows' common room is not always clear, but these were so few after 1750 that they would not have formed a significant group if excluded. What is evident is that the fellows' common room did not welcome undergraduate members. If gentlemen commoners were originally admitted as one of their privileges, in the course of the eighteenth century this right was withdrawn. Instead, as at Trinity in 1766, they were often given their separate space. At New College, the arrangements were particularly complex; the college eventually had three common rooms: one for the most senior fellows; one for the other fellows with an MA; and one for undergraduate and bachelor fellows.[49]

The one detailed glimpse of the life of a don at protestant Oxford before the creation of the common room comes in the diary of Thomas Crosfield, who went up to Queen's in 1618 and took his MA in 1625. Crosfield became a fellow of Queen's two years later and kept a diary for the thirteen years he retained his fellowship. A Latin poem, inserted under 21 June 1628, described his typical day. This began with prayers and a Latin sermon and was followed by academic work with his tutorial pupils. Before dinner (at that date a little after 10 a.m.) he attended a disputation, and he relaxed after the meal with a game of bowls (on the college green). Having blown away the cobwebs, he participated in a second disputation before attending a lecture in theology. Only then (presumably in the late afternoon) did he get down to personal study, though there is no sign that he was seriously engaged in improving his knowledge of divinity. His evenings appear to have been taken up in reading and annotating works of history, land-surveying, and poetry, and perusing the latest newsletter for information about Charles I's contentious third parliament, then in session.[50] Other entries in the diary reveal that Crosfield was a conscientious protestant but no enthusiast. He was a great sermon-goer (and giver), fasted twice

[48] Ibid., pp. 231, 233, 234, 268, 269, 270.   [49] Ibid., p. xiii.
[50] *The Diary of Thomas Crosfield*, ed. F. S. Boas (Oxford, 1935), pp. 23–5. For the time of dinner, see *sub* 6 Feb. 1627 (p. 8).

a week in Lent, and read the New Testament three times a year. Yet he was no killjoy. He liked music and possessed a pair of virginals. He also enjoyed cards, went to plays staged at the King's Arms, attended squirreling expeditions, and thoroughly approved of the college's Christmas festivities. On one occasion in February 1636, he even attended the bull-baiting in St Clement's.[51] The diary hints too that his eclectic literary interests were shared by at least one other Queen's fellow of the Caroline era. The future provost, Gerard Langbaine, it appears, possessed in his chamber a number of works that would have raised the hackles of the more puritanically minded, including Rabelais, Boccaccio, and a French translation of the *Meditations* of the sixteenth-century Spanish Franciscan Diego de Estella.[52]

Clearly Crosfield was kept busy. Even if he held no official college lectureship or university post, his teaching duties, his obligation to attend college disputations, and his attendance at a daily theological lecture ensured he had only a small amount of leisure time, which he appears not to have abused. On the other hand, he was evidently not particularly studious, even if he had enough divinity at his command to become a bachelor of theology in 1635. In an age where many saw the Thirty Years War in Europe as a war against the catholic antichrist and where the Church of England itself was dividing into hostile camps, there was little sign that the Queen's fellow was bent on making an intellectual contribution to either struggle. For this reason, it is unlikely that he would have been regarded by contemporaries as an ideal don, and unsurprising that he ended his days as rector of the rural parish of Spennithorne in Yorkshire. Whether he was a representative Oxford master in the early Stuart era is another question. Certainly he and most of his peers shared one thing in common: they published nothing. But it is only in the twentieth century that a list of publications has become the sine qua non of intellectual activity.

A century later Crosfield would have been considered a paragon simply for being relatively conscientious and self-disciplined. Obviously, in the Hanoverian era, dons not directly concerned in college or university business had much more leisure time. Only two or three masters in each college or hall had a tutorial role, the system of official lectures was in decay, and disputations were less frequent. Even if those who remained in residence were still seriously pursuing higher studies, they only had the occasional lecture to attend. In a period when fellows, if not masters in halls, were becoming more affluent, this new-found freedom was not good for the donnish soul. From the turn of the eighteenth century, evidence abounds about the life of the Oxford don and the testimony is largely negative. The common view, promoted by Whiggish satirists, society gossips, jaundiced foreign visitors, and the undergraduates themselves, was that most Oxford masters were idlers, gamblers, and topers. All Souls was judged to be a particular den of iniquity. When the Irish man

---

[51] Ibid., pp. xxi and xxv–vi, and pp. 25, 36, 41, 68, and 85 (*sub* 25 June 1628, 7 July 1629, 4 Mar. 1630, 16 Dec. 1633, and 2 Feb. 1636).

[52] Ibid., p. 68. The *Meditations* were published in 1578, the year of Estella's death. The Arminian wing of the church took an interest in Spanish mystical works: see Louis Martz, *The Poetry of Meditation: A Study in English Religious Literature of the Seventeenth Century* (London, 1962).

of letters Thomas Campbell passed through the University in 1775, he was informed by a 'gownsman' that the fellows of All Souls 'lived so luxuriantly and indolently, that they did nothing but clean their teeth all morning and pick them all evening'. Four year later, the hard-working John James was just as dismissive of the fellows of Queen's. Spending 'half their lives in poring over newspapers and smoking tobacco', they 'seem to live to no end, to be cut off from all the dearer interests of society, to possess, or at least to exert, no benevolence'.[53]

A similar view was reiterated at length by one of the masters themselves, Thomas Hearne. His diary, kept for forty years in the first part of the eighteenth century, is one long lament on the moral decline of a great institution. According to Hearne, as in an entry for 15 December 1722, Oxford's senior members were, for the most part, feckless drunks who abused their role of being in loco parentis by encouraging young bloods down the road to perdition:

> Yesterday Morning at two Clock the Duke of Beaufort (who is of Univ. College) rid out of Town with that vicious, loose Fellow, Mr Ward (commonly call'd Jolly Ward) of Univ. College. It is said they had sate up 'till that time drinking. Ward was so drunk that he vomited four times between Queen's Coll. Lane and East Gate.[54]

Hearne was an intolerant Jacobite ejected from his post at the Bodleian in 1715, so his feelings towards the many Oxford Tories with more accommodating consciences were inevitably hostile. Yet his negative portrayal of his contemporaries should not be dismissed out of hand. There is plenty of evidence in college archives to give more than a degree of credence to his anecdotes. Oxford's dons, throughout the long eighteenth century, consumed drink in considerable quantities as they relaxed in their common rooms. At Queen's in 1811 they got through 1,470 bottles of port and a further 171 of sherry and 48 of Madeira. Not surprisingly, as the drink had to be paid for (only meals were provided on the foundation), many fellows ran up large battels bills. At Magdalen in 1741–2, one William Henchman received £38 2s. 7d. for his fellowship but owed the college £91 13s. 6d.

Woodforde's diary, kept by a man who expressed contrition for an academic life lived to little purpose, provides testimony from the horse's mouth. Woodforde was hardly vicious: he was no womanizer and his idea of a good time in summer was a game of bowls, a ride on his mare, or a fishing exhibition. But he did little academic work during his stays in New College, and showed limited literary interests, beyond subscribing to the Oxford newspapers. While an assiduous chapel- and sermon-goer, he spent nearly every evening in his own or another college common room, drinking and playing whist or some other card game, often long past midnight. Even when he attended the monthly recitals at the recently founded Holywell Music Room,[55] to

---

[53] *Dr Campbell's Diary of a Visit to England in 1775*, ed. J. L. Clifford (Cambridge, 1947), p. 43; James, p. 85. For a much earlier negative comment by an undergraduate, see Dudley Ryder and William Matthews, *The Diary of Dudley Ryder, 1715–1716* (London, 1939), p. 143.

[54] Hearne, viii. 24. Ward had been a fellow of University College since 1708.

[55] Built in 1748 to a design by Thomas Camplin, vice-principal of St Edmund Hall.

which he subscribed, he imbibed handsomely beforehand. In each of the three years he was permanently based in the University, his normal annual drinks bill totted up to about £16, or 12 per cent of his income. But as he also had to stand drinks on special occasions—his election to the Weston Longville living cost him £3 5s. 6d.—and he had his own private supply of alcohol—on 31 December 1774 he bought three gallons of rum in the town for £1 13s. 6d.—the proportion of his stipend that he consumed in drink must have been considerably larger. Woodforde further wasted money gambling. Besides betting on cards, he continually lost and sometimes won money playing nothing more subtle than heads and tails:

> [1774] Aug: 10– I breakfasted, dined, supped & slept again at College. Cooke Senr., Jeffries & [Cadwallader] Coker breakfasted with me. Tossing up with Coker this morning lost 1:13:6. Coker dined & spent the afternoon with us in the MCR [masters' common room]…For fruit this afternoon in the MCR 0:1:0. I tossed up with Coker this afternoon for a Bottle of Claret for which we each pd. 0:5:0. I tossed up with him again for a Bottle of Olives and I won that—the Bottle of Olives cost 0:3:0. For port in the MCR this afternoon 0:0:6. Coker supped & spent the Evening with me in Chequer. For Rum and Water in the Chequer 0:1:0. Tossing up with Cooke Senr. & Coker this Evening lost 4:0.[56]

Woodforde may seldom have been paralytic after a night's roistering (he was no 'Jolly' Ward) but it is not hard to see why he was not the most punctilious Proctor. Rousing himself to go and check that undergraduates were no longer on the streets after 9 p.m. must have required considerable strength of will.[57]

The delinquency of the eighteenth- and early nineteenth-century don should not be exaggerated. Drinking and betting had been a problem in earlier centuries, even before the creation of the common room. Magdalen fellows, for instance, were accused of haunting taverns and gambling on several occasions in the sixteenth century, both before and after the Reformation. Seniors after 1700 were also less volatile than their predecessors. Living cheek to jowl for long periods of time in an age in which interpersonal violence was a commonplace often led to pent-up animosities which would be suddenly released in insults, calumnies, threats of violence, and downright physical harm. At Queen's in 1630, the senior fellow John Langhorne was so angered by a disciplinary fine imposed by Provost Potter for his failing to fulfil his responsibilities in chapel that he 'threatened to stiletto him'.[58] The next year, a Merton fellow inappropriately called Holyway lost control completely and murdered another who was his chamber companion. The eighteenth century was a less confrontational world where fellows had more space and had been raised, like the social elite generally, on the virtues of forbearance and politeness,

---

[56] Woodforde, p. 245. The Chequer was the college bursary where two or three fellows could eat and drink privately. Cooke, Jeffries, and Coker were also fellows of New College, though the last was still an undergraduate.

[57] For Woodforde as a Proctor, see p. 268, this volume.

[58] Boas, *Crosfield*, pp. 41 and 50, *sub* 18 Mar. 1630 and 4 Feb. 1631. Langhorne had been the only fellow not to vote for Potter's election as provost in 1626: ibid., p. xix.

popularized in the much read *Spectator* of Magdalen's Joseph Addison. They were drunk but not dangerous to others.[59]

The burden of general indolence and insobriety should also not be allowed to obscure the fact that not all dons were indolent alcoholics. In every college or hall in the eighteenth and early nineteenth century there were always a handful of hard-working and relatively ascetic masters. There were undoubtedly few Wesleys, vainly trying to set an example to their less serious colleagues. But some bookish dons were always to be found in the University. When Bodley's librarian, Joseph Bowles of Oriel, died in 1730 at the young age of 34, he left a modest collection of books numbering only 129 titles, which was valued at £13 12s. 6d. But it was the collection of a steady and serious man. Virtually all his books were religious works or editions of classical texts, and he had no modern literature except the Latin and English poems of the catholic convert Richard Crashaw. He was a man, too, who, when he relaxed, appears to have indulged in solitary pleasures, for one of the few vernacular works in his library was Walton's *Compleat Angler*.[60]

Frequently, moreover, there were masters at eighteenth-century Oxford who used their time profitably, not only pursuing the studies for which they were registered but broadening their mind. The orientalist William Jones came up to University College in 1764 and became a fellow two years later, even before he had taken his BA, in recognition of his intellectual precocity. As a fellow, he spent most of his time away from Oxford cultivating his legal career, but whenever he came into residence—mostly at Christmas and over the summer months—he devoted his time to academic study not frivolity. Writing to his patron, Viscount Althorp, in August 1772, to announce he was spending the summer in Oxford, he depicted himself totally immersed in his work: 'I study law and history seven or eight hours a day, it is scarce credible how much I read and write from seven in the morning to twelve at night, as I never go to rest earlier.'[61]

There were limits, too, to the depths to which eighteenth-century dons would sink. Despite the sexual licence of the age, lechery was seldom added to the list of charges levelled against them. Evidently some boundaries were retained, and chastity was one.[62] Too much should not be made, then, of the famous sexual scandal of 1739, which involved the unfortunate warden of Wadham, Robert Thistlethwayte.

---

[59] They were sometimes a danger to themselves. The odd master, just like the occasional undergraduate, took their own lives; e.g. Weston of St John's in 1794: Galbraith, *Stevens*, p. 166.

[60] OUA, Vice-Chancellor's Court, Inventories: HO235000, reel 005, fs 181–2. The one surprising work in his collection was the contemporary best-seller on the evils of masturbation, *Onania*. Bowles came from a relatively humble background; his father was a tailor; as a result he left little of value besides his books apart from a silver snuffbox. Hearne, obviously jealous that Bowles held a position he felt was rightly his, called him 'a most vile, wicked wretch' and claimed 'folly' and 'wickedness' had shortened his life: Hearne, x. 207 and 422. *Onania, or the heinous sin of self-pollution* first appeared in 1723 and was attributed to the Dutchman Dr Balthasar Bekker. It went through sixty printings.

[61] Cannon, *Jones*, i. 115.

[62] Even Hearne accused only a handful of senior members of lechery, most notably Dr Robert Shippen, principal of Brasenose 1710–45, who, around 1730, had purportedly debauched the pretty wife of an Oxford bookbinder: Hearne, xi. 41.

Given the close friendships that often grew up between fellows, homoeroticism of some kind must have been part and parcel of Oxford life from the beginning, especially when young adults roomed together. But its presence remains largely hidden from the historian and surfaces only on the odd occasion when an intimacy was formed or attempted that was non-consensual or between individuals of different status. At such moments, academic tolerance was always exhausted and the senior party forced to remove himself as fast as possible from the University. This was Thistlethwayte's fate when he was reported to the Vice-Chancellor for making unwelcome physical advances to a 22-year-old (and thus rather aged) undergraduate called French. Whatever had really happened remains a mystery, but Thistlethwayte's future was sealed when a servant, William Bloxley, was persuaded to testify that he had been previously sodomized by the warden. The case became a criminal matter and was transferred to the Oxford assizes. At this point, the warden thought prudence the better part of valour. Not bothering to contest the new charge, he resigned his position and headed for the continent, leaving Cambridge and the nation's wits to revel in Oxford and Wadham's discomfiture.[63] When the college, thinking the incident closed, proceeded to invest in the relatively new instrument of fire insurance, one wit had a field day:

> Well did the am'rous sones of Wadham
> Insure their house 'gainst future flame;
> They knew their crime, the crime of Sodom,
> And judg'd their punishment the same.[64]

The most obvious way of returning the community of masters to its scholarly last was to make fellowship appointments more meritocratic. As we saw in Chapter 5,[65] there was some sign that this was beginning to happen in the second quarter of the nineteenth century with the creation of open fellowships based on examination at Oriel and Balliol. But this was a drop in the ocean, and in every other college, when Victoria came to the throne, fellowships continued to be tied to a county, town, or school, and fellows appointed after a cursory examination, if any examination at all. That said, fellows in the mid-nineteenth century, though scarcely scholarly paragons, were not the inebriated ne'er-do-wells of an earlier age. If little had been done to change the appointments' system, there had been a revolution in the nation's mores in the first half of the nineteenth century that inevitably affected

---

[63] For the fullest study of the limited number of homosexual scandals at Oxford in the seventeenth and eighteenth centuries, see John McManners, *All Souls and the Shipley Case (1808–10)* (Oxford, 2002). The most recent accounts are George Rousseau, 'The Kiss of Death and the Cabal of Dons: Blackmail and Grooming in Georgian Oxford', *Journal of Historical Sociology*, 21: 4 (2008), 368–96, and George Rousseau, 'Privilege, Power and Sexual Abuse in Georgian Oxford', in George Rousseau (ed.), *Children and Sexuality: From the Greeks to the Great War* (Basingstoke, 2007), ch. 5. In the early seventeenth century, accusations of sodomy were frequently levelled at religious or political opponents. Both William Lewis, provost of Oriel, and President Anyan of Corpus, were targeted in this way in the first half of the 1620s.

[64] <http://en.wikipedia.org/wiki/Robert_Thistlethwayte> (accessed 2 Apr. 2012). For more scurrilous verse, see Rictor Norton, *Mother Clap's Molly House: The Gay Sub-Culture in England, 1700–1830* (Stroud, 2006).

[65] See pp. 157–8, this volume.

the two universities. The French Revolution had given the elite a shock, which had encouraged much of high society to sober up. The ever more powerful evangelical wing of the church had cleverly capitalized on the event, as had the other movements of religious reform that followed it. The campaign for moral and spiritual renewal led by Newman and his friends in the University in the 1830s and 1840s found a ready audience among junior and senior members that Wesley, when he preached in St Mary's a century before, had never encountered. In consequence, most fellows in the mid-nineteenth century, Tractarian, evangelical, old-fashioned high church, or new-minted broad, were a relatively sober, studious, and diligent bunch, if not necessarily particularly intellectually able. Even in the universities, the age of aristocracy was giving way to the age of the middle class.

FIGURE 8.1 'Stall' library, Merton College, 1589–90. The inspiration of the warden, Sir Henry Savile, Merton's stall library was probably the first in Europe. The spacing of the stalls was determined by the location of the windows in the medieval library and this constricted the width of the benches. Although one wing of the library was illuminated by the east window depicted in the photograph, the stalls received little light and dormer windows had to be inserted.

D. Libraries

At any time in the period, the Oxford master who took his higher studies seriously spent many hours of the day locked away in his carrel or room immersed in his books. But no scholar, even the wealthiest, could have burnished his scholarly credentials solely by his own resources. He needed access to a good library, and in this regard Oxford was particularly well endowed. His first port of call would have been the library of his college or hall (if one existed), the second, after its creation at the turn of the seventeenth century, the Bodleian. Both were principally reserved for senior members. In the first case, a fellow often had the chance to borrow a number of books and take them back to his room, though the degree to which this was permitted would have varied from college to college; in the second, books would have had to have been consulted *in situ*.[66] Over time, using an Oxford library gradually became easier. In the late middle ages, books were usually stored in chests and read on lecterns. Beginning at Merton in 1589, Oxford libraries adopted the 'stall' system where bookcases were built at right-angles to the library walls, and the books were placed on the shelves above a reading desk (see Figure 8.1). Although the most valuable books were chained until the eighteenth century, to stop them being removed, it made consulting them much more comfortable. Towards the end of the seventeenth century, books also became much simpler to find. As early as the mid-Tudor era, some colleges were appointing a fellow to take charge of the library for a small stipend, who would be expected to inform readers on its holdings. But, from 1674, locating books was revolutionized when Thomas Hyde, Bodley's librarian from 1655, published the University Library's first catalogue. Colleges purchased the catalogue, noted which books they also owned, then interleafed blank pages where they wrote down the titles of works that they but not the Bodleian possessed. This catalogue, too, was readily available. Costing 19 shillings, new readers at the Bodleian were expected to purchase a personal copy from 1692 so that they could peruse it at leisure.[67]

In the 1530s, college libraries were small and contained mainly manuscripts. By the early seventeenth century, following the printing revolution that accompanied the age of Reformation, their holdings were completely transformed. The best-supplied college libraries now contained thousands rather than hundreds of books. The colleges themselves spent little of their income before the Civil War on new acquisitions, even when they were well endowed. Magdalen's only significant investment in its library in the early part of the period was in 1571–2, when it spent £120 on buying up the library of Bishop Jewel, one of the heroes of the new Elizabethan church. The rapid growth of the Oxford college libraries from the

---

[66] For a list of books taken from New College library in the second half of the seventeenth century and the names of their borrowers, see Poole, 'Book Economy', pp. 56–82.

[67] Some colleges did have a catalogue from an early date but, normally, separate catalogues appeared only at the end of the period: Trinity's first shelf lists, for instance, date from 1771 and 1783. While books were chained, they were stored spine inwards so could not be located by casual readers.

mid-sixteenth century can mainly be attributed to the generosity of benefactors. Besides the odd volumes that were left to colleges in old members' wills, individual institutions were usually the beneficiaries of one or two sizeable bequests. Probably the largest college library at the beginning of the seventeenth century belonged to St John's. Although a new college, it was able to leapfrog its seniors, thanks in part to the gift of 1,200 books, many of them medical, that it received from a former commoner, Sir William Paddy, in 1602.[68]

The donations continued after 1650. A proper library was established in a hall for the first time in 1656, when Principal Henry Wilkinson put up the funds to construct and equip one in Magdalen Hall; this was soon filled with works of classical literature, ancient and modern philosophy, and protestant theology and piety. St Edmund Hall also had its own library by the end of the seventeenth century thanks to Principal John Mill.[69] The colleges, meanwhile, attracted ever larger benefactions, as private libraries, from the second half of the seventeenth century, grew exponentially. Christ Church was particularly blessed. In 1710, Dean Aldrich left the House 3,000 books, then Archbishop Wake a further 7,000 in 1737.[70] But the largest collection was given to All Souls in 1710 when the governor of the Leeward Islands, Christopher Codrington, left his alma mater at least 8,000 works, predominantly in French and Italian history and literature (see Figure 8.2). Some colleges, too, were able, for the first time, to go on a book-buying spree when benefactors left a specific financial bequest for this purpose. Magdalen, in 1664, had inherited possibly Europe's best collection of botany books under the will of John Goodyer, a Hampshire gentleman only tangentially connected to the college.[71] Much more useful was the sum of £1,000 given the college a year later by John Warner, Bishop of Rochester. From spending next to nothing on book purchases, the college was able annually to devote sums as high as £150 over the next fifteen to twenty years.

The state of most of Oxford's college libraries at the turn of the eighteenth century is revealed in the journal of the German traveller Zacharias Conrad von Uffenbach. Uffenbach was a book collector and bibliophile from Frankfurt who passed through Oxford in 1710 hunting for manuscripts of interest. He found the college libraries a mixed bag. New College's and Trinity's were judged wretched, Lincoln's disordered, Oriel's small, St John's merely a melange of curiosities, and Exeter's in a bad state after the fire it had suffered the year before. All Souls', too, had little to recommend it. He was aware of the recent arrival of the huge Codrington bequest but noted that,

[68] J. F. Fuggles, 'A History of the Library of St John's College, Oxford, from the Foundation of the College to 1660' (BLitt dissertation, Oxford, 1975).

[69] S. G. Hamilton, *Hertford* (London, 1903), pp. 116–17; Henry Wilkinson, *Catalogus librorum in bibliotheca Aulae Magdalenae* (Oxford, 1661); Hearne, i, 29. Magdalen Hall's library in 1661 contained works by Francis Bacon, Descartes, and the French atomist Pierre Gassendi.

[70] Brian Young, 'Henry Aldrich and Christ Church', unpublished paper given at the conference 'Henry Aldrich (1648–1710): An Oxford Universal Man', Christ Church, 21 Jan. 2011.

[71] Sarah Vowles, 'John Goodyer (c. 1592–1664) and Renaissance Botany' (BA dissertation, Oxford, 2006).

LIBRARY OF ALL SOULS COLLEGE.

FIGURE 8.2 Codrington Library, All Souls College: *Oxford Almanack* 1829, drawing C. Wild, engraving Joseph Skelton. A 'wall' library rather than a stall library, the Codrington was built between 1716 and 1720 but only ready for use in 1751. As designed by Hawksmoor and completed by James Gibbs, it had a gothic exterior and a classical interior. The library was unusual in being located on the ground floor. The statue of Codrington in the centre dressed as a Roman is by Henry Cheere.

at present, it was locked away in a separate building and the current library meagre in both its size and contents. Merton's was equally found wanting: it had a fair collection of books but they were housed in two dark, uninviting corridors. Even the new library at Queen's, built in the 1690s, was damned with faint praise. At the end of the day, for all its merits, it came a poor second to the Wren library at Trinity College, Cambridge. Only five libraries—those of Brasenose, Corpus Christi, Wadham, Christ Church (at this date still in its original building), and Magdalen— received his seal of approval: their collections were extensive and well housed. Magdalen's was particularly praised: it was housed in a building that was fairly large and bright, there were a great number of books on medicine and theology, and the medicine collection was supposedly the best of any library anywhere.[72]

Uffenbach's judgements were blinded to a degree by parti pris. He was irritated when he was unable to access manuscripts that he believed to be in a college library

[72] Zacharias Conrad von Uffenbach, *Oxford in 1710*, ed. W.H. and J.C. Quarrell (Oxford, 1928), pp. 7, 8, 15, 26, 32, 33, 40, 45, 53, 58, 61, 66, and 67.

and he only liked classical buildings. But his snapshot also reflected the predominant role played by donations in building up the individual collections. Some colleges had been much better served by their old members than others, while many collections reflected the interests of donors rather than the academic needs of the fellowship. College libraries, by the end of the seventeenth century, appear to have contained the most important recent works in the arts and sciences. But they were also all full of tomes that can have been only infrequently lifted from the shelves. Had Uffenbach returned a hundred years later, his judgement would have changed only slightly. He would have been overjoyed to visit the new libraries at All Souls, Christ Church, and Worcester, but he would have concluded that the others, even the ones he had approved of in 1710, were largely marking time. With the rapid expansion of the Republic of Letters in the eighteenth century, there was an explosion in the number of learned works on the arts and sciences appearing in print, in the vernacular, and in the new format of the learned journal. Keeping abreast of the growing literature was difficult for any non-specialist library. Most Oxford college libraries after the 1730s appear not to have tried and, in consequence, became fossilized rather than living repositories of knowledge.[73]

In that colleges usually had a growing income after 1750, the cause was not basically financial. The chief problem was that, by the early eighteenth century, the libraries were bursting at the seams and large donations could no longer be accommodated and were not solicited. If most college libraries grew at all in the last century of the period, it was only through the handful of books that the librarian cared to buy each year and the odd volume left in a bequest.[74] The new purchases too were, understandably, current theological works, seldom works of the contemporary Enlightenment, conservative or radical. A number of Oxford college libraries have a copy of the *Encyclopédie* today but they did not usually acquire Diderot and D'Alembert's chef d'oeuvre in the mid-eighteenth century.[75] Only All Souls and Christ Church with their brand-new libraries had the space to expand. The former, in particular, capitalized on its good fortune. Once Codrington's bequest had been amalgamated with the contents of the old library in 1751, the college concentrated on modernizing its collection of works in law and the humanities. By 1800, it had purchased an impressive number of books published in French, including Montesquieu's *Spirit of the Laws*, a collected Voltaire, and the works of the historian and sceptic Pierre Bayle and of the republican, Gabriel Bonnot de Mably.[76]

---

[73] Even as fossils, of course, college libraries remained significant scholarly resources. Uffenbach found Trinity 'wretched' but Samuel Johnson was a frequent visitor.

[74] A handful of libraries did still receive large bequests. When Oriel's collection was doubled by the donation of Lord Leigh in 1786 it was forced to construct a new 'senior library'.

[75] Giles Barber, 'Oxford and the Encyclopédie' (unpublished paper). The *Encyclopédie ou dictionnaire raisonné des arts, des sciences et des metiers* appeared between 1751 and 1780 in 17 volumes of text and 11 volumes of illustrations. It aimed to provide useful and up-to-date information on the sum of human knowledge.

[76] J. S. G. Simmons, *French Publications Acquired by the Codrington Library, 1762–1800* (Oxford, 1978), accession list; All Souls bought the first four volumes of the *Encyclopédie* in 1764.

Yet if most college libraries ceased to be dynamic collections in the eighteenth and first half of the nineteenth century, this was not the case with the Bodleian. When the Bodleian opened in 1602 it possessed about 5,000 books and manuscripts and was not much bigger than the largest college collections. But it quickly proved able to attract generous benefactions and, by 1675, had a collection eight times as large, thanks in particular to Archbishop Laud and the antiquarian John Selden, who left the library 8,000 books and manuscripts in 1654. Laud and Selden endowed the library with an important collection of Greek and oriental manuscripts, which were added to in the last quarter of the seventeenth century by the targeted buying policy of Thomas Hyde. At this juncture, the Bodleian had limited funds to purchase new books or manuscripts, as it was entirely reliant on the £60 a year left for the purpose by the founder in 1613. But Hyde, himself an orientalist, showed how a small budget could be put to good effect. In the 1690s especially, he organized the purchase of a number of significant private collections of Hebrew and Arabic books and manuscripts, most notably the 420 manuscripts left by the regius professor of both Hebrew and Arabic Edward Pococke, which came to the library in 1692. His endeavours, in turn, bred fresh bequests from bibliophiles, such as Narcissus Marsh, archbishop of Armagh. While the former fellow of Exeter and principal of St Alban Hall founded Dublin's first public library out of his personal collection in 1701, he gave his oriental manuscripts to the Bodleian.[77]

By the turn of the eighteenth century, the Bodleian was recognized to be a national treasure and one of the most important libraries in Europe. In the 1702 edition of Edward Chamberlayne's *Angliae Notitia*, it was praised for its 'noble, lightsome Fabrick, number of excellent Books, choice Manuscripts, diversity of Languages, liberty of Studying, [and] facility of finding any Book', and judged the equal, if not the superior, of its foreign competitors.[78] As a result, it was the Bodleian, not the college libraries, which brought foreign scholars such as Uffenbach to Oxford. Uffenbach was inevitably difficult to please. He evinced surprise that the library could be visited, if not used, by those who were not scholars. He objected to paying an 8 shilling entrance fee and having to obtain a special pass to see the best books. And he thought the organization shambolic, even finding fault with Hyde's catalogue because the books were listed alphabetically by author, presumably instead of thematically. Nor was he willing to accept that the Bodleian's collection of printed books was the nonpareil. In his view, the library put together by the dukes of Brunswick at Wolfenbüttel was better, though he did grant that the Bodleian had the finer manuscripts.[79] Later visitors were less carping. When the young antiquarian Jean-François Séguier visited the library in 1736 with his Italian patron, the Marchese di Maffei, he was suitably impressed and commented enthusiastically on a ninth- or tenth-century manuscript of Terence that he was shown,

---

[77] For his Dublin foundation, see M. McCarthy, *All Graduates and Gentlemen: Marsh's Library* (Dublin, 1980).
[78] *Angliae notitia*, 20th edn (London 1702), p. 449.
[79] Uffenbach, *Oxford*, pp. 2–6. The Wolfenbüttel library was founded in 1572 by Julius, duke of Brunswick-Lüneburg.

'with the figures of actors at the beginning of each scene'. What worried Séguier was not the library but the poor state of conservation of the Arundel marbles, gifted to the University in 1667 and kept in a nearby gallery.[80]

In the eighteenth and the first half of the nineteenth century, the Bodleian went from strength to strength. The library continued to receive large donations from private collectors or their heirs, who now not only deposited books and ancient manuscripts but also personal papers. Although, with the opening of the British Museum in 1759, there was, henceforth, a national depository for scholarly collections, some of the country's leading scholars still preferred to leave their collections to Oxford. It was certainly the case that the Bodleian received some of its most important bequests before the British Museum was established. The vast collection of 1,900 books and 5,000 volumes of manuscripts left by the former fellow of St John's and non-juror Richard Rawlinson, for instance, arrived at the library in 1756.[81] But there were even more significant gifts in the first part of the nineteenth century. The year 1809 saw the arrival in the Bodleian of the huge map collection and topographical library of one of the leading British antiquarians of the second half of the eighteenth century, Richard Gough, who had initially approached the British Museum, only to be rebuffed. This was followed in the early 1820s with the deposit of the book collection of the Shakespearian scholar Edmond Malone, which completely revolutionized the Bodleian's holdings of English literature of the sixteenth and seventeenth centuries. But the biggest and most interesting bequest came from a man who had once been the keeper of manuscripts at the British Museum, Francis Douce. When he died in 1834, Douce left to Oxford a collection of 13,000 volumes, chiefly in French and English, which included 470 incunabula and contained a unique record of the customs and pastimes of earlier ages.

After 1800, too, the Bodleian was able, for the first time, to ensure that its holdings reflected the latest scholarship. Under an Act of Parliament of 1709 both Oxford and Cambridge had a right to a copy of any new book registered by the London Stationers Company, but it was only from 1812, with a change in the law, that the Bodleian began to receive most books printed in Britain. In the interim, however, the library gained the funds to begin purchasing on a large scale itself. In the 1730s, the library was spending only £7 a year on books, far less than in Thomas Hyde's day. But the position dramatically improved in the last quarter of the eighteenth century under the prompting of the former tutor of University College, the lawyer William Scott. Realizing that the library lacked the funds to purchase

---

[80] Bibliothèque Municipale Nîmes, MS 286, pp. 58–9. Séguier later became famous for cracking the inscription on the Maison Carrée at Nîmes from studying the rivet holes. The marbles were a collection of ancient Greek sculptures and inscriptions which had belonged to Thomas Howard, 2nd earl of Arundel and Surrey and a Cambridge man. Part of the collection was retained by the family and given to Oxford in 1755. The marbles seem to have been stored, with little thought for their conservation, between the Bodleian and the Sheldonian: Chamberlayne, *Angliae Notitia*, p. 455.

[81] The other two important collections deposited before the opening of the British Museum in 1759 were the books and manuscripts of Bishop Tanner (1736) and the collection of state papers gathered by Thomas Carte (1753–4). The papers of the former university Chancellor, Edward Hyde, earl of Clarendon, also started to arrive from 1753.

works of contemporary scholarship in bulk, Scott suggested that its income should be increased by charging all members of the University an annual fee. This, the University agreed to do in 1780, and the subsequent tax brought in an income of £450, allowing the library to go on a spending spree. As Oxford's undergraduate numbers rose after 1800, so did Bodley's book-buying budget. Bulkeley Bandinel, a fellow of New College and Bodley's librarian from 1813 to 1860, was able to spend, on average, £1,800 per year from the 1820s.

Users of the Bodleian still found plenty to complain about. The library had the space to house the large donations but it took many years for the books and manuscripts to be catalogued and properly shelved. It took time as well for the library to use its new-found wealth to develop an effective buying policy, especially when so much depended on the quality and interests of the librarian. The situation was particularly bad in the years immediately following the introduction of fees, if the private chemistry instructor and later political radical Thomas Beddoes is to be believed. While residing at Pembroke College in 1787, Beddoes penned a vituperative pamphlet excoriating both the librarian and the library. Since the librarian, John Price, held a curacy eleven miles away, he was frequently absent, with the result that Beddoes could not access books on the two days of the week, Saturdays and Mondays, when he was free to read in the library. More gravely, Price was accused of purchasing imperfect, incomplete, and out-of-date works, neglecting the exciting new publications coming out of Germany, and failing to make the few journals that he bought quickly available: 'I have for these three months been asking for the *Journal de Physique* for Sept. 1786. In March last, full four months after it had arrived, the Librarian told me it was in his room.'[82]

By going into print with his complaints, Beddoes appears to have sparked off a university visitation of the library, which presumably slowly resulted in an improvement in buying practices.[83] Certainly, once Bandinel was in post, the buying policy was revolutionized. Bandinel was a discriminating bibliophile, and with the help of equally discriminating curators such as the regius professor of Greek, Thomas Gaisford, he was able to range widely in his purchases, buying new books from abroad, filling gaps, and building up the library's already significant collection of ancient manuscripts and extending it into new areas such as Sanskrit. On the other hand, turning the Bodleian into the sort of user-friendly library Beddoes desired was all but impossible to achieve given the rapid expansion in the library's holdings, however cooperative the librarian and his small staff. In 1674, when Hyde produced the first catalogue, the Bodleian possessed 40,000 books and manuscripts. By 1850, the figure had risen to 240,000 volumes. An annual list of purchases was kept from 1780, and catalogues of the Gough, Malone, and Douce collections were compiled and published in the years following their accession. But

---

[82] Thomas Beddoes, *A Memorial Concerning the State of the Bodleian Library* (n.p., 1787), p. 13. The *Journal de physique* edited by the abbé Rozier was an independent science magazine, which first appeared in 1771, publishing articles and reviews.

[83] *Narrative of Proceedings Relative to the Bodleian Library*. Report 21 June 1788 (Oxford, 1788).

even in the mid-nineteenth century many of the books and manuscripts acquired in the century before 1780 remained largely hidden from view. The Bodleian was still not a modern library.

Nevertheless, for all its deficiencies, there can be no doubt that the Bodleian in 1850 had an even higher reputation among western scholars than it had had in Uffenbach's day. In terms of its size, it certainly stood head and shoulders above other university libraries in the British Isles. The library at Cambridge had only 100,000 volumes in the 1830s, while those of Dublin and the Scottish universities were considerably smaller. Edinburgh's was the largest, with 63,000 volumes in 1838; the library of Aberdeen's Marischal College the smallest, with 11,000 in 1827.[84] In fact, the Bodleian was almost certainly the largest or one of the largest university libraries in Europe. Many old universities on the continent never developed a substantial library before 1850. The University of Paris, for instance, had no library until 1764, when it inherited the books of the Jesuits' Collège de Louis-le-Grand when the order was expelled from the kingdom. On the eve of the Revolution, its library of 17,000 volumes was only half as large as that of its most famous college, the Sorbonne.[85] Only the library of the University of Göttingen was an obvious rival to Oxford's. Founded by George II in 1733 as a new university in his kingdom of Hanover, Göttingen possessed a collection of 200,000 books as early as 1800.[86] The Bodleian, moreover, was not the only non-collegiate library in Oxford at the end of the period. Early in the seventeenth century, Henry Savile had left his mathematics books to the University to form the kernel of a specialist mathematical library.[87] More importantly, as was noted in Chapter 5, two completely new university libraries were established in 1749 and 1849, with the opening of the Radcliffe Camera and the Taylorian, the first with a book-buying budget of £200 per annum, the second with one of £100 to be devoted to the promotion of modern languages.[88]

With such resources at his fingertips, no Oxford master with a serious interest in pursuing a branch of study, be it theology or any other, had an excuse for backsliding. The fact that so few senior members passed through the Bodleian's portals in the eighteenth and the first half of the nineteenth century, even after 1780, is further evidence how few fellows were committed to learning. When the Bodleian had first opened, the Duke Humfrey reading room, if probably never full, was well attended. In 1618, the chaplain to the Venetian ambassador claimed that 'one always see fifteen or twenty gownsmen studying there most attentively and writing down the fruit of their learning'. By the mid-eighteenth century, however, the number of

---

[84] Giles Mandebrote and K. A. Manley (eds), *The Cambridge History of Libraries in Britain and Ireland*, vol. 2: *1640–1850* (Cambridge, 2006), pp. 347–8.

[85] Jacques Artier, 'Les Bibliothèques des universités et de leurs collèges', in Claude Joly (ed.), *Histoire des bibliothèques françaises*, vol. 2: *Les bibliothèques sous l'ancien régime, 1530–1789* (Paris, 1988), pp. 48 and 51. Many Paris colleges had libraries with 2–4,000 books but the Sorbonne in 1790 contained 25–36,000 volumes.

[86] William Clark, *Academic Charisma and the Origins of the Research University* (Chicago, 2006), pp. 317–21.

[87] A decision was taken in 1620 that the collections and future additions should be stored in bookcases in the room in the Bodleian quadrangle between the geometry and astronomy schools: OUS, i. 272–3.

[88] See pp. 180–1 this volume. The Radcliffe endowment was supposed to be for the purchase of books in foreign languages but no attention was paid to this.

readers had dwindled to one or two, and there were many days in the 1740s when no book orders were registered at all. Attendance was still down on the early years at the end of the period: even as late as 1845 the library received only ten readers per day in the summer term, the one time in the year when Duke Humfrey was warm enough to work in comfortably. A large proportion of the readers in the eighteenth century, furthermore, came from outside Oxford. Overseas scholars had been visiting the Bodleian from the beginning. In the twenty years before the Civil War, some 350 foreign readers were admitted, half from German-speaking lands. But in the first half of the eighteenth century, foreign scholars were the mainstay of the library: 88 per cent of the volumes ordered in December 1708, for example, were requested by seven continental scholars, six Germans, and one Frenchman. The Bodleian Library was the principal reason, besides the University's antiquity and architecture, for Oxford's international reputation as a centre of learning in the Age of Enlightenment. But its connection with the community of masters was tenuous to say the least.[89]

E. Oxford and the Republic of Letters

A rapid survey of the publications of Oxford dons while in residence or later life reveals that even the minority who went into print left little to posterity beyond sermons, religious polemic, and pastoral literature, often of indifferent quality. The large majority of Oxford masters in the period had little to do with the burgeoning Republic of Letters. They would have known of its existence, and as tutors and lecturers they were ready, from the mid-seventeenth century at least, to incorporate elements of the new science into their teaching as much as aspects of the new textual criticism. But they had little inclination to become part of the wider intellectual community. In every part of the period, however, there was always a small coterie of dons who did want to be citizens of the virtual state. Some are best described as news gatherers, senior members of the University who kept in touch with well-placed individuals around Europe and had their finger on the pulse of the latest developments. The most important such figure at the turn of the eighteenth century was Bodley's librarian, Dr John Hudson, fellow of University College, whose position allowed him to maintain a correspondence with members of the Republic who held similar positions, such as the bibliographer Lorenzo Zacagnius (Zacagni) at the Vatican.[90] Other dons were active knowledge creators who succeeded in making their own personal contribution to the advancement of the Republic's cause, and in so doing built a reputation that extended way beyond the confines of Oxford and England.

---

[89] This was also reflected in its governance. Although, under the 1610 statutes, the librarian was an elected officer of Convocation, oversight of the library was entrusted to a board of eight unelected curators, which came to comprise the Vice-Chancellor and Proctors, the regius professors of theology, law, and medicine, and the regius professors of Greek and Hebrew: OUS, i. 243 and 257.

[90] Hearne, i. 64–5.

Surprisingly, given the University's commitment to the study of Latin and Greek literary texts as part of the BA degree, no Oxford don produced a classical edition that could even begin to compare with the works of the great continental exegetes, such as Joseph Scaliger of Leiden.[91] Initially, in the century before the Civil War, there seems to have been next to no interest in forwarding classical studies. The Dutch scholar Lucas Holstenius, who visited Oxford's libraries in the 1620s to study Latin and Greek manuscripts, found he had the field to himself, for nobody in the University 'thinks of troubling them'.[92] After the Restoration, the situation improved but only marginally. There was an attempt, from the late seventeenth century, to provide undergraduates with basic editions of many Greek texts, but there were notable absences—no Plato, for instance—and the editions were hardly scholarly. In 1695 a Christ Church fellow, the Honourable Charles Boyle, produced an edition of the letters of the little-known Greek author Phalaris. His interest in the text lay in its purported moral qualities and he demonstrated little ability as a textual critic, swallowing without further consideration the idea that the letters dated from the sixth century BC. He was immediately attacked for his sloppy scholarship by the one English classicist with a European cachet at the turn of the eighteenth century, Richard Bentley, master of Trinity, Cambridge, who showed conclusively that Phalaris was a much later author. Christ Church and Oxford became a laughing stock.[93] Oxford had to wait until the first half of the nineteenth century before it sheltered a classical scholar who could command even a modicum of respect on the continent. This was Thomas Gaisford, regius professor of Greek 1811–55, whose talent for locating important but little-used manuscripts allowed him to produce a number of new editions of Greek texts which slightly altered the received version.[94]

Despite this, Oxford's right to be considered a centre of Latin and Greek scholarship by the international community was confirmed by the University's publishing record in the area of patristics. The Church of England placed great emphasis on demonstrating its affinity with the fathers of the early church, and, from the time of the Edwardian Reformation, there was always one or two Oxford theologians busy preparing editions of their works, and seeking and receiving help to complete the task from citizens of the Republic all over Europe. Three contributions were of particular note. In 1612, Savile published an important collaborative edition of Chrysostom, although most of the work was done at Eton where Merton's warden was also provost; in 1682, the dean of Christ Church and bishop of Oxford, John

---

[91] Anthony Grafton, *Joseph Scaliger, A Study in the History of Classical Scholarship* (2 vols; Oxford, 1983–93). Scaliger came to Leiden only in the last part of his life.

[92] *HUO*, iv. 262–3. Holstenius was Leiden-educated, but was a catholic and became Vatican librarian.

[93] The dispute between Boyle and Bentley fed into a wider quarrel in the Republic of Letters over the purpose of classical textual exegesis: see Floris Verhaart, 'The Public Classics: Scholarship and Education and the Rise of the Two Classical Cultures, 1670–1720' (DPhil. dissertation, Oxford, in progress). On Bentley's work more generally, see Kristine L. Haugen, *Richard Bentley: Poetry and Enlightenment* (Cambridge, MA, 2011).

[94] Hugh Lloyd-Jones, *Blood for the Ghosts: Classical Influences in the Nineteenth and Twentieth Centuries* (London, 1982), ch. 6. Except for Aristotle's *Rhetoric*, most of the ancient texts edited by Gaisford were of the second rank; he also edited several anthologies from late antiquity and a number of patristic texts. Lloyd-Jones rates him highly for industry but not for scholarship.

Fell, put his collected Cyprian of Carthage before the public; and towards the end of the period, in 1814–18, Martin Routh, the long-serving president of Magdalen, rounded off the Oxford patristic project with his much admired *Reliquiae sacrae*, an edition of fragments of all patristic authors known to have been active before the Council of Nicea (AD 325).[95]

In the early seventeenth century, a number of Oxford theologians gave further evidence of the University's linguistic credentials through their activities as biblical translators. Both English versions of the Scriptures which circulated in Elizabeth's reign were predominantly the work of Oxonians. Tyndale's pivotal contribution to the text of the protestant Geneva Bible was matched by the role of Oxford graduates in the catholic translation, which appeared at Douai in the 1570s. Both versions, though, were the work of exiles. It was Oxford's participation in the creation of the King James Bible of 1611 which demonstrated to the wider European world that the University had a powerful contingent of humanist intellectuals in residence. The translation was the work of six 'companies' of scholars based at both universities and in London. One Oxford cohort, under Rainolds, worked on the books of the Old Testament prophets, and another, under Savile of Merton, translated the gospels, the Acts of the Apostles, and the Apocalypse. Oxford MAs dispensed from residence were also involved in the London translations, notably two members of New College, the warden, George Ryves, and the future warden, Arthur Lake. While Savile's company was working from Greek originals, Rainolds and his associates were translating Hebrew texts. Their facility in tackling a series of particularly difficult books of the Bible is a tribute to the successful introduction of Hebrew into the arts and theology curriculum by the beginning of the seventeenth century.

Oxford's reputation as a centre of Hebrew scholarship was cemented even more firmly during the Interregnum and Restoration, when the University was home to two giants in the field, Edward Pococke and Thomas Smith. Pococke, of Magdalen Hall and Corpus, took up the regius chair in 1648 (see Figure 8.3). Seven years later he first came to Europe's attention when he published the six prefatory sections to the commentary on the *Mishna* by the twelfth-century Jewish scholar Moses Maimonides. This was the first of a stream of commentaries on the Old Testament and other Hebraic texts over the next forty years with which he secured his standing, while, through his teaching, he prepared the way for a number of his Oxford pupils to publish on parts of the *Mishna* itself.[96] His younger contemporary, Smith of Magdalen, staked his claim to become a citizen of the Republic a little later, in 1660, by taking up a traditional interest of Hebrew scholars since the early sixteenth century and publishing a comparative study of the Aramaic and Hebrew versions of the Old Testament. Known affectionately as 'Rabbi' or 'Tograi' because of his enthusiasm for Hebraic studies, Smith was arguably Oxford's most

---

[95] On Anglican interest in the church fathers, see Jean-Louis Quantin, *The Church of England and Christian Antiquity: The Construction of a Confessional Identity in the Seventeenth Century* (Oxford, 2009).
[96] Maimonides' fourteen-volume *Mishneh Torah* was the most important medieval codification of Talmudic law.

EDWARD POCOCK D.D. *Professor of of Hebrew &
Arabick Tongues in ye University of* Oxford *& Canon of Christ Church*

FIGURE 8.3 Edward Pococke, 1604–91, orientalist, Laudian professor of Arabic and regius professor of Hebrew: anonymous portrait. Pococke began collecting oriental manuscripts while chaplain to English merchants at Aleppo in the first half of the 1630s. He was considered one of the leading Hebraic scholars in Europe and cemented Oxford's reputation as a centre for oriental studies.

important and active member of the Republic of Letters in the second half of the seventeenth century in terms of the size of his correspondence and his continental renown.[97] In the eighteenth century, the number of prominent Hebrew scholars at Oxford declined but the creative urge was never completely spent. The lectures on Hebrew biblical poetry published in 1753 by Robert Lowth, one of the first professors of poetry, demonstrated a novel sensitivity to Hebrew verse form. The two-volume calendar of extant Hebrew manuscripts collated by the Wadham fellow Benjamin Kennicott that appeared in 1776 and 1780, were the fruits of a labour

---

[97] On Smith's life and travels, see Andrei Pipiddi, 'Knowledge of the Ottoman Empire in Late Seventeenth-Century England: Thomas Smith and Some of His Friends' (DPhil dissertation, Oxford, 1983).

worthy of Hercules: it was by no means the last word in scholarship but that it was finished at all is evidence of the extent to which Kennicott was able to engage the keepers of Europe's great libraries in his endeavours.

Oxford also made a small contribution to the understanding of other oriental languages from the mid-seventeenth century. Pococke, Smith, and several other Oxford dons were accomplished Arabic scholars, and Bodley's librarian, Hyde, knew Persian. But they had difficulty reaching an audience within or without the University. When Pococke, in 1663, published his *Historia dynastiarum*, a Latin translation of an Arabic text by the thirteenth-century Syriac bishop Bar Hebraeus, the work was largely ignored, while Hyde got his fingers burnt with his *Historia religionis veterum Persarum* in the 1690s, and most of the print run was left in his hands. Oxford orientalists enjoyed none of the patronage accorded their French counterparts in the reign of Louis XIV.[98] The situation was no better when University College's intellectual prodigy Sir William Jones turned his attention to oriental languages in the third quarter of the eighteenth century. Jones is best known as Britain's first Sanskrit scholar who helped to redirect oriental studies all over Europe at the turn of the nineteenth century, but this was a language he did not begin to study until he moved to Calcutta in 1784. While an Oxford fellow, he concentrated his attention on Arabic and Persian. He published a Persian grammar in 1771, a translation of a collection of Asian poems the following year, and, in 1774, a Latin commentary on Asian poetry. But Jones' activity had little immediate impact on oriental studies in Oxford itself and certainly did nothing to establish Oxford as a dynamic centre of the discipline, whatever the strength of the Bodleian's manuscript collection.

Oxford's contribution to the broader study of the world's ancient civilizations was equally limited. Throughout the period, most citizens of the Republic of Letters took an interest in the classical past and many prided themselves on the small refinements that they were able to make to the received narrative through their study of inscriptions and artefacts.[99] But this was not the case at Oxford. Arts students were supposed to learn something about the classical world in the course of their studies, and the holder of the Camden chair was paid to lecture on the subject each year. But Oxford's masters were largely uninterested in doing research in the field, even in the eighteenth century when not only the Bodleian but several colleges had come to possess collections of classical coins and monuments, especially Christ Church and St John's. Nor was anyone interested in synthesizing the information to be found in classical texts and producing a modern narrative history of the ancient world in the manner of the Parisian Charles Rollin.[100]

In the Age of Enlightenment, when Europe was awash with classical antiquarians, Oxford produced only two of any importance. The first, Thomas Shaw of Queen's,

---

[98] Nicholas Dew, *Orientalism in Louis XIV's France* (Oxford, 2009). For the wider context, see G.J. Toomer, *Eastern Wisdom and Learning: The Study of Arabic in Seventeenth-Century England* (Oxford, 1996).

[99] L. W. B. Brockliss, *Calvet's Web: Enlightenment and the Republic of Letters in Eighteenth-Century France* (Oxford, 2002), pp. 227–41.

[100] See p. 285, this volume.

spent the 1720s in North Africa before returning to Oxford to take up his fellowship and prepare an account of the ancient sites he had visited, which he published in 1738.[101] When Séguier of Nîmes came to Oxford in 1736, Shaw was the only Oxford don he felt the need to seek out:

> This savant has spent several years on the Barbary coast of Africa. He has gathered a quantity of remarks on this region and the antiquities that are found there. He let me see his account and drawings of an amphitheatre which is in ancient Numidia in a place called Dschem three days journey south of Tunis.[102]

The second classical antiquarian of any consequence resident in Oxford in the eighteenth century was Richard Chandler of Magdalen. In 1763, while still a scholar of the college, he published a new edition of the Parian chronicle and other classical inscriptions to be found in Oxford, under the heading *Marmora Oxoniensia*. The following year, presumably on the strength of this publication, he was commissioned by the London Dilettanti Society to go out to Asia Minor and Greece and collect inscriptions. At this date, few Europeans had had the opportunity to survey the ancient Greek sites and Chandler spent a productive two years, 1764–6, gathering material. On his return he published his *Ionian Antiquities* in 1769, and the next year was elected to a Magdalen fellowship. During the ten years he held the position he produced three significant works in as many years. His *Inscriptiones Antiquae in Asia Minori et Graecia collectae* appeared in 1774, his *Travels in Asia Minor* in 1775, and his *Travels in Greece* in 1776.[103] Chandler's activities were well known on the continent. In 1769, one of the leading antiquarians of the French Midi, Esprit Calvet of Avignon, received a tablet, picked up near Megara, bearing an interesting inscription about the first athlete to run naked in the Olympic Games, Orrippus. Calvet was convinced he had in his possession an extremely ancient inscription from the eighth century BC, which provided a fuller and more accurate account of an event recorded by the first-century AD traveller Pausanias. He was terrified though that Chandler had recorded the inscription in his travels and refused to go public before he knew for certain that it had not appeared in the much awaited collection that the Oxford don was about to put into print.[104]

In fact, Oxford's greatest contribution to the scholarly study of a dead language and culture lay in one closer to home and of a limited interest to the wider Republic of Letters: Anglo-Saxon. The study of old English had been initiated at Cambridge in the early seventeenth century but it came of age at Oxford in the years 1688 to 1715,

---

[101] *Travels, or Observations relating to several parts of Barbary and the Levant* (Oxford, 1738). Shaw became regius professor of Greek in 1741.

[102] Bibliothèque Municipale Nîmes, MS 286, p. 50. El Djem is one of the great extant amphitheatres of the Roman world.

[103] Chandler demitted his fellowship in 1780 to wed. Before quitting his fellowship and getting married Chandler began work on a new edition of Pindar based on all extant manuscripts. Though he took his new wife on a two-year honeymoon around Europe hunting for manuscripts, and had the assistance of several very prominent European Hellenists, the project was never completed.

[104] Brockliss, *Calvet's Web*, pp. 317–22, 329. The inscription is today in the Louvre. It is in fact a copy from the reign of the Emperor Hadrian.

through the efforts of a group of scholars chiefly associated with University College and Queen's, where a lectureship in Anglo-Saxon was established in 1679. The four most important scholars were the non-juror George Hickes, the future bishop of London Edmund Gibson, Edward Thwaites, who took over the Queen's lectureship in the late 1690s, and Humfrey Wanley, who was an assistant librarian at the Bodleian. Between them they published a grammar, thesaurus, and dictionary in 1689, 1699, and 1701, a calendar of extant Anglo-Saxon manuscripts in 1703–5, and a new edition of the seminal *Anglo-Saxon Chronicle* in 1692. Through death or departure, the group dissolved after 1715, but an interest in the language never entirely waned. Hearne knew no Anglo-Saxon but he oversaw the publication of the first edition of the *Battle of Maldon* and he was in touch with a number of Anglo-Saxon scholars around the country, such as the autodidact George Ballard, who was eventually given a place on the foundation at Magdalen in the 1750s as a clerk attached to the choir.[105] Paradoxically, it was only with Rawlinson's bequest of a university chair in Anglo-Saxon in 1755 that the heroic era completely came to an end. It took forty years for the chair to be set up and it was the following century before the language once again attracted serious Oxford attention.

The interest in the Anglo-Saxons was part of a wider Oxford obsession with the history of hearth and home in the second half of the seventeenth and in the eighteenth century. Initially, the University's primary concern was in recovering its own rather than the nation's past. The chief figure in this regard was the former Mertonian postmaster Anthony Wood, who devoted his adult life to writing a history of the University and preparing a biographical dictionary of its most famous sons, which appeared in 1674 and 1691–2.[106] But his was not a single-handed enterprise and he owed much to the earlier research of Brian Twyne, fellow of Corpus and the University's first archivist, whose notes he was able to use. He was also not the first university historian to get his work into print, for he was pipped at the post by Henry Savage, master of Balliol, a man whom Wood considered an amateur but whose history of the college was published six years before the *Historia*.[107] With Wood's death in 1695, however, Oxford's navel-gazing was put on hold for the following century, and the University's antiquarians turned their attention to wider themes, doubtless spurred on to spread their wings by the growing collection of British antiquities in the newly founded Ashmolean Museum, which included, from 1693, the iconic Alfred jewel.[108] An early work was Rabbi

[105] Hearne's publication was based on a fortunate transcription of the manuscript in the Cotton library in London, which had been destroyed by fire in 1731. Ballard left Anglo-Saxon manuscripts to the Bodleian.

[106] A. Wood, *Historia et antiquitates universitatis oxoniensis* (2 vols; Oxford, 1674); *Athenae Oxonienses, an Exact History of all the Writers and Bishops who have had their Education in the ancient and famous University of Oxford from the fifteenth year of King Henry VII to the end of the year 1690* (2 vols; London, 1691–2). Wood's interest in the University's history was sparked by him reading William Dugdale's *Antiquities of Warwickshire* (1656).

[107] The work which had previously circulated in manuscripts was entitled *Balliofergus*.

[108] Much of Wood's research remained unpublished until taken up and developed from the late eighteenth century by John Gutch, librarian and chaplain of All Souls and the University's registrar, and Philip Bliss, at different times fellow of St John's, Bodley's deputy librarian, and principal of St Mary Hall.

Smith's account of the customs of the Druids, which appeared in 1664.[109] But Oxford's first major contribution to the history of the nation occurred in the year Wood died, when Edmund Gibson of Queen's published a translation and extended version of William Camden's history and topography of Britain. Camden's *Britannia*, which had first appeared in 1586, was the point of departure for all seventeenth-century students of the English past. But its author had paid little attention to the period between the departure of the Romans and the Norman Conquest, and a century later it was in need of updating. Appropriately, it was one of the University's champions of Anglo-Saxon who performed the task.[110]

The three leading students of the English past resident in Oxford in the eighteenth century were Thomas Hearne, Francis Wise, and Thomas Warton the Younger. Hearne, based at St Edmund Hall in the first forty years of the century, was principally a historian of the middle ages, publishing editions of several chronicles as well as putting into print, for the first time, the works of the mid-sixteenth century antiquarian John Leland, who had done much to record England's monastic inheritance at the moment of its destruction. More importantly, Hearne maintained a huge correspondence network and was in contact with virtually every antiquarian in the country whatever their confessional allegiance.[111] Wise was Hearne's contemporary and inherited the position of Bodley's sub-librarian when Hearne was forced to demit in 1715. In contrast, he was an Anglo-Saxonist and had a less positive profile among the wider antiquarian community. Less learned than Hearne, he was also less cautious. Hearne could be credulous and tended to treat all prehistoric artefacts, including Stonehenge, as Roman. But he was not afraid to change his mind and, in the debate over the origins of the Stonesfield pavement uncovered in 1712, he ultimately judged correctly that it was not medieval: 'Upon a more mature Consideration I am perswaded 'twas a Roman Praetorium.'[112] Wise, on the other hand, could be rash, and in 1738 claimed that the Uffington White Horse commemorated Alfred's victory over the Danes, which immediately landed him in controversy with opponents who rightly claimed the monument was pre-Roman in origin.[113] Thomas Warton was the youngest and most sensitive of the three. As holder of the chair of poetry from 1755 to 1766, he was principally interested in producing a history of English literature, but he was also a careful and imaginative student of English architecture. In his notebooks, compiled around 1760, he laid out the first serious

---

[109] Thomas Smith, *Syntagma de druidum moribus ac institutis: in quo miscellanea quædam sacro-profana inseruntur…* (London, 1664).

[110] *Camden's Britannia*, trans. E. Gibson (London, 1695). For Camden's Oxford connections, see p. 240 n. 54, this volume. For an introduction to the *Britannia*, see Richard Helgerson, *Forms of Nationhood: The Elizabethan Writing of England* (London, 1992). One of Gibson's assistants was Edward Lhuyd, keeper of the Ashmolean, who laid the foundations of comparative Celtic philology in his *Archaeologia Britannica* (1707).

[111] Hearne published Leland's *Itinerary* in 9 vols in 1710–12, and his *Collectanea* in 5 vols in 1715. On the antiquarian community, see Rosemary Sweet, *Antiquaries: The Discovery of the Past in Eighteenth-Century Britain* (London, 2004).

[112] HUO, v. 763. The Stonesfield pavement was a mosaic depicting Bacchus found on an Oxfordshire farm: see Joseph Levine, 'The Stonesfield Pavement: Archaeology in Augustan England', *Eighteenth-Century Studies*, 11: 3 (1978), 340–61.

[113] On the arguments over the antiquity of ancient monuments, see esp. Stuart Piggott, *William Stukeley: An Eighteenth-Century Antiquary* (London, 1985).

chronological classification of medieval building styles, inventing his own terminology to distinguish between the different periods.[114]

Oxford's enthusiastic participation in the task of recovering its own and the nation's past was not matched by a similar readiness to assist contemporaries in developing a new understanding of man in the present. The second half of the seventeenth and the eighteenth century saw the creation of a new science of the human intellect and man in society that challenged, if never fully replaced, the Aristotelian inheritance, by purporting to build a logic, ethics, and politics on man as he was and not on what he ought to be. Oxford did produce, in John Case of St John's, one of Europe's leading Renaissance Aristotelians, a philosopher of the old school who strove to keep the peripatetic flame alight in the face of humanist criticism by producing more textually sensitive commentaries on the traditional corpus.[115] But later generations of college professors of philosophy contributed nothing positive to the development of the new psychology or ideas about man in a state of nature and the greatest good of the greatest number. Oxford was attended by four of Europe's most original philosophers of the new wave: Hobbes, Locke, Adam Smith, and Jeremy Bentham. But only Locke, who was a fellow of Christ Church until forced to flee the country in 1683, may have penned anything original and subversive while in residence.[116] Although dons were not usually hostile to the moderns in the eighteenth century, the continual use of textbooks like Sanderson's emphasize the pervading influence of Aristotelian logic and ethics.[117] A number of dons constructed courses which combined elements of the new and the old, but it was only with the publication of Richard Whately of Oriel's *Elements of Logic* in 1826 that the University had a textbook which critical outsiders felt was abreast with the times.

The same comments could be made about Oxford's contribution to the science of law, which was itself profoundly affected by the philosophical revolution. Before the Civil War, the University played a minor part in the creation of the new sciences of comparative and international law through the publications of Richard Zouche, regius professor of civil law 1620–61. But it played no role in the late seventeenth- and eighteenth-century developments in the sciences of natural and public law, nor in the early nineteenth-century historicization of Roman law, which all predominantly occurred in the German-speaking world.[118] The only sign that Oxford was

[114] Warton's history of English poetry appeared in 4 vols, 1774–81.

[115] Charles B. Schmitt, *John Case and Aristotelianism in Renaissance England* (Kingston, ON, 1983). On the different types of Renaissance Aristotelianism, see Charles B. Schmitt, 'Towards a Reassessment of Renaissance Aristotelianism', *History of Science*, 11 (1973), 159–93.

[116] Locke's *Two Treatises of Government*, which justified active resistance, was written about 1680 so was possibly composed in Oxford. But Locke was frequently on the move. Adam Smith was an exhibitioner at Balliol after studying at Glasgow.

[117] See p. 258, this volume. Another slightly more modern eighteenth-century favourite was Henry Aldrich's *Artis logicae compendium*, first published in 1692.

[118] Oxford also made no contribution to legal humanism, the Renaissance-inspired subjection of the civil and canon law texts to linguistic exegesis in order to better understand their meaning. For the role played by other universities in these developments, see Laurence Brockliss, 'Curricula', in *HUIE*, ii, 599–608.

even a part of the broader legal culture of the Age of Enlightenment was Blackstone's work on English common law. The eighteenth century saw many European states begin the process of codification to reduce a hotchpotch of customary and princely laws and decrees to a coherent and consistent system based on fundamental principles. While in residence as a fellow of All Souls, then principal of New Inn Hall, Blackstone began to bring a similar coherence to the chaos of English law. Blackstone aimed to make English law a university discipline and hoped to turn New Inn Hall, where he was principal, into a lawyers' college. He failed in his aim, but before he resigned as the first Vinerian professor in 1766, he had already published the initial volume of his *Commentaries* on English law, which set out to show that the common law, however piecemeal and unpremeditated its development, had a structure, was rational, and could be understood by any gentleman.[119]

Oxford was more seriously engaged in the development of the new science of nature that completely pushed Aristotle aside from the mid-seventeenth century. But again its involvement was limited. Throughout the period, there were always one or two individuals attached to the University who were practising and innovative experimental philosophers. The Savilian chairs of astronomy and geometry in particular were held by some of Britain's leading scientists, especially in the second half of the seventeenth and the first half of the eighteenth century, when they were occupied by John Wallis, Christopher Wren, David Gregory, Edmond Halley, John Keill, and James Bradley. Yet even the productive and original did next to no research at Oxford. Such figures took their lecturing duties seriously and even occasionally held other university offices: Wallis was also keeper of the archives. However, generally they were pluralists and spent much of the year elsewhere. The great positional astronomer James Bradley is a case in point. Bradley was Savilian professor of astronomy for forty years from 1721 to 1762, and also gave an annual private course in experimental philosophy from 1729 to 1760 at the Ashmolean. But he never observed at Oxford. His scientific research and discoveries were carried out at Wanstead, where his uncle had a private observatory; Kew, where he used the facilities of the Irish astronomer Samuel Molyneux; and Greenwich, where he was astronomer royal from 1742.

The one part of the period when there was a significant clutch of experimental philosophers actually working in Oxford was during the 1650s and early 1660s: a large enough group to be a self-conscious 'club'. Usually some twenty to thirty in number, the coterie was principally engaged in building on the physiological discoveries of William Harvey, whose discovery of the circulation of the blood had raised a series of further questions, especially about the purpose of respiration. Many of the group would become the first members of the London Royal Society, founded in 1660. The most creative among them was the Oxford MD Thomas Willis, who made an important contribution to the contemporary understanding of the physiology of the brain and the nervous system through his interpretation

[119] W. Prest, *Blackstone and His Commentaries: Biography, Law, History* (Oxford, 2009).

of sensation as a chemical process. Arguably the most important member of the group was John Wilkins, warden of Wadham and Cromwell's son-in-law, a man fascinated by machines. Although not himself a particularly original experimental philosopher, Wilkins played a crucial role in offering the warden's lodgings as a meeting place for the group and encouraging its activities when its initial leader, William Petty, left for Ireland in the winter of 1651/2. It was Wilkins who was largely responsible for encouraging an outsider, Robert Boyle, to take up permanent residence in Oxford in early 1656. Boyle was never a member of the University but it was as part of the Oxford community of experimental philosophers that he and his assistant, the MA Robert Hooke, did the experimental work on respiration and the properties of air that would lead to today's Boyle's law. While it survived, the group was innovative and often daring, no more so than in 1666 when Richard Lower, on the assumption that there was only one form of blood, tried transfusing blood from one dog to another. But both Willis, who was Sedley professor of natural philosophy from 1660 to 1673, and Boyle left for London in 1667–8 and the Oxford club collapsed. Robert Plot, the first keeper of the Ashmolean, attempted to resurrect it between 1683 and 1687 but in the absence of the necessary critical mass of experimenters, his initiative quickly fizzled out.[120]

One reason for the relatively limited role of Oxford in the realm of experimental philosophy was poor facilities. The Bodleian, the Ashmolean, and the best college libraries provided exegetes and antiquarians with the resources that they needed to learn and take the first steps in their craft. And the resource base was constantly growing. Experimental philosophers, on the other hand, were not well served. In the time of John Bainbridge, the first Savilian professor of astronomy, an observatory had been constructed in the Bodleian tower, and space was provided in the basement of the Ashmolean for anatomical dissections and chemical experiments from the 1680s.[121] But neither facility was particularly serviceable. Oxford never had a state-of-the-art anatomical theatre until Dr Lee's anatomy school was opened in 1768, and no proper site for astronomical observations before the Radcliffe Observatory was finished in 1794. The Ashmolean did not even pass muster as a chemical or physical laboratory. Experimental philosophers in the eighteenth century had fast-growing equipment and spatial needs. The Ashmolean could serve as a teaching space but was not ideal for novel or aggressive research. There were only two Oxford natural philosophers with a European research profile in the first part of the nineteenth century. The first was the reader in geology and mineralogy, William Buckland, a canon of Christ Church, whose account of the animal bones found in a cave in Kirkdale in 1821 opened up a new era in the history of

---

[120] For an introduction, Robert Frank, *Harvey and the Oxford Physiologists: A Study of Scientific Ideas* (London, 1980). Harvey, a royal physician who had studied at Cambridge and Padua, was at Oxford with Charles I in the 1640s, and was warden of Merton for a year.

[121] It is difficult to know whether the anatomy school had ever been used for dissections or was simply an osteological museum.

FIGURE 8.4 William Buckland, 1784–1856, professor of mineralogy and reader in geology: anon. Engraving. Buckland, famous for boasting that he had eaten his way through the whole of animal creation, was an enthusiastic field palaeontologist. Besides his discovery of the Kirkdale bones in 1821, he also introduced his compatriots three years later to the first dinosaur found in Britain. The drawing captures his enthusiasm for field work, which he pursued during the vacations.

palaeontology (see Figure 8.4).[122] The second was Charles Daubeny of Magdalen, who monopolized the chairs of chemistry, botany, and rural economy, and was particularly interested in vulcanology. Finding the Ashmolean basement too cramped for his needs, he was eventually forced to do what Willis and others before 1680 had done: in 1847, with the college's permission, he built his own laboratory next to the Botanic Garden (see Figure 8.5).[123]

---

[122] His contribution to science is examined in N. A. Rupke, *The Great Chain of History: William Buckland and the English School of Geology 1814–49* (Oxford, 1983). Buckland demonstrated that the animals had been eaten by an extinct species of hyena and were not the remains of bodies randomly deposited there by the biblical Flood.

[123] On his death he gave the lab and his library to Magdalen.

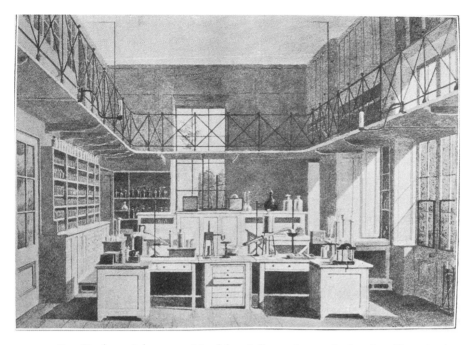

FIGURE 8.5 Daubeny Laboratory, Magdalen College, 1847: early drawing. The scientist, Charles Daubeny, had a European reputation in his several fields of interest. His correspondents included the chemist Liebig. Unlike the Old Ashmolean, the laboratory that he built for himself was light and airy. His books were stored in the gallery.

Even the Botanic Garden left much to be desired until the era of Daubeny. With its foundation in the 1620s Oxford obtained a garden far earlier than most European universities—Cambridge would not get one until 1762.[124] But it took a long time to become established as a research centre. There were a number of first-class botanists in charge of the garden in the seventeenth century, notably Jacob Bobart the Younger, who completed the catalogue of the local Oxfordshire flora begun by his predecessor, Robert Morison, and put together a herbarium of 2,000 plants created from plants grown in the garden, field trips, and exchanges with other botanists. But there was still much amiss when Uffenbach visited the site in 1710. In his view, the garden could not hold a candle to Leiden's or Amsterdam's. The classification was confused; much of the terrain was given over to growing vegetables; and only the orangery received praise.[125] The position did not greatly improve over the rest of the century. The establishment of the Sherardian chair in 1734 led to the appointment of the distinguished German botanist Johann Dillenius as its first holder, who drew a number of important visitors to the garden, including

[124] Searby, pp. 206–7. On earlier foundations: Charles B. Schmitt, 'Science in the Italian Universities', in M. P. Crosland (ed.), *The Emergence of Science in Western Europe* (London, 1975), pp. 42–4; L. W. B. Brockliss, *French Higher Education in the Seventeenth and Eighteenth Centuries* (Oxford, 1987), ch. 8, section 1.
[125] Uffenbach, *Oxford*, pp. 55–7.

Linnaeus two years later. But Dillenius died in 1747 and the chair was held for the next forty years by the relative nonentity Humphrey Sibthorp. Sibthorp, in his early years, took his post seriously and attempted to put himself and the garden on the European map by currying favour with the Göttingen botanist and physiologist Albrecht von Haller. But Haller soon lost interest in him because Sibthorp had no novel plant specimens to exchange, and the Oxford professor's burst of youthful energy expired.[126] It was only under his short-lived son, John, who in the 1780s had travelled abroad collecting material for a Greek flora, that the garden received a worthy director.

Until the late nineteenth century, however, few of Europe's experimental philosophers enjoyed lavish facilities, and most, in the early modern period, had to fashion their own working environment. A more satisfactory explanation of Oxford's relative lack of interest in experimental philosophy is to be found in its theological imperative. Oxford was not against the new science. The new cosmology and different versions of the mechanical philosophy had been introduced into the arts curriculum in the seventeenth century with little difficulty. And senior members, with a few exceptions, such as George Horne and the Hutchinsonians, had no problem accepting Newton in the following century.[127] In the first half of the nineteenth century, too, Oxford was not collectively hostile to the scientific zeitgeist, for even Newman had no objection to scientific research as long as scientists did not involve themselves with theological questions.[128] The British Association for the Advancement of Science was created in 1831 as a counterweight to what was seen as a lacklustre Royal Society. At the end of its first meeting at York, it was decided that the second in 1832, its first full gathering, would be held at Oxford chaired by Buckland. When it met, the University gave four of the scientists an honorary degree, including the Sandemanian Michael Faraday.[129]

Oxford's limited contribution to the advancement of science stemmed rather from the fact that the University's *raison d'être* throughout the Anglican era was defending and promoting the Anglican church, as it was or ought to be. It was this that occupied the energies of the most intellectually active dons, from Humphrey of Magdalen to Newman of Oriel, and led them to engage in activities that had little resonance in the Republic of Letters. It was this, too, that constrained, if it did

---

[126] Burgerbibliothek Bern, letters from Sibthorp to Haller, 1748–57 (consulted electronically); other letters are in the Fitzwilliam Museum, Cambridge. For a list, see *Repertorium zu Albrecht von Hallers Korrespondenz 1724–1777*, ed. U. Boschung, B. Braun-Bucher, S. Hächler, A. K. Ott, H. Steinke, and M. Stuber (2 vols; Basel, 2002), i. 973. Haller, known mainly today as a physiologist, had first become famous in the Republic of Letters for his work on Swiss flora: Hubert Steinke, Urs Boschung, and Wolfgang Pross (eds), *Albrecht von Haller. Leben, Werk, Epoche* (Göttingen, 2008), pp. 292–314.

[127] Indeed, Newton was seen as an ally against deism and unbelief: see John Friesen, 'Christ Church Oxford, the Ancients and Moderns Controversy, and the Promotion of Newton in Post-Revolutionary England', *HU*, XXIII: 1 (2008), 33–66.

[128] See his 'Christianity and Physical Science', and 'Christianity and Scientific Investigation', rectoral addresses given at the catholic University of Dublin in the 1850s: John Henry Newman, *The Idea of a University*, ed. Frank M. Turner (London, 1996), pp. 200–33.

[129] The BAAS returned to Oxford in 1847, 1860, 1894, and 1926. Sandemanians were a breakaway sect of the Church of Scotland who endeavoured to live like the disciples of the primitive church.

not curtail, the University's appearance in other intellectual arenas. Even dons not immediately engaged in theological polemic or spiritual exhortation were frequently immersed in research intended to support the church. Studying the Greek fathers, for instance, had an ulterior motive. The more cosmopolitan Anglican looked to the Greek and other eastern churches as allies against Rome and sometimes dreamt of union. The antiquarian study of England's history was similarly slanted, in part, to shoring up the religious status quo. Recovering the medieval and Anglo-Saxon past was a way of establishing that the Church of England had always been separate and incorrupt, while at the same time pandering to the eighteenth-century Tories' nostalgia for a disappearing world of social hierarchy and cultural uniformity.

Scholars uninterested in sustaining the Anglican church were not welcome within the University, however many might be given honorary degrees after 1700. Papists and crypto-papists were always beyond the pale, as Newman eventually discovered when he tried to reinterpret the Thirty-Nine Articles. But ultra-protestant forms of unorthodoxy were also barely tolerated, especially anti-Trinitarianism, even if their supporters continued to argue that the Bible was the Word of God. Oxford's experimental philosophers were normally openly orthodox and often in orders. But they tended to be on the tolerant wing of the church and were not always biblical literalists. Buckland, for one, had given up on the Flood by the late 1820s and became an ardent supporter of the Swiss Agassiz's glaciation theory.[130] There was always a slight question mark over experimental philosophy and its practitioners therefore, and the ambitious Oxford don was unlikely to hoist his colours to its mast. It was not coincidental that it was only in the mid-seventeenth century that experimental philosophy had a significant following. In the 1650s, Oxford was temporarily no longer an Anglican university and Church of England loyalists had to go underground. Figures like Willis, Hooke, and Wren, another member of the Oxford club, would normally have entered the church after finishing their undergraduate education; instead they took up experimental philosophy as a pis aller; their scientific creativity was one of the many unintended consequences of the king's defeat in the Civil War. Once normal service was resumed in 1660, Oxford largely turned its back on scientific research and concentrated its attentions on securing and advancing the established religion.

F. The University Press

Although Oxford's contribution to the growth of the arts and sciences in the period under review was, in many fields, at best lacklustre, its small number of publishing scholars still helped to bolster the University's profile as a centre of learning. This was because most of the works Oxford's senior members placed in the public

---

[130] Initially he had claimed that his cave discoveries did not nullify the Flood, which had still led to the eventual extinction of the hyenas and other defunct species found there.

domain came out under the University's imprint. Had their works been entrusted to London publishers, they would have appeared as the random offerings of individual scholars who happened to have an Oxford attachment. As it was, by being published by the University's press, the researches of the few appeared to be part of the collective endeavour of the University as a whole.

The invention of the printing press in the mid-fifteenth century made it possible for Europe's scholars to circulate their ideas much more widely than hitherto.[131] In the course of the following century, most universities recognized the need to establish a formal relationship with a local printer who could publish official notices and the heads of theses, provide textbooks, and put the learned works of their members before the public. Oxford appointed its first official printer in 1584 when the Chancellor, the earl of Leicester, permitted the University to give the position to Joseph Barnes, who had been active in the city as a bookseller since at least 1573. His appointment, it was hoped, would allow Oxford to play a serious part in the European-wide retrieval and collation of ancient texts. There were many important manuscripts languishing in college libraries 'shamefully covered in dust and dirt'. It was too difficult and expensive to get editions published in London but once the University had its own printer, they would soon be 'rescued from perpetual obscurity and distributed in other parts of Europe to the great credit of the whole nation'.[132]

Barnes and his successors published a number of important works by Oxford scholars in the following decades, and one of lasting significance in 1621. This was Robert Burton's *Anatomy of Melancholy*, the only book penned by a member of the University during the period to become an English classic.[133] But the University had limited control over their printers' activities and did little to further scholarship directly itself. Archbishop Laud, once elected Chancellor in 1630, had greater ambitions: he wanted the University to have its own printing press with its own agenda and not just its own printer. From 1633, the University appointed a delegacy which was to decide which manuscripts were to be published, and, under the Laudian code of 1636, Oxford was required to set up a printing office headed by a new official, the architypographus. Laud's fall from grace and the coming of the Civil War ensured that little was initially achieved. Even in the more peaceful years after parliament's victory, the University went no further in promoting Laud's project beyond purchasing sets of Arabic, Hebrew, and Anglo-Saxon type which could be lent to local printers.[134] But with the restoration of the monarchy in 1660,

---

[131] Elizabeth Eisenstein, *The Printing Press as an Agent of Change: Communications and Cultural Transformations in Early Modern Europe* (2 vols; Cambridge, 1979).

[132] Petition to the Chancellor: see Jason Peacy, '"Printers to the University" 1584–1658', in *The History of Oxford University Press*, vol. 1: *Beginnings to 1780*, ed. Ian Gadd (Oxford, 2013), p. 52. Cambridge established a right to print in 1534 but it was not immediately used: David McKitterick, *A History of Cambridge University Press*, vol. 1: *Printing and the Book Trade in Cambridge, 1534–1698* (Cambridge, 1992), pp. 22–37 and 40.

[133] Burton was a student and fellow of Christ Church from 1599 until his death in 1640. The book was printed by John Lichfield and James Short: by then there were two university printers.

[134] The University was given a good set of Greek type in 1619 by Sir Henry Savile, warden of Merton.

Laud's vision began to be implemented. The leading role was taken by John Fell, dean of Christ Church, who established a printing press in the new Sheldonian in 1668, reactivated the press delegacy, set up a type foundry, and put a lot of money and much energy into building 'a press freed from mercenary artifice, which will serve not so much as to make profits for booksellers as to further the interests and conveniences of scholars'.[135]

Fell planned an ambitious publishing programme in the humanities and the sciences, heralded, in 1672, with the appearance of Thomas Willis' *De anima brutorum*. He also had the good sense to find ways of subsidizing the infant press's learned publications. In 1636, Oxford was given the same rights as Cambridge and the King's Printer to print Bibles, almanacs, prayer books, psalters, and certain schoolbooks.[136] Rather than exercise the privilege directly, Fell gave private printers the right to set up shop in Oxford in return for an annual fee. By the time Fell died in 1690, the University Press was well established and had outgrown its initial premises. A year later, the Bible press, now run by the London Stationers' Company, had to transfer to a building in St Aldate's.[137] The space problem, however, was solved with the opening of a completely new and custom-built workshop, the Clarendon Printing House, in 1713. This owed its name to the fact it was paid for, in part, by the profits from the sale of the earl of Clarendon's *History of the Rebellion* in 1702–4. Clarendon had been Oxford's Chancellor in the 1660s and, as an act of piety, his son gave the University ownership of the book in perpetuity. The Clarendon became the centre of the press's publishing activities until the late 1820s, when the business was moved again to its present site on Walton Street (see Figure 8.6). By then it was employing some 130 compositors and pressmen against 20 in Fell's day.

In the eighteenth and the first half of the nineteenth century, Oxford University Press had two distinct branches. The Bible press published for a mass market. It was always highly lucrative and, from 1780, it ceased to be rented out and was run by the University as a partnership with an established London firm. It published Bibles, prayer books, and psalters in a wide variety of different formats that would suit all pockets, and in the first half of the nineteenth century increased its sales by a factor of ten (in 1846 it sold 1.5 million books), thanks to investment first in iron presses and stereotyping and then in new steam-driven machinery.[138] The learned press, on the other hand, was specialized, and before 1800 seldom published books with runs of more than 500 copies, and produced few best-sellers apart from Thomas Marshall's *The Catechism set forth in the Book of Common Prayer*, first published in 1679, and in its fifteenth edition by 1730–1. In the eighteenth century, the learned press's

[135] Letter to the Dutch scholar Vossius, 1671: see Vivienne Larminie, 'The Fell Era 1658–1686', in Gadd, *Oxford University Press*, p. 88. The type foundry did not last.

[136] Especially Lily's grammar (1527), which was the only authorized Latin primer for schools.

[137] The Stationers' Company was a London trade guild, incorporated in 1557, that, until the end of the seventeenth century, claimed the right to control printing in England and Wales.

[138] Throughout the eighteenth century, the press kept the production of the annual *Oxford Almanac* in its own hands. At the beginning of the 1780s it lost its privilege to print almanacs and received £500 per annum from the state in compensation. The Bible monopoly was confirmed in 1802.

FIGURE 8.6 Oxford University Press, Walton Street building: *Oxford Almanack* 1832, drawing F. Mackenzie, engraving Henry Le Keux. The new building for the learned press opened in 1830. Built on the outskirts of the city, it was an early sign that the nineteenth-century University would no longer be confined to its original site. The size and resolutely classical style of the building emphasized the Press' pretensions to be an international and not an insular publishing house.

output was steady but relatively small, on average 15.5 books per year. From 1780, the number of new books published each year rose and individual runs were usually larger. When several thousand French priests ended up interned in Britain during the French Revolution, the learned press had no scruples about supplying the exiles with 4,000 copies of the Vulgate edition of the New Testament. At no time over the century and a half did the learned press invest large amounts of capital in individual books. Although all the books of the learned press bore the University's imprint, only a small proportion was actually commissioned and paid for by the delegates.[139] Most were known as authors' books in that the author or a bookseller supported their publication, often by raising money through opening a subscription. These included some of the most important and widely read works such as Blackstone's *Commentaries on the Laws of England* (1765–9), which had netted the author more than £12,000 by the time that he sold the copyright in 1772. But it also included some very obscure works that the press agreed to take on as a special favour. Most books were aimed at the domestic or European market, but in 1725 the

---

[139] The imprint 'the University Press' was first used in 1758. Initially the imprint had been 'Printed at the Theater'.

press agreed to publish a work called *Petra scandali* on the request of the patriarch of Antioch, and most copies were dispatched to Aleppo.[140]

After Fell, the two members of the University most closely associated with the development of the Press before 1850 were Blackstone and Gaisford, the regius professor of Greek. The first led an enquiry into the Press in 1756 which aimed to professionalize its business habits and reinvigorate the Laudian vision. The second dedicated his many years as a delegate in the first half of the nineteenth century to creating a reliable collection of classical texts for the use of Oxford's growing number of undergraduates, and equipping them with a proper Greek grammar and dictionary, which led to the runaway success of Liddell and Scott.[141] Neither Blackstone nor Gaisford, though, significantly changed the Press's orientation. The output of the learned press closely mirrored the intellectual interests of the wider University. For the most part, it published scholarly works on religion, history, and ancient literature, and a lot of the religious works were on the Anglican church. Although it did not eschew vernacular publications—one of its authors' books, published in 1743–4, was a six-volume edition of Shakespeare by Sir Thomas Hanmer[142]—the press also primarily produced works in Latin. Its science list, apart from editions of ancient texts, was always poor. Although Oxford printers had been quite active publishers of works of the new science in the mid-seventeenth century, including many books by Boyle, the University Press did not follow suit. Willis' 1672 publication was a false dawn. The only original work of science published in the eighteenth century was Dillenius' *Historia muscorum* in 1740. Even in the first half of the nineteenth century when the Press was more active, its bias remained unchanged. In fact, Oxford's most original scientific minds, after 1800, preferred to publish in London. Thus, Buckland's *Reliquiae Diluvianae* (1823) and Daubeny's *Introduction to Atomic Theory* (1831) were both published by John Murray.[143]

Nonetheless, the learned press, once established, was always one of the wonders of the University. Although publications on Anglicanism usually had only a domestic audience, many of the works of Oxford's humanist scholars found their way into continental libraries and it soon had a European-wide reputation. Even the jaundiced Uffenbach on his visit in 1710 described the Press as 'far famed'.[144] By opening the Press to authors who were not resident in the colleges, moreover, the

---

[140] From a manuscript in the hands of John Gagnier, a French convert to Anglicanism, who was deputizing as the Laudian professor of Arabic.

[141] The initial print run was 3,000 in 1843; the dictionary was reprinted twice in the 1840s with print runs of 6,000 on each occasion. The press also published an abridged edition in 1843. Liddell and Scott began as a translation of Franz Passow's Greek–German lexicon. Until then, Oxford students composed their own dictionaries and commonplace books. Henry Liddell, who will be mentioned frequently in Part III of this volume, was, at this date, a tutor of Christ Church; Robert Scott was then a tutor of Balliol. Now in its ninth edition, Liddell and Scott remains the standard Greek–English dictionary.

[142] A Hanoverian Tory who had attended Christ Church.

[143] Cambridge, on the other hand, published widely in science and mathematics in the first half of the nineteenth century: see David McKitterick, *A History of Cambridge University Press*, vol. 2: *Scholarship and Commerce 1698–1872* (Cambridge, 1998), pp. 336–7.

[144] Uffenbach, *Oxford*, p. 9. His library, dispersed in 1735, contained twenty-eight Oxford books.

University was made to look more intellectually active than it was.[145] Indeed, by the mid-eighteenth century, the delegates had grasped that Oxford had everything to gain in terms of international prestige by encouraging foreigners as well as Britons to publish under its imprint. As we saw in section E, Lowth's lectures on the Psalms, which appeared in 1753, were one of the most important pieces of Hebrew scholarship to be produced by an Oxford scholar in the Age of the Enlightenment.[146] Their reception on the continent, however, was mixed and the Göttingen theologian J.-D. Michaelis, wrote a very critical response where he attacked Lowth for not putting Hebrew poetry into a broader context of oriental literature and history. Significantly, the Press felt no compunction to protect Oxford's own, and happily published the reply.[147] In the first half of the nineteenth century, Gaisford went a step further and openly solicited works from foreign scholars. Anxious to have the best scholars edit his series of classical authors, he approached a number of Dutch and Germans to prepare several of the texts, notably the Leipzig professor Karl Wilhelm Dindorf, who was responsible for editions of Euripides and Aeschylus in the early 1830s. The Press, then, was far more cosmopolitan in the first part of the nineteenth century than many within the University. In an age when Oxford seemed to be locked in an incestuous battle over Tractarianism, the Press was one part of the University which kept a window open to the outside world. It even began to introduce Oxford to the work of Germany's ancient historians when it published a translation of August Böckh's *The Public Economy of Athens* in 1828.[148]

---

[145] Marshall, for instance, was an Oxford alumnus, but in the 1670s he was chaplain to the Merchant Adventurers at Dordrecht.

[146] See p. 306, this volume.

[147] Johann David Michaelis, *In Roberti Lowth praelectiones de sacra poesi Hebraeorum notae et epimetra* (Oxford, 1763).

[148] The Press significantly did not publish the works of the Tractarians. Boekh was a professor at the new University of Berlin: see p. 326, this volume.

Conclusion

English Exceptionalism

B Y the end of the sixteenth century, Oxford and Cambridge had become very different universities from their sister institutions in Europe. Elsewhere, scholars lived where they liked, principally and often exclusively attended the higher faculties, and were taught by stipendiary professors who largely confined contact with students to their scheduled hour-long lectures. At the English universities, scholars were expected to reside in a college or hall, chiefly studied an extended arts curriculum that was delivered through college-based lectures, and, as undergraduates, had their day-to-day lives supervised, to a greater or less extent, by a personal tutor. On the other hand, there was nothing strange about the relative lack of scholarly productivity of Oxford and Cambridge dons across the seventeenth and eighteenth centuries. The large majority of professors in other universities were equally uninterested in contributing to the advancement of knowledge. Only in those institutions where medicine was strong were there likely to be found a succession of professors engaged in research of some kind.[1] The average professor saw his academic role as limited to teaching, and seldom went into print except to publish his lectures, usually on retirement. In most universities there were never more than one or two professors who were part of the wider Republic of Letters, and in many of the small institutions none at all. The lacklustre research performance of Oxford dons in the field of the new science can be attributed to confessional constraint. Their lacklustre performance more generally can be explained by the fact that fellows were theoretically studying in a higher faculty and only twenty or so of the senior members held chairs. But this tells only part of the story. The active pursuit of the advancement of knowledge, however much it found favour with growing numbers of princes, nobles, and churchmen after 1600, was not written into the early modern university's script.

The absence of any institutional commitment to research on the part of Europe's universities appears never to have worried the people and governments of catholic

---

[1] For a balanced account of the universities' contribution to the new science, see Roy Porter, 'The Scientific Revolution and the Universities', in *HUIE*, ii, ch. 13.

Europe until the second half of the nineteenth century. The *philosophes* of the French Enlightenment took a long hard look at the institution, as they subjected all social practices to scrutiny for their utility, and discovered much amiss. But what concerned them was the curriculum of the feeder schools and the faculties, not the universities' contribution to learning. The *philosophes* had no time for metaphysical speculation, often treated the Bible as no different from any other historical text, and thought the purpose of higher education was to produce effective ministers of religion, lawyers, and doctors, who would be well informed about the modern world. In consequence, they promoted the study of modern history and modern languages, wanted more time devoted to mathematics and natural science than to the other parts of the philosophy course, and believed that study in the higher faculties should be made more useful. Theology students should be taught how to be good pastors rather than how to defend confessional dogmas; the law course should be built around local and state law; and medicine should concentrate on therapeutics rather than the theory.[2] Their particular bête noire was the study of classical languages, which the *Encyclopédie* dismissed as a complete waste of time now that most works of science and literature appeared in the vernacular.[3]

Nor was the indifference to research of much interest to the French revolutionaries and Napoleon, who undertook the reform of higher education as they undertook the reform of everything else. The system that eventually emerged in France after 1800 was structurally rather than conceptually radical. The new feeder schools, the lycées, continued to provide a propaedeutic education in the arts little different from what had been given before, although more attention was given to French language and literature, history, and mathematics.[4] The independent corporate confessional universities of the Ancien Régime, on the other hand, were abolished. In their stead was established a series of state-dependent non-confessional professional schools and faculties, preparing students for the public and private professions whose curricula reflected the Enlightenment emphasis on learning in the vernacular and practical relevance.[5] But there was seldom any suggestion that the new institutions should be centres of research as well as instruction. The fact that many of the professors in the Paris-based schools were significant scientists or

---

[2] The fullest expression is Denis Diderot, 'Plan d'une université pour le gouvernement de Russie', in *Œuvres complètes*, ed. J. Assézat (20 vols; Paris, 1875–7), iii. 409–534.

[3] *Encyclopédie, ou dictionnaire raisonné des sciences, des arts et des metiers* (17 vols; Paris, 1751–65), ii. 526–8 (*sub* 'collège': the article was written by D'Alembert).

[4] In 1795, there was an attempt to set up a completely different propaedeutic course based on the Enlightenment critique but parents objected to the devaluation of Latin and Greek. For the failure of the experiment, see S. Moravia, *Il tramonto dell'illuminismo: filosofia e politica nella società francese, 1771–1810* (Bari, 1968), pp. 347–69.

[5] J. Verger (ed.), *Histoire des universités en France* (Toulouse, 1986), chs 7 and 8. The public professions at this date were the army and navy, the state engineering corps, and higher-education teaching. From 1848, there was also a school for training civil servants. On Napoleon's reforms, see Antoine Aulard, *Napoléon 1er et le monopole universitaire: origine et fonctionnement de l'Université impériale* (Paris, 1911). The imperial university was essentially a ministry of education. For the complexity of the system, see *HUO*, vi. 96 (diagram). Entrance to the state military and engineering schools was by a special examination. Entrants to the law and medical schools were expected to have a BA, and, in the second case, after 1836, also a BSc. These were granted by faculties of letters and faculties of science, which, except in Paris, were little more than graduating faculties.

scholars was an effect of their good facilities and pay. Talented scientists and scholars accepted positions in the higher-education institutions in the capital in the nineteenth century because they were prestigious state appointments, could often be held in tandem, and carried a relatively light teaching load. The Parisian medical faculty became the most famous centre of medical research in Europe in the early nineteenth century because the professors doubled as hospital physicians and surgeons and had peculiar access to patients and bodies.[6]

In Protestant Germany conversely attitudes began to change in the middle of the eighteenth century as the civil servants and bureaucrats of the petty and relatively underdeveloped northern states began to wonder whether the universities might assist them in the task of state-building. When the Hanoverian University of Göttingen was founded in 1733, it was understood from the beginning that its professors would be involved in knowledge creation as well as teaching, and, in the second half of the eighteenth century, the idea slowly gained credence in the other German protestant universities, especially among language professors.[7] The concept, however, firmly took root only at the turn of the nineteenth century when it lost its utilitarian edge and was reshaped by two of Prussia's most prominent intellectuals, Immanuel Kant and Wilhelm von Humboldt. Both men wanted the university to once again become the focus of intellectual enquiry. Kant was a professor of philosophy at the insignificant University of Königsberg, but an active member of the Enlightenment and the Republic of Letters who spent his adult life constructing a new theory of knowledge, ethics, and aesthetics. Fed up with the low status and limited drawing power of the faculty of arts to which he belonged, he published, in 1798, a critique of the existing university system, which would henceforth give it pride of place. The higher faculties, he argued, in that they trained people for particular professional roles, would always be in the business of teaching people how to fulfil those roles in the present: if they began to critique establishment codes, they became redundant. The faculties of arts, in contrast, had no professional role and should be encouraged to become dynamic centres of learning:

> It is absolutely essential that within the university there is a faculty involved in public scientific construction which, being independent of the orders of government, has the liberty, if not to give orders, at least to give a judgement on everything of scientific interest, that is to say on truth. In this faculty reason must have the authority to speak openly, for without this liberty, truth cannot be made manifest.[8]

---

[6] For an introduction, see E. Ackerknecht, *Medicine at the Paris Hospital, 1794–1848* (Baltimore, MD, 1967), and D.S. Weiner, *The Citizen-Patient in Revolutionary and Imperial Paris* (Baltimore, MD, 1993). There has been a long debate on the institutional underpinning of the fecundity of French science at the turn of the nineteenth century. The most recent account is Charles Coulston Gillispie, *Science and Polity in France: The Revolutionary and Napoleonic Years* (Princeton, NJ, 2004).

[7] Charles E. McClelland, *State, Society and University in Germany 1700–1914* (Cambridge, 1908), ch. 2; Roy S. Turner, 'University Reformers and Professional Scholarship', in Lawrence Stone (ed.), *University in Society*, vol. 2: *Europe, Scotland and the United States from the 16th to the 20th Century* (Princeton, NJ, 1975), pp. 515–29; William Clark, *Academic Charisma and the Origins of the Research University* (Chicago, 2006), pp. 126–30 and 158–79.

[8] I. Kant, *Streit der Facultäten* (1798), ed. K. Reich (Hamburg, 1959), p. 12.

Humboldt was part of the German Neohumanist and Idealist movement, whose members believed, in contrast to their Enlightenment forbears, that there were no bounds to what human reason could discover and the will achieve. His vision of the university, articulated in particular in a pamphlet of 1809, was of an institution devoted to developing the full potential of the individual and discovering the meaning of life, which would only be entered after deep immersion in Latin, Greek, and mathematics in a gymnasium or feeder school.[9] To achieve this, the professors of all faculties had to be involved in research as well as teaching, and the two had to be interconnected. Professors would be free from all constraint to follow a party line; students would be encouraged to follow any course that interested them; and professors and advanced students would meet together to discuss research findings in a new institution, the seminar. Irrespective of their field, professors and students were to be actively engaged in constructing the ultimate truth that underlay all other truths. For this to happen, the university had to be free of all confessional tests and the professors had to be appointed on merit. As merit was best discerned by a disinterested state, the university was to cease to be a self-governing corporation and become an arm of government.[10] According to Humboldt, 'it is no more advisable for teachers to govern themselves than it is for a troupe of actors to direct their own affairs'.[11]

In 1809, Humboldt was made head of the religious and education section of the Prussian Ministry of the Interior, and the following year his vision was made flesh with the foundation of a new Prussian university at Berlin. Over the next forty years, his idea also slowly took root in other German protestant universities. Humboldt's ideas were never adopted in their entirety. His commitment to the search for ultimate truth was jettisoned; the universities continued to be the site of training for the traditional professions; most students still wanted to study law; and research, especially in the natural sciences, continued to be fostered by state-sponsored academies.[12] But the notion that the university should become the locus for research in the arts and sciences became deeply embedded, as did his view that the professoriate should be state appointees. The proof of the pudding was in the eating. By the mid-nineteenth century, the universities of northern Germany

---

[9] At this stage there was no entrance qualification. The Abitur was introduced as a school-leaving certificate in Prussia in 1788, but until 1834 had to be passed only by poor students who wanted some financial support to undertake university-level studies: Clark, *Academic Charisma*, pp. 124–5.

[10] O. Vossler, 'Humboldts Idee der Universität', *Historisches Zeitung*, 178 (1954), 251–68. For an account of Humboldt's broader educational ideas, see C. Menze, *Die Bildungsreform Wilhelm von Humboldts* (Hanover, 1975).

[11] Cited in U. Muhlack, 'Die Universitäten im Zeichen von Neuhumanismus und Idealismus', in P. Baumgarten and N. Hammerstein (eds), *Beiträge zu Problemen deutscher Universitätsgrundungen der frühen Neuzeit* (Nendeln, 1978), p. 313.

[12] A third of all German students in the 1850s were still in faculties of law. On German universities generally post-1815, see McClelland, *State, Society and University*, chs 5 and 6. On the spread of the Humboldtian model, see Sylvia Paletschek, 'Verrbreitete sich ein "Humbold'sches Modell" an den deutschen Universitaten im 19. Jahrhundert?', in Rainer Christoph Schwinges (ed.), *Humboldt international: der Export des deutschen Universitäts-modells im 19. und 20. Jahrhundert* (Basel, 2001), pp. 75–104; and Sylvia Paletschek, 'Die Erfindung der Humboldtschen Universität: Die Konstruktion der deutschen Universitätsidee in der ersten Hälfte des 20. Jahrhunderts', *Historische Anthropologie*, 10 (2002), 183–205.

were home to virtually all that was intellectually interesting in Europe, and individual professors, such as the philosopher Hegel, the historians Niebuhr and Ranke, and the chemist Liebig, had founded research schools whose members would dominate their disciplines for the rest of the century. In the faculty of arts, every received text and notion was in the process of being reconceptualized and contextualized, including Scripture and Christianity.[13]

The developments in France and Germany at the turn of the nineteenth century appeared to leave Oxford untouched in subsequent decades. Oxford might have changed considerably in the late Hanoverian era. The number of matriculations rose; the examination statute of 1800 and its revision seven years later made the BA exam a more rigorous test; dons on the whole became more serious; and the level of drunkenness and rowdiness among pass men decreased as more and more undergraduates expended their energies on the river. But when Newman left Oxford in 1845, the University, in German terms, was still essentially an arts high school, where boys in their late teens and early twenties studied the Latin and Greek humanities and were introduced to logic, ethics, and the fundamentals of Christianity. The teaching was often pedestrian and the level of commitment low. Only a quarter of undergraduates ever took an honours degree and as few as 12 per cent the second BA in mathematics.[14] Indeed, ironically, for the best students who took Schools seriously, an Oxford arts education in the 1840s could be even narrower than it had been a century before. Through its array of private and public courses in a wide variety of subjects, Oxford's teaching provision had always been much wider than the official arts curriculum suggested, and talented and ambitious undergraduates in the eighteenth century, like James of Queens, had not hesitated to avail themselves of what was on offer. In the early nineteenth century, with the new professorial foundations, the public provision was even greater and clearly valued: Buckland's geology lectures were particularly popular. The growing pressure on the brighter and more dedicated students to gain a good honours degree, however, eventually had a detrimental effect on extra-curricular studies, and attendance at science lectures plummeted across the 1830s.[15] There was only one development after 1750 that reflected changes occurring in the wider university world: at some time in the second half of the eighteenth century, lectures at Oxford, both at university and college level, began to be given in the vernacular.[16]

Oxford was also not caught up in the liberal and egalitarian tide that washed over large parts of western and central Europe in the aftermath of the French Revolution

---

[13] Hegel and Ranke were at Berlin. Liebig was at Marburg. On philosophy teaching in Germany's faculties of arts across the nineteenth century, see Ulrich J. Schneider, 'The Teaching of Philosophy at German Universities in the Nineteenth Century', *HU*, xii (1993), 197–338.

[14] Calculation based on *HUO*, vi. 360 and 370 (Figure 11.1 and Table 11.A1).

[15] In the Tractarian era it was also felt that Buckland and other Oxford scientists were a threat to orthodoxy.

[16] The change is impossible to date and has been ignored by historians of Oxford. Robert Lowth, the professor of poetry, whose lectures on Hebrew poetry were published in 1753, definitely lectured in Latin. Incepting MAs still had to show they could lecture in Latin under the 1808 examination statute. From 1800, though, candidates for the BA could be addressed by the examiners in Latin or English: OUS, ii. 34 and 86–7.

and eventually engulfed even Britain and Ireland from the late 1820s. While Tory and Whig administrations abolished the confessional state, reformed the House of Commons, restructured the municipalities, and rewrote the poor law in the course of one tumultuous decade, Oxford remained locked in a past age through its tenacious defence of the Anglican monopoly and its adamantine commitment to tradition. Oxford in 1845 was still an Anglican seminary: undergraduates had to be Anglicans and fellows celibate and mostly in orders. It was also a world where custom rather than merit determined advancement, even if the power of external patrons had all but disappeared. Undergraduate scholarships were largely competitive and awarded only to those who showed some ability, but fellowships in the majority of colleges were simply handed down, on a vacancy, to a scholar in waiting. Everywhere, too, scholarships and fellowships were tied to particular counties, towns, and families, with the inevitable result that deserving candidates were unable to find a niche. Indeed, in some colleges, such as Magdalen, the automatic promotion of scholars on the foundation to a fellowship had become the commonplace even when this was not laid down in the statutes. By 1845, a few colleges, like University College, had begun to waive geographical restrictions in order to attract well-qualified outsiders. But only Oriel and Balliol, to a degree, had taken a bold step into the modern world and introduced some sort of fellowship examination, and even there, as Newman's success revealed, other factors besides merit could be weighed in the scales.

The situation at Cambridge was little different. On the surface it seemed the more forward-looking institution. In that its colleges largely awarded fellowships upon performance in a Tripos examination which privileged mathematics, it exhaled an odour of modernity. Nonetheless, it was equally only an arts school with a narrow curriculum and only a little less sectarian. Mathematics might have been king but there was limited attention paid to natural philosophy, and its dons only slowly accepted the new mathematics based on algebraic rather than geometric analysis which had been developed in France in the second half of the eighteenth century.[17] However talented the fellows, moreover, they had to be Anglicans and were seldom engaged in serious higher study or research. As much as at Oxford, fellowships were filled with the sons of landowners and clergymen living a comfortable bachelor life while awaiting a suitable living. In that they were obtained on the results of an examination, they were even more coveted, and failure was seen as a taint on a family's honour.[18]

It was Oxford, however, that became the focus of national concern. Even while Britain was fighting a war of survival against the French in the name of tradition and

[17] H. Becher, 'Radicals, Whigs and Conservatives: The Middle and Lower Classes in the Analytic Revolution at Cambridge in the Age of Aristocracy', *British Journal for the History of Science*, 28 (1995), 405–26; Andrew Warwick, *Masters of Theory: Cambridge and the Rise of Mathematical Physics* (Chicago, 2003), pp. 66–84. It was the 1820s before the new mathematics found much favour at Cambridge.

[18] Cf. the stress caused to the Hamley family in Mrs Gaskell's *Wives and Daughters* (1866), set in the late 1820s and early 1830s, when the elder son, Osborne, fails to get the fellowship everyone had expected.

hierarchy, Whigs and radicals began to agitate for its reform. By the 1820s, in some eyes, the University had become an object of vilification. When the radical William Cobbett passed through Oxford as he travelled round England, it was not the University's aesthetic appeal but its uselessness that came to mind: 'Upon beholding the masses of buildings...devoted to what they call "learning", I could not help reflecting on the drones that they contain and the wasps they send forth.'[19] With the Whigs largely in power from 1830, demands that Oxford, and Cambridge where necessary, be pulled into the modern age began to be heard in parliament. Wood's Bill in 1834 to end subscription was the first shot in what would become a growing campaign. The critics, too, had their supporters within the University. A number of Oxford dons from the mid-1820s had found their way to Germany to look at the Humboldtian university, and had returned thinking that Oxford was as antediluvian as one of Buckland's fossils. The Tractarians were appalled by developments east of the Rhine. According to Pusey, who had gone to Germany himself in 1827, the new research culture simply led to religious scepticism when even the Bible was subjected to its historicizing lens.[20] But the Tractarians' liberal opponents within the professoriate thought otherwise. Figures like Baden Powell and Thomas Arnold found German scholarship vital and liberating, and Arnold, in his short tenure of the regius chair of modern history (1841–2), introduced an Oxford audience to Niebuhr and other new historians. While the Tractarians were in the ascendant, internal calls for reform were muted. Newman's departure, however, and the humiliation of the high-church party opened the floodgates, and Oxford, somewhat belatedly but no less decisively, entered its own decade of pivotal reform.

---

[19] William Cobbett, *Rural Rides*, vol.1 (New York, 2005), p. 34.

[20] H. S. Jones, *Intellect and Character in Victorian England: Mark Pattison and the Invention of the Don* (Cambridge, 2007), p. 44. For German theological scholarship in the Humboldtian age, see Johannes Zachhuber, *Theology as Science in Nineteenth-Century Germany: From F.C. Bauer to Ernst Troeltsch* (Oxford, 2013).

PART III

The Imperial University: 1845–1945

Introduction

Reform and Resurrection

OXFORD and Cambridge, at the turn of the nineteenth century, were only two of the eight universities in the new union state of Britain and Ireland. Trinity College Dublin bore some resemblance to its English sisters. It was not a residential university but it was a pillar of Anglicanism, had no higher faculties worth the name, and had a rudimentary tutorial system. The five Scottish universities, on the other hand, had more in common with the protestant universities on the continent.[1] Their MA curriculum was similar in structure to the model laid down in the Laudian statutes, except that it was a four- rather than a seven-year course. But the Scottish universities had no college or tutorial system, the arts students were taught exclusively by professors appointed to teach a particular part of the course, and natural philosophy was always an important component. In the eighteenth and early nineteenth century, moreover, the chairs at Edinburgh and Glasgow were filled with some of the leading figures of the Scottish Enlightenment: Francis Hutcheson, Adam Smith, Adam Ferguson, Dugald Stewart, Joseph Black, and John Playfair.[2] The Scottish universities also had functioning higher faculties. As ministers of the Church of Scotland, in order to be ordained, had to demonstrate attendance at specified theology lectures, and the country's judicial system drew heavily on civil law, the country's faculties of theology and law were always well attended, while Edinburgh, in addition, boasted one of Europe's most flourishing medical schools. At the turn of the nineteenth century, a large proportion of tyro medical practitioners in Britain and Ireland spent time on the faculty benches, even if they never stayed to take a degree, and in the 1820s there were some 700 medical students in the Scottish capital.[3] The Scottish universities were far from perfect. Many of the

---

[1] Dates of foundation: St Andrews 1411; Glasgow 1451; Aberdeen 1495; Edinburgh 1582; Trinity Dublin 1592. Aberdeen developed into two rival universities: King's College established by charter within the original university in 1505 and Marischal College in 1593.

[2] The fullest study is P. B. Wood, *The Aberdeen Enlightenment: The Arts Curriculum in the Eighteenth Century* (Aberdeen, 1993).

[3] Lisa Rosner, *Medical Education in the Age of Improvement: Edinburgh Students and Apprentices, 1760–1826* (Edinburgh, 1991), ch. 6; G. Risse, *Hospital Life in Enlightenment Scotland: Care and Teaching at the Royal Infirmary of Edinburgh*

professors in all four faculties had gifted and original minds but they frequently obtained their positions through patronage, and a royal commission was established to examine the system in 1826.[4] Nevertheless, in 1800, they looked more in keeping with the age than Oxford and Cambridge, as they were no longer confessionally closed and were relatively cheap to attend, so opened the door of educational advancement to the middle classes. It was possible to survive at Glasgow in the early nineteenth century on £25 a year or £15 if frugal.

It was fitting, therefore, that the attack on Oxford as illiberal and old-fashioned was launched out of Scotland. The University had been criticized on several occasions in the second half of the eighteenth century for failing to address the idleness of many of its undergraduates, notably by Vicesimus Knox, alumnus of St John's and headmaster of Tonbridge School.[5] But the first overtly hostile attack on Oxford's BA course appeared in the *Edinburgh Review* in 1808 and 1809 in the guise of book reviews penned by Playfair and the Anglican clergyman and former fellow of New College Sydney Smith, a fervent supporter of the emancipation of slaves, women, and catholics. The *Edinburgh Review* had been set up in 1802 to fly the flag of moderation and reform in an age of reaction caused by the horrors of the French Revolution, and traditionalist Oxford was a natural target. The two reviewers sang from the same hymn sheet. The BA course at Oxford, as defined by the new examination statute of 1800, was too narrow for the modern world. Undergraduate studies should be useful. By eschewing experimental philosophy and political economy in an age of improvement and reform, an Oxford education had become redundant.[6]

Oxford did not take the Whig attack lying down. Only a year after the second review appeared, the provost of Oriel, Edward Copleston, published a long defence of the curriculum in which he emphasized its narrowness as its greatest virtue.[7] The point of an undergraduate education was not to fill the heads of the young with practical and useful information; that could come later. Rather, it should aim to form character, which was exactly what Oxford's focused curriculum was set up to do. An education built around the difficult studies of classical literature, classical logic, and ethics, and, for the better students, mathematics, trained the

---

(Cambridge, 1996). Glasgow also had a functioning medical faculty but it began to attract significant numbers of students only after 1800: see M. Moss and D. Dow, 'The Medical Curriculum at Glasgow in the Early Nineteenth Century', *HU*, VII (1988), 227–57.

[4] Roger L. Emerson, *Professors, Patronage and Politics: The Aberdeen Universities in the Eighteenth Century* (Aberdeen, 1992); Roger L. Emerson, *Academic Patronage in the Scottish Enlightenment: Glasgow, Edinburgh and St Andrews Universities* (Edinburgh, 2008). Emerson calculates that only 60 of 388 professors in the five universities in the years 1690 to 1806 were highly talented. The chief bugbear was the role of the local town council in controlling most of the Edinburgh appointments: Chris Lawrence, 'The Edinburgh Medical School and the End of the "Old Thing", 1790–1830', *HU*, VII (1989), 259–86.

[5] V. Knox, *Liberal Education: or, a Practical Treatise on the Methods of Acquiring Useful and Polite Learning* (London, 1781), pp. 320–31.

[6] The reviews were of La Place's *Traité de mécanique céleste*, and Richard Edgeworth's *Essays on Professional Education*: see *Edinburgh Review*, 11/22 (Jan. 1808), 249–84, and 15/29 (Oct. 1809), 40–53.

[7] Edward Copleston, *A Reply to the Calumnies of the Edinburgh Review against Oxford containing an account of the Studies pursued in the University*, 2nd edn (Oxford, 1810), esp. ch. 3.

mind, discouraged idle speculation, and created solid citizens who would not abuse liberty or undermine property and could profitably turn their hand to any business of life.[8] An acquaintance with the ancient historians, in particular, was essential for anyone entering public life. Through the study of Thucydides and Xenophon an undergraduate gained: 'A high sense of honour, a disdain of death in a good cause, a passionate devotion to the welfare of one's country, a love of enterprise, and a love of glory.'[9]

Copleston's argument became the standard defence of Oxford in the following decades, and was also adopted at Cambridge, whose arts course, because of its mathematical bias, was generally judged satisfactory by external critics. According to William Whewell, master of Trinity, Cambridge, writing thirty-five years later, Oxford and Cambridge's narrow curriculum was justified in that it gave instruction in what was permanent and foundational in European civilization and cultivated the intellect. No other discipline, however worthy and progressive, could be safely studied until a student had learnt Greek or geometry, and ideally both.[10] Among Oxonians, the argument was taken to its highest level by the erstwhile Oriel tutor John Henry Newman, whose seminal *The Idea of a University*, published in 1873, began as series of lectures given in Dublin in 1852. Although delivered to an Irish and Roman Catholic audience, Newman's lectures were a paean to the world that he had abandoned. Newman was no slavish defender of the classics and believed that undergraduates should study a mix of ancient and modern subjects. But he believed strongly in the virtues of a common curriculum and that the primary purpose of an undergraduate education was to develop the mind. He also believed that learning of any kind was pointless unless grounded in religion, and that there was a consequent need for undergraduates to have a personal tutor who could perform a pastoral role.[11]

Copleston's defence found favour with most Oxford dons, but there were a few in the University who thought he was defending the indefensible. The rector of Lincoln, Edward Tatham, was unimpressed with the new BA course. Tatham had long supported the need to give more weight to natural philosophy in the arts curriculum and harboured strong doubts about the new examination system. In the same year as Copleston defended the new BA course, Tatham attacked it mercilessly

---

[8] Copleston recognized that, even in 1810, not all candidates for the BA offered mathematics and physics as they were supposed to do under the revised statute of 1807. The fact that he also talked only of the mathematics exam suggests that, from the beginning, this was an examination in which physics, even mathematical physics, played only a small part.

[9] Copleston, *Reply*, p. 169.

[10] W. Whewell, *Of a Liberal Education in general and with especial reference to the University of Cambridge* (London, 1845), esp. pp. 106–7. Playfair, in 1808, had accepted that Cambridge was free of the prejudices affecting Oxford but still felt the curriculum was not ideal: there was too much rote learning: *Edinburgh Review*, 11/22 (Jan. 1808), p. 284.

[11] J.H. Newman, *The Idea of a University*, ed. F. M. Turner (London, 1996). The best account of the fight back at Oxford is Peter Slee, 'The Oxford Idea of a Liberal Education 1800–1860: The Invention of Tradition and the Manufacture of Practice', *HU*, VII (1988), 61–88. For Cambridge, see M. M. Garland, *Cambridge before Darwin: The Ideal of a Liberal Education, 1800–1860* (Cambridge, 1980), pp. 28–47.

in a printed address to Convocation, where he expressed the hope that a new curriculum would be adopted more suited 'to the present State and Advancement of Learning and Science'.[12] Tatham was a divisive figure and his disenchantment caused little heart-searching. In subsequent years, however, his views were echoed by a number of junior members, notably James Shergold Boone of Christ Church, who, in 1818–19, published a series of dialogues under the title the *Oxford Spy*, which lambasted the University for neglecting science, modern history, and modern languages. At this point the more broad-minded senior members began to take note. While Copleston and his fellow Noetics in Oriel held firm to the conviction that the justification of the Oxford arts course lay in the training it gave the mind, they recognized the need to take some of the criticisms on board. From the mid-1820s, they worked to found the study of logic and ethics on modern texts, give greater emphasis to ancient history, and make the Lit. Hum. exam more challenging. In the end, such was the power of the university conservatives in the wake of the Peel election, that the Noetics received little of what they desired when the examination statute was revised in 1830. Nonetheless, a powerful coterie within Oxford was clearly ready to meet the critics halfway.[13]

The limited revision of the examination statute in 1830 did nothing to appease the University's external foes. Fresh attacks had been made on Oxford's emphasis on the classics in various Whig magazines in the 1820s, and, in 1831, the Scot Sir William Hamilton, Edinburgh professor of civil history, tightened the screw. Hamilton had held a Snell exhibition at Balliol and had been a memorable examinee when he took the BA in 1811, but twenty years later, in the first of five articles published in the *Edinburgh Review*, he showed little gratitude for the efforts of his tutors.[14] Hamilton took the case against the curriculum as read. Instead he turned his attention to the quality of the tuition. In his view, the standard was unacceptably low because delivery of the curriculum was left to callow youths who lacked gravitas and experience. While, elsewhere in Europe, including Scotland, undergraduates were taught by professors expert in the discipline with which they were entrusted, Oxford students were left to the tender mercies of tutors wet behind the ears who had to teach the whole curriculum. The tutorial system was a hindrance not a help to learning:

---

[12] Edward Tatham, *New Address to the Free and Independent Members of Convocation* (Oxford, 1810), esp. p. 21. Tatham believed that Hebdomadal Council had been hijacked by a coterie who had forced through the new examination statute. This was one of many pamphlets in the years following 1807 in which he attacked the reform on the grounds that it was putting the clock back.

[13] The 1830 statute specifically allowed history and political theory texts to be included among the list of three authors or more on which candidates chose to be examined: see pp. 237–8, this volume.

[14] William Hamilton, 'On the State of the English Universities, with More Especial Reference to Oxford', in William Hamilton, *Discussions on Philosophy and Literature, Education and University Reform, Chiefly from the* Edinburgh Review, 2nd edn (London, 1853), pp. 401–78. That Oxford teaching was not all it was cracked up to be was implicit in a review of an Oxford edition of the geographer Strabo, written by Payne Knight, as early as 1809: see *Edinburgh Review*, 14/28 (July 1809), 429–41. Snell exhibitions were created in 1677 under the will of Sir John Snell, and allowed students from the University of Glasgow to continue their studies at Oxford. Adam Smith had had one.

As at present organized, it is a doubtful problem whether the tutorial system ought not to be abated as a nuisance. For if some tutors may afford assistance to some pupils, to other pupils other tutors prove equally an impediment...[T]he tutorial system, as now dominant in Oxford, is vicious in its application...—the tutors as now fortuitously appointed being, as a body, incompetent even to the duties of subsidiary instruction.[15]

The tutors were also intellectual lightweights:

We assert without fear of contradiction, that, on the average, there is to be found among those to whom Oxford confides the business of education, an infinitely smaller proportion of men of literary reputation, than among the actual instructors of any other University in the world.[16]

In Hamilton's eyes the effective teacher was the learned scholar who went into print.[17]

Hamilton ended his diatribe by calling on the new Whig government to set up a royal or parliamentary commission to look into the University's failings. He did not mention the German universities as a model that should be followed (although he knew all about the German Idealist tradition). But others soon did. The Utilitarians, a group of political radicals led by the former Queen's undergraduate Jeremy Bentham, who judged every institution in terms of its contribution to the happiness of greatest number, found Oxford particularly deficient. In 1833, only two years after the appearance of Hamilton's first article, one of their number weighed the two systems in the balance in the new *Quarterly Journal of Education*, and found Oxford totally wanting: 'While Germany, with far less means, is daily making rapid advances in literature, and sending forth productions of great ability, the University of Oxford is obliged to the labours of German writers for the mere class-books which she prints for the use of her "Alumni".'[18]

Over the next decades Hamilton and other Whigs continued their campaign to pull Oxford into the nineteenth century. Objections were raised not just against the Oxford curriculum and the tutorial system but increasingly against its Anglican monopoly and the restrictions governing fellowship elections, which Copleston had declared less than ideal as early as 1810.[19] The shenanigans of the Tractarians and the power that they began to wield only increased the feeling amongst outsiders that the University was in crisis. Not only were Newman and his friends viscerally committed to the academic status quo but they seemed to be pushing Oxford towards Rome. The critics soon had parliamentary support. In 1837, three years after Wood's

---

[15] Hamilton, 'State', p. 417.   [16] Ibid., p. 416.

[17] According to Hamilton, not only was the tutorial system pedagogically insane but it was also constitutionally improper: the colleges had usurped the teaching role of the University.

[18] Anon., 'Oxford Examinations', *Quarterly Journal of Education*, 5 (1833), 330–1. The review had been founded in 1829 by the Society for the Diffusion of Useful Knowledge. Another article attacking Oxford's curriculum and examination system had appeared in the journal the year before: see A. De Morgan, 'State of the Mathematical and Physical Sciences at the University of Oxford', *Quarterly Journal of Education*, 4 (1832), 191–208. For the use of classical texts edited by Germans, see p. 322, this volume.

[19] Copleston, *Reply*, pp. 183–4.

subscription bill, Hamilton's call for a royal commission was taken up in the Lords by the earl of Radnor, who accused the colleges of diverting their endowments away from the poor.[20] Initially Wellington, the University's Chancellor, was able to cool the ardour of his parliamentary colleagues. But the critics did not hold back for long. From 1843, calls for reform became part of the annual parliamentary calendar.

By then critics no longer had to turn to Scotland and Germany in search of the favoured 'other', for examples could be found closer to home. In the 1840s, Oxford and Cambridge were not the only English universities. In the second half of the 1820s, the Whig MP and legal reformer Henry Brougham succeeded in establishing a professorial, non-denominational, and non-confessional university college in London. At much the same time, the established church set up rival Anglican colleges in Lampeter, Durham, and the capital, which were much less expensive to attend than Oxford and Cambridge.[21] Initially, they offered no greater threat to the supremacy of the old universities than the dissenting academies, which had existed for over a century, or the Jesuit college set up at Stonyhurst in 1794.[22] They were too small and untried to be serious competitors. From 1836, however, the situation was radically altered with the incorporation of the University of London, which brought the two recently founded London colleges under one umbrella and established England's first non-sectarian university with the power to grant degrees in arts, law, and medicine. It had always been unlikely that many affluent English families would send their sons to the Scottish universities or Trinity College Dublin to receive a more rounded education in the arts and sciences. But the fact that the capital and richest city in the world now had its own university and two constituent colleges offering high-quality professorial tuition, as well as a number of medical schools attached to the London hospitals, changed the educational geography completely. The rapid rise in significance of the University of Berlin demonstrated the threat of new metropolitan foundations to long-standing provincial institutions. So too did the disappearance of Spain's historic University of Alcalá, subsumed into the new University of Madrid in 1836.[23] In the mid-nineteenth century, the most populous and prestigious university (or set of faculties) in every European state, bar Sweden, Portugal, and the Netherlands, was situated alongside the centre of government. Even if, in the 1840s, the University of London had yet to bed down, the omens did not look good for unreformed Oxford.

---

[20] Hamilton was not the only Whig journalist demanding a commission in the early 1830s. The former University College student Thomas Jefferson Hogg, who had been sent down with Shelley for propounding atheism, was of a similar mind: see his, 'The Universities of Oxford and Cambridge', *Westminster Review*, 15 (July 1831).

[21] University College London, founded 1826, opened 1828; Lampeter founded 1822, opened 1827; King's London founded 1828; Durham founded 1832. King's London, though an Anglican institution, had no tests. F. J. Hearnshaw, *The Centenary History of King's College, London, 1828–1928* (London, 1929); C. E. Whiting, *The University of Durham 1832–1932* (London, 1932), chs 1–2.

[22] With the French Revolution, the English colleges in France and the catholic Netherlands run by the Society were closed and the Jesuits allowed to relocate to Lancashire. On the dissenting academies, see pp. 215–16, this volume.

[23] On Alcalá's role in the diffusion of humanism, see p. 119, this volume.

Luckily for Oxford, reformers of all stripes and confessions wanted to change the University not destroy it. Hamilton had concluded that Oxford was an imperfect institution but that it was 'perfectible'.[24] Despite its perceived shortcomings, Oxford retained a solid grip on the cultural imagination of the nation's elite. The new University of London was seen as supplementing, not replacing, the country's existing university provision, and Oxford's critics were willing to play a long game in the expectation that the right conjunction of events would eventually occur. This came in the years 1845 to 1850. There was always a constituency for reform in the University in the 1830s and 1840s among the surviving Noetics and a younger generation of liberal professors and tutors, a number of whom, like Arthur Stanley of University College, had been to Germany. By the early 1840s, too, their support base had grown. The Romanist views of the Tractarians convinced many 'drys' and evangelicals of the need to reduce the power of unorthodox tutors over the minds of the young, and garnered support for broadening the curriculum in ways which would curb their influence. Newman's departure in 1845 and the subsequent defeat of the Tractarian party gave the supporters of change their head. With the appointment of the Edinburgh-educated Whig Lord John Russell as prime minister in the following year, the liberal reformers also had government squarely on their side. Most liberals in the University by the late 1840s had become convinced that only curricular reform could be effected in-house, and that root-and-branch change of the college statutes in a more liberal direction required government support. Russell was happy to oblige. In 1850, as the many outside critics had long desired, a royal commission was established to scrutinize Oxford's Ancien Régime. As Cambridge was judged to suffer from many of the same institutional failings as Oxford, although to a lesser degree, the commission's remit was extended to both universities. Within a few years it had reported and the necessary enabling legislation to cajole Oxford and Cambridge into accepting slowly but surely the norms of the Victorian liberal state had been passed.

The royal commission instituted a period of reform which completely changed the character of Oxford and Cambridge. Within half a century, they had ceased to be clerical institutions whose primary function was to provide the next generation of Anglican clergy and landowners' elder sons with an education in either classics or mathematics. Both universities remained residential and collegiate and the tutorial system flourished rather than withered. But, by the mid-1880s, college fellowships had been thrown open, the rules governing ordination and celibacy greatly eroded, and the universities opened to all faiths and none. From the late nineteenth century, too, a smaller and smaller proportion of undergraduates entered the church on going down so that, by the 1920s and 1930s, it was no more than a few per cent. On the eve of the Second World War, Oxford and Cambridge were still part of the Anglican establishment. Most junior and senior members nominally belonged to the Church of England and chapel-going continued to be encouraged, if it was

---

[24] Hamilton, 'State', p. 402.

no longer compulsory. There were also many committed Christians of different dominations in both universities, and theological studies at Oxford were in rude health.[25] But to all intents and purposes Oxford and Cambridge had become secular institutions. They had shed their Anglican identity less quickly and completely than the nation at large but they had long since ceased to be Anglican seminaries.

In response to their critics, both universities also gradually extended their undergraduate curriculum after 1850. It took time for the traditional curriculum to lose its authority and the Coplestonian belief that an undergraduate education was a mental not a practical training was never jettisoned. Nevertheless, by the beginning of the First World War, Oxford and Cambridge offered undergraduates a wide variety of courses in the arts and sciences in which they might hone their minds and take a BA. The study of Latin and Greek language and literature, which had been the mainstay of the Oxford early modern curriculum, continued to attract some of the brightest minds, but from 1887 it was no longer a compulsory part of the undergraduate course, and by 1914 only a minority specialized in the subject. By then, too, both universities had come to accept that a university was a research as well as a teaching institution. Professors were expected to extend the sum of knowledge, and fellows who were not involved in teaching and administration held their fellowship on the assumption they were involved in research. From the 1890s, both universities began to offer postgraduate diplomas and degrees. In 1917, Oxford finally established a research doctorate in the form of the DPhil.

Furthermore, by 1914, both universities had made some attempt to broaden access in response to the changing face of British society wrought by industrialization, the extension of the franchise, and the first stirrings of the women's movement. With the decision in 1868 that undergraduates need not have a college attachment and the foundation of Keble two years later, Oxford believed that it had found ways of reducing the cost of study at the University for poorer students. Then, in the early 1880s, Oxford followed Cambridge in allowing women students to enter its portals, although they were not made full members of the University and permitted to take degrees until 1920. In addition, Oxford and Cambridge became deeply involved in educational provision outside their walls. Individual colleges set up elementary schools in parishes where they held the advowson, while, from the late 1850s, the two universities began to organize the country's first national system of school-leaving examinations for secondary schools.[26] An even more important initiative was launched in 1878, when Oxford and Cambridge set up embryonic extramural departments to give the population at large a taste of higher education. Under their auspices, fellows were provided to give courses of lectures on topics of interest to local communities. For thirty years or more, the audience was a passive consumer. Shortly before 1914, however, Oxford teamed up with the burgeoning Labour movement and

---

[25] Daniel Inman, 'God in the Academy: The Reform of the University of Oxford and the Practice of Theology, 1850–1932' (DPhil. dissertation, Oxford, 2009). For comparisons with Cambridge, see Brooke, chs 4 and 5.

[26] Discussed only briefly, see p. 536, this volume.

agreed to provide much more demanding and focused courses aimed specifically at the working man, which included tutorial classes and essay work.[27]

Admittedly, neither Oxford nor Cambridge could be called modern universities by the 1930s. Although they had eventually admitted women, and a rising proportion of students between the wars came from state grammar schools and from families with limited funds, the two universities remained socially elitist. Their numbers had risen nearly fivefold since 1845 and their students came from a much broader background than hitherto, but their social tone had not changed dramatically: gentlemen's sons now rubbed shoulders with the sons and daughters of the middle class, but the large majority of students came from affluent backgrounds. In terms of their intake, too, both universities continued to be insular institutions until 1900, and even by 1940 drew few students from outside the Anglophone world. The vast majority of Oxford's junior members in the Victorian era were born and bred in England. It was only in 1902 that the University began to admit students in any numbers from beyond these shores, thanks to the scholarship scheme established under the will of the imperialist Cecil Rhodes, an Oriel man who had made his fortune in diamonds. This brought a growing number of students to Oxford from the Dominions and the United States as well as a trickle of Germans, but it did nothing to encourage other nationalities.

The background of Oxford's and Cambridge's senior members, or dons as they became known, remained even narrower. A handful of distinguished academics born in the Dominions were elected to professorships at the two universities after 1900. At Oxford, the first were the Irish Australian Gilbert Murray and the Canadian William Osler, respectively regius professors of Greek and medicine.[28] But Americans and continental Europeans were all but absent from Oxbridge senior common rooms until the second half of the 1930s. The large majority of dons throughout the period were Englishmen or women who had obtained a post in the university where they had been an undergraduate. Oxford dons were not isolated from the outside world. They travelled around Europe in the vacation, and most scientists from the late nineteenth century had spent time abroad as young researchers. Furthermore, they met continental scientists and scholars when they visited Oxford. Throughout the period, fabled continental academics, like the ancient historian Theodor Mommsen, customarily stayed in a college while researching in the Bodleian, while, from the Edwardian era, Oxford began to play host to international conferences and to invite scholars of the eminence of the

---

[27] In the eighteenth century, private lecturers had toured the provinces giving talks on experimental philosophy, for instance, and in the first half of the nineteenth century, mechanics institutes had been set up in most British cities to bring usually technical education to the working man. Adult education was a new departure for Oxford and Cambridge.

[28] Murray will be referred to later in this volume on several occasions. He was born in Australia but came to England while quite young and was an undergraduate at St John's. Osler was a real outsider, although his father had been a lieutenant in the Royal Navy. He became regius in 1905. He is often called the 'father of modern medicine' for his championship of hands-on clinical studies. The leading colonial at Cambridge in the first half of the twentieth century was the New Zealand physicist and Nobel Prize winner Ernest Rutherford.

Hellenist Ulrich von Wilamowitz-Moellendorff to give the occasional lecture.[29] All the same, the average Oxford don could scarcely be called cosmopolitan, and most arts fellows and professors knew little of the university world beyond Oxford and Cambridge.

Oxford and Cambridge's profile as research universities at the end of the period should also not be exaggerated. The quality of the research, if often high, was uneven, and many fellows, especially college tutors, produced nothing of merit. The number of postgraduate or 'advanced' students as they were known was always small. Furthermore, the two universities had different strengths reflecting their past histories: Cambridge, after 1870, quickly developed as a centre of scientific research, while Oxford, until the interwar years, showed a marked bias towards the arts. Neither, moreover, measured up to the best German universities in the first part of the twentieth century, which continued to dominate research on the continent into the Nazi era. Nor could they hold a torch to the handful of American research schools, like Johns Hopkins at Baltimore, which had been deliberately set up in imitation of the German model in the final quarter of the nineteenth century.[30] If, at the end of the 1930s, Oxford's reputation in the sciences was rising fast, this was in large part due to the appearance in its midst of a growing number of refugees from Nazi and fascist tyranny. The University sheltered a clutch of displaced academics and students during the Second World War in a wide variety of disciplines. They not only brought with them their research skills and knowledge of different research traditions, but gave the University a completely new cosmopolitan tone.

On the other hand, the international status of Oxford and Cambridge on the eve of the Second World War should not be belittled. In Britain, the British Empire, and the wider world, the two universities had acquired a cachet among the academic community bestowed on none but a handful of European and North American universities. Oxford and Cambridge in the 1930s were also viewed with approval and affection by the large majority of the English, if not British, public. Even the undergraduates were an object of interest. In the second half of the nineteenth century, the English public schools had come to place a novel emphasis on team sports: healthy minds were thought to depend upon healthy bodies. The close relationship between Oxford and Cambridge and the public schools quickly led to the same belief permeating the two universities. The Coplestonian ideal acquired a physical dimension. The undergraduate's afternoons became devoted to intercollegiate sport, especially rowing, while the most athletic were called up to represent their university in the Boat Race and the growing series of annual varsity matches. To a nation equally newly obsessed with sport, these were grand occasions which,

---

[29] Mommsen spent two weeks in Oxford in 1888 and Wilamowitz gave three lectures on Apollo about 1910: Lewis Farnell, *An Oxonian Looks Back* (London, 1934), pp. 95, 129, and 277. Between the wars, the establishment of the Zaharoff lecture allowed the modern languages faculty to bring over a French academic each year. It was funded by the Greek-born arms dealer and philanthropist Basil Zaharoff.

[30] Johns Hopkins was founded in 1876. Osler was the first physician-in-chief of the new Johns Hopkins Hospital.

from the late nineteenth century, could attract large crowds and much media attention. Even undergraduate views on matters of national importance were taken seriously by the press as the period wore on. Oxford's primary debating society, the Union, was founded as early as 1823 but was little known outside the University before the late Victorian period. In the 1930s, its debates were reported in the national press and votes on divisive issues seen as signs of national health or malaise.

Oxford's and Cambridge's position as the top universities in the British Empire in the 1930s was all the more remarkable in that they had not only to beat off the challenge of the old Scottish universities and the new University of London but also to face down competition from an ever-growing number of additional arrivals in the higher-education marketplace. All over the world after 1850, systems of higher education were expanding under the twin pressures of population growth and the perception that a university degree was professionally and economically valuable. In the United States, whose system had been long dominated by the east-coast colleges set up before independence, the years after the Civil War saw an explosion in foundations, private and state. On the continent of Europe, the university map remained largely unchanged, except in France where the faculties were once more grouped into universities in 1896. But student numbers rose dramatically every-where: Germany had 12,000 university students in 1850; it had 100,000 eighty years later. Britain and her empire were not immune to the secular trend. In the empire, a number of universities had been established in the Dominions and India by the turn of the twentieth century, starting with Toronto in 1850, Melbourne in 1855, and Calcutta, Madras, and Bombay in 1857.[31] In the mother country, there were no additional Scottish universities but a plethora of creations in the other parts of the United Kingdom. A network of university colleges was created in Ireland in 1850 and in Wales in the 1880s.[32] In England, the provision was greatly extended in the two decades before 1914 with the establishment of the London School of Economics and Imperial College in the capital, and the first civics or 'redbricks' in Bristol, Birmingham, and the north.[33] By 1939, England possessed ten independent universities, including Oxford and Cambridge, and virtually the same number of university colleges affiliated to the federal University of London established in 1898.[34]

---

[31] Toronto had begun as the Anglican King's College in 1827. There were six Australian universities founded 1850–1911. For the relations between the universities of the empire and the mother country, see T. Pietsch, *Empire of Scholars: Universities, Networks and the British Academic World, 1850–1939* (Manchester, 2013).

[32] The Irish colleges formed part of the federated Queen's University, later National University of Ireland; membership was altered in 1908 with Belfast becoming independent. The Welsh colleges, minus Lampeter, formed the federated University of Wales in 1893.

[33] The first English provincial university received its charter in 1880. The term 'redbrick' was coined by Bruce Truscot (pseudonym of E. Allison Peers), *Red Brick University* (London, 1943). See also E. Allison Peers, *Redbrick Revisited: The Autobiography of 'Bruce Truscot'*, ed. A. L. Mackenzie and A. R. Allen (Liverpool, 1996).

[34] The ten were Oxford, Cambridge, Durham, Birmingham, Bristol, Leeds, Liverpool, Manchester, Reading, and Sheffield. Several important affiliates of the University of London were not in the capital. This reflected the university's development from the 1850s as a huge examining machine: see p. 530, this volume.

The result was that Oxford and Cambridge's share of the country's student population gradually declined over the period, even if their own numbers sharply rose. There were 3,300 university students in England in 1861; in 1931 there were 37,255. The proportion attending Oxford and Cambridge in the 1930s was little more than 20 per cent.[35] Britain's other universities, too, presented a positive profile: they had been historically more welcoming to women,[36] recruited from a wider social spectrum, could attract students from the Empire and beyond,[37] and had soon developed their own successful outreach programmes. Most, moreover, had set up their own doctoral degrees at the close of the First World War and were fast developing a reputation for research. The London colleges, Manchester, Edinburgh, Glasgow, Sheffield, Liverpool, and Leeds all supported professors who produced significant work in the arts and sciences in the interwar years, although only the first three contained more than fifty research students. Significant research was also being done at Melbourne, Toronto, and other imperial universities. Oxford and Cambridge were the oldest British universities but antiquity alone gave them no automatic right to sit at the top table in an expanded imperial system. Oxford especially, because it had further to travel, had to fight hard to rise from the ashes of its pre-reform degradation.

Of course, antiquity played a part in Oxford's and Cambridge's continued success. That they emerged pre-eminent had a lot to do with their location in small towns away from the bustle and dirt of the metropolis, their attractive and often spacious historic buildings, their traditions of self-government, their library resources,[38] and, above all, their wealth. Britain's other universities were poorly endowed compared with Oxbridge, and until 1914 relied heavily on student fees. From 1920, all universities received an annual subsidy from the state, which improved their position considerably. But even then Oxford, thanks to the wealth of its colleges, still had an income more than twice as large as Manchester, the richest of the redbricks, enjoyed.[39] Antiquity, though, was not enough on its own to stop England's old universities from sharing the fate of Alcalá. As Chapters 9 to 12 will make clear, Oxford's transformation from an Anglican seminary into one of the world's top universities was ultimately the result of the persistence of a small but determined clutch of reformers across the century. They often disagreed among themselves about the best way forward. What they shared in common was a will to take Oxford by the scruff of the neck and make it a force in the new non-confessional industrial

---

[35] A. H. Halsey, *Decline of Donnish Dominion: The British Academic Professions in the Twentieth Century* (Oxford, 1992), p. 64 (graph).

[36] As early as 1874, the South Australian legislature passed a law allowing women to take degrees at the University of Adelaide.

[37] In 1921, 9–10 per cent of full-time students in Britain's universities came from overseas. There were 5,534 students from the Empire in Britain in 1936, including 2,488 from India and Africa. The LSE attracted many students from the non-settler Empire because its teachers included 'outsiders', like the socialist Harold Laski and the anthropologist Bronislaw Malinowski. Pietsch, *Empire of Scholars*, pp. 48, 178, and 182–3.

[38] In 1921, Birmingham University Library had 75,000 books; Sydney's 120,000: ibid., p. 43.

[39] In 1925–6, the University had an income of £420,000, the colleges of £492,000 (endowment and tuition fees only).

and imperial era. Much can and should be made of Oxford alumni's domination of the top posts in the government and the civil service, and the role this played in securing the University's position. It gave the University peculiar access to government grants and to the executives of the increasing number of worldwide, chiefly American, charitable trusts devoted to promoting human well-being, such as the Rockefeller Foundation, established in 1909. But this domination was not by chance. Leading Oxford figures, notably Jowett of Balliol, had helped to fix the entry system in Oxford's favour when appointment by patronage had given way to appointment by examination.

The hundred years from 1845 to 1945 form a distinctive period in the University's history. Although the First World War affected Oxford deeply, its permanent effect was limited. Oxford's commitment to scientific research was speeded up as a result, but otherwise there was no permanent structural legacy. Much more significant change would come after the Second World War. The title of this third part of the history is 'The Imperial University'. Given what has been said earlier in this introductory section about the insularity of Oxford until 1900,[40] the choice may seem bizarre, but it makes sense in the light of the reformed University's conception of its role. From the 1870s until the end of the period, most dons believed that Oxford, in some form or other, had an imperial mission. As will be made clear in Chapter 10, it was considered to be Oxford's primary function to take callow youths and turn them into intelligent, upright, and dedicated servants of a British mission *civilisatrice*, on the home front as well as abroad. The more gung-ho aspect of the vision, always questioned by some insiders, was largely jettisoned after 1918, but the concept of an education for service remained powerful throughout the 1920s and 1930s, and was absorbed by socialists as well as the politically conservative.[41] Only a minority of Oxford's graduates during the period may have literally served nation and empire, except the cohort at the beginning of the twentieth century who ended up on the Western Front. And few Oxonians could boast the imperial credentials of the Balliol undergraduate and university Chancellor Lord Curzon, who was viceroy of India from 1899 to 1905. But a significant number of Oxford men and women answered the call to the colours in various ways. Some went into politics; many others responded by joining the different branches of the home and imperial civil service; yet others went abroad as soldiers or missionaries, worked in conservation, or staffed the new overseas universities.[42] At home, Oxford graduates edited newspapers, taught in public schools, wrote school textbooks, or became involved in housing projects. In the era of the Anglican university, Oxford men were born in England and largely stayed there. In the era of the imperial university, Oxford men and women, however insular their background, were to be found living and dying all over the Empire, trying to make a difference.

---

[40] See p. 341, this volume.

[41] The alumnus of University College and Labour prime minister Clement Atlee would be a case in point.

[42] Osler and George Parkin, the first secretary of the Rhodes Trust and another Canadian, acted as recruitment agents: Pietsch, *Empire of Scholars*, p. 67.

CHAPTER 9

A Century of Reform

A. The First Steps Down the Road

THE reformers who orchestrated the campaign to modernize Oxford in the mid-nineteenth century were largely a mix of professors and tutors. Among the former, the leading light was the professor of geometry, Baden Powell, who had frequently felt the annoyance of lecturing to an empty room.[1] Among the tutors, four were particularly prominent, Benjamin Jowett of Balliol, Mark Pattison of Lincoln, and two members of University College, Arthur Stanley and Goldwin Smith. Most were liberals and Christian rationalists. Although a number, such as Stanley, were products of the newly reformed Rugby and had sat at the feet of Dr Arnold, they had none of the doctor's deep religious certainty in the truth of the resurrected Christ, and Pattison, who had originally been in the Tractarian camp, had lost his faith altogether.[2] There was one member of the group, however, who was not even on the liberal wing of the Church of England. This was Francis Jeune of Pembroke, the one ardent reformer among the heads of house. Jeune, a native of Jersey, was an evangelical. In the second half of the 1840s, thanks to the power he enjoyed as a college head, his was the public face of reform. He had become master in 1844 after several years running King Edward's School, Birmingham, and set about turning empty Pembroke into one of the most dynamic colleges in the University. In two years he had completely renovated the college and built a dining hall big enough to take 180 students, then filled the upgraded accommodation by keeping battels low.[3]

The move to reform the curriculum in earnest began in 1839. The Hebdomadal Board had realized the need to respond to the concern of Radnor and others in parliament, and suggested ways in which the BA course might be extended beyond classics to ensure undergraduates attended professorial lectures. The initiative was rejected by Convocation but spawned a number of rival reform proposals,

---

[1] For his life and career, see Pietro Corsi, *Science and Religion: Baden Powell and the Anglican Debate, 1800–1860* (Cambridge, 1988).

[2] At the end of his life, he seems to have equated God with the life of the intellect: H. S. Jones, *Intellect and Character in Victorian England: Mark Pattison and the Invention of the Don* (Cambridge, 2007), pp. 24–35 and 101–2.

[3] J. H. C. Leach, *Sparks of Reform: The Career of Francis Jeune, 1806–1868* (London, 1994), chs 2 and 3.

including one put together by Stanley and the Balliol tutor Archibald Tait.[4] While Newman and the Tractarians dominated the University stage in the first half of the 1840s, it was difficult to get attention focused on the issue of reform. The reformers were also not united: there was an important division between the tutors and the professors over the extent to which teaching should become university- rather than college-based. But with Newman's departure in 1845, and widespread feeling in the University that curricular change was necessary to keep undergraduates from the lure of Rome, the reformers recognized that time had come to strike once and for all. In the spring of 1846, the professors presented a memorandum to the Hebdomadal Board, demanding that science and the other modern subjects that they taught be included in the BA examination, or that attendance at their lectures be made compulsory. The board appointed a committee to study the proposal, which led Jeune and Osborne Gordon, tutor of Christ Church, to put forward a more radical scheme. This called for an end to awarding a BA simply on the basis of an examination in the *literae humaniores* (which, for weaker candidates, meant little more than displaying a limited acquaintance with Latin and Greek language and literature) and proposed that every candidate should also have to satisfy the examiners in one additional school, either mathematics, physics, history, or philosophy. Initially, the majority of the heads of house, aware of the bloody nose they had received a few years before, were unwilling to risk the wrath of Convocation another time. However, they eventually changed their mind when it became clear that the board was increasingly out of touch with the University. In the parliamentary election of 1847 liberal Anglicans, Tractarians, and even some evangelicals rejected the candidate favoured by most heads and voted in Gladstone, whose views on religion and trade were distinctly Peelite. Then, in March the following year, at the moment when revolution was breaking out all over Europe, fifty-nine of the sixty-three college tutors presented the board with a petition calling for the introduction of a second Schools examination in an even broader range of subjects, including theology, a school particularly championed by Jowett. Evidently there was widespread support for curricular reform among the younger fellows, whatever their party allegiance.

The heads, in consequence, bowed before the inevitable and drew up, albeit very slowly, the necessary legislation. The new statute comprised three major innovations. In the first place, the BA was divided into two parts. Responsions was now to be taken as soon as possible after matriculation, and a new examination, Moderations, introduced halfway through the course. This was to be an examination in the Holy Gospels, Greek and Latin literature, logic, and mathematics. Secondly, as Jeune and Gordon had proposed, the final examination was to be taken in two schools but with the school of Lit. Hum., which now was to give special emphasis to ancient history and philosophy, remaining compulsory: 'No one shall supplicate for the first degree without having undergone an examination in the School of Polite Literature,

[4] *Hints on the Formation of a Plan for the Safe and Effectual Revival of the Professorial System at Oxford* (1839).

and afterwards in one of the other schools, in the same or some following term, and shall have satisfied the public examiners in both schools.'[5] The heads were wary of liberalizing the curriculum too far, and especially nervous about creating a school of theology which might teach the new German biblical criticism. They therefore stuck with Jeune and Gordon's original scheme with one alteration: the mooted new schools in history and philosophy became a single school of jurisprudence and modern history. They also wanted to please the University's professoriate, so decided that no one could take either part of the second examination who 'has not attended one entire course of lectures at least of each of two professors or public lecturers' and received a certificate confirming this.[6]

The legislation was eventually presented to Convocation in March 1849. To improve its chance of passing, every attempt was made to stop the traditionally conservative non-resident MAs attending. But the statute was voted on clause by clause and the plan given approval was a mangled version of the original draft. The Hebdomadal Board was therefore forced back to the drawing board, and it was not until March 1850 that the new examination statute was finally passed in the form originally intended. The reform, however, had no time to bed down. It had hardly been passed when the board was overtaken by events outside its control. The extension of the curriculum was the least controversial of the many changes the reformers sought, and they had quickly come to the conclusion that further change from within would be well-nigh impossible. Only a royal commission would break the Gordian knot. Suspecting that the new Whig prime minister, Lord John Russell, would move, if a commission had the backing within the University, Oxford's reformers began to make overtures to the government as early as November 1847.[7] The fact that, having passed the statute, Convocation then refused to grant money to provide the laboratories and lecture rooms which the new school of natural science would need to become a reality convinced the reformers that their action was right.

B. The 1850 Commission

The reformers finally got their royal commission in 1850. In April of that year the Unitarian MP James Heywood put down a motion in the House of Commons that there be an enquiry into the state of England's two ancient universities. This time the prime minister announced that the government was prepared to act. Gladstone, as one of Oxford's two university MPs, spoke eloquently against the wisdom of outside interference, but on 18 July Russell got his way by a majority of twenty-two, and on 31 August a commission was established. This was to 'inquire into the state, discipline, studies, and revenues' of the universities and colleges of Oxford and Cambridge, and was invested with investigative but not executive powers.

---

[5] OUS, ii. 305.   [6] Ibid., 308.   [7] Geoffrey Faber, *Jowett* (London, 1957), pp. 196–7.

The team appointed to look at Oxford was a mix of former and resident members of the University, who all belonged to its liberal and reformist wing and were highly unrepresentative of the membership of the Hebdomadal Board and Convocation. The chairman was Samuel Hinds, bishop of Norwich, who had previously been vice-principal of St Alban Hall and an ally of the Noetic Richard Whately: his liberal credentials extended to him having married his cook. Serving under him were five Church of England clergymen: Tait, now the dean of Carlisle; H.G. Liddell, the headmaster of Westminster, formerly tutor of Christ Church and the co-author of the famous Greek lexicon;[8] the Savilian professor of geometry, Baden Powell; the master of Pembroke, Francis Jeune, who had played an important part in the creation and passage of the 1850 statute; and a fellow of Queen's, G.H.S. Johnson, who had formerly held the chairs of both astronomy and moral philosophy. The seventh member was a lawyer, John Dampier, vice-warden of the Stanneries of Cornwall, appointed to advise the committee on legal issues. The secretary to the committee was Arthur Stanley, fellow of University College, well-known for his broad-church religious views and an enthusiast for German scholarship (see Figure 9.1). His assistant was another fellow of the same college, Goldwin Smith, who would eventually become regius professor of modern history in 1858.[9]

The Oxford commission met for the first time on 19 October and mandated the chairman to send letters to the University and the colleges seeking cooperation. Essentially, information was sought on governance, finance, and teaching. From the beginning, however, the University refused to help, claiming parliament was acting ultra vires. Convocation voted against compliance and, in early 1851, the Hebdomadal Board obtained counsel's opinion that the commission was illegal. The majority of colleges were totally obdurate. Only five colleges (Merton, Lincoln, All Souls, Corpus, St John's, and Pembroke) and three of the surviving halls (St Edmund, St Alban, and Magdalen) provided answers to the commission's questions, and even they refused to hand over documents.[10] Most heads of house followed the nonagenarian president of Magdalen, Martin Routh, who dug in his heels on grounds of conscience: 'The President declines giving information concerning property which he is not conscious of having misused or misapplied; or surrendering Statutes for alteration or revision, which he has sworn to observe, and never directly or indirectly to procure an alteration of, or dispensation from.'[11]

As a result, the commission was forced to rely on the testimony of individual members of Convocation who looked on their endeavours more kindly and were willing to submit written evidence of the state of the University and suggest possible ways forward. Inevitably, the large majority of respondents were critics of the status quo bent on change, but few descended to simple rants. When supplemented by the commission's insider knowledge and the information about college statutes that

---

[8] See p. 321, this volume.
[9] For Smith's account of his role, see his *Reminiscences* (New York, 1911), ch. 7.
[10] Commission (1852), *Report*, p. 1.   [11] Ibid., *Evidence*, p. 334.

FIGURE 9.1 Arthur Penrhyn Stanley, 1815–81, secretary to the 1850 royal commission and professor of ecclesiastical history: Eden Upton Eddis, early 1850s. Stanley studied at Rugby and Balliol before becoming a fellow of University College. A broad churchman, he was a leading light in the University reform party in the mid-nineteenth century.

could be gleaned from the library of the British Museum, the evidence of individuals provided Hinds and his team with more than enough information to comment with authority on all aspects of contemporary Oxford except the University and colleges' finances. There were disagreements over the final recommendations but, thanks to firm chairmanship and the diligence of the secretary and his assistant, a lengthy report was ready to be put before the public in little more than a year. Moreover, the fall of the Russell government in February 1852 and its replacement by a Conservative administration under the earl of Derby did not lead to the report being buried. The Blue Book, as it was known, was published the following May with the new government's blessing and became an instant best-seller, widely commented on in the press. Even the University's venerable Chancellor, the duke of Wellington, felt compelled to give it serious attention. On 14 September 1852, he took the report to bed with him, telling his son Lord Charles Wellesley, who was present, 'I shall never get through it, Charles, but I must work on.' Sadly, the effort overwhelmed the hero of Waterloo and he died in the night.[12]

---

[12] Ward, p. 174.

The report's recommendations addressed a number of the criticisms that had been levelled at Oxford since the first decade of the nineteenth century and fell under three heads.[13] In the first place, the commission demanded a change in the University's governance to make it more representative. Government by a Hebdomadal Board that contained only the heads of house and the Proctors was felt to be an impediment to reform, so the commission suggested its extension, to include all the professors and the most senior of the tutors of all the colleges and halls. This body would now be called Congregation, would debate in English, and would have the power to set up committees called delegacies. It would continue, however, to have to submit new legislation to Convocation for approval, which would still consist of all Oxford MAs on the college books, resident and non-resident.

Secondly, the commission wanted the professoriate to have a much higher profile in order to raise the University's tone. Their numbers were to be increased, they were to be afforded by assistant professors or lecturers, and they were to be given the oversight of the delivery and examination of the curriculum through the creation of four academic boards which they would control. These would look after the higher study of theology (the one higher discipline of any significance at Oxford) and the four undergraduate schools created under the 1850 statute, now to be reduced to three: mental philosophy and philology, jurisprudence and history, and mathematics and physical science. Increasing the number of professors was to be achieved by the simple expedient of appropriating part of the income of the richest colleges and creating a new category of professorial fellow, even if this meant reducing the number of traditional fellowships.

Finally, it was the commission's firm conviction that the colleges should be opened up. At present only twenty-two of the 540 fellowships were said to be open to all comers: twelve at Oriel and ten at Balliol. The result, it was argued, was that talent was concentrated in a handful of colleges and the talented were discouraged from attending Oxford because the chance of obtaining a bursary to pursue postgraduate studies was slim.[14] Fellowships therefore were to 'be thrown open to all Members of the University, wherever born, provided they have taken the degree of Bachelor of Arts, and can produce a proper certificate of character'.[15] The only exceptions were the fellowships at New College and St John's, where it was accepted that there was no harm in retaining modified links with Winchester in the first instance and Merchant Taylors' and the other schools denoted in the founder's will in the second.[16] At the same time, it was recommended that there should be an end to any obligation to take holy orders or pursue a particular field of study, though it was accepted that fellows should continue to be celibate and 'that it would be expedient to modify rather than remove the restriction arising from the possession

---

[13] Commission (1852), *Report*, pp. 256–60, conclusion.   [14] Ibid., pp. 148–53.
[15] Ibid., p. 258.
[16] Ibid., p. 176. The commission recommended that New College fellowships should be open to anyone who had studied at Winchester, whatever college they attended, and that St John's scholarships and fellowships should be open to those who had been at any school in the city of London, not just Merchant Taylors'.

of property'. In addition, having learnt that the value of a fellowship varied across the University and could be as high as £500 per annum and as low as £20, the commission advocated that the differential should be narrowed so that no fellow should receive more than £300 and none less than £150. This was to be done by using excess income or suppressing fellowships to raise the return.[17]

The fifty or so undergraduate fellowships that still existed were to be converted into scholarships and their holders barred from being members of a college's governing body (where they had been). These and all other college scholarships were, in turn, to be opened up to all under the age of 19. Scholarships were to be increased in number; they were to be held for no more than five years; and none was to lead automatically to a fellowship without a fresh examination. Again, it was accepted that some scholarships could remain closed. Jesus could retain its Welsh link, while scholarships attached to particular schools could be preserved provided that the number was cut. Pembroke's scholarships, for instance, reserved for pupils of Abingdon School, were to be reduced from sixteen to five and filled at the rate of one per year. Moreover, 'in default of candidates of sufficient merit from that School, the Scholarship should, for that year, be disposed of like the others, after a free competition'.[18]

The commissioners also aimed to modify the intellectual and social tone of the undergraduate intake. They recommended the introduction of a common matriculation examination, the abolition of gentlemen commoners, and an end to compulsory residence in existing colleges and halls on the grounds that the cost put off many prospective entrants. Instead, 'liberty [was to] be given for the extension of the University, as well by the foundation of [new] Halls as by permitting Members of the University, under due superintendence, to live in private lodgings, without connexion with a College or Hall'.[19] On the other hand, a number of issues raised by critics in the first part of the nineteenth century were passed over with little comment. The commissioners judged the thorny question of the Anglican monopoly outside their competence. They found the curriculum still imperfect, despite the reforms of 1850, but offered no suggestions for further change, and assured the University they had no wish to make Oxford 'a Place of Professional Education, at least not for Law and Medicine'.[20] Above all, they had nothing to say about the relative merits of the tutorial and professorial systems.

This was scarcely surprising in the light of the written evidence, which suggested there was limited opposition to the tutorial system among the resident reformers. The latter pressed for a greater role for the professors, but only Henry Vaughan, regius professor of modern history, argued that tutors might be abolished and instruction left to the professors and private coaches. Balliol's Jowett thought that professorial and tutorial teaching could happily exist side by side, and that greater

---

[17] For the value of a fellowship in a number of colleges in the first half of the nineteenth century, see p. 283, this volume.
[18] Commission (1852), *Report*, p. 251. For Pembroke and Abingdon, see pp. 144 and 225, this volume.
[19] Ibid., p. 257.   [20] Ibid., pp. 54 and 72.

professorial involvement in the undergraduate curriculum could only be of benefit to the tutors, who would have less work to do and be able to devote time to study.[21] The ex-Tractarian turned reformer Mark Pattison, tutor at Lincoln, was even more fulsome in his praise of the potential of the tutorial system. In his opinion, professors should be kept away from undergraduate teaching. Their task was to advance knowledge, not to lecture. Lectures could provide only superficial knowledge and could never be tailored to the needs of the individual student. Tutorials, in contrast, if properly conducted, were the ideal way to train the young mind, which was the real purpose of university education: 'The catechetical lecture which throws the work upon the pupil himself—and which has been sneered at on that very ground as presenting the teacher in a less imposing light than as the dogmatizing deliverer of praelections—is the nearest approach we make to the Socratic principle of education.' Pattison was more than happy to give the German universities their due, accepting that their professors were at the forefront of research. But they lived on such a high intellectual plain that they could not get down to the level of the average undergraduate, and their efforts were wasted. Pattison agreed that the tutorial system in its present form was far from ideal. But it could be easily improved by increasing the number of tutors in each college and selecting them carefully according to their qualifications.[22]

C. The 1854 Act and its Consequences

Although the commission demanded substantial change, its recommendations left much of traditional Oxford intact. It might have been thought that the University would have embraced the report with alacrity. In fact, this was not the case. Within a few days of the publication of the report, fifty-six resident MAs (including three professors and twenty-five past and present tutors) called on the Hebdomadal Board to act. But the board did nothing except appoint a committee in June to consider the commissioners' recommendations, which proceeded in its deliberations with no sense of urgency. Even the fall of the short-lived Derby government at the end of 1852, and its replacement by a coalition ministry under the earl of Aberdeen, failed to spark the Hebdomadal Board into action. As the new government included Gladstone as chancellor of the exchequer, it was doubtless felt that the University would come under little pressure if it failed to give the Blue Book speedy consideration. Gladstone was not liked by the heads because of his liberal voting record on religious issues. Indeed, they had not backed his readoption at the general election of 1852. But he was thought to be solidly against direct parliamentary interference in the University's affairs and assumed to have enough influence to stop Russell and the other Whigs in the new government stirring up trouble (see Figure 9.2).

---

[21] Commission (1852), *Evidence*, pp. 37 and 86–7. On Vaughan and reform, see E.G.W. Bill, *University Reform in Nineteenth-Century Oxford: A Study of Henry Halford Vaughan, 1811–1885* (Oxford, 1973). He had been deprived of his Oriel fellowship in 1842 because he refused to take holy orders.

[22] Commission (1852), *Evidence*, pp. 48–50.

FIGURE 9.2 William Ewart Gladstone, 1809–98, undergraduate of Christ Church, university MP and prime minister. Initially opposed to government interference in Oxford, he eventually came round to the need for parliamentary legislation if reform was to be effected and drew up the 1854 bill. Though no longer the University's MP from 1865, he maintained a close association with Oxford for the rest of his life.

The colleges too did little in the following year to meet the demand that they open up their foundations and improve access. A number of colleges had begun to discuss reform even before the report was published, but supporters of change continually failed to carry the day against strong opposition. Either, as at Queen's, the fellowship was bitterly divided over ending the traditional restrictions, or the reformers' initiatives were stymied by a dyed-in-the-wool head of house. Magdalen voted by a large majority not to give the commissioners any information, but in February 1851 the college set up its own reform committee which, within a few months, had agreed on a number of radical proposals. Not only was the college to start taking commoners again but an emphasis was to be placed on attracting the poorer undergraduate by establishing a special hostel within the college where a community of sixty could live frugally. Martin Routh, however, would have none of it, as one of the reformers, James Mozley, explained in a letter to his sister of 26 April: 'The President has summarily squashed the whole scheme, on the ground of being unstatutable ... His argument is the most ridiculous you can conceive, and this he probably knows; but anything that threatens to interfere with Magdalen as it is, he cannot bear.'[23] Even where a head of house was sympathetic, attempts at reform were contested by vested interests in the wider community, as Jeune of Pembroke discovered. Committed to raising standards in the college from his appointment in 1844, Jeune had, for a long time, been attempting to stop Abingdon boys from automatically claiming a place on the foundation regardless of merit, but to no avail. He was immediately opposed by local Abingdon parents who felt that their sons' birthright was being assailed. Inevitably, then, Jeune and the two other liberal heads, Edward Cradock of Brasenose and Joseph Richards of Exeter, came to the conclusion that the only way forward was to ask parliament to pass an enabling act which would allow reform to be concluded without hindrance, something the commissioners themselves had envisaged would eventually be necessary.[24]

At first, the Aberdeen government fulfilled the Hebdomadal Board's expectations: it did nothing beyond urging the University early in 1853 to turn its attention to reform. By the beginning of 1854, however, it had begun to change its mind in the light of the Hebdomadal Board's refusal to budge. The board finally published its committee's response to the Blue Book in December 1853. This was notable only for supporting the status quo and rejecting virtually all the report's recommendations on the grounds they were destructive of discipline, study, and religion. The committee was willing to add more members of Convocation to the Hebdomadal Board or set up a new intermediate council between the two, allow some college revenue to be used to support professorial education, and permit the establishment of new halls so long as they were under control of a college. But that was all. Among the individual evidence its members received, the views of the Tractarian Pusey were particularly uncompromising. The Blue Book, in his opinion, heralded the end of the collegiate system and its replacement by a German professorial model. A system that trained the mind would be replaced by one that would simply disseminate knowledge which, in few years, would be forgotten. It was a system that he knew from his own experience to be godless and evil. German students lived in lodgings, had no moral or spiritual guidance, were not required to go to church, and had their faith undermined by sceptical lay professors. Pusey was happy for Oxford to embrace curricular reform and give undergraduates a broader intellectual foundation for their future lives. But the University must remain an arm of the Church of England: 'Only let [the foundation] be really solid, and above all, under the control of a firm, unwavering faith, to the glory of God. It will yet be well with Oxford, if she forget not her own motto, "Dominus illuminatio mea".'[25]

Furthermore, by early 1854, Gladstone himself had come to see the merits of legislation. In January 1853 he had to fight another election on his entry into the Aberdeen government.[26] As Gladstone was, in part, responsible for the demise of the Derby administration, a large majority of the heads had been again ready to back an alternative candidate, leading the University's burgess to conclude that

[23] Brockliss, p. 384.   [24] Commission (1852), *Report*, p. 260.   [25] Report (1853), *Evidence*, p. 173.
[26] At that date, on entering government, the new minister had to resign his seat and fight a by-election.

Oxford would never reform itself from above. Gladstone had also found a powerful third group within the University with whom he could, in all conscience, ally. This was the Tutors' Association, which had been formerly created at Oriel in November 1852 as the official mouthpiece of Oxford's college teachers. The Association was opposed to much in the Blue Book, but figures like James Mozley of Magdalen were not prepared to bury their heads in the sand and were willing to contemplate reform. In the course of 1853 and early 1854, the Association produced four pamphlets examining the recommendations in the report. The tutors understandably wished to retain the current tutorial system and the Proctors' control of the examinations, but they did accept compulsory attendance at professorial lectures, the establishment of private, independent halls, and the partial opening up of fellowships. They also called for a completely new Hebdomadal Board with equal representation for the heads of house, the professors and public examiners, and the tutors and resident MAs, each elected by its own constituency. These were people with whom Gladstone felt he could do business, all the more that they were a mixed group containing liberals as well as conservatives. Their views on reforming the Hebdomadal Board were also to the liking of Gladstone's close correspondent, Jeune, who backed the plan, provided that the representatives of the three categories were elected by all the resident senior members.

The Hebdomadal Board put its own very limited proposals to Convocation in February 1854. They were carried, thanks to the support of the non-resident backwoodsmen, but by then Gladstone, assisted by Jowett, was constructing a parliamentary bill which would force reform in both universities. On the one hand, this was intended to end the dominance of the college heads. At Oxford, a Hebdomadal Council, modelled on the tripartite plan supported by Jeune, would take the place of the old Hebdomadal Board, while the power of the dons would be strengthened. Convocation would continue to have the last word, but Congregation would become the University's principal deliberative and electoral body.[27] On the other hand, the bill aimed to prise open the colleges. The Balliol tutor wanted a statute that would remove the collegiate Ancien Regime of Oxford and Cambridge in one fell swoop, and, out of the complex and multifarious arrangements of the past, create a homogeneous body of statutes where those on the foundation owed their places to merit rather than patronage and vested interest. Gladstone was more cautious. Understanding that it was important to include the colleges themselves in the process, he wrote into the draft a clause for the appointment of an executive commission which would discuss with each institution the revision of its statutes in line with the bill's provisions. These too were moderate. Up to half a college's fellowships could remain closed and up to three-quarters could still be reserved for clerics, while scholarships attached to schools were protected as long as the school was sizeable. The most radical suggestion was that fellows in future should

<hr/>

[27] It will be recalled that, under the 1636 Laudian statutes, Congregation, the assembly of the resident MAs, dealt only with day-to-day academic affairs: see p. 147, this volume.

be in residence and that those who did not hold an office should provide evidence that they were engaged in study. Nothing was done in the bill to undermine the traditional role of the colleges beyond allowing new private halls to set up under licence from the Vice-Chancellor.

The bill was introduced to the Commons on 17 March and immediately encountered opposition inside and outside parliament. Conservatives thought Armageddon had arrived, while the more doctrinaire members of the commission and their supporters such as Stanley, Baden Powell, and Liddell found the bill a travesty. Oxford's Hebdomadal Board would have none of it and asked Convocation to petition against. On 31 March, however, the heads carried the day by only two votes, which suggested the tide was strongly with Gladstone. Attempts to add wrecking amendments to the bill as it passed through the Commons and Lords, if initially appearing to explode the initiative, similarly proved a damp squib, and the bill that was eventually enacted on 7 August was essentially the one that Gladstone had drafted. There was only one major alteration, but this was significant and unexpected. On 22 June, the Unitarian Heywood, who had set the reform ball rolling four years before, moved that a clause be added to the bill abolishing religious subscription for undergraduates. Although this was not part of the 1850 commission's recommendations, the amendment was enthusiastically supported in the Commons. Much to most people's surprise, it was also passed by the Lords, where the leader of the opposition, the earl of Derby, although now Oxford's new Chancellor, declined to make a stand, some said because he was anxious to get to the races.[28] As a result, when the bill became law, Oxford and Cambridge were no longer confessionally closed. Nonconformists of all stripes could take an undergraduate degree.

The Oxford commission appointed to oversee the revision of the college statutes was headed by the liberal peer the earl of Ellesmere, while its four other members were a mix of high-church lawyers and clerics. All but two of the five were old members of Christ Church. Continuity with the 1850 commission was retained through one of the five commissioners being the Queen's fellow, G.H.S Johnson, now dean of Wells, and its secretary being Goldwin Smith. Each college was asked to revise its statutes in the light of the new Act, then submit its efforts to the commission for approval. In the case of Exeter, Corpus, and Lincoln, where the governing bodies had already begun to draw up new statutes before the appointment of the commission, the necessary changes were in place as early as 1855. Elsewhere, all but one of the other colleges successfully compounded with the commissioners in 1857 and 1858. The one exception was St John's, where the president and fellows refused point-blank to cooperate and eventually had statutes imposed upon them in 1861.

---

[28] Derby, twenty years before, had supported the abolition of the religious tests, so his behaviour was consistent.

As each college was allowed to reform its statutes in a way that retained some continuity with its past, there was none of the homogeneity that Jowett had hoped for. There was only one point of commonality. None of the colleges was willing to go beyond the terms of the 1854 Act and open their fellowships to non-Anglicans, though Johnson, for one, was keen that they should. On the other hand, most colleges, on their own initiative, went further than the Act required in other ways. In the majority of instances, all fellowships, not just half, were thrown open, election based on performance in an examination, and a much smaller proportion reserved for clerics than envisaged. Lincoln was somehow permitted to insist that all but two of its twelve fellows took orders after ten years in post, but other colleges were happy to promote laicization. Only half of the fellows of University College and Merton had to be, henceforth, in orders, while Balliol waived the restriction altogether and even allowed some fellows to marry. Some colleges too could be generous. Magdalen, freed from the incubus of Routh by his long-expected death in 1854 at the age of 99, offered to use some of its great wealth to promote the cause of science in the University. Under its new 1857 statutes, ten of its forty fellowships were to be temporarily suppressed so that resources could be released to fund four Waynflete professorships in moral and metaphysical philosophy, chemistry, mineralogy, and geology, while every first, fifth, and tenth fellowship to fall vacant was to be reserved for mathematicians and scientists.[29]

It was only in the case of the handful of colleges historically associated with a particular region or school that some fellowships remained closed after 1860. But even here, vested interests were not as well preserved as the 1854 Act seemed to permit. At New College, where the foundation was now divided into forty fellows and thirty scholars in line with the recommendation of the Blue Book that insisted that all fellows should be graduates, Winchester's rights were seriously curtailed. Although, under the new statutes, half the fellowships remained closed, these were not necessarily monopolized by Wykehamists. The closed fellowships were reserved both for those who had attended Winchester School and those who had been undergraduates at the college. In that its scholarships were to be thrown open to all and it was understood that New College would start taking commoners, there was no guarantee that its fellowships would be filled with Wykehamists. At Christ Church, similarly, Westminster's rights were greatly reduced. Under Dean Gaisford the college had been totally uncooperative towards the 1850 commission on the grounds that Christ Church had never had any statutes so had nothing to reform. But in 1855 Gaisford died and the crown replaced him with one of the 1850 commissioners and most fervent supporters of reform, Henry Liddell, who had no qualms about hammering out a settlement with his successors (see Figure 9.3). Although the erstwhile headmaster of Westminster, Liddell felt no compunction in cutting the school down to size. The 101 studentships of the original foundation

---

[29] Lincoln also tried and failed to insert a heresy clause!

FIGURE 9.3 Henry Liddell, 1811–98, lexicographer, member of the 1850 royal commission, dean of Christ Church and father of Alice: artist unknown. Throughout the forty years in which he was at the centre of Oxford life, Liddell remained committed to opening up the colleges and increasing the number and authority of the university professoriate. As dean of Christ Church, however, he was unwilling to see the traditional power of the canons reduced.

were reduced to seventy-seven and divided into sixteen fellowships and sixty-one undergraduate scholarships. The fellowships were open to all, and only twenty-one scholarships reserved for the London school. That said, Liddell's reforming zeal had its limits. Under its first ever statutes promulgated in 1858, the college remained an anomaly because its governing body consisted solely of the dean and the cathedral canons. In reforming the college, Liddell did not propose, and the commissioners did not insist, that any role should be given to the fellows beyond allowing four of the most senior to take part in electing new members of the foundation. The fellows became part of the governing body only by an Act of Parliament in 1867, after three years of bitter agitation, which saw the discontented fellows appealing their cause to the University's Chancellor, the members of the 1854 commissions, the national press, and ultimately the Lords and Commons.[30]

[30] Of the eight Christ Church scholarships which fell vacant each year, three, for the next twenty years, were to be given for mathematics and natural science. At St John's, all the fellowships were opened but twenty-eight out of the thirty-three scholarships were reserved for Merchant Taylors' and other schools privileged by the founder.

D. The 1871 Act, the Cleveland Commission, and the Selborne Commission

The Oxford which emerged from the work of the 1854 commissioners was a much more meritocratic institution than the University of the age of Newman. Yet it had not undergone the revolution that its critics inside and outside had dreamed of effecting. As Pattison emphasized in his posthumous memoirs, the reform was partial:

> I do not underrate the value of what was done by the Executive Commission of 1854. The abolition of close fellowships opened the colleges to an amount of talent and energy hitherto unknown them. They had hitherto been peopled by a class of inferior men—clergymen waiting for college livings, and going through a feeble routine, which was dignified by the name of tuition to fill up the time till a living dropped in...But this sweeping away of local claims was nearly all the good that the Commission of 1854 effected.[31]

Understandably, their appetites whetted, the reformers looked for more. At first they made little progress, for it was conservatives who dominated elections to the new Hebdomadal Council in its early years. As the new college statutes protected vested interests, Oxford's character could not be changed overnight. The conservatives were not completely obdurate. The Blue Book had backed the idea of providing the science professors with decent facilities, and, in December 1854, Convocation reversed its earlier decision and agreed to build what became the University Museum, which would open in 1860.[32] But generally the conservatives hoped they could draw a line under further change. Even when one of the leading reformers, Jeune, became Vice-Chancellor in 1858, he could do nothing in his four years of office to address the many outstanding issues. Gradually, however, as more and more fellows were elected under the new dispensation, the party of reform gathered strength and, by the mid-1860s, the current of reform was once more running swiftly. Stanley, who had resigned his fellowship in 1850, came back to Oxford in 1856 as regius professor of ecclesiastical history; Goldwin Smith became regius professor of modern history two years later; Pattison was elected rector of Lincoln by a single vote in 1861; while Jowett, defeated when he had stood against Robert Scott in 1854, finally became master of Balliol in 1870.

The two most contentious issues in the 1860s and 1870s were subscription and the use of college endowments. Both were unfinished business. The Anglican monopoly had been all but swept away at undergraduate level in 1854 but, to the liberals' chagrin, heads of house, college fellows, and university professors and officials still had to be members of the established church.[33] Similarly, the fellowship reform had

---

[31] M. Pattison, *Memoirs* (London, 1885), p. 304.   [32] See pp. 489–91, this volume.

[33] Subscription could still, it seems, be demanded of scholars. The future regius professor of civil law, James Bryce, was asked to subscribe when he became a scholar at Trinity in 1857 but refused. When he became a fellow of Oriel in 1862 he refused to take holy communion.

only partly addressed the long-standing problem of the idle don. The fellowships might now be filling up with clever young laymen, but there was no guarantee they would be any more productive than their clerical forebears. Elected for life and not subject to review, there was no mechanism to stop them frittering away their time or using their college post to support the early stages of a professional career in London. Indeed, some reformers felt that deploying college endowments to support fellowships was not the best use of the money. In the light of Britain's relatively poor showing at the Paris Exhibition of 1867 and the Prussian annihilation of France three years later, there was a growing feeling that some of the colleges' wealth should be released to fund expansion in university science teaching.[34] Understandably, advance on either issue was impossible without further recourse to outside assistance. Conservatives had to be forced to surrender the vestiges of the Anglican monopoly, while college governing bodies had to be made to reveal the secrets of their finances, if any constructive reform was to ensue. The 1850 commission had met with a total blank in this regard, and college accounts remained as hidden from public gaze as the statutes before the 1840s.

The campaign to end subscription completely began as early as 1863 when Pleydell-Bouverie, the son of the earl of Radnor who had first attacked the Anglican monopoly thirty years before, unsuccessfully introduced a private bill in the Commons abolishing the surviving tests in the two universities. Although this and other bills in the ensuing years got nowhere, leading Goldwin Smith in 1866 to resign his regius professorship in disgust, the reformers kept trying and turned their attack on tests into a nationwide campaign with nonconformist support. Eventually, the great Liberal triumph in the general election of 1868 put success within their reach. Gladstone, author of the 1854 Act, who had been bounced into accepting Heywood's amendment, was initially unwilling to back further change, and as a good son of the high church claimed he would 'rather see Oxford level with the ground, than its religion regulated in the manner which would please Bishop Colenso'.[35] After 1865, however, he was no longer an Oxford University MP, and as a Peelite Conservative who had eventually moved over to the Liberals, he was a member of a party largely dependent on nonconformist votes and anxious to clip the wings of the Church of England. In 1871, now prime minister, he agreed to pilot yet another bill through parliament in the hope that its terms could be kept as moderate as possible. The Conservative leader in the Lords, the marquess of Salisbury, who was also Oxford's new Chancellor in place of the defunct Derby, attempted to soften the blow by putting forward various amendments that would

---

[34] A parliamentary select committee on scientific instruction in 1868 concluded that science teaching was being held back in the grammar schools because of its low status at the universities. The French were even more convinced that the Prussian victory was founded on its system of higher education. In fact, at this stage of industrialization, there is little evidence that there was any connection between economic and military might and the quality of science education.

[35] Mallet, iii. 332. John Colenso was the first Anglican bishop of Natal. He was persona non grata with orthodox Anglicans for defending native polygamy, contesting eternal damnation, and subjecting the Old Testament to historical and literary criticism.

have excluded college heads from the bill's provisions and required that tutors had to promise not to teach anything contrary to Scripture. The amendments, however, were voted down in the Commons and the bill passed into law. Thereafter, only candidates for theology degrees and professors of theology had to subscribe.[36]

Oxford broad churchmen, like Stanley and Jowett, were cock-a-hoop. They expected further reforms and were not disappointed. The Oxford and Cambridge Tests Act of 1871 had only just been promulgated when Gladstone, always keen that money should be properly spent, announced his intention of appointing a royal commission to look at the financial state of the two universities, the one aspect that the 1850 commission had failed to review effectively. The commission, set up in January 1872, was headed by one of the country's largest landowners, the duke of Cleveland, and had only two Oxford representatives, Bartholomew Price, fellow of Pembroke and secretary of the University Press,[37] and its strongly Liberal secretary, Charles Roundell of Merton. The Cleveland commission was tasked only with gathering information but it was clearly a prelude to future reforms. Unlike its predecessor, the commission met little opposition, for both Vice-Chancellors, prompted by Gladstone, promised complete cooperation. At Oxford, where Liddell now held the office, only New College and Lincoln refused to surrender their accounts in the form required. As a result, the commissioners had no difficulty building up a picture of income and expenditure over the ten years preceding its appointment. When the commission reported in 1874, Oxford conservatives queried some of the figures but the general findings were unchallengeable. In the first place there was a huge disparity in the combined income of the different colleges. Christ Church with £57,000 and Magdalen with £39,000 a year topped the table, while Balliol received under £11,000 and Trinity only £6,000. Christ Church and Balliol, however, had the same number of undergraduates on their books. Secondly, as everyone knew, the colleges were much better endowed than the University. While the University drew income from 7,683 acres, the colleges and halls combined boasted landed property of 184,764 acres and double the University's holdings in stock (£26,400 against £13,000). The University had a total income of only £32,000 while the colleges and halls enjoyed ten times as much: their property alone was bringing in £270,000. Both universities were judged to be using their limited funds wisely. Oxford's fifty-one professors and readers were maintained for a mere £25,000, but college fellows and heads of house were absorbing five times as much.[38]

---

[36] For the act, see *Enactments in parliament specially concerning the universities of Oxford and Cambridge … and the colleges of Winchester, Eton & Westminster*, ed. L. L. Shadwell (4 vols; OHS; Oxford, 1912), iv. 14–18.

[37] Nicknamed 'Bat', he was immortalized in Carroll's reworking of 'Twinkle, twinkle, little star …' in *Alice in Wonderland* (1865).

[38] Commission (1873), *Report*, pp. 26, 28, 29, 34, 46–7, and 201 (table). Magdalen had the largest amount of landed property, 27,000 acres. The five surviving halls contributed only £1,300 to the endowment income of the colleges and halls. New Inn and St Alban Hall had no endowment of any kind. The income figures have been largely confirmed by recent research. Magdalen's income in 1871–2 was £36,823 (of which £33,458 came from endowment).

In the light of the figures, reformers were convinced that some of the colleges' resources could be shifted towards the University without undue harm or pain, especially as the commissioners predicted that college endowment income would rise over the coming twenty years. The commissioners reported that the colleges, for the most part, administered their properties efficiently but they were confident that the return would soon be higher. This was because the colleges were in the middle of reviewing their tenancy arrangements. From the late sixteenth century, the colleges had leased their lands under a system of beneficial leases whereby tenants, in return for being totally responsible for the upkeep of the property, held a lease for a few years on a low rent, then paid a large fine to renew. While this had proved a stable and lucrative form of management in the seventeenth and eighteenth centuries and had done much to raise fellows' income, it was no longer felt to be efficient in the Victorian era as the landlord effectively lost control of the land. By the mid-nineteenth century, the preferred form of land management had shifted to rack-rent, where the landowner leased out a property at its market value and squeezed more rent from his tenants by making improvements. In the case of Oxford and Cambridge colleges, however, transferring to rack-rent had been difficult while they remained subject to the restrictive clauses of the Elizabethan Acts of Parliament governing the management of their property, and barely any had made the transition.[39] It was only from 1860 that they were released from the burden of the past. Under two new Acts of Parliament in 1858 and 1860, the two universities and their colleges were allowed to sell land for the first time, benefit from the Victorian housing boom by offering ninety-year leases to property developers, and borrow money to improve the quality of their farms or erect new buildings.[40] Most colleges leapt at the chance to modernize and, by the time of the Cleveland Commission, the transfer was in full swing. The Commission estimated that, in twenty years, the colleges would have increased the total return by £80,000, some two and a half times the University's entire income in the early 1870s.[41]

By the time the Cleveland Commission reported, a Conservative administration was in power and Oxford traditionalists must have hoped that its findings would not be acted upon. But Disraeli, the new prime minister, was no reactionary and appreciated the need to foster the sciences. He therefore introduced a parliamentary bill to set up a third royal commission on Oxford and Cambridge in February 1876 to promote further reform. As a sop to Conservative opinion, the Oxford commission was filled with moderates. Although its chairman, Lord Selborne, had been Gladstone's lord chancellor in the previous Liberal administration, he was an Anglo-catholic like his leader, while all of his six-man team, bar the All Souls

---

[39] Under the Acts of 1571 and 1572, agricultural property could not be leased for more than twenty-one years and urban property for forty. The first Oxford college to move to rack-rents was supposedly Oriel in the time of Provost Copleston: Pattison, *Memoirs*, pp. 71–2.

[40] Shadwell, *Enactments*, iii. 247–78 and 301–11. They were not allowed to hold the proceeds from sales. This was paid into a Bank of England account, which was looked after by a government committee.

[41] Commission (1873), *Report*, p. 32. The Cambridge colleges were expected to be only some £20,000 richer by the 1890s, presumably because they were more advanced in moving to rack-rent.

professor of international law, Mountague Bernard, were open or closet Tories.[42] This, though, was to be a commission with executive powers from the beginning and would work to an agenda. The commission was to be empowered to revise both the universities' and their colleges' statutes in the light of the 1871 Act and the current concern over the idleness of many senior members and the inappropriate use of collegiate wealth. How this was to be done was to be left to the commissioners. Unsurprisingly, the bill's vagueness pleased neither the right nor the left. Conservatives wanted a bill that would secure the survival of some clerical fellowships, while radical Liberals, such as Gladstone's erstwhile chancellor of the exchequer, Robert Lowe, a quondam fellow of Magdalen, wanted it written into the legislation that college endowments were to be expropriated. The bill's passage, therefore, was slow, and a new one had to be introduced the following year, which eventually received royal assent in August 1877.[43]

Within the University, there were many in both the liberal and high-church camps who hoped much good would come out of the commission. Above all, the Vice-Chancellor and the Hebdomadal Council knew what it wanted Selborne to deliver: extra money. With the scientists well ensconced in the new University Museum, Vice-Chancellor Liddell, in 1872, had set up a delegacy to improve the facilities for the arts professors by commissioning a new building for the University Schools which could accommodate the growing number of arts undergraduates who had to be examined.[44] Four years later, the task was given to the up-and coming Oxford 'Jacobethan' architect T. G. Jackson, and the foundations laid for the new Examination Schools on the High Street, which were finished six years later at the cost of £100,000.[45] Liddell, too, was anxious to expand the number of academic staff on the University's payroll. In 1873, he took advantage of a liberal majority on the Hebdomadal Council to set up a committee to consider how the professoriate might be increased and better endowed. Four years later, in spring 1877, and under Vice-Chancellor Sewell of New College, the University published its wish list. If possible it wanted to appoint a further fourteen professors and eighteen readers (more than two-thirds of the current number). To fulfil its ambitions, the University needed to increase its annual income by £15,600, half again of what it already received.

On 22 October 1877, the commission met for the first time in Oxford's Clarendon Hotel, and, like its 1850 predecessor, invited anyone who had thoughts on Oxford's long-term future to submit his views. This time it took both oral and written evidence. In the ensuing months all the old arguments were rehearsed. Some professors, like Thomas Fowler of Corpus Christi, the University's professor of

---

[42] There was some change in personnel over time. Selborne resigned to join the new Liberal government on 28 September 1880, and was replaced in the chair by Mountague Bernard.

[43] Shadwell, *Enactments*, iv. 65–92.

[44] In 1871, there were some 1,700 undergraduates in residence. Large numbers taking written exams could not be comfortably located in the old schools.

[45] For Jackson, his style and his Oxford buildings, see pp. 444–7, this volume.

logic, wanted a definite move towards a professorial regime, but the tutors, led by Jowett, held firm to the status quo. They were happy to help the University out financially and could accept a much greater role for the professoriate in under-graduate teaching but wanted the tutorial system to remain largely intact.[46] In April 1878, the commission published its own proposals in the *Oxford University Gazette*, the University's recently founded authorized journal of record, and came down firmly on the side of Jowett. The commissioners were sympathetic towards the professors and wanted to improve their position, but anticipated the transfer of a mere 1.5 per cent of college revenue to their maintenance, which would supposedly allow the creation of a further eight chairs and nine readerships. Furthermore, they were adamant that the tutorial system would remain at the heart of Oxford, insisting that they were 'unable to adopt the views of those who would desire to transfer to the University the whole, or the chief part, of the teaching work now done by the colleges'.[47]

Under the 1877 Act, the University and colleges had been permitted to undertake the revision of their statutes themselves and submit them to the commission for approval. Secure in the knowledge that their independence was no longer threat-ened, most of the colleges proceeded to do so. Negotiations with the commissioners were often long and tortuous over precise details, but, with the exception of Lincoln, all received new statutes during the course of 1880 to 1883.[48] Although Jowett still moaned that they lacked homogeneity, these new statutes were much more uniform than the ones drawn up following the 1854 Act. Building on reforms that had been earlier undertaken or broached at University College, Balliol, Merton, and New College between 1869 and 1873, fellows on the foundation were thereafter divided into two categories: official and ordinary. Official fellows were college officers, including tutors. They could be elected without examination; they could take a wife provided some were always unmarried and lived in; and they could usually hold the office for most, if not all, of their working life, and receive a pension for long service when they put it down. Ordinary fellows were fellows by examina-tion or prize fellows, as they were often called: to ensure that they did not treat the fellowship as a sinecure, they were required to demit after seven years or at least face re-election, and, in some statutes, to encourage their early departure, they still had to be celibate. There was also in most colleges, to satisfy the commissioners' desire that university staff had a college association if possible, a third category of professorial fellow created whose salary was paid by the University Chest. All official and ordinary fellows were entitled to a basic college stipend and free board and lodging (if they were single), and all could be laymen provided divine service in the college chapel was not compromised.

The new statutes specified both the maximum size of the fellowship and the maximum number of official fellows each college could have. Where fellowships

---

[46] Commission (1881), *Evidence*, esp. pp. 91–7 (Fowler).

[47] *OUG*, 26 Apr. 1878, viii. 341–4. The *OUG* has been published continually since 1870.

[48] Lincoln's statutes were not restructured because the new ones drawn up by Pattison as rector were struck down in the House of Lords on appeal by the college visitor, the bishop of Lincoln.

were small, this was usually half of the total, with the result that, across the University, the number of fellows maintained solely to pursue research was considerably reduced. Only in the case of All Souls was it accepted that prize fellows would continue to be in a large majority. All Souls was the one Oxford college that had never admitted commoners in the post-Reformation era. It had remained a college of foundationers and graduates, apart from the student servitors who had looked after the fellows' needs in the sixteenth and seventeenth centuries. The 1854 commissioners had been content to allow the college to remain a graduate institution chiefly for lawyers and it had not been forced to take undergraduates. They had insisted, however, that its fellowship examination be open only to candidates holding a First, and be an examination in law and history. Their successors under the 1877 Act, mostly lawyers themselves, were just as accommodating. In return for agreeing to support five professors and three readers, the college was allowed to remain primarily a sanctuary for prize fellows in law and history. Of the twenty-eight fellows by examination provided for under the 1881 statutes only seven were to hold renewable fellowships. But many of the others were able to remain on the books long after they had demitted. In order to retain its traditional links with the great and good, All Souls was allowed to invent two new categories of fellow: up to three non-stipendiary fellows elected for their distinction, and up to twelve receiving a stipend, to be drawn from former prize fellows whose term had come to an end but whom the college felt it was in its interest to keep on.

By the early 1880s, the commissioners had also secured agreement on a new set of university statutes which aimed to enhance the position of the professoriate without harming the colleges. The new statutes, promulgated in 1882, had little to say about the professors as teachers beyond insisting that they deliver forty-two lectures a year. Initial attempts to go further and establish a mechanism to police professorial assiduity foundered in face of opposition from the Hebdomadal Council and the national press, *The Times* declaring that the commissioners' original proposals were 'restrictions that the humblest *privatdocent* in a German university would repudiate as fatal alike to his independence and self-respect'.[49] The commissioners, however, did manage to bring the professors into the examining system by taking the appointment of examiners out of the hands of the Vice-Chancellor and Proctors and giving it to boards of study, a new institution established in 1870 on which the professors sat ex officio. The commissioners, in addition, found a way of ensuring that all professors and readers in future would be properly rewarded for their labour, by the establishment of the Common University Fund to which each college would make an annual contribution out of its endowment. Initially, this was devised as a flat rate contribution of 2 per cent, but from 1885 it was changed to a graduated tax and, by the end of the century, the richer colleges, such as Magdalen and Christ Church, faced a levy of 10 per cent on income over

---

[49] *HUO*, vii. 89.

£10,000.[50] The graduated tax, it was hoped, would provide the extra cash for expansion. Thereby, without undermining the tutorial system in any significant way, the commissioners felt they had developed an effective mechanism that would allow the University to extend the range of its teaching and ultimately develop its profile as a research institution.

E. Extension, the Foundation of Keble, and the Women Question

The Selborne Commission took evidence on many different aspects of Oxford in the 1870s. It felt no need to take further action, however, over one recommendation of the 1852 Blue Book which had not been immediately acted on—extension. In that regard there had been a broad enough consensus on the need to push forward for change to have been effected long before the commission was constituted. Extension was a policy which found favour among all groups in the University—the broad-church liberals, their Tractarian opponents, the evangelicals, and even the old guard. The evangelicals had petitioned the Hebdomadal Board as early 1845 that some way might be found of reducing the cost of an Oxford education so that less wealthy undergraduates might attend, while the Tractarians had long supported the establishment of a new college where poorer students could live frugally under a monastic discipline. Indeed, the Oriel fellow and vicar of St Mary's, Charles Marriott, known as Pusey's alter ego, was occupied from the late 1840s until his death in 1858 in trying to raise the money to build such a college.[51] Where the groups differed was over their motives. The conservative authors of the University's 1853 report on the Blue Book hoped to find room at Oxford for the indigent sons of the 'higher classes', the poorer gentry and clergy, who would be encouraged to enter the church and take Anglicanism to the urban masses.[52] The opponents of the status quo were more ambitious. Pusey, in his evidence to the University's commissioners, wanted to find space for the sons of professional families who had fallen on hard times, irrespective of their future career: 'At our Grammar-schools there are many already, who, if well trained, might render good service to our church and country, but whose parents are too "poor" to maintain them at the present average of expense.'[53] The liberals agreed, and specifically looked to attract the sons of the 'middle classes' who were destined by their fathers for a wide variety of careers that Oxford graduates had traditionally never embraced. In the liberals' opinion, there was a huge untapped market in the form of future solicitors, surgeons, general practitioners, factory managers, and engineers, who would be enticed to Oxford if they could only escape residing in a college. Such people would benefit greatly from an

---

[50] *Statutes made for the University of Oxford, and for the colleges and halls therein, by the University of Oxford Commissioners* (Oxford, 1882), pp. 108–14. The establishment of a Common University Fund had been anticipated in the 1877 Act: Shadwell, *Enactments*, iv. 72 and 75.

[51] Commission (1852), *Report*, appendix E, pp. 55–6: address and report.

[52] Report (1853), *Report*, pp. 27–8.   [53] Ibid., *Evidence*, pp. 81–2.

Oxford education, but they had hitherto not been sent to the University for financial and religious reasons, and because their fathers feared they would be put off their intended careers once they mixed with the upper classes.[54]

The 1850 commissioners had strongly backed extension and recommended that the University should welcome non-collegiate students who could lodge in the town. The 1854 Oxford and Cambridge Act, however, required the University only to pass a statute allowing the creation of new private halls under the licence of the Vice-Chancellor. The liberals, who supported the former option, were initially disheartened, and it was the evangelicals and Tractarians who seized the day, the evangelicals establishing Litton's Hall, with the intention of providing a home for like-minded protestants of all confessions, and the Tractarians attempting to revivify two existing but all but empty halls, St Alban and St Edmund, as a haven for poor scholars.[55] As neither initiative survived into the 1860s, reformers of all stamps in the University came together in 1865 to look again at the problem. A meeting at Oriel in November led to the creation of an ad hoc intercollegiate committee, which empowered subcommittees to look at four different ways forward: the Tractarians' desire for a new large-scale college or hall; the absorption of poorer students into existing societies by offering them cut-price rates; the liberals' lodging house option; and, most radical of all, Goldwin Smith's plan to establish provincial affiliates where less affluent students might be part of Oxford at a distance.

Over the next few years, all four schemes were hotly debated inside and outside the University, the liberals once again taking their cause to parliament. In March 1867, William Ewart, MP for Dumfries, who had tried to amend the 1854 Act to include the proposal, presented a private bill in the Commons permitting Oxford and Cambridge undergraduates to live in lodgings. With a Conservative administration in power under Derby, the bill was inevitably lost, but a parliamentary select committee was appointed to look into the case for extension; it sat in the following July and allowed the University's liberals, such as Jowett and the professor of chemistry, Sir Benjamin Brodie, to rehearse their arguments at Westminster.[56] The appointment of the select committee appears to have jolted the University into action. So too did the knowledge that Balliol, on Jowett's prompting, intended to go it alone and establish a college hostel where a new category of prize exhibitioner could live cheaply while receiving free tuition.[57] On the eve of the long vacation of 1867, Council gave notice that it had been won over to permitting some form of non-collegiate residence. The ensuing legislation was hotly contested and took until June of the following year to pass through Convocation. But in its eventual form it was more radical than Council had originally proposed. Rather than simply allowing undergraduates with a college affiliation to live in lodgings

---

[54] Commission (1852), *Evidence*, pp. 19, 42–3, 46–7, and 53.

[55] Litton's Hall was called after E. A. Litton, a former fellow of Oriel, who promoted the scheme.

[56] Select Committee (1867), *Evidence*, pp. 3, 7, 11, and 12.

[57] This was functioning by 1870. Balliol christened the hostel Balliol Hall. It was located in St Giles, on the site, until 2013, of the Mathematical Institute.

(an inevitable development anyway if numbers were to rise and no new buildings were to be erected), the university statute permitted the residence in the town of non-collegiates. The liberals had got what they wanted.[58]

The Delegacy for Licensing Lodgings, a two-man committee appointed by Council to examine the sufficiency of would-be non-collegiates, was soon in business, and by the end of the academic year 1868/9, forty-three had been matriculated, a third nonconformists. Thereafter, their number slowly grew, and in the 1890s and 1900s there were regularly some 200 non-collegiates in residence in any one year, a larger group than all but one or two colleges could muster. By 1914, 4,000 had passed through the University. But in various ways the experiment did not have the results some of its supporters had expected. Those who looked to turn Oxford into a professorial university hoped that the non-collegiates would be the thin end of the wedge, in that they would be forced to attend professorial lectures for their tuition and their results in Schools would show up the deficiency of the tutorial system. Most non-collegiates, however, studied for a pass degree rather than honours and relied on buying-in private tuition for their instruction, while the University, from 1877, pulled them into the tutorial system, albeit imperfectly, by appointing two lecturers to help them pass Responsions and supervise their studies. Moreover, during Jowett's Vice-Chancellorship, 1882–6, the University decided that the non-collegiates should no longer be an amorphous group but have a physical home, and funds were found to build the delegacy a headquarters, 84 High Street, which was equipped with a reading room consisting of 6,000 volumes and space for a JCR.[59] Long before this, the non-collegiates had demonstrated that they wanted to join the collegiate university rather than act as standard-bearers for an alternative model. Almost immediately on their creation as a group, they established a common identity by setting up a social centre, which, from 1874, was called St Catherine's Club after its temporary location in St Catherine's Hall, a private house opposite the Clarendon Building. The name stuck, though the club went bankrupt in 1881–2, and it was under the banner of St Catherine that the non-collegiates from 1874 went out to do battle for their collective honour in intercollegiate sports competitions.[60]

The transformation of the non-collegiates into a quasi-college was not surprising, for the wider movement for extension from the late 1860s, far from subverting the residential university, gave it a new lease of life. Attempts by individuals, and there were several, to establish small private halls in the late nineteenth century were always abortive.[61] The existing traditional university halls also all but disappeared in the following years. Magdalen Hall, the most populous in its new

---

[58] The liberals recognized that extension would only partly solve the problem of middle-class access. Jowett, for one, while not taking up Goldwin's idea of provincial affiliates, was happy to sponsor the foundation of University College, Bristol, in 1876.

[59] For the establishment of college JCRs, see pp. 457–8, this volume. From 1892 the non-collegiates also comprised a handful of pupil teachers (usually local men) who were allowed to study for an Oxford BA while attending the newly established Oxford University Day Training College.

[60] In the 1900s, the non-collegiates petitioned to become a college. For intercollegiate sporting contests, see pp. 453–6, this volume.

[61] In 1911 there were three private halls in existence: Marcon's, Pope's, and Parker's. They had thirty-one undergraduates between them.

FIGURE 9.4 Keble Chapel, interior. Designed by William Butterfield and ready for use in 1876, the chapel in its ornamentation and seating plan was unequivocal in its High Anglican allegiance. Holman Hunt's *The Light of the World* was placed in the chapel only in 1892.

buildings on Cat Street, began a second life as Hertford College from 1874, due to the munificence of the merchant banker T. C. Baring, who, by 1881, had provided it with a large enough endowment to support eighteen fellowships and thirty scholarships.[62] Its sisters, on the other hand, were judged economically unviable by the 1877 commissioners and were ordered to be subsumed in one of the colleges. Over the next two decades, when their principals died, St Alban Hall was taken over by Merton, New Inn by Balliol, and St Mary by Oriel. Only St Edmund Hall survived into the twentieth century. However, the belief pushed by the Tractarians' subcommittee in its report of 1866—that it would be possible to establish a new type of hall or college which would suit the modest pocket and extend access—soon bore spectacular fruit, and demonstrated that Oxford had no need to ditch the collegiate system in order to attract a broader clientele, even if it was not quite the clientele liberals had in mind.

The subcommittee's report reactivated Marriott's plan and suggested the creation of a college for a hundred undergraduates dedicated to frugal living and with a mixed social tone. The death, in the same year, of one of the leading lights of the Tractarian party, John Keble, another former Oriel fellow, provided the occasion to take the scheme forward even before the first non-collegiates had matriculated. Anglicanism's new high-church phalanx decided that the best memorial to their

371

---

[62] S. G. Hamilton, *Hertford* (London, 1903), ch. 8.

dead brother would be a college, and set up a committee, headed by Archbishop Longley, to raise £50,000 by subscription to turn the dream into reality.[63] Land was bought from St John's late in 1867 for £7,000, a building was commissioned to the design of the high-church gothic architect William Butterfield, and the foundation stone of the new Keble College was laid the following April. Two years later, the college was officially opened. Initially the college had no permanent chapel, library, and hall, but its low fees, no frills and budget services (rooms had standardized furniture, all meals had to be taken in common, and tips were forbidden) immediately attracted applicants, and in its first year in business many had to be turned away.

Keble was a completely new type of residential institution. It had a charter from 1870, thanks to Gladstone, and was incorporated into the University as a college in the following year, though not without opposition. But it was not a college in the traditional sense. There was no endowment, so Keble had no foundation supporting a fellowship and its income was drawn totally from its undergraduate commoners. Yet nor was it a traditional hall, for its warden, who looked after the day-to-day running of the college, was appointed by an external committee and not by the Vice-Chancellor. In addition, *pace* the secularizing intentions of the 1854 and 1871 Acts, it was an institution dedicated to a particular form of Anglicanism. Keble, according to its royal charter, was 'a College wherein sober living and high culture of the mind may be combined with Christian training based upon the principles of the Church of England'.[64] Its sobriety was ostentatiously paraded in its buildings, which were constructed of brick rather than conventional stone, and eschewed the traditional staircase for the long corridor. Its high-church Anglicanism was emphasized by its extremely ornamented chapel, opened in 1876 with a Pusey sermon, where all the seating deliberately faced the altar (see Figure 9.4). Keble accepted no non-Anglicans until the 1930s and expected its undergraduates to attend chapel twice on Sundays and regularly during the week. It was a new confessional monolith in a non-denominational, secularized university. But it had no shortage of students. By 1890 it was the fourth largest college, with 150 on its books; in 1911 it had 190, third only to New College and Christ Church. Its junior members never numerically outstripped the non-collegiates but they ran them close.

Keble's first decade coincided with a growing debate in Oxford over the rights and wrongs of finding space within the University for an entirely different excluded group. The first generation of reformers would never have thought of opening up Oxford to the female sex. But from the 1860s, the rights of women as well as men found their way onto the radical political agenda, and feminists both in Britain and on the continent began to demand female access to higher education. The relatively new University of London and its affiliated provincial colleges had no problem with

---

[63] On the old high-church wing of the Church of England that the Anglo-Catholic Tractarians replaced, see p. 211, this volume.

[64] *HUO*, vii. 744.

admitting women to their classes and, as early as 1878, London was granting them degrees.[65] At Oxford, on the other hand, there was a great deal of hostility to the idea. The Puseyites predictably thought the admission of women would turn the world upside down, but even many liberals had mixed feelings. Jowett and Goldwin Smith were particularly lukewarm. While there seems to have been no problem with allowing the wives and daughters of Oxford professors to attend the occasional lecture, or for the odd woman scholar to use the Bodleian, there was a deeprooted fear that the general admission of women would have a calamitous effect on the male undergraduates. Once surrounded by intelligent young ladies of a similar background, the men would be lured into an early marriage and would no longer be able to establish themselves in a desirable or lucrative career, which could only be achieved by a young man in his twenties who was focused and celibate.

The question of whether Oxford should admit women was first raised at the very moment the University was heavily engaged in discussing the best way to promote extension. In January 1867, Emily Davies, one of the leading campaigners for opening higher education to women, paid a visit to Oxford to enquire about the possibility of founding a female hall, the obvious way to bring women into the University without upsetting the sensitivities of the men too greatly. Although Mark Pattison, the rector of Lincoln, was supportive, Davies was confirmed in her suspicion that Oxford was not yet the ideal environment in which to launch her experiment and switched her attention to Cambridge, where, two years later, she was allowed to found what would become Girton.[66] This fact alone must have helped to move Oxford opinion in the following years, but change was also propelled by a shift in views within Oxford's Anglican establishment. With the great expansion in institutionalized secondary education for girls around the country in the 1870s, including the foundation of a day school on the University's doorstep in 1875, Oxford High, the high-church party in the University was converted to believing that the production of well-educated but godly schoolmistresses should be part of its social duty. The liberals struck first. In 1873 they established courses of extramural lectures for local women, then five years later, to ensure their continuity, created an Association for Promoting the Higher Education of Women in Oxford under the presidency of the master of University College, G. G. Bradley.[67] But the liberals did nothing to provide women with the chance to live in a formal scholarly community like male undergraduates. In this regard, it was the Tractarians and the new warden of Keble, Edward Stuart Talbot, who were in the van.

In June 1878, a group of high-church supporters of women's higher education met at Keble, with Talbot in the chair, and decided 'that it is desirable to attempt the Establishment in Oxford of a Small Hall or Hostel in Connection with the Church of England for the reception of women desirous of availing themselves of the special

---

[65] Carol Dyhouse, *No Distinction of Sex? Women in British Universities 1870–1939* (London, 1995).

[66] In 1869, her original women's college was established at Hitchen, many miles from the University. It moved to its present site in 1873.

[67] Bradley had been one of those who helped found Oxford High School.

FIGURE 9.5 Elizabeth Wordsworth, 1840–1932, first principal of Lady Margaret Hall and founder of St Hugh's College: photograph, c.1900. Wordsworth, seen here at her desk, was great-niece of the poet, daughter of the bishop of Lincoln, and a pious Anglican. Educated at home, she had a good knowledge of ancient and modern languages and was a prolific author. She founded St Hugh's with money she inherited from her father.

advantages which Oxford offers for higher Education'. A committee was set up to turn the wish into reality, containing both male and female members, which quickly got to work. By October of the following year, premises had been found in Norham Gardens; Elizabeth Wordsworth, the daughter of a headmaster-bishop, appointed as principal (see Figure 9.5); and Lady Margaret Hall (named after the greatest benefactress of higher education in England, Lady Margaret Beaufort) officially opened by the bishop of Oxford. Talbot's initiative finally galvanized the liberals into action and a rival committee was formed in February 1879 that included the low-church president of Trinity, John Percival, the broad-church idealist philosopher and Balliol tutor T. H. Green, and Mrs Humphry Ward, a member of the Arnold clan. Their response was to establish a women's hall 'in which no distinction was made between students on the grounds of their belonging to different religious denominations'. They worked even quicker, and their rival creation, Somerville, in memory of the mathematician Mary Somerville, who had died in 1872, was ready to receive undergraduates at the same time as the Anglican hall.[68]

---

[68] Citations in *HUO*, vii. 246. Lady Margaret Hall did take non-Anglicans. On Idealism and T. H. Green, see pp. 498–9, this volume.

In their first years, the two women's halls were on the fringe of the University. They were not incorporated, as Keble had been, and their charges could not attend the majority of university or college lectures or take a degree. Instead, their students chiefly attended the courses put on by Bradley's Association and were prepared for the Delegacy of Local Examinations' certificate for women over 18, one of a number of nationwide diplomas created by Oxford from the late 1850s to test the ability of school leavers. Lady Margaret Hall and Somerville, however, had no difficulty in filling their rooms, and within a short period of time it was felt that the experiment had been successful enough to merit the establishment of two more Anglican halls. St Hugh's, founded in 1886, was the creation of Elizabeth Wordsworth, while St Hilda's, opened in 1893, was the work of Dorothea Beale, principal of one of the leading girls' boarding schools, Cheltenham Ladies College. The same year also saw the formation of the Oxford Home Students Society, which catered for women attending the Association's lectures, who either lived with their parents or resided in approved digs. Unlike their male counterparts, the female non-collegiates showed little desire to gain their own institutional identity, and it was only in 1945 that they formed themselves into a society named after St Anne, the mother of the Virgin.

Initially, women students were the subject of a great deal of hostility and abuse. The idea of educating women to the highest level went against the grain of Victorian domesticity and the dominant, if contested, view of female physiology, and many junior and senior members in the early years shared the views expressed by the University's Chancellor, the marquess of Salisbury, in 1883:

> From all I hear the young ladies do not become very amiable or attractive members of society. I dare say these Colleges are useful as furnishing a diploma to ladies who wish to be Governesses: but for any other purpose I should do my utmost to dissuade any female relation over whom I had influence from going there.[69]

But majority opinion gradually swung more in the women's favour. By 1897, all colleges except Magdalen allowed female students to attend their lectures suitably chaperoned, and, from 1884, women were gradually admitted to all undergraduate examinations. Nonetheless, at the end of the Victorian era, there were still strict limits to the female presence in the University. In 1900, women could participate at least passively in the intellectual and social life of the University, and many had already done so. On the other hand, women could not matriculate, they could not receive a degree (a move to give them the right was decisively defeated in Congregation in 1895–6), and, until 1910, they were actually examined by the Delegacy of Local Examinations, who had access to the University's examination papers. Moreover, their halls sheltered a comparatively small number of undergraduates—Somerville was the largest college with eighty—and they were consciously designed

---

[69] *HUO*, vii. 251. On the debate over whether women were unsuited to long hours of study, see Hilary Marland, *'Bounding Saucy Girls': Visions and Practices of Health and Girlhood in Britain 1874–1920s* (Basingstoke, 2013), chs 1 and 2.

to replicate the domestic atmosphere in which most of the women were raised. As a result, their inhabitants had a much more frugal and constrained lifestyle than all but the most indigent of their male peers.

As they were not incorporated, the women's societies were not colleges; nor were they traditional halls run by private individuals licensed by the Vice-Chancellor. Rather, they resembled Keble without its university status and charter: they had no endowment, no fellows, and were run by a committee of trustees who appointed the principal. Yet, even if the female halls occupied a liminal position in the University at the turn of the twentieth century, their emergence proved a creative development. The champions of the admission of women to Oxford had not called for Oxford's male colleges to go co-educational: they were no more in favour of the promiscuous mixing of the sexes than their conservative opponents. What they had looked for was the establishment of a space within the University where women could live and study apart. Many non-Anglican churches, wishing to give their future ordinands some exposure to an Oxford education, found the 'In Oxford... but not of Oxford' model attractive.[70] Excluded from the confessional university before 1850, they wanted to take advantage of its dismantling, but feared contamination if the faithful resided in the secularized colleges which still remained places of Anglican worship. The women's halls therefore provided a model for others to follow.

As early as 1886, the Congregationalists, who saw themselves as the heirs of the puritans thrown out of the University in 1662, moved their training college at Spring Hill, Birmingham, to Oxford. Rechristened Mansfield College, it was initially established as a non-residential theological school on the High Street, but it soon had its own purpose-built gothic quad designed by Basil Champneys on a site to the south of the modern Science Area, which was opened in 1889. Four years later the Unitarians followed suit, relocating their Manchester College in another new building on an adjacent site built by Thomas Worthington.[71] Then, in 1926, the Baptists moved their Regent's Park College to the University. The Roman Catholics quickly followed the nonconformists. In theory, all Catholics, lay or clerical, were forbidden by the pope to attend non-confessional Oxford until 1895, but affluent members of the English congregation paid little attention to the ruling, and Oxford had its first post-Reformation Catholic fellow, Croke Robinson of New College, only a year after the 1871 Act.[72] As soon as the pope rescinded the ban the Catholic orders returned. In 1896, the Jesuits formed an Oxford community, which was eventually christened Campion Hall after the Elizabethan recusant and fellow of St John's. Three years later, the Benedictines arrived, followed by the Franciscans in 1910 and the Dominicans in 1921 who resurrected their former Greyfriars and Blackfriars

---

[70] The categorization of the female halls in 1896 by George Brodrick, warden of Merton, an opponent of deeper integration.

[71] Manchester became a fully incorporated college of the University in 1996 under the name Harris Manchester.

[72] Admittedly, he was a convert.

convents on new sites.[73] Even the evangelical Anglicans sought their special place in the sun. Wycliffe Hall was founded in 1877 as a theological college where evangelicals could train for the ministry, but with the foundation of the women's halls it soon became a hostel for spiritually athletic undergraduates seeking to shelter from the temptations of undergraduate life. It was hardly a counterpart to Keble with its nearly 200-strong undergraduate community. But the evangelicals, too, would eventually get a more extensive establishment of their own when St Peter's was founded in January 1929 through the efforts of Christopher Chavasse, rector of St Aldate's, and the financial assistance of the Rev. Percy Warrington, founder of the Allied Schools.[74]

All of the new institutions were private halls whose students could be matriculated in the University under the legislation of 1868. But three, in 1945, bore the additional appellation of 'permanent', which brought a higher status. Campion Hall and the Benedictines' St Benet's had the title from its invention in 1919, St Peter's from its opening. Together with Keble and, to a lesser extent, Lady Margaret Hall, they formed a significant denominational wedge in an otherwise secularized university. Nineteenth-century Oxford liberals had never intended that confessionalism would be replaced by competitive sectarianism. However, Britain, in the first part of the twentieth century, was still a deeply Christian society, and the creation of a series of private denominational halls ensured that Oxford played a central role in the vibrant religious conversation that still engaged some of the country's best minds.

From the late 1870s, Oxford also began to reach out to the millions of Britons who had neither the educational qualifications, nor the leisure or wealth to spend three or four years in permanent higher education. Outreach teaching in Britain's cities was promoted by most of the old and new universities and university colleges in late Victorian Britain, but Oxford was particularly committed to bringing enlightenment to the masses. In 1878, following the foundation of Keble and just before the creation of the first women's halls, the University set up a committee, chaired by Balliol's T. H. Green, to organize a system of extramural lectures around the country. The lecturers were to be Oxford dons; they would give a course of improving lectures to whomever wished to attend; and the aim was to teach the newly enfranchised how to be model and socially useful citizens. The success of the initiative across the 1880s and 1890s owed everything to the energy and commitment of individuals. Although Balliol and Corpus Christi eventually made it possible for two of the lecturers to be permanently away from Oxford by establishing fellowships specifically for extramural work, the University resolutely refused to put its hands in its own pocket and limited its involvement to establishing a permanent

---

[73] For the Benedictines, see Henry Wansbrough and Anthony Marett-Crosby (eds), *Benedictines in Oxford* (London, 1987), ch. 15.

[74] Eric H. F. Smith, *St Peter's: The Founding of a College* (Gerrards Cross, 1978). Wycliffe Hall had extended its reach to undergraduates during the principalship of Chavasse's father, Francis James, later bishop of Liverpool. St Peter's was put on a firmer financial footing at the end of the 1930s thanks to a large donation from William Morris, Lord Nuffield, one of the University's most generous benefactors: see p. 392, this volume.

Delegacy for the Extension of Teaching beyond the Limits of the University. As Hudson Shaw, one of the most enthusiastic and successful of the lecturers, complained at an Oxford conference on extension in 1887, 'We have been told over and over again that this is a missionary movement...but if it is a missionary movement then I take it that the University of Oxford is the first missionary society which ever started forth on its enterprise, and expected the people amongst whom it is to work to pay its expenses.'[75]

Despite the absence of funding, the movement was a great success once it lowered its sights and introduced short and relatively cheap courses. In 1890–1, Oxford provided 192 courses of lectures and the extramural teachers lectured to 20,248 students. Initially it was the relatively affluent who benefited, for only a quarter of the students came from the working classes. But at the beginning of the twentieth century the extramural movement succeeded in linking up directly with organized labour. From 1895, the movement's residential summer meeting, which brought hundreds of people to Oxford each year, received the blessing of the Co-operative Movement and gave Albert Mansbridge the platform to launch the Workers Educational Association in 1903. Thereafter, it was working men themselves and not the University which organized the extramural lectures on the ground. By then, too, working men had a permanent institutional presence on the fringe of the University with the opening of Ruskin Hall, later Ruskin College, in Walton Street. Named after the social reformer and Oxford professor of art, John Ruskin, the college was founded in 1898–9 by two Americans, the radical historian Charles Beard and the philanthropist Watkins Vrooman. Its aim was to provide a liberal education to working-class leaders by offering the chance of full-time residential study away from home. By 1907, Ruskin had fifty-two residents, half of them miners, and half of its income was provided by the trades unions who also chose the students.[76]

F. The Diversification of the Curriculum

As with extension, the reformers in the University had no need to call on outside assistance to effect further changes to the undergraduate curriculum. The 1850 examination statute had increased the number of Schools to four while insisting that candidates for a BA had, in future, to pass in two, 'Lit. Hum. and another. In so doing, it had seriously raised the bar. The reform had been backed by both the authors of the Blue Book and the Hebdomadal Board. But the progressives within the University wanted the new statute reopened from the beginning on the grounds that it was too demanding. On two occasions in 1857, the liberals on the new Hebdomadal Council managed to persuade their colleagues to place a motion

---

[75] *HUO*, vii. 667.
[76] Harold Pollins, *A History of Ruskin College* (Oxford, 1984). Charles Beard was one of the leading 'progressive' historians in the United States, who looked to trace the cause of major events in the country's history, such as the break with Britain, to internal social dissensions.

before Congregation that the two-school requirement be rescinded, and that under-graduates might be awarded their BA solely on their performance in a single school of their choice, as long as they had passed Classical Mods. On both occasions, the proposal was lost in Congregation, just as it was again when Vice-Chancellor Jeune had the change debated in 1859. The only revision to the curriculum in the 1850s came in the year following the 1854 Act, when Pusey and Jeune formed an alliance to accommodate the consciences of any dissenters who came up to Oxford under the new provisions. In March 1855, Congregation agreed that non-conformists need not be examined on religious knowledge in Mods and Lit. Hum. Schools but should instead offer additional texts in Greek and Latin.[77]

In 1863, the liberals tried again, this time only to be stymied by Convocation. A year later, in December 1864, still facing widespread opposition inside and outside the University, they finally succeeded, following a petition in favour of change presented to Council and signed by 103 members of Congregation, whose signa-tories included most of the professors and tutors. The vote, however, in both Congregation and Convocation was close, and the possibility of graduating in a single subject was not extended to those who took a Fourth, and was not granted to those content with gaining a pass. Despite the fact that falling matriculations suggested that the rigours of the 1850 statute was putting prospective undergrad-uates off, conservatives remained unwilling to tinker further with the BA, fearing that the limited changes heralded the beginning of the end of a common curriculum built around classical literature, history, and philosophy. Their misgivings were well founded. Having reduced the compulsory component in the curriculum to the study of Classical Mods, many reformers wanted to go further and allow under-graduates to specialize from the moment they came up. This was abundantly clear three years later in the evidence presented to the parliamentary select committee set up to look at extension. The first person to give evidence, Oxford's professor of chemistry, Sir Benjamin Brodie, insisted that the only way to increase the number of matriculands from classes who did not usually send their sons to the University was to further liberalize the curriculum. He was certain that future manufacturers and engineers would benefit from studying natural sciences at Oxford. To attract such sons of the middle classes to Oxford, however, the University had to offer them an education that would be useful to them in life, 'and a purely literary education is not of sufficient utility to induce them to come there'.[78]

As the conservative forces remained powerful in the University, removing the common classical element from the curriculum altogether took much longer than Brodie and his fellow liberalizers could have anticipated. Undergraduates taking a Fourth in their chosen subject were allowed to graduate in single honours from 1870, but it was only in 1886 that Congregation accepted that candidates for an honours degree need no longer pass Classical Mods, provided they were able to sit a

---

[77] J. H. C. Leech, *Sparks of Reform: The Career of Francis Jeune, 1806-1868* (Oxford, 1994), pp. 71–2.
[78] Select Committee (1867), *Evidence*, p. 10.

suitably rigorous intermediate examination (either a classified Mods or an easier pass-qualifying preliminary examination) in their specialist field. This had the immediate effect of reducing the length of the undergraduate course for a growing number of students, and eventually, after 1900, the majority. As the other schools created an intermediate examination that was taken at the end of the first year, the BA course for all but classicists was reduced thereafter from four years to three.

Even after the pass had been sold on Classical Mods, the University did not completely abandon its commitment to the classical inheritance. Many undergraduates in the humanities continued to be encouraged to take Classical Mods before beginning their honours course in a specialist school, even when there was an acceptable alternative. Moreover, although no longer forced to sit Classical Mods, the average undergraduate still had to pass Responsions, which, before the Great War, was little more than an examination in Latin and Greek with a bit of mathematics. At first, on its introduction, Responsions was taken early in an undergraduate's career, but by the end of the nineteenth century most colleges demanded that the examination was passed before matriculation, a requirement that was formalized in 1926 when it was adopted as the University's entrance examination for commoners.[79] Until then, the only matriculands spared the ordeal were those who held one of the increasing number of school-leaving certificates introduced from the 1850s, which the University was willing to recognize as long as the candidate had been tested in classics and maths.[80] Scholarship awards too were largely determined by prowess in classics. After the 1850s, all colleges, and not just a few, subjected applicants to a rigorous written examination, which the colleges set individually or in groups. Before the Second World War, irrespective of the subject that an undergraduate intended to study, success depended on being able to demonstrate competence in Latin and Greek. As early as 1867, Brodie, in his evidence to the parliamentary committee, complained that this stacked the odds against would-be scientists, but his claim did not lead to any action.[81] Nor was much attention paid to the growing concern of reformers from the turn of the twentieth century that the entrance requirements discouraged applications from state or state-maintained secondary schools where teaching of the classics was often deficient or non-existent. There was a broad consensus that the Oxford-educated, however extended the social origin of matriculands might become, were gentlemen, and gentlemen were identified by a love and knowledge of the culture of the classical world. The most that was conceded was that, from 1920, matriculands did not need to know any Greek.[82]

---

[79] Before this, despite the 1852 Blue Book recommendation, there was no Oxford entrance exam, although some colleges had instituted their own, e.g. Brasenose in 1901. Most commoners before 1926 were admitted on the say-so of the head of house or an admissions committee.

[80] By 1914, the University recognized fifty alternatives to Responsions, including the French baccalaureate, introduced by Napoleon as the lycée leaving exam in 1808.

[81] Select Committee (1867), *Evidence*, p. 12.

[82] There were attempts in 1877–80 and 1911 to end compulsory Greek for mathematicians and scientists.

The steady, if never total, decline in the commitment to compulsory classics from the mid-1860s was accompanied by growing curricular diversification. The first 1857 plan to reform the BA had envisaged five single honours schools rather than four, with Lit. Hum. being divided into two: a school of classical literature and philology and a school of moral philosophy and metaphysics. This never happened, and the schools' course in Lit. Hum. remained, until the 1970s, the study of ancient history and philosophy.[83] The Natural Science School, on the other hand, while retaining its separate identity, was quickly divided into a series of specialist sub-schools. From the early 1870s, undergraduates reading for science honours were allowed to specialize. They had to pass a common prelim, but thereafter could pursue a growing number of specialist tracks. By the outbreak of the First World War, they had eleven different subjects to choose from, of which the most popular in 1910–14 were chemistry, physics, and physiology (taken by future medics), followed by botany, geology, and engineering, the last only established in 1909. By then, the prelim had also ceased to be an examination in general science. At the beginning of the twentieth century, it had been divided into four parts—mathematics, mechanics and physics, chemistry, and zoology and botany—and candidates had to pass only in two.[84]

By 1914 there were also a clutch of new honours schools besides the four recognized in 1850. A Theology School was added to the undergraduate curriculum as early as 1869, when the Puseyites decided it could help the church rather than undermine it, by giving young ordinands a training they hitherto conspicuously lacked.[85] Three years later, jurisprudence and modern history were split in two; then in 1886 the School of Oriental Languages was established, divided between Indian and Semitic tongues. This was followed in 1893 with the creation of a School of English Language and Literature, consequent to a petition by 108 members of Congregation, which in turn paved the way for the School of Modern Languages erected in 1903, more than fifty years after the opening of the Taylorian to foster their study. Undergraduates who sought a pass rather than an honours degree—still 20 per cent before 1914—were also partially liberated from the tyranny of taking part of their ordinary degree in classics.[86] Pass candidates had always to take Pass or Honour Mods in classics, but from 1872 the final examination was reconstructed to embrace a wide variety of subjects, including some that could not yet be taken as

---

[83] Christopher Stray (ed.), *Oxford Classics: Teaching and Learning 1800–2000* (London, 2007). The introduction of the study of literature into the honour school of Lit. Hum was first mooted in the early 1950s by the professor of Greek, E. R. Dodds; it was finally effected by the professor of Latin, Robin Nisbet, and his faculty colleague Donald Russell.

[84] *The Student's Handbook to the University and Colleges of Oxford* (1873), p. 136; *The Student's Handbook to the University and Colleges of Oxford* (1912), pp. 142–4. In 1873 there had been only three science subjects in which honours could be taken—physics, chemistry, and biology—and the common prelim at that date was a two-part examination in mechanics and physics and in chemistry.

[85] J. D. Griffiths, 'Reform of the University of Oxford in the Nineteenth Century: A Study of Opinions of Members of the University Regarding the Establishment of an Undergraduate School in Theology' (MStud dissertation, Oxford, 2012), chs 2 and 3.

[86] In 1914, 30 per cent of Brasenose undergraduates aimed at a pass.

honours. Candidates had to demonstrate their proficiency in three different subjects, one of which had to be a language. In theory, at degree level, pass candidates could escape classics completely, provided that they offered modern languages instead. Not all new honours schools proposed, however, were adopted. As part of the University's programme of expansion, a readership in anthropology was established in 1884, the first post in the discipline in the United Kingdom, which was filled by the keeper of the University Museum, Edward Tylor. But an attempt in 1895 to establish an honour school in anthropology within the School of Natural Science was stymied because some classicists wanted to introduce the subject into Lit. Hum.[87]

To have introduced anthropology into an Oxford humanities school admittedly would have been difficult for it would have gone totally against the grain. Oxford's humanities schools, on the eve of the Great War, were anchored firmly in the past. Lit. Hum. was certainly more than the study of ancient history and philosophy. Even when William Spooner, the future warden of New College, was an undergraduate in the mid-1860s, his philosophical studies had given him a 'speaking acquaintance with Kant's Critique and Hegel's Philosophy of History' as well as a detailed knowledge of John Stuart Mill on logic and ethics. And the influence of German Idealism on the school only grew stronger in the late nineteenth century, thanks to the influence of Balliol's T. H. Green. But Lit. Hum. was still the school of Aristotle, Plato, and the pre-Socratics: it was not a school of modern philosophy. Similarly, the School of Jurisprudence taught the history of Roman, English, and international law more than the current law of the land, while the School of Oriental Languages busied itself with the classical tongues of the ancient Near East and the Indian subcontinent not demotic Arabic or Persian. The curriculum of both the Modern History and English Schools was just as resolutely geared towards a past safely out of reach. When the Modern History School was set up in 1872, the course in European history ended in 1815 and the course in English history, the centre point of the school, in 1847. Undergraduates, it was hoped, would learn how to analyse seminal constitutional documents, but they were also supposed to learn about the gradual and benign evolution of English liberties and institutions from Anglo-Saxon times, not their purported perfection in the late Victorian present. Equally, the English School, set up at the end of the nineteenth century, did not include Victorian literature in its syllabus. Many in the University thought literary studies soft and unmanly, and that if modern languages were to be taught at all in Oxford, the emphasis should be on their structure. It was conflict over the literary content of the course that scuppered an early attempt to launch a combined honour school of modern languages and English in 1886–7. The separate English School was given the green light by Congregation six years later, only when it was agreed to give the curriculum a philological emphasis by placing Anglo-Saxon and Middle English at its heart.[88]

---

[87] Anthropology, at that juncture, was considered a branch of human physiology.

[88] The first holder of the chair of English language and literature at Oxford, elected in 1885, was the German-trained Anglo-Saxon philologist Arthur Sampson Napier, formerly of Exeter College, who had no feeling for literature at all; his BA was in chemistry: see Lewis R. Farnell, *An Oxonian Looks Back* (London, 1934), pp. 51–4.

This is not to say that the humanities schools ignored their own world, for questions on examination papers in Lit. Hum. and modern history frequently encouraged candidates to draw analogies between past and present. If anything, undergraduates were encouraged to draw connections too cavalierly. But the humanities schools definitely provided no opportunity to learn about contemporary institutions or analyse modern problems. It was for this reason that, by 1914, there were calls for a new school that would fill the gap. Discussions continued throughout the war and culminated in the creation of the School of Philosophy, Politics, and Economics in 1920, which became known as Modern Greats, to distinguish it from Greats, the colloquial term for Lit. Hum. PPE initially tended to be taught historically like other arts subjects. But by the late 1930s it was beginning to forge its own identity and link the Oxford undergraduate curriculum, albeit belatedly, to the burgeoning world of the social sciences.[89] By then, too, it was not the only undergraduate subject that introduced students to the problems of mankind in the contemporary world, since, from 1930, Oxford had also a School of Geography, a hybrid discipline with a foot in both the arts and the sciences. Furthermore, from 1919, undergraduates could also study man's use and abuse of the natural world with the creation of pass schools in agriculture and forestry, which were elevated to honours status in 1937 and 1945.

For twenty years after the passage of the 1850 examination statute, Oxford's growing collection of honour schools had no institutional identity. Ad hoc committees of senior members were annually nominated by the Proctors to examine candidates on the curriculum laid down in the university statute that brought the school into being. But the schools had no formal organization. This ceased to be the case from 1872 when, under university legislation agreed on two years before, six boards of studies were created to oversee each of the schools then in existence, produce a regular lecture list, and suggest curricular alterations.[90] Initially, the boards were all part of a single faculty of arts. Under the statutes of 1882, however, which added the appointment of examiners to the list of the boards' chores, three new faculties were constituted out of the Schools of Natural Science and Mathematics, Theology, and Law, although all undergraduates continued to take

Cambridge looked on modern literary studies with the same suspicion. In the year that the attempt was first made at Oxford to set up a school of modern languages and English, Cambridge agreed to create a Tripos in medieval and modern languages. Like the Oxford English School, established in 1893, this was principally a study of language: Anglo-Saxon and Middle English and a number of foreign languages. Little attention was paid to literature. Modern English and European literature began to be seriously studied at Cambridge only from the end of the First World War when a separate English Tripos was created: Brooke, pp. 431–3 and 443–7.

[89] A move at the same time to establish a Science Greats, combining science and philosophy, failed to get the necessary support. The most important centre for the study of the social sciences in interwar Britain was the LSE.

[90] The six boards were Lit. Hum., mathematics, natural science, theology, history, and law. There was also a board for the pass school, and an eighth board was established by the end of the decade for preventive medicine, staffed by the professors of medicine and the science professors: *Oxford University Calendar* (1873), pp. 13–14; *Oxford University Calendar* (1878), pp. 13–14. Medicine was a postgraduate study: see p. 388 n.106, this volume.

a BA degree.[91] Then, in 1913, the faculty of arts itself ceased to exist when Lit. Hum., modern history, oriental languages, and English and modern languages became independent entities. PPE, on the other hand, never became a faculty. Philosophy always remained a part of Lit. Hum., while the board and the faculty of social studies, which were eventually formed in 1932, covered only politics and economics.[92] Initially, these boards dealt directly with Council. In 1912, however, a General Board of Faculties was created to oversee the whole curriculum. Chaired by the Vice-Chancellor and with representatives from the separate boards, the General Board thereafter took over Council's role in drafting curricular changes and administering the CUF scheme. It also became the main forum for forward academic thinking and organizing the still embryonic courses in graduate studies.[93]

The establishment of boards of studies did not affect the colleges' monopoly of undergraduate teaching. Some reformers wanted to put an end to college instruction altogether. Pattison, in 1868, advocated handing over the colleges' endowments to the University, using the money to expand the professoriate, turning the largest colleges into the headquarters of the different schools or faculties, and reducing the rest to simple halls of residence.[94] But such radical proposals met with minimal support. For all the curricular changes in the century following Newman's departure, Oxford remained a collegiate university. The vast majority of undergraduates applied to join a particular college, were matriculated as one of its members, and had their teaching organized by the college's tutors. Admittedly, colleges in the second half of the nineteenth century were top heavy in classics tutors and when new schools were founded there was frequently no in-house tuition available for those who wished to study for them. Undergraduates taking the Natural Science School in the first decades after 1850 had perforce to attend the lectures of science professors and their assistants if they were to receive any tuition at all, as Brodie pointed out in his evidence to the 1867 select committee.[95] But over time colleges built up their team of tutorial fellows, afforced by college lecturers, and were able to deliver most of the curriculum themselves, or by entering into bilateral agreements with their neighbours.[96] Undergraduates therefore would often attend university lectures only for very specialist parts of the curriculum. They were certainly under

[91] There was an attempt in 1877–80 to establish a separate natural science degree which would lead to a BSc and an MSc.

[92] G. N. Curzon, *Principles and Methods of University Reform* (Oxford, 1909), p. 125; C. H. Firth, *The Faculties and their Powers: A Contribution to the History of University Organisation* (Oxford, 1909). In 1885, the faculty of arts was divided into three sub-boards: Lit. Hum., oriental languages, and history; and the faculty of natural science was divided into two: natural science and medicine.

[93] See pp. 481–3, this volume.

[94] M. Pattison, *Suggestions on Academical Organisation with Especial Reference to Oxford* (Edinburgh, 1868), esp. section 5. Pattison still believed in a mix of professorial and tutorial teaching but the latter was to be provided by junior MAs in the faculty who would serve an apprenticeship before taking up a university post.

[95] Select Committee (1867), *Evidence*, p. 7. Balliol did not even have a science fellow until 1886. The 1853 report to the Hebdomadal Board also assumed science would be taught by university teachers: Report (1853), *Report*, pp. 59–60.

[96] Lecturers who were not fellows were widely used when an honour school had few takers or when a college's finances would not stretch to a full tutorial appointment.

no compulsion to do so after the 1850 examination statute was amended in 1859, and sometimes they were actively discouraged. In 1910, the lectures of the regius professor of Greek, Gilbert Murray, one of the Oxford classicists with a penchant for anthropology, were apparently blacked by many colleges because of his radical views on Ireland and empire. In fact, there was little objection to the tutorial grip on teaching and much praise, especially as the quality of the teaching after 1880 greatly improved.[97]

The tutors also dominated the new faculty boards. While the 1850 commission had imagined the curriculum being organized in the future by the professors, even if its delivery remained the preserve of the tutors, this was not how the boards set up in 1872 actually functioned. Although the professors were ex officio members, the boards under the 1882 statutes also contained an equal number of elected representatives and a smaller number of co-opted members. These two groups were usually drawn from the college tutors, who frequently formed the majority on the board or constituted its institutional memory, in that some would serve for the whole of their working life.[98] In consequence, the professors were usually unable to carry any initiative that the tutors felt threatened the status quo and collegiate teaching. At the turn of the twentieth century, the history tutors, who had organized themselves into an association as early as 1869, were regarded as a particularly reactionary bunch. When Sir Charles Firth became regius professor in 1904 he aimed to reduce the emphasis on broad outline courses and develop the curriculum in a way that would give greater weight to teaching research skills. In a forthright inaugural he lambasted the tutors for their complacency and lack of ambition, declaring that the school was: 'An excellent training for journalists ... but ... a poor test of historical ability, and a poorer preparation for the task of writing history.'[99] However, the tutors ruled the faculty roost. They accepted certain reforms, allowing schools men to present a voluntary thesis, for instance, from 1909, but they held the line against radical reform. When Firth retired from his chair in 1925, he claimed he had achieved nothing, an opinion backed up by F.M. Powicke, who took over as regius three years later and maintained that the school had not changed in the slightest since his own student days at the turn of the century.[100]

G. Curzon and the Asquith Commission

Oxford in 1900 was a very different university from the Anglican seminary of the first half of the nineteenth century. Through opening its doors to other Christian

---

[97] For Murray's dislike of imperialism, see p. 404, this volume. Tutorial teaching is discussed in Chapter 10, section C.

[98] Curzon, Principles, pp. 124–9.

[99] C. H. Firth, A Plea for the Historical Teaching of History (Oxford, 1904), p. 19.

[100] Andrea Pass, 'The Oxford Honours School of Modern History, c. 1900 to c. 1930' (BA dissertation thesis, Oxford 2007); Reba Soffer, 'Nation, Duty, Character and Confidence: History at Oxford, 1850–1914', Historical Journal, 30: 1 (1987), 77–104; J. P. Kenyon, 'Sir Charles Firth and the Oxford School of Modern History, 1892–1925', in A. C. Duke and C. A. Tamse (eds), Clio's Mirror: Historiography in Britain and the Netherlands (Zutphen, 1985).

confessions, liberalizing its undergraduate curriculum, and finding ways of extending access, it had gone some way to addressing the deficiencies identified by Whigs and radicals in the late Hanoverian age. The changes had also had the desired effect, for Oxford became a much larger university, with some 3,000 undergraduates on its books on the eve of the First World War. At the same time, these changes had been achieved without severing important links with the University's early modern past. As in an earlier period, undergraduates for the most part resided in a college or hall and received most of their teaching from college tutors. The presence of the Church of England similarly remained strong: when Magdalen Hall was transformed into Hertford in the 1870s, the new college was even allowed to have an exclusively Anglican fellowship as its founder desired.

However, Oxford in the Edwardian age was still the butt of criticism both within and without, for the world was changing fast and the University continued to look out of date to many eyes. The liminal status of women students was one ongoing problem. In 1900, Oxford and Cambridge were the only British universities which did not admit women to degrees. Another problem which was not new but had now become a burning issue was the social origins of Oxford's and Cambridge's undergraduates. Oxford had ended the traditional status divisions between its undergraduates in 1855 when it introduced a standard matriculation fee except for the sons of peers. It had also, from the 1890s, succeeded in attracting many more undergraduates from middle-class backgrounds, as Jowett and the first generation of reformers had wanted. In 1897–8, only 28 per cent of male matriculands came from landed or clerical families or had a father with a private income. A total of 64 per cent, in contrast, had fathers in business or in the professions, old and new. But if Oxford's intake had certainly broadened socially, the University was still drawing undergraduates from a narrow elite, and a large majority came from public schools. A mere 5 per cent of male matriculands in 1897–8 were lower middle or working class. Even the non-collegiates came from a privileged background.[101]

The narrow base of the University's recruitment would have escaped comment in the mid-Victorian era, but at the turn of the twentieth century Britain was a male democracy with a burgeoning labour movement which, for the most part, placed great emphasis on access to higher education.[102] Oxford, in its defence, could point to the sterling work which its lecturers of the extramural delegacy continued to do in tandem with the WEA to bring a taste of higher education to the industrial towns. But this cut little ice with a growing caucus of socialist intellectuals, like Balliol's R. H. Tawney, who hovered around the virgin Labour Party and wanted equal educational opportunity for all, and Oxford to retain its traditional political influence come the revolution:

---

[101] The women's halls had fewer undergraduates from landed and clerical backgrounds but had an even smaller percentage from poorer backgrounds. There were not huge distinctions between the colleges.

[102] It was not until 1918 that every adult male had the vote, but the majority of the electorate in 1900 was male working class.

It has always been the privilege of the older Universities...to train men for all departments of life and public administration...It seems to us that it would involve a great loss both to Oxford and to English political life were the close association which has existed between the University and the world of affairs to be broken or impaired on the accession of new classes to power.[103]

Moreover, whether Britain was about to experience the triumph of Labour or no, the potential pool of university applicants was set to grow. Britain had had a system of universal elementary education only since the 1870s, and the vast majority of children left school on reaching 13. Although state/local government bursaries had been available from the mid-1880s for the bright children of the poor to continue their education into their late teens, they had little chance of doing so, especially in England where there were few state-funded secondary schools. But all this changed in 1902 when a new Education Act provided for the creation of a network of state-maintained boys' and girls' grammar schools and allowed local authorities to purchase places in existing endowed schools. It was only a matter of time before a far greater number of 18-year-olds had reached university standard and would set their sights on higher education, especially as the 1902 Act also offered a small number of awards for those accepted.[104] Oxford could claim that, by 1910, it had responded to the changing educational environment to a small extent. Over the previous fifteen years it had raised its lower middle- and working-class intake to 10 per cent. But this seemed a derisory figure when other British universities, apart from Cambridge, were attracting far more: in the same year, Glasgow, albeit the beneficiary of the much more egalitarian Scottish educational system, drew 44 per cent of its students from this section of society.[105] To the outside world, Oxford, on the eve of the Great War, still seemed the unwelcoming elitist institution depicted in Thomas Hardy's *Jude the Obscure*, published in 1895.

A third problem was the fact that Oxford was still only an undergraduate university. Wilhelm von Humboldt had stressed that university teachers should do research as well as teach and that they should have a team of advanced students working under their direction. The Humboldtian model was never adopted in its entirety, for his concept of the unity of knowledge won limited acceptance. But the idea that universities should be centres of knowledge creation gained increasing support across the nineteenth century and not just in Humboldt's homeland. So too did the German invention of the research doctorate, a new type of higher degree awarded from the turn of the nineteenth century to young researchers who had successfully completed a piece of original work. In this regard, Oxford could not but seem deficient. Although many of its professors and readers, and some of the tutors, in 1900 were actively engaged in research, and a number, particularly scientists, had

---

[103] *HUO*, vii. 846.

[104] For an introduction, L. W. B. Brockliss and Nicola Sheldon (eds), *Mass Education and the Limits of State Building, c. 1870–1930* (Basingstoke, 2012), pp. 13–19. Still, only 15 per cent of 10- to 11-year-olds went on to secondary school in the 1930s in England.

[105] R. D. Anderson, 'Universities and Elites in Modern Britain', *History of Universities*, 10 (1991), 234–5 (tables).

spent time in Germany, there was nothing akin to an official research culture and very few postgraduate students. Before the First World War, Oxford did offer a number of taught postgraduate degrees and diplomas, most notably in medicine, which had remained, as in earlier centuries, a 'higher' discipline, while new degrees with a research focus had been established in 1895 and 1900. But there was, as yet, no Oxford research doctorate, and none would be introduced until 1917.[106] The limited attention to research had a lot to do with divisions in the reforming camp. Jowett, for one, had been totally fixated on the undergraduates and their needs. But whatever the cause, it made it difficult for Oxford to claim it was a serious modern university at the end of Victoria's reign, especially given the fact that a number of other British universities were surging ahead in the sciences. London, Manchester, and Glasgow were all centres of research. So too was Cambridge. Like Oxford, Cambridge had still to establish a modern doctorate but the Cavendish Laboratory, built in 1871–4, was already a centre of excellence in the physical sciences with numerous research pupils. In their treatment of women and the working class, neither of the traditional universities cut much of a figure, but when it came to safeguarding the future of Britain as a world power, it was clear which of the two had the stronger call on the nation's sympathy.[107]

Fortunately, the University elected a Chancellor in 1907 who was willing to endorse and foster further reform. Lord Curzon, the erstwhile viceroy of India and a product of Balliol, took office at a difficult moment (see Figure 9.6). A group of Christian socialists inside and outside the University had enlisted under the banner of the bishop of Birmingham, Charles Gore, and had begun calling for a royal commission to redress the barriers to working-class access.[108] When the election of 1906 produced a radical Liberal government, Curzon's predecessor, George Goschen, had feared the worst:

> The new House of Commons has shown immense activity during its first weeks, If they keep up the pace, depend upon it, they will have a fling at the Universities [Oxford and Cambridge] before the present Parliament expires. The Labour men are

---

[106] An Oxford BM was one of numerous degrees and diplomas given by British and Irish universities and hospitals which were recognized as a qualification to practise under the 1858 Medical Act. Candidates for the Oxford degree, rapidly increasing in numbers from 1870, had to take a BA, usually in physiology, then pass two successive examinations in medicine, one in theoretical and the other in clinical medicine, which were called the first and second BM. Until the last decade of the nineteenth century, it took eight years from the date of matriculation to qualify: four in physiology and four in medicine, and the medical component was usually studied elsewhere for lack of facilities. By the 1890s, once scientists were freed from taking Classical Mods and the physiology course had been more closely dovetailed with the syllabus of the first BM, medics could complete the first part of their medical degree at Oxford soon after taking their BA and gain their medical qualification two years faster: *The Student's Handbook to the University and Colleges of Oxford* (1873), p. 104; *The Student's Handbook to the University and Colleges of Oxford* (1892), p. 209; *The Student's Handbook to the University and Colleges of Oxford* (1912), p. 173. There was also no undergraduate music degree, though candidates could supplicate for a BMus or DMus.

[107] No British university offered a research doctorate before 1917: see p. 484, this volume.

[108] Gore had been a fellow of Trinity and, from 1884 to 1893, he was the first principal of Pusey House in Oxford, an Anglo-Catholic mission set up in St Giles on Pusey's death in 1882 to house his library and keep the Tractarian flame flying in the University.

FIGURE 9.6 George Nathaniel Curzon, 1859–1925, Viceroy of India and reform-minded University Chancellor. Curzon, educated at Eton and Balliol, had a reputation for being grand from the time he was at Oxford. Elected Chancellor in 1907, he took his role seriously and within two years had published a book detailing the changes that were needed to confirm Oxford's role as 'a focus of culture, a school of character, and a nursery of thought'.

anxious to secure room for 'Labour' in all educational establishments. If they should make a determined attack the Oxford men in the Cabinet would not be able to hold them.[109]

Curzon, however, had not returned to Britain simply to retire. In 1909 he set out his thoughts on reform in his *Principles and Methods of University Reform*, and in the eighteen years of his chancellorship worked with the reform-minded in the University to make university governance more efficient and find a way of addressing contemporary concerns.[110]

The status of women students proved relatively simple to deal with. In 1910, a Delegacy for the Supervision of Women Students was established, which kept a register of those entitled to sit the University's examinations; and in 1911 women's results were included in the Schools' lists for the first time. Then, in 1920, in a burst

[109] *HUO*, vii. 827. Goschen, an alumnus of Oriel and founding member of the Liberal Unionist Party, was in the office for only four years.
[110] To the concern of the conservatives, he resided in the University for a couple of weeks a year. His interest in reform was a surprise: he had been elected as the conservative candidate through the votes of the non-resident MAs: G. B. Grundy, *Fifty-Five Years at Oxford: An Unconventional Autobiography* (London, 1945), pp. 120–1.

of reform following the Great War, women were finally allowed to matriculate, take degrees, and become members of Congregation and faculty boards.[111] From 1925 to 1926, moreover, the women's halls became much more like the men's colleges, when they were granted royal charters which established a governing body on which the tutors had automatic representation as fellows and ended the autocracy of the heads. Admittedly, women were still not members of Oxford on the same terms as men, as was clear in 1927, when Congregation limited their number to 840. But they had definitely stepped across the threshold, a transition that would be denied their Cambridge sisters for a further twenty-five years.[112]

Curzon had less success with opening up the University to the lower middle and working classes. In August 1907, at a conference of workers' and educational organizations held in the Examination Schools under the auspices of the WEA, a committee was set up to examine how Oxford could forge closer links with working people. The subsequent report, published by OUP in 1908, proposed three major reforms. The University's outreach programme should be developed to include a series of tutorial classes where working men could become active participants in an extension course, not just passive listeners. Examined diplomas should be created which could be taken by those following the new tutorial courses, and the diplomas, along with those given by Ruskin, should be deemed sufficient proof of a capacity to study at Oxford. And the colleges should establish working-class scholarships which would be awarded by a joint university and WEA committee.[113] Curzon was happy to see the extension programme develop into a more rigorous form of education, and by 1913–14 Oxford was running eighteen tutorial extension classes.[114] But he jibbed at the other proposals. Recognizing that many within the University regarded the committee's recommendations on working-class access as an attack on meritocracy, he floated the idea instead of a new college just for the poor undergraduate, where costs would be limited. He was also convinced that the real obstacle to wider access was the lack of a common entrance examination and the insistence that freshmen knew Greek, a language either not taught or taught badly in the state grammar schools: 'In the pathway of every endeavour to open the University to wider classes or the poor, stands the vexed question of Greek in Responsions—a question which no scheme of reform can overlook, and which cannot be permanently ignored.'[115]

---

[111] One argument made against giving women full membership of the University before 1920 was that female MAs would thereby have gained the right to vote for the University's MPs at a time when they were still legally disenfranchised: Farnell, *Oxonian*, p. 280. Curzon was president of the National League for Opposing Woman Suffrage.

[112] It was only in 1950–5 that the female colleges had a governing body simply comprised of fellows. Until then, there were male members on the governing councils. Somerville had begun the process of establishing a governing body containing the tutors as official fellows in 1922. It was only in 1959 that the female colleges gained full university status.

[113] *Oxford and Working-Class Education, being the report of a joint-committee of university and working-class representatives on the relation of the University to the higher education of working people* (Oxford, 1908), ch. viii, recommendations.

[114] Other British universities were running 145.   [115] Mallet, iii. 478.

No poor man's college was established, however. The most that Curzon achieved at college level was to save St Edmund Hall, the one surviving medieval hostel, from absorption by Queen's on the resignation of its principal, and set it on the road to independence.[116] Nor did the abolition of compulsory Greek in 1920 have much of an effect on the pattern of social intake, whatever Curzon's expectation. Nonetheless, the interwar period was not one of total stasis. Thanks in large part to the much greater availability of local authority grants, male matriculands from the lower and working classes doubled to 10 per cent, and there was a modest rise from 40 to 50 per cent in the percentage of male students with fathers in education, business, and the new professions. Conversely, those from gentle backgrounds fell from 12 to 2 per cent, and those from the traditional professions fell from a third to a quarter. There was also a steady rise in the percentage of students from state schools. In 1900–13, probably less than a fifth of male undergraduates came from the state system; by 1938–9 the fraction was nearer a third.

Curzon had better fortune laying the foundations for the modern research university, which he realized depended on improving the University's finances and not just on setting up the DPhil. The new graduated tax introduced in the mid-1880s proved a great boost to the University's coffers, and by 1920 was bringing in an extra £58,000.[117] Yet the tax never produced as much income as had been hoped. The 1874 commissioners, in estimating the gains to college endowment from moving to rack-rents, did not factor in the losses that would occur from the disappearance of fines and the costs of borrowing to make improvements. They did not anticipate either the effect on rents of the great agricultural depression that hit the country from the mid-1880s, or the lengths that some colleges would go to avoid taxation. A few colleges were generous to a fault: Magdalen, which had largely escaped the agricultural downturn thanks to its large urban portfolio, and was the richest college in 1914, handed over nearly £120,000 in taxation and voluntary donations between 1910 and 1929 and frequently provided a third of the contributions to the CUF. Others, though, used the excuse of heavy debt repayments or the tax-free status of recent bequests to reduce their liability to almost nothing.[118]

College taxation alone, therefore, was only sufficient to fund a small number of new posts. The fact that, by the time Curzon died in 1925, the University had expanded its number of posts threefold to some 150, and put up several new buildings around the University Museum for teaching and research in the sciences, was chiefly made possible through Oxford's ability to attract private donations. The University had launched appeals to help fund both the Museum and the new Examination Schools, and Curzon, as soon as he became Chancellor in 1907, launched another to establish an endowment fund which generated £130,000 in a

---

[116] The Hall had been fighting for its existence with much university support from 1903.

[117] In that year, the colleges' contribution to the University was worth £77,000, when the salaries of postholders supported directly by the richer colleges are included in the total.

[118] For college income in this period, see M.J. Jones, 'The Agricultural Depression, Collegiate Finances, and Provision for Education at Oxford, 1871–1913', *Economic History Review*, 50: 1 (1997), 57–81, esp. tables and pp. 75–7.

year. More importantly, during the eighteen years of his chancellorship, Oxford benefited from a series of one-off benefactions from companies and private individuals, two of which in particular helped to put Oxford science on the map. In 1910, a building for the study of electrical science was opened opposite Keble through the generosity of the Drapers' Company; then, in the first years of the Great War, the sauce manufacturer Dyson Perrins provided the funds to establish an organic chemistry laboratory which was in use from 1916. The largesse continued into the depression years of the 1930s. At the beginning of the decade, the Rockefeller Foundation in the United States provided £600,000 of the £1 million needed to build an extension to the Bodleian. The sum was trumped in 1936 when the University received a gift of £2 million from the Oxford car manufacturer William Morris, Viscount Nuffield, to establish a research school in clinical medicine. This was Oxford's largest private donation to date, and it was added to the following year by a second gift from Morris of £1 million to develop engineering and a new subject, accountancy.[119]

The appeals and private donations, however, provided an erratic and often unpredictable financial injection which was primarily devoted to capital expenditure. By the end of the First World War, it was evident the University lacked the annual income necessary to develop as an important centre of scientific research. As it was also clear that if the University turned its back on scientific research, it would quickly drop down the pecking order, the Hebdomadal Council looked for a way to enhance its income stream and, after the war, approached the state for funding. British universities had enjoyed little central government funding before 1914, but in 1919 the state accepted that it was now part of its duty to promote higher education and set up the University Grants Committee to channel funds in their direction. Oxford immediately took the opportunity to apply. In 1920, Oxford's income was £210,000. From 1922, when the University took the king's shilling, until the outbreak of the Second World War, it received a further £100,000 per annum from the state. Combined with private bequests, this allowed the University to fund some 500 posts by 1939, mainly in the sciences. Its income, in consequence, rose from being only one-third of the combined colleges' total to more than four-fifths.[120]

There was a price for taking taxpayers' money: the University and its sister, Cambridge, equally anxious for state support, had to submit to a third commission of enquiry. Calls for a new commission had come thick and fast in the years immediately before the First World War, on the grounds that the University, whatever its other virtues, had failed to keep abreast of the new democratic spirit of the age that had informed the country's development since the 1880s. The Liberal prime minister Herbert Asquith, a Balliol man, had kept the critics, both inside and outside the University, at bay before the war and hoped that the new dynamic

---

[119] The money was not used as Nuffield wanted. see p. 486, this volume. Between 1929–30 and 1946–7, Oxford received benefactions worth £3.9 million. Before the Second World War, Oxford provided next to no instruction in clinical teaching, so candidates for the second BM had to train elsewhere.
[120] Many of the 500 posts were part-time lectureships held by college tutors, a development advocated by the Asquith Commission in 1922 but that only affected all tutors from 1947: see pp.394 and 561, this volume.

Chancellor, Curzon, would address the concerns of the new generation of reformers. It became impossible, however, to duck the issue when the University applied
for state funding in the shadow of the sacrifice of so many of the nation's young
men in the trenches. The president of the board of education between 1916 and 1922
was the erstwhile New College history tutor, H. A. L. Fisher, who dedicated his six
years in office to pushing the whole educational system in a more democratic
direction.[121] Fisher was adamant: the two universities could receive public money
only once they had been given a clean bill of health. On his insistence therefore, an
investigatory commission was set up in 1919 which reported three years later. The
Oxford section of the commission was chaired by Asquith and had a membership
that reflected the changed times. Rather than the clutch of lawyers who had graced
Selborne's commission, Asquith's team represented science, the working classes,
and the new political constituency, women. Only three were resident in Oxford:
Emily Penrose, principal of Somerville, W. G. S. Adams, Gladstone professor of
government and fellow of All Souls, and T. B. Strong, dean of Christ Church. The
commission too took evidence from a clutch of new-minted interest groups that
had gained their voice in the years since 1882, such as the Headmasters' Conference,
the National Union of Teachers, the WEA, and the Co-operative Union.[122]

In the event, both universities were dealt with kindly and it was understood that
comparisons were not to be made with other British universities. Where Oxford
was concerned, the commission went back over much of the old ground traversed
by its predecessors but had little new to add. Under Curzon's initiative the University had already put in train a number of changes in governance before the First
World War. The heads' representation on Council had been reduced, Congregation's membership circumscribed to teaching MAs, and the power of the conservative backwoodsmen clipped by reducing Convocation's ability to thwart
legislation desired by the resident senior members. In the views of the commission,
these were positive moves and they merely took them a stage further by ending the
division of Council into three constituencies and making Congregation sovereign.
The relationship between the University and the colleges was also barely touched,
although Asquith, in June 1920, set up a joint Oxford and Cambridge committee
containing representatives of both sub-commissions to look at the problem. As a
result of the war, some of the shine had gone off the German model, but several
of its members still wanted to bring all academic appointments at Oxford and
Cambridge under the control of the faculties and greatly reduce the importance of
the Oxford tutors. Strong, while accepting that the sciences were best taught
through the faculties, fought hard for the Oxford status quo, and Asquith, a good

---

[121] Fisher was the author of the 1918 Education Act, which raised the school leaving age to 14 and aimed,
without success, to provide continuing education for all until the age of 18. Fisher was also MP for the combined
universities, 1918–22: in the first part of the twentieth century, besides the MPs representing the universities of
Oxford and Cambridge, there were others sitting for the combined English, Scottish, and Welsh universities and
the University of Belfast.
[122] The other members of the Oxford section were the physicist Sir William Bragg (UCL), the mineralogist
Sir Henry Miers (Manchester, though formerly of Oxford), and Mansbridge (WEA).

college man, concurred, asserting, in the course of one discussion, that he 'felt there was a danger of exaggerating the importance of lecturing as compared with tuition'.[123] The result was a compromise that kept the tutorial system intact. The commissioners found the University's teaching staff too few and insufficiently rewarded, and recommended that professors should receive £1,200 per annum. But they said nothing about the balance between faculty and college teaching, simply suggesting that all professors be given college fellowships and all tutors a university lectureship.

There was also little of substance to emerge in regard to the new points at issue. The commissioners opposed any suggestion that Cambridge should concentrate on the sciences and Oxford on the arts, and called for fifteen acres to be set aside in the University Parks for further science buildings. When they approved Oxford's request for state funding, however, they made no recommendation that the money should be ring-fenced in any way, merely emphasizing that it could only be given to the University and not the colleges, except temporarily to the women's colleges, which were in financial difficulties.[124] The commissioners' views on the access question were just as tame. The idle rich, it was suggested, could be removed if, as Curzon desired, the University established a universal entrance examination. Otherwise, it was concluded that little could be done, given that Oxford was a residential university, beyond advocating an increase in the number of state scholarships and local authority awards and making sure that the emoluments of college scholarships were available only to the indigent. There was little enthusiasm for making college life cheaper, although this was an opinion strongly voiced by one of the witnesses, the Oxford-educated champion of workers' education R. H. Tawney, for an alternative was judged to be already at hand: 'To a far greater extent than is commonly realised, provision is already made at Oxford and Cambridge for university education at a moderate cost by the Non-Collegiate Organisations.'[125]

The executive commission established in 1923 to oversee the revision of the University's and colleges' statutes in the light of Asquith's recommendations understandably had little difficulty in completing its work. Chaired by another former viceroy of India, F. J. N. Thesiger, Viscount Chelmsford, and staffed primarily by working Oxford dons, the commissions spent the next four years getting the statutes in order. Most of the colleges in the previous forty years had made amendments to the statutes that they had received in the early 1880s. Many had received permission to increase their number of fellows and establish a retirement age. Some had set up a new category of fellow without emolument; others, with large fellowships, had specifically set aside one or two places on the foundation for young researchers, to allow them to get their feet on the academic ladder. These and more cosmetic changes were generally received by Chelmsford's commissioners approvingly, so that the new statutes issued in 1926 seldom resulted in profound rewriting. Besides insisting that any restrictions concerning marriage were completely lifted, and that

[123] *HUO*, viii. 41. [124] They were given a grant of £4,000 for ten years. [125] *HUO*, viii. 38.

all fellows, not just tutors and college officers, had pension rights, the commissioners' chief concern was to make the composition of a college's fellowship more flexible so that numbers could expand if funds permitted, and opportunities for the young be increased. The major change of 1926, therefore, was that the maximum figures laid down for each category were replaced by minimum ones.[126]

The change wrought at university level by the 1923 commission was scarcely visible. It introduced a retirement age for professors, turned Responsions into a university entrance exam, and gave the green light for what would be designated in 1934 the Science Area. But Chelmsford left little mark on Oxford's governance. As Asquith desired, the commission restricted membership of Congregation to those involved in teaching and administration and stripped Convocation of its veto where Council and Congregation were in disagreement. This, though, was the extent of the changes. The Asquith Commission had thought both the General Board of Faculties and the delegacy administering the University's finances too independent and suggested placing them under Council's control.[127] Yet nothing was done. If Chelmsford left a legacy, it lay in the impetus he gave to a closer cooperation between the University and the colleges, and between the colleges themselves. From 1926, colleges were expected to consult the relevant faculty board before making a tutorial appointment, while two intercollegiate committees were established under the new statutes, one for domestic and the other for estates' bursars.[128] But Asquith was probably more concerned about his failure to become Chancellor when Curzon died than about the limited adoption of his already minimal recommendations.[129] He had sought to make sufficient change to fend off another royal commission, and to that extent he did his work well. There were to be no further royal commissions in the twentieth century, and no detailed consideration of the overall health of the University undertaken by an internal committee for a further forty years.

[126] Again, All Souls escaped reform. The commission accepted that the college used a significant percentage of its income in different ways to support the academic life of the University. Chelmsford had been a former fellow of the college and was to become its warden.

[127] The University's finances in the early twentieth century were controlled by a delegacy consisting of the Vice-Chancellor, Proctors, and six others, known collectively as the Curators of the Chest (after the chest in which the University had kept its small income in its first centuries).

[128] Consulting the relevant faculty board made sense if tutorial fellows were to be offered a university lectureship or departmental demonstratorship, though only a limited number of arts tutors held both a college and university post before the Second World War.

[129] He was feared by the conservative forces in Convocation and he was defeated in the election for the chancellorship by George Viscount Cave, a St John's man and Conservative lord chancellor in Baldwin's first administration: Grundy, *Fifty-Five Years*, pp. 142–5.

CHAPTER 10

Undergraduates and their Education

A. Rationale

In defending the University against the attacks of the *Edinburgh Review* at the beginning of the nineteenth century, Copleston had argued that the narrowness of the Oxford BA curriculum was justified in that it fostered the undergraduate's moral and intellectual development, which was an asset more precious than knowledge. This conception of the value of an Oxford education was deeply rooted by 1850. Even after the University had agreed to extend the curriculum to include the modern subjects that Hamilton and his associates deemed 'useful', all shades of Oxford opinion believed that the University's purpose was to offer a pre-professional liberal education which would form character and train the mind. It was for this reason that Jowett and his friends were so keen to extend the intake from the middle classes. Oxford provided an education that would be of lasting benefit to many more people than a bevy of clergymen and landowners and the odd lawyer. This was a position maintained by scientists as well as arts' tutors and professors. One of the leading lights in the reform movement after 1850 was the regius professor of medicine, Sir Henry Acland, who dedicated his life to improving and extending the nation's medical services.[1] But Acland, throughout his long working association with the University, was totally opposed to the establishment of an undergraduate medical school of the Edinburgh kind. In part, this was to do with the poor hospital facilities in a small provincial town: Oxford lacked the resources to offer a complete medical education. But, as he explained to the 1850 commission, it also reflected his belief that medicine was a postgraduate study and that medical practitioners should not start their practical and clinical training before they had received a broad liberal education in the arts and sciences. The professor of chemistry, Sir Benjamin Brodie, in his evidence before the 1867 parliamentary committee on extension, concurred.[2]

---

[1] J. B. Atlay, *Sir Henry Wentworth Acland, Bart. K.C.B, F.R.S., Regius Professor of Medicine at the University of Oxford: A Memoir* (London, 1903), pp. 130–61, 197–226, 244–8, 395–7. There is no modern biography.

[2] Commission (1852), *Evidence*, pp. 235–9; Select Committee (1867), *Evidence*, p. 11.

FIGURE 10.1 Benjamin Jowett, 1817–93, Hellenist and tutor and master of Balliol. Jowett came up to Balliol in 1835 and never left until he died. A fanatical believer in the power of the tutorial system to create a race of benign supermen who would dedicate their lives to doing good, he was a college man through and through: he had no interest in turning Oxford into a research university. The drawing after Désiré François Laugée shows him holding a copy of his beloved Plato.

The idea that an Oxford undergraduate education was intended to be a preparation for an active and purposeful life was a position repeated so frequently in the century before the Second World War that it became clichéd. However, if it was a view accepted by all parties, there were differences of emphasis between the different factions, especially in the early stages of reform. Pusey and the Tractarians, following Newman, played up the religious and spiritual dimension of an Oxford education and suspected that the liberals accorded them little importance.[3] Conversely, most liberals, especially those educated at Rugby, saw Oxford as an extension of the new public school created by Thomas Arnold. An Oxford education should not be a vehicle for promoting denominational Christianity, but a conduit for sharpening the mind and character of a Christian gentleman who was ready to go out into the world and serve mankind in any capacity. Jowett had been to St Paul's, not Rugby, but this was his view to a T (see Figure 10.1). The master of

---

[3] Cf. his *Collegiate and Professorial Teaching and Discipline: in answer to professor Vaughan's strictures, chiefly as to the charges against the colleges of France and Germany* (Oxford, 1854), esp. pp. 213–16. For the genesis of this pamphlet, see Chapter 12, n.1.

Balliol was an ethical absolutist who was completely loyal to the Victorian values of his own day, which he believed had been perfected in ancient Greece: Plato and Christ tended to be merged into one in his thought. But he was also a Christian rationalist who became notorious for his historical and sceptical approach to the Scriptures through his contribution to the infamous *Essays and Reviews* of 1860. The last thing he wanted an Oxford education to do was to release doctrinal bigots on the world. What he sought, even as a young tutor, was to imbue his students with a sense of purpose and a hatred of waste, be it of time or talent:

> The heart of a young man, one would have thought, should leap within them at the feeling the future is still theirs, that whatever they do day by day is not a toilsome service to receive its penny a day, but shall bring forth fruit abundantly, turning their life from a waste into a fairly cultivated field on which the sun shines and the rains descend, and it brings forth an hundred fold, for it was sown in due season.[4]

The continued emphasis on the moral and mental value of an Oxford under-graduate education in the age of reform, however, was not without its difficulties. Copleston's argument had been specifically conceived as a justification for the study of Greats. Once undergraduates had to take only Classical Mods and eventually could escape the study of classics altogether, it was not immediately obvious that the other schools established in 1850 brought the same benefits. From the begin-ning, the natural sciences fitted uncomfortably into the schema. When Pusey gave his evidence to the University's commissioners in 1853, he came close to arguing that the sciences had no place in a liberal education, as their study was 'confined to the reception of *information* as to matters of fact, or which require the aid of the eye, as in experiments, anatomical demonstrations or the like'. They were not subjects which involved 'continued reasoning' and were therefore more suited for profes-sional than general study.[5] Jowett would have strongly disagreed, but he too tended to think of the classics, especially classical philosophy and the divine Plato, when he imagined the benefits accruing from an Oxford education. His own interest in and knowledge of the natural sciences was minimal. The establishment of a separate School of Jurisprudence in 1872 only magnified the problem. While law remained connected with modern history, it was primarily a study of the English past from the Norman Conquest to the outbreak of the War of the Spanish Succession in 1702, and the development of English law over the same period as knocked into coherent shape by Blackstone in the mid-eighteenth century.[6] It was scarcely a professional subject. But once law was a separate school, it became harder to claim it had no connection with contemporary legal practice. The additional schools created be-tween 1870 and 1930 were usually even greater objects of suspicion in the beginning.

---

[4] Geoffrey Faber, *Jowett* (London, 1957), p. 131. For Jowett's religious views, see ibid., esp. chs xl and xii. In his publications on Plato, Jowett got around Greek homoeroticism by claiming Greek, unlike Victorian, women were inadequate intellectual companions: ibid., ch. v. *Essays and Reviews*, ed. John William Parker, was a collection of seven essays which urged the Bible must be read critically, like any other book. It was an instant best-seller, but the authors were threatened with the ecclesiastical courts.

[5] Report (1853), *Evidence*, pp. 2–3.   [6] Examination Statute (1850), ch. 8, paras 26–29: OUS, ii. 316–17.

It was relatively easy to argue that theology and oriental languages were congruent with the Oxford concept of a liberal education. Promoters of other possible schools had to fight long and hard to demonstrate that the discipline they championed was suitably character-building. New schools were judged either too soft or too professional.

Where the humanities were concerned, the University solved any potential absence of fit between theory and reality by constructing syllabuses that reflected the educational ideal. Everything was done to privilege the distant past so that there could be no suggestion that teachers were cramming pupils with useful presentist knowledge. At the same time, courses were built around set texts which would, as much as possible, impart the same benefits as Greats. Modern history became essentially the study of English constitutional history, anchored firmly in the middle ages, using Stubbs' *Select Charters*, a collection of documents published in 1870 by William Stubbs, the first distinguished historian to occupy the regius chair.[7] The English School, once finally established in 1894, gave pride of place to Anglo-Saxon and Middle English, so that the students would encounter similar linguistic and textual challenges as their peers reading classics or oriental languages.[8] No humanities school, moreover, aimed to produce scholars or specialists. An Oxford education was not meant to be a training ground for the next generation of academics: that smacked too much of professionalization, the besetting sin of the German universities. Instead, the courses covered large swathes of time with the intention of giving undergraduates an overview rather than specialist knowledge.

Fitting natural science into the Oxford ethos, on the other hand, was more difficult. Scientists throughout the period took a leaf out of Acland's book and allayed colleagues' suspicions that Oxford was selling out to utility by demonstrating their broader cultural interests and endorsing Coplestonian values in lectures and speeches. Engineering became acceptable as a degree course from 1909, once it was agreed that undergraduates would not receive workshop training. But forestry and agriculture had to wait another ten years to win a place in the sun. When forestry was proposed as an honour school in 1910, the suggestion was rejected in Convocation on the grounds it was not a science but 'rather an art, or calling, or occupation'.[9] Developments in the Natural Science School from the second half of the 1880s, moreover, appeared to be taking it in a different direction from the humanities faculties. Released from taking Honour or Pass Classical Mods, science undergraduates were free to specialize once they had passed the General Science Prelim. As a result, the school seemed in danger of becoming the training ground of experts rather than gentlemen generalists. The future law lord Kenneth Diplock, up in the 1920s at University College, read chemistry before training for the bar. In a pamphlet written in 1929, he was scathing about his undergraduate studies. Oxford science undergraduates pursued fact-based, career-orientated courses and had no

---

[7] His work is briefly explored on pp. 499–500, this volume.   [8] See p. 382, this volume.
[9] *HUO*, vii. 476.

time to cultivate the mind.[10] This helps to explain why not every scientist in the University wanted to see the back of compulsory Greek: there was a fear that science undergraduates would become second-class citizens.

In fact, there was no likelihood of this happening, for, by the late nineteenth century, the mental and moral value of an Oxford education was felt to derive as much from the form of instruction and residence in a college as from the curriculum itself. Despite the criticism of inadequacy levelled at college tutors in the first half of the nineteenth century, undergraduate teaching remained firmly in their hands after 1850. By the First World War, even science teaching was largely anchored in the colleges. In the eyes of most reformers, this was essential given the *raison d'être* of the curriculum: a system based on the continual interaction between teacher and pupil was judged far more effective in developing an undergraduate's mental faculties than formal lectures, whatever the course of study. Residence of three to four years in a quasi-monastic community was also deemed to play a vital role in turning giddy youth into purposeful young men. The college was viewed as a large family where undergraduates from different schools, backgrounds, and confessions lived cheek by jowl and purportedly learnt to tolerate, respect, and cooperate with others, above all through playing intercollegiate sport. Team sports in the second half of the century, especially rowing, were an increasingly important, and sometimes all-consuming, aspect of college life. They supposedly broke down barriers, taught the advantages of working together, and fostered leadership skills, all essential lessons for life.[11]

This view of the college as a sheltered womb from which adolescents emerged as Christian gentlemen transformed by the character-building effects of playing competitive sport completely changed the way undergraduates and fellows were taught to relate to their college. Undergraduates in the past had developed a loyalty to their college simply by dint of living within its walls for a number of years. Had this not been the case, there could have been no successful appeal for funds. The publication of the class list in the first part of the nineteenth century also helped to foster a college identity among members of successful colleges like Oriel and Balliol. But the evolving concept of the college as a site of physical as well as mental exertion, where boys were turned into men in the maelstrom of intercollegiate sport, gave that loyalty a novel intensity. Undergraduates were encouraged to see their college as a special place, and to see themselves as college men first and Oxford men, even Britons, a poor second.

This conception of the transformative value of team games was not a view espoused by the first generation of reformers. Jowett, for one, had little interest in sport and believed that the pre-eminence of a Balliol education stemmed principally from the high quality of its tutorial teaching and the intellectual standards of the undergraduates. The idea that team games were character-forming came out of the reformed public schools of the mid-Victorian era that Arnold had helped to

[10] W. J. K. Diplock, *Isis; or the Future of Oxford* (London, 1929).   [11] Discussed, pp. 453–5, this volume.

promote, though it was not an Arnoldian concept and developed after the doctor was dead.[12] The public schools and the University were closely intertwined in the second half of the nineteenth century in a way that had not been the case before.[13] As public-school pupils now formed the majority of undergraduates, and fellows became public schoolmasters and vice versa, the sporting ethos rapidly spread to Oxford. At first, it was diffused by the students and younger dons, but in 1879 one of the champions of the bonding power of games became a head of house. In that year, John Percival, headmaster of Clifton, was elected president of Trinity. The Bristol school had been founded only in 1860, but under Percival it quickly developed a reputation for its messianic commitment to the ideal of education for Christian service, its insistence on hard work, and its promotion of team sports as the foundation of character. Percival also encouraged his boys to believe that their school was unique.[14]

Percival was a mixed success at Trinity. He was appalled by the idleness of many undergraduates and the lack of corporate spirit in the college, but he set out to foster it by treating undergraduates like schoolboys. He was a petty disciplinarian, quizzed undergraduates continually on their commitment to study, and, none too subtly, promoted his ideal of the Christian gentleman in his sermons, as the critic and historian Octavius Christie recalled in his memoirs:

> I have heard him in the chapel of Trinity impliedly divide his undergraduate congregation into two classes: (1) the Whites, hard-reading scholars, steady conscientious men (preferably teetotallers and non-smokers) destined to be clergymen, schoolmasters, writers on Social Reform, philanthropic manufacturers of great municipal activity, or Radical Members of Parliament; (2) the Blacks, hunting men, betting men, frequenters of billiard-rooms, taverns and houses of ill-fame...As a matter of fact, more than ninety per cent of us at Trinity were neither Black nor White, but of various hues of Grey.[15]

As a result, the erstwhile headmaster encountered opposition from both undergraduates and fellows and demitted after only eight years. Yet in that short time Percival seems to have raised the college's stock in the University considerably. More importantly, through his team-building sermons and encouragement of Trinity's sportsmen, he set out a new view of the role of a head of house as the promoter of college spirit, which later heads developed.

Percival's most fervent disciple at the turn of the twentieth century was Herbert Warren, president of Magdalen from 1885 to 1928 (see Figure 10.2). Although a Balliol undergraduate in the era of Jowett in the 1870s, he had spent four years at Clifton in his adolescence and had been smitten for life. Warren set out to turn

---

[12] John Chandos, *Boys Together: English Public Schools 1800–1864* (London, 1984), pp. 266 and 331–40.
[13] See pp. 407–8, this volume.
[14] While at Clifton, Percival had been the leading figure in the foundation of University College, Bristol; he was the author of *The Connection of the Universities and the Great Towns* (1873).
[15] Octavius Christie, *Clifton School Days (1879–1885)* (London, 1930), pp. 23–4. Christie also wrote a history of the school.

FIGURE 10.2 Herbert Warren, 1853–1930, long-serving president of Magdalen. Warren was a product of Balliol but more interested in creating rounded individuals than super intellects. He presided over Magdalen for forty years and gained a reputation, somewhat unfairly, for being a snob who loved an undergraduate lord.

Magdalen's undergraduates into Magdalen men, young adults who, in the course of their stay, would be rebaptized with a new collective identity which would be their primary identity for life. For this to happen, the college could not tolerate independent cliques or factions. Everyone had to put their hand to the common wheel and everyone should participate in college sport: Warren himself was known to row stroke on occasion. In the president's eyes, Magdalen was 'a palace' and there was no room within its portals for 'the baleful creations of vice and selfishness and sensuality'. Warren genuinely believed he had created a race apart and, in full flow, his rhetoric could reach empyreal heights:

> We can, we must, all be something … We are here, citizens, I feel, I am sure we all feel, of no mean city … It belongs to every one of us. Every one of us is a Magdalen man—the poorest, the least clever, the least conspicuous. Every one of us, every set in this place, ought to feel that. We are either worthy of it, or we are not worthy of it. Its

name, its fame is in our hands we cannot disown it ... You go carrying the name of this place with you everywhere ... people will say of you 'that is a Magdalen man, that is what they are like, he is a specimen'.[16]

At the end of the day, therefore, all Oxford undergraduates, irrespective of their subject of study, were expected to go down from the University bursting with energy, their minds and bodies honed to serve their fellow man to the best of their ability. And by the end of the nineteenth century, they were encouraged to think of operating on a global canvas. The alumni of Ancien Regime Oxford had predominantly made careers for themselves in the church and to a less extent in government, if they had careers at all. Their successors in the years before 1914 were taught the need both to have a purposeful career and to show their regenerate character by taking up the white man's burden and bringing British values to the rest of the world in the manner of Oxford's three great imperial visionaries: Cecil Rhodes, Alfred Milner, the founding father of the Union of South Africa, and George Curzon, viceroy of India.[17] Most influential dons were ardent imperialists. At their crudest, Oxonians preached the right of white Anglo-Saxons to take over the world. According to Oxford's first professor of art, John Ruskin, in his inaugural lecture of 1870, 'This is what England must do or perish. She must found Colonies as fast and as far as she is able, formed of her most energetic and worthiest men, seizing every piece she can get her feet on.'[18] In the main, however, supporters of imperialism were not jingoistic and opposed unsupervised land grabs. Jowett and his Balliol idealist colleagues, T. H. Green and Arnold Toynbee Snr, saw empire as a positive force for good, provided that the colonies were closely controlled by the state and run by officials who understood that the British were there to improve the lot of the natives. Oriel's the Reverend Lancelot Ridley Phelps, Oxford's most enthusiastic imperialist of the next generation, agreed.[19] In their eyes, Oxford's role was to provide the empire with right-minded administrators, men who would treat Indians and Africans with courtesy and understand that risking life and limb in the service of the poor and deprived of the world was the noblest of careers. An Oxford education, especially in classics, would give such men the tools to do this. Morally armed with Greek philosophy and with some sense of the problems of empire from reading Thucydides, they were suitably prepared for the adventure.[20]

Not every Oxford don at the turn of the twentieth century swallowed the concept of an Oxford education in its entirety. Most professors accepted the continued centrality of the tutorial system but even humanities professors could jib at the Oxford suspicion of specialization. An emphasis on providing a liberal and not a

---

[16] Herbert Warren, *College Unity* (Oxford, 1885), pp. 3, 21–2, 24.

[17] Milner, like Curzon, was a Balliol man.

[18] Richard Symonds, *Oxford and Empire: The Last Lost Cause?* (Basingstoke, 1986), p. 25.

[19] Phelps was an Oriel fellow from 1877, tutor from 1893, and provost from 1914 to 1929. He was a disciple of T. H. Green, a keen advocate of extension, and a Liberal with a hard-nosed view of the poor. For Green and the Oxford idealists, see pp. 498–9, this volume.

[20] Rhodes had a copy of Aristotle with him on the Veldt.

vocational education could go too far if it meant that an honours course was not a preparation for the next generation of scholars in the discipline. It was this that the regius professor of modern history, Charles Firth, found so galling about the modern history curriculum when he returned to Oxford to take up his chair in 1904.[21] A minority of dons also took issue with the global vision of service. Oxford was the alma mater of leading anti-imperialists as well as imperialists. Among the tutors, one significant opponent of imperialism was the Corpus fellow L. T. Hobhouse, the first professor of sociology at the LSE.[22] Another was Richard Congreve of Wadham, who was a follower of the French philosopher Auguste Comte. He headed a group of other Comtean Positivists in the college who adopted the Frenchman's dislike of empire and argued in numerous books and articles that India should be handed over to an international commission.[23] Among the professors, the anti-imperialist flame was kept burning in the Edwardian era by the regius professor of Greek, Gilbert Murray. Oxonian imperialists found much to admire and imitate in the classical past. A comparative study of the Roman and British empires, published in 1914 by James Viscount Bryce, the former regius professor of civil law, confidently looked forward to India being totally Europeanized by its benign rulers, just as Europe had been formerly Romanized. But Murray, Australian and Catholic by origin, drew no such comfort from his knowledge of ancient Greece. Britain was the new Athens and would be more likely to become corrupted by empire than bestow lasting benefits:

> [A]n Athenian or Englishman is bound in self respect to be in various ways better than his neighbours, worthy of his country…I cannot help seeing in modern England as in ancient Athens a dangerous extension of this: an argument that because Englishmen are superior creatures therefore they should be allowed a little extra latitude.[24]

The First World War only strengthened the position of internal critics. The country's obvious need for more specialist scientists, the huge slaughter, the break-up of the United Kingdom, and the stirrings of nationalist discontent in the empire encouraged a new generation of dons, many of whom had served in the trenches, to doubt some of the much vaunted benefits of an Oxford education. It was usually accepted in the interwar years that Oxford should be a transformative intellectual experience and that an undergraduate would best flourish within the caring embrace of the right college. But the old idea that an undergraduate curriculum should eschew the practical and the contemporary was no longer so readily subscribed to. Many

---

[21] See p. 385, this volume. Pattison had preached the merits of specialization as early as 1868, claiming it to be the key to the development of the mental faculties, especially judgement.

[22] Hobhouse was another, albeit critical, disciple of Green, who opposed the Boer War. He became a supporter of the interventionist liberalism of Lloyd George and Asquith.

[23] Comte looked for a solution to mankind's many social problems through the creation of a science of society akin to the physical sciences, and had a vision of the future where all races were bound together in harmony by a religion of humanity.

[24] From a letter to John Buchan working with Milner in South Africa, cited in Symonds, *Oxford and Empire*, p. 92.

dons still revelled in the 'uselessness' of their subject. G. H. Hardy, who held the Savilian chair of geometry in the 1920s, delighted in telling audiences that pure mathematics brought no public benefit whatsoever. But aversion to vocational learning, especially among scientists, was lessening in the interwar years, as were objections to presentism.[25] It was recognized by the 1930s that most Oxford graduates would have to go out into the world and earn a living, and that an Oxford degree, for all its intellectual value, did not automatically lead to a good career. Students then were encouraged to think ahead when choosing their course and were alerted to the fact that in many cases they should expect to undertake specific vocational training after going down.[26] It also came to be widely accepted that an Oxford undergraduate course should at least offer the chance to develop research skills. The most radical curricular development occurred in chemistry. Such was the pressure for high-quality scientists during the First World War that, in 1916, it was agreed to make Oxford's most popular natural science school a four-year course with two parts, the second devoted to a personal research project.[27]

Also greatly, if not entirely, eroded was the conviction that Oxford was in the business of creating Christian gentlemen. The need for undergraduates to demonstrate that they were acquainted with the basic tenets of Christianity survived the abolition of subscription in 1854, for a divinity examination was retained in both Classical Mods and Schools. When Classical Mods ceased to be a compulsory exam for all undergraduates in 1887, Christian undergraduates, regardless of their denominational background, were still expected to show they were biblically literate: none could thereafter graduate unless they had passed a new divinity examination, commonly called 'Divvers'. In the aftermath of the Great War, many dons felt the exam had no place in a modern university. Before 1914, there were few senior members who were not committed Christians. After the experience of the trenches, many younger dons returned to Oxford having lost what little faith they had: some embraced humanism, a few Marxism. Although the majority of senior members elected to fellowships in the 1920s and 1930s seldom went so far and remained largely Christian in outlook, they were equally unwilling to embrace the muscular Christianity of the pre-war generation and preferred to keep their religious beliefs to themselves. In such a different atmosphere, it is not surprising that, in 1931, once the old guard had retired or died, 'Divvers' was abolished. Even the fervent Christians to be found in Christ Church—between the wars a bastion of conservatism of all kinds—were not overly concerned. 'Divvers' was already treated by undergraduates and their examiners in a relatively light-hearted way before the First World War. In the 1920s it was treated with disrespect even by believers. The poet John Betjeman, a Magdalen undergraduate who, in adult life, became a fervent Anglican, somehow managed to fail 'Divvers' twice in 1928. His irreverent response to his first failure was

---

[25] Admittedly, the undergraduate course in agriculture was in theory not practice.
[26] *Handbook to the University of Oxford* (Oxford, 1932), 'Callings and Careers', p. 283ff.
[27] This became the unique selling point of Oxford chemistry as no other university followed suit.

to write an article for a student magazine which contained tips for those wanting to pass without effort—special cut-out cuffs bearing details from the Old and New Testaments—and a spoof exam paper whose questions included: 'Where is Rugby mentioned in the Bible?'

Most tutors, after 1918, still expected that their charges would make something of themselves and contribute to the general good. But there was little sense, once Warren and his generation had passed on, that an Oxford education was training missionaries who would reshape the world. The imperial vision was certainly all but dead. In the years 1895 to 1914, the empire had been a topic of constant debate in the *Oxford Magazine*, the dons' weekly journal established in 1883. In the years following 1918 the subject dropped from sight.[28] What survived from the pre-war era was the belief that an Oxford education provided a training of the mind and that the tutorial system was the key to its efficacy. Most post-war tutors were dedicated teachers and were no more willing than their predecessors to allow undergraduate teaching to become predominantly lecture-based, or the colleges simple halls of residence. Indeed, as all colleges increased their tutorial provision between the wars, especially in the sciences, thanks in part to the willingness of the University to use its government funding to take up part of the cost, the tutorial system became ever more deeply embedded. Some tutors, though, were not just interested in teaching the young to think but wanted to open young minds in new and subversive ways. The most notorious was Maurice Bowra, who tutored in Classics Mods at Wadham from 1922 to 1938 and deliberately pulled into his web the most talented arts students of the interwar years. Bowra was not interested in training citizens but subversives who would mock the establishment and learn to live as the Greeks had really done, physically and intellectually. In many respects, Pusey, Jowett, or even Copleston would still have felt a close affinity with the Oxford of the 1930s, but they would have been appalled by the 'Bowristas' and their rejection of conventional Christian morality.[29]

B. Recruitment and Distribution

The number of adolescents who sought to have their minds whetted by the Oxford tutorial system grew steadily after 1860. In 1842 there had been only 1,222 undergraduates in residence. By 1913, the figure had almost tripled to 3,000, and by 1939–40 it had risen again to about 4,400, of whom 850 were women. The expansion was primarily fuelled by upper-middle-class families deciding to send their sons (and, from the 1880s, their daughters) to the University for the first time,

---

[28] Some old members remained locked in the past. Sir George Whitehead, who lost two sons in the war, gave money to Trinity in 1924 to establish a travelling scholarship which would teach men to 'think Imperially': Hopkins, p. 364.

[29] Leslie Mitchell, *Maurice Bowra: A Life* (Oxford, 2009), esp. ch. 7. Bowra's own *Memories 1898–1939* (London, 1966) provide a clear account of his appreciation of the Greek inheritance but are coyer about the activities and prejudices of his circle.

just as Jowett and like-minded reformers had wanted. Limited educational opportunities and the absence of full-cost government grants meant that few undergraduates, even between the wars, came from the lower-middle and working classes.[30] But the University was never as successful in attracting the offspring of the substantial middle classes as the liberals had hoped. The proportion of young men entering business or the professions who had been to any university, let alone Oxford or Cambridge, before the Second World War always remained low. An increasing number would have needed to pass professional exams to be fully qualified, but few, apart from clergymen, medical practitioners, and barristers, were expected to have received a higher education. The large majority of people in middle-class occupations, even on the eve of the Second World War, left school at 15 or 16 and trained on the job: their families saw little point in wasting £200 to £300 a year on an expensive Oxford liberal education. As a result, the University was well aware that, by the late 1930s, Oxford had reached the limits of its possible expansion within the existing system of supply and demand, especially with the birth rate falling among the better off. Significantly, even under the more rigorous entrance procedures of the interwar era, scarcely any prospective undergraduates were turned down: there was virtually a perfect fit between the number of applicants and the number of places the colleges had to offer.

The large majority of male undergraduates, all but those from the poorest families, had much the same educational background. In the first half of the nineteenth century, about a third of matriculands had attended one of the nine most famous English secondary schools, which later became known as the Clarendon schools.[31] The rest had been to a wide variety of grammar schools and private academies, and many had been tutored at home. In the first decades of the twentieth century, in contrast, the large majority of male undergraduates, between 65 and 70 per cent, had had a common schooling at one of the hundred or so recognized public boarding schools that had been founded or re-established in the mid-Victorian era on Arnoldian lines, and attracted the sons of upper- and well-to-do middle-class families in droves. In 1902–4 only 13 per cent of the intake came from schools in receipt of a government grant, and the fraction never rose above a quarter even in the interwar years. Before 1914, moreover, some 40 per cent of male matriculands were drawn from a small group of twenty-two schools, above all Eton, Winchester, and Rugby. Some colleges were particularly exclusive. At University College in 1894–7 two-thirds of its freshmen were drawn from the Clarendon schools alone, and only five of the number had attended a grammar school; while Balliol, which under Jowett had had lots of grammar-school boys, drew 24 per cent of its intake in 1894–1903 from Eton and Harrow. The dominance of a handful of Clarendon schools was greatly reduced between the wars when most male colleges recruited predominantly from the less

---

[30] See pp. 387 and 390–1, this volume.
[31] Eton, Harrow, Winchester, Rugby, St Paul's, Shrewsbury, Westminster, Charterhouse, and Merchant Taylors'. They were given the name after the Clarendon Commission, a royal commission set up in 1861 to look at their governance.

prestigious public schools and took in a growing number of state-school pupils. But the elite schools never lost their grip entirely. New College was always full of Wykehamists, while Magdalen, always one of the posh colleges, still drew 48 per cent of its undergraduates from the Clarendon schools in 1928 and over a third just from Eton and Winchester. Only unfashionable colleges, like Worcester, Jesus, Lincoln, Queen's, Wadham, and St Edmund Hall, were relatively free of their influence, and only the non-collegiates contained a large proportion of non-public-school men: 47 per cent in 1895–8.

The importance of the public schools to Oxford's recruitment over the period emphasizes that it remained largely an English as well as an elitist university before the Second World War. Indeed, if a larger proportion of undergraduates were drawn from the north and east of the country than in the pre-modern era, it still relied heavily on the southern and western counties for its intake: London and the south-east alone usually produced a third of matriculands each year.[32] In contrast with earlier centuries, however, Oxford, by the turn of the twentieth century, attracted students from other nations as well. A small Scottish, and an even smaller Irish presence from the 1870s—illustrated if not epitomized by Oscar Wilde's sojourn at Magdalen—suggested that late Victorian Oxford was now, in some regard, a British and not just an English university, while the Edwardian era witnessed the arrival of the first significant cohort of foreign students. Their representation quickly expanded, so by 1939 Oxford had welcomed students from most parts of the world at one time or another. The large majority always came from the white dominions and the USA. Among male matriculands in 1920–1, fully a third were born to parents domiciled outside Britain, but only 2 per cent were from neighbouring Europe and a further 3 from non-Anglophone countries.[33]

Australians, Canadians, and South Africans, though not many Americans, had begun to turn up at Oxford before 1900. One of the first was the Canadian G.M. Wrong, who stayed at Balliol for a short time in the late 1870s and went on to become the first professor of history at the University of Toronto. Their numbers, though, were very small before the establishment of the Rhodes Scholarship scheme in 1902. Cecil Rhodes dreamt of binding together the British and German empires and the USA in one grandiose Anglo-Saxon alliance that would dominate the world for the general good (see Figure 10.3). To help realize his vision, he established, under his will, a trust fund to allow students from South Africa, Canada, Australasia, America, and Germany to come to Oxford to enjoy its advantages. Candidacy was not to be limited by race or religion, and the scholars had to have already demonstrated they were academic, sporty, and men of character to ensure that they obtained the maximum benefit from their studies.[34] Rhodes' bequest was

---

[32] Lawrence Stone, 'The Size and Composition of the Oxford Student Body 1580–1910', in Lawrence Stone (ed.), *The University in Society*, vol. 1: *Oxford and Cambridge* (Princeton, NJ, 1975), p. 102 (table).
[33] In the same year all but 6 per cent of female matriculands were British.
[34] There were also a few scholarships for natives of the West Indies but none for Indians.

FIGURE 10.3 Cecil John Rhodes, 1853–1902, imperialist and university benefactor. Rhodes was not an impressive undergraduate while up at Oriel, but through the establishment of the Rhodes Scholarship scheme under his will, he played a leading role in laying the foundations of the modern international university.

munificent and by 1906 there were already 161 scholars in residence enjoying a maintenance allowance of £300 per annum: seventy-one from the British colonies, seventy-nine from the United States, and eleven from Germany. Unlike college places more generally, the Rhodes scheme was heavily oversubscribed. Half of the 2,000 applicants in the first few years did not even have the right qualifications to be considered by the local institutions and committees entrusted with the task of selection.

As similar bursary schemes were not available for nationals from other parts of the world, representation from other countries was sporadic and usually limited to the rich and highly connected. Besides numerous Indian princes lured to Oxford from the 1890s by the thought of mixing with the scions of the British aristocracy, there were always one or two exotic catches who were the delight of the heads who had landed them, like the Russian Prince Felix Yusupov, one of the assassins of Rasputin, who matriculated from University College in 1909, or the Japanese Prince Chichibu, who was netted for Magdalen by Warren in 1926. Poorer students from distant places, such as the Syrian Christian Edward Atiyah, who found his way to Brasenose in 1923 armed with a letter of recommendation from Lord Allenby, the Egyptian High Commissioner, were very rare.[35]

Foreign students seem to have been generally made welcome. There were some initial fears that the Rhodes scheme would erode Oxford's commitment to under-graduate education since most of the scholars would already have a degree from their home university and want to undertake postgraduate work. The Oxford Union Society even passed, by a huge majority, a motion thoroughly condemning the move. The fears, however, were quickly put to rest. Rhodes had made clear that his scholars were to follow a BA course, and only the Germans, who were the products of a very different university system, wanted to move on to higher studies.[36] There was little religious or racial discrimination. It was the Rhodes scholars from the American south not the English natives who were disconcerted when a Harvard African-American was elected in 1907.[37] The one group that did suffer prejudice in some colleges were Indians from the subcontinent. Jowett encouraged them to come to Oxford, and between 1871 and 1893 as many as forty-nine matriculated. But Trinity and Magdalen were notoriously racist for most of the period. The two sons of the Nawab of Moorshedabad were eventually accepted at Trinity in 1893, when their headmaster at Rugby, the erstwhile President Percival, pleaded their cause, but nearly twenty years later P. T. Rajan, a pupil at the Leys School Cambridge, was not so fortunate. Writing to Rajan's headmaster, President Herbert Blakiston made his position crystal clear: 'I should add that we have not had an Indian at this college for nearly twenty years, and are not anxious to encourage Indian students to come to Oxford.'[38]

For the most part, regardless of the rhetoric about the uniqueness of each institu-tion and the need to choose a college with care, most undergraduates, wherever they hailed from, ended up at college because either their father, other relatives, or family friends had been there, or it was recommended by their school. Colleges never specialized. Some colleges became associated with a particular subject, such as Corpus for classics, but the majority took students to read for any school in the undergraduate curriculum. Few students, therefore, ever selected a college for its subject profile, even if some colleges had a fuller complement of tutors than others. Nor was there usually much need to apply to a particular college to enhance the chances of winning a scholarship. The 400 open scholarships available for the intellectually gifted in 1914 were unevenly distributed, as they had been in the past. But apart from Balliol, colleges pooled their resources from the end of the nineteenth century and organized the scholarship examination in groups, dividing the best candidates between them.[39] Some colleges certainly had a better academic record

---

[35] Atiyah left an account of his time at Oxford: *An Arab Tells his Story: A Study in Loyalties* (London, 1946).
[36] The first three German Rhodes to arrive in 1903 were immaculately dressed in top hats and frock coats, and clicked their heels in unison when they met the Trust's secretary.
[37] Oxford's first black graduate was the University College student Christian Cole of Sierra Leone, who took his degree in 1877.
[38] Hopkins, p. 344. He eventually went to Jesus.
[39] There were a further 100 closed scholarships connected with particular schools.

than others. For most of the period Balliol was the college to which the intellectually ambitious gravitated; Magdalen, for all of Warren's bluster, one for those with more modest aspirations. But every college had a leaven of gifted students, however small, and few undergraduates can have been directed towards an Oxford college on purely intellectual grounds. Parents were more likely to have been influenced by the religious tone of the establishment. When Magdalen's dean of divinity, J.M. Thompson, got in trouble for his ultra-rationalist views on miracles in a book published in 1911, the vice-provost of Lancing was soon writing to Warren to inform him that nervous parents were thinking twice about sending their sons to such a godless institution.[40]

As there were only two new male colleges founded before the First World War, whatever college a male undergraduate eventually elected to enter was sure to have a much larger student population than in the years before 1850. In 1842, the number of undergraduates in residence in any one college ranged from seventeen to 154; in 1911, the smallest college, St Edmund Hall, had 46, the largest 230. But there were significant changes in the pecking order. In the early 1840s, four colleges, three among the best endowed, had had scarcely any students—Magdalen, Corpus, New College, and Merton. All four began to admit large numbers of undergraduates after 1860, in particular New, which had a mere twenty-two students in residence in the early 1840s and was the most populous Oxford college seventy years later. Other colleges also expanded at a rapid rate, especially Jesus, which, thanks to the careful exploitation of its traditional Welsh connections, had 124 undergraduates on its books on the eve of the Great War, almost four times as many as in the early years of Victoria's reign. In contrast, several colleges failed even to double in size. Exeter had always been one of the most frequented colleges in the early modern period and was the second largest society in 1842 with 111 undergraduates. It was still the seventh largest in 1911, or sixth if the non-collegiates are excluded, but it had managed to increase the numbers on its books merely to 154. The poor showing of colleges like Exeter reflected their relative poverty. As undergraduates in the new era of expansion expected much better accommodation than their early seventeenth-century predecessors, colleges had to put up new buildings to ensure a fair share of the demand.[41] Only rich colleges had the means to do this without strain, and even then undergraduates had to spend part of their stay at Oxford living out, which was permitted under the legislation admitting non-collegiates.

In all colleges, the undergraduates were extremely unevenly distributed by subject of study. Oxford was always firmly an arts university before the Second World War, and the admission of women only confirmed the bias. In the five years between 1855 and 1860, a paltry 8.1 per cent of honours degrees were awarded to candidates offering natural science. The percentage had risen to 13.7 in the period 1910–14 but it was still only 14.6 in 1938, seven points less than the combined figure for law and PPE, the latter a new subject but already sharing 11.3 per cent of the figure. Honours in natural science, moreover, were only ever earned in significant numbers in three of the sub-schools: physics, chemistry, and physiology. All the rest attracted barely any candidates. Arts candidates too were never evenly distributed among the growing number of schools. Initially when undergraduates were free to graduate in just one school, Greats remained the subject of choice, and as late as the Edwardian era, 48 per cent of Oxford graduates took their degree in either the honour or pass schools, a far higher proportion than the 23 per cent who graduated in modern history, its nearest rival. But the days of classics' dominance were fading and modern history was coming up fast on the rails. In 1873, only sixty candidates took the school, but in 1904, 165 men and twenty-two women did so, and the number taking honours exceeded the number of classicists. Modern history's position as the University's favourite honour school was confirmed in the years following the Great War. In 1923, 29.1 per cent of all undergraduates took honours in the school against 14.8 per cent in Greats, 10.7 per cent in English, and 7.7 per cent in modern languages, the two subjects with particular appeal to women students. However, by 1938, modern history had dropped back in turn. It was still the largest school in the University, with 20.9 per cent of honours graduates, but it had lost many potential students in the interim to the new school of PPE.

By 1938, virtually every Oxford undergraduate took an honours degree. The proportion of undergraduates taking honours surpassed the proportion gaining a pass degree in the mid-1860s, and the two curves continued to diverge until the Great War. By then, only 16 per cent of matriculands emerged with an unclassified degree, and Balliol, New College, Corpus, and St John's had virtually eliminated the species. Only the women's societies and the odd men's college, such as Brasenose, where 30 per cent still aimed at a pass in 1913–14 resisted the lure of specialization. But between the wars the proportion fell quickly and only 3 per cent of undergraduates took a pass in 1935–9. On the other hand, on the eve of the Second World War there still remained a significant minority of undergraduates who left Oxford with no degree at all. In the period 1850–1914, the percentage of undergraduates who never took a BA stayed stubbornly around the 30 per cent mark. The percentage fell in the interwar years, but in the first half of the 1930s, 10 to 15 per cent of male and female matriculands never sat a final examination, and 9 per cent never faced the examiners at any point.

The disappearance of the pass men was not accompanied by a dramatic improvement in the honours results. Before the Second World War, scientists habitually outperformed arts students in the schools, but no subject had particularly sparkling results. The proportion of first-class degrees awarded in all subjects in 1900 was 12 per cent, and the figure barely shifted over the next forty years; nor did the proportion of Thirds, which hovered between 35 to 38 per cent both before and after the First World War. Only the emergence of the Second as the University's favourite class from the first decade of the twentieth century (replacing the Third) suggested that standards were slowly rising. But dramatic improvement was not to be expected while there was a little sign that places were fought over. The disappearance of the pass men reflected policy rather than improvement in the intellectual calibre of

Oxford's intake. With more and more underpowered undergraduates being corralled into taking honours, the proportion of Thirds and Fourths inevitably remained high.[42] For the large majority of undergraduates, too, who had no desire to become scholars and academics, the incentive was lacking, even if they had the talent, to work hard for a First. Given the limited attention paid to a higher-educational qualification in recruiting by most British professions before the Second World War, the average male undergraduate with family connections knew he would have no difficulty in entering a professional career, whatever his degree result. In these circumstances, it is more surprising that an eighth of the undergraduates in every annual cohort had a mind with an edge that tutors could sharpen for examination success, and the wit and the will to submit it to the tutorial whetstone.

C. The College System

College teaching in the first half of the nineteenth century was the responsibility of about fifty college tutors. In the middle of the nineteenth century, the average college had a teaching staff of three: two tutors in classical literature, logic and moral philosophy, and the Greek New Testament; and one in maths. With the extension of the curriculum and the rapid increase in the number of undergraduates after 1860 this number was no longer sufficient. Some reformers had envisaged that the new subjects introduced under the 1850 examination statute could be taught by the professors, but Oxford's commitment to college-based teaching was so strong that, from the 1870s, there was general agreement that some form of tutorial provision had to be made for any new discipline added to the undergraduate curriculum. Pusey in the early 1850s had thought it proper that students reading natural science should be taught through professorial lectures, given the factual nature of the subject. Acland in 1867, though sharing none of Pusey's anti-science prejudices, agreed. In his evidence before the parliamentary select committee of that year, he insisted that science instruction should be permanently based in the new University Museum. Neither had anticipated the tenacity of the college system. Science undergraduates were soon brought under tutorial direction. Magdalen appointed its first tutor in natural science as early as 1868, and Merton and Trinity a few years later in 1872 and 1873. As a result, the number of college tutors offering instruction on every part of the expanding curriculum grew as fast as the undergraduate body, and, until the interwar years, always outstripped the number of university appointments. There were some 150 tutorial fellows in post in 1908, and 214 in 1922; the corresponding figures for the University's postholders were 110 and 143.

In contrast with the first half of the nineteenth century, undergraduates were not always tutored by fellows in their own college, or indeed by fellows at all, so the real

---

[42] It would be wrong, however, to view the pass degree as simply the preserve of the idle and the stupid. As a degree that demanded a wide range of knowledge, it could be attractive to students of all abilities. Cf. the comments in F.H. Lawson, *The Oxford Law School, 1850–1965* (Oxford, 1968), pp. 41, 42, and 45.

number of college teachers was even greater. The men's colleges always had in-house tutors in classics and philosophy who were on the foundation, and most, before the First World War, had a tutor and fellow in modern history. However, the number of students reading one of the other subjects in any one college was often too few or too subject to periodic fluctuation to merit appointing an official fellow in the discipline, given the state of many colleges' finances and the fact that, from the early 1880s until 1926, the number of official fellowships was limited under the statutes.[43] Even a rich college like Magdalen, that could appoint up to thirteen official fellows on the eve of the Great War, did not immediately have tutorial fellows in the small schools. In 1914, the college had four classics and two science fellows and a fellow each in modern history and mathematics. It was only between the wars, especially once the *numerus clausus* was abolished in 1926, that the college really began to expand, appointing its first law fellow in 1921, its first English fellow in 1925 (C. S. Lewis), four more historians (one in ancient history), another science fellow, and eventually fellows in politics and economics.[44] Poorer colleges still had very few tutorial fellows in the 1920s and 1930s. Wadham, for instance, did have a law fellow from 1926 but its only science tutor and fellow before the Second World War was T. C. Keeley, elected in 1924 as tutor in physics.

Where there was no college tutorial fellow in a subject, the undergraduates were taught by a part- or full-time lecturer who was paid either an annual retainer or a capitation fee. This was the simplest way for a college to cover its tutorial obliga- tions while minimizing the expense, for the lecturer could be stood down if there were no clients. Some of these lecturers could be ordinary fellows in the college who might look after a couple of pupils while holding a professorial fellowship or pursuing research. Many were fellows elsewhere. Magdalen's first full-time tutor in modern history, C. R. L. Fletcher, was initially a fellow of All Souls when appointed in the mid-1880s.[45] Some, however, were no more than freelance lecturers who worked for several colleges. When the English honours school was created, University College, in 1898, gave the task of looking after their handful of under- graduates reading the subject to an old member, Ernest de Sélincourt, who himself had read classics. For the next ten years, until he took up a chair at Birmingham, de Sélincourt looked after virtually every member of the infant school in the University, but he never had a college fellowship.

The formal part of a tutor's role in the first half of the nineteenth century was to give lectures on the different parts of the traditional curriculum. These were not ex cathedra monologues but college classes where a group of undergraduates were taken through a text or an exercise they had already supposedly prepared. Class lectures still remained an important part of a tutor's job a century later but had changed their character and were much more formal, though the best were

---

[43] See pp. 366–7 and 394–5, this volume.

[44] Before the Great War, an ordinary fellow, the future head of house, George Gordon, looked after the handful of undergraduates reading English literature. No tuition was supplied in oriental languages.

[45] He became a fellow of Magdalen in 1889. Fletcher was an imperialist ultra. See p. 516 n. 102, this volume.

delivered off the cuff. Moreover, they were no longer given only to undergraduates of the tutor's college. As syllabuses became more specialized, colleges in the last decades of the nineteenth century dealt with the problem of coverage by forming alliances and putting on joint lecture courses. This was a solution supposedly pioneered by Gladstone's son-in-law, E. C. Wickham of New College, in 1868. The history tutors took collaboration one stage further. Faced with a wide-ranging syllabus and increasing numbers of students, they formed the Modern Historians' Association in 1891, which coordinated tutorial lectures across the University.[46] Between the wars, most science tutors gave up lecturing in college altogether and moved to the Science Area. As they were now generally university lecturers and demonstrators as well as college tutors, they were contracted to give classes to all undergraduates in their discipline, and usually only the departments had the appropriate facilities.[47]

The less formal part of the tutor's role in the age of Copleston and Newman had been to look after the pastoral and academic development of a group of under-graduates placed under his charge. This was always considered the key feature of the Oxford tutorial system and remained the case in the century of reform. The role, though, became much more onerous and time-consuming. Tutors, before the mid-nineteenth century, seldom set written work. It was the custom in the 1830s for the undergraduates as a body to be given an essay or theme to do each week, but the responsibility for setting and marking their efforts usually lay with the dean.[48] It was only in the 1840s, on the eve of Newman's departure, that the task began to be usurped by some of the younger tutors, who developed it into a much more individually tailored exercise. Jowett of Balliol, who became a tutor in 1842 and held the office for nearly thirty years, was the most famous of these pioneering spirits. Although a shy man with a high-pitched voice who punctuated his con-versation with long silences, he became a demi-god in the eyes of many of his pupils simply because of the attention he paid them and the confidence he had in their abilities if they worked hard. His uniqueness appears to have lain above all in his dedication. Jowett gave his all to the job, and was ready to offer advice on pupils' work day or night, even if he was not their official tutor and they were not natural scholars. Jowett's principal aim was not exam success, though he nurtured many a Balliol First, but to match the rhetoric with the reality of the tutorial system. According to George Brodrick, a future warden of Merton, Jowett was an expert in honing his pupils' intellects:

> His greatest skill consisted, like that of Socrates, in helping us to learn and think for ourselves...No other tutor, within my experience, has ever approached him in the depth and extent of his pastoral supervision, if I may so call it, of young thinkers, and

---

[46] Another view is that joint courses were the creation of Mandell Creighton of Merton and Robert Laing of Corpus. Collaboration was less common in Lit. Hum., where there was a superfluity of teachers.

[47] There were more than 100 postholders in science in 1937.

[48] Mark Pattison, *Memoirs* (London, 1885), pp. 112–13.

it may truly be said that in his pupil-room, thirty, forty and fifty years ago, were disciplined many of the minds which are now exercising a wide influence over the nation.[49]

Jowett and like-minded tutors in the mid-nineteenth century raised the tutorial bar to new heights and the coach gradually became superfluous for honours men.[50] They did not, though, invent the modern tutorial, where undergraduates on their own, in pairs, or a small group turn up at an appointed time, once or twice a week, to discuss prepared work with their tutors.[51] This seems to have been a development of the 1870s, when Jowett had become master of Balliol and had finally put down his tutorial office. It was in this decade that college tutors, for the first time, were formally contracted to deliver a number of lectures each week and to devote a specified number of hours to private tuition. In the case of W.L. Courtney, who became a classics lecturer at New College in 1876, the balance was six hours of lectures and twelve of tutorials. But by the end of the century, with the growth of intercollegiate lecturing, tutorial work was taking up more and more of a tutor's time. Where tutorials were scheduled to last no more than twenty minutes or half an hour, the teaching load was not overwhelming. Another classicist, Herbert W. Greene of Magdalen, who took Mods pupils individually twice a week for Greek and Latin verse composition in the 1890s and 1900s, got through his twenty or more individual tutorials a week in about eight hours. Historians, however, gave hour-long tutorials from the beginning and had a teaching week that was longer than a public schoolmasters'. H. A. L. Fisher, New College's tutor in history in 1891, was lecturing only twice a week but giving eighteen hours of tutorials. Thirteen years later, in 1912, Magdalen's senior history tutor, C. Grant Robertson, complained that he and his two colleagues had an even greater teaching load: each was giving twenty-four weekly tutorials.[52] The load for many tutors diminished in the interwar years, when those who gained a part-time university post were allowed to cut their college hours to twelve. But not all benefited. A. S. Russell was the Christ Church chemistry tutor from 1920 to 1955. He purportedly spent twenty-five hours a week giving tutorials and a further thirty as a laboratory demonstrator.[53] Inevitably, many

[49] Faber, *Jowett*, p. 167. Another pioneer was Pattison, who would see tutees individually from 8 to 10 p.m. each night: Pattison, *Memoirs*, p. 263; see also his definition of a tutor's duties: ibid., pp. 215–16.

[50] The honours coach existed until about 1880. Pass men were still being coached in 1900. Lewis Farnell, later rector of Exeter, coached for seven hours a day in the late 1870s while attempting to gain a college fellowship. G. B. Grundy, tutor in ancient history at Brasenose from 1904 to 1917, earned a living from coaching in 1897: L. R. Farnell, *An Oxonian Looks Back* (London, 1934), pp. 71–6; G. B. Grundy, *Fifty-Five Years at Oxford: An Unconventional Autobiography* (London, 1945), p. 86. Many tutors before 1900 found the idle among the pass men difficult to handle.

[51] One-to-one tutorials in the first part of the twentieth century were known as 'private hours', a term still common in Christ Church in the 1960s.

[52] Charles Oman, tutor in modern history at New College, had twenty-five pupils in the second half of the 1880s whom he took one at a time and only had Sundays off: Oman, *Memories of a Victorian at Oxford and of Some Early Years* (London, 1941), pp. 136, 148–9.

[53] John Mabbott, a philosophy tutor at St John's, was also still doing twenty-five hours' tutorial teaching a week in the 1920s: John Mabbott, *Oxford Memories* (Oxford, 1986), p. 49. Bowra, who became a Mods classics tutor at Wadham in 1922, was more fortunate: he was expected to give up to eighteen tutorials a week but in the summer term usually gave only nine: *Memories*, p. 148.

tutors found it impossible to complete their teaching within a normal working day, all the more so that, by the end of the nineteenth century, early afternoons were reserved for student recreation. In consequence, tutors, family men or no, could teach late into the evening. Some became famed for their stamina. The first economics fellow appointed by University College, the guild socialist and atheist G. D. H. Cole, elected in 1925, was already in his thirties when he took up his appointment, but he would schedule tutorials for 10.30 at night.

The heavy tutorial load after 1870 meant that tutors had little free time in term. What they had was further eaten up by other newly minted duties. In the Ancien Regime University most administrative matters regarding teaching were left to the head of house, but by the end of the nineteenth century these had largely become the responsibility of a new institution, the tutorial board, established in all colleges under the statutes of the early 1880s. Consisting of the head of house and the official fellows of the college, the tutorial board met several times a term to discuss academic policy, oversee the tutorial budget, sanction new appointments, maintain academic discipline, and organize the admission of scholars on the foundation; normally only the selection of commoners remained in the hands of the head. The board greatly extended the tutors' influence but it steadily embroiled them in more work. As its remit broadened at the turn of the twentieth century, one of their number became its permanent secretary or senior tutor and others found themselves sitting on the subcommittees it soon spawned. Examining duties also steadily increased. In the interwar period, tutors not only had to help set and mark the scholarship and commoners' entrance examinations each year but also administer written in-house examinations or 'collections' at the beginning of each term, an innovation of the 1920s set up to monitor undergraduates' progress and give them some practice in taking Schools.[54] On top of this, dedicated tutors were expected to spend some of their leisure time with their pupils. The most assiduous, like William Stallybrass and Maurice Platnauer at Brasenose between the wars, helped them celebrate their sporting triumphs, mixed with them in their student societies, hosted musical dinners, and virtually every night kept open house, plying students with drink and conversation into the early hours.[55]

Even the vacations did not bring total release for the unmarried. In the first half of the nineteenth century, a tutor might occasionally go off on holiday with one of his pupils to whom he had taken a particular shine. By the end of the century, it was commonplace for tutors to take quite large groups of undergraduates away on a reading party for several weeks, usually at their own expense, either at Easter or in

---

[54] These were based on the previous term's work. The traditional formal oral collections at the end of the term (see p. 256, this volume) continued as before but became an occasion for tutors to comment on progress rather than an opportunity for students to show off their paces. In addition, tutors would periodically have to be university examiners as well.

[55] Some tutors came close to the ideal without liberally dispensing alcohol. The fullest account of a tutor's life was left by Clement Webb, a classics tutor at Magdalen for thirty years, whose diary reveals a man generous with his time but not bibulous: see Bodleian MSS Eng. Misc. d.1105–32, e. 1139–96, f. 649–50: journals 1887–1954. On the development of student societies in this period, see pp. 456ff, this volume.

the summer. Jowett was a great promoter of such excursions, and every year in the long vacation for some forty years, even when master, brought together favoured pupils and his intellectual friends for vigorous physical and mental exercise in some rural paradise. Jowett did not invent the practice as he seems to have thought— Pattison took select pupils on vacation study trips in the 1840s and Hugh Clough refers to a university reading party in his pastoral, *The Bothie of Tober-na-Vuolich*, written in 1848.[56] But it was the Balliol tutor who made them fashionable. As transport links improved, the excursions became more adventurous. Jowett had favoured Scotland, though he sometimes went no further afield than Malvern. Beginning in 1891, Balliol's long-serving modern history tutor, 'Sligger' Urquhart, well known in term times for holding court into the early hours, would take his pupils off to his chalet in the French Alps.[57]

Undergraduates whom tutors taught individually, socialized with, and accompanied on holiday often ceased to be pupils and became friends for life. But this did not always happen. No tutor or team of tutors had the expertise to cover the whole syllabus by the late nineteenth century, so it became customary for undergraduates to have tuition on the more specialized papers in other colleges, just as they attended lectures elsewhere. Where this happened, teacher–pupil relations remained more distant. Out-college tuition was particularly prevalent in the different branches of the Natural Science School. Even if a college had a full-time science tutor (fellow or lecturer)—and there were only thirteen in the whole University in 1892—it was often the case that, for many undergraduates, in-house teaching stopped with the Natural Science Prelim. Magdalen had had two science tutors in the Edwardian era, but at the end of the First World War found itself with only one—and sixty undergraduates reading the subject. The surviving tutor, Robert Gunther, is remembered today as a prolific historian of science and the man behind the foundation in 1935 of Oxford's Museum of the History of Science. But Gunther, who began teaching at Magdalen in 1894, was a fellow in zoology, a school with very few students. To make matters worse he had not kept abreast of his own subject, so while he remained in post virtually every Magdalen science undergraduate reading for an honours degree had to be sent out.[58]

The new female societies were particularly dependent on out-college tuition. Resident female dons were not part of the vision of the AEW, which had hoped to keep the organization of women's education in its own hands, and it was not until 1892, when Somerville appointed Lilla Haigh, that a women's college had an in-house tutor. The women's colleges too never had the funds before the Second

[56] Clough was an Oriel fellow who resigned his fellowship in 1848 having lost his faith.

[57] Faber, *Jowett*, pp. 186–9; Pattison, *Memoirs*, p. 262; Cyril Bailey, *Francis Fortescue Urquhart* (1936), pp. 60–85 and 154–81. Urquhart died in 1934. On interwar reading parties, see Mabbott, *Memories*, pp. 121–2. Goldwin Smith remembered summer reading parties from the 1840s but is unclear whether tutors were present: *Reminiscences* (New York, 1910), pp. 69–70.

[58] Not surprisingly he was eventually forced to resign so that someone more appropriate could be appointed. For his life, A. E. Gunther, *Early Science in Oxford*, vol. 15: *Robert T. Gunther: A Pioneer in the History of Science* (Oxford, 1967).

World War to build up a bank of tutors, so were forced, from their foundation, to rely on the charity of male colleges.[59] Once women were allowed to take university exams in 1884, there was little problem with getting them admitted to college lectures.[60] Tutorial provision, however, was more difficult to organize. Male and female students were not permitted to have tutorials together, which meant it was often difficult before the First World War to find the latter tuition. Margaret Lee, one of the first to read for the English School, had an unremitting diet of lectures: 'Nobody was coached either in Language or Literature unless they chanced to excite the interest of Professor Napier, who would then invite them to his study on Headington Hill to "discuss difficulties".'[61] On the other hand, the philosopher Hilda Oakley, reading Greats at the end of the nineteenth century, was taught by some of the best minds in the University, including Balliol's Edward Caird.

Whether the standardized tutorial of the post-Jowett era always had the intellectual results the master of Balliol believed to be possible is highly unlikely. After 1850, accounts written by former undergraduates of their years at Oxford are legion. Although they tend to display much more interest in the peculiar quirks and mannerisms of their tutors than in the tutorial itself, they provide plenty of evidence that the quality and experience varied tremendously. Interviews conducted at the end of the twentieth century with undergraduates from the 1920s and 1930s confirm this impression. Given the differences in tutors' ages and experience, this was not surprising. Some were young graduates with a good result in Schools who were hardly older than the undergraduates; others were former public schoolmasters with many years' experience in teaching juveniles; while many had been giving tutorials for most of their adult life: once fellows no longer had to take orders and could marry, being a college tutor ceased to be an interim occupation and became a permanent career.

The format of the tutorial was predictable. Written work was almost never taken in either before or after the event, so the undergraduate received no recorded feedback.[62] Instead, the common practice was for pupils to read out their essay or demonstrate their solution to problems on a blackboard. J. M. Thompson of Magdalen, understandably no longer dean of divinity, who was a modern history tutor in the interwar years, was remembered as quirky because he would read a student's essay silently to himself, occasionally throwing out comments, an understandably unnerving experience for the author. Once the undergraduate had revealed what he or she had achieved over the week, the tutor would offer positive and critical comments and initiate discussion which probably lasted about forty minutes. This was the creative part of the tutorial where tutor and pupil or pupils supposedly engaged in Socratic exchange, and tutors deployed very different styles of interrogation. Some tutors were kindly;

---

[59] There was only one female maths tutor in all five women's colleges in the 1930s.

[60] See p. 375, this volume.   [61] *HUO*, vii. 283. For Napier, see p. 382, n.88, this volume.

[62] For an exception, see Bowra, *Memories*, pp. 109–10. Bowra was sent to Gilbert Murray for Greek composition and Murray always corrected his efforts beforehand. Murray's assiduity was all the more commendable in that he was a professor and had no tutorial obligations.

others took no prisoners. The historian, socialist, and Oxford clergyman A. J. Carlyle, who tutored in history, politics, and English for several colleges for forty years from the 1890s, appears to have been a tartar. Returning from a tutorial with the vicar of St Martin's and All Saints, a St Hugh's student confessed in her diary to feeling 'in a somewhat headless condition hav[ing] had this part of the anatomy bitten off by A. J. C.'.[63]

Whether undergraduates drew greater intellectual benefit from being cosseted or bullied presumably depended on the individual. Either approach could develop the mind. It depended greatly on what the tutor set out to achieve. Many ageing tutors, especially before the Great War, simply went through the motions. When the future Scottish advocate T. B. Simpson arrived at Magdalen to read classics in 1911, he was expecting great things from his Mods tutor, Alfred Godley, who was a reputed poet and scholar. But Godley was profoundly disappointing, even on first acquaintance. Expecting Byron, Simpson encountered 'a long, lanky, gone-at-the-knees, out-at-the-elbow, broken-down-looking man, without a spark of life in his expression'. Godley's teaching confirmed he was past it: 'He was content to let us go over the ground we had already traversed at school, "crambe repetita", since the method saved him the trouble of making suggestions, his pupils that of breaking new ground.' Even the proses he set were out of the ark and handed down:

> I often used to speculate on the real origin of the College essays. Some of them must have been hundreds of years old, and a higher critic could doubtless have detected traces of translation from the original Latin. Here and there a daring innovator would insert a new sentence but the corpus of the essays, dated on the whole, from Wolsey's time.[64]

Other, more conscientious, tutors also fell short of the Jowett ideal because they were more interested in creating disciples than in training minds. Both Arnold Toynbee and T. H. Green were Jowett's own appointments and the master's close friends but neither sought to develop a student's critical faculties before anything else. Toynbee was a preacher not a teacher, who enthused his pupils with a desire to go out into the world and imitate Christ's mission to the poor. Green was a systematizer and wanted to pass on his own Idealist ethical philosophy to his charges.[65] Yet other tutors, probably the majority, were guilty of cramming their students rather than stimulating thought. Their goal by the end of the tutorial was to impart enough new information for the recipient to tackle the topic successfully in an exam, even if this meant turning the tutorial into a mini-lecture. Undergraduates liked the approach but in later life, on reflection, could see it hardly encouraged independent thinking.

Jowett's real heirs were those who had no agenda and insisted that new insights and understanding had to be the undergraduate's own, the result of existential discovery in response to the tutor's probing. The truly Socratic tutor, however,

[63] HUO, vii. 283.   [64] Brockliss, pp. 452–3.   [65] Faber, Jowett, pp. 355–7.

FIGURE 10.4 Harold Joachim, 1868–1938, Idealist philosopher, tutor, and Wykeham professor of Logic. One of the most demanding tutors of the early twentieth century, Merton's Joachim was notorious for getting his pupils to think.

was intellectually demanding and even the brightest students were often intimidated, especially if every position an undergraduate advanced was shot down. G. R. G. Mure had the good fortune to be tutored in Greats at the beginning of the Great War by the Merton philosopher Harold Joachim, probably the pick of the tutorial bunch (see Figure 10.4). But it was only looking back, once Mure himself had become a philosopher, that he realized how he had benefited. His initial reaction in 1914 had been far from positive:

> Certainly I sensed a more powerful intellect than any I had met before, but for a long time I got little from the discussion of my weekly essay but a most humbling conviction of my own futility. That is of course a common enough experience among beginners in philosophy; Oxford philosophy tutors are by a sound tradition relentless in trying to make their pupils think and see little place for mercy in their destructive criticism. What I found quite shattering was Joachim's habit of taking a sentence or two from one's essay and assuming with a more than Socratic courtesy that one must have meant something definite when one wrote them. It soon became evident that one had not. He would suggest this or that meaning as seriously as if he were trying to interpret an obscure sentence in Aristotle. One quickly collapsed under this technique, and he would say, 'Perhaps you were a little confused', and pass on to explain how it might have been better put. After four terms I was still frankly in a

muddle, and the prospect of final schools filled me with apprehension. Examinations were not a subject one could discuss with Joachim. They seemed to him, however necessary, to be a great evil for both the victim and the executioner.[66]

Unsurprisingly, the most demanding tutors were not usually the best loved given the limited intellectual abilities of many who came under their care. But they knew what they were about and took pride in their assiduity. The first modern historian in Magdalen to stretch the minds of his pupils was the medievalist Bruce McFarlane, who joined the tutorial team as the fourth tutor in 1928. After the Second World War he came to be worshipped by his more discerning students, but in the 1930s his efforts were sometimes derided. When, in 1936, his long-term confidante, Helena Wright, a gynaecologist and pioneering sex therapist, questioned the point of a tutorial system that in its interwar incarnation seemed principally interested in sharpening intellect not perfecting the whole man, McFarlane leapt to its defence and set down one of the few first-person accounts of what the Socratic tutor in the first half of the twentieth century aimed to achieve:

> Do you really think my tutorials in the past have just been chunks of information which a dictaphone could produce as well? I may not have been much interested in their personalities apart from their work... but a tutorial has always been the contact of mind with mind, an argument not instruction... The whole point of the tutorial method of education is to put the pupil through his intellectual exercises, not to fill him up with potted knowledge. What I haven't done sufficiently, I am ready to admit, is to consider the personal reasons for the mental idiosyncrasies of my pupils; I've taken their essay as you might take an article in a paper, tried to understand it (no easy exercise this when it's being read to you & you have to keep all the points in your head until the end), suggest its logical weaknesses, its faults of approach & treatment, welcome its merits & then pose the arguments against its conclusions. I'd like to see the dictaphone to do this... [T]he majority are capable of keeping their end up & learning each week to think & write better. Because I've not concerned myself with the moral or spiritual welfare of my young, don't delude yourself into supposing that I've been doing nothing. I've little doubt that I've been a good tutor.[67]

Incremental improvement, however, required more than an assiduous tutor. To give of their best in their weekly work, undergraduates had to be able to prepare properly. College or professorial lectures played an important part here, but as the lectures and tutorials were not necessarily coordinated, arts undergraduates especially needed access to books. Before 1850, the amount of required reading and the range of available texts were small. Undergraduates could purchase what they needed from Oxford's booksellers. But research in all areas expanded rapidly from the mid-nineteenth century, resulting in a dramatic increase in the number of scholarly and scientific journals and the publication of more and more detailed

---

[66] G. H. Martin and J. R. L. Highfield, *A History of Merton College, Oxford* (Oxford, 1997), pp. 328–9. An account of Mure's more congenial tutors is given on pp. 326–8.

[67] MCA, MC: P27/C1/231, 17 Nov. 1936. McFarlane corresponded with Wright two or three times a week for thirty years. His letters to her are in the Magdalen College Archives and closed until at least 2050.

monographs. By the First World War, the keenest and cleverest students needed access to well-stocked libraries if they were to take a first-class degree. In this regard, both the University and colleges were initially ill-placed to meet the new demand. Both the Bodleian and the college libraries had been traditionally closed to all but high-status undergraduates, and though several colleges had set up independent collections for undergraduates in the late seventeenth and eighteenth century, they had not always survived. Provision for undergraduates therefore had to start virtually from scratch.

The University did little before the Second World War to remedy the deficiency. Undergraduates could consult Bodley's copyright collection from the turn of the twentieth century when the Radcliffe Camera was turned into a reading room for them, and they could also use the Taylorian and Codrington. They equally had access to a growing number of faculty and institute libraries that began to take shape in the Edwardian era out of the personal collections of professors.[68] These, though, like the Bodleian and the other specialist libraries that existed by 1914, were essentially research collections and of limited use to undergraduates.[69] Understandably, given the focus of undergraduate teaching, it was the colleges that filled the gap, albeit slowly. Virtually every college in the 1870s made some attempt to open its fellows' library to junior as well as senior members. They provided an undergraduate reading room, hired a deputy librarian or clerk who would fetch books on request at appointed times, and occasionally allowed books to be borrowed. But the initiative was far from ideal. Opening hours were restricted—it was 1897 before Trinity's library was open for four hours a day—and many colleges paid little attention to the needs of undergraduates when buying books. Even when the reading room was lined with relevant works that undergraduates could take from the shelves themselves and read *in situ* or borrow, the experiment did not always come up to expectations. Christ Church fitted up a proper reading room in 1884 and provided a grant of £100 to purchase a set of classical texts and cheap editions of 'standard authors, English and foreign, prose and poetry, as may be judged useful'. Though the committee set up to run the room had a grant of £35 per annum to make fresh purchases, the venture was a mixed success. Too many books disappeared and the suggestion that all volumes should be confined to the reading room was countered with the objection that it smelt and was too hot at one moment and too cold at another.[70]

What undergraduates needed was their own library, but this was not usually seen as a college priority before 1914. Magdalen opened its fellows' library to under-graduates in 1874; then, at the turn of the twentieth century, allowed three of its undergraduate schools—classics, modern history, and law—to set up their own undergraduate libraries, which were largely the creation of student subscriptions

---

[68] For the first institutes, see pp. 489 and 493–4, this volume.

[69] The different research libraries are listed in G. N. Curzon, *Principles and Methods of University Reform* (Oxford, 1909), p. 184. Their development and metamorphosis in some cases into undergraduate lending libraries is charted in Paul Morgan, *Oxford Libraries Outside the Bodleian: A Guide*, 2nd edn (Oxford, 1980).

[70] Curthoys, p. 279.

and gifts. When Compton Mackenzie read modern history in the college in the 1900s, he was asked to contribute two guineas towards the cost of buying the original *Dictionary of National Biography*. It was only in 1920 that the college's thoughts turned to establishing a single independent undergraduate library when the then fellow librarian, R. T. Gunther, submitted a memorandum to the governing body accusing Magdalen of neglecting what should have been its primary concern given its importance. It was twelve years, however, before Gunther's dream was realized, and it only became possible when Magdalen College School vacated its college site and moved to Cowley Place, with the building of Longwall quad. This left an empty building on the south side of the quad which had been the old school hall. Designed by J. C. Buckler and opened only in 1851, it was handed over to Sir Giles Gilbert Scott to convert into a library.

Most colleges provided their arts undergraduates with reasonable access to books by the end of the period. Where collections remained deficient, students fell back on the Union Society, whose well-stocked library remained a godsend for hard-pressed undergraduates long after the 1930s. What the colleges could not deliver en bloc were the practical facilities their science students needed. Only six colleges ever had their own laboratories, which were largely used for teaching and research in chemistry. Christ Church and Magdalen's were inherited, the first originally Dr Lee's anatomical laboratory, the second built in 1847 by Charles Daubeny in the Botanic Garden for his personal research.[71] The others were purpose-built. Balliol had a laboratory as early 1853, which was extended in the 1880s; Trinity's, the Millard, was opened in 1886; while Queen's and Jesus' were erected in 1900 and 1907. As these laboratories catered only for in-house pupils or students from colleges with which there was an arrangement, many science undergraduates had to attend practical classes organized departmentally on the Science Area.[72] Between the wars, moreover, the college laboratories had difficulty in keeping going as centres of teaching and research in the face of much better-funded facilities in the University and began to fold. Magdalen's closed in 1923 and all were shut by 1947. By the end of the period, therefore, the University had a virtual monopoly over practical instruction in natural science, just as it did in lecturing. The centrality of the college as a teaching institution loomed so large in the Oxford imagination in 1939 only because 85 per cent of undergraduates were studying arts and social sciences.

D. Undergraduate Careers

Most Oxford undergraduates in the second half of the nineteenth and first half of the twentieth century spent three or four years at the University and were then released into the world. On going down, whatever the subject they had studied, they

---

[71] See pp. 276 and 314, this volume.

[72] The Millard was named for the benefactor, Thomas Millard, who had funded Trinity's first science tutorship. Balliol and Trinity shared their facilities. Until 1904, each laboratory operated independently, but thereafter resources and pupils were pooled so that each could concentrate on a different branch of chemistry.

purportedly possessed the skills and moral fibre to excel in any career they chose to enter. Historically Oxford had been a training ground for the Anglican church and, to a moderate degree, the English bar. Other undergraduates who passed through its care were bound for a life of leisure, punctuated by service on the local bench and, in some cases, service in parliament and the government. Liberals and Puseyites alike, in the mid-nineteenth century, had greater ambitions for the Oxford of the future. Liberals in particular looked forward to a time when Oxford's graduates would be found in every walk of commercial and professional life, while a later generation of imperialists dreamt of Oxford men ruling the world at home and abroad. The reality inevitably fell some way short of the aspiration. Oxford men were always thinly spread in middle-class occupations that continued to recruit straight from school, while women students had limited career options of any kind. Nonetheless, the reformers' expectations were partially fulfilled: Oxford graduates by 1900 were to be found in a much wider range of careers than hitherto.

Oxford's clerical past was not immediately discarded, for some Oxford colleges initially continued to turn out Anglican clergyman in large numbers. Unsurprisingly, in the first twenty years following Keble's foundation in 1870, 450 out of its 879 matriculands took holy orders. But after 1900, the proportion of graduates year on year becoming clergymen fell fast across the University. In 1875, a quarter of Magdalen men were bound for the church; in 1895, less than a fifth; and, by 1928, barely any. Instead, most Oxford graduates found a niche in either the private professions, or secondary-school teaching, or government service (both civil and, to a lesser extent, military). Very few, before the Second World War, ended up in business, except those who joined the handful of companies, mainly in the chemical and pharmaceutical industries, which had research departments. Even the sons of businessmen often had no intention of entering the family firm. The father of the future Field Marshal Earl Haig was a whisky distiller, but Haig, who came up to Brasenose in 1880, had set his sights on entering the army while still at Clifton.

Among the private professions, the bar lost none of its traditional sheen and attracted a broad spectrum of undergraduates, not simply those who had studied jurisprudence. After 1850, however, Oxford men gradually found their way into all the recognized Victorian private professions as the curriculum expanded, including those that did not require a degree.[73] Medicine, for instance, became a much more popular option for the University's students once it became possible to specialize in physiology at undergraduate level and study for the whole of the first BM at Oxford;[74] so too did engineering after it became an honours subject in 1909. Even a few prospective solicitors were enticed to the University, such as Willie Elmhirst, who came up to Worcester shortly before the First World War.[75] After 1900,

---

[73] For the Victorian professions and their entry requirements, see H. Byerley Thompson, *The Choice of a Profession* (London, 1857).

[74] See Chapter 9, n. 106, this volume.

[75] Elmhirst, who died in the Great War, kept a record of his first year at Oxford: *A Freshman's Diary 1911–12* (Oxford, 1969).

moreover, Oxford graduates began to infiltrate occupations whose professional credentials were still not firmly established, such as publishing and journalism. It was figures like Corpus' C. P. Scott and Magdalen's Geoffrey Dawson, long-standing editors of the *Manchester Guardian* and *The Times*, who helped to establish journalism as a respectable career.[76]

Secondary-level teaching was not a new occupation for Oxford graduates, as many from poorer backgrounds had always been grammar schoolmasters or private tutors to the rich. But with a few notable exceptions (the antiquarian William Camden, who had been usher and headmaster of Westminster for many years, was one), they had been clergymen who were teaching while awaiting a benefice or because they had failed to get one. Oxford graduates who flooded into secondary-school teaching from the mid-nineteenth century were primarily laymen who looked to make a permanent career in the profession, chiefly in the transformed public schools. It was a popular career choice too among women students, who found positions in the new girls' boarding schools and schools of the Girls Public Day School Trust (GPDST).[77] In the women's case, a teaching or teaching-related career was almost inevitable if they needed a job, and most did: they had virtually no access before the First World War to any other profession except medicine. At least two-thirds of Oxford women, whose careers between 1881 and 1913 are known, found employment as teachers, educational administrators, researchers, librarians, or archivists.[78] But for men the motivation must have been more complex, a mix of a genuine love for their subject, the appeal of the relatively cloistered atmosphere of the public school or the academy, and the attraction of a steady pensionable salary.

Only a small proportion of Oxford alumni entered higher education. Although young Oxford graduates with a few years' research experience found academic posts throughout the expanding university system as well at Oxford itself, positions remained relatively few. University pay and conditions were also much less attractive than many alternative careers (including teaching in a public school). Quite a large proportion of women students became academics but only a few high-flying males. Eighteen Magdalen students gained a First in modern history between 1900 and 1930 but only one entered the profession. This was Henry Alcock, who graduated in 1908 and went on to become a non-publishing professor of history and economics at Queensland from 1922 to 1948. Another, Richard Atkinson, had an academic-related career as assistant keeper at the Public Record Office, and a third became a schoolmaster. But the rest disappeared into a wide spectrum of careers that had no direct connection with their studies. One became a Benedictine

[76] C. P. Scott was an anti-imperialist like his fellow Corpuscle, Hobhouse, whom he employed on his newspaper.

[77] The GPDST dates from 1872.

[78] Before they were allowed to graduate, Oxford's women often had to take a BA at another university first in order to gain a good teaching position. Women were allowed to enter the top grade of the civil service from 1919.

| | | | | | | H = Home Civil Service. I = Indian Civil Service. |

Service for which Entered.	Order in Examination.	Name.	University.	College.	Status.	University Honours.
H I C	1	Blackett	Oxford	University	Scholar	2 Mods., 1 Lit. Hum.
H I C	2	Henderson, J. F.	Oxford	Brasenose	Scholar	1 Mods., 1 Lit. Hum.
H I C	3	Haig	Oxford	New	Scholar	2 Mods., 1 Lit. Hum.
H I C	4	Barnes	Cambridge	Trinity	Scholar	3rd Wrangler
H C	5	Batterbee	Oxford	Hertford	Scholar	1 Mods., 1 Math. Mods., 2 Lit. Hum.
H	6	Robinson	Oxford	New	Commoner	2 Mods., 3 Lit. Hum.
H	7	Chrystal	Oxford	Balliol	Exhib.	2 Mods., 2 Lit. Hum.
H	8	Phillips, S. H.	Cambridge	St. John's	Scholar	3rd Wrangler, 1 Nat. Sci. Trip.
H I C	9	Bromley	Oxford	Magdalen	Demy	1 Mods., 1 Lit. Hum.
H I	10	Salt r.	Oxford	Brasenose	Scholar	1 Mods., 1 Lit. Hum.
H C	11	Thorp	Oxford	Wadham	Scholar	1 Mods., 2 Lit. Hum., Goldsmith's Exhib.
H	12	Simon	Oxford	Balliol	Scholar	1 Mods., 2 Lit. Hum., Ireland & Craven Scholarships, Hon. Mention Hertford
H I C	13	Minnis	{ Royal Ireland	Queen's, Galway }	Scholar	Univ. Scholarship in Mod. Lang., 1st in Mod. Lang. at B.A. Exam.
H I	14	Strickland	Oxford	New	Scholar	2 Mods., 1 Lit. Hum.
I	15	Booth-Gravely	{ Edinburgh Oxford	Trinity	Scholar	2 Mods., 1 Lit. Hum.
H I C	16	Phillips, E. H.	Cambridge	Sid. Sussex	Scholar	1 Cl. Trip. (Div. 3)
I	17	Broomfield	Cambridge	Christ's	Scholar	1 Cl. Trip. (Part I, Div. 1), 2 Hist. Trip. (Part II)
H I C	18	Burdon	Oxford	University	Scholar	1 Mods., 3 Lit. Hum.
H I C	19	Tanner	Cambridge	Clare	Scholar	8th Wrangler, 1 Nat. Sci. Trip. (Part I)
H I C	20	Robertson	Cambridge	Queens'	Scholar	1 Cl. Trip. (Part I, Div. 2)
H I C	21	Gwynn	Dublin	Trinity	Scholar	Gold Medallist in Classics and Mod. Lit.
H I C	22	Jamieson	Cambridge	King's	Scholar	1 Med. and Mod. Lang. Trip.
H I C	23	Covernton	Oxford	St. John's	Scholar	1 Mods., 1 Lit. Hum.
H I C	24	Lindsay	Oxford	Worcester	Exhib.	2 Mods.
H I	25	Perham	Cambridge	Christ's	Scholar	1 Cl. Trip. (Part I, Div. 2)
H I C	26	Soames	Oxford	Merton	Postmaster	1 Mods., 1 Lit. Hum.
H	*27	Kaudel	Manchester	Owens C.	Scholar	1 Class. Hon. School, Univ. Scholar
H I C	28	Milne	Aberdeen		Bursar	M.A. (Honours in Classics)
H I C	29	Dawes	Cambridge	Sid. Sussex	Scholar	1 Cl. Trip. (Div. 3)
H I C	30	Worsley	Oxford	Balliol	Commoner	2 Mods., 3 Lit. Hum.

FIGURE 10.5 Oxford's success in the annual civil service examinations: *Oxford Magazine*, 26 October 1904. The examinations for entrance to the top grade of the home and Indian civil service were designed to advantage Oxford graduates. They made the most of their good fortune and every year in the late Victorian and Edwardian era headed the lists.

abbot, another became a singer, and two fulfilled the regius professor Charles Firth's jaundiced view of the value of Oxford history, and became journalists.[79]

The lure of state and especially imperial employment seems to have been greater in some colleges than others. Balliol men, appropriately enough, given Jowett's concept of the purpose of an Oxford education, appear to have been particularly attracted to government service. Admittedly, in the first years of Jowett's mastership, this was not a Balliol graduate's obvious choice: between 1874 and 1883 only 5 per cent of the college's students found a career with the state, compared with 12 per cent who joined the church and 30 per cent who entered the law. But the British and imperial state at this juncture was still small, and thereafter the number of entrants mushroomed. By 1904, there were 164 former members of Balliol in the home civil service, and a staggering 226 in its Indian equivalent, plus a further twenty attached to the colonial service and six serving as administrators in Egypt and Sudan. Many of these, moreover, held top positions and three had been successively viceroys of India, including Curzon. Magdalen graduates, on the other hand, showed much less

[79] Pass, 'Oxford Honours School', p. 39.

enthusiasm for a career with the state, except as soldiers. Each year only a trickle of the college's graduates entered any branch of the civil service at home or overseas. The college certainly educated some top mandarins. President Gordon, Warren's successor, could boast in 1929 that four members of the Council of India and the secretary to the viceroy were Magdalen men. It was also the alma mater of the future king-emperor Edward VIII, who, had he turned out as Warren had hoped, would have been the greatest imperial servant of them all. But even the Prince of Wales' presence at the college in 1910–12 did not turn the thoughts of Magdalen men to state service in large numbers. Warren's last year as president was 1928. Of the undergraduates who matriculated in that year and whose career is known, only one entered the home and one the colonial service. The college's alumni who did take up a state service often did sterling service as administrators: Sir Douglas Dodds-Parker, who came up in 1927, became a colonial civil servant on going down and immediately found himself, in his early twenties, responsible for a tract of the Sudan as big as Britain. But the Dodds-Parkers of this world were isolated figures dotted around the empire, while Balliol graduates formed a visible clique wherever the Union flag was unfurled.[80]

A large proportion of Oxford's graduates who entered state service before the First World War had read classics. This reflected the school's dominant share of the undergraduate body. But it was also the consequence of the entry process. Traditionally, appointments to government positions were by patronage, but from 1870 admission to the home civil service was reorganized and entry was determined by written examination. This was open to all, but intentionally favoured those who had been to Oxford and Cambridge, and especially those who had read Greats, on the grounds that those trained in moral philosophy and ancient history would make first-rate administrators.[81] As Jowett had been a member of the royal commission that had recommended the new entry process in 1854 the bias was predictable. But his views had coincided with the committee's as a whole and were completely endorsed by the report's co-author, the Conservative MP Sir Stafford Henry Northcote. Northcote, another Balliol man, believed a classical education should be the foundation of all walks of life:

> I attribute my own success, such as it has been, entirely to the power of close reasoning which a course of Thucydides, Aristotle...&c., engenders or developes [sic.], and to the facility of composition which arises from classical studies. There is nothing that can compensate for the want of being able to follow out a train of reasoning, rejecting immaterial and irrelevant issues, and keeping close to the matter in hand.[82]

[80] Interview with the late Dodds-Parker, 31 Aug. 2001 (tape and transcript, Magdalen College Archives).

[81] Heather Ellis, 'Efficiency and Counter-Revolution: Connecting University and Civil Service Reform in the 1850s', *History of Education* 42. 1(2012), esp. pp. 9–12. See also Farnell, *Oxonian*, p. 268. The commission had devised an exam which mirrored Schools: candidates had to pass in two of four categories: one category was classical literature, another political economy, law, and moral philosophy: the first was the Mods course; the second, half of Greats.

[82] Ellis, 'Efficiency', p. 18.

Late Victorian and Edwardian Oxford men made the most of the opportunity and dominated the examinations, the celebration of their success in the *Oxford Magazine* becoming an annual ritual. Oxford men took seventeen out of the first twenty places in 1899, ten out of the first twelve in 1904 (see Figure 10.5), seven out of the first ten in 1908, and all of the first seven in the following year. In 1902, 75 per cent of successful candidates had been to Oxford and Cambridge. Graduates from other British or imperial universities gained next to no look in.[83]

Entrance to the Indian civil service was similarly rigged in favour of the traditional universities from the mid-1890s. The ICS had admitted by examination long before India became the direct responsibility of the British government, but had always had a pre-university entry, and attempts by Jowett and others to bring the ICS into line with the home civil service only slowly bore fruit. In the mid-1870s it was decided that entrants on selection should attend Oxford and Cambridge for two years' preparatory study before going abroad; this allowed Jowett to ensure that as many as possible resided in Balliol, where they could learn the virtues of hard work and sacrifice for the common good. Then in 1892, shortly before the master's death, the ICS placed a premium on graduates and established an examination that again privileged classicists. Oxford once more seized the day, and between 1892 to 1914 won half the places on offer.[84] Success was so assured that, in the Edwardian era, according to Arnold Toynbee Jnr, Balliol came to see the ICS as the automatic career choice for the uncommitted:

> At my college in Oxford…before 1914, any freshman who had no clear idea of what he wanted to do after he went down was put down for the Indian Civil Service by the dons as a matter of routine. An I.C.S. career was assured to any Balliol man who could not do better than that. And the contract that a successful candidate for the I.C.S. concluded with the Government of India gave the new recruit security for the rest of his life.[85]

No one has ever calculated what proportion of Oxford's undergraduates became British or imperial administrators across the period 1850 to 1945.[86] Definite figures exist, however, for the number before the First World War who spent at least two

---

[83] The Scottish universities complained at what they felt was unfair treatment.

[84] Phiroze Vasunia, 'Greek, Latin and the ICS', *Cambridge Classical Journal: Proceedings of the Cambridge Philological Society*, 51 (2005), 35–71. In 1896, the examinations to the home and Indian civil services were merged. Entrance by examination to the civil service of Britain's other Asian colonies was only introduced in 1906. There was never an examination for the Egyptian and Sudanese services. As a result, the Sudan civil service tended to take the less intellectual and more athletic Oxonians: see A. Kirk-Greene, *The Sudan Civil Service: A Preliminary Profile* (Oxford, 1982). Dodds-Parker took a Second in 1930.

[85] Arnold Toynbee, *Experiences* (London, 1969), p. 106. Arnold Toynbee Jnr was the nephew of the Balliol Idealist. He was research professor in international affairs at the LSE between the wars and shared none of his uncle's Christian concern for the plight of the poor. Oxford remained a centre for training recruits to the ICS until Indian independence: before the First World War all passed through the hands of Phelps of Oriel, who taught them political economy.

[86] The ICS was no longer quite as attractive after 1930 as Indians began to be appointed to high positions. Grundy claimed to no longer recommend it to pupils. Parents did not like their sons to be subordinate to natives: Grundy, *Fifty-Five Years*, pp. 139–41. Oxford graduates who did go out to India between the wars, such as Oriel's Hugh Lambrick, often began to question the value of an Oxford education once they were on the ground.

years in the Empire serving in some capacity or other, not just as administrators but as doctors, teachers, and missionaries. Between 1874 and 1914, the percentage of undergraduates who did this from Balliol, Corpus, Keble, and St John's was 27.1, 21.9, 20.4, and 16.7 respectively.[87] Oxford women also did their bit: as many as sixty-six of Somerville's undergraduates in the first thirty-five years of its history went out to the Empire to work, generally as teachers. These were impressive figures, and testify to the successful inculcation of the imperial vision. It must not be thought, however, that the large majority of undergraduates who preferred to enter a private profession rather than seek employment with the British state or an overseas mission had no concept of service. Jowett and the Oxford idealists like Green and Toynbee Snr may have given the impression that a career as a public servant or a missionary worker was the only really worthwhile occupation. But most Oxford fellows and heads of house had a broader view that Warren, in particular, articulated. While Magdalen's president shared the belief that Oxford graduates should dedicate their lives to improving the lot of the mass of mankind, he felt this task should not be monopolized by the state and its surrogates. All professional people should contribute, and Magdalen old members, wherever they ended up, could benefit the greater community by spreading the service ethos throughout the workplace. It was some version of this view, a heady mix of the Aristotelian conception of the active life and the protestant idea of the holiness of every calling, that all Oxford graduates took out into the world on the eve of the Great War.[88]

E. Ultimate Sacrifice

Most undergraduates up at Oxford at the beginning of the twentieth century had barely had time to settle into their chosen career and make a difference before they found themselves in uniform fighting for king and country; some never even finished their degree. Patriotism was always part of the service ethic, and it was a commonplace for undergraduates in the Edwardian era to join the University's Officer Training Corps when they were up.[89] So when war was declared with Germany in August 1914 there was no possibility that Oxford would stand aloof. On the contrary, Oxford men, fellows, and college servants, as well as current undergraduates, flocked to the colours, and the University quickly emptied out. Within a month, an ad hoc committee set up by Vice-Chancellor Thomas Banks Strong, dean of Christ Church, had processed 2,000 applications to join up.

Thereafter, for the duration of the war, the only male undergraduates left in residence were the odd foreign national, such as the American T. S. Eliot, who spent

---

[87] In 1921, 13.5 per cent of the subscribers to Oriel's alumni magazine were overseas. In the early twentieth century, Orielenses were particularly prominent in the Sudanese political service. For alumni magazines, see p. 474, this volume.

[88] Green's influence was at its height during the period 1885–1914, after the posthumous publication of his lectures.

[89] The Oxford OTS was set up after the Boer War and developed out of the Oxford Volunteer Corps: Farnell, *Oxonian*, pp. 148–57.

FIGURE 10.6 The Examination Schools as a hospital during the First World War: photograph, Christmas 1915. As Schools was no longer required for lectures and examinations, the building was quickly taken over by the military to house some of the wounded. The photograph comes from a collection taken by one of the nurses, Isabel Mabel Wace.

a year at Merton, or the certified unfit, such as Balliol's Aldous Huxley, whose bad eyesight kept him out of the forces.[90] The colleges did not become deserts, for stripped of their undergraduates they were commissioned for war work. Trinity and Lincoln served as billets for military cadets and the Millard Laboratory became a bathhouse; while Merton's St Alban's Quad was taken over by nurses staffing the hospital established in the Exam Schools and University College (see Figure 10.6). Other societies welcomed Belgian and Serbian refugees, including Wycliffe Hall, where 150 were lodged. Some Oxford graduates refused to get caught up in the war euphoria, notably the socialist G. D. H. Cole, who spent the war away from the University writing books about the creation of a new social order. Others, while accepting that the war was just, like the anti-imperialist Gilbert Murray, were happy to use their influence to ease the lot of high-placed conscientious objectors. In the main, however, Oxford was solidly behind the war effort.[91]

All told, 15,000 Oxford men served in the Great War. As most were platoon commanders and subaltern officers who were the first to go over the top, they suffered disproportionately. About 12 per cent of the soldiers who served in the armies of Britain and her allies died in the conflict but one in five of the Oxford

[90] A number of female undergraduates also abandoned their studies to take up war work, most famously the writer Vera Brittain, who left Somerville after a year to serve as a Voluntary Aid Detachment nurse overseas. Her experience is immortalized in her *Testament of Youth* (1933).

[91] On conscientious objectors at Oxford, see David Roberts, 'Magdalen Conscientious Objectors' (unpublished paper, lent by the author). Only 4 out of 1,000 Magdalenses refused to serve.

contingent. The slaughter was particularly horrendous among the old members of colleges, with an abnormally large proportion of classicists and public-school men. Only 15 per cent of Jesus' alumni died but Corpus had a death rate of one in four.[92] The cohort who matriculated in 1913 had the greatest losses, almost 30 per cent being killed, a death rate equivalent to the ravages of the Black Death. Among those who gave their lives there were many tales of heroism, and every college, by the time the war was over, could boast a clutch of old members who had been honoured for their singular bravery. The most highly decorated of them all was Trinity's Noel Godfrey Chavasse, the only member of Britain's armed forces in the First World War to be awarded the VC twice (see Figure 10.7).

Chavasse, the son of the bishop of Liverpool, came up to Oxford with his twin brother, Christopher, in 1905. An Olympic athlete as well as a first-class student, he moved on to Liverpool to complete his medical studies, where he graduated in 1912. As a medical officer with the Liverpool Scottish regiment, he served on the Western Front throughout the war, praised for his pioneering work as a field hygienist as well as for his bravery. He won the MC at Hooge in June 1915; then was awarded the VC at Guillemot on the Somme in August 1916 for saving the lives of at least twenty men while under heavy enemy fire. In the following August he was badly injured by a shell at the third battle of Ypres but continued to assist the wounded until he himself collapsed and subsequently died. For this final act of devotion to duty, simply related in the citation, he was posthumously granted a Bar to his VC:

> Though severely wounded early in the action whilst carrying a wounded soldier to the dressing station, Captain Chavasse refused to leave his post, and for two days not only continued to perform his duties, but in addition went out repeatedly under heavy fire to search for and attend to the wounded who were lying out.
>
> During these searches, although practically without food during this period, worn with fatigue and faint with his wound, he assisted to carry in a number of badly wounded men, over heavy and difficult ground.
>
> By his extraordinary energy and inspiring example he was instrumental in rescuing many wounded who would have otherwise undoubtedly succumbed under the bad weather conditions.[93]

Chavasse, by the time he died at the young age of 32, had certainly made a difference.

Many of the 15,000 who served kept in touch with their old college as they fought overseas. It had always been common for former undergraduates out in the Empire to keep tutors and heads of house abreast of their progress in bringing enlightenment to the benighted. Oriel's L. R. Phelps, fellow and later provost, kept in touch with former pupils in India for some fifty years, while Fisher of New College was in

---

[92] Jesus did, though, produce one of the most colourful and celebrated military officers of the war in Lawrence of Arabia. T. E. Lawrence read modern history at the college between 1907 and 1910 before becoming an archaeologist in the Near East. When he enlisted in 1914 he was seconded to military intelligence in Cairo.

[93] Hopkins, p. 354.

FIGURE 10.7 Noel Godfrey Chavasse (1884–1917), undergraduate at Trinity College, army doctor and double VC. Chavasse was a pupil of Magdalen College School, Oxford. There is a fulsome memorial to his work as a medical officer in the Royal Army Medical Services museum at Mychett.

close contact with the Oxford men around Milner in the 1900s attempting to establish a British South Africa.[94] But the communication to and fro spawned by the war was singular in its intensity. Officers of the college seem to have felt a responsibility for the young men they had nurtured to do their duty, and the young officers on the Western Front or in other theatres of the war turned to the college as to a peaceful haven beyond the maelstrom. Warren of Magdalen, as can be imagined, took the responsibility particularly seriously. In the course of the war, he wrote lengthy letters of condolence to the parents of all 187 Magdalen men who fell in the conflict, and compiled his own tribute to their sacrifice in the form of a biographical register.[95] From the letters he received in reply from grieving mothers and fathers, the president had clearly got to know his charges as individuals and was always able to recall some attribute or other of their dead son. The letters he received from soldiers at the front, on the other hand, suggest he was also a man to whom many believed they could open their mind.[96] Some letters were gung-ho and expressed a 'Boys Own' delight in warfare but many were rueful and reflective.

[94] Phelps' correspondence is held at Oriel.   [95] MCA, MS 876.
[96] MCA, PR32/C3: a collection of about 1,000 letters.

In August 1916, Roy Machon, still only in his mid-twenties (he had come up to the college as an exhibitioner in 1910), sent the president a particularly despondent assessment of modern warfare. He wished he could tell Warren that he was happy, but this was impossible:

> War now is only a combat between the resources on either side of the scientific means to kill... War is really very impersonal now. And heroism may be there (and of course the men are wonderful, and more prove heroes than not when their time comes), but it takes very unheroic forms.'[97]

What kept Machon and others going were memories of their time at Magdalen, a golden age to which they all looked back at nostalgically.[98]

The war finally over, Oxford, like the rest of the nation, had to decide how to commemorate its war dead appropriately. The University, in 1920, published a roll of service, but it is indicative of the adamantine collegiate character of early twentieth-century Oxford that there was no university war memorial. The colleges erected their own. As the slaughter of the war had shaken the Christian convictions of many fellows as well as many old members, there was often heated debate over what form, beyond a simple tablet listing the fallen in or adjacent to the chapel, the memorial should take. Some colleges opted for a memorial cross. Others, anxious to be inclusive, thought the most positive memorial would be to appeal for funds from old members to erect a new building in honour of the dead. These initiatives, too, did not always meet with approval. Christ Church was forced to fall back on constructing a memorial garden when its building appeal failed. Both Trinity and New College, however, did eventually put up memorial libraries. Trinity's was ready by 1928 after a relentless fundraising campaign that saw President Blakiston, who drew up the basic neoclassical design, write 1,200 of the 1,300 begging letters himself. Progress in New College was considerably slower. It took until 1938 to create a large enough building fund of £23,500, and the library was not finished until the early years of the Second World War.

The limited response to appeals for funds was unsurprising in the post-war climate. The war had left little desire among many Oxford graduates to celebrate the colossal sacrifice in any form, so even initiatives that promised to bring direct benefit to future generations were not always successful. The disillusionment was largely shared by the undergraduates in the 1920s and early 1930s. Raised in a Britain whose best brains were devoted to building a future based on international co-operation through the League of Nations, and taught by dons who in many cases had escaped physically but were not mentally and emotionally unscarred from the conflict, it is understandable that most would have concurred with Dr Johnson that 'patriotism was the last refuge of the scoundrel'.[99] Few undergraduates in these years would have said that they hated their country, but, just like the dons, the majority

---

[97] Ibid., no. 815: Machon to Warren, 25 Aug. 1916.   [98] Ibid., no. 818: Machon to Warren, 18 Sept. 1917.
[99] One of the most articulate critics of the war, the poet Edmund Blunden, who had come up as a mature student after the war, became Merton's tutor in English in 1931.

had misgivings about Britain holding onto its empire by force or acting as the world's policeman.

Undergraduate disillusionment peaked on 9 February 1933 when the Union Society debated the motion that 'This House will in no circumstances fight for its King and Country'. Kenelm H. Digby of St John's, who in the following year went off to Sarawak as a district officer, spoke in favour of the motion; K. R. F. Steel Maitland of Balliol spoke against. Digby, like so many of his generation, thought the way forward was being shaped in Moscow and appealed to the audience accordingly:

> It is no mere coincidence that the only country fighting for the cause of peace, Soviet Russia, is the country that has rid itself of the war-mongering clique. The justification urged for the last war was that it was a war to end war. If that were untrue it was a dastardly lie; if it were true, what justification is there for opposition to this motion tonight.

His words struck a powerful chord. Despite an appeal by the All Souls prize fellow and future Conservative politician Quintin Hogg, that Digby's views were more likely to cause war than stop it, the motion was won by 275 votes to 153. Immediately Oxford became a pariah in the popular press, and the *Daily Express* was incandescent:

> There is no question but that the woozy-minded Communists, the practical jokers, and the sexual indeterminates of Oxford have scored a great success in the publicity that has followed this victory... Even the plea of immaturity, or the irresistible passion of the undergraduate for posing, cannot excuse such a contemptible and indecent action as the passing of that resolution.

Purportedly, Cambridge threatened to cancel the Boat Race.[100]

However, Hitler became chancellor of Germany ten days later, and the views of both dons and students began to change. By the time of the Munich crisis in September 1938 there was probably no greater willingness to die for king and country, but a considerable part of the University had come round to accepting the value of meeting fascism with force. In the Oxford city by-election of October 1938, which pitted the now pro-appeasement Quintin Hogg against the anti-appeaser A. D. Lindsay, master of Balliol, the University was split down the middle. Hogg eventually emerged victorious but six months later the balance had shifted. In February 1930, the Union had opposed the introduction of peacetime conscription, but on 27 April it was demanded by a full house, voting 423 to 326 in its favour.[101]

---

[100] 'King and Country debate', <https://en.wikipedia.org/wiki/The_King_and_Country_debate> (accessed 3 Sept. 2012). More details in Martin Ceadel, 'The King and Country Debate, 1933: Student Politics, Pacifism and the Dictators', *Historical Journal*, 22: 2 (1979), 397–422. After the debate, a box containing 275 white feathers was delivered to the Union. There were very few committed communists, or fascists for that matter, in Oxford in the 1920s and 1930s. The branch of the Communist Party that the novelist Graham Greene joined in 1923, while up at Balliol, served both the city and the University: see his *A Sort of Life* (London, 1971), p. 132.

[101] For a recent account of the election, see *Oxfordshire Limited Edition* (magazine of the OT), Sept. 2013, pp. 77–81.

When war broke out for a second time in September 1939, the University rallied to its country's call as in 1914. The War Office set up a recruitment office in the Clarendon Building and 2,362 young men under the age of 25 came forward out of a pool of 3,000. Even Gilbert Murray, idealized between the wars as a demi-god for his work with the League of Nations, found the outbreak of war stirring.[102] This time, though, the undergraduates joined up for a cause, not for a country, as the Battle of Britain ace Richard Hillary and a commoner at Trinity explained: '[Volunteering] required no heroics but gave us the opportunity to demonstrate in action our dislike of organised emotion and patriotism.'[103] In contrast with the earlier conflict as well, the colleges continued to perform some sort of academic function throughout the war. Scientists and medics were in great demand, so many volunteers in 1939 were sent back to college to finish their degree, while, until the call-up age was reduced to 18 in 1942, freshmen continued to come into residence for a couple of years and take advantage of the chance to take a specially shortened honours course.[104] Thereafter, too, tutors not swept up in war work were kept busy with the introduction of six-month short-term courses with no entry qualifications for service cadets.[105] Nevertheless, the Second World War still upset the rhythm of academic life from the beginning, as whole or parts of colleges were requisitioned for war purposes. Balliol was initially taken over by the Royal Institute for International Affairs; Magdalen was colonized by an RAF maintenance command which included WAAFs; and Lincoln filled up with nurses. Colleges therefore had to double up: Balliol's undergraduates moved to Trinity and Lincoln's to Exeter, while Christ Church took in students from Pembroke and Brasenose, and University College those of Merton and Keble.

The Second World War also cost Oxford dear in loss of life, although many of Oxford's brightest alumni, women as well as men, and many Oxford dons found positions as government scientists or advisers and intelligence officers, so largely escaped the fighting. Typical was the young Merton JRF, Hugh Trevor Roper, later regius professor of modern history, who first worked as a code-breaker for MI8, the Radio Security Service, and then joined MI6.[106] However, the death toll among Oxford alumni was still high, and this time the roll of honour included a sprinkling of women as well as men. An estimated 1,719 Oxonians lost their lives in the conflict compared with 2,857 in the Great War.[107] The death rate reflected the fact that so many Oxford graduates served with the RAF in the Second World War, where the

---

[102] A full account of Murray's work with the League of Nations can be found in Christopher Stray (ed.), *Gilbert Murray Reassessed: Hellenism, Theatre and International Politics* (Oxford, 2007), ch. 11.

[103] Richard Hillary, *The Last Enemy* (London, 1943), p. 28.

[104] The special shortened war degree was introduced in Michaelmas 1939. It was not initially to be an honours degree but was upgraded in Michaelmas 1940. Many undergraduates never fulfilled the number of terms needed so had to come back after the war if they wanted to graduate.

[105] There were also very short weekend and weekly courses put on for members of the allied forces.

[106] Immediately the conflict ended, Major Trevor-Roper was given the task of finding out what had happened in Berlin in the last days of the war, which led to his book *The Last Days of Hitler* (1947).

[107] Eight former members of St Hugh's lost their lives by enemy action, mostly in bombing raids: Vera Brittain, *The Women at Oxford: A Fragment of History* (London, 1960), p. 200.

chances of survival were much less than in the other two services. An early victim was the legendary rugby player and Brasenose man Alexander Obolensky, 'The Flying Prince', killed at the age of 24 on 29 March 1940 when he crash-landed his plane in a training exercise. His death was typical of many in a war that was the first to be fought by men in machines rather than by men on foot. In contrast with the 1914–18 conflict, death by accident, misadventure, and 'friendly' fire was a commonplace, carrying off as many as a quarter of Magdalen's share of the deceased.[108] But life, whether squandered in the Flanders mud or snuffed out by a British shell, was just as much a waste and loss of future promise. Jowett, in the mid-nineteenth century, expected the hearts of young undergraduates to 'leap within them at the feeling that the future is still theirs'. In the first half of the twentieth century, the hearts of 4,500 Oxford men and a few women ceased to beat long before most of them had any chance to bring forth the abundant fruit that Jowett had urged them to set as their goal. For far too many Oxford undergraduates in the first half of the twentieth century, an Oxford education was not a preparation for life but a preparation for death.

---

[108] R. Hutchins and R. Sheppard, *The Undone Years: Magdalen College Roll of Honour 1939–47 and Roll of Service 1939–1945 and Vietnam* (Oxford, 2004). For Obolensky's rugby heroics, see p. 536, this volume.

CHAPTER 11

Oxford Life

A. An Expensive Education

IN the mid-nineteenth century, according to the 1850 commission, a four-year stay at Oxford cost from £370 to £450 for board, lodging, and instruction. By 1914, although retail prices had been largely stable in the interim, this amount had risen by about 25 per cent. When Chancellor Curzon investigated the cost of an Oxford education in the 1900s, he found that the average college charge for an undergraduate in residence was between £120 and £130 per annum, to which had to be added a further £8 to £12 for 'clubs, fees, and dues, and tips to servants'. However, as all but classicists now spent only three years in residence, the outlay was much the same.[1] And it remained so on the eve of the Second World War. Charges rose rapidly with the inflation that accompanied the Great War and its aftermath, but they fell back from the mid-1920s, and in 1939 were not much higher than they had been in the Edwardian era. The average male undergraduate up in the 1930s would have had an annual battel's bill of from £150 to £180 for his room, meals, tuition, and various establishment charges.[2]

To reformers of all stripes at the beginning of the period, the sum was excessive and condemned Oxford to being a university for the social elite. In 1846, evangelical critics wanted the cost lowered to £60 per annum. The 1850 commissioners went further and believed it should be possible to reduce the outlay on a four-year course to £200. Jowett concurred. In his evidence to the commission, he claimed that poorer undergraduates could live in Oxford for only £30 to £60 a year if colleges were to set up affiliated halls where meals and tuition were free.[3] In the following decades some attempt was made to provide a cheaper education for a minority, and by the time Curzon was Chancellor there were two alternatives. An undergraduate who sought to save money could either attend Keble, which had been deliberately set up to undercut the other colleges, or register as a non-collegiate and live in digs

---

[1] Commission (1852), *Report*, p. 33; George N. Curzon, *Principles and Methods of University Reform: Being a Letter Addressed to the University of Oxford* (Oxford, 1909), p. 70. The 1850 costs include books. The fourth year was not a complete year. It may be necessary to add a further £25 to Curzon's estimate if his figure does not include the annual cost of tuition which he gives on p. 71: £22–5 college fee and £2 10s. university fee.

[2] *Handbook to the University of Oxford* (Oxford, 1933), pp. 318–19 (general) and 399–448 (costs college by college).

[3] Commission (1852), appendix E, pp. 55–6; *Evidence*, pp. 30–40.

or one of the small private halls. Undergraduates, on Keble's inception in 1870, faced an annual standing charge of £81, and the figure was only £4 higher in 1909. Non-collegiates, on the other hand, Curzon revealed, could cover the cost of board, lodging, tuition, and examination for as little as £52.[4]

This was only the basic cost of keeping someone at Oxford. In addition, money had to be found for clothes, wine, tobacco, and entertainment, not to mention the expenses that could be incurred in travelling during the six months of the year an undergraduate was 'down'. As in earlier periods, some undergraduates burnt money, while others lived frugally. The commission of 1850 thought the total cost of a four-year course would seldom be less than £600; Thorold Rogers, a few years later, thought it was often nearer £1,000.[5] This must have been close to the top of the range. In the first half of the twentieth century, £200 a year would usually prove sufficient, and an allowance of £350 was thought princely. At New College in the early 1930s the future secretary of the TUC, George Woodcock, recalled few of his fellow undergraduates with an income of more than £250. Rhodes scholars were given £300 per annum when the scheme was set up at the turn of the twentieth century, but this had to last the whole year (see Table 6).

Even at the lower end of the market, an Oxford education before the Second World War was always hard to finance for all but the richest families. As we saw in Chapter 9, the social profile of the undergraduate population broadened quite significantly across the period, even if Oxford remained elitist.[6] It is difficult to see how this could possibly have happened, were it not for the fact that many under-graduates were in receipt of some form of extra-parental financial support. By the 1900s, the colleges, between them, offered 504 scholarships and 230 exhibitions. The first were strictly academic prizes and awarded irrespective of family circum-stances; the second, like the twenty-four attached to Jowett's Balliol Hall, were intended for those of slender means.[7] Scholarships were usually worth £80 per annum, exhibitions from £30 to £70. As 300 of the scholarships were in classics and a further 122 were restricted to particular schools or localities, the lion's share always went to public-school pupils. Nonetheless, Curzon claimed that, in 1909, even the large majority of scholarships were in the hands of those who needed the money.[8] By then the hard-pressed could also seek support from their Local Educational Authority. Set up in 1902 to oversee state primary and secondary education, these bodies were further empowered to offer scholarships to university students from families of limited means. Initially such scholarships were rare, but in the interwar period they became more plentiful. In 1937, 1,100 of Oxford's undergraduates, some 25 per cent, women as well as men, were in receipt of a local authority bursary.

---

[4] Curzon, *Principles*, pp. 53 and 70. A non-collegiate would need a further £10 to pay the entrance fee and dues to the delegacy but would not need more than £70 to cover all expenses. A total of £52 was the cost of board, lodging, and tuition at Ruskin: ibid. p. 58.

[5] Commission (1852), *Report*, p. 33; J.E. Thorold Rogers, *Education in Oxford: Its Methods, Its Aims, Its Rewards* (London, 1861), pp. 203–4. Rogers, a free-trade economist and Liberal politician, was the Drummond professor of economics and fellow of All Souls from 1762 to 1867.

[6] See pp. 386–7 and 391, this volume.   [7] See p. 369, this volume.

[8] Curzon, *Principles*, pp. 81–2.

Oxbridge in the 1930s also monopolized the small number of scholarships given by the central government Board of Education for those who had attended schools wholly or partly assisted by the taxpayer.

However, the financial support available only ever covered part of an undergraduate's expenses. Scholarships, especially a college one, might go a long way to paying a frugal undergraduate's bills but parents still had to make up the shortfall. This was why there were so few representatives of the working classes at Oxford before 1939. Average pay in the 1930s was £4 per week, so only the very fortunate like Woodcock, who was a graduate of Ruskin and had his full costs covered by the University's extramural delegacy, could ever dream of attending.[9] Even among middle-class undergraduates there was always a number who could not make ends meet, for family circumstances could dramatically change during the course of their stay. To ensure that such students could finish their degree, colleges, in the first half of the twentieth century, maintained hardship funds. Scholarship holders who had no need of the £80 were encouraged to forgo all or part of the payment so that the money saved could be distributed among the needy.[10] Colleges too would find other ways of helping the relatively indigent. The future master of the rolls, Alfred 'Tom' Denning, entered Magdalen in 1916 to read mathematics from Andover Grammar School. He was the fourth son of a respectable draper from Whitchurch and had limited parental support. Although he had a college exhibition worth £30 and a Hampshire county scholarship worth £50, he had less than he needed and was forced to economize by renting a modest room and skimping on coal: 'Father could not help. But I determined to accept it—and manage the best I could. Go without if need be.' Luckily, President Warren came to his assistance: 'The President was very good to me. He helped me at every turn. Owing to him my exhibition of £30 a year became a demiship of £80 ... He got the Goldsmiths' Company of London to grant me an exhibition of £30 [as well]. So I was able to get through.'[11]

B. Accommodation and Buildings

A male undergraduate who came up to Oxford in the century after 1845 and lived in a college would have usually occupied a set of rooms comprising a bedroom and sitting room. Some colleges offered students the chance to rent a single room or even a three-roomed set, but neither was common. Even the founding fathers of Keble, anxious to cut student costs, assumed that the inhabitants of the new college would a need a pair of rooms. The new women's colleges, in contrast, assumed that young ladies' spatial requirements were more modest. Not only did they drop the traditional staircase model—Lady Margaret Hall, like Keble, had corridors, while

---

[9] In 1924, the Delegacy of Extra-Mural Studies replaced the Delegacy for the Extension of Teaching beyond the Limits of the University. In the interwar years, the delegacy had the funds to award a handful of scholarships to bright students who had not had a conventional education, so could not apply to Oxford through the usual channels.

[10] Curzon, *Principles*, p. 83.   [11] A.T. Denning, *Denning, the Family Story* (London, 1981), p. 34.

Somerville believed that women students should be accommodated in homely houses not quads—but they also divided the rooms into bedsits. In the old colleges, where rooms were of different shapes and sizes, the best rooms were occupied by those with the largest purse, for rents were charged on a sliding scale. Francis Needham, Lord Newry, who went up to Christ Church in 1860, could command one of the best sets in Tom Quad and had a living room large enough to serve as the present-day graduate common room. Poorer students found themselves living under the eaves in misshapen rooms with low beams and little light. When the impoverished Edward Atiyah arrived at Brasenose from Syria in 1923, he could afford only to rent 'the cheapest set … in College', a pair of attic rooms on staircase VII.[12]

Whatever their size or shape, college rooms came ready-furnished. Individual tenants might add the odd piece of furniture to the existing stock, but for the most part items were passed down from student to student. In most colleges, undergraduates paid a furniture rent to the college for a basic kit of table, chairs, bedstead and mattress, washstand, mirror, fireplace utensils, and crockery. In the posh male establishments, each undergraduate was judged to be the owner of the furniture during his time in residence and the incoming tenant paid his predecessor for the movables that he inherited, the amount based on a valuation made by the home or domestic bursar.[13] Inevitably, sets in smarter colleges were more profusely appointed. On arriving at Magdalen in 1901, the novelist Compton Mackenzie occupied a pair of rooms in St Swithun's III. The home bursar presented him with an inventory of the furnishings and requested he pay £31 4s 3d to the previous incumbent. The furnishings were carefully itemized:

> Sitting Room. Set Fire Irons. Bordered Carpet. Rug. Set ash tables. Ash Chiffonier. Easy chair. Study chair. 4 Cane seat chairs. Roller Blind. Brass Window Poles. Pr. Chenille curtains. Brass Rod and Tapestry Curtains in recess. Wicker chair. Settee in cretonne. Bamboo table. Chimney Shelf. 2 Rods and 2 Curtains over doors. Walnut writing table.
> Bedroom. Bedstead. Matting palliasse. Mattress. Bolster and Pillow. 2 Blankets and Quilt. Polpine Chest of Drawers. Washstand. Dressing Glass. Blind. [clothes] Horse. 4 pieces ware. Waste pail.[14]

Although undergraduates lived among hand-me-downs, there were few who passed up the opportunity to personalize the space they occupied. Students had already begun to do this in the eighteenth century, as we saw in Chapter 7.[15] But Britain by the mid-nineteenth century was the world's first industrial society and there were many more possible ways of making an individual mark on a room. The evidence from sketches and photographs points to sitting rooms becoming more and more cluttered with personal items as the Victorian period wore on. In the 1860s and 1870s decoration was muted and taste conservative. Students

[12] Edward Atiyah, *An Arab Tells His Story: A Study in Loyalties* (London, 1946), p. 104.
[13] Information about the arrangement in each college is given in the different editions of *The Student's Handbook to the University and Colleges of Oxford*, which was first printed in 1873.
[14] Compton Mackenzie, *My Life and Times, Octave Three, 1900–1907* (London, 1964), pp. 59–60.
[15] See pp. 262–3, in this volume

FIGURE 11.1 The sitting-room of the Exeter undergraduate Basil G. Nevinson: photograph 1873. Nevinson appears to have had a love of landscapes. The piano with the piece of Bach on its stand suggest he was a serious musician.

favoured a light-coloured wallpaper with a faint geometrical pattern; hung up quiet landscapes on the walls; and had one or two comfortable chairs. They might decorate their living room with the odd grandiose and luxurious item but they appear not to have gone out of the way to impress. A photograph of the sitting room occupied by an Exeter undergraduate in 1873 suggests that the occupant had devoted limited time to its embellishment. The arrangement of the gown and mortar board in the background reveals a man with a sense of humour, but apart from the pictures, the only obvious personal furnishings are the tablecloth, chaise longue and cushions, and the china on the dresser (see Figure 11.1). By 1900, on the other hand, many students were fussier about their surroundings, especially those under the influence of the arts and crafts movement of William Morris and Edward Burne-Jones, themselves Oxford alumni.[16] Objects were everywhere. Wallpaper decorated with prominent flowers was now in the ascendant, but, as pictures threatened to cover the walls, was only partly visible. Photos littered every surface; so too did flowers, cut or paper, and luxuriant throws. Many undergraduates, furthermore, emphasized their individuality by aiming to shock or amuse. A photograph of the room Richard Slater occupied in University College in 1901 reveals, at its centre, a parasol sparing the blushes of a naked hearth (see Figure 11.2).

[16] Both were at Exeter.

FIGURE 11.2 The sitting room of the University undergraduate Richard Slater: photograph 1901. The mantelpiece is decorated with what look like family photographs, though two appear to be men in costume. A photograph of a sports team has been hung above the bookcase.

The interwar years saw the undergraduates dividing into camps. Some serious scholars presented a puritanical face. The sitting room occupied by the Magdalen Rhodes scholar Thornton Page in the mid-1930s, was ostentatiously bare except for a desk, bookcase, armchair, sofa, and the odd poster on the walls.[17] Other undergraduates, usually the rich, cultivated eccentricity, like Evelyn Waugh's Sebastian Flyte, who was appropriately located in aristocratic Christ Church:

> His room was filled with a strange jumble of objects—a harmonium in a gothic case, an elephant's foot waste-paper basket, a dome of wax fruit, two disproportionately large Sèvres vases, framed drawings by Daumier—made all the more incongruous by the austere college furniture and the large luncheon table.[18]

[17] MCA, B/1/79A (collection of photographs).
[18] E. Waugh, *Brideshead Revisited* (Harmondsworth, 1970), p. 33. In contrast, the room of the narrator, Charles Ryder, reflected its occupier's as-yet-unformed and middle-brow taste: ibid., p. 29. Ryder had been given an allowance of £550 by his father, rather than the £350 advised by the college head—further evidence of his parvenu background: ibid., p. 27. Waugh himself was at Hertford in the 1920s.

Most undergraduates, however modest their means, attempted to make their rooms suggest that they were people worth getting to know. Atiyah might have rented the cheapest rooms in Brasenose in 1923 but he had come armed with mementoes from home and souvenirs he had collected while crossing Europe to get to Oxford. He was determined to make a splash and demonstrate his cultivated taste:

> I had the walls repapered and the furniture re-covered. I bought an extra chair and lampshades, and I succeeded in wheedling a new rug out of the Bursar. From home I had brought with me a leopard skin which I spread over my book case, and on that was installed a small bust of Dante imported from Florence. My Michelangelo and Leonardo prints were then suitably arranged around the walls; and in the towering shadow of the Radcliffe Camera I sat for the first time in a room of my creation, and found it good.[19]

The belief that male undergraduates should be housed in two-room sets placed an increasing strain on college accommodation as numbers rapidly expanded. The problem could be met after 1868 by allowing students to live out, but as living within the college curtilage was felt to be an essential part of the Oxford experience, the only solution was to erect new buildings. The years between 1860 and the outbreak of the Great War saw one of the great periods of Oxford's physical expansion. Not only did these decades witness the construction of the University's new schools in the High Street and the erection of buildings for Keble, the women's colleges, and a number of affiliated halls, but virtually every existing male college bar Wadham put up a new quad or range. The colleges employed a variety of architects of national renown. In the mid-1860s, Christ Church used Thomas Deane to design the Meadow Buildings, while Balliol employed Alfred Waterhouse to erect their new range fronting the Broad (see Figure 11.3). In the 1870s it was neither of these, but William Butterfield, who was commissioned to put up Keble, while New College asked the most famous Victorian architect of them all, George Gilbert Scott, to build the four-storey western range along Holywell Street. In the following decade, the changes were rung again. At the beginning of the 1880s, St John's employed Gilbert Scott Jnr to erect a new front on St Giles, while Magdalen gave the task of designing St Swithun's on the site formerly occupied by Magdalen Hall to George Bodley and Thomas Garner. New College, on the other hand, deserting Scott Snr, gave the task of building the eastern range of Holywell Buildings and its connecting tower to Basil Champneys, the architect of Mansfield, the Indian Institute,[20] and the first part of Lady Margaret Hall.

There was one architect, however, who was taken up in the 1870s and still finding work in Oxford in the Edwardian era. This was Thomas Graham Jackson. Jackson was a solicitor's son and evangelical Christian who was an undergraduate, then,

---

[19] Atiyah, *Arab Tells His Story*, p. 126.
[20] The Indian Institute was planned as a centre for teaching Indian civil service probationers and Indian students: see p. 429, this volume. It was to have a comprehensive collection of books and newspapers and house a museum of Indian objects. The foundation stone was laid in 1883 and it took twelve years to complete.

FIGURE 11.3 Broad Street frontage, Balliol College, mid-1860s: architect Alfred Water-house. At this date Waterhouse was only beginning to catch the nation's eye. His early work had been done in Manchester to much acclaim and he had only moved to London in 1865. The Balliol building was his first commission for an Oxford or Cambridge college.

from 1864 to 1878, a prize fellow, of Wadham. Although a pupil in the practice of G. G. Scott in the late 1850s, he had quickly fallen out of love with the medieval gothic style that his master had done so much to promote. Instead, he favoured a more eclectic approach that drew its inspiration from the Italian Renaissance more than the late middle ages and was an echo of the buildings of late Elizabethan and Jacobean Oxford. His designs were therefore very different from those of most of his contemporaries working in Oxford, who all, with the exception of Champneys, who could work in different styles, were dedicated gothicizers. Jackson also preferred to work in the golden Clipsham stone of Rutlandshire rather than the more friable but traditional grey stone of the Headington quarries. In consequence, he was thought to be doing something new. Not surprisingly, his eclecticism found particular favour with the reformers in the University, like Jowett, who saw his 'Jacobethan' style as a modern yet traditionalist answer to the 'catholic' and benighted gothic championed by so many other Victorian architects.[21]

---

[21] Jackson himself was in the reformers' camp though an evangelical.

Jackson's first large commission in Oxford was the new Examination Schools, which he was awarded in 1876 on the back of liberal support. The massive neo-Jacobean building, completed in 1883, divided Oxford opinion along party lines. Conservatives and Anglo-catholics hated it. The modernizers praised the building to the skies, and Jackson was immediately asked by more progressive heads of house to turn his attention to designing new college buildings. In the course of the 1880s, Jackson was responsible for a vast new range at Trinity, the Grove Building at Lincoln, a small range at Corpus, an extension to Somerville, and Balliol's King's Mound, a stand-alone house, initially intended to become Balliol Hall, in Mansfield Road. He also, in 1887–9, gave the new Hertford College an identity it had hitherto lacked. Hertford was as much an Anglican, and thus as old-fashioned a foundation, as Keble. It had no wish, however, to be seen as a clone of its slightly older Anglo-catholic relation, and it looked to establish its distinctiveness in stone. Its principal from 1877 to 1922, the reform-minded Henry Boyd, sought Jackson's help, and the architect duly obliged. In closing the existing site with a new range fronting Cat Street, he erected an architectural gem which remained true to the classical inspiration of the buildings erected by William Garbett for Magdalen Hall in the early 1820s. At the same time, he gave the resulting quad its own idiosyncratic character through adding a five-sided protruding staircase to the internal wall of the frontage, which transported Hertford to the banks of the Loire (see Figure 11.4).[22]

Jackson continued to work for Hertford over the next two decades and eventually built its second quad on the other side of New College Lane, connected by the Bridge of Sighs. In later years, however, his versatility was particularly shown in his work at Brasenose, where in two phases, 1886–90 and 1907–11, he oversaw the construction of a new High Street frontage. The architect was anxious to produce a building that was both true to the original sixteenth-century parts of the college and in keeping with nearby St Mary's Church. His solution was to design an internal façade that was 'Jacobethan' and an external one that had many more late medieval elements. Indeed, had Jackson had his way (but the college demurred) the homage to an earlier age would have been even clearer. The façade was broken by a traditional Oxford crenellated tower with a pointed archway on the High Street and a rounded one on the college side. Jackson had wanted to top the arch with a complicated spire in imitation of the spire above the entrance to Aberdeen's King's College.

The new college buildings added in the decades before 1914 were expensive items. Keble cost a colossal £150,000 to build from scratch, but even the addition of a new range could easily require £15–£20,000. On top of this, the period was one of constant restoration and improvement to existing college buildings in response to the ravages of time, changing fashion, and scientific progress. Crumbling stonework

---

[22] See Figure 11.4. Pevsner, who did not appreciate Jackson, dubbed the Hertford staircase 'the bastard child of Blois': Jennifer Sherwood and Nikolaus Pevsner, *Oxfordshire* (Harmondsworth, 1974), p. 139. For the original buildings, see p. 176, this volume.

FIGURE 11.4 Renaissance staircase, Hertford College, 1887–9: architect Thomas Graham Jackson. Jackson was the most sought-after architect in late Victorian and Edwardian Oxford who could work sensitively and imaginatively in various styles. He also received a number of important commissions at Cambridge. Like George Gilbert Scott Jnr, he was an academic architect who wrote about architecture as well as practised.

and rotting beams were the subject of continual attention; several chapels were given gothic makeovers, starting with Exeter's and Balliol's in the 1850s, which were rebuilt by Scott Snr and Butterfield (see Figure 11.5);[23] while at the turn of the twentieth century all colleges rapidly installed electricity and took the first tentative steps to providing fitted bathrooms. Brasenose, which entrusted everything to Jackson, seems to have run up a bill with the architect of £45,000.[24] Some colleges found a benefactor to cover the cost: Balliol's Waterhouse Building was erected through the generosity of Hannah Brackenbury, a spinster who claimed to be a collateral relative of the founder. Others, such as Trinity, which paid for a third of its two Jackson ranges with subscriptions, sought support from old members. But richer colleges, such as Magdalen, covered all of the cost from endowment income and by taking out loans, as they were allowed to do under the 1858 legislation.[25]

[23] For Scott Snr's building, see Figure 11.5. Butterfield's building was not judged a success.
[24] He had already been employed at Brasenose earlier in the 1880s.
[25] The one and a half ranges of Magdalen's St Swithun's cost £30,000.

FIGURE 11.5 Exeter College chapel, 1850s: architect George Gilbert Scott: engraving of H. Le Keux 1860. George Gilbert Scott's creation was a pastiche of the mid-thirteenth-century Paris church of Sainte-Chapelle on the Île de la Cité. The old chapel that it replaced had been built in 1623–4. Many of the fellows were High Anglicans and wanted something less austere and puritanical.

As the agricultural depression caused the colleges' landed income to fall by as much as a half in the 1870s and 1880s, dreams of expansion and renewal often had to be scaled back. The result was that, despite the building boom, there was never enough accommodation for the rising number of undergraduates, and it became normal, from the end of the nineteenth century, for students in all colleges to spend at least a year, usually their second, in digs. The situation was made worse by the huge influx of undergraduates after the First World War and the continued expansion of the undergraduate population in the 1920s and 1930s. The more enterprising colleges built anew. Magdalen erected Longwall in 1929 and Longwall Corner (outside the curtilage) in 1935; Balliol renovated and extended Holywell Manor House in the early 1930s; while Merton at the beginning of the Second World War opened a new building on Rose Lane, which was designed by Sir Hubert Worthington in a restrained neoclassical style suited to the depression decade (see Figure 11.6).[26] But such interwar initiatives were few and never sufficient, and living out became an accepted part of Oxford life until the end of the twentieth century.

[26] Longwall was built by Sir Giles Gilbert Scott, son of Gilbert Scott Jnr.

FIGURE 11.6 Rose Lane Building, Merton College, early 1930s. architect Hubert Worthington The son and half-brother of distinguished architects, Worthington was a pupil of Edwin Lutyens. Less brutal than much 1930s architecture, there was still an air of austerity about his buildings. He was appointed Slade lecturer in architecture at Oxford in 1929.

Renting rooms in the town after spending the first year in college was a tremendous shock to the male undergraduate system. While living in, whatever their background, male undergraduates enjoyed the services of their staircase scout and his 'boy' who catered to their every whim. In the morning, he brought them hot water to wash in, made up the fire, cleared away the detritus of the night before, made the bed, and fetched breakfast. During the day, if needed, he ran errands or helped his charges to get ready to entertain friends. The scout was also the freshman's mentor and councillor: he knew the college lore and how to extricate his 'young gentlemen' from the consequences of their youthful excesses.[27] In digs, on the other hand, undergraduates ceased to be treated like lords and had to learn to fend for themselves: landladies were expected to provide meals and laundry services, but they were not slaves and would not tolerate disruptive behaviour. The social gain of living in town, however, almost certainly outweighed any temporary discomfort or restraint. Taking digs in the city did not end, overnight, the separation

[27] The centrality of the staircase scout was always emphasized in student memoirs: e.g. J. Brett Langstaff, *Oxford 1914* (New York, 1965), pp. 43 and 65. Scouts received tips on top of their college salary for extra services. For an overview of their role, see D.C.M. Platt, *The Most Obliging Man in Europe: Life and Times of the Oxford Scout* (London, 1986).

of town and gown that had existed since the University began. But the experience did begin to break down barriers between the two at a time when the development of the car industry was fast releasing the city from the University's grip, and it was no longer uncommon in the 1930s to find both undergraduates and townsmen and women attending the same function in Oxford Town Hall. More importantly, in the short term, the commonality of the experience of living out helped to end the isolation of the small but not insignificant group of non-collegiates, known disrespectfully in the late nineteenth century as 'toshers' or trash. In this regard, collegiates and non-collegiates in digs lived in a similar fashion. They both took their Oxford identity from a physical site—the college or Jackson's non-collegiate building, erected on the corner of the High and Merton Street, in 1886–8—but in neither case did it define their existence.[28]

C. An Undergraduate's Day

Until the Second World War, Oxford male undergraduates in or out of residence, were bound by a set of rules which, in general outline, had been laid down many centuries before. Out on the street, they were judged to be different from other adolescents. As scholars and gentlemen, they had to be more carefully policed in order that they did not demean themselves or dishonour their parents. They were not allowed to stay out of college overnight: college gates were shut at 9.10 p.m. and lodging-house doors locked at 10; they could not wear what they liked but were expected to don a cap and gown when attending lectures, entering university buildings such as the Bodleian, or simply wandering about the town at certain times of the day; and they were forbidden altogether, or except under licence, various pleasures permitted other citizens, especially the right of those over 18 to enter a public house. In contrast, within their college or digs, restrictions on undergraduate dress and behaviour were largely relaxed. Undergraduates had to wear their gown in chapel and hall, or when calling on their tutor, but they were otherwise free to dress as they liked. Equally, they could consume as much alcohol as they could afford and, within limits, let off steam. Nonetheless, even within college, they were still subject to a bevy of written and unwritten rules concerning deference to elders, attendance at chapel, dining in hall, keeping pets, and tending window boxes. As in earlier periods, too, undergraduates who transgressed the rules faced a day of reckoning with the college dean, the Proctors, and in the most heinous cases, the Vice-Chancellor in his court.

In the course of the period, the rules controlling conduct outside the college, while never abolished, were partially redrawn. Thus, while gate-hours always remained, it was accepted that undergraduates could stay out till midnight.

---

[28] For the decision to create a non-collegiate headquarters, see p. 370, this volume. Jackson was inevitably given the commission, as the reformers' favourite architect.

Similarly, if academic dress had always to be worn whenever students and dons came together formally, the licence to wear mufti out in the town was slowly extended. In 1883, a cap and gown were required before 1 p.m. and after sunset; by 1912, they had to be worn only after 8 p.m. in winter and 9 p.m. in summer. The restrictions on what a student might get up to outside college were also liberalized to a degree. They were always forbidden to attend hotels, restaurants, and public houses simply to drink, but between the wars it was recognized that they could frequent such places provided they had a meal. The range of restrictions also changed with the times. In 1883, the university regulations still had a medieval ring. Undergraduates were allowed neither 'to smoke in the streets; nor to engage in any games of chance; nor to take part in or subscribe money for horse-races or shooting matches'. They were also not allowed to 'keep a horse or to drive a vehicle of any kind' without the consent of their college and the Proctors. But by the outbreak of the First World War the University felt the need to outlaw a new set of temptations. On the banned list in 1912, only race meetings remained from an earlier date. Instead, the University was now anxious that undergraduates should not be lured into billiard halls before 1 p.m. or attend private or public subscription dances without proctorial approval.[29] Ownership of a horse was also no longer a worry. The problem now was the motor car and motorcycle. Proctorial permission had equally to be sought if an undergraduate desired to 'learn or practise aviation'. Yet the fear of dances and billiard halls equally proved ephemeral. Only car ownership without a permit remained off limits in the 1930s.[30]

College restrictions were also eased over time. The insistence that undergraduates attended chapel each morning had to be eased from the moment that colleges admitted non-conformists. Non-Anglicans were allowed to line up for roll-call instead. But by the 1880s several colleges, notably Balliol, had extended this right to all undergraduates, and by the First World War it was the custom virtually everywhere.[31] Over time, too, it no longer became necessary to put in a daily appearance. At the beginning of the twentieth century, undergraduates usually had to attend roll-call or chapel only three times a week, and between the wars some colleges abandoned the practice altogether or gave up treating absentees harshly. In the interwar years, the requirement to dine each night in college similarly often went by the board. Attendance remained the default position, but in most colleges undergraduates were allowed to order dinner in their rooms with the dean's permission or sign out a number of nights a week. Undergraduates in their year out were often no more than occasional visitors to their college. George Woodcock recalled that, at New College in the 1930s, they 'might come into college only for tutorials.

---

[29] Attempts in the early 1920s by American students to get dances going where undergraduates might mix with town girls was immediately scotched by Vice-Chancellor Farnell of Exeter: G. B. Grundy, *Fifty-Five Years at Oxford: An Unconventional Autobiography* (London, 1945), pp. 137–8.

[30] *The Student's Handbook to the University and Colleges of Oxford* (Oxford, 1883), p. 23; *Student's Handbook* (Oxford, 1912), p. 92; *Student's Handbook* (Oxford, 1937), p. 348.

[31] An exception was Lincoln.

The only common meal was dinner in hall and it was possible to sign off from that on three of the seven nights in the week.'[32]

Provided a male undergraduate accepted these limitations on his movement and conduct, he was free to live as he wished. Apart from waiting on his tutor when required, the college made no other statutory demands on his time and next to no formal effort outside the ritual of termly collections to ensure he kept his nose to the grindstone. There was equally minimal interest in ensuring that an undergraduate took regular meals. Keble expected all students to breakfast and lunch as well as dine in the college hall. But this was unique. Normally, a male undergraduate took other meals during the day in his own or a friend's room, or ate out if he could afford to, while poorer students took advantage of the system and ate nothing.[33] Meals taken in an undergraduate's college room were usually simple fare, supplied by the buttery on demand and charged to battels. Lunch was normally bread, cheese, and beer. But on special occasions when an undergraduate entertained his friends, it could be a bespoke feast ordered in advance from the kitchens, its sumptuousness and consequent cost dependent on the individual pocket. An opportunity to drink heavily as well as eat to excess, such meals went on for hours, with the scout acting as waiter, and became an excuse to idle away the day.[34]

Mornings were supposed to be set aside for work—hence the ban on attending billiard halls before 1 p.m.—and even the less able and committed usually made some pretence at getting down to study. Most spent the large part of the morning engaged in reading or preparing for a tutorial, either in their rooms or a library. Mornings were also when lectures in and outside the college were scheduled, but students then, as today, had difficulty in maintaining attendance. When the future archbishop of Canterbury Randall Thomas Davidson came up to Trinity in October 1868 he listened to eleven lectures a week in his first term, and on some days to three in succession. But Davidson was cramming for Responsions and his steadfastness was seldom replicated by undergraduates who had completed their matriculation requirements. Arts students, in particular, whatever their good intentions, quickly dropped out. Edward John Buxton was an earnest undergraduate at New College in the first half of the 1930s, who religiously attended the lectures of the college's ancient historian, C. E. 'Tom Brown' Stevens. When the two met up again in 1949, on Buxton becoming a fellow in English at the college, Stevens joshed him about his assiduity: 'The first lectures, I gave, you were in the audience; after about four weeks, you *were* the audience.'[35]

---

[32] Buxton and Williams, p. 133. Many undergraduates ate out as often as they could because they found the quality of hall food poor. The novelist Angus Wilson, up at Merton in the early 1930s, was an habitué of The George, a restaurant on the corner of George Street and Cornmarket: Mark Davies, 'The Great Unknown Novelist', OT, 21 Nov. 2013, p. 35.

[33] They also skipped dinner if they could sign out. C. T. Atkinson, later modern history tutor at Exeter, often ate nothing all day while up from 1893–8: see Bodleian, MS Eng. Misc.e.1141, fol. 2 (diary of Clement Webb).

[34] Waugh depicts Sebastian and his friends lunching on plovers' eggs and lobster Neuberg: *Brideshead Revisited*, pp. 33–4.

[35] Buxton and Williams, p. 141. Stevens was known as 'Tom Brown' supposedly because his mother had sent him to Winchester in a Rugby uniform. He moved on to become a fellow at Magdalen.

The afternoons after lunch were for physical relaxation. Until the 1860s, most undergraduates, like earlier generations, would have whiled away the time walking in Oxford and the immediate countryside chatting with their friends. However, the publication of Matthew Arnold's *Thyrsis* in 1867, which nostalgically recalled his rambles to the south of the city with his friend Hugh Clough twenty years before, was a threnody to a past age.[36] By then, a significant proportion of the student body was devoting its afternoons to college-based team games where undergraduates trained for or took part in intercollegiate contests. In the 1860s, these were essentially limited to two: rowing and cricket. But by 1900, thanks to the belief of many dons that team sports were character-building and good for creating college spirit, their number had expanded to include not only soccer and rugby but a variety of individual sports that were also organized around intercollegiate contests, such as athletics, boxing, and lawn tennis. By the Edwardian era, too, those who eschewed intercollegiate competition could still take physical exercise by taking part in social sports such as golf or beagling, the latter particularly associated with the richer elements of Christ Church, Magdalen, and New College.[37] But it was the intercollegiate sports that always claimed the attention of most undergraduates, even between the wars when the virtues of athletic manliness and playing the game had lost much of their Victorian allure. What undergraduates prized as much, if not more, than a good degree, was to be in a team that won 'cuppers' (as all intercollegiate competitions except rowing were called) or in a crew that went 'head of the river'.[38]

Throughout the period, rowing was the most popular and favoured team sport, where there were, as now, two intercollegiate competitions each year: Torpids and Eights. The first, held in Hilary Term from 1852, was a competition for novice crews;[39] the second and more serious contest took place in May and was a central part of Commem week.[40] Both competitions lasted several days and were organized in the same way. The boats were assembled in line astern in an order determined by their performance the previous year or day, and in the course of the race attempted to catch up and 'bump' the boat in front. The crew that emerged as 'head of the river' at the end of the contest was feted like royalty. Rowing was a well-established part of the Oxford scene in the second quarter of the nineteenth century, but from the 1860s far greater numbers of undergraduates began to participate in the sport and every college had a boat club. Rowing too, from this date, became more competitive. Initially it had been common for an enthusiast to fill a college boat with his friends, regardless of their aptitude. This, though, became virtually impossible with

---

[36] Arnold, like Clough, had been a fellow at Oriel in the 1840s; he was the son of Arnold of Rugby.

[37] M. C. Curthoys and H. S. Jones, 'Oxford Athleticism, 1850–1914: A Reappraisal', *History of Education*, 24: 4 (1995), 305–17. In the period 1850–70 individual colleges had sports days but there was no athletics intercollegiate competition. For the development of golf at Oxford, see Grundy, *Fifty-Five Years*, pp. 165–6.

[38] Cuppers was called after the trophy received by the winners.

[39] The competition was called Torpids from the word 'torpor': the races had originally lacked the vim of the Eights.

[40] Commem week was the week in which the University remembered its benefactors at Encaenia: see p. 148, this volume. By the mid-nineteenth century, Encaenia itself was only one of many social events that occurred in the week: see pp. 475–6, this volume.

FIGURE 11.7 Trinity Eight, head of the river, 1842: hand-coloured print. Although Trinity's glory days were just before and after the Second World War, its boat club had known success a century before. The print could be used by any college as a permanent memorial to victory on the river. The vests of the oarsmen were left blank so the college colours could be painted on.

the introduction from 1856 of the keel-less boat, which was difficult to balance and required practice and teamwork. As few schools offered the chance to row, good oarsmen had henceforth to be identified when they came up and gradually trained over their stay. This only helped to raise standards, foster intercollegiate competition, and encourage the formation of more than one crew per college, which necessitated, from 1874, the creation of divisions to make the races manageable.[41] The introduction of sliding seats in the latter part of the century took the professionalism further. Every undergraduate was encouraged to have a go and see if they had what it took. By the end of the nineteenth century, a majority of the undergraduate body rowed competitively at some stage of their career, and most students were obsessed by their college's ranking on the river. A number of colleges were particularly successful at the sport. Brasenose, University, New College, and Magdalen all had their glory years in Eights during the period, and Trinity set a record in the late 1930s and 1940s when it was head of the river for six consecutive contests (see Figure 11.7). Magdalen's first eight gained a particular reputation for consistency. Although its boat club was not formed until 1859, by 1928 Magdalen had been in the first three on the river every May for fifty years except one, when it dropped to fourth. Its crews had also won numerous competitions at other venues, especially at Henley, whose regatta, by the late nineteenth century, was an international event. In

---

[41] Divisions were first introduced in Torpids. It was not until 1908 that a college could enter more than one crew in Eights: Roger Hutchins, 'Well-Rowed Magdalen': A History of Magdalen College Boat Club 1859–1993 (Oxford, 1993), p. 10.

a single year, 1907, Magdalen won three Henley trophies: the Stewards', Visitors', and Wyfold Cups.[42]

Rowing prospered because revered by the dons above other sports. Since so few undergraduates had rowed at school, it proved to be particularly integrative and democratic. Non-conformists in particular seem to have found it a good way to become an accepted member of college. For this reason it was promoted by many liberals. Balliol's A. L. Smith, the scion of the non-sporty Christ's Hospital, was so keen on the sport that he acquired an eight and a four for Ruskin. When a college's senior members turned their backs on the river, performance could plunge. Brasenose was head on 110 nights over the years 1839 to 1891, which was twice as many as their nearest rival. When Charles Heberden became principal in 1889, he blamed rowing for the college's poor academic record and withdrew his patronage. Not until 1928 was the college head of the river again, and it slumped to twenty-second place in one year of Heberden's reign, bottom of the second division.[43]

Rowing's democratic credentials were further burnished towards the end of the nineteenth century once participation became cheap. Initially, the members of the different sports clubs had funded their own activities, and the rowing fraternity had frequently run up heavy debts. Not only did boat clubs have the cost of renting or buying and storing the college boat or boats, but from the middle of the nineteenth century they also incurred the added expense of maintaining a second-hand barge by the river bank, where oarsmen could change before rowing and where members of the college could gather to cheer on their crews: Brasenose had one as early as 1846.[44] Rowing, then, was scarcely a sport for the indigent. From the 1880s, however, the colleges, beginning with Balliol, brought their different sporting clubs together under a single umbrella, called the Amalgamated Clubs, whose treasurer was a fellow. Thereafter, a fixed annual subscription was collected from every junior member and divided up according to a club's need, with the result that team sport was brought within the reach of everyone. From then on, the colleges also agreed to subsidize the costs of college sport to a certain extent and sometimes to pay part of the subscriptions of the poorer students. In consequence, the colleges, by 1900, had begun to provide much needed infrastructure, establishing proper sports fields, building pavilions, and commissioning leading architects to design brand-new barges which became statements of college identity. Magdalen had a barge designed by Edwin Lutyens in 1887, while Trinity spent £3,260 on buying and fitting out a new sports field in 1898.[45]

Apart from cricket in summer, which could go on long into the evening, most sports and games only took up a couple of hours of the undergraduate day and

[42] Ibid., ch. 3.   [43] Curthoys and Jones, 'Oxford Athleticism', p. 308.
[44] Many had been formerly owned by the London livery companies.
[45] Curthoys and Jones, 'Oxford Athleticism', p. 308; Hutchins, 'Well-Rowed Magdalen', p. 20 and plate VI. Exeter's Amalgamated Clubs was founded in 1881, Lincoln's and Magdalen's in 1887, and Christ Church's and Oriel's in 1889. By the 1920s, the new barges began to be replaced by more permanent structures, but there were no boathouses before the late 1930s, so boats still had to be stored elsewhere.

were over by teatime. The late afternoon and evening after dinner were the principal parts of the day set aside for tutorials, so one or two times a week most undergraduates had to return to their books on leaving the river or playing field. If a meeting with their tutor was not imminent, however, only the most studious students devoted much or any of the rest of the day to private study. For the majority, the hours between 4 p.m. and bedtime, punctuated by dinner, were usually dedicated to socializing. As in an earlier period, a lot of time was passed simply relaxing and talking with friends, while often imbibing considerable amounts of alcohol. But most undergraduates, by the turn of the twentieth century, also spent several evenings a week in the more structured atmosphere of a private college club. Undergraduate societies before 1850 were virtually unknown outside Brasenose and Christ Church, where several had come into existence in the late Georgian era, such as the Phoenix and Loder's.[46] By 1900 they were legion.

Among the first clubs to be set up and always the most exclusive were dining societies, which allowed a few well-heeled and socially well-connected members of the college to gather together from time to time to indulge their taste for excessive drinking and eating in a more formal fashion, which involved bizarre toasts and secret rituals. Merton had a dining society, the Myrmidons, from as early as 1865; Brasenose's Octagon, where members dined off octagonal plates, was established in the following year; Trinity's Claret Club in 1870; and University College's Shaker Club in 1876.[47] By the end of the century, however, most colleges also possessed at least one undergraduate club which catered for the intellectual as well as for the gourmand. This was usually a debating society where the more serious undergraduates of the college would first listen to, then discuss, a paper on a contemporary topic read by one of the members.[48] Most were conservative in their politics but this did not stop their members from addressing a wide range of topics. In the year 1899/1900, Magdalen's Waynflete Society discussed inter alia the 'Black Art', the merits and demerits of Ruskin Hall, agriculture, the Boers, Gladstone, tree-growing, and 'The Modern Jew', the last an occasion for the voicing of highly anti-Semitic sentiments about recent immigration from eastern Europe. In addition, some colleges, by the Edwardian era, had societies specifically devoted to the arts. Most were staid musical clubs whose activities reflected current middlebrow taste and which only occasionally entertained their college peers with more substantial fare. Few college societies ever reached the heights scaled by Christ Church's Philharmonic Society when it performed Brahms' cantata *Rinaldo* in the college hall in 1885.[49] On the other hand, there was nothing staid or conservative about Brasenose's Pater Society, founded in 1907 by an undergraduate called Goodyear.

---

[46] The Phoenix was the oldest: see p. 267, this volume. Loder's dated from 1814.

[47] Lincoln did not have a dining society until 1905.

[48] Some debating clubs had members from more than one college: The Raleigh, already active in the mid-1870s, drew members from Oriel, Exeter, and Trinity: Lewis Farnell, *An Oxonian Looks Back* (London, 1934), p. 55.

[49] For the standard fare, see the programme of Magdalen's Maltese Glee Club in 1865 and a Merton concert in 1887, transcribed in *HUO*, vii. 438–9.

Named after Walter Pater, a Brasenose fellow who had devoted his life to attacking the aesthetic status quo, the Pater Society was dedicated to the avant-garde in all its forms, held talks on Fauvism and post-Impressionism, and had its own magazine entitled *Rhythm*.[50]

Between the wars, the number of college clubs proliferated. New College boasted twelve in Woodcock's day, 'ranging from the serious to the frivolous and from the orthodox to the eccentric', including the XX Club, whose members gave witty speeches 'almost invariably delivered in an attempted imitation of the style of some famous past or present parliamentary or after-dinner speaker'.[51] Many of the new clubs proved short-lived but some put down firm roots, especially the one ubiquitous new creation in the 1920s and 1930s: the college dramatic society. College drama had been frowned upon before the First World War, in part because undergraduates preferred to perform light comedy pieces rather than Shakespeare and Greek tragedy. Attempts to establish comic theatre at Christ Church at the start of the period were met by a decree from the Vice-Chancellor, Francis Leighton, in 1869, banning all student drama within his jurisdiction. The ban never held, but very few colleges ever had a dramatic society before 1914, and college drama flourished only in the more liberal post-war atmosphere, when male colleges were allowed to use members of the women's halls for female roles. Undergraduate taste had not evolved in the meantime, and the most popular fare in the 1930s were blood-curdling melodramas, such as *Maria Marten, or the Murder in the Red Barn*.

Attendance at a college club was usually by invitation and membership depended on election. There was one college society, however, which was open to all under-graduates: the JCR. There had been several attempts before 1850 to set up a common room for undergraduates in imitation of the rooms set apart for fellows in the latter part of the seventeenth century. But these had always been private clubs or exclusively for scholars on the foundation, and, in the mid-nineteenth century, the few that existed fell into bad odour with the college authorities who disliked their exclusivity. In 1867, a new form of JCR was constituted at Magdalen where the old demies' common room was turned into a club for all, and the initiative was gradually adopted elsewhere, especially in the 1880s once the college authorities got behind the scheme and agreed to supply a room. After Lincoln established a JCR in 1892, only Corpus was left without one. Run by elected committees, the new JCRs provided a number of services which were paid for by the subscriptions collected each year from the whole undergraduate body. Essentially, the JCR was a reading room where undergraduates could enjoy a wide range of newspapers and maga-zines. But it also laid on a hearty breakfast for those who wanted one, had tea and coffee on tap throughout the day, and acted as an 'undergraduate shop' where students could order their cigarettes and wine without going into the town. Furthermore, if not yet normally a centre of communal agitation against the college authorities, it played an important role in fostering the college's collective

---

[50] On Pater's scholarship, see pp. 495–6, this volume.   [51] Buxton and Williams, p. 135.

spirit by organizing regular entertainments for junior members after hall. Known as 'smokers' or 'afters', these were light-hearted musical soirées where anyone with a modicum of musical talent was encouraged to perform before his peers. To ensure the smooth performance of these several functions and keep the room clean and tidy, the JCR had its own team of servants. At their head was the JCR steward, a long-serving figure of mythical proportions, known to generations of undergraduates for his knowledge of college lore and sound advice.

JCRs, however, were not always as egalitarian as they seemed on the surface. At Magdalen until long after the Second World War, the JCR steward occupied a small room adjacent to the JCR where, in an evening after hall, a small group of favoured undergraduates would gather under his paternal eye to drink and converse. The originator of the tradition was Richard Gunstone, who hailed from a family of college servants and was steward for thirty years until retiring in 1914. 'Gunner', as he was called, was a college character, renowned for his racy humour, his readiness to dispense wisdom, and his banana trick, which entailed pouring a small glassful of spirits into a bottle, lighting the fumes, placing a banana on the neck of the bottle, and watching it slowly being drawn inside. He looked after and educated his boys while they were in residence and continued to write to them once they were down, keeping them informed of college success and gossip. There was no formal invitation to Gunner's Room but no undergraduate who lacked the right social or sporting credentials dared cross the threshold.[52]

For most undergraduates most of the time, the college was the centre of their social world and was intended to be so. Yet by 1900 few undergraduate would not have spent some leisure time outside its ambit, mixing with students from other colleges in university-wide activities. The establishment of clubs and societies across the period was a university as well as a college phenomenon, and by the turn of the twentieth century the University had a far wider range of undergraduate clubs and societies than even the larger colleges could boast. As in the colleges, the most notorious were elite dining societies, such as the Bullingdon, which had begun life in the late eighteenth century as a cricket club but, in the Edwardian era, represented the 'acme of exclusiveness at Oxford; it is the club of the sons of nobility, the sons of great wealth'.[53] The vast majority, however, offered undergraduates the opportunity to pursue interests and ambitions which the colleges either neglected or for which they only partially catered. The colleges celebrated unity and self-effacement; the university clubs and societies provided a platform for the pursuit of individual ambition. The bevy of university sporting clubs attracted the most gifted athletes, who found intercollegiate sport too tame, while the raft of subject-based clubs, such as the Junior Scientific Club or the Alembic Club, provided a congenial meeting

---

[52] Richard Sheppard, *The Gunstones of St Clements* (Oxford, 2003). Needless to say, the Prince of Wales was a regular visitor while up at Magdalen. On one occasion, George V observed the banana trick: Duke of Windsor, *A King's Story: The Memoirs of the Duke of Windsor* (New York, 1951), p. 96.

[53] *New York Times*, 1 June 1913.

place for academic high-flyers.[54] It was also only within the University that the tyro politician could find a home. Edwardian Oxford was a largely conservative institution but it was not divorced from the growing polarization and complexity of British political life and was soon awash with political societies at the university level. The future Conservative prime minister Harold Macmillan, up at Balliol from 1912 to 1914 and still unsure of his party affiliation, joined three: the Tory Canning, the Whig Russell, and the socialist Fabian Society.[55]

Before 1914, furthermore, the University was the natural home of the serious musician and thespian. The activities of the University Musical Union, founded in 1884, and the Bach choir, established in 1896, demonstrated that music-making in Oxford could rise above the mundane, while the Oxford University Dramatic Society, licensed by the Vice-Chancellor in 1885 and allowed to import women actors, proved undergraduates could tackle Greek tragedy and Shakespeare. OUDS productions were far from perfect—in an out-of-doors performance of *Twelfth Night* in 1902, Sir Toby, Sir Andrew and Fabian robbed Malvolio of most of his best scene by entering early—but they demonstrated that student theatre could rise above the burlesque and laid the ground for the flowering of college drama in the 1920s.[56] It was towards the University, too, that undergraduates with a journalistic and literary bent would gravitate both before and after the First World War. Colleges occasionally supported an in-house magazine but it was only at university level that a permanent undergraduate newspaper, *Isis*, was eventually established. Founded in 1892 by Mostyn Turtle Piggott, it remained, until the end of the period, a relatively light-hearted commentator on university affairs, as its first editor had intended: 'We shall endeavour to be humorous without being ill-humoured, critical without being captious, militant without being malevolent, independent without being impertinent, and funny.' Its hallmark was its 'Isis Idols', regular pen-portraits of the most prominent undergraduates, both athletes and scholars.[57] Before 1914 *Isis* had no rivals, but from 1920 it had to compete for the undergraduates' attention with a more serious publication, *Cherwell*, set up, according to one of its founding editors, Balliol's George Edinger, as a radical alternative: 'We were feeling for a new Oxford...We were anti-convention, anti-Pre War values, Pro-Feminist. We did not mind shocking and we often did.'[58] But *Cherwell*'s radicalism lay more in its literary pretensions than its political views, and between the wars at least it never supplanted *Isis* as the undergraduates' voice. In many respects, it was simply the most successful of a

---

[54] The Alembic Club was founded in 1901 for chemistry enthusiasts. It ceased meeting regularly in the 1960s: see <http://socialarchive.iath.virginia.edu/ark:/99166/w6n9g9vmc> (accessed 1 September 2015).

[55] Charles Williams, *Harold Macmillan* (London, 2009), p. 27. Russell was the prime minister who appointed the 1850 commission.

[56] Humphrey Carpenter, *OUDS: A Centenary History of the Oxford University Dramatic Society 1885–1985* (Oxford, 1985); Mackenzie, *Life and Times*, p, 103. Groups of actors from across the University also sometimes put on a Greek tragedy in Greek; supposedly the first was Aeschylus' *Agamemnon*, played at Balliol Hall in 1879: Farnell, *Oxonian*, p. 78.

[57] <https://en.wikipedia.org/wiki/The_Isis_Magazine> (accessed 1 September 2015): a quote from the first number.

[58] <https://en.wikipedia.org/wiki/Cherwell_%28newspaper%29> (accessed 25 July 2013).

UNION SOCIETY, OXFORD, DEBATING HALL.

FIGURE 11.8 Debating chamber, Oxford Union Society, 1879: architect Alfred Waterhouse. The Union Society was founded in 1823 but moved to its present site only in 1857 when it took possession of a set of buildings designed by Benjamin Woodward off St Michael's Str. The original debating chamber, now the old library and famous for its Pre-Raphaelite murals, soon proved too small. Waterhouse, then at the height of his fame having landed the commission to erect London's Natural History Museum, was asked to design a free-standing debating chamber in the gardens.

series of literary magazines, usually short-lived and ephemeral, that were published in Oxford in the first part of the twentieth century by earnest undergraduates anxious to attract the attention of the country's literary lions.[59]

As with the colleges, the most prestigious university sport was rowing. Not only was it the first to be organized—the Oxford University Boat Club was formed in 1839—but it was also, for a long time, the only one to stage a regular contest with Cambridge. While the Boat Race was first held in 1829 (even before the club was founded) and became an annual event from 1856, there was no regular Oxford and Cambridge cricket match before the 1870s, and varsity matches in other sports such as a rugby, football, hockey, and boxing had to await the end of the century.[60] By then, the singular status of the University's leading sportsmen was fully recognized, and they had their own elite club in Vincent's. The club had been founded in 1863 by the Brasenose oarsman W. B. Woodgate, and was initially intended as a society for

[59] Typical of the genre was Compton Mackenzie's *The Oxford Point of View*, which he edited from 1902 to 1904. For the early numbers, see his *Life and Times*, pp. 96–100 and 117–20. In 1921, an overtly political magazine, the Bolshevik *Free Oxford*, was published by undergraduates but was shut down by Vice-Chancellor Farnell for preaching terror: Farnell, *Oxonian*, p. 296.

[60] The first Boat Race was an informal contest held at Henley. It occurred when two school friends, one at Oxford and the other at Cambridge, agreed to get together a crew from each university to race one another.

his friends. It only became specifically associated with the University's premier athletes after 1870 when the first Blues were awarded.[61]

The most famous non-sporting university club was the Oxford Union. Set up as a debating society in 1823, it was initially of limited significance and became firmly established only from 1879, with the construction of a purpose-built debating chamber, on its present site, to a design by Waterhouse (see Figure 11.8). If this plunged the society into debt, it made the Union an attractive stage on which political heavyweights could strut their stuff, and the quality of the debates and numbers attending rose quickly. Although the debates tended to be dominated by Liberals, in contrast to college debating societies, the tone in the 1890s and 1900s was generally flippant and Conservative members turned up in commanding numbers whenever controversial issues were discussed. Predictably, the Union voted against women's suffrage in 1908, although only by 31 votes in a poll of 689. More surprisingly, the Union came out against both the creation of Ruskin and the admission of Rhodes scholars, the opening speaker on the latter occasion claiming that 'all the world will send us its worst specimens'.[62] After 1900, there were also continual majorities in support of motions calling for some form of conscription. It was only after the First World War that the Union swung against militarism, culminating in the 'King and Country' debate of 1933.[63]

The Union Society came to be seen as the one extra-collegiate social institution at the heart of undergraduate life. Membership was a virtual necessity, if only to use its well-equipped library. Joining other university societies and clubs was a matter of personal taste. Some undergraduates, especially those who arrived at Oxford as part of a peer group forged at school, preferred to be university rather than college men and deliberately spent their leisure hours beyond the college gate. Typical was the explorer Wilfred Thesiger, who spent little time at Magdalen in the early 1930s but concentrated on winning a boxing Blue and mixing with fellow old Etonians.[64] Most undergraduates, however, were college men through and through who ventured out into the wider university only in order to fill a particular void. The craving could be spiritual as well as academic, political, or aesthetic. The religious undergraduate who found, for confessional or personal reasons, his college chapel not to his taste would seek spiritual solace in the services held in one of the city's parish churches (which catered for all forms of Anglican opinion), or, from the turn of twentieth century, in one of the chaplaincies and halls run by the catholics and non-conformists, or in the synagogue in Richmond Road. Other undergraduates, more secular and non-denominational in their religious tastes but keen on dressing-up, would join the Oxford masons. The University's Apollo Lodge was particularly well supported from the beginning of the period: when Woodgate was up at Brasenose in the early 1860s, a third of his year were members.[65]

---

[61] 'An Oxford Institution Set to Toast Its 150th Anniversary', *OT*, 13 June 2013, pp. 28–9.
[62] *HUO*, vii. 810. For an overview, see Christopher Hollis, *The Oxford Union* (London, 1965).
[63] See p. 435, this volume.   [64] Interview, 16 Nov. 2001.
[65] Oscar Wilde joined the Lodge in 1875.

The daily life of the non-collegiate male undergraduate was not greatly different from his collegiate peers'. Anxious to be seen as a 'college-in-waiting', the non-collegiates organized a JCR in the cellar of their High Street headquarters and took part in intercollegiate sporting contests under the name of St Catherine's. From 1905, they had their own sports ground, and from 1908 a second-hand barge. Women undergraduates, however, if part of the University, were never totally integrated, especially before the First World War. Admittedly, those living inside a hall quickly developed a vibrant recreational life: they formed their own sports teams, organized competitions between the women's colleges, and soon had JCRs and a wide range of college clubs, including, in Somerville's case, a parliament where women assumed male personae. Nonetheless, before 1914, even within their hall, women students were always more trammelled than men. They had much less freedom to take meals where they pleased: they were not battelled for what they ate but paid for full board in advance. They were also expected to conform to con-temporary views of female propriety. The female halls opened at a moment when a national debate was raging over how much it was safe for women to exercise, and certain sports were felt to be a little rough. The council that ran Lady Margaret Hall feared its students might appear unladylike: it tried to ban hockey and expected its charges to go to bed early and eschew cigarettes and alcohol.[66] Beyond the college, women students were definitely more constrained. Every effort was made to keep them apart from the male undergraduates outside lectures, from fear that promis-cuous mixing of the sexes would encourage early and ruinous marriage. Women were allowed to attend university events as spectators, join the Bach choir, and attend Union debates in the gallery as guests. But they could seldom take part in other university societies, even as guests, and to go anywhere they had to have their principal's consent and be chaperoned.

Even once women became full members of the University in 1920, the position changed only slowly. Most societies remained male preserves. Thus, individual women students were allowed to act with OUDS by invitation from 1926, but could join as members only from 1964.[67] The sole clubs women were permitted to join on an equal footing with men were the new mixed societies, which had begun to develop shortly before the Great War. These, though, were scarcely independent associations: until 1949 they required the women principals' blessing. Women, moreover, were still not free to mix as they pleased. The system of permissions and chaperonage took a long time to fade away. It was not until 1935 that a female student could visit a male undergraduate in his rooms unaccompanied by another female, and even then she had to leave before evening hall. The constraints on women receiving male guests were never removed. At best, on the eve of the Second World War, a male undergraduate could visit a female student in her college

[66] For the debate on women and exercise, see Hilary Marland, *Health and Girlhood in Britain, 1874–1920* (Basingstoke, 2013), ch. 4.
[67] Before 1939 they also had to compete for roles with professional actresses.

at set times on Sundays, when, at St Hugh's, 'the bed was ceremoniously wheeled into the corridor'.[68] Although these rules affected the freedom of movement of both sexes, it was women students who were the more closely policed.

Despite the constraints, the women, between the wars, made the most of their limited opportunities. Had they not done so, the rapid development of college drama in the 1920s would have been impossible. On the other hand, the growing right of female students to participate, in some form, in university societies under-mined the vibrant collegiate and intercollegiate life they had established in their halls before 1914. Lady Margaret Hall's essay club and debating society had died by 1924; Somerville's parliament and 'Going Down Play' had gone by the early 1930s; so too had *Fritillary*, the college's magazine; while women's interest in sport also declined rapidly in the 1930s. It was as if women undergraduates had been able to become full members of the University only by turning their backs on its essence: collegiality.

D. Behaviour and Discipline

Oxford undergraduates were adolescents on the edge of adulthood, and the rules that the University and colleges expected them to live under were frequently honoured only in the breach. The occasional student, such as Magdalen's Terence Hodgkinson up in the first half of the 1930s, was upright to a fault, unless he lied to his diary.[69] But most male undergraduates repeatedly fell foul of the authorities. Throughout the period, they cut chapel or roll-calls, flouted gate-hours, broke the rules on wearing gowns, visited the city's pubs, and kept horses, and later motor cars, without permission. The more brazen also visited prostitutes and experimen-ted with narcotics, like Ernest Dowson of Queen's in the late 1880s, later a leading light in the decadent movement.[70] Women students, if generally more closely watched and less deviant, could be just as transgressive in their own way, especially in the interwar era when the rules about consorting with male undergraduates came to be seen as oppressive. The pioneering female journalist Anne Scott-James found Oxford's regulations 'idiotic and annoying', and left Somerville after two years, disillusioned, albeit with a first in Classical Mods. In the interim, she can hardly have found the regulations too restricting because she had managed to receive three proposals of marriage.[71]

Male undergraduates were also perpetually rowdy, boorish, and sometimes vicious. The undergraduate year in all colleges was constantly punctuated by celebrations of all kinds where alcohol was consumed in large quantities: coming-of-age parties,

---

[68] *HUO*, viii. 362.

[69] MCA, MC: P174/J1/1–10: diaries, 1930–40. He had been at school at Uppingham, wrote to his mother virtually every day, and ended up in the secret service during the war—at which point he abandoned his diary.

[70] Thomas Wright, 'Ernest Dowson at Oxford', OM, 8th week, TT (1999), 13–15. Queen's students at the end of the nineteenth century were notoriously delinquent. St John's Street and South Parks Road were the pick-up points for prostitutes.

[71] Adams, p. 215.

club dinners, national anniversaries, and so on. Whatever the event, the celebrations nearly always resulted in broken furniture, smashed windows, and damaged flower-beds. Dining society meetings were always riotous occasions. The Bullingdon had a particular reputation for riot and invariably lived up to it. In 1894, its members managed to break all the windows in Christ Church's Peckwater Quad. But the celebrations that followed a college going head of the river were the most likely to get completely out of control because of the large numbers caught up in the festivities, which always began with a bibulous bump supper. On such occasions, undergraduates particularly liked building bonfires and letting off fireworks, and the damage could be considerable, not to mention the danger to life and limb. Exeter, in the period, was not among the noted rowing colleges, so when it went head for the third year running in 1884, its undergraduates set out to have a night to remember. The fellow left to police proceedings, Lewis Farrell, could still vividly recall the chaos decades later:

> The *pièce de resistance* was a large bonfire in the main quadrangle which was then ungrassed: quaint fodder was brought to feed the monster (rumour mentioned a grand piano, whose tone the owner disliked), and the fire-worshippers showed their zeal by dancing round it and leaping through the flames: as the evening went on, this became more and more a heroic feat. Meantime continual volleys of soaring rockets threatened the skies, and in their fall descended...on the roofs of the adjacent Bodleian. The Exonians then living in the house called Exeter Hall at the corner of Ship Street had their own special *diablerie*. Some skilled engineers among them had constructed a bridge of double wires from one of their topmost windows and attached it to the parapet opposite where fellow revellers attended to it: along this they ran out a flat-bottomed bath full of terrifying combustibles, so that it hung suspended over the Turl fifty feet below: then with well-directed fiery missiles they kindled it, and the effect was on the scale of a volcanic eruption. Unfortunately some of the burning stuff fell into the street, and the citizens who had assembled in crowds to see the spectacle felt aggrieved, and ungratefully broke every window of our college that was affording them so much entertainment gratis.[72]

Undergraduates did not need the excuse of a formal occasion to cause mayhem, however. It was a common feature of student life during the period that an under-graduate who wanted to be marked out by his peers as a leader had to devise a 'rag', a disruptive and unruly incident that would amuse their comrades and annoy authority. Compton Mackenzie's none too successful contribution to the genre in his second term was to buy a pig in Iffley, get it into Magdalen secretly by hauling it up on a rope through a window of a friend's room, grease the animal, then let it loose in Chaplain's Quad. Unfortunately for Mackenzie, 'the pig refused to run' and simply lay down and grunted: 'After a while I had to admit the rag was a complete

---

[72] Farnell, *Oxonian*, p. 136. Farnell was still a relatively new fellow. He almost had a death on his hands when a visitor from Trinity fell into the bonfire and had to be dragged out by his heels.

fiasco, and we all retired to our rooms, leaving the pig to wander about until it made its way into the deer park where one of the gardeners found it next morning.'[73]

Most rags, like Mackenzie's, were harmless, but one or two each year were specifically aimed at individuals who were not felt to be sufficiently collegiate in their behaviour. Although Warren and other heads of house were always anxious to stress college unity, their anxiety was testimony to the fact that every college had its divisions and cliques. Northerners and southerners frequently viewed each other with suspicion; so too did philistines and intellectuals and public- and grammar-school boys; while the politically conservative and the politically radical could share a mutual loathing and incomprehension which could often lead to violence. At Brasenose in 1870, Llewellyn Jones, the son of a leading Chartist, had his room trashed after speaking up for the Fenians in a college debate on Irish nationalism: 'I found my bedding lying soaked in water at the bottom of three flights of stairs and my room wrecked.' Life was even harder for the communist Ieuan Thomas, at Merton in the mid-1920s, who reportedly 'had his books burnt twice and his wardrobe four times in a single term'.[74]

Above all, a war simmered between college sportsmen and a minority of under-graduates who affected to despise athletic endeavour, dressed unconventionally, and appeared obsessed with avant-garde poetry, art, and music. To the 'hearties', the 'aesthetes' were a slur on the college's escutcheon who, from time to time, had to be put in their place for the common good. Before the First World War, the victims of their rage were limited in number and unsavoury events were few. After 1918, in contrast, the aesthetes were a larger and more self-conscious group who ostenta-tiously refused to conform. One of their leaders in the mid-1920s was the writer and dilettante Harold Acton, who read PPE at Christ Church. Acton would deliberately provoke the college hearties by standing on a balcony of Meadow Buildings and reciting T. S. Eliot's new avant-garde poem *The Waste Land* through a megaphone. In consequence, he and his friends were deemed fair game. Brasenose was notoriously intolerant. When John Betjeman, who had excoriated the hearties' excesses in his poem *The 'Varsity Students' Rag* (1927), entered its portals, he affected a limp in the hope he would arouse pity rather than contempt. In his own college, Magdalen, Betjeman survived by playing the buffoon. Had he not done so, his life would have been miserable, for Magdalen's hearties could be unforgiving. In 1931 a young poet had his rooms trashed, while, in the following year, an undergraduate 'with Oscar Wildish propensities' had his grand piano broken up and his suits thrown on a bonfire after a bump supper. The clashes between the two sides, however, became less frequent after the Crash of 1928. The aesthetes were less visible in the 1930s because their fathers could no longer afford to support their extravagant lifestyle.[75]

---

[73] Mackenzie, *Life and Times*, pp. 102–3. There were also female rags.

[74] Crook, pp. 262–3; A. J. P. Taylor, *A Personal History* (London, 1983), pp, 68–9.

[75] C. M. Bowra, *Memories 1898–1939* (London, 1966), pp. 155–6; Brockliss, p. 670; Michael Ignatieff, *Isaiah Berlin: A Life* (London, 1998), p. 47. Oscar Wilde, at Magdalen in the 1870s, had never been victimized for his aestheticism: he boxed and rowed.

Undergraduates chiefly targeted their peers, but in the second half of the nineteenth century, if not thereafter, they occasionally turned on senior members who had incurred their wrath. Where the fellowship collectively was felt to be at fault, college property would be vandalized. One night in May 1870 members of Christ Church's Loder's Club, supposedly annoyed by the dismissal of a friendly porter, stole the statues from the college library and put their trophies on public view, lit by bonfires. A quarter of century later, in 1893, after the House's undergraduates had been banned from attending a ball at Blenheim, the offended daubed slogans around the Great Quadrangle denouncing the dean and cut the bell rope of Great Tom as a protest against gate-hours. More often, though, the target was individual dons who had caused displeasure. Fellows were never manhandled (undergraduates knew their place) but their windows could be broken and the outer door of their set of rooms sealed. At University College in March 1868, three fellows, as well as an undergraduate, had the outer doors of their rooms screwed up. The dean escaped the same fate only because he heard 'the noise made in the act of fixing the screws in the door' and was able to 'prevent its being fastened'.[76] At the same college, twelve years later, it was decided at a dinner to do the same to the door of the Senior Proctor, Albert Chavasse.

Visitors were also sometimes subjected to similar chastisement. When the socialist George Bernard Shaw addressed a meeting in Magdalen in the 1890s, the event was mobbed and opponents screwed up the door. Unpopular college servants, on the other hand, did not usually face the same humiliations, as undergraduates recognized the need to treat their inferiors with respect. In the first half of the twentieth century, however, with a more cosmopolitan intake, not all undergraduates knew the rules. After a particularly bibulous boat club dinner at Magdalen in the 1930s, the college's head porter was tarred (with honey) and feathered (with a burst pillow) in his lodge: the outrage was perpetrated by an Australian and an American.

When dealing with breaches of the rules and rowdiness of all kinds, the college authorities had three principal weapons at their disposal: fines, gating, and rustication. For the most part, these weapons were exercised with tact and moderation. In women's colleges retribution could sometimes be fierce. In 1924 another Somervillian journalist, Dilys Powell, was sent down for two terms simply for climbing into college after a secret meeting with a male undergraduate. In men's colleges, in contrast, even persistent infringement of the college rules or the grossest misbehaviour seldom invited more than a fine or gating. First-time offenders were simply told to pull their socks up, drunks believed when they promised future reform, and only the most vicious miscreant was treated harshly by rustication. Even trashing a student's rooms usually incurred little or no penalty. Honouring the rules in the breach was expected and winked at, provided undergraduates were happy to dip

[76] Darwall-Smith, p. 384.

into their pockets to atone for their sins, as a notice put up in Trinity regarding bad behaviour in hall made clear: 'Gentlemen coming from homes where bread-throwing is habitual and finding difficulty in conforming suddenly to the unfamiliar ways of a higher civilisation, will be permitted to continue their domestic pastime, on a payment of 5/- a throw during the first year. After that the charge will be doubled.'[77]

In Evelyn Waugh's account of college discipline at the beginning of *Decline and Fall* (1928), the dons' insouciance was principally put down to venality. He imagines them rubbing their hands with glee as they contemplate the fines they will be able to impose after the Bollinger [Bullingdon] Club has wrecked the college in the aftermath of its annual dinner:

> 'There must be fifty of them at least', said Mr Postlethwaite. 'If only they were all members of the College! Fifty of them at ten pounds each. Oh my!'
> 'It'll be more if they attack the Chapel', said Mr Sniggs. 'Oh, please God, make them attack the Chapel'.[78]

This was unfair. For the most part deans and heads of house recognized they were dealing with young adults, not schoolboys, and knew they had to temper mercy with discipline if they were to exercise control. A dean, according to the Magdalen fellow A. D. Godley, writing of the imaginary St Blasius at the end of the nineteenth century, had to learn to 'ride on the breaking wave of anarchy' and to accept that the general good was best preserved by promoting the lesser evil: 'It is better not to drive vicious propensities below the surface. No doubt it is wrong to play football in the Principal's garden; but how much better and healthier than to play cards in one's room.'[79] Deans who did try to enforce the letter of the law lost the undergraduates' respect. In the early 1880s at Merton, discipline was in the hands of a don called E. A. Knox, who would put out of residence any undergraduate caught climbing in. When, in 1880, he rusticated five Mertonians for simply removing the bedclothes of a fellow student, the undergraduates were so incensed that they appealed to the visitor. Unsurprisingly, 'Hard Knox', as he was known, was heartily disliked, and when he appeared in chapel for the last time in 1884, after receiving a living, the hymn 'Now thank we all our God' was sung with particular gusto.[80]

Waugh was nearer the mark when he suggested that the dons by and large sympathized with the perpetrators rather than with the victims of mayhem. There was a readiness among the college authorities after 1880 to clamp down on egregious drunkenness, but nothing else. The conservative majority had little time for aesthetes and radicals who threatened to subvert college unity and college spirit,

[77] Hopkins, p. 319.
[78] *Decline and Fall*, (London, 1977), p. 13 (published as the first in an omnibus edition of six Waugh novels).
[79] A. D. Godley, *Reliquiae*, ed. C. R. Fletcher (Oxford, 1926), p. 151.
[80] G. H. Martin and J. R. L. Highfield, *A History of Merton College, Oxford* (Oxford, 1997), pp. 312–13. At Merton the dean has the title principal of postmasters.

and arguably saw the targeted rag as an exercise in acculturation. The victims would never have been sent down for indecency, as happened to the unfortunate scholar Pennyfeather, in *Decline and Fall*, who was caught in the quad and debagged by the Bollinger Club on the rampage, but they would have certainly been expected to take their humiliation like a man.[81]

There was a limit, however, to the dons' tolerance. They certainly drew the line at disrespect to themselves. When the Proctor's door was screwed up at University College in 1880, retribution was swift. The master summoned all the undergraduates to the hall the next day and peremptorily informed them that: 'The College is sent down, and members must leave by 4 o'clock today. Any gentleman who likes to give in his name as having had nothing to do with the disgraceful affair of last night may stay up.'[82] As a result, some forty undergraduates packed their bags and left, carrying a letter written by the master to their parents. The affair was resolved a week later only when the chief architect of the villainy, one Samuel Sandbach, who immediately after the event had gone off to a yeomanry camp, was contacted by one of his peers, told of the fallout from his prank, and came forward to confess his crime.

The dons would also not tolerate rowdiness and incivility outside the college. Within the curtilage undergraduates were allowed off the leash, on the assumption, presumably, that licensed irresponsibility was character-forming for both victim and perpetrator. Outside, they had to behave as the gentlemen they were or would become, and were expected to set an example to their inferiors, especially when away from Oxford altogether and beyond the clutches of the Proctors. Disorderly conduct while travelling by train was particularly frowned upon. The University had been reluctant to have the railway come to Oxford, fearing that undergraduates would acquire a new freedom to roam. It was not day-trippers to London, however, that caused the problems but sports teams returning from away fixtures. God's Wonderful Railway was understandably the most commonly vandalized part of the network, but teams on tour were travelling the country by the end of the century and their commitment to gentlemanly behaviour sadly lessened the further they were away from their alma mater. In March 1892, Trinity's rugby team narrowly missed being sued by the Great Northern Railway Company, which accused one member of indecent exposure and others of damaging a first-class compartment. The college moved swiftly to keep the complaint out of court. The president gave the team four days to find £85 to pay off the company, and sent down two players for the rest of the year and four till the end of term. Only the six of the team who declared their innocence on the word of a gentleman escaped any punishment.

---

[81] In 1886, a cross-college meeting was held to discuss outlawing the worst excesses of student carnival, but it broke up without agreement: Farnell, *Oxonian*, p. 139.
[82] Darwall-Smith, p. 402.

E. Dons

In many respects, the character of the senior membership over the hundred years after 1850 changed more profoundly than the undergraduate body's. In the first half of the nineteenth century, the large majority of college fellows were in Anglican orders, all were celibate, and virtually all were believers. Under the new statutes promulgated following the three royal commissions, fellowships were slowly opened up to laymen, non-Anglicans, and the married. Although the new provisions took time to take effect, given the number of fellows elected under the old statutes who survived long into the second half of the nineteenth century, the character of the senior membership had been transformed by 1914. On the eve of the Great War most fellows were still nominally Anglican and barely any were Roman Catholic.[83] A total of 52 per cent, on the other hand, were married, and a mere one in five were in orders; the percentage of married dons would have been higher still but for the fact that, before the 1920s, colleges insisted that some of the tutors were bachelors. Between the wars clerical fellows virtually disappeared. Magdalen, one of the largest fellowships, still had five of its thirty-three fellows in orders in 1926, but two were in their seventies and one, J. M. Thompson, had been all but defrocked for his views on miracles, and had lost his faith.[84]

Laicization was accompanied by professionalization. In the past, fellows had been young men in their twenties and early thirties, more or less seriously engaged in higher study or tutoring while they waited for a college living or a rich wife to fall into their lap. There was no academic profession as such, and many senior members, including many involved in teaching, spent large parts of the year away from Oxford involved in other activities. By 1900, senior members were a more scholarly and visible bunch, even if the younger amongst them still dreamt of marrying well. In term time, tutors and fellows with university posts were completely absorbed in their teaching duties, while the ordinary fellows actively pursued research and were usually absent from the University only when the life of the mind called them elsewhere. Pursuing a political, legal, or literary career while holding a fellowship, though not unknown, was becoming increasingly difficult, as was joining the London glitterati. The senior member was metamorphosing into the don, a recognized species distinct from the other professions and occupations which Oxford alumni entered, and a term well established in the English lexicon by the 1880s.[85] The senior member in this new manifestation, on the other hand, was just as inbred as his predecessors. Before the Second World War, few Oxford fellows had been educated elsewhere, and a disproportionate number came from Balliol. So dominant was the college as the undergraduate academic powerhouse in the age of

---

[83] The only catholic don with a high profile before the Great War was 'Sligger' Urquhart of Balliol.

[84] His journey into unbelief is traced in his verse autobiography: J. M. Thompson, *My Apologia* (privately published, 1940).

[85] The emergence of the species is traced in Arthur Engel, *From Clergyman to Don: The Rise of the Academic Profession in Oxford* (Oxford, 1983).

Jowett that a quarter of all of those elected to fellowships across the University from 1860 to 1878 had passed through its portals. Many fellows, too, once dons could marry, belonged to formidable Oxford dynasties whose tentacles extended into the farthest reaches of academic life.[86]

Under the initial reform of the college statutes in the 1850s, there had been no attempt to limit the tenure of a fellowship, and many individuals elected in the third quarter of the nineteenth century opted to remain fellows for life. Brasenose's last surviving 'lifer', William Stocker, died in 1949, aged 98. From the early 1880s, however, more and more ordinary and official fellows demitted long before they were required to do so by the statutes, and in early middle age began a fresh life outside the college. Most quondam fellows took up university posts, either in Oxford or Cambridge or at one of the new universities, or migrated to a senior post in a major public school. A few also went into educational administration. A fellowship at All Souls, however, was often a passport to greater things, as the college retained its traditional links with the legal and political establishment. Twenty of the 132 fellows elected to the foundation between 1850 and 1914 later entered parliament, one (Lord Salisbury) became prime minister, and another, archbishop of Canterbury.

The chief factor encouraging fellows to move on was pay. As a result of the reform of the college statutes between 1857 and 1882 and the move to rack-renting, the traditional practice of paying the fellows a dividend based on the annual surplus and sharing out tenancy fines which had led to gross inequalities in income was abandoned. Thereafter, all fellows received the same annual stipend of about £200 until the years following the outbreak of the First World War, which saw the figure increased in line with inflation. This was a reasonable but not generous income for a professional man. The position was improved in the 1920s and 1930s in some colleges, when fellows' stipends began to be paid on an ascending scale according to length of service and status. But this only led to new inequalities. At University College in the mid-1930s the senior fellow, the philosopher A. L. S. Farquharson, elected in 1899, received £500 per annum, the most junior, the political scientist John Maud, £350.[87]

Only dons who had a university or college position as well as a fellowship and drew a second salary were well off. Heads of house were usually the best paid: they seldom had incomes less than £1,500 at any point after 1850. But university professors gradually caught them up. Professors could receive salaries as low as £200 in the mid-Victorian era but in the first part of the twentieth century they normally received an annual payment of between £1,000 and £1,200, plus an extra allowance of £200 from 1924 if they had departmental responsibilities.[88] By then

---

[86] Noel Annan, *The Dons: Mentors, Eccentrics and Geniuses* (London, 2000), esp. pp. 304–41, 'Annexe: The Intellectual Aristocracy' (on both Oxford and Cambridge).

[87] Robin Darwall-Smith, email communication, 16 Oct. 2012.

[88] The 1850 commission believed that professors should not receive less than £800, though many did: Commission (1852), *Report*, p. 109. Asquith treated £1,200 as the benchmark for professorial salaries.

the growing number of junior academic staff were also reasonably well remunerated: in the 1930s, readers of any kind received £500 while demonstrators in the
science departments earned from £350 to £750. College tutors could also do very
well for themselves, though the level of remuneration varied greatly according
to age and the number of pupils they looked after. Before the First World War,
Magdalen's tutors were paid between £100 and £600; after 1926, from £200 to £700.
At the bottom end, tutorial salaries were not attractive, but at the top they could
produce a combined salary as high as a professor's. In 1877, Walter Pater at
Brasenose had an income of nearly £900: £537 from his tutorship, £199 as college
dean, and £230 as a fellow. In the 1930s, many experienced tutors, like Maurice
Bowra at Wadham, received £1,000 or more and could increase the sum by agreeing
to examine in Schools.[89] (See Table 11.)

Even handsomely paid dons, however, were not necessarily in clover. With free
board and lodging (albeit only a sitting room and bedroom), plenty of good food
and drink (albeit batteled), and the constant attention of a college servant, bachelor
dons who lived in continued to enjoy a life of relative luxury, regardless of the level
of their stipend. The married, or those who were single but decided to live out, were
not so well placed, even if the cost of housing in real terms was much less than
today. A number of colleges softened the blow by letting out houses they owned in
Oxford to fellows at a low rent. A.L. Smith, for instance, while a Balliol tutor, lived
with his wife and his brood of daughters in the newly built King's Mound in
Mansfield Road. But many living-out fellows were forced to search for accommodation on the open market. The most affluent dons took up residence on Boars Hill,
an undeveloped wooded knoll a few miles to the south-west of the city, which had
been the favourite haunt of the young Matthew Arnold and his friends and was
within striking distance of the University by foot, bicycle, or car. Made fashionable
at the turn of the twentieth century when H.W. Moore built a summer retreat there
for the president of Trinity in 1887–8, it was soon dotted with academic villas, one
of which, Yatscombe, was occupied by the professor of Greek, Gilbert Murray,
between the wars.[90] Boars Hill, though, was an option only open to the few. The
large majority of dons, especially the freshly married, could only dream of living in
such grandeur and plumped instead for North Oxford.

Until the second half of the nineteenth century, the land directly to the north of
St Giles, largely owned by St John's, was given over to agriculture. In the 1850s, the
college threw it open to development. The first houses bordering the University
Parks went up in the early 1860s, and by 1900 the area between St Giles and
Summertown on either side of the Woodstock and Banbury roads had been
covered in housing. The development of the suburb began ten years before most
fellows were free to marry, so it was never intended to be a donnish enclave and

---

[89] Bowra, *Memories*, p. 338. There is evidence that professorial fellows in some colleges had their fellows'
stipend reduced between the wars. Postholders are still paid extra for examining today.
[90] Boars Hill was nicknamed Parnassus in 1920 because the poets Bridges, Masefield, Graves, and Blunden all
lived there.

dons were always in a minority. All the same, the suburb's propinquity to the city centre ensured from the beginning that there were members of the University purchasing the new properties. An early resident was the regius professor of modern history, Goldwin Smith, who, in 1862, moved into 7 Norham Gardens, the first house erected on land north of the University Parks. By 1881, when the initial stage of development was complete, the dons were present in North Oxford in strength. Of the 266 heads of household listed in the national census of that year for the central area of the expanding suburb, forty-nine were connected with the University.[91]

The better-paid Oxford don who took advantage of the right to marry from the 1870s could live well in the new houses going up in North Oxford but could not afford to spend lavishly in an age when it was assumed that a respectable middle-class household always kept at least one servant. Many, though, made the best of their position and in the late Victorian era deliberately forged a distinctive middle-class identity that was at once both restrained and avant-garde. Humphry Ward was an undistinguished fellow and tutor of Trinity. In 1872 he married Mary Arnold, a granddaughter of Dr Thomas, and moved out of college. The newly-weds quickly became part of a close-knit North Oxford society, as his spouse, in later life a best-selling novelist, fondly recalled:

> Nobody under the rank of a Head of College, except a very few privileged Professors, possessed as much as a thousand a year. The average income of the new race of married tutors was not much more than half that sum. Yet we all gave dinner parties and furnished our houses with Morris papers, old chests and cabinets, and blue pots. The dinner parties were simple and short... Most of us were very anxious to be up-to-date, and in the fashion, whether in aesthetics, in house-keeping, or education. But our fashion was not that of Belgravia or Mayfair, which we scorned! It was the fashion of the movement which sprang from Morris and Burne-Jones... And when we had donned our Liberty gowns we went out to dinner, the husband walking, the wife in a bath chair... Everybody was equal, nobody was rich, and the intellectual average was naturally high.[92]

Once children began to be born, life got more difficult. Even the better-off Oxford don living in college property could find the cost of keeping up appearances worrisome, as is evident from the chequered fortune in the 1920s of Magdalen's Edward Murray Wrong. Wrong was a Canadian, the son of the first professor of history at the University of Toronto, who in the 1900s had followed in his father's footsteps and gone to Balliol. In the mid-1920s he was ostensibly financially well placed as a tutor in modern history, the Beit lecturer in colonial history, and secretary to the college's tutorial board. With his fellow's stipend he must have had a salary close to or in an excess of £1,000. He also had an allowance from his

---

[91] T. Hinchcliffe, *North Oxford* (New Haven, CT, and London, 1992), pp. 160–1 and 167–8. Hinchcliffe is the standard account of the development of the area.

[92] Crook, pp. 277–8, citing Mrs Humphry Ward, *A Writer's Recollections* (London, 1918), pp. 119–20, 152.

father, and had got his feet firmly under the Oxford table by marrying a daughter of the master of Balliol, A. L. Smith. But Wrong's correspondence with his father shows he was a troubled man. Even the delight of renting one of the college's most desirable properties, Holywell Ford, did not lighten the gloom. He had a growing family of six and found money was always tight in autumn before next year's salary arrived in the spring. 'September–November is always a lean season for tutors', he wrote to his father in July 1927, 'when one sells stocks and shares, hoping to buy something back in March next + not always succeeding.' To compound matters, Wrong fell ill. At this juncture, sick tutors were expected to pay for their own replacement, and Wrong feared his family would suffer. A year later, he was dead and his wife left bereft. For all her Oxford connections, she received little local support and the children were whisked away to be brought up in Canada.[93] It is unsurprising that many dons sympathized with the plight of the likes of Alfred Denning when poverty or its threat too often stalked their own lives.

F. College Families

The laicization of college fellowships did nothing to undermine the ideal of the tutor–undergraduate relationship fostered by Newman and his successors. Married or unmarried, tutors were expected to be paragons of collegiality who dined in hall each evening and at least before the 1920s took an interest in all aspects of the junior members' lives and not just in their academic progress. The perfect don supported college teams on the sports field or river, graced college undergraduate societies, and burnished his charges' social and conversational skills by being frequently (sometimes nightly) 'at home' in the evening and plying them liberally with drink. The women's colleges frowned on the use of alcohol as a social lubricant but took social mixing to an extreme. The ritual of chaperonage in its early manifestation meant that female students and dons were inevitably thrown together much more frequently than their male counterparts. But this was seen as a positive good by most female dons, however boring it might have been to hear the same lecture for the umpteenth time. Anxious to replicate the intimacy of middle-class domestic life in their new societies, the female dons went out of their way to rub shoulders with their students at every opportunity. At Somerville between the wars undergraduates were not only regularly invited to dine on high table with the dons but were expected to 'volunteer' about once a week to breakfast with them as well. Undergraduates also had to provide tea for their tutors once a term.

It was further expected that dons and students would continue to mix with one another long after undergraduates had left the college. There had always been one

---

[93] MCA, MC: P95/MS1/1: 31 July 1927 (typed extract). Wrong replaced his brother-in-law, A. L. F. Smith, as tutor in 1919, the year he gained the Beit. For his life, R. Mitchison, 'An Oxford Family', in E. C. Hodgkin (ed.), *Arthur Lionel Forster Smith, 1880–1972: Chapters of a Biography* (n.p. 1979). Also correspondence and conversations with one of his sons. His widow remarried and taught history at Worcester in the 1960s.

mechanism whereby a college kept in touch with a cross-section of its old members. MAs who wanted to enjoy the rights of membership of Convocation had to keep their names on their college's battels book. By the end of the nineteenth century, however, every college, including the women's societies, endeavoured to retain an association with all of its erstwhile junior members. This was principally done through the annual gaudy. Most colleges held an annual feast as an act of thanksgiving for the benefactions received over the years, but guests were traditionally limited to members of the foundation and their invited friends. In the course of the 1870s, Balliol, Magdalen, and other leading colleges began to transform the event into an annual reunion to which old members were also invited, commoners as well as scholars and former fellows, and by 1900, when Trinity finally adopted the practice, the modern gaudy had become a commonplace. As the number of old members swelled, it became impossible for everyone to attend each year and invitations had to be staggered. To maintain contact in the interim, colleges, at the turn of the twentieth century, encouraged the formation of old members' associations that had their own annual dinners and events, usually in London. These, too, had been forming informally from the 1870s, but the colleges now gave them their imprimatur and their popularity rapidly grew. At the same time, the colleges also started to publish a short annual newsletter which detailed the chief achievements of the college of the previous year. Initially restricted to remarks about the current undergraduates, the reports were soon extended to contain information about the old members themselves and, in the First World War, when the colleges emptied out, were reduced to little more than a poignant list of the fallen.

To a certain extent, the new interest in former undergraduates reflected the colleges' need for funds. Most could put up the new buildings required to house the growing number of undergraduates only by appealing for donations from old members. Unsurprisingly, unendowed Keble purportedly even antedated Balliol and Magdalen in establishing an annual reunion, while Somerville set up an old members' association and an annual report, called the *Oxford Correspondent*, as early as 1888. However, there was more to the initiative than mercenary considerations. To Warren and other heads at the turn of the twentieth century, when undergraduates entered a college, they became part of a new family, where they were transmogrified into a new form of being unique to their alma mater and forged an association with their contemporaries for life. To the more critical Oxonian, this was tosh. When C. S. Lewis became a fellow of Magdalen in 1926, having been an undergraduate at University College, he found Warren's emphasis on the 'special needs' of its undergraduates absurd: 'as if they were different from any others!'[94] But the belief was deeply internalized by the majority. Many of Warren's correspondents during the Great War, such as the medical officer H. G. G. Mackenzie, believed they were much better equipped to face their ordeal because they were Magdalen men: 'I feel sure you must realise that the war is showing that there has been an alchemy at work in

[94] C. S. Lewis, *Collected Letters*, vol. 1: *Family Letters 1905–1931*, ed. W. Hooper (London, 2000), p. 645.

Magdalen which has touched the ordinary mortal and transformed it into gold—All honour, I think, to the man who ruled the laboratory.'[95]

In consequence, from their arrival at Oxford, undergraduates learnt that they had a specific college identity which gave them a superior edge. This explains the intensity of intercollegiate rivalry, played out off as well as on the river and sports field. When colleges were neighbours, rags were frequently inter- rather than intra-college events. The hostility between Balliol and Trinity JCRs, which dated from at least the 1890s, was proverbial. Balliol revelled in its intellectual and cosmopolitan reputation, Trinity in its Anglo-Saxon heartiness, and both colleges frequently traded insults and invaded the other's curtilage. Trinity was particularly incensed by its neighbour's readiness to admit coloured students, and a favourite chant on the eve of the First World War was 'Balliol, Balliol, bring out your black men!' Even the female societies quickly developed or were apportioned separate identities, which came to be worn as a badge of pride. In a magazine article written in July 1929, the novelist Winifred Holtby, an old member and later benefactor of Somer-ville, recalled the adage about the women's colleges current in her undergraduate days immediately following the Great War: 'LMH for Young Ladies, St Hilda's for Games, St Hugh's for Religion and Somerville for Brains', or 'Freaks' in the version espoused by Somerville's rivals.[96]

The construction of a lifelong collegiate attachment went hand in hand with a concomitant weakening of any residual university identity. Being an Oxonian, as opposed to a Cantabrigian, was annually celebrated outside Oxford through the Boat Race and the growing number of varsity matches in the latter part of the nineteenth century, but the most visible affirmation of 'Oxfordness' in the University's internal calendar—Commem week—quickly lost most of its historic signifi-cance as the colleges put on their own events. Until the 1870s, Commem was the one moment in the year when dons, undergraduates, and many old members came together to emphasize their unity. Through a series of university-sponsored events culminating in Encaenia in the Sheldonian, where the undergraduates were licensed to misbehave and did so, both junior and senior members showed off Oxford to their families, especially to their mothers and sisters, who, for a few days, were allowed access to a male preserve. The merging of Commem with Eights week in the mid-nineteenth century only strengthened the 'togetherness' of an occasion which was affectionately satirized by Cuthbert Bede in *The Adventures of Mr Verdant Green* (1853), and more appreciatively recalled by an outsider, Charlotte Yonge, in *The Daisy Chain* (1856).[97] As late as 1877, when the University was visited by another outsider, Henry James, Commem was still a magical moment. Encaenia was less

[95] MCA, MC: PR32/C3/823: Mackenzie to Warren, 16 Sept. 1918. Mackenzie had matriculated in 1888, three years into Warren's reign. Warren would have liked to have cemented old members further into college life by giving them a vote in the election of the head of house and some fellowships: see Bodleian Library, MS. Top. Oxon. b.104, fos 199–209: memo to the Asquith Commission.
[96] Hopkins, p. 309; Adams, p. 233: there were other versions current among male undergraduates: ibid., p. 1.
[97] For another positive account of Commem, see Thomas Hughes, *Tom Brown at Oxford* (1861), chs xxv–xvii.

riotous than it had been twenty years before but it was still 'a carnival of chaff' where the undergraduates present were allowed to hoot, stamp, and cat-call as the great and good received their honorary degree:

> Each of them when the little speech is ended, ascends the steps leading to the chair; the Vice-Chancellor bends forward and shakes his hand, and the new D.C.L. goes and sits in the blushing row of his fellow-doctors. The impressiveness of all this is much diminished by the boisterous conduct of the collegians, who superabound in extravagant applause, in impertinent interrogation of the orator's Latinity.[98]

James, however, witnessed an institution in its dotage. In the following years Commem week lost most of its significance. Show Sunday, the custom at the beginning of the week for the whole University, with their guests, to parade around Christ Church meadows had gone by the late 1870s; the mid-week Nuneham picnic, the Masonic Garden Party (in different colleges), and the Masonic Ball (in the Corn Exchange) lost their allure; and only the Show of Boats on the Monday (when all the crews in the subsequent Eights rowed up and down the course to the applause of a huge crowd) lingered on into the 1890s. Instead colleges held their own balls in-house—University College had agreed to hold one every three years as early as 1875—and Encaenia became a ceremony for the more serious dons.[99]

As the colleges rose in self-importance, in one important regard they, not the University, even became the face of Oxford in the outside world. The last decades of the nineteenth century saw the emergence on both sides of the Atlantic of a movement within the churches, universities, and private schools to bring young middle-class men and women into the poorest areas of the big cities as volunteer teachers and social workers. Oxford dons played a privileged part in the initial stages of what was called the Settlement Movement through their role in the creation of Toynbee Hall and Oxford House, two of the most famous settlement houses in the East End, the first non-denominational and named after the Balliol tutor and social reformer Arnold Toynbee Snr, who died in 1883, the second a high Anglican establishment.[100] It was not the University, however, but the colleges that set up an institutionalized presence among the poor of London. Christ Church had a mission in Poplar as early as 1882; University College one in Battersea and Magdalen one in Shoreditch two years later; and Trinity a fourth in Stratford from 1888. The college missions organized boys' and girls' clubs, children's country holidays, and sometimes housing schemes funded by loan capital. They were explicitly college foundations, funded by current and past students, where their more altruistic members might live for one or

---

[98] Henry James, *Portraits of Places* (London, 1883), ch. xi, 'Two Excursions', p. 243.

[99] The university Masonic lodge took the name Apollo in 1820. It sponsored a grand ball from 1855 and a musical garden party from 1857.

[100] Toynbee Hall was run by Samuel Barnett. The warden of Keble, Edward Talbot, was one of those behind the rival high Anglican establishment. High Anglican critics thought Toynbee Hall was not focused enough on addressing the moral weaknesses of the poor: see *The Crawford papers: the journals of David Lindsay twenty-seventh earl of Crawford and tenth earl of Barcarres, 1871–1940, during the years 1892–1940*, ed. John Vincent (Manchester, 1984), pp. 14–15.

FIGURE 11.9 Edward Prince of Wales receiving his share certificate as a member of Magdalen's St Pancras House Improvement Society: photograph 1926. The prince, known as 'the Pragger Wagger' by his undergraduate contemporaries, matriculated from Magdalen on 15 October 1912. He remained a loyal member of the college thereafter. The photograph shows him being handed his certificate by the missioner, Fr Basil Jellicoe, during a visit to a refurbished home of a tenant in Clarendon St, Somers Town, Euston.

two months offering succour to the destitute under the supervision of a clergyman in charge. The fact that these were college initiatives only encouraged old members to open their wallets. Magdalen's mission was based in Somers Town, Euston, from 1908 to 1940, where it extended its activities to include a House Improvement Society. Within a few years, in the 1920s, the society had raised enough money to provide 660 new flats, thanks in part to the patronage of the college's most illustrious old member, the Prince of Wales, who was a frequent visitor to the mission (see Figure 11.9).[101]

The University made no attempt to redress the balance until the end of the period when it belatedly formed the Oxford Society in 1932 in anticipation of a future appeal. On its formation, Lewis Farnell of Exeter, who had served as Vice-Chancellor in the early 1920s and always been conscious of the need to bolster the centre's authority, was confident that it would create a new and larger corporate

---

[101] The Prince of Wales was proud to have been a Magdalen man but claimed never to warm to Warren: Windsor, *A King's Story*, p. 94.

spirit among Oxford's alumni: 'We may look forward to the obliteration in the future of the old rivalry between college and university, so that the term "college-man" [in the sense of a champion of college separatism] will be no more heard.'[102] But Farnell was over-optimistic. When the appeal was launched in 1937, it was relatively successful and raised £500,000 in two years—Oxford alumni never forgot they had been part of a university as well as a college. But the society never attracted broad support, even though it eventually had branches all over the world. Old members were college men and women first and few wished to belong to a university association. Over the next fifty years, fewer than 14 per cent of the eligible joined.

---

[102] Farnell, *Oxonian*, pp. 343–4.

CHAPTER 12

Towards the Research University

A. Learning, Scholarship, and Research

THE reformers of the mid-nineteenth century were principally interested in finding ways to make the appointment to fellowships more meritocratic and to widen undergraduate access. They manifested no obvious enthusiasm for making the new Oxford a centre of research as well as teaching along the lines of the German Humboldtian universities. In this respect, Jowett would have been in perfect agreement with Newman and his allies, whose idea of a university was succinctly expressed by Pusey in a pamphlet attacking reform in 1854:

> The problem and special work of an University is, not how to advance science, not how to make discoveries, not to form new schools of mental philosophy, nor to invent new modes of analysis; not to produce works in Medicine, Jurisprudence, or even Theology; but to form minds religiously, morally, intellectually, which shall discharge aright whatever duties God, in His Providence, shall appoint them.[1]

By the late 1860s, however, some reformers, though never Jowett, had begun to shift their ground and, to the dismay of *The Times* of 8 March 1867, the first shoots of a research culture had been sighted at both Oxford and Cambridge. The 'Thunderer' stood by the traditional view of a university which, it was confident, was shared by 'Englishmen in general'. Research and teaching were as chalk and cheese: 'The men who are the most skilful and bold in speculation are not the best teachers.' It was with alarm that the newspaper had discovered that the German disease had crossed the North Sea and was affecting the quality of the education offered in the old universities: 'It is a growing subject of discontent among the public that the tutors and professors of both our universities are becoming more and more absorbed in their own scientific pursuits.'[2]

---

[1] E. B. Pusey, *Collegiate and Professorial Teaching and Discipline: In answer to Professor Vaughan's Strictures, chiefly as to the charges against the colleges of France and Germany* (Oxford, 1854), pp. 213–15. Vaughan, as regius professor of history, was anxious to extend the role of the professoriate. Pusey's pamphlet was a reply to Vaughan's *Oxford reform and Oxford professors: a reply to certain objections urged against the report of the Queen's Commissioners* (London, 1854).
[2] *The Times*, 8 Mar. 1867, cited in Mark Pattison, *Suggestions on Academical Organisation with Especial Reference to Oxford* (Edinburgh, 1868), p. 135.

FIGURE 12.1 Mark Pattison, 1813–84, rector of Lincoln and supporter of a professorial university. Pattison was the antithesis of Jowett and wanted to create university departments out of the bigger colleges and turn the rest into halls of residence. He did not, however, see the University as a research institution and his own scholarly achievements were limited. The portrait is of a weary and defeated character. He was thought, perhaps wrongly, to be the inspiration for George Eliot's Casaubon.

To contemporaries, there was no doubt who was the leader of the new 'research' party in the 1860s: Mark Pattison, erstwhile Tractarian, college tutor and rector of Lincoln from 1861 (see Figure 12.1).[3] Pattison laid out the case for the Oxford don being more than a teacher in his *Suggestions on Academical Organisation* of 1868, in which he demanded that the bulk of undergraduate teaching should be entrusted to re-energized university professors and lecturers. What was needed, if an Oxford education was to be worth the value that its supporters placed on it, was a revolution in its organization so that undergraduates sat at the feet of men of science and learning rather than tyros. Lincoln's rector stood squarely behind the system he had seen operating in the German universities on his many visits to the continent from the 1850s. Professors were no longer to be appointed on the grounds of their liberal or conservative churchmanship but purely on academic merit and by people who could assess their learning objectively. Tutors would still exist—every undergraduate would still be given a tutor on matriculation. But tutors were to be the bottom rung of a new academic ladder, and none could be

[3] On Pattison's significance, see Goldwin Smith, *Reminiscences* (New York, 1910), p. 85.

appointed who had not pursued a further three years of study in his discipline, following the BA.

In insisting that dons should be learned, Pattison had no wish to turn Oxford into a hive of research, whatever his critics believed. Just like his opponents, conservatives or reformers, his primary interest lay in training the undergraduate mind in the most effective way possible. He was not interested in research for its own sake but as a way of making undergraduate education more professional and effective. Indeed, while he insisted university teachers should be men of science, he did not expect them to be creative minds expanding the frontiers of knowledge:

> The university is to be an association of men of science. But it is not for the sake of science that they are associated. Whether or no the State should patronise science, or promote discovery, is another question. Even if it should, a university is not the organ for this purpose. A professoriate has for its duty to maintain, cultivate and diffuse extant knowledge. This is an everyday function which should not be confounded with the very exceptional pursuit of prosecuting researches or conducting experiments with a view to new discoveries.[4]

Extending the boundaries of knowledge was the role of academies not universities.

Nevertheless, if Pattison and his supporters in the 1860s did not separate learning from teaching, they sowed the seeds for the emergence of a more independent conception of the role of research in the coming years. A key part in the development was played by the Selborne Commission. Pattison had been disenchanted with the earlier reforms because the fellowships set up under the 1850s statutes were effectively sinecures. They were held for life and carried no obligation to study. Many ambitious young men regarded them simply as resting places while they looked for a place in public life.[5] Under the new college statutes, drawn up by the commissioners in the early 1880s, such freeloading was discouraged. The new category of ordinary fellows who had gained their position as a result of success in an examination could still spend their time as they chose, but they were elected for a fixed term. If they wanted to be re-elected, it became generally accepted that they had to submit evidence of their research achievements, often in the form of testimonials from outsiders.[6]

Towards the end of the nineteenth century, university postholders also started to view their role differently. In his evidence to the Selborne Commission, the White professor of moral philosophy and former Balliol tutor T. H. Green suggested that the solution to the ongoing debate about the teaching role of the professors and readers was to take them out of undergraduate education altogether and let them

---

[4] Pattison, *Suggestions*, pp. 171–2, 212–13, 226–7, 265.

[5] Ibid., p. 98. In his posthumous *Memoirs* (London, 1885), pp. 88–90, Pattison claimed never to have heard any serious conversation in an Oxford common room since the mid-century reforms.

[6] For examples of the process of re-election on the eve of the Great War, see MCA: FECM/1/1, Magdalen College Fellowship Committee Minute Book, 1910–25. Ordinary fellows, who did not undertake research, became the target of criticism: see George N. Curzon, *Principles and Methods of University Reform: Being a Letter Addressed to the University of Oxford* (Oxford, 1909), pp. 94–100.

concentrate on teaching specialist courses to high-flyers and graduates who sought a fellowship.[7] As there were no official postgraduates to instruct at this juncture, except in medicine, the proposal was revolutionary. It required the creation of a graduate school and the commitment of university postholders to active research. It took time for the idea to take root, but by 1900 most professors and readers had accepted that they were researchers as well as teachers, and a few had begun to form research teams and run research seminars. In the van was a group of thirty dons particularly committed to developing 'the character of the University as a home of learning and science', who, from 1889, formed 'a militant dining club' to promote their ideas. Its aim inter alia was 'to strengthen the influence of the professoriate and to diffuse the ideal of research throughout the college teaching staff'.[8]

By 1900, too, the University had its first research degrees. The year 1895 saw the establishment of the BLitt and the BSc, which required a dissertation on a subject of special study and eight terms of residence. Five years later the University instituted the DLitt and DSc, which could be awarded to anyone who had been on their college's books for twenty-six terms on the submission of original work in the form of books or articles. The 1890s and 1900s further witnessed the setting up of eight postgraduate diplomas in education, geography, economics (from 1909, economics and political science), forestry, engineering and mining, anthropology, classical archaeology, and agriculture or rural economy, which offered BAs the chance to do a further year of specialist study.[9] In addition, the BCL was resurrected as a second degree course of two years in length that could be taken by students who had initially studied elsewhere; this proved particularly popular with Rhodes scholars.[10] Some colleges, moreover, began to provide support for graduate students in the form of senior scholarships, while most encouraged their brighter undergraduates, especially scientists, to spend a year abroad during or after their undergraduate studies, and often extended their undergraduate studentship to allow them to do so.

However, Oxford's new research culture, in the first decade of the twentieth century, was still a frail and lopsided plant. What research was going on was chiefly in the arts; compared with Cambridge, which had already built up an international reputation for its scientific work, Oxford was lagging a long way behind.[11] The number of students, moreover, drawn to the University to read for a graduate qualification was still very small. There were possibly no more than a hundred

---

[7] Commission (1881), *Evidence*, pp. 201–5.

[8] For its creation and membership, see Lewis R. Farnell, *An Oxonian Looks Back* (Oxford, 1934), p. 275. Farnell of Exeter claimed to be its initiator: he was an historian of Greek religion and the author of a six-volume work on the subject.

[9] The first was education in 1896; the last agriculture in 1909.

[10] The BCL had continued to exist throughout the reform period but ceased to attract many candidates once law became a separate honour school in 1872. From the 1850s it could be taken only by those who had an Oxford BA, and was normally awarded in the twenty-seventh term after matriculation.

[11] Even in the arts, there were few research seminars. In modern history there were just two, one run by the regius professor, Firth, and the other by the professor of jurisprudence, Paul Vinogradoff, on social and legal history.

registered on the University's books in any year, and the large majority were on diploma courses that could be taken by those who had never gained a first degree but were judged to be sufficiently educated. Hardly anyone took the DLitt or DSc or even the lower bachelor degrees in the first years of their existence, and as late as 1912–13 there were only twelve BLitts and seven BScs awarded. The diplomas too, whatever their intellectual content, were given on performance in a conventional examination and not by submitting a thesis. And they were principally in practical subjects. Even anthropology, along with classical archaeology the least practical on the surface, was thought to be principally useful as training for those going out to administer the British Empire.[12]

Furthermore, there were few stipendiary positions for young researchers after the first years of research. The colleges and the University appear to have been supporting about thirty advanced students in some form in the 1900s, usually for one or two years. But there were few purely research positions that they or any other young postgraduates could take up thereafter. Not only was there no expansion in the number of ordinary or prize fellowships between the 1880s and 1914 but colleges suffering from the agricultural depression and accumulated debt due to costly building projects left many fellowships vacant in order to save money.[13] At most, half a dozen were released each year.[14] What positions there were also tended to go to researchers in the arts, older scholars, or simply the celebrated who could enhance a college's reputation: hence the suggestion, as early as 1892, by one of the most vocal advocates of raising the level of Oxford science, Edwin Ray Lankester, the Linacre professor of comparative anatomy, that the University should establish its own fixed-term research fellowships in zoology and botany for bright young scholars, paid for by specific college contributions.[15]

Nonetheless, by 1914, research was firmly on the University's agenda. According to Chancellor Curzon in 1909, it was no longer a question of whether research should be part of Oxford's remit but how research might best be encouraged, for it was 'now an accepted axiom that it is a portion of the duty of the oldest Universities to train their members for the exploration of remote as well as the survey of well-trodden fields'. In contrast to Pattison, Curzon saw the two functions as completely separate: 'They represent distinct though not antagonistic ideals of the work of a university, and they appeal to different intellectual types.' He gave the 1877 commissioners their due for identifying the need to promote research but he found their provision insufficient for the modern age: 'The strides made in advanced study have

---

[12] This continued to be the case to 1939 and beyond. On the eve of the Great War, anthropology (set up in 1905) had the lion's share of the diploma students.

[13] This was permitted under the statutes which, before 1926, laid down the maximum number of fellows each college should have, not the minimum.

[14] Curzon, *Principles*, pp. 95–6 and 182. Curzon calculated there were ninety-five ordinary fellows in post for seven years at a time, but most would be re-elected.

[15] *An Appeal to the Governing Bodies of Colleges within the University of Oxford* (Oxford, 1892). Lankester was a leading member of the informal dining club of thirty senior members devoted to university reform: see Farnell, *An Oxonian Looks Back*, pp. 270–1.

been so enormous that what was thought liberal in 1882 is now generally regarded as halting and inadequate.' In consequence, contemporary criticisms of Oxford as research shy were justified, though the position was not as bad as some cared to imagine. The Chancellor's view of the way forward was for the University and the colleges to discuss and devise a research policy, something that had hitherto never been done. His hope was that the result of this discussion would be agreement by the colleges to 'set apart for Research purposes a certain number of Fellowships with a rotation of subjects prescribed by the University', and the measured establishment of senior scholarships to support those starting out in postgraduate work. More, too, was to be done to give all professors, not just scientists, the space and facilities to train graduate students, and particular attention should be paid to increasing their number. At the same time, Curzon recognized that there was a limit to what could be achieved given Oxford's historic role. In Curzon's opinion, Oxford must continue to be the 'national training ground for those of our youth who aspire to a broad and liberal education', and should never expect to match the leading universities across the Atlantic in its research focus: 'We cannot hope…to emulate either those American Universities, like the Johns Hopkins University at Baltimore, which exist for post-graduate study alone, or those Universities of the more ordinary type, like Harvard, which have nevertheless more than 350 post-graduate students.'[16]

Curzon's dream of the colleges financially underpinning an expansion in research was dashed in the following decade by the Great War, which left the University deserted in a period of soaring prices. All the same, the commitment of his Oxford supporters to his wider research agenda remained undiminished. Recognizing, like many other members of the British establishment, that investment in scientific research would be essential if Britain was to be a great military and economic power after the war, Curzon's allies moved to ensure that Oxford was better prepared to do its bit in the future. The introduction in 1916 of a research component into the undergraduate chemistry degree has been mentioned in Chapter 10.[17] The second significant innovation during the war years was the creation of the DPhil. In 1917, representatives of Britain's universities met to discuss whether or not the country should follow the Americans and introduce a research doctorate. Supporters in Oxford took advantage of the heightened interest in the question, and in the same year persuaded Congregation to set up the new degree.[18] After the war, the Asquith Commission kept up the momentum. The commission had been triggered by the University's request for state funding to maintain and develop the work of its scientific departments, and the commissioners believed firmly that the regeneration

---

[16] Curzon, *Principles*, pp. 17, 180, 181, and 186–7.   [17] See p. 405, this volume.

[18] It was hoped that its introduction would attract more Americans postgraduates to the University. Unable to get an academic job in the States without a doctorate, few had been hitherto interested in pursuing research at Oxford: see John Mabbott, *Oxford Memories* (Oxford, 1986), p. 145. For the broader development of doctoral studies on this side of the Atlantic, see Renate Simpson, *How the PhD Came to Britain: A Century of Struggle for Postgraduate Education* (Guildford, 1983). PhDs had been established in Canadian universities from the 1890s to discourage Canadians from going to the United States to study: T. Pietsch, *Empire of Scholars: Universities, Networks and the British Academic World, 1850–1939* (Manchester, 2013), pp. 53–4.

of the nation's industry could only come through training more scientists. Above all, it wanted Oxford to catch up with Cambridge as a centre for science. Although the commission offered little advice on how this might be done beyond building more specialist labs, it did take the debate about Oxford's role as a research university a further step forward. A number of dons had made it clear in their evidence that college teachers were underpaid. Asquith's way out of this dilemma was to suggest the creation of joint appointments: all tutors should ideally also hold a university lectureship. This immediately led to a re-evaluation of the tutor's role. According to Asquith, in making appointments both the University and the colleges should use the same criteria. Research should not just be expected of professors and readers. Tutors too should be chosen from those with an ability to increase as well as impart knowledge. They were no longer to be interchangeable with public schoolmasters.

Admittedly, the tutor as researcher was not an unknown phenomenon before the First World War. As early as 1910, H. W. C. Davis, a fellow and tutor in modern history at Balliol from 1902 to 1921, threatened to resign unless the college reduced his teaching hours so that he could get on with his own work. The college graciously met him halfway and lowered his tutorial load to twenty hours on the grounds that his research and writing was 'work itself directly beneficial to the College, and conducive to its reputation as a place of advanced study'.[19] That said, a tutor like Davis was an oddity before 1914: most tutors were exhausted by the end of the academic year and could not wait to get away from Oxford for a long period of recuperation, preferably in the Swiss Alps. It took the Asquith Commission to produce a serious change in the tutorial culture. Coupled with the appointment of a new generation of tutors after the war who embraced the research ethic, the report effected a sea change in attitudes within a decade. By the 1930s, the majority had come to accept their dual role and had an area of research expertise. Colleges responded by slowly reducing tutors' hours, even when they did not hold a university lectureship and college post in tandem, and offering the possibility of taking sabbaticals.

Young tutors now expected that their research needs would be properly catered for. Leslie Sutton became a fellow and tutor in chemistry at Magdalen in 1935, a position he held until 1973. Like many of his contemporaries who took up a tutorial appointment in the years before the Second World War, Sutton had already established a reputation as a researcher. He had been elected to the foundation as an ordinary fellow in 1932 and spent the next three years away from Oxford working with Linus Pauling at Caltech. Before accepting the tutorial position, Sutton penned a long letter to Magdalen's president, George Gordon, explaining his view of the role. Customarily, he believed, a tutor had to spend 75 per cent of his time on teaching and associated duties; if he was lucky he had 25 per cent left for research. Sutton saw himself as a researcher first and foremost and hoped the proportion could be reversed. He was happy to see the weekly tutorial continue but thought that, except at the beginning and end of the course, teaching could be farmed out to young researchers. He saw no reason, either, why pupils could not be seen in small groups rather than individually. In his opinion, Oxford tutors were a self-satisfied insular bunch and needed to see more of the world. Sabbaticals ought to be made compulsory: 'Fellows should not merely be *allowed* to take off one year in seven, as I believe they are at present, in some Colleges, they should be *made* to do so: they should be escorted to the boat.'[20]

Not only did research gain a new respectability between the wars but the number of active researchers also grew sharply. In the 1900s, when college tutors were employed only to teach, there were no more than 200 Oxford dons obliged to promote the advancement of knowledge: 110 university professors, readers, and lecturers, plus some ninety college-funded postgraduates and fellows. By 1945, when virtually all university and college postholders were expected to do research and the University's academic staff had expanded fivefold, the figure was close to 800. This was composed of some 350 full-time university postholders, 250 college tutors (many of whom were also part-time university lecturers or demonstrators), and upwards of 200 other college-funded researchers. Besides a sizeable body of ordinary fellows, re-electable to retirement, this last figure now included a growing contingent of junior researchers. By 1939, senior scholarships were awarded by the majority of colleges and not just one or two, while most colleges were also funding a couple of fixed-term and non-renewable research fellowships specifically for scholars beginning their academic career, as they were encouraged to do under the new statutes of the mid-1920s.[21]

The number of research students similarly increased rapidly after 1920. Although enthusiasm for the new doctorate was initially muted and there were no new diploma courses invented until 1938, which saw the launch of the diploma in public and social administration, the number of registered postgraduate students climbed swiftly. From 100 in 1909, the figure had reached 536 in 1938–9 and 1,071 ten years later. Postgraduates still remained a small proportion of the total student body (11 per cent in 1938–9; 14 per cent in 1948–9), and at least two-thirds of the number were working in the humanities and social sciences. All the same, 300 of the cohort in the late 1930s were studying for a research degree, not a diploma, and of the 180 registered for the DPhil, eighty-three were scientists. (See Table 4.) At a time when few research grants were available, the expansion was impressive. Even as early as 1934, Oxford had more full-time postgraduates than any other British university except Cambridge.

The University was also expecting the number to grow rapidly in the future in one particular field at least. In 1937 when Lord Nuffield offered to fund a new college for accountancy and engineering, Vice-Chancellor Lindsay and the then registrar, the smooth-talking and forward-thinking Douglas Veale, persuaded him to change his mind. What Oxford wanted, and what Nuffield agreed to fund, was a graduate only college which would cater for the burgeoning social sciences.[22]

[20] MCA: FD/11, *sub* L. E. Sutton. MS letter L.E. Sutton to President Gordon, 5 May 1934.

[21] The figures are not precise. Most JRFs were in any subject but a few were reserved for specialists, like the post in Egyptology established by University College in 1936.

[22] There still remained a great deal of suspicion that postgraduates would undermine the University's *raison d'être* as a school for sharpening the minds of undergraduates, as the Rhodes House secretary (C. K. Allen) explained in a report to the Rhodes Trust in 1933/4: written communication from Richard Sheppard (n.d.).

B. Resources

It was no coincidence that Oxford's research profile before the Second World War was heavily weighted towards the arts and social sciences. Not only were most of the university and colleges' teaching resources traditionally invested in instructing undergraduates in the humanities, but researchers in the arts were peculiarly blessed in their research facilities. In the Bodleian, in particular, they had access to an exceptional collection of books and manuscripts on their doorstep that ineluctably grew larger and larger. Between 1850 and 1914 its holdings expanded fourfold, from 250,000 to 1 million items. Between the wars, even if the librarian never received 10 per cent of the government grant to the University as the Asquith Commission desired, its holdings almost certainly doubled again thanks to its copyright status.[23] In addition, arts researchers, by the end of the period, had a growing number of specialist libraries at their disposal. In the mid-nineteenth century, there had been only two: the Taylorian, a library that concentrated on the literature and culture of continental Europe, and the Codrington, already noted for its collections in history and law. Sixty years later, there were a further ten or twelve of varying size, including the libraries attached to the Indian Institute (1884–5), the department of geography (1899), and the faculty of modern history (1908). By this date too, several colleges possessed specialist collections, such as Oriel's library of comparative philology and the Maitland library for socio-legal studies accommodated in All Souls.[24] Yet other specialist libraries were created in the interwar years, most notably the library of Rhodes House, opened in 1929, which was devoted to American and British imperial history. Most of these specialized libraries had been established as independent, free-standing institutions, though in the 1920s and 1930s some of the more recent were brought under the Bodleian's control. This both reduced the dangers of duplicate purchases and allowed the overstretched Bodleian to transfer many of its books to more suitable locations.

Oxford's material collections in the first part of the twentieth century were fewer in number but just as rich. In 1850, the University's collection of art and artefacts, housed partly in the Bodleian and partly in the Ashmolean Museum in Broad Street, was a hotchpotch of items in a poor condition of preservation and largely uncatalogued. On the eve of the Second World War, virtually everything had been removed from the two sites and the original Ashmolean had become the University's Museum of the History of Science, largely constituted from a collection of scientific instruments given to Oxford by Lewis Evans in 1924.[25] The Ashmolean's natural history collection had been transferred to the new University Museum when it opened in 1860; so too had its

The University appointed a registrar to assist the Vice-Chancellor from at least the early sixteenth century. The role developed as the University expanded after 1850 and the Asquith Commission wanted the registrar to become involved in all areas of the central administration. But when Veale was appointed in 1930, he headed a team of only eight.

[23] Sir Edmund Craster, *History of the Bodleian Library 1845–1945* (Oxford, 1952), p. 345.
[24] Curzon, *Principles*, p. 184.
[25] Evans was a successful businessman who had studied chemistry at UCL.

FIGURE 12.2 Arthur Evans, 1851–1941, archaeologist of Knossos and founder of the new Ashmolean. Evans turned his attention to Crete and Knossos only after the early death of his wife and the island's liberation from Ottoman control. His excavation of the palace in 1900–3 and his discovery of a Minoan civilization that predated Mycenae put Oxford archaeology on the international map.

ethnographical material, which, from 1890, was housed along with the much larger eclectic collection given to Oxford by Augustus Henry Pitt-Rivers in 1883, in a specially built annex bearing his name.[26] On the other hand, Oxford's classical sculptures (the Arundel marbles) and the University's collection of largely classical and post-classical antiquities and coins had been gradually transferred around 1900 to the University Galleries in Beaumont Street, which became the new Ashmolean Museum.[27]

The leading figure in the transformation of the University Galleries was the field archaeologist Arthur Evans, Lewis' more famous brother, who became keeper of the old Ashmolean in 1884 (see Figure 12.2).[28] Evans had shown a precocious interest in archaeology even while studying modern history at Brasenose, and by the early 1880s, still only 30, he had built up a solid reputation in his subject, based on his work in the Balkans. From the moment that he took up his post, Evans was intent on creating a new art and archaeology museum for Oxford. Having found in Charles Drury Edward Fortnum a benefactor willing to finance an extension to

[26] Pitt-Rivers was an army officer, ethnologist, and archaeologist with a large private income. Born Augustus Henry Lane Fox, he had to change his surname when he inherited the estates of a Pitt-Rivers cousin.
[27] For the creation of the University Galleries, see p. 181, this volume.
[28] On Evans, see Joan Evans, *Time and Chance: The Story of Arthur Evans and His Forebears* (London, 1943).

the Beaumont Street building and bequeath the University his collection of classical and Renaissance art, he badgered the University into agreeing to amalgamate the Ashmolean and the University Galleries in 1892.[29] Evans was keeper of the Ashmolean until 1908 when he was replaced by another Oxonian field archaeologist, David Hogarth, who gave way in turn, in 1927, to Edward Leeds. Under their directorship the new museum became, as Evans had always wanted, a centre for the study of the pre-classical as well as the classical world, especially after it became the home of the new Institute for Egyptological and Near Eastern Archaeological Research in 1939.[30] Thanks too to the many bequests and gifts the directors received from their archaeological friends, the collection was also greatly increased and enriched with specimens from many different epochs and cultures. In Evans' day, 2,000 accessions were being added annually. This was a period when no attempt was made to stop archaeologists working on classical and pre-classical sites from removing what they found, so the museum acquired numberless peerless treasures. The Pitt Rivers also expanded rapidly in the first half of the twentieth century. Its founder had initially bequeathed the University 15,000 specimens. The museum owned 1 million by 1939.

Arts researchers in Oxford then had an embarrassment of riches. Their only problem was that the collections and holdings were expanding so fast that they were rapidly filling up the available space. The Bodleian was particularly affected, all the more that it was now being heavily used. Whereas in earlier centuries the Bodleian had been little more than a book depository, by 1914 it had become a research Mecca for scholars from inside and outside the University. Even undergraduates, to the number of 275 a day, were using its resources. As a result, the library was faced not simply with finding somewhere to put its growing number of books but also its growing number of readers. Valiant attempts were made by a succession of librarians to address the problem, but it was only under Arthur Cowley, in charge from 1919 to 1931, that the nettle was firmly grasped. Cowley realized the Bodleian had to find additional premises, and initiated discussion over whether to extend the existing library or build anew on a greenfield site. In contrast to Cambridge, Oxford unwisely went for the first option. Rather than establish a brand-new library fit for the age of research, it was eventually agreed to build a second Bodleian on the corner of the Broad and Parks Road, which would be capable of storing 5 million books. Sir Giles Gilbert Scott was commissioned to design the new building, and, through the generosity of the Rockefeller Foundation, it was possible to begin construction in the summer of 1937. The extension was ready by 1940 but it was not officially opened until after the Second World War, in 1946.[31]

The scientists, in contrast, had no research facilities to speak of at the beginning of the period, and until the outbreak of the First World War had to fight hard to

[29] Fortnum was an entomologist as well as an art lover who had farmed when young in Australia. He was one of the first people in England to appreciate and invest in the work of minor Renaissance artists.
[30] 'A Treasure Trove of Antiquity', *OT*, 27 Mar. 2014, p. 4.
[31] Craster, *Bodleian Library*, pp. 318–48. For Oxford's problems with book storage at the beginning of the twenty-first century, see p. 642, this volume.

FIGURE 12.3 Interior, the University Museum, 1860: architects Thomas Deane and Benjamin Woodward. The opening of the Museum was the beginning of a new chapter in the study of the natural sciences at Oxford, but it was intended as a teaching rather than a research institution. This reflected the view of most Oxford dons in the mid-nineteenth century, both traditionalists and reformers, that the University's principal role was to instruct the young.

wring money out of the University to create them. Until at least the 1880s, many members of Congregation and Convocation harboured a suspicion that research in natural science was a godless enterprise and should not be encouraged. This was manifest right at the beginning of the period when the University agreed only reluctantly to fund a new building to house the new Natural Science School and provide the science professors with rooms, lecture theatres, and laboratories, as the 1850 commissioners had recommended. Constructed between 1855 and 1860 to a design by the Dublin practice of Thomas Deane and Benjamin Woodward, the University Museum, viewed from the inside, was a very modern building: the roof over its central quad suspended on iron pillars was a marvel of the industrial age (see Figure 12.3). But the building was also arguably intended to put the scientists in their place. Deliberately sited outside the area of the traditional University on what was then pristine countryside, it was built in the gothic style to remind its users of the University's medieval Christian roots. The chemical laboratory attached to its south side was even intended to be an echo of the abbot's kitchen at Glastonbury.[32]

---

[32] H. M. Vernon and K. D. Ewart, *A History of the Oxford Museum* (London, 1909). The design was promoted by the Museum's chief advocate, the regius professor of medicine, Henry Acland, and one of the country's leading historians of art with a love of the middle ages, John Ruskin: see their *The Oxford Museum* (London, 1859), which went through several editions.

In the year the Museum opened, moreover, the tension between the arts and the sciences was brought particularly into focus when the former naval surgeon Thomas Huxley and Oriel's Samuel Wilberforce, bishop of Oxford, debated the merits of Darwinian evolution before the annual gathering of the British Association for the Advancement of Science, held that year in the University. Too much importance has been attributed to the insults purportedly traded between the two relating to Huxley's simian ancestry, and their different positions were more subtle than traditionally reported. However, there can be no doubt that what was at stake was the unimpeachable authority of the biblical description of the Creation in Genesis.[33]

The University Museum had been built as a teaching institution on the assumption that there would never be many college tutors in natural science, and it was inadequate as a centre for serious research. It had a good library, called the Radcliffe Library, as it was managed by the trustees of the original Radcliffe bequest, but apart from the abbot's kitchen, there was next to no space for investigatory work in the other sciences. In 1870 and 1875, the deficiency was remedied to a certain extent with the opening of the Clarendon Laboratory for physics and the new University Observatory: the one abutting the Museum to the north, the other on an independent site to the north-east to a design by Charles Barry Junior.[34] Three years later, chemistry was also given a boost when an extension was added to the abbot's kitchen. But thereafter progress was slow. An independent physiology building was established in 1883 at the cost of £10,000 on the north-east corner of the Museum but only in the face of great opposition in Convocation, which was appalled by the fact that the professor of physiology, John Burdon-Sanderson, was a keen vivisectionist.[35] Then, in the mid-1890s, a building to house the department of human anatomy was tacked on to the east end of the Pitt Rivers, and another for comparative anatomy added to the Museum to the north, the work of the architect H. W. Moore. This was the limit of the University's capital investment in scientific research in the late Victorian and Edwardian eras. Even money to finance improvements to the existing plant was only grudgingly bestowed and, once given, deemed sufficient. In 1882, R. B. Clifton, the professor of experimental philosophy, obtained a grant of £4,000 from Council to install a generator in the Clarendon. As a result, in 1902, when the Museum was connected to the mains electricity, the Clarendon was not, and it was still unconnected in 1919.

This meant that the bevy of new science professors and readers created after 1870 frequently had to find research space where they could. A second chair in physics was created in 1900 but there was no room in the Clarendon for the holder,

---

[33] John Headley Brooke, 'The Wilberforce–Huxley Debate: Why Did It Happen', *Farmington Papers*, SC15 (2001); Allan Chapman, 'Monkeying about with History: Remembering the "Great Debate" of 1860', *OM*, 0th week, TT (2010), 10–12. Darwin's *Origin of the Species* had appeared only the year before, so the debate was about a theory hot off the press. Twenty-five years later, Huxley, now a respected scientist, received an Oxford DCL.

[34] Roger Hutchins, *British University Observatories, 1772–1939* (Aldershot, 2008).

[35] His chief opponent in the University was Bodley's librarian, E. W. B. Nicholson: see Matthew Simpson, '"A duty from which I cannot deviate": Bodley's Librarian and the New Laboratory', *OM*, 2nd week, TT (2008), 4–7.

J. S. E. Townsend, to develop his research on gaseous ions. He and his research team had to borrow a room in the Observatory and set up their experiments in a tin hut. Science tutors who aspired to do research had to fend for themselves, for the University felt under no obligation to support them. What original work they did was performed in one of the five college teaching laboratories.[36] The situation began to improve only in the years immediately before the First World War. In 1903, the London Drapers Company had paid for the Museum's Radcliffe Library to be rehoused in a new building close by.[37] In 1906–8 a separate building was created for the new graduate discipline of forestry (later shared with agriculture) on the west side of Parks Road at its junction with South Parks Road. Two years later Townsend was finally installed in his own electrical laboratory in a building to the north of the Clarendon, funded again by the Drapers Company. Then in 1914 engineering found an independent home on a site to the north of Keble where Parks Road meets the Banbury Road. This was followed during the war, in 1916, with the opening of Oxford's first purpose-built chemical laboratory, paid for by the sauce makers Dyson Perrins. Located to the south of the Museum in a new building which fronted South Parks Road, it allowed organic chemistry at least to escape from the abbot's gothic cage (see Figure 12.4).

The flurry of activity, however, thereafter petered out, and in the 1910s new-comers still had to box and cox. When pharmacology was established as a separate department in 1914, the reader found space in an attic. Further significant expansion awaited the interwar period, and a novel commitment to seeking external funding to improve the facilities for science on what was now dubbed the Science Area.[38] The first fruits of this new commitment were realized in 1927. That year saw an electrical wing added to the engineering building, the opening of a biochemistry laboratory largely funded by the Rockefeller Foundation, and the establishment of the school of pathology on a virgin site at the east end of South Parks Road, paid for out of bequest of £100,000 left by Sir William Dunn five years before.[39] There was then a ten-year lull until 1937, when the University drew up ambitious plans for peppering the whole of the Science Area with sufficient buildings to accommodate every science, including mathematics, and fund-raising began in earnest. New building began again apace. By autumn 1939, thanks to the University's appeal of 1937 and the efforts of the then director of the Clarendon, F. A. Lindemann, Oxford had a much needed modern physics laboratory ready to replace its antiquated predecessor, which was scheduled to be inherited by geology.[40] Three years later, largely through the generosity of Lord Nuffield, the University was also able to open

---

[36] Keith J. Laidler, 'Chemical Kinetics and the Oxford College Laboratories', *Archive for History of Exact Sciences*, 38: 3 (1988), 217–38. For the establishment of the college labs, see p. 424, this volume.

[37] The library was taken over by the Bodleian in 1927, and when the building was renovated and extended in 1934 it became the Radcliffe Science Library.

[38] The size of the original Science Area was reduced in 1937 after the University agreed with the city that there would be no further intrusion on the Parks: see the maps in Jack Morrell, *Science at Oxford 1914–1939. Transforming an Arts University* (Oxford, 1997), pp. 39 and 44.

[39] Scottish-born philanthropist and creator of a large trading empire.

[40] Most of the old Clarendon was pulled down in 1946. To make the new Clarendon a reality, the University still had to sell £77,000-worth of securities.

FIGURE 12.4 The Dyson Perrins Organic Chemistry Laboratory, South Parks Rd, opened 1916. Once science professors began to take interest in doing research, the inadequacies of the Museum became obvious. When W. H. Perkin arrived from Manchester in 1913 to take up the Waynflete chair in chemistry, he immediately began to look for funds to build a new laboratory. Charles William Dyson Perrins who became chairman of the family company, Lea Perrins, had been educated at Charterhouse and Queen's. The building was designed by Paul Waterhouse, Alfred's, son who worked in a classical idiom.

its long desired laboratory in physical or inorganic chemistry, which the Asquith Commission had demanded be built as early as 1922.[41]

The full programme of 1937 was inevitably put on hold with the outbreak of the Second World War but much had been achieved since 1918. By 1942, virtually every science, except zoology, had some sort of home of its own outside the Museum. Within the departmental structure of the faculties of natural science and medicine, moreover, several research teams were now housed in specialist institutes of the kind beloved by German scientists, the first established with state funding in 1924 to promote agricultural engineering.[42] The footprint of Oxford's scientists had

---

[41] Nuffield gave £100,000 and ICI £10,000.
[42] Oxford's first institute was the Indian Institute in the 1880s, but this was conceived as a teaching not a research institution. The first arts research institute was the one for Egyptology referred to on p. 489, this volume.

also been extended beyond the Science Area and reached the western side of the Banbury Road. Thanks to the Nuffield bequest for an Institute of Medical Research and a School of Clinical Medicine in 1935–6, Oxford researchers were now firmly ensconced in the Radcliffe Infirmary.[43] (See Map 5.)

This interwar expansion in facilities was all the more important in that there was no concomitant expansion in the number of science departments. There were nineteen non-medical science chairs at the end of the First World War and only a further three (one in the new science of biochemistry) thirty years later. In consequence, the University in the interim moved from a position where only a minority of science professors had reasonable research facilities to one where the majority did. At the same time, the development of the system of part-time departmental and university demonstratorships meant that many college tutors now had research space within the Science Area, and the college laboratories largely became redundant.[44] Only the Balliol–Trinity lab, a large enterprise, which, in 1922, had five staff, including four college fellows, and twelve rooms and fifty-five bench places, continued to have a significant research profile under the leadership of the chemist and future Nobel laureate Cyril Hinshelwood.

What the science professors and readers still lacked were the resources to keep their labs running from day to day. The annual sum received from the University, even when bolstered by the government grant, was insufficient. The cost of equipment and the pay of researchers not on the university payroll had normally to be found from private funds. Some scientists with large private incomes kept their research afloat by dipping into their own capacious pockets, like the metallurgist W. Hume-Rothery, who worked in the inorganic chemistry lab in the 1930s. Others made the most of inadequate apparatus. But as equipment costs soared, especially in physics as it entered the atomic age, and research teams grew in size, most heads of department went looking for external funding from philanthropists, industry, the Royal Society, or the government's Department of Scientific and Industrial Research, set up in 1916 to promote scientific discovery during the First World War. As a result, professors were forced to devote much of their time to painstaking lobbying. Lindemann was a master of the art and trebled the income of the Clarendon between 1919 and 1938. By the late 1930s, he had built up a formidable team of researchers working on low-temperature physics. Even he, though, rapidly ran out of funds to keep it together, and was fearful that, when the new Clarendon opened, he would inherit an empty shell. In the event, it was the outbreak of war which threw him a lifeline. For all the improvements in their environment, interwar scientists still had a difficult life and needed to cultivate a range of skills which researchers in the arts seldom required.

[43] The foundation of the school was intended to allow medical students to train in Oxford while studying for the second BM: see p. 388, n.106, this volume.

[44] There were sixteen science readers and 119 science posts in Oxford in the late 1930s.

C. The Humanities

Oxford arts research had a rising profile in the forty years before 1914. Admittedly, among the professors and readers in the smaller arts subjects there was only one figure of international stature. This was the Sanskrit expert Friedrich Max Müller, Oxford's first professor of comparative philology from 1868 until his death, who did pioneering work on the Vedic scriptures, which he used to underpin his somewhat heretical ideas about the common origins of Aryan religions.[45] But the dominant faculties of Lit. Hum. and modern history sheltered a bevy of serious and substantial scholars, many of whom were tutors. The range and originality of their scholarship remained limited, for researchers were constrained in various ways by the contemporary view of their discipline as training for citizenship, or had to battle against it. Yet, if the scholars in neither faculty took full advantage of the riches in Oxford's libraries and collections, they succeeded in putting the University on the intellectual map. In the second half of the nineteenth century, Britain, unlike other western countries, had no national academy for the humanities and social sciences, so was unable to send representatives to international meetings organized by the arts academies in America and Europe. When the British Academy was finally established in 1902, its fellowship was dominated, for the rest of the period, by Oxford dons or the Oxford-trained.[46]

In the case of Lit. Hum., the disciplinary constraints were most evident in the work done on classical language and literature. To Jowett and virtually every Oxford classicist, the culture of the classical world, especially classical Greece, had an eternal significance that largely precluded their study in an objective and scholarly fashion. Greek literature, philosophy, and history contained the moral and practical lessons that the Victorian elite needed to learn to take their destined place in the world. Britain was the new Greece and London the new Athens. Aspects of ancient Greek culture which appeared not to fit with Victorian concepts of propriety, such as homosexuality and paedophilia, were carefully sanitized. Thus Jowett refused to accept that Plato's *Symposium* and *Phaedrus*, two texts he adored, suggested in any way that male friendship might find fulfilment in a physical union. Rather, he always insisted that: 'The love of which [Plato] speaks is the mystical love of men for one another, the union of two souls in a single perfect friendship.' It was the pure love of Jonathan for David.[47] The one Oxford classicist to resist this approach before 1900 was the Brasenose tutor Walter Pater, who celebrated rather than finessed the difference between the Greeks and the Victorians, lauding the former's

---

[45] Lourens P. van den Bosch, *Friedrich Max Müller: A Life Devoted to the Humanities* (Leiden, 2002). Müller retired in 1875 but continued to hold the chair. He was one of the few continental Europeans to be found in the University in the second half of the nineteenth century. He had been trained at Leipzig and took up a post at Oxford as deputy profesor of modern languages when the Taylorian was founded: see p. 245, this volume.

[46] In 1908, forty-five of the nintety-two fellows were present or former Oxford dons or Oxford-educated scholars; in 1927, the figure was fifty-eight out of 107. Based on *Proceedings of the British Academy*, sub anno, list of members.

[47] Geoffrey Faber, *Jowett: A Portrait with Background* (London, 1957), pp. 88 and 90–1.

pagan spirit and lust for beauty in all its forms, especially in his infamous conclusion to his *Studies in the History of the Renaissance*, published in 1873. But Pater's supporters were to be found among undergraduates, such as Oscar Wilde, who revelled in the tutor's rejection of Victorian taste and adopted his yearning for a new exuberant aesthetic. The Brasenose tutor had few followers among the senior members of the University: in fact, in April 1875 he was denounced from Christ Church by the bishop of Oxford, for promoting unbelief.[48] Pater's approach to the classical world, moreover, was as present-oriented as Jowett's for all their obvious disagreement.[49]

As a result, Oxford's contribution to the study of classical languages and literature was meagre before the turn of the twentieth century, and by no stretch of the imagination could stand comparison with the work of German scholars.[50] In 1843, the appearance of Liddell and Scott's renowned Greek dictionary had suggested that Oxford classics, which had long been able to claim only Gaisford as a figure of substance, was on the verge of a new era.[51] But the following decades produced little of merit beyond an endless list of scholarly editions for the use of undergraduates. It was only with the arrival of Gilbert Murray at New College in 1905, and his appointment to the chair of Greek in 1908, that classical studies began to take a more objective turn. Murray, who had previously been at Glasgow, had come under the influence of the Cambridge ritualist anthropologist Sir James Frazer, and believed the latter's ideas could be used to elucidate Greek drama and poetry. Murray still greatly admired the culture of classical Athens but his ancient Greece was no longer a pre-Christian utopia but an historic society emerging from its primitive roots. That a new era had dawned with his arrival was soon in evidence. Murray's more measured approach to the Greek past was emphasized in 1907 with his publication of *The Rise of the Greek Epic*, then in 1911 with his *Four Stages of Greek Religion*.[52]

Jowett's view of the contemporary significance of the classical past had an equally stultifying effect on Greek history, where there was no specific professor before 1910 and the creation of the Wykeham chair, and the major publications of the pre-war period were undergraduate textbooks and editions prepared by college tutors. Roman history, however, escaped his dead hand to a certain extent with the appointment of Henry Francis Pelham to the Camden chair in 1889. Pelham, an Exeter man with some of Pattison's attitudes to scholarship, presided over the

---

[48] S. Evangelista, 'Walter Pater's Teaching in Oxford: Classics and Aestheticism', in Christopher Stray (ed.), *Oxford Classics: Teaching and Learning, 1800–2000* (Oxford, 2007), ch. 5. Wilde was an 'aesthete' at Oxford, not a homosexual. Some judged Pater a poor teacher, and his lectures showed no appreciation of developments in archaeology: Farnell, *Oxonian*, p. 76; G. B. Grundy, *Fifty-Five Years at Oxford* (London, 1945), pp. 81 and 84.

[49] Faber, *Jowett*, pp. 379–84. Jowett, shortly before he died, praised Pater's *Plato and Platonism* (1893). Pater had been Jowett's pupil.

[50] As was recognized by contemporary critics; e.g. Richard B. Haldane, *Education and Empire* (London, 1902), p. 31.

[51] For Gaisford, see p. 304, this volume.

[52] Christopher Stray (ed.), *Gilbert Murray Reassessed: Hellenism, Theatre and International Politics* (Oxford, 2007), esp. chs 3–6.

largest collection of ancient historians anywhere in the world. If much of the work published on ancient Rome during his tenure also took the form of textual commentary, it was of high quality, and Pelham fostered original research. He himself never emerged from the shadow of the German early-nineteenth-century colossus Mommsen, but he allowed other ancient historians in the University to do so, notably Warde Fowler of Lincoln, who developed a formidable knowledge of Roman social history. In addition, Pelham encouraged Oxford's ancient historians to see the value of archaeology, a science still in its infancy but where again the Germans were taking the lead.[53]

Jowett also had no time for archaeology and could see little point in Heinrich Schliemann's excavations of the site of Troy. Unsurprisingly, when one of Britain's leading archaeologists of the ancient world, Arthur Evans, put himself forward for Oxford's new chair in the subject in 1883, at the very moment Jowett was Vice-Chancellor, he was unsuccessful. As his father-in-law had warned him, Jowett and his tribe were like the opponents of the humanists of old:

> They are the obscurantists and answer exactly to the *Trojans* of the 16th century. As men fought then for the *knowledge* of Greek and the Jowetts of that day opposed them, so we fight for the *use* of Greek, for the proper place of Greek in the history of the world, and the Jowetts of this day—the cribmongers—oppose us.[54]

But Evans was rich and tenacious and was not to be denied. The following year he was appointed keeper of the Ashmolean, *pace* Jowett, and, as we have seen in the previous section of this chapter,[55] set about putting Oxford archaeology on the map. Jowett was not amused, but he faded from the scene too quickly to have much influence on the outcome, and Evans, over time, had his way. Pelham, once elected to the Camden chair, proved a powerful ally. As a result, field archaeology before the First World War became one of the most fruitful areas of Oxford's research activities, even if much of the most exciting work continued to be done outside the university world altogether by people like the Egyptologist Flinders Petrie.[56] Besides Evans himself, whose excavations at Knossos in the first decade of the twentieth century made him world famous, two figures were particularly significant from the next generation: Francis Haverfield and David Hogarth. Haverfield, who, after Oxford, became a schoolteacher at Lancing, was elected the Camden professor of Roman history in succession to Pelham in 1907, and spent the next seven years excavating the Romano-British site at Corbridge on Hadrian's Wall, and laying the foundation of modern Romano-British archaeology. His credo was summed up in his 1907 Ford lectures: 'Today the spade is mightier than the pen; the shovel and the pick are the revealers of secrets.'[57] David Hogarth, a Magdalen fellow from 1886, was

---

[53] He was another founding member of Farnell's dining society.
[54] Evans, *Time and Chance*, pp. 261–2. His father-in-law was the then regius of modern history, E. A. Freeman.
[55] See pp. 488–9, this volume.   [56] Petrie eventually held a chair at UCL from 1892.
[57] *HUO*, vii. 355. For his life and work, see Richard Hingley, 'Francis John Haverfield (1860–1919): Oxford, Roman Archaeology and Edwardian Imperialism', in Stray, *Oxford Classics*, ch. 10. His excavation techniques could be cavalier: see Grundy, *Fifty-Five Years*, p. 156.

FIGURE 12.5 Thomas Hill Green, 1836–82, Balliol tutor, White's professor of moral philosophy, and father of Oxford idealism. Green was one of Oxford's most prominent Liberals and social reformers. He promoted universal manhood suffrage and women's education and campaigned against the demon drink. His posthumously published lectures insisted that human beings could be morally improved.

a leading archaeologist of the Mediterranean world and the Near East who had dug with both Petrie and Evans, and been the second director of the British School at Athens established in 1887. He continued his fieldwork after taking up the Ashmolean post, and in the years before the Great War was particularly involved with the excavation of Carchemish, an important Hittite centre, where he was helped by the Magdalen senior demy and later fellow of All Souls, T. E. Lawrence.

Oxford's reaction to the development of a research tradition in archaeology was to cut all but the first Olympiad out of the Greek history curriculum set for Lit. Hum. schools, so that it could remain a text-based subject.[58] Scholarly developments in philosophy, in contrast, were initially less troublesome. The study of philosophy in Greats was founded on the text-based study of Aristotle and Plato, but it was understood, in the age of Jowett, that their ideas were to be interrogated with the help of the moderns. The moderns, too, were not necessarily opposed to the ancients, as the school of philosophy developed in the 1870s by Oxford's first resident philosopher of note for many centuries, Balliol's T. H. Green, demonstrated (see Figure 12.5). Green and his followers were philosophical idealists who strongly

[58] Robin Collingwood, *An Autobiography* (Oxford, 1939), pp. 82–3.

believed that the study of philosophy was an education in active citizenship. Green reacted negatively to the dominant late Victorian theory of ethics and politics based on a mixture of the utilitarianism of John Stuart Mill and the neoDarwinianism of Herbert Spencer, and, in the 1870s and 1880s, developed an alternative and much more positive view of humankind. Human beings were not competing, self-centred individuals but potentially cooperative Christ-like creatures, and the state, as Aristotle, Kant, and Hegel had all understood, should be a vehicle for maximizing human potential rather than an instrument for controlling the worst aspects of human nature.[59] There was clearly nothing here to challenge the dominant curricular ethos, even when Green's most creative disciple, Francis Herbert Bradley, who lived in Oxford and was a fellow of Merton but never taught at the University, historicized his ideas and argued that Green's cooperative ethic only became germane with the birth of industrial society.[60]

By the turn of the twentieth century, on the other hand, Oxford philosophy had become more subversive, as Green's school spawned a counter party who cut philosophy adrift from its moral moorings. The majority of Oxford philosophers did not subscribe to Green's ideas. He and his supporters were dismissed as well-meaning dreamers and their idealist philosophy looked at critically by a group who called themselves realists. The leader of this second school was the professor of logic, John Cook Wilson, who rejected any connection between knowledge and action. The realists, who had an affinity with the Cambridge philosopher G. E. Moore, still saw philosophy as a peculiarly important study for teaching people how to think through analysing the truth content in propositions, but they were in essence sceptics. Before the First World War, however, their views were not widely known outside Oxford because they published little. As Cook Wilson once explained to Robin Collingwood, a philosopher whose objection to the realists was made abundantly public in the interwar period, this was because he was continually changing his mind: 'If I published, every book I wrote would betray a change of mind since writing the last. Now, if you let the public know that you change your mind, they will never take you seriously.'[61]

In the case of modern history, scholars were forced to work within the telos of an undergraduate curriculum that was primarily the invention of the first holder of the regius chair to engage in serious archival research, William Stubbs (see Figure 12.6). From a poor background, Stubbs had gone up to Christ Church as a servitor before the age of reform and then joined the church. He had cut his teeth as a historian

---

[59] Green's works were published posthumously, notably his *Prolegomena to Ethics*, 1882.

[60] Bradley argued that right behaviour was what was right in a particular civilization. Other Oxonian members of Green's school were R.L. Nettleship, William Wallace, Bernard Bosanquet, Edward Caird, and Clement Webb. Recent studies include A. Vincent and R. Plant, *Philosophy, Politics and Citizenship: The Life and Thought of the British Idealists* (Oxford, 1984), and J. Patrick, *The Magdalen Metaphysicals: Idealism and Orthodoxy at Oxford 1901–45* (Macon, GA, 1985) [a number of Green's supporters, including Webb, were associated with Magdalen].

[61] Collingwood, *Autobiography*, p. 19. For the two schools, see ibid., ch. 3. Cook Wilson had no more time than Green for Mill's work. As a young tutor in logic at Oriel in the late 1870s, he criticized the utilitarian mercilessly: Farnell, *Oxonian*, p. 45.

FIGURE 12.6 William Stubbs, 1825–1901, regius professor of modern history and father of the Oxford history school. He helped create the separate modern history school in 1872, gave it its English history focus and laid down the narrative of the English past it should uphold. He put down his chair in 1884 on being appointed bishop of Chester and thereafter gave up historical research.

while a humble parish priest by preparing and publishing editions of medieval rolls.[62] Made regius professor through Lord Derby's influence in 1866, he had proceeded to associate the new faculty of modern history with his personal narrative of the English past, based on a belief that the key to the present lay in the middle ages. Stubbs' narrative stressed the early but steady and gradual institutionalization of English/British liberty under the law. In his *Select Charters* (1870) he published a series of documents that traced the development of the English/British constitution from the German forests to the reign of Edward I. In his *Constitutional History of England* (3 vols, 1873–8) he offered a coherent, archive-based account of how the English/British had emerged as a unitary nation dedicated to freedom between the Anglo-Saxon period and the fifteenth century, and how its liberties had been protected in parliament.[63]

---

[62] He eventually contributed nineteen volumes to the series *Chronicles and Memorials of Great Britain and Ireland in the Middle Ages*.

[63] James Campbell, *Stubbs and the English State* (Reading, 1988).

Stubbs' narrative was not new except in its scholarly underpinning, which came from his early encounter with the German historical tradition. The story had first surfaced in the early seventeenth century among parliamentary opponents of the early Stuarts and was deeply embedded in popular political culture. But it was nonetheless highly significant. The two most popular Victorian historians writing in the same heroic tradition, Thomas Babington Macaulay in the mid-nineteenth century, and Stubbs' contemporary, S. R. Gardiner, professor at King's College, London, traced the beginnings of Britain's contemporary liberties to the struggle between the Stuarts and their parliaments, not to the middle ages. Stubbs' narrative emphasized the Englishness of the story.[64]

Stubbs' reading of the national past was quickly internalized by the University's modern historians. By the time he resigned his chair in 1884 to become a bishop, he had given the young undergraduate discipline a focus that allowed it to challenge Lit. Hum. as the training ground of the nation's elite. By learning of their country-men's long-standing commitment to freedom, undergraduates would understand what was peculiar, precious, and engrained about being English/British, and be fitted for a future as civil servants and administrators of empire. English medieval history both legitimized Britain's hegemonic role in the world and suggested that role would be exercised benignly. Once established as the curriculum's leitmotiv, scholars within the faculty were not expected to deviate from the orthodoxy. Research was supposed to reinforce Stubbs' argument not undermine it, and his pupils duly obliged. Stubbs produced a whole clutch of medievalists who followed in his footsteps, most notably T. F. Tout, fellow of Pembroke and professor of history at Manchester from 1890 to 1925. Tout had different views from his master when it came to undergraduate teaching: he valued learning research techniques at an early stage and introduced a compulsory dissertation. But he maintained the flame, merely placing the emphasis on the development of English administration in the middle ages rather than on the growth of parliament, a shift apparently caused by his introduction to contemporary French historiography.[65]

By the Edwardian era, the modern history faculty was becoming a scholarly force. It boasted its own publishing organ, the *English Historical Review*, founded in 1886, the country's first academic history journal, and an annual series of research lectures on British history established under the will of one of Stubbs' friends, James Ford. It had not, however, escaped from Stubbs' clutches. Gardiner, on putting down his chair at King's, spent the last twenty years of his life in Oxford as an ordinary fellow, first at All Souls and then at Merton. But his presence did little to dent Stubbs' influence. Nor did the appointment of Firth as regius in 1904. Although Firth was a

---

[64] J. G. A. Pocock, *The Ancient Constitution and the Feudal Law: A Study of English Historical Thought in the Seventeenth Century: A Reissue with a Retrospect* (Cambridge, 1987); John Burrow, *A Liberal Descent: Victorian Historians and the English Past* (Cambridge, 1981). S. R. Gardiner had been an undergraduate at Christ Church.

[65] P. R. H. Slee, *Learning and a Liberal Education: The Study of Modern History in the Universities of Oxford, Cambridge and Manchester, 1800–1914* (Manchester, 1986); Reba N. Soffer, *Discipline and Power: The University, History and the Making of an English Elite 1870–1930* (Stanford, CA, 1994).

seventeenth-century historian and in some ways Gardiner's disciple—his originality lay in the positive role he gave to Cromwell in the national narrative—he was no iconoclast.[66] In consequence, it was difficult for those who did not subscribe to Stubbs' continuity thesis to obtain a post at Oxford. A number of young historians whose loyalty was suspect had to move on. Oxford historians of the national story also had to be English, as the young Lewis Namier discovered. Marked down as unsound for his Polish and Jewish background, he failed to get an All Souls fellowship on the eve of the First World War, despite being judged intellectually superior to the rest of the field. Many years later, now working as a private scholar, Namier confirmed his untrustworthiness by publishing an account of parliament on the accession of George III which painted a picture of an institution dominated by jobbery and family connections rather than by a love of freedom.[67]

The First World War largely put paid to the idea that an Oxford education in Lit. Hum. or modern history was an education for citizenship. Thereafter, the two subjects could claim to be doing nothing different from any other Oxford school: they were training undergraduates to think. The undermining of the old certainties affected research across the humanities. Oxford's interest in textual and literary criticism was even greater between the wars than before, and was now extended beyond the Bible and the classical age to all manner of medieval and early modern texts, many hitherto unpublished. Some used the freedom to set up new idols. Bowra wrote extensively on the pre-Attic Greece of Pindar, which he extolled as an age of aristocracy where the body was worshipped as well as the mind.[68] But all scholars displayed a novel commitment to context. This was exemplified in the burgeoning scholarship of a new generation of professors and tutors of the School of English literature, in particular by J. R. R. Tolkien's edition of *Sir Gawain and the Green Knight* (1925) and his British Academy lecture of 1936 on *Beowulf*.[69]

The philosophers and historians were particularly emancipated by no longer having to engage with their faculty telos. The former gained an unaccustomed freedom to engage sympathetically with the novel work being done by their colleagues on the continent. Oxford's reduction of philosophy to the analysis of language was not fully completed until after 1945, with the publication of Gilbert Ryle's seminal *The Concept of Mind* (1949). But already in the 1930s there were plenty of signs that the University's young philosophers were coming under the influence of the Viennese school of logical positivism, represented in Britain by Wittgenstein, who had moved to Cambridge in 1929. The most prominent member of the new

---

[66] Esp. his *Oliver Cromwell and the Rule of the Puritans in England* (London, 1900).

[67] L. B. Namier, *The Structure of Politics at the Accession of George III* (2 vols; London, 1929). Namier briefly taught at Balliol after the First World War.

[68] Leslie Mitchell, *Maurice Bowra: A Life* (Oxford, 2009), ch. 4. For Bowra's own account of classics in interwar Oxford, see his *Memories* (London, 1966), ch. 11.

[69] Tolkien became Rawlinson professor of Anglo-Saxon in 1925. From the mid-1930s he turned his attention to imaginative literature. The first serious literary critic to gain an appointment at Oxford was Sir Walter Alexander Raleigh, a fellow of Merton in 1904 and a Cambridge man.

guard at this juncture was not Ryle, then a tutor at Christ Church, but his college colleague and erstwhile pupil Alfred (Freddie) Ayer, whose *Language, Truth and Logic* was published in 1936. The new linguistic philosophers deliberately cultivated a separate persona and formed an informal community. From the mid-1930s, the coterie met to discuss their ideas in the rooms of another young heretic, Isaiah Berlin, a prize fellow at All Souls from 1932.[70]

The historians also had their young Turks. The faculty's commitment to English history remained unchanged. Research too continued to be focused on the middle ages under the leadership of the regius professor from 1925, Maurice Powicke. However, scholars who took up their posts from the late 1920s were much more interested in how English society held together in a particular reign or century than in the evolutionary history of key institutions.[71] Typical in this regard was Bruce McFarlane, tutor at Magdalen from 1928, whose expertise lay in the fourteenth and fifteenth centuries. One of a small number of Oxford academics between the wars to come under the influence of Marxism, both as a political philosophy and a historical methodology, McFarlane dismissed the independent power of ideas, so dear to the liberal tradition. Instead, he promoted the view that successful kingship in the age of 'bastard feudalism', a term earlier invented by the Corpus historian Charles Plummer, was determined purely by the skilful and ruthless use of royal power to control ambitious, self-interested magnates.[72] Power and violence also fascinated McFarlane's senior colleague, J. M. Thompson, who was one of a handful of Oxford historians between the wars to develop an interest in the history of continental Europe. Surplus to requirements as a tutor of philosophy after the Great War, he was reborn as a tutor for modern history, who decided to take as his subject the French Revolution. By the time he retired in 1938, he had become the country's leading authority on the upheaval. Although Thompson was not an archival historian, his works on French history, such as his biography of Robespierre (1935), were based on close reading of the growing number of printed sources and a good acquaintance with the latest French research. It was thanks to him that the pioneering work of the great French historians of the first half of the twentieth century, Aulard, Mathiez, and Lefebvre, became better known to an English-speaking readership.

There was only one significant Oxford scholar in the 1920s and 1930s who continued to bat on the side of the old order. This was the philosopher and ancient historian Robin Collingwood, who was a tutor at Pembroke from 1912 until he became the Waynflete professor of metaphysics in 1935. Collingwood believed there had to be a connection between logical thought and action or mankind was

---

[70] Noel Annan, *The Dons: Mentors, Eccentrics and Geniuses* (London, 2000), p. 211. Berlin fell out of love with logical positivism after 1940. For a consideration of Berlin's intellectual contribution, see p. 650, this volume.

[71] Admittedly the most significant attack on the old form of history in this period, Herbert Butterfield's *Whig Interpretation of History* (1931), came out of Cambridge.

[72] McFarlane published little. He popularized the term 'bastard feudalism' in two articles in 1944 and 1945. For the McFarlane school, see R. H. Britnell and A. J. Pollard (eds), *The McFarlane Legacy: Studies in Late Medieval Politics and Society* (Stroud, 1995).

doomed. Cook Wilson and his successors had a lot to answer for. If human beings had no ideals or principles to live by, they became the slaves of passion and emotion, and would fall under the spell of demagogues:

> If the realists had wanted to train up a generation of Englishmen and Englishwomen expressly as the potential dupes of every adventurer in morals or politics, commerce or religion, who should appeal to their emotions and promise them private gains which he neither could procure them nor even meant to procure them, no better way of doing it could have been discovered.[73]

Collingwood also insisted that history, as the study of human actions in the past through the interpretation of evidence, was an indispensable science for the modern politician. It was the key to human self-knowledge and the control of human affairs, and without it politicians blundered in the dark as they had at Versailles:

> [F]or sheer ineptitude the Versailles treaty surpassed previous treaties as much as for sheer technical excellence the equipment of twentieth-century armies surpassed those of previous armies. It seemed almost as if man's power to control 'Nature' had been increasing *pari passu* with a decrease in his power to control human affairs.[74]

Throughout the 1930s, Collingwood strove to fight the rise of the European dictators (and the pusillanimity of Baldwin and Chamberlain) by erecting a new philosophical idealism. Sadly, he died relatively young (in 1942) and his project was never completed. For most of the 1930s he treated philosophy and history as separate sciences, while always maintaining that the philosophical classics had to be studied in context if they were to be understood. By the end of his life, he had implicitly collapsed philosophy into history. Collingwood believed that history, rightly conceived, was a new discipline forged in the late nineteenth century by archaeologists like Arthur Evans as much as by historians. In its new form, as an endeavour to understand human action in the past by getting inside the heads of the perpetrators (be they princes or potters), the best history written in his own day was as deserving of the name of science as philosophy or physics. It was a science of a different kind, however, and its principles needed to be elucidated. This he endeavoured to do in his posthumous *Idea of History*. In the seventeenth century, the development of the natural sciences had had a revolutionary impact on the science of philosophy. The new science of history was destined to have a similar effect. Had Collingwood had time, he planned to overhaul 'all philosophical questions in the light of the results reached by the philosophy of history in the narrower sense'. Had he done so, it is difficult to see how he could not have been any less sceptical about absolute ethics and metaphysics than his realist opponents.[75]

Collingwood's conviction that man's understanding of nature had far outstripped his understanding of himself received sympathetic attention only from Oxford's

---

[73] Collingwood, *Autobiography*, pp. 48–9.　　[74] Ibid., p. 91.
[75] *The Idea of History*, ed. Jan van der Dussen (Oxford, 1994), pp. 6–7. For Collingwood's definition of history, see Collingwood, *Idea*, pp. 7–10.

diminishing coterie of committed Christians who shared his pessimism, such as the evangelical English don C. S. Lewis. A rising star in the 1930s for his work on medieval allegory, Lewis made his own fears for a world devoid of a Christian compass crystal clear in 1945 when he published his science fiction novel *That Hideous Strength*. This was a roman à clef whose sociologist anti-hero was T. D. (Harry) Weldon, a Kantian scholar and free-thinking Magdalen freemason. Weldon liked to destroy the old to create anew: he terrified his tutorial pupils by demolishing any argument they tried to bring forward, and during the war helped to terrify the Germans by acting as an adviser to 'Bomber' Harris.[76]

D. The Sciences

Even given its limited resources, late Victorian and Edwardian Oxford's contribution to the development of the natural sciences was lamentable. The tone was set by the holders of the two most important science chairs in physics and chemistry, R. B. Clifton and W. Odling. Clifton bestirred himself to get the Clarendon set up and then sat on his laurels until he retired, aged 80, in 1915, while Odling, who occupied the Waynflete chair until 1912, did nothing at all.[77] The professors in the smaller sciences were rather more active but seldom had an international reputation and there was often no continuity. Burdon-Sanderson presided over a burst of research into electro-physiology while he held the chair of physiology in the 1880s, but under his successor, Francis Gotch, the department slept.[78] Among the other science professors, only the professor of mineralogy, H. A. Miers, appointed in 1895, who worked in the field of crystallography, was a figure of substance.[79] Indeed, it could be argued that what little exciting work was being done in late Victorian and Edwardian Oxford in the sciences was largely located outside the Museum complex in college and private laboratories. The University's most important physiologist in this period, for instance, was Burdon-Sanderson's nephew, J. S. Haldane, who came to Oxford from Edinburgh in 1887, became a fellow of New College, and did pioneering work on the physiology of respiration in his private home, now the site of Wolfson College.

The one obvious exception was in the area of electricity and magnetism. J. S. E. Townsend, appointed to the new Wykeham chair of experimental physics in 1900, had to wait ten years for a purpose-built laboratory but he quickly built up an important research team working on electrical discharges in gases. On the eve of the Great War, the most innovative member of the lab was H. G. J. 'Harry' Moseley, a former undergraduate at Trinity, who had come back to Oxford in late 1913 after

---

[76] Weldon left Bomber Command before the attack on Dresden.

[77] The young Clifton had been more dynamic, see G. Gooday, 'Precision Measurement and the Genesis of Teaching Laboratories in Victorian Britain' (PhD dissertation, Kent, 1986), ch. 6.

[78] Terry M. Romano, *Making Medicine Scientific: John Burdon Sanderson and the Culture of Victorian Science* (Baltimore, MD, 2002).

[79] He later moved to Manchester and served on the Asquith Commission.

working for three years with Ernest Rutherford at Manchester. Still in his mid-twenties, Moseley returned to his Alma Mater with a formidable reputation as a researcher. By showing earlier in the year that different chemical elements produced distinctive X-ray wavelengths when bombarded with electrons, he had brought a new predictive rigour to the periodic table. Sadly he died at Gallipoli in 1915 fighting with the Royal Engineers. Had he lived, he was destined for a stellar scientific career.[80]

Positive mention, too, must be made of anthropology, even if the discipline straddled the arts and the sciences. The readership in anthropology, established in 1884, was one of three new creations in that year intended to strengthen the University's commitment to human and comparative anatomy and physiology. The appointment to the post of E. B. Tylor, hitherto a private scholar until he became keeper of the University Museum the year before, proved a good investment and put Oxford anthropology on the map. Tylor was Britain's leading evolutionary anthropologist, who eschewed the Eurocentrism so common among his contemporary ethnographers. In a series of seminal works, published both before and during his tenure, he forged an ambitious and unitary account of human cultural development, which attributed differences in the level of civilization to different cultural arrangements rather than race or mental immaturity.

A number of Oxford's science departments continued to perform poorly between the wars. A case in point was geology under the leadership of W. J. Sollas, who was appointed in 1897 and held the chair for forty years until 1936. Despite the presence of William Arkell, who was the country's foremost authority on the Jurassic, Oxford earth sciences remained largely moribund. Little, too, went on at the Dunn School of Pathology until the late 1930s, despite its high-quality facilities, while attempts to get experimental psychology off the ground with the foundation of an institute for the subject in 1936 proved largely abortive. The work of the Institute of Agricultural Engineering was even compromised by scandal. In 1931, its director, B. J. Owen, was found to be cooking the books, and Oxford was sued by Sugar Beet and Crop Driers for £750,000 as compensation for the dud patents that Owen had sold the company under the University's name. Other departments gave promise of leaving the doldrums only to become becalmed again after a short burst of activity. This was particularly true of mathematics, where a much-needed boost came with the appointment of a leading Cambridge mathematician, G. H. Hardy, to the Savilian chair in 1920. Hardy, famous for his work on the theory of functions, connected Oxford with the best mathematicians on the continent and the United States and persuaded the University to set up a small mathematical research institute in 1930. But he returned to Cambridge in the following year, and it was left to one of the mathematics tutors, the Balliol topologist Henry Whitehead, to keep the research flame burning on the eve of the Second World War.

---

[80] Moseley had studied natural sciences and graduated with a First in 1910. An exhibition displaying his life and achievements was mounted in the summer of 2015 in the Museum of the History of Science, Oxford, entitled ''Dear Harry...'' Henry Moseley. A Scientist Lost to War'.

However, the duds apart, Oxford science finally came of age between the wars. Oxford's standing in the life sciences was given a fillip even before the First World War when the University appointed Charles Sherrington to the chair of physiology in 1913. Sherrington, a Cambridge man who had previously been at Liverpool, was already a renowned experimental neurophysiologist. At Oxford in the 1920s and early 1930s, he continued his work, built up an able team of experimenters that included the Australian J.C. Eccles, and created the world's foremost animal physiology laboratory. His most notable achievement in the 1920s was the isolation and functional analysis of the motor unit, a spinal neurone orchestrating the activity of a large number of muscle fibres. It was for this that he received the Nobel Prize for Medicine in 1932. Sherrington, though, was only one of several distinguished Oxford scientists working on different aspects of the three kingdoms. R. A. Peters, another Cambridge man and the first holder of the new chair in biochemistry, headed up a team in the late 1920s and 1930s investigating the vitamin B complex; the professor of anatomy, W. E. Clark, and his star researcher, the South African S. Zuckerman, spent the 1930s researching the functional affinities between human beings, monkeys, and apes; while a clutch of botanists and zoologists developed the new science of ecology.

A. G. Tansley, elected to the Vine chair of botany in 1927 and the purported inventor of the term ecosystem, was Oxford's outstanding public figure in the new field. But the really innovative work was done by zoologists. The most creative mind in the department in the 1920s was the New College tutor Julian Huxley, who was a great believer in experimental fieldwork and was an expert on bird courtship. He then passed the torch to his pupil C. S. Elton. The latter was particularly dynamic. Having published the classic account of animal ecology in the year that Tansley became a professor, Elton spent the 1930s giving the subject an institutional base in the Bureau of Animal Population, set up initially on a shoestring in 1932. The botanists and zoologists, moreover, were not just interested in ecology but did important work in another new field, genetics. They were also unafraid to branch out on their own. When, in the late 1930s, the young P. B. Medawar, a future Nobel laureate, discovered his work on cell growth using tissue techniques did not find favour with the Linacre professor of the interwar period, Edwin Goodrich, he moved out of the Department of Zoology and found research space in the Dunn School of Pathology.[81]

The University similarly attempted to kick-start chemical research by importing research stars. In 1913, the same year that Sherrington came to Oxford, the University headhunted from Manchester the services of the German-trained organic chemist W. H. Perkin and agreed to the establishment of a new laboratory. Six years later, an attempt was made to revitalize inorganic chemistry with the

---

[81] Medawar had broad intellectual and reformist social interests and was close to many leading contemporary philosophers. For his intellectual odyssey, see his autobiography, *Memoirs of a Thinking Radish* (Oxford, 1986).

appointment of the Merton-educated Frederick Soddy, then professor at Aberdeen, to Dr Lee's chair. Of the two, Soddy had the greater scientific reputation through his investigation into the chemistry of the radio elements and the formulation of the theory of isotopes, made public in 1913. But it was Perkin who would put Oxford chemistry on the map. Although Soddy was awarded Oxford's first Nobel Prize in 1921 for his isotope work, he thereafter abandoned research, perhaps the only Oxford scientist in the interwar years unnerved, like Collingwood, by the gap between scientific potential and human progress.[82] Perkin, on the other hand, revelled in the opportunity to build up organic chemistry at Oxford and was unabashed by the University's traditional distaste for marketable research. His own work was not ground-breaking: throughout his career, he primarily focused on understanding the structure of naturally occurring organic substances by the well-tried method of degradation and synthesis, and he paid little attention to theoretical chemistry beyond finding empirical support for Baeyer's strain theory. But by the time Perkin retired in 1930, he was able to bequeath to his successor, Robert Robinson, a respected and well-supported organic laboratory, albeit one staffed largely by outsiders.

Robinson was Perkin's favourite son. He had trained under him at Manchester before taking up a series of academic positions elsewhere, and he shared Perkin's research interest in the structure of natural substances, especially alkaloids and colouring matters. In comparison, he was a much more imaginative designer of experiments and was even more successful in filling his lab with researchers from all round the world: Australia, New Zealand, Sweden, Switzerland, and even Japan. In consequence, he was highly productive. Between 1931 and 1938, he and his collaborators published a paper a fortnight. The outside world thought highly of his work and in 1947 he became Oxford's second chemistry Nobel. But in an important respect, his research in the 1930s was not at the cutting edge. Robinson used the same technique of degradation and synthesis as Perkin and ignored alternative methods of analysis that were being developed, in particular turning his back on using measurements of dipole moments and X-ray crystallography. Despite Robinson's scepticism, however, both techniques were well established in Oxford by the outbreak of the Second World War. Dipole moments were championed within the Dyson Perrins itself by the Magdalen chemist Leslie Sutton, whose stint at Caltech had made him an advocate of all things new, while X-ray crystallography was gaining traction thanks to the research of the Somerville science tutor, Dorothy Hodgkin. Hodgkin, née Crowfoot, was Oxford's one significant female scientist between the wars and would eventually be awarded the Nobel Prize for Chemistry in 1964 for her contribution to understanding the structure of various complex molecules, notably vitamin B12 (see Figure 12.7). In the 1930s, she was working in the

---

[82] Soddy, in middle age, was a utopian and friend of H. G. Wells. In 1912, he published a book entitled *Matter and Theory: How Scientific Discoveries Could Produce a Garden of Eden* (1912). He was disillusioned by the Great War. See L. Merricks, *The World Made New: Frederick Soddy, Science, Politics, and Environment* (Oxford, 1996).

FIGURE 12.7 Dorothy Hodgkin, 1910–94, OM, biochemist and Nobel laureate. Hodgkin remains Oxford's only female laureate. Her research into the structure of complex molecules spanned thirty-five years and was crowned in 1969 with her discovery of the structure of insulin. Hodgkin was an anti-Imperialist and social reformer and too close to the Communist party for the Americans' liking. The photograph depicts Hodgkin with her husband in their garden.

mineralogy, not the chemistry, department, studying protein structures in a room in the University Museum. Crystallography was transferred to chemistry only in 1941 when the mineralogy department ceased to exist on the death of Professor Bowman.

Innovative chemical research, moreover, was not limited to the Science Area, for, between the wars, important work was also being conducted in the Balliol–Trinity lab (see Figure 12.8). In the 1920s, under its director H. B. Hartley, the Balliol chemistry fellow, the laboratory was home to several research programmes in physical chemistry. The one that soon became dominant was headed by Cyril Hinshelwood, the Trinity science tutor and a Hartley pupil. Hinshelwood worked on chemical kinetics or the precise mathematical description of chemical reactions, and won his own Nobel in 1956 for work carried out in 1927–8 on identifying the upper and lower limits of the pressure range at which gaseous explosions occur. He had none of the advantages of Perkin and Robinson: his facilities were poor (his two laboratories over the period had been a lavatory and a bathhouse), he could attract few foreign collaborators except Rhodes scholars, and he was immersed in undergraduate teaching. But he turned the tutorial system to his own advantage by getting fourth-year chemists to work with him on specific projects, and even extracted publishable work from two undergraduates who took Thirds in finals. Indeed, the set-up pleased him, for when he was appointed Lee's professor in 1937 he

FIGURE 12.8 The Chemistry Laboratory, Trinity College: Cyril Hinshelwood, water-colour, 1930s? Besides being one of the University's leading chemists before and after the Second World War, Hinshelwood was also a keen amateur painter. His painting of the laboratory in which he did his research shows an affection and warmth for his workplace which is clear even in a black-and-white reproduction.

moved reluctantly. Hinshelwood, more than anyone, demonstrated that under-graduate teaching and fruitful research could be successfully amalgamated.[83]

The rejuvenation of physics, on the other hand, was spearheaded by one man, Frederick Lindemann, later Lord Cherwell (see Figure 12.9).[84] Lindemann was of mixed German-American parentage and had studied at Berlin under W. H. Nernst, the German physical chemist who formulated the third law of thermodynamics. He had come to Britain at the start of the First World War and worked at the Royal Air Force Laboratory at Farnborough, where he became the first person to explain why planes could go into a fatal spin. Appointed to head the Clarendon in 1919, he was determined to turn the laboratory into a rival of the Cavendish and make Oxford the world centre for low-temperature physics, his own particular research interest. His method of doing this was singularly different from that of Oxford's other leading scientists in the interwar era. He did little active research himself after the early 1920s but concentrated on building up a team of experimentalists and finding the funds to support them. In the 1920s, he had very little success, for the low-temperature programme was stymied by his lab's inability to make the liquefier,

[83] Laidler, 'Chemical Kinetics', pp. 239–81.
[84] The standard biography is Adrian Fort, *Prof: The Life of Frederick Lindemann* (London, 2003).

FIGURE 12.9 Frederick Lindemann, 1st Viscount Cherwell, 1886–1957, CH, PC, professor of experimental philosophy and director of the Clarendon Laboratory. Lindemann held his chair for nearly forty years. A fundraiser and talent-scout rather than a creative scientist, he turned the Clarendon into one of the world's leading laboratories. During the Second World War, he was Churchill's favourite scientist and advocated the saturation bombing of German towns.

built by Nernst's head mechanic, work. As a result, the Clarendon failed to attract foreign scientists, and only the pioneering study of ozone in the upper atmosphere by G. M. B. Dobson, university lecturer in meteorology, suggested that there were glory days ahead.[85] In the 1930s, however, Lindemann's approach paid off, as he immediately realized how events in Germany could benefit Oxford science.

The rise to power of Hitler in 1933, and the removal of Jewish and left-wing intellectuals from their German university posts, opened up the possibility of bringing to Britain some of the world's leading scientists. Most of Oxford's science professors showed little interest in finding a billet for German refugees and failed to grasp the opportunity, in part a reflection of residual anti-Semitism in some quarters of the University.[86] The Freiburg biochemist Hans Krebs, for instance, was

---

[85] Dobson actually worked in his own lab on Boars Hill. He had an independent income.

[86] A few dons had fascist sympathies: Provost Lys of Worcester admired Mussolini and put him up for an honorary degree. Officially, the University was hostile to the Axis powers and in 1937 refused to send a delegation to celebrate the 200th anniversary of the foundation of Göttingen: Mitchell, *Bowra*, p. 219.

anxious to come to Oxford in 1933, wrote to Peters seeking support, and came straight to the University on his arrival in England. But Peters vacillated and Krebs went off to Cambridge where he received a warm welcome, and then to Sheffield, eventually returning to Oxford only in 1954, now a newly crowned Nobel laureate, to take up the chair in biochemistry.[87] Lindemann, in contrast, was galvanized by the possibility of augmenting his team with foreign exiles and even before the Nazi takeover had persuaded one of the leading German experts in superconductivity and superfluidity, K. A. G. Mendelssohn, who had trained at Berlin but worked in Breslau, to come to Oxford and produce the first liquid helium in Britain. In spring 1933, Lindemann went on the offensive. Having secured from ICI a promise of funding, he toured Germany in his chauffeur-driven Rolls trying to recruit Jewish experimentalists. In the end, he brought a further five to the Clarendon, including three other Breslau scientists: Mendelssohn's mentor, Franz Simon, the Hungarian Nicholas Kurti, and Heinz London, a post-doc, the first two specialists in low-temperature physics.

Lindemann also wanted to colonize Oxford with German theoretical physicists but here he was less successful. The University, with his help, had already enticed one German star into its midst when Einstein had visited Oxford in spring 1931 and lectured on relativity. In the summer of that year, it looked as if he had been captured for good when he was offered a five-year research studentship by Christ Church, to the horror of J. G. C. Anderson, professor of classical art and archaeology, who called the appointment 'unpatriotic'.[88] But Oxford was only a point of transit. Einstein was soon off to Princeton and lectured for the last time in the University in June 1933.[89] Lindemann wanted to replace him with an equally big fish, and on his visit to Germany that spring began negotiations with the Austrian Erwin Schrödinger, professor of theoretical physics at Berlin, whose expertise was the quantum theory of wave mechanics. Schrödinger was a Roman Catholic, not a Jew, but disliked the Nazis' anti-Semitism. He accepted the offer to come to Oxford and was made a fellow of Magdalen for five years in November 1933, with a small research grant. Having immediately on his arrival been awarded the Nobel, it appeared that Lindemann had bagged a winner. But he too proved a bird of passage. Schrödinger disliked living off charity and Oxford was unnerved by his unconventional domestic arrangements. In 1936, after two and a half years, he moved to Graz, though he retained some sort of association with Magdalen until 1938.[90]

[87] Hans Krebs, *Reminiscences and Reflections* (Oxford, 1981); F. L. Holmes, *Hans Krebs* (2 vols; Oxford, 1991–3). His innovatory work was principally done while a lecturer at Sheffield University.

[88] OT, 29 Mar. 2012, p. 191. The dean replied: 'Einstein's attainments and reputation are so high that they transcend national boundaries, and any university in the world ought to be proud of having him.'

[89] Paul Kent, 'Einstein at Oxford', OM, 2nd week, MT (2005), 8–10.

[90] MCA: CMR/2/1/: College *Acta*, esp. 16 May and 3 Oct. 1934. He received an annual research grant of £150. The standard biography is W.J. Moore, *Schrödinger: Life and Thought* (Cambridge, 1989). See also P. Hoch and E. J. Joxen, 'Schrödinger at Oxford: A Hypothetical National Cultural Synthesis which Failed', *Annals of Science*, 44: 6 (1987), 593–616.

Lindemann's recruits did him proud. Although only Simon, who was made a reader in 1936, got a permanent post at the University before the war and the rest relied on grants from ICI and other well-wishers, the refugees knuckled down to their reduced position and within a few years the Clarendon's status had been revolutionized. Both Simon and Mendelssohn built up productive research groups in their specialist areas and, by the late 1930s, Oxford had overtaken Leiden and Berkeley as the centre for magnetic cooling research. Another exile, Heinrich Kuhn, who had come from Göttingen, did high-quality work on experimental spectros-copy with D. A. Jackson, a self-financing member of the Clarendon lab who had been working in the field since he had come to Oxford from Cambridge in 1927. The presence of the exiles drew both foreigners and home students to the Clarendon and, on the eve of the Second World War, the laboratory supported a research team of twenty-three. It was their successful elevation of Oxford physics that, more than anything, persuaded the University of the need for a new Clarendon in 1937. Ultimately, though, none of this could have happened without Lindemann, who got no assistance from the other professor of physics, Townsend. The latter may have helped to establish a research tradition in physics before the First World War but afterwards he achieved nothing of note. Throughout the 1930s, research in the electrical laboratory chugged along on a small scale under a professor out of touch with contemporary developments. Although knighted early in 1941 for his services to science, his career came to an abrupt end a few months later when he was forced to resign or face the sack for refusing to help the war effort by teaching servicemen.

Oxford's emergence as a centre of scientific research was not simply the work of a small group of innovative and entrepreneurial professors, readers, and tutors. The fact that the leading lights of interwar Oxford science were headhunted from outside is evidence that the University, even before the First World War, was aiming to raise its game, while the report of the Asquith Commission confirmed that the state viewed this as a national necessity. Individuals counted, as Soddy's limp contribution emphasized, but Oxford's research scientists were working with the grain of the times. The distance travelled between the wars should not be oversold. In 1939 Cambridge was still the most significant centre of scientific research in Britain by a long margin, just as there were many other British universities with a solid research tradition. Without the University of Manchester, Oxford chemistry would never have taken off. There again, Oxford's progress was impressive. Oxford in 1939 might only have been ranked fifth in terms of the number of staff it employed in science and technology; it was out-trumped by London, Cambridge, Manchester, and Leeds.[91] But it had raised its science research profile while remaining predominantly an arts university and without even increasing the proportion of the undergraduate body reading a science. This made it unique among Britain's institutions of higher education of the day.

---

[91] Oxford had 119 scientists in post against Cambridge's 186.

E. The University Press and Research

Oxford's emergence as a research university in the first half of the twentieth century was greatly assisted by the continual expansion of its University Press. In 1845, the Press had few academic rivals: most universities had printers but few their own printing house. A hundred years later this was no longer the case, and the Press could quickly have lost its pre-eminence. But thanks to energetic oversight by a series of secretaries to the delegates, in particular 'Bat' Price (1868–84) and Charles Cannan (1898–1919),[92] good management, and a readiness to seize the main chance, the Press rose to the challenge. As early as 1896 it was employing 800 people in its offices, printing house, bindery, foundry, warehouse, and paper mill, and by the 1930s it was publishing 200 new titles a year.[93] Between the wars, the Press's position as the world's leader in academic publishing went unchallenged. It was also a global business. Not only was the Press selling its books all round the world, but in North America and the British Empire it had established its own relatively autonomous branches with a licence to print as well as distribute. OUP New York was opened in 1896; OUP Canada and Australia in 1904 and 1908; and OUP India and South Africa in 1912 and 1915. Cambridge, too, had its own thriving press during the period. But its overall output was small beer compared with Oxford's and its only major overseas outlet was in North America.[94]

As in the first centuries of its history, OUP continued to be two businesses, the one dealing with a mass market, the other the provision of learned books with limited appeal. By 1900, however, they were much more integrated. In 1862, the partnership that ran the Bible business took over the management of the learned press as well.[95] Then, in the following year, the Delegates appointed the London publisher Alexander Macmillan to head up the publishing side of the Press's operations and offer advice on commercial expansion. This he did with aplomb for the next seventeen years, until he was summarily dismissed in 1880 for being too independent and using Oxford's name to promote his own business ventures.[96] At this juncture, the Delegates decided that they wanted to bring the Press much more under their direct control. In 1881 they dissolved the Bible partnership and, for the first time in the University's history, took charge of both sides of the Press's activities. Thereafter, the Bible and learned presses were gradually merged, although the reorganization was not fully completed until 1905–7, when the Oxford printing

---

[92] Until 1897, a tutor at Trinity.

[93] Paper-making and book-binding were new ventures for the Press taken up at the beginning of the period. The Press controlled the paper mill at Wolvercote from 1855 and totally owned it from 1871. It had its own bindery from 1867. The Wolvercote mill was never able to meet all the Press's demand for paper.

[94] David McKitterick, *A History of Cambridge University Press*, vol. 3. *New Worlds for Learning, 1873–1972* (Cambridge, 2004), chs 6–7, 9, and 12–13.

[95] For the partnership, see p. 319, this volume.

[96] He had done this to effect with the publication of *Alice's Adventures in Wonderland* in 1865. Its author, Charles Dodgson, aka Lewis Carroll, was mathematics tutor at Christ Church, and his children's book had come out under the Oxford imprint. But Macmillan had borne the production and distribution costs and shared the profits with the author.

house assumed responsibility for printing all titles that appeared under the Press's name, and the newly christened London Business was given the task of binding as well as distributing its books. The books produced by the Oxford printing house were always of a high quality. Prior to the First World War, the works became much more efficient, with electrification and the introduction of Linotype and Monotype composing machines, but this never led to quality being sacrificed for profit. When the Delegates, towards the end of the period, so much as hinted that greater attention should be paid to the bottom line, John Johnson, the University's printer from 1925 to 1946, fought tooth and nail to maintain traditional standards.[97]

Even before the end of the nineteenth century, the commercial side of the business no longer limited its activities to selling Bibles and prayer books. In an era of rising population and imperial expansion, the market for Bibles and prayer books remained strong, and the University continued to benefit from its privileged position in the market.[98] But profits began to decline from the 1860s, as Oxford and the other Bible publishers cut the unit cost in response to the demand from Bible societies for cheaper versions, and the Bible press was forced to diversify to stay in the black.[99] One money-spinner was the publication of a new translation of the Bible, sponsored by the Convocation of the Church of England, for which Oxford and Cambridge were given the copyright. So successful was the Revised Version which appeared in 1881 and 1885 that, by the end of the century, sales of Bibles and prayer books topped the 3 million mark.[100] More important for the future, however, was the decision in the mid-1860s to move into educational publishing. The Press, in the first half of the nineteenth century, had overseen the publication of classical texts for the use of undergraduates, but it had taken a very limited interest in producing schoolbooks. The introduction of nationwide school-leaving examinations from the 1860s inevitably encouraged curricular standardization, and the Press sensed an opportunity.[101] The Delegates established a School-Book Committee as early as November 1863, and two years later the Press published its first textbook, A. W. Williamson's *Chemistry for Students*. Thereafter, the Clarendon Press Series, as it became known, expanded quickly. Between 1865 and 1900, 861 works appeared under its label. A third were classical texts, but there was a respectable number of works in French and German, a clutch of high-quality science books, a few historical works, and a large collection of English literature from the middle ages to the Romantics.

---

[97] As a result, despite the monopoly that the printing house theoretically held, many Press books from the beginning of the twentieth century were not printed there. The house had to bid against other printers for the Press's business and was undercut. Johnson had not had a printer's training but was an Oxford papyrologist. He was an inveterate collector of ephemera, which was given to the Bodleian when he died.

[98] From the 1630s, Oxford was one of the few publishers allowed to print Bibles: see p. 319, this volume.

[99] The Society for the Promotion of Christian Knowledge and the British and Foreign Bible Society existed to bring the good news to the poor and the heathen and wanted cheap, lightweight, small-format Bibles and prayer books.

[100] A number of Oxford theologians helped in the translation.

[101] For Oxford's role in the creation of school-leaving examinations, see p. 536, this volume.

Educational publishing by the beginning of the twentieth century was a crowded field and the series thereafter stagnated. The impetus, however, was not lost, for the Press's burgeoning commercial department found new markets to exploit. The Press showed its continued commitment to serving the needs of schoolchildren and university students studying classics by launching the highly successful Oxford Classical Texts in 1898, and continuing to provide them with dictionaries and grammars, including the evergreen Liddell and Scott and its Latin equivalent, Lewis and Short, first published in 1879.[102] In the 1930s, the Press also moved into the niche but expanding market of learning English as a second language when it produced its first Oxford English Course, constructed so it could be adapted for use anywhere in the world. But the Press's main commercial target in the first part of the twentieth century was the middle-class reader at home. In 1900, the Press became a presence in the lucrative anthology market by bringing out the *Oxford Book of English Verse*, edited by Arthur Quiller-Couch, the first of many ever more specialized collections with which the Press flooded the bookshops in the coming decades.[103] Then, in 1906, it took its first steps into the potentially more extensive market for European and English prose literature by buying the World's Classics Series from the bankrupt firm of Grant Richards. By the end of the period, the Press had found a further way of quenching the middle-class thirst for English-language literature by offering useful contextual and biographical information about authors and their works in the form of the literary companion. The first, the *Oxford Companion to English Literature*, penned by Sir Paul Harvey and precursor to many others, appeared in 1932.[104] Nor were the middle-classes' children forgotten. As early as 1907, the Press did a deal with Hodder & Stoughton to publish books for a younger reader-ship. Children's books were a leap in the dark, but in the 1930s the Press struck gold with the 'Biggles' novels of W. E. Johns. Oxford dons might be wearying of the rhetoric of duty and sacrifice that they had embraced with enthusiasm before 1914, but the Press was happy to publish an author who claimed his books taught 'the spirit of teamwork, loyalty to the Crown, the Empire, and to rightful authority'.[105]

The aim of the learned press continued to be to place before the public works of scholarship and science that would, at best, break even. As in previous centuries, the majority of the works it published were by scholars and scientists who were either Oxford-educated or college fellows, but the list quickly ceased to be dominated by classics and theology and, by the end of the period, covered most academic

---

[102] Lewis and Short began life as a dictionary prepared in the United States for an American publisher. The Press also published an extremely successful, if racist and jingoistic, school history in Charles Fletcher and Rudyard Kipling's *History of England*, which appeared in 1911 in a print run of 25,000. It was reprinted until 1950.

[103] It went through twenty-one impressions and had sold half a million copies by 1939. Quiller-Couch had been an undergraduate at Trinity, Oxford. After a career as a journalist and writer, he became professor of English literature at Cambridge in 1912.

[104] The author was a diplomat. In 1935 he was responsible for the *Oxford Companion to Classical Literature*.

[105] Ron Heapy, 'Children's Books', in W. Roger Louis (ed.), *The History of Oxford University Press*, vol. 3: *1896–1970* (Oxford, 2013), p. 475. The Press also became involved in music publishing with the opening of its music department in the early 1920s. Composers on its list include Walton, Vaughan Williams. and the young Benjamin Britten.

disciplines except law and the social sciences. Theological publications also ceased to be only Anglican in orientation. By 1900, the Press was publishing works of the new biblical criticism that Pusey and the Tractarians had so despised,[106] as well as key meditations on religion by prominent non-conformists, such as the Unitarian James Martineau, for forty-five years professor at Manchester College.[107]

Before the First World War, the Press mainly published scholarly editions and translations of texts, linguistic dictionaries, and collections of edited documents or personal letters. Sometimes the publications formed part of a series. In 1875, the philologist Friedrich Müller was appointed to edit a collection of translations of key non-Christian religious texts, known as Sacred Books of the East, which eventually extended to forty-nine volumes.[108] Usually, the Press published isolated works of scholarship. Typical examples were Skeat's *Complete Works of Chaucer* (1894–5), Payne Smith's Latin–Syriac dictionary (1868–91), and P. S. Allen's edition of the correspondence of Erasmus, which began to come out in 1906 and was finally concluded in 1958.[109] When such publications occasionally sold well, they did so because they found an undergraduate as well as a scholarly audience. William Stubbs' *Select Charters*, published by the Press in 1870, was initially taken on as a contribution to historical scholarship. But, as was noted in section C of this chapter,[110] it became a staple of the new modern history curriculum and was constantly revised and updated. As a result, it had gone through eight editions by 1895.

In emphasizing scholarly editions and dictionaries, the Press, before 1914, was continuing in a time-honoured tradition. If its output was now much larger than hitherto and the concept of authors' books had all but disappeared, the learned press was still locked in a publishing policy laid down in the age of John Fell. Significantly, in contrast to its Cambridge rival, it made little attempt to get into the fast-developing academic journal market beyond taking on the *Annals of Botany* in 1887. Even publishing the papers of learned societies was deemed beyond its remit unless they were local, like the Oxford Historical Society, founded in 1884.[111]

After 1914, the Press continued to be chary of academic journals but began to spread its wings and invest more heavily in specialized monographs, especially in history and literature. This development was crucial in cementing Oxford's reputation as a centre for research in the humanities. Many authors were not based in the University, as was the case with the formidable literary scholar E. K. Chambers, whose *The Elizabethan Stage* and *Shakespeare: A Study of Facts and Problems*, were published by the Press in 1923 and 1930. The fact, though, that authors both inside

---

[106] See p. 329, this volume.

[107] In 1888–9 and 1900 the Press brought out his two-volume *Study of Religion*.

[108] Some caused controversy because they appeared to favour oriental religions over Christianity, and there was never a translation of the Koran.

[109] W. W. Skeat was the Cambridge professor of Anglo-Saxon; Robert Payne Smith was a previous Oxford regius professor of divinity; and Allen was a former undergraduate at Corpus Christi, Oxford, and fellow of Merton from 1908.

[110] See pp. 500–1, this volume

[111] The first work published for the OHS was *Register of the University of Oxford*, vol. 1, ed. Revd C. W. Boase (1885).

and outside the University published their research under the OUP imprint, suggested that Oxford was at the cutting edge of contemporary debate.[112] The value of the new initiative was all the greater in that some works were immediately recognized to be revolutionary. This was true of Frank Stenton's *The First Century of English Feudalism, 1066–1166*, which appeared in 1932; it was also true of Ronald Syme's *The Roman Revolution*, published seven years later. A book that turned its back on the usual constitutionalist approach to the fall of the Roman Republic in favour of a Namierite study of family connections, it completely transformed the subject.[113]

For the Press's history list, the 1930s was a particularly important decade, with the decision to launch a fourteen-volume *Oxford History of England* edited by the Oriel fellow G. N. Clark. The Press had previously shied away from a similar series and the lead had been taken by other publishers, including Cambridge, whose *Cambridge Modern History*, covering Europe and the world in the period 1450–1910, had appeared between 1902 and 1912. In 1929, however, the Press finally bit the bullet. The books in the series were supposed to pay serious attention to social and economic history as well as political history and foreign policy, but otherwise they were conceived as stand-alone single-authored volumes, in contrast to Cambridge's multi-authored approach. Clark got together a strong team, consisting of Oxford-educated historians or classicists, and the series soon began to appear. Clark's own on the later Stuarts was published in 1934, and a further six volumes had been published by 1939.[114]

The interwar years also saw a much greater commitment to publishing in the natural sciences. Before 1914, the Press had put out in translation a number of important German works on physiology and zoology, such as August Weismann's *Essays upon Heredity and Kindred Biological Problems* in 1889.[115] But the only significant works that it had published by British scientists were James Clerk Maxwell's *Treatise on Electricity and Magnetism* (1873) and J. J. Thomson's *Notes on Recent Researches in Electricity and Magnetism* (1893).[116] Oxford's heightened commitment to scientific research in the 1920s and 1930s was soon reflected in the Press's list. The natural sciences remained under-represented among its learned publications until the second half of the twentieth century, but the bias was less pronounced, and the Press, for the first time, agreed to set up a number of science series, albeit with mixed

---

[112] Chambers had been educated at Corpus Christi, Oxford, but was a career civil servant at the Board of Education.

[113] Stenton was professor of history at Reading; the book started out as the Ford lectures for 1929. Syme was a fellow of Trinity, Oxford, when he wrote the book; he later became the Camden professor of ancient history. For Namier's prosopographical approach, see p. 502, this volume.

[114] Brian Harrison, '"An Ambitious Venture": Oxford University Press and *The Oxford History of England*', in S. J. Brown, F. Knight, and J. Morgan-Guy (eds), *Religion, Identity and Conflict in Britain: From the Restoration to the Twentieth Century. Essays in Honour of Keith Robbins* (Farnham, 2013), pp. 233–60. Oddly, given Oxford's strength in the subject, the Press did not commission an ancient history series. This was left to Cambridge.

[115] The inspiration behind their publication was Burdon-Sanderson, Waynflete professor of physiology. Weismann, often considered second only to Darwin as an evolutionary biologist, was professor at Freiburg im Breisgau.

[116] Neither, of course, were Oxford men. Maxwell held chairs at Aberdeen and King's, London, Thomson at Cambridge.

results. The attempt by Julian Huxley of New College and D. L. Hammick of Oriel to develop a Clarendon Science Series proved disappointing—only five volumes were published between 1923 and 1935, although one was the important *Animal Biology* by J. B. S. Haldane (1927).[117] But the Press had much better fortune with the International Series of Monographs on Physics, proposed by two fellows of Trinity, Cambridge, in 1927. The high quality of the series was set from the beginning. The first volume to appear was P. A. M. Dirac's *Principles of Quantum Mechanics* in 1930.[118]

The Press's new interest, between the wars, in monograph publication did not curtail its traditional commitment to editions and dictionaries, which continued to appear apace. Indeed, it was not until 1928 that the Press brought to fruition its most ambitious and extensive excursion into lexicography, the *Oxford English Dictionary*. This had been conceived as early as 1857 and had been initially patronized by the Philological Society. The Press took over the project in 1879 and the first fascicle appeared in 1884. The *OED* was a mammoth undertaking that pulled in large numbers of people besides the editorial team led by Sir James Murray. It was perhaps the world's first experiment in crowdsourcing.[119] According to Cannan, writing to Murray in 1905, the *Dictionary* was probably 'the largest single engine of research working anywhere in the world'.[120] It was only possible because the Press was willing to commit large sums of money, drawn from its commercial profits, to keep the project going. Understandably, the Press was quick to look for a return on its heavy investment and soon produced the *Shorter OED* in 1933 for the educated reader, and updated new editions of its earlier dictionaries the *Concise*, *Pocket*, and *Little Oxford*.[121] But the *OED* was not a one-off. It was a reflection of a growing belief of the Delegates that the Press existed to promote and sustain scholarly projects of national importance which would otherwise never see the light of day because of their cost and complexity. For this reason, in 1917, the Press accepted the gift of the *Dictionary of National Biography* (1885–1900), formerly published by Smith, Elder, and agreed to provide ten-yearly supplements. It also underpinned new and commercially unviable publishing projects: in 1933, it gave the lexicographer and Oxford don C. T. Onions, who had just finished overseeing the preparation of the *Shorter OED*, the awesome task of compiling the *Oxford Dictionary of English Etymology*, which was only completed in 1966.[122]

The Press, from the late nineteenth century, was therefore not just a publisher of academic research but a sponsor and patron of learning in its own right. It was as much an Oxford research institution as the Clarendon Laboratory, and by 1939

[117] Haldane, at that juncture, was reader in biochemistry at Cambridge.
[118] Dirac of Cambridge would share the Nobel Prize with Schrödinger in 1933. Another successful series was in engineering science, set up in 1932.
[119] Simon Winchester, *The Surgeon of Crowthorne: A Tale of Madness, Murder and the Meaning of Words* (London, 1998); Simon Winchester, *The Meaning of Everything: The Story of the Oxford English Dictionary* (Oxford, 2003). Murray had been a schoolteacher and a banker.
[120] Alan Bell, 'Scholarly and Reference Publishing', in Louis, *Oxford University Press*, p. 328.
[121] The *Concise* and *Pocket* appeared in 1911 and 1924.
[122] Onions had worked on the *OED* with Murray from 1895.

it was vitally important in sustaining the University's credentials as a centre of scholarship. It would continue to play this productive supporting role throughout the six years of disruption that followed the outbreak of the Second World War. Paper during these years was rationed, labour was scarce, and all but 5 per cent of the Press's output was war work. But it continued to publish a reduced number of academic books, such as Stenton's *Anglo-Saxon England* in 1943, and it was able to provide financial assistance to several world-class scholars, rendered stateless by Nazi tyranny.[123]

F. The Second World War

As a result of the growth of Oxford science, the University was ready, as war clouds gathered for a second time, to play its part in defeating the enemy in the laboratory. The role of Oxford scientists in winning the First World War was minimal. War work went on in various laboratories relating to dyes, drugs, and methods of countering poison gas. But only the professor of pathology, Georges Dreyer, made a significant contribution when he showed that the 'enteric fever' suffered by troops at the front was paratyphoid not typhoid, and persuaded the War Office to inoculate against the disease. Some Oxford scientists did leave the University to work in government establishments but their number was few. Townsend's laboratory supplied eight of its research team, but the Clarendon only one. Many of those who left, moreover, were lost to Oxford for good, such as the tutorial fellow of Oriel, Henry Tizard, who had studied along with Lindemann under Nernst in Berlin. Judged to be one of Oxford's scientific hopes for the future, Tizard did return temporarily from work with the air force, but was soon lured away to study the detonation characteristics of different engine fuels at a private laboratory at Shoreham. After the war, he became a scientific civil servant, then rector of Imperial College in 1929, and spent the 1930s helping to coordinate Britain's air defences.[124] The Second World War was very different. While the classicists, historians, mathematicians, and philosophers, such as Gilbert Ryle, disappeared to Bletchley Park and different government ministries, most scientists stayed put and got on with research that would help the war effort.

In the main, the contribution of Oxford scientists to defeating the Nazis was solid rather than spectacular. Every department did its bit, but most did nothing that stands out with hindsight. The work of Peters' biochemistry laboratory is a case in point. During the war Peters and his colleagues did research in a variety of areas: the treatment of burns; the blood signature of the anti-malarial, mecrapine; nutrition (especially into the amount of vitamin C that humans required); and the effects of toxic substances. In the end, however, if the biochemists did sterling service, they

---

[123] Stenton's book was part of the *Oxford History of England* series.
[124] R. W. Clark, *Tizard* (London, 1965). He later came back to Oxford as president of Magdalen, his original college.

FIGURE 12.10 Sir Howard Florey, 1898–1968, OM, life peer, co-developer of penicillin, Nobel Prize winner, and provost of Queen's: portrait by Henry Carr, 1968. After studying medicine at Adelaide, Florey came to Oxford as a Rhodes scholar but took his PhD at Cambridge. In 1941, the first person to be treated by Florey and his team with penicillin died because the dose administered was insufficient, so the initial trial was conducted on children who could be cured with a smaller amount.

had only one noteworthy achievement: the development by Peters and two of his colleagues of dimercaptopropanol (or BAL: British Anti-Lewisite), a drug that countered the severe dermatitis resulting from treating venereal disease with arsenotherapy.[125] This was important but hardly earth-shattering. In this regard, only two of Oxford's departments could be placed in the top league: the Dunn School of Pathology and the Clarendon.

The Dunn School of Pathology had been revitalized as a research centre with the appointment of the Australian Rhodes scholar Howard Florey as professor in 1935 (see Figure 12.10). Florey, a protégé of Sherrington, had several projects on the go before the outbreak of the war, but the one that proved particularly fruitful was his investigation of lysozyme, an enzyme found in mucus that was known to neutralize certain bacteria. By 1940 a team led by Ernst Chain, a Jewish refugee who had come to Oxford in the year that Florey took up his chair, had identified how the enzyme worked and had begun to work on other non-toxic anti-bacterial substances,

---

[125] Lloyd A. Stocken and Margery Ord, 'The Department in Wartime, 1939–1945' (unpublished paper). For the biochemistry department's work on nutrition, see J. Ewin, *Fine Wines and Fish Oil: The Life of Hugh Macdonald Sinclair* (Oxford, 2001).

notably penicillin. The potential of penicillin had been suggested by Alexander Fleming, professor of bacteriology at the University of London, in a paper published in 1929, and when the Scot's work came to Chain's notice early in 1938, he immediately grasped its importance. Florey's entrepreneurial skills in securing funding from the Rockefeller Foundation ensured the penicillin project was up and running by the outbreak of the war. His managerial flair, too, ensured that the team he had brought together continued to work effectively in the early years of the war and could undertake the first small-scale clinical trial at the Radcliffe Infirmary. By July 1941, research had advanced to the stage where a small quantity of the new purified and stabilized drug could be taken to the United States and the process of mass manufacture begun. In consequence, when the allies landed in France in June 1944, the invasion force had sufficient penicillin to save the lives of many of the wounded. Oxford's association with the therapeutic revolution, moreover, did not finish with the work of the Dunn School. In 1945, the year when Florey and Chain shared with Fleming the Nobel Prize for Medicine in recognition of their research, Dorothy Hodgkin identified the structure of penicillin.

The Clarendon's significant contribution came through its limited role in the theoretical and experimental work lying behind the invention of the atomic bomb. Lindemann wanted the University to become a leader in nuclear as well as low-temperature physics but he had little success in establishing a research team from Jewish exiles. The Hungarian nuclear physicist Leó Szilárd had been brought over in 1935 with a promise of a three-year grant from ICI, but he had left for America in 1938, while a possible replacement, the Austrian Lise Meitner—who had been working with Otto Hahn, the 'father of nuclear chemistry', on nuclear fission in Berlin—had gone off to Stockholm instead. At the beginning of the war, therefore, Oxford was not the obvious place in which to establish the British government's programme to build an atomic bomb, and the Maud Committee, in 1940, gave the work to Birmingham, Liverpool, and Cambridge. Initially, too, Lindemann did not attempt to bring the Clarendon into the project. Lindemann was a long-term friend and ally of Churchill, and when the latter was created First Lord of the Admiralty at the beginning of the war, he made the Oxford professor his personal scientific adviser. The Clarendon was immediately handed over to the navy for war work, and the majority of the researchers in the laboratory spent the war designing and developing microwave radar for aircraft and ships. The foreign members of the Clarendon, however, were not allowed to participate in the research for security reasons, and offered their services, unofficially, to colleagues in other universities working on the nuclear programme. Thereby, Simon, Kurti, Kuhn, and Arms (one of Simon's DPhil students) came to play a leading part in perfecting the diffusion method of separating isotopes of uranium, work undertaken in part in the Jesus laboratory. Later in the war all four went off to the States to join the Manhattan Project, though only one Oxford physicist, J. L. Tuck, an import from Manchester working before the war on electron acceleration, was employed at Los Alamos making the bomb.

The pressure of war completely skewed the traditional balance of Oxford's research effort. The research of the University's postholders in the arts and social sciences came to a virtual halt, as even the dons left permanently in Oxford, and not just returning from time to time, were frequently caught up in war work of some kind. The socialist G. D. H. Cole, for instance, was made director of the Nuffield College Social Reconstruction Survey in November 1940 and spent the next three years, until the treasury grant ran out, organizing private conferences on issues relating to trade, employment, and education. Yet research into the humanities and social sciences did not completely atrophy with the outbreak of war. The spread of Nazi and fascist tyranny across the continent brought scholars in the arts to the University, as well as refugee scientists. German exiles had helped to rejuvenate Oxford science in the 1930s; now refugees from the Axis powers and Franco's Spain helped to keep research in the arts alive during the Second World War.[126]

Gilbert Murray had been as keen as Lindemann to bring Jewish or non-Aryan scholars to Britain,[127] and he quickly became involved with the nationwide Society for the Protection of Science and Learning that was set up in May 1933 through the efforts of Sir William Beveridge, then director of the LSE, but from 1937 master of University College.[128] Settling refugee arts scholars in Oxford, however, was more difficult than finding billets for scientists who could attract funding from companies like ICI. The LSE immediately urged its academic staff to give a small proportion of their salary to an Academic Assistance Fund that could support less biddable exiles, but Oxford initially made no such move and its contribution to sheltering refugees was minimal. In the two years that followed the Nazi takeover only six displaced scholars with an arts background found some sort of home in Oxford.

Five were taken in by colleges. One, the 60-year old international lawyer Albrecht Mendelssohn Bartholdy, was made a fellow of Balliol, thanks to his friendship with Lindsay. Two others, the historian of ideas Ernst Cassirer, who had formerly been a professor of philosophy at Hamburg, and Jacob Marschak, the so-called father of econometrics, spent 1933–5 as lecturers of All Souls.[129] A fourth, the educationalist Elisabeth Blochmann, was made tutor in German at Lady Margaret Hall;[130] while the fifth, the philosopher Raymond Klibansky, was given common room rights at Oriel.[131] The last of the six, the extremely prestigious classical scholar Eduard Fraenkel, late of Freiburg, was the only one to step almost immediately into a permanent university post when he was elected to the chair of Latin, attached to

---

[126] Their story is told collectively and individually in Sally Crawford and Katharina Ulmschneider (eds), *Ark of Civilisation* (forthcoming).

[127] In Germany, non-Aryan was the Nazi term for Christians of Jewish descent or tainted by Jewishness.

[128] Until 1936 the society was called the Academic Defence Council. For a general account, see Norman Bentwich, *Rescue and Achievement of Refugee Scholars* (The Hague, 1953).

[129] OUA, PSL/3/file 1/no. 10: warden of All Souls to Vice-Chancellor, 30 Jan. 1939. Cassirer moved on to Gothenburg before migrating to the United States; Marschak became the first director of Oxford's new Institute of Statistics.

[130] Blochmann had been professor of social and theoretical pedagogy at Halle.

[131] OUA, UR6, PSL/3/file 1/no. 21: provost of Oriel to Vice-Chancellor, 30 Jan. 1939. Klibansky was a specialist in ancient Greek philosophy who had been a lecturer at Heidelberg.

FIGURE 12.11 Eduard Fraenkel, 1888–1970, Jewish exile, professor of Latin and renovator of Oxford classics: photograph. As professor of Latin, Fraenkel brought a Germanic rigour to the philological analysis of classical texts. His painstaking, line-by-line exegesis in his seminars was proverbial. He was no dry-as-dust scholar, however. Although totally dependent on his wife—he committed suicide immediately following her death—he had been a notorious ladies' man in middle age.

Corpus Christi, at the end of 1934 (see Figure 12.11). Fraenkel's election was a coup but it might easily not have happened. The Plautus scholar had been keen to settle in Oxford, given its traditional reputation in his discipline, and had initially been given a handout of £50 by Corpus in August 1934. Almost immediately, however, he had been offered a fellowship at Trinity College, Cambridge, and it looked as if Oxford had lost him. Luckily, the Latin chair was vacant and the electors, thanks above all to a powerful letter of support from the Cambridge Latin professor, A. E. Housman, were moved to recommend his appointment.[132]

The situation improved rapidly in 1938–9 when several colleges finally decided to contribute to the Society for the Protection of Science and Learning by offering to provide grants to support academic refugees, regardless of their standing, and asking the society to nominate beneficiaries. Under the prompting of Vice-Chancellor George Gordon, a keen advocate of assisting exiles from the continent, these individual initiatives quickly gave way to a university-wide assistance programme, and an Oxford Committee for Refugee Scholars was set up in February

---

[132] Stephanie West, 'Eduard Fraenkel Recalled', in Stray, *Oxford Classics*, pp. 204–5 and 207; OUA, UR6, PSL/3/file 1/no. 21, nos 28 and 28A: president of Corpus to Vice-Chancellor, 1 Feb. 1934; Corpus Christi College Archives, MS 551/A.I.2, no numbering: Hugh Last to Fraenkel, 13 Aug. 1934. There was some internal opposition to Fraenkel's appointment.

1939 to coordinate the response.[133] All parts of the University were encouraged to do their bit, with the result that, instead of the half-dozen or so who had originally found shelter in Oxford, the number of refugee scholars in the humanities and the social sciences supported during the war years rose to forty or fifty. Most survived through charity. Either a college or a number of colleges agreed to provide the £200 a year thought necessary to keep an exiled scholar in modest comfort, or funds were found from an external source. The former professor of Roman history at Turin, Arnaldo Momigliano, already famous in Oxford for his seminal biography of the Emperor Claudius, was eventually maintained on a grant from the Rockefeller Foundation. But a minority, usually the most prestigious scholars, were more fully integrated into Oxford life by being given employment. Several were found jobs in the Bodleian or at the University Press. The rest found a billet in a college. Only one of the new arrivals, the Austrian Byzantine musicologist and composer Egon Wellesz, looked after by Lincoln, became a fellow.[134] The others were given college lectureships, so that they could cover the gap in teaching left by tutors away on war work: Merton employed the Roman lawyer Fritz Pringsheim, formerly of Freiburg;[135] Corpus the Callimachus scholar Rudolf Pfeiffer.[136]

However sustained, the scholars exiled in Oxford during the war were all engaged in original research. Indeed, this was a condition of their support. Those who were relatively junior academics often registered for a DPhil, like the historian Franz Carsten, who came to Oxford in 1939 from Berlin by way of Amsterdam, and was maintained at Wadham on a newly founded senior scholarship worth £150 per annum. Carsten had been working as a private scholar on the manorial economy of north-east Germany, and once in Oxford registered for a doctorate. By 1942, despite a short spell as an internee (the fate of most of Oxford's refugees), he successfully submitted his thesis and won the Royal Historical Society's Alexander Prize.[137] The senior exiles got on with their specialist studies, frequently bringing lasting benefits to future Oxford scholars as they did so. Paul Kahle, formerly professor of oriental philosophy at Bonn, continued his pioneering work on the history of the Hebrew text of the Old Testament, while being employed by the Bodleian to perfect its catalogue of Arabic manuscripts. The Königsberg Hellenist Paul Maas, an expert on Greek poetry, who had escaped from Germany at the last minute, was taken on by the Press as an editorial consultant and helped to complete the latest revision of

---

[133] OUA, UR 6/PSL/2, file 1, no. 18: Council minute, 13 Feb. 1939.

[134] He was a Christian of Jewish descent.

[135] Pringsheim's time at Oxford in discussed at length in Tony Honoré, 'Fritz Pringsheim (1882–1967)', in Jack Beatson and Reinhard Zimmermann (eds), *Jurists Uprooted: German-Speaking Emigré Lawyers in Twentieth-Century Britain* (Oxford, 2004), pp. 206–28. Pringsheim was not dismissed until 1936 because of his war record. He did not find living in Oxford agreeable.

[136] Pfeiffer lost his post at Munich in 1937 because he was married to a Jew. Klibansky also had a lectureship at Oriel.

[137] *The College Record* [Wadham] (Jan. 1999), p. 75 (reference supplied by Cliff Davies). A few younger refugees had registered as advanced students immediately after the Nazi takeover. The philosopher Theodor Adorno, for instance, spent the years 1933–6 at Merton working on a book on Husserl under the supervision of Gilbert Ryle.

Liddell and Scott.[138] The archaeologist Paul Jacobsthal, who arrived in Oxford from Marburg in 1937 and was employed by Christ Church as a college lecturer, handsomely repaid his host's investment by crowning his stay with the publication of his seminal *Early Celtic Art* in 1944.[139] Above all, Felix Jacoby was able to spend the war beavering away at his monumental collection of text fragments of the Greek historians, which had first begun to appear in print in 1923. Jacoby, originally a professor at Keil, had arrived in England in 1939 and at first had had to earn a living by giving tutorials and lectures. Thanks to the generosity of Christ Church and OUP, however, he was able to devote his time completely to research.[140]

Wellesz, Pfeiffer, Blochmann, and Jacobsthal followed Fraenkel into permanent Oxford jobs when the war was over.[141] All the other historians, literary scholars, and social scientists, had to move on. Some, like Kahle, went back to Germany.[142] Others, especially the younger ones, found positions in British or American universities: Carsten took up a lectureship at London's Westfield College in 1947, while Momigliano, after initially going back to Turin, gained a post at Bristol before becoming professor of ancient history at UCL in 1951 and enjoying a new career as an authority on the history of historiography. But wherever they ended up, they left a permanent mark on the humanities at Oxford. The handful of big fish netted in the 1930s had a specific impact on the study of ancient texts and artefacts. Fraenkel's presence revolutionized Oxford's classical scholarship: his textual rigour, exemplified in his multi-volume edition of Aeschylus' *Agamemnon*, which appeared in 1950, made even Gilbert Murray blanch. More importantly, the wartime refugees, in general, simply by their numbers and presence, broke down the erstwhile insularity of Oxford's arts faculties. The University's leading scientific research teams in the 1930s contained representatives from all over the globe, and many of the professors had spent time on the continent or in America, even if few were foreign nationals. Oxford's arts faculties attracted second BAs and some postgraduates from the Empire and the USA. But there were few postholders who had any experience of the academic world outside the University: they were nearly all British by birth, protestant by background, and public-school and Oxford educated. Isaiah Berlin, a Jew born in Riga, was exceptional only in his religion and native

---

[138] Bowra, *Memories*, p. 300; OUA, UR6/PSL/2/file 1, nos 111–26, various letters March to April 1940 concerning Maas' financial position and the plight of his Danish protestant wife, still abroad.

[139] The book remains the standard text on the subject. In January 2012, Jacobsthal's experiences as a refugee were the subject of an exhibition at Oxford's City Museum: 'Persecution and Survival: A Wartime Refugee Story'.

[140] Jacoby also received support from several university trust funds: see OUA, UR6 PSL/1/file 1, no. 149, letter, H. T. Wade-Gery (professor of ancient history) to the Vice-Chancellor, *c.* June 1945: account of Jacoby's income during the war. Jacoby was a Christian convert who had actually voted for Hitler. His *Die Fragmente der griechischen Historiker*, although still unfinished at his death, is considered one of the greatest feats of Hellenist scholarship of the twentieth century.

[141] Jacoby never became a postholder but continued to be looked after by Christ Church and the Lit. Hum. board until the mid-1950s, when he received a German pension. Wellesz held a lectureship in the newly established faculty of music set up in 1944, which he had largely helped to found.

[142] Pfeiffer and Blochmann, too, eventually returned home.

land.[143] The refugees invigorated the arts faculties with a huge breath of continental air that savoured of different university systems and scholarly traditions. St John's even harboured a former professor at the Sorbonne, Claude Schaeffer, a distinguished Middle East archaeologist and officer in the Free French Navy, who had escaped to England in 1941.[144]

The humanities at Oxford were never the same again, all the more so that, as the elder generation of refugees moved on, a younger cohort, who had come to Britain in their teens and thought themselves British, but had a much more international perspective, moved in. The future holder of the Chichele chair in medieval history, Karl Leyser, came to England in the mid-1930s, when he was 17, and finished his education at St Paul's before coming up to Oxford. Although he had fought in the Black Watch during the war, his Britishness only went so far. When he became a postgraduate after the war, he initially started work on the Good Parliament of Edward III's reign. But once elected a fellow of Magdalen in 1950, he defied tradition and insisted on doing research into medieval Germany rather than cutting his teeth, like his peers, on the English late middle ages.[145]

---

[143] Only two of Magdalen's forty-three fellows in 1938–9 had been born abroad and only one was a graduate of a foreign university. Bowra, more mobile than most humanities' dons, spent time at Harvard just before the war; *Memories*, ch. 13.

[144] Mabbott, *Memories*, p. 111.   [145] Information from Roger Highfield of Merton.

Conclusion

Oxford in Context

THE University of Oxford at the end of the Second World War was a very different institution from its namesake of a hundred years before. Student numbers had expanded almost fivefold and women had been admitted, while the undergraduate curriculum had been greatly broadened, its teaching enriched by the development of the tutorial system, and its organization entrusted to an ever-expanding number of faculties. At the same time, Oxford had come to support a small but growing number of postgraduates, many attracted from abroad, and the majority of the dons had become engaged in some form of research, even if they were not always anxious to publish their work. As a result, Oxford in 1945 had an unquestioned international reputation, something that could never have been said of the insular, confessional university in the age of Newman. The city in which the University was embedded had equally been reinvented in the course of the period, especially between the wars. The town's population little more than doubled between 1841 and 1921, from 24,000 to 57,000. But over the next twenty years it rose to over 100,000 with the rapid expansion of Pressed Steel and the Morris car plant at Cowley, which was already employing 5,000 workers by 1927.[1] In consequence, Oxford filled up with immigrants from other parts of the country, notably Wales, and the town became one of the three most prosperous places in the country. Lord Nuffield's legacy was therefore twofold. On the one hand, he provided the University with much needed resources to develop as a world-respected centre of learning and research; on the other, he broke the city's dependence on the University and transformed the relations between the two.

Nevertheless, the University of Oxford emerged from the Second World War with many of its traditional features intact. Both the University and the colleges had greatly extended their physical footprint over the previous century, but the majority

---

[1] Alan Crossley (ed.), *The Victoria History of the County of Oxford*, vol. 4: *The City of Oxford* (Oxford, 1969), p. 182. E. W. Gilbert, 'The Industrialisation of Oxford', *Geographical Journal*, 109 (1947), 1–25. The 1 millionth car rolled off the assembly line on 22 May 1939: photograph in *OT*, 13 Dec. 2012, p. 38.

of the new buildings, except in the Science Area, were redolent of Oxford's medieval and early modern past. It was still, too, a self-governing university and one where the dons, through their parliament, Congregation, had re-emerged as the sovereign power. The relationship between the University and its colleges had not fundamentally changed either. The colleges no longer dominated the University as they had a century before, but they were still the centre of undergraduate teaching and undergraduate life, and, until 1953, their combined annual income remained higher than the University's. Oxford's students, moreover, were just as elitist and self-referential as they had ever been. For all the efforts to improve access, the large majority of undergraduates continued to come from well-to-do families, while the new emphasis on college spirit and lasting loyalty ensured that most Oxford graduates, whatever their background, emerged from the University armed with a new college-primed identity. As Goldwin Smith remarked in his memoirs about the reforms of his own day, ending the confessional monopoly had not changed the University a jot: 'The Non-conformists had not, as the defenders of tests feared, swallowed up old Oxford; old Oxford had rather swallowed the Non-conformists. The spirit of the place, aided by its aesthetic and historic influences had prevailed.'[2]

Oxford's development between 1845 and 1945 was broadly mirrored in the history of its sister institution in the Fens. Cambridge had suffered from the same confessional insularity and curricular narrowness at the beginning of the Victorian age and was subject to the same four royal commissions of 1850, 1872, 1877, and 1919. Cambridge, too, had widened access to a degree, broadened its undergraduate curriculum, enhanced its delivery through the establishment of the tutorial or supervision, set up a plethora of faculties, and embraced research, while always retaining its right of self-government. As its undergraduate curriculum had been traditionally centred on mathematics rather than classics, Cambridge understandably developed much more quickly than Oxford as a centre of scientific research in the late nineteenth century. In other fields, however, it may even have lagged behind on the eve of the Great War. The returns to a reforms committee set up by the Fenland university in 1911 suggest that, in most departments, research was not high on the agenda or was stymied by lack of time, space, or finance.[3] Any gap between the two universities in the sciences, furthermore, was greatly diminished between the wars. What did distinguish Cambridge from Oxford in 1945 was the relationship between the university and the colleges. As a result of the Asquith Commission, the fees of Cambridge students were paid to the university not to the college, which immediately gave the university a much higher income and allowed an expansion in the number of junior university postholders. The Cambridge colleges continued to select the undergraduates and organize their tutorial supervision, but the colleges and university made separate appointments and the faculties/departments kept control of the curriculum: there was nothing like the joint-appointment system

---

[2] Goldwin Smith, *Reminiscences* (New York, 1910), p. 382.
[3] G. R. Evans, 'Teaching and Research—Then', OM, oth week, TT (2001), 6–8.

that was beginning to develop at Oxford. Cambridge was also much slower in making women full members of the university. Though the university's first female colleges had antedated those at Oxford by several years, only in 1947 did Cambridge admit women to degrees.

The significant changes that both Oxford and Cambridge had undergone, however, did not mean that either had drawn structurally closer over the previous century to the model of the university favoured on the continent. As in the mid-nineteenth, so in the mid-twentieth century, there were two types of European university: the German and the French, the first adopted in other parts of central and eastern Europe, the second in the Latin world. The German system derived from the Humboldtian belief that universities should be centres of research as well as teaching, that the first should enliven the second, and that university teachers should be free within their discipline to teach as they liked. Where it departed from the Humboldtian idea was that German universities made no pretence that knowledge was a seamless unified whole, and the connection between research and teaching was frequently jejune, however significant and original the research undertaken.[4] The French system was still based on the reforms of Napoleon. Since the recreation of individual universities in 1896, it was no longer the system set up by the emperor. But as the prestigious and now more numerous Paris-based schools which trained for the state professions remained independent and had the better resources, the new universities were always second-class citizens. It was these *grandes écoles* too which continued to shelter the best research minds, even if, from the 1860s, greater emphasis was placed on *universitaires* being researchers as well as teachers.[5]

Neither the German nor the French universities had much in common with the two ancient English universities. They were totally dependent on the state for their finances; they had little self-government (hence the ease with which the German universities were purged by the Nazis); they maintained the traditional four- or fivefold faculty organization; their teaching was entirely lecture-based; beyond the odd student hostel, undergraduates were left to fend for themselves and establish their own social institutions; there was no mixing between academic staff and students; and there was no conception of the university as a site of citizen training. Undergraduates in both systems, moreover, principally chose their discipline

---

[4] For a detailed study of one German university in the first part of the twentieth century, see Notker Hammerstein, *Die Johann Wolfgang Goethe-Universität, Frankfurt am Main: von der Stiftungsuniversität zur staatlichen Hochschule*, vol. 1: *1914 bis 1950* (Frankfurt, 1989). Frankfurt was a new university founded in 1912.

[5] Jacques Verger (ed.), *Histoire des universités en France* (Toulouse, 1986), ch. 8; G. Weisz, *The Emergence of Modern Universities in France, 1863–1914* (Princeton, NJ, 1983); Robert Fox, *The Savant and the State: Science and Cultural Politics in Nineteenth-Century France* (Baltimore, MD, 2012); Mary Jo Nye, *Science in the Provinces: Scientific Communities and Provincial Leadership in France, 1860–1930* (Los Angeles, CA, 1986). Research in the French higher-education system was largely coordinated through external state institutions, such as the École Pratique des Hautes Études (1868) to which the brightest *universitaires* were affiliated. For a European university that was first under German and then French control, see John E. Craig, *Scholarship and Nation Building: The Universities of Strasbourg and Alsatian Society, 1870–1939* (Chicago, 1984).

with an eye to a specific career. Although lip service was paid in the German universities to the idea that undergraduates reading an arts or science subject in the philosophical faculty did so for love, most, just like their French peers, were gaining their meal ticket to a job in a secondary school.[6] In consequence, the better-off and more ambitious students were to be found in law and medicine. There was only one significant similarity between Oxbridge and its continental cousins in 1945. The French and German universities equally showed limited interest in promoting the applied sciences or technical studies: no German university even had an engineering department before the First World War. On the continent, there was no difficulty in acquiring a high-quality technical education, especially in Germany's polytechnics. But the Technische Hochschule served an entirely separate and socially less elevated clientele from the universities.[7]

Oxford and Cambridge in 1945 were also distinctive universities in the wider anglophone world, where again they were set apart from the two dominant models: the provincial-imperial and the Scoto-American. The first, prevalent in England, Wales, and Ireland, and throughout the British Empire, mimicked Oxford and Cambridge in offering undergraduates classified honours degrees in a wide variety of subjects normally based on three years' study. But there was little other structural similarity. The urban redbricks and their cousins across the world were run by senates and councils on which the professors shared power with outsiders and the rest of the academic staff had little representation. Their academic organization was both old-fashioned and formal: they kept the traditional medieval structure, multiplied departments not faculties, and delivered the curriculum through formal lectures and seminars. Most of the English civic universities had small endowments and were not totally reliant on fees and the government grants which were available from 1889. Yet they had neither the will nor the resources to reconstitute Oxbridge, even though many professors and lecturers were Oxbridge educated.[8] The civics had also been set up to provide cheap higher education for local students who would live at home and study useful, practical subjects, and this commitment continued to be honoured with some success, even between the wars when they began to attract a nationwide intake and, in some subjects, had established strong research schools.[9] Residential accommodation was provided to a certain extent, but there was no attempt to replicate the collegiate experience of Oxford and Cambridge, even at Durham, which had pretensions to be the northern

---

[6] France had separate faculties of letters and science from 1808; in Germany the arts and the sciences continued to be organized under one faculty umbrella.

[7] Robert Fox and Anna Guagnini (eds), *Education, Technology and Industrial Performance in Europe, 1850–1939* (Cambridge, 1993).

[8] Jill Pellew, 'A Metropolitan University Fit for Empire: The Role of Private Benefaction in the Early History of the London School of Economics and Political Science and Imperial College of Science and Technology, 1895–1930', *HU*, XXVI: 1 (2012), 202–45. The government gave a grant in aid to eleven university colleges in 1889.

[9] Elizabeth J. Morse, 'English Civic Universities and the Myth of Decline', *HU*, XI (1992), 177–204.

Oxbridge. In consequence, students at these universities came from a broad social background.[10]

In the main, the provincial and imperial universities began life as simple colleges of higher education, technical colleges, or teacher training colleges and only slowly gained the right to give degrees.[11] Most, too, took the first steps down that road by becoming part of a federation. Many placed themselves under the wing of the University of London, which, from 1858, was empowered to grant degrees to external candidates and not just to members of its two original constituent colleges, King's and University College. The rest, for the most part, were either grouped or grouped themselves under new umbrella institutions set up to examine for degrees and diplomas, such as Queen's University (later the Royal, and then the National University) of Ireland, the three original universities of India, the University of New Zealand, the Universities of McGill and Toronto, the University of Wales, and the Victoria University for the north of England. In the empire, only Australia's state universities were founded as independent entities from the beginning.[12] There had been suggestions in the 1860s that Oxford should develop in a similar way and become the mother institution of urban colleges dotted around England. But the idea found limited support within the University, and it was London, at the turn of the twentieth century, that grasped the opportunity of becoming the federal university par excellence, bringing under its wing an ever-growing number of educational institutions in the capital and beyond, and creating central institutions for fostering pioneering research.[13] Although the Victoria University broke up at the beginning of the twentieth century and many of London's satellites gained their independence between the wars, the federal ideal remained alive, even in England, and was still seen as the ideal mechanism for rearing the fledgling university of the future at the end of the Second World War. In 1945, four of the redbricks—Nottingham, Southampton, Leicester, and Hull—had yet to win their spurs and escape the control of the University of London.

The Scoto-American model had no connection with Oxbridge at all. The Scots in the mid-nineteenth century were confident in the superiority of their universities over Oxford and Cambridge and remained wedded to their traditional organization. There was limited academic self-government and the curriculum was modernized only slowly. Until the end of the nineteenth century, Scottish undergraduates continued to take an ordinary or general degree in arts whose content was carefully prescribed, and only then proceeded to one of the higher faculties if they wished to

---

[10] Robert D. Anderson, 'Universities and Elites in Modern Britain', *HU*, X (1991), 235 (table, Wales) and 239 (table, Birmingham and Nottingham).

[11] The archetype was the University of Manchester, which began life as Owen's College in 1851.

[12] In England, the University of Birmingham, founded in 1900, was the first higher-education college to move straight to university status; then Bristol in 1909.

[13] The University of London became an educational as well as an examining institution under an Act of Parliament of 1898, which gave it the right to monitor the courses given by its affiliates. This led to the establishment of boards of studies and faculties which established common courses for the growing number of colleges under its aegis in London.

study theology, law, or medicine. Honours degrees were established in 1892 but the ordinary degree remained popular. Honours degrees, too, were only semi-specialized and the course lasted for four years rather than three. The first two years were general and remained prescriptive, and in the last two honours courses were taken in two of the subjects already studied. The Scottish universities, with the majority of students drawn from the immediate locality, were also little influenced by the purported character-building aspects of an Oxbridge collegiate system: there was no attempt to set up residential universities where undergraduates would be turned into citizens, although a minority of day students proved as adept as their Oxbridge counterparts in creating an independent student culture of clubs and societies. The relatively undemanding nature and cheapness of the ordinary degree helped the Scottish universities to educate a larger proportion of the age cohort than their counterparts in the rest of the United Kingdom, albeit still only 2 per cent in 1910–11, and to attract a socially diverse clientele and a large number of women.[14] But the commitment to prescriptive generalism was not particularly beneficial to the development of a Scottish research culture in the arts and sciences, as the low level of much of the teaching did not make a university post attractive to the most creative minds. Although Scotland produced some leading British scientists in the period, only Lord Kelvin, who was sheltered by Glasgow for fifty years, and Macquorn Rankine did really productive work in the country's universities.[15]

The universities of the United States took the cult of generalism to an extreme. The pre-independence colleges had been largely formed on the Scottish model, and this remained so in the nineteenth century in regard to undergraduate education. Germany also had an important part to play in the way the system developed, for many Americans went to do advanced study there after 1850 and came under the sway of the Humboldtian ideal.[16] But American universities were never directly controlled by the state in the German manner, as many (including the most famous) were private foundations, and those set up by the individual states were not treated as part of the state bureaucracy. In nearly all American universities or university-level colleges, power normally rested with the board of governors chaired by the president, a lay body on which the academic faculty had little representation. The Scottish legacy was primarily seen in the structure of the curriculum. In all the many state and private universities that dotted the continent by 1945, undergraduate degrees remained general, and professional training in law, medicine, and so on was undertaken after gaining a BA, often at a different university.[17] However, in the

---

[14] Anderson, 'Universities and Elites', pp. 233–4. At Aberdeen in 1920 almost half the students were women: Lindy Moore, *Bajanellas and Semilinas: Aberdeen University and the Education of Women, 1860–1920* (Aberdeen, 1991).

[15] For the slow development of historical studies in the Scottish system, see Robert D. Anderson, 'University History Teaching and the Humboldtian Model in Scotland, 1858–1914', *HU*, XXV: 1 (2010), 138–84.

[16] In 1911, 22 per cent of students at Göttingen were American: Ben Wildavsky, *The Great Brain Race: How Global Universities are Reshaping the World* (Princeton, NJ, 2010), p. 19.

[17] Princeton students had no choice but to go elsewhere. It was the one Ivy League university that had no medical or law school.

United States, above all through the influence of Charles William Eliot, president of Harvard from 1869 to 1908, there was little attempt to prescribe a core under-graduate curriculum and an elective system prevailed. Although some sort of specialization was permitted in the final years of the four-year degree, students were usually encouraged to take whatever courses took their fancy.[18] The profes-sors, too, could largely teach what they liked, which ensured the wealthiest uni-versities could easily attract the best researchers if they wished to build a reputation as research universities and develop a graduate school.[19] The American universities also made no distinction between theoretical and practical subjects, unlike their European and British counterparts. Anything could be taught, and was, in the new state-funded universities founded after the Civil War, where local agricultural and industrial needs received a higher priority than established curricular subjects and increasing the number of students in tertiary education was far higher on the political agenda by the interwar period than in the Old World.[20] As a result, there was no template. American universities took many forms, especially as they were independent institutions with no external quality control. As one president of a state university boasted in the 1930s, there was 'no intellectual service too undigni-fied for them to perform'.[21]

The Ivy League universities, with their high fees, exclusive fraternities and soro-rities, and reluctance to admit Jews and even Roman Catholics before the Second World War, were in many ways more elitist than Oxford and Cambridge. But they were never Oxbridge clones. Only Princeton, through its preceptorial system, promoted by Woodrow Wilson, and Yale, with its residential colleges and archi-tectural borrowings, attempted to create an undergraduate university that bore some resemblance to Oxford and Cambridge.[22] Nor were the plethora of expensive liberal arts colleges that sprang up along the east coast Oxbridge lookalikes: they offered a much more personal undergraduate experience and they were influenced by the old English universities but they were not the same. The American universities' heavy expenditure on promoting student sports from the late nine-teenth century was also no more than a partial homage to Oxbridge. American universities everywhere saw themselves as part of their locality and believed their role was to provide a wide variety of facilities—recreational and artistic as well as

---

[18] Richard Norton Smith, *The Harvard Century: The Making of a University to a Nation* (Cambridge, MA, 1986), ch. 1; Sheldon Rothblatt, *The Modern University and its Discontents* (Cambridge, 1997), pp. 27–49. Also Morton and Phylis Keller, *Making Harvard Modern: The Rise of America's University* (Oxford, 2001).

[19] Roger L. Geiger, *To Advance Knowledge: The Growth of American Research Universities 1900–1940* (Oxford, 1986). Not all of America's leading universities quickly developed a graduate school. There was particular opposition at Princeton University. The Institute of Advanced Study at Princeton, established in 1930, was and is an independent foundation. It was not a graduate school but a research institute, and its academic staff had no teaching responsibilities.

[20] David O. Levine, *The American College and the Culture of Aspiration, 1915–1940* (Ithaca, NY, 1986).

[21] Rothblatt, *Modern University*, p. 47. The plasticity of American universities was noted by Goldwin Smith as early as 1910: see his *Reminiscences*, p. 115.

[22] James Axtell, *The Making of Princeton University: From Woodrow Wilson to the Present* (Princeton, NJ, 2006); Reuben A. Holden, *Yale: A Pictorial History* (New Haven, CT, 1967), esp. ch. 4.

educational—that the local community lacked.[23] What the American universities, especially the Ivy League, did take directly from Oxbridge was the custom of tapping alumni for funds, and they soon outpaced their teacher: by 1945 the top universities had professional alumni associations which were helping them build up enviable endowments, and, unlike Oxford and Cambridge, they were not competing for alumni loyalty with rivals within.

In 1945, therefore, Oxford and Cambridge were as unique as they had been a century before. Despite the many adjustments that they had made to the demands of modernity in the interim, some commentators thought they were still passé. At the turn of the twentieth century, the Scottish imperialist Viscount Haldane believed they should be left simply to stew in their old-fashioned juice. What Britain needed were higher-educational institutions that would promote national wealth in the way Germany's universities and technical high schools supposedly did. Speaking at Liverpool in 1901, Haldane saw the future as lying with the new University of London, still a 'somewhat unruly infant in swaddling clothes' but potentially 'the educational centre of our empire', if only the state would establish a new postgraduate research college there.[24] And his views were not changed by the First World War. In 1921, in an address at the capital's leading science and technology academy, Imperial College, he returned to the same theme:

> The University of London...ought to be the chief centre of learning for the entire empire, perhaps the chief centre for learning of the entire world. Here ought to be concentrated the highest talent, the highest level in that passion for excellence... the highest atmosphere, such as only can come in a great capital at the heart of a great country.[25]

Haldane's negative view of Oxbridge, however, was not shared by the British public. Although the vast majority of Britons at home and abroad never went near Oxford and Cambridge in their lives, ordinary men, and many women, from the late nineteenth century felt an affinity with the two universities and often a loyalty to one or the other. This had nothing to do with the rising intellectual calibre of the two institutions but reflected the nation's novel obsession with competitive sport. As team sports ceased to be the property of the public schools and became the property of everyman, the annual contests between Oxford and Cambridge became national events, their significance stoked by a popular press which taught the public to associate heroism and valour with sporting achievement. Both the Boat Race on the Tideway and the annual varsity cricket match at Lords attracted thousands of spectators enthusiastically supporting either side. As many Oxbridge sportsmen before the Second World War were good enough to be picked for county and

[23] R. A. Smith, *Sports and Freedom: The Rise of Big Time College Athletics* (Oxford, 1988); D. Chu, *The Character of American Higher Education and Intercollegiate Sport* (Albany, NY, 1989).

[24] Richard B. Haldane, *Education and Empire* (London, 1902), pp. 34–6.

[25] Cited in Pellew, 'Metropolitan University', p. 204. Imperial had been founded in 1908 from a number of existing technical schools.

national teams, their derring-do in a broader arena only cemented the love affair of the English, in particular, with the two traditional universities. Thanks to the help of heavy press coverage, millions thrilled to the deeds of Wadham's C. B. Fry in the 1890s, who, as an undergraduate, played football for the Corinthians, equalled the world long-jump record, and began a spectacular cricketing career that led to his captaining England in later life. After the invention of the newsreel, the public could even see their heroes in action. In January 1936, with the aid of Pathé News, a nation cheered as Brasenose's Prince Obolensky ran three-quarters of the length of the field to score the first of his two tries in England's first ever victory over the All Blacks.[26]

The more politically knowledgeable were also aware that Haldane was wrong to dismiss Oxford and Cambridge as useless dinosaurs. Even if they had done little directly to promote Britain's national wealth before 1939 and most of their scientific research had been theoretical, they had made a contribution in other ways, not least through their interventions in the wider field of educational provision. The role played by individual colleges in developing primary schools in parishes where they held the advowson was small beer compared with the part played by the churches generally in preparing the ground for the 1870 Act, which established a national system of elementary education in England and Wales. But this could hardly be said of the two universities' contribution to the promotion of adult education.[27] In addition, both had been at the forefront of the movement to improve and standardize secondary schooling in England and Wales through evaluating pupils' progress by a common system of external examination. As early as 1857, through the encouragement of the educational reformer T. D. Acland, Oxford had set up a Local Examinations Delegacy, which offered a diploma to boys, and, from 1869, also to girls, in secondary day schools, and that could be taken by different age cohorts. Then, in 1873, the University had teamed up with Cambridge and established an examining board for the public schools threatened with state-imposed exams after the Taunton Commission.[28] By the First World War, Oxford and Cambridge were not alone in the field, for London University and the new provincials soon set up their own boards in imitation. But the two universities were always the dominant force in the provision of secondary-school examinations and were largely responsible, through their influence in government, for stopping the state from taking over the system.[29] Educational outreach in all its forms was seen by Oxford and

[26] <http://en.wikipedia.org/wiki/Alexander_Obolensky> (accessed 17 Jan. 2013). Oxford also produced the first captain of the England football team. This was Cuthbert Ottaway, who led the First ever national side in a match against Scotland in 1872. Ottaway came up to Brasenose from Eton in 1869 as a scholar and gained a First in Honour Mods. He represented Oxford in varsity matches in five different sports.

[27] See pp. 377–8, this volume.

[28] The Taunton Commission was set up in 1864 to investigate the 782 endowed grammar schools not covered by the earlier Clarendon Commission. It reported in 1868 and criticized many of the schools for the inadequacy of their curriculum and the poor use of resources.

[29] Basic information in John Roach, *Public Examinations in England 1850–1900* (Cambridge, 1971), and John Roach, 'Examinations and the Secondary Schools 1900–1945', *History of Education*, 8: 1 (1979), 45–58. T. D. Acland was an ex-fellow of All Souls and an MP who was the brother of Henry, regius professor of medicine. Initially, far more secondary-school pupils took Cambridge's exams than Oxford's but numbers were even on the eve of the First World War.

Cambridge as both a duty and a way of 'increasing their popularity and the general sense of their values', to quote the Balliol fellow Frederick Temple in a letter of 1857.[30] As a public relations exercise, the strategy proved highly successful.

It was not only Oxbridge's contribution to educational reform over the years that encouraged the British elite in all its myriad forms to keep faith with the two universities. What always gave Oxford and Cambridge their pre-eminent place in the eyes of the elite was what principally differentiated the two universities from their competitors at home and abroad: the structure and *raison d'être* of their undergraduate education. Whether a three-year attachment to an Oxbridge college, subject to its gothic architecture, bucolic surroundings, and the rigours of the tutorial system, really did hone the intellect and make a young man or woman a fit tool of empire, or, between the wars, a true citizen of the world, must remain moot. But it was generally agreed to be so, both by those who had passed through the two universities, and by the many who had not. Even trade union leaders were willing to believe that an Oxbridge education was something special and valuable. All might have rightly felt that much more could have been done both before and after the First World War to open up the two universities to the working classes. Nor can they have been happy that large numbers of Oxbridge undergraduates— 200 from Christ Church alone—volunteered to break the General Strike in 1926. But trade unionists usually fell under the universities' educational charm if they once entered their portals. Oxford had a particular allure to those who had only known the grime of industrial cities. Ramsay MacDonald was exceptional in his suspicion, however prescient, that opening up Oxford to the working classes would be the death knell of working-class culture.

It was the humanity and informality of an Oxford undergraduate education that appealed to foreign visitors as well. When the Canadian humourist Stephen Leacock visited Oxford in 1921 he affected not to understand how the tutorial system worked its magic: 'I gather that what an Oxford tutor does is to get a little group of people together and smoke at them. Men who have been systematically smoked at for four years turn into ripe scholars.' But he was convinced that an Oxford education was extraordinary and to be prized: 'Oxford gives something to its students, a life and a mode of thought which in America as yet we can emulate but not equal.'[31] The German Rhodes scholar, Adolf Schlepegrell, writing in the *Daily Telegraph* in 1934, was more serious but just as convinced that the tutorial system transmogrified the student soul. Schlepegrell recognized that there was more to Oxford than its undergraduates and that the University was now a seat of learning. He also understood that many tutorials were unstimulating, where 'pupils discreetly look at their watches as at school'. Nonetheless, together with its student clubs and societies and the care taken over a student's progress, an Oxford undergraduate education was special:

---

[30] *HUO*, vii. 661. Temple was later archbishop of Canterbury.
[31] 'Oxford As I See It', in J. B. Priestley (ed.), *The Bodley Head Leacock* (London, 1957), pp. 159 and 161.

The Oxford man has probably the best general education to be got in the world. Through himself and through the influence he has on people with whom he comes into contact, he is a most valuable asset to society. The German can only get this general education of a high standard if his home can provide it; there is no university where he can acquire it.

His universities can make him an expert or a scholar, but there is no place where he can go for that part of the general education which is so valuable in his later life. It is Oxford's secret.[32]

---

[32] *Daily Telegraph*, 12 Sept. 1934. Schlepegrell went up to University College in 1931.

PART IV

The World University: 1945–2015

Introduction

Higher Education in Britain since 1945

THE gradual expansion of higher education in the first half of the twentieth century had a limited effect on Oxford. The University took an interest in what was happening at Cambridge but paid scant attention to developments at London or the new civic universities. Many Oxford graduates found posts in the redbricks, and Oxford was happy to poach the occasional provincial star. But by and large the new universities were not considered as rivals. As most graduates of the redbricks went into teaching, the new universities offered no threat to Oxford and Cambridge's near monopoly of the best positions in the state and private professions. Nor did the fact that, in the 1920s and 1930s, Oxford was receiving an annual subsidy from the government significantly reduce its independence. The two ancient universities had to accept the Asquith Commission in return for receiving state support, but the commissioners demanded only minimal changes to their governance. Oxford was expected to use the government grant to build up its science provision; otherwise, it remained free to develop between the wars as it sought fit. By 2014, on the other hand, as the University as an institution entered its ninth century, the situation was very different. Oxford was still an independent, self-governing corporation, but it was now merely one, albeit large, cog in a vast state-controlled higher-education machine, and its own interests were not necessarily congruent with those of the government of the day.

The system of higher education that developed in Britain after 1945 was much bigger and far better financed than its pre-war precursor, and the system kept on growing. Except for a period in the 1980s, post-war governments both on the left and right were committed to building and sustaining a publicly funded system of higher education, which would allow all those who had the minimum entrance qualifications the chance of attending a university or tertiary college.[1] This was seen not simply as only just in a democratic society but also an

---

[1] Since the introduction of A-levels in England, Wales, and Northern Ireland in the early 1950s, entrants to a higher-education course at 18 need a minimum of a pass into two subjects. Scotland has its own 'highers'

economic desideratum, especially after 1990 when the potential for economic growth began to be ever more closely associated with the size of the nation's graduate pool. The economic needs of the nation equally encouraged the British state, from 1945, to pump money into the universities to promote research and develop postgraduate education. As a result, in the course of the second half of the twentieth century, Britain's higher-education system moved from being on the periphery of the service economy to being at its heart.

The utilitarian attitude of successive post-war governments was greatly encouraged by the two independent enquiries into the future of higher education, conducted in 1963 and 1996. Admittedly, the first, chaired by Lord Robbins of the LSE, still paid lip service to Newman's idea of the university and claimed that higher education had a key role in 'the transmission of a common culture and common standards of citizenship'. Nonetheless, it was adamant that higher education was first and foremost an economic good, both for the individual student, whose earning power was increased, and for the nation, whose progress 'depends to a much greater extent than ever before on skills demanding special training'.[2] The second enquiry, headed by a retired civil servant, Sir Ron Dearing, could see only the practical benefits of a university education. The committee had been set up at the very moment the new information technology was beginning to transform the world economy, and this completely coloured its conclusions. The chance to attend university should be extended as widely as possible, students should be taught transferable skills, and graduates could expect to return to higher education in the course of their working life to retool:

> The education and skills of our people will be our greatest national resource in the global world of tomorrow. They must be developed to internationally excellent standards if we are to prosper. A high quality workforce will secure continued and increasing investment in the UK by industry and commerce ... [H]igher education's relative importance is increasing, both in developing the levels of capability that are needed in the world of work and in providing an underpinning research base.

Research, too, had to have a practical value. Robbins had appreciated the Humboldtian vision of the search for truth as its own reward, but Dearing reduced the advancement of knowledge to the needs of UK plc:

> In research, we see higher education taking a more active role in relating the outcomes of research and scholarship to the wider needs of society. We see industry and commerce, and a wide range of public bodies who have need of research, reciprocally making greater use of the knowledge and expertise which resides in higher education.

---

system. To accommodate students from abroad and those from British schools who take foreign qualifications, there are also a number of alternative routes.

[2] Robbins, pp. 6–7. Robbins worried that English undergraduate degrees were too specialized. He liked the Scottish general degrees: see pp. 532–3, this volume.

All subjects had an economic utility: 'Research in the arts and the humanities contributes to growing industries in tourism, entertainment and leisure.'[3]

Convinced that unprecedented investment in higher education was both fair and necessary, British governments in the years between 1945 and 2013 presided over a massive expansion of the system. In 1938–9, the number of students in full-time higher education in the United Kingdom stood at 69,000, of whom fewer than 2,000 were involved in postgraduate study; in 2012–13 there were 1.4 million full-time undergraduates in the system and 300,000 postgraduates. The expansion had a dramatic effect on the proportion of 18-year-olds in higher education. In 1938–9, only 1.7 per cent of the cohort went on to higher education; by the end of the period, it was more than 40 per cent. The expansion further profoundly altered the gender and social profile of the student body. In 1962, fewer than half as many girls as boys went onto tertiary education; by 1995–6 they were a majority. The sons and daughters of poorer families were also much more visible, even if it was the middle classes who benefited most from the expansion in student numbers. Only 2 per cent of the children of skilled manual workers born in 1940 went onto university; 10 per cent of those born forty years later did so.[4]

The expansion occurred in three stages (see Table 10). In the twenty-five years following the war, numbers in full-time higher education rose tenfold to reach 440,000 in 1970–1. The rapid expansion of the system then came to an abrupt halt in the 1970s, as first Britain's post-war economic growth faltered under the impact of the 1973 oil crisis, and then the Conservative government that came to power in 1979 under Margaret Thatcher refused to commit more resources. Too many students, it believed, were pursuing irrelevant or subversive courses in the arts and social sciences rather than benefiting the nation by studying science and technology. Numbers continued to rise slowly throughout the 1970s and 1980s but by 1985–6 had reached only 596,000. In 1987, however, the Conservative education secretary, Kenneth Baker, was won over to the view that Britain needed more graduates in all disciplines if it were to remain a great economic power, and the brakes were taken off. By 1997, when a new Labour administration took office, full-time numbers had doubled again to 1.1 million. In 2001, the Labour government promised that 50 per cent of 18-year-olds would be in higher education by the end of the decade. The target was never reached because of the financial crash of 2008, but by 2012–13 there were still nearly twice as many full- and part-time students as in 1993.

In 1938–9, the 69,000 students were working for degrees given by eighteen different universities whose combined current and capital expenditure was £7 million.[5] In 2012–13, the 2.3 million full- and part-time students were spread among 165 higher education institutions (HEIs), as degree-giving bodies were now called, and the university system consumed in total £29.1 billion, seventy times more in real terms than before the war. About three-quarters of the total was

---

[3] Dearing, pp. 11 and 77.   [4] Robbins, pp. 16 and 68; Dearing, pp. 21–3.
[5] The number was eighteen if the University of London is treated as a single institution.

provided by the state, either in the form of direct grants or indirectly through the research councils; the rest came from endowment and other, usually private, funding bodies. The universities at the end of the period were huge conglomerates and employed nearly 400,000 people. Half were academics; half administrators, librarians, secretaries, counsellors, and clerks.[6] The size of the support staff emphasized how much the responsibilities of higher-education institutions had grown as the system expanded. They were needed not just to facilitate core teaching and research, but to respond to novel external pressures. At the beginning of the millennium, legions of administrators were required to ensure compliance with the profusion of top-down directives concerning health and safety at work, employee rights, and student welfare, spawned by the European Union, the government, and its phalanx of educational agencies.

Sussex, York, Warwick, and four other universities established in the late 1950s and early 1960s, began life as new institutions built on greenfield sites. Another brand-new institution was the trailblazing Open University, set up at Milton Keynes in 1969 by the then Labour government as a distance learning and research university for part-time and older or mature students. All the other new HEIs started out as colleges of higher education, technical colleges, or teacher training colleges, which were eventually given the status of universities.[7] A number, like the University of Nottingham, a former affiliate of the University of London, won their spurs shortly after the Second World War. But the majority became universities only after 1990. The largest group comprised the polytechnics. These were the brainchild of Anthony Crosland, a Labour secretary for education in the 1960s who had favoured building high-grade technology and technical training into a separate higher-education sector which would offer part-time and full-time degree courses and ape similar, historically highly successful, institutions on the continent.[8] By 1973, there were thirty in existence, and their courses, diplomas, and degrees were validated by a new governing body, the Council for National Academic Awards.[9] The polytechnics, however, had never stuck to their technical last as Crosland had wanted, and by the early 1990s several were offering courses in the arts and social sciences no different from those at the universities. In 1992 a new Conservative education secretary, Kenneth Clarke, concluded that their separate institutional existence was pointless and had them rechristened as universities. The university

---

[6] Information from <http://en.wikipedia.org/wiki/List_of_universities_in_the_United_kingdom_by_size> (accessed 31 October 2013): colleges and institutes of the University of London and the University of Wales are listed individually; <http://www.hesa.ac.uk> (accessed 17 July 2014). HESA is the Higher Education Statistical Agency. The exact percentage of the total supplied by the public purse is unclear: official figures do not distinguish between grants from the government research councils and grants from charities, such as the Wellcome Trust, or industry. Before 1965, when the Social Science Research Council (from 1983 the Economic and Social Science Research Council) was created, all research funding councils were for the sciences; the oldest was the Medical Research Council founded in 1920. Besides the 165 HEIs there were some 700 further education colleges or their equivalents offering higher-education courses leading to a degree from an HEI.

[7] Like the earlier civics.

[8] *A Plan for Polytechnics and Other Colleges: Higher Education in the Further Education System* (London, 1966).

[9] A CNAA had been called for by Robbins, but to look after the lower-level technical colleges: see Robbins, ch. 8. He had wanted the teacher training colleges brought under the universities.

system was transformed overnight. In 1995–6 there were 115 universities instead of the thirty-one when Robbins was published.

The huge expansion was made possible only because there was a rapidly growing student market. The state facilitated this by ensuring more and more children stayed on at school to gain the necessary entrance qualifications: it raised the school leaving age to 15 after the war, to 16 in the 1960s, and finally to 18 at the end of the period.[10] It also agreed, until the 1990s, to pay the students' tuition fees and provide them with generous maintenance grants based on the salary of their father or guardian. Without this, it would have been very difficult to coax large numbers of lower-middle- and working-class students into the system. But there were other factors at play as well. Crucial was a change in the job market. From the late 1960s, for the first time, entrants to virtually all the professions had to have a degree, so more and more young people had to go to university before beginning a career.[11] The decline in manufacturing and the explosion in the number of professional positions as the economy became dominated by the service sector from the 1980s only cemented the trend. Female emancipation also played an important part. Had it not become normal for young women from the 1970s to build independent careers, their presence at university would never have increased in the way it did. And the expansion fed on itself. The growing number of undergraduates spawned ever larger numbers of postgraduates as the best jobs went to those who stayed on in higher education to gain specialist advanced diplomas and degrees.[12]

Britain's dramatic expansion of tertiary education in the second half of the twentieth century was mirrored in every developed country, for the conviction that higher education was a national as well as personal good was universal. Only the pace of the timing and the source of funding differed. In the Soviet Union (until its collapse in the early 1990s) and continental Europe (both east and west) higher education was resourced almost entirely from public funds, whether or not an institutional distinction was made between pure and applied knowledge, as in Germany, or the university system played second fiddle to elite national training schools, as in France. The white British Commonwealth aped Britain and developed a system that was essentially publicly financed and controlled but encouraged private investment in individual institutions. The United States, in contrast, continued to sustain its traditional mix of state and private universities and colleges, in which a small number of private institutions, by assiduously cultivating their alumni, became exceptionally rich. But, however organized, most of the original

---

[10] In 1938, only 4 per cent of 17-year-olds were still in education. In 1962, only 7 per cent left school with two or more A-levels or their equivalent; in 1994, 28 per cent did so in England: Dearing, p. 57.

[11] Until then only the church, the bar, medicine, and secondary-school teaching demanded that entrants had had a higher education (and in England and Wales teachers could train in a teacher training college). Other professions usually recruited straight from school. This was why so many graduates of redbricks before the war went into teaching; there were limited other openings, especially for women.

[12] Robbins called for a 50 per cent rise in the number of postgraduates on the grounds that knowledge in all fields had become so extensive that only the rudiments could be taught at first-degree level. But the real need was to increase the number of postgraduates studying the sciences and social sciences.

industrialized nations had reached the position, by the year 2000, where from 30 to 50 per cent of 18-year-olds were in higher education compared with a few per cent sixty years earlier. China and the other fast-industrializing states at the beginning of the new millennium were rapidly following in their footsteps. By 2012, the world's 17,000 universities were enrolling 153 million students, a leap of more than 50 per cent in nine years.[13]

On the other hand, the manner in which the United Kingdom's new national system was organized and controlled was a very British story. Until the early 1990s, pre-war conditions prevailed and, as in the past, government largesse was dispensed through the University Grants Committee (UGC). The UGC, largely independent of government authority and staffed with academics representing their universities, proved a benign watchdog. It was happy to oversee the system's expansion and made little attempt to interfere with university autonomy. Until 1970, relations between the universities and its paymaster were particularly cordial. Every five years each university had to draw up and cost a plan of action. Though they were nearly always expansionist, most universities got what they wanted. Money for new buildings, laboratories, libraries, and personnel was freely available, and the staff–student ratio became steadily more favourable. Thereafter, as the economic skies darkened and money got tighter, relations became less cosy. Action plans now had to be produced annually and the UGC was no longer so accommodating. All the same, it remained the universities' friend and made little attempt to shape the internal life of the institutions under its care.

The easy life finally came to an end while Kenneth Baker was education secretary. The Thatcher government felt that the professions, as much as the trades unions, were a conspiracy against the public, and that the teaching professions in particular, whose members were largely employed by the state or by state-supported institutions, were in need of close scrutiny. There was a general feeling in Whitehall that increasing amounts of public money had been given to universities since the Second World War without due attention paid to the purpose or quality of their research and teaching. In 1988, Baker replaced the long-standing UGC with the Universities Funding Council, which, four years later, when the polytechnics became part of the university system, was transformed into three separate Higher Education Funding Councils for England (HEFCE), Wales, and Scotland. The UFC and its successors were directly accountable to a minister for higher education rather than the treasury, and comprised a mixed body of academics and businessmen to ensure that Britain's economic needs were properly considered.[14] Baker also

---

[13] Ben Wildavsky, *The Great Brain Race: How Global Universities are Reshaping the World* (Princeton, NJ, 2010), p. 37.

[14] The revolution in the structure of higher education begun in the late 1980s was given statutory underpinning in two principal pieces of legislation: the 1988 Education Act (which, for the first time, prescribed a national curriculum for schools in England and Wales) and the 1992 Further and Higher Education Act. The key background document is Kenneth Baker's White Paper, *Higher Education: Meeting the Challenge* (London, 1987). With the establishment of devolved governments in Scotland and Wales in 1997, responsibility for the Scottish and Welsh funding councils passed to Edinburgh and Cardiff. Northern Ireland has its own system.

instituted the first external audits of British higher education. These were intended to ensure that, in the future, government money would be rationally distributed, and to bring, in the minister's view, much needed transparency and competition to the system. As a sop to university sensitivity, the audits were conducted by academics, but they began immediately and have been repeated at intervals ever since. The first national research audit took place in 1989;[15] the first teaching audit occurred in the early 1990s. Initially, direct responsibility for both lay with the funding councils, but from 1997 the teaching audit was farmed out to the Quality Assurance Agency (QAA).[16]

The Research Assessment Exercise (RAE) ranked university departments or their equivalents according to the quality and extent of their research output. The teaching audits introduced a novel culture of targets and norms, which was already well known in the business world and Whitehall. Every aspect of a university's life was put under the microscope. The gender, class, and ethnic profile of its students were 'norm referenced'.[17] Its curriculum, examination system, and student-contact provision were tested on the anvil of so-called 'best practice'. Even its system of governance was scrutinized according to a standardized ideal. While the government ministry that was given ultimate control over higher education frequently changed after 1990, there was no let-up in the degree to which politicians and educational bureaucrats endeavoured to micro-manage the system.[18] Where there was some difference of opinion, was over how to divide the spoils when it came to research. Dearing, in 1996, feared that the RAE would lead to government funds being lavished on a small number of institutions who came out top. Like Robbins before him, he wanted it to be possible for all academics to be 'research active' if they so desired. Labour's education secretary, Charles Clarke, in a White Paper of 2003 disagreed. He preferred to concentrate resources on the elite and argued that the lion's share of research funding should go to departments judged best by the RAE.[19] Despite much opposition to the idea, the education's secretary's position became the new orthodoxy. Today, of the 165 universities, only 20 or so are significant centres of research and form a sector apart. Virtually all are members of the Russell Group, a collection of pre-Robbins universities, including Oxford and Cambridge, with particularly high research aspirations, which came together in 1994 to emphasize their distinctive needs and nature.[20]

---

[15] Others took place in 1992, 1996, 2001, 2008, and 2014. The audit was initially called the Research Selectivity Exercise, then the RAE, and, in 2014, the Research Excellence Framework. There was a trial run in 1986.

[16] On the ideas and activities of the QAA in its first years, see Roger Brown, 'The New UK Quality Framework', *Higher Education Quarterly*, 54: 4 (2000), 323–42.

[17] Dearing, pp. 21 and 23, was particularly keen to improve the attendance rates of students from unskilled and partly skilled backgrounds and those from ethnic minorities. Robbins made no mention of the needs of immigrants' children. The large-scale immigration to the United Kingdom which has been such a significant feature of post-war history had already begun by the time of his report, but it hardly registered on the political radar.

[18] Micro-management was a further factor swelling the universities' support staff.

[19] Dearing, p. 38; Department of Education and Skills, *The Future of Higher Education*, Cm. 5735 (Jan. 2003).

[20] For a list see <http://en.wikipedia.org/wiki/Russell_Group> (accessed 31 January 2013). It was called after the London hotel in which the group was first formed.

Britain's fast-growing number of universities found coping with outside intrusion all the more difficult in that they were being expected to do more with less. Robbins judged that the expansion in undergraduate and postgraduate numbers could be realized without harm to the students. His report expected the favourable staff–student ratio to be maintained; the quality of teaching and learning to be improved by better use of lectures, small-group teaching, and written work; and a rapid growth in student accommodation on campus to happen.[21] The cost to the exchequer would be huge, but the country would be able to bear it as long as the government was willing to double the percentage of GDP spent on higher education from 0.8 to 1.6 per cent. In the event, no government ever came near to meeting Robbins' target. Public expenditure on higher education as a percentage of GDP actually fell between 1980 and 1988. Although it had risen by the mid-1990s to just under 1.2 per cent, this was small beer for what was needed in the second period of rapid expansion.

The cost was partly kept down by gradually phasing out maintenance awards. Each year from 1990, the maximum amount a student could receive was cut and a system of top-up loans introduced to fill the gap. But expenditure was also reduced by cutting in real terms the per capita fee that the state had paid universities for the previous thirty years to cover the cost of a student's tuition.[22] In consequence, it was impossible to maintain traditional staffing levels. During the Conservative government of 1979 to 1997, the amount of money spent on each student deteriorated by 47 per cent and the staff–student ratio fell from one to nine to one to seventeen. Research funding also suffered. In the ten years to 1994–5, expenditure by the government's funding bodies and research councils on research and development equally decreased in real terms.[23] Furthermore, the money was divided more unevenly, as most of the money the UGC had had for research was transferred to the research councils to be distributed according to success in the RAE.

The Dearing Report of 1996 recognized that the funding cuts were having a serious effect on staff morale and advocated an end to free higher education. The British government was committing roughly the same proportion of GDP to the sector as other EU states, so it was unrealistic to expect a dramatic increase in public funding. Robbins had discussed but dismissed the suggestion that students should pay for their tuition. Dearing grasped the nettle. Not only should maintenance grants be completely scrapped and replaced by loans but all graduates should pay back 25 per cent of the cost of their studies across their working lives. It was impossible to expect the state to fund an individual's tuition entirely once participation rates rose to 45 per cent (his suggested target) or higher. Nor was it fair on non-graduate taxpayers.[24]

---

[21] By 1963, only 20 per cent of students in higher education were living at home, against 40 per cent in 1939.
[22] The fee was intended to cover teaching costs and the depreciation of buildings and equipment. The amount varied according to the university and the type of course studied; science and medical students attracted a higher fee.
[23] Dearing, p. 39.   [24] Ibid., pp. 46–7; Robbins, pp. 212–14.

To the horror of many of their supporters, Labour was also not averse to demanding that students should contribute to their education in order to keep the cost of expansion to the minimum and avoid paying the extra £2 billion annually that Dearing thought was needed.[25] Starting in 1998, the government introduced a student fee, and from the following year abolished maintenance grants entirely. At first the annual tuition charge was only £1,000 per year, but from 2006 higher-education institutions were allowed to claim up to £3,000 from their students, and from 2013 as much as £9,000.[26] As the fee was means-tested from its inception and, from 2013, not paid beforehand but redeemed in the form of a graduate tax, it was hoped that the innovation would not deter poorer students.[27] Indeed, in the spirit of Dearing, the Labour government made increasing the participation rate of students from poorer homes a priority. From 2006, no institution was allowed to charge the new variable fee unless they had demonstrated to an educational quango, the Office for Fair Access (OFFA), that they had put in place mechanisms for broadening their social intake.

Confronted by post-war governments keen to finance the expansion of higher education, Oxford, like Cambridge, had little choice but to accept the money on offer. On the one hand, most senior members of the University wanted to play a part in post-war reconstruction by increasing undergraduate numbers and opening up Oxford to pupils from state schools in much greater numbers. On the other, they were anxious that the University should continue to develop as a world-class centre of research, which meant welcoming many more postgraduates, creating posts in new and specialist disciplines, and investing heavily in nuclear physics and other cutting-edge sciences. The University's endowment was far too small, and the colleges' insufficient, to bear the colossal costs that such a step change would incur. As the UGC was more than happy to assist Oxford to expand and maintain its position as one of the world's leading universities, it would have been folly not to become much more dependent than hitherto on the state's bounty.

Until the 1970s, it seemed that Oxford had made a good bargain. Thanks to government funding, the University was able to more than double its student numbers, firmly establish its postgraduate arm, and cement its reputation in scientific research, while still retaining its traditional bias towards the arts. Oxford had to plead its cause before the UGC and submit a quinquennial plan, but, like other universities, its ambitions were usually indulged. In the 1950s and 1960s, the government and the civil service continued to be dominated by Oxbridge graduates, so there was little opposition to the two universities being handsomely supported by the public purse. Oxford was also quick to forestall criticism. Robbins, in 1963,

---

[25] By 2002, the share of GDP spent by the government on higher education had fallen to 0.83 per cent.

[26] Useful account in <http://en.wikipedia.org/wiki/Tuition_fees_in_the_United_Kingdom> (accessed 31 January 2013). Tuition fees were not introduced in Scotland, whose own devolved government, from 1997, controlled higher education.

[27] It was also assumed, wrongly, that higher-education institutions would not charge the maximum but try to attract good students by setting a lower fee.

was not hostile to Oxford and Cambridge but found that all was not completely well: they were too elitist, had too tight a grip on the nation's research and life, and were not always efficiently managed. Oxford responded swiftly with its own committee of enquiry, the Franks Commission, which reported in 1966 on how the University might better meet its responsibilities in an age of social democracy while remaining world class.[28] The University also reacted rapidly to the challenges presented by the youth and feminist movements that were fast gaining momentum inside and outside the University in the late 1960s. Within a few years, junior members' views were sought and listened to and Oxford colleges had begun the process of going co-ed.

Oxford had no problems either with keeping on good terms with the other members of the burgeoning public system. As Britain's universities expanded in number and size, they found their academic staff preponderantly among Oxford and Cambridge postgraduates and fellows, who took with them a positive and roseate view of their alma mater. Oxford and Cambridge were seen as a higher-education ideal to which the rest of the system would aspire if they could. When the new greenfield universities were set up at the turn of the 1960s, Oxbridge served as a model. Scholars with deep-rooted affection for the old English universities frequently played an important role in their early development, and there was talk of improving on the original. Sussex, for instance, owed much to the former Worcester historian Asa Briggs, who moved to a chair at the new university in 1961. For the next sixteen years, he was continually at the centre of the new university's gestation, serving as dean of the school of social studies, pro-vice-chancellor, and finally vice-chancellor, before returning to his old college as provost in 1976.[29]

By the 1980s, however, the bargain began to look less attractive. As government money became tight and the UGC less obliging, the environment became more competitive and other universities less willing to accept Oxford's and Cambridge's leadership. Everyone wanted the largest possible share of a shrinking cake. A number of universities that the Thatcher government felt to be too weighted to the arts and social sciences suffered catastrophic cuts to their income.[30] This was not Oxford's fate, despite its subject balance, but it still had to tighten its belt and freeze a large number of posts. As there was little sign that the good days would return, the University was forced to rethink its strategy to shore up its position. For several years, Oxford dithered as to the best way forward. Finally, at the end of the 1980s, it decided that the only solution was to lessen its dependence on the state. The University would continue to be part of Britain's public system of higher education but it would gain greater freedom for manoeuvre by seeking private money to fund capital projects and build up its endowment.

---

[28] Cambridge followed suit with its own commission.

[29] Briggs is the author of a five-volume history of the BBC. He was a fellow of Worcester for ten years after the war, before taking a chair at Leeds.

[30] Curiously, most were on or near to Britain's eastern shoreline.

Staying within the public system meant accepting ever greater government scrutiny of its activities in the new world of the RAE and QAA. But Oxford gambled on coming out on top in any competitive national audit, as did Cambridge, who took a similar line. Acceptance of the new audit culture was expected to reap financial dividends. Not all the dons agreed. Many, perhaps most, remained committed to the pre-war belief that an undergraduate degree was a mental training, not a passport to a specific career. Ever more suspicious of the government's crude economic agenda for higher education, some, by the early 1990s, took up a cry, first occasionally heard in the 1960s, that the University should cut itself adrift from the state entirely and become a British Harvard.[31] This, though, was not and is still not the majority position. Most senior members felt and feel that the University could never raise sufficient private money to allow it to sustain its position as a world leader, especially in the sciences and medicine, which require large-scale investment in buildings and equipment.

Over the next twenty years, the decision proved to be the right one. Oxford competed successfully within the new regulatory system and maximized its government income.[32] It was also able to gain far more than its fair share of the huge sums of private money that industry and charities like the Wellcome Trust made available for research after 1900. The University equally proved an adept fundraiser. It still remained heavily dependent on the state. Even in 2006 the HEFCE block grant accounted for 30 per cent of its income.[33] But huge sums of money were donated to put up new buildings, establish new research centres, and fund postgraduate scholarships. The colleges played their part as well. Besides in turn finding the private capital to build new residential blocks and improve student facilities, they also built up their endowment to underpin the tutorial system, which even the £9,000 undergraduate fee could not properly sustain at the end of the period.[34]

Thereby, Oxford was able to grow and flourish and retain its place at the top table. Growing government concern from the late 1980s that higher education should be cost-effective, and a post-industrial obsession with consumer choice, led to the United Kingdom's universities being continually ranked by the press and other bodies in terms of research output, the quality of their undergraduate teaching, the provision of facilities, graduate starting salaries, and so on. International rankings too became a commonplace at the beginning of the new century in

---

[31] E.g. Nevil Johnson, 'Time for a Declaration of Independence', OM, 4th week, HT (1993), pp. 12–13 and 16. For such views in the 1960s, see p. 558, this volume.

[32] The RAE has adopted several different ranking mechanisms. In 1988/9, 70 per cent of the University's forty-six units of assessment received the top grade; in 1996, 75 per cent. In 2008, 32 per cent of the units of assessment were awarded a 4* (world-leading) and 70 per cent a 3* (world-leading and intellectually excellent in the United Kingdom): see p. 645, this volume.

[33] [University of Oxford] *Corporate Plan 2005–6 to 2009–10*, supplement 1* to OUG, no. 136, Sept. 2005, p. 20.

[34] Historically, tutorial fellowships had been supported by undergraduate fees. This continued to be the case after 1945 when the state took over paying the fees of the large majority of undergraduates. The colleges' fee income became less secure and predictable after 2000: see pp. 587–9, this volume.

response to globalization and global student mobility.[35] On all criteria, Oxford and Cambridge invariably scored well. Oxford was never out of the top three in national and the top ten in international polls, coming as high as second in the Times Higher Education World University Rankings, 2011–12. In a global ranking system dominated by the richest American private universities, Oxford and Cambridge were usually not just the only British, but the only European, institutions acknowledged to be in the top flight.[36]

All the same, Oxford's decision to stay within the public system, however wise, was not always a comfortable choice. It had continued to grow and flourish—its undergraduates and postgraduates numbered 25,000 by the end of the period—but it had frequent altercations with the hand that continued to feed it. Britain's higher-education system in 2000 was large, diverse, and complex. Some HEIs were major research universities; others had no research profile to speak of at all. Some offered undergraduates degrees only in traditional academic subjects; others a portfolio of specialist career-orientated courses, such as Northumbria's degree in call-centre studies. HEFCE had to balance and promote the needs of them all. Oxford was only one demanding fish in the shoal. For all its expansion since 1945, the University's junior members comprised a mere 1.5 per cent of the nation's student population and its share of the higher-education budget was a paltry 3.3.[37] Oxford dons too were greatly diminished as a fraction of the United Kingdom's academic workforce. There were now three times as many as before the war, but this was scarcely 2 per cent of the whole.[38] Although high in the world rankings, Oxford could hardly expect special treatment. The Labour government that came to power in 1997 agreed. Pledged to waging war on the dead hand of tradition supposedly holding back modern Britain, Oxford and Cambridge were seen as part of the problem. As far as the government, HEFCE, and most other universities were concerned, Oxford and Cambridge were minnows with an inflated sense of entitlement. From the mid-1990s, there was growing resentment within higher education, the press, the civil service, and government of Oxbridge's historic dominance. Critics objected to their continued monopoly of top positions in the state and private professions, the cost to the public purse of their personalized system of college-based undergraduate teaching, their Newmanite ambivalence to the utilitarian ideal, and the democratic and cumbersome nature of their governance, which offended

---

[35] Wildavsky, *Brain Race*, ch. 4, 'College Rankings Go Global'. Some 4 million of the 153 million students in 2012 were studying in a foreign country; in 2009, 10 per cent of students abroad were based in the United Kingdom: ibid., p. 15.

[36] <http://en.wikipedia.org/wiki/Russell_Group> (accessed 31 January 2013), p. 10. One of the first world rankings, which placed Oxford and Cambridge second equal, appeared in 1988–9 in the *Asian Wall Street Journal*. In the 2013 QS World University Rankings, which ranks by subject rather than university, Oxford had fifteen subjects ranked in the top ten and four first places: philosophy, geography, modern languages, and English. Cambridge had three firsts and twenty-seven out of thirty subjects in the top ten. Harvard was top in ten subjects; Imperial had ten subjects in the top ten, and the LSE seven. *The Times*, 8 May 2013.

[37] <http://en.wikipedia.org/wiki/List_of_universities_in_the_United_Kingdom_by_size> (accessed 31 Jan. 2013); <http://en.wikipedia.org/wiki/Russell_Group> (accessed 31 January 2013): data on research income.

[38] <http://www.hesa.ac.uk> (accessed 7 April 2013). There were 80,000 permanent full-time academics in the British higher-education system in 2011/12.

contemporary ideas of corporate best practice. The critics demanded change and the Labour government was ready to use legislation to force compliance.

The response of the Vice-Chancellor and Oxford's central administration to the unaccustomed harassment was to stress the folly of undermining one of the nation's few blue-ribbon institutions because it stood out from its peers, but, where necessary, to seek compromise and accommodation. In the case of governance, the centre was keen to demonstrate that it had read the runes and to anticipate outside concerns by initiating reform itself. Two years before Labour gained office, Congregation agreed to establish an internal commission of enquiry, headed by Vice-Chancellor Peter North, to assess Oxford's size and shape and suggest how its administration might be made more effective. The commission's report, published in 1997, became the blueprint for the many changes to Oxford's governance that were introduced or proposed across the next decade. The central administration's aim was to make the University more efficient and proactive while retaining the sovereignty of Congregation. Many senior members, however, feared that their historic powers of scrutiny and control were being marginalized. Although the initial reforms were accepted, the proposals for further rationalization brought forward by Vice-Chancellor John Hood in 2005–6 were bitterly opposed and eventually defeated. By attempting to forestall outside criticism, the central administration ended up dividing the University in two.

Oxford in 2014 retained many links with the pre-war era: both undergraduates and postgraduates were attached to residential colleges; undergraduate teaching continued to be based round tutorials; and the University was still ultimately run by the dons. But in most respects, as the chapters in Part IV will show, it was an entirely different institution. It was numerically five times as large; it had as many postgraduates as undergraduates; its postgraduates and dons came from all round the world; and it was no longer a male preserve. Its footprint in the city and beyond was also much more extensive. At the same time, the relationship between the University and its constituent colleges had profoundly altered. Although the University grew in size and wealth between the wars, the colleges still retained their traditional independence and authority. By the end of the period, the relationship had been reversed as Oxford's ever-expanding focus on research effected a permanent shift in the balance of power.

Research was the University's province, not the colleges, which continued to devote the lion's share of their resources to undergraduate teaching. The rapid development of Oxford's research arm in the post-war decades meant that, by the 1980s, the University had become a financial and administrative giant. The large sums of research money that Oxford attracted after 1990, and the new welfare and audit culture, turned it into a leviathan. In 2014, the University employed 1,722 academic postholders, 4,087 postdoctoral researchers, and 3,074 administrative staff.[39] The leviathan was not slow to demonstrate its power. Part of the impetus

---

[39] UOG, supplement (1) to n. 5051, 26 Feb. 2014, p. 340.

for governance reform came from the central administration's desire to bring the colleges more closely under its wing. From 1980, if not before, the ability of individual colleges to control their own affairs was steadily reduced and by the end of the period even undergraduate admissions were being partly policed by the faculties. Some powerful figures in the sciences and medicine began to suggest that the college system was passé and a hindrance to the University's development; central administrators began to dream of administering and perhaps appropriating the colleges' endowments.[40] The fact that today Oxford officially describes itself as a collegiate university is evidence of how far the balance of power has shifted. Between the wars, the world did not need reminding of the fact: it was a given.

Oxford's success in the competitive environment spawned by the RAE brought additional problems. While the 1,700 postholders on the University's payroll in 2014 held college fellowships, the vast majority of the postdocs and admin staff did not. The majority, too, were not members of Congregation. This inevitably led to jealousies and conflicts of interest. Staying ahead in the competitive race also shaped recruitment. The University was committed to increasing the number of female dons but this was difficult in a research world where senior academics in most subjects were male.[41] Another recurring headache was how to attract and retain the best minds of either sex, given the cost of housing in Oxford, the small number of stipendiary professorships, and the constraints of the pay scales adopted in the 1950s. The problems were much discussed in the final years of the period but few solutions were found.

Furthermore, Oxford was always short of the money that it needed to fulfil its ambitions. The University was able to attract large private donations, but the proportion of its income that it drew from endowment never rose above 10 per cent and even dipped towards the end of the period. It never came near to matching the richest American private colleges. In 2012, Harvard's income was eight times as large as the University and colleges' combined.[42] Going cap in hand to donors and alumni for money also brought problems. The University at first had difficulty connecting with its old members since it had made limited attempts in the past to keep in touch.[43] The colleges had always fostered relations with their alumni, but they too had to do this much more assiduously by keeping old members closely informed about college life and organizing a continual series of events, not just the occasional gaudy. Big donors with no historic connection with Oxford had to be handled especially carefully. Well aware of the way that Nuffield's desire to establish a college for accountancy and engineering had been ignored, they often wanted some say in how their money was spent. Oxford, to a degree, became a victim of pet

---

[40] It was felt that the University's and the colleges' endowments would be better administered if pooled.
[41] In 2013 women were 25 per cent of Oxford's academic staff and only 18 per cent of professors: 'Oration by the Vice-Chancellor', supplement 1 to OUG no. 5036, 16 Oct. 2013, p. 74.
[42] Harvard's endowment grew by over 50 per cent between 2001 and 2012.
[43] For the small membership of the Oxford Society, see pp. 477–8, this volume.

projects. The University did not seek to establish a school of twenty-first-century studies. It was the donor, James Martin, who sought out Oxford.[44]

Oxford's emergence as an academic colossus fundamentally affected its relations with the city and the wider British public. In 2014, the University's buildings were no longer confined to the area around the Bodleian but were spread all over the city and beyond. Town–gown relations were better than they had been traditionally but the feuds of the past were replaced by new quarrels. In a small city, to the annoyance of many, the University was everywhere, putting up architecturally insensitive buildings and destroying quiet residential neighbourhoods.[45] Conversely, to the British public, Oxford was no longer a permanent presence in the family parlour. It was understood to be an intellectual hothouse whose students won the lottery of life; radio and television made a handful of Oxford dons household names; and there was a much better chance by the end of the period that members of the public knew of at least one young person from their neighbourhood who had gone to Oxford. But the relationship was distant and no longer warm, and most people had little understanding of the University's academic pre-eminence.[46]

What had bonded the two together at the end of the nineteenth century had been sport. But Oxford's (and Cambridge's) claim to be at the centre of the nation's sporting life was at an end by the early 1960s. Sport remained an important part of college life throughout the period, but few Oxford men (or women) stepped straight into the national side, the University's teams looked weak compared with good county sides, and varsity contests, except the Boat Race, lost a public following.[47] In 1954, an Oxford student took the world by storm when Roger Bannister ran the first sub four-minute mile on the Iffley Road track.[48] But this turned out to be Oxford's sporting swansong. As college admissions became more meritocratic, the standard of male sport declined; the great expansion in the number of female students dropped it further. In a nation even more obsessed by sport than hitherto, Oxford ceased to be a team to follow.[49]

---

[44] See pp. 602 and 628, this volume.

[45] Conflict was intensified as there were two universities in Oxford by the end of the period: see pp. 710–12, this volume.

[46] For informed analysis of breaking news, TV and radio tended to rely on academics attached to the colleges of the University of London, rather than Oxford and Cambridge dons.

[47] The Boat Race in the television age became an annual event in the sporting calendar and the recording rights were sold round the world. The crews remained of a high calibre because the continued mystique of the event encouraged American rowing internationals in particular to do postgraduate work at Oxbridge. Oxford had three Olympic gold medallists in the 2014 race. In 1987, a quarrel between the coach, Dan Topolski, and five American internationals in the blue-boat squad led to the Americans walking out and a novice crew rowing to victory. Topolski's best-selling book about the affair was turned into the film *True Blue* (1996).

[48] Bannister, of Exeter college, went on to be a neurologist and returned to Oxford as master of Pembroke: for his life, see his *Twin Tracks: The Autobiography* (London, 2014).

[49] Britain's universities continued to attract talented athletes but they tended to gravitate to places that offered specialist sports facilities and courses in sports science, like Loughborough, granted university status in 1966. The only sport where Oxford alumni were still a significant presence in the national squad was rowing. The most famous Oxford oarsman at the beginning of the twenty-first century was Sir Matthew Pinsent, four-time winner of an Olympic gold medal in the coxless pairs.

Many members of the public gained a new acquaintance with Oxford in the second half of the period. Through visiting the city as tourists, and its frequent use as a backdrop to television drama, Britons fell in love with its buildings.[50] But this was an affection for the Oxford of the past, not the present. Significantly, it was the colleges, whose power and influence was waning, that they were charmed by. In the popular mind, Oxford at the beginning of the twenty-first century was not the home of sporting heroes with whom the public identified and sought to emulate but the home of too-clever-by-half boffins and eggheads with whom one would sup, if one had to sup all, with a long-handled spoon.[51]

[50] The evergreen detective series *Morse* was first shown in 1987 and continues today in different manifestations. Colin Dexter, the author of the Morse books, was a Cambridge graduate who worked for many years as assistant secretary to the University's Delegacy of Local Examinations.

[51] The British public's long-standing suspicion of intelligence, exemplified in the views of my own ancestors, continues to run deep. At the end of the final episode of the highly popular TV comedy *Blackadder Goes Forth* (1989), set in 1917, the cast prepares to go over the top, having failed to engineer a plan of escape. The self-serving use of intelligence and its limited value at times of real need are laid bare in a cutting reference to 'a fox who's just been appointed Professor of Cunning at Oxford University'. The comedy's co-writer, Richard Curtis, is a Christ Church man.

CHAPTER 13

External Pressures and Internal Responses

A. The Post-War Era

THE years from 1945 to 1965 were a halcyon period of growth and prosperity for the University of Oxford. The opening up of academic secondary education to many more children from less affluent backgrounds swelled the pool of potential Oxford entrants, and the University was happy to let undergraduate numbers gradually increase to accommodate the growing demand. By 1964–5, there were 7,300 undergraduates in residence, over 60 per cent more than on the eve of the war, and 40 per cent were grammar-school pupils.[1] Oxford also accepted that, in a world that placed a new premium on research in the arts and sciences, its reputation, both nationally and internationally, depended on building up its postgraduate provision. It was in these two decades that Oxford finally came of age as a research university, however significant individual achievements had been in the interwar years. In 1938–9, postgraduates had been less than a tenth of the student population. By 1964–5, the intake had expanded more than fourfold to 2,150 and the postgraduate share of the total was almost a quarter. (See Table 4.) The postgraduate in arts needed little beyond the good library facilities which already largely existed. The postgraduate scientist, on the other hand, needed lab space, and only physics, chemistry, and pathology were suitably housed. The development of the Science Area, curtailed because of the war, therefore continued apace and, by the early sixties, new buildings had been constructed for the other sciences.[2] The scientists also required a host of new ancillary facilities to support their activities. A sign of how the world of research was changing was the establishment of the Computing Laboratory in 1957.

The expansion was made possible by government largesse. No longer queasy about accepting state funding, Oxford warmly embraced successive governments' readiness to finance the expansion of higher education and promote research, and drew ever more heavily on the bounty of the UGC for both capital and current

---

[1] Robbins, p. 80.   [2] Listed on p. 635, this volume.

expenditure. In 1934–5 the University had an income of £452,000 and received 20 per cent from the treasury. Thirty years later, that income had rocketed to £6.3 million, four times higher in real terms, and Oxford relied on the state for over 80 per cent of its funds.[3] The University continued to receive generous benefactions that allowed development into new research areas. The establishment in 1954 of Queen Elizabeth House, for instance, the University's centre for British colonial studies, was made possible by a gift of £100,000 from Sir Ernest Oppenheimer. But its significant building projects of the era relied heavily on the UGC. Although the Rockefeller Foundation contributed to the one important humanities building put up in the twenty years after the war, the St Cross Building for Law and English, begun in 1961, the majority of the money was supplied by the taxpayer.[4] Few dons ever doubted the wisdom of coming to rely more and more heavily on state funding. When the Worcester College economist and educationalist John Vaizey hinted in the *Oxford Magazine* of 7 November 1963 that the University might eventually have to go private like Harvard if it wanted to retain its international standing, his guarded suggestion fell on deaf ears.[5]

The UGC supplied the means. But it did not supply the vision. Oxford's rapid expansion in the post-war era was principally the responsibility of a small group of energetic college heads who controlled the University's affairs. They were not usually the members of the University best known to the general public.[6] But they were the real architects of Oxford's continued pre-eminence. Some, like William Stallybrass of Brasenose and Maurice Bowra of Wadham (Vice-Chancellors in 1947–8 and 1951–4) were already significant figures in Oxford life before the war and ensured links with the past were not completely broken.[7] Others came to prominence for the first time in the era, such as the two Australians Sir Kenneth Wheare and Dame Lucy Sutherland. Wheare, Gladstone professor of government, rector of Exeter, and Vice-Chancellor 1964–6, was a man solidly rooted in Oxford who travelled little and spent the post-war era immersed in university administration. He was a member of Council from 1947 to 1967, sat on the UGC from 1959 to 1963, and chaired the Rhodes Trust from 1962 to 1969.[8] Sutherland, a respected historian of the eighteenth century and principal of Lady Margaret Hall, noted for her rapid speech, was the first woman to become a leading light in the University (see Figure 13.1). Although never elected to the top job, she represented Oxford on the UGC from 1964 to 1969 and was the University's first female pro-Vice-Chancellor. The heads of house were ably seconded

---

[3] Franks, i. 283. This gives a figure of 75 per cent for 1962–3 but this does not include the student fees paid by the state.

[4] The buildings put up by the colleges, on the other hand, relied heavily on private donors: see p. 671, this volume.

[5] OM, 7 November 1963, p. 63. Vaizey was responding to the criticisms of Oxford by Robbins. Vaizey later became professor of economics at Brunel and vice-chancellor of Monash.

[6] For these, see pp. 658–9, this volume.

[7] For Bowra as an enfant terrible, see pp. 406 and 502, this volume. Stallybrass was a conservative figure fixated on college sport. Yet as Vice-Chancellor he understood the need to develop Oxford as a science university.

[8] Wheare had studied PPE as a Rhodes scholar. He sat on the city council between 1940 and 1957 and was later chancellor of the University of Liverpool.

FGIURE 13.1 Dame Lucy Sutherland, 1903–80, historian, principal of Lady Margaret Hall, and University politician: photograph. Sutherland, of Australian parentage, was a fellow and tutor at Somerville between the wars before moving to Lady Margaret Hall. Her particular passion was the East India Company and she might have been the first female regius professor of modern history if she had not put her college before her faculty.

by the two registrars of the era. The unobtrusive Sir Douglas Veale continued to weave his magic until 1958 when he was replaced by Sir Folliott Sandford. Another career civil servant, Stanford was just as unobtrusive and diligent, though he lacked his predecessor's creative touch.[9]

The coterie of college heads who shaped Oxford's post-war future carried through the expansion without changing the University's structure to any extent. The University was much the same institution in 1966 as thirty years earlier. Executive power continued to lie with the Vice-Chancellor and Council, while Congregation remained sovereign, though its meetings were so poorly attended that a system of postal voting had to be introduced in 1960 to extend participation. The University also remained a predominantly male institution. The quota on the number of female students was lifted in 1957, but they were actually a smaller

[9] He would not have seen the opportunity presented by Nuffield's desire to found a college: see p. 486, this volume.

percentage of the undergraduate student body in 1965–6 than in 1928–9, down to 13 from 15 per cent.[10] The University's collegiate character went equally unchallenged. The traditional requirement that undergraduates and graduates should be attached to a college, society, or hall, regardless of whether they were resident inside or outside its walls during their sojourn, was cemented rather than relaxed, while the colleges remained independent of the University and largely of one another. From 1946, there was an additional forum in the Senior Tutors' Committee where matters of shared interest might be discussed, but the colleges clung jealously to their traditional rights and eschewed joint decision-making. The University, too, remained poorly endowed compared with the colleges, even if its income from the early 1950s was higher than theirs combined.[11]

The University did make some moves towards interfering with college independence but they chiefly related to admissions and were scarcely radical. In 1960, Congregation accepted the recommendation of the Chilver Committee that Latin should be abolished as an entrance requirement for scientists. Two years later, in 1962, following the report of the Hardie Committee, the scholars' and commoners' entrance examinations were merged on the grounds that the calibre of candidates had risen in the past decade, and the Colleges' Admissions Office was set up to oversee the process.[12] If anything, competition between the colleges remained just as strong as it had ever been. Indeed, it gained greater weight in the public mind from 1963 when *The Times* first published a list ranking college performance in Schools. Known as the Norrington Table after the president of Trinity, Sir Arthur Norrington, who suggested a refined weighting of the results, it helped to embed more widely the idea that Oxford was a confederation rather than a federation of colleges.[13] So too did the popular TV quiz show *University Challenge*, aired for the first time in the same year, in which teams from Oxford and Cambridge colleges took on other universities.[14]

The expansion in numbers was also largely managed within the existing college framework, though it put huge pressure on colleges that could not afford new buildings. Some institutions enjoyed a change of status: Keble became a full college in 1952, as did St Edmund Hall and St Peter's in 1957 and 1961; while Mansfield became a permanent private hall in 1955, and Greyfriars and Regent's Park in 1957.[15] There were only five entirely new foundations over the twenty years, however. Now

---

[10] Franks, i. 54 (table).

[11] Ibid., i. 283. In 1962–3, the University's share of the total income of both the University and the colleges was 73 per cent. In 1964, the colleges' endowment income was five times higher than the University's.

[12] The first committee was chaired by Guy Chilver, ancient historian at Queen's, the second by W. F. R. Hardie, president of Corpus.

[13] Norrington, Vice-Chancellor 1960–2, had been assistant secretary, then secretary, to the Delegates of the University Press.

[14] An Oxford college, New, won for the first time in 1965: <https://en.wikipedia.org/wiki/University_Challenge> (accessed 8 August 2013).

[15] Greyfriars ceased to be a PPH in 2008. By then Blackfriars had joined the number in 1994, Wycliffe Hall in 1996, and the Anglo-catholic St Stephen's House (formerly an Anglican theological college founded by the Tractarians in 1876) in 2003.

that poorer students could receive grants to cover their fees and maintenance, there was no longer a need to provide for undergraduates who could not afford a college attachment, so the two non-collegiate societies lost their *raison d'être*. The Oxford Home Students Society for women, St Anne's, was opened as a residential college in 1952 and received its charter in 1959. Its male counterpart, St Catherine's, made the transition ten years later, through the determination of the historian and former New College tutor Sir Alan Bullock, who became its first master. Thanks to Bullock's efforts and enthusiasm, a greenfield site in Holywell Great Meadow was acquired from Merton, £2.5 million raised from public and private sources, and the Danish architect Arne Jacobsen commissioned to design a modern and minimalist building that was begun in 1960.[16] The three other foundations were graduate-only institutions. There was no suggestion that the upsurge in graduate numbers should lead to the establishment of a separate non-residential community. Postgraduates had to be members of a college as well as a faculty. Yet, as it was accepted that not all graduates, especially newcomers to the University, would want to live in a mainly undergraduate environment, no objection was raised to the creation of separate societies. Nuffield, the oldest, had been set up before the war but did not move to its present buildings until 1960; St Antony's was founded in 1950 as a result of a gift from Antonin Besse, an Aden merchant, and was established from the beginning on the Woodstock Road; while Linacre, opened in 1962, was a University initiative and located initially on a site in St Aldate's.[17]

For fifteen years, the UGC made no attempt to use its financial muscle to corral Oxford into changing its traditional structures and bring it more into line with other British universities, bar Cambridge. Indeed, immediately after the war, the UGC ensured the long-term survival of the collegiate and tutorial system by agreeing to fund a huge expansion in the number of university lectureships. Between the wars, most college tutors were paid by their college to provide tutorials and intercollegiate lectures. Some, on the other hand, especially in the sciences, had been given university lecturing posts and had part of their salary paid from the Chest. From 1949, the UGC agreed that the scheme could be extended to all 286 tutorial fellows who gave intercollegiate lecturers. They would henceforth be known as Common University Fund lecturers and the cost would be borne by the public purse.[18] The arrangement suited both the University and the colleges. The colleges saved money on individual tutors, so were able to expand their number to meet the growing undergraduate intake, while the University's faculties gained closer control over the delivery of the curriculum.

---

[16] Bullock was one of the few forgers of modern Oxford with a high public profile thanks to his *Hitler: A Study in Tyranny* (1952). He became Vice-Chancellor in 1979.

[17] It moved to Cherwell Edge, its present site, in 1977.

[18] It will be recalled that, from the late nineteenth century, college lectures ceased to be simply for those who resided in the college and began to be thrown open to all junior members: see pp. 414–15, this volume. From 1950 it was agreed that all future tutorial fellows would become CUFs from the second year of their tenure. There were still some college-only appointments, but nothing akin to Cambridge, where a system of university-only or college-only appointments, begun after the First World War, continued to pertain.

In 1960, however, the UGC indicated it might eventually extract its pound of flesh by announcing an enquiry into Oxford's teaching methods. This came to nothing, and the UGC appeared to give its wholehearted support to the college system when, contrary to its usual practice of only financing university capital projects, it gave £650,000 towards building St Catherine's.[19] The appointment of the Robbins Committee in the following year, on the other hand, suggested that more serious trouble might lie ahead. Robbins, it was feared, would find Oxford out of kilter with the rest of the British higher-education system and demand significant changes to its collegiate structure.

In the event, Robbins was not overly critical when he reported in 1963. He had three chief complaints about Oxford and Cambridge. In the first place, the universities were not drawing enough pupils from state schools. Even if 39 per cent of Oxford undergraduates now came from the state system, this was far removed from the 70 per cent share of other universities in England and Wales, and was actually no more than 30 per cent when male entrants alone were considered.[20] Much closer liaison between the colleges and the maintained schools was advised. Secondly, the ancient universities were too attractive. In terms of pay and conditions, they were much more appealing than elsewhere and were consequently creaming off the country's academic talent. He had no quarrel with the two traditional universities as elite institutions but wanted more competition in the system and other universities given a chance to shine. The best way forward, he felt, was for potential competitors to receive huge capital grants to create a more level playing field, and for the Oxbridge pay scale to be brought into line with the rest of the system:

> It is not a good thing that Oxford and Cambridge should attract too high a proportion of the country's best brains and become more and more exclusively composed of a certain kind of intellectual elite . . . [W]hat is needed is not only greater equality of opportunity to enter Oxford and Cambridge but also rather more equality of attraction between them and at least some other institutions.[21]

Thirdly, and most importantly, Robbins made it clear that the universities' system of governance that required the agreement of both the colleges and Congregation or senate before major decisions could be taken was defective:

> We recognise fully the distinctive merits of the college system. It gives to both senior and junior members a strong focus of loyalty within a large institution, and allows the virtues of academic self-government to be widely diffused. But the number of times when it is necessary to except Oxford and Cambridge from general statements about British universities, the difficulty both universities have in reaching rapid decisions on matters of policy with their present constitutional arrangements, and the general obscurity in which so many of their administrative and financial arrangements are

---

[19] St Catherine's had been mooted since 1957 and the University requested money for its development in its 1959–64 quinquennial plan. The University refused to ask the UGC for money to aid the development of Mansfield.

[20] Robbins' figures were much too low: see p. 574, this volume, and Table 2.   [21] Robbins, pp. 80–1.

shrouded are not compatible with a situation in which they, like other universities, are largely dependent on public funds. Continuance of such anomalies may well endanger not only their own welfare but also the effectiveness of the whole system of higher education in this country, of which they are and should be so splendid a part.

Both universities were to be given the opportunity to address the issue. However, 'if Oxford and Cambridge are unable satisfactorily to solve these problems within a reasonable time, they should be the subject of independent inquiry.'[22]

The two universities took the warning to heart. Although they had a friend in the Conservative prime minister, Harold Macmillan, who had been Chancellor of Oxford since 1959, there was a general election in the offing which might well bring a less sympathetic Labour government to office. Even before Robbins reported, Oxford had begun to look at the mote in its own eye. Besides the Hardie Committee on admissions, a second, chaired by the warden of Merton, A. R. W. Harrison, had been set up in 1962 to look at how teaching and research might be more closely integrated in a system where the colleges were primarily associated with teaching and the faculties with research. Robbins' comments prompted further action. On 3 February 1964, Hebdomadal Council appointed a committee headed by the provost of Worcester, Lord Franks, 'to consider the recommendations and criticisms in the Robbins Report and arising out of it which particularly affect Oxford'. The provost's committee quickly concluded that the University must appoint its own investigatory commission 'to inquire into and report upon the part which Oxford plays now and should play in the future in the system of higher education in the United Kingdom, having regard to its position as both a national and an international University'. Council accepted the recommendation, and on 18 March set up a commission of six senior members, four men and two women, with Franks in the chair and a deputy registrar, B. G. Campbell, acting as secretary.[23] The University also established two other committees to look at specific issues. One, the Kneale Committee, was empowered to look into the undergraduate examination structure to see what improvements might be made.[24] The other, the Norrington Committee, chaired by the president of Trinity, was asked to pick up where Harrison had left off and explore the vexed question of university lecturers with no college attachment. Oxford's expansion as a research university meant that there were many new university lecturers by the early 1960s in areas not specifically covered by the undergraduate curriculum. Although it was now de rigueur for new tutorial fellows to have or be given a university lectureship, there was no concomitant agreement that all university lecturers should be elected to a college fellowship. In 1962, non-fellows formed 43 per cent of Congregation's membership.[25]

---

[22] Robbins, p. 224. Robbins was later unfairly accused of wanting to make all universities equal when he reiterated his views in his *The University in the Modern World, and Other Papers on Higher Education* (London, 1966): see *The Times*, 25 Apr. 1966, p. 11.

[23] Franks, i. 11–13.

[24] Called after its chair, William Calvert Kneale, White's professor of moral philosophy, and a leading Oxford analytical philosopher: for Oxford philosophy post-war, see pp. 648–9, this volume.

[25] From 1961, the non-fellows had an informal committee looking after their interests which became the Oxford Collegiate Society in June 1963.

B. The Franks Report and its Aftermath

Oliver Franks was the perfect insider to head Oxford's first internal audit. Initially a humdrum tutor in philosophy at Queen's who had moved to a chair at Glasgow in the early 1930s, Franks had exchanged academic life for government service during the war and never looked back. He had played an important role in setting up the Marshall Plan, helped to create NATO, and spent two years in Washington as the British ambassador. Before becoming provost of Worcester in 1962, he had also been chairman of Lloyds Bank. Franks was renowned for being profoundly reasonable and publicly austere. There was no other head of house in the 1960s with his prestigious pedigree, and the findings of his commission were guaranteed to command respect in Whitehall and beyond.[26]

Over the next two years, the Franks Commission met on 189 occasions and received both oral and written evidence (see Figure 13.2). The material that was gathered and eventually placed in the OUA was a lasting tribute to the thoroughness of the enquiry and formed a snapshot of unprecedented detail of every aspect

FIGURE 13.2 The Franks Commission, first oral hearing, October 1964: photograph. The photograph shows the chairman and his committee of six. The committee was reasonably representative of the University's different constituencies. From left to right: Sir Robert Hall, an economist and principal-elect of Hertford; Miss M. G. Ord, a biochemist and tutor at Lady Margaret Hall; Sir Maurice Shock, politics tutor and estates bursar of University College; Lord Franks; Sir Lindor Brown, Waynflete professor of physiology; Mrs J. Floud, a sociologist and fellow of Nuffield; and J. Steven Watson, a historian and student and fellow of Christ Church.

[26] He later became chancellor of the new University of East Anglia.

of the University's life. The commission's report contained 170 recommendations and was submitted to Council on 29 March 1966. It was wide-ranging and considered nearly every aspect of the University's life.[27] The tone was critical but always defensive. On the one hand, Robbins was right. Oxford's governance was inefficient for the needs of the second half of the twentieth century and should be streamlined. On the other, he was wrong in wanting to spread the cream more widely and reduce Oxford's attraction. While the commission recognized that Oxford was part of a British higher-education system and was morally and financially accountable to the British public, it believed that Robbins had not fully grasped the University's special needs. Oxford was an international university 'comparable to the great centres of learning in Europe and across the Atlantic, attracting scholars and students of the highest quality from all parts of the world'. To retain this position, it could not be just another British research university excelling in one or two branches of knowledge: it had to 'exhibit research and teaching of distinction...over a wide field'. No move should be undertaken that diluted its activities and Oxford pay should be raised rather than reduced. Oxford's status had to be protected in order to sustain Britain's reputation in the world of science and scholarship.[28]

The report therefore set out to transform Oxford into a university that would pass muster with its external critics but still be head and shoulders above the large majority of its British competitors. This was to be done not by wholesale change, but by working with the grain of the existing system. There was to be no revolution. The report did not debate at length the purpose of higher education beyond asserting that 'a university is concerned, on the one hand, with the advancement of knowledge, and, on the other, with the training of young people'.[29] What it was anxious to do was to identify the essential characteristics of the University of Oxford in the present and suggest how these could be best preserved and fostered.

First of all, Oxford was to remain an independent society of learning. It was not to develop into the American 'multiversity' recently trumpeted by Clark Kerr of the University of California, where higher education directly served the needs of the local or national community.[30] Knowledge was a national good and cooperation with bodies like the National Health Service was legitimate, but 'new ideas of a fundamental nature' would never germinate if contact with the outside world was too close. Dons must continue, for their own good, to live in an ivory tower, so that they could think in the long term.[31]

Secondly, the commission insisted that Oxford should remain a democratic and collegiate university where dons were not locked into their subject speciality and dictated to by a distant bureaucracy but participated in decision-making at all

---

[27] It contained nothing about Oxford's libraries. These were the subject of a separate enquiry chaired by Robert Shackleton, a fellow in French at Brasenose, expert on the Enlightenment, and later Bodley's librarian.
[28] Franks, i. 29–30.   [29] Ibid., p. 21.
[30] Clark Kerr, *The Uses of the University* (Cambridge, MA, 1963). Kerr, an economist turned administrator, was president of the University of California, 1958–67.
[31] Franks, i. 43.

levels: 'In the last resort we rest on the view that the nature of teaching and research is such that both will be better done if those engaged on these activities feel that they can be fully associated with the determination of university policy if they wish to be.'[32] But the maintenance of the collegiate system meant that the University should not become too big. A college would lose its unity and identity if the total number of senior and junior members in any college were to rise above 500, and there was a limit to the number of colleges Oxford could successfully support. Few more could be safely accommodated. Not only were there geographical constraints on further expansion but cooperation between essentially autonomous units would break down if their number was allowed to go on increasing willy-nilly. The University now had some 10,000 students: according to the commission, 13,000 was the optimum for the future.[33]

Thirdly, Oxford should be, as it was now, a university of undergraduates and postgraduates. A Fabian pamphlet in 1959 had suggested that the way forward was for Oxford to become a graduate-only university and the possibility was also raised in the Robbins Report. The Franks Commission had no truck with this idea. It was taken as a given that teaching and research were complementary, and that they could never be separated without loss. The trick was to get the balance between the two right, and here Oxford was wanting. Research was not an add-on: '[It] is not something which academics do in the spare time they have left over from teaching, but ... the first priority in their lives, giving meaning to the rest of their activities.' In Oxford, however, CUF tutors and lecturers were frequently teaching more than fifteen to sixteen hours a week. This was twice as much as the national average and impoverished both the University's research and teaching. The University must take the imbalance in hand. Progress could be made by increasing the number of postholders; placing a fourteen-hour cap on teaching obligations of all kinds, including graduate supervision; and ensuring dons took their sabbatical entitlement: 'It is not so much the total of hours spent in teaching each week which affects results so much as the need to have unbroken days and blocks of time for it.'[34]

Little was thought to be amiss with Oxford's undergraduate education. An expansion in the number of students reading the natural and social sciences was predicted, and a plea was made for increasing the numbers studying the applied sciences, especially engineering, where Oxford looked weak nationally.[35] On the other hand, the traditional method of selecting undergraduates by a separate Oxford entrance examination met with complete approval. Although all other universities, apart from Cambridge, chose students on their A-level performance, there was no need for Oxford to follow their lead. A-levels were an uncertain predictor and the sensible way forward was for a common university entrance examination to be devised for all applicants to the British university system.[36] Just

[32] Ibid. pp. 191–2.   [33] Ibid., pp. 45–6.   [34] Ibid., pp. 30, 105–6, 130, 138–9, 214, and 225.
[35] Only 3 per cent of Oxford students were taking a course in the applied sciences compared with 15 per cent across the UK. Franks wanted to increase the number studying engineering to 500: ibid., pp. 49–50.
[36] Ibid., pp. 80–2.

as sacrosanct was the time-honoured method of delivering the undergraduate curriculum by single or paired tutorials. The number of tutorials could be safely reduced to one a week, so that tutor and student were not overburdened, and care was to be taken that they were used to teach pupils to think rather than impart knowledge. The commission also agreed with Robbins that room should be found for classes and lectures as well as lab work. But the tutorial based on private preparation beforehand was the hallmark of an Oxford education: 'We intend that reading and writing, rather than listening, should continue to be the salient characteristics of the Oxford system.'[37]

The commission was more concerned about postgraduate studies. At present, provision was too small. Oxford needed to train more postgraduates, both to come into line with national policy and to ensure the expanding university system at home and abroad was properly staffed. Robbins believed that 30 per cent of the student population should be postgraduates. To reach and surpass this target, assuming its undergraduate numbers only grew slowly, Oxford would have to increase its postgraduates by at least 60 per cent over the next 15 to 20 years, to between 3,500 and 4,000 students. The selection and support of the postgraduates should also be better organized. Graduates should be initially admitted by a faculty, not by a college, as still frequently occurred in the arts; efforts should be made to seek good candidates from other universities and abroad by advertising; financial support should be found for those without research council or government awards; and the progress of all graduates should be properly monitored at college and university level. Furthermore, graduate needs were not properly catered for in the old undergraduate colleges: this had to be addressed.[38]

The most urgent issue that had to be tackled in the commission's view was governance. Since 1945, a lot of changes had occurred silently as the University grew in size and its administration became more complex under the pressure of an internally and externally generated increase in business. In theory, Council, the Chest, and the General Board were equal partners under a semi-detached Vice-Chancellor, but in fact Council had become the dominant body and the Vice-Chancellor, though also a head of house, was now a full-time executive officer and liaison between Oxford and the outside world. This change needed statutory warranty. As things stood, none of the three parties understood their precise role and there was a tendency for the different parts of the university administration to be reactive rather than proactive in an age where forward planning was much more important. There were also unnecessary administrative complexities and peculiarities. Congregation was asked to give its verdict on trivial curricular issues but had no sight of the five-year plan drawn up by Council for the UGC, while the need to consult each college over any initiative which touched on college interests led to huge delays in decision-making. According to the evidence given by Wadham's warden, Maurice Bowra, the

---

[37] Ibid., pp. 102–16. [38] Ibid., pp. 49–50, 92–3, 119–24.

fact the system worked at all was 'a miracle of good temper' and 'goodwill'.[39] All could be rectified, however, if the system was rationalized.

Under the recommendations of the commission, the pre-eminent administrative role of the Hebdomadal Council was to be formally recognized. Henceforth, it was to contain twenty-four members, eighteen elected by Congregation and six, including the Vice-Chancellor and the Proctors, ex officio. Its remit was to plan for the future and administer the University through its many committees, which would include the General Board and a new Chest Committee. Congregation would still be sovereign, for it was the foundation upon which Oxford's claim to be a 'republic of equals' rested. But its competence was to be clearly outlined. Its powers would be electoral, legislative, consultative, and interrogatory. Only Council would have the power to present legislation, but Congregation could confirm or reject draft statutes and would be the forum in which major issues were debated and disputes resolved. Congregation's position, too, would be strengthened by putting an end to Convocation's residual right to interfere in its decisions. At the same time, the colleges would be brought properly into the central decision-making apparatus by the creation of a Council of Colleges. At present, the colleges had little influence over university policy because they did not speak with one voice and were 'in danger of becoming no more than endowed halls of residence'. The new intercollegiate forum, normally summoned by the Vice-Chancellor, would allow the colleges to become a force in the University by giving them a mechanism through which to express a collective point of view.[40]

To ensure that the new structure worked smoothly, the central administration, headed by the reorganized Hebdomadal Council, was to be made more coherent and effective by clarifying the roles of the Vice-Chancellor, the registrar, and the General Board. The Vice-Chancellor was to serve for four years rather than two, which was judged a term 'long enough to enable a man to use the instruments we have designed for him', but not 'so long that he becomes remote from the interests of academic life'.[41] He was to be designated by a nominating committee and need no longer be a college head. The registrar was to be his right-hand man in charge of a unified secretariat. The General Board was to become the chief academic administrative body, hold the purse strings, and not be overloaded with petty work. While hitherto it had had only limited sway over the quasi-independent faculty boards, it was to be given real teeth. In order that the General Board had 'a less blurred view of, and more effective control over, the whole academic scene', the number of faculty boards was to be reduced to five: theology, philosophy, history, and music; languages and literature; social studies including law; physical sciences, including mathematics; and biological sciences including medicine: 'The present divisions correspond roughly to the undergraduate Honours Schools, but not to the interests of postgraduate research nor to the fields of knowledge as advance and

[39] Ibid., p. 215.   [40] Ibid., pp. 230–1, 235, and 262–5.   [41] Ibid., p. 237.

interpretation proceed.' General Board members would be elected from the five faculties: they 'would understand the points of view of sectional groups' but would not be 'committed to them'.[42] The old faculties would become sub-faculties and be responsible for day-to-day academic business.

The commission also concluded that, for Oxford to fulfil its *raison d'être* effectively, an attempt had to be made to reduce the great difference in wealth between the richest and poorest colleges. The wealth discrepancy had grown rather than diminished over the years, with the foundations since the late nineteenth century. Of the thirty-one colleges existing at the time of the report, Christ Church was the richest, with a gross endowment income in 1964 of £301,325; St Peter's the poorest, with a mere £6,364. The University had already signalled its concern about the imbalance when it decided in 1963 to give £2,000 per annum to the five women's colleges and the four poorest men's. The commission decided it was time to address the problem in earnest: 'Hitherto it has been the weakness of the collegiate system in Oxford that a number of colleges have been insufficiently endowed to achieve the level of financial security necessary for the unfettered and unharassed performance of their academic tasks.' The solution was to use the fruits of college taxation, introduced in the 1880s, to build up the endowment of the poorer institutions. Now that the colleges' combined income was less than the University's, there was no longer a need for an annual transfer of funds from one to the other. Instead, the money could be used over a twenty-year period to raise the endowment of the twelve poorest colleges and the three new graduate societies to £40,000 per annum, a figure already attained by all the colleges founded before 1800 except Worcester and Pembroke.[43] Franks rejected the idea that the colleges' resources might be pooled. If there were an equal distribution of wealth, colleges would lose the incentive to improve their income by their own efforts, there would be less opportunity to innovate, and they would no longer feel independent. But the present situation could not go on and the colleges collectively had a responsibility for the well-being of their poorer brothers and sisters.

In May 1966, the Franks Report was discussed in Congregation, then, over the next two years, a series of statutes was placed before it to turn the recommendations into law. Many suggestions were taken up. The Vice-Chancellor's tenure was extended, Hebdomadal Council's powers and composition restructured, the role of Congregation clearly defined, and the redirection of the college contribution approved without difficulty.[44] But the dons would not accept everything Franks wanted. Congregation was ready to have its powers clarified and Convocation neutered but it wanted more power over the executive than Franks had envisaged. Above all, it insisted on the right to elect the Vice-Chancellor, the power to amend or reject Council's decrees and regulations, and the ability to compel Council to

[42] Ibid., pp. 247, 254, and 260.   [43] Ibid., pp. 284 and 290 (table).
[44] There was a lot of discussion prior to the report about the exact details of the new contributions system: see University Archives PRP/1/2/1: Report of Evidence by Colleges, 27 May 1965.

bring forward legislation when a resolution had been passed by a majority of at least seventy-five. The role of the postal vote was also reinforced. In cases of disagreement between the executive and the legislature, a vote could be ordered either by Council or fifty or more members of Congregation.

Two of the key recommendations aimed at streamlining decision-making were equally turned down. There was complete refusal to reorganize the academic side of the University in the name of efficiency. In consequence, the General Board's role, if anything, became more difficult to perform not less. From 1967, it had a full-time vice-chairman and its membership, elected by Congregation, was reduced to sixteen, with equal representation in arts and sciences. But it still had to liaise with a disparate group of independent disciplinary faculties and a growing number of stand-alone committees for interdisciplinary subjects such as Byzantine studies.[45] The colleges also valued their independence too dearly to accept the Council of Colleges. Instead, a Conference of Colleges was set up in November 1966, where representatives could chew over matters of mutual interest but which had no power to bind its constituent members. Nothing was done about All Souls either. Under the conservative rule of the sterile and complex John Sparrow—a Bowrista, but always publicly on the side of convention—All Souls had remained stuck in its pre-war past, a dining club for the intellectually precocious, high court judges and top politicians.[46] Franks looked on a college that had no students as a contradiction in terms and gave it three years to come up with a coherent plan which would show that it was an academic benefit to the University. In the event, little pressure was put on it to change its spots, and All Souls continued to be a college of fellows, albeit one that now spent some of its wealth on an extensive visiting fellowship scheme.[47]

Congregation was even less impressed with the findings of the Norrington and Kneale committees that reported independently a year earlier, in 1965. Kneale had two basic recommendations: the University should develop joint honours degrees; and Schools should be divided into a two-part exam as at Cambridge, to lessen the load in the final year and allow students to change subject after part 1.[48] The dons were willing to contemplate the development of joint honours degrees and the first were introduced in 1969, but reform of the examination system was dismissed out of hand. The problem of the lecturer without a college attachment addressed in the Norrington Report was also put to one side. In 1965 it was agreed that two more

---

[45] There were sixteen faculties in 1966: anthropology and geography, biological sciences, English language and literature, law, Lit. Hum., mathematics, medieval and modern European languages, medicine, modern history, music, oriental studies, physical sciences, physiological sciences, psychological studies (since 1959, the only post-war creation), social sciences, and theology. These were divided into various sub-faculties and departments.

[46] On Sparrow, see Noel Annan, *The Dons: Mentors, Eccentrics and Geniuses* (London, 1990), ch. 10. A man who 'quite procrastinated life away', Sparrow was a practising lawyer of some distinction but wrote nothing of substance.

[47] Franks, i. 145–7. There was a coterie of reform-minded fellows in All Souls in the first half of the 1960s but they had difficulty getting Sparrow to act on their wishes: see Isaiah Berlin, *Building. Letters 1960–1975*, ed. Henry Hardy and Mark Pottle (London, 2013), pp. 186–90, 194, and 217.

[48] W. C. Kneale, *Report of the Committee on the Structure of the First and Second Public Examination* (Oxford, 1965).

graduate societies should be set up, Iffley and St Cross, which, together with Linacre, it was hoped, would mop up a large proportion of the unattached.[49] No attempt, however, was made to compel colleges to take in the rest. The problem was largely solved from 1973 when it was agreed that, in future, all appointments to newly created university lectureships should come with the prospect of a fellowship. But it was 1987 before the 'entitlement' issue, as it was known, was finally put to bed. As there were always a number of new university lectureships for which it was difficult to find a college association, an element of compulsion was introduced. A rota of colleges was established, and any new lectureship that had failed to arouse a college's interest was allocated to the next on the list.[50]

The University of Oxford was perhaps the austere Franks' sole passion. His love for his alma mater was obsessive. The principal aim of his report was to safeguard the University's traditional core against outside attack by making it more efficient and opening it up to a wider constituency. But there was a clear limit to how far Oxford would accept restructuring, even to keep the enemy from the gate. Most dons had a limited knowledge of the problems of the central administration and were content with the status quo. Congregation was happy to give legislative recognition to changes that had occurred informally over the preceding twenty years, but it was reluctant to restructure the administrative hierarchy and simplify the relationship between the University and the colleges in the name of efficiency. At the end of the 1960s, Oxford and Cambridge (where the Bridges Syndicate had led to similar limited reforms) were still organized very differently from other British universities. In consequence, as Oxford grew larger and larger its structural problems were certain to inflate.

C. Access

Besides discussing undergraduate and postgraduate numbers and suggesting changes to the subject balance, Franks also voiced concern about the low proportion of women and working-class students at Oxford. In both respects, Oxford and Cambridge were unusual. In other British universities both women and working-class students formed about 30 per cent of the intake, but at Oxford the figures were only 16 and 13 per cent.[51] The imbalance, Franks believed, had to be corrected. No ideal figure was given for the proportion of working-class undergraduates, but it was hoped that women would form a quarter of the junior members by the mid-1980s. In the event, raising the representation of women students, not just to a quarter but to a half of the total, proved relatively easy in the coming decades. The poor showing of students from disadvantaged backgrounds, on the other hand, was

---

[49] The one to be located at 10 St Cross Road, the other at Court Place, Iffley.
[50] For the background to the 1973 decision, see J. H. E. Griffiths, *Report of the Committee on the Long-Term Problem of Entitlement* (Oxford, 1970).
[51] Franks, i. 78. The percentage of working-class students at Cambridge was even lower: 9 per cent.

a problem with which the University struggled for the rest of the twentieth century and beyond.

Franks suggested that the profile of women at Oxford could be improved by founding another women's college and increasing numbers in the rest. His report did not anticipate that the problem would be solved in the 1970s by the undergraduate colleges going co-ed. The idea was not completely foreign to Oxford. The three new graduate colleges had been mixed for several years, while New College, in 1964, had voted to amend its statutes so that women might be admitted.[52] But Franks was only too well aware that a recommendation would not have commanded support in mid-1960s Oxford, so passed over the possibility in silence. This was a miscalculation, for the report appeared at a moment when a wind of cultural and social change was beginning to blow through the British establishment and the broader public, which rapidly transformed attitudes to single-sex education and gender roles as to so much else. Within a few years, the cause of co-education began to be taken up in Oxford JCRs and found growing support among senior members. By Michaelmas of 1970 it was clear that a revolution was in the offing.[53]

On 3 December 1970, representatives of sixteen men's colleges met in Queen's to discuss the possibility of admitting women en masse. This in turn led to a report by a group of colleges favourable to change suggesting how it might be done, and the decision of five of them to go ahead and admit female students and fellows. The University's response to the initiative was cautious. Although arguably it was up to the individual societies whether to break with tradition, it was recognized that opening up male colleges to women could reduce undergraduate applications to the women's societies. As the latter opposed the move en bloc, their interests had to be protected. It was therefore agreed that the five trailblazers could go ahead only with Congregation's approval. This was gained in May 1972 when the supporters of co-education won both the debate in the House and the subsequent postal vote, and Wadham, in the van from the beginning under Warden Stuart Hampshire, Hertford, Brasenose, Jesus, and St Catherine's were allowed to open their doors to women in October 1974.[54] Balliol, meanwhile, though not one of the five, had agreed on 6 December 1971 to admit women fellows, if not junior members, as soon as they could get the Privy Council to effect a change in the statutes, and in 1973 elected the first female fellow of a male college, Carol Clark, an expert in French literature.

There was then a hiatus, for it had also been agreed in May 1972 that no other college would follow suit for a further five years. Despite the passage of the Sex Discrimination Act by the Labour government at the end of 1975—which made Oxford look legally as well as culturally out of line—the moratorium was

[52] Nuffield and Linacre admitted women from their foundation, St Antony's from 1962. New College was not the first of the old Oxford colleges to vote on the issue. A motion to change All Souls' statutes had been put and lost two years before: Berlin, *Building. Letters*, pp. 80–2.

[53] University College's JCR petitioned for change as early as November 1968. From 1967, Balliol and St Anne's graduates mixed together in a building they shared in Holywell Ford.

[54] Hampshire, one of Oxford's leading philosophers in the 1950s, returned to Wadham from Princeton in 1970.

honoured. The Rhodes trustees took advantage of the Act to admit women as well as men as scholars, but it was only in October 1979 that the experiment of co-education was extended in the colleges. Initially, in June 1977, it had been decided among the men's colleges that a further eight of their number would admit women from the end of the decade. But by then virtually every men's college wanted to do so, and none was willing to wait any longer if they were not selected for the second wave. First University College, then Magdalen, broke ranks and declared that once the moratorium was over they would admit women regardless. The agreement, in consequence, could not hold, with the result that all the remaining male single-sex colleges, except Oriel and Christ Church, went co-ed from October 1979, along with two female colleges, St Anne's and Lady Margaret Hall, who had abandoned their earlier principled opposition. Most of the laggards soon came round. Christ Church admitted women from the following year; Oriel and St Hugh's went mixed from 1986; while Somerville took in men from 1994. Only St Hilda's steadfastly stood out against the Zeitgeist and did not succumb until 2008.[55]

The conflict on a governing body while the issue of co-education was being debated could often be bitter, and opponents used all the tricks in the book to frustrate change. Magdalen's tutorial board voted 22 to 10 on 18 June 1971 that the college 'should seek to be one of the initial group to become co-residential'.[56] The decision was then passed to the college meeting of 13 October, where the motion in favour of change was put by the left-wing historian A. J. P. Taylor, who argued that the admission of women was the next logical step in Magdalen's slow transition from its origins as a clerical seminary. Taylor's supporters were overconfident of victory, and one of their number, the economist Keith Griffin, was told he had no need to hurry back from Geneva. As a result, when the college voted, the necessary two-thirds majority was secured by a whisker, the fellows dividing thirty-two to sixteen. At this point, President James Griffiths, who opposed co-education, declared a tie, and used his casting vote to cause the motion to fall. Worn down by a lengthy and acrimonious meeting, the fellows, who included at least one legal luminary, failed to spot the sleight of hand and Magdalen's chance of being in the first wave was lost. Taylor, always a champion of change, was apoplectic. 'I can't quite remember what he said,' a former prize fellow told his biographer, 'but I recall feeling myself in proximity to a diminutive volcano.'[57]

Once a decision was taken, however, the transition went as smoothly as could be expected, and for the most part the newcomers were welcomed, as Carol Clark recalled.[58] The coming of co-education dramatically improved the University's

---

[55] The permanent private halls also gradually went co-ed. St Benet's had still not admitted women undergraduates in 2015 but was looking to do so: *OT*, 26 March 2015, p. 23.

[56] MCA: TBM/1/13: papers and minutes, 18 June 1971.

[57] Kathleen Burk, *Trouble Maker: The Life and History of A.J.P. Taylor* (London, 2002), p. 338. A vote requiring a two-thirds majority cannot of course be tied. Griffin later became president in the year Magdalen first welcomed women. For Taylor's significance as a historian, see p. 648, this volume.

[58] <http://www.balliol.ox.ac.uk/sites/default/files/WomensAnniversaryforWebsite.pdf> (accessed 25 July 2014): on women at Balliol 1979–2009.

gender balance among junior members within a decade. The first wave of colleges had been allowed to take in only a hundred women students, but no restraints were imposed after 1979 and most colleges increased their female cohort as fast as they could. Between the years 1973–4 and 1984–5 the proportion of women undergraduates at Oxford doubled to above 30 per cent and the proportion of postgraduates went up by a half. By 1993–4, the first figure stood at 41 per cent and the second at 36. By 2012–13, the gender imbalance had all but disappeared. The female share of the undergraduate and graduate intake had stabilized around 46 per cent and 44 per cent respectfully (see Tables 1 and 4).[59]

Broadening the social profile of Oxford's undergraduate body to an acceptable level proved more difficult because the problem was redefined and became hard to address without compromising admission standards. Initially, the target had been working-class representation. But the traditional working class was fast disappearing from the 1980s as the economy became more and more dependent on services, so attention switched to the children of poorer families generally. Precisely identifying the new target audience was extremely difficult in social terms, as many graduates working in the state professions were poorly paid, many skilled manual workers well rewarded, and single parents, whatever their social and educational background, often in dire straits. In consequence, both the University and its critics settled on school background as the best indicator of a student's social circumstances. This was a crude indicator given the fact that many affluent parents sent their children to state schools, and many children from relatively poor families had scholarships to independent schools, as the public schools were officially called from 1973. But it was a conveniently easy variable to measure.

At the time of Franks, state-school representation seemed to be rising fast thanks to the post-war explosion in secondary education and the easy availability of grants. (See Table 2.) State-school pupils formed 32 per cent of the male intake in 1938–9 but 57 per cent in 1965–6. As it was assumed their share would continue to rise, little thought was given as to how their representation might be improved. In the 1970s, however, progress halted and state-school share of the intake began to decline. By 1989–90, only 44.5 per cent of entrants came from the maintained sector, far less than in 1958.[60] The slippage had nothing to do with Oxford. In the course of the 1970s, the majority of state grammar schools were abolished in favour of a comprehensive system of secondary education, which led to certain subjects, such as classics, modern languages, and physics, being de-emphasized.[61] At the same time, many prestigious direct-grant schools, which had previously sent large numbers of pupils to Oxford and Cambridge and historically been part of the state

---

[59] OU, *Annual Reports*, 1994 and 2012, pp. 31 and 9.

[60] The percentages do not correspond exactly to the figures in the 'offers by sector' column in Table 2 because the latter excludes overseas and non-conventional admissions. In 1989, these accounted, unusually, for 7.5 per cent of the intake: see p. 578, this volume.

[61] Grammar schools were retained only in Northern Ireland and by a handful of English LEAs, including Kent.

sector, went independent, thereby helping the public schools improve their academic performance.[62] The state-schools' share, however, began to fall below the 50 per cent mark just at the moment that consensus had been reached as to its value as an indicator of social access, and Oxford got the blame. It was seen as evidence of the University's residual elitism. By the early 1980s, it was clear that Oxford could no longer sit idly by in the hope that the traditional dominance of the independent schools would wither away. Political pressure from outside, if not a sense of social justice within, demanded that something be done.

As the University sought to admit the best students, most dons were reluctant to lower admissions requirements to increase the state-school intake. Instead, realizing that many well-qualified state-school pupils did not apply to Oxford, it attempted to augment the University's appeal. Oxford had two strategies. One was to reach out to the schools. Believing that part of the problem lay in prejudice and fear of the unknown, the University has striven over the past thirty years, often in the face of ill-informed press and political commentary, to dispel popular myths about its bias towards the independent schools and the social snobbery of the students and dons. At the outset, it was left to individual colleges to offer short-term fellowships to schoolteachers, produce an attractive prospectus, and organize school visits and open days with the assistance of the colleges' admissions office. But from the 1990s, the University and the faculties became more enterprising, and in recent years, in a sensible attempt to coordinate and maximize the various initiatives, each college has been allotted an area of the country in which to evangelize.[63] Much, too, has been done to minimize the mystery of Oxford through the personal initiative of the philanthropist Sir Peter Lampl. A grammar-school boy of Czech background who came up to Corpus shortly after the Franks Report, Lampl, in the early 1990s, concluded, rightly or wrongly, that the children of immigrants no longer stood any chance of getting into Oxford or any other top British university. His solution was to fund an annual summer school at Oxford, where bright children whose parents had never been to university could spend a week in a college attending seminars and mixing with students already there. The venture proved highly successful and led Lampl to found the Sutton Trust, an educational charity dedicated to improving social mobility, which, in recent years, with government help, has extended the summer school to other universities in the Russell Group.[64]

---

[62] Direct-grant schools were independent of local authority control and received their funds directly from central government. In 1964–5, they accounted for 17 per cent of male entrants: Franks, i. 72. Robbins' claim that only 30 per cent of Oxford male students came from state schools in the early 1960s was only true if the pupils from the direct-grant schools were excluded.

[63] In recent years, colleges have also become more imaginative. Pembroke has developed links with schools in London, Cheshire, and Manchester, which act as hubs to host regular events for students and teachers from the local regions, led by the college's academics and admissions staff. Gifted but disadvantaged students from these regions are also selected to take part in Pembroke's special access scheme: see Peter Claus, 'A University Settlement Movement for Our Times: The Pembroke Access Scheme', OM, 8th week, TT (2013), 10–12; 'Pembroke Reaches Out', BP, May 2014, p. 12.

[64] Since 2010, the University has run its own summer school, which is very popular. Of the 750 who attended the 2012 school, 197 were offered an Oxford place in December 2012: The Times, 28 Feb. 2013, p. 17.

The second strategy was to make the admissions process more congenial to state-school applicants. This had been suggested in 1966 by Franks, who thought the entrance examination, as it existed, was inherently unfair. Most public-school applicants took the examination during their seventh term in the sixth form, while most grammar-school candidates, whose schools had no facility for staying on after A-level, did so towards the end of the fourth term. Public-school candidates were obviously advantaged, and Franks' solution was to introduce two-section examination papers, one for fourth-term and one for seventh-term entrants.[65] When, in the early 1980s, the University belatedly got round to addressing Franks' concerns, a different approach was tried. As the problem was not just one of age but the differential in the amount of coaching public- and state-school pupils would receive before taking the examination, the fair way forward, it was felt, was to allow state-school pupils to enter Oxford without taking the exam at all. Beginning with the admissions round of December 1987, a two-mode entry was introduced: all pre-A-level candidates had to take the entrance examination; all post-A-level candidates would be judged on their A-level performance and an interview. The intention was to have the best of both worlds: state-school pupils would no longer be disadvantaged, and late developers in the sixth form would not be denied the possibility of coming to Oxford. So that post-A-level candidates would not feel discriminated against, the award of scholarships and exhibitions on performance in the exam was abolished. Instead, colleges made awards following the results of the first public examination.[66]

The new dispensation, however, proved as unsatisfactory as the old to Oxford's growing chorus of media and political critics, and, from the admissions round of 1996, on the advice of a committee chaired by the academic lawyer Ruth Deech, principal of St Anne's, the entrance examination was scrapped altogether.[67] This, too, did not prove to be a lasting solution. By the year 2000 so many school pupils were gaining top grades at A-level, as standards rose or the exams became easier (there was no consensus), that there were few British-educated candidates applying to Oxford who were not predicted to obtain three As.[68] This placed a much greater weight than had traditionally been the case on performance in the interview, which again was thought to give an advantage to applicants from independent schools and educated, affluent homes. The colleges went out of their way to make candidates feel welcome and make interviews as predictable and stress-free as possible. But complaints continued and the dons themselves felt that, on the margins, decisions were arbitrary. By 2010, many faculties were again setting examinations and tests, which were used primarily as a way of filtering out weaker candidates. The wheel had come full circle, though the system was definitely fairer and less daunting.

---

[65] Franks, i. 85.

[66] The changes had been promoted four years before in a report on undergraduate admissions chaired by Sir Kenneth Dover, president of Corpus Christi: *Report of the Committee on Undergraduate Admissions* (Oxford, 1983).

[67] Deech had been the college's law tutor for many years. She went on to head the Human Fertilisation and Embryology Authority and receive a peerage.

[68] A total of 45,000 candidates gained three As at A-level in 2010. Three As became the University's standard entry requirement.

Although candidates continued, as always, to be admitted by a college, it was possible now to apply simply to Oxford and be allocated to the list of a college with below the average number of applicants in the subject specified. Within different subjects, too, attempts were made to equalize college lists. By redistributing candidates around the colleges according to the number of places each college offered in a given school, candidates were not disadvantaged by applying to a popular college. If the admissions process could still seem bemusing, this was due to the fact that each faculty got round the problem of A-level grade inflation in different ways and the faculty-based tests took many forms.[69]

The great efforts directed at improving the state/private-school balance did not reap the spectacular dividends that the University expected. The ratio improved across the 1990s, and by 1999 state-school pupils always made up more than half of the British-educated students admitted. Progress thereafter, though, was slow and the balance of the mid- to late 1960s had only just been regained by the end of the period. What Oxford did achieve was to increase the number of applicants. Back in the 1960s there were seldom more than two candidates per place in the men's colleges. By the late 1980s, there were still only three across the University. In 2014, when the annual number of applicants had soared to over 17,000, the figure had risen to nearly six, and even higher in certain subjects.[70] But this was a development that Oxford's critics ignored. It was the failure to raise the proportion of state-school entrants to a level anywhere near the proportion of secondary-age pupils in state schools that remained the focus of concern, in particular with the Labour government that came to power in 1997. A percentage that stayed in the low 50s for most of the 2000s was judged inadequate when state-school pupils made up 65 per cent of students gaining three As.[71]

The relative ease with which Oxford raised the percentage of women students was unsurprising. Most male dons accepted the case for increasing the female presence in the University. The minority who were uneasy with the idea of co-education were soon reconciled to the idea once they grasped that it would have a positive effect on standards. Few tutors bridled at the prospect of replacing weaker male undergraduates with first-class women, and none wanted to see their college slip down the Norrington ranking by failing to join the bandwagon.[72] There was no difficulty either in recruiting many more women of a high calibre. Intelligent middle-class girls wanted the same opportunities as their brothers, and their parents

---

[69] We have now entered the world of the super A grade or A*. Oxford is not yet demanding three A* but Cambridge and other top universities are, so it is only a matter of time before Oxford succumbs. In summer 2012, 8 per cent of A-levels were graded A* and 27 per cent of entries received an A.

[70] <http://www.ox.ac.uk/about/facts-and-figures/admissions-statistics> (detailed tables) (accessed 8 September 2015).

[71] The Times, 9 June 2000, p. 23, letter from the minister of education, Tessa Blackstone. There was also concern that candidates from independent schools stood a slightly better chance of being offered a place: in the 2010 round, 24.7 per cent of applicants from the private sector were successful but only 19.9 per cent from maintained schools.

[72] The female colleges, conversely, thought that they would lose all their best students if the male societies were allowed to go co-ed. In the first years of the Norrington Table, the women's societies had always done well.

recognized the social and economic advantages that would accrue from having their daughters as well as their sons attending Oxford.[73] Attracting a larger proportion of state-school pupils was much more difficult. Pupils from independent schools might be only 35 per cent of the cohort gaining 3 As each year but they continued to dominate the top grades in certain subjects, as in the 1970s. It was also hard to attract the brightest state-school pupils from disadvantaged areas whose potential would have shone through at interview. Despite all the University's efforts, there remained a strong distrust of Oxford among both pupils and their schools. Most state comprehensives had only the occasional exceptional student; when he or she was turned down by Oxford, as happened frequently once the number of candidates per place rose, the school understandably felt slighted.

The University's difficulties in complying with the Labour government's wishes were only compounded by its desire to expand its international footprint. Traditionally, Oxford colleges had taken few undergraduates from outside the United Kingdom, except Rhodes scholars taking a second BA or the odd Third World student subsidized by the junior members.[74] After 2000, however, the University began to look outwards, announcing in its corporate plan for 2005/6–2009/10 an intention to 'implement a vigorous programme of international recruitment'.[75] The new initiative was quickly successful. In the 2011 admissions exercise, 31.2 per cent of applications came from outside the UK and 16.6 per cent of the places went to foreigners. This inevitably depressed the maintained sector's share of the intake. Although 57 per cent of successful home applicants in the 2011 round were state-school educated, they formed only 47 per cent of the undergraduates admitted in October 2012.

D. The North Report

Oxford's readiness in the 1970s and 1980s to embrace co-education and attend seriously to the under-representation of pupils from the state sector demonstrated the University's ability to respond positively to a changing world, just as in the age of Jowett. It showed the same adaptability in the 1990s when forced to contend with the Conservative government's new managerial attitude to higher education. Despite some misgivings, Oxford embraced the new audit culture and played the game with success, with the result that it fared much better than most British universities in an age of government financial austerity. Success in the first RAEs and the early teaching audits meant that the University continued to enjoy its customary share of the state's expenditure on higher education, even if the cake

---

[73] Most well-to-do families were perfectly happy to let their daughters take advantage of the career opportunities that opened up for women after 1970. It maximized the chance of a family retaining its social position, and was a godsend for the many one-child families with only a daughter.

[74] Before the 1990s, overseas students were seldom more than 5 per cent of the intake and frequently lower. The one significant exception was Balliol, which had had many foreign undergraduates on its books as early as the 1950s.

[75] *Corporate Plan 2005–6 to 2009–10* (Oxford, 2005), pp. 10 and 11 (draft for Congregation).

was not getting bigger. At the same time, it was able to sustain a high staff–student ratio, since it came under little pressure to expand its undergraduate numbers, unlike the sector in general. Above all, Oxford had no difficulty attracting research funds in a much more competitive era. Between 1970–1 and 1995–6, the government's annual core grant to the University rose by less than 20 per cent in real terms. The funds that Oxford drew from the research councils, charities, and industry, on the other hand, quadrupled in value. (See Table 8.)

In consequence, though the state turned Britain's system of higher education upside down at the turn of the 1990s, Oxford navigated the stormy conditions with relative aplomb. It was certainly not blown off course from pursuing its own programme of development and reform according to an agenda broadly laid down by Franks. By the mid-1990s, most of Franks' recommendations had been implemented. The central administration had been streamlined, if not as completely as the commission had hoped; the collegiate system had been strengthened through the transference of some £70 million from the richer to the poorer colleges; and the tutorial system, *pace* Robbins and fiscal exigency, had been preserved. The University had certainly grown faster than the commission had desired, for there were 15,000 students on the books in 1995–6, not the 13,000 anticipated. But the expansion had occurred in the form that Franks had advocated. It was post-graduate not undergraduate numbers that had grown rapidly. Now totalling close to 4,500, postgraduates formed almost 30 per cent of the student body, just the proportion Franks had advised.[76]

Moreover, as the commission had equally wanted, postgraduates were much better looked after and integrated into the collegiate university than thirty years before. An important Committee of Inquiry into Graduate Provision, chaired by the warden of Merton and historian John Roberts, and which reported in 1986, led to significant improvements at both faculty and college level in graduates' care and facilities, especially in undergraduate colleges.[77] For those who did not want to mix with undergraduates, furthermore, there were now seven graduate colleges rather than two. The St Cross and Iffley societies had been duly established in the mid-1960s. The former initially occupied a building near St Cross Church before moving to St Giles in 1981; the latter, renamed Wolfson College after the businessman and philanthropist Sir Isaac Wolfson, was set up in leafy North Oxford, first in a house on the Banbury Road and then from 1974 in brand-new premises on a riverside site at the end of Linton Road, largely paid for by the Wolfson and Ford Foundations (see Figure 13.3).[78] In 1979 and 1983, two more graduate colleges, the sixth and seventh, had come into being. The sixth, Green College, was founded on the old

---

[76] Franks, i. 49.

[77] 'Report of the Committee of Inquiry into Provision for Graduate Students' (1987). It was followed by a working party report in 1990. Roberts, a long-serving Merton tutor in modern history, had been Vice-Chancellor of Southampton when the Conservative axe fell in the early 1980s.

[78] Ford committed $4.5 million and Wolfson $1.5 million. For an account of the foundation, see M. Ignatieff, *Isaiah Berlin: A Life* (London, 1998), ch. 17. Berlin was the first principal of the college.

FIGURE 13.3 Wolfson College: the most palatial of the graduate colleges. Ready for use in 1974, Wolfson was a college built in a modern style but with traditional echoes. Designed by Powell and Moya architects, it was divided into three quadrangles and the concrete exterior was softened by the deliberate preservation of the mature trees on the site and its riverside location. Distinctions between junior and senior members were eroded by the creation of a single common room and the absence of a high table.

Radcliffe Observatory site through the generosity of two American friends of the University, Cecil H. Green and his wife Ida.[79] The seventh, Templeton College, located at Egrove Park on the outskirts of Oxford, had begun life in 1969 as the home of the Oxford Centre for Management Studies, but gained its new name and status following a donation from the American-born mutual-fund investor Sir John Templeton, a former Rhodes scholar.[80]

Over the intervening thirty years, Oxford had also become much more heavily involved in areas of education that Franks had never discussed. On the one hand, the Department of Educational Studies in Norham Gardens had developed from doing little more than prepare graduates for the PGCE and validating the BEd degree studied in local training colleges into one of the country's leading research centres for all levels of schooling, including pre-schools.[81] On the other, the University had

---

[79] Green was the founder of Texas Instruments.

[80] Wolfson and Green were incorporated almost immediately but Linacre and St Cross only became full members of the University in the 1980s and Templeton in 1995.

[81] The University had been involved in teacher training since 1892 when it opened the Oxford University Day Training School for elementary school pupil teachers. As a result of the Robbins Report, teacher training colleges

transformed its commitment to extension. Oxford had continued to play a part in workers' education in the two decades after the Second World War but its commitment had lessened in a changed environment where demand was slackening owing to widening educational opportunities for the young, growing prosperity, and the new consumer culture built around the television and the car. But as the number of adults hungry for their first taste of academic instruction diminished, a new market emerged among the growing population of educated men and women with the time and inclination to develop new intellectual and cultural interests in later life. Such people were frequently keen to re-enter higher education on a part-time or casual basis, and by the mid-1990s the University had responded creatively to this new constituency. The Delegacy for Extra-Mural Studies became the Department for External Studies and was brought under the control of the General Board from 1971. Metamorphosing into the Department for Continuing Education, it dropped most of its outreach teaching outside Oxfordshire and Buckinghamshire and concentrated on its residential summer schools and in-house courses and colloquia. At the same time, it offered those who attended its Oxford courses the possibility of taking part-time diplomas or degrees. With help from a grant from the Kellogg Foundation in 1982, the department was also able to create much better facilities at its base in Rewley House, where external studies had been located since early in the century. In 1988–9, the Department for Continuing Education enrolled 9,300 students.

As more and more of the department's clients were studying for a qualification, the University was anxious that such students should feel part of the wider collegiate university. In 1990, Rewley House was made a constituent college of the University. Rechristened Kellogg College in 1994 in honour of the cereal manufacturer who had generously supported many Oxford initiatives over the years, the new college was eventually physically divided from the department when it moved to a site on the Banbury Road in 2004.[82] The University did not neglect the needs of full-time mature students either. From 1990, adults over 21 who wanted to be full-time undergraduates at Oxford and wished to live apart from their younger peers also had a place of their own when the Unitarians' ailing Manchester College, hitherto loosely attached to Oxford, became a permanent hall for mature students. Six years later, it too was made a constituent college of the University and was renamed Harris Manchester after the carpet retailer, Lord Harris of Peckham, who had provided a substantial benefaction to effect the change of status. This was not the only former non-conformist society to change its status in the mid-1990s. In the

---

were renamed colleges of education and their students allowed to take a BEd if they stayed on for a fourth year after gaining their teaching diploma. The degree had to be validated by a university. From the 1980s, all teachers who qualified without first attending a university had to have a BEd. In 1969, Oxford's Department of Education and the Institute of Education, founded in 1951, joined together to become the Department of Educational Studies, under first an educational delegacy and then a committee and board. A sign of its growing significance was the creation of the University's first chair in education in 1989. From 2007 it has become again the Department of Education. See <http://www.education.ox.ac.uk/about-us/timeline-history/> (accessed 8 September 2015).

[82] In 2012, Kellogg College had 190 and 580 full- and part-time students; the Department of Continuing Education now had a roll of 15,000.

FIGURE 13.4 Sir Peter North, b. 1936, academic lawyer, principal of Jesus, Vice-Chancellor and chair of the North Commission. North was tutor for law at Keble from 1965–76 before developing a more public career. While chairing the North Commission, he was a busy man. He was also in charge of the government's review body looking at the rules relating to parades and marches in Northern Ireland which reported in January 1997, a year before the Good Friday Agreement.

previous year, Mansfield, the former Congregationalist academy turned permanent private hall, finally became an incorporated college.[83]

Yet if Council, by the mid-1990s, could congratulate itself on weathering the audit storm and even catching the prevailing wind and surging ahead, it was not complacent. The University was now, in many different respects, a much bigger institution than in Franks' day, and it was felt that it was time to initiate a second wide-ranging internal audit, taking advantage of the fact that there was no obvious outside pressure for this to be done. In March 1994, Council appointed a new commission of enquiry under the chairmanship of the principal of Jesus and current Vice-Chancellor, Peter North, an academic lawyer with a keen sense of the possible and good diplomatic skills (see Figure 13.4).[84] Its remit was wide-ranging but its terms of reference precise:

> To review such aspects of the operation and structure of the collegiate University and its decision-making machinery as it considers appropriate, including current issues concerning the relationship between different bodies, and between the University and the colleges, and the colleges themselves, the distinctive role of each body, the balance

---

[83] Tony Cross, 'An Idea Whose Time Had Come: The Mature Students Project at Harris Manchester College', OM, 8th week, TT (2003), 5–6.
[84] In the course of the enquiry, he was given the further task by the government of chairing the review body of the Independent Review on Parades and Marches in Northern Ireland. He was knighted in 1998.

between undergraduate and graduate teaching, and between teaching and research, the position of different categories of senior members within the collegiate University, and related matters.

The commission was expected to pay due attention to the recommendations made by various ad hoc university committees already looking at some of these aspects, and report back with its own to Council, the General Board, and Congregation.[85]

The committee consisted of eight people plus the secretary, six representatives of Oxford and two outsiders—the principal of Newnham College, Cambridge, and the rector of Imperial College, London. This was a sign of the times: Oxford could no longer conduct even an internal review in isolation. For the commission's conclusions to be credible in the eyes of government and the wider higher-education system, it had to be seen to be seeking advice from the outside world. The commission went out of its way to take external soundings. In the course of the enquiry, a study of Oxford's governance was commissioned from the education consulting group Coopers & Lybrand; an independent consultant, Dr Harry Atkinson, was asked to prepare a detailed study of the governance of Oxford and five other universities in the UK; and the consultants KMPG were hired to furnish a report on financial modelling.[86] Everything was also done to solicit the opinion of Congregation and junior members and keep the broader University informed of the current state of the commission's deliberations by sending out questionnaires seeking answers to specific questions and publishing interim reports.[87]

The commission was ready to report by early 1997 but held back from publishing its conclusions until the end of the year in order to take into account the findings of the Dearing Committee, which appeared in July. The appointment by the Conservative government in May 1996 of a commission to investigate the future of British higher education tout court upset the North enquiry's agenda, just at the moment it was finalizing its ideas. North had begun with the assumption that Oxford had adapted to the new age of financial stringency and greater government intervention relatively successfully, and now had the leisure to think about internal reform in a more stable educational landscape. The Dearing Committee threatened to herald a further period of upheaval and change, and there was the particular fear that its recommendations could easily torpedo the commission's efforts if it laid down sector norms and goals very different from those that North intended to propose. At the very least, it would be necessary to adjust the commission's report in the light of Dearing's conclusions.

The report, in consequence, did not appear until November. The commission recommended significant changes in the University's governance but was careful to present the reforms as enhancing rather than undermining Oxford's collegiate and

---

[85] North p. vii.   [86] Ibid., pp. 1–4.
[87] The two most important interim publications were *Commission of Enquiry: Framework Document* (Oxford, Jan. 1995), and *Commission of Enquiry: Consultative Paper on the University's Objectives. Structure, Size and Shape* (Oxford, Feb. 1996).

democratic traditions. The starting point was the same as Franks'. The University's governance was too unwieldy, Byzantine, and secretive to facilitate the strategic planning and rapid decision-making that was required if Oxford were to remain world-class in teaching and learning. Council had no control over academic matters or a vision for the future, so Oxford's growth was haphazard; the General Board was overwhelmed with petty business sent up from the faculties, and had no control over the University's income from research grants, which was now bigger than its own budget; and Congregation did not work as it should: much of its business was so perfunctory that the membership was largely passive and could not even be bothered to carry out its electoral responsibilities. The solution drew heavily on the advice given by Coopers & Lybrand. The way forward was to entrust policy-making at the top to a single body, delegate its implementation and day-to-day administration to a lower tier, and reignite interest in Congregation by reducing its scope. The consultants had suggested that Congregation should be confined to an electoral and occasional advisory role and take no part in decision-making.[88] Wisely, the commission did not go down this road. It contented itself with recommending that Congregation's electoral role be diminished, the number of votes in the House needed to make a resolution binding be increased, and its right to elect the Vice-Chancellor be handed to a nominating committee. It also suggested that Congregation grow in size by extending membership to a further tranche of the huge number of academic-related staff.[89]

The report focused, above all, on streamlining the University's administration. The Vice-Chancellor should be appointed for five years with a possibility of serving for a further two, and the office no longer be restricted to a member of Congregation; there should be a new twenty-five-member council, including three student representatives with voting rights and two externals; the new Council should have direct oversight of the University's resources, its current academic policy, and future development, helped by several subcommittees, which would include a Planning and Resource Allocation Committee (PRAC) and an Educational Policy and Standards Committee (EPSC); and the General Board, no longer capable of doing the job for which it had been set up ninety years before, should be replaced by a new administrative tier subordinate to the new Council:

> The General Board should be abolished and three new academic boards should be established beneath the new Council, inheriting from the General Board such responsibilities as are not assumed by the new Council.
> One board should cover clinical medicine, a second biological and physical sciences, and a third humanities and social sciences...
> The academic boards should each have full responsibility, under the Council, for the management and administration of the subject areas within their sphere of responsibility. This would include in particular responsibility for submitting annually

---

[88] Coopers & Lybrand, 'University of Oxford Governance', Mar. 1996, paras 707–712.
[89] North, pp. 68–77.

to the Council an updated long-term strategic plan and an annual operating statement; this plan should be approved by the Council each year and should provide the framework for each academic board's work during that year.

The boards should be responsible for managing the detailed allocation of resources, for strategic planning and for quality assurance of the educational provision made under their aegis.[90]

The three boards were to be headed by full-time deputy vice-chancellors, who along with a fourth representing the University's academic support services (principally the libraries, museums, and computing centre) would be ex officio members of the new Council. They would be appointed by an electoral board, like a professor, could be outsiders, and would serve for a five-year renewable term. Little was said about the subject-specific committees which would be under the academic boards, but it was assumed that the science board in particular would see what scope there was in the extant complex mix of faculties, sub-faculties, and departments for rationalization.

Apart from the governance reforms, North had little to recommend that was radical. Congregation was to remain sovereign and would elect twelve of the twenty-five members of the new Council; the traditional role of the Proctors and Assessor,[91] and their right to attend any university committee including the new Council, its committees, and the academic boards, was confirmed;[92] and it was judged necessary that Oxford should remain part of the publicly funded British higher-education system on the grounds that it would take a hundred years to raise the extra £2 billion endowment needed to cover the funds presently received from the state.[93] The commission was willing to entertain further expansion in numbers, but recommended only a modest growth, given the resource implications, the limitations of space, and the need to protect Oxford's collegiate ethos.[94] It was also adamant that the University should continue to contain a mix of undergraduates and postgraduates; that Oxford should continue to offer single and joint honours undergraduate degrees, eschewing the modular route taken by some British universities; and that the graduates should continue to be spread among the colleges rather than collected into a graduate school.[95]

While the commission recognized there was room for improvement in the way undergraduates and graduates were served, it had little to say that had not been earlier voiced by Franks. The tutorial system was judged to be non-negotiable since it made 'a significant contribution to maintaining Oxford's standard of excellence in

---

[90] Ibid., pp. 83–94, 107–8, and 116–17.
[91] An Assessor was first elected to assist the Proctors in 1963 and initially served as a representative of the women's colleges. With the introduction of co-education, the Assessor has become, to all intents and purposes, a third Proctor.
[92] North, p. 118.
[93] Ibid., pp. 220–1. Some dons thought that the commission had not given enough attention to the pros and cons of going private: see 'An Open Letter to the Chairman of the North Commission', OM, 2nd week, HT (1997), 5–6.
[94] North, pp. 28–30.   [95] Ibid., ch. 3 and pp. 156–7 and 177.

teaching'.[96] But it was not to be overused as a substitute for classes, which were a more efficient way of communicating information. It was also important that faculties be more energetic in overseeing the delivery of the curriculum by defining best practice and monitoring the performance of dons. Thought too should be given to spreading the examination load across three years and diversifying the forms of assessment, while booklets should be prepared in each faculty containing factual information on 'standard marking practices, syllabuses, examinations and norms for numbers of tutorials', which would 'give guidance on the aims of a tutorial and the role of the tutor'.[97]

The report gave little consideration to how the University and the colleges might cooperate more effectively.[98] Coopers & Lybrand had argued that one committee of the new Council should be a university/college board, which could be 'a court of appeal for the resolution of any conflicts which arose between subject units and College interests' and would largely replace the Senior Tutors' Committee.[99] As in the case of Congregation, the consultants' advice in this regard was ignored. The commission agreed that the colleges and the University needed bringing closer together in order for Oxford to function efficiently. But it felt that this could be done less provocatively simply by having six of the twelve members of the EPSC appointed in some manner by the Conference of Colleges, and by the Conference and other bodies representing the colleges summoning university officers to their meetings.[100] The commission was more interested in reducing the differences between the colleges than in reshaping their relations with the University. As there still remained a huge disparity in wealth between the richest and poorest colleges, the college contributions scheme was to continue, and the colleges founded since the late 1980s added to the list of beneficiaries. In addition, as the exam results suggested that undergraduates in the richest colleges were better taught, everything should be done to ensure that all the colleges were equally attractive to aspiring tutorial fellows. Housing allowances (which differed greatly between colleges) and other tutorial perks were to be abolished, and all tutorial fellows given a small pay rise in lieu.[101]

Part of the commission's reticence with regard to University–college relations can be put down to the Dearing Committee. Dearing in no way shaped North's conclusions. Most of the recommendations were included in the draft proposals put out for discussion in the course of 1996.[102] But Dearing's fingerprints were everywhere, not least in a promise to do more on access, a commitment to promote lifelong learning through the work of the Department for Continuing Education

---

[96] Ibid. p. 163.   [97] Ibid., ch. 9, esp. p. 152.

[98] It did have views on the joint-appointment system: see pp. 624–5, this volume.

[99] Coopers & Lybrand, 'University of Oxford Governance: Summary Report' (Mar. 1996)', para. 29; Coopers & Lybrand, 'University of Oxford Governance', paras 719–20.

[100] North, pp. 89 and 120–1.

[101] Ibid., pp. 223–37. In the post-war era, tutorial fellows received a housing allowance when they lived out, in lieu of their right to free board and lodging in college.

[102] See p. 583, n. 87, this volume.

and Kellogg College, and the recommendation that greater consideration be given to ensuring that Oxford graduates had the key communication and analytical skills they would need to succeed in life.[103] The commission was also anxious to emphasize that the new governance structures were in the spirit of Dearing, if very different from his committee's conception of best practice. As envisaged, the new Council would be predominantly a committee of academics, largely elected by Congregation, which would remain the sovereign body. This hardly squared with Dearing's insistence that, in all universities, the council should be the ultimate decision body and have a lay majority.[104] But the North Commission defiantly defended its corner:

> We accept fully the need for clarity in identifying the institution's governing body, and for openness and accountability in the way in which executive bodies operate. We do not accept, however, that there is only one single effective way in which these objectives can be achieved. We have considered the objectives set out in the Dearing Report, and believe they can be delivered in Oxford within the broad framework of its present constitution, particularly if the changes we propose...are adopted.[105]

Yet Dearing was more than a point of reference. Through his call for the college fee to be reviewed, he made it impossible for North to suggest deeper changes to the existing structures that acted as an interface between the University and the colleges. From the early 1960s, when it became mandatory for local authorities to pay the tuition costs of students from their area, Oxford and Cambridge had received a larger per capita sum to support their undergraduate teaching than other universities because both the universities and the colleges were allowed to collect a student fee.[106] There had been moves by the state in the late 1980s to lessen the perceived inequity by reducing Oxford's UGC grant by a sum equivalent to 42 per cent of the money received by the colleges.[107] Dearing queried whether there should be a separate fee at all, and, by the time North was published, negotiations were already in train between the two universities and an incoming Labour government largely hostile to the fee's continuation.[108] The consequences for Oxford if the college fee were to go were momentous. As per capita undergraduate funding for tuition had been largely frozen for a decade and maintenance grants were fast disappearing, the colleges were already relying more and more on their endowment income to maintain the level of tutorial provision and board and lodging. Were the college fee to be abolished—a sum equivalent to a third of the return on total college

---

[103] North, pp. 36, 37, and 168–9. For the Dearing Committee's view on developing key skills, see Dearing, ch. 9.

[104] Dearing, pp. 236 and 239 (recommendation 54).   [105] North, p. 70.

[106] Before 1850, undergraduates had only paid a tutorial fee to the college; by 1914 they were also paying a small fee to the University; in the post-war era the college fee always remained the larger of the two, though the University's role in undergraduate science teaching, in particular, increased.

[107] Initially, universities and, at Oxbridge, the colleges set their own tuition costs and billed local authorities accordingly. But the government in the 1960s began to insist on common costs, albeit differentiating between the arts and the sciences. From the early 1970s, Oxford colleges all had to charge the same.

[108] Dearing, p. 300. At a Labour Party conference in July 1997, Gordon Brown promised to end the college fee.

endowment would be taken out of the University—the poorer colleges especially would stand no chance of retaining the tutorial system and undergraduate provision might quickly be reduced to faculty-based lectures and classes. At the same time, since the state's financial contribution to undergraduate education would now be completely in the hands of the central administration, the relationship between the University and the colleges was guaranteed to be altered profoundly. The North Commission understandably, therefore, had nothing concrete to say about the future in this regard. It was not in charge of the script.[109]

E. Restructuring the Collegiate University

The debate over the college fee came to a head in the month the North Report was published. The new chancellor of the exchequer, Gordon Brown, was keen to end the fee and he had a willing ally in the minister of higher education, Tessa Blackstone, who, at the beginning of the 1997/8 academic year, asked HEFCE to find a way forward. Oxford and Cambridge came out fighting. Asked by HEFCE to produce a written defence of the college fee by late October, they duly obliged, arguing that a continuation of the present system was essential if their global reputation for teaching excellence was to be preserved and that the combined fee constituted value for money, given the much higher tuition charges of their American competitors.[110] Oxford's and Cambridge's many supporters in the establishment also rallied in their defence, and the rights and wrongs of the college fee were discussed in the House of Lords on Wednesday, 12 November, as a result of a motion put down by Lord Beloff, erstwhile Gladstone professor of government and emeritus fellow of All Souls.

In the debate, Oxford's corner was robustly defended by a galaxy of well-wishers led by the University's Chancellor and former Labour home secretary, Roy Jenkins.[111] The government's mind, however, was not to be changed, especially as there was broad support for an end to the college fee in the rest of the higher-education system and in the media. HEFCE's report also called for change. The status quo was untenable. The blow might be softened by giving Oxford and Cambridge 'special factor funding' in acknowledgement of the expense of the college system, but in future the student fee should be paid to the two universities alone. The die was therefore cast. In a subsequent short debate in the House of Commons on 19 November, Kim Howells, the government's spokesman, promised that nothing would be done to harm the two universities that between them had

---

[109] North, p. 62.

[110] Oxford's reply is summarized in *OUG*, supplement (1) to no. 4452 (5 Nov. 1997), pp. 327–31. The status quo was robustly defended in North's valedictory oration as Vice-Chancellor: see *OUG*, no. 4449 (16 Oct. 1997), p. 172.

[111] Jenkins read PPE at Balliol in the 1930s. Although very grand, he was the first Chancellor not to be a grandee: he was the son of a Labour MP and former coal miner. As home secretary in the Wilson government, he had been responsible for several significant liberal reforms. He became Chancellor in 1987 on the death of Macmillan.

produced sixty-nine Nobel Prize winners, but pointed out that they were not the only centres of excellence and their needs had to be looked at in the round: 'I would like a lot more Nobel prizes to be won by other universities as well.' He also pulled the rug from under the universities' defence by raising again the question of access: the combined fee could hardly be called a public good when the proportion of state-school pupils among the undergraduates had not increased for thirty years.[112]

With the government's mind made up, the two universities were left with making the best possible terms. Prime Minister Blair, an Oxford alumnus, was more sympathetic to their cause than his Scottish chancellor of the exchequer, and a compromise was hammered out in the course of 1998. By March 1998, it was evident that Oxford and Cambridge would not lose the college fee immediately but that the change would be phased in over several years, and that with the various teaching premiums the two universities could bid for, they would lose, at the most, £12 million at the end of the day rather than the £35 million originally feared.[113] Oxford's new Vice-Chancellor, Colin Lucas, master of Balliol, continued to express disquiet that the new arrangements threatened both college autonomy and teaching provision (see Figure 13.5). Nonetheless, there was a general feeling among members of Congregation that the University had escaped lightly. There was initially talk of recouping the loss in public funds by charging Oxford students top-up fees, in addition to the £1,000 a year all university students in England and Wales would have to pay. But the move was stymied by the government, which made such initiatives illegal. The future now was clear. The Oxford colleges would have to make economies and dig deeper into their endowment income to support the tutorial system in its current form, while the University, henceforth invested with total control over the student fee, would have to work out a mechanism for dividing up the money between the faculties and the colleges.

It was in this new context that the recommendations of the North Report began to be discussed. On receiving the North Report, Council established working parties to put flesh on its recommendations. The Joint Working Party on Governance, comprising representatives of Council, the General Board, and the colleges, presented its first report in October 1998.[114] Essentially, it maintained North's proposals, recognizing that they would bring much needed efficiency gains. But it modified them significantly. First, it handed back to Congregation the power of

---

[112] *OUG*, no. 4455 (20 Nov. 1997), p. 394 (Lords' debate); *Hansard* (House of Commons debates), 27 Nov. 1997, column 282. For examples of media hostility to the fee, see *The Times*, 8 Nov. 1997, p. 22, and *The Guardian*, 12 Nov. 1997, p. 21 (articles by Simon Jenkins and Ian Corfield). Howell's comment on access took no account of the changed educational landscape since 1970 and the improvement in the independent/state-school ratio in the 1990s.

[113] Oxford's potential loss was mooted to be £19 million, but the figure was arguably higher: see the draft paper circulated by the deputy registrar to all heads of house on 13 October 1997, p. 2. The lowest estimate was £12.5 million which, it was suggested, would require endowment to the value of £250 million to replace: see *OM*, 2nd week, HT (1997), 5. For the putative settlement, see 'Note of Meeting of Vice-Chancellor with Heads of House on 18 March 1998 on Issue of College Fees' and accompanying letter from the Vice-Chancellor to the heads of all societies.

[114] First Report of the Joint Working Party on Governance, Supplement (1) to *OUG*, No. 4487, 21 Oct. 1998.

electing the Vice-Chancellor, albeit on the recommendation of North's nominating committee. Secondly, it decided that the student representatives on Council should have only observer status, and that the appointment of the two co-opted external members should be ratified by Congregation.[115] Thirdly, it reduced the college presence on the EPSC but made the chair of the Conference of Colleges a member of the new Council and gave the colleges representation on all its major committees. Finally, paying heed to disquiet within the University that the replacement of the General Board by three academic boards subordinate to Council would seriously disadvantage the arts when it came to lobbying for resources, it was proposed that the arts board should be split in two: one for humanities and the other for the social sciences. At the same time, the biological sciences were attached to medicine rather than physics, the academic boards were rechristened divisions, and their heads became simple chairs not deputy vice-chancellors.

The working party's document was then sent to the University's various constituencies for discussion and comment, the responses were collated, and a second report was presented to Council in March 1999.[116] The second both developed and refined the first. The broad responsibilities of the centre, divisions, and faculty boards were more carefully defined, college representation on Council and some of its committees enhanced, and two alternative models for the divisional structure adumbrated. It was now proposed, following representations from the relevant faculties and departments, that there should be three science divisions, with the biological sciences separated from medicine and joined with anthropology and geography to form a Life and Environmental Sciences Division. Whether there were to be one or two arts divisions was to be left to Congregation, as the faculties concerned were divided on the issue. But either way, the representation of the arts and sciences on the new Council was to be equal with six (ex officio and elected) members each. Otherwise, the second report followed the first. The working party reported a broad consensus in favour of the new Council, its committee structure, the creation of divisions, and the extension of the Vice-Chancellor's office to five or seven years. Thirty years after Franks, and in a much more competitive and complex environment, the University had come round to accepting the need to reform the decision-making process.

The second report and its recommendations in the form of resolutions were discussed and voted on in Congregation on 11 May 1999. The debate in the House began with a ringing endorsement of the proposals by Vice-Chancellor Lucas:

> I do believe that a reform along the lines proposed today is necessary. The higher education context, both nationally and internationally is changing rapidly. We have to defend, strengthen and enhance our reputation and our real activity as a great

[115] Junior members already had observer status on the existing Council. This right had been achieved in the early 1970s as part of the 'student revolution' of those years: see pp. 668–9, this volume.
[116] Second Report of the Joint Working Party on Governance, supplement (1) to no. 4506, OUG. 24 March 1999.

FIGURE 13.5 Sir Colin Lucas, b. 1940, historian, master of Balliol, Vice-Chancellor and implementer of the North recommendations. As a historian of the French Revolution Lucas made a significant contribution to the undermining of the traditional class-based interpretation built around the rise of the bourgeoisie. As Vice-Chancellor he had not only to oversee the introduction of the North reforms but fight the University's corner with a hostile Labour government.

international university. We have to continue to provide the environment and support that we all need in our different disciplines not merely to sustain the quality of our research and teaching, but above all to innovate. We have to act, and we have to act creatively, within a context of local regulation, financial stringency accompanied by intensifying funding complexity, and the rapid appearance of alternative forms of the organisation and delivery of higher education both nationally and worldwide. Wise and informed strategy leading to choices nimbly made will lead us forward in a higher education world that will never return to what it was fifteen, let alone thirty, years ago.[117]

The speakers that followed the Vice-Chancellor largely concurred. The fear was expressed that there was a democratic deficit in the proposals. While North and the joint working party had ensured a strong representation of elected members of Congregation on Council, it was felt that they might be crowded out by the growing number of ex officio members, and there was a call for direct elections

[117] General Resolutions Concerning Governance, *OUG*, supplement (1) to no. 4511 (Wed. 19 May 1999) (verbatim report), p. 1238b.

to reserved positions on its committees.[118] There were also worries that the needs of postgraduates might still be overlooked in the new governance structures. But generally there was broad support for the resolutions and they were easily carried.[119]

The votes in the House were then confirmed by a postal ballot of members of Congregation, the resolutions were turned into legislation, and the new structures came into being in October 2000. Over the next five years, the new Council and divisions gradually bedded down, with continuity provided both by Vice-Chancellor Lucas, who remained in office until October 2004, and by the new divisional heads, who were mainly drawn from insiders with significant adminis-trative experience. Their task was not easy, as many aspects of the new administra-tive system still had to be worked out. Devising a transparent resource allocation method acceptable to all the University's constituencies/cost centres proved par-ticularly difficult. The second working party report laid down the principles that should underlie the mechanism but it was left to another committee to work out the details. Various complex algorithms were developed, tried, then further refined over the coming years, but the RAM or JRAM (Joint Resource Allocation Model) as it came to be known, was still controversial at the end of the decade.[120] By and large, however, the new structures worked well, commanded consent, and allowed the University to think much more carefully about its future direction, as was clear from the new five-year corporate plan that Council presented to HEFCE in July 2005. This was the third such plan that Oxford had had to construct since the creation of the funding council, and it was far more cogent and precise in its aims and objectives than its precursors.[121] The University's primary aim was to remain one of the world's leading universities while retaining its collegiate identity, broad spectrum of disciplinary interests, traditional mix of undergraduates and graduates, and tutorial system. To achieve this, the plan set out clear objectives in the fields of research, learning and teaching, external collaboration, ancillary services, the treatment and retention of staff, the use of space, and the generation of additional resources.

As in the 1990s, the post-North University was not free to develop its academic strategy without reference to the outside world. The new corporate plan was inevitably conditioned by the Labour government's 2003 White Paper on Educa-tion, its continual pronouncements on widening access, and its wish to see closer

---

[118] Ibid., p. 1240 (intervention of Fergus Millar, Camden professor of ancient history).

[119] Ibid., p. 1248 (votes). There was some difference of agreement over the composition of the two arts boards: ibid., pp. 1242–3 (intervention of Hugh Williamson, regius professor of Hebrew).

[120] Nothing had been agreed on by 2004 except the complexity of the task. A Joint Resource Allocation Working Group met from the beginning of 2005, which developed a mechanism whereby the sum transferred to the colleges each year (known in Oxford as the Quantum) would take account of both undergraduate and graduate teaching and a college's contribution to the University's research effort. Their deliberations, after much wrangling, led to the JRAM, introduced in 2007–8. This was responsible for allocating, between the different parts of the University, the HEFCE core grant, the money received by Oxford for its success in the RAE, and the undergraduate and postgraduate fee income.

[121] *Corporate Plan* 2005–6 to 2009–10.

links between business and higher education, given particular voice in the Lambert Report, which chastised Oxbridge for a lack of entrepreneurialism.[122] Admissions were always a point of conflict. In December 1999, even before the new governance structures had come into being, the University had been hit by the Laura Spence affair. Spence was a comprehensive-school pupil from Northumberland who applied to read medicine at Magdalen but was rejected despite stellar A-level predictions. When her fate came to the attention of the media, the chancellor of the exchequer, Gordon Brown, pounced on the decision as prima facie evidence of Oxford's unacceptable bias against state-school candidates. Although the accusation was unfair, the mud stuck, and Oxford and Magdalen had to expend energy and time defending their admissions policy throughout the following year.[123] A veil had hardly been drawn over the affair when, in March 2002, the University found itself once again the subject of hostile comment about its admissions policies after a journalist's sting. Two fellows of one of the University's poorest colleges, Pembroke, had been enticed to hint that undergraduate places might be bought.[124]

Inevitably, allaying criticisms over admissions became the University's priority and the central administration set up two working parties in 2002 and 2004–5 to see how the process could be made more acceptable to outsiders without compromising the colleges' rights.[125] The University's new corporate plan built on their recommendations and had a strong admissions and access strategy. By then, the University had been given permission to charge the new maximum fee of £3,000, and the strategy reflected the changing landscape. The plan pledged that the best applicants would be admitted, 'irrespective of origin, circumstance, and college choice'. It promised, through Oxford's agreement with OFFA, to promote 'applications from under-represented groups, using targets based on the populations achieving the required entry standard in appropriate A-level subjects'. And it boasted that, when the new higher fee was introduced in the academic year 2006/7, the University would 'be offering one of the most generous bursary schemes in the country for undergraduates from the UK, through the Oxford Opportunity Bursary Scheme'.[126]

Colin Lucas was the right man to oversee the implementation of the North Report and draw the sting of a hostile government. A Balliol history tutor for many years before becoming an administrator, he had the trust of the dons and understood their sensitivities. He recognized how many Oxford decisions were finalized over the dinner table and was a convivial host. He could be steely, as

---

[122] *Lambert Review of Business–University Collaboration: Final Report* (London, 2003). Its author, Richard Lambert, was former editor of the *Financial Times*, and had been charged with the review in 2002 by Gordon Brown.

[123] Spence did not come from a particularly poor home and her case exemplified the inadequacy of using school background as a designator of disadvantage. Brown never apologized. For his handling of the affair, see Tom Bower, *Gordon Brown* (London, 2005), pp. 306 and 308.

[124] OT, 29 Mar. 2002.

[125] For greater faculty involvement in admissions at the end of the period, see pp. 575–7, this volume.

[126] *Corporate Plan*, pp. 10–11. The University promised to give awards of up to £13,000 to students from economically disadvantaged backgrounds. For further information, see pp. 663–4, this volume.

befitted a historian of the French Terror, but he was also an adept negotiator who had cut his teeth as a Chicago dean. Unsurprisingly, he and his able lieutenants successfully managed the transition.[127]

F. The Hood Coda

On Lucas' watch, Council, the divisions, and the colleges worked successfully together to create a collegiate university that was both fit for purpose in the twenty-first century and true to the broader principles laid down by Franks and North. When Lucas was replaced in October 2004 by the New Zealander John Hood, Oxford's first Vice-Chancellor not to be a resident member of the University on his election, the outlook seemed fair (see Figure 13.6). The University had retained its high rating in the 2001 RAE, Oxford was awash with new buildings, and the financial position was healthy. Hood was an engineer with a mixed background in industry and academia, who had been a Rhodes scholar at Worcester thirty years earlier and won plaudits as the Vice-Chancellor of Auckland. It was assumed that he would build on the achievements of his predecessor. In the event, his time in

FIGURE 13.6 John Hood, b. 1952, Oxford's first Vice-Chancellor appointed from outside. Hood had been at Oxford for a short time in the mid-1970s reading for an MPhil in Management and excelling at sport. Returning home to New Zealand, he had a business career before becoming an academic administrator. In his five years at Oxford, he tried and failed to bring the University more in line with other British higher-education institutions by separating institutional from academic governance and introducing a much greater degree of external oversight.

[127] He was knighted in 2002.

office was unhappy, though not unproductive. The outlook was still fair five years later when Hood stood down. But in the interim the University had torn itself apart over further refining the new administrative structures that had been almost universally welcomed at the end of the 1990s.

In May 1999, Congregation had resolved that the working of the new structures would be reviewed after five years.[128] In October 2004, Council asked Congregation to allow the review to be brought forward in order that it might take place during the new Vice-Chancellor's first year in office. Congregation concurred and a committee headed by Hood set to work under terms of reference that asked for particular attention to be paid to the relationship between Council, its committees, the divisional boards, and the colleges. The committee began its task by inviting comments from around the University on the strengths and weaknesses of the new governance arrangements and discovered three main areas of dissatisfaction. The colleges had yet to be effectively brought into the decision-making process; individuals felt a greater remoteness from decision-making than hitherto; and the roles and responsibilities of high-level committees were not clearly articulated, leading to duplication of effort. In the light of the responses, the committee drew up a Green Paper outlining a possible way forward, which was published in March 2005.[129] This suggested abolishing the new Council and dividing institutional from academic governance. Institutional governance would be entrusted to a small Board of Trustees comprised of outsiders who would be responsible for the broad financial, legal, and regulatory arrangements of the University and would be the public face of Oxford. Academic governance would be handed to a 150-strong Academic Council, chaired by the Vice-Chancellor and containing the heads of the divisions and major departments (including OUP), all college heads, forty elected members of Congregation, and six student representatives. Its committees would include a colleges committee, which would replace the autonomous Conference of Colleges.[130]

When put out for consultation, the Green Paper's proposals were received critically by virtually all parts of the University. There were objections to the external composition of the Board of Trustees and its powers, even though the membership was ultimately subject to confirmation by Congregation. And there was widespread feeling that the proposed Academic Council was far too big to operate effectively. It would become the tool of the University's senior management team (Vice-Chancellor, divisional heads, and so on), however representative of the University's different constituencies it appeared to be on the surface.[131] There was also the suspicion that the integration of the colleges into the governance structure was

---

[128] Passed 83 to 0: see General Resolutions Concerning Governance, OUG, supplement (1), no. 4511, 19 May 1999, pp. 1237 and 1248.

[129] 'Oxford's Governance Structure: A Green Paper', OUG, supplement (*3) to vol. 135 (Mar. 2005).

[130] Ibid., pp. 7–9 (including diagram, p. 8).

[131] By 2000, the term senior management team had become a shorthand in the business and educational world to describe the small group of people at the top of an institution who controlled its day-to-day activity. In many institutions this was a designated group of people; Oxford has never had a senior management team as such.

the thin end of the wedge: the colleges' voice would effectively be neutered and their historic autonomy lost.[132] The review committee therefore went back to the drawing board and had a second Green Paper ready for discussion by the end of September.[133] The new paper incorporated responses to most of the criticisms. Institutional and academic governance remained divided, but the Board of Trustees and the Academic Council were renamed and their composition radically revised. The board became a council and, in the first instance, was to consist of an equal number of internal and external members under the University's Chancellor. The Academic Council became a board and its membership was slashed to thirty-six, of whom fourteen would be ex officio (the Vice-Chancellor, pro-Vice-Chancellors,[134] heads of division, and the Proctors and Assessor) and twenty-two elected (ten by Congregation, ten by the colleges, and two by students). In addition, the Conference of Colleges was resurrected as an autonomous body with its own committees, and the role of Congregation in electing members of the Council of Trustees on the recommendation of an independent nominations committee dominated by insiders clarified.[135]

The new Green Paper was much better received than the first, but when the fresh proposals were discussed in Congregation on 1 November 2006 a lot of hostility was evinced over the composition of the new Council, especially over the decision that, after five years, membership should be split 8:7 in the externals' favour and that an external should be in the chair. Nevertheless, after minor tweaking, following a new round of consultations, the proposals of the second Green Paper became the White Paper circulated to the University in Trinity Term 2006, and were the basis for the legislation reforming the University's governance placed before Congregation on 14 November.[136] In the interim, both supporters and opponents of the proposals vigorously campaigned to carry the day: the *Oxford Magazine* gave space to both points of view but in its editorials largely opposed the change, while the Vice-Chancellor very publicly placed his weight behind the reform in his annual October oration.[137] When Congregation assembled at the appointed time, the Sheldonian was packed to the rafters and its members bitterly divided. In the event there had to be two meetings of the House. On 14 November, the debate was largely confined to an amendment proposed by the provost of Oriel and the master of University College, the former cabinet secretary Lord Butler, that it

---

[132] Among the many critical documents produced at the time, see in particular the collected responses of the colleges circulated by Sir Michael Scholar, president of St John's, for the meeting of the Conference of Colleges on 10 May 2005.

[133] 'Governance Discussion Paper', MT 2005: OUG, supplement (*2) to vol. 136 (Sept. 2005).

[134] While North's recommendation that the divisional heads be made deputy-vice-chancellors was turned down, a number of pro-vice-chancellors had been appointed under the new governance arrangements to oversee certain areas of the University's activities such as research. They were the appointees of the Vice-Chancellor and not elected by Congregation.

[135] See 'Governance Discussion Paper', MT 2005, diagram, p. 23.

[136] *White Paper on University Governance* (Oxford, 2006).

[137] OUG, supplement (1) to no. 4781 (4 Oct. 2006), pp. 96–7. See also the interview he gave to the University's staff magazine: *BP*, 26 Oct. 2006, p. 9.

should be left to Congregation in the future to decide whether there should be a lay or academic majority of the Council of Trustees. Both were stalwart supporters of the proposals and the amendment was meant to sugar the pill. But it was carried by only 652 to 507, and the size of the task confronting the Vice-Chancellor and his allies if they were to win the day at the next meeting two weeks later became crystal clear.[138] The meeting on 22 November was equally large and it quickly became evident that the Vice-Chancellor was in trouble. Speaker after speaker insisted that the proposals were undemocratic and would not work as intended, so should be shelved. The verdict was inevitable. They were voted down 730 to 456 and the decision ratified on a subsequent postal vote by a similar proportion.[139]

The chief reason for the Vice-Chancellor's defeat was that the case for creating a new fifteen-man Council which would head the University under Congregation had not been effectively made. The separation of institutional and academic governance was needed, it was argued, for both internal and external reasons. On the one hand, the University was now such a huge and complex entity and the demands made upon it so great that a single overarching body could not cope. On the other, the change was required to bring Oxford into line with the sector norm. The Nolan Committee on Standards in Public Life of the mid-1990s, Dearing, and the Lambert Report had all emphasized that universities should be headed by a small council with a majority of lay members who would bring much needed expertise and an independent point of view to their administration. Their view was endorsed by the Committee of University Chairmen, HEFCE, and the Privy Council, and was in the process of being enshrined in the new Charities Law, which required tax-exempt charities, like the University, to have a lay-dominated governing body.[140] Most members of Congregation could understand the need to divide institutional and academic governance but they feared that the change would lead to Oxford being run by outsiders who would bring a managerial and balance-sheet mentality to the world's third oldest institution of higher learning. Nor did they believe that, at the end of the day, Oxford would be forced down this road simply because it was now deemed best practice. The opposition's fears may have been groundless or grossly exaggerated but the feeling was visceral, as Professor D. G. Fraser of Worcester's speech before Congregation in the debate of 14 November emphasized:

> The issue of governance is quite simple. It was summed up for me by a quietly-spoken colleague. He said there are two issues: (1) it is dangerous to concentrate too much power in the hands of too few individuals; (2) why should we give up something good, merely to conform to some sector norm?

---

[138] *OUG*, supplement (1) to no. 4788 (22 Nov. 2006) (verbatim debate). Butler continued to puff his proposal prior to the second meeting: see 'Oxford Dons Will Always be Masters of their Own Destiny', at <http://www.telegraph.co.uk/comment/personal-view/3634702/Oxford-dons-will-always-be-masters-of-their-own-destiny.html> (accessed 29 November 2006).

[139] *OUG*, supplement (1) to no. 4791 (7 Dec. 2006) (verbatim debate).

[140] See esp. *White Paper*, pp. 16–22, 'changes in the external regulatory environment'. Hood stressed the peculiarity of a unicameral system in an email sent to all members of Congregation on 3 May 2005.

He is right. The White Paper fails Oxford on both counts. It removes power from academics and places it firmly in the hands of an all-powerful University Executive, with no adequate system of checks and balances...

Only three years ago, Cambridge University rejected proposals similar to those now contained in the White Paper. It has retained its independence, excellence and vitality. HEFCE has made no move to persuade it to think again. In contrast, Oxford's Working Party now proposes to introduce an executive-led style of corporate governance and management of academics like that so comprehensively rejected by Cambridge...

The proposal is similar to the top-down management introduced into the National Health Service. And I am very glad that so many medical colleagues have chosen to attend today. They will know that managers now seek routinely to impose decisions on clinicians that are contrary to their best medical judgement.[141]

However, even if the case had been better presented, several ancillary factors would have made it difficult for the Vice-Chancellor to obtain a majority. To begin with, the review committee had appeared secretive and unmindful of constitutional propriety. Submissions to the committee prior to the first Green Paper had not been made publicly available and its publication had not swiftly led to a debate in Congregation.[142] The first Green Paper was published, moreover, at a time when members of Congregation were being asked to consider another important document, which related to Oxford's academic strategy and was part of the process of drawing up the new corporate plan. Though commended for tackling a wide range of policies and problems, the document provoked a great deal of hostility because it seemed, among other things, to ignore the role of the colleges and recommend top-down monitoring of academics' performance.[143] Council was thought to be moving too fast and to be indifferent to collegiality and tradition. It was also felt to be too quick to ignore well-intentioned and sound advice, a feeling that only gathered force during the following eighteen months as it became clear that the central administration, while preaching the virtues of efficiency, had been guilty of financial mistakes of its own. Two highly expensive computer systems, OSIRIS and ISIDORE, had been purchased against the informed advice of a number of senior members and had proved to be a massive waste of money. By the time the proposals of the White Paper reached Congregation, the atmosphere had been soured. There was a

---

[141] OUG, supplement (1) (22 Nov. 2006), p. 409. The great growth in managers in the NHS and their search for efficiency was a sore point with doctors.

[142] OM, no. 237, 0th week, TT (2005), 1–2 (editorial). The paper appeared in March and there was no debate until the tenth week of Trinity, when many dons were caught up examining or already immersed in research.

[143] Conference of Colleges, 'Response to the Academic Strategy Green Paper', 10 Mar. 2005: COF 05/12; draft. That there was cause for alarm appeared to be confirmed when a number of scientists, during the Easter vacation, received pro forma letters from divisional heads seeming to threaten dismissal unless they increased their research output: Peter Matthews, 'Why be a Don? Reflections on a Changing World', OM, no. 237, 0th week, TT (2005), 4–5.

widespread feeling, however unfair, that the senior management team was out of touch.[144]

The aftermath of the Congregation debate was an anti-climax. At first it looked as if Fraser was wrong and the sky would fall in. On 10 January 2007, HEFCE's chief executive, David Eastwood, wrote to the Vice-Chancellor expressing concern over the vote. Eastwood, a former modern history tutor at Pembroke, who had moved to Swansea in the mid-1990s, did not mince his words:

> The University has accepted that its Council is its single governing body responsible for academic and strategic matters (albeit that Congregation remains the supreme legislative assembly) but has rejected a particular proposal that would have delivered a lay majority. HEFCE takes the view that its investment of public funds must be subject to effective governance oversight, and that this oversight needs to be largely external and demonstrably free from potential conflicts of interest.[145]

HEFCE appeared to expect imminent action to retrieve the situation but none was taken, and the funding council did not pursue the matter robustly.[146] Nor did the Vice-Chancellor and the review committee come up with a new set of governance proposals that might have been successfully commended to Congregation, so the University continued to be governed for the rest of the Hood era, as it still is today, through the structures introduced in 2000. Oxford in 2014 is the university of Franks and North, not of Hood.[147] Apart from the merger of Green and Templeton Colleges in October 2008, the only significant change to the structure of the collegiate university under his watch was the disappearance of the Life and Environmental Sciences Division. Always the smallest of the five, it imploded in the course of the governance review when the biochemists announced that they were joining medicine where they felt more at home. The biological sciences were then attached to maths and physics while geography and anthropology were moved to the social sciences.[148] Oxford had returned to the four-faculty model of the medieval universities, although in its early twenty-first-century form theology, once the queen of the sciences, was now a mere appendage of the humanities.

---

[144] There was also an ongoing disagreement between the central administration and the colleges during 2005–6 over the amount by which the Quantum would be increased.

[145] HEFCE letter.

[146] In late July 2007 it was made clear, in the Final Report of the HEFCE Assurance Service, which had visited Oxford on 17–19 January 2006 to look at the University's governance structure, that it was up to Oxford to demonstrate how its 'corporate governance arrangements meet requirements for effectiveness and scrutiny given the very limited involvement of external individuals in its corporate governance'.

[147] The University's Audit and Scrutiny Committee was given the task of reviewing governance. In Hilary 2009, the Audit and Scrutiny Committee produced a defence of Oxford's system of governance which was sent to HEFCE. The document suggested ways of strengthening the externals' presence on Council and Council committees. But members of the committee were divided and the suggestions were not taken forward. The collapse of the world's banking system in 2008 somewhat diminished the case for the value of independent externals. For a discussion, see the editorial and articles by Laurence Whitehead and Alan Ryan in OM, 2nd week, HT (2009), pp. 1–2 and 3–7.

[148] Voted through Congregation in June 2006: see OUG, no. 4772 (25 May 2006), pp. 1109–10. The Mathematics and Physics Division was renamed the Division of Mathematical, Physical and Life Sciences.

Hood's failure was a personal tragedy. He had come to Oxford keen to help it consolidate its position as a leading world university, and he quickly became convinced, rightly or wrongly, that this demanded further centralization and rationalization of the administration. But he appeared to lack his predecessor's appreciation of the dons' deep-rooted attachment to self-government. He was a spare, ascetic man who drove himself hard. He knew his own mind and seemed impatient with opponents, though, to his credit, he was gracious in defeat. In character, he was reminiscent of Newman. Hood's term as Vice-Chancellor ended in 2009 and he did not apply for an extension. He was replaced by another outsider, Andrew Hamilton, a chemist and FRS with a Cambridge doctorate who had previously been provost of Yale. Hamilton, a more self-effacing figure, opted for the quiet life, and the University settled down to working with the administrative reforms of the Lucas era rather than dramatically revising them.

G. Rebalancing the Finances

While John Hood's attempts to restructure Oxford's governance came to nothing, his efforts to improve Oxford's financial position by organizing the University's largest fund-raising appeal to date were destined to be a great success and ensured his Vice-Chancellorship ended on a positive note. Many of Oxford's colleges had been asking old members for donations to carry out specific projects from the second half of the seventeenth century, but the University first began to seek money from its alumni in the first half of the twentieth, and then far from vigorously. With the change in government policy after the Second World War, the University showed little interest in continuing down the fund-raising road. There was every expectation that the UGC would find most of the money needed to fuel the University's expansion. The University did not cease to receive important benefactions and donations in these years to support a variety of projects, but there was little attempt at targeted fund-raising. The two appeals launched by the University in the twenty years before Franks were for the one item of expenditure the UGC could not be expected to support: the renovation of the colleges' historic buildings. The appeal of 1957–8 brought in £1.6 million, and the second in 1963 a further £800,000. Only Alan Bullock, among the leading lights in the University in the post-war era, recognized that the good times might not last and that Oxford should try to build up its endowment. But his advice was ignored.

Even the economic downturn, following the oil crisis of 1973, and the election of a Conservative government in 1979 determined to control higher-education expenditure did nothing to dent optimism. By the end of the 1980s, however, opinion in the University had begun to shift. The cuts in higher-education funding announced by the Conservatives in 1981 did not dramatically affect Oxford, for the University was largely spared the axe. But as the UGC grant barely grew in real terms across the 1970s and 1980s, Oxford began to experience financial difficulties. It was forced to retrench as early as 1981; then cut back expenditure by 10 per cent over the five years between 1986–7 and 1990–1. Faced by the potential loss of some 200 permanent posts, Council realized there was a need to look for funds elsewhere, and in the course of 1988 launched Oxford's first serious financial appeal. At the same time, it established a proper External Relations/Development Office to organize it. The change of direction owed much to the perspicacity of the Vice-Chancellor and warden of All Souls, Sir Patrick Neill, a distinguished QC who had little time for donnish unworldliness. Announcing the pending appeal in his annual oration, Neill made clear that this was a new but necessary departure:

> No other course offers any real prospect of rescuing Oxford from its over-dependence on increasingly earmarked state financing…To those who will not join us in these efforts or who think it wrong to try I would say only this: that they must resign themselves to the role of a tragic chorus bemoaning the unfoldings of an implacable fate and, incidentally, providing further copy for that already substantial academic tome—the Oxford Book of Whingeing.[149]

The appeal was scheduled to run for six years, and by the time it was wound up in 1994, Oxford had raised £340 million.[150] It was judged so successful that the University decided to continue the appeal even after it was officially closed, with the result that a further £329 million had been raised by 1997, including £23 million given by the Saudi-Syrian businessman Wafic Saïd to establish a business school that would rival the best in America.[151] But by 2000 even more private investment was needed to cover the increasing calls upon Oxford's income. Though the government grant began to increase again in real terms from the mid-1990s, it did not do so for long and was never enough. To an important degree, Oxford was the victim of its own success. By increasing its research income fourfold in real terms between 1987–8 and 2010–11, it only incurred new and additional expenditure, for the research councils and charities did not cover the overhead costs of employing some 3,000 research staff. And when, belatedly, the position in this regard partially improved, the University was hit with an entirely different expense. As a result of its access agreement with OFFA, Oxford had to provide opportunity bursaries to help offset the tuition and maintenance costs of poorer students.[152] Merely to stand still, Oxford had to plumb the generosity of its alumni and friends ever more deeply. To

---

[149] 'Oration by the Vice-Chancellor', in *OUG*, supplement (3) to no. 4090 (Jan. 1988), p. 383. Neill, made Lord Neill of Bladen in 1998, referred to a paper on the dangers of over-reliance on the state written as early as 1932 by Lionel Curtis of All Souls. A total of 127 posts were abolished between 1981 and 1990 under the two retrenchment plans, and further sixty-seven were slated for abolition. At the same time, paradoxically, the University gained a further one hundred posts through deliberate expansion in computing and engineering in particular, and under the government's so-called 'new-blood' initiative, which gave money to allow universities to take on young talent. The colleges stepped in to cover the losses in some cases. The External Relations Office quickly became an important part of the central administration. In 1996–7, it had an annual budget of £2.23 million and a staff of forty-seven: *OUG*, supplement (1) to no. 4392 (26 Feb. 1996), p. 810.

[150] *The Times*, 8 Oct. 1994, p. 2. The target had been 220 million.

[151] 'Oration by the Vice-Chancellor', in *OUG*, supplement (3) to no. 4449 (15 Oct. 1997), p. 171. Oxford already had a business school that was beginning to develop: see p. 629, this volume. Saïd was not an Oxford graduate.

[152] Towards the end of the 2000s, the government research councils agreed to pay overheads but not the private charities, such as the Wellcome Trust.

expand into new areas, the University had to find a clutch of benefactors as liberal as Wafic Saïd.

On 1 August 2004, the University mooted a new appeal, this time for the staggering amount of £1.25 billion. No other university in the United Kingdom, even Cambridge, had ever attempted to raise such a sum, and it was left to John Hood to ensure its success. Hood proved an effective ambassador for the University. By the time the campaign was officially launched in March 2008, the University had already received £575 million.[153] Progress was stymied by the world banking crash in the following autumn, but two years later, within a few months of Hood giving way to Hamilton, two-thirds of the target had been reached. And despite the slowness of the economic recovery, money continued to flow in. In March 2012, the campaign passed its initial goal, and it was decided to create a new target of £3 billion.[154] Three years later the University was raising £200 million a year, the total had reached the £2 billion mark, and it was assumed that the campaign would acheive its goal by 2020.[155]

A significant proportion of the funds raised came from relatively small donations. Even by the time of the official launch, 20,000 individuals, foundations, and other organizations had made a contribution, the vast majority in gifts of £25,000 and below.[156] But there had also been a handful of extraordinary benefactions from philanthropists whose connections with Oxford were often tangential. An expert in systems design, the businessman James Martin, gave $100 million in 2005 to set up the James Martin 21st Century School;[157] in 2010, the Russian-American businessman Leonard Blavatnik proffered £75 million to establish a School of Government;[158] and in 2012, two huge benefactions were received for student support. In February interior designer Mica Ertegun gave £26 million to set up the Mica and Ahmet Ertegun Graduate Scholarship Programme in the Humanities; while in July Michael Moritz, the Welsh-born and Christ Church-educated venture capitalist, promised £75 million to support undergraduates from homes with an income of less than £16,000. Given the increasing financial problems faced by both undergraduates and graduates, the Ertegun and Moritz bequests were especially welcome. According to the University's Chancellor in 2012, Christopher Patten,[159] the Erteguns were the new Bodley and Ashmole. 'Oxford wasn't created by the state', he declared on 29 February. 'Oxford was created by a million and one private

---

[153] <http://www.philanthropy-impact.org/news/oxford-university-campaign-reaches-%C2%A31bn-through-%E2%80%98donor-centric%E2%80%99-approach> (accessed 8 September 2015).

[154] [University of Oxford] *Annual Review* 2011/12, p. 3, 'Vice-Chancellor's Welcome'.

[155] <http://www.ox.ac.uk/news/2015-05-12-fundraising%20-campaign-reaches-£2-billion-and-counting> (accessed 14 May 2015); *The Times*, 12 May 2015, p. 22

[156] 49,246 gifts by 2015. In 2013–14, 18 per cent of Oxford alumni donated.

[157] This was relaunched five years later as the Oxford Martin School by another donation from the businessman of $50 million in the form of matching funding. Martin read physics at Keble. For the school's activities, see p. 628, this volume.

[158] Initially housed in temporary quarters in Merton Street, it moved to a new building in Walton Street at the end of 2015. The University provided £26 million towards the cost.

[159] The Conservative politician Lord Patten, last governor of Hong Kong, was elected Chancellor in 2003 on the death of Lord Jenkins. He was another Balliol man who had read modern history.

acts of generosity. On a rare day [it was a leap year] we are announcing something that is very rare indeed…the largest gift for the support of students in the Humanities in Oxford's 900 year history.'[160]

Benefactions, however, have not been the only sources of Oxford's growing financial independence in the last twenty-five years. Long before the Lambert Report criticized Oxford and Cambridge for neglecting links with business, the University had entered the marketplace and was earning money through Isis Innovation, a subsidiary set up in 1987 to help the University's scientists commercially exploit discoveries arising from their research in return for a percentage of the profits.[161] More importantly, Oxford received an increasing income flow from the one commercial company it directly owned: the University Press. Thanks to good management and the success of its educational and non-academic publishing arms, the Press was producing a healthy profit by the end of the twentieth century.[162] As a result, at the turn of the millennium, OUP was contributing £6 million a year to the University and making periodic one-off donations to swell the University's coffers.

Much of the money collected after 1990 was used for capital expenditure and research, as was the intention. Perhaps less than a half went into building up the University's relatively small endowment. By the time of the White Paper on governance in 2006 this was worth some £600 million, perhaps three times its value between the wars in real terms. Five years later, despite the recession engendered by the banking crash, its value had risen to over a billion thanks, inter alia, to a gift of £203.5 million from OUP. By 2014, as the appeal gained momentum, it had nearly reached £1.5 billion (Table 9).[163] But the endowment still produced only a minute proportion of the University's recurrent needs. In 2001–2 it comprised 7 per cent of the University's income but in 2013–14 only 5.6 per cent. (See Table 8.) If the University was no longer so dependent on the state as it had been forty years before—only 50 per cent of its income in 2010–11 came from HEFCE and publicly funded research grants and fees—it had not yet established a firm independent foundation.[164] Admittedly, compared with other British universities, Oxford was in a healthy position, for only Cambridge had a larger endowment and most had little wealth of their own or none at all.[165] But Oxford's American rivals were in a different league. In 2014 Harvard's endowment stood at $35.9 billion and Yale's at

---

[160] <http://www.ox.ac.uk/media/news_stories/2012/110712> (accessed 25 Feb. 2013, but website no longer extant). Oxford promised to match it, creating a fund of £300m. About 1,000 students would benefit. Mica Ertegun's late husband was the founder of Atlantic records: <http://oxfordstudent.com/2012/03/01who-on-erte-is-mica-ertegun> (accessed 25 Feb 2013). Blavatnik and Ahmet Ertegun, like Saïd, were not Oxford alumni.

[161] See pp. 657–8, this volume.

[162] According to the *White Paper on University Governance*, p. 38, OUP had a £400 million turnover in 2004–5: it had a £100 million reserve in 2002: letter, OM, 8th week, TT (2002), 14.

[163] OUP also gave £62 million in 2003–4 to allow the University to buy the Radcliffe Infirmary site once it was vacated by the local health authority: see p. 639, this volume. The interwar valuation is based on the assumption that the return on endowment was between 3 and 5 per cent.

[164] In fact, in percentage terms, the University's reliance on the state had not changed dramatically over the period it had been seriously fund-raising: in 1988–9, the University's income from the block grants, fees, and the research councils was already down to 62 per cent.

[165] <https://en.wikipedia.org/wiki/List_of_UK_universities_by_endowment> (accessed 8 September 2015).

$23.9 billion.[166] Depending on the fluctuating exchange rate, Oxford today has about 6 per cent of the wealth that America's premier university enjoys.

On the other hand, Oxford's endowment profile is much improved when college wealth is taken into account. University income overtook combined college income in the early 1950s, but the colleges still have a much larger endowment, despite twenty years of highly successful fund-raising on the part of the Development Office. Like the University, the colleges, in the last twenty-five years, have continually sought to attract private money to enhance their endowment, erect new buildings, and provide student support. It is impossible to chart accurately the growth in college wealth since the Second World War for, until recently, information related only to their endowment return. All the same, a reasonable estimate can be made. In 1964, when the colleges' combined gross endowment income was £2.7 million, the value of their endowment was in the region of £54 million to £80 million. By 1997 this had risen to £1 billion, and by 2013–14 to nearly £3.5 billion. If the estimate for 1964 is roughly correct, then college wealth since the time of Franks has virtually trebled in real terms (Table 9).[167]

Adding the wealth of the University and colleges together, Oxford in 2014, had an endowment worth just under £5 billion.[168] Although a much more respectable total, this is still relatively small beer in American terms. In that year at least twelve American institutions of higher education had a larger endowment than Oxford and its colleges.[169] Oxford's decision, therefore, to remain part of Britain's public system of higher education is understandable. Even today, HEFCE's core grant could not be easily jettisoned. In the 1970s, Oxford was fast becoming a state university. What twenty-five years of vigorous fund-raising by the University and colleges had done was not to return it to the independence it enjoyed before 1919—even combined, the endowment income of the University and colleges is not nearly as large as the HEFCE grant. But fund-raising had given Oxford a flexibility that most British universities did not enjoy, and allowed it to retain some degree of control over the development and expansion of its plant and activities, especially after 2000, when the government's core grant once more barely rose in real terms.[170]

---

[166] <http://en.wikipedia.org/wiki/List_of_colleges_and_universities_in_the_United_States_by_endowment> (accessed 25 Feb. 2013).

[167] Franks, i. 290: estimate based on a 3 to 5 per cent return; The Times, 5 May 1997, p. 8; White Paper, p. 38. For the spread of endowment wealth between the colleges, see pp. 720–1, this volume.

[168] Cambridge at this date had a combined endowment of £5.9 billion. Source: as in note 165. The same source credits Oxford with a combined income of only £4.3 billion.

[169] Source: as in note 166 (assuming an exchange rate of 1.5 dollars to the pound).

[170] From 1999/2000 to 2011/12 the real value of the HEFCE grant rose 12.6 per cent.

CHAPTER 14

Students, Staff, and Research

A. Undergraduates

IN 1938–9 there were about 4,500 undergraduates studying at Oxford. In the late 1940s, with an influx of students returning to finish their studies or beginning them late, the intake rose by 40 per cent. In the following sixty years, numbers slowly doubled from about 6,000 in 1948–9 to nearly 12,000 in 2012–13 (Table 1). This was a much smaller increase than that experienced by most of Britain's universities, both old and new. Manchester, in 1934–5, had 2,500 undergraduates; today it has 27,000.[1] Oxford's modest expansion reflected its determination to remain a collegiate and residential university where an undergraduate would continue to enjoy the academic benefits of the weekly tutorial. Despite the rapid development of a mass system of higher education in the United Kingdom from the late 1980s, Oxford came under no pressure to increase its numbers at a faster rate or even increase them at all. The perennial concern in the second half of the period was not the number of undergraduates at Oxford but the proportion of women and the students' background. Oxford's readiness to embrace co-education and positively encourage applications from state schools had completely altered the gender and school profile of the undergraduate community by the end of the period. From being only 15 per cent of undergraduates in 1948–9, women were almost on equal terms with men from 2002–3, while the ratio of state- to independent-school pupils offered places moved from 34:66 for men and 47:53 for women on the eve of the Second World War to 57.5:42.5 for both men and women in December 2011 (Tables 1 and 2).[2] At the same time, in the new multicultural and rights-conscious Britain of the early twenty-first century, Oxford succeeded in reaching out to minority groups. In the 2007 admissions round, 17 per cent of applicants to Oxford were from black or minority ethnic backgrounds, while 6 per cent were registered as suffering from some form of physical or mental disability.[3]

---

[1] Manchester's total was boosted in 2004 when it merged with the University of Manchester Institute of Technology. Nonetheless, a tenfold increase since the war seems to be the norm for the old redbricks.

[2] Albeit with a downturn in the 1970s and 1980s. For a discussion, see Chapter 13, section C.

[3] 'Undergraduate Admission Statistics 2008 Entry', p. 5 (tables): *OUG*, supplement (2*) to vol. 139 (March 2008). Oxford was still not thought to be doing enough. In 2010, the University was accused of institutional racism. Some ethnic minorities, notably the Chinese, performed exceptionally well in

What is much harder to ascertain is whether the social character of Oxford's undergraduate intake seriously changed over the forty years following the Franks Report. Between the wars, only 10 per cent of the fathers of male students were clerks, skilled workers, small shopkeepers, or semi- and unskilled workers. The vast majority were in business, teaching, and the professions. After 1945, the proportion of male undergraduates from working-class or petty bourgeois backgrounds rose sharply with the admission of growing numbers of grammar-school boys: in the years 1946–67, 19.4 per cent of the cohort came from relatively humble backgrounds. What has happened since Franks is much less clear because detailed information is lacking, but there is reason to believe that the position has not greatly altered. An analysis of the social background of undergraduates coming up to Magdalen in 1968 and 2003 found that the proportion which could be described as petty bourgeois or working class actually declined in the intervening years: from 12.5 per cent to 9 per cent. At both moments, a generation apart, nearly every student had a business, media, or professional background. Even more interestingly, only 9 per cent of Magdalen freshers in 2003 did not have at least one close relative with experience of higher education of some kind, while 11 per cent had fathers, and 14 per cent one sibling who had attended either Oxford or Cambridge. Admittedly, this does not mean that all Oxford's students today were reared in luxury. In 2012, the University estimated that 15 per cent of undergraduates came from households with combined incomes below £25,000, and a quarter from households with less than £42,600. The first was equivalent to the national wage, the second sufficient for a modest but not an extravagant lifestyle.[4] On the other hand, the Magdalen evidence does suggest that, regardless of gender, schooling, or ethnicity, early twenty-first-century Oxford's undergraduates were a largely homogeneous group in terms of culture and educational expectations.

This homogeneity was also reflected until the recent past in the undergraduates' geographical background. Historically, Oxford was never a national university for it drew most of its students from the south and west of England, and the position has not radically changed over the last sixty years. At present, its undergraduates come from all over the United Kingdom, but Scotland remains heavily under-represented and the dominant group hails from London and the south-east.[5] What has altered over the last two decades is the proportion of undergraduates who are not British nationals. In 1964–5 foreign students formed only 5.9 per cent of the undergraduate body and were mostly from the Commonwealth and the USA. From the mid-1990s,

admissions, but searching through the published statistics, the Labour politician David Lammy discovered that black candidates, especially those from a West Indian background, found it much more difficult to gain a place. See <http://www.theguardian.com/commentisfree/2010/dec/06/the-oxbridge-whitewash-black-students> (accessed 15 Aug. 2013).

[4] 'Financial Support for Undergraduates' (2012): circulated university document. A study of the United Kingdom's universities in 2013 revealed that 13 per cent of Oxford students came from families with an income less than £16,000: OT, 15 June 2013, p. 24.

[5] For the situation in 2012–14: <http://www.ox.ac.uk/about/facts-and-figures/admissions-statistics/undergraduate2014> (UK region) (accessed 8 September 2015).

however, there was a deliberate effort by many British universities to recruit foreign undergraduates as a useful money-raising exercise, at a time when the per capita government fee for home students was falling in real terms, and Oxford felt it had to follow suit. Attracting a much larger number of high-quality overseas candidates was signalled as a goal in the corporate and strategic plans of the following decade, even if this meant reducing the number of British students at Oxford, and was judged essential if Oxford were to remain in the world's premier league.[6] The strategy quickly paid dividends. In 2014, 18 per cent of Oxford undergraduates came from abroad and their composition was entirely changed from Franks' day. EU students now made up 42 per cent of the total, and the largest contingent of overseas students came from the Chinese People's Republic (360) followed by Germany (161).[7]

As in previous centuries, the undergraduates since the Second World War have been divided up unevenly between the colleges. While all colleges grew in numbers over the period, there remained a distinct hierarchy. In 1948–9, the most populous college was New with some 350 undergraduates, followed by Balliol, Brasenose, Christ Church, Exeter, Magdalen, and Wadham, with just under 300 each. The smallest colleges were Corpus and St Peter's with barely 130 each, and Hertford with 150. In 2011–12, the pecking order was rather different. The largest college was now St Catherine's, the old non-collegiate society, with 506 undergraduates (see Figure 14.1), and a further twelve numbered over 400. These included Wadham, Christ Church, Magdalen, and New College, which had been large institutions throughout the twentieth century, together with three colleges which had been relatively small in the late 1940s—Worcester, St Edmund Hall, and St John's—as well as the female non-collegiate society St Anne's, and three of the four former women's colleges. Corpus, in addition, was no longer the smallest college. It remained tiny with only 238 undergraduates, but Harris Manchester, the college for mature students, had only 100, and Mansfield, another new college, 210.[8]

There was also a significant shift across the sixty years in what undergraduates chose to study. Throughout the period, Oxford continued to emphasize the fact that the primary value of its undergraduate education was intellectual. All courses, whether an art (a humanity or social science) or a science, were intended to promote independent and critical thinking: they provided undergraduates with a set of interchangeable skills and were not necessarily propaedeutic to a specific career. Even law was seen as an academic not a professional subject.[9] However, with the growing emphasis, from the time of Robbins if not before, that Britain's universities

---

[6] Franks, ii. 25; 'International Graduate Student Recruitment': International Office, 12 Feb. 1997; [University of Oxford], *Corporate Plan 2005–6 to 2009–10* (2006), pp. 10–11; 'University of Oxford: Strategic Plan 2008–2009 to 2012–2013': OUG, supplement (1) to no. 4845 (21 May 2008), p. 1106.

[7] <http://www.ox.ac.uk/about/facts-and-figures/student-numbers> (accessed 8 September 2015).

[8] Franks, ii. 30; 'Student Numbers, 2011', OUG, supplement (1) to no. 4978 (15 Feb. 2012), p. 323.

[9] For recent statements, see Keith Thomas, 'What Are Universities For?', *Times Literary Supplement*, 7 May 2010, pp. 13–15; Laurence Brockliss, 'In Search of the New Newman', and David Palfreyman, 'The Oxbridge Legacy', in OM, no. 319, 0th week, HT (2012), 4–9.

FIGURE 14.1 St Catherine's College: the Oxford college with the most undergraduates in 2011–12. View of the original front entrance. Offspring of the old St Catherine's Society, the college was only founded in 1960s. Its buildings, designed by the Danish architect Arne Jacobsen, completely broke with tradition. There was no quadrangle, no tower, no gates and not the slightest reference to Oxford's gothic past.

had a crucial role to play in fostering economic growth, the study of mathematics and natural science was granted a novel value in the Oxford curriculum. The Kneale Committee in 1965 suggested that undergraduates should be encouraged to take mathematics in their first public examination, as the subject had replaced classics as the cultural cement of the modern age.[10] This was seen as a step too far, but, from the beginning of the period, the University was happy to work with the Zeitgeist, all the more as, with the replacement of the Higher School Certificate by A-levels in 1953, it soon became clear that the post-war generation of sixth-formers was swinging away from the arts. Sensing an expanding market, Oxford responded accordingly. At the end of the 1950s, the University decided to give greater emphasis to the life sciences and not just concentrate on mathematics, chemistry, and physics, while Franks, in 1966, counselled promoting the applied sciences as well.[11] The result was a decline over the period in the proportion of students studying the humanities and the social sciences. In 1948–9, 75 per cent of Oxford undergraduates were reading arts; by 1965 6 this figure had dropped to 67 per cent. From the 1970s,

[10] For its remit, see p. 563, this volume.   [11] See p. 566, this volume.

the figure stabilized at just above 60 per cent, then fell again by a further five points between 2004 and 2012. In December 2012 there were 4,082 full-time undergraduates in the Humanities Division, 3,493 in MPLS, 2,122 in Social Sciences, and 1,663 in Medical Sciences. Oxford could no longer be called an arts university.[12]

The growth in undergraduate numbers was matched by a doubling of the number of honour schools that a student might take: from twenty to forty-eight.[13] The increase was not the result of a dramatic expansion in the number of single honours courses. Oxford remained true to its long-standing conviction that an undergraduate education was an academic training par excellence, and was never tempted to establish a legion of more practical courses, such as nursing studies, in imitation of many universities, especially the old polytechnics. Oxford never even developed a single honours course in sociology or economics.[14] There was certainly a modest growth in the number of single honour schools across the period: two new schools in the arts—Fine Art (1977) and History of Art (2004)—and six in the sciences—Forestry (1945), Biochemistry (1949), Metallurgy (1956), Experimental Psychology (1970), Pure and Applied Biology (1982), and Computation (1994). But as several science schools had disappeared by the 1990s, the gain was marginal: Forestry was merged with Agriculture in 1971 before both were closed down from 1983; Metallurgy and Geology came together in 1984 to form Earth Sciences; while Pure and Applied Biology, Botany, and Zoology were subsumed in Biological Sciences from 1990.

The primary reason for the expansion in choice was the development of a wide array of joint honour schools in response to the Franks Report, which had felt that 'the present range of subjects studied in Oxford' was 'artificially narrow'.[15] Immediately after the war, in 1947, an honours course had been set up that bridged the arts/science divide—Psychology, Philosophy, and Physiology—while the first joint schools that were established, such as Physics and Philosophy in 1965 and Human Sciences (a mix of anthropology, zoology, and biology) in 1969, followed this template. But Franks was keen that 'Oxford should concentrate on, and experiment with, combinations of related or overlapping subjects, where knowledge of one field has relevance to the other', and this became the established convention. From 1970, very few of the twenty or so joint degrees established over the next forty years bridged the arts/science divide, and the large majority brought together cognate disciplines in the humanities and the social sciences, as in the case of Classics and English, set up in 1988, or History and Politics, created at the end of the 1990s. Had this not been so, the arts share of the undergraduate intake would have fallen below parity by the end of the period.

---

[12] Franks, ii. 15; Table 3; 'Student Numbers, 2012', Table 2 *OUG*, supplement (1) to no. 5017 (6 Mar. 2012), p. 408.
[13] According to the list in *OUG*, supplement (3) to no. 4783 (18 Oct. 2006), pp. 241–2.
[14] Sociology at undergraduate level was first available as an optional paper in PPE Schools in 1964.
[15] Franks, i. 34.

The rising profile of undergraduate science did not displace the traditional dominance of the large arts schools (Table 3). Modern History had by far the largest number of undergraduates in 1951, followed at some distance by Modern Languages, PPE, Jurisprudence, and English. Modern History still had the largest cohort of first years in 2005, even though, in the interim, the number of undergraduates beginning the course had fallen from 340 to 252, while the other four continued to follow in its wake, though now breathing hard on its heels. PPE had temporarily taken poll position in the 1990s but none of the science schools had ever run the arts leviathans close. Nor had diversification altered the pecking order in the sciences. Chemistry was always the largest science school, boasting an intake of a hundred in 1951 and about 180 at the turn of the millennium. Only Physics, which had more than trebled its numbers over the sixty years, threatened to challenge its supremacy. Even Lit. Hum. had not been pushed to one side. If smaller than several science schools by the end of the period, it still had a substantial presence, with over 100 students starting the degree each year. History's decline, moreover, can be exaggerated. When its five joint schools are added to the total, it was just as large at the end of the period as at the beginning.[16]

There was a similar predictability about the subject distribution within the colleges. Undergraduates had never been distributed evenly by subject. Long before the war, colleges had become associated with certain subjects more than others as Oxford's schools first developed, and this continued to be the case. No college specialized—it was an unwritten law that the Oxford system was characterized by undergraduates reading different subjects rubbing shoulders with one another in their leisure hours. But nor was it expected that colleges should present a similar subject profile. Although the proportion of undergraduates reading for science schools grew everywhere, colleges mostly maintained their historical differences, which could give one or two disciplines within a college a prominence completely out of kilter with the university norm. Corpus Christi was a small college which always had a large cohort of classicists; Magdalen was a large college with exceptional numbers of historians and PPEists but no geographers; Wadham took a disproportionate share of students reading oriental studies; while Merton usually had the largest number of physicists and St Edmund Hall the biggest group of biochemists. St Catherine's, the most populous undergraduate college at the end of the period but only established in the early 1960s, was as idiosyncratic as its older sisters. In deference to the business community that provided much of the money for its foundation, it recruited more than half of its undergraduates from the sciences from its inception.

Past practice also continued to exercise a powerful hold over the basic structure of an Oxford undergraduate education. Throughout the period, the average undergraduate followed an honours course that demanded three years of residence, was

---

[16] By the end of the period, Modern History had been rechristened History to avoid confusion among state-school applicants, who might wonder why the course began with the fall of the Roman Empire.

largely examined by a series of conventional three-hour papers, and led to a BA whatever the school. Around 2000, a number of science schools instituted four-year courses in imitation of Lit. Hum. and Chemistry, and which led in their case directly to a master's qualification, but there was no attempt to introduce a BSc.[17] Custom, too, for a long time maintained a tight grip over the syllabus of the large art schools. In the pre-Franks era, undergraduates reading Greats, English, or modern history would have followed a course scarcely changed from the day the individual schools were created, however differently taught. Candidates for the Lit. Hum. school could not offer literature options, the English course stopped in 1830 and still emphasized the study of language, and modern historians continued to be largely fed on a diet of English, not even British, history, from the Anglo-Saxon invasions to a moving but never contemporary present. It was only from the late 1960s that change began to be effected in response to a growing attack from younger postholders and student activists that undergraduate study should reflect current intellectual concerns and geopolitical realities. Even then, profoundly remodelling the curriculum was a slow and painful task. The traditional syllabus was usually flexible enough to permit the introduction of new approaches or subject areas within an existing course component, but it was hard to get them accepted in their own right. It was not until the 1990s that the English and modern language faculties became reconciled to adding the study of film to their under-graduate portfolio.[18]

In the face of changing market forces, arts faculties could respond imaginatively. Lit. Hum. kept up its numbers when ancient Greek ceased to be taught in state schools by allowing undergraduates to study the language from scratch. Modern languages did the same in the case of Russian and other minority European languages. But reforming the curriculum was a different matter. As at the University, so at the faculty level great emphasis was placed on consensus, and, too, many tutors, often in post for twenty or thirty years, had a vested interest in retaining the status quo. Furthermore, once the traditional edifice had begun to be torn down, it proved difficult to rebuild. The faculty of modern history began unpicking its prescriptive curriculum in the mid-1980s but it was still arguing over the shape of its more flexible successor at the end of the 1990s, as the regius professor, Sir John Elliott, lamented at his farewell dinner in 1997: 'I have regretted, and continue to regret, that the altering of our syllabus and teaching arrangements remains such a Sisyphean task. It should be easier than it is to put on new subjects, and discard those that have done long service and are due for honourable retirement.'[19]

---

[17] The only undergraduates who did not receive a BA at the end of their three-year course were students in fine art, who took a BFA, and theology students from 2000 on the BT course. Medical students, until 2003, gained a BA in physiological sciences and, from 2004, a BA in medical sciences; they then, as in the previous era, went on to study for the first and second BM.

[18] The ball was set rolling by Lit. Hum., which was reformed to include literary options in 1968.

[19] Sir John Elliott, 'Text of Farewell Speech at Retirement Dinner', 10 July 1997, pp. 8–9 (photocopy circulated to all faculty members). Elliott is a historian of early modern Spain and the Spanish Empire, who initially specialized in the reign of Philip IV. He held chairs at London and Princeton before coming to Oxford.

Tellingly, it was to be under his successor that the faculty finally agreed to introduce a compulsory thesis, a hundred years after its adoption had been urged by Firth.[20]

Curricular conservatism, however, did not put prospective students off. There were 5,853 candidates for the admission round of December 1965; in 2010, applications reached a high point of 17,343 (Table 2). The growing competition for places markedly raised the intellectual quality of the undergraduate body. In the pre-Franks era, Oxford was graced with many talented scholars but its male commoners, selected on their performance in a less taxing exam and frequently chosen for their sporting prowess or their family's past association with the college, were not always dazzling intellectuals.[21] Admissions tutors in the post-Franks age had a much wider choice and were able to cream off a high proportion of the country's most talented 17-year-olds. In assessing candidates, emphasis came to be based exclusively on academic performance to date and potential, and old members' children had to compete on the same terms as everyone else. In an earlier age, heads of house had played an important role in selecting commoners and had not always been moved by purely academic considerations. Post-Franks, the preferences of the heads of house were no longer of consequence, as Asa Briggs, provost of Worcester, pointed out to an interviewer in 1986:

> I do not have anything to do with admissions to this college, nor in fact do most heads of college … I get letters from old members of the college about their sons and daughters, and I know perfectly well if I were, for whatever reason, to press the claim of somebody … I would be counterproductive, even though there are people who would be very helpful to the college for benefactions and things of that sort … When I was in college in 1955, the provost [was] a very powerful figure in relation to admissions, which was one of his main interests. When I got back here, to my very great surprise, I found that the provost had nothing to do with admissions. It was a total change.[22]

The great growth in applications allowed Oxford to become a meritocracy for the first time.[23]

The effect of increased competition on standards can be seen in the improving A-level scores of Oxford's undergraduates. In the mid-1960s, only 26.8 per cent of male undergraduates had top A-level grades in two or three subjects; but in 1983 around 82.4 per cent of all candidates admitted had three As or better; and from the

---

[20] As of 2015, the faculty is attempting yet again to construct a curriculum that reflects the new global age and the current state of historical study but is meeting fierce opposition.

[21] Female candidates were equally not always subject to a testing academic interview. One applicant to read history in 1957 was 'given a ball of wool and knitting needles and told to knit a square', which would be joined with others to 'form a blanket for Hungarian refugees': letter, *The Times*, 31 July 2014, p. 25.

[22] Cited in Soares, p. 209. Admittedly, some heads used their influence wisely: Bowra at Wadham in the 1950s and 1960s strove hard to raise the intellectual level of the college: Leslie Mitchell, *Maurice Bowra: A Life* (Oxford, 2009), p. 245.

[23] Until the mid-1980s, top public-school heads could usually find a place for a solid but uninspiring candidate: see the many instances in John Rae, *The Old Boys' Network: A Headmaster's Diaries 1970–1986* (London, 2009).

turn of the twenty-first century, no one, unless they had special mitigating circumstances, could be admitted at 18 who had not got three As or their equivalent in another school-leaving exam.[24] The effect can also be seen in the Schools results. After the war barely anyone was admitted simply to read for a Pass degree but the intellectual calibre of honours students was not always high. In 1955, only 6.9 per cent of finalists took a First, while 34 per cent took a Third or below. From the mid-1960s, however, the tail began to decline: the Fourth was abolished in 1967 and by the end of the decade over 75 per cent of undergraduates gained a Second or above. When, in 1986, the Second, as in most other universities, was divided into two divisions, about a third of finalists still found themselves on the wrong side of the line, but the proportion quickly fell. The Third had all but vanished by the mid-1990s and the 2:2 ten years later. The percentage of Firsts, on the other hand, steadily grew. Ten per cent in 1970, it was 17 per cent twenty years later, and 30 per cent in 2012.[25] Admittedly, other factors were at work here. A rapidly rising percentage of Upper Seconds and Firsts was a common feature of the whole university system after 1990. It reflected a greater dedication to study in an age of increased competition for jobs and a move away from traditional forms of assessment. But in Oxford's case, where the system of examination remained largely unchanged, the growing competition for places was the primary cause.[26]

How well an individual student did while at Oxford depended to a degree on his or her college. Since the creation of undergraduate schools in the second half of the nineteenth century, there had always been an element of competition between the colleges, but this quickened as the quality of the students improved. From 1964, the rivalry was formalized with the publication of the first Norrington Table, which allowed the public as well as the dons to study the relative performance of different colleges year on year. Although annual positions could fluctuate widely, by and large the richest colleges were always in the top half of the league. There were few years when Magdalen, Merton, New College, and St John's, if not Christ Church, were not in the top ten. Only Balliol and Wadham, of the more modestly endowed colleges, consistently held their own against their wealthier brethren, while only the old women's colleges suffered a radical shift in fortune. Before the mid-1970s, they largely put the men to shame: Somerville and St Anne's were invariably in the top flight. With the coming of co-education they found it difficult to attract the best candidates and were usually condemned to the bottom, along with St Peter's and Pembroke.[27]

---

[24] At present, 98 per cent of undergraduates at Oxford have three As or better: <http://www.ox.ac.uk/about_the_university/facts_and_figures> (accessed 15 Aug. 2013).

[25] Final Honour Schools' results from 1990 can be found at <http://www.ox.ac.uk/gazette/statisticalinformation/#d.en.6208> (final honour schools) (accessed 8 September 2015). In 2012, 37 per cent of candidates in schools in the MPLS division gained a First.

[26] At the end of the period most of the University's schools still had only one or two papers that were not assessed by a three-hour examination.

[27] For the positions in the years 2006–12, see <http://www.wikipedia.org/wiki/Norrington_Table> (accessed 15 Aug. 2013).

Until the 1990s, the disparity in performance caused little comment. The academic competition between the colleges was felt to be one of the positive features of the collegiate university. But as Oxford came more and more under scrutiny from outsiders looking for signs of irregularity in any aspect of its governance, the dominance of the wealthy colleges began to raise concern. Rightly or wrongly it was felt that their students' comparative success reflected better library resources, more generous financial aid, and better and more intense teaching: the best tutors purportedly clustered in colleges that offered the best benefits.[28] For several years at the turn of the millennium, the University responded to the disquiet by ceasing to publish the league table, but this only buried the problem: it did not stop the circulation of an unofficial version nor quieten the criticisms.[29]

B. Postgraduates

All over the world after 1945 the number of students in some form of postgraduate study exploded. Western states promoted research in the natural and social sciences and medicine as a national good, and were even ready to underpin research in the humanities to a degree. The expansion was also encouraged towards the end of the century in Britain and elsewhere by the development of a mass system of higher education: many graduates found that their first degree had a limited market value and that further study in a specialist or professional skill was necessary to secure decent employment. Oxford, like Cambridge, was well placed, with its brand name and good library and laboratory facilities, to capitalize on the growing demand, and was anxious from the beginning of the period to expand its postgraduate education. The result was a spectacular expansion in its postgraduate numbers, though one mirrored in many other British universities to a greater or less extent. While Oxford's undergraduate numbers doubled over the sixty years following the Second World War, the postgraduate total expanded ninefold. Little more than a thousand in 1948–9, postgraduates numbered 9,857 in 2012–13. As a result, their proportion of the junior membership steadily rose. Less than 15 per cent in 1948–9, postgraduates formed 20 per cent of the total in 1963–4, 30 per cent in 1995–6, and 44 per cent in 2012–13 (Table 4). It can be only a matter of time before postgraduates outnumber undergraduates. Although a working group of Council in 2011 noted that the balance between the two was about right, there continues to be pressure for further expansion at divisional level for financial reasons, as long as numbers can be increased without appointing more academic staff.[30]

---

[28] On the range of benefits, see pp. 705–6, this volume.

[29] Attacks came from inside as well as out, and from undergraduates as well as dons. For an early criticism, see OM, no. 4, TT (1991), 1–2. The author suggested the table encouraged overteaching and took dons away from research.

[30] 'Report from the Strategic Plan Review Implementation Group (SPRIG)', 2011, pp. 9–10 (document passed to the Conference of Colleges and then the colleges). According to the report, the ratio of undergraduates to graduates was similar to the pattern of other major British and American state universities, so there was no need to change it further. It was also suspected that the postgraduate bubble was on the point of bursting.

As in the case of the undergraduates, there was a steady swing in the postgraduate intake towards the sciences and medicine across the period. Between 1945 and 2012–13, the proportion of Oxford's postgraduates studying the humanities and the social sciences declined from two-thirds to little more than a half. Nevertheless, the swing was not sufficiently strong to undermine completely Oxford's historic bias towards the arts. The largest postgraduate group in 2012–13 was formed by the Social Sciences Division, where the number was nearly as many as in MPLS and medical sciences combined (3,539 against 3,777). It was also the only division where postgraduates outnumbered the undergraduates (by a factor of almost two to one). For most of the period, moreover, the largest cluster of doctoral students was always to be found in modern history/history. It was only in 2011 that the faculty was finally knocked off its perch. As a result, even in the 2010s, Oxford's postgraduate numbers in the sciences, though large numerically (no other British university apart from Cambridge had so many) still looked low when judged in terms of their percentage share. Only chemistry and engineering were very large research schools. Oriental studies had more doctoral pupils than biochemistry (Table 5).

The relative balance between the divisions was profoundly affected at the close of the period by the proportion of their students taking a taught postgraduate course rather than studying for a research degree. Between the wars, 45 per cent of Oxford's small postgraduate community were on taught courses working towards a diploma, the largest group, 36.8 per cent of the total, studying for a DipEd.[31] After 1945, the proportion of postgraduates on taught courses steadily fell. Although the University expanded its taught graduate provision with the creation of many new programmes, most notably the two-year BPhil in philosophy, established in 1947, the rapid growth in the number of doctoral students caused the percentage of postgraduates taking taught courses to fall to 30 per cent by the time of Franks. Over the next thirty years it fell even further. Though new programmes continued to be invented and a number of the old diploma courses gained an increased cachet with the creation of the MSc in 1971, which allowed them to be upgraded to a master's, only 24 per cent of postgraduates were on a taught course in the early 1990s. The situation changed dramatically thereafter, however, as Oxford moved to gain a share of the burgeoning market in one- and two-year postgraduate courses, and the research councils began to insist that no one could proceed to read for a doctorate without first taking a master's degree. Within a few years, numbers on taught postgraduate courses had mushroomed, and by 2010–11 their proportion of the total was back to the pre-war level (Table 4). As Oxford was happy to invest in the contemporary obsession with postgraduate managerial and business training, the growth was particularly significant in the Social Sciences Division: 65 per cent of the division's postgraduates were on taught courses at the end of the period, of

---

Applications in 2009–10 had stood at 20,000 (higher than undergraduate applications) but there had then been a 7 per cent drop in the following year.

[31] Diploma of education; the former name for the PGCE.

whom 8 per cent were pursuing an MBA, a qualification unobtainable at Oxford before 1993. In medical sciences, in contrast, the figure was only 14 per cent.[32] To cope with the new era, Oxford, along with Cambridge and Trinity College Dublin, had to invent a degree hitherto unknown in the university world, the MStud. As an Oxford MA remained a degree that any Oxford BA could take twenty-one terms after matriculation, a new master's degree had to be created for the legion of new taught courses in the humanities and social sciences for which an MSc was inappropriate.[33]

Although a growing proportion of postgraduates were members of the new graduate societies—16 per cent in the mid-1960s; 30 per cent at the end of the period—the large majority were always attached to an undergraduate college.[34] Pre-Franks, postgraduates in undergraduate colleges were never more than 10 to 20 per cent of the junior members. But by the end of the period, due to the rapid rise in their numbers, they formed a significant presence everywhere. In 2012–13, in most undergraduate colleges, postgraduates accounted for at least 30 per cent of students, and in three cases they were in a majority.[35] As a result, it became customary after 2000 to drop the undergraduate label and call the thirty colleges that took both undergraduates and postgraduates 'combined' or 'mixed' societies. Nonetheless, apart from Nuffield, the graduate colleges always had the largest contingents of advanced students. In 2012–13, St Cross, Wolfson, and Green Templeton had more than 500 graduate students each, while only one former undergraduate college, Balliol, had more than 300.[36]

The historic Oxford ideal was that a college should house a mixed disciplinary community, so from the moment postgraduates were attached to the existing colleges between the wars there was no attempt to establish disciplinary clusters. Four of the postgraduate colleges, however, were specifically founded with a subject focus: St Antony's welcomed graduates working on modern history, international affairs, and the extra-European world, while Nuffield, despite the intention of its founder, was home to social scientists, Green to students of clinical medicine, and Templeton to graduates studying business management.[37] Some members of the University thought that this should be the template for the future where graduates were concerned, and there was talk in the University, post-North, of encouraging the other colleges, both graduate and mixed, to build their postgraduate community around cognate disciplines. The idea, though, never commanded much support and

---

[32] OUG, supplement (1) to no. 5017, vol. 143, 6 Mar. 2013, p. 408; <http://www.sbs.ox.ac.uk/degrees/mba/our_students> (accessed 15 Aug. 2013, but site no longer extant). From the 1990s, it was felt that no one could learn how to manage the resources of large private and state corporations efficiently and productively without specialist training. Only dealers in the City were frequently deployed on the trading floor without a higher-education qualification. For Oxford's investment in business studies, see p. 629, this volume.

[33] There were forty-two MStud courses in 2005: see 'Report of the Working Party on Taught Graduate Courses' (2005), Tables. By then there were barely any diploma students and no more DipEd/PGCE students than there had been in 1951–2: see OUG, supplement (2) to no. 4783 (18 Oct. 2006), p. 234. The MStud also exists at the Australian National University.

[34] There were seven graduate colleges from 1983: see pp. 561, 570–1, and 579–80, this volume.

[35] Franks, ii. 30 (data 1948/9 to 1964/5); 'First Report from the Graduate Issues Group' (Dec. 2012), p. 2.

[36] OUG, supplement (1) to no. 5017, vol. 143 (6 Mar. 2013), p. 409.

[37] Green did take students in other subjects. For Nuffield's original intentions, see p. 486, this volume.

the customary approach pertained.[38] Indeed, many colleges did not even attempt to weight postgraduate admissions towards subjects in which their undergraduate numbers were strong.

Even before the publication of the Roberts Report on graduate provision in the late 1980s, the mixed colleges worked hard to integrate their postgraduates into college life and demonstrate that their collegiate attachment was academically and socially beneficial.[39] Whether in a mixed or a graduate college, however, the postgraduates always formed a community apart. Undergraduates and postgraduates belonged to different tribes. Postgraduates were older and more mature than the traditional Oxford junior member; many were married, especially in the first part of the period.[40] They were resident in Oxford for most of the year; and the focus of their academic life was the Bodleian or one of the other of the University's libraries, the faculty seminar, and the departmental laboratory. However much part of their college—and many developed a deep college loyalty—postgraduates were inevitably detached to some degree. They were much more likely than undergraduates to identify closely with the faculty and the department, especially as it was the University that had admitted them in the first place, while their college affiliation was often a matter of chance.[41]

Undergraduates and postgraduates also came from different backgrounds. It was not that they had distinctive social origins or gender profile, for in this respect there was little difference between the two groups.[42] It was rather that postgraduates, throughout the period, were a much more cosmopolitan group. The large majority of undergraduates were British and arrived at Oxford with the prejudices and cultural experiences of the average British teenager. From the beginning, Oxford's postgraduate community was recruited internationally and, by 1964–5, 30 per cent came from overseas. From then on the percentage steadily grew until, in the 2000s, it reached a plateau between 55 and 60 per cent (Table 4). The overseas contingent also became more ethnically and culturally diverse. In 1964–5, the large majority came from the English-speaking world and were the beneficiaries of the Rhodes Trust and other scholarship schemes: 48 per cent of the group came from the Commonwealth, mostly Australians and Canadians, and 28 per cent from the USA. By the end of the period, the overseas postgraduates came from all over the world. In 2006–7, there were 4,169 foreign nationals in full-time postgraduate study

---

[38] Franks had promoted disciplinary clusters to a degree and had argued that postgraduates should be admitted only to colleges with a fellow in their subject: Franks, i. 122.

[39] See p. 682, this volume. [40] Thirty-five per cent in 1964: Franks, ii. 200.

[41] By 1980, candidates for a postgraduate degree could not apply directly to a college but had first to be admitted by a faculty or department. Only then was their dossier passed to a college. Candidates could specify a college but most outsiders who plumped for a mixed college did not get their first choice. They tended to opt for the most famous, where competition for places was fierce.

[42] Social background: survey of members of Magdalen MCR 2014; only 18.8 per cent did not have either a mother or a father who had been through higher education, and 59.4 per cent had both; more than 90 per cent had fathers who had worked or were working in professional occupations. Gender: Franks, ii.15; <http://www.ox.ac.uk/media/global/wwwoxacuk/localsites/gazette/documents/supplements2014-15/Student_Numbers_2014_-_(1)_to_No_5083.pdf> (Table 1: students by course, type and sex 2009–2014) (accessed 8 September 2015).

at Oxford, drawn from more than 120 countries. A total of 1,041 were denizens of the EU, the large majority doing doctoral research and 30 per cent of the total coming from Germany. The remaining 3,128 came from more than a hundred other nation states scattered around the world. Americans, Australians, and Canadians were still an important group, and Americans were the largest contingent by far (818). But the Americans now only formed 19.6 per cent of the overseas cohort, and the second largest contingent were the Chinese (354).[43]

As the more advanced doctoral students might be involved in teaching under-graduates at college and faculty level, one group of postgraduates was even further removed from the undergraduate community. Oxford always prided itself on the extent to which its undergraduate teaching was in the hands of the dons. According to North, Oxford must not go down the American road and entrust face-to-face teaching to postgraduates, so that postholders could get on with their research: 'It is partly on this principle that Oxford's reputation for excellent undergraduate teach-ing rests, and we cannot allow it to be diluted to any degree.'[44] Nevertheless, from the 1950s, senior doctoral students were commonly called upon to fill in when tutors were on leave, and by the end of the period the University was keen that all of the cohort should have the chance to teach in order to enhance their prospects of gaining an academic job.[45] Limited training in conducting tutorials and classes was provided by the University's education department, and in some faculties postgrad-uates were not allowed to teach until they had gained experience by shadowing a don for a term. Only a minority had the opportunity to teach—tutorial teaching was largely in the gift of the tutor on leave—and there was a tendency to employ Oxford graduates who had, earlier in life, taken the course. But the fact that every doctoral pupil was potentially a tyro teacher suggested that the allegiance of the senior section of the postgraduate community lay predominantly with the dons.[46]

The development of a large postgraduate community of students at Oxford in the second half of the twentieth century profoundly altered the character of the University. With nearly half its junior members identifying with their faculty or department at least as much as their college, Oxford University, for the first time since the medieval era, could be said to have its own student constituency. The transformation was another factor in swinging the balance of power in the University's favour. More importantly, the multinational and multicultural nature of the postgraduate community was an essential element in making Oxford a much more outward-looking and dynamic institution. In the increasingly mobile

[43] Franks, ii. 25; <http://www.ox.ac.uk/media/global/wwwoxacuk/localsites/gazette/documents/statisticalinformation/studentnumbers/2007/table4b.pdf> (accessed 8 September 2015): this is the last year for which information is easily available. The new importance of China was emphasized by the decision taken in 2015 to elect a number of Chinese Rhodes scholars each year: *Oxford Times*, 9 April 2015, p. 5.

[44] North, p. 132. From the late 1980s, lecturers had to demonstrate at interview that they would be effective undergraduate teachers.

[45] It also gave them the chance to see if they enjoyed teaching.

[46] For a further distinction between one group of postgraduates and the undergraduates, see p. 627, this volume.

post-war world, overseas graduates flocked to Oxford because of its history, its facilities, and the perceived quality of its research degrees and the research of the University's senior members. But overseas students gave as much as they received by offering Oxford a novel and stimulating access to alternative cultural traditions, educational systems, and cognitive practices that left a permanent mark on all sections of the academic community. Their presence was the key to turning Oxford into a world university.

C. The Academic Staff

As with any other university in the modern era, the fourfold expansion in student numbers across the period was accompanied by a dramatic rise in the size of the academic staff. Immediately after the war, in 1948–9, there had only been 573 academic members of staff on the University's payroll. By 1964–5, the figure stood at around 1,120, and thirty years later, 3,500. By 2013 it had grown to 5,809 (Table 7). In the first part of the period, the growth had occurred principally in the number of university lecturers. Once the UGC had agreed, in 1950, that all tutorial fellows could be given a part-time university lectureship in order to reduce the cost to their college, the number of tutorial fellows quickly expanded, especially in the sciences, where student numbers were growing fast, while the development of graduate studies into areas not covered by the undergraduate curriculum necessitated the creation of more and more full-time posts. In 1948–9 there had been only 573 part- or full-time university postholders; by 1964–5 that number had risen to 973. There- after, the number of professors, readers, and lecturers grew more slowly. Their combined total was still only some 1,350 in 1995–6 and 1,700 at the end of the period. Post-Franks, the expansion mainly occurred in the number of academic- related research staff. Before 1939, several science professors had a team of senior researchers working under their supervision and paid for by government, philan- thropists, or industry. But their numbers were few. Oxford's success in attracting a large share of the increasing amount of research money on offer from the mid- 1970s resulted in a rapid growth in the number of postdoctoral researchers on relatively short-term contracts. In 1964–5 there were about 150 members of the University's academic staff who were not employed in a teaching post. In 1975 there were 400 contract research staff, 2,000 in 1995–6, and 4,087 in 2013. By 2005, they formed two-thirds of all academic staff, a higher proportion than any other uni- versity in the United Kingdom.[47]

The changing balance of the academic establishment over the period threw up continual problems that the University struggled to address. The chief worry in the early 1960s was the large group of university lecturers who were principally servicing postgraduates and had no college attachment. Colleges, after the war, were usually happy to provide a new professorial appointee with a fellowship and

---

[47] *Corporate Plan*, p. 5 (para. 41).

vied with one another for the privilege.[48] They were much less willing to give fellowships to lecturers, mostly scientists, who would play little role in teaching the college's undergraduates. The problem was solved over the next twenty years, as we have seen in Chapter 13, by the creation of new graduate colleges and the eventual establishment of the entitlement scheme.[49] There were still anomalies, however. Although, from the 1950s, nearly all Oxford's lecturers were paid on the same age-related scale, regardless of whether their post was funded by the University alone or jointly with a college, the tutorial fellows among them received various extra college benefits, which could lead to a considerable salary differential.[50] The North Commission suggested the way forward was to abolish the most significant benefit, the housing allowance, and adjust the lecturer pay scale upwards so that all postholders below professor and reader would receive the same amount.[51] The suggestion, however, met with little support in the mixed colleges, and the most that could be agreed was that university lecturers who were fellows but not tutorial fellows would receive a salary supplement if they did a few hours' tutorial teaching or carried the same teaching load as their tutorial colleagues.[52]

The problem of academic staff with no college attachment was once more on the University's agenda from the mid-1990s, as the number of research staff swelled. The elite of the group, who had permanent research positions, could usually find a college fellowship, especially if they had an Oxford background. The rest, though, on short-term contracts, had no chance of negotiating an attachment on their own initiative. On this, the colleges could not be swayed despite the University's best intentions.[53] The number that needed to be integrated was so large that the problem could not be resolved by creating another couple of societies and there was real fear that existing fellowships would be swamped and lose their coherence. Even the suggestion that research staff could be made members of a senior common room was largely cold-shouldered. All the University could do in the end was improve the social facilities for all its members of staff, academic and non-academic, by providing a new building on Mansfield Road for the University Club, which opened in

---

[48] Colleges that already had a number of professorial fellows tended to be passed over in favour of those with barely any.

[49] See pp. 570–1, this volume.

[50] After the Second World War, the existing pay scales were homogenized. Whereas beforehand there had been a scale for university lecturers and a separate scale for college lecturers and tutors drawn up by each individual college, a single age-related scale was created in the early 1950s with an end point at the age of 55 (45 from 1966). Either the University paid the whole salary, or in the case of a tutorial fellow, paid a part and the college made up the rest. Today the scale is not age related and new appointments can be made at the top point. For subjects with their own pay scale: see p. 705, this volume.

[51] North (1997), p. 235. An earlier university working party report on the problem in 1995 revealed that there were 185 university lecturers who were not tutorial fellows and that most were in the graduate colleges; it was suggested the anomaly could be ended by creating a separate salary scale for them with a higher end point: OUG, 10 July 1995, p. 1368.

[52] 'Revision of Arrangements for the Grading and Salary Progression of University Staff', annexe to a letter to heads of house from the deputy head of personnel services, 25 Apr. 2006, p. 4. On average, towards the end of the period, university lecturers with a tutorial post earned £10,000 more per annum pensionable salary than simple university lecturers.

[53] *Corporate Plan*, pp. 16 and 17 (para. 113).

FIGURE 14.2 Oxford University Club, Mansfield Rd, opened 2004. By 2013 there were some 4,000 contract research staff and most had no college attachment. The University Club provided them with a social centre, especially those who were new to Oxford and were not part of a large research team. The University Club began life in 1946 as a social centre for unattached dons and postgraduates. From 1950 it had been based in Halifax House on South Parks Road.

2004 and offered good-quality meals and the possibility of accommodating guests relatively cheaply. It was a welcome but inadequate substitute for a college attachment. As a third of research staff were entitled to be members of Congregation, the failure to make the group part of the collegiate university could potentially have significantly affected university politics.[54] Just as in the early 1960s, Oxford academics at the end of the period were divided into two interest groups. Nonetheless, as the 2006 vote on governance demonstrated, the division did not obviously strengthen the hand of the central administration, at least in the short term.

The University had more success in addressing another problem that reared its head in the 1990s: career development. The historic separation between university and college posts meant that there was no obvious career ladder at Oxford. Not only were there relatively few professorships and readerships in the second half of the twentieth century, but, as many were the result of donor whim rather than academic strategy, they were frequently, especially in the arts, in narrow specialist fields that had limited connection with the undergraduate curriculum. College

---

[54] A total of 1,358 research staff could be members of Congregation in 2013: *OUG*, supplement (1) to no. 5051 (26 Feb. 2014), p. 340.

tutors, who were usually chosen because their research interests were in the main-stream, were unlikely ever to hold one. This caused few problems for a large part of the period. As college tutors often earned more than professors when the housing allowance was taken into account, most were happy to spend their working lives holding a joint post. The landscape was changed, however, when the number of professorial posts in the country was vastly inflated by the expansion in the university system and the national professorial salary scale collapsed with the competition between universities for RAE talent.[55] Tutors and non-tutors among the lecturing staff began to be enticed elsewhere, hitherto an infrequent occurrence, and the University was forced to respond.[56] From 1996, it became possible for lecturers and academic staff of all kinds to apply for the ad hominem title of reader or professor, which was awarded subsequent to external peer-group review of an individual's research. In the first year alone, 162 new professors and ninety-nine readers were created, and within a few years some of the science faculties, where the lust for titles was particularly great, were beginning to look top-heavy.[57] This, though, was not felt to be problematic given the age and research profile of Oxford's academic staff. More contentious was the fact that an ad hominem award was a mark of distinction and brought no financial benefit and change of duties.[58] After a lengthy discussion, which began in 2005 and was only concluded in 2014, it was eventually decided that ad hominem professors would receive a small increase in salary and be allowed to apply for extra merit pay, as was already the case with the holders of titular chairs.[59]

Some progress was equally made in the last decade of the period in tackling a more specific concern that the teaching obligations of the different types of uni-versity lecturer had become too inflexible to meet the needs of a university with a fast-growing graduate cohort. By the 1990s, there were essentially three types of lecturer: those who were required to teach for the University alone (ULNTFs); those, usually scientists, who were primarily funded by the University but contracted to provide their college with seven tutorial hours a week (ULTFs); and those, the majority of mathematicians and postholders in arts subjects, who drew one-third

---

[55] After the war a national pay scale for university lecturers, senior lecturers, readers, and professors was accepted by all universities except Oxford and Cambridge. The two oldest universities, from the beginning, had their own pay scales, which mirrored the universities' national scale with a small premium. At Oxford, the lecturer scale tracked the national senior lecturer scale. From the 1990s, universities began to buy and retain talent by offering professors, in particular, individual packages that gave them a salary far above the top of the scale. Breaches in the national scale were also encouraged by the ending of the binary system, as the polytechnics and colleges of education had their own distinctive pay scales.

[56] Restructuring the Oxford career ladder was under discussion from 1993 when Council issued a consulta-tion paper and Vice-Chancellor Sir Richard Southwood, Linacre professor of zoology, raised the issue in his leaving oration: OM, 5th week, TT (2009), p. 5 (republished extract of the text in OUG, 5 Oct 1993).

[57] Many science dons believed that they were not taken seriously in the United States without a professorial title.

[58] The small number of ad hominem titles awarded before 1996 had led to a change in duties.

[59] 'Merit Pay and Titles for Academics', OUG, supplement (2) to no. 5036 (16 Oct. 2013), pp. 77–80. There was considerable opposition to merit awards being given to professors of any kind on the grounds that growing disparity in pay between the well remunerated and the rest was undermining collegiality: 'Ethical Pay', OM, 0th week, TT (2013), 1–3.

of their salary from the Chest and owed their college twelve hours of teaching (CUFs).[60] The CUFs were a particularly problematic group in light of the changing complexion of the junior membership. Even into the 1980s, college tutors and lecturers in the arts were not required to take graduate pupils. It was understood that their teaching role was to supply the lectures and tutorials needed to maintain the undergraduate curriculum. With the explosion in taught graduate courses, not to mention the growing number of doctoral pupils, the division of labour could not hold, and many arts tutors had to devote a considerable part of their week during term time to servicing graduate needs. Oxford tutors had historically invested a large amount of time in teaching undergraduates. Franks discovered that, even in the mid-1960s, 20 per cent of CUFs were committing between seventeen and twenty hours per week to the task.[61] By the time of the North Commission thirty years later, few CUFs gave more than twelve tutorials per week. But with a growing postgraduate burden, more demanding undergraduates, and a much greater emphasis on research output, there was widespread recognition that the number of hours spent in face-to-face teaching was still too high and was extending the length of a working week to unhealthy levels.[62]

A possible way forward was to hand over face-to-face teaching to graduate assistants, as in the United States. North rejected this suggestion out of hand: Oxford's high reputation for undergraduate teaching rested on the fact that students were taught by leading academics in their field, so the dons must continue to be tutors.[63] His solution was the creation of a single flexible lecturer contract with a fixed teaching commitment where the balance of obligation between college and university/undergraduate and postgraduate teaching might be reviewed every five years and changed on mutual agreement according to new needs and an individual's preference. Every lecturer would have to provide eighteen units of teaching a week, where one unit would be equivalent to one hour of tutorial or class teaching or an hour's dissertation supervision, and a lecture would equate to three.[64] Selling the new common contract to the colleges, however, was much more difficult and deliberations were still ongoing at the end of the period.[65] What was agreed on, slowly, and faculty by faculty, was that the number of tutorial hours required of a CUF could be safely reduced to eight without harming the undergraduates, provided tutorials were always paired and the number per course slightly reduced. This may not have freed up time for research in term time, as was the purported intention, but it did allow CUFs to find more space for graduate teaching beyond their contractual requirement. Finally, too, as part of the package improving the position of ad hominem professors, the University established a single category

---

[60] See List of Abbreviations. The last name was an anomaly. The university part of a CUF's salary was not paid for out of college taxation but by the recurrent UGC grant, for post-Franks college taxation went to build up the endowment of the poor colleges.

[61] Franks, i. 138–9; ii. 284–5.

[62] North, p. 132, table: estimated hours per week by different types of postholder in 1964 and 1996.

[63] Ibid.   [64] North, pp. 139–40.

[65] By 2009, there was widespread agreement that a move to a single category of lecturer was desirable: 'Duties of Academics, and Related Issues: Consultation Document from the Task Force on Academic Employment', *OUG*, supplement (1) to no. 4874 (11 Mar. 2009), pp. 746–55.

of university lecturer. From October 2014, all lecturers became associate professors.[66]

The University, from the mid-1990s, further helped to ease pressure on hard-pressed lecturers by buying them out of some or sometimes all of their teaching obligations so that they could get on with their research or take up administrative jobs in their faculty. Others won buy-outs from the various grant-giving bodies that introduced teaching-relief schemes towards the end of the period. This, though, only helped to increase the amount of tutorial teaching that was done by post-graduates and postdocs, who were paid by the hour. North was right to emphasize the important role played by senior academics in undergraduate teaching in con-trast with many other British universities, but he skated over the crucial contribu-tion of freelance tutors who had always been needed to cover tutorial fellows on sabbatical leave or teach on courses for which it was difficult to find a qualified postholder. Their number across the period is impossible to know precisely but the North Commission came up with a figure of 1,250 in 1996, only fifty less than the University's official academic establishment at the time.[67] When the University bought out a tutorial fellow's teaching completely in the last decades of the period, it was usual to make a full-time stipendiary replacement which could be dressed up as a career development position. Most buy-outs, however, just swelled the number of supply teachers employed by the colleges. To an important degree, undergraduate teaching at Oxford in the age of the RAE was maintained by a floating contingent of freelance labour. This was a staffing problem that the Uni-versity never felt compelled to address.

In 1945, Oxford's dons had been largely divided into two groups, those who taught for the University and those who were college-based. By 2015, a new and deepening divide had emerged between the academic and academic-related staff, but the dons had been slowly transformed into a single community. The evolution was never complete even by 2000, because the colleges continued to shelter a large number of junior and sometimes senior research fellows with no university attach-ment,[68] and there was still a sizeable group of tutorial fellows with no university lectureship because the University's half of the joint post had been abolished or suspended during the cuts of the 1980s.[69] But a homogeneity of sorts had been created, which was further promoted by the gradual evolution of a common process of appointing to joint positions. In the first twenty years after 1945, colleges continued to elect to tutorial fellowships without reference to the University. Posts were not always advertised and candidates frequently grilled over dinner rather than

---

[66] Source as in note 59. This was to adopt the American system where academic staff were divided into assistant, associate, and full professors. Several British universities had already gone down this road.

[67] North, p. 7. Many were into middle age. For family reasons or love of the city, they had stayed in Oxford rather than seek a permanent academic post elsewhere.

[68] Senior research fellows were to be particularly found in All Souls. In 2013 there were 403 JRFs distributed across thirty colleges; 125 were stipendiary posts; 41 carried teaching responsibilities: 'Report on 2013 Survey of JRF Appointments in Colleges', Nov. 2013 (paper prepared for the Conference of Colleges, CONF 13/73).

[69] They became a problematic group in 2014: should they too have the title of associate professor?

in a separate interview with a panel. The successful candidate either already had a university post, commonly the case in the sciences, or was given one relatively quickly without further to-do. After 1970, the process became much more rigorous and the two sides joined forces. Thereafter, the task of making a new joint appointment was entrusted to a joint committee, which was weighted towards the college or faculty according to the balance of teaching duties.[70] The appointment to university posts at all levels became much more professional eventually. Professorial appointments, which were in the hands of electoral boards whose composition was laid down by statute, long remained mysterious events beyond outside scrutiny.[71] But by the end of the period, even the regius chairs, which were in the gift of the crown, were disposed much more openly. In 1997, the regius professor of modern history was chosen by a committee for the first time, but the post was not publicly advertised and none of the individuals considered was interviewed. Fourteen years later, the chair was announced like any other post and the four short-listed candidates had to present their credentials to a faculty meeting.

By the end of the period, Oxford dons were also part of a much more outward-looking profession. Between the wars, it had been the tendency for college tutors in particular to be recruited from within Oxford. Most Oxford dons were Oxford educated and had taught nowhere else. This changed rapidly after 1970. On the one hand, in the arts especially, few new lecturers had not already spent a number of years teaching in another university. On the other, Oxford dons ceased to be almost exclusively British. Although many foreigners came to Oxford in the 1930s to escape Nazi persecution, few found permanent posts. Outsiders, however, became much more visible after Franks, whose report tellingly said nothing about the national provenance of the academic staff. At the beginning of the twenty-first century, Oxford's academic staff had an international profile almost as broad as its postgraduate body. In 2008–9, 38 per cent were citizens of countries other than the United Kingdom, many from non-anglophone parts of the world.[72] The national mix of college fellowships was completely transformed. As late as 1969–70, thirty-seven of Magdalen's fifty-four fellows were Oxford BAs and only eight were not British by birth. By 2006–7, the first figure had fallen to nineteen out of sixty-six, and the second had risen to twenty-three and included twelve of the thirty-seven tutors (in the arts as well as the sciences).

In one important respect, however, the dons of the first decade of the twenty-first century were still locked in the past. While the junior members had become a mixed body of men and women, this was much less true of their teachers. In 2014 on average, in the higher-education institutions of the United Kingdom, women

---

[70] Recent changes have given faculty assessors in CUF appointments a greater but not majority say.

[71] Outsiders relied for information on the readiness of electors to leak proceedings, as they frequently did. Cf. the account of the election of the Chichele professor of medieval history in 1969 in Richard Davenport-Hines and Adam Sisman (eds), *One Hundred Letters from Hugh Trevor-Roper* (Oxford, 2014), pp. 186–92.

[72] 'University of Oxford; Strategic Plan 2008–2009 to 2012–2013', OUG, supplement (1) to no. 4845 (21 May 2008), p. 1098.

formed 44.5 per cent of the academic staff. At Oxford, only 25 per cent of academics were women, and in clinical medicine the figure was as low as 13 per cent, no different from the percentage of female dons across the whole University before co-education. Women were particularly under-represented at the titular professorial level, ranging from 5.8 per cent in MPLS to 17.4 per cent in social sciences.[73] The introduction of the Recognition of Distinction exercise in the late 1990s showed signs of helping to rectify the imbalance: between 1998 and 2014, 34 per cent of readerships and 25 per cent of professorial titles were awarded to women. It was also the case that women made a better showing among younger academics. All the same, given its commitment to gender equality, the University judged the imbalance unacceptable, and, over the course of the 2000s it tried to increase the number of female postholders by launching various initiatives such as its Career Development Programme, which aimed to help women move from temporary research posts to permanent teaching positions. However, as women applied for Oxford posts in far smaller numbers than men, progress continued to be slow.[74] Even the election of female heads of house in a number of the former male colleges—the first was the former fellow of St Hugh's and Jane Austen expert Marilyn Butler, as rector of Exeter in 1993—did little to dent male dominance.[75]

D. Institutes, Schools, Centres, and Units

Oxford's undergraduate university in the second half of the twentieth century was organized along traditional lines. Students were admitted to a college to read for a particular honours degree and the college largely looked after their teaching, while the curriculum they followed and its examination was organized by the cognate faculty, sub-faculty, or department. As Oxford developed into a large research university with increasing numbers of postgraduates and postdocs, a different structure evolved to meet the changing circumstances. It was not just that the college was of limited significance to postgraduates and of no significance whatsoever to most research staff, but a faculty/departmental system which had evolved to cope with undergraduate instruction did not fit the needs of a research university. The research university was at the cutting edge of knowledge creation: postgraduates and postdocs worked in novel and specialist areas which had not yet entered the undergraduate curriculum, while their work cut across traditional disciplinary boundaries, not only between individual arts and individual sciences but also

---

[73] <https://www.hesa.ac.uk/pr212> (accessed 8 September 2015); <http://www.learning.ox.ac.uk/resources/equality/facts> (accessed 8 September 2015); <http://www.admin.ox.ac.uk/media/global/wwwadminoxacuk/localsites/personnel/documents/factsandfigures/staffingfigures2014/Data_for_2014_booklet.pdf> (charts 14–19) (accessed 8 September 2015).

[74] *Corporate Plan*, p. 17; <http://www.learning.ox.ac.uk/resources/equality/facts> (accessed 13 Mar. 2013).

[75] It remains to be seen whether the situation will change radically over the next seven years. In May 2015 Council nominated Professor Louise Richardson to be the next Vice-Chancellor after Andrew Hamilton, who demitted his office at the end of 2015 and returned to the United States. Professor Richardson, formerly principal of the University of St Andrews, took up the post on 1 January 2016. An expert on terrorism, she was educated at Trinity College Dublin, UCLA, and Harvard.

between the arts and sciences *tout court*. By the end of the period, therefore, postgraduates and postdocs were frequently grouped into specialist clusters reflecting their particular focus of interest and these clusters were often accorded a separate institutional identity. When given the title of institute or school, the clusters were usually stand-alone institutions subject directly to the General Board or, after its abolition, a division. If called a centre, the cluster was normally part of an institute or department, and if christened a unit, a subdivision of a faculty. But the names and the exact lines of reporting were of limited importance compared with the significance of their existence. Institutional clustering gave many postgraduates and postdocs a peculiar identity which separated them fundamentally from the undergraduate university and drew them together in a way that eroded the customary distinction between junior and senior members.

Oxford already had a few research institutes before the Second World War, such as, the Institute of Economics and Statistics, the Nuffield Institute of Medical Research, and the Grey Institute of Field Ornithology.[76] From the early 1950s there were further foundations, starting with the establishment of Queen Elizabeth House in 1953 as a centre for colonial studies.[77] But for the first forty years of the period the foundations were sporadic and had no obvious focus. It was only with the rapid growth in the University's research income and the concomitant increase in its research staff towards the end of the 1980s that their number took off. Over the next two decades, the establishment of three or four new centres, units, or institutes was announced every year, and between 2004 and 2010 as many as fifty were formed. From the time of North, the development had the full backing of the University, which saw the creation of institutionalized research clusters as the most efficient mechanism for promoting interdisciplinary research, viewed henceforth as the holy grail: 'Whilst their organisational structures vary, such centres provide a focal point which brings together researchers in different disciplines from different departments. They can also more readily support the cost of expensive research equipment than can individual departments.'[78]

In the final twenty years of the period, institutionalized research clusters bearing different names and of varying degrees of size and significance were created across the disciplinary spectrum. Some, like the European Humanities Research Centre set up by the Modern Languages Board in 1994, were funded in the first instance completely out of the faculty or departmental budget. Others relied solely on targeted government funding in the manner of the Centre for Excellence in Preparation for Academic Practice, founded in 2005 as part of the Department of Education. But the institutions with the highest profile were those that owed their

[76] The first two were set up in 1935, the third, named after Edward, Viscount Grey, Chancellor 1928–33, in 1938.

[77] In 2006, it changed its name to the Department of International Development (Queen Elizabeth House) to take account of its wider remit in a post-colonial world.

[78] North, p. 201. On the University's commitment to interdisciplinary research, see 'Strategic Plan, 2008–2009 to 2012–2013', p. 1101 (para. 57), and 'University of Oxford: Draft Strategic Plan, 2013–18', *OUG*, supplement (1) to no. 5007 (28 Nov. 2012), p. 189 (priority 2).

inception to a private benefaction or enjoyed a range of public and private funding, such as the Institute of Molecular Medicine, founded in 1989 through the efforts of the later regius professor of medicine, Sir David Weatherall.[79] Intended as a forum in which clinicians and non-clinicians could work side by side in the study of disease, it was established with the help of the Medical Research Council, the Imperial Cancer Research Fund, and a number of private charities. Within seven years of its foundation, the institute was attracting grants of £12 million a year, had produced over 1,500 research papers on a wide variety of medical disorders including AIDS and tropical disorders, and won a Queen's Anniversary Prize for Higher and Further Education.[80] It was private generosity too that allowed Oxford to develop its most imaginative cross-disciplinary institutional initiative, the James Martin 21st Century School, created overnight in the summer of 2005. Martin's large benefaction was to support the study of key problems affecting the contemporary world, such as migration, ageing, and climate change. The technology entrepreneur was an optimist whose motto was 'We can make any world we want'. By 2015, 300 researchers in 20 academic disciplines were working under the Institute's umbrella, fired by its founder's guiding maxim.[81]

Some of the specialist research institutions established before 1990 found space in colleges, such as the Middle East Centre, established at St Antony's in 1957, or the Centre for Socio-Legal Studies, set up at Wolfson in 1972 to explore how legal rules affect the people they were supposed to serve. A few others, notably the Centres for Hebrew and Islamic Studies, founded in 1972 and 1985, were not within the University at all but independent associate institutions that looked after their own accommodation.[82] But the majority of the new creations, both before and after 1990, were located on university premises and were shunted from pillar to post as buildings became vacant. Understandably, the aim of the largest schools and institutes was to have a specially designed building of their own which would provide a permanent site and add to their lustre. But few found the necessary funding and there could be a long period of transition. The Institute of Molecular Medicine was housed in its own purpose-built quarters from the beginning as it had the wherewithal to absorb, adapt, and extend the building that had previously housed the Nuffield Institute of Medical Research in the new John Radcliffe Hospital on Headington Hill.[83] In contrast, it was nearly forty years before Oxford's

---

[79] Weatherall is an expert on the thalassemias, blood disorders associated with abnormalities in the production of globin.

[80] <http://www.imm.ox.ac.uk/about> (accessed 15 Aug. 2013). The institute is now named after Weatherall.

[81] The Institute's original intention was not to underpin a particular project permanently but to provide seed-corn funding to help establish new research centres. As the projects supported initially by the Martin School failed to find independent financing, it proved necessary to use its funds to maintain many of them indefinitely. On the school's activities, see OT, 8 Aug. 2013, p. 29 and 2 April 2015, p. 35. For Martin and his donation, see p. 602, this volume.

[82] North did not believe unaffiliated institutions should be allowed to proliferate: North, pp. 201–2.

[83] This gave it 6,000 square feet of lab space, which was further extended in 2002–4. The Nuffield Institute had originally been established on the Radcliffe Observatory site but moved to the new John Radcliffe Hospital at Headington when it opened in the late 1970s. It was incorporated into the new Institute of Molecular Medicine.

Business School was satisfactorily located. The school began its existence in 1965 when the University established an independent Centre for Management Studies and set up a BPhil, and from 1969 it was based in a new set of buildings on the edge of the city which would eventually become Templeton College. From 1990, however, once the University had decided to invest more heavily in business studies, renamed the centre a school, and established a two-year MBA intended to rival the best in the United States, the location was no longer ideal and the hunt began to find a donor to provide a building to fit the new school's ambition.[84] Wafic Rida Saïd generously agreed to give the University £20 million in 1996 to forward the scheme, but a great deal of contention arose over the location of the new building in particular, so it was not until 2001–2 that the Saïd Business School was able to move in. In the end, though, the Business School got what it wanted. Replete with spire, the new building, designed by Sir Jeremy Dixon, gave the Saïd School its indelible architectural signature (see Figure 14.3).[85]

The proliferation of research centres of one kind or another was a commonplace in all British universities in the last part of the twentieth century where research became a central and costly part of the annual budget. Oxford was only different from most other universities with a high research profile because of the wide range of its research commitments, the huge number of centres that this generated, and its evident obsession with the concept. According to the history faculty website, just a single arts faculty had fourteen research centres under its jurisdiction in 2013. But only three or four of these, including the oldest, the Wellcome Unit for the History of Medicine, established from 1972 on the Banbury Road, had a physical presence. The rest were virtual centres formed by clusters of scholars working in the same research field who ran seminars and organized conferences under a titular umbrella.[86]

Oxford's fascination with research centres added a further layer of complication to the day-to-day life of most dons. Before the Second World War, Oxford academics were employed by either the University or a college, and this largely determined their perspective on matters of mutual concern. Once the University, in the 1950s, took over the direct payment of the lecturing part of a college tutor and lecturer's salary, most dons owed service to two masters and had to learn how to adjust their views according to the hat they were wearing at a given moment. The ubiquity of research centres by the end of the period meant that many in the

---

[84] The school was moved to temporary premises in the Radcliffe Infirmary in 1994. The first MBA students joined the school in Michaelmas 1996: [University of Oxford], *Development News*, June 1997, no. 3, supplementary page.

[85] Templeton continued to be used by the Business School as its Executive Education Centre. The postgraduates living there were transferred to Green when the two colleges merged. See p. 599, this volume. Within fifteen years the new building was insufficient for the Business School's needs. In 2015, it was proposed that the school should expand its premises by taking over and developing the city's old power station at Osney: *OT*, 2 July, 2015, p. 5.

[86] <http://www.history.ox.ac.uk/research/centres/a-z.html> (accessed 15 March 2013). The Wellcome Unit was originally supported by the Wellcome Trust. The Trust continues to fund research projects but no longer maintains the building.

FIGURE 14.3 Saïd Business School, opened 2001: architects Edward Jones and Sir Jeremy Dixon. Its eventual location next to the station gave the Business School a peculiar importance as the first part of the University that many tourists would see. Its open front design—people waiting for buses in St Frideswide's Square could watch students at work in the library—equally emphasized that the Business School and the University were open to the world. Inside, the School's seriousness was suggested by its Spartan and functional rooms. On the other hand, its spire linked it clearly to the rest of the University and its open-air amphitheatre at the rear demonstrated that business and the arts were not antithetical.

academic community were having to don and doff three hats not just two, with the consequent potential for growing intra-departmental and faculty tension, especially where a centre's activities were cross-disciplinary and cross-divisional. Oxford, from the 1960s, was constant in its determination to be a mixed university with under-graduates and graduates and not become a research school, and few of its academics demurred. But this did not make for an easy existence and placed added pressure on the non-academic staff of the collegiate university, who had to keep the different boilers of the educational powerhouse stoked and functioning.

E. The Non-Academic Staff

Oxford in 2012–13 had four or five times the number of academics and students as before the Second World War, and an income that was higher in real terms by a factor of forty (Table 8). In the ordinary course of affairs, such substantial growth would have had a concomitant knock-on effect on the size of the University's non-academic staff. Just to cope with the basic needs of an academic community that had grown to 28,000 (22,177 undergraduates and postgraduates and 5,809 staff), the University needed vastly more administrators, secretaries, finance officers, librarians, curators, and lab assistants. This was not the only factor informing the growth of the University's bureaucracy across the period, however. In the last quarter of the twentieth century, the University was required to shoulder an ever-growing number of additional responsibilities and duties that ensured that the numbers on its payroll expanded much faster than could have ever been envisaged at the time of Franks.

In the first place, the University took on novel pastoral commitments. Traditionally, what pastoral care existed was the colleges' province, and the University limited its involvement in the non-academic life of junior members to providing a rudimentary recruitment agency which had been set up at the beginning of the century. From 1970s, in contrast, it was running a serious careers advisory bureau for both undergraduates and graduates, and providing an expanding counselling service.[87] In time, too, this support system was extended to the University's staff (academic and non-academic) whose well-being their employer was now required by law to protect and promote. As social legislation affecting the workplace snowballed after 1990, the support services grew in response and completely new arms of the administration were created, such as the Equality and Diversity Unit, to implement the deluge of equality, right-to-work, and health-and-safety legislation which the government of the day and the EU chose to impose on businesses and charities.

Secondly, staff numbers from the late 1980s were inflated by the need to cope with the new audit culture, service the hunt for private-sector funding, maintain the new divisions, and support the activities of a more proactive Council. The changed environment spawned a number of new administrative offices that expanded their remit over the years. The External Relations Office was set up in 1988 to facilitate the first appeal for funds, but ten years later had become the University's interface with the public and not just the alumni,[88] while the Staff Development Office, initially a vehicle to introduce academics to current best practice in various aspects of their duties, was soon, post-Dearing, running a teaching diploma for entrants to the profession. In a similar vein, the Research and Commercial Services Office, established to centralize the process of applications to outside bodies for research grants and offer advice, quickly grew tentacles as the funding opportunities mushroomed, and virtually every faculty and department had its own research development officer by 2010.

Lastly, administrative expansion was fuelled by the rapid diffusion of the new technology. When Oxford University Computing Services was set up in 1970, it

---

[87] Timothy Weston, *From Appointments to Careers: A History of the Oxford University Careers Service* (Oxford, 1994), ch. 5. As late as the early 1960s, the *Handbook to the University of Oxford* (Oxford, 1962), p. 277, claimed there was no need for a student counselling service because tutors provided it.
[88] *The External Relations Office: A Guide* (Oxford, 1997).

formed a specialist service within the Computing Laboratory. As early as 1978, however, it became a separate department on the Banbury Road, and by the end of the century even individual arts faculties had their own computing officers.[89] As the use of the word processor became ubiquitous among the University's staff, academic and non-academic, it required an ever-growing number of personnel to oversee the purchase, installation, and care of computers, offer programming advice, and organize the digitization of key teaching and research resources. Digitizing Oxford's vast library resources, a task undertaken in the first part of the 1990s, somewhat belatedly compared with other universities, was particularly labour-intensive.[90]

The great growth in the University's support staff was accompanied by an equally sharp rise in the number of porters, cleaners, gardeners, caterers, and so on needed to keep both the academy and its administration afloat. Relatively low paid, poorly unionized, often transient, and increasingly recruited from ethnic minorities, they were the one part of the University whose voice was seldom heard. Yet their presence was essential. They were the hidden underbelly of the great leviathan without whom Oxford would have failed to function.

It seems likely that, in 1945, the University's non-academic staff numbered no more than one or two hundred. Their number grew relatively slowly until 1970, expanded more quickly between 1970 and 1990, and then rose steeply over the last twenty years of the period, far outstripping the modest rise in permanent academic posts. Unfortunately, it is impossible to corroborate the assumption because the statistics are not publicly available. What is certain is that non-staff numbers rose rapidly in the first decade of the twenty-first century. In 1995–6, the University employed 3,292 full-time non-academic staff, and the total scarcely changed over the next eight years. Thereafter, numbers rose by 90 per cent in ten years. From 3,184 in 2003–4, they had risen to 4,128 in 2007–8, and to 5,995 in 2013–14 (Table 7). By that date, non-academic staff outstripped academic staff by several hundred and dwarfed postholders by more than three to one. There were 1,400 administrators employed on professional or clerical grades, nearly 600 working in IT, 170 librarians, and 1,700 ancillary workers keeping the University above the waves.[91]

By the end of the period, many dons felt that such a rapid expansion of the University's bureaucracy was unjustified and that the tail was beginning to wag the dog. The former Christ Church economist Peter Oppenheimer, for one, thought the rise could largely be attributed to a mix of incompetence and duplication,

---

[89] 'Report of the Review Committee for the Computing Services' (May 1997), esp. pp. 3–4.

[90] The first steps were taken at the Bodleian in early 1988: see 'Oration by the Vice-Chancellor', *OUG*, supplement (3) to no. 4090 (14 Jan. 1988), p. 393 (paras 43–4). On 17 October 1993, the 1 millionth entry was recorded on OLIS (Oxford Integrated Library System): *Oxford University Annual Report 1993/94*: *OUG*, supplement (*2) to vol. 125 (Mar. 1995), p. 17.

[91] Particularly rapid expansion occurred in the number of top administrators: in 1995 there were 279; in 2013 1,429: see OM, 0th week, MT (2013), 1. The number of administrators on professional or clerical grades increased by 11.7 per cent between July 2012 and July 2013 and a further 8.5 per cent between July 2013 and July 2014: <https://www.admin.ox.ac.uk/media/global/wwwadminoxacuk/localsites/personnel/documents/factsandfigures/staffingfigures2014/Table_1.pdf> (accessed 8 September 2015).

offering as a particular illustration the fact that the Equality and Diversity Unit employed thirty staff. On learning that the biggest cost of staff time in the unit was supporting over 1,000 disabled students, he considered his case made:

> Much support received by these students is provided by their colleges and departments – which arrange access and accommodation as well as medical and other ancillary services for them – and by tutors and supervisors who guide their academic work (after admitting them to the University in the first place). What material addition to the process is made by 4.6 extra administrators … remains unclear.[92]

Dons working within the administration, on the other hand, felt that the expansion was essential if the University was to function effectively. As Ralph Walker, first head of the Humanities Division, made clear in his valedictory address of July 2006, more administrators were needed, not fewer:

> The myth that the Administration is well-funded while the rest of the University starves has never had any basis in truth, at least in my time. We are extraordinarily lucky in the high standard of administrators that we have, but at faculty level, at divisional level, and at the level of the University Offices we are badly short staffed. Those who complain about the dilatoriness of officers have little idea of the volume of business they have to deal with, nor the length of time that many of them work beyond their official hours.[93]

This was a typical difference of opinion between outsiders and insiders. In normal times the expansion might have raised little comment but it occurred in a decade when there was disquiet over dons' salaries and undergraduates were being asked to contribute to the cost of their studies for the first time. Oppenheimer estimated that the numbers employed just in the central administration grew from 612 to 1,020 across the years 1999 to 2008. Had the rise not occurred, 'the pay of Oxford's 4,000 academic staff in 2008 could have averaged £4,000 per annum more than it actually did'. The University's view was that Oxford's administration offered value for money. Taking 2007–8 as the baseline year, Oxford's non-academic staff, as a percentage of all staff on the University's payroll, was the third lowest among the Russell Group at 47.27 per cent. At Warwick at the same date, they formed 61.27 per cent of the total.[94]

Neither side brought the colleges into the argument. Had the number of college staff been included in the figures, then the ratio would not have looked so positive. Most colleges employed more than a hundred staff in the first decade of the twenty-first century, so the total number of non-academic personnel in the collegiate

---

[92] Letter, OM, 8th week, MT (2009), p. 17. Oppenheimer had already taken the University to task in a number of articles in the *Oxford Magazine* in the course of the year.

[93] Email letter to all members of the division, 31 July 2006.

[94] Peter Oppenheimer, 'Confronting Executive Hypertrophy', OM, 0th week, HT (2009), p. 6; Julie Maxton, 'Supporting the University's Activities: The Development of its Administration from 2004 to Date' (26 June 2009), p. 2. Maxton was the University's first female registrar. By 2013, non-academic staff as a percentage of all university staff stood at 50.8 per cent.

633

university at the end of the period was nearer 10,000 than 6,000.[95] The colleges, however, were seldom put in the dock alongside the University for wasting resources. Although the colleges came under the same external pressures as the University after 1970, there was only a modest increase in the number of college employees over the period. Rather, their composition changed. At the beginning of the twentieth century, colleges had very few administrators but large numbers of manual workers serving as porters, scouts, gardeners, bicycle boys, and maintenance men, or based in the kitchen and buttery. A hundred years later, the numbers of manual staff were still in the majority but there were far more white-collar workers, men and women, working in the bursary, college office, library, computing room, and development office. Magdalen employed 116 non-academic staff in 1945 and 130 to 140 in 2006, many of them part-time. In the interim, the number of scouts had been drastically reduced and the number of office staff increased from two to twenty-eight.

The great expansion in the Oxford white-collar workforce at all levels of the collegiate university brought with it a further problem of representation that played into the governance debate. Like the academics, the non-academic secretariat had its own hierarchies and divisions but equally a legitimate interest in the University's future. Yet only the top administrators were members of Congregation and/or college fellows, and the large majority were just as disenfranchised as research staff on short-term contracts.[96] At the end of the period, as at the beginning, Oxford took pride in being a self-governing university, as the dons, as teachers, research supervisors, and elected officials, ran the University at all levels. But in 1945 the dons had been unquestionably the *senior pars* of the University. By 2011, the twin effects of bureaucratization and the research imperative had left them a minority among the University's employees. Oxford in 2011 was an oligarchy rather than a democracy, which was only grist to the mill of those who wanted to bring its governance in line with the sector norm.

F. Buildings

A university of 22,000 students and 12,000 academic and non-academic staff required much more working space than one less than a sixth of the size on the eve of the Second World War. In 1945, the University had limited spatial needs. It principally occupied two major sites: the Bodleian and its surrounding buildings, including the Clarendon, which contained the university administration; and the area adjacent to the University Museum, which had been developed between the wars as the Science Area. The arts faculties had no distinctive homes, and their small

---

[95] According to 'Draft Strategic Plan 2013 18', p. 192 (para. 61), Oxford employed 18,000 people across the collegiate university, presumably academics as well as non-academics. The 2006 *White Paper on University Governance*, p. 6, gave a total figure for non-academic staff, including OUP, of 15,000.

[96] In 2013, 1,258 of the 5,995 non-academic staff were eligible for Congregation: source as in n. 54, p. 621, this volume.

libraries and even smaller administration were housed randomly all over central Oxford. As most arts dons had teaching rooms in college and no obvious other space needs, there appeared no call for purpose-built faculty accommodation. As Oxford expanded, however, more and more space was needed for seminar rooms, libraries, and eventually computers and printers, and the University's requirements exploded. Finding additional properties to house the growing demand became a constant headache. More and more property was acquired in the city centre, and most arts faculties, as well as the new specialist institutes, departments, units, and centres, were periodically moved around to meet their changing needs. As a result, Oxford's footprint lay much more heavily on the city by 2012 and the University was no longer located on two principal sites. While many parts of the University continued to be rammed pell-mell into buildings of all ages, shapes, and sizes, and were housed all over town, Oxford at the end of the period had been effectively transformed into a six- or seven-site university, as the central administration slowly tried to impose order on the distributional chaos (Maps 6 and 7).

Immediately after the war in 1946, the University increased its presence on the Bodleian site with the opening by George VI of the New Bodleian, located on the corner of Broad Street and Parks Road. Thereafter, for the next two decades, the University concentrated its attention on improving its science facilities around the Museum, to keep abreast of the growing numbers of undergraduates and graduates and the new national focus on scientific research. Buildings were erected for sciences which did not yet have their own and new ones set up in expanding subject areas. On the Science Area proper a forestry building was opened in 1950, one for botany the following year and a new physiology building in 1953; while in 1959, with the completion of the metallurgy building, expansion began on the land between Parks Road and Banbury Road to the north of Keble, which was dubbed the Keble Triangle. The improvement programme continued into the following decade with the opening of three buildings designed by Basil Ward: a microbiology and a new biochemistry building in 1961 and 1964 on the Science Area, and new premises for engineering in 1963 on the Keble Triangle (see Figure 14.4). The programme culminated in 1971 with the opening of Sir Leslie Martin's zoology and psychology building on the corner of South Parks Road and St Cross Road, and the completion, after many years in gestation, of a nuclear physics laboratory, whose architect was Arup Associates, on the corner of Keble and Banbury Roads (Map 5).

But even in the 1960s there was evidence that the University was beginning to spread its wings. In 1961 it was decided to relocate the law and English faculties and the Institute of Statistics in a brand-new building on the corner of St Cross and Manor Road, near the new college of St Catherine's. Another creation of Sir Leslie Martin, it was opened in 1965.[97] In 1961, too, the University's central administration began to migrate from the Clarendon Building to larger facilities. Initially, the Chest

---

[97] The Institute of Statistics has had many homes since its establishment in the 1930s: G. D. N. Worswick, 'The Peripatetic Institute', Dec. 1990 (typed manuscript).

FIGURE 14.4 Engineering Science Building, opened 1963. Engineering was one of Oxford's fastest growing sciences in the 1950s. Its new building was the work of the firm of Basil Ward and was one of the more daring modernist designs erected in the University in the 1960s. The city council thought the building out of keeping with the local environment and resolved not to allow similarly tall buildings in the future. The photograph is taken from the Banbury Road.

and other sections of the administration that moved out in the 1960s were housed in existing buildings. Then in 1968 the University took the plunge to move the whole central administration to Wellington Square on the edge of North Oxford and house it in a completely new building which was ready for occupation by the early 1970s (see Figure 14.5).[98] Neither development, however, had an immediate successor. The University initiated no further new building outside its two core sites until the 1990s. As funding for large-scale capital expenditure from the UGC dried up, the University had to pull in its horns. Even small-scale building on the core sites was minimal. The only important development on the Science Area in the 1970s after the completion of the zoology building was the underground extension to the Radcliffe Science Library, built between 1972 and 1975.

[98] Thereafter, 'Wellington Square' became synonymous with the central administration.

FIGURE 14.5 University Offices, Wellington Square, opened early 1970s. The transfer of the central administration from the Clarendon to a new building close to the University Press was a significant moment in the displacement of the University from its traditional heartland. The unprepossessing modernist building continues to be the home of the Vice-Chancellor and the Proctors and the meeting-place of Council.

Nonetheless, from the late 1970s further dispersal took place which was largely out of the University's hands. While Oxford had become an important centre of medical research by the end of the war, with the establishment of an Institute of Social Medicine to complement the institute set up with Nuffield's money in the 1930s, it only slowly developed a postgraduate school of clinical medicine in the 1950s and 1960s. Oxford's one significant hospital, the Radcliffe Infirmary, was situated only a short distance from the Science Area at the bottom of Woodstock Road, but it lacked the beds and laboratories to support a thriving clinical school, so tutors in the 1950s sent their best pupils to London to take the second part of their medical degree. By the end of the 1960s, the University had found ways to make the best of a poor hand: intake to the second BM had risen to fifty and a bridge course had been added to the pre-clinical curriculum which gave Oxford's medical students an early exposure to clinical studies.[99] But clinical medicine at Oxford was still far

---

[99] Oxford's post-war medical course remained divided into three parts: the BA and the first and second BMs: see p. 388, n. 106, this volume.

FIGURE 14.6 John Radcliffe Hospital, opened 1979. Thereafter the new hospital on Headington Hill was the chief centre for specialist medical services in the region. The old Radcliffe Infirmary on the Woodstock Road continued to provide some facilities until the 2000s but was completely redundant from 2006 when a west wing was added to the John Radcliffe which included a children's hospital, an ear, nose and throat hospital, and an eye hospital.

from world class. What gave the school the boost it desperately needed was the completion of the new 1,000-bed John Radcliffe Hospital in 1979 on Headington Hill (see Figure 14.6).[100] The opening of the JR pulled most of the University's medics into its orbit and created a novel opportunity to expand the faculty's research base. Clinical training immediately transferred to the new hospital, and Oxford's growing number of medical scientists soon followed in their wake, while others relocated to two other hospitals relatively close to the JR, the Churchill (for cancer) and the Warneford (for mental disease).[101] By the end of the period, medicine had become largely detached from the heartland of the University, especially with the eventual closure of the Radcliffe Infirmary in 2006 and the opening of the JR's Children's Hospital and Ear, Nose and Throat wing.

The University accepted this development and made no attempt to reverse it. Instead, it concluded that subject-specific concentration was the future. Bringing to an end decades of ad hoc extension in the city centre, it decided in the late 1980s that the arts faculties and their cognate institutes, centres, and units should also be grouped together as far as possible on specific sites. Optimistic that it would be

---

[100] The hospital was built in two stages: the maternity wing opened in 1971.

[101] The Churchill, founded in 1940, was named after the war leader's wife. The Warneford, which had been formerly the Oxford asylum, was set up in 1826; it owed its name to Samuel Warneford, rector of Bourton-on-the-Water, who gave the asylum £70,000 in 1843.

possible to find private funds to put up new buildings for the humanities and social sciences, Oxford developed what became known as the three-site strategy. In its first version, endorsed by Congregation in November 1991, the three sites were centred on the Bodleian, the Ashmolean, and Manor Road.[102] The first would accommodate modern history and English, principally in the Indian Institute, where the historians had been established since 1968;[103] the second, through the creation of a new building and adapting existing ones would serve Lit. Hum. and oriental studies as well as modern languages ensconced in the Taylorian; while the last, already home to the St Cross Building, would house law and the various social sciences, which, at that juncture, were located in the former Oxford High School for Boys (today known as the Old Boys High School) on George Street.[104] The second version, in play from the end of the 1990s, was much more ambitious. From 1997 it became clear that the local health authority would vacate the Radcliffe Infirmary and that the site might be purchased by the University. Once this was acquired in 2003, a new possibility emerged. The plans for the Bodleian area were jettisoned and it was agreed that all the humanities faculties, except the Ruskin School of Art and Classics, which would remain on the Ashmolean site, would be relocated on the Woodstock Road. The Radcliffe Infirmary site would not be for the exclusive use of the new Humanities Division for it was also to serve mathematics, but it was hoped that the area could finally provide all the teaching, study, and recreational space that its member faculties needed. The faculties would retain their separate identity but most of the facilities would be pooled and a giant humanities library, containing the contents of twelve existing collections and augmented to serve the needs of postgraduates, would be built.[105]

Raising the funds to make the three-site strategy a reality began immediately as part of the University's initial funding appeal, but it was 2001 before the first new buildings—the Sackler Library for the study of ancient Mediterranean civilization, the Rothermere American Institute, and the Saïd Business School—were opened.[106] And progress continued to be slow. By autumn 2004 a new Manor Road building had been constructed on a former Territorial Army site, which became the home of an integrated social sciences library. But development of the Radcliffe Infirmary site

---

[102] Vice-Chancellor Southwood's farewell oration, 1993, reprinted extract in OM, 5th week, TT (2009), 4–5; 'University of Oxford Development Office Programme', OUG, supplement (1) to no. 4392 (26 Feb. 1996), p. 809.

[103] The Indian Institute had lost its original purpose with the ending of empire.

[104] The University had purchased the site from the city when the school moved to new buildings.

[105] Email letter from Vice-Chancellor Hood to all members of Congregation, 30 March 2005; 'A University Library for the Twenty-First Century', OUG, supplement (1) to no. 4743 (22 Sept. 2005), p. 45; email letter from Ralph Walker, head of humanities to all postholders in the division, 1 January 2006; Humanities Divisional Board, report of meeting 20 Jan. 2006. The Ruskin School has been located for many years at 74 High Street. There has been talk of its moving to a site at Osney.

[106] The Sackler was founded by a donation from the late Dr Mortimer Sackler, an American physician who made a fortune in pharmaceuticals; its appropriately classical building was designed by ADAM Architecture. The Rothermere Institute is supported by the foundation of the family that owns the Daily Mail. Its building was designed by Kohn Pedersen Fox Associates.

(now called the Radcliffe Observatory Quarter or ROQ), complex because of the need to retain the Grade II-listed façade of the eighteenth-century hospital, had only just started by the end of the period. The administrative arm of the Humanities Division had moved into the original infirmary building and the Oxford Research Centre in the Humanities set up, but none of the humanities faculties had moved on to the site. Argument was still going on as to the layout and facilities it would eventually contain, and the planned humanities library remained on the drawing board. Only one new building had been constructed—for the Institute of Mathematics (see Figure 14.7).[107] As a result, the English faculty continued to be based in the St Cross building, and history had been able to gain more space only by relocating from the Indian Institute to the Old Boys Grammar School when the Social Sciences Library had been transferred to Manor Road.[108] Even the successful location of the different components of the Social Sciences Division on the St Cross site was incomplete. The Saïd Business School was nowhere near Manor Road. Originally intended to be built nearby on Mansfield Road, opposite the new American Institute, lengthy wrangling over the site led to its being constructed on the other side of the city by the station.[109] The only part of the revised clustering strategy that had been satisfactorily concluded by 2012 was the plan to create a physical site for the study of the ancient world centred on the existing Ashmolean Museum, which was realized in three stages: the construction of the Sackler Library, the opening of the Ioannou Centre for Classical and Byzantine Studies in a house on St Giles in 2006 (which contained the classics faculty),[110] and the extensive renovation and expansion of the Museum itself between 2006 and 2009, and again in 2011.

Yet, although the three-site strategy did not evolve as quickly as some people hoped, other building projects advanced apace in the final decade of the period to the benefit of research in the humanities and the social sciences as well as the sciences. Research facilities on the Science Area were greatly enhanced by the opening of a £60 million chemistry research laboratory in 2004, which could hold 600 researchers, and new buildings for biochemistry and the biomedical

---

[107] To make way for new buildings, the old hospital site had been cleared except for the original eighteenth-century building, which was also to house the Department of Health Care Sciences: OT, 21 Nov. 2013, p. 22. The new Mathematical Institute, the work of Rafael Viñoly Architects, was opened in 2013.

[108] It had been hoped that faculties would be moving to the site by 2010: Ralph Walker, head of the Humanities Division, email letter, 1 Jan. 2006. The Martin School now occupies the Indian Institute and its interior has been redesigned: see 'HQ for Oxford's Revolution', OT, 3 Dec. 2013, p. 10.

[109] Vice-Chancellor North sent a letter to all members of Congregation announcing the Saïd bequest on 16 July 1996. The original location of the new building was vetoed by Congregation on 5 November 1996 because it was a greenfield site whose use would reduce student sports facilities in the centre of Oxford. When an alternative brownfield site, at that point a car park, was found, Congregation overturned its decision on 17 June 1997, but there were still dissident voices: 'Saïd Business School, Verbatim Proceedings in Congregation', OUG, supplement (2) to no. 4442 (23 June 1997).

[110] Named after the Cypriot industrialist the late Stelios Ioannou, whose family were founding benefactors of the centre.

FIGURE 14.7 Andrew Wiles Building, Mathematical Institute, Radcliffe Observatory Quarter, opened 2013: architects Rafael Viñoly Architects. The two wings of the building are joined by a glass vestibule which allows the old Radcliffe Observatory to become part of the design. The building was named after Sir Andrew Wiles, Royal Society research professor at Oxford, who proved Fermat's last theorem.

sciences in 2008, the latter delayed for several years by animal rights protesters.[111] Scientists too benefited from the University's decision in 1998 to buy a research and development site at Begbroke near Woodstock, and develop it as an out-of-town science park for collaborative and space-intensive projects which did not need to be in Oxford itself.[112] The University also put money into the Headington Hill complex. In the mid-2000s, it purchased several brownfield sites close to the Churchill to ensure that the medical faculty could make the most of its close links with the city's hospitals by improving its research and library facilities. By 2015, the Old Road Campus, as the area was known, housed a number of new medical research institutes, including the Li Ka Shing Centre for Health Information and Discovery, named for the Hong Kong businessman who gave £20 million towards its foundation. The first building of the Centre, the Target Discovery Institute, which aims to

---

[111] The Chemistry Research Laboratory was opened by the Queen: see *BP*, vol. 4, no. 7, (26 Feb. 2004), p. 1. Both the chemistry and biomedical sciences buildings were located on the south side of South Parks Road. In 2011, the University was also given permission to erect a new physics building on the Science Area, due to be completed in 2017: *OT*, 19 March 2015, p. 8.

[112] *Corporate Plan* 2005-6 to 2009-10' (2005), p. 19.

help pharmaceutical companies better direct their research into cures for cancer and inflammatory diseases, was opened in 2013. The second building, which will be home to the Oxford 'Big Data' Institute, was given planning permission in August 2014. It will cost £45 million to erect and employ 400 people in the analysis of medical statistics.[113]

Researchers in the arts, on the other hand, at the end of the period were the beneficiaries of a significant enhancement of the Bodleian's services. The computerization of library catalogues in the 1990s, and the creation in 2000 of an integrated library service, had made the Bodleian and Oxford's many specialist research and subject libraries much easier to use than in earlier decades. But, as a report of 2005 emphasized, the Bodleian itself, which had been relatively untouched since 1946, was in desperate need of an upgrade: it wanted more book space, open-shelf access, and better conservation facilities for its manuscripts.[114] The first requirement was solved by erecting a new book repository at Swindon which replaced the primitive book store used since the 1970s at Nuneham Courtenay. Completed in September 2010, it contained 5.3 million items by the following summer (see Figure 14.8). The second was met, if only in part, by creating an underground reading room linking the Radcliffe Camera to the Bodleian, opened in July 2011. Named the Gladstone Link after the nineteenth-century prime minister, it had 120 seats and 270,000 items on open shelves accessed through rolling stacks.[115] The third requirement was tackled by renovating the New Bodleian so that the library's special collections could be properly looked after. The renovation, to a design by Wilkinson Eyre Architects, was completed in summer 2014, and the library reopened at the beginning of the new academic year under the new name of the Weston Library, as a mark of thanks to the Garfield Weston Foundation that had provided £25 million towards the cost.[116] The junior members' recreational needs were not forgotten either in the drive to improve the research environment. From 2004, thanks to an enabling gift from the American hedge-fund manager Lief Rosenblatt, the University finally had a swimming pool on its Iffley Road sports complex.[117]

As more and more of Oxford, both within and beyond the city centre, came under the University's ownership, the size of its urban footprint swelled. In 2008, including the Begbroke Science Park, the University's estate comprised over

---

[113] In 2017 or 2018, the University also plans to open a Precision Cancer Medicine Institute on the site: OT, 30 October 2014, p. 27.

[114] 'A University Library for the Twenty-First Century. A Report to Congregation by the Curators of the University Libraries', OUG, supplement (1) to no. 4743, 22 September 2005. By Nov. 2015 the Bodleian contained 12 million books, six times as many as in 1945.

[115] Bodley librarian's report, OUG, supplement (1) to no. 4985 (25 Apr. 2012), pp. 453–64. Gladstone purportedly invented the rolling stack.

[116] For the donation, see 'Oxford Thinking: Report on the Progress of the University's £1.25 Billion Funding Campaign to 31 January 2010'. Weston was a Canadian businessman. The Weston Library was officially opened in spring 2015. The library contains a café and exhibition galleries so that the Bodleian's treasures can be displayed to the public.

[117] Corporate Plan, p. 19. In 2016, the facilities on the Iffley Road site will be enhanced by the opening of a new indoor sports hall, named for Acer Nethercott, a former cox of the blue boat and Olympian who died at a young age in 2013: OT, 29 January 2015, p. 12.

FIGURE 14.8 Bodleian Book Repository, Swindon, opened 2010: architects, Peter Brett Associates. It was originally intended to build the repository on Osney Mead industrial estate on the western side of Oxford but the plan was thwarted by conservationists and environmentalists who feared that the building would be a blot on the landscape and damage the flood plain. The new repository is about thirty miles from the Bodleian and books are delivered twice a day.

520,000 square metres, an area 44 per cent greater than ten years before.[118] Such a rapid physical expansion brought a new problem. As Oxford became a multi-campus university, its traditions of self-government and collegiality were threatened. Dons based far from the historic centre found it difficult to play their expected role in college and university affairs. The medics on Headington Hill were particularly detached as a group. Located several miles to the north-west of the Sheldonian and controlling the largest divisional share of research funds, they seemed to be fast forming a separate entity.[119] Indeed, it is difficult to see how Oxford could have held together after 2000 but for the new technology, which allowed dons to receive the papers for meetings digitally and, where necessary, participate in decision-making from a distance.

Oxford's physical expansion also made it more difficult to distinguish the University from the city. Oxford had always been at the heart of the city in a way that was less true of Cambridge but by the end of the period it was invading residential

---

[118] 'Plan 2008–2009 to 2012–2013' (2008), p. 1108. The expansion is set to continue. In the fifteen years from 2010 to 2025, the University expects to spend £1.8 billion on its building programme: OT, 22 May 2014, p. 32.

[119] It was said that the structural reforms advocated by the North Report were necessitated, above all, by the new weight in the University of the medical sciences. They enjoyed too large a share of the university cake to be simply one of sixteen faculties represented on the General Board.

areas. This inevitably caused friction.[120] But the tension was mitigated by the quality of the new buildings that the University sponsored. For the forty years when the expansion was mainly subsidized by the UGC, the emphasis was on cost and function. There was limited attention paid to aesthetic appeal, and most of the early buildings erected were dismissed as concrete modernist eyesores, especially Ward's Engineering and Biochemistry blocks, which were too tall and bulky to harmonize with their neighbours. The best of a bad bunch was considered to be Martin's Zoology and Psychology Building, which was a low-rise construction famed for its paternoster lift and imaginative and flexible internal design. Many of the buildings erected after 2000, however, were architectural gems that did much to enhance Oxford's urban landscape. The still unfinished Islamic Centre on Marston Road with its distinctive minaret and dome and cool white stone was a case in point. So too was the extension to the Ashmolean designed by Rick Mather, that doubled the display space and turned a dreary old-fashioned museum into a light and spacious cathedral to ancient material culture.[121] But the nonpareil was the Saïd Business School—the work of Sir Jeremy Dixon. With its floor-to-ceiling glass frontage, protected by solid stone wings, and its interior garden, flanked at the far end by an open-air amphitheatre, it had nothing in common with Oxford's old college buildings beyond its spire. Far from hiding the school's activities from public view, it invited citizens and tourists alike to join the tyro masters of the universe as they toiled over their books in the first-floor library overlooking St Frideswide's.[122] Aspirational and worldly, it was the antithesis of the Cistercians' Rewley Abbey, on whose ruins it was raised. As Vice-Chancellor Lucas recognized in his annual oration of 2001, the school spoke of the future to the city as much as the University:

> It is evident that this development is a powerful impetus to the regeneration of this area of West Oxford which one can see beginning to take shape. In this, the University is continuing its historic and creative function in both contributing to the physical aspect of the city and being a positive influence on its prosperity.[123]

G. Research

Oxford's ability, from the Second World War, to attract large numbers of post-graduate students and expanding amounts of research money was possible only because of the calibre of its academic staff. While the University placed great store

---

[120] See pp. 711–12, this volume.

[121] Some of the best buildings were to be found on the Science Area, but were largely hidden from view as they were squeezed in between existing buildings. The finest was the biochemistry building designed by Hawkins\Brown architects.

[122] The only ancient college which encouraged ordinary mortals to peer inside was Trinity. When its new quad was built in the late seventeenth century, it was deliberately constructed as a three-sided building so that the interior would be open to the public gaze through a large gate at the end of the garden on today's Parks Road. Information supplied by Clare Hopkins.

[123] 'Oration by the Vice-Chancellor', OUG, supplement (1) to no. 4597 (10 Oct. 2001), p. 181. The new building is affectionately described in an article in OT, 16 Mar. 2001, p. 17.

on undergraduate teaching being maintained by the dons, it also always expected its postholders, irrespective of whether they had a joint or full-time appointment, to undertake research—and high-quality research at that—as part of their academic duties. In the 1950s and 1960s many college tutors remained reluctant to place the fruits of their labour before the public and were content to air their ideas with pupils and colleagues. But in the new 'publish or perish' culture of the RAE, modesty was no longer considered an academic virtue and scarcely anyone was appointed to a post at Oxford after 1990 who had not begun to establish an academic reputation in print. Most appointees as lecturers and tutors in the second half of the period were men and women in their thirties who had already won their spurs in another university, and were judged to be potential leaders of their research fields in the future. Although Oxford and Oxfordshire were expensive places to live, the University seldom failed to attract candidates of high quality for an advertised position. Conditions of work, the good facilities, and the University's historic name ensured that there was no shortage of young academics, British and increasingly non-British, who dreamt of moving to Oxford, even if the traditional salary premium ceased to carry much weight once national pay scales collapsed. As a result, Oxford in 2012 was a huge and vibrant research university.

Before the late 1980s, there was always the suspicion among many outsiders that Oxford's reputation as a research university was overstated. Clearly the University had its intellectual stars, and each year half a dozen or so of its senior members were and continued to be elected fellows of the Royal Society and the British Academy. All the same, it was felt that there was a lot of donnish dead wood and that some of the most innovative developments were occurring in the newer universities founded after the war. The establishment of the RAE, whatever its shortcomings, gave the lie to any belief that Oxford traded on past glories. From its inception, Oxford and Cambridge were always placed at the top of the ladder in terms of both the range and depth of their research output. In the 2008 exercise, the last before it was rebranded as the REF, 32 per cent of Oxford's research activity was judged world-leading and 70 per cent world-leading or internationally excellent, a higher proportion than any of its United Kingdom competitors. Of the forty-eight units of assessment or different disciplinary heads under which a university's research was evaluated, Oxford topped the list in seventeen and was second in six. More importantly, Oxford submitted a greater number of staff than any other higher-education institution involved in the RAE. Of the 1,600 postholders, a total of 85 per cent were judged to have published work of a high enough standard for entry. But, besides the postholders, many of the contract research staff and the 200 or so junior research fellows supported by the colleges were also thought worthy of submission. As a result, Oxford entered a total of 2,246 individuals.[124]

---

[124] <http://www.ox.ac.uk/research/rae_2008_results/> (accessed 8 Apr. 2013). For earlier results, see p. 551, n. 32, this volume.

In the thirty years following the Second World War, Oxford stars in the humanities and social sciences were liberally distributed through the faculty firmament. Admittedly, some disciplines partly lost their earlier sheen. Fraenkel's retirement in 1951 and C. S. Lewis' departure to a Cambridge chair in 1954 were heavy blows to Lit. Hum. and English. The first had been pivotal in the revitalization of British classical scholarship, the second, after Tolkien had decided to dedicate his life to imaginative fiction, in the continued development of the contextual school of English literary studies.[125] Nonetheless, there was scarcely any faculty or sub-faculty in the arts which did not have at least one figure of pre-eminence who put the discipline at Oxford on the international map, as the positivist and utilitarian Herbert Hart did for law through his many works on legal philosophy.[126] Three disciplines, moreover, could boast figures whose influence could be described as transformational: anthropology, modern history, and philosophy.

Oxford anthropology, still a relatively new discipline, had been in the doldrums between the wars, but with the appointment of Edward Evans-Pritchard in 1946 to head the new Institute of Social Anthropology, the subject flowered. Already famous for his study of the mystical beliefs of the Azande, E-P, as he was known, brought to Oxford the enthusiasm for fieldwork which characterized the LSE, where he had trained under Bronislaw Malinowski.[127] For twenty-three years, making good use of the department's connections with the colonial service, he spearheaded a successful crusade to turn Oxford into one of the world's leading centres of social anthropology. E-P broke with the biological determinism of his mentor, who saw tribal rituals as an expression of basic human needs. Instead, eschewing grand theory, he taught his pupils to seek the internal coherence of tribal belief systems and social practices through careful and sensitive observation. He spawned a bevy of illustrious acolytes, above all Mary Douglas, whose own researches took a more comparative turn, epitomized by her cross-cultural study of taboo as a system, *Purity and Danger* (1966).[128]

Modern history had not been similarly becalmed between the wars, but as a discipline it had remained closely marked by the Whiggish assumptions of an earlier age. It was not until the Second World War was over that the young Turks of the

---

[125] Fraenkel and his stimulating influence were not completely lost to the University for he continued to run his seminar in the 1950s. Lewis held his Cambridge chair until shortly before his death in 1963: in the last fifty years his reputation as a children's author and Christian apologist has largely obscured his contribution to literary scholarship.

[126] His best-selling work was *A Concept of Law* (1961), a beginner's guide to jurisprudence which carefully distinguished law from force and morality. Hart, professor of jurisprudence from 1952 to 1960, was Britain's leading legal philosopher of his generation. Before the war Oxford's law faculty had shown little interest in legal theory. See Nicola Lacey, *A Life of H. L. A. Hart: The Nightmare and the Noble Dream* (Oxford, 2004).

[127] E-P's *Witchcraft, Oracles and Magic among the Azande* was published in 1937. E-P had been an undergraduate at Exeter where the rector, R. R. Marett, was interested in anthropology. The LSE was at the heart of British anthropology in the first half of the twentieth century.

[128] Mary Douglas moved to University College London in the early 1950s and then to the United States in 1977: for her life and work, see R. Farndon, *Mary Douglas: An Intellectual Biography* (London, 1999). For E-P's influence, see Mary Douglas, *Edward Evans Pritchard* (London, 2003).

1930s came into their own and were able to undermine the faculty's obsession with England's constitutional narrative. Most of the radicals were touched by the Marxist theory of history and believed that political events were mere epiphenomena. The faculty's remit should be the past in all its aspects, as advocated in the 1930s by the founders of the French Annales School, Marc Bloch and Lucien Febvre, with their concept of *histoire totale*. As early as 1952, the new guard displayed their confidence by creating a new historical journal, *Past and Present*, which deliberately turned its back on the high political history promoted by the *English Historical Review*, and became the country's primary organ for publishing the latest work on the rapidly developing fields of social and cultural history.[129] For the first ten years after the war the force for change continued to be found among the college tutors, not the faculty's professors. From 1957, however, the new focus of research became firmly embedded in the faculty when one of the young Turks, the well-connected, urbane, but often prickly, Hugh Trevor-Roper, tutor at Christ Church, was made regius professor. Four years later, the revolution was complete when another of their number, the medievalist Richard Southern, tutor at Balliol, became Chichele professor of modern history.[130]

Trevor-Roper was an early modern historian of Britain and Europe fascinated by the interplay between politics, religion, and science in the post-Reformation world, who rejected economic explanations for political and social change as too simple, and took the independent role of ideas in human action seriously. Like Collingwood, he believed that history was a science and would only advance by 'hypothesis and criticism, not by accumulation and piety; through the laboratory, not the museum; by public controversy, not secret relic-worship'.[131] His delight was to frame provocative but illuminating hypotheses which immediately engendered debate, as in 1959 when he floated the idea that the many civil wars and uprisings that bedevilled Europe and the British Isles in the mid-seventeenth century had the same underlying cause: a clash between 'court' and 'country'.[132] Trevor-Roper maddened many of his more Marxisant colleagues with his emphasis on the power of ideas, but, interested in all periods of the past and always ready to encourage the young, he was the ideal figure to preside over the faculty's permanent

---

[129] Christopher Hill, R. H. Hilton, and E. J. Hobsbawm, 'Past and Present: Origins and Early Years', *Past and Present*, 100: 1 (1983), 3–14. For Bloch, Febvre, and their successors, see Peter Burke, *The French Historical Revolution: The Annales School 1929–89* (Cambridge, 1990).

[130] On Trevor-Roper, see Adam Sisman, *Hugh Trevor-Roper* (London, 2010). Southern announced his arrival on the historical stage in 1953 with his widely read *The Making of the Middle Ages*. His specialist interest was St Anselm.

[131] Davenport-Hines and Sisman, *One Hundred Letters*, pp. 59–60: in a letter of 13 December 1956 to Sir John Masterman, provost of Worcester, where he berates the faculty's professors for either writing nothing or doing little beyond editing obscure texts. Southern showed his contempt for the historian as editor in his augural lecture.

[132] There was a cleavage within the ruling class between those who monopolized the state's resources and those left in the wilderness who suffered from a loss of status and declining incomes. The article first appeared in *Past and Present*. For the ensuing debate, see Trevor Aston (ed.), *Crisis in Europe, 1560–1660* (London 1965). Trevor-Roper was predominantly an essayist. He found completing full-length books difficult, although several of the manuscripts that he had laid aside have been published posthumously.

change in direction.[133] During his tenure as regius professor, Oxford's historians became the most dynamic in the country and arguably the world in terms of the range and diversity of their research.

Several of the most original members of the faculty in the 1950s and 1960s were historians of early modern England, like Trevor-Roper. The Balliol tutor Christopher Hill made his name bringing to life English puritanism; Lawrence Stone of Wadham wrote an *histoire totale* of the English aristocracy; while Keith Thomas of St John's, one of the stars of the generation that came up after the war, used the insights of social anthropology to pioneer the study of English witchcraft.[134] But English history in general flourished in these two decades, as did the study of the European past, hitherto a poor relation. Initially, the emphasis fell on nineteenth- and twentieth-century Europe thanks to the dominant presence of Magdalen's A. J. P. Taylor, a captivating lecturer and publishing phenomenon. In some ways Taylor belonged to the old school in that his interest lay in diplomatic and political history, but his published work gained widespread respect through its command of detail, broad sweep, and originality. Like Trevor-Roper, he also knew how to provoke, particularly raising hackles in 1960 when he argued that Britain would not have had to go to war against Germany in 1939 had it avoided its reckless guarantee of Poland's integrity.[135] By 1970, the faculty's research net was cast more widely. Inspired by figures like the young Peter Brown, whose positive reading of the late Roman Empire was about to take the world by storm, and the Balliol tutor Richard Cobb, an expert on the French Revolution from below, the faculty's doctoral students were rapidly colonizing key periods in Europe's pre-industrial past as well.[136]

Oxford philosophy, too, had not been dormant between the wars, but again it was only after 1945 that Gilbert Ryle (see Figure 14.9) and his friends were able to impose their particular brand of analytic philosophy on the sub-faculty. In the twenty years after the war, Ryle, John L. Austin, Paul Grice, Bernard Williams, and Peter Strawson sought to construct a philosophy of language which developed the original insights of Wittgenstein and the Viennese School in a completely novel

---

[133] Trevor-Roper had a particular interest in Nazi Germany and the history of espionage following his wartime experiences: see p. 436, this volume. In 1983, after he had ceased to be regius, his reputation took a fall when he authenticated the forged Hitler diaries.

[134] E.g. Christopher Hill, *Society and Puritanism in Pre-Revolutionary England* (London, 1964); Lawrence Stone, *The Crisis of the Aristocracy, 1558–1641* (Oxford, 1965); K. T. Thomas, *Religion and the Decline of Magic: Studies in Popular Beliefs in Sixteenth- and Seventeenth-Century England* (London, 1971). Hill published several books on English puritanism from 1958; he had earlier been a member of the communist party and he remained wedded to a Marxist approach to the English Civil War. Stone's book was published after he had moved to Princeton.

[135] For his work, see Chris Wrigley, *A. J. P. Taylor: A Radical Historian of Europe* (London, 2006). Taylor was principally interested in modern Germany and the Austrian Empire. For his views on 1939, see his *Origins of the Second World War* (London, 1961). The other significant modern Europeanist in Oxford in the 1950s and 1960s was Raymond Carr, the historian of modern Spain.

[136] Brown cut his teeth with a biography of St Anselm in 1967; his *The World of Late Antiquity* appeared in 1971; he left Oxford in 1975. Cobb became a Balliol tutor in 1962, then professor of modern history in 1971. Before joining Balliol he had spent many years as a private scholar in France. His colourful life was continually refashioned in a number of publications beginning with *A Second Identity: Essays on France and French History* (1969). His most famous book, *The Police and the People: French Popular Protest, 1789–1820*, appeared in 1970.

FIGURE 14.9 Gilbert Ryle, 1900–76, doyen of British ordinary language philosophers: photograph. Ryle was educated at Brighton College and Queen's, Oxford. His principal work, *The Concept of Mind*, appeared in 1949. The photograph depicts him in uniform during the Second World War. He held a commission in the Welsh Guards and like many Oxford dons worked in intelligence.

direction.[137] Whereas the logical positivists of the Viennese School had concentrated on understanding which statements had meaning and which had not, the Oxford philosophers discovered meaning and performative power everywhere. They rejected the Viennese belief that only statements that could be empirically verified made sense, by showing that in everyday speech words like reality and real had meaning when uttered, although the meaning was plastic and unstable. Their account of the philosophy of ordinary language made Oxford the most important centre of analytic philosophy in the world and further enhanced the University's reputation in linguistics, which had been forged at the beginning of the twentieth century by the compilers of the *OED* and the nascent English School. Their principal organ of dissemination was the philosophy journal *Mind*, founded in 1876, which Ryle edited from 1947 to 1973. But their influence came through their teaching and their contribution to faculty seminars and informal discussion groups as much as their published work, and Austin's most famous work on speech acts was published only after his early death.[138] Key was Ryle's creation of the two-year BPhil in the late 1940s, which introduced a number of leading American and Australian philosophers to the Oxford school.

---

[137] Ryle was the Waynflete professor of metaphysical philosophy; Austin held White's chair in moral philosophy; Grice, Williams, and Strawson were tutors at St John's, New College, and University College; Strawson, from 1968, held the Waynflete chair.

[138] *How to do Things with Words*, ed. J. O. Urmson (Oxford, 1962). Based on his Harvard lectures of 1955.

Oxford's philosophers were a far from united company and this helps to explain their vitality. Logical positivism was never completely swept from the field, especially after its foremost British champion, A. J. Ayer, returned to Oxford in 1959.[139] Some of the sub-faculty, too, continued to see value in the works of the leading philosophers of the past studied in Greats and PPE, while one of their number, Isaiah Berlin, broke with analytical philosophy altogether (see Figure 14.10).[140] Berlin spent the war in New York as a diplomat entertaining Americans with his sparkling conversation and impressing the British government with his acuity. He returned to All Souls committed to becoming a historian of political philosophy. For the rest of his life, he sought a foundation for his own liberal individualism in the writers of the past. His favourite authors were the Romantics, who, to his mind, best understood Kant's 'crooked timber of humanity': man lived in time, his values were ever changing, the heart usually ruled the head, and there was no utopian solution to the human condition. Individuals should therefore be left to make their own lives and their own mistakes as long as they did not hurt others. His ideal world was an Oxford college, shorn of its hierarchies and stuffiness, where its members were free to argue eternally about everything under the sun. Not surprisingly, he leapt at the chance to become the first president of Wolfson in 1966 and construct a college from scratch. Wolfson was Berlin's perfect community where scientists rubbed shoulders with researchers in the arts and postgraduates, and dons mixed on equal terms in fine buildings and bucolic surroundings.[141]

In the physical sciences, the brightest stars in the firmament in the first half of the period were Oxford's three Nobel laureates in chemistry, who spent all or a significant part of their working lives in the University. Robert Robinson was honoured in 1947, Cyril Hinshelwood in 1956, and Dorothy Hodgkin in 1964. Robinson retired in 1955 and Hinshelwood in 1964 but Somerville's Hodgkin, the only British woman to ever become a science laureate, continued to hold her Wolfson research professorship until 1977.[142] Nobels were also won by several incumbent postholders in medicine and the life sciences in the thirty years following the Second World War. Chain and Florey were crowned in 1945 for their role in the discovery of penicillin, Rodney Porter in 1972 for determining the structure of an anti-body, and Nikolaas Tinbergen (see Figure 14.11) one year later for elucidating the individual and social behaviour of animals. Chain left Oxford for a post at Rome

---

[139] As Wykeham professor of logic. His nomination was opposed on the electoral board by Ryle and Austin: see Isaiah Berlin, *Enlightening. Letters 1946–1960*, ed. Henry Hardy and Jennifer Holmes (London, 2011), pp. 675 and 678–80. For Ayer at Oxford before the war, see pp. 502–3, this volume.

[140] Another, Herbert Hart, jumped ship. Hart taught philosophy at New College after the war and turned to jurisprudence only because he felt that he would never be in the top flight. Bernard Williams also moved away from ordinary language philosophy on leaving Oxford in 1959.

[141] Michael Ignatieff, *Isaiah Berlin: A Life* (London, 1998), chs 13–17. Berlin was made professor of social and political theory in 1957. Unlike most post-war liberal intellectuals, he had little time for the Enlightenment, which he claimed preached a one-dimensional view of human beings and which he blamed for totalitarianism. He was not blind, on the other hand, to the Romantics' penchant for system-building. For his own account of his relations with Oxford in the 1950s and 1960s, see Berlin, *Enlightening*, and Isaiah Berlin, *Building: Letters 1960–1975*, ed. Henry Hardy (London, 2013).

[142] On their contribution, see pp. 508–10, this volume.

FIGURE 14.10 Sir Isaiah Berlin, 1909–97, OM, historian of ideas and broadcaster. Through his radio talks on political ideas, Berlin became one of the best known Oxford dons in the 1950s. During and after the war, he was able to gain first-hand experience of the two new super-powers and became a committed supporter of the United States. It was at Bryn Mawr in 1952 that he sketched out his theory of negative and positive liberty. The photograph was taken in a BBC Radio studio in 1959.

only three years after his elevation but the other three, like their chemistry colleagues, had illustrious Oxford careers. Florey remained professor of pathology until 1962 before becoming provost of Queen's; Porter, Cambridge-trained, was Whitley professor of biochemistry from 1967 to 1985; while Tinbergen, a Dutchman, was a fellow and tutor of Merton from 1950 to 1966, before becoming professor of animal behaviour from 1966 to 1976. Oxford's other Nobel Prize winner in science in these years was Hans Krebs, Porter's predecessor in the Whitley chair, who received the award for his work in the 1930s on the urea and citric acid cycle. As was pointed out in Chapter 12, Krebs had already won his Nobel when he moved to Oxford in 1954. But he spent the last twenty-five years of his life in the University and the Radcliffe Infirmary putting biochemistry firmly on the Oxford map.[143]

The Nobel laureates, however, were only the tip of a creative iceberg. Oxford won no Nobel prizes in physics but the department had a solid international reputation, particularly in nuclear physics. Before the war this was a field largely ignored at Oxford but it was built up rapidly from 1956, when Denys Wilkinson was brought from Cambridge and the number of academic staff involved in the area grew from

---

[143] See pp. 511–12, this volume. Three other Nobel Prize winners in science in the first half of the period had spent much or part of their research career in Oxford but left long before they were honoured: the Spaniard Severo Ochoa (1959), Peter Medawar (1960), and the Australian John Eccles (1963). Ochoa, who had been a demonstrator and research assistant at the Nuffield Institute from 1938 to 1941 received the prize for synthesizing RNA (ribonucleic acid); Eccles was a neurologist trained by Sherrington.

FIGURE 14.11 Nikolaas Tinbergen, 1907–88, animal behaviourist and Nobel Prize winner. Tinbergen came to Oxford from the Netherlands after the Second World War. His pioneering *The Study of Instinct* appeared in 1951. He was one of the first migrants from the continent of Europe who was not a refugee to gain a permanent post at Oxford and his appointment was a sign of the much more cosmopolitan nature of the post-war University. The photograph emphasizes his commitment to fieldwork.

twenty to 135 in the space of six years. By the early 1970s, Oxford was Europe's leading centre of research in the field, the department divided between those working on traditional nuclear physics and those involved with the developing field of particle physics.[144] Metallurgy too quickly developed an international profile in the 1950s, thanks to the efforts of William Hume-Rothery, who became the first professor in 1957, while zoology, which had lost much of its pre-war lustre, revived from 1961 when another Cambridge man, John Pringle, was made Linacre professor, and set up new areas of research such as molecular biology. It was between 1950 and 1975, moreover, that several stars of the future had their early scientific training and

---

[144] In 2001, the Nuclear Physics Laboratory, now home to the sub-department of Astrophysics and Particle Physics, was named after him.

first academic posts, even if they later moved on to other universities. Sir John Gurdon, who won the Nobel Prize for Medicine in 2012 for his discovery that mature cells can be converted to stem cells, spent most of his career at Cambridge. But he was a Christ Church undergraduate in the 1950s, who came up from Eton to read classics before transferring to zoology. For his DPhil he studied nuclear transplantation in the frog Xenopus with Michael Fischberg, then, after a spell at Caltech, returned to Oxford to the Zoology Department as an assistant lecturer from 1962 to 1971. It was at Oxford as a young researcher that he performed the crucial experiments which made his name.[145]

Distinguishing Oxford's most creative and original minds from those whose research was merely competent and solid is much more difficult for the second half of the period. Certainly, the University has entertained many figures of distinction among its postholders, who have taken the research of their predecessors in new and fruitful directions. The American Ronald Dworkin did this in the field of legal philosophy, where he undermined Hart's positivist approach and brought morality back into law. So too did the analytical philosophers Sir Michael Dummett and Derek Parfit, who developed influential positions on the issues of realism and personal identity.[146] Enough time has not yet passed, however, to determine whose books and articles will be considered seminal by future generations or whose discoveries, proofs, or explanations completely revolutionized their research area. Moreover, in the world of medicine and science, it has become harder than ever before to isolate the prince from the attendant lord. As developments in computerization and imaging made it possible to investigate the organic and inorganic world in ways completely unimaginable fifty years before, much more work came to be undertaken by research teams working collaboratively as the only way of bearing the cost in terms of machinery, time, and labour. Oxford's experimental physicists, in particular, worked in research teams that crossed university and national boundaries; their research from the 1970s, much more than before, was frequently focused outside Oxford altogether, at purpose-built government-funded international sites such as the European Organization for Nuclear Research (CERN) near Geneva, or more locally at Britain's Atomic Energy Research Establishment at Harwell and the Joint European Torus (JET) project at Culham.[147] In the modern era of collaborative research, which, by the end of the period, was beginning to embrace the humanities and social sciences as well, assessing the particular contribution of an Oxford researcher in a heralded breakthrough is often as hard for the outsider as evaluating the strength of the claim itself.

[145] One of his key articles was published in 1962: J. B. Gurdon, 'The Developmental Capacity of Nuclei Taken from Intestinal Epithelium Cells of Feeding Tadpoles', *Journal of Embryology and Experimental Morphology*,10 (1962), 622–40.
[146] Dworkin, a Rhodes scholar, followed Hart in the chair of jurisprudence. Dummett, former Wykeham professor of logic, was a fellow of All Souls, as is Parfit. The present generation of British analytical philosophers are often called post-Dummettian.
[147] CERN was set up in 1954; JET in 1973. One of Oxford's leading scientists in the 1970s and 1980s, the fusion physicist Sir Christopher Llewellyn Smith, was director of CERN from 1994 to 1998.

The many honours collected by Oxford dons in recent decades also offer only a limited guide. In 2012 about one-eighth of the academic staff had been honoured nationally: there were one hundred fellows of the British Academy, eighty fellows of the Royal Society, some seventy fellows of the Academy of Medical Sciences and nine fellows of the Royal Academy of Engineering, not to mention a clutch of knights and the odd peer.[148] Only a handful of postholders in the second half of the period, on the other hand, had been awarded high international recognition for their research, a surer predictor of future greatness. International prize winners were not absent from the academic staff. Five, since 1987, have received the prestigious Balzan Prize, either while in post or shortly after retirement: the historians Sir Richard Southern and Sir John Elliott (in 1987 and 1999); the animal ecologist Robert Baron May in 1998; the Hellenist Martin West in 1999; and the French literary scholar Terence Cave in 2009.[149] It was an evident sign, too, of a renaissance in mathematics in these years that, in the 1980s, three of the professors at the Mathematical Institute—Michael Atiyah, Simon Donaldson, and the American Daniel Quillen—were holders of the Fields Medal, the prestigious international award given every four years by the International Mathematical Union to young mathematicians with a major achievement behind them.[150] But in comparison with the post-war decades, there was a striking absence of Nobel laureates, as British politicians keen to cut Oxford down to size periodically pointed out. Three economists, Sir James Mirrlees, the American Joseph Stiglitz, and the Indian Amartya Sen,[151] the geneticist Sir Paul Nurse,[152] and two or three visiting fellows in physics and chemistry were awarded the prize after their association with Oxford had ended, but there was no Nobel laureate on the university payroll after Rodney Porter retired in 1985. Indeed, in the last twenty-five years, only one laureate has

[148] <http://www.ox.ac.uk/research> (accessed 9 Apr. 2013); <http://www.ox.ac.uk/about_the_university/> (accessed 9 Apr. 2013). By 2012, Oxford's academic and academically related staff had also won eight Queen's Anniversary Prizes for Higher Education, more than any other university. Prize winners included OUP in 2007 for successfully bringing to conclusion the new edition of the [Oxford] *Dictionary of National Biography* and the University's museums, libraries, and archives in 2009.

[149] The Balzan Prize is awarded by the Balzan Foundation (named after an Italian newspaper proprietor) to outstanding contributions in the fields of the humanities, the natural sciences, and culture (especially the promotion of the brotherhood of man). Both West and May were also awarded the Order of Merit. West had a long connection with Oxford, although holding a chair for many years in London. May, an Australian, had no links with the University until 1988 when he won a Royal Society research professorship, which he held jointly at Imperial and Oxford. Dworkin won the prize in 2012, fourteen years after demitting his professorship.

[150] Atiyah (1966) and Donaldson (1986) were at Oxford when they were awarded the medal.

[151] James Mirrlees (laureate 1996) taught at Oxford from 1969 to 1995; Joseph Stiglitz (2001) and Amartya Sen (laureate 1998) were consecutively Drummond professors 1976–9 and 1980–8. Mirrlees won the prize for his contribution to economic modelling in the face of incomplete information; Stiglitz for his analysis of the inbuilt inefficiency of markets; and Sen for his work in welfare economics. Sen's influential *Poverty and Famines: An Essay on Entitlement and Deprivation* (1981), which outlined his belief that the poor had to be provided with 'capabilities' if they were to function successfully, was published while he was at Oxford. An earlier Drummond professor, the Keynesian macroeconomist J. R. Hicks, won the Nobel Prize in Economic Science in 1972. One other economist with loose Oxford associations has also been a recent laureate: Michael Spence (2001).

[152] Nurse, Iveagh professor of microbiology 1988–93, was awarded the prize in 2001 for his co-discovery of the protein molecules which control the division of cells in the cell cycle. He became the president of the Royal Society in 2010. When he had applied to Oxford to be an undergraduate, he had been rejected because he lacked a foreign language; his PhD was from East Anglia.

been a resident member of any kind of the University. This was the American Baruch S. Blumberg, master of Balliol 1989–94, who received the prize in 1976 for his work in identifying and finding a vaccine for the Hepatitis B virus. Only the future will tell whether, at the very time when Oxford's contribution to science and scholarship was more extensive and wide-ranging than in the whole of its 800-year history, the University proved incapable of fostering and sustaining genius. It was perhaps a sign that the University itself was concerned about the verdict of posterity that, at the very end of the period, Oxford's professor of pharmacology, Baroness Susan Greenfield, evinced an interest in running a research project to uncover the neurological basis of exceptional talent.[153]

Yet if it is impossible at this juncture to make an objective assessment of the quality of the University's research over the last thirty years, it is clear that there are two principal ways in which its balance has significantly shifted. The rising profile of the social sciences, especially in the fields of social policy, development studies, and international relations, is one. The other is the rapid expansion of medicine and the biomedical sciences, which have moved from being on the periphery of the University's research culture to its heart. Oxford may have played a key role in the war years in developing penicillin, and continued to shelter talented researchers thereafter, such as the maverick nutritionist Hugh Sinclair, who pioneered interest in the dangers of consuming fatty foods.[154] But as late as 1965, both pre-clinical and clinical medicine absorbed only a small part of Oxford's resources. Fewer than 10 per cent of postholders were medics and only 20 per cent of the small number of research staff totally dependent on outside funding. By the end of the period, not only had the new Medical Division, including biochemistry, spread all over Headington Hill, as we saw in section D, but medicine now absorbed the lion's share of the University's income. In 2010–11, the Medical Division might still comprise only 15 per cent of the academic staff but it commanded 60 per cent of Oxford's research money. With a research income of £235 million and a research staff (assistants, technicians, and others) of 1,666, it put the other three divisions in the shade. In contrast, MPLS, whose faculties and departments had engrossed most of the money for research and buildings in the first part of the period, could muster a research income of only £93 million and a research staff of 813. Moreover, some of the funds controlled by MPLS were also being used for a medical end, as several scientists in the Department of Engineering were engaged in devising more effective medical apparatus.[155]

The novel predominance of medicine was part of a worldwide trend and reflected the West's obsession with health and longevity in the post-industrial age, an obsession only enhanced by the successful sequencing of the human genome at the beginning of the twenty-first century. Medicine's advance was particularly

---

[153] Greenfield is a neuroscientist. She has been director of the Royal Institution of Great Britain. Her seat in the House of Lords is unconnected with her scientific distinction.

[154] J. Ewin, *Fine Wines and Fish Oil: The Life of Hugh Macdonald Sinclair* (Oxford, 2001).

[155] Franks, ii. 255–6; <http://www.ox.ac.uk/research> (accessed 9 Apr. 2013).

striking at Oxford because, historically, the University had limited its interest to pre-clinical studies. Even after the war, clinical research did not fully take off until Richard Doll, already a national name for his discovery of the link between smoking and lung cancer, became regius professor in 1969.[156] In consequence, Oxford, for the first time, became one of the world's leading centres of medical research. The University not only continued to be strong in areas, such as neuroscience, where it had had a long-standing commitment. But it quickly became deeply involved in the new and very expensive sciences of molecular pathology and gene therapy as well as the clinical study of virtually every disease, the search for new vaccines, and the discovery of better drug delivery mechanisms.[157] Most research has had both a theoretical and practical side, as the work of the geneticist and ion channel physiologist Frances Ashcroft exemplifies. Ashcroft, director of the Oxford Centre for Gene Function at the end of the period, and the 2012 winner of the L'Oréal-UNESCO Award for women in science, has dedicated her life to a better scientific understanding of type II diabetes and neonatal diabetes. As a result of her work, it has been possible for children born with diabetes to control the disease through taking tablets rather than suffering insulin injections.

H. Outreach

The practical orientation of much of the work of the Medical Division was part of a wider shift in the University's research culture in the later part of the period. Oxford, at the beginning of the nineteenth century, had stood firm against the utilitarians' belief that higher education should be practically useful, and insisted that a university's goals should be moral and intellectual. This prejudice against practical knowledge remained, to a powerful degree, even in the second half of the twentieth century as Oxford evolved into a university devoted to both teaching and research. Franks was happy to see Oxford develop close links with the outside world, but he was adamant that the University should keep it at a distance.[158] Most of his Oxford contemporaries agreed. There was a suspicion in many quarters of Oxford academics, whatever their discipline, who got too close to industry or government, such as Balliol's Thomas Balogh, who became chief economic adviser to the new Wilson administration in 1964.[159] Even in the 1990s there was hostility to the enlargement of the Oxford Business School on the grounds it was too close to the marketplace.[160] By then, though, the atmosphere was rapidly changing. By the end of the period, it was widely accepted that Oxford's research should be judged by

---

[156] Doll's pioneering research was done at the Central Middlesex Hospital.

[157] A new area in which Oxford is making an important contribution today is optogenetics, or the use of light to turn on and off nerve cells at will with millisecond temporal precision. One of the pioneers in the field is Gero Miesenböck, Waynflete professor of physiology, who has won several international prizes for his work.

[158] Franks, ii. 43.

[159] Balogh, later Lord Balogh, had been connected to Balliol from before the war. He was one of the founding members of the Institute of Statistics.

[160] This latent hostility lay behind much of the opposition to the Saïd Building in 1996–7.

its utility as much as its advancement of knowledge, and that it was a marketable asset to be exploited. In the 2005 corporate plan, developing 'interactions with business, the public sector and government' was a key part of what was called Oxford's enterprise and collaboration strategy, now seen as the University's 'third-leg' activity after teaching and research.[161] Again, Oxford was only responding to the spirit of the age. On the one hand, government by the mid-1980s had come to believe that the primary purpose of university research was not intellectual curiosity but wealth creation. On the other, lacking the means to fund ever more costly research projects, the state passed the torch to industry, which inevitably had its own practical agenda. After 2000, even historians were expected to show the social value of their research proposals.[162]

Oxford, however, did not just bow before the utilitarian god. It quickly moved to bring benefit to itself and its medics and scientists from the new dispensation. Oxford academics of an earlier generation had not always been averse to making money out of their research or developing its practical potential. But they had often found it difficult to get the funding they needed. Florey, in the 1940s, had to go off to the United States to find the capital to mass-produce penicillin on failing to find a backer in Britain. His pupil, the philanthropist and fellow of Lincoln Sir Edward Penley Abraham, had better luck with cephalosporin in the 1950s only because by then governments and pharmaceutical companies had realized the importance of antibiotics.[163] It took entrepreneurial flair to go it alone. The only Oxford scientist in the 1950s and 1960s to set up a successful manufacturing and design company was Martin Wood, senior research officer at the Clarendon Laboratory, who founded Oxford Instruments in his garden shed in 1959 to exploit his work on high-field magnets. In 1987, two years after Sir Keith Joseph, the minister for education and science, had announced that universities would in future be permitted to market the research of their staff, Oxford decided to help oil the works and created its own technology transfer company, which was christened Isis Innovation in the following year. The company's primary purpose was and is to help Oxford academics file patents and identify potential industrial partners in return for a share in the profits. It has proved a tremendous success. In the years 2000–5 alone, it 'filed over 300 patent applications, signed 250 licence and consultancy deals, and established 50 spin-out companies, raising £185 million of external investment'.[164] Through Isis Innovation's assistance, Oxford scientists

[161] Corporate Plan 2005–6 to 2009–10', pp. 12–13.

[162] Not all were content with the development: see R. J. P. Williams, 'Science in the University', OM, no. 186, 2nd week, HT (2001), 3.

[163] Through the income from his patents, Abraham was able to donate £30 million to his college and the Dunn School of Pathology by 2000.

[164] Peter Hirsch and Catherine Quinn, 'Isis Innovation: How Did it Start?', OM, 8th week, TT (2008), 8–14; Corporate Plan, p. 12 (para. 87). Isis Innovation was originally called OURADO. The University was forced to assert its intellectual property right after several dons and lab assistants had benefited substantially from the commercial exploitation of work done with its equipment. The University can assert ownership only when the rights of exploitation are not already tied, as is usually the case in research sponsored by commercial companies.

and medics have become involved in the manufacture of a wide variety of products from one-touch ovens to high-performance materials. But its most illustrious creation is Oxford Molecular Ltd, established in an empty hut in September 1989 with the aim of supplying software to pharmaceutical and biotechnology companies who needed to model complex molecular structures. The brainchild of the chemist Professor Graham Richards, a pioneer in deploying computer graphics to study molecular interaction, Oxford Molecular began with a working capital of £30 million. By the time it floated on the Stock Exchange five years later, it was worth £200 million.[165] The collegiate University also made it possible for the commercial potential of scientific and medical discoveries to be tested and developed close to home by providing academics and their sponsors with the necessary space to rent. In October 1989, Magdalen set up a joint-venture company with the Prudential to create the Oxford Science Park on college land east of the city ring road; then, ten years later, the University followed suit by purchasing the site at Begbroke. One of the first spin-out companies to take advantage of the Magdalen initiative was Oxford Molecular.[166]

This new willingness to embrace the utilitarian research agenda of the outside world, if never complete and, in the humanities' case, usually highly contrived, was coupled with a similarly novel attitude to the importance of disseminating the work of the research university among the wider public. Oxford had played a key role in the development of adult learning at the end of the nineteenth century and many tutors had penned school textbooks. But there was little belief before the Second World War that it was part of an Oxford don's research brief to reach out beyond a specialist audience to the ordinary man in the street and package the fruits of his or her wisdom in a way that would entertain and inform a mass audience. In the 1950s, several prominent dons were inveigled into giving erudite talks on the BBC's Third Programme. Isaiah Berlin in autumn 1952 even became an overnight celebrity for his six hour-long lectures on political theory from Helvétius to de Maistre.[167] That, though, was as far as it went. There was little sign that Oxford academics en masse were anxious to lift the veil on their research activities. In general, it was felt that to popularize was to trivialize. Significantly, only one Oxford don in the post-war era, the historian A. J. P. Taylor, reached out to the British public through the new medium of television, fast supplanting the radio in most British homes by the late 1950s (see Figure 14.12). Taylor could talk to camera for half an hour without the slightest hesitation and swiftly became a household name. But Taylor, who, through his books as well as his TV appearances, sought to give a generation that had lived

---

[165] 'Isis Innovation Ltd', brochure, Mar. 1997, p. 3. In the three years from 1998 to 2001 alone Isis Innovation helped to create twenty companies worth £9.5 million, while Cambridge, over the same period, generated only eight, with a value of £5 million: BP, 19 Apr. 2001, p. 2.

[166] There have recently been additional initiatives. The Saïd Business School has a centre where members of the University from any background can develop business ideas, called Launchpad, and the Careers Services runs innovation workshops in The Shed: 'Welcome to Entrepreneurial Oxford', BP, May 2014, p. 8.

[167] Ignatieff, Berlin, p. 205. Other Oxford broadcasters included Evans-Pritchard, Hart, and Trevor-Roper. Their talks were often printed in the corporation's weekly magazine, The Listener.

FIGURE 14.12 A. J. P. Taylor, 1906–90, historian and broadcaster: June Mendoza, oil on canvas, no date. Taylor was a brilliant communicator who would schedule his lectures for 9 a.m. but still speak to a crowded room. His innumerable works on European history in the nineteenth and early twentieth century, which combined erudition with narrative power, won a large audience among the general public as well as generations of students.

through the Second World War some insight into the long-term historical context that had produced it, was derided by many of his academic colleagues as a journalist and renegade.[168] It was not until 1966, in the Romanes lecture of that year, that a member of the Oxford establishment came out strongly in favour of the Oxford don becoming a missionary. This was the unlikely figure of the classicist and warden of Wadham, Sir Maurice Bowra, who had dedicated his life to preaching the virtues of an aristocracy of the mind. Bowra was an elitist's elitist but he recognized that the public had developed an appetite for knowledge, their imagination fired by discoveries such as the Dead Sea Scrolls, and believed that their curiosity was entirely laudable: 'It is a sign that the people is becoming eager to educate itself, and it helps to bridge the many gulfs which separate social groups from one another. It breaks the brutal monotony of leisure and stirs the intelligence

---

[168] See the comments in A. J. P. Taylor, *A Personal History* (London, 1983). Taylor wrote frequently for the newspapers. So too did Trevor-Roper, who suffered the same obloquy.

to work in fields outside its daily necessities.' Bowra also understood that popularizing knowledge without vulgarizing it required 'special gifts of understanding and clarity' that dons should not be shy of acquiring.[169]

Bowra's words alone did not create a change in the University's attitude towards the popularization of knowledge but they demonstrated that a thaw had set in. The change legitimated the Department for Continuing Education's move, in the last decades of the twentieth century, to put on a profusion of courses on all manner of academic subjects for the interested man in the street, in addition to its diploma programme. The thaw also encouraged the University to view with more affection its museums and other collections and look to their enhancement and embellishment, especially the Ashmolean, the jewel in the crown. While Oxford was content to hide its research activities from the general public, the museums were at best a scholarly and scientific resource, and at worst an encumbrance. A novel interest in outreach gave them a new lease of life as the University's most obvious interface with the wider world. Visitors were welcomed and counted; attempts were made to make the collections more accessible and informative, especially to the young; and the museums developed their own programme of talks and courses. In the 2005 corporate plan, the museums were trumpeted as 'a catalyst for life-long learning and cultural recreation'.[170]

Outreach, however, was not limited to institutional initiatives. From the 1970s, younger academics, won to the cause of proselytizing, took it upon themselves to introduce the latest work in their field to the masses. Some gave talks to schools and local societies; others, notably socially concerned scientists, began to publish works of popularization in the form of articles helping to allay, in part at least, the popular image of the Oxford don as aloof and incommunicative. Gradually more and more Oxford dons stepped outside their ivory tower, at least for a moment or two. From 1990, any reticence about appearing on radio and television quickly disappeared. The new trend was, to some degree, a further reflection of the broader changes in Britain's research culture. The demand of grant-giving bodies that research should have some demonstrable public benefit led humanities' dons in particular, with little definite to offer, to promise that their findings would be given due media exposure. But it was primarily the result of the tremendous upsurge in the number of TV and radio programmes devoted to the arts and sciences. Whereas in previous decades, such programmes had been sporadic, though usually much loved, they were now ubiquitous to the extent of the same subjects being frequently reprised at a short interval by different programme makers. As a result, there were few postholders in any of the four divisions who had not, at some time or another, made a podcast or had at least a bit part in a TV or radio programme, and a handful had headed a series.

---

[169] Maurice Bowra, *A Case for Humane Learning: The Romanes Lecture Delivered in the Sheldonian Theatre 17 November 1966* (Oxford, 1966), pp. 22–3. For all his belief in the natural superiority of the Bowristas, Bowra was in some ways a social radical: he despised the British class system. The Dead Sea Scrolls were found between 1946 and 1956.

[170] *Corporate Plan 2005–6 to 2009–10*', p. 14.

As in the 1950s and 1960s, Oxford towards the end of the period had one media don on its academic staff who was a household name. This was the zoologist Richard Dawkins of New College, renowned, indeed infamous, as the proselytizing acolyte of both Darwinianism and unbelief.[171] Dawkins was a force of nature reminiscent of A. J. P. Taylor in his prime but more combative and less avuncular, and had been one of the first of the University's scientists to accept the importance of opening up the latest thinking in his discipline to the general public.[172] His skills as a communicator were evident from the moment he published *The Selfish Gene* in 1976. A robust and highly accessible adaptation of Darwin's ideas that also allowed room for moral freedom, it became an instant best-seller which has been reissued many times. His later books, particularly *The God Delusion*, which has so far sold 2 million copies, proved just as successful if more controversial. In the history of Oxford's recent past, Dawkins stands above all as a figure for the University's changed commitment to outreach. Although provocative, Dawkins did not exist on the margins like A. J. P. Taylor. From 1995 to 2008, when he retired, he was the first holder of the University's chair for the public understanding of science.[173]

---

[171] For his own account of his life, see *An Appetite for Wonder: The Making of a Scientist* (London, 2013).

[172] Although British television today is awash with historians, no Oxford don in post has picked up the mantle of A. J. P. Taylor. One omnipresent face on British television, however, Simon Schama, was a fellow and tutor in modern history at Brasenose in his younger days, albeit for a year.

[173] Another Oxford science don who has always been keen to take her subject to the public is Frances Ashcroft, whose books include *Life at the Extremes* (London, 2000) and *The Spark of Life: Electricity in the Human Body* (London, 2012).

CHAPTER 15

The Oxford Experience

A. Student Support

O N the eve of the Second World War, an Oxford undergraduate who lived moderately needed no more than £250 per annum to meet the costs of tuition and his or her living expenses. By the close of the period, this figure had risen to £15,000, while an equally careful postgraduate, in residence for nine or twelve months each year rather than six, faced a bill closer to £20,000 (Table 6). In real terms, the cost had not risen greatly—perhaps little more than 10 per cent for an undergraduate. But the relative amounts spent on tuition and living had fundamentally changed. Living in Oxford got cheaper over the period, even though junior members, by the 2000s, had many more material wants than their grandparents and expected to live far more comfortably. The cost of tuition, on the other hand, rocketed, and in real terms was six times higher in 2013 than in 1939. In the 1950s and 1960s, the combined college and university fee paid by undergraduates and graduates rose only in line with inflation: £30 in 1939, it was still only about £170 thirty years later. Thereafter, it steadily rose. In 1997–8, the undergraduate and graduate fee ranged from £4,000 to £6,000, depending on the type of course followed. By 2012–13, in a period of relatively low inflation, the postgraduate fee had increased by a half, while the amount collected for most undergraduates had more than doubled. And this was only the cost to home and European Union students whose education was heavily subsidized by the University. So-called overseas students, who were required from 1970 to pay full fees, were charged considerably more: at the end of the period they needed at least £30,000 to cover their tuition, board and lodging, and other expenses.[1]

The rise in tuition fees after 1970 was fuelled by the steady improvement in the University's library and laboratory facilities, the huge new expense incurred by the information technology revolution, and spiralling staff costs. The last was not the result of mouth-watering increases in dons' pay, for academic salaries scarcely

---

[1] Under European law, EU students had to be charged the same as Britons. According to the University, the real cost of educating an Oxford undergraduate in 2013 was £16,000 p.a.: 'Oration by the Vice-Chancellor', OUG, supplement (1) to no. 5036 (16 Oct. 2013), p. 73. The most expensive course in 2013 was the MBA where all students paid the same fee. The University and college fee for one year's study came to £44,150.

kept abreast of inflation in the later part of the period. Rather the rise, especially after 1990, reflected the rapid expansion in the number of the University's administrative and ancillary staff, discussed in Chapter 14. Undergraduate fees in the 2000s were helping to support not only a bevy of counsellors and equal opportunity officers but also the increasing number of technicians and assistants needed to maintain the large community of postdoctoral researchers whose grants paid their own salaries but initially did not cover the University's overheads.[2] The colleges, too, were not immune from responsibility. Even if the growth in their non-academic establishment was moderate in comparison, their employment costs rose sharply. By 1997, according to one estimate, college administrative costs alone stood at £1,200 per undergraduate.[3]

Fortunately, for many undergraduates and graduates across the period, the costs of their stay at Oxford were largely underwritten by the taxpayer and private benefactions. Had this not been the case, the background of Oxford's students would have remained as exclusive as in the past. As public support for university study became much more bountiful following the Second World War, many undergraduates from poorer backgrounds had their stay completely covered by outside sources from the beginning. A Jewish refugee who came to Britain as a child in the 1930s and studied at Oxford between 1946 and 1951 recalled that he had more than enough to survive on, as long as he was careful: he received grants of £550 from his college and £942 from the Ministry of Education.[4] By the late 1960s, following the state's decision earlier in the decade that virtually all UK students were entitled to free university education and some sort of maintenance from the public purse, nearly every Oxford undergraduate, male and female, was in receipt of financial assistance. Magdalen was reputed to be one of the more socially elitist colleges, but even there only 12 per cent of its freshmen in 1968 had to pay their own way. The rest had at least their fees paid for them and a minimum maintenance grant of £50. A total of 42 per cent received a grant in excess of £300 and 16 per cent the maximum of £395.[5]

For the next two decades, Oxford's undergraduates benefited, like the rest of the country's students, from the liberality of the public purse. By the turn of the twenty-first century, however, the purse had snapped shut: the automatic entitlement to a maintenance grant was slowly brought to an end across the 1990s, and from 1998–9 students were also expected to contribute towards their tuition costs. As Oxford, like most other universities, charged the maximum permitted from the introduction of the variable fee in 2006, its undergraduates, at the end of the period, were paying an annual sum of £9,000, albeit in the form of a government loan.[6] Only the

[2] See p. 601, this volume.
[3] Chris Goodall, 'Softening the Blow: If College Fees Go', OM, 8th week, MT (1997), 7.
[4] Letter to author, 27 Sept. 2012. Equivalent to £40,000 in 2011.
[5] Franks, ii. 27, found only 5.9 per cent of students in 1965 had no outside support at all.
[6] In the case of humanities and social sciences students £9,000 was deemed to be the full fee, and Oxford received no additional per capita allowance for their tuition. In the case of science and medical students the University continued to collect a small per capita grant from the state.

poorest students were cushioned. Under the system that came into operation in 2012–13, 15 per cent of Oxford's undergraduates received a discount on their fee liability and 25 per cent some sort of maintenance grant from the state and an additional bursary provided by the University, the amount in either case determined on a sliding scale according to their parents' income. This brought down the cost of an Oxford education considerably. Anyone from a family with an income of less than £16,000 had to find only £3,850 in the first year and £7,350 and £10,250 in the second and third years to cover their tuition and living expenses.[7] Thanks to the Moritz-Heyman bequest, moreover, a hundred of the poorest undergraduates had even this sum completely covered, so they would be able to leave Oxford debt-free.[8] The great majority of Oxford's undergraduates, on the other hand, were destined henceforth to go out into the world with a large financial burden around their shoulders, even if they lived modestly. At worst, without parental support, they would leave owing at least £45,000, of which some £3,000 to £7,500 would have been borrowed at commercial rates of interest.[9] At best, if their parents were affluent and could give them the money needed to pay their living expenses, they would go down owing the state £27,000.

Postgraduates similarly found the state less than munificent in funding their courses towards the end of the period, but in their case the public purse had only ever been half open. The government committed itself to supporting a small number of American and Commonwealth postgraduate scholars under the 1953 Marshall Aid Commemoration Act and the 1959 bilateral agreement between Commonwealth states to offer bursaries to each other's students. But it was wary of becoming too deeply involved in postgraduate funding in the immediate post-war era. It was not until 1955 that the Ministry of Education deigned to support British postgraduates at all, and it was still far from bountiful in the mid-1960s. At the time of Franks, only 40 per cent of Oxford postgraduates received some form of public grant.[10] Most of the rest were supported by their family or friends or by various businesses or charities: the Rhodes Trust alone funded some eighty foreign postgraduates in the first part of the period, though many of these were taking a second BA rather than a higher degree. The British state increased its investment in the late 1960s and 1970s, acting on the recommendation in Robbins,[11] but grants for postgraduate study were never automatic and were always awarded only to those with the best undergraduate examination performance. Administration of the awards was also left to the British Academy and the various research councils set up in the interwar and post-war years, which had different methods of distributing

---

[7] 'Financial Support for Undergraduates': document prepared for the use of colleges by the deputy registrar (14 Sept. 2012). In 2013 some sort of maintenance grant and Oxford bursary was available to all undergraduates whose parental income was less than £42,500.

[8] For this bequest, see p. 602, this volume.

[9] Undergraduates at all universities in 2012–13 had the right to take out a government maintenance loan ranging from £3,500 to £5,200 per annum according to parental income.

[10] Franks, ii. 27.   [11] See Robbins, ch. 8, esp. p. 105.

the money they were given by the state.[12] The science councils allocated a number of awards to different university departments and left it to the department to decide whom to favour. The British Academy, in contrast, gave studentships to individual postgraduates, who were free to hold their award at whichever university would accept them.

From the mid-1980s, public funding became harder to obtain once more, as competition grew and the government became less liberal with its resources. Only the opportunities for foreign graduates were extended, with the establishment of the Overseas Research Students Awards Scheme in 1979 and the Foreign Office's Chevening scholarships in 1984.[13] By the mid-1990s the situation was parlous, especially in the social sciences and the humanities. According to the North Report in 1997, a mere 22 per cent of applicants to the Humanities Research Board of the British Academy had been successful in the previous year, although 81 per cent had Firsts. North feared for the future:

> From this combination of experiences there emerges a university-wide conclusion that Oxford must take action to ensure that the unavailability or unpredictability of public funding for graduate students does not result in a situation in which either faculties or departments have to place inappropriate restrictions on the number of graduate students they recruit, or less able, but privately-funded applicants are admitted because some of the most highly qualified candidates have to turn down a place for lack of funding.[14]

The University duly took action by seeking funds to set up its own bursary scheme—one that would be open to scholars of all nationalities not simply those from the United Kingdom and the European Union, who were eligible for research council funding. By the late 1990s, the University had already established a number of small schemes of its own, such as the scholarships named after the banker Joseph Scatcherd, which were first awarded in 1996–7 and allowed nine students from the European continent to come to Oxford to study and nine to go abroad.[15] Oxford also benefited from the various schemes to aid students from eastern Europe, funded by the financier George Soros.[16] But the Rhodes Scholarships remained the only large in-house scholarship fund. All this changed after 2001 when OUP undertook to use part of its profits to build up a graduate bursary fund. By the end of the period, some £37 million had been committed and the University's Clarendon scholarships were supporting both the fees and living costs of some 120 to 150 graduates, nearly twice as many as were funded by the Rhodes Trust.[17] The number

---

[12] There were seven research councils in 2013. Until the creation of the Arts and Humanities Research Board (later Council) in the 1990s, government used the British Academy as a surrogate research council.

[13] Oxford was a major beneficiary of the new awards. In 1995, it had 160 Chevening scholars: *OUG*, 2 Nov. 1995, p. 283.

[14] North, p. 191.

[15] Made possible by a £7 million bequest from his daughter, Jane Ledwig Rowohlt: *OUG*, 16 Nov. 1995, p. 345.

[16] Some also funded undergraduate study.

[17] <http:/en.wikipedia.org/wiki/Clarendon_bursary> (accessed 22 August 2013).

of beneficiaries, too, was further augmented by new private benefactions which swelled the number of scholarships on offer, notably the gift of Mica and Ahmet Ertegun, who pledged £26 million in 2012 to support a foundation of thirty-five humanities scholars.[18] The colleges also played their part. For many years, the colleges had been helping a small number of postgraduates with their fees and living expenses, if usually only partly.[19] In the first decade of the new millennium, most began to fund-raise in earnest for graduate bursaries. Some were able to establish scholarships that covered the total cost of study; others contributed to an initiative established right at the end of the period whereby a college could agree to underwrite part of the cost of a Clarendon, Marshall, or research council award, thereby allowing a greater number of graduates to be supported under these schemes than would otherwise have been the case.[20]

Despite the great efforts of the University to find funding for its ever-growing number of graduate students, the task remained far from complete at the end of the period. According to the University's updated strategic plan of May 2008, 30 per cent of master's and 59 per cent of doctoral students were fully funded by public or private bursaries, but the percentage varied across the divisions and only 40 per cent of those pursuing a DPhil in the humanities and social sciences were totally supported.[21] This meant that more than half the postgraduate community, nearly 5,000 students, were still heavily reliant on, sometimes completely, a combination of their own or their families' resources and bank loans to get through their studies.[22] And parental help was less readily available. In the 1980s and 1990s when the state still paid for undergraduate education, parents had sometimes remortgaged their houses so that their sons or daughters could read for a DPhil. By 2012, when many parents, especially those on middling incomes, were making unprecedented sacrifices to ensure that their offspring were not too greatly mired in debt when they finished their first degree, postgraduates were increasingly on their own. It was extremely difficult, and generally discouraged, for Oxford undergraduates to undertake more than the odd hour of paid labour per week in term time. Many postgraduates, however, relied on casual earnings to survive and it was not unknown for the more impoverished to spend several hours a day on the checkout at Marks and Spencer.[23]

---

[18] See p. 602, this volume.

[19] From the 1950s, most colleges had a few prestigious bursaries, such as Merton's Harmsworth senior scholarships.

[20] 'Invitation to Offer College Partnership Awards with the Clarendon Fund, UK Research Council Studentships and Marshall Scholarships'. Document circulated by the head of graduate funding, 1 June 2012.

[21] 'University of Oxford: Strategic Plan 2008–2009 to 2012–2013'. *OUG*, supplement (1) to no. 4845 (21 May 2008), p. 1105. For a less optimistic figure, see 'Student Number Planning Committee: Report to Council on Student Number Planning April 2011', p. 4.

[22] Some enterprising students sought public sponsorship by advertising for donations: see *The Times*, 25 July 2014, p. 18.

[23] In 2013, the University considered fund-raising to support its postgraduates a priority and announced a campaign to create a further 130 scholarships: 'Oration by the Vice-Chancellor', UOG, Supplement (1) to No 5036, 16 October 2013, p. 74.

B. Student Emancipation

Oxford's junior members, between the wars, were treated like overgrown school-children. Expected to keep to gate-hours, allowed to mix socially with students of the opposite sex only on strict conditions, deterred from visiting city pubs, subject to decanal discipline, and allowed no role in the government of their college, they lived in an environment that replicated the public-school world from which so many of them had come. Little was formally changed in the twenty-five years that followed the end of the Second World War, except that pubs ceased to be completely out of bounds and gowns no longer had to be worn in the town. In the 1950s, Oxford contained large numbers of junior members in their early twenties, undergraduates as well as postgraduates, for it was common to do National Service before coming up. Despite this, little attempt was made to remodel the disciplinary regime. For the most part, measures were taken that allowed the rules to remain in force but also to be easily circumvented. Proctors and deans began to turn a blind eye to all but the most egregious examples of drunkenness and impropriety, and some college officers even encouraged rule-breaking. On arriving at Balliol in 1956, one of the first things that the blind Indian writer, Ved Mehta, learnt from the college chaplain, was how to get round gate-hours regardless of his disability: 'You know, there's a college rule that no one is supposed to be outside college after midnight...But if you ever are, there is a window on the ground floor of Staircase X. Any undergraduate can show you how to climb in.'[24] Scouts, too, did not usually peach on male undergraduates who entertained a female guest in their room overnight.[25] In female colleges, though, the regulations could be enforced with venom. As late as 1961, St Hilda's expelled an undergraduate discovered with a man in her room once the gates were closed.

By the mid-1960s, Oxford's junior members were less willing to be treated as children, even as children permitted a long leash. Nor were they willing to be treated as a race apart. They no longer tolerated being addressed as young ladies or gentlemen and demanded to be called students like everyone else in higher education. As early as 1961, they took the first step down the road of collective action when they formed, on their own initiative, a student council with the brief to monitor and produce reports on aspects of junior members' lives. The Oxford University Students' Representative Council, as it was known, showed little inclination to challenge the system outright in the ensuing years. Some of its constituents, more quickly in tune with the new spirit of rebellion and self-importance that was sweeping through the youth of the western world in the 1960s, were less coy. When the Franks Commission did not support students being represented on university committees, a group of radicals, including the president of the Balliol JCR, Michael Burton, petitioned the Privy Council. As the student movement

---

[24] Ved Mehta, *Continents of Exile: Up at Oxford* (London, 1992), p. 75. This is the fullest published personal account of student life in the 1950s.
[25] John Carey, *The Unexpected Professor: An Oxford Life in Books* (London, 2014), ch. 5 (electronic version).

gathered pace in the United States and France, the radicals took their protest to the streets. The Proctors' jurisdiction was particularly disliked and provoked the first hostile demonstration against university discipline in June 1968. The University moved swiftly to meet the students' grievances, and immediately set up a committee under the respected jurisprudent Herbert Hart to look at relations between junior members and the central University. When the committee published its report in the following year, the students got most of what they wanted. Besides accepting that students should have a limited voice in university decision-making at all levels, the committee recommended the establishment of a new disciplinary court, with both junior and senior representatives, which would replace the traditional jurisdiction of the Proctors in cases of major breaches of university discipline. In subsequent years, similar changes were introduced in the colleges, Balliol taking the lead, Christ Church lagging behind. By the early 1970s, gate-hours had been abolished; students were usually issued with gate keys so that they could go in and out when they wanted; rules about having guests in student rooms overnight had gone by the board; decanal jurisdiction had been partly replaced by student-dominated tribunals; and junior members had a voice if not a vote on governing body and college committees that dealt with matters concerning their interests.[26]

The University and the colleges also bowed to the student demand that the traditional dress code be relaxed. On all formal academic occasions until the mid-1960s undergraduates were expected to wear gowns, and female students a respectable skirt or dress. As late as 1966, women taking Schools were warned by the Proctors to keep their hemline low: 'Extravagantly short skirts are incompatible with the intended sobriety of sub-fusc and we consider that examiners may reasonably take exception to them.'[27] Within a few years the authorities had thrown in the towel: by the end of the 1970s, gowns, except for formal hall and university examinations, were worn only by the eccentric, and it was acceptable for women to dress in trousers rather than a skirt, even when wearing sub-fusc, provided the trousers were black with a crease. Somewhat surprisingly there was never much demand for sub-fusc itself to be abolished: examinations continued to be seen as an occasion worth getting dressed up for. From the 1950s, if not before, it was common for undergraduates to add their own informal garnish to the official costume by placing a carnation in their buttonhole. By the 1990s this was de rigueur and an elaborate convention had developed as to the right colour to sport at different stages of the examination.[28]

The changes were effected relatively painlessly because the students were pushing at an open door. Many female dons themselves chafed at the requirement to lecture

---

[26] For an account of the changes from a don's point of view, see Anthony Kenny, *A Life in Oxford* (London, 1997), pp. 47–8, 51–2, and 77.

[27] Adams, p. 318 (proctorial letter to the women's colleges).

[28] For an explanation of the invented ritual, see *Oxfordshire Limited Edition*, Aug. 2013, p. 113 (magazine of the *OT*). As early as the 1960s it was common for female students to sport a rose given them by their boyfriend: private communication from Brian Harrison.

or examine in a skirt, while hardly any senior member was willing to defend gate-hours: St Catherine's had been built in the early 1960s without any gates, while most colleges, even before the Hart Report, had followed the lead taken by Somerville as early as 1964 and started distributing late gate keys to those with a good excuse for being out after curfew. Moreover, from 1970, when the age of majority was reduced from 21 to 18, the colleges were no longer in loco parentis and lost any right to control how students spent their leisure hours or were accoutred provided there was no harm or inconvenience to others. Student representation on university and college committees was more controversial. Conservatives felt that granting the demand would undermine their role as trustees and tried to hold back the tide. John Mabbott, president of St John's, claimed to have taken the wind out of the students' sails until his retirement in 1969, simply by showing them how little of the business of the college's governing body related to education.[29] But even in 1968, a poll of senior members across the University found a majority in favour of the initiative, and, once introduced, it was broadly felt to be a positive development at all levels. The new disciplinary apparatus proved to be the one largely ephemeral innovation. The junior members usually had the choice of whether to face decanal correction or the new tribunal. As the latter tended to be a more rigorous upholder of the letter of the law than the deans, student malefactors voted with their feet and the tribunals had normally fallen into abeyance by the late 1970s.

The students' desire from the mid-1960s to be free from past constraints also extended to commensality. Students in the second half of the period were used to a much more varied and continental diet than all but the most aristocratic of their forebears, and many, especially women, were now vegetarians. Earlier generations had sometimes complained about the quality of hall food, especially during and after the Second World War, when food was rationed and cooks experimented with whale meat and other dubious delicacies, but they had usually accepted the concept of formal hall and its role in bringing students of different backgrounds together. A more radical and independent generation wanted to eat where and when they wished, and were as impatient of the concept of formal hall as their pre-war predecessors had been of morning roll-call. Again the colleges largely met their desires. From the 1970s, the majority gave up providing a formal student hall each evening and replaced it with a cafeteria service. Magdalen, aiming to save money after the war, had sold the pass as early as 1948. Increasingly, too, it was accepted that students living in should have the chance to cook their own meals, so new accommodation blocks were built with well-appointed kitchens and existing staircases adapted where possible.[30]

---

[29] John Mabbott, *Oxford Memories* (Oxford, 1986), p. 141. Mabbott pointed out that St John's had had a joint consultative committee of junior and senior members from 1919.

[30] Formal hall was never completely abandoned. Most colleges in the 2000s continued to lay on a formal student hall at least once a week. These were usually well attended and students dressed for the occasion. For the present situation at University College, see Robin Darwall-Smith, email communication, 2 Apr. 2014.

FIGURE 15.1 Sit-in at the Clarendon Building, February 1970. The occupation of administrative buildings was a common tactic of student militants in the late 1960s and the first half of the 1970s. Oxford suffered less than most and the sit-ins soon fizzled out. The files supposedly kept by the Proctors on student activists which sparked off the 1970 sit-in were never discovered.

What did alienate most dons was when the junior members forsook peaceful demonstrations for change and invaded university property, putting the well-being of non-academic staff at risk. This happened for the first time in the last week of February 1970 when a party of students occupied the Delegates' Room in the Clarendon Building in search of the files purportedly kept on troublemakers (see Figure 15.1). It happened again in November 1973, when the Examination Schools were taken over for a week, and for a third and fourth time in March 1974, when attempts were made to storm the Indian Institute and the new university offices in Wellington Square. The last three acts of bravura were part of a renewed flurry of student militancy around the country and were engendered by various issues of the day, such as the miners' strike against the Heath government. But in Oxford's case they were also connected with the desire of many undergraduates to replace the Students' Representative Council, considered toothless, with a more powerful central students' union, akin to those in other universities. It is testimony to the University's willingness to listen that the students got what they wanted, even in the face of provocation. OUSU (Oxford University Students' Union) was set up in 1974.[31]

Released from the closely regulated life of earlier generations, Oxford junior members from the 1970s were able to enjoy their new freedom in unprecedented

[31] OUSRC had been formally recognized by the University following the Hart Report.

comfort. The quality of existing accommodation in most colleges in the 1950s and 1960s remained much the same as it had been pre-war. Sitting rooms might no longer be heated by coal fires but the electric or gas appliances which replaced them seldom provided sufficient warmth in winter, while separate bedrooms had no heating at all and visiting the toilet or having a bath often required a trek outdoors and across the quad. By the late 1960s, however, most colleges were able to offer more appealing accommodation, as the increase in student numbers encouraged the construction of new residential blocks of bedsits in order to extend the supply of rooms. The lead was taken by Wadham, which knocked down a collection of cottages and outhouses off Holywell Street to create the Goddard Building as early as 1953. From the end of the decade, other colleges followed suit and launched appeals for the necessary funds. Some of these new buildings were architectural gems, such as the imaginative 'beehive' created by the Architects Co-Partnership for St John's and put up in 1958–60 (see Figure 15.2). Others, notably the New College block with its back to Longwall, built in 1961–2 to a design by David Roberts, were modernist horizontal monstrosities. Yet whatever their architectural value, they were all much more comfortable to live in, with better heating and better sanitary facilities, and pointed to a less ascetic future.[32] So too did the new colleges built from scratch over the two decades: St Antony's, Nuffield, St Catherine's, and Wolfson. The last in particular was handsomely appointed. Slowly, from the 1970s, older college buildings also began to be thoroughly renovated and improved. By the end of the period, most students living in college were comfortably ensconced in centrally heated bedsits with good internet access and in close proximity to well-appointed bathrooms and kitchens.

The transformation reflected growing expectations. Post-war college accommodation quickly looked austere in an era that saw the standard of living of all classes steadily rising. Initially, it was only Americans at Oxford who were appalled by the sanitation and discomfort.[33] By the 1980s it was home students too. By then there were few junior members who had not grown up in a centrally heated home with instant access to hot water and showers, and they were far less willing than an earlier generation to get through the winter by putting on more clothes. Their parents, too, as the short-lived era of generous maintenance grants came to an end, wanted to see value for the money that they were being forced to spend on their offspring. The parents of female students in the new mixed colleges could be particularly vocal about the facilities. It was perfectly acceptable for their sons to rough it but they expected their daughters to have the same creature comforts that they were used to at home.

The older colleges had another reason for making their buildings more attractive. When inflation took off in the 1970s and it became harder to balance the books, all

---

[32] Not all the new accommodation took the form of bedsits. Trinity's Cumberbatch Building, opened in 1966, still had sets.

[33] One female American in the 1950s was so cold that she literally toasted her legs on her electric fire and was hospitalized for ten days: Mehta, *Up at Oxford*, p. 75.

FIGURE 15.2 'The Beehive', St John's College, 1958–60: Architects Co-Partnership. Many colleges put up new residential buildings in the 1960s. Most were uninteresting or even brutal concrete blocks. St John's erected a building that enhanced rather than detracted from the existing quad by using a simple geometric pattern redolent of the cells in a honeycomb.

colleges sought to augment their income during the long vacation by taking advantage of Oxford's attraction as a venue for the burgeoning conference and summer-school trade. By 2013, many colleges had become quasi-hotels and were offering bed and breakfast to tourists. It was a competitive environment and the colleges with the best facilities had the fullest order book and made the most money. As a result, the new college buildings that continued to be put up with gusto in the final decades of the period inside and outside the curtilage were usually built to a high specification and with an eye to the wider market. En suite facilities became de rigueur. Magdalen's Grove Quad, erected in the mid-1990s to a design by the anti-modernist architect Demetri Porphyrios, cost over £12 million to build. With its mixed neo-gothic and neoclassical façade and its rather cold American oak interior, it could best be described as 'monastic chic': it offered the summer visitor anxious to experience historic Oxford the illusion of living in a gloomy anchorite's cell without the discomfort.[34]

The result of fifty years of building and refurbishment was that the large majority of junior members at the start of the new millennium could enjoy the benefits of

---

[34] Unfortunately, there were problems with the design, and in 2015–16 the college undertook expensive internal and external repairs.

living in for the duration of their stay, despite the quadrupling of numbers. In the 1950s and 1960s most undergraduates spent one year in lodgings, while postgraduates nearly always lived out. Trinity was so hard-pressed for space in 1957 that it decided to limit the time undergraduates could have a room in college to between four and five terms.[35] Gradually the position improved. University College was able to house all of its undergraduates as early as 1973 with the erection of a new building in North Oxford known as Stavertonia.[36] Elsewhere progress was slower, but by the late 1990s nearly every college could offer accommodation to any undergraduate or postgraduate who wanted it. According to the University's 2005 corporate plan, 80 per cent of junior members were living in.[37] The turnaround was advantageous to the average student anxious to reduce costs, as maintenance grants were replaced by loans. Until the early 1970s, students living out were expected to rent a room in a 'recognized' lodging house, which guaranteed a reasonable level of quality, even if the landlady was essentially a college spy. But as any restrictions on student choice were lifted once colleges were no longer in loco parentis, junior members found themselves subject to the rigour and horrors of the marketplace. As commercial rents in Oxford were high and accommodation frequently of a low standard, the large majority of students were only too pleased to reside permanently in college.

While junior members became more independent and comfortably housed after 1970, they ceased to be cosseted in other ways. In the first two decades of the period, male undergraduates still had their staircase scout, who acted as part personal servant, part counsellor in adversity. The best were still gentlemen's gentlemen, as an undergraduate from a northern grammar school who came up in 1958 was amazed to discover. In his third year, he was looked after by a scout who served tea to his girlfriend, insisted on cleaning his shoes and tying his tie before he went out to a dinner, and actually appeared outside the Examination Schools with a silver tray bearing champagne when he finished his finals.[38] But scouts became harder to replace after 1945 as the continued commercial and industrial expansion of the city provided a surfeit of better-paid jobs in offices and factories, while the colleges, by the mid-1960s, were happy to dispense with their services: fires no longer had to be laid, water no longer had to be fetched, and waiting in hall was on the point of becoming redundant. A new generation of students, too, largely unused to servants and opposed to deference of any kind, were keen to see the back of the institution, and many dons, such as Trinity's domestic bursar, Robin Fletcher, agreed: 'A case

---

[35] Forty-five per cent of Oxford students were living out in 1968.

[36] After the street in which the building is located. University College had also been one of the first to improve the quality of its existing accommodation. Washbasins were put in most rooms and lavatories and bathrooms on most staircases in the mid-1950s.

[37] *Corporate Plan 2005–6 to 2009–10* (Oxford, 2006), p. 19. The figure included those living in the small amount of university accommodation. Until the very end of the period there were still several colleges where undergraduates had to spend a year out. Pembroke could finally house all of its 360 undergraduates only in 2013 when it opened its new Rokos Quad: *OT*, 25 Apr. 2013, p. 4.

[38] Taped interview, 22 Feb. 2002.

might be made for the privileged of tomorrow learning something about staff relations, but having their shoes cleaned and their crockery washed for them may well be the worst possible introduction.'[39] In consequence, quite quickly over the course of the late 1960s and 1970s, ostensibly on the grounds of the financial savings that could be made, male scouts, as they retired, were replaced by local women who worked part-time. Students continued to have their beds made and their rooms cleaned, but female scouts were not at their beck and call: they were assigned a number of staircases or corridors and there was a definite limit to the amount of mess that they would agree to clear up. Most, too, went home at lunchtime and had no further duties in the college. When a large number of staff was needed to wait in hall, the colleges used contract labour supplied by agencies. Students in the second half of the period were adults and had to look after themselves.

Junior members after 1970 took their new status seriously. Anxious to flex their adult muscles, they were much readier than hitherto to stick up for their own interests and confront the colleges' governing bodies with their grievances. Having won independence from the restrictions of the past with little difficulty, they were willing to cross swords with senior members over all manner of decisions. In June 1998, after the governing body of St Edmund Hall had clashed with the popular principal, Sir Stephen Tumim, and precipitated his resignation, more than a third of the college's 350 students passed a motion of no confidence in the fellowship and proceeded to stage a quiet protest on the college lawn.[40] But the perennial points of conflict with senior members in all colleges after 1970 were rent rises and the often indifferent quality of college food. In the 1950s, the dissatisfied had an outlet for their ire in the JCR suggestions' book, but collective action was rare and the oversensitive were not admired. One semi-professional Magdalen complainant so annoyed his peers that, on one occasion, he was put in his place by a note appended to his latest entry: 'P.S. The marmalade was cold this morning.'[41] After 1970, in contrast, junior members were much more critical. Students welcomed the chance to live in but they wanted to do so on the best possible terms. Although colleges tried to keep room rents and kitchen charges down, they still had to be raised each year at least in line with inflation and restructured from time to time to keep control of spiralling deficits on the house account. The annual negotiations with the students over the size of the increase became wars of attrition that continually led to threats to withhold battels payments and occasional battels strikes. There was a limit, however, to how far a college could be held to ransom. As battels debtors could not officially graduate until a change of the regulations in 2014, strikes did not usually run into Trinity Term and were frequently concluded with a compromise that gave the college what it wanted. Paradoxically, rent strikes often did a college no damage at all. When Balliol's junior members withheld their rent in Michaelmas 1980, the strikers, showing maturity and common sense, paid their battels into a

[39] Hopkins, p. 427.
[41] Brockliss, p. 648.
[40] *The Times Higher Education*, 19 June 1998, p. 15.

strike fund. When the strike ended in December, the money in the account plus accumulated interest was paid over to the college. As the then master, Anthony Kenny, noted in his memoirs, 'since strikers tended to pay their battels into the fund more promptly than the average indolent undergraduate settled his debts with the Bursar', Balliol on this and similar occasions ended up better off.[42]

Undergraduates and postgraduates in 2015 were still in a state of dependence despite all the changes. Although they were consulted on college decisions that had a bearing on their day-to-day lives, they had only a limited power of veto.[43] Moreover, for all their freedom from earlier restrictions, they were still corralled, but in a different way. Students before the 1980s left their rooms open, wandered unchallenged from college to college in the daytime, and had no qualms about going out at night on their own. Students at the turn of the twenty-first century were encouraged to believe that they lived in a dangerous world. As student rooms were now full of expensive consumer goods, such as hi-fi equipment, word processors, and mobile phones, junior members were exhorted to be ever vigilant against opportunistic theft. Students themselves had to be protected from the predatory advances of their peers and strangers. For their own protection, new restrictions were placed on their behaviour and movement which would have shocked an earlier generation. Minute regulations were drawn up governing interpersonal relations, women students were given rape alarms, and colleges became security-conscious. Identity checks were made on those who entered a college's portals, and locked doors were fitted at the foot of staircases that could be opened only by swipe cards.

C. Forms of Study

Throughout the period, the tutorial remained at the centre of undergraduate instruction and was continually lauded by all shades of opinion in the University as a vehicle of instruction that made Oxford unique and was the cause of its worldwide reputation as a teaching institution. Through weekly or twice-weekly meetings with a senior academic to discuss a piece of written work, Oxford undergraduates were taught to think critically and argue their corner in a way that was considered to give them the intellectual edge over the products of other universities, barring Cambridge. But the tutorial's omnipresence in the undergraduates' academic life did not escape criticism. The Franks Commission in 1966 confirmed its centrality but concluded that it should not be relied on entirely: 'Even with an intensive use of the vacation it must…remain true that a syllabus cannot be "covered" by the tutorial system alone. It is necessary to make use of other means of formal instruction. These other means are lectures, classes and laboratory work.' The same point

[42] Kenny, *Life*, p. 130.
[43] They did not usually have voting rights on the governing body, and were asked to leave before the fellows discussed financial matters or appointments. In some colleges, matters of 'reserved business' remained a subject of conflict until the end of the period.

was made by North, and in the University's corporate plans drawn up at the beginning of the new millennium. These stressed that the tutorial was invaluable for honing an undergraduate's powers of analysis but did little to develop the communicative skills needed in the modern workplace 'such as collaboration and teamwork which may best be fostered in other pedagogical settings'.[44] As a result, from the 1990s especially, greater attention was paid to providing lecture courses that would support tutorial work, more papers came to be taught through a mix of classes and tutorials, and the overall number of tutorials that an undergraduate received in the course of a three- or four-year sojourn at Oxford was slightly reduced.

This, however, was as far as it went. Individual voices in the later part of the period, both inside and outside the University, which called for a more radical rethink, were always resisted. Even the rapid development of new ways of disseminating knowledge with the invention of the World Wide Web were not thought to devalue the case for the tutorial but rather the reverse. Denis Noble, the Burton Sanderson professor of cardiovascular physiology, was ready to argue in 2001 that science students needed only four tutorials a term: 'I do not think it is unreasonable to ask that, if a student is going to command an hour of prime time with his tutor, he should devote a couple of weeks to developing a really substantial document to discuss, not a hastily word-processed concoction.' But he defended the value of the tutorial to the hilt and saw it as the pedagogical tool of the future not the past: '[A]s more routine knowledge is acquired through electronic methods, the need for stimulating personal contact through tutorial interaction becomes *more* important not less...Oxford already has a great tradition in precisely the kind of teaching that will be needed to complement the increasingly impersonal methods of the twenty-first century.'[45]

How far tutorials in this period as in any other measured up to the ideal is hard to say. Franks complained that the tutorial, by the mid-1960s, had frequently become a cramming exercise, and North, thirty years later, concurred. Rather than being a vehicle for making undergraduates argue and think, it was being used as an expensive way of teaching them about how to impress future examiners.[46] There was some justice in the observation. Tutorials, especially at the end of a long day, could degenerate into mini-lectures, where the voice of the undergraduate was scarcely heard. For the most part, though, tutorials were wide-ranging and interactive encounters, where both tutor and pupil were challenged, and the tutor could sometimes be worsted. Beneficiaries remembered and appreciated the experience, even if they inevitably preferred some dons to others and felt that some tutors were just going through the motions. Its value was acknowledged in countless memoirs

---

[44] Franks, i. 103; 'Plan 2008–2009 to 2012–2013', p. 1099. Also North, pp. 133 and 165; *Corporate Plan 2005–6 to 2009–10*', p. 47.

[45] Denis Noble, 'Science, Tutorials, and Colleges', OM, 4th week, HT (2001), 5–6.

[46] Franks, i. 103; North, pp. 165–7.

and oral recollections, where tutors were praised to excess, even by those close to the event who could not be accused of being deceived by nostalgia.[47] It was also confirmed in the last decade of the period by students still in residence, who were asked to fill in anonymous termly reports on their tutors' performance as part of a new cultural obsession with feedback and customer service. Consequently, Oxford scored better than other top British universities when it came to student satisfaction with their teaching. In a National Student Survey of 2012, the only area in which Oxford undergraduates felt the system fell down was in the clarity and detail of the oral and written comments that they received on their essays.[48]

The tutorial of 2015, on the other hand, was not the tutorial of the 1950s. In the decade following the war, tutors set a student an essay title or some mathematical problems to answer, then largely left them to it. Advice about books and articles that might be consulted was minimal, and typed reading lists all but unknown. The undergraduate as a singleton or part of a pair duly returned at the allotted time, essay or solutions in hand, and laid out the fruits of his or her labour before the listening tutor. Most written work was never handed in to be marked; and only essays or solutions not discussed in the tutorial were scrutinized after the event and handed back with minimal comment. Tutorial styles varied. Most tutors listened to the student without comment. Others, such as A. J. P. Taylor, continually interrupted. As a result, the whole hour in his presence could be absorbed simply in getting to the end of the essay, especially as he spent much of the time on the phone fielding criticisms of his latest newspaper article.[49] Some tutors were kind and supportive and plied their pupils with sherry. Others could push the Socratic method to the limit. In their commitment to getting their pupils to think clearly and weigh evidence, they could leave their charges cowed and feeling unworthy. Somerville's Isobel Henderson once returned an essay to an English student in the 1950s with the command, 'Now tear this up and write what *you* think.'[50] Many tutors were downright eccentric. When the future Corpus historian James Howard-Johnston came up in the early 1960s he was regaled with stories of a don 'who rolled himself up in a carpet as he listened to essays', of another, always on the move, 'who taught in the train', and a third so still and taciturn that it was impossible to tell whether he was asleep or awake.[51]

By 2015, tutorials were less anarchic and more predictable (see Figure 15.3). From the late 1960s, typed bibliographies were a commonplace. As the literature on all subjects expanded rapidly over the period, it soon became impossible for any tutor to keep it in his or her head. The time-honoured custom of reading an essay aloud was also eventually abandoned. The editor of the *Oxford Magazine* defended

---

[47] E.g. Darius Guppy, *Roll the Dice* (London, 1996), pp. 46–7. Guppy published his memoirs only a few years after going down.

[48] 'Communication from Education Committee to Senior Tutors Committee: National Student Survey 2012', pp. 7–8.

[49] Interview, 22 Feb. 2005.   [50] Adams, p. 336.

[51] James Howard-Johnston, 'In Praise of the Tutorial', OM, 2nd week, HT (2006), 4.

FIGURE 15.3 A tutorial at the turn of the twenty-first century. The photograph depicts a tutorial in philosophy given by Elizabeth Fricker (on the right), fellow and tutor of Magdalen, in her ground-floor rooms in the Cloister. Philosophy tutorials are unusual in that they still tend to be one-to-one.

the practice as late as 1997 on the grounds it allowed the undergraduate to 'set the precise terms of the debate'.[52] But by then the practice was becoming obsolete. In the 1980s, younger tutors began demanding that work was handed in early, so that it could be read beforehand and the whole hour devoted to discussing the topic. The advent of word processors only hastened the change, as typed essays could be read much more quickly. The main area of disagreement at the end of the period was whether a student's work should be given a mark or simply returned with comments outlining its strength and deficiencies. The insistence from the 1980s, too, that new tutors should undergo some form of in-house teacher training, indeed, ideally by the end of the period take a two-year teaching diploma organized by the University's Department of Education, further ensured that tutors were much more alert to the need to respect their pupils' dignity and to encourage rather than mock. The audit culture did the rest, forcing the colleges and faculties to set down and publicize, for the benefit of students, definitions of teaching best practice to which dons could be expected to subscribe.[53] The upshot was the eccentric Oxford don became a thing of the past and tutorial styles much more uniform. Even so, there always remained room for creativity. At the base of every tutorial was always a piece

[52] 'Special Treatment', OM, 4th week, MT (1997), 1.
[53] Following the North Report this was part of the brief of the new EPSC and the divisional boards: see North, ch. 8, esp. recommendation 42 (p. 149).

of written work, but tutors experimented with its structure. While most tutorials were paired and lasted for the traditional hour, some tutors, convinced that many topics were now too complex to explore in the conventional format, took pupils in groups or four or five and saw them for two hours or more, thereby dissolving the distinction between the tutorial and the class.

Postgraduates, in contrast, were largely taught in a manner common across the university world. Students preparing a dissertation at doctoral and master's level had a personal supervisor who saw them individually to discuss progress and suggest ways of moving forward, but the meetings were not tutorials: they were not weekly events based round a piece of written work (although a piece of written work was often the reason for meeting); their aim was to talk over what students had discovered rather than to teach them to think; and the master–pupil relationship was often reversed. Taught postgraduate courses were mainly built around weekly seminars. Students were expected to prepare for the seminar by reading recommended books and articles and one or more of the group would be asked to introduce the topic by presenting a short paper. Some arts courses made provision for tutorials and essay writing but most did not. Master's students usually had to submit one or two long pieces of work as part of the examination of their degree, but most had no weekly essays or one-to-one meetings, except to discuss possible topics for the assessed essays.

It was also the case that, until 2000, the quality of postgraduate tuition frequently left much to be desired. In the science departments, doctoral students were usually part of a team working with a professor or lecturer on a problem of mutual interest, so pupil and supervisor were constantly in contact and there was little chance that a researcher would be neglected. In the arts faculties, however, there were continual complaints before the 1990s that supervisors were reluctant to meet with their pupils, offered little advice, and were often uninterested in their work. There were many excellent arts supervisors throughout the period who inspired permanent, even obsessive, loyalty and affection, but it could often be a matter of chance to whom a student was assigned.[54] There was a widespread feeling among the older dons that, at Oxford, arts postgraduates studied on their own and had no need to be given formal instruction in research skills, as they were in the United States. These were picked up casually from contemporaries and occasional encounters with one's supervisor. Unsurprisingly, the standard of teaching on taught postgraduate courses was often lamentable. Rosa Ehrenreich was an American Marshall scholar who came up to Christ Church to read for an MPhil in European politics in the early 1990s. She was less than enamoured by the experience, even though this was one master's course where there was tutorial provision. The reading was unstructured, she was not given the chance to write her own research papers, and she was

---

[54] For the lottery of postgraduate supervision in the English faculty in the late 1950s see Carey, *Unexpected Professor*, ch. 6. Carey himself was well served by Helen Gardner of St Hilda's, perhaps the most highly regarded scholar in the faculty after the departure of C. S. Lewis.

given little idea by her tutor how to improve her work. She insisted, too, that her disillusionment was widely shared among foreign students, especially Americans:

> In a survey commissioned by Rhodes House in 1992, about two thousand former Rhodes Scholars, of all nationalities, described their Oxford days. In a preliminary tabulation of results, twenty-one percent rated the quality of teaching at Oxford average; fourteen percent described it as bad or very bad.[55]

Ehrenreich's response was extreme but it reflected the difficulty Oxford had in providing high-quality postgraduate education in the arts at all levels for most of the period. As the number of postgraduates rose, much of this education had to be entrusted to joint postholders. Fully committed as college tutors and used to a particular form of instruction, most had neither the time to devote to postgraduate students nor much idea of how to cope with older students who wanted both access to Oxford academics and the freedom to work on their own. It did not help either that the growth in postgraduate numbers tended to lower their overall calibre, as James Howard-Johnston pointed out in 2006:

> The competition for graduate places has nothing like the intensity of that for undergraduate places. While there are, of course, many stars, I doubt whether they amount to more than 30% of the total. All too many of the remainder have in effect bought their places. They can afford the fees. The liveliness, open-mindedness, and variegation of character and interests, which are characteristic of undergraduates, are often missing.[56]

There was usually no problem with the intellectual ability of students on long-established master's courses such as the BPhil and BCL. But in many cases in the later part of the period, Oxford dons were being asked to look after doctoral and master's students who required handling very differently from most undergraduates.

By the time Howard-Johnston uttered the unutterable, the University had begun seriously to address the problem. Having decided to go on expanding postgraduate numbers, it evidently behoved the central administration to think of ways of bridging the teaching deficit. The University's initial moves were responses to the 1987 Roberts Report on graduate provision, and led to a set of guidelines being issued to both postgraduates and dons outlining a research supervisor's duties. Follow-up working parties in 1990 and 1994 suggested how the colleges could play a fuller part in monitoring their graduates' progress. The mixed colleges had already established a separate tutor for graduates to look after graduate problems, University College as early as 1962. The working parties now advocated colleges holding graduate collections and each graduate being assigned a college adviser who would monitor the student's progress and be available 'for consultation on

---

[55] Rosa Ehrenreich, *A Garden of Paper Flowers: An American at Oxford* (London, 1994), esp. pp. 105 and 119 and 140–1.

[56] Howard-Johnston, 'Tutorial', p. 5.

academic or other matters which a student felt could not be taken to a supervisor'.[57] North, in 1997, proposed new ways of improving the graduate's lot. Besides reiterating the need for the colleges to establish a properly functioning college advisory system, his committee made several fresh recommendations. These included the establishment of faculty directors of graduate studies where these did not exist, the establishment of supervisorial norms to ensure that postholders were not overburdened, and the appointment of supplementary supervisors where possible to enhance student–academic contact. The committee also suggested the introduction of a faculty and departmental self-reporting scheme 'so that students in each year, including the first year, of their graduate work, would have their opportunity to comment on their progress and on their experiences of Oxford'.[58]

Consequently, by the end of the 1990s, it was difficult for postgraduate students to slip through the net and doctoral supervision had greatly improved. Only the quality of many of the taught master's courses, the area in which the University was expanding fast, continued to cause concern. By the end of the period, however, this too had been effectively tackled. On the one hand, much closer attention went into organizing individual courses and ensuring that the materials the students needed were easily available. On the other, postholders involved in master's teaching became fully committed. Younger dons who had undergone in-house training now had a far better understanding of how to motivate a class of different ability levels, while many were also less pressed for time because they were giving fewer undergraduate tutorials each week.[59]

D. Student Life

As in their teaching, there were important elements of continuity with an earlier age in the junior members' leisure lives. Oxford continued to be a university where students played hard. As they had done before the war, talented athletes joined the University's sporting clubs, budding journalists offered their services to *Cherwell* and *Isis*, while aspirant politicians flung themselves into the Union Society or the newly created OUSU. The large majority of students, however, still built their leisure life around their college. Admittedly, virtually all Oxford students in 2015 spent more time in the town than in 1945. The right to frequent pubs from the start of the period, the growing attraction of the commercial cinema from the 1980s, and the craze for 'clubbing' in the 2000s meant that only the most reclusive students did not pass one or two evenings a week outside their immediate college environs. Many students, too, after 1970, maintained close contact with friends beyond the

---

[57] 'Report of the Working Party on Graduate Provision' (1990), paras 18–25; 'The Graduate Studies Committee's Follow-Up to the Working Party on Graduate Provision' (1994), annexe C, *sub* 'college tutors for graduates' and 'college advisers'. For the original Roberts Report, see p. 579, this volume.

[58] North, pp. 182–6. The committee conducted a graduate survey that suggested that the college advisory system was not working and that students, even in the sciences, had limited contact with academic staff.

[59] See p. 623, this volume.

University and disappeared at weekends. Nonetheless, for all but the exceptional, their college, which continued to host a range of events and support an array of clubs and societies, remained the focus of their day-to-day lives.

The massive expansion in postgraduate numbers had little effect in this regard. Postgraduates in mixed colleges were simply absorbed into the existing clubs and societies, while the new graduate colleges immediately set up their own and wholeheartedly entered into the tradition of intercollegiate competition. Postgraduates, in that they were older, sometimes married, and frequently looked to an academic career, obviously had separate interests and needs. But the mixed colleges, from the late 1950s, recognized that they formed a distinctive community and found ways of making them feel at home. Postgraduates were given their own common room—the first MCR was established at Lincoln in 1958; they were permitted their own representatives on governing body and other college committees; they had a growing opportunity to apply for travel grants and bursaries; and they were granted peculiar access to senior members through formal invitations to high table and regular MCR/SCR events. They were also given the chance to live apart, as colleges began to build separate postgraduate accommodation towards the end of the period. The special attention reaped its reward. As an OUSU review of 2012 revealed, doctoral students in particular saw their college 'as a refuge from their degree...and the saving grace of the Oxford experience'. It was essential for maintaining a good work–life balance and helped keep sane those who were having difficulties with their research.[60]

Co-education equally did nothing to shift the centrality of the college. The newcomers, women or men, met with little resistance, as we saw in Chapter 13, and were easily integrated into college life at all levels.[61] Where, in the case of sports, there were obvious reasons why teams could not be mixed, the newcomers simply formed their own clubs with college support. In fact, women's sport was invigorated by the advent of co-education. Beforehand, women's teams had few opponents. Now they had as many as the men, and teams from the surviving women's colleges in the 1980s revelled in the opportunity of putting their sisters from the newly mixed foundations in their place. Women, by the end of the period, had their own intercollegiate competitions in all manner of traditionally male domains, even rugby. But it was women's rowing that was the most visible beneficiary of the disappearance of the single-sex college. The Oxford University Women's Boat Club was founded in the 1920s but was disbanded between 1953 and 1964 for lack of funds. In 2015 most colleges were able to put out two or more women's crews in Torpids and Eights (see Figure 15.4).[62]

---

[60] Cited in 'First Report from the Graduate Issues Committee', paper circulated from Education Policy Support, Dec. 2012.

[61] See pp. 573–4 this volume.

[62] For a brief account of women's rowing at Oxford, see Roger Hutchins, *Well-Rowed Magdalen: A History of Magdalen College Boat Club 1859–1993* (Oxford, 1993), pp. 101–12. Mixed colleges with large MCRs occasionally fielded postgraduate teams.

FIGURE 15.4 St Hilda's College First Eight, summer 1981. By 1980 women's races were a well-established part of Torpids and Eights. St Hilda's First Eight had won the Oriel Regatta in 1977; it was second on the river in 1981.

This did not mean that college life remained unchanged across the period. From the birth of the Oxford college in the thirteenth century, the chapel and its daily services had been its heart. That heart had begun to beat less strongly from the late nineteenth century but the chapel continued to be significant for the majority of students in the 1930s, even if attendance at roll-call several days of the week was preferred to morning prayers. After the 1950s, chapel attendance at any time of the day quickly became a minority preference. This largely reflected the growing retreat from organized religion among the wider population as well as Oxford's growing multi-confessional and multicultural intake. But in some colleges the decline was encouraged in the second half of the period by the character of the dean or chaplain. Many of the chaplains appointed from the 1970s were on the liberal or unorthodox wing of the Church of England. They made great efforts to get onto the wavelength of the young and some junior members warmed to them. Many practising Anglicans among the Christian rump, however, preferred to be ministered to by more traditional clergy, and the evangelicals in particular preferred to worship at St Aldate's. Typical of the new breed was the well-meaning and scholarly Timothy Gorringe, chaplain and tutor in theology at St John's 1986–95. Gorringe was an admirer of Karl Barth, liberation theology, and all things eastern. He included Mahatma Gandhi among the saints; the walls of his house were covered with batik Indian wall hangings; his children talked to each other in Tamil (he had spent a lot of time in Madurai, India); and lunch at his house was usually curry eaten with one's fingers while sitting on the floor. Inevitably, chapel attendance was

683

low. The Intercollegiate Christian Union was so incensed by Gorringe's theology that they banned members from attending his services.[63] What saved many college chapels towards the end of the period was the appointment, for the first time, of female chaplains, who, however academic, often seemed less alien than many of their male counterparts.

On the other hand, the college JCR (and the new MCR) took on a much greater importance in students' daily lives. Between the wars the JCRs in the male colleges were glorified gentlemen's clubs where the rich and idle gathered in the afternoons to take tea. This continued to be the case to a large extent in the 1950s, which led to many students from state schools feeling excluded. At Magdalen, the JCR steward, R. C. Bond, still had a private room where he served the student elite pre-prandial cocktails, just as 'Gunner' had done fifty years before.[64] By the late 1960s, however, the student common rooms in all colleges were much more inclusive and proactive under the influence of the contemporary youth revolution, social liberalization, and Oxford's broadening intake. In a way that was quite unprecedented, the JCRs in particular became an arena for collective agitation over student grievances and a platform for political activism. Bringing their members together socially, too, became a much greater part of the common rooms' remit. Besides taking over the organization of the traditional Commem balls, the common rooms put on regular, sometimes weekly, 'bops' and college events, and ran their own bar where junior members gathered to continue drinking after closing time. The first seems to have been Trinity's Beer Cellar, opened in summer 1967.[65] Towards the end of the period, the common rooms also did their best to integrate new students into the college on their arrival by organizing a host of activities in freshers' week.[66]

College societies equally became much more inclusive than hitherto. The sports clubs, especially the boat clubs, had always had an open door and welcomed anyone who showed an interest or modicum of talent. Many of the more intellectual societies between the wars, however, were closed and elitist: membership was by recommendation and election. Here, similarly, there was little change in the 1950s. When Mehta was at Balliol in the second half of the decade, he belonged to two prestigious academic societies. Both were closed and dominated by students from public schools. The Leonardo consisted of thirteen self-selected undergraduates who met on every second Friday to listen to papers on the arts or the sciences while drinking mulled claret; the Arnold and Brackenbury was the college debating

[63] Email communication, 6 Apr. 2014. Gorringe, author of several respected works of theology, moved on to be professor of theology at Exeter University.

[64] For 'Gunner', see p. 458, this volume. For afternoon tea in the Balliol JCR in the 1950s, see Mehta, *Up at Oxford*, pp. 130–1.

[65] For the politicization of the common rooms, see pp. 693–4, this volume. The smoking concerts of the Edwardian era seem to have died between the wars.

[66] Until the late 1980s, Oxford first years were plunged immediately into work on their arrival. This was felt too abrupt a transition, however, and, in common with other universities, freshers were given a whole week to settle in before they began their studies. Towards the end of the period, the common rooms also sought to put candidates who came up for interview in the annual admissions at their ease by organizing events in the evening.

society, limited to thirty members.[67] By the end of the period such elitism was no longer acceptable in an Oxford whose students were dedicated social egalitarians. Most colleges had far more student societies in 2015 than in 1945. Besides the drama and music clubs that had sprung up between the wars and continued to flourish, there were new ones devoted to film and the visual arts, and an increasing number of subject-specific societies for history, law, medicine, and so on.[68] All were open. Even the subject-specific societies encouraged students in different disciplines to attend. Usually only college dining and drinking societies remained closed, and they no longer had the status and stature of an earlier era. Although they survived into the twenty-first century, they were generally frowned upon by both junior and senior members, and many were clandestine and ephemeral.[69]

By the 1990s, the rhythm of student life was also not as predictable as it had been. The traditional structure of the student day still pertained: lectures in the morning, competitive sport in the afternoon, and society meetings in the evening. But there was no longer a moment or moments in the day when the college assembled en masse to parade its unity. Morning roll-calls ended with the war, and, from 1970, as was noted in section B, afternoon and evening ceased to be separated by compulsory hall. Indeed, many students towards the end of the period could no longer divide their day into distinct segments. Tutorials and university classes might be scheduled for any time in the afternoon, while so many crews sought to use the river that practice sessions were frequently held at first light before breakfast. The under-graduates' working year expanded as well. Although it was always expected that students would undertake further reading in the vacations,[70] it was understood that once the eight-week term was ended they were free to do as they liked. Rather than immerse themselves in private study, many from all backgrounds took on casual employment during the holidays, so that they could earn enough money to take advantage of the falling cost of foreign travel from the mid-1960s and see the world.[71] This remained possible in 2015, but with the introduction of assessed essays and theses in lieu of the traditional three-hour examination, academic work spilled over into the vacations. Future employers, too, expected recruits to have garnered some experience before they applied for a job. Many Oxford students after 2000 spent part of the long vacation of their second year as unpaid interns.

None of these developments, however, undermined the central role of the college in an Oxford student's life. In 2015, despite the huge expansion in the University's support services, it was still the college that was the student's first port of call when trouble struck. Each college at the close of the period had its own NHS doctor,

---

[67] Mehta, *Up at Oxford*, pp. 175–93 and 268. The Arnold and Brackenbury were originally two separate societies, the first more serious than the second in the topics discussed.

[68] Some subject-specific societies had a long history. Keble's history society, the Tenmantale, seems to have been founded with the college: email communication, 6 Apr. 2014.

[69] See pp. 691–2, this volume. Open societies in the period charged no subscription. Just like the sports clubs, they were funded through the college's amalgamated clubs, which received a small portion of the college fee.

[70] See p. 675, this volume.

[71] Before this only the rich undergraduates had been able to travel abroad in the summer.

offered an expanding range of welfare services on top of the tutorial system, and maintained a liberal hardship fund to look after students who had financial problems. Even where a student needed to access specialist services supplied by the University, the college acted as the conduit. As a result, college loyalties were as strong as ever, irrespective of the far greater standardization in teaching and facilities. As in the first half of the twentieth century, the colleges worked to cement this loyalty for life, all the more diligently in that they looked to old members far more than previously to fund new buildings and bursaries. By 2000, the colleges had entered an era of permanent 'giving', one fund-raising campaign running into the next. A college's old members therefore were assiduously cultivated. From the 1970s, if not before, the old members' associations set up at the end of the nineteenth century began to be professionally run, and colleges often anticipated the University in establishing their own development office.[72] Gaudies ceased to be the chief point of contact between the colleges and their former students. Frequent alumni events were organized in and outside Oxford, and each year old members received an ever larger college magazine detailing the history of their alma mater over the previous twelve months. Old members responded generously. The result was a spectacular rise in the endowments of most colleges and ambitious plans for the future. In 2004, Oriel, for instance, set out a long-term programme to double its endowment to £80 million by its 700th anniversary in 2026.[73]

The vibrancy and security of college life during the period meant that most students, undergraduates or postgraduates, quickly adapted to Oxford life, whatever their background and culture. Settling down at Oxford was never easy for foreigners. The novelist V. S. Naipaul, who came to University College from the Caribbean in 1950, was initially very lonely. Even the self-assured Rosa Ehrenreich, daughter of a New York columnist, confessed to being terrified.[74] Home students, too, could fail to adjust completely. Even once the youth revolution of the 1960s had greatly eroded the class differences between the young, there were always some junior members who found Oxford overwhelming and alienating and escaped from the University as fast as they could once term was over. A student survey in 1992–3 found that a staggering 40 per cent of undergraduates had contemplated quitting at one time or another, and, sadly, scarcely a year went by without one or two student suicides.[75] But the colleges created an environment in which most could flourish and one that was flexible enough to change with the times.

This was essential for the survival of the college as an idea. From the late 1960s, junior members arrived at Oxford with a novel belief in their own importance, a suspicion of authority, and eagerness to experiment with different lifestyles which had been largely denied them at home and school. Far from buckling under the pressure, the college system adapted to the new world with considerable success.

---

[72] See p. 631, this volume.
[73] For more on college wealth at the end of the period, see pp. 720–1, this volume.
[74] V. S. Naipaul, *Letters between a Father and a Son* (London, 1999); Ehrenreich, *Garden*, pp. 89 and 270.
[75] On suicide at Oxford, see the novel by Alan Judd, *The Noonday Devil* (Glasgow, 1988).

The new temptations and possibilities made student life everywhere far more complex and challenging than hitherto. The college offered junior members a non-judgemental environment in which they could enjoy and explore their new-found independence as long as they did not impede the liberty of others, and receive support when things went wrong. Students showed their appreciation. Whenever they could, the vast majority preferred to live in, and not just because rents were comparatively low. As a result, Oxford, along with Cambridge, always had a much smaller undergraduate dropout rate than other British universities. In 2010–11, it was only 1.5 per cent, a fifth of the national figure.[76]

E. A Revolution in Manners

The social and cultural changes of the 1960s and 1970s had a profound impact on junior members' day-to-day lives. It not only brought Oxford students a novel independence and gave students everywhere a sense of entitlement born of the belief that they were the custodians of progress, but it also spawned new forms of sociability. Although the differences between the first and second half of the period can be exaggerated, and there was always a significant minority who preferred to live in a manner reminiscent of earlier generations, there can be no doubt that the social life of the average junior member was transformed after 1970: sex became readily available, so too did recreational drugs, while students were finally liberated from the tyranny of college cooking.

Physical intimacy between junior members of the same or opposite sex had certainly not been absent from post-war Oxford. But contemporary mores and the college rules governing visitors and staying out overnight meant that there were limited opportunities for sexual encounters between men and women at least. Somervillians in the early 1960s were even discouraged from kissing their boy-friends goodbye outside the college gates. The huge gender imbalance until the 1970s also meant that, in many ways, Oxford remained a single-sex university, with women students scarcely intruding on the world of many men. Indeed, they often remained second-class citizens, allowed to participate in the most distinguished university societies but on men's terms. Margaret Thatcher might have become president of the Oxford University Conservative Association the year after the war, but the Union Society did not allow women to become full members until 1962 and OUDS was even slower to give women their due.[77] Everything changed from the late 1960s when the barriers against pre-marital intercourse were permanently pulled down with the advent of the pill and the spread of more relaxed attitudes to sex in society as a whole. Students' relationships with members of the opposite

---

[76] Hilary Baxter, 'Why Do So Many Students Drop Out of Higher Education?', OM, 2nd week, TT (2013), 11. Cambridge's figure was equally good.

[77] For one student's perception of sexual activity in late 1950s Oxford, see Mehta, *Up at Oxford*, pp. 219–20. For a nostalgic fictional account of women at Oxford in the early 1960s, see Caroline Seebohm, *The Last Romantics* (London, 1986).

sex became their own affair and colleges quickly withdrew from attempting to enforce the rules about overnight guests in rooms. Co-education barely affected the equation, for the revolution was already complete. It merely made it more likely that male students found partners among the female junior members and that many students settled into domestic bliss long before they went down. Same-sex relationships took longer to be treated with the same indifference, for many junior members, even in the 1970s, still found homosexuality a cause for ribald comment in private. But by the end of the 1980s there can have been few Oxford students who did not feel free to express their sexuality openly, whatever its nature. By the early 1990s, OUSU and most JCR committees not only had a woman's officer but also representatives for the lesbian, gay, bisexual, and transgender undergraduate communities.

The consumption of illegal substances, on the other hand, was a novel phenomenon. Male students had downed large quantities of alcohol for generations, and most students, male and female, had a nicotine habit in the 1950s and early 1960s.[78] But the wide variety of other narcotics and stimulants that had been consumed in Bohemian circles since the early nineteenth century began to make an appearance at Oxford only from the mid-1960s. Cannabis was always the most widely used substance, but there were also, from the beginning, much harder drugs in circulation, such as LSD and heroin. Drug-taking was a much thornier problem for the colleges to deal with because the substances were illegal and their abuse led to the occasional fatality. When the victims had a high profile, such as Olivia Channon of Christ Church, daughter of a government minister, who died of an overdose in 1986 only hours after finishing her finals, the press as well as the police became instantly involved.[79] Initially the colleges' reaction to anyone caught with drugs could be heavy-handed. Even cannabis-takers could end up being sent down for repeated offences. But from the 1970s it became usual to turn a blind eye unless drug-taking was affecting a student's academic performance or grossly upsetting others. It was only when students moved from being consumers to 'pushers' that the colleges felt forced to step in. In 1977–8, Magdalen swiftly closed down a drugs business that was found to be operating out of one of its student houses on the High Street.[80]

Eating out was equally a novel departure. Before the 1970s taking meals in the town would have been difficult, even if it had been encouraged. During and after the war, students had eked out the meagre college fare by filling up at the Lyons Corner House in the town. But by the 1960s there were still no restaurant in the city where a

---

[78] After the war women could also drink in college. Women's colleges dropped their ban on alcohol and allowed beer and cider at parties in the students' common rooms.

[79] Rosie Johnston, who bought the heroin at the dead girl's behest, became the centre of media attention. A second-year student at Manchester College at the time, she was eventually sent to prison for nine months. Darius Guppy, a friend of Channon, thought the sentence unjust: *Roll of the Dice*, p. 52.

[80] On the freedom to 'trip out' in the college ten years before, see Duncan Fallowell, 'Amazing Places' (typed MS), pp. 5–6. In 2015, hard drugs were not seen as an Oxford problem but there were fears about the abuse of modafinil and ritalin to aid concentration: *OT*, 15 May 2014, p. 29.

FIGURE 15.5 Doner kebab van, High Street, March 2015: 4 a.m. The decline of compulsory hall encouraged an explosion in the number of Oxford's ethnic restaurants. These, though, were usually outside the historic centre of the University. Immigrants from Turkey and the eastern Mediterranean realized that students wanting a quick meal at any time of the night would welcome the chance to purchase a snack on their doorstep. In the 1990s, licensed doner kebab vans appeared all over the city centre, much to the horror of many fellows.

student on a moderate budget could buy a decent meal.[81] The arrival in Oxford of immigrants from many different parts of the world, just at a time when compulsory hall was on the decline, revolutionized the gastronomic map. By the end of the period, there were countless ethnic restaurants the length and breadth of the city serving reasonable food at competitive prices, and the Cowley Road to the east of Magdalen Bridge had become Oxford's equivalent of Manchester's 'Curry Mile'.[82] Oxford's many pubs also took advantage of the potential student market and ceased to be purely drinking establishments. Furthermore, for those students seeking a quick snack in the evening and unconcerned about the quality of the offering, the city centre by the 1990s boasted a legion of fast food outlets. The most notorious and controversial were the ubiquitous doner kebab vans that nightly took up residence outside some of Oxford's most beautiful buildings, to the dismay of the dons and delight of junior members (see Figure 15.5). Purportedly the best at

---

[81] There had always been good restaurants in the city for those who could afford it. In the 1920s and early 1930s both the novelist Angus Wilson and the poet John Betjeman frequented the George, which was on the corner of George St and Cornmarket: *OT*, 21 Nov. 2013, p. 35. The affluent students of the post-war era ate out at the Capri and the Elizabeth outside Christ Church. In the late 1950s there was one Indian restaurant in Walton Street, the Bombay.

[82] There were purportedly 360 restaurants in Oxford in 2013.

the end of the period was Hassan's van in the Broad, which even parents found enticing:

> My daughter at Trinity recommended Hassan's. The other night we left a pub and went by a number of others but came back to Hassan's, a Trinity College tradition. Glad we did. I told server I loved lamb and would take his recommendation. Got big plate of shaved lamb with sauce over chips. Massive meal. Delicious and a great time.[83]

Conservative dons who lingered on into the second half of the period saw this new era of sociability as an age of dross. Yet it had an important positive side. Oxford students after 1970 were much more numerous than hitherto but they were less rowdy and destructive in college. After a bibulous evening in the 1950s, students often went on the rampage within the curtilage, just as they had between the wars. At Christ Church, the socially most exclusive college, young bloods continued to pride themselves on breaking as many windows in Peckwater Quadrangle as their fathers and grandfathers had done. At more cerebral Balliol the exclusive Annandale dining society would end the evening by urinating on the dividing wall with Trinity and singing anti-Trinity songs. But no college was exempt. Boat clubs were the worst offenders. Victory on the river was always the occasion for a celebration bump supper followed by a ritual boat-burning in which all the junior members took part and misrule was given its head. Dons frequently colluded in the mayhem. When Keble went head in the early 1960s, John Carey, the college's young English tutor, suggested that the bonfire's flames be fuelled with furniture from the college's main lecture room.[84]

In the second half of the period, incidents of collective student rowdiness were much reduced, if they never disappeared altogether. Throwing food at college dinner parties, even when senior members were present, remained a commonplace, to the annoyance of the staff who had to clean up the mess. Hurling insults at members of neighbouring colleges over the dividing wall similarly remained a regular occurrence. But such incidents were largely harmless rituals which lacked the venom and imagination of rags of an earlier period. The last truly coup de théâtre in the long-standing rivalry between Balliol and Trinity occurred in 1963 when Balliol students turfed the floor of the Trinity JCR and planted daffodils (see Figure 15.6).[85] Boat-burning too continued but the event became subject to the constraints of health and safety. After an incident in 1986, Oriel even imposed a ban on the traditional sport of leaping over the flames.[86] Where the old order

---

[83] <http://www.tripadvisor.co.uk/ShowUserReviews-g186361-d1316919-r161171964-Hassan_s_Kebab_Van-Oxford_Oxfordshire_England.html> (accessed 9 September 2015).

[84] Mehta, *Up at Oxford*, p. 2/1; Carey, *Unexpected Professor*, chs 6 and 7.

[85] Balliol students in the early 2000s would still sing anti-Trinity songs, often outside Trinity's main gate, whenever Balliol beat Trinity at sport, and after college bops: email communication, 7 Apr. 2014.

[86] Good order occasionally broke down. In 1990 University College held a bump supper to celebrate success on the river but Oriel students swiped the boat due to be burnt while the boat club was eating and the sacrifice

FIGURE 15.6 Trinity College's JCR planted with daffodils by Balliol students, 1963. Balliol's coup appears not to have been avenged. The feud between the two colleges continued into the new millennium. In 1996, Balliol's Harry Lime Society painted Trinity boathouse green in honour of Lime's creator, the Balliol alumnus Graham Greene.

survived in anything like its pre-war form was in the exclusive university and college dining societies. Although some were closed down, like Brasenose's Vampires, others continued periodically to trash restaurants and nightclubs as they had always done. The Bullingdon's nefarious activities were frequently in the news, as in December 2004 when its members raised Cain at the White Hart at Fyfield. But exclusive dining clubs were only for the extremely wealthy. Even in 1984, the cost of a Bullingdon Club dinner was £400 per head.[87]

The relative restraint of the second part of the period reflected a new age in which both junior and senior members no longer saw the college as a space apart with its own rules, some more restrictive, others more liberal, than the world outside. Student liberation inevitably put an end to student licence, except for a small minority who wanted to have their cake and eat it.[88] Co-education also cemented the change, for rowdiness, vulgarity, and excess had been a characteristic of the old

had to be 'liberated' by force: email communication, 2 Apr. 2014. Oriel still burnt a boat when it went head in 2015: OT, 18 June 2015, p. 31.

[87] OT, 10 Dec. 2004, p. 2; Guppy, *Roll the Dice*, pp. 40–3.

[88] It did not put an end to undergraduate drunkenness, however, which remained a perennial problem, especially in freshers' week, when first years, sometimes little used to drinking alcohol, overindulged. By 2015 it was agreed by junior and senior members that the amount of alcohol on offer at events sponsored by the JCRs and student societies would be limited.

male Oxford. Women in former men's colleges could certainly be just as childish as men. Christ Church in the early 1990s had an all-female drinking society called the Misdemeanours, where the members and their male guests, once suitably inebriated, would be given animal personae and required to crawl around the floor making suitable noises and looking for their opposite number to kiss. But female students by and large found such antics, whether initiated by men or women, demeaning and shallow and expected single-sex dining and drinking clubs to treat their invitees with respect. The college authorities agreed. A Keble all-male dining society was closed down in the early 1990s when a dinner was followed by a serious sexual assault on a female guest.[89] Indeed, the female students in most of the new mixed colleges proved remarkably adept at weaning their male peers off the chauvinistic culture of the past. Once admitted into the former male colleges, they were quickly elected onto the JCR and MCR committees where they used their power to get male students to see the world from a woman's point of view. Wadham feminists in the late 1980s even managed to get their male counterparts to accept that menstruation was a tool of masculine oppression: the college agreed to offer female students free sanitary products and divide the cost between all junior members.[90]

The new junior member of the late 1960s and 1970s was also a much more political animal. Oxford students in the post-war era were already politically more engaged than their pre-war counterparts. In 1959 it was estimated that just under a half were politically active. But most students expressed their views behind closed doors at the Union Society or the University's political clubs. The only time they took to the streets in any numbers in Oxford to protest against government policy was in 1956 over the invasion of Suez, when members of Ruskin College marched to the Martyrs Memorial, while running the gauntlet of Brasenose students who pelted them with tomatoes and sang Rule Britannia. It was thought rather bad form for students, still for the most part unable to vote, to take the initiative in publicly criticizing the government.[91] It was perfectly legitimate for students to join the Campaign for Nuclear Disarmament (CND), set up in 1957 by a number of clerics and academics, including A. J. P. Taylor, and take part in public protest organized by their seniors. It was quite another to go it alone.[92] When a special H-bomb issue of *Isis* was produced on 26 February 1958 outlining the case for unilateral nuclear disarmament, the British establishment was not amused. Two of the undergraduate

[89] Ehrenreich, *Garden*, pp. 157–70 and 228.

[90] Some male sports clubs still had a chauvinistic reputation at the end of the period. In October 2013, the Pembroke College Rugby Football Club was in trouble with the college authorities for circulating an email about an impending club function involving female freshers entitled 'Free Pussy'. *The Times*, 26 Oct. 2013, p. 5. The following month, a St Hugh's drinking society, The Black Cygnet, was condemned for organizing a 'fox hunt' with female students as 'prey': ibid., 15 Nov. 2013, p. 40.

[91] Ruskin's students of course were mature adults. The young ladies of Somerville more decorously passed a motion of no confidence in the government, which was relayed to the prime minister by telegram.

[92] The previous year several students in term time had travelled to Hungary with medical supplies for people caught up in the rising against the Soviets. They were rusticated or gated when they returned: Berlin, *Enlightening*, p. 552; copy of letter to Robin Darwall-Smith, 9 Aug. 2013; <http://www.independent.co.uk/life-style/> (accessed 18 September 2015).

contributors, William Miller and Paul Thompson, ended up being imprisoned for three months under the Official Secrets Act for writing about British intelligence operations on the Soviet borders. [93] The situation barely changed in the early 1960s with the first stirrings of the youth revolution.[94] Even as late as 1965, Oxford students expressed their disquiet over the escalating war in Vietnam by holding an eight-hour teach-in in the calm surroundings of the Union Society.[95]

By the late 1960s, in contrast, many Oxford students, like their brothers and sisters all over the western world, felt that it was their duty to make a stand against tyranny and exploitation both at home and abroad, targeting in particular America's role in the Vietnam War, South Africa under the apartheid regime, the treatment of Britain's miners, and the oppression of the catholic minority in Northern Ireland.[96] The most radical and messianic gained control of college JCRs and MCRs and normal domestic business began to be swamped by political debates, while university-wide street protests against government policy became a commonplace. The radicals also sought to impose their presence on their colleges. College buildings were rechristened and new mascots adopted: Wadham's back quad was renamed after Ho Chi Minh, while Balliol adopted a tortoise known as Rosa (after Rosa Luxemburg). Jesus students, on the other hand, showed their contempt of the college's governing body by electing a goldfish as JCR president and requiring the head of house, Sir John Habakkuk, to discuss student matters with their elected official through the assistance of a JCR interpreter.[97]

Individuals as well as issues were targeted. In the 1950s it would have been considered the height of impoliteness to attempt to prevent or disrupt a club meeting or social gathering on the grounds that the invited guest had unacceptable views. In the late 1960s and early 1970s not only politicians seen to be on the far right, such as Enoch Powell, but also middle-of-the-road government ministers, Labour and Conservative, found themselves spirited into buildings through howling mobs.[98] Even the prime minister was not exempt. When Balliol SCR invited Edward Heath, the college's former organ scholar, to dine in June 1971, students

---

[93] In a poll of the University's students in 1958 only 350 unequivocally supported the bomb.

[94] During the Cuban Missile Crisis of October 1962, barely 200 Oxford undergraduates attended a political rally protesting against a possible American invasion of the island.

[95] The Union Society was not afraid to court controversy on a wide variety of issues at this point in time. On 3 December 1964, a guest speaker at a debate on extremism in defence of liberty was the black American militant Malcolm X, who had been invited by the Union president, the Jamaican Eric Abrahams. A few months later the Union was addressed by another black civil-rights activist, James Baldwin. The invitation to Malcolm X was connected with a student campaign against racism aimed at university-approved landladies who refused to accept black lodgers: Stephen Tuck, *The Night Malcolm X Spoke at the Oxford Union: A Transatlantic Story of Antiracist Protests* (Berkeley, CA, 2014). In the same week Abrahams was asked to rule on the more trivial question of whether women might attend the pending Union ball in topless dresses: *OT*, 4 December 2014, p. 38.

[96] An undergraduate poll in 1968 showed 57 per cent favoured American withdrawal from Vietnam.

[97] Email communications, 4 and 7 Apr. 2014; *Proceedings of the British Academy*, 124 (2004), 107 (obituary of Habakkuk); *OT*, 23 July 2015, p. 28 (letter). Wadham students ended bops by crying 'Free Nelson Mandela'. Balliol's tortoise was last seen in 2004.

[98] Enoch Powell, a leading figure in the Tory party, became a hate figure on the country's campuses after his 'Rivers of Blood' speech in April 1968, when he prophesied that black immigration would lead to social breakdown.

inside and outside its walls took the opportunity to vent their spleen over the renewal of the Simonstown Agreement, which allowed the Royal Navy to use a base in South Africa. The night before the prime minister arrived, junior members painted obscenities on the plate-glass windows of the SCR and daubed graffiti on walls. When the fellows crossed the quad to dinner with their illustrious guest, fights broke out between protestors and officers from Special Branch who had been summoned by the dean to help police the expected protest. According to Balliol's master, Anthony Kenny, the prime minister himself was surprised by the strength of feeling: 'As we crossed the quad between the scufflers, I found myself next to Heath. "This is a new experience for us," I said, "but I expect you're quite used to this kind of thing." "Never seen anything like it before in my life," he replied.'[99]

Once OUSU was established, however, a lot of the heat and venom went out of student protest even if raucous demonstrations against the policies of the government of the day continued at regular intervals until the end of the period, resulting in university buildings on the route being occasionally closed for the afternoon to prevent their occupation.[100] From the mid-1970s, moreover, the left no longer had it all its own way, as conservatives and moderates began to put up candidates in college and OUSU elections and radicals no longer automatically dominated student committees.[101] A turning point in Magdalen came as early as December 1974 when the JCR debated the bombing of a Birmingham pub by the IRA the previous month. The undergraduates voted nem. con. to condemn the attack, but more significantly rejected a motion that the JCR throw their weight behind the campaign to remove British troops from Northern Ireland. Even a motion that a message of sympathy be sent to a leading CND activist, Pat Arrowsmith, imprisoned for inciting troops to disaffection, was narrowly defeated. By the 1980s there were strong signs that, in committee elections for OUSU and leading university clubs, college as much as political affiliation was determining voting loyalties. There was no lack of political commitment—throughout the decade female students were frequent visitors to the Women's Peace Camp established at Greenham Common in 1981 in protest against siting cruise missiles at the local RAF base. But few students any longer saw student protest as a vehicle for changing the world or believed that political activity should be placed before academic work. This remained the case at the close of the period. The only issue that could get large numbers of Oxford students out on the streets in the 2000s was one dear to their own hearts: the introduction of student fees.[102]

The relative depoliticization of student life from the 1990s was emphasized in how students chose to represent themselves in their college newsletters, which began

---

[99] Kenny, *Life*, pp. 54–5.

[100] Student protest could be intimidating in Oxford until the mid-1980s. Brian Harrison recalls the difficulty of attending seminars in All Souls run by Conservative politicians at the height of the confrontation between the miners and Margaret Thatcher.

[101] A poll in 1970 revealed that 37 per cent of Oxford's students supported Labour, 33 per cent the Tories, and 12 per cent the Liberals.

[102] Probably the last bastion of the hard left was Wadham's JCR (called, naturally, the Student Union), which only lost control in the mid-1980s.

to be published from the late 1960s. While, in the first half of the 1970s, the periodic JCR newsletter depicted junior members as deeply engaged with the world's problems, its successor, twenty years later, reduced student life to a depressing mix of sex and alcohol. Only drug-taking, for obvious reasons, was not alluded to. Valentine's Day issues were particularly scurrilous. St Hilda's relatively mild *Quadrangle* for February 1992 mainly comprised a first-years' guide to men and a gossip page by 'Bigmouth' aimed to titillate. This targeted inter alia 'a voracious Hildebeast' who had passed an innocent night with a man simply talking, then made up for the lapse the following week by being discovered in flagrante delicto with another 'in someone's front garden at 5 am'.[103] Admittedly *Cherwell* and *Isis*, the University student newspapers, remained serious purveyors of information and politically correct opinion across the period, but they too frequently slid into prurience. Among the articles posted on the *Cherwell* website at the beginning of Trinity Term 2013 were some topical pieces on the Vice-Chancellor's salary and a recent animal rights demonstration in Oxford. Accessed through the 'Lifestyle' button, on the other hand, was an article entitled 'Creaming Spires: Week 2', where the reader was offered an account of the art of foreplay under the suitable byline 'Penny Tration'.[104]

This new infantile image no more reflected the values and behaviour of the average Oxford student than the radical posturing of an earlier generation. In reality, Oxford men and women at the turn of the twenty-first century were no more hedonistic and self-centred than they had ever been. The expensive, glitzy, and loud biennial or triennial Commem balls were the most visible expression of the contemporary pleasure culture. But the fact that the profits, if any, went to charity was also evidence that Oxford student life was Janus-faced. Church- and chapel-going might have declined dramatically between the beginning and the end of the period, but many Oxford students, with or without religious belief, continued to commit time and energy to helping the poor and underprivileged in many different ways. The college missions atrophied between the wars but, by the end of the period, they had been replaced by a host of new initiatives usually pioneered by the students themselves. Many of these initiatives were focused on the local community but not all were narrowly based. In the mid-1990s, one enterprising group made repeated trips to Bosnia and other parts of the former Yugoslavia torn apart by ethnic conflict, bringing material aid to the victims and lightening their spirits with a performance of *A Midsummer Night's Dream* in mime.[105] The large majority of undergraduates, too, applied themselves much more diligently to their studies than

---

[103] PDF image received 8 Apr. 2014. In 2004, the Valentine's Day issue of Balliol's *John de Balliol* appeared under the tasteless title John de Labiall. Most of these publications were never archived but University College Library contains good runs of *Martlet Pie* and *Univoc*, the college newsletters from the 1970s and 1980s.

[104] <http://www.cherwell.org> (accessed 29 April 2013).

[105] Their initiative was applauded by senior members in contrast to the largely negative reception that greeted their predecessors who had taken medical aid to Hungary forty years earlier: see p. 692, n. 92, this volume.

hitherto. What was surprising about Oxford students at the end of the period was that they were ever able to commit so much time to sport, drama, music, and the Union Society when they were so conscientious about their academic work. Unfortunately, the persona of idleness and debauchery was so successfully adopted in these decades that outsiders were easily taken in. The sententious American Rosa Ehrenreich inevitably confounded image with reality. What appalled her about Oxford in the early 1990s was that her fellow students were unfeeling 'oiks', who 'seemed mired in apathy and indifference'. Harvard students dedicated themselves to community service. Oxford students enjoyed themselves at the taxpayers' expense and were uninterested in the plight of the poor.[106] She was completely deceived. The majority of Oxford students in her day, as in 2015, cared deeply both about their studies and the ills of the world, but they were not doctrinaire.

F. Careers

In the last twenty years of the period, most Oxford students worked extremely hard because they wanted to enter a career that would bring both intellectual satisfaction and financial reward. As late as the 1970s, it was sufficient to have been at Oxford to land a good job: in most careers, degree classification counted for little. By the end of the twentieth century, as the number of British graduates with good degrees rose substantially and employers could pick and choose, this was no longer the case. Most professions would not look at a graduate, even from Oxford, who had not gained an upper second. Putting extra-curricular activities before academic work and emerging with a gentleman or lady's third was no longer a wise option, regardless of the school an undergraduate hailed from. In courses in the humanities and the social sciences, the introduction of assessment by long essays and theses alongside traditional three-hour exams also meant it was no longer possible to scrape a reasonable degree by cramming hectically for the last few months before finals. The position was no different for postgraduates, especially those on taught courses, who were similarly put under much closer scrutiny than hitherto and forced to work to deadlines.

What happened to Oxford's undergraduates immediately on their going down is clearly documented across the period thanks to the annual surveys compiled by the Oxford Careers Service, which existed from 1960. These reveal that the students split into two distinct and relatively equal groups: those who immediately entered into paid employment and those who went on to further study. The first group found employment in a variety of careers. A small proportion of any annual cohort, no more than 7 or 8 per cent, went into the public sector and began work in central and local government and the NHS; others entered publishing and the different branches of the media or went straight into teaching in independent schools. But the largest number went into industry, commerce, or chartered accountancy, which

---

[106] Ehrenreich, *Garden*, pp. 191–6.

habitually absorbed 20 to 30 per cent of the total. The second group was divided between graduates who continued in academic study at either masters or doctoral level and those who began specific professional training for the bar, medicine, and teaching. The proportion in the first category slowly grew over the period. In the early 1960s, no more than 16 per cent of the total took their academic education to a higher level but by 2004 the figure had risen to more than a quarter.[107] The readiness of at least a third and sometimes a half of Oxford's graduates to continue in some sort of full-time training marked Oxford out from most other universities. Elsewhere, the large majority of graduates immediately entered the workforce, and the proportion remaining in higher education of some kind began to climb only in the final decades of the period, when the rapid expansion of the country's under-graduate population encouraged many students to gain an additional qualification in the hope that this might improve their job chances.[108]

The longer-term career orientation of Oxford's graduates cannot be quantified with the same precision, for this has been studied in depth only for the first half of the period. Between 1952 and 1967 about a third of male graduates eventually settled for a career in education, another third in industry or commerce, while the rest worked for the state or in the traditional professions of the church, law, and medicine. How far this distribution was replicated among both male and female graduates towards the end of the period is impossible to say.[109] A survey of Magdalen's alumni between 1968 and 1997 suggests that it changed as business and commerce lost ground to the traditional professions and the media. A third of Magdalenses continued to find a billet in some form of education, but only 20 per cent ended up in banking, business, chartered accountancy, and management consultancy, while nearly a third were lawyers and medics, and 10 per cent journalists or working in the wider media and the arts.

What is incontrovertible is that particular careers fell out of favour. Unsurprisingly, the decline of Britain's industrial base and the growing importance of finance and the new information technology were quickly reflected in the career choice of Oxford's graduates. As late as 1981, 10.9 per cent of Schools' candidates had gone straight into industry; by 1997 the percentage had nearly halved and far more were entering chartered accountancy and some form of banking (272 against 156).[110] It was the recruitment to secondary-school teaching, however, that suffered the most vertiginous fall as the profession lost status, opportunities for women broadened, and Oxford students increasingly saw their future as living and working in London. In 1946–52, between 15 and 20 per cent of Oxford male graduates, and probably more than 30 per cent of the female cohort, became schoolteachers. By the turn of

---

[107] Franks, ii. 191; Oxford University Careers Service, *Careers Review, 2004–2005* (Oxford, Dec. 2005), p. 6.

[108] Franks, ii. 191; Timothy Weston, *From Appointments to Careers: A History of the Oxford University Careers Service* (Oxford, 1994), pp. 190–1 (figs for 1971, 1981, 1991); *Careers Review, 2004–2005*, p. 5; Jonathan Black, 'It's Not All the City', OM, 0th week, MT (2013), 15–16 (latest figures).

[109] Oxford graduates today have, on average, three different employers in the first ten years after going down.

[110] Weston, *Careers*, p. 190; Oxford University Careers Service, *Report 1996–97* (Oxford, n.d.), p. 33.

the century the profession had completely lost its appeal. It was still holding up in 1971 when nearly 15 per cent of the year's graduates entered teacher training. Thereafter it collapsed. In 1997 only 2.3 per cent of Oxford graduates were attracted to the career, and even fewer in 2004. A large proportion of Oxford undergraduates still went into teaching eventually in the last decades of the period, but they were now almost entirely to be found in tertiary education.[111]

The fate of Oxford's postgraduates is even harder to determine accurately because so many came from overseas and the Careers Service has managed to log the initial destination of only 30 to 40 per cent. Obviously, the biggest employer of doctoral students was the educational sector, but towards the end of the period this absorbed no more than a half of those Oxford DPhils who immediately began paid work. The rest were scattered among a wide variety of professional and commercial careers. The two-thirds of master's students who took a job as soon as they went down similarly colonized a range of occupations, but in their case the largest group—as many as 60 per cent—found employment in industry and commerce, especially in management consultancy.[112] The one group of overseas students for which detailed information exists is the Rhodes scholars. Interestingly, for all the hopes of the founder of the scheme that its beneficiaries would dedicate their lives to government service, their career choices closely mirrored those of Oxford's undergraduates. Between 1951 and 1997, 32 per cent went into education, 20 per cent into law, 15 per cent into business, and only 10 per cent ended up serving the state.[113]

There was nothing exceptional in the career orientation of Oxford's alumni across the period. A similar range of occupations was filled by graduates from all British universities and the changing emphasis was reflected everywhere. Any differences from the national norm were differences of degree. There were always some careers, such as the higher ranks of the civil service, law, or accountancy, that recruited a disproportionate number of Oxford students.[114] But where careers rose or fell in popularity across the period, Oxford closely followed the secular trend. Over the years 1971 to 1991, a lower proportion of Oxford graduates went into industry than the national average and a higher proportion into commerce, but in both cases the changes in the respective popularity of these careers across the two decades was a national not simply an Oxford phenomenon. In the first case, entrants from all universities declined by 50 per cent; in the second, they rose threefold to a high point in 1987 before falling rapidly with the onset of the

---

[111] Weston, *Careers*, pp. 190–1 and 193 (graph); *Report 1996–97*, p. 33; *Careers Review, 2004–2005*, p. 6. At the end of the period, intake into secondary-school teaching recovered a little with the introduction of Teach First, a scheme that allowed graduates to go straight into teaching in inner-city areas without a PGCE. Oxford had ninety entrants to the scheme in 2012, about 3 per cent of the cohort. This was roughly the same number who began a PGCE. Figures for 2009–11 also reveal that a further 5 per cent of the cohort went directly into academia or education: this would have included those who took up administrative or clerical positions as well as a group who chose to teach in the independent sector where a teaching diploma was similarly not required: Black, 'It's Not All the City', p. 215; Black, email communication, 10 Sept. 2014.

[112] *Careers Review, 2004–2005*, pp. 8–9.

[113] Thomas J. Schaeper, *Cowboys into Gentlemen: Rhodes Scholars, Oxford, and the Creation of an American Elite* (New York, 1998), ch. 14, esp. p. 279 (table 2).

[114] As many as 10 per cent of Schools candidates entered the law in 1997, more than double the national rate.

recession in the late 1980s and early 1990s. Similarly, Oxford's desertion of school teaching was not greatly out of line with national trends before the second half of the 1990s. Twenty per cent of British graduates in 1971 started a PGCE on finishing their course; this figure was down to 5 per cent in 1991; then rose to some 8 per cent at the turn of the millennium.[115]

Where Oxford's alumni were exceptional was in the disproportionately large number who, in later life, reached the top of the career ladder or came to national prominence in the fields of the arts and politics.[116] The high flyers were always a minority of the University's graduates but they pervaded virtually every area of national life. Despite the massive expansion of higher education in Britain in the second half of the twentieth century, Oxford lost none of its traditional pre-eminence in the British establishment, continuing to produce an extraordinary number of learned academics, vice-chancellors, permanent secretaries, high court judges, successful writers, MPs, and government ministers.

Oxford's contribution to the literary arts was greater than it had ever been. The University's alumni had always played an important part in English literary culture. From Oriel's Sir Walter Raleigh through University's Shelley and Balliol's Matthew Arnold to Merton's T. S. Eliot and Christ Church's Auden, Oxford had produced a succession of the nation's leading poets. But before the Second World War it had educated few novelists or playwrights of note. The Victorian novel was largely the creation of men and women who had not passed through any university. The emergence of Evelyn Waugh and Graham Greene in the interwar years suggested the dearth was about to end, but no one could have anticipated the extent to which Oxford graduates, several of them dons, such as St Anne's Iris Murdoch, came to dominate the English novel in the second half of the twentieth century.[117] Only William Golding (at Brasenose before the war) and Naipaul gained the Nobel Prize for Literature during the period, but Oxonians repeatedly carried off lesser literary awards.[118] Oxford's alumni excelled at all literary genres. Philip Larkin of St John's headed a galaxy of Oxford post-war poets;[119] Tolkien virtually invented the fantasy quest; miner's son Dennis Potter, up at New College in the mid-1950s, was a pioneer of serious TV drama;[120] the members of Beyond the Fringe and Monty Python (albeit creations in which Cambridge shared equal billing) revolutionized

---

[115] Weston, *Careers*, pp. 192–7 (graphs); *Report 1996–97*, p. 22. Nationally, of course, given the huge expansion in undergraduate education since 1990, the number of graduates taking a PGCE remained stable; among Oxford graduates, the number plummeted.

[116] Of the 2,318 graduates of 20 UK universities who could be classed as extremely rich, 401 had been at Oxford: *OT*, 2 May 2013, p. 28.

[117] Murdoch was a philosophy fellow at St Anne's.

[118] Not all the best British novelists in the second half of the twentieth century went to Oxford but a considerable proportion did. Ian McEwan was at Sussex and several were the products of the University of East Anglia's creative writing course set up by Malcolm Bradbury.

[119] The University's third Nobel literary laureate, Seamus Heaney, cannot be legitimately claimed as an Oxford poet. He was professor of poetry, 1989–94, but never studied at the University.

[120] His plays included *Stand Up, Nigel Barton!* (BBC, 1965), a critical account of a working-class student's time at Oxford.

satirical comedy;[121] while Jeffrey Archer, who entered Brasenose to study for a diploma in education in 1963, demonstrated that Oxonians could write best-selling page-turners.[122]

Oxford's dominance on the political stage was just as extraordinary. Given that, by the end of the period, the University educated only a tiny proportion of the country's students, the number of Oxonians in government ought to have fallen rapidly after the mid-1970s when politicians educated before the war quit the scene. But this was not the case. Besides being the alma mater of three prime ministers in the second half of the period—Margaret Thatcher, Tony Blair, and David Cameron—Oxford was also the breeding ground for scores of cabinet ministers. In the Cameron coalition government, which came to power in 2010, five were drawn from Magdalen alone, including the chancellor of the exchequer, foreign secretary, and attorney general.[123] The House of Commons similarly continued to be dominated by Oxonians. Of the 650 or so MPs elected in 1992, 118 had been educated on the Isis and eighty-three on the Cam, compared with sixteen at Glasgow, and fourteen at Edinburgh and London. In 2005 nothing had changed, except the colour of the majority party, which was now red rather than blue. A total of 108 MPs were Oxford men and women, fifty-one Tories, forty-three Labour, and the rest Liberal Democrats. Virtually every Oxford college had a representative, even newcomers like Mansfield, where the Rhondda's MP, Chris Bryant, had been a student.[124] In contrast with earlier ages, moreover, Oxford's influence extended far beyond the British establishment. Besides populating the anglophone world with academics, as had already begun to happen in the first part of the twentieth century, post-war Oxford also played a part in educating many of its leaders. Since 1960 Oxford has produced prime ministers for India, Pakistan, Canada, and Australia, and, most famously, in William Jefferson Clinton, who came to University College in 1968 as a Rhodes scholar, a president of the United States. Clinton retained fond memories of his Oxford days and packed his government with Oxonians, including secretary of labour Robert Reich, assistant secretary of state for African affairs Susan Rice, and the roving ambassador Strobe Talbott.[125]

Some commentators towards the end of the period found the continued dominance in public life of Oxford and, to a smaller extent, Cambridge, despite all the social and cultural changes of the second half of the twentieth century, an affront to democracy and meritocracy. It was deemed a conspiracy whereby Oxbridge insiders

---

[121] The Oxford members of *Beyond the Fringe* were Exeter's Alan Bennett and Magdalen's Dudley Moore. Bennett went on to be a prolific writer for the stage and TV. The Oxford Pythons were Brasenose's Michael Palin and St Edmund Hall's Terry Jones.

[122] Oxford produced important children's authors, too, notably C. S. Lewis in the 1950s and Exeter's Philip Pullman in the 1990s. Their works contain diametrically opposite views on traditional Christianity. Oxonians contributed much less to the other arts but the University nursed several members of successful pop groups.

[123] This was an uncommon privilege for Magdalen, not known for producing cabinet ministers.

[124] *The Times*, 11 Apr. 1997, p. 17; Oxford University Society email, 12 May 2005, to members of the University: 'General Election May 2005: Public Affairs Overview'.

[125] All three were Rhodes scholars: Rice was at New College, Talbot at Magdalen, and Reich at University College.

at the top of the British establishment deliberately selected and nurtured their successors from their old universities and ignored the talent raised in other universities, to the detriment of national efficiency.[126] Defenders of the ancient universities disagreed. As the two universities at the end of the twentieth century were taking the cream of the nation's students, it was both inevitable and just that they should continue to garner the glittering prizes.

Both parties could muster strong arguments in support of their point of view. An Oxford degree definitely gave the University's graduates a head start in life. While Oxford graduates entered the same kinds of professional employment as their peers from other universities, they tended to be taken on by the very best firms and practices in London, which made it that much easier for the high-flying and ambitious to reach the top. They also did suspiciously well in competitive examinations for entry to government service: in 1993–4, a typical year, Oxford supplied 5 per cent of the applicants but took 20 per cent of the places.[127] On the other hand, the advantages an Oxford degree brought could not simply be put down to the University's long-standing connections with the establishment. As universities awarded more and more first-class degrees in the final decades of the period, the currency became devalued. In the eyes of employers, only a handful of universities, in particular Oxford and Cambridge where a good degree was seen as the result of hard work and rigorous examination, were felt to offer solid coin.

The Labour government that won power in 1997 accepted the accusations of 'cronyism' levelled against Oxford and Cambridge and vowed to reduce their influence in the top professions and the civil service by positive discrimination if necessary. In the event, the rhetoric was not matched by action. What was never commissioned was a study of the beneficiaries of the old universities' undoubted influence to see if there was a clear-cut relationship between family wealth and position and an undergraduate's future career. Oxford, in the final decades of the period, drew its undergraduates from a wide cross-section of British society. Few may have come from families with no experience of university education but a significant group came from households with a relatively low income. Were Oxford entrants to the top stream in the civil service and the best legal and financial firms drawn indiscriminately from all sections of the University's undergraduate community, there would have been limited grounds for complaint. Oxford students might have had a distinctive edge over their competitors in the jobs market but the University's connections and historic image could be seen as a positive force for social mobility in ensuring that clever students from poorer backgrounds had no trouble gaining the recognition in the workplace that their talents deserved. Conversely, if the beneficiaries of the 'old-boy' (or 'girl') network were the sons and daughters of parents already firmly implanted in the British establishment, Oxford

---

[126] Walter Ellis, *The Oxbridge Conspiracy: How the Ancient Universities Have Kept their Stranglehold on the Establishment* (London, 1994).

[127] *The Times*, 25 Sept. 1994, p. 3.

was guilty as charged. The University's influence at the end of the period was working, as it had largely always done, to sustain the status quo. All the University was doing was validating that the establishment's offspring had the intellectual capacity to inherit their place in the sun.

As no statistical study of the background of the beneficiaries was undertaken, the reality remains unknown. Anecdotal evidence, however, suggests that, in the final decades of the period, family wealth and career choice were not unconnected. As the status and income of Oxford dons declined in comparison with the top professions, few Oxford graduates from affluent families, male or female, were tempted to register for a DPhil.

G. The Dons

The creation of the joint-appointment scheme after the Second World War gave most dons a novel financial security. Once all tutors had lectureships, few were bedevilled with the money worries that had beset Murray Wrong.[128] Oxford dons in the post-war era were never in clover. Only the very richest, like Lindemann, who remained in charge of the Clarendon until 1956, could afford servants, and many were delighted when they could buy a refrigerator.[129] But Oxford academics were paid more than their peers in the university sector and their salaries easily kept abreast of the modest inflation of the 1950s and early 1960s. Moreover, there were plenty of ways of earning a little extra, especially examining in Schools, which supposedly brought in enough to buy a motor car. As a result, more and more dons took advantage of the relatively low cost of housing in the 1950s and 1960s to marry early and move out of college. By the time of Franks, only a quarter of Oxford's tutors and 5 per cent of professors, readers, and other fellows lived in, while 58 per cent of the University's academic staff lived more than a mile away from the city centre and 17 per cent outside Oxford altogether.[130] The move to the suburbs had an inevitable effect on traditional commensality. Most dons left their workplace in the early evenings to return to the family hearth and attended only dinner and dessert a few nights each week. The custom of dining in hall had so far declined by the end of the 1950s that most colleges instituted a communal lunch where tutors especially could meet each day to discuss matters of common concern.[131]

On the other hand, the continuities with the interwar period remained strong and the Second World War only temporarily altered the rhythms of college life. For

---

[128] See pp. 472−3, this volume.

[129] Cf. the reminiscences of Beatrix Walsh, wife of a Merton philosophy tutor, who lived at 6 Merton Street from 1950 to 1960: OM, 2nd week, MT (1997), 5−8. She did employ au pairs.

[130] Franks, ii. 394−5. In women's colleges 50 per cent of tutors lived in. Some married fellows lived in college housing but this could be of indifferent quality. Cf. John Carey's description of the difference between the accommodation provided by Keble (appalling) and St John's (luxurious) in the first half of the 1960s: Carey, *Unexpected Professor*, chs 6 and 7.

[131] This was helped by the fact that the Oxford colleges persuaded the Inland Revenue to accept that fellows could take two meals a day free of charge; at Cambridge it was usually only one.

senior members, whether they lived in or out, the college as a society and place of work was a peculiarly privileged milieu, all the more precious in that it was piece of old England that was fast disappearing. The English country house was dying under the weight of post-war taxation and the lack of staff. But in the Oxford male colleges staircase scouts were still on hand to run errands, the staff treated the dons like demi-gods, and the fellows called each other by surname. Dinner in hall continued to be a particularly heady brew of tradition, formality, and luxury that few, even on the left in politics, could resist. Fellows sometimes sat in order of election; black tie was frequently worn; guests of the opposite sex were frowned upon, and only very occasionally permitted; and the courses were lavish and the drink good. As there was little pressure to publish or perish and the amount of administration remained fairly light, most dons had little objection either to the less glamorous demands of college life and willingly took their turn sitting on college committees and holding college offices. Understandably, there was little job dissatisfaction. For most dons, the 1950s and early 1960s were a golden age.

In the twenty years following the Second World War, too, most dons continued as before to see senior and junior members as parts of a single college family and felt it their duty to introduce their pupils to life as well as study. If some limited their relationship with junior members to a weekly academic encounter, albeit enlivened with sherry, the majority, especially those who lived in, went out of their way to take the young under their wing. Undergraduates were encouraged to talk about themselves in tutorials; tutorial drinks parties and luncheons were commonplace; reading parties continued to be organized in the summer months; and most heads of house made an effort to know every student individually. Keble's warden in the 1960s, Austin Farrer, was particularly well informed: 'Farrer had this extraordinary capacity of making you feel that he knew everything about you. I was told, and witnessed at first hand, that this was partly because he spent at least an hour in prayer in the chapel each morning, partly with cards of every undergraduate in front of him, praying for us, each and every one.'[132] Heads of house, and not just the younger fellows, were also usually happy to see their charges letting off steam. Oriel's long-serving provost, Kenneth Turpin, liked nothing better than a good food fight in hall. Not surprisingly, students of the era mostly remembered the dons whom they encountered with great affection. It made little difference whether the tutorial teaching was particularly illuminating.

But there was a darker side to post-war fraternization, probably more than had been the case in earlier periods. Dons seldom treated junior members equally. If the hand of friendship was extended to all, a minority were given special treatment. Dons had their favourites and many undergraduates felt left out in the cold. Heads of house could be the worst offenders. Maurice Bowra of Wadham would invite small groups of freshmen in turn to dinner in the lodgings where they would be treated to his sparkling conversation and regaled at length on the centrality of

---

[132] Email communication, 14 Apr. 2014.

poetry and the other arts to the maintenance of a civilized society. For the majority this was the one and only occasion they were given to sit at the feet of the great man. Only the few who responded positively to his wit and aesthetic enthusiasms were picked out as tyro 'Bowristas' and invited back for more.[133] Magdalen's Tom Boase, a historian of art by background, was just as selective. He prided himself in taking every undergraduate on an outing once during their stay. But he sized up the student in advance and the nature of the treat was determined by an individual's perceived artistic sensibilities. Sensitive souls had a night at the opera; philistines were taken to the circus. There appears to have been little agreement either of how close a friendship between a senior and junior member could legitimately go. It is hard to believe that there were not instances of male dons who slept with their male pupils, yet none so far has publicly surfaced. Canon John Kelly, principal of St Edmund Hall from 1951 to 1979, was famously fond of young sportsmen but probably never did more than put a hand on a firm thigh.[134] Female students, on the other hand, definitely had sexual relationships with male bachelor dons, and some treated it as an inevitable rite of passage.[135]

From the mid-1960s, this cosy, incestuous, and slightly sinister world began to fall apart. The youth revolution bred a generation of students who were highly suspicious of cross-generational relationships and largely shied away from socializing with their tutors and other dons. Older tutors continued to invite their charges to lunch or supper parties at their own homes but younger fellows, who were themselves the children of '68, were usually far more reticent. By the 1980s, most students found such occasions, however well intentioned, embarrassing. Co-education only further encouraged dons and students to go their separate ways. In the second half of the period tutors were anxious to treat all of their pupils even-handedly. 'Favouritism', like any other form of special treatment, was now heavily frowned upon. As most married male tutors were understandably wary of getting too close to their female students, they felt they had to keep the same distance with their male charges.[136]

The new puritanism of the last decades of the period virtually put the lid on all unofficial intercourse between dons and students. The University and the colleges drew up codes of conduct that defined almost any form of unsolicited human contact as harassment and encouraged victims to complain. Physical intimacy

---

[133] Leslie Mitchell, *Maurice Bowra: A Life* (Oxford, 2009), p. 248.

[134] <http://www.oxfordtimes.co.uk/news/gray_matter/4295343.Kelly_s_eye_for_the_handsome_headmaster> [OT, 16 Apr. 2009] (accessed 11 September 2015). There is evidence from surviving letters at present closed to the public that at least one homosexual don in the 1950s and early 1960s fantasized about his male pupils in graphic detail, but whether he slept with any of them remains a mystery.

[135] Married dons could also not always keep their hands to themselves. In the 1940s, Fraenkel continually harassed his female pupils, whom he insisted on taking singly in the evenings: John Stray, paper to the Oxford Philological Society, 28 Feb. 2014.

[136] Co-education also diminished the tutors' pastoral role as women students were usually unwilling to talk to male tutors about their personal problems. Initially, in the absence of female fellows, the wives of college heads stepped into the pastoral breach, but they usually belonged to an older generation and had limited understanding of young women raised on Germaine Greer and *Cosmopolitan*.

between junior and senior members was considered totally inappropriate. Where, even in the late 1980s, the ageing college Lothario could still ply his trade with relative impunity, by the end of the period a snatched peck on the cheek in a public bar could send a senior member on his way to early retirement, the hounds of the student press baying at his ears. Heads of house and deans continued to entertain junior members in groups, and tutors always said an official farewell to their tutees with a schools dinner. But, apart from college societies where junior and senior members sometimes mixed, there were few other forms of social fraternization. Undergraduates and postgraduates retained fond memories of their tutors and supervisors and were hugely appreciative in the main for the help and encouragement they had received in their academic work, but very few became friends for life with a senior member.

The life of Oxford dons towards the end of the period was also less comfortable than at the beginning. From the end of the 1970s, Oxford salaries, like academic salaries everywhere, if roughly keeping pace with inflation, steadily fell behind those of comparable professional groups supported by the state, such as top civil servants and judges. While the country overall got considerably richer in the twenty-five years prior to the 2008 financial crash, the pay of university teachers marked time. Between 1981–2 and 1998–9 the real earnings of a university lecturer in Britain rose by 1.1 per cent; average earnings by 36.6 per cent. Within Oxford too divisions began to open up. After the war, age-related salary scales were drawn up for professors, readers, and tutors and lecturers, which established a pay differential between the professoriate and other senior dons but not a substantial one. The pay scales reflected the fact that Oxford was a democratic not a hierarchical university. From the late 1980s, however, the scales began to be eroded.

Medics had always had been paid separately. By the end of the period, this was also true of the academic staff of the Business School who inhabited a universe of their own, while many statutory professors were receiving considerable ad hominem payments in addition to their ordinary pay in recognition of their stellar contributions to research. The tutors' and lecturers' scale held fast but it ceased to be age-related, and many dons in their thirties were appointed at the topmost point. Great differences, too, developed between the colleges.[137] It was the custom to pay tutors who lived out a housing allowance in lieu of their right to free board and lodging in college. Initially this had been modest but, in the second half of the period, it began to be used by the richer colleges as a way of increasing tutorial salaries. According to the North Report, the housing allowance a tutor received in the mid-1990s varied between £2,000 and £8,000.[138] By 2013, the variation was much less—the range went from £5,300 to £12,750—but was just as wide when a

---

[137] The system of merit pay was forced on Oxford and other universities by the government in 1987. By 1999, 140 of Oxford's 180 statutory professors were receiving merit pay: 'Reward', OM, 8th week, HT (1999), 1. On pay scales and merit pay, see p. 622, this volume.

[138] North, pp. 227–31.

large number of other benefits, such as research allowances, health care, and gym membership were added in. At the end of the period, a tutor and lecturer's combined salary at the top of the scale was £60,000. In addition, the lowest remunerated tutors received an extra £6,670; the best £21,910.[139] Oxford's Vice-Chancellor meanwhile had joined the country's financial elite. When Colin Lucas occupied the position in 1997, he was one of the lowest paid university chief executives in the country, earning some £100,000 a year. Andrew Hamilton in 2013, in contrast, enjoyed a salary of £330,000, which, with pension and other benefits, was the equivalent of £424,000, and Oxford had leaped to the head of the ladder.[140] The result was growing resentment and jealousy. Tutors in the poorer colleges understandably felt aggrieved. The cost of housing was a particular problem. As the city was constrained from further expansion by its green belt, and a growing proportion of its residents were London commuters, the price of property rose faster than the national average. From the mid-1980s, only dons with high-earning partners or an independent income could afford to live in Oxford, and most newly appointed postholders with young children were forced to settle in modest houses beyond the ring road and build a social life outside the University.[141]

The attack on pension rights that began in 2008 at the time of the financial crash only lowered morale further. University teachers from the late 1970s had been part of a typical public-sector inflation-proofed final-salary pension scheme which ensured academics would retire in reasonable comfort. In 2008, however, the Universities Superannuation Scheme began a round of consultations which aimed to reduce the rising costs caused by increased longevity by raising employee contributions and introducing a potentially less lucrative pension entitlement based on career average earnings for new entrants. Congregation expressed its opposition both in a debate in the Sheldonian on 30 November 2010 and in the subsequent ballot. But the final-salary scheme was closed to newcomers in the following years, and from April 2016 a completely new pension scheme was introduced for all academic staff, ensuring old age could no longer be entertained with the same equanimity.[142] The University itself did not help matters. Compulsory retirement at 65 was abolished by the state from October 2011 and employees had the right to continue in work as long as they were capable of doing the job. Potentially, then, academics could mitigate any adverse changes to their pension entitlement by staying in post. The

---

[139] 'Review of Fellows' Allowances and Joint Equity Scheme: Allowances − Mixed Colleges Only' (attached table): Magdalen College, Bursarial Committee Papers, 1 May 2013.

[140] *OT*, 18 Apr. 2013, p. 7.

[141] Their lifestyle too was totally different from their better-off colleagues', whose younger children, as in pre-war days, continued to be looked after by nannies, albeit usually in a share scheme with other families. The number of dons living some distance from Oxford only further reduced dining in: male dons who, before the war, would have dined in most evenings in term and given tutorials afterwards were now expected to help with the chores and children in the evening.

[142] From 2016 benefits accrued under the final-salary scheme were frozen until retirement (though still inflation-proofed) and a new two-section scheme set up to which academics contributed a higher proportion of their salary than hitherto. The first section was an average-earnings scheme under which benefits were accrued salaries of up to £55,000 (subject to annual adjustment in line with inflation); the second was akin to a private pension scheme where a portion of a member's salary over £55,000 was paid into a pension pot and invested. 'Report of Proceedings in Congregation 30 Nov. 2010', *OUG*, supplement (1) to no. 4937 (8 Dec. 2010); USS, 'Changes to USS—an update', document circulated to members, 17 Aug. 2015.

University concluded, however, that allowing male academics to hang on to their jobs for ever would make it difficult to increase the representation of women and ethnic minorities. Along with Cambridge, Oxford sought and was granted an opt-out from the law, so that it could introduce a compulsory retirement age of 67.[143]

Not all the changes to the dons' pay and conditions could be blamed on the Conservative governments of Thatcher and Major, but it was the Conservatives who bore the brunt of their ire. In the immediate post-war era, Oxford and Cambridge academics had been fairly evenly split in their political affiliations. At the time of Suez, some 370 senior members of the University, including professors and heads of house, strongly signalled their opposition to the government's action.[144] But there were plenty of dons who supported the invasion. Somerville's fellows were so divided over the affair that it was never mentioned within the confines of the SCR. Little had changed by the mid-1960s. Prior to the general election of 1964, 38 per cent of Oxbridge teachers supported the Conservatives, 40 per cent Labour, and 15 per cent the Liberals. By 1989, after ten years of the Thatcher government and its crusade to reduce the Higher-Education Bill, support for the Conservatives had collapsed to 15 per cent, lower even than in the other universities and the polytechnics.[145] Oxford showed how far the pendulum had swung as early as January 1985 when Congregation voted, by 738 votes to 319, to reject Council's motion that the prime minister, an old member of Somerville, be awarded an honorary degree as custom demanded. The move was a deliberate snub and reflected widespread disenchantment with the government's policies on education and science. Even supporters held their nose when they voted in favour.[146] Thereafter, the Conservatives' position among the dons never recovered. The growing intervention of the state in the University's affairs after 1990 only confirmed the negative impression. The Conservatives seemed to wish to turn Oxford into an instrument of economic growth and reduce the dons to minor civil servants. Not that the Labour party benefited greatly as a result. Since the Blair and Brown governments at the end of the period adopted the same utilitarian and dirigiste approach to higher education and were scarcely more generous, most dons fell into the arms of the Liberal Democrats, the one major party before 2010 that had no experience of office in the modern era and was consequently happy to sympathize with the dons' feelings of injured *amour-propre*.

Yet if being an Oxford don at the end of the period was not what it once was, it remained an enviable existence. Tutors had pleasant rooms to teach in. The intellectual calibre of undergraduates was very high, and relations between students and dons, if more distant, remained amicable. Above all, every don was still part of a

---

[143] 'Consultation on Maintaining an Employer Justified Retirement Age on the Abolition of the Default Retirement Age: Communication from the Personnel Committee': document circulated Apr. 2011. Conf/11/O4. Most older academics already had the contractual right to retire at 67.

[144] *OT*, 9 Nov. 1956, p. 7.

[145] A. H. Halsey, *Decline of Donnish Dominion: The British Academic Profession in the Twentieth Century* (Oxford, 1992), p. 237.

[146] Kenny, *Life*, ch. 17 (an account by a member of Council); *OT*, 11 Apr. 2013, pp. 4–5 (a retrospective); *OT*, 2 May 2013, p. 32 (letter from Professor Denis Noble, who took the lead in opposing the honorary degree). Two foreign politicians had been rejected for an honorary degree in the 1970s: *OT*, 18 Apr. 2013, p. 33 (letter by Professor Raoul Franklin).

small self-governing college community with its own special identity. For most academics, the privilege and responsibility of belonging to an Oxford college was more than compensation for falling salaries and government interference. No two colleges had exactly the same form of governance; no two colleges had exactly the same internal feuds; none was alike in its dining arrangements; and all had their idiosyncratic traditions and customs. Through regularly coming together at lunch and in college meetings, and taking part in annual rituals and feasts, college fellows developed a shared identity that transcended their many differences and, in the case of the older colleges, forged a bond between the present generation and its predecessors that the pace of change in the post-industrial world could not dissolve. The Britain of 1900 and 2000 were light years apart but All Souls, the most idiosyncratic of all Oxford colleges in still having no students, had no hesitation at the beginning of 2001 in holding its centennial ritual of 'hunting the mallard' to commemorate a wild duck that was purportedly disturbed by builders excavating the front quadrangle in the 1440s and adopted as the college emblem. After a sumptuous dinner on Sunday 14 January, 118 fellows and past fellows paraded around the college behind 'Lord Mallard', the classics don Dr Martin West, who was carrying a wooden duck on a pole and singing the Mallard song:

> The Griffin, Bustard, Turkey and Capon
> Let other hungry mortals gape on,
> And on their bones with stomach fall hard,
> But lett All Souls men have their Mallard.
> *O by the blood of King Edward,*
> *O by the blood of King Edward,*
> *It was a swapping, swapping Mallard!* (See Figure 15.7.)[147]

The words and refrain were ridiculous and the event childish. But it caught precisely why the majority of Oxford dons remained, until the end of the period, largely satisfied with their lot and unwilling to move on, for all the relative deterioration in their social and financial position.[148]

H. Town and Gown

Besides being members of the University and a college or hall, Oxford dons and students also belonged to the wider community of the city. In some respects, the interdependence of town and gown in this final period diminished. The huge reduction in the number of staircase scouts and the disappearance of the college landlady as living out was deregulated meant that, by the end of the period, few junior members established close relations with Oxford citizens any longer, unless

---

[147] *Daily Telegraph*, 15 Jan. 2001, p. 3.
[148] Most of the old colleges have an annual foundationers' dinner which links past and present. Queen's has several, including the Needle and Thread dinner, usually held on New Year's Day, where 'each guest is handed a needle and thread and told: "Take this and be thrifty"': *OT*, 2 Jan. 2014, p. 33.

FIGURE 15.7 'Hunting the Mallard', All Souls, 2001. The rowdy centennial commemoration of the discovery of a wild duck while the college was being built in the mid-fifteenth century exemplifies Oxford's ability to compromise with the present while remaining true to the past. In 2001, the duck was wooden; in 1801, the fellows pursued and slaughtered a live duck and its blood was added to the red wine imbibed on the occasion.

they became friends with the porters.[149] On the other hand, town and gown remained as closely interlocked as ever, thanks to the great growth in the University's administrative and technical staff from the 1970s, which provided the local population, with the requisite skills, burgeoning job opportunities. In 2009, the University employed 8 per cent of the local workforce. Its presence, moreover, helped to create and sustain many other jobs in the area. The 4 million tourists at the end of the period who flocked to Oxford each year to look at the Bodleian and the University's museums and historic colleges supposedly kept as many as 5,300 people in work.[150] More importantly, the University's prominent role in scientific research encouraged the development, from 1990, of a wide variety of knowledge-based industries both in and around Oxford, which ended the city's dependence on the car industry, the key to its interwar wealth. According to the draft version of the University's 2013–18 strategic plan, 60 per cent of jobs in Oxford were now in 'knowledge-intensive activities', many the result of its spin-out companies and collaboration with industry.[151]

[149] For the collapse in the traditional close relationship between the college and families in the town, see Brian Harrison, 'College Servants in Corpus Forty Years Ago', *Oral History*, 40: 2 (2012), 40–58.

[150] 8Ei/University of Oxford (8076), p. 1: the University's response to the government's draft plan published in May 2009 for development in south-east England ([June] 2009). The figure for the number of tourists was a conservative one. Oxford City Council's website today gives 9.5 million: <http://www.oxford.gov.uk/PageRender/decC/Population_statistics_occw.htm> (accessed 6 May 2013).

[151] 'University of Oxford Draft Strategic Plan 2013–18', OUG, supplement (1) to no. 5007 (28 Nov. 2012), p. 192 (para. 61).

Nonetheless, as in earlier periods, relations between the University and the City Council were not always harmonious. The University no longer had any authority over the town and after the war had finally lost its independent representation in parliament.[152] But there were new frictions caused by the sheer number of students. Oxford city in 1931 had 80,000 inhabitants, including students. By 2011, the number had almost doubled but the proportion of its citizens in full-time education had rocketed. Between the wars, students formed only one out of seventeen in the population; by the end of the period they formed at least one out of five and probably one out of four. Not only had the numbers attending the University of Oxford quadrupled since the war but there was now a second university in the city, Oxford Brookes, located on Headington Hill, which had begun life as the Oxford College of Technology in 1956, become a polytechnic in 1970, and gained university status in 1992.[153] In 2013, the two universities had 45,000 students between them, most living within the city's boundaries. This gave the city population a peculiar age profile. Britain's population was ageing fast towards the end of the period, but Oxford had a disproportionately large number of young people. According to the 2001 census, a quarter of its working-age population were students, a higher percentage than anywhere else in England and Wales.[154] As so many among the postgraduates were from abroad, the two universities also helped to skew the ethnic balance of the city, where one in five rather than one in eight were non-white or from minority backgrounds in 2009. Given the shortage of housing in Oxford, the presence of so many students helped to inflate rents in the city and created ill-feeling, especially in east Oxford, where they were to be found in large numbers. The situation began to be eased to a limited degree only after 2000, once the senior university was able to house the large majority of its students in college accommodation.[155]

There was also frequent friction between the council and the two universities, especially the University of Oxford, over development plans. In the post-war era, the University and the city were thrown into opposing camps over the council's plans to alleviate Oxford's traffic problem. Anxious to end congestion in the High Street, plans were drawn up early in the 1940s to construct a relief road from Magdalen Bridge to Folly Bridge across Christ Church meadows. The plans were debated on and off throughout the 1950s, and by the early 1960s the Conservative council had placed its weight behind a scheme designed by Sir Geoffrey Jellicoe, who proposed to sink the road in a cutting like a ha-ha so that it would be heard but not seen, except at night when it would be brightly lit (see Figure 15.8). In the 1950s, the University's opposition was muted. Well aware that there was an alternative

---

[152] The University kept its own city councillors until 1974.

[153] Called after John Henry Brookes, the man responsible for forming the Oxford College of Technology through the merger of the Oxford School of Art, where he had been head since 1928, and the Oxford City Technical School: see Bryan Brown, *John Henry Brookes: The Man who Inspired a University* (Oxford, 2015).

[154] <http://www.oxford.gov.uk/PageRender/decC/Population_statistics_occw.htm> (accessed 6 May 2013).

[155] See p. 673, this volume. As late as 1987–8, nearly 4,000 of Oxford's students lodged in the town. After 2000, the tension was primarily caused by the expanding number of Brookes' students.

FIGURE 15.8 Christ Church Meadows road plan, 1963. Shortly after the Jellicoe Plan was revealed, Congregation voted against the road by 120 votes to 11. The Oxford Preservation Trust also campaigned for it to be shelved and the plan was debated in the national press. The photograph shows Jellicoe pointing to the road on a model (seen at the bottom of the photograph). It would have passed behind St Hilda's and Magdalen College School before joining Iffley Road.

plan on the table which would have put a relief road through the University Parks, Congregation on two occasions gave the Christ Church scheme guarded approval. Jellicoe's ha-ha, however, concentrated minds, and the University succeeded in having the plan shelved when it was discussed at a public enquiry in 1965. Christ Church meadows were too idyllic to sacrifice to the motor car. The scheme continued to be in play until the early 1970s. It was scotched only when the council itself, now Labour controlled, decided that a better solution to Oxford's congestion was to encourage the use of public transport and pedestrianize the city centre, which was slowly, if never fully, achieved.[156]

More normally, the friction arose over the University's and the colleges' plans for expansion. The City Council thought it its duty to protect the Oxford skyline and on several occasions thwarted the University's desire to build high. The plan to construct a twenty-five-storey modernist tower to house zoology was firmly sat upon in 1962, as was the desire, fifty-five years later, to solve the Bodleian's storage problems by erecting another tall building on the Osney Mead industrial estate off

---

[156] For succinct accounts, see Mark Barrington Ward, 'That 60-Year Debate over the World's Finest Bus Lane', OT, 28 May 1999, p. 17, and Mark Barrington Ward, 'Real Story of "Jellicoe's Road"', OT, 7 Nov. 2013, p. 11. For additional information, see, Damian Fantato, 'The Road that Never Was', OT, 24 Oct. 2013, p. 10, and the letter by Bruce Ross-Smith in OT, 7 Nov. 2013, p. 34. For the original recommendation of the meadows' relief road, see Thomas Sharp, Oxford Replanned (London, 1948), published for Oxford City Council.

the Botley Road.[157] Moreover, when the council was willing to be accommodating, the growing number of conservationist lobby groups in and around the city frequently stepped into the breach, the long-standing Oxford Preservation Trust to the fore.[158] In the 1990s, the Saïd Business School had initially taken a long time to win approval because Congregation objected to its being located on the Mansfield Road sports ground. When the decision was taken to place the school on a brownfield site to the north of St Frideswide Square, huge opposition this time arose from conservationists, who were concerned about the fate of a Grade-II-listed wooden building which had originally been the station for the old London and North Western Railway.[159] As conservation lobby groups in the city mushroomed at the turn of the new millennium, the objections grew. In 2013, the University was fighting two battles at once. Lovers of Port Meadow were demanding that a new accommodation block at Castle Mill overlooking the area and given the go-ahead by the city council should be lowered to protect the view, while various groups, including the residents of Jericho, were opposing the erection in Walton Street of the new home for the Blavatnik School of Government on the grounds it would look like 'a concrete marshmallow' and be three metres taller than Carfax Tower.[160] At the end of the period, several colleges too faced criticism over the design of buildings they hoped to put up. Zaha Hadid's new three-storey building for St Antony's Middle East Centre, nicknamed the 'Softbridge', raised the hackles of the Victorian group of the Oxfordshire Architectural and Historical Society for its futuristic vision, while Worcester was in trouble with the Oxford Preservation Trust for planning fill-in buildings on its central site that would turn their back on the city.[161]

These quarrels, however, were between the council and the lobbyists and the University and the colleges. They were not the classic town–gown struggles of the old days which had been fought out on the streets. Such tribal clashes still occurred in the post-war era. In the 1950s, Guy Fawkes Night each year always saw sporadic outbursts of violence between the two sides. But such incidents grew rarer and rarer.[162] They had been principally occasioned by the fact that Oxford's students

---

[157] The building was constructed at Swindon instead: see p. 642, this volume.

[158] Set up in 1928 to preserve Oxford's green spaces and the local countryside. Its great achievements were the purchase of South Park, Headington, and the establishment of the green belt round the city in 1955.

[159] The station had been closed in 1951. The problem was solved by transporting the building in its entirety to Quainton in Buckinghamshire in February 2000.

[160] *OT*, 14 Feb. 2013, p. 3; 4 Apr. 2013, p. 10; 16 May 2013, p. 10; 24 October 2013, p. 3; 31 October, pp. 8 and 32. The Port Meadow block was a university not a college initiative. On both counts, the University triumphed over its opponents. The University agreed to improve the landscaping of the Port Meadow block but not to reduce its height and won the backing of Congregation and the junior members for its stance. The Blavatnik building was also not scaled back: *OT* 5 Feb. 2015, p. 11; 12 Feb, 2015, p. 1; 11 June 2015, p. 1. Congregation was asked to give its opinion on the Port Meadow flats by senior members who opposed the development. For the University's case, see <http://www.ox.ac.uk/about/organisation/university-officers/vice-chancellor/congregation-and-castle-mill> (accessed 3 September 2015).

[161] *OT*, 23 Aug. 2012, p. 3 and 31 Jan. 2013, pp. 28–9. Worcester gained permission for its scheme in spring 2014; the same month St Cross' plans for expansion in St Giles were turned down: *OT*, 3 Apr. 2014, 6, and 10 Apr. 2014, p. 32. The 'Softbridge', a twisting, concave, metallic building, joins together an Edwardian and Victorian house on the St Antony's site. It was opened in 2015.

[162] Guy Fawkes Night had always been an occasion when the town went on the rampage. In the late 1950s, department stores still shuttered their windows to prevent vandalism.

were set apart from the mass of young people in the city. They dressed differently, spoke differently, answered to different laws, and seemed to have bottomless purses thanks to the easy credit they could command of local tradesmen. By the 1970s, most of these differences had been extinguished. The youth revolution was classless and affected town and gown alike. Once freed from the shackles of gate-hours, academic dress, and dining-in, Oxford's students, in their clothing, demeanour, and tastes, were usually indistinguishable from their peers. Even accents were less revealing, as southern students flattened their vowels and the Oxford burr began to be replaced by Estuary English. Not surprisingly, the ritual clashes between town and gown on Guy Fawkes Night went out with the 1950s. There were still tensions. College Commem balls, ever more raucous and luxurious, were an annual reminder that some youths were more gilded than others. But apart from Magdalen's coup in booking the Rolling Stones in 1964 (see Figure 15.9), ball committees never had the money to hire the hottest talent and the groups who kept Oxford's citizens awake on the odd summer night were yesterday's men and women. When the bands of the moment came to Oxford in the 1960s and 1970s, they played in the Town Hall and the Carfax Assembly Rooms, as the Beatles did on 16 February 1963, and could be enjoyed by all.[163] In the final decades of the period, the only real point of contention was over the unseemly celebrations outside Schools in the exam season. It had always been the custom for undergraduates to assemble in the High Street to welcome their friends as they finished their final examination. But in the 1990s the welcome got out of hand. Flour, tins of baked beans, and champagne began to be poured over the heads of the emerging students, much to the distress of passing young mothers with babies and toddlers. The Proctors soon took note of the swelling discontent: candidates were required to exit the Schools via Merton Street and all celebrations were banned until the students had returned to college.

In addition, there was much that the town had to thank the University for besides attracting tourists and jobs. Across the second half of the twentieth century, the small city of Oxford grew into a vibrant cultural centre. In 2015, like any other wealthy English provincial town, it had a plethora of amateur music and drama societies, plus several performing arts schools and private galleries. But the city was also home to a number of cultural institutions of national and international renown. It boasted two successful professional theatres—the New, which brought opera as well as musicals to Oxford, and the Playhouse, established in Beaumont Street from 1938, which put on a wide range of classical and modern plays and, from 1956 to 1974, had its own resident company, the Meadow Players.[164] It had five highly regarded museums—the Ashmolean, the Museum of Natural History, the

---

[163] Trevor Hayward, *Rocking in Oxford: A Personal History of the 1960s and 1970s Music Scene* (Oxford, 2009). The Stones performed in the Town Hall on 4 January 1964. The Beatles did visit the University specifically a few months later, on 5 March 1964, but only to be entertained in the principal's lodgings at Brasenose and visit Vincent's. They were there at the invitation of Brasenose's Jeffrey Archer, who had inveigled the group into supporting his campaign to raise £500,000 for Oxfam: *OT*, 22 Nov. 2012, p. 38 and 6 Mar. 2014, pp. 24–5.

[164] Administered by Frank Hauser, the company contained most of the best young actors of the day.

<table>
<tr><td>

CABARET MARQUEE

10.00
The Falling Leaves

10.50
The Rolling Stones

11.40
The Falling Leaves

12.15
The Rolling Stones

1.05
The Falling Leaves

1.50
Sadler, Arnold and Gould

2.00
Freddie and the Dreamers

2.35
Sadler, Arnold and Gould

2.40
John Lee Hooker

3.20
The Rolling Stones

4.10
The Falling Leaves

5.15
Tubby Hayes and his Band

THE BALLROOM

10.00
Ian Stewart and his Orchestra

1.05
John Mayall and the Blues Breakers

3.15
Ian Stewart

</td><td>

JAZZ MARQUEE

10.00
Johnny Dankworth and his Band

11.50
Tubby Hayes

1.10
Johnny Dankworth

2.15
Tubby Hayes

3.15
Tubby Hayes

4.50
Johnny Dankworth

CLOISTERS NIGHT CLUB

10.00
Clem and John

11.00
Tomaso y Latinos

12.35
Mellotones

1.55
Tomaso y Latinos

3.15
Mellotones

4.20
Tomaso y Latinos

The Mellotones are playing in St. John's quad to welcome guests from 10.00 till 11.45.

The committee wishes to thank Ajax Entertainments for their help in securing the artists playing at the Ball.

</td></tr>
</table>

FIGURE 15.9 Magdalen College Commemoration Ball programme 1964 featuring the Rolling Stones. Commem balls in the 1960s seldom featured the hottest talent. Magdalen booked the Stones for the 1964 ball before the group had become famous. The Stones were held to their contract and had to break off their successful first tour of the States to perform for a fee which did not cover their travel expenses.

Pitt Rivers, the Museum of Science, and Modern Art Oxford.[165] And, in Blackwell's, it had one of the world's most famous bookshops. Each year, too, the city hosted Oxfordshire Artsweeks devoted to the visual arts (started in 1981), a literary festival (begun in 1996), a 'Venturefest' (continuous since 1999) where engineers, scientists, and entrepreneurs come together to discuss their ideas, and its own Fringe modelled

---

[165] The last, established in Pembroke Street in 1965, was known as the Museum of Modern Art Oxford until 2002.

on Edinburgh's (first held in 2007). It is difficult to see how such a cultural cornu-
copia could have been developed and sustained without the presence of the University, ably abetted towards the close of the period by Brookes. Although Oxford
city's cultural vitality had its origins in the inspiration of a number of visionary
individuals largely outside the two universities, the critical mass was provided by the
large number of students and academics living in or close to the town.

More importantly, the University of Oxford was directly involved in the town's
emergence as a beacon of culture. In the case of the development of the city's world-
class museums, the University's role was central, for all but Modern Art Oxford
were under its control. Before the war, the collections in the University's care, except
the Ashmolean's art collection, were principally objects of academic study.[166] The
metamorphosis of its four museums into ever more popular public attractions in
the second half of the period was the result of the University's willingness and
ability to raise the necessary funds to extend and renovate their premises.[167]
Equally, the University helped keep the Playhouse in business on two occasions
when its management got into financial difficulties, first by purchasing the theatre's
lease in 1961 and then by setting it up as a charity under the Oxford Playhouse Trust
in 1989. It was the University, too, that guaranteed the success of Oxford's various
festivals by allowing the Sheldonian, the Bodleian, and other buildings to be used as
venues. In music it went even further, establishing in 2002 its own orchestra in
residence, the Oxford Philomusica.[168] The colleges played their part as well in
boosting the arts in the city. The three choral foundations—Christ Church, Magdalen, and New College—continued to maintain world-class chapel choirs; St Hilda's
in 1995 opened the Jacqueline du Pré Music Building, the first purpose-built concert
venue in Oxford since the Holywell Music Room (see Figure 15.10);[169] some colleges
at the end of the period set up their own arts festivals; while most colleges allowed
their buildings and gardens to be used by outsiders for a range of artistic events.

The University and the colleges also made an effort to cultivate Oxford's citizens
on a more day-to-day level. The Department for Continuing Education showed the
way through its outreach activities; the University's museums followed suit by
fostering visits by local schools; and even the Saïd Business School revealed a
human face by hosting exhibitions of city children's art. The colleges did their bit
by allowing local residents to visit without charge and inviting the public to view

---

[166] For the history of these collections, see pp. 179, 309, and 487–9, this volume.

[167] The University's museums did receive a grant from central government but only to cover their running
costs. For the renovation of the Ashmolean, see p. 640, this volume. The most recent museum to be renovated
is the Museum of Natural History, whose Victorian glass roof was cleaned in 2013–14: *OT*, 6 Feb. 2014, p. 25.
Much of the university museums' transformation must be put down to the energy and determination of a series
of dynamic directors, such as the Ashmolean's Christopher Brown.

[168] *OT*, 15 May 2014, 'Weekend' section, p. 2.

[169] Details at <http://www.st-hildas.ox.ac.uk/about/about-jacqueline-du-pré-music-building> (accessed 12
September 2014). The renowned cellist had been an honorary fellow of the college. Oxford city has no concert
hall of its own beyond the town hall and orchestral concerts are usually held in the Sheldonian.

FIGURE 15.10 The Jacqueline du Pré Music Building, St Hilda's College, opened 1995. It was designed by architects van Heyningen and Haward with acoustics by Arup Acoustics. It included practice rooms as well as 200-seat auditorium. The building hosts regular lunchtime recitals, educational events, plays, art exhibitions and conferences.

their gardens on special days. The town responded by seeing parts of the University as common property: with the opening of Rick Mather's extension at the end of 2009, advertisements on the city buses called on the inhabitants to visit 'Your Ashmolean'.

As a result, town and gown, from the 1970s, got on better than they had ever done. Of course, it was primarily a middle-class Oxford to which the University was reaching out at the end of the period. But Oxford town, through the creation of the huge number of white-collar jobs that the University had helped to spawn, was a much more middle-class city. This was another reason why town–gown friction had eased. When students and dons went to the cinema or theatre, joined the forlorn hope that trekked out to the Kassam Stadium to watch Oxford United, or simply went shopping in the city centre, they rubbed shoulders with people much like themselves.[170] Oxford and the University were no longer places apart, the former little known to the latter except as a supplier of servants and service and a beneficiary of charity. Town and gown had a shared identity as voters, taxpayers, and consumers, and were bound together in a shared dislike of tourists. Senior

---

[170] The enthusiasm for clubbing shared by young adults of all backgrounds in the early twenty-first century brought town and gown particularly close together.

members were also members of the city and, as such, could be at the forefront of protest against any threat by the University or the colleges to the Oxford skyline.[171] For students and dons, Oxford city and its environs were as much their home as the University and the colleges. The town and the surrounding county had finally become a positive part of the Oxford experience.

[171] Colleges showed little solidarity with each other's plans for expansion. When Ruskin moved to its new location, its old Walton Street building was acquired by Exeter. When the college unveiled its plans to construct a new building on the site, Worcester joined the Oxfordshire Architectural and Historical Society in objecting to the planning application. The Jericho Community Centre, on the other hand, liked the new plans: OT, 25 Apr. 2013, p. 20, and 23 May 2013, p. 7.

Conclusion

Future Prospects

OXFORD, on the eve of the Second World War, was the second largest of the United Kingdom's universities and contained more than a tenth of the country's students in full-time education. In 2013, it was more than four times as big but was now only the thirtieth in size and its share of the student population had fallen below 1.5 per cent. In the interim, Oxford had changed dramatically. In 1939 it had been predominantly an undergraduate university focusing on the arts and educating British, mainly English, students. Its students had come largely from the upper stratum of the middle class and only a small proportion were women. By the end of the period, a much greater emphasis was placed on the sciences, Oxford's postgraduate and undergraduate populations were nearly equal, and the majority of postgraduates came from abroad. The students were still largely middle class, but members of the professional and commercial classes were now a majority of the working population and the University recruited from across the spectrum. Women too formed virtually 50 per cent of the undergraduate and postgraduate intake, even if they still remained a small proportion of postholders. The University's physical footprint was also much larger and it had become a significant force in the British economy. Oxford was now a multi-campus university spread throughout the city and beyond, and its medics, scientists, and social scientists had close links with government and industry. Most importantly, through the quantity and quality of the work of its academic staff (dons and postdocs), Oxford had an undisputed reputation as one of the world's leading research universities, consistently ranked in the top ten, alongside Cambridge, Harvard, Stanford, Berkeley, MIT, Caltech, Columbia, Princeton, and Chicago.

Oxford had not risen to this pinnacle from nowhere. It had already attained a high profile as a centre of research in the arts and sciences in the 1930s, but it had come late to the race, and many other universities in the United States and Europe, even in Britain, appeared much better placed to consolidate their reputation. Although the predominance of American institutions among the elite could have been anticipated, given the wealth and size of the United States, no one would have predicted that only Oxford and Cambridge among the European giants would have been deemed worthy of a seat at the top table. The achievement was all the more remarkable in that the British establishment was constantly ambivalent about the success of its two ancient universities. Some in Whitehall and Westminster thought they were national assets that should be protected and cherished. Others, starting with Robbins in 1963, thought they should be cut down to size as they undermined the politically correct belief that all British universities, even in the inflated system of the present, were equal.

Oxford's and Cambridge's rise to the top was undoubtedly helped by the fact they were the two oldest universities in the anglophone world. They had a patina of greatness automatically conferred upon them by their antiquity. But longevity is not everything. Caltech became a member of the Association of American Universities only in 1934. Neither Oxford nor Cambridge could have been placed in the modern pantheon had they not contributed significantly to their own elevation. After the war, both had to accept that the modern research university would be built on the sciences and could only be created with government money. Had either drawn the line at further state funding in 1945, they would quickly have been reduced to the status of quaint liberal arts colleges, and rivals like Imperial, UCL, Manchester, and Edinburgh would have taken their place as the pre-eminent British universities.[1] As it was, both took advantage of the UGC's willingness in the 1950s and 1960s to fund virtually any initiative a university put forward to build up the plant and academic staff they needed to flaunt their credentials as world-class centres of scientific research. Oxford's ability to grasp the spirit of the age and act on it was particularly impressive. Cambridge was already a science university in 1939 but Oxford had to change direction.

The two ancient seats of learning had to be equally ready to adapt again from the mid-1980s once the state's financial commitment to the research university faltered. What gave Oxford and Cambridge the edge over the leading universities of continental Europe and most British universities was the speed with which they reacted to the new conditions and went looking for private money to ensure that their research base was not just secure but enhanced. Both were peculiarly well placed to do this: their location, antiquity, and historic reputation made them attractive to high-profile donors, while many of their alumni were either wealthy, well-connected, or in positions of influence. But the successful rebalancing of the two universities' income, which their potential rivals on this side of the Atlantic were unable to imitate, was achieved only through the foresight and efforts of successive Vice-Chancellors and their support teams.

It was also sensible to embrace the RAE, for all the administrative burdens it placed on academic and non-academic staff alike. Under the RAE, government research funds were divided up according to departmental (or unit of assessment)

---

[1] Imperial and UCL remain the main challengers today: Imperial attracted more research income than Cambridge in 2010–11.

research ratings. As Oxford and Cambridge emerged at the top of virtually every discipline they sustained, they received the lion's share of government money, thereby allowing them to draw even further ahead of their rivals. And success bred success. Having built up proven centres of research excellence in the sciences, it was unsurprising that, when more and more 'soft' research money was made available by the research councils from the 1990s, Oxford and Cambridge dons proved adept competitors and scooped the pool.[2]

Both universities were able to transform themselves into world-beaters without abandoning their traditional structures of governance. While their American rivals, like other British universities, were ultimately run by outsiders, Oxford and Cambridge remained ultimately controlled by the dons. Attempts were made across the period to limit or redefine the power of Oxford's Congregation or Cambridge's Senate but the dons always kept a close guard over their sovereignty. Nor, in the first decade of the twenty-first century, despite considerable external pressure to conform to the 'sector norm', would they agree to set up an elected council, which had a majority of non-academic members, to act in their name.[3] Oxford and Cambridge also remained collegiate universities: all junior members had to have a college affiliation, and undergraduate teaching continued to be centred around tutorials or supervisions organized at college level. The chief difference between the two was that Cambridge, from the 1920s, did not go down the road of dual appointments. University lecturers had no college teaching duties as part of their contract and many were not even college fellows. The colleges continued to make their own independent teaching arrangements, which meant senior academics were not always closely involved in undergraduate education.

Admittedly, the balance of power between the two universities and their constituent colleges had changed. For various reasons—the size of their post-war income, the rise in postgraduate numbers, the abolition of the college fee, and the connivance of government—the universities were now in the driving seat. However, the emasculation of their colleges was only relative. At Oxford the colleges were still 50 per cent wealthier than the University in terms of endowment, and a number of colleges were extremely rich. The colleges were fund-raising just as enthusiastically as the University towards the end of the period, and as college loyalties were as strong as ever, they usually had first call on their alumni's generosity. No Oxford college in 2013 came near to rivalling the wealth of Trinity, Cambridge, but St John's, which owned North Oxford and whose finances had been particularly well managed since 1945, and Christ Church, were worth over £300 million, and four others—All Souls, Merton, Queen's, and Magdalen—more than

---

[2] According to the Dearing Report in 1997, five universities in England received a third of the available research funds, and 50 per cent of research council grants went to individuals in twelve universities: Dearing, p. 40.

[3] The Cambridge Senate plays a more active role in administering the university than Congregation. 'In Oxford Council decisions are presented to Congregation as enacted unless challenged—the role of Congregation is routinely one of rubber-stamping—in Cambridge Council merely proposes, the Regent House [where Senate meets] disposes': OM, 8th week, HT (2014), p. 3.

£150 million. The wealth of Oxford's colleges was a powerful factor in maintaining strong college identities in the face of the growing authority of Wellington Square, as it was visibly used to ensure that their junior members, whatever their background, had the fullest opportunity to make the most of their student years. For this reason, even the richer colleges were happy to continue to support the process of redistribution introduced by Franks, which proved a successful initiative. Although some colleges were still poor in 2013—Mansfield, Linacre, and Harris Manchester had endowments worth less than £10 million—most of those initially targeted for help in 1966, through a combination of college taxation and their own efforts, had flourished. St Anne's and St Hilda's now had endowments close to £50 million.[4]

Oxford's and Cambridge's ability to retain their democratic and collegiate traditions and still rise to the top was significant. The system had many imperfections. Postholders tended to be conservative and vote for the status quo on controversial issues, while the need to square both the dons' parliament and the colleges made decision-making cumbersome. In both universities there was also the problem of the growing numbers of research and non-academic office staff who had no representation. Nonetheless, despite its shortcomings, the model appeared to be able to function in an era of academic globalization without any obvious harm to the two universities' international standing. This testified to its durability and adaptability. Having survived in some shape or form from the late middle ages, it continued to prove a model for all seasons and a powerful counterweight to the claim that only a top-down corporate and bureaucratic model could create success in a highly competitive academic marketplace. Its shortcomings were also offset by its attractions. Democratic collegiality was one of the factors that helped to explain Oxbridge's high ranking. Academics from around the world were attracted by the collegiate ideal of small self-governing communities of scholars from different disciplines engaged in fruitful dialogue, even if the reality was more mundane. They liked too the idea of having a say in decision-making at all levels, even if, for the most part, they became closely engaged only when important issues were at stake. Neither university had enough money to compete with American campuses in a bidding war for academic stars but both offered peculiarly satisfying working conditions.[5]

Of course, it would be wrong to make an absolute distinction between Oxbridge and other British universities in 2013. Both remained part of the national system of

---

[4] <http://en.wikipedia.org/wiki/Colleges_of_the_University_of_Oxford> (accessed 10 September 2015), p. 4. Accurate valuations of the colleges' endowments became available only from the start of the new millennium. The ranking has scarcely changed over the last fifteen years: see 'The Oxford College Accounts: League Table, 2001', at <http://www.akme.btinternet.co.uk/oclxleg4.html> (accessed 10 June 2005, but website no longer extant; author's print-out; figures derived from the published college accounts). Trinity College, Cambridge, was worth £620 million in 2008 and is possibly worth more than £800 million today. For a discussion of its wealth, see Robert Neild, *Riches and Responsibility: The Financial History of Trinity College, Cambridge* (Cambridge, 2008), esp. ch. 5.

[5] Venki Ramakrishnan, Nobel laureate in chemistry in 2009, claimed that he had taken a 40 per cent pay cut when he moved to Cambridge in 1999. But he had done so because 'Britain offered the most stable environment for my work': *The Times*, 8 May 2013, p. 22.

higher education and relied heavily on public money to fund posts, infrastructure, and research. In important respects, too, the history of Oxford and Cambridge over the previous twenty-five years had not been strikingly different from that of other members of the Russell Group. All of Britain's leading universities had seen a rapid growth in the number of postgraduates, especially on taught courses; all had sought to find private money to support research and infrastructure development; all had become much bigger physical institutions; and all had strengthened their ties with the private sector. Indeed, Warwick, one of the new greenfield universities of the 1960s, had gone out of its way to woo business and industry from its foundation (much to the disgust of its sisters). On the other hand, the distinctiveness of Oxford and Cambridge cannot be refuted. Their collegiate structure, the personalized system of their undergraduate teaching, and their greater success in fund-raising and garnering research grants immediately set them apart.

Membership of a self-governing college fellowship with its rituals and esprit de corps eroded any illusion that Oxbridge dons were part of a single uniform British academic profession. Durham, historically, and York and Lancaster, among the new universities of the 1960s, had developed a quasi-collegiate structure, but their colleges were never more than halls of residence and the college loyalty of both students and staff was of little weight. For many Oxbridge dons, the college was the centre of their academic life. For all, it was a cushion that kept them relatively satisfied with their lot as pay and conditions deteriorated from the 1980s. As a result, most Oxbridge dons felt little solidarity with their colleagues in other universities. Membership of the Association of University Teachers, the academics' trades union, was weak in comparison, and the level of militancy low.

The tutorial and supervisorial systems similarly distinguished Oxbridge's undergraduates from their peers. In most universities before the 1980s there had been some attempt to give students a degree of individual attention alongside lectures and classes, and several of the new universities of the 1960s had hoped that they would be able to imitate Oxbridge in this regard. But as staff–student ratios deteriorated with the great expansion in undergraduate numbers in the 1990s, and many academics looked to reduce their teaching commitments in order to get on with research, personal contact between staff and students in many universities became perfunctory. In some departments, students never encountered a postholder until their final year, and teaching was handed over to assistants. At Oxford and Cambridge, in contrast, undergraduates continued to be cosseted, even if socializing with tutors and supervisors became less commonplace. Neither university came under pressure to expand undergraduate numbers, the staff–student ratio remained unchanged as the colleges used their wealth to protect tutorial posts under threat, and students were taught from the beginning by senior academics.

As magnets for money, Oxford and Cambridge were in a league of their own. Already far wealthier than the other British universities before they and their colleges began to fund-raise in earnest, they had pulled out of sight by the end of the period. In 2011 Oxford and Cambridge were worth £3.9 billion and £4.3 billion respectively. Their nearest rival was the University of Edinburgh with an endowment of £236.5 million. Imperial College, London, equally prestigious as Oxbridge as a science university, had accumulated only £75.6 million; while Warwick, for all its closeness to the private sector, had a mere £4.9 million.[6] The disparity when it came to raising research funds was less acute but still significant. In 2010–11, among the twenty-four members of the Russell Group, Oxford stood alone with a research income of £376.7 million; Imperial, Cambridge, and University College London tied for second place with £280–300 million; while the rest were a long way behind. Ten, headed by Manchester, commanded a research income between £100 and £200 million; the remainder were under £100 million, the lowest the LSE with £24 million.[7] Oxford, moreover, had a source of wealth that no other university shared, even Cambridge. The latter was able to attract large sums from the extremely wealthy Bill and Melinda Gates Foundation, built on the profits of Microsoft. But Oxford, in the University Press, had its own goose that laid golden eggs every year.

It would be equally wrong to conclude that Oxford had hit on a winning formula that would guarantee the University's place at the top table long into the future. Remaining among the top ten universities in the world is certain to become more and more difficult in the next twenty-five years. It can be only a matter of time before one or more Chinese universities join the elite. The People's Republic has yet to count a Nobel Prize winner among its citizens but its ambitions in that regard are clear.[8] Oxford may even find itself being challenged more fiercely at home by some of the Russell Group, despite their inferior resources. If the pecking order in science in Britain today was determined by the number of Nobel laureates a university had on its staff, it would be Manchester, with three, which would be at the top.[9] The University's current five-year plan, which covers the years 2013 to 2018, reveals that the central administration is content (understandably) with the status quo, but Oxford would be wise to consider whether its present position, both in and outside the national system, will continue to serve its ambition in the long term to be one of the world's leading universities.[10]

This may be the moment for Oxford to revisit the possibility of becoming a private university. Given the state of the government's finances as the country emerges from the longest recession since the 1930s, and the growing amounts of money needed to keep the NHS afloat with an ageing population, it seems unlikely that any government in the future will be able to lavish increasing sums on higher education. Oxford might have greater flexibility to expand in the way that it wants if

[6] <http://en.wikipedia.org/wiki/List_of_UK_universities_by_endowment> (accessed 26 February 2013). The Warwick figure is for 2009.

[7] <http://en.wikipedia.org/wiki/Russell_Group> (accessed 31 January 2013).

[8] Cong Cao, 'Chinese Science and the "Nobel Prize" Complex', *Minerva*, 42 (2004), 151–72. It has been predicted that five Chinese universities will join the world's top 20 by the 2030s: see *The Times*, 25 November 2014, p. 8.

[9] <http:// www.manchester .ac.uk/discover/history-heritage/history/**nobel-prize** (accessed 10 September 2015).

[10] 'University of Oxford Strategic Plan, 2013–2018', *OUG*, supplement (1) to no. 5025 (22 May 2013), pp. 579–84.

it were to cut itself adrift from the national system. At the very least, it would no longer be under pressure to show the immediate practical benefit of its research to UK plc, and could make up its own mind how far to emphasize 'third-leg' activities.[11] The usual response to the suggestion is that the University is still highly dependent on state funding and that it could never raise the necessary extra endowment it would need to make this possible. At first glance this seems to be incontrovertible. Oxford still receives 50 per cent of its income from HEFCE and the national research councils. The University would need to increase its endowment by upwards of £8 billion simply to cover the HEFCE grant of £200 million.[12] However, in the light of the University's confidence that it can raise £3 billion in the present campaign to fund a variety of novel ventures and obligations, it may not be outside the realm of possibility to raise such a sum, if the advantages of independence were carefully and plausibly explained to alumni and donors. There are several ways in which money might be raised: many American universities raise capital by selling bonds.

As it is, Oxford is likely to find its present status far less congenial in the coming years. It is hard to see how the University can continue to benefit as handsomely from being a member of the national system of higher education as it has hitherto. At present, Oxford and Cambridge get the best of both worlds. Their endowment and good facilities help them to dominate each round of the RAE: this provides the income to do more high-quality research which in turn attracts more private funds. For the two universities, it is a virtuous circle. To outside observers, it is manifestly unfair. Public money is flowing towards those in clover rather than those in need. In a national system, limited funds should be distributed more equitably and with an eye to sustaining national research priorities rather than maintaining Oxford and Cambridge's international eminence. It can only be a matter of time before the other members of the Russell Group put this point forcibly to government, and the government of the day, whatever influence the two universities can bring to bear, accepts that Oxford and Cambridge should have less of a call on the public's research purse.

It is also certain that an Oxford inside the national system will continue to be pressed hard about undergraduate access and the expense of its teaching provision. At present, the central administration is committed to keeping undergraduate numbers steady, broadening access, and maintaining the tutorial system. At the same time, it calculates that each student's education has to be subsidized to the

---

[11] See Chapter 14, section H, this volume. One of the world's leading private research universities, Johns Hopkins at Baltimore, has always deliberately fostered scientific research for its own sake, played a very limited role in promoting technological change, and stood aloof from the marketplace: M. P. Feldman and Pierre Desrochers, 'Truth For its Own Sake: Academic Culture and Technology Transfer at Johns Hopkins', *Minerva*, 42 (2004), 105–26. Other American research universities have become aggressively commercial: see B. Clark, *Creating Entrepreneurial Universities* (New York, 1998).

[12] On the assumption of a 2–3 per cent return. Fifty per cent is a very high figure even for many of America's state universities, which receive their core funding from the local state government. A highly respected state university, such as the University of Wisconsin, draws only 18.6 per cent of its income from the state government: <http://www.uwsa.edu/our/publicat/factbook.pdf> (accessed 19 September 2014).

tune of £7,000 a year and worries that the figure may grow if a new government were to cut the student fee/loan. Attempting to square the circle cannot go on forever. Even if there is no appetite in the University for exploring the viability of going it alone, there is a definite need to think more constructively about Oxford as an undergraduate university.

To abandon undergraduate teaching altogether, as is sometimes mooted, has the attraction of ending the problems of access and funding at one stroke. Moreover, the success of the present postgraduate colleges demonstrates that an Oxford without undergraduates could continue to function perfectly satisfactorily as a residential collegiate university: indeed, it could be pointed out that its original colleges were graduate institutions. Nonetheless, the proposal is unlikely to attract widespread support within Oxford. It demands too radical a break with the last five centuries; expanding the number of postgraduates in lieu would be difficult without lowering entry requirements and establishing many more bursaries; and there would be a detrimental effect on fund-raising. Too many of Oxford's post-graduates, especially doctoral students, become relatively indigent academics. The wealth of America's Ivy League has been built on the donations and bequests of their undergraduate alumni.

A more sensible way of finessing the access problem would be for Oxford and Cambridge to admit undergraduates after they had already done a year in higher education elsewhere. Were the two universities to recruit only from students already in the system who had demonstrated their ability to do high-quality university-level work, the accusations of bias levelled against the present admissions system would no longer have purchase. Tutorial time would be freed up, too, to improve the quality of master's teaching. Obviously, such a radical change would require an equally radical shake-up in the structure of British higher education. It would have to be remodelled along the lines of the State University of California where students under the California Master Plan of 1960 begin their undergraduate studies in a wide variety of different higher-education institutions and the best transfer, on the basis of their results, to one of the elite campuses, such as Berkeley.[13] Getting other universities to accept a transfer system would be extremely difficult, but it might be possible to win the backing of the Russell Group if all of its members were included in the scheme. HEFCE might be interested as well, were Oxford also to show that it was thinking creatively about the cost of its undergraduate provision.

This is the area where change could be most easily effected as it is an in-house affair, and the conversation has already begun to an extent. Some senior members of the University, often administrators or holders of titular chairs, would like to see

[13] The modern University of California was principally the creation of Clark Kerr, head of the Berkeley campus, 1952–8, then president of the state university, 1958–67, until he was removed in a coup backed by the state governor, Ronald Regan. For his own assessment of his achievements, see Clark Kerr, *The Gold and the Blue: A Personal Memoir of the University of California, 1949–67* (2 vols; Berkeley, CA, 2001–3). In a report on higher education in California in the early 1990s, the OECD treated the state as a separate country and its university as a national system: see Sheldon Rothblatt (ed.), *The OECD, the Master Plan, and the California Dream: A Berkeley Conversation* (Berkeley, CA, 1992). Other American states have developed versions of the California Master Plan.

the tutorial system abolished on the grounds it is a luxury and a hangover from a past age. It is deemed expensive, wasteful of dons' time, and thought to bring little intellectual benefit. Oxford's undergraduates are highly intelligent and committed, and do not need the stimulation and support of the tutorial to succeed; if the nation has the resources to provide some of its undergraduates with one-to-one or one-to-two teaching, then the money should be directed towards the less able.[14] There is much to commend this point of view. A recent survey of Oxford alumni twenty years after graduation found that they considered the tutorial system, for all its purported benefits, to have been of limited importance in their future lives.[15] That said, there can be no doubt that Oxford undergraduates find the best tutorials demanding, informative, and exciting, and appreciate the chance to argue and fly kites, which is much more difficult in a large class and impossible in a lecture. Dons, too, often find that they learn from tutorials: undergraduates suggest new avenues to explore and help them refine and cement their ideas.

The best way forward would be to modify the tutorial rather than abandon it. Critics forget that the Oxford tutorial, as this book has shown, is in a constant state of development. The tutorial of today is not the tutorial of the 1930s, let alone of the age of Jowett. Individual tutors are continually thinking of ways of making tutorials more effective. There is no reason to think that effectiveness and efficiency are at odds. Repeating tutorials on the same topic can numb the best tutor's brain: taking four students together rather than seeing them separately or in pairs is likely to be a more satisfactory pedagogical experience for both sides, provided everyone present is brought into the conversation and individuals can have some private time with the tutor, if they wish. All that is needed for a successful group tutorial is that the undergraduates do the work set, that they talk together during the week so as to bond, and that they produce written work in advance so that the tutor knows the point they have reached. There should be ways, therefore, of reducing the under-graduate teaching bill without sacrificing the tutorial. Even if the University were forced to cut academic posts following a fall in fee income and a subsequent rise in the subsidy, adaptation would still not be impossible.[16]

It may be the case, however, that the University's future will ultimately be determined not by its internal or external critics but by forces that are posed to destabilize and reconfigure the global field of higher education. Oxford, like most British universities, has been keen to take advantage of the growing global demand for high-quality higher education and has recruited more and more of its

[14] This seems to be the view of the current head of the Humanities Division.

[15] Jonathan Black, email communication, 11 Sept. 2014.

[16] Some members of the University believe it is the central administration not the academic staff that should bear the cost of future cutbacks as it is the ever-expanding central bureaucracy that has swelled the cost of an undergraduate education: see *The Times*, 11 Oct. 2013, 'Oxford's Fees': letter of Peter Oppenheimer. There would be great savings if Oxford and Brookes pooled some of their administrative costs. Discussing ways in which the two universities might be fully amalgamated, as Manchester and UMIST merged in 2004, may also make sense if the financial situation became very bleak. As many colleges are busy raising funds to endow the college part of joint posts, there may soon be a financial cushion to mitigate the worst effects of a change in government policy.

postgraduates from abroad. The structure of the global market in higher education, however, is changing rapidly and the attractions of Oxford may soon diminish. As more and more students in the developing world have sought a higher-education qualification from the west, the more entrepreneurial universities, like NYU, have realized that the best way to maximize their share of the market is to set up campuses overseas that provide the same top-level education as the home academy. The more this happens, the fewer students from India, China, and so on will feel the need to travel.[17]

The attraction of Oxford to British undergraduates is also under threat. The new technology is already transforming the way in which information is delivered and processed at all levels of education. It has the potential to make the residential university redundant. Reading materials, lectures, tutorials, even lab work can now be accessed or conducted online. The successful universities of the future are likely to be virtual spaces whose students live at home and study at their own convenience, often while in paid employment. The academic fees may remain as high but there will no longer be any need for British undergraduates to take on upwards of £24,000 of debt in order to fund their maintenance. At present there seems to be little interest in reshaping the British university system along virtual lines. Too much money has been invested in student accommodation and teaching facilities over the last sixty years for such a revolutionary overhaul to command support, and local economies have come to depend on student consumers. But it can only be a matter of time before a less favoured institution, probably one of the old polytechnics, sees a market opportunity.

MOOCs (massively open online courses) are already taking off in the United States with MIT leading the way.[18] As yet, they do not lead to a credit equivalent to one gained by a student who takes the course *in situ*, but they do lead to a certificate stating that the course material has been mastered. It is difficult to believe that any move towards virtual higher education would not be warmly supported by British governments of any colour anxious to increase the participation of 18-year-olds from poorer backgrounds and instil the habit of lifelong learning in a world where few can expect to hold the same job for life. It was Britain, after all, that pioneered the concept of distance learning with the Open University, founded in 1969, which now has five times as many students as the most populous residential university, Manchester.[19] Britain, furthermore, already has a prototype for the future in the University of Highlands and Islands. Established as a higher-education institute in 2001 and given university status in 2011, it provides a mix of on-site and virtual learning in a regional context and today has 7,000 students.[20]

---

[17] Ben Wildavsky, *The Great Brain Race: How Global Universities are Reshaping the World* (Princeton, NJ, 2011), ch. 2.
[18] Ibid., pp. xvii–xviii.
[19] A total of 200,000 against 40,000: <http://en.wikipedia.org/wiki/List_of_universities_in_the_United_Kingdom_by_enrollment> (accessed 31 January 2013).
[20] The University of the Highlands and Islands is the brainchild of engineer Sir Graham Hills, and was conceived as a university that would combine virtual and traditional forms of learning before the web was invented: see Graham Hills, *Report to the Advisory Steering Group Co-ordinated by Highland Region Council and Highland*

So far Oxford had shown little sign of addressing these challenges. It has made no moves to create a campus overseas, though several British universities have already gone down the road, including Nottingham, which has been established at Ningbo in China since 2005.[21] Nor has there been any discussion hitherto about greatly expanding the University's undergraduate intake by moving even partially into virtual learning.[22] Indeed, Oxford remains a remarkably closed institution in a global age. It has always been keen to bring distinguished outsiders within its orbit. Every summer since the eighteenth century it has bestowed honorary degrees on the great and good. If Congregation snubbed Margaret Thatcher, it was happy to make a number of her political contemporaries doctors of law in the following years, whether or not they had any Oxford association: King Juan Carlos of Spain in 1986, Crown Prince Naruhito of Japan in 1991, the president of Ireland Mary Robinson in 1993, and President Bill Clinton in 1994. Oxford's colleges, too, since the war, have set up visiting fellowship schemes which allow scholars and scientists from all round the world to spend some time in the University. But Oxford has so far been reluctant to embrace wholeheartedly the EU's ERASMUS programme, which is intended to allow its citizens to move freely from one university to another, gathering credits towards an undergraduate or postgraduate degree.[23] While it will accept several hundred visiting students each year, including Americans doing a year abroad, it is resolute that Oxford undergraduates cannot normally take courses elsewhere that will count towards their honours degree. An Oxford degree can be gained only by study at Oxford.[24] The University belongs to the Coimbra Group of 'historic' European universities, which was established in 1987 to promote collaboration between its members at all levels and allow a common response to initiatives emanating from the EU.[25] Yet the group's activities are certainly not at the forefront of the Vice-Chancellor's mind. Oxford, in many respects, is a very aloof institution.

Admittedly, the University might well be able to survive with its research profile intact, even if its undergraduate and postgraduate numbers were decimated. Oxford has the plant, the academic personnel, and basic endowment in the

---

and Island Enterprise (June 1992). By entering into a partnership with a wide variety of educational institutions and research centres in the region, it was offering distance-learning courses as early as 1995. Hills saw this as the future: 'The idea of students trooping to a centre and taking knowledge as they would water from a well: that is going.' See The Scotsman Magazine, 3 Apr. 1995, pp. 12–13. By 1995, hi-tech distance learning was also being developed at Exeter and the University of Ulster.

[21] In 2005 there were 100 branch campuses worldwide; in 2010, 162.

[22] Edinburgh seems to be the British University most willing to invest in MOOCs at the present time.

[23] European Community Action Scheme for the Mobility of University Students, or ERASMUS, was set up in 1987. Between 1994 and 2007 it was part of the EU's Socrates I and II programmes and is now incorporated into its lifelong learning programme. In 2006, over 15,000 students took part in the scheme, although this was only 1 per cent of the cohort.

[24] A peculiar anomaly was the study of Japanese. Until recently Oxford students spent their first year at Sheffield because there was no available tuition. There is a bilateral exchange agreement with Princeton that allows a handful of Oxford students to study in the States for a term and count the work they do there towards their degree.

[25] 'Information Note: Coimbra Group'. Document sent to heads of department and units from the Director of the External Relations Office, 2 March 1998.

combined wealth of the University and the colleges, to turn itself into a larger and grander version of Germany's Max Planck Institutes, which dominate the research field in central Europe. Yet it would be a very different Oxford and one that had cut itself off from its past. It has always been a university, not a learned academy of the kind that appeared for the first time in Europe in the late seventeenth century. It might be argued that this is a doomsday scenario, that Oxford, simply through its location and facilities, will always attract students, however much the British university system as a whole may be revolutionized by virtual learning. If this is the case, though, it is likely that the students who will continue to attend the University will be the rich and the connected. Oxford will retain its historic commitment to the residential university but at the expense of its sixty-year campaign to democratize access.

In the mid-nineteenth century, Goldwin Smith dreamt of extending the benefits of Oxford education to a much wider constituency by establishing affiliated institutions in the provinces. In that way the University would be at the apex of a rejuvenated higher-education system. His ideas were not taken up by the Oxford reformers, but found an echo from the late nineteenth century in the colleges, affiliated to several of the new northern universities, and in London's system of external examinations. Goldwin Smith's dreams of a benevolent monopoly were a fantasy in an age of chalk and talk, poor library resources, and relatively slow communications. Oxford had no way of ensuring that its affiliates provided a blue-ribbon service. Today, in the digital age, it is quite possible to see how a university that grasps the nettle and provides a high-quality virtual education could quickly come to dominate the field and use its fast-expanding fee income to recruit more and more academic stars. Oxford today appears to have two alternatives. It can stand aside and let the world of higher education be reshaped around it, or it can take the lead and potentially enjoy a future where its influence is even greater than it is at present—and where the carping about the social profile of its undergraduates would be finally laid to rest. Taking the second road would not mean abandoning Oxford's historic mission. The virtual university is the modern equivalent of the extension movement in which the University has always played such an important role. In fact, the Department for Continuing Education, at present frequently looked down upon as a Cinderella service, may well provide the University with a template for future development. The Department is already using the digital technology imaginatively and conducting online tutorials.

Crystal ball gazing is a dangerous occupation, and historians are notoriously bad at forecasting the future. All the same, Oxford would be unwise to rest on its laurels, and the Vice-Chancellor and Council would be advised to plan for a less stable and uncomfortable future than the one assumed in the current strategic plan.[26] It may

---

[26] 'University of Oxford Strategic Plan 2013–2018', *OUG*, supplement (1) to no. 5025 (22 May 2013). Only paras 9 and 40 (pp. 579–80 and 582) touch on digital learning and the emphasis is apparently on expanding the use of the new technology as an educational tool *within* the physical University. The initial draft of the plan was even less specific: 'University of Oxford Draft Strategic Plan 2013–18', *OUG*, supplement (1) to no. 5007 (28 Nov.

be that Oxford in the late twenty-first century will still be the Oxford of today. On the other hand, if the new technology produces the changes in higher education predicted and the University responds creatively, it may well be a very different institution, a community of teacher-researchers spread out over the world, digitally interacting with students living at home, and organizing and carrying out collaborative research projects wherever funding and need take them. Physically a much smaller entity, the University of Oxford may primarily be a brand name authenticating the quality of the teaching and research delivered under its auspices. Its administrative core might no longer be located in Oxford city at all. If such a scenario were ever to materialize, maintaining the principal factors of continuity that link Oxford today with its pre-modern past—democratic governance and collegiality—would be a challenge indeed.[27]

2012), p. 191 (paras 45 and 51). The extent to which the Department for Continuing Education is pushing the boundaries of virtual and distance learning was evident from its director's intervention in the Congregation debate on the initial draft: *OUG*, supplement (1) to no. 5016 (27 Feb. 2013), pp. 391–2. The University's current plan does aim to give more Oxford students an opportunity to study abroad (p. 581, para. 33) but does not say how; the draft plan suggested the emphasis would be on summer courses (p. 190, para. 42).

[27] The first indication that Oxford might be about to embrace the concept of the virtual university was given at the end of July 2013 when postholders were invited by Council's Education Committee to fill in a questionnaire aimed at gauging the extent of interest in developing open online courses. 'Education Committee noted the rising interest and increasing activity in developing MOOCs. It recognised that the University needed to reach a view on whether and if so how to engage with MOOCs, that this was a strategic matter for Council, and that any consideration of MOOCs needed to be situated within the wider discussion of the University's Digital Strategy.' Covering letter circulated 29 July 2013 as attachment to email. However, the matter was discussed on Council in the course of Trinity Term and it was concluded that 'engagement with large-scale MOOCs is not an immediate educational priority for the University given what the University already provides in this area'. Source: <https://www1.admin.ox.ac.uk/council/201213/vcbriefingfortrinityterm2013/> (accessed 24 September 2013). Nothing further has been heard of the Education Committee's questionnaire.

Chronology

1324	Foundation of Oriel College
1327	Richard of Wallingford designs his *equatorium* or cosmological slide rule
1328	Bradwardine's *De proportionibus velocitatum in motibus*
1341	Foundation of Queen's College
1344	Bradwardine completes his *De causa Dei*
1345–55	Swineshead's *Liber calculationum*
1355	The St Scholastica's Day riot and extension of the University's privileges; city to atone annually
1367	Pope gives the University the right to elect its Chancellor without reference to the bishop of Lincoln
1369–72	Wyclif lectures on the Bible and *Sentences*
1375–6	Wyclif lectures on the theme *De civili dominio*
1377–8	Wyclif composes *De veritate sacrae scripturae*
1379	Foundation of New College
1382	Wyclif condemned by the church and leaves Oxford
c.1410	All scholars ordered to live in halls or colleges
1411	Visitation of Archbishop Arundel
1412	University requires all graduates in future to take an oath condemning Lollardy
1427	Foundation of Lincoln College
1431	New statutes governing the study of arts
1438	Foundation of All Souls College
Post-1450	The Chancellor becomes non-resident and his role is performed by a deputy whom he appoints (from 1549 called the Vice-Chancellor)
1458	Magdalen College established on the site of St John's Hospital
1480	Foundation of Magdalen College School; Magdalen College statutes: first to permit scholars not on the foundation to be residents; first to establish stipendiary lecturers whose lectures were open to all
1480s	Aularian statutes
1480–1550	Decline of the halls and the rise of the colleges as the residence of the majority of scholars
1488	Completion of the Divinity School and Duke Humfrey's Library
1497	Foundation of the Lady Margaret Beaufort chair of theology, the University's first stipendiary post
1498	Colet lectures privately at Oxford on Paul's *Epistle to the Romans*
1500–1600	Establishment of arts teaching to the bachelor's level in colleges
1509	Foundation of Brasenose College
1517	Foundation of Corpus Christi College
1518	Thomas More writes to the University bemoaning its hostility to Greek
1523	The humanist Vives lectures in Oxford
1525	Foundation of Cardinal College (short-lived)
1530	Convocation agrees that Henry VIII's marriage is invalid

1535	Royal visitation conducted by Cromwell's agents; teaching of canon law forbidden; Greek encouraged; colleges and convents of monks and friars closed
1540	Regius chairs of theology, Greek, Hebrew, civil law, and medicine established
1546	Foundation of Christ Church
1548–9	Royal visitation; Edwardian statutes; protestantization of college chapels
1550	Linacre lectures in medicine set up
1550–1650	Emergence of the tutorial system within colleges and halls as a way of policing and fostering the intellectual and moral development of pre-BA-level students in arts
1552	University census of the numbers residing in colleges and halls
1553	College chapels recatholicized
1555	Foundation of Trinity and St John's Colleges; burning of Latimer and Ridley
1556	Burning of Cranmer; legatine visitation of Cardinal Pole and new statutes
1559	Royal visitation; college chapels reprotestantized, though catholic presence survives
1564–5	New statutes
1566	Visit of Elizabeth I
1570	Office of Vice-Chancellor is restricted to heads of house and canons of Christ Church
1571	Act of Parliament confirming the University's privileges; foundation of Jesus College
1571–2	Acts of Parliament limiting the length of time for which college properties could be leased
1574	Robert Parsons of Balliol, one of the last catholic fellow-travellers at Oxford, leaves
1576	Act of Parliament permitting colleges to collect a third of the rent due on a property in kind
1581	University matriculation statute ordering all scholars of 16 or over to subscribe to the Thirty-Nine Articles and the royal supremacy; Calvinists in the ascendant
1589–90	Merton's new library constructed
1592	Visit of Elizabeth I
1602	Bodley's Library opened
1604	University MPs instituted
1605	Visit of James I
1608	William Laud of St John's in his doctoral thesis breaks the Calvinist consensus by claiming only bishops could ordain
1608–10	Merton's Fellows' Quad constructed
1610	Foundation of Wadham College; Oxford's scholars required to take an oath of allegiance to the crown
1613	The consecration of Wadham's 'ornate' chapel reveals the dawn of a new religious aesthetic; orthodox Calvinist Robert Abbot of Balliol attacks Arminians
1613–24	Construction of the Schools' Quadrangle
1618	Sedley bequest for a chair in natural philosophy

1619	Savile bequest for chairs in geometry and astronomy
1621	White bequest for a chair in moral philosophy; Danby bequest for a physic garden
1622	Camden bequest for a chair in ancient history
1624	Foundation of Pembroke College (formerly Broadgates Hall); Tomlins' readership in anatomy founded
1626	Crown forbids discussion of predestination; Heather bequest for a chair in music
1628	Convocation loses right to elect Proctors; Sheldon denies the pope is antichrist
1629	Embellishment of Lincoln's chapel begun
1630	Laud, bishop of London, elected Chancellor
1631	Establishment of the Hebdomadal Board: Convocation and Congregation marginalized; St John's Canterbury Quad begun; altar re-established at Magdalen
1636	Royal Charter; Laudian Code (a summation of existing statutes); visit of Charles I; regius professorship in Arabic founded
1640	Convocation House completed
1641	Laud demits as Chancellor; partial dismantling of Laudian innovations in college chapels
1642	King and court take up residence in the University as the Civil War begins
1642–3	College plate and silver surrendered to the King
1647	University exempted from the assessment ordinance
1648	Parliamentary visitation (commission sits till 1652)
1649	Oxford's club of experimental philosophers, promoted by Wilkins of Wadham, begins to meet
1650–1850	Gradual dwindling of the number of scholars taking higher degrees in theology, civil law, and medicine
1651	Cromwell becomes Chancellor
1653	Cromwellian visitation (commission sits till 1659)
1654	The room above Convocation House becomes the Selden End of Bodley's Library when it receives Selden's books
1656	Robert Boyle comes to Oxford
1660	Restoration visitation (until 1662)
1661	Privy Council confirms all the University's privileges
1662	Royal declaration on avoiding theological controversy
1664	Construction of the Sheldonian begun
1668	Boyle leaves Oxford; Oxford's club of experimental philosophers comes to an end; the University's press is physically established in the Sheldonian's cellars
1669	Construction of the Sheldonian completed
1677	Construction of the Ashmolean begins
1679	Anglo-Saxon lectureship established at Queen's
1682–3	Construction of New College's Garden Quad
1683	James, duke of York visits; university statute backing non-resistance; the destruction of suspect books; completion of the Ashmolean; Oxford Philosophical Society begins to meet

1684	Tom Tower, Christ Church, completed
1686	Obadiah Walker, master of University College, converts to catholicism
1687	Oxford Philosophical Society ceases to meet; James II visits (Feb.); expulsion of Magdalen's fellows and demies for disobedience (Nov.)
1688	reinstatement of Magdalen's fellows and demies (Oct.)
1690	Arthur Bury of Exeter unmasked as an anti-Trinitarian
1693–6	Queen's library constructed
1696	William III visits
1699	Lord almoner's professor of Arabic initiated
1700–7	Additions to New College
1702	Queen Anne visits
1707–14	Peckwater Quad, Christ Church, constructed
1708	Chair of poetry founded by Henry Birkhead
1710	Rebuilding of Queen's begun (completed 1770)
1714	Foundation of Worcester College (formerly Gloucester Hall); the Act is replaced by Encaenia
1715–17	Jacobite riots; Oxford becomes associated with opposition to the Hanoverians
1716	Work begun on All Souls' Codrington Library (completed 1756)
1717	Whig plans to reform Oxford mooted
1724	First regius professor in modern history appointed
1729	Wesleys' Holy Club formed
1730s	Magdalen's New Building constructed
1731	Crewe bequest: funds an annual oration and entertainment at Encaenia
1734	Sherardian chair in botany activated (set up 1728); Construction of the Radcliffe Camera begun
1736	Colleges limited by Act of Parliament in the number of advowsons they could hold
1740	Charter for Hertford College (formerly Hart Hall)
1741	Wesley attacks Oxford for immorality in a sermon at St Mary's
1748	Holywell music room opened
1749	Radcliffe Camera opened
1754	Newdigate becomes one of the University's MPs (till 1780)
1755	Vinerian chair in common law founded
1758	Blackstone judges that the University has the right to make its own statutes, *pace* the Laudian Code
1766	Dr Lee's readership in anatomy established at Christ Church
1768	Methodists removed from St Edmund Hall; Christ Church anatomy school opened
1769	Chancellor's medals for Latin verse and prose composition instituted
1770	Opening of the Radcliffe Infirmary

1772	Lord North becomes Chancellor (until 1792); Oxford comes in from the political cold; construction of the Radcliffe Observatory begun
1772–4	Quarrel over subscription within the University and parliament
1775–8	Canterbury Quad, Christ Church, constructed
1780	First Bampton lectures; foundation of the Lichfield chair of clinical medicine at the Radcliffe Infirmary
1781	Foundation of the Phoenix dining club, Brasenose, Oxford's first
1786	George III visits
1794	Radcliffe Observatory finished
1795	Rawlinson chair of Anglo-Saxon activated (founded 1755)
1796	Sibthorp's bequest for a chair in rural economy
1800	New examination statute establishing a stiffer oral examination for the BA which becomes known as 'Schools'; best candidates ranked
1803	Aldrichian chairs in chemistry, anatomy, and the practice of medicine established
1806	Institution of the Newdigate prize in English poetry
1807	Examination statute revised: two honour classes created; students could be honoured in both Lit. Hum. (classics, ancient history, logic, and moral philosophy) and Mathematics (mathematics and physics); they gradually become separate schools: Lit. Hum. has to be taken first; Mathematics is taken by the high-flying minority
1808	Responsions introduced (Little-Go); initially a first-year exam, then usually taken before coming up.
1810	Copleston's defence of the University against Whig assertions in the *Edinburgh Review* that the Oxford undergraduate course was out of date as it paid no attention to modern subjects and experimental philosophy; Crewe reader in experimental philosophy established (bequest of 1749)
1813	Reader in mineralogy established by a gift of the Prince Regent
1815	First Eights races
1816	Hertford College dissolved
1818	Reader in geology established by a gift of the Prince Regent
1820s	Introduction of written examinations for the BA
1823	Oxford Union Society founded
1825	Third class in honours created; city released from its St Scholastica Day obligation
1826	Drummond chair of political economy founded
1829	Peel by-election after the University's MP sides with catholic emancipation and resigns his seat to test Oxford opinion; Peel is defeated
1830	Examination statute further revised: introduction of the fourth class in honours
1831	Hamilton's attack in the *Edinburgh Review* on Oxford's college-based teaching in arts and his call for the institution of a professorial system

1833	Keble's Assize sermon; heralds the arrival of the Tractarians on the Oxford stage
1834	Parliamentary campaign to end subscription begins with the tabling of Wood's Bill
1836	Tractarians and orthodox Anglicans in the University oppose the appointment of the Noetic Renn Hampden as regius professor of divinity
1839–40	Attempt by the heads of house to introduce modern subjects taught by professors into the undergraduate curriculum is defeated in Convocation
1840	Chair of rural economy activated
1841	Newman's Tract 90 declaring that the Thirty-Nine Articles could be understood in a catholic sense
1842	Chairs of pastoral theology and ecclesiastical history established; introduction of the voluntary theological exam (attempt to provide Oxford MAs entering the church with a theological qualification for the first time)
1844	Ward of Balliol stripped of his degrees for writing a book supporting Roman Catholicism
1845	Newman leaves Oxford for Rome
1846	Heads of house memorandum on the liberalization of the curriculum
1847	Chairs in modern languages and the interpretation of Holy Scripture set up; Jowett of Balliol agitates for a royal commission to reform all aspects of Oxford
1848	Tutors call for liberalization of the curriculum
1849	Taylorian opens
1850	New undergraduate schools in Natural Science and Law and Modern History established; Lit. Hum. school still to be taken initially by all; introduction of Lit. Hum. Moderations at the end of the second year; royal commission established with investigatory powers only
1852	Commission report, known as the Blue Book: above all, calls for opening up fellowships and scholarships to proper competition; does not attack the tutorial system and college-based teaching
1854	Act of Parliament abolishes subscription for undergraduates, replaces the Hebdomadal Board with an elected Hebdomadal Council, re-empowers Congregation as the seat of legislation but allows Convocation to retain spoiling powers, and sets up a new commission with powers of compulsion to reform college statutes; University agrees to the creation of a Natural History Museum
1857–8	The colleges, except St John's, draw up new statutes opening up fellowships and scholarships
1857	Local Examinations Delegacy set up
1858	Universities and Colleges Estates Act: land could be sold for the first time, though proceeds had to be held by the Board of Agriculture; building leases could be granted for up to ninety-nine years rather than forty

1860	University Museum opened: replaces the Ashmolean as the centre of the University's science teaching and research; BAAS meeting held at Oxford, Wilberforce–Huxley debate about Darwinianism; further Universities and Colleges Estates Act allows colleges to borrow to make up for loss of fines on moving to rack-rents
1863	Vincent's Club established
1864	Single-subject specialization permitted but undergraduates still needed to pass Mods in Lit. Hum.
1868	Undergraduates allowed to live in lodgings and have no college attachment; Pattison of Lincoln's *Suggestions on Academical Organisation with Especial Reference to Oxford* published: a call to end the collegiate university, turn the larger colleges into faculty centres, and create halls of residence out of the others
1869	Non-collegiate society for men formed
1870	Opening of the Clarendon Laboratory, the first purpose-built physics lab in Britain; establishment of Keble College; foundation of the Theology School
1871	University Tests Act: ends subscription for fellows and professors; Ruskin School of Art set up
1872	Cleveland Commission set up by parliament to look at university and college finances; Law and Modern History became separate schools; separate pass degree constituted for those who did not want to read for honours: candidates had to take three subjects from a list that included French and German; six boards of study created to oversee the curriculum but not examining (Lit. Hum., law, history, mathematics, natural science, theology): professors ex officio members
1873	Establishment of the Oxford and Cambridge Schools Examination Board
1874	Cleveland Commission reported revealing the great discrepancy in income between the University and the colleges; Hertford College refounded (formerly Magdalen Hall)
1875	Opening of new observatory in the Parks
1877	Oxford and Cambridge Act: appointment of the Selborne Commission to overhaul university and college statutes in the light of the 1871 Act and fears that many fellows were time-servers: no objection to college-based teaching; Wycliffe Hall opened for evangelicals
1878	Oxford extension movement starts (eventually, in the twentieth century, becomes the Department for Continuing Education)
1879	First women's societies: Lady Margaret Hall and Somerville opened
1880–3	College statutes revised: introduction of the distinction between official fellows (tutors chiefly) and ordinary fellows (by examination); end of all subscription; official fellows allowed to marry in most cases; professors given college attachment; colleges to contribute to university income
1882	New university statutes: six boards of study replaced by four faculties or faculty boards (arts, natural science, law, and theology), which are given control of examinations (formerly in the hands of the Vice-Chancellor and Proctors); the arts faculty to consist of two sub-faculties of Lit. Hum. and modern history;

natural science faculty to consist of two sub-faculties: natural science and mathematics, and medicine; professors ex officio members of the boards

1883   University taxation introduced: each college to pay a percentage of its endowment return to the University (from 1885 a graduated tax based on college wealth); new Examination Schools opened on the High Street (as a base for the humanities); *Oxford Magazine* begins publication (till 1970; restarted 1985); creation of 'Divvers', a compulsory second-year examination in Holy Scripture

1884   Pusey House (Anglo-catholic) opened; readership in anthropology established (first in UK); Toynbee Hall (London) founded; Temple supports Darwin in the Bampton lectures; women begin to be admitted to university examinations

1885   Geology part of the Natural Science School; chair in English language and literature established; OUDS founded

1886   Mansfield College moves to Oxford (Congregationalist training college); St Hugh's founded; readership in geography created; Indian Institute opened (mooted in 1881); Oriental Studies Honours School established and a new sub-faculty board of the faculty of arts created; Natural Science School split into different branches and undergraduates allowed to specialize; undergraduates taking the Natural Science School released from the need to do Classical Mods, provided they take the Preliminary Examination in Natural Science (which quickly becomes a specialist rather than a general examination in the branch of science to be offered in Schools)

1889   Manchester Unitarian College moves to Oxford

1890   Pitt-Rivers ethnographic bequest (1883) housed in new building attached to the University Museum

1892   *Isis* founded; Oxford University Day Training College established for pupil teachers

1893   St Hilda's founded; Society for Oxford Home Students (female) opened

1894   School of English set up; archaeological material in the Old Ashmolean transferred to the New Ashmolean

1895   BLitt and BSc established

1895   Astronomy and mineralogy part of the Natural Science School

1895–6   Congregation refuses to admit women to degrees

1896   Educational Diploma set up; the Jesuits establish a presence in Oxford (Campion Hall from 1918)

1897   The Benedictines return to Oxford

1899   Ruskin Hall founded (from 1903, Ruskin College)

1900   DLitt and DSc created; second chair of physics established

1901   Department of Pathology opened

1902   Rhodes Scholarships established; chair of agriculture created

1903   Honour School of Modern Languages created; Radcliffe Science Library moved from the University Museum to a separate building

1904   Beit chair in imperial history founded

1905	Diplomas in anthropology, forestry, and scientific engineering and mining mooted and organizing committees created; India Forestry Service School transferred to Oxford
1907	Oxford University Appointments Committee officially recognized (in existence since 1892); first chair in engineering established; Gore calls for royal commission on grounds of Oxbridge failing to adapt
1908	Committee of the University and the WEA produce *Oxford and Working Class Education*; merger of the University Galleries and the New Ashmolean to form the Ashmolean Museum of Art and Archaeology
1909	Diploma in agriculture set up; Honour School of Engineering established (within the Natural Science School)
1910	The Franciscans back in Oxford; Drapers' Company provides a grant for an electrical laboratory
1911	Women's results included in Schools' lists for the first time
1912	General Board of Faculties set up which largely controls academic policy until its abolition at the end of 1999; Barnett House (Centre for Social Studies) set up; Department of Pharmacology established with its own reader; Agricultural Institute set up
1912–13	First state grant to Oxford for the Department of Engineering
1913	St Edmund Hall (last surviving medieval hall) saved from absorption by Queen's; Institute of Agricultural Economics established; faculty of arts divided into four faculties (Lit. Hum., modern history, oriental languages, and modern languages and English)
1914	Department of Social Anthropology established; purpose-built engineering laboratory opened
1916	A fourth, research, year introduced into the undergraduate degree in chemistry; Committee of Advanced Studies set up; Dyson Perrins Organic Chemistry Laboratory opened
1917	DPhil established; women admitted to medical studies
1918	Jesuit and Benedictine hostels gain permanent private hall status
1919	Royal commission set up to look into Oxbridge under Asquith as price of receiving permanent financial assistance from the state; pass schools in Agriculture and Forestry established
1920	Compulsory Greek abolished for matriculands; full membership of the University granted to women (could take degrees as well as sit the examinations); creation of the Honour School of PPE; theology degrees opened to non-Anglicans; biochemistry chair established (fourth in the country)
1921	The Dominicans return to Oxford
1922	Royal commission reports, but demands minimal reforms including the recognition of Congregation's sovereignty: no attempt to undermine the tutorial system; Oxford henceforth receives an annual state subsidy
1923	Universities of Oxford and Cambridge Act: establishes executive commission to oversee changes demanded by Asquith

1924	Elections to Council made more democratic; state-funded Agricultural Engineering Research Institute established at Oxford (until 1942); Lewis Evans' gift of collection of scientific instruments placed in Old Ashmolean
1925	First secretary to the faculties appointed; college statutes renewed: most significant change, the number of fellows in different categories is no longer capped
1925–6	Women's colleges gain royal charters
1926	Uniform admissions procedure for first time: Responsions becomes an entrance examination for those not taking the colleges' scholarship examination; non-academic members of Convocation no longer able to thwart the will of the majority in Congregation; creation of a faculty board in English; Regent's Park College (Baptist) moves to Oxford
1927	Quota placed on the number of women students; Dunn School of Pathology opened (bequest of William Dunn, 1922); biochemistry building opened (largely funded by the Rockefeller Foundation); electrical wing of the engineering laboratory opened
1928	St Peter's becomes a permanent private hall
1929	Rhodes House built
1930	Creation of the School of Geography
1931	Non-collegiate society for men officially renamed St Catherine's Society, with its own building in St Aldate's; abolition of 'Divvers'
1932	Faculty board of social studies created; Bureau of Animal Population established; Oxford Society founded for old members
1933	'King and country debate' in the Union
1934	Science Area designated; embryonic Institute of Mathematics set up
1935	Museum of History of Science incorporated (old Ashmolean); Nuffield Institute of Medical Research opened; Institute of Economics and Statistics set up; closure of Radcliffe Observatory (moved to Pretoria)
1936	Institute of Experimental Psychology opened; Diploma in public and social administration established; Nuffield bequest for clinical medicine; Natural Science Moderations introduced to encourage natural scientists not to specialize from the beginning
1937	University appeal for inter alia an extension to the Bodleian and a new physics laboratory; Nuffield bequest to promote engineering and accountancy: University perverts the bequest and decides to establish a new postgraduate college for the social sciences which becomes Nuffield College; creation of the School of Rural Economy
1938	Edward Grey Institute of Field Ornithology set up; the appeasement city election
1939	Griffith Institute for Egyptology set up attached to the Ashmolean; Department of Forestry created; New Clarendon opened; Oxford branch of the Association of University Teachers established
1941	Diploma in experimental psychology established

1942	New physical chemistry laboratory opened (thanks to Nuffield); Society of Oxford Home Students (female) becomes St Anne's Society
1944	Honour School of Music established
1945	Honour School of Forestry established (agreed upon 1938)
1946	Opening of the new Bodleian by George VI (though finished by 1940); Institute of Colonial Studies established; beginning of the CUF scheme (college tutors in arts giving intercollegiate lectures to be brought on to the university payroll as part-time university lecturers)
1947	Honour School of PPP created; BPhil established
1948	Maison Française opened
1949	Honour School of Biochemistry created; extension of CUF scheme to all intercollegiate lecturers; building of Nuffield College begins
1950	Forestry building opened; St Antony's College founded (first fully functioning graduate college); University's direct representation in parliament abolished
1951	Botany building opened
1952	St Anne's receives charter to become women-only college; Keble becomes a full college; the publication of separate lists of men's and women's results in Schools abandoned
1953	Physiology building opened; Queen Elizabeth House established as a centre for colonial studies; colleges allowed to invest in equities with ministerial permission; St Antony's receives charter
1955	Mansfield becomes a permanent private hall
1956	Honour School of Metallurgy established
1957	Quota lifted on number of women students; University launches its Historic Buildings Appeal; Computing Laboratory set up; Regent's Park and Greyfriars become permanent private halls; St Edmund Hall incorporated as a college; Oxford's Middle East Centre opened in St Antony's
1958	First MCR established at Lincoln; *Isis* H-bomb issue; chair in metallurgy created
1959	University's Chilver Committee on entrance requirements reports; metallurgy building completed (first building on Keble triangle); Oxford Instrument Company founded (first successful spin-out company); all the women's colleges become full members of the University with rights of self-government; faculty board of psychological studies set up
1960	Postal voting introduced to Congregation; St John's Beehive building (first modernist college building) completed; compulsory Latin for science matriculands abolished
1961	St Peter's Hall given collegiate status and charter; arrival of Opus Dei in Oxford
1962	Merging of scholars' and commoners' entrance exam following the Hardie Report; colleges' admissions office set up; St Catherine's opened (established 1960 out of the St Catherine's Society of Non-Collegiate Students); Linacre House set up as a non-collegiate society for graduates in St Aldate's; St Antony's charter changed so that it can take women; Nuffield's buildings completed

1963   Nuffield receives charter; Student Representative Council set up; eleven-storey engineering building mooted; separate faculty of mathematics established

1964   St Catherine's buildings completed; first reader in sociology appointed; new biochemistry building; Norrington Table begins; Oxford and Cambridge join UCCA but retain own entrance exams; amendment of 1925 Universities and Colleges Estates Act, gives more freedom to manage finances and acquire equities without ministerial permission; New College votes by two-thirds majority to amend statutes and allow women

1964–5   Franks Commission sits to look into all aspects of the collegiate University to forestall a possible government commission, responding to criticisms of Oxbridge in the 1963 Robbins Report on higher education

1965   St Cross Building (for law and English) opened on what becomes known as the St Cross site; Kneale Committee Report (on changing the format of Oxford examinations); Honour School in Engineering Science and Economics established; Iffley, later Wolfson, and St Cross Colleges opened as graduate societies; Manchester College given society status; teach-in at the Union Society on Vietnam; Congregation votes all senior members of the University entitled to a college fellowship

1966   Franks Report calls for expansion in graduate numbers, more science students, more working class students, joint degrees, a shake-up of the University's administration to speed up decisions, and the diversion of university taxation to build up the endowments of poorer colleges: the tutorial system must be preserved, though room for more seminar and lecture-based teaching; Shackleton Report on library provision (not dealt with by Franks); Institute of Mathematics gets own building; establishment of Conference of Colleges, watered-down version of joint decision-making body wanted by Franks

1967   End of the fourth class degree; beginning of college taxation to increase college endowments

1968   Honour Schools in Physics and Philosophy and Mathematics and Philosophy created; Proctors mobbed by students seeking an end to the existing disciplinary structure; Hart committee on university discipline and representation largely gives students what they demand; decision taken to move the University's administration to Wellington Square

1970   Honour Schools in Human Sciences and Experimental Psychology set up; student sit-in in the Clarendon Building (heart of the university administration), sparked by a belief that the administration kept files on student troublemakers

1971   Zoology and psychology building completed; nuclear physics laboratory opened; combined Honour School of Agriculture and Forestry created; MSc introduced as a graduate qualification

1972   Debate in Congregation on co-education; Centre for Socio-Legal Studies established at Wolfson; Hebrew Studies Centre created as an affiliate of the University; University's counselling service set up

743

1973	Five male colleges go co-ed (first female students admitted 1974); student occupation of the Examination Schools in pursuit of an all-Oxford Student Union; Balliol elects a female fellow
1974	University representation on the city council abolished; entitlement statute came into being (to ensure all University postholders had a college fellowship); student attempt to occupy the Indian Institute and the university offices in Wellington Square; Wolfson's new buildings complete
1976	Rhodes Trust opens scholarships to women
1977	Congregation accepts report of review committee giving go-ahead to expanding the number of co-educational colleges; women allowed to become Proctors; Honour School of Fine Art established; Linacre moved to Cherwell Edge
1978	Oxford University Computing Service created; BFA established
1979	All men's colleges, except Christ Church and Oriel, go mixed, along with Lady Margaret Hall and St Anne's; Green College established (for graduates)
1981	Oxford fields the first female cox in the boat race; St Cross moves into Pusey House
1982	Abolition of the School of Agriculture and Forestry; creation of the Honour School of Pure and Applied Biology
1983	Dover Report on undergraduate admissions, calling for applicnts to be allowed not to take the entrance exam and be admitted on their A-level performance; Templeton College founded outside the University as a school of business studies
1985	Prime Minister Thatcher denied an honorary degree by Congregation; Oxford Centre for Islamic Studies set up in St Cross; the *Oxford Magazine* revived
1986	First UGC RAE (trial run); division of the second class degree; Linacre receives charter and becomes college
1987	Roberts Report on postgraduate provision, which is judged highly unsatisfactory in terms of academic supervision and social provision; directors of graduate studies appointed by each faculty board
1988	Campaign for Oxford launched (£220 million sought over five years); External Relations Office set up: Oxford is the first British university to launch a major appeal; creation of ISIS Innovation (originally OURADO) for exploitation of know-how arising from research funded by UK research councils or other bodies where rights not tied
1989	First real RAE; installation of the first Vice-Chancellor not to be a head of house in the modern era (Sir Richard Southwood); Institute of Molecular Medicine founded; Manchester becomes a permanent private hall for mature students
1990	Honour School of Biology created; end of the Honour Schools of Botany and Zoology; Congregation agrees to set up a graduate school of management studies at Templeton; establishment of the Centre for Cognitive Neuroscience
1991	Honour School of Archaeology and Anthropology created; publication of Oxford's first 'mission statement' drawn up at the behest of the UFC
1992	Second RAE

1994	North Commission set up to revisit the Franks Report and advise on the reform of university governance; Deech Report calls for the abolition of the Oxford entrance examination in the expectation that this will encourage applications from state schools; campaign for Oxford wound down: £340 million raised; Department for Continuing Education becomes Kellogg College
1995	Templeton receives its charter and becomes a graduate college specializing in business studies; Mansfield College incorporation
1996	Coopers & Lybrand report on governance for the North Commission: identifies four problems: staff retention, quality of teaching, good use of research money, heavy dependence on government funds; first external audit of Oxford's teaching by the QAA; third RAE; entrance examination abolished; site for Saïd Business School rejected by Congregation; Wycliffe Hall becomes a permanent private hall; Manchester College for mature students becomes Harris Manchester and receives its charter
1997	North Report calling for the establishment of a new Council with power over both institutional and academic policy and the replacement of the General Board by three academic boards (arts, science, and medicine), subject to the new Council: Congregation to remain sovereign and the tutorial system to be preserved; review of computing services: calls for greater use of local services with subject-specific computer officers and area-specific computer units; working party on access created; new scheme for the creation of ad hominem readers and professors begins; alternative site for the Saïd Business School accepted by Congregation; Centre for Brazilian Studies set up; HEFCE demands the University responds to criticism of the separate college fee in Dearing's *Higher Learning in Society*
1998	North Report discussed in Congregation; Joint Working Party on Governance set up and largely supports implementation of the main planks of the North Report: suggests creating two academic boards (now called divisions) for the arts (humanities and social sciences); Oxbridge loses separate college fee (henceforth HEFCE pays per capita fees to the University and a proportion distributed to the colleges); all Oxford home and EU undergraduates pay a fee of £1,000 p.a. to the University, following government legislation permitting this
1999	Second report of Joint Working Party on Governance: increases college representation on the new Council, suggests the number of science boards be increased to three by separating the physical and life sciences, and leaves it to Congregation to decide whether the arts faculties should be collected into one or two divisions; Congregation accepts the modified proposals and votes for two arts divisions
2000	New governance proposals implemented: establishment of new Council and five academic divisions
2001	Opening of the Saïd Business School, the Sackler Library, and the Rothermere American Institute; fourth RAE
2002	Second Deech Report on admissions calls for greater university control over admissions; new building for economics opened on the St Cross site; Peter

Medawar Building for Pathogen Research opened on South Parks Rd; Portuguese Studies Centre established

2003   OUP transfers to the University a one-off capital gift of £74 million; purchase of the redundant Radcliffe Infirmary site as a possible centre for the humanities

2004   New university appeal for £1.25 billion mooted; consultation document on academic strategy; draft of the University's corporate plan for HEFCE (2004–9); Clarendon Fund established to support 100 graduates; Elizabeth II opens a new chemistry laboratory; Oxford has its first Vice-Chancellor who is not a member of the University when elected by Congregation (John Hood of the University of Auckland)

2005   Oxford's access agreement with OFFA to establish the Oxford Opportunity Bursary Scheme in 2006–7 (in return for being allowed to charge students a higher tuition fee of £3,000; agreement required under 2004 Higher Education Act permitting the increase); Green Papers on Governance drawn up by a committee asked to report on the working of the governance reforms instituted in 2000: papers call for wholesale restructuring at the top with the creation of separate bodies for institutional and academic affairs, the first either completely or potentially dominated by outsiders; great opposition in Congregation to both papers, though Congregation to remain sovereign; continued discussion of academic strategy and finalization of the University's corporate plan for HEFCE (2005/6–2009/10); report of a further working party on undergraduate admissions advocating a greater role for faculties and departments; masterplan for the Radcliffe Infirmary site: to contain a humanities library and facilities for most of the humanities faculties and mathematics; James Martin 21st Century School set up with large donation from businessman

2006   HEFCE Assurance Review of the University; White Paper on Governance, little changed from the second Green Paper: voted down by Congregation; much greater responsibility for admissions given to the University and establishment of a common framework; reduction of the number of divisions to four: Humanities, Social Sciences, Mathematical, Physical and Life Sciences, and Medicine; attempt to finalize the JRAM; new student fee of £3,000 p.a. introduced

2007   Final report of HEFCE Assurance Service on Oxford (negative on governance but no repercussions)

2008   Official launch of new appeal; University's strategic plan for HEFCE (2008/9–2012/13); merger of Green and Templeton Colleges; fifth RAE; new biology and biomedical sciences buildings opened

2009   Turnbull Committee's review of governance in light of HEFCE dissatisfaction: accepts Congregation's verdict on the plan to separate institutional and academic decision-making at the top and recommends strengthening the presence of externals on Council and Council's committees: as the committee was divided in its recommendations, no action is taken; New Bodleian to be refurbished and renamed the Weston Library; Oxford's second Vice-Chancellor to be appointed from overseas (Andrew Hamilton of Yale)

2010   University appeal reaches £817 million; report on establishing a new career structure for Oxford academics presented; proposed changes to dons' superannuation system rejected in Congregation; Bodley's new book storage facility at Swindon completed; new Bodleian underground reading room, the Gladstone Link, opened; James Martin School renamed the Oxford Martin School and relaunched with another large donation from its founder (includes the Oxford Institute for the Future of the Mind)

2012   Appeal target reached and a new target of £3 billion announced; *The Times* 'Good University Guide' ranks Oxford the best university in the UK for the eleventh year running: in *The Times Higher Education* world rankings Oxford is judged the best in Europe; University is permitted to opt out of a law ending a default retirement age for men and women, and sets its own retirement age for academics as 67; Mica Ertegun benefaction to establish Ertegun House and the Mica and Ahmet Ertegun Graduate Scholarship Programme; Moritz bequest to support poor students; Blavatnik donation to establish a School of Government; Ruskin College relocates to Old Headington (original site bought by Exeter College in 2010)

2013   New strategic plan for HEFCE (2013/14–2017/18); quarrel with residents and conservationists over graduate accommodation built by the University on the edge of Pool Meadow and the proposed site of the Blavatnik School of Government; Congregation accepts that all postholders will have the title of professor; Li Ka Shing Centre for Health Information and Discovery opened on the Old Road Campus, Headington

2014   Weston Library opened; the Oxford 'Big Data' Institute given planning permission; first REF

2015   Oxford's first female Vice-Chancellor announced (in office from 1 January 2016): professor Louise Richardson (principal of the University of St Andrews); fund-raising campaign reaches £2 billion mark; Zaha Hadid's new three-storey building for St Antony's Middle East Centre opened; end of dons' final-salary superannuation scheme announced (from April 2016)

MAPS

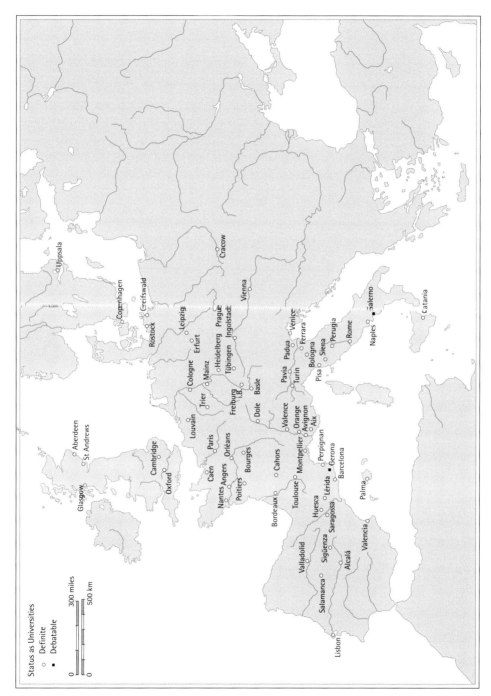

MAP 1. Europe's Universities in 1500

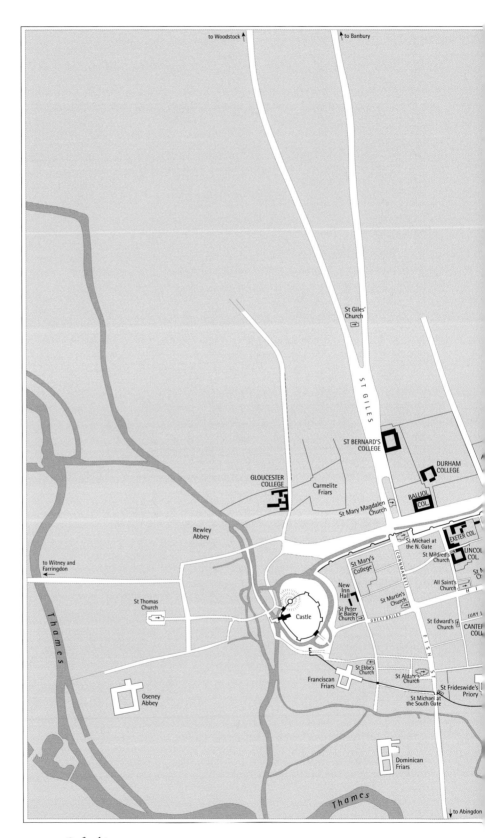

MAP 2. Oxford in 1500

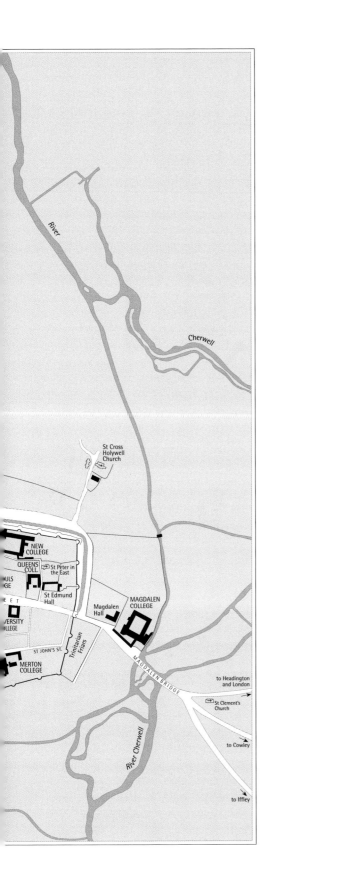

River

Cherwell

St Cross
Holywell
Church

NEW
COLLEGE

QUEENS
COLL.

St Peter in
the East

ULS
GE

St Edmund
Hall

Magdalen
Hall

MAGDALEN
COLLEGE

VERSITY
LLEGE

ST JOHN'S ST.

Trinitarian
Friars

MERTON
COLLEGE

MAGDALEN BRIDGE

to Headington
and London

St Clement's
Church

River Cherwell

to Cowley

to Iffley

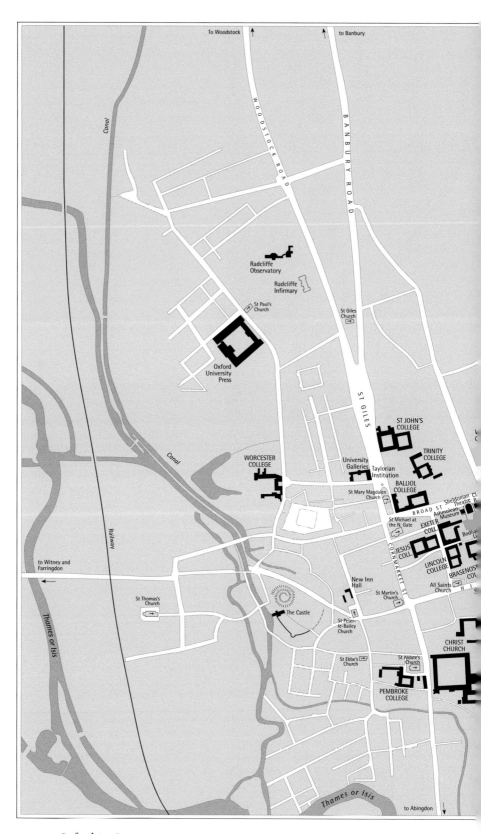

MAP 3. Oxford in 1850

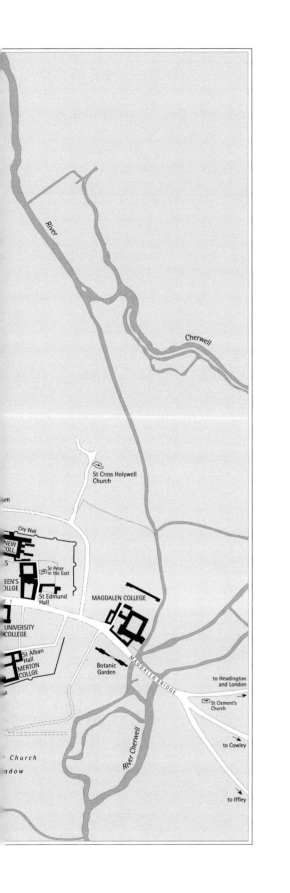

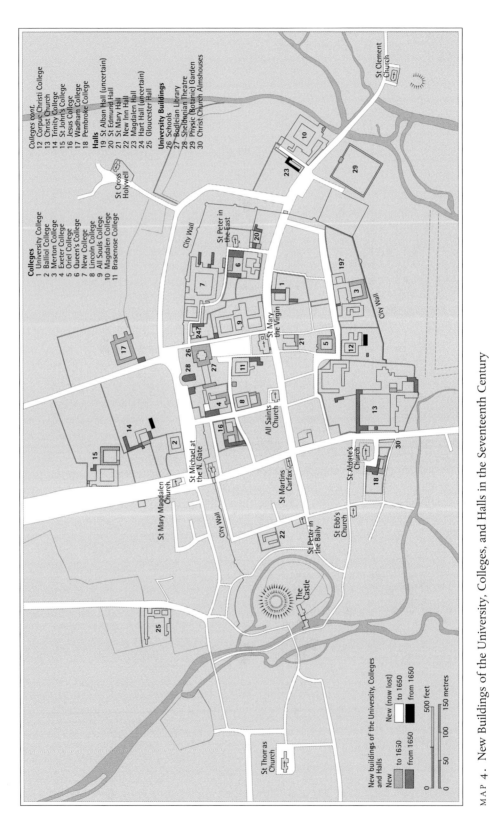

MAP 4. New Buildings of the University, Colleges, and Halls in the Seventeenth Century

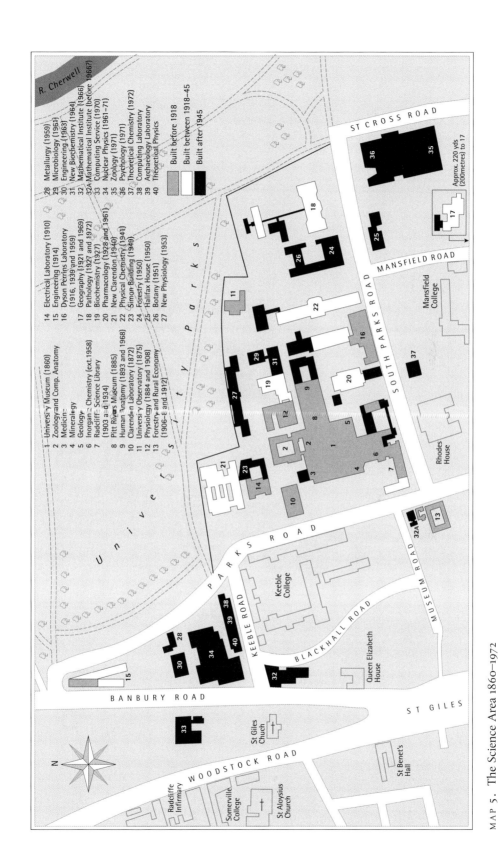

MAP 5. The Science Area 1860–1972

1 University Museum (1860)
2 Zoology and Comp. Anatomy
3 Medicine
4 Mineralogy
5 Geology
6 Inorganic Chemistry (ext.1958)
7 Radcliffe Science Library
   (1903 and 1934)
8 Pitt Rivers Museum (1885)
9 Human Anatomy (1893 and 1968)
10 Clarendon Laboratory (1872)
11 University Observatory (1875)
12 Physiology (1884 and 1908)
13 Forestry and Rural Economy
   (1906–8 and 1912)

14 Electrical Laboratory (1910)
15 Engineering (1914)
16 Dyson Perrins Laboratory
   (1916, 1939 and 1959)
17 Geography (1921 and 1969)
18 Pathology (1927 and 1972)
19 Biochemistry (1927)
20 Pharmacology (1928 and 1961)
21 New Clarendon (1940)
22 Physical Chemistry (1941)
23 Simon Building (1949)
24 Forestry (1950)
25 Halifax House (1950)
26 Botany (1951)
27 New Physiology (1953)

28 Metallurgy (1959)
29 Microbiology (1961)
30 Engineering (1963)
31 New Biochemistry (1964)
32 Mathematical Institute (1966)
32A Mathematical Institute (before 1966?)
33 Computing Service (1970)
34 Nuclear Physics (1961–71)
35 Zoology (1971)
36 Psychology (1971)
37 Theoretical Chemistry (1972)
38 Computing Laboratory
39 Archaeology Laboratory
40 Theoretical Physics

Built before 1918
Built between 1918–45
Built after 1945

Approx. 220 yds
(200 metres) to 17

R. Cherwell

University Parks

ST CROSS ROAD

MANSFIELD ROAD

Mansfield College

SOUTH PARKS ROAD

Rhodes House

PARKS ROAD

Keeble College

MUSEUM ROAD

KEEBLE ROAD

BLACKHALL ROAD

Queen Elizabeth House

BANBURY ROAD

St Giles Church

ST GILES

Radcliffe Infirmary

Somerville College

St Aloysius Church

St Benet's Hall

WOODSTOCK ROAD

N

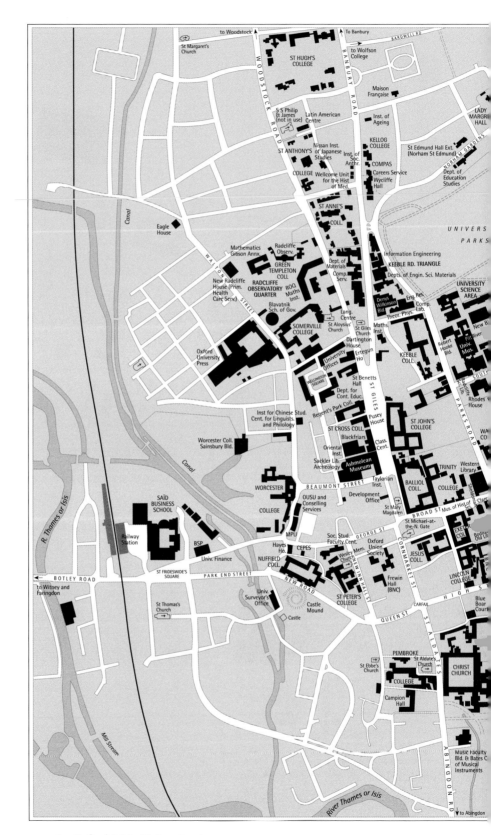

MAP 6. Oxford: Main University Area 2015

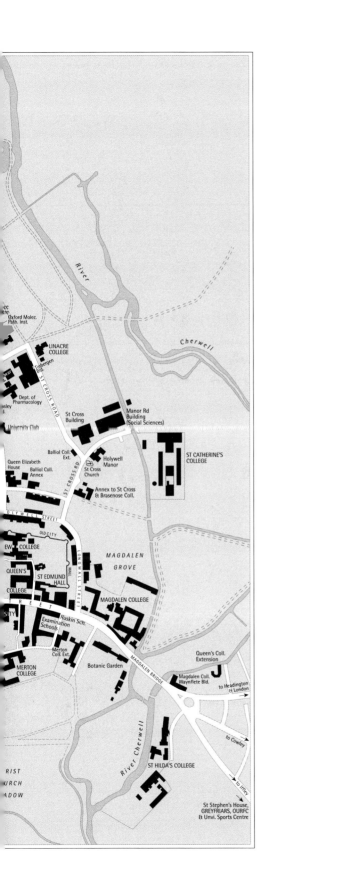

Oxford Molec.
Path. Inst.

LINACRE
COLLEGE

ST CROSS ROAD

Tinbergen
Bld.

Dept. of
Pharmacology

University Club

St Cross
Building

Manor Rd
Building
(Social Sciences)

Cherwell

River

Balliol Coll.
Ext.

Queen Elizabeth
House

Balliol Coll.
Annex

ST CROSS RD

Holywell
Manor

St Cross
Church

ST CATHERINE'S
COLLEGE

Annex to St Cross
& Brasenose Coll.

HOLYWELL STREET

OLD CITY

EW COLLEGE

QUEEN'S
COLLEGE

ST EDMUND
HALL

LONGWALL STREET

MAGDALEN

GROVE

MAGDALEN COLLEGE

STREET

SITY

Ruskin Sch.

Examination
Schools

Merton
Coll. Ext.

MERTON
COLLEGE

Botanic Garden

MAGDALEN BRIDGE

Queen's Coll.
Extension

Magdalen Coll.
Waynflete Bld.

to Headington
& London

River Cherwell

to Cowley

ST HILDA'S COLLEGE

to Iffley

RIST
URCH
ADOW

St Stephen's House,
GREYFRIARS, OURFC
& Unvi. Sports Centre

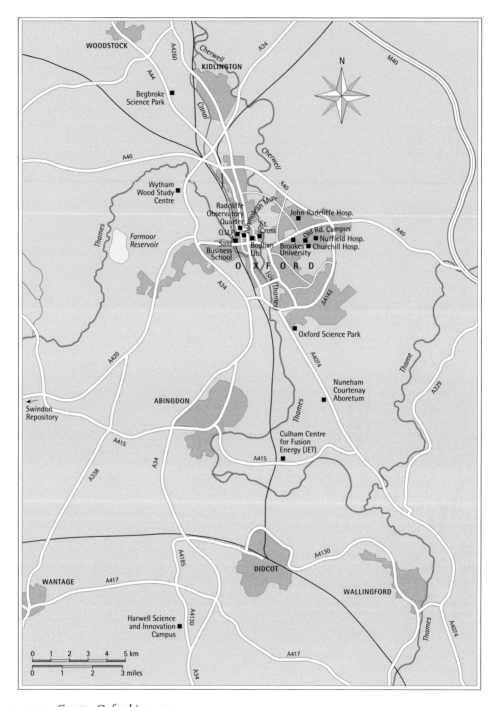

MAP 7. Greater Oxford in 2015

Tables

TABLE 1 Student Numbers, c.1300–2015

	Undergraduates	Women as percentage of all undergraduates	Postgraduates	Total
c.1300				2,000+
c.1450				1,700+
1552				1,015
1566				1,764
1605				2,254
1612				2,920
1634				3,305
1700				1,850
1842	1,222			1,800
c.1860	2,000			
1890	2,676			
1914	3,097		100	
1923/4	3,709	18	439	4,163
1938/9	4,391	17	536	5,023
1948/9	6,159	15.1	1,071	7,294
1958/9	7,436	13.9	1,263	8,699
1964/5	7,297	16.3	2,153	9,450
1986/7	9,370	Not Found	3,394	13,124
1991/2	10,326	40.5	3,962	14,288
1993/4	10,462	40.8	4,276	14,738
1995/6	10,823	41	4,413	15,236
2000/1	10,978	44.9	4,931	16,411
2002/3	11,096	46.7	5,626	19,097
2007/8	11,917	47.3	7,580	20,014
2011/12	11,752	45.9	9,621	21,872
2012/13	11,832	45.8	9,857	22,177
2014/15	11,703	46.5	10,173	22,348

Note: (1) Totals from c.1300 to 1842 include senior members. (2) Totals from 1923/4 onwards usually include a number of ancillary/visiting students who cannot be classified as either undergraduates or postgraduates. (3) The percentage of women students for 1923/4 and 1938/9 refers to all women students, not just female undergraduates.

Sources: T. H. Aston, 'Oxford's Medieval Alumni', *Past and Present*, 74 (1977), 6–8; *HUO*, iii. 153–4; *HUO*, iv. 44; *HUO*, vii. 159; Mallet, iii. 469n; Franks, ii. 12, 13, and 15; *OUG*, relevant years (annual statistics until 2007/8 were published as a supplement every July; available online from 1991 at <http://www.ox. ac.uk/gazette/statisticalinformation/#d.en.6208)>; <http://www.admin.ox.ac.uk/ac-div/statistics& reporting/studentstatistics/oneyearsummary> (annual statistics from 2009); <http://www.ox.ac.uk/ about/facts-and-figures/student-numbers> (as of December 2014).

TABLE 2 Undergraduate Admissions by Gender and School Type, 1958–2011

Dec.	Total appl.	M	MA	W	WA	I	Mt	O	Offers by sector
1900–13									18:82
1938			1,235		258				Mn 34:66
									Wn 47:53
1958			2,056		325				Mn 46:54
									Wn 62:38
1965	5,853	4,011	1,912	1,842	443				Mn 58:42
									Wn 68:32
1969									56.1:43.9
1979									49.9:50.1
1985	8,130	4,782	1,883	3,348	1,237				
1987	7,190	4,189	1,828	3,001	1,242				
1989									48.1:51.9
1994	9,787	5,372	1,895	4,008	1,380	43.9%	33.2%	20.8%	48.1:51.9
1998	9,320	5,054	2,000	4,266	1,720	47.7%	39.6%	21.2%	48.4:51.5
1999	9,340	4,661	1,637	4,679	1,584	40.6%	34.7%	19.6%	51.8:48.1
2002	11,793	5,873	1,681	5,920	1,600	33.8%	27.4%	15.7%	51.7:48.3
2004	12,496	6,282	1,690	6,214	1,524	32.1%	25.6%	12.8%	51.4:48.6
2010	17,343	8,665	1,678	8,478	1,508	24.7%	19.9%	9.8%	57.7:42.3
2011	17,241	8,764	1,732	8,477	1,501	25.0%	20.1%	9.9%	57.5:42.5

Note: Appl. = applicants; figures do not exist before the creation of the Central Admissions Office; M = number of male applicants; MA = number of men accepted; W = number of women applicants; WA = number of women accepted; I = percentage of applicants from UK independent schools offered a place; Mt = percentage of applicants from UK maintained schools (including direct grant) offered a place; O = percentage of applicants from other educational backgrounds (usually overseas) offered a place; offers by sector: percentage of maintained to independent schools places offered in a given admissions round (ratio 1938, 1958, 1965 gives the figure for those actually admitted and separate figures for men (Mn) and women (Wn); ratio 1900–13 is for men taking a degree in arts).

Sources: HUO, viii. 53 and 756; Franks, i. 72 and ii. 58–9 and 71; OUG, relevant years (usually December supplements); <http://www.ox.ac.uk/gazette/statisticalinformation/#d.en.6208> (data back to 1990).

TABLE 3 Number of Undergraduates Matriculating to Read for an Honour School, 1951–2012 (Selected Honour Schools and Overall Total)

MT	BS	C	E	J	LH	M	MH/H	ML	PPE	P	PS	All HS (% Sc)
1951		100	176	183	132	75	340	220	187	52	53	1,704 (21.4)
1961		176	230	190	178	115	313	223	251	167	63	2,271 (31.6)
1971		187	236	196	161	181	291	225	245	176	97	2,610 (38.4)
1981		190	292	252	148	200	295	251	289	184	102	3,010 (37.2)
1991	104	181	264	259	137	189	300	213	312	179	112	3,158 (39.3)
2001	93	179	251	274	119	180	262	206	272	172	159	3,335 (38.2)
2004	96	173	258	253	112	179	241	185	266	175	177	3,281 (39.5)
2005	92	179	251	238	118	177	252	205	250	170	130	3,290 (42.9)
2012												11,360 (45.4)

Note: MT: Michaelmas Term; BS = Biological Sciences; C = Chemistry Part 1; E =English; J = Jurisprudence; LH = Lit. Hum.; M = Mathematics; MH/H = Modern History/History; PPE: Philosophy, Politics, and Economics; P = Physics; PS = Physiological Sciences (includes Pre-Clinical Medicine); HS = Honour Schools; Sc = Science and Medicine (joint schools that straddle the divide, except Psychology, Philosophy, and Physiology, are counted as arts).

NB: The information for 2012 relates to the total number of full-time undergraduates in the current four divisions (Humanities; Social Sciences; Mathematics, Physics and Life Sciences; and Medicine).

Sources: <http://www.ox.ac.uk/gazette/statisticalinformation/#d.en.6208> (student numbers supplements 1991–2005, table 5, and 2012, table 2; from 2007, the OUG no longer provided information about the number of undergraduates matriculating to read individual honours schools.

TABLE 4 Postgraduate Numbers, 1914–2015

	Total number	PGR	PGT	W	O	H & SS	PGs/AS
1914	100						
1928/9	357					86.6%	7.8%
1938/9	536	300	236			72.4%	11%
1948/9	1,071			13.3%		66.9%	14.8%
1958/9	1,263			13.2%		67.6%	14.5%
1964/5	2,153	1,487	666	15.0%	29.4%	60%	22.8%
1971/2	2,805						
1981/2	2,868						
1986/7	3,394					62.8%	
1991/2	3,962	3,027	935	35.6%	41.8%	56.6%	27.7%
1993/4	4,276	2,937	1,339	36.4%	43.6%	52.8%	29%
1995/6	4,413	3,067	1,346	38.6%	44.5%	57.3%	29%
2001/2	5,188	3,166	2,022	41.9%	53%	53.7%	31.2%
2005/6	6,768	4,169	2,599	44%	57.6%	50.9%	36.7%
2011/12	9,621	5,371	4,250	44.1%	60.5%	54.9%	44%
2012/13	9,857	5,518	4,330	43.5%	55.5%	54.1%	44.5%
2014/15	10,173	5,637	4,536	43.6%	62.0%	53.7%	45.5%

Note: PGR = postgraduate research degree; PGT = postgraduate mainly taught degree; W = women as percentage of total number; O = overseas students (including those from the EU) as percentage of total; H & SS: humanities and social science students as percentage of total; PGs/AS: postgraduates as a percentage of all students. The figures for PGR students between 1938/9 and 2005/6 are estimates based on those registered as studying for a DPhil and a variety of other degrees with a dominant research component, which have been introduced over the years, such as the MLitt: it is only recently that the University has divided postgraduates into the categories PGR and PGT.

Sources: Franks, ii. 13, 15, 23, 25; Jack Morrell, *Science at Oxford 1914–1939: Transforming an arts university* (Oxford,1997), p. 29; <http://www.ox.ac.uk/gazette/statisticalinformation/#d.en.6208> (since 1991; information about foreign graduates only until 2007); <http://www.ox.ac.uk/about/facts-and-figures/student-numbers> (live site only gives information for the current academic year).

TABLE 5 Faculties and Sub-Faculties with More than 100 Full-Time Doctoral Students in December 2013 (plus Biochemistry)

	1991	2000	2006	2010	2011	2013
Biochemistry	n/a	n/a	145	92	75	72
Chemistry	n/a	n/a	214	269	272	254
Clinical Medicine	45	99	174	227	n/a	157
Computer Science	n/a	n/a	85	118	125	118
Engineering Science	n/a	n/a	220	247	237	253
English	106	143	192	160	172	154
Geography & Environment	51	59	123	106	120	138
History	131	185	273	278	257	247
Law	23	68	106	165	157	138
Materials	n/a	106	91	122	131	144
Mathematics	117	100	132	167	174	178
Medieval & Modern Languages	50	57	90	117	109	120
Oriental Studies	38	55	123	109	103	115
Politics	n/a	n/a	130	170	149	129
Zoology	n/a	n/a	121	120	126	129

Note: Figs for chemistry include organic and inorganic. Figs for English include English (before 1500) and English language and literature. Figs for geography in 1991 and 2000 include anthropology. Figs for history in 2013 include history, history of art, history of science and medicine, and economic and social history. n/a: figures unavailable. In these years, the subject was subsumed in a wider category; thus politics in 1991 and 2000 was subsumed in social sciences.

Sources: <http:// www.ox.ac.uk/gazette/statisticalinformation/#d.en.6208> (1991–2005); <http://www.admin.ox.ac.uk/ac-div/statistics/student statistics/detailed tables/2006–2013> (website no longer extant).

TABLE 6 Annual Cost of Study at Oxford c.1400–2013

Date	Undergraduate tuition fee	Postgraduate tuition fee	Tuition, board and lodging	All costs	All costs in 2011 prices
1400–1500	10s.			£2 10s.–£7	£1,566–£4,384
1500–1600	£1			£4–£8	£1,185–£2,371
1640	£8			£8–£45	£1,171–£6,585
1700–1800				£24–£120	£3,098–£15,490
1800–50	£12 12s.			£150–£300	£10,100–£20,210
1850	£16 16s.–£20 4s.		£114–£173	£185–£309	£16,230–£27,110
1909	£24 10s.– £27 10s.		£128–£142	£200–£350	£17,110–£29,940
1939	£30		£150–£180	£250–£300	£12,670–£15,260
1946	£40			£250	£9,048
1969	£170			£550	£7,827
1997	£3,866–£5,916	£4,006		£8,000	£11,950
2013–14	£9,000	£6,600–£8,600		£15,000–£20,000	£14,100–£18,800

Note: The figures for 1997 and 2013–14 give the costs for students from the UK and the EU. Postgraduate figures for 2013–14 are for the DPhil and the cheaper masters' courses and include the separate college fee. Overall costs for 2013–14 are based on the University's figures for board, lodging, and so on at the lower end of the scale. Overseas students could expect to spend much more. So too could those taking an MBA where home, EU, and overseas students were charged a university tuition fee of £41,000 in 2013–14. The figures for the nineteenth century do not cover the cost of a coach, who could charge £30 a term. In the final column, the annual cost has been converted into 2011 prices using the RPI data provided by the website: <http://www.measuringworth.com/ukcompare>.

Sources: The table is drawn from many different sources and is intended to be indicative. A detailed breakdown of the cost of study at Oxford in 2013 was found at <http://www.ox.ac.uk/feesandfunding/fees-funding/> (accessed 8 April 2013, but website no longer extant) . Figures for 2015–16 are available at <http://www.ox.ac.uk/students/fees-funding/fees-funding/fees> (information backdated to 2005/6 in the second case).

765

TABLE 7 University Personnel (Academic and Non-Academic), 1908–2013

	College tutors and other academics with no university attachment	University postholders	University research staff	University non-academic staff (figure in brackets: top administrators)	Total (figure in brackets includes colleges and OUP staff)
1908	150	110			
1922	214	143			
1927		150			
1938/9		504			
1948/9		573			
1958/9		842			
1964/5	154	973	c.150		
c.1975			c.400		
1995/6	1,250	1,376	2,118	3,292 (279)	6,786
2003/4				3,184	7,183
2005		c.1,500	c.3,000	c.3,500	8,210 (15,000)
2007/8		c. 1,500	c.3,000	4,128	8,706
2013/14		1,722	4,087	5,995 (1,258)	11,804

Note: (1) The number of university non-academic staff in 2003/4 and 2007/8 does not include library and museum staff, who formed 13 per cent of the non-academic total in 2011. (2) The number of university postholders in 1995/6 includes 103 classed as unestablished, so presumably impermanent members of staff. (3) The number of top administrators in 2013/14 is based on the number of non-academic staff who were eligible to be members of Congregation.

Sources: G. N. Curzon, *Principles and Methods of University Reform* (Oxford, 1909), p. 121; Morell, p. 77; Mallet, iii. 488; Franks, ii. 32, 39, and 236; North, pp. 7 and 18; *Corporate Plan 2005–6 to 2009–10*, p. 5 (para. 41); Governance Discussion Paper (MT, 2005), p. 4; White Paper on University Governance (TT, 2006), pp. 6 (para. 22) and 37; Julie Maxton, 'Supporting the University's Activities: The Development of Its Administration from 2004 to Date' (2009), p. 2 (internal Oxford document); <http://www.admin.ox.ac.uk/media/global/wwwadminoxacuk/localsites/personnel/documents/factsandfigures/staffingfigures2014/Table_1.pdf>; OM, 0th week, MT, 2013, p. 1; OUG, supplement (1) to no. 5051, 26 Feb. 2014, p. 340 (gives number of research staff and non-academic staff eligible for membership of Congregation).

TABLE 8 University Income, c.1250–2013, in £1,000s

	Endowment	Fees	UGC/HEFCE grant	Research grants and contracts (government/research councils/charities/business)	Total (2011 prices in brackets)
c.1250					0.005 (4.53)
c.1500					0.1 (68.3)
1873					32 (2,438)
1907					76 (6,597)
1920					210 (6,922)
1934/5	147	46	97	27	452 (25,700)
1953/4	317	206	[1,400]		2,000 (44,700)
1963/4	447	408	4,200	1,300	6,400 (110,000)
1970/1	897	550	9,000	3,500	14,000
1980/1	4,000	10,000	34,000	15,000	63,000
1987/8	6,600	14,300	52,000	40,800	115,000 (253,000)
1993/4	22,200	38,000	70,000	85,000	240,000
1997/8	22,000	38,500	88,500	114,500	305,000
2001/2	29,000	112,000	135,000	150,000	426,000 (569,000)
2004/5	24,000	68,000	159,000	184,000	530,000
2007/8	42,600	110,000	186,000	285,000	767,000
2008/9	37,100	123,000	195,000	341,000	863,000
2010/11	31,300	152,700	200,000	377,000	920,000
2011/12	36,700	173,000	204,000	409,000	1,016,000
2013/14	30,300	235,900	182,200	478,300	1,174,000 (1,079,000)

Note: The figures for total annual income are inflated by a variety of miscellaneous items, such as donations from OUP.

Sources: Commission (1873); Jack Morrell, *Science at Oxford 1914–1939: Transforming an Arts University* (Oxford, 1997), p. 436; Franks, i. 40; HUO, viii. 679–81; Oxford University/University of Oxford Annual Report/Review 1993/4–2011/12; <http://www.ox.ac.uk/about_the_university/facts_and_figures/financial_statements.html> (data 1999/2000–2010/11, but this website is no longer extant); <http://www.ox.ac.uk/sites/files/oxford/field/field_document/Financial_Statements.pdf> (online version of Oxford's annual financial statement since 2010/11).

TABLE 9 University and Colleges' Endowment Wealth 1964–2013/14 in £1,000s

	University	2011 prices	Colleges	2011 prices	Total
1964			54,000–80,000	897,900–1,330,000	
1988			900,000		
1989	200,000	408,300			
1997			1,000,000		
2001	470,000		1,900,000		2,370,000
2004/5	558,300		2,200,000		2,758,300
2005/6	628,800		2,400,000		3,028,800
2006/7	688,600		2,700,000		3,388,600
2009/10	628,000		2,700,000		3,328,000
2010/11	856,000		2,850,000		3,706,000
2011/12	1,037,000	1,037,000	2,900,000	2,900,000	3,937,000
2013/14	1,488,000	1,378,000	3,500,000	3,216,000	4,988,000

Sources: HUO, viii. 671–2; *The Times*, 5 May 1997, p. 8; 'The Oxford Colleges' League Table for Financial Year Ended 31 July 2001 Ranked by Estimated Assets' (<http://www.akme.btinternet.co.uk/oclxleg4. html; based on the Oxford college accounts; website no longer extant; author's print-out); White Paper 2006, p. 38; 'Aggregated College Accounts: Statement of Financial Activities: Years Ended 2006, 2007, 2010, 2011, 2012' (<http://www.ox.ac.uk/about_the_university/facts_and_figures/ financialstatementsoftheOxfordcolleges>; site no longer extant); 'University Financial Statements 1999/2000–2010/11' (<http://www.ox.ac.uk/about_the_university/facts_and_figures/university_finan-cial_statement>; site no longer live); <http://www.ox.ac.uk/about/organisation/finance-and-funding/financial-statements-of-the-Oxford-Colleges-2013-14> (annual financial statements from 2006/7); <http://www.ox.ac.uk/sites/files/oxford/field/field_document/Financial_Statements.pdf> (online version of Oxford's annual financial statement since 2011/12 with information back to 2007/8).

TABLE 10 Number of Students in UK Institutions of Higher Education, 1900/1–2012/13

	Oxford	FT students in UK universities	FT students in other UK HEIs	FT students in all UK HEIs	Postgraduates in FT education as percentage of total	PT students in HEIs
1900/1	3,000	20,000	5,000	25,000		
1924/5		42,000	19,000	61,000		
1938/9	5,000	50,000	19,000	69,000	2%	
1954/5		82,000	40,000	122,000		
1962/3		118,000	98,000	216,000	6%	
1970/1	11,000	236,000	204,000	440,000		
1979/80				510,000	12%	
1985/6	13,000			596,100		300,000
1992/3				822,800		600,000
1995/6	15,000			1,100,000	14%	500,000
2011/12	22,000			1,721,400	18%	775,245
2012/13	22,000			1,682,110	17.6%	668,000

Note: FT = full-time; PT = part-time; HEI = higher educational institution. NB: Open University students are counted as part time.

Sources: Robbins, table 3; Robert Stevens, *University to Uni: The Politics of Higher Education in England since 1944* (London, 2004); pp. 4, 15, 57, 75; North, p. 10; Dearing, p. 18; <http://www.hesa.ac.uk>.

TABLE 11 Stipends and Salaries of Oxford Fellows, Tutors, and Lecturers 1700–2013

	Low	High	2011 prices
Fellows			
1700	£40	£60	£4,900–£7,400
1750	£50	£70	£6,450–£9,000
1840	£252	£403	£18,700–£29,900
Fellows and tutors			
1877		£900	£69,500
1930	£350	£1,200	£18,160–£62,250
CUF & lecturer scale			
1950	£800		£21,550
1957		£1,000	£19,130
1963	£1,900	£2,975	£31,400–£49,170
1969	£1,790	£3,895	£22,920–£49,880
1978	£4,910	£9,388	£21,600–£41,200
1994	£19,052	£32,879	£28,270–£48,780
2013	£43,312	£58,157	£40,730–£54,690

Note: Before 1950 and the creation of the joint university–college scale this table is only indicative. The pre-1840 values are for fellows' stipends only; they do not include the additional sum that could be earned by a college tutor; in the first half of the nineteenth century when most colleges employed only three tutors, a tutor's salary would easily have given a fellow another £200 a year. The figures throughout the table include only stipends and salaries. Were the value of free board and lodging, judged to be worth about £9,000 today, and various other benefits to be factored in, then the totals would be higher. What is clear for the post-war era is that the top point of the university lecturer/CUF scale has kept pace with inflation since the 1960s, but the purchasing power of the average don at the top of the scale in 2013 is only about 12 per cent greater than it was fifty years ago, though GDP per capita has tripled.

Sources: Various; since 1950, information has been taken from the minutes and papers of the Magdalen College Governing Body.

Further Reading

General

Anderson, Robert David, *European Universities from the Enlightenment to 1914* (Oxford, 2004).

Clark, William, *Academic Charisma and the Origins of the Research University* (London, 2006).

Cobban, A. B., *The Medieval Universities: Their Development and Organisation* (London, 1975).

Rashdall, Hastings, *The Universities of Europe in the Middle Ages*, ed. F. M. Powicke and A. B. Emden (3 vols; Oxford, 1936).

Ridder-Symoens, H. de (ed.), *A History of the University in Europe*, vol. 1: *Universities in the Middle Ages* (Cambridge, 1992).

Ridder-Symoens, H. de (ed.), *A History of the University in Europe*, vol. 2: *Universities in Early Modern Europe (1500–1800)* (Cambridge, 1996).

Rüegg, Walter (ed.), *A History of the University in Europe*, vol. 3: *Universities in the Nineteenth and Early Twentieth Centuries (1800–1945)* (Cambridge, 2004).

Rüegg, Walter (ed.), *A History of the University in Europe*, vol. 4: *Universities since 1945* (Cambridge, 2011).

Britain and the Anglophone World

Anderson, Robert D., *Education and Opportunity in Victorian Scotland: Schools and Universities* (Oxford, 1983).

Anderson, Robert D., *Universities and Elites in Britain since 1800* (Cambridge, 1995).

Beloff, Michael, *The Plateglass Universities* (London, 1968).

Cobban, A. B., *The Medieval English Universities: Oxford and Cambridge to c. 1500* (Cambridge, 1988).

Deer, C. M. A., *Higher Education in England and France since the 1980s* (Oxford, 2002).

Halsey, A. H., *Decline of Donnish Dominion: The British Academic Profession in the Twentieth Century* (Oxford, 1992).

Jones, David R., *The Origins of Civic Universities: Manchester, Leeds and Liverpool* (London, 1988).

Pietsch, T., *Empire of Scholars: Universities, Networks and the British Academic World, 1850–1939* (Manchester, 2013).

Sanderson, Michael, *The Universities and British Industry, 1850–1970* (London, 1972).

Simpson, Renate, *How the PhD came to Britain: A Century of Struggle for Postgraduate Education* (Guildford, 1983).

Stevens, Robert, *University to Uni: The Politics of Higher Education in England since 1944* (London, 2004).

Vernon, Keith, *Universities and the State in England 1850–1939* (London, 2004).

Veysey, Laurence, *The Emergence of the American University* (Chicago, 1965).

Whyte, William, *Redbrick: A Social and Architectural History of Britain's Civic Universities* (Oxford, 2015).

University of Oxford

The History of the University of Oxford

Volume I: *The Early Oxford Schools*, ed. J. I. Catto (Oxford, 1984).
Volume II: *Late Medieval Oxford*, ed. J. I. Catto and T. A. R. Evans (Oxford, 1992).
Volume III: *The Collegiate University*, ed. James McConica (Oxford, 1986).
Volume IV: *Seventeenth-Century Oxford*, ed. Nicholas Tyacke (Oxford, 1997).
Volume V: *The Eighteenth Century*, ed. L. S. Sutherland and L. G. Mitchell (Oxford, 1986).
Volume VI: *Nineteenth-Century Oxford, Part 1*, ed. M. G. Brock and M. C. Curthoys (Oxford, 1997).
Volume VII: *Nineteenth-Century Oxford, Part 2*, ed. M. G. Brock and M. C. Curthoys (Oxford, 2000).
Volume VIII: *The Twentieth Century*, ed. Brian Harrison (Oxford, 1994).

The History of Oxford University Press

Volume I: *Beginnings to 1780*, ed. Ian Gadd (Oxford, 2013).
Volume II: *1780–1896*, ed. Simon Eliot (Oxford, 2013).
Volume III: *1896–1979*, ed. Wm. Roger Louis (Oxford, 2013).

Other Works

Batson, Judy G., *Her Oxford* (Nashville, 2008).

Chester, Daniel N., *Economic, Political and Social Studies in Oxford 1900–85* (London, 1986).

Ellis, Heather, *Generational Conflict and University Reform: Oxford in the Age of Revolution* (Leiden and Boston, MA, 2012).

Evans, G. R., *The University of Oxford: A New History* (London, 2010).

Fauvel, John, Flood, Raymond, and Wilson, Robin, *Oxford Figures: 800 Years of the Mathematical Sciences* (Oxford, 2000).

Fox, Robert, and Goody, Graeme (eds), *Physics in Oxford, 1839–1939: Laboratories, Learning and College Life* (Oxford, 2005).

Goldman, Lawrence, *Dons and Workers: Oxford and Adult Education since 1850* (Oxford, 1995).

Hood, Christopher, King, Desmond, and Peele, Gillian, *Forging a Discipline: A Critical Assessment of Oxford's Development of the Study of Politics and International Relations in Comparative Perspective* (Oxford, 2014).

Inman, Daniel, 'God in the Academy: The Reform of the University of Oxford and the Practice of Theology, 1850–1932' (D.Phil. dissertation, Oxford, 2009).

Kenny, Anthony (ed.), *The History of the Rhodes Trust, 1902–1999* (Oxford, 2001).

Leff, Gordon, *Paris and Oxford in the Thirteenth and Fourteenth Centuries: An Institutional and Intellectual History* (London, 1968).

Mallet, Charles Edward, *A History of the University of Oxford*, vol. 1: *The Medieval University and the Colleges Founded in the Middle Ages*; vol. 2: *The Sixteenth and Seventeenth Centuries*; vol. 3: *Modern Oxford* (London, 1927).

Morrell, Jack, *Science at Oxford 1914–1939: Transforming an Arts University* (Oxford, 1997).

Ord, Margery G., and Stoken, Lloyd A., *The Oxford Biochemistry Department 1920–2006* (Oxford, 2006).

Prest, John, *The Illustrated History of Oxford University* (Oxford, 1993).

Rivière, Peter (ed.), *A History of Oxford Anthropology* (Oxford, 2007).

Roberts, Pamela, *Black Oxford: The Untold Stories of Oxford University's Black Scholars* (Oxford, 2013).

Soares, Joseph A., *The Decline of Privilege: The Modernisation of Oxford University* (Stanford, CA, 1999).

Stone, Lawrence, 'The Size and Composition of the Oxford Student Body, 1580–1910', in Lawrence Stone (ed.), *The University in Society*, vol. 1: *Oxford and Cambridge from the 14th to the Early 19th Century* (Princeton, NJ, 1974), pp. 3–110.

Symonds, Richard, *Oxford and Empire: The Last Lost Cause?* (Basingstoke, 1986).

Ward, W. R., *Victorian Oxford* (London, 1965).

Whyte, William, *Oxford Jackson: Architecture, Education, Status, and Style 1835–1924* (Oxford, 2006).

Williams, Robert J., Chapman, Allan, and Rowlinson, J. S. (eds), *Chemistry at Oxford: A History from 1600 to 2005* (Cambridge, 2009).

Oxford Colleges

Adams, Pauline, *Somerville for Women: An Oxford College 1879–1993* (Oxford, 1996).

Bill, E. G. W., *Education at Christ Church Oxford 1600–1800* (Oxford, 1988).

Brockliss, L. W. B. (ed.), *Magdalen College Oxford: A History* (Oxford, 2008).

Buxton, John, and Williams, Penry (eds), *New College Oxford 1379–1979* (Oxford, 1979).

Catto, Jeremy (ed.), *Oriel College: A History* (Oxford, 2013).

Crook, J. Mordaunt, *Brasenose: The Biography of an Oxford College* (Oxford, 2008).

Curthoys, Judith, *The Cardinal's College: Christ Church, Chapter and Verse* (London, 2012).

Darwall-Smith, Robin, *A History of University College Oxford* (Oxford, 2008).

Davies, C. S. L., and Garnett, Jane, *Wadham College* (Oxford, 1994).

Green, S. J. D., and Horden, Peregrine (eds), *All Souls under the Ancien Regime: Politics, Learning and the Arts, c. 1600–1850* (Oxford, 2007).

Green, S. J. D., and Horden, Peregrine (eds), *All Souls and the Wider World: Statesmen, Scholars and Adventurers, c. 1850–1950* (Oxford 2011).

Green, Vivian H. H., *The Commonwealth of Lincoln College 1427–1977* (Oxford, 1979).

Hopkins, Clare, *Trinity: 450 Years of an Oxford College Community* (Oxford, 2005).

Jones, John, *Balliol College: A History*, 2nd edn (Oxford, 1997).

Kaye, Elaine, *Mansfield College Oxford: Its Origin, History and Significance* (Oxford, 1996).

Kelly, J. N. D., *St Edmund Hall: Almost Seven Hundred Years* (Oxford, 1989).

Maddicott, John, *Founders and Fellowship: The Early History of Exeter College, Oxford, 1314–1592* (Oxford, 2014).

Martin, G. H., and Highfield, J. R. L., *A History of Merton College, Oxford* (Oxford, 1997).

Schwartz, Laura, *A Serious Endeavour: Gender, Education and Community at St Hugh's, 1886–2011* (London, 2011).

Cambridge

Brooke, Christopher N. L., *A History of the University of Cambridge*, vol. 4: *1870–1990* (Cambridge, 1993).

Brooke, Christopher N. L., *A History of Gonville and Caius College* (Woodbridge, 1996).

Cunich, Peter, Hoyle, David, Duffy, Eamon, and Hyam, Ronald, *A History of Magdalene College, Cambridge 1428–1988* (Cambridge, 1994).

Leader, Damian Riehl, *A History of the University of Cambridge*, vol. 1: *The University to 1546* (Cambridge, 1988).

Linehan, Peter (ed.), *St John's College Cambridge: A History* (Woodbridge, 2011).

Morgan, Victor, *A History of the University of Cambridge*, vol. 2: *1546–1750* (Cambridge, 2004).

Searby, Peter, *A History of the University of Cambridge*, vol. 3: *1750–1870* (Cambridge, 1997).

Twigg, John, *A History of Queens' College, Cambridge 1448–1986* (Woodbridge, 1987).

Other British and Irish Universities

Anderson, Robert D., Lynch, Michael, and Phillipson, N. T., *The University of Edinburgh: An Illustrated History* (Edinburgh, 2003).

Bamford, T. W., *The University of Hull: The First Fifty Years* (Oxford, 1978).

Dahrendorf, Ralf, *A History of the London School of Economics and Political Science 1895–1995* (Oxford, 1995).

Harte, Negley, *The University of London, 1836–1986: An Illustrated History* (London, 1986).

Ives, E., Drummond, D., and Schwartz, L., *The First Civic University: Birmingham, 1880–1908: An Introductory History* (Birmingham, 2000).

Kennerley, Alston, *The Making of the University of Plymouth* (Plymouth, 2000).

McDowell, R. B., and Webb, D. A., *Trinity College Dublin 1592–1952: An Academic History* (Cambridge, 1982).

Mathers, Helen, *Steel City Scholars: The Centenary History of the University of Sheffield* (London, 2005).

Morgan, Prys, *The University of Wales, 1939–1993* (Cardiff, 1997).

Moss, Michael, Munro, J. Forbes, and Trainor, Richard H. (eds), *University, City and State: The University of Glasgow since 1870* (Edinburgh, 2000).

Nicholls, C. S., *The History of St Antony's College, Oxford, 1950–2000* (Basingstoke, 2000).

Pullan, Brian, with Abendstern, Michele, *A History of the University of Manchester, 1951–1973* (Manchester, 2000).

Sanderson, M., *The History of the University of East Anglia* (London, 2002).

Thompson, F. M. L. (ed.), *The University of London and the World of Learning, 1836–1986* (London, 1990).

Williams, J. Gwynn, *The University of Wales, 1893–1939* (Cardiff, 1997).

INDEX OF PERSONS

Abbreviations

A person's dates are followed where applicable or known by their most significant relationship to the University of Oxford, then by their defining characteristic

GENERAL INDEX

827

2017. 01. 25   60.00 (30.00)